Setting Yourself up for...
SUCCESS

 W9-BGC-363

MAKE THE MOST OF CLASS

1. Attend class. Regular attendance is a key to success.
2. Make sure you have a book and a notebook for homework and notes.
3. Take notes in class. At a minimum, write down what your instructor writes on the board.
4. If you have tried to solve a problem, but need help, ask a question in class when it is appropriate. Many times other students have the same question.
5. Get to know someone in class. Learning is enhanced when you can talk to someone about math.
6. Did you miss something in class? The **Video Lectures on CD or DVD*** offer a short lecture for each section of your text and are taught by math instructors. These videos will help you review material you may have missed in class or found confusing.

HELP IS HERE WHENEVER YOU WANT IT!

1. Find out your instructor's office number and office hours.
2. Ask if there is a tutor room on campus and find out the hours when tutors are available. The tutors at the Math Tutor Center are available by phone, fax, email, or interactive web, and offer instant, live, one-on-one help with your course. For more information, visit www.mathtutorcenter.com.
3. Before going to office hours or the tutor room, organize your questions. Be sure you try a problem before you ask your instructor or tutor to help you.
4. Don't know why you got the wrong answer? The **Student's Solutions Manual*** contains complete, worked-out solutions (not just answers) to every odd-numbered exercise problem and to ALL the review and test problems in the book.
5. Need some more practice? The **Worksheets for Classroom or Lab Practice*** include extra practice problems for every section of the book.

MASTERING THE EXAM

1. Try the **Pass the Test CD**, found in the front of your book. It contains video clips of an instructor working through the complete solution for all exercises from the chapter tests in your book. **Pass the Test** also includes vocabulary flashcards, tips for time management, and a Spanish glossary.
2. Find a consistent time and place to study every day rather than "pulling an all-nighter" before the exam.
3. Keep all your homework and notes in a notebook. Reading your notes and going through your homework assignments will make reviewing for the exam easier.
4. Find out from your instructor which topics will be covered on the exam.
5. **Tab Your Way to Success** by using the color-coded Post-It® tabs provided in the back of the book to mark important pages of the text that you may want to return to for review, instructor help, or test preparation.
6. When you think you are ready for the exam, pick a few problems from your assignments *at random*. If you can work them, without any help, you are well on your way to being ready.
7. Carefully show your work whenever possible on your exam.
8. Relax and visualize doing well.

You can SUCCEED in Math!

* *These items and others can be purchased at www.mypearsonstore.com*

PEARSON

ALWAYS LEARNING

Gary K. Rockswold • Terry A. Krieger

Intermediate Algebra with Applications and Visualization

Second Custom Edition for Portland Community College

Taken from:
Intermediate Algebra with Applications and Visualization, Third Edition
By Gary K. Rockswold and Terry A. Krieger

Cover Art: Photograph Courtesy of Will Freeman.

Taken from:

Intermediate Algebra with Applications and Visualization, Third Edition
by Gary K. Rockswold and Terry A. Krieger
Copyright © 2009 by Pearson Education, Inc.
Published by Addison Wesley
Boston, Massachusetts 02116

Pearson Learning Solutions, 501 Boylston Street, Suite 900, Boston, MA 02116
A Pearson Education Company
www.pearsoned.com

Printed in the United States of America

6 7 8 9 10 V092 16 15 14

000200010271680697

DT

ISBN 10: 1-256-84594-9
ISBN 13: 978-1-256-84594-2

CONTENTS

3 LINEAR EQUATIONS AND INEQUALITIES   149

6 RATIONAL EXPRESSIONS AND FUNCTIONS   403

7   RADICAL EXPRESSIONS AND FUNCTIONS   497

8 QUADRATIC FUNCTIONS AND EQUATIONS

PREFACE

Intermediate Algebra with Applications and Visualization, Third Edition, more than any other conventional textbook, connects the real world to mathematics in ways that are both meaningful and motivational to students. Students using this textbook will have no shortage of realistic and convincing answers to the perennial question, "When will I ever use this?" The early introduction of graphs allows instructors to use graphs and other visualizations to marshal a host of applications of mathematical concepts to galvanize students' attention and comprehension. Real data, graphs, and tables play an important role in the course, giving meaning to the numbers and equations that students encounter. This approach increases students' interest and motivation and, consequently, the likelihood of success.

This textbook is one of three textbooks in a series that includes *Beginning Algebra with Applications and Visualization*, Second Edition, and *Beginning & Intermediate Algebra with Applications and Visualization*, Second Edition.

APPROACH

We introduce mathematical concepts by moving from the concrete to the abstract, using relevant applications to support students' comprehension of abstract mathematical ideas. We have included a diverse collection of unique, up-to-date applications to buttress students' understanding of difficult concepts. Additionally, we present mathematical concepts using multiple representations, giving students a variety of perspectives for learning the same material—something especially helpful because students have various learning styles.

The primary purpose of the text, of course, is to teach mathematical concepts and skills. Building skills is an objective of every section. Problem-solving skills, which will help students succeed in more advanced mathematics courses, are given a strong emphasis. Throughout the text, problem solving is frequently combined with real-world applications to capture and maintain students' interest while reinforcing problem-solving habits. Standard mathematical definitions, theorems, symbolism, and rigor will prepare students for higher-level courses should they choose to pursue them.

CHANGES INCORPORATED INTO THIS EDITION

This edition contains important changes resulting from numerous comments and suggestions from instructors, students, and reviewers. We have made the text more visual by using more color and adding many photos. The following exciting features have been added to enhance students' learning of mathematical skills and concepts. To emphasize how mathematics can be used in everyday life, **A Look into Math** appears at the start of every section and **Real-World Connections** are highlighted throughout the text. **Now Try Exercises** appear after every example, and **Thinking Generally** concept exercises appear in most exercise sets. There are also new **Cumulative Review** exercise sets for chapters that previously did not have them, and Chapter Tests have been updated and are now more comprehensive.

The examples and the exercises have also been updated and expanded throughout the text:

- There are **more than 1000 new exercises**, including additional graphing calculator exercises.
- **Approximately 50 new examples** have been added, many of them multi-part, with an emphasis on solving word problems, factoring, and radicals.
- **Data in applications have been updated** throughout and many new topics have been added, including applications about iPods, global warming, and video games, giving instructors familiar with the text a fresh, rich set of practice material to work with.

ORGANIZATION

CHAPTER 1: Starting with this chapter, hundreds of applications involving data have been updated to make the text even more current.

CHAPTER 2: Increased emphasis on numerical, graphical, symbolic, and verbal representations of functions is included. This theme of multiple representations has increased importance throughout the text.

CHAPTER 3: Starting with this chapter, there is more emphasis on having students distinguish between expressions and equations. More applications and word problems involving linear equations have been included. In Section 3.1 exercises for finding x- and y-intercepts have been added.

CHAPTER 4: More explanation of how to graph a line by using x- and y-intercepts has been included in this chapter. Section 4.5 now includes new subsections that discuss systems of equations with no solutions or infinitely many solutions.

CHAPTER 5: Section 5.6, Summary of Factoring, is new to this edition. Arithmetic operations on functions is now introduced in Section 5.1 and is reviewed in later chapters with other types of functions. Multiplying functions has been added to Section 5.2.

CHAPTER 6: Addition, subtraction, multiplication, and division of functions are included. There is now more emphasis on students deciding whether they are simplifying a rational expression or solving a rational equation.

CHAPTER 7: There are more explanations, examples, and exercises related to radicals and rational exponents in this chapter.

CHAPTER 8: It is possible to cover Chapter 8 directly following Chapter 5 without loss of continuity. A new subsection on graphing the equation $y = ax^2 + bx + c$ has been added to this chapter.

CHAPTERS 9–11: Features, such as A Look into Math and Real-World Connections, continue to give meaning to the mathematics that students learn. Additional exercises and examples are provided to enhance a student's opportunity to learn these important concepts.

FEATURES

MATH IN THE REAL WORLD

CHAPTER OPENERS
Each chapter opens with an application that motivates students by giving them insight into the relevance of that chapter's mathematical concepts.

MATH IN THE REAL WORLD

CHAPTER **2**

Linear Functions and Models

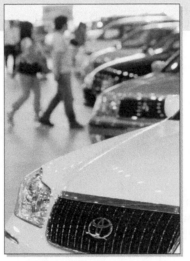

Every day our society creates enormous amounts of data, and mathematics is an important tool for summarizing those data and discovering trends. For example, the table shows the number of Toyota vehicles sold in the United States for selected years.

Year	1998	1999	2000	2001	2002
Vehicles (millions)	1.4	1.5	1.6	1.7	1.8

Source: Autodata.

These data contain an obvious pattern: Sales increased by 0.1 million each year. A scatterplot of these data and a line that models this situation are shown in the figure. In this chapter you will learn how to determine the equation of this and other lines. (See Section 2.2, Example 6.)

2.1 Functions and Their Representations
2.2 Linear Functions
2.3 The Slope of a Line
2.4 Equations of Lines and Linear Models

No great thing is created suddenly.
—EPICTETUS

73

XV

MATH IN THE REAL WORLD

NEW!
A LOOK INTO MATH
Nearly every section begins in the context of the practical world that motivates the math topic that follows.

4.3 SYSTEMS OF LINEAR INEQUALITIES

Solving Linear Inequalities in Two Variables ■ Solving Systems of Linear Inequalities

A LOOK INTO MATH ▷ People often walk or jog in an effort to increase their heart rates and get in better shape. During strenuous exercise, older people should maintain lower heart rates than younger people. A person cannot maintain precisely one heart rate, so a range of heart rates is recommended by health professionals. For aerobic fitness, a 50-year-old's heart rate might be between 120 and 140 beats per minute, whereas a 20-year-old's heart rate might be between 140 and 160. Systems of linear inequalities can be used to model these situations.

Solving Linear Inequalities in Two Variables

▶ REAL-WORLD CONNECTION   Figure 3.15 shows the distances that two cars are from Chicago, Illinois, after x hours while traveling in the same direction on a freeway. The distance for Car 1 is denoted y_1, and the distance for Car 2 is denoted y_2.

Figure 3.15 Distances of Two Cars

When $x = 2$ hours, $y_1 = y_2$ and both cars are 150 miles from Chicago. To the left of the dashed vertical line $x = 2$, the graph of y_1 is below the graph of y_2, so Car 1 is closer to Chicago than Car 2. Thus

$$y_1 < y_2 \quad \text{when} \quad x < 2.$$

To the right of the dashed vertical line $x = 2$, the graph of y_1 is above the graph of y_2, so Car 1 is farther from Chicago than Car 2. Thus

$$y_1 > y_2 \quad \text{when} \quad x > 2.$$

NEW!
REAL-WORLD CONNECTION
Where appropriate, the authors expand on specific math topics and their connections to the everyday world.

GROUP ACTIVITY
WORKING WITH REAL DATA

Directions: Form a group of 2 to 4 people. Select someone to record the group's responses for this activity. All members should work cooperatively to answer the questions. If your instructor asks for the results, each member of the group should be prepared to respond.

Sport Utility Vehicles (SUVs) SUVs became increasingly popular during the 1990s. The table lists the number of SUVs sold in various years.

Year	1992	1994	1996	1998	2000
SUVs (millions)	1.1	1.5	2.1	2.7	3.2

Source: Autodata Corporation.

 (a) Make a scatterplot of the data. Discuss any trend in SUV sales. Let $x = 0$ correspond to 1992.
(b) Estimate the slope m of a line that could be used to model the data.
(c) Find an equation of a line $y = mx + b$ that models the data.
(d) Interpret the slope m as a rate of change.
(e) Use your results to estimate SUV sales in 1997 and 2001. Answers may vary.

GROUP ACTIVITIES: WORKING WITH REAL DATA
This feature occurs after select sections (1 or 2 per chapter) and provides an opportunity for students to work collaboratively on a problem that involves real-world data. Most activities can be completed with limited use of class time.

PRACTICE

EXAMPLES

New to this edition, every example directs students to practice exercises patterned after that example for practice and immediate reinforcement of that skill.

EXAMPLE 4   Solving linear inequalities graphically

Use Figure 3.14 to find the solution set to each equation or inequality.

(a) $-\frac{1}{2}x + 1 = 0$ (b) $-\frac{1}{2}x + 1 > 0$ (c) $-\frac{1}{2}x + 1 < 0$

Solution

(a) The graph of $y = -\frac{1}{2}x + 1$ in Figure 3.14 crosses the x-axis at $x = 2$. Thus the solution set is $\{x \mid x = 2\}$.

(b) The graph is *above* the x-axis when $x < 2$. Thus the solution set is $\{x \mid x < 2\}$.

(c) The graph is *below* the x-axis when $x > 2$. Thus the solution set is $\{x \mid x > 2\}$.

Now Try Exercise 49

Figure 3.14

EXERCISES

The exercise sets lead from basic concepts to skill-building, writing, applications, and conceptual mastery.

2.2 Exercises

MyMathLab   Math XP   PRACTICE   WATCH   DOWNLOAD   READ   REVIEW

CONCEPTS

1. The formula for a linear function is $f(x) =$ _____.

2. The formula for a constant function is $f(x) =$ _____.

3. The graph of a linear function is a _____.

4. The graph of a constant function is a _____ line.

5. If $f(x) = 7x + 5$, each time x increases by 1 unit, $f(x)$ increases by _____ units.

6. If $f(x) = 5$, each time x increases by 1 unit, $f(x)$ increases by _____ units.

19.   20.

CONTINUOUS REVIEW EXERCISES

After every two sections, *Checking Basic Concepts* presents a brief set of exercises that students can use for review of recently studied concepts.

CHECKING BASIC CONCEPTS
SECTION 3.5

Write answers in interval notation whenever possible.

1. Solve $\left|\frac{3}{4}x - 1\right| - 3 = 5$.

2. Solve the absolute value equation and inequalities.
   (a) $|3x - 6| = 8$
   (b) $|3x - 6| < 8$
   (c) $|3x - 6| > 8$

3. Solve the inequality $|-2(3 - x)| < 6$. Then solve $|-2(3 - x)| \geq 6$.

4. Use the graph to solve the equation and inequalities.

   $y = |2x - 4|$

   (a) $|2x - 4| = 2$ (b) $|2x - 4| \leq 2$
   (c) $|2x - 4| \geq 2$

PRACTICE

NEW!
THINKING GENERALLY
New to this edition, most exercise sets include open-ended conceptual questions encouraging students to synthesize what they've learned.

Exercises 71 and 72: Solve the inequality graphically. Approximate boundary numbers to the nearest thousandth.

71. $\pi(\sqrt{2x} - 1.2) + \sqrt{3x} > \dfrac{\pi + 1}{3}$

72. $3.1x - 0.5(\pi - x) \le \sqrt{5} - 0.4x$

73. *Thinking Generally* Let y_1 be a (nonconstant) linear function. If $y_1 < b$ when $x > a$, then solve $y_1 > b$.

74. *Thinking Generally* Let y_1 be a (nonconstant) linear function and $y_1 = 0$ when $x = a$. What are the possible solution sets to $y_1 \le 0$?

GRAPHING CALCULATOR EXERCISES
The icon is used to denote an exercise that requires students to have access to a graphing calculator.

TECHNOLOGY NOTE: Asymptotes, Dot Mode, and Decimal Windows

When rational functions are graphed on graphing calculators, pseudo-asymptotes often occur because the calculator is simply connecting dots to draw a graph. The accompanying figures show the graph of $y = \dfrac{2}{x-2}$ in connected mode, dot mode, and with a *decimal*, or *friendly*, *window*. In dot mode, pixels in the calculator screen are not connected. With dot mode (and sometimes with a decimal window) pseudo-asymptotes do not appear. To learn more about these features consult your owner's manual.

$[-6, 6, 1]$ by $[-4, 4, 1]$ $[-6, 6, 1]$ by $[-4, 4, 1]$ $[-4.7, 4.7, 1]$ by $[-3.1, 3.1, 1]$

Connected Mode   Dot Mode   Decimal Window

TECHNOLOGY NOTES
Occurring throughout the book, optional Technology Notes offer students guidance, suggestions, and cautions on the use of a graphing calculator.

NEW!
TAB YOUR WAY TO SUCCESS
Forty reusable color-coded Post-It® tabs encourage students to mark important pages of the text for review, extra help, test preparation, etc.

CONCEPTS

MATH FROM MULTIPLE PERSPECTIVES
Throughout the text, concepts are presented by means of verbal, graphical, numerical, and symbolic representations to support multiple learning styles and problem-solving methods.

MAKING CONNECTIONS
This feature occurs throughout the text and helps students relate previously learned concepts to new concepts, pointing out the interrelatedness of mathematical topics.

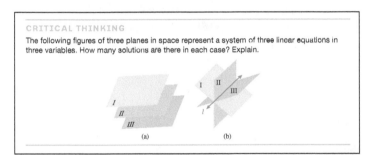

CRITICAL THINKING
One or more Critical Thinking exercises are included in most sections. They pose questions that can be used for classroom discussion or homework assignments.

PUTTING IT ALL TOGETHER
This helpful feature appears at the end of each section to summarize techniques and reinforce the mathematical concepts presented in the section.

CHAPTER MASTERY

CHAPTER SUMMARY

For a quick and thorough review, each chapter is condensed into key terms, topics, and procedures accompanied by illuminating examples to assist in test preparation.

CHAPTER 2   SUMMARY

SECTION 2.1   FUNCTIONS AND THEIR REPRESENTATIONS

Function   A function is a set of ordered pairs (x, y), where each x-value corresponds to exactly one y-value. A function takes a valid input x and computes exactly one output y, forming the ordered pair (x, y).

Domain and Range of a Function   The domain D is the set of all valid inputs, or x-values, and the range R is the set of all outputs, or y-values.

Examples: $f = \{(1, 2), (2, 3), (3, 3)\}$ has $D = \{1, 2, 3\}$ and $R = \{2, 3\}$.

$f(x) = x^2$ has domain all real numbers and range $y \geq 0$. (See the graph below.)

Function Notation $y = f(x)$ and is read "y equals f of x."

Example: $f(x) = \frac{2x}{x-1}$ implies that $f(3) = \frac{2 \cdot 3}{3 - 1} = \frac{6}{2} = 3$. Thus the point $(3, 3)$ is on the graph of f.

CHAPTER 2   REVIEW EXERCISES

SECTION 2.1

Exercises 1–4: Evaluate $f(x)$ for the given values of x.

1. $f(x) = 3x - 1$ $\qquad$ $x = -2, \frac{1}{3}$

2. $f(x) = 5 - 3x^2$ $\qquad$ $x = -3, 1$

3. $f(x) = \sqrt{x} - 2$ $\qquad$ $x = 0, 9$

4. $f(x) = 5$ $\qquad$ $x = -5, \frac{7}{5}$

Exercises 5 and 6: Do the following.

   (a) *Write a symbolic representation (formula) for the function described.*
   (b) *Evaluate the function for input 5 and interpret the result.*

5. Function P computes the number of pints in q quarts.

6. Function f computes 3 less than 4 times a number x.

7. If $f(3) = -2$, then the point _____ lies on the graph of f.

8. If $(4, -6)$ lies on the graph of f, then $f(\_\_) = \_\_\_$.

15. Use the table to evaluate $f(-1)$ and $f(3)$.

x	-1	1	3	5
$f(x)$	7	3	-1	-5

16. A function f is represented verbally by "Multiply the input x by 3 and then subtract 2." Give numerical, symbolic, and graphical representations for f. Let $x = -3, -2, -1, \ldots, 3$ in the table of values, and let $-3 \leq x \leq 3$ for the graph.

Exercises 17 and 18: Use the graph of f to estimate its domain and range.

17.

18.

CHAPTER REVIEW EXERCISES

For extra practice of any topic, students can use these exercises to gain confidence that they've mastered the material.

EXTENDED AND DISCOVERY EXERCISES

These capstone projects at the end of every chapter challenge students to synthesize what they've learned and apply it in other college courses.

CHAPTER 2   EXTENDED AND DISCOVERY EXERCISES

1. *Developing a Model*   Two identical cylindrical tanks, A and B, each contain 100 gallons of water. Tank A has a pump that begins removing water at a constant rate of 8 gallons per minute. Tank B has a plug removed from its bottom and water begins to flow out—faster at first and then more slowly.
   (a) Assuming that the tanks become empty at the same time, sketch a graph that models the amount of water in each tank. Explain your graphs.
   (b) Which tank is half empty first? Explain.

 2. *Modeling Real Data*   Per capita personal incomes in the United States from 1990 through 2000 are listed in the following table.

Year	1990	1991	1992	1993

   (c) Use f to estimate per capita income in 1998.

3. *Graphing a Rectangle*   One side of a rectangle has vertices $(0, 0)$ and $(5, 3)$. If the point $(0, 5)$ lies on one side of this rectangle, as shown in the figure, write the equation of each line.

CHAPTER TEST

Students can reduce math anxiety by using these tests as a rehearsal for the real thing.

CHAPTER 2   TEST Pass Test Video solutions to all test exercises

1. Evaluate $f(4)$ if $f(x) = 3x^2 - \sqrt{x}$. Give a point on the graph of f.

2. Write a symbolic representation (formula) for a function C that calculates the cost of buying x pounds of candy at \$4 per pound. Evaluate $C(5)$ and interpret your result.

3. Sketch a graph of f.
   (a) $f(x) = -2x + 1$ (b) $f(x) = x^2 + 1$
   (c) $f(x) = \sqrt{x + 3}$ (d) $f(x) = |x + 1|$

4. Use the graph of f to evaluate $f(-3)$ and $f(0)$. Determine the domain and range of f.

8. Determine if $f(x) = 6 - 8x$ is a linear function. If it is, write it in the form $f(x) = ax + b$.

9. Find the slope of the line passing through $(-3, 7)$ and $(6, -2)$.

10. Determine the slope of the line shown in the graph.

11. Write the slope–intercept form of a line satisfying the conditions.
    (a) x-intercept -2, y-intercept -4
    (b) Passing through $(-5, 2)$ and perpendicular to the line passing through $(-2, 5)$ and $(-1, 3)$
    (c) Passing through $(1, -2)$ and $\left(-5, \frac{3}{2}\right)$.

PASS THE TEST CD

Included with every new copy of the book, the Pass the Test CD includes the following resources: video clips of an instructor working through the complete solutions for all Chapter Test exercises for each chapter; vocabulary flashcards; tips for time management; and a Spanish glossary.

CUMULATIVE REVIEWS

Starting with Chapter 2 and appearing in all subsequent chapters in this edition, these reviews help students see the big picture of math by staying fresh with topics and skills they've already learned.

CHAPTERS 1–3   CUMULATIVE REVIEW EXERCISES

Exercises 1 and 2: Classify each real number as one or more of the following: natural number, whole number, integer, rational number, or irrational number.

1. $-7, -\frac{3}{5}, 0, \sqrt{5}, \frac{8}{5}, 5.\overline{12}$

2. $-\frac{6}{3}, \frac{0}{9}, \sqrt{9}, \pi, 4.\overline{6}$

Exercises 3 and 4: State whether the equation illustrates an identity, commutative, associative, or distributive property.

3. $8x - 2x = 6x$

4. $(6 + z) + 3 = 6 + (z + 3)$

Exercises 5 and 6: Use properties of real numbers to evaluate the expression mentally.

5. $11 + 26 + (-1) + 14$

6. $7 \cdot 98$

7. Plot the numbers $-4, -\frac{5}{2}, 0,$ and 3 on a number line.

8. Find the opposite of $-5y - 4$.

16. Identify the domain and range of the relation $S = \{(-2, 4), (0, 2), (1, 4), (3, 0)\}$.

Exercises 17 and 18: Evaluate the given formula for $x = -2, -1, 0, 1,$ and 2. Plot these ordered pairs.

17. $y = -2x + 1$ 18. $y = \dfrac{x^3 + 4}{2}$

19. Sketch the graph of $f(x) = x^2 - 3$ by hand.

20. Find the domain of $f(x) = \dfrac{4}{x}$.

Exercises 21 and 22: Use the graph or table to evaluate $f(0)$ and $f(-2)$.

21.

STUDENT SUPPLEMENTS

INSTRUCTOR SUPPLEMENTS

Student's Solutions Manual
- Contains solutions for the odd-numbered section-level exercises (excluding Writing About Mathematics and Group Activity exercises), and solutions to all Concepts exercises, Checking Basic Concepts exercises, Chapter Review Exercises, Chapter Test exercises, and Cumulative Review Exercises.

  ISBNs: 0-321-52350-4, 978-0-321-52350-1

Video Lectures on CD or DVD
- Complete set of digitized videos on CD-ROM or DVD for student use at home or on campus.
- Presents a series of lectures correlated directly to the content of each section of the text.
- Features an engaging team of instructors who present material in a format that stresses student interaction, often using examples and exercises from the text.
- Ideal for distance learning and supplemental instruction.
- Video lectures include English captions.

  CD ISBNs: 0-321-52354-7, 978-0-321-52354-9
  DVD ISBNs: 0-321-54273-8, 978-0-321-54273-1

Math XL Tutorials on CD
- Provides algorithmically generated practice exercises that correlate at the objective level to the content of the text.
- Includes an example and a guided solution to accompany every exercise and video clips for selected exercises.
- Recognizes student errors and provides appropriate feedback; generates printed summaries of students' progress.

  ISBNs: 0-321-52356-3, 978-0-321-52356-3

Pass the Test: Chapter Test Solutions on CD
- Contains video clips of an instructor working through the complete solution for all Chapter Test exercises.
- Additional resources include tips for time management, vocabulary flashcards, and a Spanish glossary.

Automatically included in every new copy of the textbook.

Math Tutor Center
The Math Tutor Center is staffed by qualified mathematics instructors who provide students with tutoring on examples and odd-numbered exercises from the textbook. Tutoring is available via toll-free telephone, toll-free fax, e-mail, and the Internet. White Board technology allows tutors and students to actually see problems worked while they message in real time over the Internet during tutoring sessions.

Annotated Instructor's Edition
- Contains Teaching Tips and provides answers to every exercise in the textbook excluding the Writing About Mathematics exercises.
- Answers that do not fit on the same page as the exercises themselves are supplied in the Instructor Answer Appendix at the back of the textbook.

  ISBNs: 0-321-51330-4, 978-0-321-51330-4

Instructor's Solutions Manual
- Provides solutions to all section-level exercises (excluding Writing About Mathematics and Group Activity exercises), and solutions to all Checking Basic Concepts exercises, Chapter Review Exercises, Chapter Test exercises, and Cumulative Review Exercises.

  ISBNs: 0-321-52345-8, 978-0-321-52345-7

Instructor and Adjunct Support Manual
- Includes resources designed to help both new and adjunct faculty with course preparation and classroom management.
- Offers helpful teaching tips and additional exercises for selected content.

  ISBNs: 0-321-52355-5, 978-0-321-52355-6

Printed Test Bank and Instructor's Resource Guide
- The Test Bank contains three free-response test forms per chapter, one multiple-choice test form per chapter, and one free-response and multiple-choice final exam.
- The Resource Guide contains three sets of Cumulative Review Exercises that cover Chapters 1–3, 1–6, and 1–9 and notes for presenting graphing calculator topics, as well as supplemental activities.

  ISBNs: 0-321-52344-X, 978-0-321-52344-0

TestGen
- Enables instructors to build, edit, print, and administer tests.
- Features a computerized bank of questions developed to cover all text objectives.
- Creates multiple but equivalent versions of the same question or test with the click of a button.
- Instructors can modify questions or add new questions.
- Tests can be printed or administered online.

The software and testbank are available for download from Pearson Education's online catalog.

Worksheets for Classroom or Lab Practice

- Extra practice exercises for every section of the text with ample space for students to show their work.
- These lab- and classroom-friendly workbooks also list the key topics and vocabulary terms for every text section, along with vocabulary practice problems.

ISBNs: 0-321-54271-1, 978-0-321-54271-7

Pearson Math Adjunct Support Center

The Pearson Math Adjunct Support Center is staffed by qualified mathematics instructors with more than 50 years of combined experience at both the community college and university level. Assistance is provided for faculty in the following areas:

- Suggested syllabus consultation
- Tips on using materials packed with your book
- Book-specific content assistance
- Teaching suggestions including advice on classroom strategies

  For more information, visit www.aw-bc.com/tutorcenter/math-adjunct.html

MathXL® www.mathxl.com

MathXL is a powerful online homework, tutorial, and assessment system that accompanies Pearson Education textbooks in mathematics and statistics. With MathXL, instructors can create, edit, and assign online homework and tests using algorithmically generated exercises correlated at the objective level to the textbook. They can also create and assign their own online exercises and import TestGen tests for added flexibility. All student work is tracked in MathXL's online gradebook. Students can take chapter tests in MathXL and receive personalized study plans based on their test results. The study plan diagnoses weaknesses and links students directly to tutorial exercises for the objectives they need to study and retest. Students can also access supplemental animations and video clips directly from selected exercises. MathXL is available to qualified adopters. For more information, visit our Web site at www.mathxl.com, or contact your sales representative.

MyMathLab® www.mymathlab.com

MyMathLab is a series of text-specific, easily customizable online courses for Pearson Education textbooks in mathematics and statistics. Powered by CourseCompass™ (our online teaching and learning environment) and MathXL® (our online homework, tutorial, and assessment system), MyMathLab gives instructors the tools they need to deliver all or a portion of their course online, whether students are in a lab or working at home or elsewhere. MyMathLab provides a rich and flexible set of course materials, featuring free-response exercises that are algorithmically generated for unlimited practice and mastery. Students can also use online tools, such as video lectures, animations, and a multimedia textbook, to independently improve their understanding and performance. Instructors can use MyMathLab's homework and test managers to select and assign online exercises correlated directly to the textbook, and they can create and assign their own online exercises and import TestGen tests for added flexibility. MyMathLab's online gradebook—designed specifically for mathematics and statistics—automatically tracks students' homework and test results and gives the instructor control over how to calculate final grades. Instructors can also add offline (paper-and-pencil) grades to the gradebook. MyMathLab is available to qualified adopters. For more information, visit our Web site at www.mymathlab.com or contact your sales representative.

InterAct Math® Tutorial Web site: www.interactmath.com

Get practice and tutorial help online! This interactive tutorial Web site provides algorithmically generated practice exercises that correlate directly to the exercises in the textbook. Students can do an exercise as many times as they like with new values each time for unlimited practice and mastery. Every exercise is accompanied by an interactive guided solution that provides helpful feedback for incorrect answers, and students can also view a worked-out sample problem that steps them through an exercise similar to the one they're working on.

ACKNOWLEDGMENTS

Many individuals contributed to the development of this textbook. We thank the following reviewers, whose comments and suggestions were invaluable in preparing *Intermediate Algebra with Applications and Visualization*, Third Edition.

Raul Aparicio, *Blinn College–Brenham Campus*
Alina Coronel, *Miami-Dade College–Kendall Campus*
Emmett Dennis, *Southern Connecticut State University*
James Deveney, *Virginia Commonwealth University*
Debbie Garrison, *Valencia Community College–East Campus*
Joan Van Glabek, *Edison Community College–Collier Campus*
Cynthia Gubitose, *Southern Connecticut State University*
Shawna Haider, *Salt Lake Community College*
Kristy Hill, *Hinds Community College–Raymond Campus*
Mike Kirby, *Tidewater Community College–Virginia Beach Campus*
Kim Luna, *Eastern New Mexico University*
Rhonda MacLeod, *Tallahassee Community College*
Toni McCall, *Angelina College*
Glenn Noé, *Brookdale Community College*
Mario Scribner, *Tidewater Community College–Virginia Beach Campus*
Robert Shankin, *Santa Fe Community College*
Yvette Stepanian, *Virginia Commonwealth University*
Carol Walker, *Hinds Community College–Raymond Campus*
Elizabeth White, *Trident Technical College*

Elina Niemelä, Bob Bohland, David Atwood, Paul Lorczak, Jessica Rockswold, and Namyong Lee deserve special credit for their help with accuracy checking. Without the excellent cooperation from the professional staff at Addison-Wesley Publishing Company, this project would have been impossible. Thanks go to Greg Tobin and Maureen O'Connor for giving their support. Particular recognition is due Randy Welch and Lauren Morse, who gave essential advice and assistance. The outstanding contributions of Kathy Manley, Joe Vetere, Jay Jenkins, Nathaniel Koven, Antonio Arvelo, and Ceci Fleming are greatly appreciated. Special thanks go to Kathy Diamond, who was instrumental in the success of this project.

Thanks go to Wendy Rockswold and Carrie Krieger, whose unwavering encouragement and support made this project possible. We also thank the many students and instructors who used the previous editions of this textbook. Their suggestions were insightful and helpful.

Please feel free to send us your comments and questions at either of the following e-mail addresses: gary.rockswold@mnsu.edu or terry.krieger@roch.edu. Your opinion is important to us.

Gary K. Rockswold
Terry A. Krieger

Real Numbers and Algebra

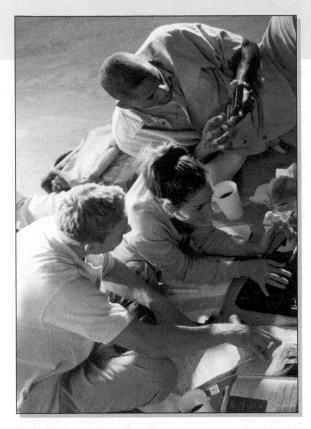

"Why do I need to learn math?" This question is commonly asked by students across the country. A recent cover story in *Business Week* helped explain the answer to this question. In fact, according to James R. Schatz, chief of the mathematics research group at the National Security Agency, "There has never been a better time to be a mathematician."

The world is moving into a new age of numbers. Mathematics is being used to represent all types of information, including digital music and photographs. Mathematics is the *language of technology* and businesses are relying more and more on mathematics. The Internet programs Yahoo! and Google both use a significant amount of mathematics to search millions of items in only tenths of a second. Even consumer behavior is being represented and analyzed mathematically. A company, called Umbria, is breaking down English messages into mathematics and then looking for consumer trends. Mathematicians are in high demand and "top mathematicians are becoming a new global elite." However, the United States needs to produce more mathematics majors—only about 10,000 citizens obtain a math major each year.

Decisions made by students to avoid mathematics can have lifelong ramifications that affect their vocations, incomes, and lifestyles. For example, if you switch majors to avoid mathematics, your decision may prevent you from pursuing your dreams. Like reading and writing, mathematics is an essential component for realizing your full potential.

> The human mind has never invented a labor-saving device greater than algebra.
>
> —J. W. Gibbs

Source: Stephen Baker with Bremen Leak, "Math Will Rock Your World," *Business Week*, January 23, 2006.

1.1 DESCRIBING DATA WITH SETS OF NUMBERS

Natural and Whole Numbers ▪ Integers and Rational Numbers ▪ Real Numbers ▪ Properties of Real Numbers

A LOOK INTO MATH ▷

The need for numbers has existed in nearly every society. Numbers first occurred in the measurement of time, currency, goods, and land. As the complexity of a society increased, so did its numbers. One tribe that lived near New Guinea counted only to 6. Any number higher than 6 was referred to as "many." This number system met the needs of that society. However, our highly technical society could not function with so few numbers. For example, cell phones, iPods, and digital cameras have created a need for a wide variety of numbers. (**Source:** *Historical Topics for the Mathematics Classroom, Thirty-first Yearbook,* NCTM.)

In this section we discuss numbers that are vital to our technological society. We also show how different types of data can be described with sets of numbers.

Natural and Whole Numbers

One important set of numbers found in most societies is the set of **natural numbers**. These numbers comprise the counting numbers and may be expressed as

$$N = \{1, 2, 3, 4, 5, 6, \ldots\}.$$

Set braces, { }, are used to enclose the elements of a set. Because there are infinitely many natural numbers, three dots show that the list continues in the same pattern without end. A second set of numbers, called the **whole numbers**, is given by

$$W = \{0, 1, 2, 3, 4, 5, \ldots\}.$$

Natural numbers and whole numbers can be used when data are not broken into fractional parts. For example, Table 1.1 lists the number of bachelor's degrees awarded during selected academic years. Note that either natural numbers or whole numbers are appropriate to describe the data because a fraction of a degree cannot be awarded.

TABLE 1.1   **Bachelor's Degrees Awarded**

Year	1979–1980	1989–1990	1999–2000	2004–2005
Degrees	929,417	1,051,344	1,237,875	1,352,000

Source: Department of Education.

EXAMPLE 1   Describing iPod size

The amount of memory in an iPod is usually measured in gigabytes (GB), where 1 GB is equal to 1,073,741,824 (or approximately 1 billion) bytes of memory.
(a) How many bytes of memory would a 4 GB iPod have?
(b) Would the amount of memory in an iPod be better described by a natural number or a fraction? Explain your answer.

Solution

(a) $4 \times 1{,}073{,}741{,}824 = 4{,}294{,}967{,}296$ bytes.

(b) A natural number is better because a fraction of a byte is not allowed.

Now Try Exercise 1

Integers and Rational Numbers

The set of **integers** is given by

$$I = \{\ldots, -3, -2, -1, 0, 1, 2, 3, \ldots\}.$$

The integers include both the natural numbers and the whole numbers. During the eighteenth century, negative numbers were not readily accepted by all mathematicians. Such numbers did not seem to have any physical meaning. However, today when a person opens a personal checking account for the first time, negative numbers quickly take on meaning. There is a difference between a positive and a negative balance.

A **rational number** is any number that can be expressed as the ratio of two integers: $\frac{p}{q}$, where q is not equal to 0 because we cannot divide by 0. Rational numbers can be written as fractions and include all integers. Some examples of rational numbers are

$$\frac{8}{1}, \quad \frac{2}{3}, \quad -\frac{3}{5}, \quad -\frac{7}{2}, \quad \frac{22}{7}, \quad 1.2, \quad \text{and} \quad 0.$$

Note that 1.2 and 0 are both rational numbers because they can be written as $\frac{12}{10}$ and $\frac{0}{1}$.

Rational numbers may be expressed in decimal form that either *repeats* or *terminates*. The fraction $\frac{1}{3}$ may be expressed as $0.\overline{3}$, a repeating decimal, and the fraction $\frac{1}{4}$ may be expressed as 0.25, a terminating decimal. The overbar indicates that $0.\overline{3} = 0.3333333\ldots.$

▶ REAL-WORLD CONNECTION   Integers and rational numbers are used to describe things such as temperature. Table 1.2 lists equivalent temperatures in both degrees Fahrenheit and degrees Celsius. Note that both positive and negative numbers are used to describe temperature.

TABLE 1.2   **Fahrenheit and Celsius Temperature**

°F	°C	Observation
−89	$-67.\overline{2}$	Alcohol freezes
−40	−40	Mercury freezes
0	$-17.\overline{7}$	Snow and salt mixture freezes
32	0	Water freezes
100	$37.\overline{7}$	A very warm day
212	100	Water boils

EXAMPLE 2   Classifying numbers

Classify each number as one or more of the following: natural number, whole number, integer, or rational number.

(a) $\frac{6}{3}$ **(b)** -1 **(c)** 0   **(d)** $-\frac{11}{3}$

Solution

(a) Because $\frac{6}{3} = 2$, the number $\frac{6}{3}$ is a natural number, a whole number, an integer, and a rational number.

(b) The number -1 is an integer and a rational number but not a natural or a whole number.

(c) The number 0 is a whole number, an integer, and a rational number but not a natural number.

(d) The fraction $-\frac{11}{3}$ is a rational number as it is the ratio of two integers. However, it is not a natural number, a whole number, or an integer.   Now Try Exercise **27**

Real Numbers

Real numbers can be represented by decimal numbers. Every fraction has a decimal form, so real numbers include rational numbers. However, some real numbers cannot be expressed by fractions. They are called **irrational numbers**. If a square root of a positive integer is not an integer, then it is an irrational number. The numbers $\sqrt{2}$, $\sqrt{15}$, and π are examples of irrational numbers. They can be expressed by decimals but *not* by decimals that either repeat or terminate. Examples of real numbers include

$$2, \quad -10, \quad 151\frac{1}{4}, \quad -131.37, \quad \frac{1}{3}, \quad -\sqrt{5}, \quad \text{and} \quad \sqrt{11}.$$

CALCULATOR HELP

To evaluate π and square roots, see the Appendix (page AP-1).

Any real number may be approximated by a terminating decimal. We use the symbol $\approx$, which means **approximately equal**, to denote an approximation. Each of the following real numbers has been approximated to three *decimal places*.

$$\pi \approx 3.142, \quad \frac{2}{3} \approx 0.667, \quad \sqrt{200} \approx 14.142$$

Figure 1.1 shows the relationships among the different sets of numbers. Note that each real number is either a rational number or an irrational number but not both. The natural numbers, whole numbers, and integers are contained in the set of rational numbers.

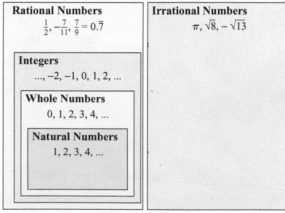

Figure 1.1 The Set of Real Numbers

EXAMPLE 3 Classifying numbers

Classify each real number as one or more of the following: a natural number, an integer, a rational number, or an irrational number.

$$5, \quad -1.2, \quad \frac{13}{7}, \quad -\sqrt{7}, \quad -12, \quad \sqrt{16}$$

Solution

Natural numbers: 5 and $\sqrt{16} = 4$

Integers: 5, -12, and $\sqrt{16} = 4$

Rational numbers: 5, $-1.2, \frac{13}{7}, -12$, and $\sqrt{16} = 4$

Irrational number: $-\sqrt{7}$ Now Try Exercise **21**

Even though a data set may contain only integers, decimals are often needed to describe it. One common way to do so is to find the **average**. To calculate the average of a set of numbers, we find their sum and divide by the number of numbers in the set.

EXAMPLE 4 Analyzing test scores

A student obtains the following test scores: 81, 96, 79, and 82.
(a) Find the student's average test score.
(b) Is this average a natural, a rational, or a real number?

Solution
(a) To find the average, we find the sum of the four test scores and then divide by 4:

$$\frac{81 + 96 + 79 + 82}{4} = \frac{338}{4} = 84.5.$$

(b) The average of these four test scores is both a rational number *and* a real number but is not a natural number.   Now Try Exercise **91**

CRITICAL THINKING

Is the sum of two irrational numbers ever a rational number? Explain.

Properties of Real Numbers

Several properties of real numbers are used in algebra. They are the identity properties, the commutative properties, the associative properties, and the distributive properties. These properties are essential to understand algebra. If a person does not know "the rules of the game," then it is very difficult to use algebra correctly to solve problems.

IDENTITY PROPERTIES   The **identity property of 0** states that, if 0 is added to any real number a, the result is a. The number 0 is called the **additive identity**. For example,

$$-3 + 0 = -3 \quad \text{and} \quad 0 + 18 = 18.$$

The **identity property of 1** states that, if any number a is multiplied by 1, the result is a. The number 1 is called the **multiplicative identity**. Examples include

$$-7 \cdot 1 = -7 \quad \text{and} \quad 1 \cdot 9 = 9.$$

We can summarize these results as follows.

IDENTITY PROPERTIES

For any real number a,

$$a + 0 = 0 + a = a$$

and

$$a \cdot 1 = 1 \cdot a = a.$$

COMMUTATIVE PROPERTIES   The **commutative property for addition** states that two numbers, a and b, can be added together in any order and the result is the same. That is, $a + b = b + a$. For example, if a person is paid \$5 and then \$7 or paid \$7 and then \$5, the result is the same. Either way the person is paid a total of

$$5 + 7 = 7 + 5 = \$12.$$

There is also a **commutative property for multiplication**. It states that two numbers, a and b, can be multiplied in any order and the result is the same. That is, $a \cdot b = b \cdot a$. For example, 3 groups of 5 people or 5 groups of 3 people both contain

$$3 \cdot 5 = 5 \cdot 3 = 15 \text{ people.}$$

We can summarize these results as follows.

COMMUTATIVE PROPERTIES

For any real numbers a and b,

$$a + b = b + a$$

and

$$a \cdot b = b \cdot a.$$

5 layers

4

3

Figure 1.2

ASSOCIATIVE PROPERTIES   The commutative properties allow us to interchange the order of two numbers when we add or multiply. The associative properties allow us to change how numbers are grouped. For example, we may add the numbers 3, 4, and 5 as follows.

$$(3 + 4) + 5 = 7 + 5 = 12$$
$$3 + (4 + 5) = 3 + 9 = 12$$

In either case we obtain the same answer, which is the result of the **associative property for addition**. Note that we did not change the order of the numbers; rather, we changed how the numbers were grouped. There is also an **associative property for multiplication**, which is illustrated as follows.

$$(3 \cdot 4) \cdot 5 = 12 \cdot 5 = 60$$
$$3 \cdot (4 \cdot 5) = 3 \cdot 20 = 60$$

3 layers

5

4

Figure 1.3

We can stack cubes as shown in Figures 1.2 and 1.3 to illustrate the associative property for multiplication. The stacks are shown with either 5 layers of 12 cubes or 3 layers of 20 cubes. In both cases there is a total of 60 cubes in the stack.

We can summarize these results as follows.

ASSOCIATIVE PROPERTIES

For any real numbers a, b, and c,

$$(a + b) + c = a + (b + c)$$

and

$$(a \cdot b) \cdot c = a \cdot (b \cdot c).$$

NOTE: Sometimes we omit the multiplication dot. Thus $a \cdot b = ab$ and $5 \cdot x = 5x$.

EXAMPLE **5**   Identifying properties of real numbers

State the property of real numbers that justifies each statement.
(a) $4 \cdot (3x) = (4 \cdot 3)x$ **(b)** $(1 \cdot 5) \cdot 4 = 5 \cdot 4$ **(c)** $5 + ab = ab + 5$

Solution
(a) This equation illustrates the associative property for multiplication, with the grouping of the numbers changed. That is, $4 \cdot (3x) = (4 \cdot 3)x = 12x$.
(b) This equation illustrates the identity property of 1 because $1 \cdot 5 = 5$.
(c) This equation illustrates the commutative property for addition; the order of the terms 5 and ab changed.
         Now Try Exercises **33, 35, 39**

DISTRIBUTIVE PROPERTIES   The **distributive properties** (see Figure 1.4) are used frequently in algebra to simplify expressions. An example of a distributive property is

$$3(6 + 5) = 3 \cdot 6 + 3 \cdot 5.$$

It is important to multiply the 3 by *both* the 6 and 5, not just the 6. This distributive property is valid when addition is replaced by subtraction. For example,

$$3(6 - 5) = 3 \cdot 6 - 3 \cdot 5.$$

We can summarize these results as follows.

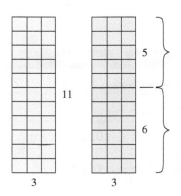

$3(11) = 3 \cdot 6 + 3 \cdot 5$

Figure 1.4

DISTRIBUTIVE PROPERTIES

For any real numbers a, b, and c,

$$a(b + c) = ab + ac$$

and

$$a(b - c) = ab - ac.$$

NOTE: Because multiplication is commutative, the distributive properties may be written as

$$(b + c)a = ba + ca \quad \text{and} \quad (b - c)a = ba - ca.$$

EXAMPLE **6**   Applying the distributive properties

Apply a distributive property to each expression.
(a) $5(4 + x)$ **(b)** $10 - (1 + a)$ **(c)** $9x - 5x$ **(d)** $5x + 2x - 3x$

Solution
(a) $5(4 + x) = 5 \cdot 4 + 5 \cdot x = 20 + 5x$
(b) $10 - (1 + a) = 10 - 1(1 + a) = 10 - (1 \cdot 1) - (1 \cdot a) = 9 - a$
(c) $9x - 5x = (9 - 5)x = 4x$
(d) Because each term contains an x, apply the distributive properties to all three terms:

$$5x + 2x - 3x = (5 + 2 - 3)x = 4x.$$ Now Try Exercises 63, 67, 75, 81

1.1 PUTTING IT ALL TOGETHER

Data and numbers play a central role in a diverse, technological society. Because of the variety of data, it has been necessary to develop different sets of numbers. Without numbers, data could be described qualitatively but not quantitatively. For example, we might say that the day seems hot, but we would not be able to give an actual number for the temperature. The following table summarizes some of the sets of numbers.

Concept	Comments	Examples
Natural Numbers	Are referred to as the *counting numbers*	$1, 2, 3, 4, 5, \ldots$
Whole Numbers	Include the natural numbers	$0, 1, 2, 3, 4, \ldots$
Integers	Include the natural numbers and the whole numbers	$\ldots, -2, -1, 0, 1, 2, \ldots$
Rational Numbers	Include integers and all fractions $\frac{p}{q}$, where p and q are integers (q is not equal to 0), and all repeating and terminating decimals	$\frac{1}{2}, -3, \frac{128}{6}, -0.335, 0,$ $0.25 = \frac{1}{4},$ and $0.\overline{3} = \frac{1}{3}$
Irrational Numbers	Include real numbers that cannot be expressed *exactly* by a fraction (rational number)	$-\pi, \sqrt{2},$ and $\sqrt{7}$
Real Numbers	Any number that can be expressed in decimal form, including the rational numbers and the irrational numbers	$\pi, \sqrt{3}, -\frac{4}{7}, 0, -10,$ $0.\overline{6} = \frac{2}{3}, 3,$ and $\sqrt{15}$

Real numbers have several important properties, which are summarized in the following table.

Property	Definition	Examples
Identity (0 and 1)	The identity for addition is 0 and the identity for multiplication is 1. For any real number a, $a + 0 = a$ and $a \cdot 1 = a$.	$5 + 0 = 5$ and $5 \cdot 1 = 5$
Commutative	For any real numbers a and b, $a + b = b + a$ and $a \cdot b = b \cdot a$.	$4 + 6 = 6 + 4$ and $4 \cdot 6 = 6 \cdot 4$
Associative	For any real numbers a, b, and c, $(a + b) + c = a + (b + c)$ and $(a \cdot b) \cdot c = a \cdot (b \cdot c)$.	$(3 + 4) + 5 = 3 + (4 + 5)$ and $(3 \cdot 4) \cdot 5 = 3 \cdot (4 \cdot 5)$
Distributive	For any real numbers a, b, and c, $a(b + c) = ab + ac$ and $a(b - c) = ab - ac$.	$5(x + 2) = 5x + 10,$ $5(x - 2) = 5x - 10,$ and $5x + 4x = (5 + 4)x = 9x$

 Exercises

 MyMathLab Math XL PRACTICE WATCH DOWNLOAD READ REVIEW

CONCEPTS

1. Which numbers are in the set of natural numbers and which are in the set of whole numbers?

2. Which numbers are in the set of integers? Give an example of an integer that is not a natural number.

3. Which numbers are in the set of rational numbers? Give an example.

4. Which numbers are in the set of real numbers? If a number is a real number but not a rational number, what type of number must it be? Give an example of a real number that is not a rational number.

5. Give an example of the commutative property for addition.

6. Give an example of the commutative property for multiplication.

7. Why is the number 1 called the multiplicative identity?

8. Why is the number 0 called the additive identity?

9. Give an example of the associative property for multiplication.

10. Give an example of a distributive property.

11. Earning $100 and then $50 is equivalent to earning $50 and then $100. What property of real numbers does this illustrate?

12. A marching band with 10 rows and 8 people in each row has the same number of members as a different marching band with 8 rows and 10 people in each row. What property of real numbers does this illustrate?

CLASSIFYING NUMBERS

Exercises 13–20: Classify the number as one or more of the following: natural number, integer, rational number, or real number.

13. 26,461 (Number of Subway franchises in 2006)

14. 3.8 (Percent of mathematics majors who go on to obtain a Ph.D.)

15. $\frac{89}{3687}$ (Fraction of 18- to 19-year-old males who are married in the U.S.)

16. 4 (Pounds of garbage the average person produces each day)

17. 7.5 (Average number of gallons of water a person uses each minute while taking a shower)

18. 2.57 (Average number of people per household in 2003)

19. $90\sqrt{2}$ (Distance in feet from home plate to second base in baseball)

20. −71 (Wind chill when the temperature is −30°F and the wind speed is 40 miles per hour)

Exercises 21–26: Classify each real number as one or more of the following: natural number, whole number, integer, rational number, or irrational number.

21. $-5, 6, \frac{1}{7}, \sqrt{7}, 0.2$ **22.** $-3, \frac{2}{9}, \sqrt{9}, -1.37$

23. $\frac{3}{1}, -\frac{5}{8}, \sqrt{5}, 0.\overline{45}, \pi$ **24.** $0, \frac{50}{10}, -\frac{23}{27}, 0.\overline{6}, -\sqrt{3}$

25. $-2, \frac{1}{2}, \sqrt{9}, 0.\overline{26}$ **26.** $\sqrt{4}, \sqrt{6}, \frac{4}{2}, 0.26$

Exercises 27–32: For the measured quantity, state the set of numbers that is most appropriate to describe it. Choose from the natural numbers, integers, or rational numbers. Explain your answer.

27. Shoe sizes   **28.** Populations of states

29. Gallons of gasoline   **30.** Speed limits

31. Temperatures given in a winter weather forecast in Montana

32. Number of compact discs sold

PROPERTIES OF REAL NUMBERS

Exercises 33–46: State whether the equation is the result of an identity, a commutative, an associative, or a distributive property.

33. $b + 0 = b$ **34.** $1 \cdot 5 = 5$

35. $4 + a = a + 4$

36. $(5 + 1) + 8 = 5 + (1 + 8)$

37. $8(9x - 3) = 8 \cdot 9x - 8 \cdot 3$

38. $4(3 + 5a) = 4 \cdot 3 + 4 \cdot 5a$

39. $4 \cdot (10 \cdot 6) = (4 \cdot 10) \cdot 6$

40. $x \cdot 5 = 5x$

41. $3 \cdot (6 \cdot 2) = (6 \cdot 2) \cdot 3$

42. $bac = abc$

43. $4(x - 3) = (x - 3)4$

44. $4 \cdot (5x) = 20x$

45. $5(x - 3) - 2(x - 3) = 3(x - 3)$

46. $4 - (a - b) = 4 - a + b$

Exercises 47–54: Use a commutative property to write an equivalent expression.

47. $4 + a$ **48.** ba

49. $a \cdot \frac{1}{3}$ **50.** $100 + x$

51. $1 + x$ **52.** $b \cdot 5$

53. yx **54.** $b + a$

Exercises 55–62: Use an associative property to write an equivalent expression.

55. $4 + (5 + b)$ **56.** $(x + 2) + 3$

57. $5(10x)$ **58.** $(a \cdot 5) \cdot 4$

59. $(x + y) + z$ **60.** $-3(4x)$

61. $(x \cdot 3)4$ **62.** $(a + 6) + 5$

Exercises 63–84: Use a distributive property to write an equivalent expression.

63. $4(x + y)$ **64.** $-3(a + 5)$

65. $(x - 7)5$ **66.** $(11 + b)a$

67. $-(x + 1)$ **68.** $-(a - 2)$

69. $ax - ay$ **70.** $4a + 4b$

71. $12 + 3x$ **72.** $2 - 4x$

73. $3x + 7x$ **74.** $\frac{1}{2}z + \frac{3}{2}z$

75. $8t - 2t$ **76.** $y - \frac{2}{3}y$

77. $x - \frac{3}{4}x$ **78.** $13r - 6r$

79. $3 - (1 - 2z)$ **80.** $5 - (1 - 4y)$

81. $3z + 4z + z$ **82.** $5z + 4z + 2z$

83. $10t - t - 4t$ **84.** $20t - 2t - t$

Exercises 85–90: Use a distributive property to evaluate the expression two different ways.

85. $7(11 - 3)$ **86.** $(5 + 9)12$

87. $13(16 + 23)$ **88.** $4(12 - 8)$

89. $5(19 - 7)$ **90.** $(8 + 12)9$

Exercises 91–96: Calculate the average of the list of numbers. Classify the result as a natural number, an integer, or a rational number.

91. $3, 4, 5, 8$ **92.** $5, 8, 10, 23, 9$

93. $45, 33, 52$

94. $3.2, 7.5, 8.1, 12.8, 13.4$

95. $121.5, 45.7, 99.3, 45.9$

96. $99.88, 39.11, 85.67, 23.86, 19.11$

Exercises 97–104: Use properties of real numbers to evaluate the expression mentally.

97. $8 + 3 + 2 + 7$ **98.** $52 + 103 + 48 + 97$

99. $\frac{2}{9} \cdot 8 \cdot 9 \cdot \frac{3}{8}$ **100.** $\frac{1}{2} \cdot \frac{1}{3} \cdot \frac{1}{4} \cdot 2 \cdot 3 \cdot 4$

101. $4 \cdot 16 - 4 \cdot 6$ **102.** $7 \cdot 12 + 7 \cdot 3 + 7 \cdot 5$

103. $\frac{4}{5}\left(\frac{5}{2} + 5 + \frac{15}{4}\right)$

104. $37 - 19 + 63 - 31$

105. Thinking Generally The fraction $\frac{ab}{ac}$ can be simplified as follows:
$$\frac{ab}{ac} = \frac{a}{a} \cdot \frac{b}{c} = \frac{b}{c}.$$
Give a property of real numbers used in this simplification.

106. Thinking Generally Is the product of two irrational numbers always an irrational number? Explain.

APPLICATIONS

107. *iPods* Would eight 4 GB iPods store more songs than four 8 GB iPods? Explain the property of real numbers that your calculation illustrates.

108. *Digital Images* If an image downloaded from the Internet is 240 pixels across by 360 pixels high and a different image is 360 pixels across by 240 pixels high, how do the total numbers of pixels in the images compare? What property of real numbers does this result illustrate?

109. *Higher Education* The following table lists the total higher education enrollment for selected years.

Year	1998	2000	2003	2005
Students (millions)	14.5	15.4	16.3	16.5

Source: Department of Education.

(a) What was the enrollment in 2003?
(b) Mentally estimate the average enrollment for this 4-year period.
(c) Calculate the average enrollment. Is your estimate from part (b) in reasonable agreement with your calculated result?

110. *Federal Budget* The following table lists the spending by the federal government for selected years.

Year	2001	2002	2003	2004	2005
Budget ($ trillions)	1.9	2.0	2.2	2.3	2.5

Source: Office of Management and Budget.

(a) What was the budget in 2003?
(b) Mentally estimate the average budget for this 5-year period.
(c) Calculate the average budget. Is your estimate from part (b) in reasonable agreement with your calculated result?

111. *Circumference* The circumference C of a circle is given by $C = 2\pi r$, where r is the radius of the circle. State if the formula is valid for calculating C.
(a) $C = 2r\pi$
(b) $C = 2(\pi r)$
(c) $C = 2\pi + 2r$

112. *Geometry*   The area A of a rectangle equals the product of its length L and width W. What property states that either formula, $A = LW$ or $A = WL$, is correct?

W

L

113. Is subtraction either commutative or associative? Explain, using examples.

114. Is division either commutative or associative? Explain, using examples.

GROUP ACTIVITY
WORKING WITH REAL DATA

Directions: Form a group of 2 to 4 people. Select someone to record the group's responses for this activity. All members of the group should work cooperatively to answer the questions. If your instructor asks for your results, each member of the group should be prepared to respond.

1. *New Windchill Factor*   Before November 1, 2001, the windchill factor was based on wind speeds taken 33 feet above ground level. Today wind speeds are measured 5 feet above the ground, which corresponds to the typical height of a person's face. The following table lists the current windchill factor for different wind speeds when the temperature is 0°F.

Windchill Temperatures at 0°F

Wind Speed (mph)	0	5	10	15
Windchill (°F)	0	−11	−16	−19

Wind Speed (mph)	20	25	30
Windchill (°F)	−22	−24	−26

Source: National Weather Service.

(a) Find the windchill factor when the wind speed is 20 miles per hour and the temperature is 0°F.
(b) For each 5-mile-per-hour increase in the wind speed, does the windchill factor decrease by the same amount? Explain.
(c) Estimate the windchill factor when the wind speed is 40 miles per hour. Explain your reasoning.
(d) Look up the true value for part (c) on the Internet.

2. *New Windchill Factor*   The following table lists the current windchill factor for different temperatures when the wind speed is 15 miles per hour.

Windchill Temperatures with a 15-mph Wind

Temperature (°F)	−30	−20	−10	0
Windchill (°F)	−58	−45	−32	−19

Temperature (°F)	10	20	30
Windchill (°F)	−7	6	19

Source: National Weather Service.

(a) Find the windchill factor when the temperature is −20°F and the wind speed is 15 miles per hour.
(b) Is the windchill factor always a fixed number of degrees less than the actual temperature? Explain.
(c) Estimate the windchill factor when the temperature is −40°F. Explain your reasoning.
(d) Look up the true value for part (c) on the Internet.

1.2 OPERATIONS ON REAL NUMBERS

The Real Number Line ▪ Arithmetic Operations ▪ Data and Number Sense

A LOOK INTO MATH ▷ Real numbers are used to describe data. To obtain information from data we frequently perform operations on real numbers. For example, exams are often assigned a score between 0 and 100. This step reduces each exam to a number or *data point*. We might obtain more information about the exams by calculating the average score. To do so we perform the arithmetic operations of addition and division.

In this section we discuss operations on real numbers and provide examples of where these computations occur in real life.

Figure 1.5 The Number Line

The Real Number Line

You can visualize the real number system by using a number line, as shown in Figure 1.5. Each real number corresponds to a point on the number line. The point associated with the real number 0 is called the **origin**.

If a real number a is located to the left of a real number b on the number line, we say that a is **less than** b and write $a < b$. Similarly, if a real number a is located to the right of a real number b, we say that a is **greater than** b and write $a > b$. Thus $-3 < 2$ because -3 is located to the left of 2, and $2 > -3$ because 2 is located to the right of -3. If $a > 0$, then a is a **positive number**, and if $a < 0$, then a is a **negative number**.

Figure 1.6

The **absolute value** of a real number a, written $|a|$, is equal to its distance from the origin on the number line. Distance may be either a positive number or zero, but it cannot be a negative number. As the points corresponding to 2 and -2 are both 2 units from the origin, $|2| = 2$ and $|-2| = 2$, as shown in Figure 1.6. The absolute value of a real number is *never* negative.

EXAMPLE **1**   Finding the absolute value of a real number

Find the absolute value of each real number.
(a) 9.12   **(b)** $-\frac{3}{4}$ **(c)** $-\pi$
(d) $-a$, if a is a positive number
(e) a, if a is a negative number

Solution
(a) $|9.12| = 9.12$ **(b)** $\left|-\frac{3}{4}\right| = \frac{3}{4}$
(c) $|-\pi| = \pi$ because $\pi \approx 3.14$ is a positive number.
(d) If a is positive, $-a$ is negative and $|-a| = a$.
(e) If a is negative, $-a$ is positive. Thus $a < 0$ implies that $|a| = -a$. For example, if we let $a = -5$, then $|-5| = -(-5) = 5$.   Now Try Exercises **17, 21**

The absolute value of a number can be defined as follows.

$$|a| = a \qquad \text{if } a > 0 \text{ or } a = 0, \text{ and}$$
$$|a| = -a \qquad \text{if } a < 0.$$

Arithmetic Operations

The four arithmetic operations are addition, subtraction, multiplication, and division.

Addends
$\overbrace{3 + 5} = 8$
           $\searrow$
              Sum

ADDITION AND SUBTRACTION OF REAL NUMBERS   In an addition problem, the two numbers added are called **addends**, and the answer is called the **sum**. In the addition problem $3 + 5 = 8$, the numbers 3 and 5 are the addends and 8 is the sum.

The **additive inverse** or **opposite** of a real number a is $-a$. For example, the additive inverse of 5 is -5 and the additive inverse of -1.6 is $-(-1.6)$, or 1.6. When we add opposites, the result is 0. That is, $a + (-a) = 0$ for every real number a.

EXAMPLE 2   Finding additive inverses

Find the additive inverse or opposite of each number or expression. Then find the sum of the number or expression and its opposite.

(a) 10,961   (b) π (c) $-\dfrac{3}{4}$ (d) $6x - 2$

Solution
(a) The opposite of 10,961 is $-10,961$. Their sum is $10,961 + (-10,961) = 0$.
(b) The opposite of π is $-\pi$. Their sum is $\pi + (-\pi) = 0$.
(c) The opposite of $-\frac{3}{4}$ is $\frac{3}{4}$. Their sum is $-\frac{3}{4} + \frac{3}{4} = 0$.
(d) The opposite of $6x - 2$ is $-(6x - 2) = -6x + 2$. Their sum is

$$6x - 2 + (-6x) + 2 = 6x + (-6x) - 2 + 2 = 0.$$

Now Try Exercises 31, 37

▶ REAL-WORLD CONNECTION   When you add real numbers, it may be helpful to think of money. A positive number represents being paid an amount of money, whereas a negative number indicates a debt owed. The sum

$$8 + (-6) = 2$$

would represent being paid \$8 and owing \$6, resulting in \$2 being left over. Similarly,

$$-7 + (-5) = -12$$

would represent owing \$7 and owing \$5, resulting in a debt of \$12.
To add two real numbers we may use the following rules.

ADDITION OF REAL NUMBERS

To add two numbers that are either *both positive* or *both negative*, add their absolute values. Their sum has the same sign as the two numbers.

To add two numbers with *opposite signs*, find the absolute value of each number. Subtract the smaller absolute value from the larger. The sum has the same sign as the number with the larger absolute value. The sum of two opposites is 0.

The next example illustrates addition of real numbers.

EXAMPLE 3   Adding real numbers

Evaluate each expression.
(a) $-3 + (-5)$ **(b)** $-4 + 7$ **(c)** $8.4 + (-9.5)$

Solution
(a) The addends are both negative, so we add the absolute values $|-3|$ and $|-5|$ to obtain 8. As the signs of the addends are both negative, the sum has the same sign and equals -8. That is, $-3 + (-5) = -8$. If we owe \$3 and then owe an additional \$5, the total amount owed is \$8.

(b) The addends have opposite signs, so we subtract their absolute values to obtain 3. The sum is positive because $|7|$ is greater than $|-4|$. That is, $-4 + 7 = 3$. If we owe \$4 and are paid \$7, the result is that we have \$3 to keep.

(c) $8.4 + (-9.5) = -1.1$ because $|-9.5|$ is 1.1 more than $|8.4|$. If we are paid \$8.40 and owe \$9.50, we still owe \$1.10.   Now Try Exercises 55, 57

Addition of positive and negative numbers occurs at banks if deposits are represented by positive numbers and withdrawals are represented by negative numbers.

EXAMPLE 4   Balancing a checking account

The initial balance in a checking account is \$157. Find the final balance if the following represents a list of withdrawals and deposits: -55, -19, 123, -98.

Solution
We find the sum.

$$157 + (-55) + (-19) + 123 + (-98) = 102 + (-19) + 123 + (-98)$$
$$= 83 + 123 + (-98)$$
$$= 206 + (-98)$$
$$= 108$$

```
┌─────────────────────┐
│ 157+(-55)+(-19)+     │
│ 123+(-98)           │
│                 108 │
│ 157-55-19+123-98    │
│                 108 │
└─────────────────────┘
```

Figure 1.7

The final balance is \$108. This result may be supported by evaluating the expression with a calculator. See Figure 1.7, where the sum has been calculated two different ways. Instead of adding the opposite of a number, we can also subtract.   Now Try Exercise 61

$$8 - 5 = \underset{\text{Difference}}{3}$$

The answer to a subtraction problem is called the **difference**. When you're subtracting two real numbers, it sometimes helps to change the subtraction problem to an addition problem.

TECHNOLOGY NOTE:
Subtraction and Negation

On graphing calculators, two different keys typically represent subtraction and negation. In the first calculation in Figure 1.7, we used the negation key, and in the second calculation, we used the subtraction key.

SUBTRACTION OF REAL NUMBERS

For any real numbers a and b,

$$a - b = a + (-b).$$

To subtract b from a, add a and the opposite of b.

EXAMPLE 5   Subtracting real numbers

Evaluate each expression.

(a) $-12 - 7$ **(b)** $-5.1 - (-10.6)$ **(c)** $\dfrac{1}{2} - \left(-\dfrac{2}{3}\right)$ **(d)** $3t - 7t$

Solution

(a) $-12 - 7 = -12 + (-7) = -19$

(b) $-5.1 - (-10.6) = -5.1 + 10.6 = 5.5$

(c) $\dfrac{1}{2} - \left(-\dfrac{2}{3}\right) = \dfrac{1}{2} + \dfrac{2}{3} = \dfrac{3}{6} + \dfrac{4}{6} = \dfrac{7}{6}$

(d) $3t - 7t = (3 - 7)t = -4t$

Now Try Exercises 58, 59, 81

MULTIPLICATION AND DIVISION OF REAL NUMBERS In a multiplication problem, the two numbers multiplied are called the **factors**, and the answer is called the **product**. In the problem $3 \cdot 5 = 15$, the numbers 3 and 5 are factors and 15 is the product. The **multiplicative inverse** or **reciprocal** of a nonzero number a is $\frac{1}{a}$. The product of a nonzero number a and its reciprocal is $a \cdot \frac{1}{a} = 1$. For example, the reciprocal of -5 is $-\frac{1}{5}$ because $-5 \cdot -\frac{1}{5} = 1$, and the reciprocal of $\frac{2}{3}$ is $\frac{3}{2}$ because $\frac{2}{3} \cdot \frac{3}{2} = 1$. To multiply positive or negative numbers we may use the following rules.

Factors
$\overbrace{3 \cdot 5} = 15$
    Product

MULTIPLICATION OF REAL NUMBERS

The product of two numbers with *like* signs is positive. The product of two numbers with *unlike* signs is negative.

EXAMPLE 6 Multiplying real numbers

Evaluate each expression.

(a) $-11 \cdot 8$ (b) $\dfrac{3}{5} \cdot \dfrac{4}{7}$ (c) $-1.2(-10)$ (d) $(1.2)(5)(-7)$

Solution

(a) The product is negative because the factors -11 and 8 have unlike signs. Thus the product is $-11 \cdot 8 = -88$.

(b) The product is positive because both factors are positive. Thus $\frac{3}{5} \cdot \frac{4}{7} = \frac{3 \cdot 4}{5 \cdot 7} = \frac{12}{35}$.

(c) As both factors are negative, the product is positive. Thus $-1.2(-10) = 12$.

(d) $(1.2)(5)(-7) = (6)(-7) = -42$

Now Try Exercises 63, 65, 77

In the division problem $20 \div 4 = 5$, the number 20 is the **dividend**, 4 is the **divisor**, and 5 is the **quotient**. This division problem can also be written as $\frac{20}{4} = 5$. Division of real numbers can be defined in terms of multiplication and reciprocals.

Divisor
$20 \div 4 = 5$
Dividend Quotient

DIVISION OF REAL NUMBERS

For real numbers a and b, with $b \neq 0$,

$$\frac{a}{b} = a \cdot \frac{1}{b}.$$

That is, to divide a by b, multiply a by the reciprocal of b.

The expression $b \neq 0$ is read "b **not equal to** 0." Note that division by 0 is always *undefined*. For example, suppose that we try to define $12 \div 0$ to be equal to some number k. Then $\frac{12}{0} = k$ and k must satisfy $0 \cdot k = 12$ because a division problem can be checked by using multiplication. (For example, $\frac{12}{3} = 4$, so $3 \cdot 4 = 12$.) But the product of 0 and any number k is 0, not 12. Thus there is no reasonable value for k, so division by 0 is undefined.

NOTE: The quotient of two numbers with *like* signs is positive, and the quotient of two numbers with *unlike* signs is negative.

EXAMPLE 7   Dividing real numbers

Evaluate each expression.

(a) $-12 \div \frac{1}{2}$ (b) $\dfrac{\frac{2}{3}}{-7}$ (c) $\dfrac{-4}{-24}$ (d) $6 \div 0$

Solution

(a) $-12 \div \frac{1}{2} = -12 \cdot \frac{2}{1} = -24$

(b) $\dfrac{\frac{2}{3}}{-7} = \frac{2}{3} \div (-7) = \frac{2}{3} \cdot \left(-\frac{1}{7}\right) = -\frac{2}{21}$

(c) $\dfrac{-4}{-24} = -4 \cdot \left(-\frac{1}{24}\right) = \frac{4}{24} = \frac{1}{6}$

(d) $6 \div 0$ is undefined because division by 0 is not possible.   Now Try Exercises 67, 75

Many calculators have the capability to perform arithmetic on fractions and express the answer as either a decimal or a fraction. The next example illustrates this capability.

EXAMPLE 8   Performing arithmetic operations with technology

Use a calculator to evaluate each expression as a decimal and as a fraction.

(a) $\frac{1}{3} + \frac{2}{5} - \frac{4}{9}$ (b) $\left(\frac{4}{9} \cdot \frac{3}{8}\right) \div \frac{2}{3}$

Solution

(a) From Figure 1.8,

$$\frac{1}{3} + \frac{2}{5} - \frac{4}{9} = 0.2\overline{8}, \quad \text{or} \quad \frac{13}{45}.$$

In Figure 1.8, the second calculation uses the "Frac" feature. This feature displays the answer as a fraction, rather than a decimal.

NOTE: Generally it is a good idea to put parentheses around fractions when you are using a calculator.

(b) From Figure 1.9, $\left(\frac{4}{9} \cdot \frac{3}{8}\right) \div \frac{2}{3} = 0.25$, or $\frac{1}{4}$.

```
(1/3)+(2/5)-(4/9
)
          .2888888889
(1/3)+(2/5)-(4/9
)▶Frac
              13/45
```
Figure 1.8

```
((4/9)*(3/8))/(2
/3)
             .25
((4/9)*(3/8))/(2
/3)▶Frac
             1/4
```
Figure 1.9

CALCULATOR HELP

To express answers as fractions, see the Appendix (page AP-2).

Now Try Exercises 87, 89

Data and Number Sense

In everyday life we commonly make approximations involving a variety of data. To make estimations we often use arithmetic operations on real numbers.

EXAMPLE **Developing number sense**

A rectangular birthday cake serves exactly 24 pieces of cake. Suppose that a similar cake is twice as wide and twice as long. How many pieces does the second cake serve?

Solution

Let L be the length and W be the width of the first cake. Then the area of this rectangular cake is $A = LW$. The length of the second cake is $2L$ and the width is $2W$. The area of this cake is $A = 2L \cdot 2W = 4LW$, or four times the area of the first cake. Thus, the second cake can serve $4 \cdot 24 = 96$ pieces of cake.   Now Try Exercise 111

EXAMPLE 10 **Determining a reasonable answer**

It is 2823 miles from New York to Los Angeles. Determine mentally which of the following would best estimate the number of hours of driving time required to travel this distance in a car: 50, 100, or 120 hours.

Solution

Speed equals distance divided by time. Dividing by 100 is easy, so start by dividing 100 hours into 2800 miles. The average speed would be $\frac{2800}{100} = 28$ miles per hour, which is too slow for most drivers. A more reasonable choice is 50 hours because then the average speed would be double, or about 56 miles per hour.   Now Try Exercise 115

EXAMPLE 11 **Estimating a numeric value**

Table 1.3 lists the number of subscribers of cellular telephones in selected years. Estimate the number of subscribers in 2005.

TABLE 1.3   Cellular Phone Subscribers

Year	2001	2002	2003	2004	2005
Subscribers (millions)	128	141	159	182	?

Source: Cellular Telecommunications Industry Association.

Solution

The data show that the number of subscribers has had annual increases of 13, 18, and 23 million from 2001 to 2004. Note that in each successive year the increase is 5 million more than the previous year. That is, $13 + 5 = 18$ and $18 + 5 = 23$. Following this pattern, we might expect there to be $23 + 5 = 28$ million more subscribers in 2005 than in 2004. Thus, one estimate is that there were $182 + 28 = 210$ million cell phone subscribers in 2005. Other estimates are possible.   Now Try Exercise 119

1.2 PUTTING IT ALL TOGETHER

The following table summarizes some of the information presented in this section.

Operation	Definition	Examples
Absolute Value of a Real Number	For any real number a, $|a| = a$ if $a > 0$ or $a = 0$, and $|a| = -a$ if $a < 0$.	$|-5| = 5$, $|3.7| = 3.7$, and $|-4 + 4| = 0$
Additive Inverse (Opposite)	The opposite of a is $-a$.	4 and -4 are opposites. -5 and $-(-5) = 5$ are opposites.
Addition of Real Numbers	See the highlighted box: Addition of Real Numbers on page 14.	$3 + (-6) = -3$, $-2 + (-10) = -12$, $-1 + 3 = 2$, and $18 + 11 = 29$
Subtraction of Real Numbers	We can transform a subtraction problem into an addition problem: $a - b = a + (-b)$.	$4 - 6 = 4 + (-6) = -2$, $-7 - (-8) = -7 + 8 = 1$, $-8 - 5 = -8 + (-5) = -13$, and $9 - (-1) = 9 + 1 = 10$
Multiplication of Real Numbers	The product of two numbers with *like* signs is positive. The product of two numbers with *unlike* signs is negative.	$3 \cdot 5 = 15$, $-4(-7) = 28$, $-8 \cdot 7 = -56$, and $5(-11) = -55$
Division of Real Numbers	For real numbers a and b with $b \neq 0$, $$\frac{a}{b} = a \cdot \frac{1}{b}.$$	$-3 \div \frac{3}{4} = -3 \cdot \frac{4}{3} = -4$ and $\frac{5}{2} \div \left(-\frac{7}{4}\right) = \frac{5}{2}\left(-\frac{4}{7}\right) = -\frac{20}{14} = -\frac{10}{7}$

1.2 Exercises

CONCEPTS

1. If $a > b$, then a is located to the _____ of b on the number line.

2. If $a < 0$, then a is located to the _____ of the origin on the number line.

3. The product of two negative numbers is a _____ number.

4. The sum of two negative numbers is a _____ number.

5. The quotient of a positive number and a negative number is a _____ number.

6. If $a < 0$ and $b > 0$, then the difference $a - b$ is a _____ number.

7. The additive inverse of a is _____.

8. The multiplicative inverse, or reciprocal, of $\frac{a}{b}$ is _____ for $a \neq 0$.

9. If $a < 0$ and $b < 0$, then $\frac{a}{b}$ is a _____ number.

10. The opposite of $a + b$ is _____.

THE REAL NUMBER LINE AND ABSOLUTE VALUE

Exercises 11–16: Plot each number on a number line. Be sure to include an appropriate scale.

11. $0, 4, -3, 1.5$

12. $10, 20, -5, -15$

13. $100, 300, -200, 50$

14. $-0.4, 0.2, 0.5, -0.1, 0$

15. $-\frac{3}{2}, \pi, \frac{1}{3}, 2$

16. $-2, -\frac{1}{2}, 1, \frac{7}{3}$

Exercises 17–24: Evaluate the absolute value.

17. $|-6.1|$

18. $|17|$

19. $|8 - 11|$

20. $|2 \cdot 8 - 23|$

21. $|x|$, where $x > 0$

22. $|x|$, where $x < 0$

23. $|x - y|$, where $x > 0$ and $y < 0$

24. $|x + y|$, where $x < 0$ and $y < 0$

Exercises 25–30: State whether only positive numbers are typically used to measure the given quantity or whether both positive and negative numbers are used. Explain your reasoning.

25. Area

26. Distance

27. Temperature

28. A person's net worth

29. Gas mileage of a car

30. Elevation relative to sea level

ARITHMETIC OPERATIONS

Exercises 31–42: Find the additive inverse, or opposite, of the number or expression.

31. 56

32. $-\frac{5}{7}$

33. -6.9

34. 12.8

35. $-\pi + 2$

36. $a + b$

37. $a - b$

38. $-x + 3$

39. $-(x - y)$

40. $-1 - x$

41. $z - (2 - z)$

42. $2z - (1 + 2z)$

Exercises 43–54: Find the multiplicative inverse, or reciprocal, of the number or expression.

43. 3

44. $\frac{3}{8}$

45. $-\frac{2}{3}$

46. 1.5

47. π

48. $-\frac{x}{y}$

49. $a + 3$

50. $x - 1$

51. $-\frac{2a}{b}$

52. $-\frac{2b}{3a}$

53. $\frac{1}{x - 7}$

54. $\frac{3}{x + y}$

Exercises 55–84: Perform the following arithmetic operations and simplify.

55. $4 + (-6)$

56. $-10 + 14$

57. $-7.4 + (-9.2)$

58. $-8.4 - 10.3$

59. $-\frac{3}{4} - \left(-\frac{1}{4}\right)$

60. $\frac{1}{5} - \left(-\frac{3}{10}\right)$

61. $-9 + 1 + (-2) + 5$

62. $-5 + 7 - (-2) + 3$

63. $-6 \cdot -12$

64. $-(8 \cdot -4)$

65. $-\frac{1}{2} \cdot \frac{5}{7} \cdot \frac{1}{3}$

66. $-\frac{6}{7} \cdot -\frac{5}{3}$

67. $-\frac{1}{2} \div -\frac{3}{4}$

68. $-5 \div \frac{4}{5}$

69. $\frac{3}{4} \div (-2)$

70. $-\frac{4}{5} \div \frac{7}{10}$

71. $-\frac{8}{2}$

72. $-\frac{45}{9}$

73. $-25 \div -5$

74. $8 \div 0$

75. $\frac{1}{0}$

76. $\frac{0}{7}$

77. $-4 \cdot 7 \cdot (-5)$

78. $-2 \cdot -6 \cdot 6 \cdot -1$

79. $6 \cdot \frac{2}{3} \cdot 3 \cdot \left(-\frac{1}{6}\right)$

80. $\left(\frac{4}{5} \cdot \frac{5}{8}\right) \div \frac{1}{2}$

81. $4x - 9x$

82. $\frac{1}{2}x - \frac{3}{4}x$

83. $z - 4z + 2z$

84. $5z - 3z - 6z$

Exercises 85–92: Evaluate the expression.

85. $-23.1 + 45.7 + (+34.6)$

86. $102 - (-341) + (-112)$

87. $\frac{1}{2} + \frac{2}{3} - \frac{5}{7}$

88. $-\frac{8}{13} + \frac{1}{2} - \frac{2}{5}$

89. $-\frac{3}{4} \cdot \frac{4}{5} \div \frac{5}{3}$

90. $\left(\frac{3}{4} \div (-11)\right) - \frac{2}{5}$

91. $\frac{1}{2}\left(\frac{4}{11} + \frac{2}{5}\right)$

92. $-\frac{5}{13} + \left(\frac{3}{5} \div \frac{2}{17}\right)$

DATA AND NUMBER SENSE

Exercises 93–100: Mentally estimate the average of the list of numbers. Check your estimate.

93. 9, 5, 15, −9

94. 12, 8, 27, −7

95. −2, 12, 7, −17

96. 45, 55, 65, 35

97. 101, 99, −42, 82

98. −4, 2, 5, −8, 5, 24

99. Thinking Generally a, b, a, b, a, b

100. Thinking Generally $a, 2a, 3a, 4a, 5a$

Exercises 101–110: Mentally evaluate the expression.

101. $-2 + 8 + 3 + 2 - 11$

102. $-22 + 43 - 78 + 7$

103. $103 - 44 + 97 - 56$

104. $10 + 11 + 12 - 11 - 11 - 11$

105. $\frac{1}{5} \cdot \frac{2}{3} \cdot \frac{1}{7} \cdot \frac{1}{9} \cdot 5 \cdot \frac{3}{2} \cdot 7 \cdot 9$

106. $\frac{1}{2} \cdot \frac{1}{3} \cdot \frac{1}{4} \cdot (-4) \cdot (-3) \cdot (-2)$

107. $\left(\frac{1}{2} - \frac{1}{3}\right) + \left(\frac{1}{3} - \frac{1}{4}\right) + \left(\frac{1}{4} - \frac{1}{5}\right) + \left(\frac{1}{5} - \frac{1}{6}\right)$

108. $\frac{1}{2} \div \frac{1}{3} \cdot \frac{1}{3} \div \frac{1}{4} \cdot \frac{1}{4} \div \frac{1}{5} \cdot \frac{1}{5}$

109. Thinking Generally $a \cdot b \cdot c \cdot \frac{1}{a} \cdot \frac{1}{b} \cdot \frac{1}{c}$

110. Thinking Generally $b - a(b + c) + ab + ac$

APPLICATIONS

111. *Storage in a Box* A rectangular box contains 200 cubic inches. If a similar box has the same height but double the length and triple the width, how many cubic inches does this box contain? (*Hint:* Volume = Length × Width × Height.)

112. *Water in a Lake* A lake covers 400 acres, has an average depth of 20 feet, and contains 350 million cubic feet of water. Estimate how many cubic feet of water there are in a lake that covers 200 acres and has an average depth of 10 feet.

113. *Filling a Pool* A hose fills a rectangular swimming pool in 2 days. Suppose that a similar swimming pool has the same average depth but is four times longer and two times wider. How long will it take to fill this swimming pool?

114. *Fudge in a Pan* A single batch of fudge fills a circular pan as illustrated in the figure. How many batches of fudge are needed to fill a similar pan that has twice the diameter? (*Hint:* $A = \pi r^2$.)

115. *Buying a Computer* An advertisement for a computer states that it costs $202 down and $98.99 per month for 24 months. Mentally estimate which of the following represents the cost of the computer if it is purchased under these terms: $2600, $3200, or $3800. Explain your reasoning. Find the actual cost.

116. *Leasing a Car* To lease a car costs $1497 down and $249 per month for 36 months. Mentally estimate the cost of the lease. Find the actual cost.

117. *Cybercrimes* The number of reported hacking incidents for U.S. business computer systems has risen dramatically. The following table lists reported hacking incidents.

Year	1998	1999	2000	2001	2002
Rate	3734	9859	21,756	52,658	82,094

Source: Carnegie Mellon University.

(a) Has the number of hacking incidents increased by a fixed number each year? Explain.

(b) What was the average number of hacking incidents over this 5-year period?

(c) If current trends continue, estimate the number of hacking incidents for 2003. Then discuss any difficulties that you may have encountered in making this estimate.

118. *Cigarette Consumption* Although smoking in the United States has declined since 1980, it has continued to grow globally. The table on the next page lists the global cigarette consumption.

Year	1950	1960	1970	1980	1990	2000
Cigarettes (trillions)	1.7	2.2	3.1	4.4	5.4	5.5

Source: Department of Agriculture.

(a) In 1960 the world population was 3 billion people. How many cigarettes were consumed per person?

(b) In 2000 the world population was 6 billion people. How many cigarettes were consumed per person?

(c) Estimate cigarette consumption in 1985. Explain your reasoning.

(d) Is cigarette consumption likely to increase or decrease between 2000 and 2010? Explain your reasoning.

119. *Cable Modems*   Cable modems provided by the cable TV industry give high-speed access to the Internet. The following table lists the number of cable modem subscribers for selected years.

Year	2005	2006	2007	2008
Subscribers (millions)	15.1	17.3	19.5	21.7

Source: Federal Communications Commission.

(a) Discuss any trends in cable modem subscribers from 2005 through 2008.

(b) Estimate the number of subscribers in 2010. Explain your reasoning.

120. *Digital Subscriber Lines*   Local phone companies provide digital subscriber lines (DSL) for high-speed Internet access. This technology competes directly with cable modem service provided by cable TV companies. The following table lists the number of digital subscriber lines for selected years.

Year	2005	2006	2007	2008
DSL users (millions)	19.7	22.0	23.7	25.0

Source: Federal Communications Commission.

(a) Discuss any trends in DSL from 2005 through 2008.

(b) Estimate the number of subscribers in 2010. Explain your reasoning.

WRITING ABOUT MATHEMATICS

121. Suppose that $a \neq b$. Explain how a number line can be used to determine whether a is greater than b or whether a is less than b. Give examples.

122. Explain why a positive number times a negative number is a negative number.

CHECKING BASIC CONCEPTS
SECTIONS 1.1 AND 1.2

1. Identify each number as one or more of the following: a natural number, an integer, a rational number, or a real number.
   (a) -9 (b) $\frac{8}{4}$ (c) $\sqrt{5}$ (d) 0.5

2. Identify the property of real numbers that each equation illustrates. Write the property, using variables.
   (a) $3 + 4 = 4 + 3$
   (b) $-5 \cdot (4 \cdot 8) = (-5 \cdot 4) \cdot 8$
   (c) $4(5 + 2) = 4 \cdot 5 + 4 \cdot 2$
   (d) $4x - (5 - x) = 4x - 5 + x$

3. Evaluate each expression.
   (a) $-3 + 4 + (-5)$
   (b) $5.1 \cdot (-4) \cdot 2$
   (c) $-\frac{2}{3} \cdot \left(\frac{1}{4} \div \frac{2}{5}\right)$

4. A small lake covers 400 acres, has an average depth of 15 feet, and contains about 2 billion gallons of water. Estimate the number of gallons in a lake that covers 1200 acres and has an average depth of 30 feet.

1.3 INTEGER EXPONENTS

Bases and Positive Exponents ■ Zero and Negative Exponents ■ Product, Quotient, and Power Rules ■ Order of Operations ■ Scientific Notation

A LOOK INTO MATH ▷ Technology has brought with it the need for both small and large numbers. The size of an average virus is 5 millionths of a centimeter, whereas the distance to the nearest star, Alpha Centauri, is 25 trillion miles. To represent such numbers we often use exponents. In this section we discuss properties of integer exponents and some of their applications. (***Source:*** C. Ronan, *The Natural History of the Universe.*)

Bases and Positive Exponents

The area of a square that is 8 inches on a side is given by the expression

$$\underbrace{8 \cdot 8}_{2 \text{ factors}} = 8^2 = 64 \text{ square inches.}$$

Exponent
8^2
Base

The expression 8^2 is an **exponential expression** with **base** 8 and **exponent** 2. Exponential expressions occur frequently in a variety of applications. For example, suppose that an investment doubles its initial value 3 times. Then its final value is

$$\underbrace{2 \cdot 2 \cdot 2}_{3 \text{ factors}} = 2^3 = 8 \qquad \text{Doubles 3 times}$$

times as large as its original value. In general, if n is a positive integer and a is a real number, then

$$a^n = a \cdot a \cdot a \cdot \,\cdots\, \cdot a. \qquad (n \text{ factors of } a)$$

Table 1.4 contains examples of exponential expressions.

TABLE 1.4

Expression	Base	Exponent
2^3	2	3
6^4	6	4
7^1	7	1
0.5^2	0.5	2
x^3	x	3

4
4 Squared
Figure 1.10

Read 0.5^2 as "0.5 squared," 2^3 as "2 cubed," and 6^4 as "6 to the fourth power." The terms *squared* and *cubed* come from geometry. If the length of a side of a square is 4, then its area is

$$4 \cdot 4 = 4^2 = 16$$

square units, as illustrated in Figure 1.10. Similarly, if the length of an edge (side) of a cube is 4, then its volume is

$$4 \cdot 4 \cdot 4 = 4^3 = 64$$

4
4 Cubed
Figure 1.11

cubic units, as shown in Figure 1.11.

EXAMPLE 1   Writing numbers in exponential notation

Using the given base, write each number as an exponential expression. Check your results with a calculator.

(a) 10,000 (base 10)   **(b)** 27 (base 3)   **(c)** 32 (base 2)

Solution
(a) $10,000 = 10 \cdot 10 \cdot 10 \cdot 10 = 10^4$
(b) $27 = 3 \cdot 3 \cdot 3 = 3^3$
(c) $32 = 2 \cdot 2 \cdot 2 \cdot 2 \cdot 2 = 2^5$

   These values are supported in Figure 1.12, where we evaluated exponential expressions with a calculator, using the (^) key.

CALCULATOR HELP

To calculate exponential expressions, see the Appendix (page AP-1).

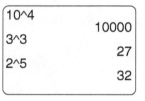

```
10^4
              10000
3^3
                 27
2^5
                 32
```

Figure 1.12

Now Try Exercise 17

▶ **REAL-WORLD CONNECTION**   Computer memory is often measured in bytes. A *byte* is capable of storing one letter of the alphabet. For example, the word "math" requires four bytes to store in a computer. Bytes of computer memory are often manufactured in amounts equal to powers of 2, as illustrated in the next example.

EXAMPLE 2   Using exponents to analyze computer memory

In computer technology, 1 K (kilobyte) of memory is equal to 2^{10} bytes, and 1 MB (megabyte) of memory is equal to 2^{20} bytes. Determine whether 1 K of memory is equal to 1000 bytes and whether 1 MB is equal to 1,000,000 bytes.   (*Source:* D. Horn, *Basic Electronics Theory.*)

Solution
Figure 1.13 shows that $2^{10} = 1024$ and that $2^{20} = 1,048,576$. Thus 1 K represents slightly more than 1000 bytes and 1 MB is more than 1,000,000 bytes.

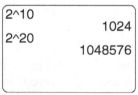

```
2^10
              1024
2^20
           1048576
```

Figure 1.13

Now Try Exercise 127

Zero and Negative Exponents

Exponents can be defined for any integer. If a is any nonzero real number, we define

$$a^0 = 1.$$

For example, $3^0 = 1$ and $\left(\frac{1}{7}\right)^0 = 1$. We can also define a^{-n}, where n is a positive integer, as

$$a^{-n} = \frac{1}{a^n}.$$

Thus $5^{-4} = \frac{1}{5^4}$ and $y^{-2} = \frac{1}{y^2}$. Using the previous definition, we obtain

$$\frac{1}{a^{-n}} = \frac{1}{\frac{1}{a^n}} = \frac{a^n}{1} = a^n.$$

Thus $\frac{1}{2^{-5}} = 2^5$ and $\frac{1}{x^{-2}} = x^2$. If a and b are nonzero numbers, then

$$\frac{a^{-n}}{b^{-m}} = \frac{\frac{1}{a^n}}{\frac{1}{b^m}} = \frac{1}{a^n} \cdot \frac{b^m}{1} = \frac{b^m}{a^n}.$$

Thus $\frac{4^{-3}}{z^{-2}} = \frac{z^2}{4^3}$. This discussion leads to the following properties for integer exponents.

INTEGER EXPONENTS

Let a and b be nonzero real numbers and m and n be positive integers. Then

1. $a^n = a \cdot a \cdot a \cdot \cdots \cdot a$ (n factors of a)
2. $a^0 = 1$ (*Note:* 0^0 is undefined.)
3. $a^{-n} = \dfrac{1}{a^n}$ and $\dfrac{1}{a^{-n}} = a^n$
4. $\dfrac{a^{-n}}{b^{-m}} = \dfrac{b^m}{a^n}$
5. $\left(\dfrac{a}{b}\right)^{-n} = \left(\dfrac{b}{a}\right)^n$

EXAMPLE **3** Evaluating expressions

Evaluate each expression.

(a) 3^{-4} (b) $\dfrac{1}{2^{-3}}$ (c) $\left(\dfrac{5}{7}\right)^{-2}$ (d) $\dfrac{1}{(xy)^{-1}}$ (e) $\dfrac{2^{-2}}{3t^{-3}}$

Solution

(a) $3^{-4} = \dfrac{1}{3^4} = \dfrac{1}{3 \cdot 3 \cdot 3 \cdot 3} = \dfrac{1}{81}$ (b) $\dfrac{1}{2^{-3}} = 2^3 = 2 \cdot 2 \cdot 2 = 8$

(c) $\left(\dfrac{5}{7}\right)^{-2} = \left(\dfrac{7}{5}\right)^2 = \dfrac{7}{5} \cdot \dfrac{7}{5} = \dfrac{49}{25}$ (d) $\dfrac{1}{(xy)^{-1}} = (xy)^1 = xy$

$\qquad\qquad\qquad\qquad\qquad\qquad\qquad\qquad$ Base is xy.

(e) Note that only t and *not* $3t$ is raised to the power of -3.

$$\frac{2^{-2}}{3t^{-3}} = \frac{t^3}{3(2^2)} = \frac{t^3}{3 \cdot 4} = \frac{t^3}{12}$$

$\qquad\qquad$ Base is t.

Now Try Exercises **25, 31**

Powers of 10 are important because they are used in mathematics to express numbers that are either small or large in absolute value. Table 1.5 may be used to simplify powers of 10. Note that, if the power decreases by 1, the result decreases by a factor of $\frac{1}{10}$.

CRITICAL THINKING

Use Table 1.5 to explain why it is reasonable for 10^0 to equal 1.

TABLE 1.5   **Powers of Ten**

Power of 10	10^3	10^2	10^1	10^0	10^{-1}	10^{-2}	10^{-3}
Value	1000	100	10	1	$\frac{1}{10}$	$\frac{1}{100}$	$\frac{1}{1000}$

Product, Quotient, and Power Rules

We can calculate products and quotients of exponential expressions *provided their bases are the same*. For example,

$$3^2 \cdot 3^3 = \underbrace{(3 \cdot 3)}_{2 \text{ factors}} \cdot \underbrace{(3 \cdot 3 \cdot 3)}_{3 \text{ factors}} = 3^5. \qquad 2 + 3 = 5$$

This expression has a total of $2 + 3 = 5$ factors of 3, so the result is 3^5. To multiply exponential expressions with like bases, add exponents. Thus

$$x^3 \cdot x^4 = \underbrace{(x \cdot x \cdot x)}_{3 \text{ factors}} \cdot \underbrace{(x \cdot x \cdot x \cdot x)}_{4 \text{ factors}} = x^7. \qquad 3 + 4 = 7$$

THE PRODUCT RULE

For any number a and integers m and n,

$$a^m \cdot a^n = a^{m+n},$$

Note that the product rule holds for negative exponents. For example,

$$10^5 \cdot 10^{-2} = 10^{5+(-2)} = 10^3.$$

EXAMPLE 4   Using the product rule

Multiply and simplify. Use positive exponents.

(a) $10^2 \cdot 10^4$ **(b)** $7^3 \, 7^{-4}$ **(c)** $x^3 x^{-2} x^4$ **(d)** $3y^2 \cdot 2y^{-4}$

Solution
(a) $10^2 \cdot 10^4 = 10^{2+4} = 10^6 = 1{,}000{,}000$ Add exponents.

(b) $7^3 \, 7^{-4} = 7^{3+(-4)} = 7^{-1} = \dfrac{1}{7}$

(c) $x^3 x^{-2} x^4 = x^{3+(-2)+4} = x^5$

(d) $3y^2 \cdot 2y^{-4} = 3 \cdot 2 \cdot y^2 \cdot y^{-4} = 6y^{2+(-4)} = 6y^{-2} = \dfrac{6}{y^2}$

Note that 6 is *not* raised to the power of -2 in the expression $6y^{-2}$.

Now Try Exercises 33, 35

Consider division of exponential expressions. Here

$$\frac{6^5}{6^3} = \frac{6 \cdot 6 \cdot 6 \cdot 6 \cdot 6}{6 \cdot 6 \cdot 6} = \frac{6}{6} \cdot \frac{6}{6} \cdot \frac{6}{6} \cdot 6 \cdot 6 = 1 \cdot 1 \cdot 1 \cdot 6 \cdot 6 = 6^2. \qquad 5 - 3 = 2$$

Because there are two more 6s in the numerator, the result is $6^{5-3} = 6^2$. Thus, to divide exponential expressions with like bases, subtract exponents.

THE QUOTIENT RULE

For any nonzero number a and integers m and n,

$$\frac{a^m}{a^n} = a^{m-n}.$$

Note that the quotient rule holds for negative exponents. For example,

$$\frac{2^{-6}}{2^{-4}} = 2^{-6-(-4)} = 2^{-2} = \frac{1}{2^2}.$$

However, you may want to evaluate this quotient as

$$\frac{2^{-6}}{2^{-4}} = \frac{2^4}{2^6} = \frac{1}{2^2}.$$

NOTE: The quotient rule can also be used to justify that $a^0 = 1$. For example, $\frac{3^2}{3^2} = \frac{9}{9} = 1$ and by the quotient rule $\frac{3^2}{3^2} = 3^{2-2} = 3^0$. Thus $3^0 = 1$.

EXAMPLE 5   Using the quotient rule

Simplify each expression. Use positive exponents.

(a) $\dfrac{10^4}{10^6}$ (b) $\dfrac{x^5}{x^2}$ (c) $\dfrac{15x^2y^3}{5x^4y}$ (d) $\dfrac{3a^{-2}b^5}{9a^4b^{-3}}$

Solution

(a) $\dfrac{10^4}{10^6} = 10^{4-6} = 10^{-2} = \dfrac{1}{10^2} = \dfrac{1}{100}$ Subtract exponents.

(b) $\dfrac{x^5}{x^2} = x^{5-2} = x^3$

(c) $\dfrac{15x^2y^3}{5x^4y} = \dfrac{15}{5} \cdot \dfrac{x^2}{x^4} \cdot \dfrac{y^3}{y^1} = 3 \cdot x^{2-4}y^{3-1} = 3x^{-2}y^2 = \dfrac{3y^2}{x^2}$

(d) $\dfrac{3a^{-2}b^5}{9a^4b^{-3}} = \dfrac{3b^5b^3}{9a^4a^2} = \dfrac{b^8}{3a^6}$

Now Try Exercises 39, 43

How should we evaluate $(4^3)^2$? To answer this question consider

$$(4^3)^2 = 4^3 \cdot 4^3 = 4^{3+3} = 4^6. \qquad 3 \cdot 2 = 6$$

Similarly,

$$(x^4)^3 = x^4 \cdot x^4 \cdot x^4 = x^{4+4+4} = x^{12}. \qquad 4 \cdot 3 = 12$$

These results suggest that, to raise a power to a power, multiply the exponents.

RAISING POWERS TO POWERS

For any real number a and integers m and n,

$$(a^m)^n = a^{mn}.$$

EXAMPLE **6**   Raising powers to powers

Simplify each expression. Use positive exponents.

(a) $(5^2)^3$ **(b)** $(2^4)^{-2}$ **(c)** $(b^{-7})^5$ **(d)** $\dfrac{(x^3)^{-2}}{(x^{-5})^2}$

Solution

(a) $(5^2)^3 = 5^{2 \cdot 3} = 5^6 = 15{,}625$ Multiply exponents.

(b) $(2^4)^{-2} = 2^{4(-2)} = 2^{-8} = \dfrac{1}{2^8} = \dfrac{1}{256}$

(c) $(b^{-7})^5 = b^{-7 \cdot 5} = b^{-35} = \dfrac{1}{b^{35}}$

(d) $\dfrac{(x^3)^{-2}}{(x^{-5})^2} = \dfrac{x^{-6}}{x^{-10}} = \dfrac{x^{10}}{x^6} = x^4$

Now Try Exercises 45, 55

How can we simplify the expression $(2x)^3$? Consider

$$(2x)^3 = 2x \cdot 2x \cdot 2x = (2 \cdot 2 \cdot 2) \cdot (x \cdot x \cdot x) = 2^3 x^3.$$

This result suggests that, to cube a product, cube each factor.

RAISING PRODUCTS TO POWERS

For any real numbers a and b and integer n,

$$(ab)^n = a^n b^n.$$

EXAMPLE **7**   Raising products to powers

Simplify each expression. Use positive exponents.

(a) $(6y)^2$ **(b)** $(x^2 y)^{-2}$ **(c)** $(2xy^3)^4$ **(d)** $\dfrac{(2a^2 b^{-3})^2}{4(ab^3)^3}$

Solution

(a) $(6y)^2 = 6^2 y^2 = 36y^2$ Base is $6y$.

(b) $(x^2 y)^{-2} = \dfrac{1}{(x^2 y)^2} = \dfrac{1}{(x^2)^2 y^2} = \dfrac{1}{x^4 y^2}$

(c) $(2xy^3)^4 = 2^4 x^4 (y^3)^4 = 16x^4 y^{12}$

(d) $\dfrac{(2a^2 b^{-3})^2}{4(ab^3)^3} = \dfrac{2^2 a^4 b^{-6}}{4a^3 b^9} = \dfrac{4a^4}{4a^3 b^9 b^6} = \dfrac{a}{b^{15}}$

Now Try Exercises 47, 57

The expression $\left(\frac{a}{b}\right)^3$ can be simplified as

$$\left(\frac{a}{b}\right)^3 = \frac{a}{b} \cdot \frac{a}{b} \cdot \frac{a}{b} = \frac{a^3}{b^3}.$$

This result suggests the following rule.

RAISING QUOTIENTS TO POWERS

For nonzero numbers a and b and any integer n,

$$\left(\frac{a}{b}\right)^n = \frac{a^n}{b^n}.$$

EXAMPLE 8 Raising quotients to powers

Simplify each expression. Use positive exponents.

(a) $\left(\frac{3}{x}\right)^3$ **(b)** $\left(\frac{1}{2^3}\right)^{-2}$ **(c)** $\left(\frac{3x^{-3}}{y^2}\right)^4$ **(d)** $\left(\frac{3x^2}{4y^2z}\right)^3$

Solution

(a) $\left(\frac{3}{x}\right)^3 = \frac{3^3}{x^3} = \frac{27}{x^3}$

(b) $\left(\frac{1}{2^3}\right)^{-2} = \left(\frac{2^3}{1}\right)^2 = \frac{(2^3)^2}{1^2} = 2^6 = 64$

(c) $\left(\frac{3x^{-3}}{y^2}\right)^4 = \frac{3^4(x^{-3})^4}{(y^2)^4} = \frac{81x^{-12}}{y^8} = \frac{81}{x^{12}y^8}$

(d) $\left(\frac{3x^2}{4y^2z}\right)^3 = \frac{3^3x^6}{4^3y^6z^3} = \frac{27x^6}{64y^6z^3}$

Now Try Exercises **49, 61**

EXAMPLE 9 Simplifying expressions

Write each expression using positive exponents. Simplify the result completely.

(a) $\left(\frac{y^{-3}}{3z^{-4}}\right)^{-2}$ **(b)** $\frac{(rt^3)^{-3}}{(r^2t^3)^{-2}}$

Solution

(a) $\left(\frac{y^{-3}}{3z^{-4}}\right)^{-2} = \left(\frac{3z^{-4}}{y^{-3}}\right)^2 = \left(\frac{3y^3}{z^4}\right)^2 = \frac{9y^6}{z^8}$

(b) $\frac{(rt^3)^{-3}}{(r^2t^3)^{-2}} = \frac{(r^2t^3)^2}{(rt^3)^3} = \frac{r^4t^6}{r^3t^9} = \frac{r}{t^3}$

Now Try Exercises **67, 69**

Order of Operations

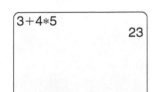

Figure 1.14

When we evaluate the expression $3 + 4 \cdot 5$, is the result 35 or 23? Figure 1.14 shows that a calculator gives a result of 23. This is because multiplication is performed before addition.

Because it is important that we evaluate arithmetic expressions consistently, the following rules are used. (Two people should evaluate the same expression the same way.)

ORDER OF OPERATIONS

Using the following order of operations, first perform all calculations within parentheses and absolute values, or above and below the fraction bar. Then use the same order of operations to perform the remaining calculations.

1. Evaluate all exponential expressions. Do any negations *after* evaluating exponents.
2. Do all multiplication and division from *left to right*.
3. Do all addition and subtraction from *left to right*.

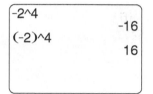

Figure 1.15

Be sure to evaluate exponents before performing negation. For example,

$$-2^4 = -(2 \cdot 2 \cdot 2 \cdot 2) = -16, \quad \text{but} \quad (-2)^4 = (-2)(-2)(-2)(-2) = 16.$$

These results are supported by Figure 1.15.

EXAMPLE 10   Evaluating arithmetic expressions

Evaluate each expression. Use a calculator to support your results.

(a) $5 - 3 \cdot 2 - (4 + 5)$ **(b)** $-3^2 + \dfrac{5 + 7}{2 + 1}$ **(c)** $4^3 - 5(2 - 6 \cdot 2)$

Solution
(a)
$$\begin{aligned}
5 - 3 \cdot 2 - (4 + 5) &= 5 - 3 \cdot 2 - 9 \\
&= 5 - 6 - 9 \\
&= -1 - 9 \\
&= -10
\end{aligned}$$

(b) Assume that both the numerator and the denominator of a fraction have parentheses around them.

$$\begin{aligned}
-3^2 + \frac{5 + 7}{2 + 1} &= -3^2 + \frac{(5 + 7)}{(2 + 1)} \\
&= -3^2 + \frac{12}{3} \\
&= -9 + \frac{12}{3} \qquad \text{Do exponents before division.} \\
&= -9 + 4 \\
&= -5
\end{aligned}$$

(c)
$$\begin{aligned}
4^3 - 5(2 - 6 \cdot 2) &= 4^3 - 5(2 - 12) \\
&= 4^3 - 5(-10) \\
&= 64 - 5(-10) \\
&= 64 + 50 \\
&= 114
\end{aligned}$$

```
5-3*2-(4+5)
              -10
-3²+(5+7)/(2+1)
               -5
4^3-5(2-6*2)
              114
```

Figure 1.16

These results are supported by Figure 1.16.

Now Try Exercises 81, 85, 89

Scientific Notation

▶ REAL-WORLD CONNECTION   Numbers that are large or small in absolute value occur frequently in applications. For simplicity these numbers are often expressed in scientific notation. As mentioned at the beginning of this section, the distance to the nearest star is 25 trillion miles. This number can be expressed in scientific notation as

$$25{,}000{,}000{,}000{,}000 = 2.5 \times 10^{13}.$$

In contrast, a typical virus is about 5 millionths of a centimeter in diameter. In scientific notation this number can be written as

$$0.000005 = 5 \times 10^{-6}.$$

A calculator set in *scientific mode* expresses these numbers in scientific notation, as illustrated in Figure 1.17. The letter E denotes a power of 10. That is, $2.5\text{E}13 = 2.5 \times 10^{13}$ and $5\text{E}-6 = 5 \times 10^{-6}$.

```
25000000000000
               2.5E13
.000005
               5E-6
```

Figure 1.17

CALCULATOR HELP

To display numbers in scientific notation, see the Appendix (page AP-2).

SCIENTIFIC NOTATION

A real number a is in **scientific notation** when a is written as $b \times 10^n$, where $1 \le |b| < 10$ and n is an integer.

Use the following steps to express a positive (rational) number a in scientific notation.

WRITING A POSITIVE NUMBER IN SCIENTIFIC NOTATION

1. Move the decimal point in a number a until it represents a number b such that $1 \le b < 10$.
2. Count the number of decimal places that the decimal point was moved. Let this positive integer be n. (If the decimal point is *not* moved, then $a = a \times 10^0$.)
3. If the decimal point was moved to the left, then $a = b \times 10^n$.
    If the decimal point was moved to the right, then $a = b \times 10^{-n}$.

NOTE: The scientific notation for a negative number a is the additive inverse of the scientific notation of $|a|$. For example, $5200 = 5.2 \times 10^3$, so $-5200 = -5.2 \times 10^3$.

Table 1.6 shows the values of some important powers of 10.

TABLE 1.6   **Important Powers of 10**

Number	10^{-3}	10^{-2}	10^{-1}	10^3	10^6	10^9	10^{12}
Value	Thousandth	Hundredth	Tenth	Thousand	Million	Billion	Trillion

EXAMPLE 11   Writing a number in scientific notation

Express each number in scientific notation.
(a) 360,000   (Dots in 1 square inch of some types of laser print)
(b) 0.00000538   (Time in seconds for light to travel 1 mile)
(c) 10,000,000,000   (Estimated world population in 2050)

Solution

(a) Move the assumed decimal point in 360,000 *five places* to the *left* to obtain 3.6.

$$3.6\,0\,0\,0\,0.$$

The scientific notation for 360,000 is 3.6×10^5.

(b) Move the decimal point in 0.00000538 *six places* to the *right* to obtain 5.38.

$$0.0\,0\,0\,0\,0\,5.38$$

The scientific notation for 0.00000538 is 5.38×10^{-6}.

(c) Move the decimal point in 10,000,000,000 *ten places* to the *left* to obtain 1.

$$1.0\,0\,0\,0\,0\,0\,0\,0\,0\,0.$$

The scientific notation for 10,000,000,000 is 1×10^{10}. Note that positive powers of 10 indicate a large number, whereas negative powers of 10 indicate a small number.

Now Try Exercises 95, 99

MAKING CONNECTIONS

Scientific Notation and Moving the Decimal Point

When a *positive* number a is expressed in scientific notation, a negative exponent on 10 indicates that $a < 1$, thus a is relatively small, and a positive exponent on 10 indicates that $a \geq 10$, thus a is relatively large. This can be helpful when converting from scientific notation to standard notation or vice versa. For example, to write the number 3.4×10^7 in standard form, we move the decimal point in 3.4 seven places. Because the exponent on 10 is positive, the resulting number should be relatively large. Moving the decimal point to the right results in 34,000,000. To express the number 0.00087 in scientific notation, we move the decimal point four places to obtain 8.7. Because the number 0.00087 is relatively small, the exponent on 10 will be negative. The resulting scientific notation is 8.7×10^{-4}.

In the next example we convert numbers from scientific notation to **standard form**, or decimal form.

EXAMPLE 12   Writing a number in standard form

Write the number in standard (decimal) form.
(a) 2×10^8 (Number of years for the sun to orbit in the Milky Way)
(b) 9.1×10^{-2} (Fraction of deaths worldwide caused by injuries in 2002)

Solution

(a) Because the exponent of 10 is *positive*, move the assumed decimal point in 2 to the *right* 8 places to obtain 200,000,000.

(b) Because the exponent of 10 is *negative*, move the decimal point in 9.1 to the *left* 2 places to obtain 0.091.

Now Try Exercises 103, 109

Arithmetic can be performed on expressions in scientific notation. For example, multiplication of the expressions 8×10^4 and 4×10^2 may be done by hand.

$$
\begin{aligned}
(8 \times 10^4) \cdot (4 \times 10^2) &= (8 \cdot 4) \times (10^4 \cdot 10^2) && \text{Properties of real numbers} \\
&= 32 \times 10^6 && \text{Add exponents and simplify.} \\
&= (3.2 \times 10^1)(10^6) && \text{Write in scientific notation.} \\
&= 3.2 \times 10^7 && \text{Add exponents.}
\end{aligned}
$$

Division may be performed as follows.

$$
\begin{aligned}
\frac{8 \times 10^4}{4 \times 10^2} &= \frac{8}{4} \times \frac{10^4}{10^2} && \text{Property of fractions} \\
&= 2 \times 10^2 && \text{Subtract exponents.}
\end{aligned}
$$

CALCULATOR HELP
To enter numbers in scientific notation, see the Appendix (page AP-3).

▶ **REAL-WORLD CONNECTION** The next example illustrates how scientific notation is used in applications.

EXAMPLE 13 Analyzing the federal debt

In 2005, the federal debt held by the public was 4.72 trillion dollars, and the population of the United States was 296 million. Approximate the national debt per person.

Solution
In scientific notation 4.72 trillion equals 4.72×10^{12} and 296 million equals 296×10^6, or 2.96×10^8. The per person debt held by the public is given by

$$
\frac{4.72 \times 10^{12}}{2.96 \times 10^8} \approx \$15{,}946.
$$

Figure 1.18 supports this result.

Now Try Exercise 125

```
(4.72*10^12)/(2.
96*10^8)
        15945.94595
```

Figure 1.18

CRITICAL THINKING
Estimate the number of seconds that you have been alive.

1.3 PUTTING IT ALL TOGETHER

The following table summarizes important properties of exponents, where a and b are nonzero real numbers and m and n are integers.

Property	Definition	Examples
Bases and Exponents	In the expression a^n, a is the base and n is the exponent. *Note:* 0^0 is undefined.	$3^4 = 3 \cdot 3 \cdot 3 \cdot 3 = 81$, $\quad 7^0 = 1$, $2^{-3} = \dfrac{1}{2^3} = \dfrac{1}{2 \cdot 2 \cdot 2} = \dfrac{1}{8}$, and $-3^2 = -9$

continued on next page

continued from previous page

Property	Definition	Examples
The Product Rule	$a^m \cdot a^n = a^{m+n}$	$8^4 \cdot 8^2 = 8^{4+2} = 8^6$ and $5^6 \cdot 5^{-3} = 5^{6+(-3)} = 5^3$
The Quotient Rule	$\dfrac{a^m}{a^n} = a^{m-n}$	$\dfrac{6^7}{6^4} = 6^{7-4} = 6^3$ and $\dfrac{7^{-4}}{7^{-2}} = 7^{(-4-(-2))} = 7^{-2} = \dfrac{1}{7^2}$
The Power Rules	1. $(a^m)^n = a^{mn}$ 2. $(ab)^n = a^n b^n$ 3. $\left(\dfrac{a}{b}\right)^n = \dfrac{a^n}{b^n}$	1. $(2^2)^3 = 2^6$ 2. $(3y)^4 = 3^4 y^4$ 3. $\left(\dfrac{x^2}{y}\right)^4 = \dfrac{x^8}{y^4}$
Quotients and Negative Exponents	1. $\dfrac{1}{a^{-n}} = a^n$ 2. $\dfrac{a^{-n}}{b^{-m}} = \dfrac{b^m}{a^n}$ 3. $\left(\dfrac{a}{b}\right)^{-n} = \left(\dfrac{b}{a}\right)^n$	1. $\dfrac{1}{x^{-2}} = x^2$ 2. $\dfrac{z^{-3}}{y^{-5}} = \dfrac{y^5}{z^3}$ 3. $\left(\dfrac{4}{t}\right)^{-2} = \left(\dfrac{t}{4}\right)^2 = \dfrac{t^2}{4^2}$
Scientific Notation	A positive number a is in scientific notation when a is written as $b \times 10^n$, where $1 \le b < 10$ and n is an integer.	$52{,}600 = 5.26 \times 10^4$ and $0.0068 = 6.8 \times 10^{-3}$

1.3 Exercises

MyMathLab   Math XL PRACTICE   WATCH   DOWNLOAD   READ   REVIEW

CONCEPTS

1. Identify the base and the exponent in 8^3.

2. Evaluate 97^0 and 2^{-1}.

3. Write 7 cubed, using symbols.

4. Write 5 squared, using symbols.

5. Are the expressions 2^3 and 3^2 equal? Explain.

6. Are the expressions -4^2 and $(-4)^2$ equal? Explain.

7. $7^{-n} = $ ____   8. $6^m \cdot 6^n = $ ____

9. $\dfrac{5^m}{5^n} = $ ____   10. $(3x)^k = $ ____

11. $(2^m)^k = $ ____   12. $\left(\dfrac{x}{y}\right)^m = $ ____

13. $\dfrac{1}{x^{-n}} = $ ____   14. $\dfrac{a^{-n}}{b^{-m}} = $ ____

15. $\left(\dfrac{y}{z}\right)^{-n} = $ ____   16. $5 \times 10^2 = $ ____

PROPERTIES OF EXPONENTS

Exercises 17–22: (Refer to Example 1.) Write the number as an exponential expression, using the base shown. Check your result with a calculator.

17. 8   (base 2)   **18.** 1000   (base 10)

19. 256   (base 4)   **20.** $\frac{1}{16}$ (base 2)

21. 1   (base 6)   **22.** $\frac{1}{125}$ (base 5)

Exercises 23–32: Evaluate each expression.

23. (a) 4^3 (b) 3^4

24. (a) 2^{-3} (b) 7^{-2}

25. (a) $\dfrac{1}{4^{-2}}$ (b) $\dfrac{1}{3^{-3}}$

26. (a) 5^0 (b) $\dfrac{1}{6^0}$

27. (a) $\left(\dfrac{2}{3}\right)^3$ (b) $\left(-\dfrac{2}{3}\right)^{-3}$

28. (a) $\left(-\dfrac{1}{2}\right)^4$ (b) $\left(-\dfrac{3}{4}\right)^3$

29. (a) $\dfrac{3^{-2}}{2^{-4}}$ (b) $\dfrac{4^{-3}}{5^{-2}}$

30. (a) $\dfrac{4^{-2}}{2^3}$ (b) $\dfrac{3^3}{5^{-2}}$

31. (a) $\dfrac{1}{2x^{-3}}$ (b) $\dfrac{1}{(ab)^{-1}}$

32. (a) $\dfrac{1}{3b^{-2}}$ (b) $\dfrac{2^{-3}}{b^{-1}}$

Exercises 33–38: Use the product rule and positive exponents to simplify the expression.

33. (a) $3^5 \cdot 3^{-3}$ (b) $x^2 x^5$

34. (a) $10^{-5} \cdot 10^2$ (b) $y^4 y^{-3}$

35. (a) $(-3x^{-2})(5x^5)$ (b) $(ab)(a^2b^{-3})$

36. (a) $6z^2(-z^3)$ (b) $(a^2b^{-3})(2ab^3)$

37. (a) $5^{-2}5^3 2^{-4} 2^3$ (b) $2a^3 \cdot b^2 \cdot 4a^{-4} \cdot b^{-5}$

38. (a) $2^{-3} 3^4 3^{-2} 2^5$ (b) $3x^{-4} \cdot 2x^2 \cdot 5y^4 \cdot y^{-3}$

Exercises 39–44: Use the quotient rule and other properties of exponents to simplify the expression. Use positive exponents to write your answer.

39. (a) $\dfrac{4^3}{4^2}$ (b) $\dfrac{10^{-3}}{10^{-5}}$

40. (a) $\dfrac{5^4}{5^{-7}}$ (b) $\dfrac{6^{-5}}{6}$

41. (a) $\dfrac{b^{-3}}{b^2}$ (b) $\dfrac{24x^3}{6x}$

42. (a) $\dfrac{x^0}{x^{-5}}$ (b) $\dfrac{10x^5}{5x^{-3}}$

43. (a) $\dfrac{12a^2b^3}{18a^4b^2}$ (b) $\dfrac{21x^{-3}y^4}{7x^4y^{-2}}$

44. (a) $\dfrac{-6x^7y^3}{3x^2y^{-5}}$ (b) $\dfrac{32x^3y}{-24x^5y^{-3}}$

Exercises 45–50: Use the power rules to simplify the expression. Use positive exponents to write your answer.

45. (a) $(3^2)^4$ (b) $(x^3)^{-2}$

46. (a) $(-2^2)^3$ (b) $(xy)^3$

47. (a) $(4y^2)^3$ (b) $(-2xy^3)^{-4}$

48. (a) $(-2a^2)^3$ (b) $(a^{-1}b^5)^{-2}$

49. (a) $\left(\dfrac{4}{x}\right)^3$ (b) $\left(\dfrac{2x}{z^4}\right)^{-5}$

50. (a) $\left(\dfrac{-3}{x^3}\right)^2$ (b) $\left(\dfrac{2xy}{3z^5}\right)^{-1}$

Exercises 51–74: Use rules of exponents to simplify the expression. Use positive exponents to write your answer.

51. $\dfrac{12m^2n^{-5}}{8mn^{-2}}$ **52.** $\dfrac{15m^{-1}n}{5m^{-2}n^3}$

53. $(2x^3y^{-2})^{-2}$ **54.** $(4x^{-4}y)^2$

55. $\dfrac{(b^2)^3}{(b^{-1})^2}$ **56.** $\dfrac{(a^3)^{-1}}{(a^{-3})^{-2}}$

57. $\dfrac{(-3ab^2)^3}{(a^2b)^2}$ **58.** $\dfrac{(-2ab)^3}{(ab)^2}$

59. $\dfrac{(-m^2n^{-1})^{-2}}{(mn)^{-1}}$ **60.** $\dfrac{(-mn^4)^{-1}}{(m^2n)^{-3}}$

61. $\left(\dfrac{2a^3}{6b}\right)^4$ **62.** $\left(\dfrac{-3a^2}{9b^3}\right)^4$

63. $\left(\dfrac{t^{-3}}{t^{-4}}\right)^2$ **64.** $\left(\dfrac{r^{-2}}{2r^{-1}}\right)^{-4}$

65. $\dfrac{8x^{-3}y^{-2}}{4x^{-2}y^{-4}}$ **66.** $\dfrac{6x^{-1}y^{-1}}{9x^{-2}y^3}$

67. $\left(\dfrac{2t}{-r^2}\right)^{-3}$ **68.** $\left(\dfrac{t^2}{3r}\right)^{-1}$

69. $\dfrac{(r^2 t^2)^{-2}}{(r^3 t)^{-1}}$

70. $\dfrac{(2rt)^2}{(rt^4)^{-2}}$

71. $\dfrac{4x^{-2} y^3}{(2x^{-1} y)^2}$

72. $\dfrac{(ab)^3}{a^4 b^{-4}}$

73. $\left(\dfrac{-15r^2 t}{3r^{-3} t^4}\right)^3$

74. $\left(\dfrac{4(xy)^2}{(2xy^{-2})^3}\right)^{-2}$

ORDER OF OPERATIONS

Exercises 75–94: (Refer to Example 10.) Evaluate.

75. $4 + 5 \cdot 6$

76. $4 - 5 - 9$

77. $2(4 + (-8))$

78. $500 - 10^3$

79. $5 \cdot 2^3$

80. $\dfrac{4 + 8}{2} - \dfrac{6 + 1}{3}$

81. $\dfrac{-2^4 - 3^2}{4} + \dfrac{1 + 2}{4}$

82. $\dfrac{(-4^2 + 1)}{\frac{2}{3}}$

83. $\dfrac{1 - 2 \cdot 4^2}{5^{-1}}$

84. $6 \div 4 \div 2$

85. $4 + 6 - 3 \cdot 5 \div 3$

86. $-3(25 - 2 \cdot 5^2) \div 5$

87. $\dfrac{-3^2 + 3}{3}$

88. $\dfrac{2 \cdot 4 - 7}{7}$

89. $-4^2 + \dfrac{15 + 2}{8 - 7}$

90. $1 - 3 \cdot 4^3$

91. $|7 - 2^2 \cdot 3|$

92. $\dfrac{4^2 - |5 - (-6)|}{-2^2}$

93. $\sqrt{4^2 + 3^2}$

94. $\sqrt{13^2 - 12^2}$

SCIENTIFIC NOTATION

Exercises 95–102: Write in scientific notation.

95. 2,447,000   (U.S. deaths in 2002)

96. 132,000   (New York City AIDS cases in 2001)

97. 26.9 billion   (Dollars spent on health care in 1960)

98. 1.7 trillion   (Dollars spent on health care in 2003)

99. 0.051   (Fraction of the population expected to spend time in prison)

100. 0.156   (Fraction of people without health insurance)

101. 0.000001   (Approximate wavelength of light in meters)

102. 0.00244   (Fraction of people who died from heart disease in 2002)

Exercises 103–110: Write in standard (decimal) form.

103. 5×10^5

104. -7.85×10^3

105. 9.3×10^6

106. 2.961×10^2

107. -6×10^{-3}

108. 4.1×10^{-2}

109. 5.876×10^{-5}

110. 9.9×10^{-1}

Exercises 111–116: Evaluate the expression. Write your answer in both scientific notation and standard form.

111. $(2 \times 10^4)(3 \times 10^2)$

112. $(5 \times 10^{-4})(4 \times 10^6)$

113. $(4 \times 10^{-4})(2 \times 10^{-2})$

114. $\dfrac{6 \times 10^4}{2 \times 10^2}$

115. $\dfrac{6.2 \times 10^3}{3.1 \times 10^{-2}}$

116. $\dfrac{2 \times 10^{-2}}{8 \times 10^{-5}}$

APPLICATIONS

117. *GPS Clocks*   The Global Positioning System (GPS) is made up of 24 satellites that allow individuals with a GPS receiver to pinpoint their positions on Earth. Every 1024 weeks the clocks in the GPS satellites reset to zero. The first time this resetting occurred was on August 21, 1999.   (**Source:** Associated Press.)
(a) Find an exponent k so that $2^k = 1024$.
(b) Estimate the number of years in 1024 weeks.

118. *Astronomy*   Light travels at 186,000 miles per second. The distance that light travels in 1 year is called a *light-year*.

(a) Calculate the number of miles in 1 light-year. Write your answer in scientific notation.

(b) Express your answer from part (a) in standard notation.

(c) Except for the sun, the nearest star is Alpha Centauri. Its distance from Earth is about 4.27 light-years. How many miles is this?

(d) If a rocket flew at 50,000 miles per hour, how many years would it take to reach the star Alpha Centauri?

119. *Volume* If the sides of a cube have length a, then its volume is $V = a^3$. Find the volume of a cube with sides of length $2a$.

120. *Area* If the sides of a square have length a, then its area is $A = a^2$. Find the area of a square with sides of length $3a$.

121. *Area* Find the area of the square.

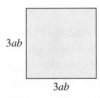

122. *Volume* Find the volume of the cube.

123. *Calculating Interest* If P dollars are deposited in a savings account paying 5% annual interest, the amount A in the account after x years is given by the formula $A = P(1.05)^x$. Find A for the values of P and x at the top of the next column.

(a) $P = \$500; x = 2$ years
(b) $P = \$1000, x = 4$ years

124. *Calculating Interest* If P dollars are deposited in a savings account paying r percent annual interest, then the amount A in the account after x years is given by the formula $A = P(1 + \frac{r}{100})^x$. Find A for the given values of P, r, and x.

(a) $P = \$200, r = 10\%, x = 7$ years
(b) $P = \$1500, r = 8\%, x = 15$ years

125. *Federal Debt* (Refer to Example 13.) In 1990, the federal debt held by the public was \$2.19 trillion, and the population of the United States was 249 million. Approximate the national debt per person.

126. *Federal Debt* In 1980, the federal debt held by the public was \$710 billion, and the debt per person was \$3127. Approximate the population of the United States in 1980.

127. *Computer Memory* (Refer to Example 2.) If a computer has 256 MB of memory, how many bytes is this? Express your answer in standard form.

128. *Computer Memory* One gigabyte of computer memory equals 2^{30} bytes. Write the number of bytes in 1 gigabyte, using standard notation.

129. *World Population* The following table lists populations of selected countries in 1996 and their projected populations in 2025. Rewrite the table below, expressing each population in scientific notation.

Country	1996	2025
China	1,255,100,000	1,480,000,000
Germany	82,400,000	80,900,000
India	975,800,000	1,330,200,000
Mexico	95,800,000	130,200,000
United States	265,000,000	332,500,000

Source: United Nations Population Fund.

130. *World Population* If current trends continue, world population P in billions may be modeled by the equation $P = 6(1.014)^x$, where x is in years and $x = 0$ corresponds to the year 2000. Estimate the world population in 2010 and 2025. (*Source:* United Nations Population Fund.)

131. Give the product and quotient rules for exponents and an example of each.

132. A student evaluates three expressions:

$$-4^2 \text{ as } 16; \quad 6 + 4 \cdot 2 \text{ as } 20; \quad \text{and}$$
$$20 \div 4 \div 2 \text{ as } 10.$$

Correct the errors and explain the mistakes.

GROUP ACTIVITY
WORKING WITH REAL DATA

Directions: Form a group of 2 to 4 people. Select someone to record the group's responses for this activity. All members of the group should work cooperatively to answer the questions. If your instructor asks for your results, each member of the group should be prepared to respond.

1. *Walk to the Moon*   The distance to the moon is about 2.37×10^5 miles. Walking at 4 miles per hour, estimate the number of hours it would take to travel this distance. How many years is this?

2. *Salary*   Suppose that for full-time work a person earns 1¢ for the first week, 2¢ for the second week,

4¢ for the third week, 8¢ for the fourth week, and so on for 1 year.
(a) Discuss whether you think this pay scale would be a good deal.
(b) Estimate how much this person would make the last week of a 52-week year.

1.4   VARIABLES, EQUATIONS, AND FORMULAS

Basic Concepts ■ Modeling Data ■ Square Roots and Cube Roots ■ Tables and Calculators (Optional)

A LOOK INTO MATH ▷   Most of the mathematics that people have discovered throughout the ages can be derived by using only pencil and paper, not from science and measured data. However, one of the amazing aspects of mathematics is that it can be used in countless applications that improve our quality of life. In fact, this ability of mathematics to describe the real world is so amazing that Nobel Laureate Eugene Wigner wrote the article "The Unreasonable Effectiveness of Mathematics in the Natural Sciences." Without mathematics, we would not have compact disc players, cars, warm buildings, or accurate weather forecasts. Mathematics can even be used to predict the increase in sea level if the polar ice caps were to melt. (See Exercise 1 in the Chapter 1 Extended and Discovery Exercises.) In this section we introduce some of the mathematical concepts that are used to model our world.   (***Source:*** Eugene Wigner, *Communications of Pure and Applied Mathematics,* February 1960.)

Basic Concepts

▶ **REAL-WORLD CONNECTION**   Suppose that we want to calculate the distance traveled by a car moving at a constant speed of 30 miles per hour. One method would be to make a table of values, as shown in Table 1.7.

TABLE 1.7

1-hour increase

Elapsed time (hours)	1	2	3	4	5	6
Distance (miles)	30	60	90	120	150	180

30-mile increase

Note that for each 1-hour increase the distance increases by 30 miles. Many times it is not possible to list all relevant values in a table. Instead, we use *variables* to describe data. For example, we might let elapsed time be represented by the variable t and let distance be represented by the variable d. If $t = 2$, then $d = 60$; if $t = 5$, then $d = 150$. In this example, the value of d is always equal to the value of t multiplied by 30. We can *model* this situation by using the *equation* or *formula* $d = 30t$. The values for distance in Table 1.7 can be calculated by letting $t = 1, 2, 3, 4, 5, 6$ in this formula.

A **variable** is a symbol, such as x, y, or t, used to represent any unknown number or quantity. An **algebraic expression** can consist of numbers, variables, arithmetic symbols $(+, -, \times, \div)$, exponents, and grouping symbols, such as parentheses, brackets, and square roots. Examples of algebraic expressions include

$$6, \quad x + 2, \quad 4(t - 5) + 1, \quad \sqrt{x + 1}, \quad \text{and} \quad LW. \qquad \text{Expressions}$$

An **equation** is a statement that two algebraic expressions are equal. An equation *always* contains an equals sign. Examples of equations include

$$3 + 6 = 9, \quad x + 1 = 4, \quad d = 30t, \quad \text{and} \quad x + y = 20. \qquad \text{Equations}$$

The first equation contains only constants, the second equation contains one variable, and both the third and fourth equations contain two variables. A **formula** is an equation that can calculate one quantity by using a known value of another quantity. (Formulas can also contain known values of more than one quantity.) Formulas show relationships between variables. The formula $y = \frac{x}{3}$ computes the number of yards in x feet. If $x = 15$, then $y = \frac{15}{3} = 5$. That is, in 15 feet there are 5 yards.

EXAMPLE 1   Writing and using a formula

If a car travels at a constant speed of 70 miles per hour, write a formula that calculates the distance d that the car travels in t hours. Evaluate your formula when $t = 1.5$ and interpret the result.

Solution
Traveling at 70 miles per hour, the car will travel a distance of $d = 70t$ miles in t hours. Evaluating this formula at $t = 1.5$ results in

$$d = 70(1.5) = 105.$$

After 1.5 hours the car has traveled 105 miles.   Now Try Exercises 25, 63

EXAMPLE 2   Writing formulas

Write a formula that does the following.
(a) Finds the circumference C of a circle with radius r
(b) Calculates the pay P for working H hours at $9 per hour
(c) Converts Q quarts to C cups

Solution
(a) The circumference of a circle is $C = 2\pi r$, where $\pi \approx 3.14$.
(b) Pay equals the product of the hourly wage and the hours worked. Thus $P = 9H$.
(c) There are 4 cups in each quart, so $C = 4Q$.

Now Try Exercise 15

EXAMPLE 3   Evaluating formulas from geometry

Evaluate each formula for the given value(s) of the variable(s). See Figure 1.19.
(a) $A = \pi r^2, r = 4$ Area of a circle
(b) $P = 2L + 2W, L = 8$ and $W = 4$ Perimeter of a rectangle
(c) $V = s^3, s = 3$ Volume of a cube

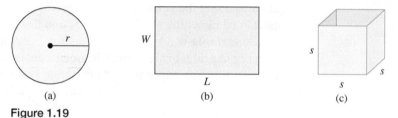

(a)   (b)   (c)

Figure 1.19

Solution
(a) $A = \pi(4)^2 = \pi(16) = 16\pi$ Let $r = 4$.
(b) $P = 2(8) + 2(4) = 16 + 8 = 24$ Let $L = 8$ and $W = 4$.
(c) $V = 3^3 = 3 \cdot 3 \cdot 3 = 27$ Let $s = 3$.

Now Try Exercises 29, 35, 39

Modeling Data

 REAL-WORLD CONNECTION   Faster moving automobiles require more distance to stop. For example, at 60 miles per hour it takes about four times the distance to stop as it does at 30 miles per hour. Highway engineers have developed formulas to estimate the braking distance of a car.

EXAMPLE 4   Calculating braking distance

The braking distances in feet for a car traveling on wet, level pavement are shown in Table 1.8. Distances have been rounded to the nearest foot.

TABLE 1.8   **Braking Distances**

Speed (mph)	10	20	30	40	50	60	70
Distance (feet)	11	44	100	178	278	400	544

Source: L. Haefner, *Introduction to Transportation Systems.*

(a) If a car doubles its speed, what happens to the braking distance?
(b) If the speed is represented by the variable x and the braking distance by the variable d, then the braking distance may be calculated by the formula $d = \frac{x^2}{9}$. Verify the distance values in Table 1.8 for $x = 10, 30, 60$.

(c) Calculate the braking distance for a car traveling at 90 miles per hour. If a football field is 300 feet long, how many football field lengths does this braking distance represent?

Solution

(a) When the speed increases from 10 to 20 miles per hour, the braking distance increases by a factor of $\frac{44}{11} = 4$. Similarly, if the speed doubles from 30 to 60 miles per hour, the distance increases by a factor of $\frac{400}{100} = 4$. Thus it appears that, if the speed of a car doubles, the braking distance quadruples.

(b) Let $x = 10, 30, 60$ in the formula $d = \frac{x^2}{9}$. Then

$$d = \frac{10^2}{9} = \frac{100}{9} \approx 11 \text{ feet},$$

$$d = \frac{30^2}{9} = \frac{900}{9} = 100 \text{ feet, and}$$

$$d = \frac{60^2}{9} = \frac{3600}{9} = 400 \text{ feet.}$$

These values agree with the values in Table 1.8.

(c) If $x = 90$, then $d = \frac{90^2}{9} = 900$ feet. At 90 miles per hour the braking distance equals three football fields stretched end to end.   Now Try Exercise **65**

In the next example we find a formula that models data in a table.

CRITICAL THINKING

Write a formula that calculates the time T for a bike rider to travel 100 miles moving at x miles per hour. Test your formula for different values of x.

EXAMPLE **5**   Finding a formula

The data in Table 1.9 can be modeled by the formula $y = ax$. Find a.

TABLE 1.9

x	y
1	3
2	6
3	9
4	12
5	15

Solution

Each value of y is 3 times the corresponding value of x, so $a = 3$. We can also find a symbolically. If $x = 1$, then $y = 3$. We can substitute these values into the equation.

$$y = ax \qquad \text{Given equation}$$
$$3 = a \cdot 1 \qquad \text{Let } x = 1 \text{ and } y = 3.$$
$$3 = a \qquad \text{Identity}$$

Thus $a = 3$. The formula $y = 3x$ models the data in Table 1.9.   Now Try Exercise **47**

Square Roots and Cube Roots

The number b is a **square root** of a number a if $b^2 = a$. For example, one square root of 9 is 3 because $3^2 = 9$. The other square root of 9 is -3 because $(-3)^2 = 9$. We use the symbol $\sqrt{9}$ to denote the *positive* or **principal square root** of 9. That is, $\sqrt{9} = 3$. The following are examples of how to evaluate the square root symbol. A calculator is sometimes needed to approximate square roots.

$$\sqrt{16} = 4, \quad -\sqrt{100} = -10, \quad \sqrt{3} \approx 1.732, \quad \pm\sqrt{4} = \pm 2$$

The symbol "$\pm$" is read "plus or minus." Note that ± 2 represents the numbers 2 or -2.

The number b is a **cube root** of a number a if $b^3 = a$. The cube root of 8 is 2 because $2^3 = 8$, which may be written as $\sqrt[3]{8} = 2$. Similarly, $\sqrt[3]{-27} = -3$ because $(-3)^3 = -27$. Each real number has *exactly one* real cube root.

EXAMPLE 6   Finding square roots and cube roots

Evaluate each expression.
(a) $\sqrt{3^2 + 4^2}$ **(b)** $\sqrt[3]{64}$ **(c)** $\sqrt[3]{-2^3 - 19}$

Solution

CALCULATOR HELP

To calculate square roots and cube roots, see the Appendix (page AP-1).

(a) $\sqrt{3^2 + 4^2} = \sqrt{9 + 16} = \sqrt{25} = 5$. *Note:* $\sqrt{3^2 + 4^2} \neq \sqrt{3^2} + \sqrt{4^2} = 3 + 4 = 7$.

(b) $\sqrt[3]{64} = 4$ because $4 \cdot 4 \cdot 4 = 4^3 = 64$.

(c) $\sqrt[3]{-2^3 - 19} = \sqrt[3]{-8 - 19} = \sqrt[3]{-27} = -3$ because $(-3)(-3)(-3) = -27$.

Now Try Exercises 9, 10, 33

EXAMPLE 7   Finding lengths of sides

Find the length of a side s for each geometric shape.
(a) A square with area 100 square feet
(b) A cube with volume 125 cubic inches

Solution

(a) The area of a square is $A = s^2$. Thus $s = \sqrt{100} = 10$ feet because $10^2 = 100$.

(b) The volume of a cube is $V = s^3$. Thus $s = \sqrt[3]{125} = 5$ inches because $5^3 = 125$.

Now Try Exercises 83, 85

MAKING CONNECTIONS

Square Roots and Cube Roots

The square root of a negative number is not a real number. However, the cube root of a negative (or positive) number is a real number. For example, $\sqrt{-8}$ is not a real number, whereas $\sqrt[3]{-8} = -2$ is a real number.

▶ **REAL-WORLD CONNECTION**   Roots of numbers often occur in biology, as illustrated in the next example.

EXAMPLE 8   Analyzing the walking speed of animals

When smaller animals walk, they tend to take faster, shorter steps, whereas larger animals tend to take slower, longer steps. For example, a hyena is about 0.8 meter high at the shoulder and takes roughly 1 step per second when walking, whereas an elephant 3 meters high at the shoulder takes 1 step every 2 seconds. If an animal is h meters high at the shoulder, then the frequency F in steps per second while it is walking can be estimated with the formula

$F = \frac{0.87}{\sqrt{h}}$. The value of F is referred to as the animal's *stepping frequency*. (**Source:** C. Pennycuick, *Newton Rules Biology*.)

(a) A Thomson's gazelle is 0.6 meter high at the shoulder. Estimate its stepping frequency.

(b) A giraffe is 2.7 meters high at the shoulder. Estimate its stepping frequency.

(c) What happens to the stepping frequency as h increases?

Solution

(a) $F = \frac{0.87}{\sqrt{0.6}} \approx 1.12$. A Thomson's gazelle takes about 1.12 steps per second when walking.

(b) $F = \frac{0.87}{\sqrt{2.7}} \approx 0.53$. A giraffe takes roughly half a step per second when walking, or 1 step every 2 seconds.

(c) As h increases, the denominator of $\frac{0.87}{\sqrt{h}}$ also increases, so the ratio becomes smaller. Thus, as h increases, the stepping frequency decreases.   Now Try Exercise **71**

Tables and Calculators (Optional)

Many calculators are able to generate tables. To generate a table, we specify the formula, the starting x-value (TblStart), and the increment (Δ Tbl) between x-values. The calculator generates the required table automatically, as demonstrated in the next example.

EXAMPLE **9**   Using the table feature

Make a table for $y = \frac{x^2}{9}$, starting at $x = 10$ and incrementing by 10. Compare this table to Table 1.8 in Example 4.

Solution

In Figure 1.20 the desired table is generated. Note that, if values are rounded to the nearest foot, the values in Figure 1.20(c) agree with those in Table 1.8.

CALCULATOR HELP

To display a table of values, see the Appendix (page AP-3).

```
Plot1  Plot2  Plot3
\Y₁■X^2/9
\Y₂=
\Y₃=
\Y₄=
\Y₅=
\Y₆=
\Y₇=
```

(a)

```
TABLE SETUP
 TblStart=10
  ΔTbl=10
Indpnt: Auto Ask
Depend: Auto Ask
```

(b)

X	Y₁	
10	11.111	
20	44.444	
30	100	
40	177.78	
50	277.78	
60	400	
70	544.44	

Y₁■X^2/9

(c)

Figure 1.20

Now Try Exercise **61**

1.4 PUTTING IT ALL TOGETHER

The following table summarizes some of the important topics discussed in this section.

Concept	Comments	Examples	
Variable	Represents an unknown quantity	x, y, z, A, V	
Algebraic Expression	Can consist of numbers, variables, operation symbols, exponents, and grouping symbols but *no* equals sign	$2x - 8$ $3 - (5y + 6)$ s^3 $2L + 2W$	
Equation	A statement that two algebraic expressions are equal—*always contains an equals sign*	$5x = 10$ $y = 2x + 1$ $n + 5 = 3 - n$ $z^2 + 1 = 17$	
Formula	An equation used to calculate one quantity, using known values of other quantities—shows relationships between variables	$A = \pi r^2$ $C = 2\pi r$ $V = s^3$ $P = 2L + 2W$ $A = \frac{1}{2}bh$	Area of a circle Circumference of a circle Volume of a cube Perimeter of a rectangle Area of a triangle
Square Root	The *positive* or *principal square root* of a is written $\sqrt{a}$. The square root of a negative number is not a real number.	$\sqrt{25} = 5$ $\pm\sqrt{100} = \pm 10$ $-\sqrt{16} = -4$	
Cube Root	The cube root of a is written $\sqrt[3]{a}$	$\sqrt[3]{-8} = -2$ because $(-2)^3 = -8$. $\sqrt[3]{64} = 4$ because $4^3 = 64$.	

1.4 Exercises

MyMathLab

CONCEPTS

1. A(n) _____ is a symbol used to represent an unknown number or quantity.

2. A(n) _____ is a statement that says two algebraic expressions are equal.

3. An equation always contains a(n) _____ sign.

4. A(n) _____ is an equation that can be used to calculate one quantity by using known values of another quantity.

5. Identify the variables in the equation $x^2 + y^2 = 9$.

6. Give an example of an equation with no variables.

7. Give an example of an equation with one variable.

8. Give an example of an equation with two variables.

9. $\sqrt{9} = $ _____   10. $\sqrt[3]{-8} = $ _____

11. If $b > 0$, then $\sqrt{b^2} = $ _____.

12. $\sqrt[3]{b^3} = $ _____

13. If $y = 2x$ and $x = 3$, then $y = $ _____.

14. If $A = s^2$ and $s = -2$, then $A = $ _____.

WRITING FORMULAS

Exercises 15–24: Write a formula that does the following.

15. Converts x miles to y feet

16. Converts x quarts to y gallons

17. Finds the area A of a square with a side of length s

18. Finds the surface area A of a cube with a side of length s

19. Determines the number of seconds y in x hours

20. Determines the gas mileage G of a car that travels m miles on g gallons of gas

21. Determines the area A of a triangle with base b and height h

22. Determines the perimeter P of a square with side s

23. Finds the area A of a circle with diameter d

24. Finds the circumference C of a circle with diameter d

USING DATA, VARIABLES, AND FORMULAS

Exercises 25–42: Evaluate the formula for the given value(s) of the variable(s).

25. $y = 5x$ $x = 6$

26. $y = \frac{x}{10}$ $x = 30$

27. $y = x + 5$ $x = -3.1$

28. $d = 5 - 4t$ $t = -1.5$

29. $d = t^2 + 1$ $t = -3$

30. $z = 3k^2 - \frac{3}{4}$ $k = \frac{1}{4}$

31. $z = \sqrt{2k}$ $k = 18$

32. $y = \sqrt{5 - x}$ $x = 1$

33. $y = -\frac{1}{2}\sqrt[3]{x}$ $x = \frac{1}{8}$

34. $M = \sqrt[3]{1 - p}$ $p = 65$

35. $N = 3h^3 - 1$ $h = \frac{1}{3}$

36. $S = 1 - \frac{1}{2}w^3$ $w = -2$

37. $P = |5 - w|$ $w = 4.7$

38. $D = |2t - 5|$ $t = 2.5$

39. $A = \frac{1}{2}bh$ $b = 3, \quad h = 6$

40. $P = 2L + 2W$ $L = 9, \quad W = 7$

41. $V = \pi r^2 h$ $r = \frac{1}{2}, \quad h = 5$

42. $S = 2\pi r(r + h)$ $r = 2, \quad h = 8$

Exercises 43–46: Select the formula that best models the data in the table.

43.
x	1	2	3	4	5
y	2	4	6	8	10

(i) $y = x + 2$, (ii) $y = 2x$, (iii) $y = 4x - 2$

44.
x	-2	-1	0	1	2
y	4	1	0	1	4

(i) $y = x^2$, (ii) $y = x + 6$, (iii) $y = 2x$

45.
x	-4	-2	0	2	4
y	4	2	0	2	4

(i) $y = x^2$, (ii) $y = x$, (iii) $y = |x|$

46.
x	-27	-1	0	8	64
y	-3	-1	0	2	4

(i) $y = \sqrt[3]{x}$, (ii) $y = \frac{x}{4}$, (iii) $y = \sqrt{x}$

Exercises 47–50: (Refer to Example 5.) Find a value of the variable a so that the equation models the data.

47. $y = ax$

x	-2	-1	0	1	2
y	6	3	0	-3	-6

48. $y = ax$

x	-10	-5	5	10	15
y	-15	-7.5	7.5	15	22.5

49. $d = t - a$

t	0	1	2	3	4
d	-2	-1	0	1	2

50. $N = aw^2$

w	0	2	4	6	8
N	0	-4	-16	-36	-64

Exercises 51–56: Complete the table for each x-value, using the formula.

51. $y = 2.5x - 0.5$

x	0	2	4	6	8
y					

52. $y = \frac{1}{2}x^2$

x	0	2	4	6	8
y					

53. $y = |5x|$

x	-3	-1	1	3
y				

54. $y = \sqrt{x + 2}$

x	-2	-1	2	7
y				

55. $y = \sqrt[3]{x} - 2$

x	-1	0	1	8
y				

56. $y = x^3 - 4x$

x	-2	0	1	2
y				

Exercises 57 and 58: **Thinking Generally**   *Use the formula to complete the table for each x-value. Assume that the variable a represents a positive number.*

57. $y = \sqrt{x + 1}$

x	a	$a - 1$	$a^2 - 1$
y			

58. $y = 2x + 1$

x	a	$\frac{3}{2}a$	$\frac{1}{2}a - \frac{1}{2}$
y			

Exercises 59–62: Use a calculator to make a table for the given formula. Let x = 1, 2, 3, … ,7.

59. $y = x + \sqrt[3]{x}$

60. $y = \dfrac{1}{\sqrt{x}}$

61. $y = \sqrt{7 - x}$

62. $y = \dfrac{x^3 - 2x}{3}$

APPLICATIONS

63. *Modeling Motion*   The following table lists the distance y traveled by a car in t hours. Find an equation that models these data.

Elapsed time (hours)	1	2	3	4
Distance (miles)	60	120	180	240

64. *Diving and Water Pressure*   The world's record for descending below the surface of the ocean on a single breath is in excess of 400 feet by Francisco Ferreras. During his descent his heart rate slows from 60 beats per minute on the surface to 4 beats per minute at 400 feet. He is able to hold his breath for 7 minutes. These dives are dangerous because of the extreme water pressure. The water pressure P in pounds per square inch at a depth of x feet can be calculated with the formula $P = 0.445x$.
   (a) Calculate the water pressure at a depth of 400 feet.
   (b) The world's deepest diving mammals are sperm whales, which can dive to a depth of 7000 feet.

Calculate the water pressure at this depth.
(**Source:** G. Carr, *Mechanics of Sport.*)

65. *Braking Distance*   (Refer to Example 4.) The braking distance d for a car traveling at x miles per hour on *dry,* level pavement is $d = \frac{x^2}{12}$.   (**Source:** L. Haefner.)

(a) Make a table of braking distances for speeds of 10 to 70 miles per hour in increments of 10 miles per hour.

(b) What is the braking distance for a car traveling at 40 miles per hour?

(c) What happens to the braking distance when the speed doubles?

(d) At 60 miles per hour how much farther does it take the car to stop on wet pavement than on dry pavement? $\left(\text{Hint: For wet pavement } d = \frac{x^2}{9}.\right)$

66. *Songs on an iPod*   A 4 GB iPod can hold about 1000 songs, whereas a 60 GB iPod can store 15,000 songs.   (**Source:** Apple Corporation.)

(a) Find a formula that calculates the number of songs S that can be stored on x gigabytes.

(b) How many songs can be stored on a 30 GB iPod?

67. *Bicycle Speed Records*   The fastest speed attained on a bicycle is 223.3 feet per second. This speed was attained by the bicyclist following a pace vehicle. The bicyclist thus experienced less wind resistance and was carried along by the draft or "suction" created by the pace vehicle. The formula $M = \frac{15}{22}x$ converts feet per second to miles per hour. Find the speed of this record in miles per hour.   (**Source:** G. Carr.)

68. *Pollution and Lawn Mowers*   A person using a gas-powered lawn mower for 1 hour pollutes the air as much as a person driving a car for 340 miles. (**Source:** Minnesota Pollution Control Agency.)

(a) Find a formula that calculates the hours H of lawn mowing that create the same amount of pollution as x miles of driving.

(b) How many hours of lawn mowing pollute the same as 850 miles of driving?

69. *Wing Span and Weight*   A bird's weight W is frequently related to the length L of its wing span. For one species of bird the formula $W = 1.1L^3$ could be used to predict a bird's weight W in kilograms for a wing span of L meters.   (**Source:** C. Pennycuick.)

(a) If a bird has a wing span of 0.75 meter, estimate its weight.

(b) If a bird has a wing span of 1.5 meters, estimate its weight.

(c) If the wing span of a bird doubles, what happens to its weight?

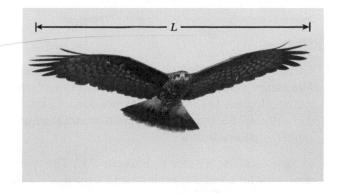

70. *Wing Span and Weight*   (Refer to Exercise 69.) The formula $L = \sqrt[3]{16W}$ relates the weight W of one species of bird in pounds to its wing span L in feet.

(a) Estimate the wing span L when $W = 5$ pounds.

(b) Does a doubling of the weight W double the wing span? Explain.

71. *Stepping Frequency*   (Refer to Example 8.) The formula $F = \frac{0.87}{\sqrt{h}}$ gives the stepping frequency F of an animal with a shoulder height h. Suppose that an animal has four times the shoulder height of another animal. How do their stepping frequencies compare?

72. *Birds*   The surface area of a bird's wings S is frequently related to its weight W. For one species of bird, the formula $S = 0.11\sqrt[3]{W^2}$ could be used to predict the surface area S in square meters of a bird's wings for a weight W in kilograms.   (***Source:*** C. Pennycuick.)
  (a) If a bird weighs 0.5 kilogram, estimate the area of its wings.
  (b) If a bird's weight doubles, does the area of its wings also double?

73. *Escape Velocity*   To escape the gravity of a planet or a moon, a spacecraft must reach the *escape velocity*, which we denote E. The larger the planet or moon, the greater the escape velocity is. But for a spacecraft simply to attain a circular orbit, a slower velocity C is necessary. The relationship between E and C is modeled by $E = \sqrt{2}C$. Use this formula to approximate the missing values in the following table. (***Source:*** H. Karttunen, *Fundamental Astronomy.*)

Planet	Venus	Earth	Moon	Mars
C (mph)	16,260			8050
E (mph)		25,040	5360	

Source: M. Zeilik, *Introductory Astronomy and Astrophysics.*

74. *Escape Velocity*   (Refer to the preceding exercise.) The escape velocity for the largest planet in our solar system, Jupiter, is 136,000 miles per hour. Calculate the velocity necessary for a circular orbit around Jupiter.   (***Source:*** M. Zeilik.)

75. *Escape Velocity*   (Refer to Exercise 73.) The speed necessary for a circular orbit around Saturn is 57,000 miles per hour. Find the escape velocity for Saturn. (***Source:*** M. Zeilik.)

76. *Animals and Trotting Speeds*   (Refer to Example 8.) The relationship between the shoulder height h in meters and an animal's stepping frequency F in steps per second while *trotting* is given by $F = \frac{1.84}{\sqrt{h}}$. (***Source:*** C. Pennycuick.)

  (a) Estimate the stepping frequency for a trotting buffalo that is 1.5 meters high at the shoulders.
  (b) What happens to an animal's stepping frequency while trotting as its shoulder height increases?

77. *Pulse Rate in Animals*   According to one model, the rate at which an animal's heart beats varies with its weight. Smaller animals tend to have faster pulses, whereas larger animals tend to have slower pulses. The pulse rate of an animal can be modeled by the equation $N = \frac{885}{\sqrt{W}}$, where N is the number of beats per minute and W is the animal's weight in pounds. (***Source:*** C. Pennycuick.)
  (a) Estimate the pulse for a 25-pound dog.
  (b) Estimate the pulse for a 1600-pound elephant.

78. *Pulse Rate in Animals*   (Refer to the preceding exercise.) Suppose that an animal has half the pulse rate of another animal. How do the weights of these animals compare?

79. *Area of an Equilateral Triangle*   An equilateral triangle has three sides equal in length. Its area A is given by $A = \frac{\sqrt{3}}{4}s^2$, where s is the length of a side, as shown in the accompanying figure. Calculate the areas for the given values of s.

  (a) $s = 2$ feet   **(b)** $s = 4$ meters

80. *Equilateral Triangle*   (Refer to the preceding exercise.) What happens to the area of an equilateral triangle if the length of a side triples?

81. *Circumference of a Circle*   The circumference C of a circle is given by $C = 2\pi r$, where r is the radius. Calculate the circumference of each circle with the given radius.
  (a) $r = 14$ inches   **(b)** $r = 1.3$ miles

82. *Area of a Circle*   The area A of a circle is given by $A = \pi r^2$, where r is the radius. Calculate the area of each circle with the given radius.
  (a) $r = 12$ inches   **(b)** $r = 6$ feet

Exercises 83–86: Determine the length of a side for each geometric shape.

83. A square with an area of 81 square inches

84. A square with an area of 121 square meters

85. A cube with a volume of 27 cubic meters

86. A cube with a volume of 64 cubic feet

87. *Inline Skating*   During a strenuous skating workout, an athlete can burn 336 calories in 40 minutes.
(**Source:** *Runner's World.*)

(a) Write a formula that calculates the calories C burned from skating 40 minutes a day for x days.

(b) How many calories could be burned in 30 days?

88. *Inline Skating*   (Refer to the preceding exercise.) If a person loses 1 pound for every 3500 calories burned, write a formula that gives the number of pounds P lost in x days from skating 40 minutes per day. How many pounds could be lost in 100 days?

WRITING ABOUT MATHEMATICS

89. Explain the difference between an *algebraic expression* and an *equation*.

90. Give an example of a formula that models an application and identify each variable. Explain how to use the formula.

CHECKING BASIC CONCEPTS
SECTIONS 1.3 AND 1.4

1. Evaluate each expression.
  (a) 2^4 **(b)** $3^{-2} \cdot 2^0$

  (c) $\dfrac{2^4}{2^2 \cdot 2^{-3}}$ **(d)** $x^3 x^{-4} x^2$

  (e) $\left(\dfrac{2x^3}{y^{-4}} \right)^2$

2. Evaluate each expression.
  (a) $4 + 5 \cdot (-2)$ **(b)** $\dfrac{1+3}{-4+3}$

  (c) $2^3 - 5(2 - 3 \cdot 4)$

3. Express each number in scientific notation.
  (a) 103,000   **(b)** 0.000523   **(c)** 6.7

4. Express each number in standard form.
  (a) 5.43×10^6 **(b)** 9.8×10^{-3}

5. *Indoor Air Pollution*   Ventilation is an effective method for removing indoor air pollution. The formula $y = 900x$ calculates the cubic feet per hour of air that should be circulated in a classroom containing x people. Make a table showing the ventilation necessary for classes containing 10, 20, 30, and 40 people. How much ventilation is necessary per person? (**Source:** American Society of Heating, Refrigerating, and Air-Conditioning Engineers, ASHRAE.)

1.5 INTRODUCTION TO GRAPHING

Relations ■ The Cartesian Coordinate System ■ Scatterplots and Line Graphs ■
The Viewing Rectangle (Optional) ■ Graphing with Calculators (Optional)

A LOOK INTO MATH ▷   Computers, the Internet, and other types of electronic communication are creating large amounts of data. The challenge for society is to use these data to solve important problems and create new knowledge. Before conclusions can be drawn, data must be analyzed. A powerful tool in this step is visualization. Pictures and graphs are capable of communicating large quantities of information in short periods of time. A full page of computer graphics typically contains a hundred times more information than a page of text.

The map in Figure 1.21 shows the average date of the first 32°F temperature in autumn. Imagine trying to describe this map by using *only* words. In this section we discuss how graphs are used to visualize data.   (***Source:*** J. Williams, *The Weather Almanac*.)

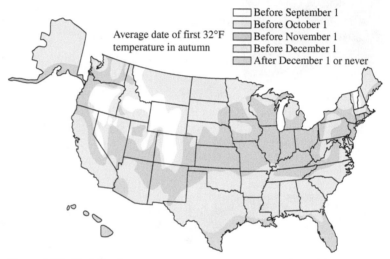

Average date of first 32°F
temperature in autumn

☐ Before September 1
☐ Before October 1
☐ Before November 1
☐ Before December 1
☐ After December 1 or never

Figure 1.21 First Frost

Relations

▶ **REAL-WORLD CONNECTION**   Table 1.10 lists monthly average wind speeds in miles per hour for San Francisco. In this table January corresponds to 1, February to 2, and so on, until December is represented by 12. For example, in April the average wind speed is 12 miles per hour.

TABLE 1.10 Average Wind Speeds in San Francisco

Month	1	2	3	4	5	6	7	8	9	10	11	12
Wind Speed (mph)	7	9	11	12	13	14	14	13	11	9	8	7

Source: J. Williams, *The Weather Almanac*.

If we let x be the month and y be the wind speed, then the **ordered pair** (x, y) represents the average wind speed y during month x. For example, the ordered pair $(2, 9)$ indicates that in February the average wind speed is 9 miles per hour, whereas the ordered pair $(9, 11)$ indicates that the average wind speed in September is 11 miles per hour. *Order is important* in an ordered pair.

The data in Table 1.10 establish a *relation*; that is, each month is associated with a wind speed in an ordered pair (**month, wind speed**). This relation can be represented by a set S, which contains 12 ordered pairs:

$$S = \{(1, 7), (2, 9), (3, 11), (4, 12), (5, 13), (6, 14),$$
$$(7, 14), (8, 13), (9, 11), (10, 9), (11, 8), (12, 7)\}.$$

RELATION

A **relation** is a set of ordered pairs.

If we denote the ordered pairs in a relation (x, y), then the set of all x-values is called the **domain** of the relation and the set of all y-values is called the **range**. In Table 1.10 the domain is

$$D = \{1, 2, 3, 4, 5, 6, 7, 8, 9, 10, 11, 12\},$$

which corresponds to the 12 months. The range is

$$R = \{7, 8, 9, 11, 12, 13, 14\},$$

which corresponds to the monthly average wind speeds. Note that an average wind speed of 14 miles per hour occurs more than once in Table 1.10, but it is listed *only once* in the range set R. The same is true for the values 7, 9, 11, and 13.

EXAMPLE 1   Finding the domain and range of a relation

Find the domain and range for the relation given by

$$S = \{(-1, 5), (0, 1), (2, 4), (4, 2), (5, 1)\}.$$

Solution
The domain D is determined by the first element in each ordered pair, or

$$D = \{-1, 0, 2, 4, 5\}.$$

The range R is determined by the second element in each ordered pair, or

$$R = \{1, 2, 4, 5\}.$$ Now Try Exercise 7

▶ REAL-WORLD CONNECTION   We are all well aware that tuition and fees go up each year. In the next example, we describe this interaction between the year and the cost as a relation.

EXAMPLE 2   Analyzing tuition and fees

Table 1.11 (on the next page) lists the average cost of tuition and fees at *public* colleges from 2001 through 2004. Express this table as a relation S. Identify the domain and range of S.

TABLE 1.11   **Tuition and Fees**

Year	2001	2002	2003	2004
Cost	$3725	$4081	$4694	$5132

Source: The College Board.

Solution

Let the year be the first element in the ordered pair and the cost of tuition and fees be the second element. Then relation S is given by the following set of ordered pairs.

$$S = \{(2001, 3725), (2002, 4081), (2003, 4694), (2004, 5132)\}$$

The domain of S is

$$D = \{2001, 2002, 2003, 2004\}$$

and the range of S is

$$R = \{3725, 4081, 4694, 5132\}.$$

Now Try Exercise **15**

It is possible for a relation to contain *infinitely many* ordered pairs. For example, let the equation $y = 2x$ define a relation S, where x is any real number. Then S contains infinitely many ordered pairs of the form $(x, 2x)$, such as $(-2, -4)$, $(3, 6)$, and $(0.1, 0.2)$.

EXAMPLE **3**   Analyzing iPod memory

The formula $S = 250m$ identifies a relationship between the memory m of an iPod in gigabytes and the number of songs S that can be stored on it. Give four ordered pairs in this relation.

Solution

One way to determine four ordered pairs is to assign the variable m four different values. For example, when $m = 4$, $S = 250(4) = 1000$. The ordered pair $(4, 1000)$ means that a 4 GB iPod can hold 1000 songs. Table 1.12 lists this ordered pair along with three additional ordered pairs: $(8, 2000)$, $(20, 5000)$, and $(30, 7500)$.

TABLE 1.12

m	4	8	20	30
S	1000	2000	5000	7500

Now Try Exercise **21**

The Cartesian Coordinate System

We can use the **Cartesian coordinate system**, or *xy*-plane, to visualize or *graph* a relation. The horizontal axis is the *x*-axis and the vertical axis is the *y*-axis. The axes intersect at the **origin** and determine four regions called **quadrants**. They are numbered I, II, III, and IV counterclockwise, as illustrated in Figure 1.22. We can plot the ordered pair (x, y) by using the *x*-axis and the *y*-axis. For example, the point $(1, 2)$ is located in quadrant I, 1 unit to the right of the origin and 2 units above the *x*-axis, as shown in Figure 1.23.

Figure 1.22 The xy-plane

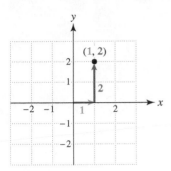

Figure 1.23 Plotting a Point

Similarly, the ordered pair $(-2, 3)$ is located in quadrant II, $(-3, -3)$ is in quadrant III, and $(3, -2)$ is in quadrant IV. See Figure 1.24. A point lying on a coordinate axis does not belong to any quadrant. The point $(-2, 0)$ is located on the x-axis, whereas the point $(0, -2)$ lies on the y-axis.

Figure 1.24 Plotting Points

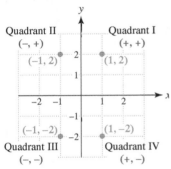

Figure 1.25

CRITICAL THINKING

If a is negative, then what quadrant does the point $(a, -a^2)$ lie in?

For any point (x, y) with x and y nonzero, we can determine the quadrant in which it is located. For example, the point $(1, 2)$ lies in quadrant I because both x and y are positive, whereas $(-1, -2)$ lies in quadrant III because both x and y are negative. The point $(-1, 2)$ lies in quadrant II where x is negative and y is positive, and $(1, -2)$ lies in quadrant IV where x is positive and y is negative. These concepts are illustrated in Figure 1.25, where $(+, +)$ indicates that $x > 0$ and $y > 0$ for any point (x, y) in quadrant I. Other quadrants and ordered pairs can be interpreted similarly.

EXAMPLE **4**   Plotting points

Plot the data listed in Table 1.13. State the quadrant containing each point or the axis on which each point lies.

TABLE 1.13

x	-3	0	1	4
y	1	4	-2	3

Solution

We plot the points $(-3, 1)$, $(0, 4)$, $(1, -2)$, and $(4, 3)$ in the xy-plane, as shown in Figure 1.26 on the next page. The point $(-3, 1)$ is in quadrant II, $(1, -2)$ is in quadrant IV, and $(4, 3)$ is in quadrant I. The point $(0, 4)$ lies on the y-axis and does not belong to any quadrant.

Figure 1.26

Now Try Exercise 17

EXAMPLE 5   Graphing points given an equation

Evaluate $y = x^2 + 1$ for $x = -2, -1, 0, 1,$ and 2. Plot the resulting ordered pairs.

Solution

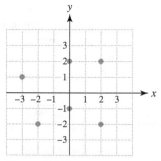

Figure 1.27

Start by evaluating the formula $y = x^2 + 1$ for each x-value.

$$x = -2: \quad y = (-2)^2 + 1 = 5$$
$$x = -1: \quad y = (-1)^2 + 1 = 2$$
$$x = 0: \quad y = 0^2 + 1 = 1$$
$$x = 1: \quad y = 1^2 + 1 = 2$$
$$x = 2: \quad y = 2^2 + 1 = 5$$

The points $(-2, 5), (-1, 2), (0, 1), (1, 2),$ and $(2, 5)$ are plotted in Figure 1.27.

Now Try Exercise 47

EXAMPLE 6   Determining the domain and range

Use the graph in Figure 1.28 to determine the domain and range of the relation.

Figure 1.28

Solution

The relation shown in Figure 1.28 includes the points $(-3, 1), (-2, -2), (0, 2), (0, -1), (2, 2),$ and $(2, -2)$. The domain of this relation consists of the x-values of these ordered pairs, or $D = \{-3, -2, 0, 2\}$. The range of this relation consists of the y-values of these ordered pairs, or $R = \{-2, -1, 1, 2\}$.

Now Try Exercise 27

Scatterplots and Line Graphs

If distinct points are plotted in the xy-plane, the resulting graph is called a **scatterplot**. Figure 1.28 is an example. A scatterplot of a different relation is shown in Figure 1.29, where the points $(1, 2), (2, 4), (3, 5), (4, 6), (5, 4),$ and $(6, 3)$ have been plotted. Its domain is $D = \{1, 2, 3, 4, 5, 6\}$, and its range is $R = \{2, 3, 4, 5, 6\}$.

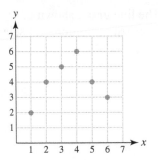

Figure 1.29 A Scatterplot

▶ **REAL-WORLD CONNECTION** The next example illustrates how to make a scatterplot from real data.

EXAMPLE **7** Making a scatterplot of gasoline prices

Table 1.14 lists the average price of a gallon of gasoline for selected years. Make a scatterplot of these data.

TABLE 1.14 **Average Prices of Gasoline**

Year	1955	1965	1975	1985	1995	2005
Price (per gallon)	29¢	31¢	57¢	120¢	121¢	227¢

Source: Department of Energy.

Solution

Plot the points $(1955, 29), (1965, 31), (1975, 57), (1985, 120), (1995, 121),$ and $(2005, 227)$. The x-values vary from 1955 to 2005, so we label the x-axis from 1955 to 2005. The y-values vary from 29 to 227, so we label the y-axis from 0 to 250. (Note that labels on the x- and y-axes may vary.) Figure 1.30 shows these points as plotted and labeled. Note that the double hash marks // on the x-axis indicate that there is a break in the scale, which starts at 0 and then jumps to 1955.

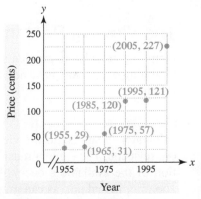

Figure 1.30 Price of Gasoline

Now Try Exercise **35**

▶ REAL-WORLD CONNECTION   Sometimes it is helpful to connect the data points in a scatterplot with straight line segments. This type of graph emphasizes changes in the data and is called a **line graph**.

EXAMPLE 8   Interpreting a line graph

The line graph shown in Figure 1.31 depicts the total number of all types of college degrees awarded in millions for selected years.   (*Source:* Department of Education.)

Figure 1.31 College Graduates

(a) Did the number of graduates ever decrease during this time period? Explain.
(b) Approximate the number of college graduates in the year 1970.
(c) Determine the 10-year period when the increase in the number of college graduates was greatest. What was this increase?

Solution
(a) Yes, the number decreased slightly between 1950 and 1960. For this time period, the line segment slopes slightly downward from left to right.
(b) In 1970, about 1.1 million degrees were awarded.
(c) The greatest increase corresponds to the line segment that slopes upward most from left to right. This increase occurred between 1960 and 1970 and was about $1.1 - 0.5 = 0.6$ million graduates.   Now Try Exercises 39, 75

The Viewing Rectangle (Optional)

Graphing calculators provide several features beyond those found on scientific calculators. Graphing calculators have additional keys that can be used to create tables, scatterplots, and graphs.

▶ REAL-WORLD CONNECTION   The **viewing rectangle**, or **window**, on a graphing calculator is similar to the viewfinder in a camera. A camera cannot take a picture of an entire scene. The camera must be centered on some object and can photograph only a portion of the available scenery. A camera can capture different views of the same scene by zooming in and out, as can graphing calculators. The *xy*-plane is infinite, but the calculator screen can show only a finite, rectangular region of the *xy*-plane. The viewing rectangle must be specified by setting minimum and maximum values for both the *x*- and *y*-axes before a graph can be drawn.

Figure 1.32

We use the following terminology regarding the size of a viewing rectangle. **Xmin** is the minimum *x*-value along the *x*-axis, and **Xmax** is the maximum *x*-value. Similarly, **Ymin** is the minimum *y*-value along the *y*-axis, and **Ymax** is the maximum *y*-value. Most graphs show an *x*-scale and a *y*-scale with tick marks on the respective axes. Sometimes the distance between consecutive tick marks is 1 unit, but at other times it might be 5 or 10 units. The distance represented by consecutive tick marks on the *x*-axis is called **Xscl**, and the distance represented by consecutive tick marks on the *y*-axis is called **Yscl** (see Figure 1.32).

This information about the viewing rectangle can be written as [Xmin, Xmax, Xscl] by [Ymin, Ymax, Yscl]. For example, $[-10, 10, 1]$ by $[-10, 10, 1]$ means that Xmin $= -10$, Xmax $= 10$, Xscl $= 1$, Ymin $= -10$, Ymax $= 10$, and Yscl $= 1$. This setting is referred to as the **standard viewing rectangle**. The window in Figure 1.32 is $[-3, 3, 1]$ by $[-3, 3, 1]$.

EXAMPLE 9   Setting the viewing rectangle

Show the viewing rectangle $[-2, 3, 0.5]$ by $[-100, 200, 50]$ on your calculator.

Solution
The window setting and viewing rectangle are displayed in Figure 1.33. Note that in Figure 1.33(b) there are 6 tick marks on the positive *x*-axis because its length is 3 units and the distance between consecutive tick marks is 0.5 unit.

CALCULATOR HELP

To set a viewing rectangle, see the Appendix (page AP-4).

(a)

$[-2, 3, 0.5]$ by $[-100, 200, 50]$

(b)

Figure 1.33

Now Try Exercise 61

Graphing with Calculators (Optional)

Many graphing calculators have the capability to create scatterplots and line graphs. The next example illustrates how to make a scatterplot with a graphing calculator.

EXAMPLE 10   Making a scatterplot with a graphing calculator

Plot the points $(-2, -2)$, $(-1, 3)$, $(1, 2)$, and $(2, -3)$ in $[-4, 4, 1]$ by $[-4, 4, 1]$.

Solution

We entered the points $(-2, -2)$, $(-1, 3)$, $(1, 2)$, and $(2, -3)$ shown in Figure 1.34(a), using the STAT EDIT feature. The variable L1 represents the list of x-values, and the variable L2 represents the list of y-values. In Figure 1.34(b) we set the graphing calculator to make a scatterplot with the STATPLOT feature, and in Figure 1.34(c) the points have been plotted. If you have a different model of calculator you may need to consult your owner's manual.

CALCULATOR HELP

To make a scatterplot, see the Appendix (page AP-4).

(a)

(b)

$[-4, 4, 1]$ by $[-4, 4, 1]$

(c)

Figure 1.34

Now Try Exercise 69

▶ REAL-WORLD CONNECTION   In the next example, a graphing calculator is used to create a line graph of sales of cordless telephones.

EXAMPLE 11   Making a line graph with a graphing calculator

Table 1.15 lists numbers of cordless telephones sold for selected years from 1990 through 2005. Make a line graph of these sales in an appropriate viewing rectangle. Then interpret the line graph.

TABLE 1.15   **Cordless Phone Sales**

Year	1990	1995	2000	2005
Phones (millions)	10.1	19.5	39.0	38.3

Source: Cellular Telecommunications Industry Association.

Solution

Plot the points $(1990, 10.1)$, $(1995, 19.5)$, $(2000, 39.0)$, and $(2005, 38.3)$. The x-values vary from 1990 to 2005, and the y-values vary between 10.1 and 38.3. We selected the viewing rectangle $[1988, 2007, 5]$ by $[0, 50, 10]$, although other viewing rectangles are possible. The viewing rectangle should be large enough to show all four data points without being too large. A line graph can be created by selecting this option on the graphing calculator.

CALCULATOR HELP

To make a line graph, see the
Appendix (page AP-4).

Figures 1.35(a) and 1.35(b) show the data entries and plotting scheme. Figure 1.35(c) shows the resulting graph. It reveals that sales have increased dramatically and then decreased slightly during this time period.

(a)

(b)

[1988, 2007, 5] by [0, 50, 10]

(c)

Figure 1.35

Now Try Exercise 77

1.5 PUTTING IT ALL TOGETHER

Graphs are frequently used in mathematics, science, and business as a way to summarize and understand data better. The xy-plane is commonly used to visualize relations.

Concept	Explanation	Example
Relation	A set of ordered pairs	$S = \{(1, 2), (-2, 3), (4, 2)\}$
Domain and Range	If a relation consists of a set of ordered pairs (x, y), then the set of x-values is the domain and the set of y-values is the range.	If $S = \{(1, 2), (-2, 3), (4, 2)\}$, then $D = \{-2, 1, 4\}$ and $R = \{2, 3\}$.
Cartesian Coordinate System or xy-plane	Has four quadrants, two axes, and an origin Used to plot points and graphs	(graph showing four quadrants with axes, origin, Quadrant II, Quadrant I, Quadrant III, Quadrant IV)
Scatterplot	A scatterplot results when individual points are plotted in the xy-plane.	(scatterplot graph)
Line Graph	A line graph is similar to a scatterplot except that line segments are drawn between consecutive points.	(line graph)

1.5 Exercises

CONCEPTS

1. What is a relation?

2. What are the domain and range of a relation?

3. Sketch the *xy*-plane and identify each of the following: the *x*-axis, the *y*-axis, the origin, and the four quadrants.

4. Sketch an example of a scatterplot and a line graph.

5. Do the ordered pairs (1, 2) and (2, 1) represent the same point in the *xy*-plane?

6. In what quadrant does the point $(-1, -1)$ lie?

RELATIONS AND THE RECTANGULAR COORDINATE SYSTEM

Exercises 7–12: Identify the domain and range of S.

7. $S = \{(1, 2), (3, -4), (5, 6)\}$

8. $S = \{(0, 4), (0, 6), (3, -1), (4, 0)\}$

9. $S = \{(-2, 3), (-1, 2), (0, 1), (1, 0), (2, 1)\}$

10. $S = \left\{\left(\frac{1}{2}, -\frac{3}{4}\right), \left(-\frac{5}{8}, \frac{4}{7}\right), \left(\frac{1}{2}, \frac{3}{4}\right), \left(\frac{8}{7}, \frac{3}{4}\right)\right\}$

11. $S = \{(41, 67), (87, 53), (41, 88), (96, 24)\}$

12. $S = \{(-1.2, -1.1), (0.8, 2.5), (1.5, -0.6)\}$

Exercises 13–16: Express the relation S in the table as a set of ordered pairs. Then identify the domain and range.

13.

x	1	3	5	7	9
y	3	7	11	15	19

14.

x	−2.1	−1.5	0.7	1.3	2.9
y	9.6	7.4	3.3	−2.0	−8.8

15. U.S. unemployment rate in percent

x	2000	2001	2002	2003	2004
y	4.0	4.2	5.8	6.0	5.5

Source: Department of Labor.

16. U.S. population in millions

x	1800	1840	1880	1920	1960	2000
y	5	17	50	106	179	281

Source: U.S. Census Bureau.

Exercises 17–20: Plot the points in the table in the xy-plane. State the quadrant containing each point or the axis on which each point lies.

17.

x	1	−3	0	−1
y	2	0	−2	3

18.

x	2	−4	−2	0
y	6	−4	0	−5

19.

x	10	−30	50	−20
y	50	20	−25	−25

20.

x	0.2	0.4	0.6	0.8
y	3	1	−1	−3

Exercises 21–26: (Refer to Example 3.) Find four ordered pairs that belong to the relation determined by the given equation. Answers may vary.

21. $y = 4x$ **22.** $y = 3x + 5$

23. $A = 4 - t^2$ **24.** $R = 3t^2$

25. $z = \dfrac{1}{r^2 + 1}$ **26.** $z = \dfrac{2}{5 - r}$

Exercises 27–32: Express the relation shown in the graph as a set of ordered pairs. Identify the domain and range.

27.

28.

29.

30.

31. Billions of dollars spent on military personnel in the United States; answers may vary slightly. (*Source:* Department of Defense.)

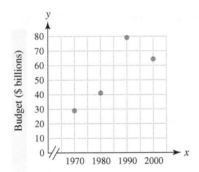

32. Reported cases of tetanus in the U.S.; answers may vary slightly. (***Source:*** Department of Health and Human Services.)

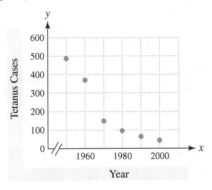

33. Thinking Generally If the ordered pairs (a, b) and (b, a) represent the same point in the xy-plane, what can be said about a and b?

34. Thinking Generally In what quadrant does the point $(-b, b)$ lie, if b is negative?

SCATTERPLOTS AND LINE GRAPHS

Exercises 35–38: Complete the following.
  (a) Find the domain and range of the relation.
  (b) Determine the minimum and maximum of the x-values; of the y-values.

(c) Label appropriate scales on the x- and y-axes.
(d) Make a scatterplot of the data by hand.

35. $\{(0, 2), (-3, 4), (-2, -4), (1, -3), (0, 0)\}$

36. $\{(1, 1), (3, 0), (-4, -4), (5, -2), (0, 3)\}$

37. $\{(10, 50), (-30, 40), (20, -50), (30, 20)\}$

38. $\{(5, 15), (25, 20), (10, 10), (-10, 30), (-20, -10)\}$

Exercises 39–42: Make a line graph of the data.

39. $(0, 2), (1, 4), (2, 5), (4, 4), (5, 2)$

40. $(-2, 4), (-1, 1), (0, 0), (1, 1), (2, 4)$

41. $(4, 4), (8, -4), (12, 8), (16, 0), (20, -8)$

42. $(10, 20), (20, 30), (30, 40), (40, 60), (50, 30)$

Exercises 43–46: Make a line graph of the data.

43.

x	0	1	2	3
y	-2	-1	0	3

44.

x	-2	-1	0	1	2
y	0	3	4	3	0

45.

x	0	1	2	3
y	-3	0	3	0

46.

x	0	1	4	9
y	0	1	2	3

Exercises 47–58: (Refer to Example 5.) Evaluate the formula for $x = -2, -1, 0, 1,$ and 2. Plot the resulting ordered pairs.

47. $y = 3x$ **48.** $y = -2x$

49. $y = -x + 2$ **50.** $y = 2x + 4$

51. $y = -\frac{1}{2}x$ **52.** $y = \frac{1}{2}x + 1$

53. $y = x^2 - 1$ **54.** $y = \frac{1}{2}x^2$

55. $y = -x^2$ **56.** $y = 2x^2$

57. $y = |x|$ **58.** $y = \sqrt{x} + 2$

GRAPHING CALCULATORS

 Exercises 59–64: Show the given viewing rectangle on your graphing calculator. Predict the number of tick marks on the positive x-axis and the positive y-axis.

59. Standard viewing rectangle

60. $[-12, 12, 2]$ by $[-8, 8, 2]$

61. $[0, 100, 10]$ by $[-50, 50, 10]$

62. $[-30, 30, 5]$ by $[-20, 20, 5]$

63. $[1980, 1995, 1]$ by $[12000, 16000, 1000]$

64. $[1900, 1990, 10]$ by $[1700, 2800, 100]$

Exercises 65–68: Express the relation S shown in the graph as a set of ordered pairs.

65. $[-3, 3, 1]$ by $[-2, 2, 1]$ **66.** $[-6, 6, 1]$ by $[-4, 4, 1]$

67. $[-5, 5, 1]$ by $[-3, 3, 1]$ **68.** $[1900, 2000, 20]$ by $[0, 500, 100]$

Exercises 69–74: Use your calculator to make a scatterplot of the relation after determining an appropriate viewing rectangle.

69. $\{(4, 3), (-2, 1), (-3, -3), (5, -2)\}$

70. $\{(5, 5), (2, 0), (-2, 7), (2, -8), (-1, -5)\}$

71. $\{(20, 40), (-25, -15), (-20, 25), (15, -25)\}$

72. $\{(-13, 12), (3, 10), (-15, -4), (12, -9)\}$

73. $\{(100, -100), (50, 200), (-150, -140), (-30, 80)\}$

74. $\{(-125, 75), (45, 65), (-53, -67), (150, -80)\}$

APPLICATIONS

Exercises 75–80: Graphing Real Data   Each table contains real data.

(a) Make a line graph of the data.
(b) Comment on any trends in the data.

75. Head Start participation y in thousands during year x

x	1970	1980	1990	2000	2004
y	480	380	540	860	906

Source: Department of Health and Human Services.

76. Sales y of CDs in millions during year x

x	1990	1992	1994	2000	2005
y	290	410	660	1273	705

Source: Recording Industry Association of America.

77. Welfare beneficiaries y in millions during year x

x	1993	1995	1997	1999	2003
y	14.1	13.7	10.9	7.0	5.0

Source: Administration for Children and Families.

78. Medicaid recipients y in millions during year x

x	1975	1981	1990	1995	2003
y	3.6	3.4	3.2	4.2	5.0

Source: Health Care Financing Administration.

79. Asian-American population y in millions during year x

x	1998	2000	2002	2004	2006
y	10.5	11.2	12.0	12.8	14.0

Source: U.S. Census Bureau.

80. Internet usage in millions of users y during year x

x	1991	1993	1997	2001	2004
y	7.5	20.1	57.0	143	201

Source: The Internet Society.

WRITING ABOUT MATHEMATICS

81. Explain how the domain and range of a relation can be used to determine an appropriate viewing rectangle for a scatterplot.

82. Explain the difference between a scatterplot and a line graph. Give an example of each.

CHECKING BASIC CONCEPTS

1. State the domain and range of the relation given by $S = \{(-5, 3), (1, 4), (2, 3), (1, -1)\}$.

2. Plot the following points in the xy-plane. State the quadrant containing each point or the axis on which each point lies.
   (a) $(1, 4)$ (b) $(0, -3)$
   (c) $(2, -2)$ (d) $(-2, 3)$

3. Evaluate $y = 2 - x^2$ for $x = -2, -1, 0, 1,$ and 2. Plot the resulting ordered pairs.

4. The following table lists the number of people in millions living below the poverty level for five selected years. Make a line graph of these data. Comment on any trends in the data.

Year	1960	1970	1980	1990	2000
Number	40	25	29	34	31

Source: U.S. Census Bureau.

CHAPTER 1   SUMMARY

SECTION 1.1 ■ DESCRIBING DATA WITH SETS OF NUMBERS

Sets of Numbers

Natural Numbers $N = \{1, 2, 3, 4, \dots\}$

Whole Numbers $W = \{0, 1, 2, 3, \dots\}$

Integers $I = \{\dots, -2, -1, 0, 1, 2, \dots\}$

Rational Numbers   Can be written as $\frac{p}{q}$, where p and $q \neq 0$ are integers; includes repeating and terminating decimals

Examples: $\frac{1}{2}, -3, 6, \sqrt{9}, 0.\overline{7}, 0.123$

Irrational Numbers   A real number that is not rational

Examples: $\pi, \sqrt{11}, -\sqrt{3}$

Real Numbers   Any number that can be written in decimal form

Examples: $-\frac{2}{3}, 0, 12.6, \sqrt{11}, \pi$

Properties of Real Numbers

Identity Properties

$$a + 0 = a \qquad\qquad a \cdot 1 = a$$

Commutative Properties

$$a + b = b + a \qquad\qquad a \cdot b = b \cdot a$$

Associative Properties

$$(a + b) + c = a + (b + c) \qquad (a \cdot b) \cdot c = a \cdot (b \cdot c)$$

Distributive Properties

$$a(b + c) = ab + ac \qquad\qquad a(b - c) = ab - ac$$

Real Number Line   The number line is used to graph real numbers.

Origin

$$\xleftarrow{\hspace{1cm}} \underset{-3}{\,|\,} \underset{-2}{\,|\,} \underset{-1}{\,|\,} \overset{\text{\tiny/}}{\underset{0}{\,|\,}} \underset{1}{\,|\,} \underset{2}{\,|\,} \underset{3}{\,|\,} \xrightarrow{\hspace{1cm}}$$

Absolute Value $|a|$ equals a if $a > 0$ or $a = 0$, and $-a$ if $a < 0$.

Examples: $|-4| = 4$, $|7| = 7$, and $|\pi - 7| = 7 - \pi$ because $7 > \pi$

Arithmetic Operations

Addition   **Examples:** $-3 + 4 = 1$, $3 + (-4) = -1$, and $-3 + (-4) = -7$

Subtraction   Use $a - b = a + (-b)$.

                            Examples: $-5 - 6 = -5 + (-6) = -11$ and
                            $4 - (-3) = 4 + 3 = 7$

Multiplication   The product of two numbers with like signs is positive. The product of two numbers with unlike signs is negative.

                            Examples: $3 \cdot (-4) = -12$ and $-5 \cdot (-6) = 30$

Division   Use $\dfrac{a}{b} = a \cdot \dfrac{1}{b}$.

                            Examples: $\frac{1}{2} \div -\frac{4}{5} = \frac{1}{2} \cdot -\frac{5}{4} = -\frac{5}{8}$ and

                            $-\frac{3}{2} \div 6 = -\frac{3}{2} \cdot \frac{1}{6} = -\frac{3}{12} = -\frac{1}{4}$

Exponential Expression

$$\text{Base} \rightarrow 6^2 \leftarrow \text{Exponent}$$

Integer Exponents   Let n be a positive integer and a be a nonzero number.

$$a^n = a \cdot a \cdot a \cdot \,\cdots\, \cdot a \quad (n \text{ factors of } a)$$
$$a^0 = 1 \;(\text{Note: } 0^0 \text{ is undefined.})$$
$$a^{-n} = \frac{1}{a^n}$$

Examples: $4^3 = 4 \cdot 4 \cdot 4 = 64$, $5^0 = 1$, and $2^{-3} = \dfrac{1}{2^3}$

Properties of Exponents
Product Rule $a^m \cdot a^n = a^{m+n}$

                            Example: $z^3 \cdot z^5 = z^8$

Quotient Rule	$\dfrac{a^m}{a^n} = a^{m-n}$
	Example: $\dfrac{x^5}{x^7} = x^{-2} = \dfrac{1}{x^2}$
Power Rules	$(a^m)^n = a^{mn}, \ (ab)^n = a^n b^n, \ \text{and} \ \left(\dfrac{a}{b}\right)^n = \dfrac{a^n}{b^n}$
	Examples: $(5^2)^3 = 5^6, \ (2x)^3 = 8x^3, \ \text{and} \ \left(\dfrac{2x}{y}\right)^3 = \dfrac{8x^3}{y^3}$
Negative Exponents	$\dfrac{1}{a^{-n}} = a^n, \ \dfrac{a^{-n}}{b^{-m}} = \dfrac{b^m}{a^n}, \ \text{and} \ \left(\dfrac{a}{b}\right)^{-n} = \left(\dfrac{b}{a}\right)^n$
	Examples: $\dfrac{1}{2^{-3}} = 2^3, \ \dfrac{x^{-4}}{y^{-3}} = \dfrac{y^3}{x^4}, \ \text{and} \ \left(\dfrac{2}{5}\right)^{-4} = \left(\dfrac{5}{2}\right)^4$

Order of Operations

Using the following order of operations, first perform all calculations within parentheses and absolute values, or above and below the fraction bar. Then use the same order of operations to perform the remaining calculations.

1. Evaluate all exponential expressions. Do any negation *after* evaluating exponents.
2. Do all multiplication and division from *left to right*.
3. Do all addition and subtraction from *left to right*.

Example: $-2^4 - 2 \cdot 3 = -16 - 2 \cdot 3 = -16 - 6 = -22$

Scientific Notation   A number a written as $b \times 10^n$, where $1 \le |b| < 10$ and n is an integer.

Examples: $23{,}400 = 2.34 \times 10^4$ and $0.0034 = 3.4 \times 10^{-3}$

SECTION 1.4 VARIABLES, EQUATIONS, AND FORMULAS

Terminology

Variable	Symbol that represents an unknown quantity
	Examples: $x, y, z, A,$ and T
Algebraic Expression	Can consist of numbers, variables, operation symbols, exponents, and grouping symbols but *no* equals sign
	Examples: $3z, \ (x - y)^3, \ 4a + 3b, \ 5,$ and $|x - 2|$
Equation	A statement that two algebraic expressions are *equal*—always contains an equals sign
	Examples: $2 + 4 = 6, \ 2x = 8,$ and $x^2 + 2 = 10$
Formula	An equation used to calculate one quantity by using known values of other quantities
	Examples: $P = 2W + 2L$ and $A = \pi r^2$

Square Root   The number b is a square root of a number a if $b^2 = a$.

Example: The square roots of 36 are 6 and -6.

Principal Square Root   The positive square root of a number, denoted $\sqrt{a}$

Examples: $\sqrt{4} = 2$, $\sqrt{100} = 10$, and $\sqrt{81} = 9$

Cube Root   The number b is a cube root of a number a if $b^3 = a$.

Examples: $\sqrt[3]{8} = 2$, $\sqrt[3]{-27} = -3$, and $\sqrt[3]{64} = 4$

SECTION 1.5 ■ INTRODUCTION TO GRAPHING

Relation   A set of ordered pairs

Example: $S = \{(-2, 3), (0, 3), (1, 2)\}$

Domain and Range   In a relation consisting of ordered pairs (x, y), the set of x-values is the domain and the set of y-values is the range.

Example: For $S = \{(-2, 3), (0, 3), (1, 2)\}$, $D = \{-2, 0, 1\}$ and $R = \{2, 3\}$.

The Cartesian Coordinate System (*xy*-plane)

Points   Plotted as (x, y) ordered pairs

Four Quadrants   I, II, III, and IV; the axes do not lie in a quadrant.
                                        NOTE: The point $(1, 0)$ does not lie in a quadrant.

xy-plane

Scatterplot

Line Graph

CHAPTER 1   REVIEW EXERCISES

SECTION 1.1

Exercises 1 and 2: Classify each real number as one or more of the following: natural number, whole number, integer, rational number, or irrational number.

1. $-2, 9, \frac{2}{5}, \sqrt{11}, \pi, 2.68$

2. $\frac{6}{2}, -\frac{2}{7}, \sqrt{6}, 0.\overline{3}, \frac{0}{4}$

Exercises 3–8: State whether the equation illustrates an identity, commutative, associative, or distributive property.

3. $a \cdot 1 = a$ **4.** $4 \cdot x = x \cdot 4$

5. $(a + 1) + 4 = a + (1 + 4)$

6. $a(b + 2) = a \cdot b + a \cdot 2$

7. $3(t + 2) - r(t + 2) = (3 - r)(t + 2)$

8. $4x + 8x = 12x$

9. Use identity properties to simplify $1 \cdot (a + 0)$.

10. Use a commutative property to write $x \cdot \frac{1}{4}$ as an equivalent expression.

11. Use an associative property to write $8(10x)$ as an equivalent expression.

12. Use a distributive property to write $5z - 3z$ as an equivalent expression.

Exercises 13 and 14: Evaluate the expression two different ways by applying a distributive property.

13. $5(8 + 11)$ **14.** $3(9 - 5)$

Exercises 15 and 16: Calculate the average of the list of numbers.

15. $6, 9, 3, 11, 5, 20$

16. $3.2, 6.8, 6.1, 10.8, 1.7$

Exercises 17–20: Use properties of real numbers to evaluate the expression mentally.

17. $12 + 23 + (-2) + 7$

18. $\frac{3}{2} \cdot \frac{2}{5} \cdot \frac{5}{7} \cdot \frac{7}{3}$

19. $5 \cdot 23 + 5 \cdot 7$ **20.** $45 - 34 + 55 - 66$

SECTION 1.2

21. Plot the numbers $-3, 0, 2,$ and $\frac{7}{2}$ on a number line.

22. Evaluate the expression $|-7.2 + 4|$.

23. Find the additive inverse of $-\frac{2}{3}$.

24. Find the multiplicative inverse of $\frac{4}{5}$.

25. Find the opposite of $-2x + 3$.

26. Find the reciprocal of $-\frac{1}{a + b}$.

Exercises 27–36: Evaluate the expression.

27. $-5 + (-7) + 8$ **28.** $-9 + 11$

29. $-12 - (-8)$ **30.** $\frac{1}{2} + (-2) + \frac{3}{4}$

31. $\frac{2}{3} \div (-4) - \frac{1}{3}$ **32.** $-\frac{7}{11} + \frac{\frac{1}{5}}{\frac{2}{9}}$

33. $-7 \cdot 4 \cdot -\frac{1}{7}$ **34.** $\frac{3}{4} \cdot \frac{4}{7} + 1$

35. $4x + 5x$ **36.** $2z - 3z + 8z$

37. Use a calculator to evaluate $\frac{1}{5} - \frac{3}{7} + \frac{\frac{2}{13}}{\frac{4}{5}}$.

38. Mentally evaluate $-4 + 9 + 4 + 11 - 6 + 16$. Mentally estimate the average of these numbers.

SECTION 1.3

39. Identify the base and the exponent for 4^{-2}.

40. Use a calculator to decide if 3^π and π^3 are equal.

Exercises 41–48: Evaluate the expression.

41. -2^4 **42.** $(-2)^4$

43. 9^0 **44.** $\left(\frac{2}{3}\right)^{-3}$

45. 4^{-3} **46.** $\frac{1}{5^{-2}}$

47. $\frac{5^{-3}}{3^{-2}}$ **48.** $\frac{1}{2 \cdot 4^{-2}}$

Exercises 49–64: Simplify the expression. Write the result using positive exponents.

49. $4^3 \cdot 4^{-5}$ **50.** $10^4 \cdot 10^{-2}$

51. $x^7 x^{-2}$ **52.** $\frac{3^4}{3^{-7}}$

53. $\frac{5a^{-4}}{10a^2}$ **54.** $\frac{15a^4b^3}{3a^2b^6}$

55. $(2^2)^4$ **56.** $(x^{-3})^5$

57. $(4x^{-2}y^3)^2$ **58.** $(4a)^5$

59. $\left(\frac{5x^3}{3z^4}\right)^3$ **60.** $\left(\frac{-3x^4y^3}{z}\right)^{-2}$

61. $\left(\frac{3a^{-4}}{4b^{-7}}\right)^2$ **62.** $\left(\frac{3m^2n^{-4}}{9m^3n}\right)^{-1}$

63. $\left(\frac{rt}{2r^3t^{-1}}\right)^{-3}$ **64.** $\left(\frac{3r^2}{4t^{-3}}\right)^2$

Exercises 65–70: Evaluate each expression by hand.

65. $2 + 3 \cdot 9$ **66.** $4 - 1 - 6$

67. $5 \cdot 2^3$ **68.** $\frac{2 + 4}{2} + \frac{3 - 1}{3}$

69. $20 \div 4 \div 2$ **70.** $\frac{3^3 - 2^4}{4 - 3}$

Exercises 71 and 72: Write in scientific notation.

71. 186,000

72. 0.00034

Exercises 73 and 74: Write in standard form.

73. 4.5×10^4

74. 9.23×10^{-3}

SECTION 1.4

Exercises 75 and 76: Write a formula for the following.

75. Converting x feet to y inches

76. Finding the total area A of 6 circles all with radius r

Exercises 77–82: Evaluate the formula for the given value(s) of the variable(s).

77. $y = 12x$ $x = 3$

78. $d = \sqrt{t - 3}$ $t = 67$

79. $N = h^2 - \frac{3}{4}$ $h = \frac{3}{2}$

80. $P = w^3 - 2$ $w = -2$

81. $A = \frac{1}{2}bh$ $b = 4, h = 5$

82. $V = a^2b$ $a = 3, b = 3$

83. Select the formula that models the data in the table.

x	1	2	3	4	5
y	−1	1	3	5	7

    (i) $y = x - 2$,   (ii) $y = 3x - 4$,
    (iii) $y = 2x - 3$

84. Find a value for a so that $y = ax$ models the data.

x	−2	0	2	4	6
y	−3	0	3	6	9

85. Use $y = x^3 + 1$ to complete the table.

x	−2	−1	0	1	2
y					

86. Use a calculator to make a table of $y = \sqrt{\frac{x - 1}{x + 1}}$. Let $x = 1, 2, 3, \ldots, 7$.

SECTION 1.5

87. Identify the domain and range of the relation $S = \{(-1, 1), (2, 3), (3, -6), (3, 7)\}$.

88. Express the relation shown in the graph as a set of ordered pairs. Identify the domain and range.

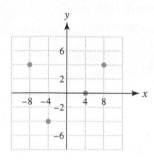

Exercises 89–92: Evaluate the formula for $x = -2$, $-1, 0, 1$, and 2. Plot the resulting ordered pairs.

89. $y = -3x$

90. $y = \frac{1}{2}x - 1$

91. $y = x^2$

92. $y = \dfrac{5}{x^2 + 1}$

Exercises 93 and 94: Plot the points in the table. State the quadrant containing each point or the axis on which the point lies.

93.

x	−2	−1	0	2
y	2	−3	1	−1

94.

x	−15	−5	10	20
y	−5	0	20	−10

Exercises 95 and 96: Show the viewing rectangle on your graphing calculator. Predict the number of tick marks on the positive x-axis and the positive y-axis.

95. $[-9, 9, 1]$ by $[-6, 6, 3]$

96. $[-20, 20, 5]$ by $[-12, 12, 4]$

Exercises 97 and 98: Make a scatterplot of the relation. Identify the domain and range.

97. $\{(0, 4), (-1, 2), (3, 3), (4, -1), (2, 0)\}$

98. $\{(-10, 10), (50, 20), (-20, -30), (45, -25)\}$

APPLICATIONS

99. *Mayors' Salaries*   The following table lists the four highest mayors' salaries in 2002.

City	Chicago	New York	Houston	Detroit
Salary	$170,000	$165,000	$160,500	$157,300

Source: U.S. Conference of Mayors.

(a) Mentally estimate which of the following represents the average salary: $141,500, $163,200, or $168,750.

(b) Check your estimate by finding the actual average.

100. *Calculating Interest* If P dollars are deposited in a savings account paying 1% annual interest, the amount A in the account after t years is $A = P(1.01)^t$. Find A for the given values of P and t.
(a) $P = \$2500, t = 1$ year
(b) $P = \$800, t = 2$ years

101. *Speed of Earth* Earth orbits the sun in a nearly circular orbit with a radius of 93,000,000 miles.
(a) Calculate the distance in miles traveled by Earth in 1 year. Write your answer in scientific notation. (*Hint:* $C = 2\pi r$.)
(b) Estimate the speed of Earth around the sun in miles per hour.

102. *Modeling Motion* The following table lists the distances in miles traveled by a car for various elapsed times. Find an equation that models these data.

Elapsed Time (hr)	2	4	6	8
Distance (mi)	80	160	240	320

103. *Heart Beat in Animals* The rate N at which an animal's heart beats varies with its weight. This relation can be modeled by $N = \frac{885}{\sqrt{W}}$, where N is in beats per minute and W is the animal's weight in pounds. Estimate the pulse for a 16-pound cat and a 144-pound person. (*Source:* C. Pennycuick, *Newton Rules Biology.*)

104. *Graphing Real Data* The following data show the poverty threshold y for a single person from 1960 through 2000. Make a line graph and comment on any trends in the data.

x	1960	1970	1980	1990	2000
y	$1490	$1954	$4190	$6652	$8794

Source: U.S. Census Bureau.

105. *Area* Find the area of a square whose sides have length $4ab$.

106. *Volume* Find the volume of a cube whose sides have length $5z$.

CHAPTER 1 TEST 🎓Pass the Test Video solutions to all test exercises

1. Classify each of the real numbers as one or more of the following: natural number, whole number, integer, rational number, or irrational number.

$$-5, \frac{2}{3}, -\frac{1}{\sqrt{5}}, \sqrt{9}, \pi, -1.83$$

2. State whether each equation illustrates an identity, commutative, associative, or distributive property.
(a) $a + 0 = a$ (b) $4(12x) = 48x$
(c) $5(2 + 3x) = 5(3x + 2)$
(d) $a(x - y) = ax - ay$

3. Use identity, commutative, associative, and/or distributive properties to simplify the expression.
(a) $0 + (a \cdot 1) \cdot 1$ (b) $2x - 5x + 4x$
(c) $2(x \cdot 3) + 2x$ (d) $(a + b)a - ab$

4. Calculate the average for 34, 15, 96, 11, and 0.

5. Plot the numbers $-1.5, 0, 3,$ and $\frac{3}{2}$ on a number line.

6. Evaluate each expression.
(a) $\left| \frac{1}{2} + \frac{2}{3} - \frac{8}{3} \right|$
(b) $12 + (-3) + 18 + (-7)$
(c) $\frac{1}{2} \cdot \frac{2}{3} \cdot \frac{3}{4} \cdot \frac{3}{2} \cdot 2$
(d) $\frac{1}{2} + \frac{2}{3} - \frac{3}{2} + \frac{1}{3}$

7. Find the multiplicative inverse of each expression.
(a) $-\frac{5}{4}$ (b) $\frac{2}{b+1}$

8. Evaluate each expression.
(a) $-\frac{1}{2} + \frac{2}{3} \div 3$ (b) $-4 + \frac{\frac{2}{3}}{-\frac{1}{4}}$
(c) $5 - 2 \cdot 5^2 \div 5$ (d) $(6 - 4 \cdot 5) \div (-7)$

9. Evaluate each expression.

(a) 5^{-2} (b) π^0 (c) $\left(-\frac{2}{5}\right)^4$

(d) $\frac{6^{-2}}{2^{-4}}$ (e) $\frac{1}{5^{-3}}$ (f) $2^2 \cdot 2^{-4}$

10. Simplify each expression. Use positive exponents.

(a) $x^6 \cdot x^{-4} \cdot y^3$ (b) $\dfrac{16x^{-2}y^8}{6xy^{-7}}$

(c) $(2yz^{-2})^3$ (d) $\left(\dfrac{15x^4}{10xy^{-2}}\right)^{-2}$

11. Write 5.2×10^{-4} in standard form.

12. Write 3,400,000 in scientific notation.

13. Write a formula that converts x minutes to H hours.

14. Evaluate the formula $y = \sqrt{x+1} + x$ for $x = 3$ and $x = -1$.

15. Identify the domain and range of the relation. $S = \{(-3, 2), (-1, 3), (2, 3), (2, -4)\}$.

16. Plot the points in the table. State the quadrant containing each point or the axis on which the point lies.

x	-2	-1	0	1	2
y	3	-2	2	-1	1

17. Express the relation shown in the graph as a set of ordered pairs. Identify the domain and range.

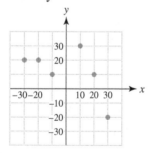

18. Make a scatterplot of the data. Write an equation that models the data.

x	1	2	3	4
y	1.25	2.50	3.75	5.00

19. Use your calculator to make a scatterplot of S after determining an appropriate viewing rectangle.

$S = \{(-15, 5), (10, 20), (-10, 15), (0, 0), (5, 35)\}$

20. *Temperature*   The formula $C = \frac{5}{9}(F - 32)$ can be used to convert degrees Fahrenheit, F, to degrees Celsius, C. If the outside temperature is 5°F, find the equivalent temperature in Celsius.

21. *Alcohol Consumption*   In 1994, about 211 million people in the United States were age 14 or over. They consumed, on average, 2.21 gallons of alcohol per person. Use scientific notation to estimate the total gallons of alcohol consumed by this age group. (*Source*: Department of Health and Human Services.)

22. *Radius of a Circle*   If a circle has area A, then its radius r is given by $r = \sqrt{\frac{A}{\pi}}$. Find the radius of a circle with an area of 25 square feet. Approximate this radius to the nearest hundredth of a foot.

23. *Modeling Motion*   The following table lists the distances in miles M traveled by a car for various elapsed times t. Find an equation that models these data.

Elapsed Time (hr)	4	6	10
Distance (mi)	244	366	610

CHAPTER 1   EXTENDED AND DISCOVERY EXERCISES

1. *Global Warming*   If the global climate were to warm significantly as a result of the greenhouse effect or other climatic change, the Arctic ice cap would start to melt. This ice cap contains an estimated 680,000 cubic miles of water. More than 200 million people currently live on land that is less than 3 feet above sea level. In the United States several large cities have low average elevations. Three examples are Boston (14 feet), New Orleans (4 feet), and San Diego (13 feet). In this exercise you are to estimate the rise in sea level if this cap were to melt and determine whether this event would have a significant impact on people.

(a) The surface area of a sphere is given by the formula $4\pi r^2$, where r is its radius. Although the shape of the earth is not exactly spherical, it has an average radius of 3960 miles. Estimate the surface area of the earth.

(b) Oceans cover approximately 71% of the total surface area of the earth. How many square miles of the earth's surface are covered by oceans?

(c) Approximate the potential rise in sea level by dividing the total volume of the water from the ice cap by the surface area of the oceans. Convert your answer from miles to feet.

(d) Discuss the implications of your calculation. How would cities such as Boston, New Orleans, and San Diego be affected?

(e) The Antarctic ice cap contains 6,300,000 cubic miles of water. Estimate how much sea level would rise if this ice cap melted.   (*Source:* Department of the Interior, Geological Survey.)

2. *Injuries at Work*   The following table lists the injuries per 100 full-time workers in private industry.

Year	1992	1995	1998	2001
Injuries	8.3	7.3	6.4	5.4

Source: Bureau of Labor Statistics.

Explain your reasoning for each of the following.
(a) Make a scatterplot of the data. Discuss how the injury rate has changed over this period of time.
(b) Estimate the injury rate in 1989.
(c) Assuming that trends continue, estimate the injury rate in 2004.
(d) Would it be valid to try to estimate when the accident rate will reach 0? Explain.

3. *Body Mass Index*   Many studies have tried to find a recommended relationship between a person's height and weight. The following steps may be used to compute the body mass index (BMI). Federal guidelines suggest that $19 \leq BMI \leq 25$ is desirable. (*Source:* Associated Press.)
Step 1: Multiply the weight W in pounds by 0.455.
Step 2: Multiply the height H in inches by 0.0254.
Step 3: Square the result in Step 2.
Step 4: Divide the answer in Step 1 by the answer in Step 3.

The result is the person's BMI. Write a formula to calculate the BMI given the height H and weight W of a person. Let y represent the BMI.

Exercises 4–6: Body Mass Index   (Refer to the previous exercise.) Compute the BMI for each individual.

4. 119 pounds, 5 feet 9 inches (Steffi Graf, tennis player) (*Source:* J. Monroe, *Steffi Graf*).

5. 160 pounds, 6 feet 1 inch (Venus Williams, tennis player) (*Source:* CBS SportsLine.)

6. 300 pounds, 7 feet 1 inch (Shaquille O'Neal, professional basketball player) (*Source:* The Topps Company, Inc.)

Exercises 7–10: Modeling Data with Formulas   Find values for a and b so that the formula models the data.

7. $y = ax + b$

x	−3	−1	1	3
y	5	2	−1	−4

8. $y = a\sqrt{x} + b$

x	1	4	9	16
y	1	−1	−3	−5

9. $y = ax^2 + bx$

x	1	2	3	4
y	1	3	6	10

10. $y = b(a^x)$

x	0	1	2	3
y	3	6	12	24

Linear Functions and Models

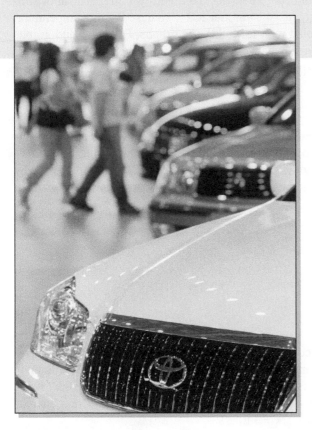

Every day our society creates enormous amounts of data, and mathematics is an important tool for summarizing those data and discovering trends. For example, the table shows the number of Toyota vehicles sold in the United States for selected years.

Year	1998	1999	2000	2001	2002
Vehicles (millions)	1.4	1.5	1.6	1.7	1.8

Source: Autodata.

These data contain an obvious pattern: Sales increased by 0.1 million each year. A scatterplot of these data and a line that models this situation are shown in the figure. In this chapter you will learn how to determine the equation of this and other lines. (See Section 2.2, Example 6.)

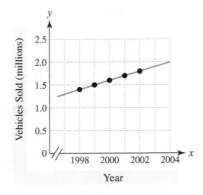

No great thing is created suddenly.

—Epictetus

2.1 FUNCTIONS AND THEIR REPRESENTATIONS

Basic Concepts ▪ Representations of a Function ▪ Definition of a Function ▪ Identifying a Function ▪ Tables, Graphs, and Calculators (Optional)

A LOOK INTO MATH ▷ In Chapter 1 we showed how to use numbers to describe data. For example, instead of simply saying that it is *hot* outside, we might use the number 102°F to describe the temperature. We also showed that data can be modeled with formulas and graphs. Formulas and graphs are sometimes used to represent *functions*, which are important in mathematics. In this section we introduce functions and their representations.

Basic Concepts

▶ REAL-WORLD CONNECTION   Functions are used to calculate many important quantities. For example, suppose that a person works for $7 per hour. Then we could use a function f to calculate the amount of money the person earned after working x hours simply by multiplying the *input* x by 7. The result y is called the *output*. This concept is shown visually in the following diagram.

For each valid input x, a function computes *exactly one* output y, which may be represented by the ordered pair (x, y). If the input is 5 hours, f outputs $7 \cdot 5 = \$35$; if the input is 8 hours, f outputs $7 \cdot 8 = \$56$. These results can be represented by the ordered pairs $(5, 35)$ and $(8, 56)$. Sometimes an input may not be valid. For example, if $x = -3$, there is no reasonable output because a person cannot work -3 hours.

We say that y *is a function of* x because the output y is determined by and *depends* on the input x. As a result, y is called the *dependent variable* and x is the *independent variable*. To emphasize that y is a function of x, we use the notation $y = f(x)$. The symbol $f(x)$ does not represent multiplication of a variable f and a variable x. The notation $y = f(x)$ is called *function notation*, is read "y equals f of x," and means that function f with input x produces output y. For example, if $x = 3$ hours, $y = f(3) = \$21$.

FUNCTION NOTATION

The notation $y = f(x)$ is called **function notation**. The **input** is x, the **output** is y, and the *name* of the function is f.

$$\overset{\text{Name}}{\underset{\text{Output} \qquad \text{Input}}{y = f(x)}}$$

The variable y is called the **dependent variable** and the variable x is called the **independent variable**. The expression $f(4) = 28$ is read "f of 4 equals 28" and indicates that f outputs 28 when the input is 4. A function computes *exactly one* output for each valid input. The letters f, g, and h are often used to denote names of functions.

Figure 2.1 Function Machine

▶ REAL-WORLD CONNECTION   Functions can be used to compute a variety of quantities. For example, suppose that a boy has a sister who is exactly 5 years older than he is. If the age of the boy is x, then a function g can calculate the age of his sister by adding 5 to x. Thus $g(4) = 4 + 5 = 9$, $g(10) = 10 + 5 = 15$, and in general $g(x) = x + 5$. That is, function g adds 5 to every input x to obtain the output $y = g(x)$.

Functions can be represented by an input–output machine, as illustrated in Figure 2.1. This machine represents function g and receives input $x = 4$, adds 5 to this value, and then outputs $g(4) = 4 + 5 = 9$.

Representations of a Function

▶ REAL-WORLD CONNECTION   A function f forms a relation between inputs x and outputs y that can be represented verbally, numerically, symbolically, and graphically. Functions can also be represented with diagrams. We begin by considering a function f that converts yards to feet.

VERBAL REPRESENTATION (WORDS)   To convert x yards to y feet we must multiply x by 3. Therefore, if function f computes the number of feet in x yards, a **verbal representation** of f is "Multiply the input x in yards by 3 to obtain the output y in feet."

NUMERICAL REPRESENTATION (TABLE OF VALUES)   A function f that converts yards to feet is shown in Table 2.1, where $y = f(x)$.

A *table of values* is called a **numerical representation** of a function. Many times it is impossible to list all valid inputs x in a table. On the one hand, if a table does not contain every x-input, it is a *partial* numerical representation. On the other hand, a *complete* numerical representation includes *all* valid inputs. Table 2.1 is a partial numerical representation of f because many valid inputs, such as $x = 10$ or $x = 5.3$, are not shown in it. Note that for each valid input x there is exactly one output y. *For a function, inputs are not listed more than once in a table.*

SYMBOLIC REPRESENTATION (FORMULA)   A *formula* provides a **symbolic representation** of a function. The computation performed by f to convert x yards to y feet is expressed by $y = 3x$. A formula for f is $f(x) = 3x$, where $y = f(x)$. We say that function f is *defined by* or *given by* $f(x) = 3x$. Thus $f(2) = 3 \cdot 2 = 6$.

GRAPHICAL REPRESENTATION (GRAPH)   A **graphical representation**, or **graph**, visually associates an x-input with a y-output. The ordered pairs

$$(1, 3), (2, 6), (3, 9), (4, 12), (5, 15), (6, 18), \text{ and } (7, 21)$$

from Table 2.1 are plotted in Figure 2.2(a). This scatterplot suggests a line for the graph f. For each real number x there is exactly one real number y determined by $y = 3x$. If we restrict inputs to $x \geq 0$ and plot all ordered pairs $(x, 3x)$, then a line with no breaks will appear, as shown in Figure 2.2(b) on the next page.

TABLE 2.1

x (yards)	y (feet)
1	3
2	6
3	9
4	12
5	15
6	18
7	21

(a)

Figure 2.2

(Figure 2.2)

(a) Function

(b) Function

(c) Not a Function

Figure 2.3

MAKING CONNECTIONS

Functions, Points, and Graphs

If $f(a) = b$, then the point (a, b) lies on the graph of f. Conversely, if the point (a, b) lies on the graph of f, then $f(a) = b$. Thus each point on the graph of f can be written in the form $(a, f(a))$.

DIAGRAMMATIC REPRESENTATION (DIAGRAM) Functions may be represented by **diagrams**. Figure 2.3(a) is a diagram of a function, where an arrow is used to identify the output y associated with input x. For example, input 2 results in output 6, which is written in function notation as $f(2) = 6$. That is, 2 yards are equivalent to 6 feet. Figure 2.3(b) shows a function f even though $f(1) = 4$ and $f(2) = 4$. Although two inputs for f have the same output, each valid input has exactly one output. In contrast, Figure 2.3(c) shows a relation that is not a function because input 2 results in two different outputs, 5 and 6.

MAKING CONNECTIONS

Four Representations of a Function

Symbolic Representation $f(x) = x + 1$

Numerical Representation   ***Graphical Representation***

x	y
-2	-1
-1	0
0	1
1	2
2	3

Verbal Representation f adds 1 to an input x to produce an output y.

▶ REAL-WORLD CONNECTION   In the next example we calculate sales tax by evaluating different representations of a function.

EXAMPLE 1   Calculating sales tax

Let a function f compute a sales tax of 7% on a purchase of x dollars. Use the given representation to evaluate $f(2)$.

(a) **Verbal Representation**   Multiply a purchase of x dollars by 0.07 to obtain a sales tax of y dollars.
(b) **Numerical Representation**   Shown in Table 2.2
(c) **Symbolic Representation** $f(x) = 0.07x$
(d) **Graphical Representation**   Shown in Figure 2.4
(e) **Diagrammatic Representation**   Shown in Figure 2.5

TABLE 2.2

x	$f(x)$
$1.00	$0.07
$2.00	$0.14
$3.00	$0.21
$4.00	$0.28

Figure 2.4 Sales Tax of 7%

Figure 2.5

Solution
(a) Multiply the input 2 by 0.07 to obtain 0.14. The sales tax on $2.00 is $0.14.
(b) From Table 2.2, $f(2) = \$0.14$.
(c) Because $f(x) = 0.07x$, $f(2) = 0.07(2) = 0.14$, or $0.14.
(d) To evaluate $f(2)$ with a graph, first find 2 on the x-axis. Then move vertically upward until you reach the graph of f. The point on the graph may be estimated as $(2, 0.14)$, meaning that $f(2) = 0.14$ (see Figure 2.6). Note that it may not be possible to find the exact answer from a graph. For example, one might estimate $f(2)$ to be 0.13 or 0.15 instead of 0.14.

Figure 2.6

(e) In Figure 2.5, follow the arrow from 2 to 0.14. Thus $f(2) = 0.14$.

Now Try Exercises 19, 31, 51, 57, 59

EXAMPLE **2**   Evaluating symbolic representations (formulas)

Evaluate each function f at the given value of x.

(a) $f(x) = 3x - 7$ $x = -2$

(b) $f(x) = \dfrac{x}{x + 2}$ $x = 0.5$

(c) $f(x) = \sqrt{x - 1}$ $x = 10$

Solution

(a) $f(-2) = 3(-2) - 7 = -6 - 7 = -13$

(b) $f(0.5) = \dfrac{0.5}{0.5 + 2} = \dfrac{0.5}{2.5} = 0.2$

(c) $f(10) = \sqrt{10 - 1} = \sqrt{9} = 3$ Now Try Exercises **21, 29**

▶ **REAL-WORLD CONNECTION**   There are many examples of functions. To give more meaning to a function, sometimes we change both its name and its input variable. For instance, if we know the radius r of a circle, we can calculate its circumference by using $C(r) = 2\pi r$. The next example illustrates how functions are used in physical therapy.

EXAMPLE **3**   Computing crutch length

People who sustain leg injuries often require crutches. A proper crutch length can be estimated without using trial and error. The function L, given by $L(t) = 0.72t + 2$, outputs an appropriate crutch length in inches for a person t inches tall.   (*Source: Journal of the American Physical Therapy Association.*)

(a) Find $L(60)$ and interpret the result.

(b) If one person is 70 inches tall and another person is 71 inches tall, what should be the difference in their crutch lengths?

Solution

(a) $L(60) = 0.72(60) + 2 = $ **45.2**. Thus a person 60 inches tall needs crutches that are about 45.2 inches long.

(b) From the formula, $L(t) = 0.72t + 2$, we can see that each 1-inch increase in t results in a 0.72-inch increase in L. For example,

$$L(71) - L(70) = 53.12 - 52.4 = 0.72.$$ Now Try Exercise **77**

In the next example we find a formula and then sketch a graph of a function.

EXAMPLE **4**   Finding representations of a function

Let function f square the input x and then subtract 1 to obtain the output y.

(a) Write a formula, or symbolic representation, for f.

(b) Make a table of values, or numerical representation, for f. Use $x = -2, -1, 0, 1, 2$.

(c) Sketch a graph, or graphical representation, of f.

Solution

(a) **Symbolic Representation**   If we square x and then subtract 1, we obtain $x^2 - 1$. Thus a formula for f is $f(x) = x^2 - 1$.

TABLE 2.3

x	$f(x)$
-2	3
-1	0
0	-1
1	0
2	3

(b) *Numerical Representation*   Make a table of values for $f(x)$, as shown in Table 2.3. For example,

$$f(-2) = (-2)^2 - 1 = 4 - 1 = 3.$$

(c) *Graphical Representation*   To obtain a graph of $f(x) = x^2 - 1$, plot the points from Table 2.3 and then connect them with a smooth curve, as shown in Figure 2.7. Note that we need to plot enough points so that we can determine the overall shape of the graph.

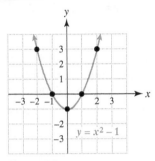

Figure 2.7

Now Try Exercise 61

Definition of a Function

A function is a fundamental concept in mathematics. Its definition should allow for all representations of a function. *A function receives an input x and produces exactly one output y,* which can be expressed as an ordered pair:

$$(x, y).$$

Input ↗   ↖ Output

A relation is a set of ordered pairs, and a function is a special type of relation.

FUNCTION

A **function** f is a set of ordered pairs (x, y), where each x-value corresponds to exactly one y-value.

The **domain** of f is the set of all x-values, and the **range** of f is the set of all y-values. For example, a function f that converts 1, 2, 3, and 4 yards to feet could be expressed as

$$f = \{(1, 3), (2, 6), (3, 9), (4, 12)\}.$$

The domain of f is $D = \{1, 2, 3, 4\}$, and the range of f is $R = \{3, 6, 9, 12\}$.

MAKING CONNECTIONS

Relations and Functions

A relation can be thought of as a set of input–output pairs. A function is a special type of relation whereby each input results in exactly one output.

▶ **REAL-WORLD CONNECTION**   In the next example, we see how education can improve a person's chances for earning a higher income.

EXAMPLE **5**   Computing average income

The function f computes the average 2004 individual income in dollars by educational attainment. This function is defined by $f(N) = 18{,}900$, $f(H) = 25{,}900$, $f(B) = 45{,}400$, and $f(M) = 62{,}300$, where N denotes no diploma, H a high school diploma, B a bachelor's degree, and M a master's degree.   (***Source:*** U.S. Census Bureau.)
(a) Write f as a set of ordered pairs.
(b) Give the domain and range of f.
(c) Discuss the relationship between education and income.

Solution
(a) $f = \{(N, 18900), (H, 25900), (B, 45400), (M, 62300)\}$.
(b) The domain of function f is $D = \{N, H, B, M\}$, and the range of function f is $R = \{18900, 25900, 45400, 62300\}$.
(c) Education pays—the greater the educational attainment, the greater are annual earnings.

Now Try Exercise **37**

EXAMPLE **6**   Finding the domain and range graphically

Use the graphs of f shown in Figures 2.8 and 2.9 to find each function's domain and range.
(a)   **(b)**

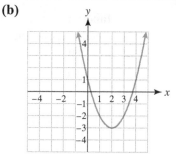

Figure 2.8   Figure 2.9

Solution
(a) The domain is the set of all x-values that correspond to points on the graph of f. Figure 2.10 shows that the domain D includes all x-values satisfying $-3 \le x \le 3$. (Recall that the symbol $\le$ is read "*less than or equal to*.") Because the graph is a semicircle with no breaks, the domain includes all real numbers between and including -3 and 3. The range R is the set of y-values that correspond to points on the graph of f. Thus R includes all y-values satisfying $0 \le y \le 3$.

Figure 2.10

(b) The arrows on the ends of the graph in Figure 2.9 indicate that the graph extends indefinitely left and right, as well as upward. Thus D includes all real numbers. The smallest y-value on the graph is $y = -3$, which occurs when $x = 2$. Thus the range is $y \geq -3$. (Recall that the symbol $\geq$ is read "*greater than or equal to*.")

Now Try Exercises 79, 83

Symbolic, numerical, and graphical representations of three common functions are shown in Figure 2.11. Note that their graphs are not lines. Use the graphs to find the domain and range of each function.

Absolute value: $f(x) = |x|$

x	-2	-1	0	1	2
$|x|$	2	1	0	1	2

Square: $f(x) = x^2$

x	-2	-1	0	1	2
x^2	4	1	0	1	4

Square root: $f(x) = \sqrt{x}$

x	0	1	4	9
$\sqrt{x}$	0	1	2	3

(a)

(b)

(c)

Figure 2.11

CRITICAL THINKING

Suppose that a car travels at 50 miles per hour to a city that is 250 miles away. Sketch a graph of a function f that gives the distance y traveled after x hours. Identify the domain and range of f.

The domain of a function is the set of all valid inputs. To determine the domain of a function from a formula, we must determine x-values for which the formula is defined. This concept is demonstrated in the next example.

EXAMPLE 7   Finding the domain of a function

Use $f(x)$ to find the domain of f.

(a) $f(x) = 5x$ **(b)** $f(x) = \dfrac{1}{x - 2}$ **(c)** $f(x) = \sqrt{x}$

Solution
(a) Because we can always multiply a real number x by 5, $f(x) = 5x$ is defined for all real numbers. Thus the domain of f includes all real numbers.

(b) Because we cannot divide by 0, input $x = 2$ is not valid for $f(x) = \frac{1}{x-2}$. The expression for $f(x)$ is defined for all other values of x. Thus the domain of f includes all real numbers except 2, or $x \neq 2$.

(c) Because square roots of negative numbers are not real numbers, the inputs for $f(x) = \sqrt{x}$ cannot be negative. Thus the domain of f includes all nonnegative numbers, or $x \geq 0$.

Now Try Exercises **89, 93, 97**

Identifying a Function

Recall that for a function each valid input x produces exactly one output y. In the next three examples we demonstrate techniques for identifying a function.

EXAMPLE 8 Determining whether a set of ordered pairs is a function

The set S of ordered pairs (x, y) represents the monthly average temperature y in degrees Fahrenheit for the month x in Washington, D.C. Determine whether S is a function.

$$S = \{(\text{January}, 33), (\text{February}, 37), (\text{March}, 45), (\text{April}, 53), (\text{May}, 66), (\text{June}, 73),$$
$$(\text{July}, 77), (\text{August}, 77), (\text{September}, 70), (\text{October}, 51), (\text{November}, 48),$$
$$(\text{December}, 37)\}$$

(**Source:** A. Miller and J. Thompson, *Elements of Meteorology*.)

Solution
The input x is the month and the output y is the monthly average temperature. The set S *is* a function because each month x is paired with exactly one monthly average temperature y. Note that, even though an average temperature of 37°F occurs in both February and December, S is nonetheless a function.

Now Try Exercise **121**

EXAMPLE 9 Determining whether a table of values represents a function

TABLE 2.4   Determine whether Table 2.4 represents a function.

x	y
1	-4
2	8
3	2
1	5
4	-6

Solution
The table does not represent a function because input $x = 1$ produces two outputs: -4 and 5. That is, the following two ordered pairs both belong to this relation.

Same input x

$(1, -4)$ $(1, 5)$

Different outputs y

Now Try Exercise **123**

VERTICAL LINE TEST   To determine whether a graph represents a function, we must be convinced that it is impossible for an input x to have two or more outputs y. If two distinct points have the same x-coordinate on a graph, then the graph cannot represent a function. For example, the ordered pairs $(-1, 1)$ and $(-1, -1)$ could not lie on the graph of a function because input -1 results in *two* outputs: 1 and -1. When the points $(-1, 1)$ and $(-1, -1)$ are plotted, they lie on the same vertical line, as shown in Figure 2.12(a). A graph passing through these points intersects the vertical line twice, as illustrated in Figure 2.12(b).

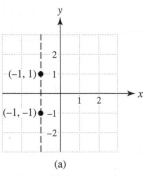

(a)   (b)

Figure 2.12

To determine whether a graph represents a function, visualize vertical lines moving across the *xy*-plane. If each vertical line intersects the graph *at most once*, then it is a graph of a function. This test is called the **vertical line test**. Note that the graph in Figure 2.12(b) fails the vertical line test and therefore does not represent a function.

VERTICAL LINE TEST

If every vertical line intersects a graph at no more than one point, then the graph represents a function.

EXAMPLE 10   Determining whether a graph represents a function

Determine whether the graphs shown in Figures 2.13 and 2.14 represent functions.

(a)   (b)

Figure 2.13   **Figure 2.14**

Figure 2.15 Passes Vertical Line Test

Solution

(a) Any vertical line will cross the graph at most once, as depicted in Figure 2.15. Therefore the graph *does* represent a function.

(b) The graph *does not* represent a function because there exist vertical lines that can intersect the graph twice. One such line is shown in Figure 2.16 on the next page.

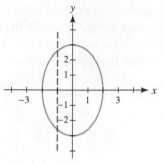

Figure 2.16 Fails Vertical Line Test

Now Try Exercises 113, 115

Tables, Graphs, and Calculators (Optional)

We can use graphing calculators to create graphs and tables, usually more efficiently and reliably than with pencil-and-paper techniques. However, a graphing calculator uses the same techniques that we might use to sketch a graph. For example, one way to sketch a graph of $y = 2x - 1$ is first to make a table of values, as shown in Table 2.5.

We can plot these points in the xy-plane, as shown in Figure 2.17. Next we might connect the points, as shown in Figure 2.18.

TABLE 2.5

x	y
-1	-3
0	-1
1	1
2	3

Figure 2.17 Plotting Points

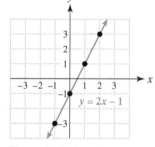

Figure 2.18 Graphing a Line

In a similar manner a graphing calculator plots numerous points and connects them to make a graph. To create a similar graph with a graphing calculator, we enter the formula $Y_1 = 2X - 1$, set an appropriate viewing rectangle, and graph as shown in Figures 2.19(a) and (b). A table of values can also be generated as illustrated in Figure 2.19(c).

CALCULATOR HELP

To make a graph, see the Appendix (page AP-5). To make a table, see the Appendix (page AP-3).

(a)

$[-10, 10, 1]$ by $[-10, 10, 1]$

(b)

(c)

Figure 2.19

2.1 PUTTING IT ALL TOGETHER

One important concept in mathematics is that of a function. A function calculates exactly one output for each valid input and produces input–output ordered pairs in the form (x, y). A function typically computes something, such as area, speed, or sales tax. The following table summarizes some concepts related to functions.

Concept	Explanation	Examples
Function	A set of ordered pairs (x, y), where each x-value corresponds to exactly one y-value	$f = \{(1, 3), (2, 3), (3, 1)\}$ $f(x) = 2x$ A graph of $y = x + 2$ A table of values for $y = 4x$
Independent Variable	The *input* variable for a function	*Function* *Independent Variable* $f(x) = 2x$ x $A(r) = \pi r^2$ r $V(s) = s^3$ s
Dependent Variable	The *output* variable of a function. There is exactly one output for each valid input.	*Function* *Dependent Variable* $y = f(x)$ y $T = F(r)$ T $V = g(r)$ V
Domain and Range of a Function	The domain D is the set of all valid inputs. The range R is the set of all outputs.	For $S = \{(-1, 0), (3, 4), (5, 0)\}$, $D = \{-1, 3, 5\}$ and $R = \{0, 4\}$. For $f(x) = \frac{1}{x}$ the domain includes all real numbers except 0, or $x \neq 0$.
Vertical Line Test	If every vertical line intersects a graph at no more than one point, the graph represents a function.	This graph does *not* pass this test and thus does not represent a function.

A function can be represented verbally, symbolically, numerically, and graphically. The following table summarizes these four representations.

continued on next page

continued from previous page

Type of Representation	Explanation	Comments
Verbal	Precise word description of what is computed	May be oral or written Must be stated *precisely*
Symbolic	Mathematical formula	Efficient and concise way of representing a function (e.g., $f(x) = 2x - 3$)
Numerical	List of specific inputs and their outputs	May be in the form of a table or an explicit set of ordered pairs
Graphical, diagrammatic	Shows inputs and outputs visually	No words, formulas, or tables Many types of graphs and diagrams are possible.

2.1 Exercises

CONCEPTS

1. The notation $y = f(x)$ is called _____ notation.

2. The notation $y = f(x)$ is read _____.

3. The notation $f(x) = x^2 + 1$ is a _____ representation of a function.

4. A table of values is a _____ representation of a function.

5. The set of valid inputs for a function is the _____.

6. The set of outputs for a function is the _____.

7. A function computes _____ output for each valid input.

8. What is the vertical line test used for?

9. Name four types of representations for a function.

10. If $f(3) = 4$, the point _____ is on the graph of f. If $(3, 6)$ is on the graph of f, $f(\underline{\quad}) = \underline{\quad}$.

11. **Thinking Generally**   If $f(a) = b$, the point _____ is on the graph of f.

12. **Thinking Generally**   If (c, d) is on the graph of g, then $g(c) = \underline{\quad}$.

13. **Thinking Generally**   If a is in the domain of f, then $f(a)$ represents how many outputs?

14. **Thinking Generally**   If $f(x) = x$ for every x in the domain of f, then the domain and range of f are _____.

Exercises 15–18: Determine whether the phrase describes a function.

15. Calculating the square of a number

16. Determining your age to the nearest whole number

17. Listing the students who passed a given math exam

18. Listing the children of parent x

REPRESENTING AND EVALUATING FUNCTIONS

Exercises 19–30: Evaluate $f(x)$ at the given values of x.

19. $f(x) = 4x - 2$ $x = -1, 0$

20. $f(x) = 5 - 3x$ $x = -4, 2$

21. $f(x) = \sqrt{x}$ $x = 0, \frac{9}{4}$

22. $f(x) = \sqrt[3]{x}$ $x = -1, 27$

23. $f(x) = x^2$ $x = -5, \frac{3}{2}$

24. $f(x) = x^3$ $x = -2, 0.1$

25. $f(x) = 3$ $x = -8, \frac{7}{3}$

26. $f(x) = 100$ $x = -\pi, \frac{1}{3}$

27. $f(x) = 5 - x^3$ $x = -2, 3$

28. $f(x) = x^2 + 5$ $x = -\frac{1}{2}, 6$

29. $f(x) = \dfrac{2}{x + 1}$ $x = -5, 4$

30. $f(x) = \dfrac{x}{x - 4}$ $x = -3, 1$

Exercises 31–36: Do the following.

  (a) *Write a formula for the function described.*

  (b) *Evaluate the function for input 10 and interpret the results.*

31. Function I computes the number of inches in x yards.

32. Function M computes the number of miles in x feet.

33. Function A computes the area of a circle with radius r.

34. Function C computes the circumference of a circle with radius r.

35. Function A computes the square feet in x acres. (*Hint:* There are 43,560 square feet in one acre.)

36. Function K computes the number of kilograms in x pounds. (*Hint:* There are about 2.2 pounds in one kilogram.)

Exercises 37–40: Write each function f as a set of ordered pairs. Give the domain and range of f.

37. $f(1) = 3, f(2) = -4, f(3) = 0$

38. $f(-1) = 4, f(0) = 6, f(1) = 4$

39. $f(a) = b, f(c) = d, f(e) = a, f(d) = b$

40. $f(a) = 7, f(b) = 7, f(c) = 7, f(d) = 7$

Exercises 41–50: Sketch a graph of f.

41. $f(x) = -x + 3$ **42.** $f(x) = -2x + 1$

43. $f(x) = 2x$ **44.** $f(x) = \frac{1}{2}x - 2$

45. $f(x) = 4 - x$ **46.** $f(x) = 6 - 3x$

47. $f(x) = x^2$ **48.** $f(x) = \sqrt{x}$

49. $f(x) = \sqrt{x + 1}$ **50.** $f(x) = \frac{1}{2}x^2 - 1$

Exercises 51–56: Use the graph of f to evaluate the given expressions.

51. $f(0)$ and $f(2)$ **52.** $f(-2)$ and $f(2)$

 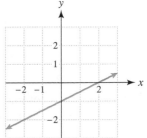

53. $f(-2)$ and $f(1)$ **54.** $f(-1)$ and $f(0)$

 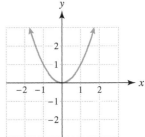

55. $f(1)$ and $f(2)$ **56.** $f(-1)$ and $f(4)$

 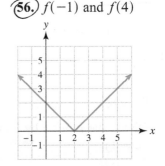

Exercises 57 and 58: Use the table to evaluate the given expressions.

57. $f(0)$ and $f(2)$

x	0	1	2	3	4
$f(x)$	5.5	4.3	3.7	2.5	1.9

58. $f(-10)$ and $f(5)$

x	-10	-5	0	5	10
$f(x)$	23	96	-45	-33	23

Exercises 59 and 60: Use the diagram to evaluate f (1990). Interpret your answer.

59. The function f computes average fuel efficiency of new U.S. passenger cars in miles per gallon during year x.   (*Source:* Department of Transportation.)

60. The function f computes average cost of tuition at public colleges and universities during academic year x.   (*Source:* The College Board.)

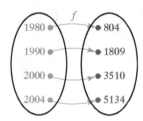

Exercises 61–64: Express the verbal representation for the function f numerically, symbolically, and graphically. Let x = −3, −2, −1, . . . , 3 for the numerical representation (table), and let −3 ≤ x ≤ 3 for the graph.

61. Add 5 to the input x to obtain the output y.

62. Square the input x to obtain the output y.

63. Multiply the input x by 5 and then subtract 2 to obtain the output y.

64. Divide the input x by 2 and then add 3 to obtain the output y.

Exercises 65–68: Express the function f numerically and graphically. Let x = −3, −2, −1, . . . , 3 for your numerical representation and use the standard window for your graph.

65. $f(x) = \sqrt{x + 3}$ **66.** $f(x) = x^3 - \frac{1}{2}x^2$

67. $f(x) = \dfrac{5 - x}{5 + x}$ **68.** $f(x) = |2 - x| + \sqrt[3]{x}$

Exercises 69–74: Give a verbal representation for f(x).

69. $f(x) = x - \frac{1}{2}$ **70.** $f(x) = \frac{3}{4}x$

71. $f(x) = \dfrac{x}{3}$ **72.** $f(x) = x^2 + 1$

73. $f(x) = \sqrt{x - 1}$ **74.** $f(x) = 1 - 3x$

75. *Cost of Driving*   In 2005, the average cost of driving a new car in the United States was about 50 cents per mile. Symbolically, graphically, and numerically represent a function f that computes the cost in dollars of driving x miles. For the numerical representation (table) let $x = 10, 20, 30, \ldots , 70$.   (*Source:* Associated Press.)

76. *Federal Income Taxes*   In 2005, the lowest U.S. income tax rate was 15 percent. Symbolically, graphically, and numerically represent a function f that computes the tax on a taxable income of x dollars. For the numerical representation (table) let $x = 1000, 2000, 3000, \ldots , 7000$, and for the graphical representation let $0 \le x \le 30{,}000$.   (*Source:* Internal Revenue Service.)

77. *Home Prices*   The average price P of a single-family home in thousands of dollars from 1990 to 2000 can be approximated by $P(x) = 5.7(x - 1990) + 150$, where x is the year. Evaluate $P(1995)$ and interpret the result.   (*Source:* U.S. Census Bureau.)

78. *Median Family Income*   The median income I of a family in thousands of dollars from 2000 to 2005 can be approximated by $I(x) = 1.4(x - 2000) + 51$, where x is the year. Evaluate $P(2003)$ and interpret the result.   (*Source:* U.S. Census Bureau.)

IDENTIFYING DOMAINS AND RANGES

Exercises 79–86: Use the graph of f to estimate its domain and range.

79.

80.

81.

82.

83.

84.

85.

86.

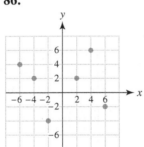

Exercises 87 and 88: Use the diagram to find the domain and range of f.

87.

88.

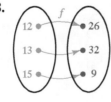

Exercises 89–102: Find the domain.

89. $f(x) = 10x$

90. $f(x) = 5 - x$

91. $f(x) = x^2 - 3$

92. $f(x) = \frac{1}{2}x^2$

93. $f(x) = \dfrac{3}{x - 5}$

94. $f(x) = \dfrac{x}{x + 1}$

95. $f(x) = \dfrac{2x}{x^2 + 1}$

96. $f(x) = \dfrac{6}{1 - x}$

97. $f(x) = \sqrt{x - 1}$

98. $f(x) = |x|$

99. $f(x) = |x - 5|$

100. $f(x) = \sqrt{2 - x}$

101. $f(x) = \dfrac{1}{x}$

102. $f(x) = 1 - 3x^2$

103. *Accidental Deaths* Function f computes the number of accidental deaths y per 100,000 people during year x. (**Source:** Department of Health and Human Services.)

$f = \{(1910, 84.4), (1930, 80.5), (1950, 60.3),$
$\quad (1970, 56.2), (1990, 36.9), (2000, 35.5)\}$

(a) Evaluate $f(1950)$ and interpret the result.
(b) Identify the domain and range of f.
(c) Describe the trend in accidental deaths from 1910 through 2000.

104. *Motor Vehicle Registrations* The following table lists motor vehicle registrations y in millions during year x. Let $y = f(x)$.

x	1920	1940	1960	1980	2000
$f(x)$	9	32	74	156	216

Source: American Automobile Manufacturers Association.

(a) Evaluate $f(1940)$ and interpret the result.
(b) Identify the domain and range of f.
(c) Represent f with a diagram.

IDENTIFYING A FUNCTION

Exercises 105–108: Determine whether the diagram could represent a function.

105.

106.

107.

108.

109. *Average Precipitation*   The table lists the monthly average precipitation P in Las Vegas, Nevada, where $x = 1$ corresponds to January and $x = 12$ corresponds to December.

x (month)	1	2	3	4	5	6
P (inches)	0.5	0.4	0.4	0.2	0.2	0.1

x (month)	7	8	9	10	11	12
P (inches)	0.4	0.5	0.3	0.2	0.4	0.3

Source: J. Williams.

(a) Determine the value of P during May.
(b) Is P a function of x? Explain.
(c) If $P = 0.4$, find x.

110. *Wind Speeds*   The table lists the monthly average wind speed W in Louisville, Kentucky, where $x = 1$ corresponds to January and $x = 12$ corresponds to December.

x (month)	1	2	3	4	5	6
W (mph)	10.4	12.7	10.4	10.4	8.1	8.1

x (month)	7	8	9	10	11	12
W (mph)	6.9	6.9	6.9	8.1	9.2	9.2

Source: J. Williams.

(a) Determine the month with the highest average wind speed.
(b) Is W a function of x? Explain.
(c) If $W = 6.9$, find x.

Exercises 111–120: Determine whether the graph represents a function. If it does, identify the domain and range.

111.

112.

113.

114.

115.

116.

117.

118.

119.

120.

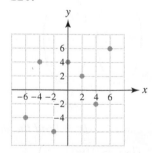

Exercises 121–124: Determine whether S is a function.

121. $S = \{(1, 2), (4, 5), (7, 8), (5, 4), (2, 2)\}$

122. $S = \{(4, 7), (-2, 1), (3, 8), (4, 9)\}$

123. *S* is given by the table.

x	5	10	5
y	2	1	0

124. *S* is given by the table.

x	−3	−2	−1
y	10	10	10

GRAPHICAL INTERPRETATION

Exercises 125 and 126: The graph represents the distance that a person is from home while walking on a straight path. The x-axis represents time and the y-axis represents distance. Interpret the graph.

125.   **126.**

WRITING ABOUT MATHEMATICS

127. Give an example of a function. Identify the domain and range of your function.

128. Explain in your own words what a function is. How is a function different from other relations?

129. Explain how to evaluate a function by using a graph. Give an example.

130. Give one difficulty that may occur when you use a table of values to evaluate a function.

2.2 LINEAR FUNCTIONS

Basic Concepts ■ Representations of Linear Functions
■ Modeling Data with Linear Functions

A LOOK INTO MATH ▷   In mathematics, functions are used to model real-world phenomena, such as electricity, weather, and the economy. Because there are so many different applications of mathematics, a wide assortment of functions has been created. In fact, new functions are invented every day for use in business, education, and government. In this section we discuss an important type of function called a *linear function*.

Basic Concepts

▶ **REAL-WORLD CONNECTION**   Suppose that the air conditioner is turned on when the temperature inside a house is 80°F. The resulting temperatures are listed in Table 2.6 for various elapsed times. Note that for each 1-hour increase in elapsed time, the temperature decreases by 2°F.

TABLE 2.6   House Temperature

1-hour increase

Elapsed Time (hours)	0	1	2	3	4	5
Temperature (°F)	80	78	76	74	72	70

2°F decrease

A scatterplot is shown in Figure 2.20, which suggests that a line models these data.

CALCULATOR HELP

To make a scatterplot, see the Appendix (page AP-4).

Figure 2.20 Temperature in a Home

Over this 5-hour period, the air conditioner lowers the temperature by 2°F for each hour that it runs. The temperature is found by multiplying the elapsed time x by -2 and adding the initial temperature of 80°F. This situation is modeled by $f(x) = -2x + 80$. For example,

$$f(2.5) = -2(2.5) + 80 = 75$$

means that the temperature is 75°F after the air conditioner has run for 2.5 hours. A graph of $f(x) = -2x + 80$, where $0 \le x \le 5$, is shown in Figure 2.21. We call f a *linear function* because its graph is a *line*. If a function is *not* a linear function, then it is a **nonlinear function.**

Figure 2.21 A Linear Function

LINEAR FUNCTION

A function f defined by $f(x) = ax + b$, where a and b are constants, is a **linear function**.

For $f(x) = -2x + 80$, we have $a = -2$ and $b = 80$. The constant a represents the rate at which the air conditioner cools the building, and the constant b represents the initial temperature.

▶ REAL-WORLD CONNECTION   In general, a linear function defined by $f(x) = ax + b$ changes by a units for each unit increase in x. This **rate of change** is an increase if $a > 0$ and a decrease if $a < 0$. For example, if new carpet costs \$20 per square yard, then the linear function defined by $C(x) = 20x$ gives the cost of buying x square yards of carpet. The value of $a = 20$ gives the cost (rate of change) for each additional square yard of carpet. For function C, the value of b is 0 because it costs \$0 to buy 0 square yards of carpet.

NOTE: If f is a linear function, then $f(0) = a(0) + b = b$. Thus b can be found by evaluating $f(x)$ at $x = 0$.

EXAMPLE 1   Identifying linear functions

Determine whether f is a linear function. If f is a linear function, find values for a and b so that $f(x) = ax + b$.

(a) $f(x) = 4 - 3x$ (b) $f(x) = 8$ (c) $f(x) = 2x^2 + 8$

Solution
(a) Let $a = -3$ and $b = 4$. Then $f(x) = -3x + 4$, and f is a linear function.
(b) Let $a = 0$ and $b = 8$. Then $f(x) = 0x + 8$, and f is a linear function.
(c) Function f is not linear because its formula contains x^2. The formula for a linear function cannot contain an x with an exponent other than 1.   Now Try Exercises 9, 11, 13

EXAMPLE 2   Determining linear functions

Use each table of values to determine whether $f(x)$ could represent a linear function. If f could be linear, write a formula for f in the form $f(x) = ax + b$.

(a)

x	0	1	2	3
$f(x)$	10	15	20	25

(b)

x	−2	0	2	4
$f(x)$	4	2	0	−2

(c)

x	0	1	2	3
$f(x)$	1	2	4	7

Solution
(a) For each unit increase in x, $f(x)$ increases by 5 units so $f(x)$ could be linear with $a = 5$. Because $f(0) = 10$, $b = 10$. Thus $f(x) = 5x + 10$.
(b) For each 2-unit increase in x, $f(x)$ decreases by 2 units. Equivalently, each unit increase in x results in a 1-unit decrease in $f(x)$, so $f(x)$ could be linear with $a = -1$. Because $f(0) = 2$, $b = 2$. Thus $f(x) = -x + 2$.
(c) Each unit increase in x does not result in a constant change in $f(x)$. Thus $f(x)$ does not represent a linear function.   Now Try Exercises 21, 23, 25

Representations of Linear Functions

The graph of a linear function is a line. To graph a linear function f we usually start by making a table of values and then plot three or more points. We can then sketch the graph of f by drawing a line through these points, as demonstrated in the next example.

EXAMPLE 3   Graphing a linear function by hand

Sketch a graph of $f(x) = x - 1$. Use the graph to evaluate $f(-2)$.

Solution

Begin by making a table of values containing at least three points. Pick convenient values of x, such as $x = -1, 0, 1$.

$$f(-1) = -1 - 1 = -2$$
$$f(0) = 0 - 1 = -1$$
$$f(1) = 1 - 1 = 0$$

Display the results, as shown in Table 2.7.

   Plot the points $(-1, -2)$, $(0, -1)$, and $(1, 0)$. Then sketch a line through the points to obtain the graph of f. A graph of a line results when *infinitely* many points are plotted, as shown in Figure 2.22.

   To evaluate $f(-2)$, first find $x = -2$ on the x-axis. See Figure 2.23. Then move downward to the graph of f. By moving across to the y-axis, we see that the corresponding y-value is -3. Thus $f(-2) = -3$.

TABLE 2.7

x	y
-1	-2
0	-1
1	0

Figure 2.22

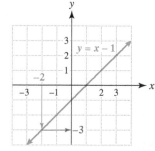

Figure 2.23 $f(-2) = -3$

Now Try Exercises 35, 53

CRITICAL THINKING

Two points determine a line. Why is it a good idea to plot at least three points when graphing a linear function by hand?

EXAMPLE 4   Representing a linear function

A linear function is given by $f(x) = -3x + 2$.
(a) Give a verbal representation of f.
(b) Make a numerical representation (table) of f by letting $x = -1, 0, 1$.
(c) Plot the points listed in the table from part (b). Then sketch a graph of $y = f(x)$.

Solution

(a) *Verbal Representation*   Multiply the input x by -3 and then add 2 to obtain the output.

(b) *Numerical Representation*   Evaluate the formula $f(x) = -3x + 2$ at $x = -1, 0, 1$, which results in Table 2.8. Note that $f(-1) = 5, f(0) = 2$, and $f(1) = -1$.

(c) *Graphical Representation*   To make a graph of f by hand without a graphing calculator, plot the points $(-1, 5)$, $(0, 2)$, and $(1, -1)$ from Table 2.8. Then draw a line passing through these points, as shown in Figure 2.24.

TABLE 2.8

x	$f(x)$
-1	5
0	2
1	-1

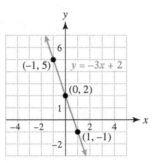

Figure 2.24

Now Try Exercise 67

In the next example a graphing calculator is used to create a graph and table.

EXAMPLE 5   Using a graphing calculator

Give numerical and graphical representations of $f(x) = \frac{1}{2}x - 2$.

Solution

Numerical Representation   To make a numerical representation, construct the table for $Y_1 = .5X - 2$, starting at $x = -3$ and incrementing by 1, as shown in Figure 2.25(a). (Other tables are possible.)

Graphical Representation   Graph Y_1 in the standard viewing rectangle, as shown in Figure 2.25(b). (Other viewing rectangles may be used.)

CALCULATOR HELP

To make a table, see the Appendix (page AP-3). To make a graph, see the Appendix (page AP-5).

(a)

$[-10, 10, 1]$ by $[-10, 10, 1]$

(b)

Figure 2.25

Now Try Exercise 71

Mathematics in Newspapers

Think of the mathematics that you seé in newspapers. Often percentages are described *verbally*, numbers are displayed in *tables*, and data are shown in *graphs*. Seldom are *formulas* given, which is an important reason not to study only symbolic represéntations.

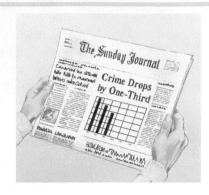

Modeling Data with Linear Functions

▶ **REAL-WORLD CONNECTION**   A distinguishing feature of a linear function is that when the input x increases by 1 unit, the output $f(x) = ax + b$ always changes by an amount equal to a. For example, the number of doctors in the private sector from 1970 to 2000 can be modeled by

$$f(x) = 15{,}260x - 29{,}729{,}000,$$

where x is the year. The value $a = 15{,}260$ indicates that the number of doctors has increased, on average, by 15,260 each year.   (*Source:* American Medical Association.)

The following are other examples of quantities that are modeled by linear functions. Try to determine the value of the constant a.

- The wages earned by an individual working x hours at \$8 per hour
- The distance traveled by light in x seconds if the speed of light is 186,000 miles per second
- The cost of tuition and fees when registering for x credits if each credit costs \$80 and the fees are fixed at \$50

When we are modeling data with a linear function defined by $f(x) = ax + b$, the following concepts are helpful to determine a and b.

MODELING DATA WITH A LINEAR FUNCTION

The formula $f(x) = ax + b$ may be interpreted as follows.

$$f(x) \quad = \quad ax \quad + \quad b$$

(New amount) = (Change) + (Fixed amount)

When x represents time, *change* equals (rate of change) × (time).

$$f(x) \quad = \quad a \quad \times \quad x \quad + \quad b$$

(Future amount) = (Rate of change) × (Time) + (Initial amount)

▶ **REAL-WORLD CONNECTION**   These concepts are applied in the next three examples.

EXAMPLE **6**   Modeling car sales

Table 2.9 shows numbers of Toyota vehicles sold in the United States. (Refer to the introduction to this chapter.)

TABLE 2.9   **Toyota Vehicles Sold (millions)**

Year	1998	1999	2000	2001	2002
Vehicles	1.4	1.5	1.6	1.7	1.8

Source: Autodata.

(a) What were the sales in 1998?
(b) What was the annual increase in sales?
(c) Find a linear function f that models these data. Let $x = 0$ correspond to 1998, $x = 1$ to 1999, and so on.
(d) Use f to predict sales in 2004.

Solution
(a) In 1998, 1.4 million vehicles were sold.
(b) Sales have increased by 0.1 million (100,000) vehicles per year. Because this rate of change is the same each year, we can model the data *exactly* with a linear function.
(c) Initial sales in 1998 ($x = 0$) were 1.4 million vehicles, and each year sales increased by 0.1 million vehicles. Thus

$$f(x) \quad = \quad 0.1 \quad \times \quad x \quad + \quad 1.4$$

(Future sales) $=$ (Rate of change in sales) $\times$ (Time) $+$ (Initial sales),

or $f(x) = 0.1x + 1.4$.
(d) Because $x = 6$ corresponds to 2004, evaluate $f(6)$.

$$f(6) = 0.1(6) + 1.4 = 2 \text{ million vehicles}$$

Note that the actual sales in 2004 were 2 million vehicles, so the estimate is accurate.

Now Try Exercise **91**

In the next example we model tuition and fees.

EXAMPLE **7**   Modeling the cost of tuition and fees

Suppose that tuition costs $80 per credit and that student fees are fixed at $50. Find a formula for a linear function that models tuition and fees.

Solution
Total cost is found by multiplying $80 (rate or cost per credit) by the number of credits x and then adding the fixed fees (fixed amount) of $50. Thus $f(x) = 80x + 50$.

Now Try Exercise **83**

In the next example we consider a simple linear function that models the speed of a car.

EXAMPLE 8   Modeling with a constant function

A car travels on a freeway with its speed recorded at regular intervals, as listed in Table 2.10.

TABLE 2.10   Speed of a Car

Elapsed Time (hours)	0	1	2	3	4
Speed (miles per hour)	70	70	70	70	70

(a) Discuss the speed of the car during this time interval.
(b) Find a formula for a function f that models these data.
(c) Sketch a graph of f together with the data.

Solution
(a) The speed of the car appears to be constant at 70 miles per hour.
(b) Because the speed is constant, the rate of change is 0. Thus

$$f(x) \quad = \quad 0x \quad + \quad 70$$
$$(\text{Future speed}) = (\text{Change in speed}) + (\text{Initial speed})$$

and $f(x) = 70$.
(c) Because $y = f(x)$, graph $y = 70$ with the data points

$$(0, 70), (1, 70), (2, 70), (3, 70), \text{ and } (4, 70)$$

to obtain Figure 2.26.

Figure 2.26 Speed of a Car   Now Try Exercise 79

The function defined by $f(x) = 70$ is an example of a *constant function*. A **constant function** *is a linear function* with $a = 0$ and can be written as $f(x) = b$. Regardless of the input, a constant function always outputs the same value, b. Its graph is a horizontal line.

▶ REAL-WORLD CONNECTION   The following are two applications of constant functions.

• A thermostat calculates a constant function regardless of the weather outside by maintaining a set temperature.
• A cruise control in a car calculates a constant function by maintaining a fixed speed, regardless of the type of road or terrain.

2.2 PUTTING IT ALL TOGETHER

A linear function is a relatively simple function. A clear understanding of linear functions is essential to the understanding of functions in general.

Concept	Explanation	Examples
Linear Function	Can be represented by $f(x) = ax + b$	$f(x) = 2x - 6$, $a = 2$ and $b = -6$ $f(x) = 10$, $a = 0$ and $b = 10$
Constant Function	Can be represented by $f(x) = b$	$f(x) = -7$, $b = -7$ $f(x) = 22$, $b = 22$
Rate of Change for a Linear Function	The output of a linear function changes by a constant amount for each unit increase in the input.	$f(x) = -3x + 8$ decreases 3 units for each unit increase in x. $f(x) = 5$ neither increases nor decreases. The rate of change is 0.

The following table summarizes symbolic, verbal, numerical, and graphical representations of a linear function.

Type of Representation	Comments	Example
Symbolic	Mathematical formula in the form $f(x) = ax + b$	$f(x) = 2x + 1$, where $a = 2$ and $b = 1$
Verbal	Multiply the input x by a and add b.	Multiply the input x by 2 and then add 1 to obtain the output.
Numerical (table of values)	For each unit increase in x in the table, the output of $f(x) = ax + b$ changes by an amount equal to a.	1-unit increase x: 0, 1, 2 $f(x)$: 1, 3, 5 2-unit increase
Graphical	The graph of a linear function is a line. Plot at least 3 points and then sketch the line.	Graph of $y = 2x + 1$

2.2 Exercises

MyMathLab   PRACTICE   WATCH   DOWNLOAD   READ   REVIEW

CONCEPTS

1. The formula for a linear function is $f(x) =$ _____.

2. The formula for a constant function is $f(x) =$ _____.

3. The graph of a linear function is a _____.

4. The graph of a constant function is a _____ line.

5. If $f(x) = 7x + 5$, each time x increases by 1 unit, $f(x)$ increases by _____ units.

6. If $f(x) = 5$, each time x increases by 1 unit, $f(x)$ increases by _____ units.

7. If $C(x) = 2x$ calculates the cost in dollars of buying x square feet of carpet, what does 2 represent in the formula? Interpret the fact that the point (10, 20) lies on the graph of C.

8. If $G(x) = 100 - 4x$ calculates the number of gallons of water in a tank after x minutes, what does -4 represent in the formula? Interpret the fact that the point (5, 80) lies on the graph of G.

IDENTIFYING LINEAR FUNCTIONS

Exercises 9–16: Determine whether f is a linear function. If f is linear, give values for a and b so that f may be expressed as $f(x) = ax + b$.

9. $f(x) = \frac{1}{2}x - 6$

10. $f(x) = x$

11. $f(x) = \frac{5}{2} - x^2$

12. $f(x) = \sqrt{x} + 3$

13. $f(x) = -9$

14. $f(x) = 1.5 - 7.3x$

15. $f(x) = -9x$

16. $f(x) = \frac{1}{x}$

Exercises 17–20: Determine whether the graph represents a linear function.

17.

18.

19.

20.

Exercises 21–28: (Refer to Example 2.) Use the table to determine whether $f(x)$ could represent a linear function. If it could, write $f(x)$ in the form $f(x) = ax + b$.

21.

x	0	1	2	3
$f(x)$	−6	−3	0	3

22.

x	0	2	4	6
$f(x)$	−2	2	6	10

23.

x	−2	0	2	4
$f(x)$	6	3	0	−3

24.

x	0	3	6	9
$f(x)$	8	4	2	1

25.

x	−2	−1	0	1
$f(x)$	−5	0	20	40

26.

x	−2	−1	0	1
$f(x)$	6	3	0	−3

27.

x	1	2	3	4
$f(x)$	0	2	4	6

28.

x	1	2	3	4
f(x)	0	1	3	7

EVALUATING LINEAR FUNCTIONS

Exercises 29–34: Evaluate $f(x)$ at the given values of x.

29. $f(x) = 4x$ $x = -4, 5$

30. $f(x) = -2x + 1$ $x = -2, 3$

31. $f(x) = 5 - x$ $x = -\frac{2}{3}, 3$

32. $f(x) = \frac{1}{2}x - \frac{1}{4}$ $x = 0, \frac{1}{2}$

33. $f(x) = -22$ $x = -\frac{3}{4}, 13$

34. $f(x) = 9x - 7$ $x = -1.2, 2.8$

Exercises 35–40: Use the graph of f to evaluate the given expressions.

35. $f(-1)$ and $f(0)$

36. $f(-2)$ and $f(2)$

37. $f(-2)$ and $f(4)$

38. $f(0)$ and $f(3)$

39. $f(-3)$ and $f(1)$

40. $f(1.5)$ and $f(0.5\pi)$

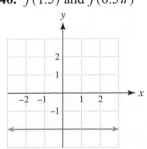

Exercises 41–44: Use the verbal description to write a formula for $f(x)$. Then evaluate $f(3)$.

41. Multiply the input by 6.

42. Multiply the input by -3 and add 7.

43. Divide the input by 6 and subtract $\frac{1}{2}$.

44. Output 8.7 for every input.

REPRESENTING LINEAR FUNCTIONS

Exercises 45–48: Match $f(x)$ with its graph (a.–d.).

45. $f(x) = 3x$ **46.** $f(x) = -2x$

47. $f(x) = x - 2$ **48.** $f(x) = 2x + 1$

a.   **b.**

c.   **d.**

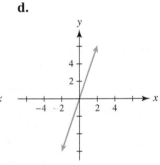

Exercises 49–58: Sketch a graph of $y = f(x)$.

49. $f(x) = 2$ **50.** $f(x) = -1$

51. $f(x) = -\frac{1}{2}x$ **52.** $f(x) = 2x$

53. $f(x) = x + 1$ **54.** $f(x) = x - 2$

55. $f(x) = 3x - 3$ **56.** $f(x) = -2x + 1$

57. $f(x) = 3 - x$ **58.** $f(x) = \frac{1}{4}x + 2$

Exercises 59–64: Write a symbolic representation (formula) for a linear function f that calculates the following.

59. The number of pounds in x ounces

60. The number of dimes in x dollars

61. The distance traveled by a car moving at 65 miles per hour for t hours

62. The long-distance phone bill *in dollars* for calling t minutes at 10 cents per minute and a fixed fee of $4.95

63. The total number of hours in a day during day x

64. The total cost of downhill skiing x times with a $500 season pass

65. **Thinking Generally**   For each 1-unit increase in x, $y = ax + b$ with $a > 0$, y increases by _____ units.

66. **Thinking Generally**   For each 1-unit decrease in $y = cx + d$ with $c < 0$, x increases by _____ units.

Exercises 67–70: Do the following.

    (a) Give a verbal representation of f.
    (b) Make a numerical representation (table) of f for $x = -2, 0, 2$.
    (c) Plot the points listed in the table from part (b). Then sketch a graph of f.

67. $f(x) = -2x + 1$ **68.** $f(x) = 1 - x$

69. $f(x) = \frac{1}{2}x - 1$ **70.** $f(x) = \frac{3}{4}x$

Exercises 71–74: Do the following.

    (a) Make a numerical representation (table) of f for $x = -3, -2, -1, \ldots, 3$.
    (b) Graph f in the window $[-6, 6, 1]$ by $[-4, 4, 1]$.

71. $f(x) = \frac{1}{3}x + \sqrt{2}$ **72.** $f(x) = -\frac{2}{3}x - \sqrt{3}$

73. $f(x) = \frac{x + 2}{5}$ **74.** $f(x) = \frac{2 - 3x}{7}$

MODELING

Exercises 75–78: Match the situation with the graph (a.–d.) that models it best, where x-values represent time from 1995 to 2005.

75. The cost of college tuition

76. The cost of 1 gigabyte of computer memory

77. The distance between Chicago and Denver

78. The total distance traveled by a satellite orbiting Earth if the satellite was launched in 1995.

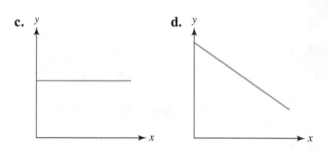

APPLICATIONS

79. *Thermostat*   Let $y = f(x)$ describe the temperature y of a room that is kept at $70°$F for x hours.
    (a) Represent f symbolically and graphically over a 24-hour period for $0 \le x \le 24$.
    (b) Construct a table of f for $x = 0, 4, 8, 12, \ldots, 24$.
    (c) What type of function is f?

80. *Cruise Control*   Let $y = f(x)$ describe the speed y of an automobile after x minutes if the cruise control is set at 60 miles per hour.
    (a) Represent f symbolically and graphically over a 15-minute period for $0 \le x \le 15$.
    (b) Construct a table of f for $x = 0, 1, 2, \ldots, 6$.
    (c) What type of function is f?

81. *Distance*   A car is initially 50 miles south of the Minnesota–Iowa border traveling south on Interstate 35. Distances D between the car and the border are recorded in the table for various elapsed times t. Find a linear function given by $D(t) = at + b$ that models these data.

t (hours)	0	2	3	5
D (miles)	50	170	230	350

82. *Estimating the Weight of a Bass*   Sometimes the weight of a fish can be estimated by measuring its length. The table lists typical weights of bass having various lengths.

Length (inches)	12	14	16	18	20	22
Weight (pounds)	1.0	1.7	2.5	3.6	5.0	6.6

Source: Minnesota Department of Natural Resources.

(a) Let x be the length and y be the weight. Make a line graph of the data.

(b) Could the data be modeled accurately with a linear function? Explain your answer.

83. *Solid Waste*   In 1960, the average American disposed of 2.7 pounds of garbage per day, whereas in 2003 this amount was 4.3 pounds per day. (*Source:* Environmental Protection Agency.)

(a) Find a linear function f that calculates the amount of garbage disposed of by a person in 1960 after x days. Find $f(60)$ and interpret the result.

(b) Repeat part (a) for 2003 with a linear function g.

84. *Rain Forests*   Rain forests are forests that grow in regions receiving more than 70 inches of rain per year. The world is losing about 49 million acres of rain forest each year. (*Source:* New York Times Almanac.)

(a) Find a linear function f that calculates the change in the acres of rain forest in millions in x years.

(b) Evaluate $f(7)$ and interpret the result.

85. *Mobile Malware*   As the number of smart mobile telephones has increased, so has the number of malicious software viruses that affect these devices. In 2006 the total number N of *malware* viruses detected from January to July could be modeled by the formula $N(x) = 16x + 136$, where $x = 1$ corresponds to January, $x = 2$ to February, and so on. (*Source:* Hypponen, Mikko, "Malware Goes Mobile," *Scientific American*, November 2006.)

(a) Use the window [1, 7, 1] by [0, 300, 100] to graph f.

(b) Discuss any trend in the graph.

(c) Evaluate $f(3)$ and interpret your result.

(d) What does the number 16 in the formula indicate?

86. *Temperature and Volume*   If a sample of a gas, such as helium, is heated, it will expand. The formula $V(T) = 0.147T + 40$ calculates the volume V in cubic inches of a sample of gas at temperature T in degrees Celsius.

(a) Evaluate $V(0)$ and interpret the result.

(b) If the temperature increases by $10°C$, by how much does the volume increase?

(c) What is the volume of the gas when the temperature is $100°C$?

87. *Temperature and Volume*   (Refer to the preceding exercise.) A sample of gas at $0°C$ has a volume V of 137 cubic centimeters, which increases in volume by 0.5 cubic centimeter for every $1°C$ increase in temperature T.

(a) Write a formula $V(T) = aT + b$ that gives the volume of the gas at temperature T.

(b) Find the volume of the gas when $T = 50°C$.

88. *Cost*   To make a music video it costs $750 to rent a studio plus $5 for each copy produced.

(a) Write a formula $C(x) = ax + b$ that calculates the cost of producing x videos.

(b) Find the cost of producing 2500 videos.

89. *Weight Lifting*   Lifting weights can increase a person's muscle mass. Each additional pound of muscle burns an extra 40 calories per day. Write a linear function that models the number of calories burned each day by x pounds of muscle. By burning an extra 3500 calories a person can lose 1 pound of fat. How many pounds of muscle are needed to burn 1 pound of fat in 30 days? (*Source:* Runner's World.)

90. *Number of Doctors*   The number N of doctors in the private sector from 1970 to 2000 can be approximated by $N(t) = 15{,}260t + 333{,}200$, where t is in years and $t = 0$ corresponds to 1970.
  (a) Evaluate $N(0)$ and $N(30)$ and interpret each result.
  (b) Explain what the numbers 15,260 and 333,200 represent in the formula.

91. *Baseball*   The table shows the average length of a major league baseball game in minutes for various years.

Year	2000	2001	2002
Length (minutes)	180	176	172

Source: Elias Sports Bureau.

  (a) What was the average length in 2000?
  (b) By how many minutes did the average length change each year?

(c) Find a linear function f that models these data. Let $x = 0$ correspond to 2000.
(d) Use f to predict the average length in 2004.

92. *Wal-Mart Sales*   The table shows Wal-Mart's share as a percentage of overall U.S. retail sales for various years. (This percentage excludes restaurants and motor vehicles.)

Year	1998	1999	2000	2001	2002
Share (%)	6	6.5	7	7.5	8

Source: Commerce Department, Wal-Mart.

  (a) What was Wal-Mart's share in 1998?
  (b) By how much (percent) did Wal-Mart's share increase each year?
  (c) Find a linear function f that models these data. Let $x = 0$ correspond to 1998.
  (d) Use f to estimate Wal-Mart's share in 2005.

WRITING ABOUT MATHEMATICS

93. Explain how you can determine whether a function is linear by using its
  (a) symbolic representation,
  (b) graphical representation, and
  (c) numerical representation.

94. Describe one way to determine whether a set of data points can be modeled by a linear function.

CHECKING BASIC CONCEPTS
SECTIONS 2.1 AND 2.2

1. Find a formula and sketch a graph for a function that squares the input x and then subtracts 1.

2. Use the graph to the right to do the following.
  (a) Find the domain and range of f.
  (b) Evaluate $f(0)$ and $f(2)$.
  (c) Is f a linear function? Explain.

3. Determine whether f is a linear function.
  (a) $f(x) = 4x - 2$
  (b) $f(x) = 2\sqrt{x} - 5$
  (c) $f(x) = -7$
  (d) $f(x) = 9 - 2x + 5x$

4. Graph $f(x) = 4 - 3x$. Evaluate $f(-2)$.

5. Find a formula for a linear function that models the data.

x	0	1	2	3	4
$f(x)$	-1	$-\frac{1}{2}$	0	$\frac{1}{2}$	1

6. The median age in the United States from 1970 to 2000 can be approximated by

$$f(x) = 0.264x + 27.7,$$

where $x = 0$ corresponds to 1970, $x = 1$ to 1971, and so on.
  (a) Evaluate $f(20)$ and interpret the result.
  (b) Interpret the numbers 0.264 and 27.7.

2.3 THE SLOPE OF A LINE

Slope ▪ Slope–Intercept Form of a Line ▪ Interpreting Slope in Applications

A LOOK INTO MATH ▷

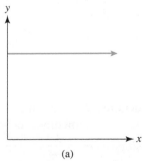

Figure 2.27 shows some graphs of lines, where the x-axis represents time.

Which graph might represent the amount of gas in your car's tank while you are driving?

Which graph might represent the temperature inside a refrigerator?

Which graph might represent the amount of water in a pool that is being filled?

To answer these questions, you probably used the concept of slope. In mathematics, slope is a real number that measures the "tilt" of a line in the xy-plane. We assume throughout the text that lines are always straight. In this section we discuss how slope relates to the graph of a linear function and how to interpret slope.

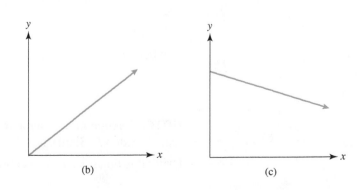

(a)   (b)   (c)

Figure 2.27

Slope

▶ **REAL-WORLD CONNECTION**   The graph shown in Figure 2.28 illustrates the cost of buying x pounds of candy. The graph tilts upward from left to right, which indicates that the cost increases as the number of pounds purchased increases. Note that for every 2 pounds purchased, the cost increases by \$3. We say that the graph *rises* 3 units for every 2 units of *run*. The ratio $\frac{\text{rise}}{\text{run}}$ equals the *slope* of the line. The slope of this line is $\frac{3}{2}$, or 1.5. That is, for every unit of run along the x-axis, the graph rises 1.5 units. A slope of 1.5 indicates that candy costs \$1.50 per pound.

Figure 2.28 Cost of Candy

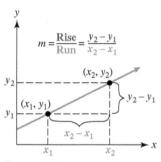

Figure 2.29

A more general case is shown in Figure 2.29 where a line passes through the points (x_1, y_1) and (x_2, y_2). The **rise** or **change in y** is $y_2 - y_1$, and the **run** or **change in x** is $x_2 - x_1$. The slope m is given by

$$m = \frac{\text{rise}}{\text{run}} = \frac{y_2 - y_1}{x_2 - x_1}.$$

NOTE: The expression x_1 has a **subscript** of 1 and is read "x sub one" or "x one." Thus x_1 and x_2 denote two different x-values. Similar comments can be made about y_1 and y_2.

SLOPE

The **slope** m of the line passing through the points (x_1, y_1) and (x_2, y_2) is

$$m = \frac{y_2 - y_1}{x_2 - x_1},$$

where $x_1 \neq x_2$. That is, slope equals *rise over run*.

NOTE: *Change in x* is sometimes denoted Δx and equals $x_2 - x_1$. The expression Δx is read "delta x." Similarly, *change in y* is sometimes denoted Δy and equals $y_2 - y_1$. Using this notation, we can express slope as $m = \frac{\Delta y}{\Delta x} = \frac{y_2 - y_1}{x_2 - x_1}$.

EXAMPLE 1   Calculating the slope of a line

Find the slope of the line passing through the points $(-4, 1)$ and $(2, 4)$. Plot these points and graph the line. Interpret the slope.

Figure 2.30

Solution
Begin by letting $(x_1, y_1) = (-4, 1)$ and $(x_2, y_2) = (2, 4)$. The slope is

$$m = \frac{y_2 - y_1}{x_2 - x_1} = \frac{4 - 1}{2 - (-4)} = \frac{3}{6} = \frac{1}{2}.$$

A graph of the line passing through these two points is shown in Figure 2.30. A slope of $\frac{1}{2}$ indicates that the line rises 1 unit for every 2 units of run. This slope is equivalent to 3 units of rise for every 6 units of run.

Now Try Exercise 31

We would calculate the same slope in Example 1 if we let $(x_1, y_1) = (2, 4)$ and $(x_2, y_2) = (-4, 1)$. In this case the calculation would be

$$m = \frac{y_2 - y_1}{x_2 - x_1} = \frac{1 - 4}{-4 - 2} = \frac{-3}{-6} = \frac{1}{2}.$$

If a line has **positive slope**, the line *rises* from left to right. In Figure 2.31 the rise is 2 units for each unit of run, so the slope is 2. If a line has **negative slope**, the line *falls* from left to right. In Figure 2.32 the line *falls* 1 unit for every 2 units of run, so the slope is $-\frac{1}{2}$. Slope 0 indicates that a line is horizontal, as shown in Figure 2.33. If (x_1, y_1) and (x_2, y_2) are two points on a vertical line, $x_1 = x_2$. In Figure 2.34 the run is $x_2 - x_1 = 0$, so a vertical line has **undefined slope** because division by 0 is undefined.

Figure 2.31 Positive Slope

Figure 2.32 Negative Slope

Figure 2.33 Zero Slope

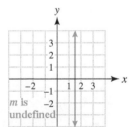

Figure 2.34 Undefined Slope

EXAMPLE 2   Calculating slope

Find the slope of the line passing through each pair of points, if possible
(a) $(-1, 4), (8, 4)$ **(b)** $\left(-\frac{3}{4}, \frac{1}{4}\right), \left(-\frac{3}{4}, \frac{5}{4}\right)$ **(c)** $(a, 3b), (3a, 5b)$

Solution

(a) For $(-1, 4)$ and $(8, 4)$, $m = \dfrac{y_2 - y_1}{x_2 - x_1} = \dfrac{4 - 4}{8 - (-1)} = \dfrac{0}{9} = 0.$

(b) For $\left(-\frac{3}{4}, \frac{1}{4}\right)$ and $\left(-\frac{3}{4}, \frac{5}{4}\right)$, $m = \dfrac{y_2 - y_1}{x_2 - x_1} = \dfrac{\frac{5}{4} - \frac{1}{4}}{-\frac{3}{4} - \left(-\frac{3}{4}\right)} = \dfrac{1}{0}$, which is undefined.

(c) For $(a, 3b)$ and $(3a, 5b)$, $m = \dfrac{y_2 - y_1}{x_2 - x_1} = \dfrac{5b - 3b}{3a - a} = \dfrac{2b}{2a} = \dfrac{b}{a}.$

Now Try Exercises **17, 19, 27**

EXAMPLE **3**   Sketching a line with a given slope

Sketch a line passing through the point $(0, 4)$ and having slope $-\frac{2}{3}$.

Solution

Start by plotting the point $(0, 4)$. Because $m = \dfrac{\text{change in } y}{\text{change in } x}$, a slope of $-\frac{2}{3}$ indicates that the y-values *decrease* 2 units each time the x-values increase by 3 units. That is, the line *falls* 2 units for every 3-unit increase in the run. The line passes through $(0, 4)$, so a 2-unit decrease in y and a 3-unit increase in x results in the line passing through the point $(0 + 3, 4 - 2)$ or $(3, 2)$, as shown in Figure 2.35.

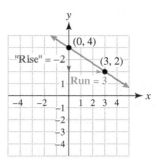

Figure 2.35

Now Try Exercise **35**

Slope–Intercept Form of a Line

Because $f(0) = 3$ and $f(1) = 5$, the graph of $f(x) = 2x + 3$ is a line that passes through $(0, 3)$ and $(1, 5)$, as shown in Figure 2.36. Therefore the slope of this line is

$$m = \frac{5 - 3}{1 - 0} = 2.$$

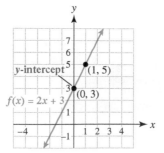

Figure 2.36

Note that slope 2 equals the coefficient of x in the formula $f(x) = 2x + 3$. In general, if $f(x) = ax + b$, the slope of the graph of f is $m = a$. For example, the graph of $f(x) = 6x - 5$ has slope $m = 6$, and the graph of $f(x) = -\frac{4}{5}x + 1$ has slope $m = -\frac{4}{5}$.

The point $(0, 3)$ lies on the graph of $f(x) = 2x + 3$ and is located on the y-axis. The y-value of 3 is called the *y-intercept*. A **y-intercept** is the y-coordinate of a point where a graph intersects the y-axis. To find a y-intercept let $x = 0$ in $f(x)$. If $f(x) = ax + b$, then

$$f(0) = a(0) + b = b.$$

Thus if $f(x) = -4x + 7$, the y-intercept is 7, and if $f(x) = \frac{1}{2}x - 8$, the y-intercept is -8.

Because $y = f(x)$, any linear function is given by $y = mx + b$, where m is the slope and b is the y-intercept. The form $y = mx + b$ is called the *slope–intercept form* of a line.

SLOPE–INTERCEPT FORM

The line with slope m and y-intercept b is given by

$$y = mx + b,$$

the **slope–intercept form** of a line.

EXAMPLE 4   Graphing lines

Identify the slope and y-intercept for the three lines $y = \frac{1}{2}x - 2$, $y = \frac{1}{2}x$, and $y = \frac{1}{2}x + 2$. Graph and compare the lines.

Solution

The graph of $y = \frac{1}{2}x - 2$ has slope $\frac{1}{2}$ and y-intercept -2. This line passes through the point $(0, -2)$ and rises 1 unit for each 2 units of run (see Figure 2.37). The graph of $y = \frac{1}{2}x$ has slope $\frac{1}{2}$ and y-intercept 0, and the graph of $y = \frac{1}{2}x + 2$ has slope $\frac{1}{2}$ and y-intercept 2. These lines are parallel, and the vertical distance between adjacent lines is always 2.

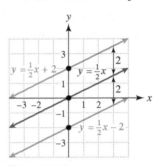

Figure 2.37

Now Try Exercise 45

EXAMPLE 5   Using a graph to write the slope–intercept form

For each graph shown in Figures 2.38 and 2.39, write the slope–intercept form of the line.

(a)

Figure 2.38

(b)

Figure 2.39

Solution

(a) The graph passes through $(0, -2)$, so the y-intercept is -2. Because the graph rises 3 units for each unit increase in x, the slope is 3. The slope–intercept form is $y = 3x - 2$.

(b) The graph passes through $(0, 2)$, so the y-intercept is 2. Because the graph is a horizontal line, its slope is 0. The slope–intercept form is $y = 0x + 2$, or more simply, $y = 2$.

Now Try Exercises 53, 55

EXAMPLE 6   Finding the slope–intercept form

TABLE 2.11

x	y
−1	1
0	?
2	10

The points listed in Table 2.11 all lie on a line.
(a) Find the missing value in the table.
(b) Write the slope–intercept form of the line.

Solution
(a) The line passes through $(-1, 1)$ and $(2, 10)$ so its slope is

$$m = \frac{10 - 1}{2 - (-1)} = \frac{9}{3} = 3.$$

For each unit increase in x, y increases by 3. When x increases from -1 to 0, y increases from 1 to $1 + 3 = 4$. Therefore the missing value is 4.
(b) Because the line passes through the point $(0, 4)$, its y-intercept is 4. The slope–intercept form is $y = 3x + 4$.   Now Try Exercise 67

Interpreting Slope in Applications

▶ REAL-WORLD CONNECTION   When a linear function is used to model physical quantities, the slope of its graph provides certain information. Slope can be interpreted as a **rate of change** of a quantity, which we illustrate in the next four examples.

EXAMPLE 7   Interpreting slope

The distance y in miles that an athlete riding a bicycle is from home after x hours is shown in Figure 2.40.
(a) Find the y-intercept. What does the y-intercept represent?
(b) The graph passes through the point $(2, 6)$. Discuss the meaning of this point.
(c) Find the slope–intercept form of this line. Interpret the slope as a rate of change.

Figure 2.40 Distance from Home

Solution
(a) The y-intercept is 30, which indicates that the athlete is initially 30 miles from home.
(b) The point $(2, 6)$ means that after 2 hours the athlete is 6 miles from home.
(c) The line passes through the points $(0, 30)$ and $(2, 6)$. Thus its slope is

$$m = \frac{6 - 30}{2 - 0} = -12,$$

and the slope–intercept form is $y = -12x + 30$. A slope of -12 indicates that the athlete is traveling at 12 miles per hour *toward* home. The negative sign indicates that the distance between the athlete and home is *decreasing*.   Now Try Exercise 79

EXAMPLE 8   Interpreting slope

Water is being pumped into a 500-gallon tank during a 10-minute interval. The amount of water W in the tank after t minutes is given by $W(t) = 40t + 100$, where W is in gallons.
(a) Evaluate $W(0)$ and $W(10)$. Interpret each result.
(b) Graph W for $0 \leq t \leq 10$.
(c) What is the slope of the graph of W? Interpret this slope.

Solution
(a) $W(0) = 40(0) + 100 = 100$; $W(10) = 40(10) + 100 = 500$. Initially, there are 100 gallons of water in the tank. After 10 minutes, there are 500 gallons and the tank is full.
(b) Because $W(0) = 100$ and $W(10) = 500$, plot the points $(0, 100)$ and $(10, 500)$. Function W is linear, so connect these points with a line segment. See Figure 2.41.

Figure 2.41

(c) The slope is 40, which indicates that water is being pumped into the tank at a rate of 40 gallons per minute.   Now Try Exercise 85

EXAMPLE 9   Interpreting slope

If a sample of a gas is heated, it will expand. The expression $V(t) = 0.183t + 50$ gives the volume V of a sample of helium in cubic inches at a temperature of t degrees Celsius.
(a) Find the slope of the graph of V.
(b) Interpret the slope as a rate of change.

Solution
(a) The slope of the graph of $V(t) = 0.183t + 50$ is $m = 0.183$.
(b) A slope of $m = 0.183$ means that the sample of helium increases in volume by 0.183 cubic inch for each $1°C$ increase in temperature.   Now Try Exercise 86

EXAMPLE 10   Analyzing growth of Wal-Mart

Table 2.12 on the next page lists numbers of Wal-Mart employees.
(a) Make a line graph of the data.
(b) Find the slope of each line segment in the graph.
(c) Interpret these slopes as rates of change.

TABLE 2.12   **Wal-Mart Employees (millions)**

Year	1997	1999	2002	2007
Employees	0.7	1.1	1.4	2.2

Source: Wal-Mart.

Solution

(a) To make a line graph start by plotting the points (1997, 0.7), (1999, 1.1), (2002, 1.4), and (2007, 2.2). Connecting these points with line segments results in Figure 2.42.

CRITICAL THINKING

An athlete runs away from home at 10 miles per hour for 30 minutes and then jogs back home at 5 miles per hour. Sketch a graph that shows the distance between the athlete and home.

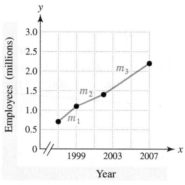

Figure 2.42 Wal-Mart Employees

(b) The slopes of the line segments in Figure 2.42 are

$$m_1 = \frac{1.1 - 0.7}{1999 - 1997} = 0.2, \quad m_2 = \frac{1.4 - 1.1}{2002 - 1999} = 0.1, \quad \text{and}$$

$$m_3 = \frac{2.2 - 1.4}{2007 - 2002} = 0.16.$$

(c) Slope $m_1 = 0.2$ means that, on average, the number of Wal-Mart employees increased by 0.2 million (or 200,000) per year between 1997 and 1999. Slopes m_2 and m_3 can be interpreted similarly.   Now Try Exercise 75

2.3 PUTTING IT ALL TOGETHER

The graph of a linear function is a line. The "tilt" of a line is called the slope and equals rise over run. A positive slope indicates that the line *rises* from left to right, whereas a negative slope indicates that the line *falls* from left to right. A horizontal line has slope 0 and a vertical line has undefined slope. The following table summarizes some basic concepts about slope and slope–intercept form.

Concept	Explanation	Example
Slope	The slope of the line passing through the points (x_1, y_1) and (x_2, y_2) is given by $$m = \frac{\text{rise}}{\text{run}} = \frac{y_2 - y_1}{x_2 - x_1}, \quad (x_1 \neq x_2).$$ Rise = change in y; run = change in x	The slope of the line passing through $(-2, 3)$ and $(1, 5)$ is $$m = \frac{5 - 3}{1 - (-2)} = \frac{2}{3}.$$ If the x-values increase by 3 units, the y-values increase by 2 units.
Slope–Intercept Form for a Line	The slope equals m, and the y-intercept equals b. $$y = mx + b$$	If $y = \frac{1}{2}x + 1$, the slope of the graph is $\frac{1}{2}$ and the y-intercept is 1. 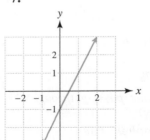
Slope as a Rate of Change	The slope of the graph of a linear function indicates the rate at which a quantity is either increasing or decreasing.	From 1981 to 2000, average public college tuition and fees can be modeled by $$f(x) = 136x + 772,$$ where $x = 1$ corresponds to 1981. The slope of the graph of f is $m = 136$ and indicates that, on average, tuition and fees increased by \$136 per year between 1981 and 2000.

2.3 Exercises

MyMathLab   PRACTICE   WATCH   DOWNLOAD   READ   REVIEW

CONCEPTS

1. Slope is equal to *change in* _____ over *change in* _____.

2. If two points have the same y-coordinates but different x-coordinates, then the slope of the line passing through these points is _____.

3. A line with positive slope _____ from left to right.

4. A line with slope 0 is a _____ line.

5. A line with undefined slope is a _____ line.

6. The form $y = mx + b$ is called the _____ form for a line.

SLOPE

Exercises 7–12: Find the slope of the line.

7.

8.

9.

10.

11.

12.

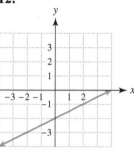

Exercises 13–30: Find the slope of the line passing through the two points.

13. $(1, 2), (2, 4)$

14. $(-3, 2), (2, -3)$

15. $(2, 1), (-1, 3)$

16. $\left(-\frac{3}{5}, -\frac{4}{5}\right), \left(\frac{4}{5}, \frac{3}{5}\right)$

17. $(-3, 6), (4, 6)$

18. $(-3, 5), (-5, 5)$

19. $\left(\frac{1}{2}, -\frac{2}{7}\right), \left(\frac{1}{2}, \frac{13}{17}\right)$

20. $(-1, 6), (-1, -4)$

21. $\left(\frac{1}{3}, -\frac{4}{3}\right), \left(\frac{1}{6}, \frac{1}{3}\right)$

22. $\left(-\frac{1}{2}, \frac{3}{2}\right), \left(2, \frac{1}{2}\right)$

23. $(1989, 10), (1999, 16)$

24. $(1950, 6.1), (2000, 10.6)$

25. $(2.1, 3.6), (-1.2, 4.3)$

26. $(12, -34), (14, 64)$

27. Thinking Generally $(2a, b), (3a, 4b)$

28. Thinking Generally $(-a, -b), (b, a)$

29. Thinking Generally $(a + b, 0), (a, b)$

30. Thinking Generally $(a, b), (b, a)$

Exercises 31–34: Do the following.

  (a) *Find the slope of the line passing through the given points.*
  (b) *Plot these points and graph the line.*
  (c) *Interpret the slope.*

31. $(-1, 2), (3, -1)$

32. $(-2, -2), (1, 3)$

33. $(0, 2), (-3, 0)$

34. $(-1, 2), (1, 2)$

Exercises 35–42: Sketch a line passing through the given point with slope m.

35. $(0, -2), \quad m = 3$

36. $(0, 1), \quad m = -1$

37. $(0, 4), \quad m = -\frac{1}{2}$

38. $(0, -3), \quad m = \frac{2}{3}$

39. $(-1, 1), \quad m = -2$

40. $(2, 1), \quad m = \frac{1}{2}$

41. $(2, -3), \quad m = \frac{1}{2}$

42. $(-2, 3), \quad m = -\frac{3}{5}$

Exercises 43–52: Do the following.

  (a) *Find the slope and y-intercept of the line.*
  (b) *Graph the equation.*

43. $y = x + 2$

44. $y = x - 2$

45. $y = -3x + 2$

46. $y = \frac{1}{2}x - 1$

47. $y = \frac{1}{3}x$

48. $y = -2x$

49. $y = 2$

50. $y = -3$

51. $y = -x + 3$

52. $y = \frac{2}{3}x - 2$

Exercises 53–58: Use the graph to express the line in slope–intercept form.

53.

54.

55.

56.

57.   **58.**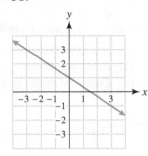

Exercises 59–62: Write the slope–intercept form for a line satisfying the following conditions.

59. Slope 3, y-intercept -5

60. Slope $-\frac{2}{3}$, y-intercept 7

61. Passing through $(1, 0)$ and $\left(0, -\frac{3}{2}\right)$

62. Passing through $(0, 4)$ and $(-2, 0)$

Exercises 63–66: Let f be a linear function. Use the table to find the slope and y-intercept of the graph of f.

63.

x	0	1	2	3
$f(x)$	-2	0	2	4

64.

x	-1	0	1	2
$f(x)$	5	10	15	20

65.

x	-2	-1	1	2
$f(x)$	18	11	-3	-10

66.

x	-4	-2	2	4
$f(x)$	6	3	-3	-6

Exercises 67–70: Let $f(x)$ represent a linear function.

   (a) *Find the missing value in the table.*
   (b) *Write the slope–intercept form for f.*

67.

x	0	1	2
$f(x)$	-1	1	?

68.

x	1	2	3
$f(x)$	12	8	?

69.

x	-2	0	4
$f(x)$	2	?	11

70.

x	0	5	20
$f(x)$	?	10	40

INTERPRETING SLOPE

Exercises 71–74: Modeling   Choose the graph (a.–d.) that models the situation best.

71. Money that a person earns after x hours, working for $10 per hour

72. Total acres of rain forests in the world during the past 20 years

73. World population from 1980 to 2005

74. Square miles of land in Nevada from 1950 to 2005

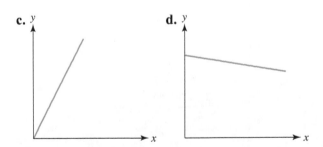

Exercises 75–78: Modeling   Each line graph on the next page represents the gallons of water in a small swimming pool after x hours. Assume that a pump can either add water to or remove water from the pool.

   (a) *Estimate the slope of each line segment.*
   (b) *Interpret each slope as a rate of change.*
   (c) *Describe what happened to the amount of water in the pool.*

Exercises 75–78: See instructions on page 115.

75.

76.

77.

78.

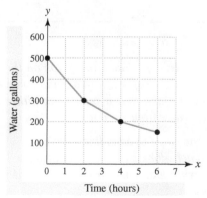

Exercises 79 and 80: **Modeling Distance**   *An individual is driving a car along a straight road. The graph shows the distance that the driver is from home after x hours.*

(a) *Find the slope of each line segment in the graph.*
(b) *Interpret each slope as a rate of change.*
(c) *Describe both the motion and location of the car.*

79.

80.

Exercises 81–84: **Sketching a Model**   *Sketch a graph that models the given situation.*

81. The distance that a bicycle rider is from home if the rider is initially 20 miles away from home and arrives home after riding at a constant speed for 2 hours

82. The distance that an athlete is from home if the athlete runs away from home at 8 miles per hour for 30 minutes and then walks back home at 4 miles per hour

83. The distance that a person is from home if this individual drives (at a constant speed) to a mall, stays 2 hours, and then drives home, assuming that the distance to the mall is 20 miles and that the trip takes 30 minutes

84. The amount of water in a 10,000-gallon swimming pool that is filled at the rate of 1000 gallons per hour, left full for 10 hours, and then drained at the rate of 2000 gallons per hour

APPLICATIONS

85. *Older Mothers* The number of children in thousands born to mothers 40 years old or older is modeled by $f(x) = 4x - 7910$, where x is the year with $1990 \leq x \leq 2005$. (**Source:** National Center for Health Statistics, 2006.)
   (a) Estimate the number of children born to older mothers in 1993.
   (b) Graph f. Describe the graph.
   (c) What is the slope of the graph of f?
   (d) Interpret the slope as a rate of change.

86. *Number of Radio Stations* The number of radio stations on the air from 1950 to 2001 may be modeled by

$$f(x) = 201.7x - 390,477,$$

where x is the year. (**Source:** National Association of Broadcasters.)
   (a) How many radio stations were on the air in 1980?
   (b) What is the slope of the graph of f?
   (c) Interpret the slope as a rate of change.

87. *Commercial Banks* From 1987 to 2004 the number N of federally insured banks could be approximated by

$$N(t) = -358.4t + 13,723,$$

where t is the year and $t = 0$ corresponds to 1987.
   (a) How many federally insured banks were there in 2002?
   (b) What is the slope of the graph of N? Interpret this slope as a rate of change.
   (c) What is the y-intercept of the graph of N, where $y = N(t)$? Interpret this intercept.

88. *Population Density* From 1900 to 2000 the population density D of the United States in people per square mile could be approximated by

$$D(t) = 0.581t + 21.5,$$

where t is in years and $t = 0$ corresponds to 1900.
   (a) Find population density in 1900 and 2000.
   (b) What is the slope of the graph of D? Interpret this slope as a rate of change.
   (c) What is the y-intercept of the graph of D, where $y = D(t)$? Interpret this intercept.

89. *Cost of Carpet* The graph shows the cost of buying x square yards of carpet. Find the slope of this graph and interpret the result.

Carpet (square yards)

90. *Cost of Removing Snow* The graph shows the cost of removing x tons of snow. Find the slope of this graph and interpret the result.

Snow Removed (tons)

91. *Filling a Swimming Pool* A 20,000-gallon swimming pool is being filled at a constant rate. Over a 5-hour period the water in the pool increases from $\frac{1}{4}$ full to $\frac{5}{8}$ full. At what rate is water entering the pool?

92. *Rock Music* In 1987 rock music accounted for 46% of all music sales. By 2004 this amount had decreased to 24%. (**Source:** Recording Industry Association of America.)
   (a) Let x represent the number of years after 1987. Find values for a and b so that $f(x) = ax + b$ models these data.
   (b) Estimate this percentage in 1995 and compare it with the actual value of 34%.

93. *Rap and Hip Hop Music*   In 1987 rap and hip hop music accounted for only 3.8% of all music sales. By 2004 this amount had increased to 12.1%.   *(Source: Recording Industry Association of America.)*

   (a) Let x represent the number of years after 1987. Find values for a and b so that $f(x) = ax + b$ models these data.

   (b) Estimate this percentage in 2000 and compare it with the actual value of 9.7%.

94. *Speed of an Airplane*   An airplane on a 1200-mile trip is flying at a constant rate. Over a 2-hour period the location of the plane changes from covering $\frac{1}{3}$ of the distance to covering $\frac{7}{8}$ of the distance. What is the speed of the airplane?

95. *U.S. Average Family Income*   In 1990, the average family income was about \$37,000, and in 2005 it was about \$60,000.   *(Source: Department of the Treasury.)*

   (a) Let $x = 0$ represent 1990, $x = 1$ represent 1991, and so on. Find values for a and b so that $f(x) = ax + b$ models the data.

   (b) Estimate the average family income in 2000.

96. *Minimum Wage*   In 1980, the minimum wage was about \$3.10 per hour, and in 2005 it increased to \$5.15.   *(Source: Department of Labor.)*

   (a) Let $x = 0$ represent 1980, $x = 1$ represent 1981, until $x = 25$ represents 2005. Find values for a and b so that $f(x) = ax + b$ models the data.

   (b) If this trend continues, what should be the minimum wage in 2020?

WRITING ABOUT MATHEMATICS

97. Describe the information that the slope m of a line gives. Be as complete as possible.

98. Could one line have two different slope–intercept forms? Explain your answer.

GROUP ACTIVITY
WORKING WITH REAL DATA

Directions: Form a group of 2 to 4 people. Select someone to record the group's responses for this activity. All members should work cooperatively to answer the questions. If your instructor asks for the results, each member of the group should be prepared to respond.

Sport Utility Vehicles (SUVs)   SUVs became increasingly popular during the 1990s. The table lists the number of SUVs sold in various years.

Year	1992	1994	1996	1998	2000
SUVs (millions)	1.1	1.5	2.1	2.7	3.2

Source: Autodata Corporation.

 (a) Make a scatterplot of the data. Discuss any trend in SUV sales. Let $x = 0$ correspond to 1992.

   (b) Estimate the slope m of a line that could be used to model the data.

   (c) Find an equation of a line $y = mx + b$ that models the data.

   (d) Interpret the slope m as a rate of change.

   (e) Use your results to estimate SUV sales in 1997 and 2001. Answers may vary.

2.4 EQUATIONS OF LINES AND LINEAR MODELS

Point–Slope Form ▪ Horizontal and Vertical Lines ▪ Parallel and Perpendicular Lines

In 1999, there were approximately 100 million Internet users in the United States, and this number grew to about 200 million in 2005. This growth is illustrated in Figure 2.43, where the line passes through the points (1999, 100) and (2005, 200). In this section we discuss how to find the equation of the line that models these data. To do so we start by discussing the *point–slope form* of a line.

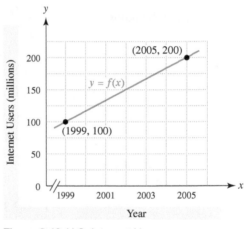

Figure 2.43 U.S. Internet Users

Point–Slope Form

If we know the slope m and y-intercept b of a line, we can write its slope–intercept form, $y = mx + b$. The slope–intercept form is an example of an **equation of a line**. The point–slope form is a different form of the equation of a line.

Suppose that a (nonvertical) line with slope m passes through the point (x_1, y_1). If (x, y) is a different point on this line, then $m = \frac{y - y_1}{x - x_1}$ (see Figure 2.44). We can use this slope formula to find the point–slope form.

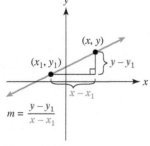

Figure 2.44

$$m = \frac{y - y_1}{x - x_1} \qquad \text{Slope formula}$$

$$m(x - x_1) = y - y_1 \qquad \text{Multiply each side by } (x - x_1).$$

$$y - y_1 = m(x - x_1) \qquad \text{Rewrite the equation.}$$

$$y = m(x - x_1) + y_1 \qquad \text{Add } y_1 \text{ to each side.}$$

The equation $y - y_1 = m(x - x_1)$ is traditionally called the *point–slope form*. We frequently think of y as being a function of x, written $y = f(x)$, so the equivalent form $y = m(x - x_1) + y_1$ is also referred to as the point–slope form.

POINT–SLOPE FORM

The line with slope m passing through the point (x_1, y_1) is given by

$$y = m(x - x_1) + y_1,$$

or equivalently,

$$y - y_1 = m(x - x_1),$$

the **point–slope form** of a line.

EXAMPLE **1**   Using the point–slope form

Find the point–slope form of a line passing through the point $(1, 2)$ with slope -3. Does the point $(2, -1)$ lie on this line?

Solution
Let $m = -3$ and $(x_1, y_1) = (1, 2)$ in the point–slope form.

$$y = m(x - x_1) + y_1 \qquad \text{Point–slope form}$$
$$y = -3(x - 1) + 2 \qquad \text{Substitute.}$$

To determine whether the point $(2, -1)$ lies on the line, substitute 2 for x and -1 for y in the equation.

$$-1 \stackrel{?}{=} -3(2 - 1) + 2 \qquad \text{Let } x = 2 \text{ and } y = -1.$$
$$-1 \stackrel{?}{=} -3 + 2 \qquad \text{Simplify.}$$
$$-1 = -1 \qquad \text{The point satisfies the equation.}$$

The point $(2, -1)$ lies on the line because it satisfies the point–slope form.

Now Try Exercises **15, 27**

We can use the point–slope form to find the equation of a line passing through two points.

EXAMPLE **2**   Applying the point-slope form

Find an equation of the line passing through $(-2, 3)$ and $(6, -1)$.

Solution
Before we can apply the point–slope form, we must find the slope.

$$m = \frac{y_2 - y_1}{x_2 - x_1} \qquad \text{Slope formula}$$

$$= \frac{-1 - 3}{6 - (-2)} \qquad \text{Substitute.}$$

$$= -\frac{1}{2} \qquad \text{Simplify.}$$

We can use either $(-2, 3)$ or $(6, -1)$ for (x_1, y_1) in the point–slope form. If we choose $(-2, 3)$, the point–slope form becomes the following.

$$y = m(x - x_1) + y_1 \qquad \text{Point–slope form}$$

$$y = -\frac{1}{2}(x - (-2)) + 3 \qquad \text{Let } x_1 = -2 \text{ and } y_1 = 3.$$

$$y = -\frac{1}{2}(x + 2) + 3 \qquad \text{Simplify.}$$

If we choose $(6, -1)$, the point–slope form with $x_1 = 6$ and $y_1 = -1$ becomes

$$y = -\frac{1}{2}(x - 6) - 1.$$

Note that, although the two point–slope forms look different, they are equivalent equations because their graphs are identical. **Now Try Exercise 31**

Example 2 illustrates the fact that the point–slope form *is not* unique for a given line. However, the slope–intercept form *is* unique because each line has a unique slope and a unique y-intercept. If we simplify both point–slope forms in Example 2, they reduce to the same slope–intercept form.

$$y = -\frac{1}{2}(x + 2) + 3 \qquad y = -\frac{1}{2}(x - 6) - 1 \qquad \text{Point–slope forms}$$

$$y = -\frac{1}{2}x - 1 + 3 \qquad y = -\frac{1}{2}x + 3 - 1 \qquad \text{Distributive property}$$

$$y = -\frac{1}{2}x + 2 \qquad y = -\frac{1}{2}x + 2 \qquad \text{Identical slope–intercept forms}$$

We can use the *slope–intercept form*, $y = mx + b$, instead of the point–slope form to find the equation of a line, as illustrated in the next example.

EXAMPLE 3 Applying the slope–intercept form

Find the equation of the line that passes through the points $(-3, 9)$ and $(1, 1)$.

Solution
First, find the slope of the line.

$$m = \frac{y_2 - y_1}{x_2 - x_1} = \frac{1 - 9}{1 - (-3)} = -\frac{8}{4} = -2$$

Now substitute -2 for m and $(-3, 9)$ for x and y in the slope–intercept form. The point $(1, 1)$ could be used instead.

$$y = mx + b \qquad \text{Slope–intercept form}$$

$$9 = -2(-3) + b \qquad \text{Let } y = 9, m = -2, \text{ and } x = -3.$$

$$9 = 6 + b \qquad \text{Simplify.}$$

$$3 = b \qquad \text{Solve for } b.$$

Thus the slope–intercept form is $y = -2x + 3$. **Now Try Exercise 43**

▶ REAL-WORLD CONNECTION   In the next example we model the data presented in the introduction to this section.

EXAMPLE 4   Modeling growth in Internet usage

In 1999, there were approximately 100 million Internet users in the United States, and this number grew to about 200 million in 2005 (see Figure 2.43).
(a) Find values for m, x_1, and y_1, so that $f(x) = m(x - x_1) + y_1$ models these data.
(b) Interpret m as a rate of change.
(c) Use f to estimate Internet usage in 2007.

Solution
(a) The slope of the line passing through (1999, 100) and (2005, 200) is

$$m = \frac{200 - 100}{2005 - 1999} = \frac{100}{6} = \frac{50}{3}.$$

Thus, by choosing the point (1999, 100) for the point–slope form, we can write

$$f(x) = \frac{50}{3}(x - 1999) + 100.$$

(b) Slope $m = \frac{50}{3} \approx 16.7$ indicates that the number of Internet users is increasing by about 16.7 million users per year.
(c) $f(2007) = \frac{50}{3}(2007 - 1999) + 100 \approx 233$ million.   Now Try Exercise 91

MAKING CONNECTIONS

Modeling and the Dependent Variable x

From Example 4, $f(x) = \frac{50}{3}(x - 1999) + 100$ models the number of Internet users in the United States. In this formula x represents the actual year. We could also model Internet users with $g(x) = \frac{50}{3}x + 100$, where $x = 0$ corresponds to 1999, $x = 1$ to 2000, and so on. Then to estimate the Internet users in 2007, we let $x = 8$.

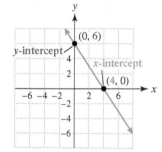

Figure 2.45 x-intercept 4; y-intercept 6

If a line intersects the y-axis at the point (0, 6), the y-intercept is 6. Similarly, if the line intersects the x-axis at the point (4, 0), the x-intercept is 4. This line and its intercepts are illustrated in Figure 2.45. The x-coordinate of a point where a graph intersects the x-axis is called the **x-intercept**. The next example interprets intercepts in a physical situation.

EXAMPLE 5   Modeling water in a pool

A small swimming pool containing 6000 gallons of water is emptied by a pump removing 1200 gallons per hour.
(a) How long does it take to empty the pool?
(b) Sketch a linear function f that models the amount of water in the pool after x hours.
(c) Identify the x-intercept and the y-intercept. Interpret each intercept.
(d) Find the slope–intercept form of the line. Interpret the slope as a rate of change.
(e) What are the domain and range of f?

Solution
(a) The time needed to empty the pool is $\frac{6000}{1200} = 5$ hours.
(b) Initially the pool contained 6000 gallons, and after 5 hours the pool was empty. Thus the graph of f is a line passing through $(0, 6000)$ and $(5, 0)$, as shown in Figure 2.46.
(c) The x-intercept is 5, which means that after 5 hours the pool is empty. The y-intercept of 6000 means that initially (when $x = 0$) the pool contained 6000 gallons of water.
(d) To find the equation of the line shown in Figure 2.46, we first find the slope of the line passing through the points $(0, 6000)$ and $(5, 0)$.

$$m = \frac{y_2 - y_1}{x_2 - x_1} \qquad \text{Slope formula}$$

$$= \frac{0 - 6000}{5 - 0} \qquad \text{Substitute.}$$

$$= -1200 \qquad \text{Simplify.}$$

The slope is -1200 and the y-intercept is 6000, so the slope–intercept form is

$$y = -1200x + 6000.$$

The pump *removed* water at the rate of 1200 gallons per hour.
(e) The domain is D: $0 \le x \le 5$, and the range is R: $0 \le y \le 6000$.

CRITICAL THINKING

Can the graph of a function have more than one y-intercept? Explain. Can the graph of a function have more than one x-intercept? Explain.

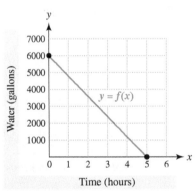

Figure 2.46 Water in a Pool

Now Try Exercise 88

In the next example we introduce a method for modeling linear data by hand.

EXAMPLE 6   Modeling linear data by hand

Find a line $y = mx + b$ that models the data in Table 2.13.

TABLE 2.13

x	10	20	30	40	50
y	15	24	30	39	45

Solution

STEP 1: *Carefully make a scatterplot of the data*   Be sure to label properly the *x*- and *y*-axes. For these data in Table 2.13 we can label each axis from 0 to 60 and have each hash mark represent 10 units. A scatterplot of the data is shown in Figure 2.47.

TABLE 2.13   (Repeated)

x	y
10	15
20	24
30	30
40	39
50	45

Figure 2.47

Figure 2.48

STEP 2: *Sketch a line that models the data*   You may want to use a ruler for this step. In Figure 2.48 a line is drawn that passes through the first and fourth data points. Your line may be slightly different. Note that the line does not have to pass through any of the data points.

STEP 3: *Choose two points on the line and find the equation of the line*   The line in Figure 2.48 passes through (10, 15) and (40, 39). Therefore its slope is

$$m = \frac{39 - 15}{40 - 10} = \frac{24}{30} = \frac{4}{5}.$$

The equation of the line is

$$y = \frac{4}{5}(x - 10) + 15 \quad \text{or} \quad y = \frac{4}{5}x + 7.$$

Note that answers may vary because the data are not exactly linear.

Now Try Exercise 97

MAKING CONNECTIONS

Modeling, Lines, and Linear Functions

If a set of data is modeled by $y = mx + b$, then the data are also modeled by the linear function defined by $f(x) = mx + b$ because $y = f(x)$. In Example 6 the data set is modeled by $y = \frac{4}{5}x + 7$, so it is also modeled by $f(x) = \frac{4}{5}x + 7$.

Horizontal and Vertical Lines

The graph of a constant function is a horizontal line. For example, the graph of $f(x) = 3$ is a horizontal line with *y*-intercept 3, as shown in Figure 2.49. Its equation may be expressed as $y = 3$, so every point on the line has a *y*-coordinate of 3. In general, the equation $y = b$ represents a horizontal line with *y*-intercept *b*, as shown in Figure 2.50.

Figure 2.49   **Figure 2.50**

A vertical line cannot be represented by a function because different points on a vertical line have the same x-coordinate. The equation of the vertical line depicted in Figure 2.51 is $x = 3$. Every point on the line $x = 3$ has an x-coordinate equal to 3. In general, the equation of a vertical line with x-intercept h is $x = h$, as shown in Figure 2.52.

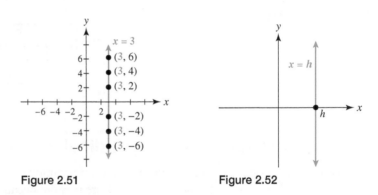

Figure 2.51   **Figure 2.52**

EQUATIONS OF HORIZONTAL AND VERTICAL LINES

The equation of a horizontal line with y-intercept b is $y = b$.

The equation of a vertical line with x-intercept h is $x = h$.

EXAMPLE 7   Finding equations of horizontal and vertical lines

Find equations of the vertical and horizontal lines that pass through the point $(-3, 4)$. Graph these two lines.

Solution
The x-coordinate of the point $(-3, 4)$ is -3. The vertical line $x = -3$ passes through *every* point in the xy-plane with an x-coordinate of -3, including the point $(-3, 4)$.

Similarly, the horizontal line $y = 4$ passes through *every* point with a y-coordinate of 4, including the point $(-3, 4)$. The lines $x = -3$ and $y = 4$ are graphed in Figure 2.53 on the next page.

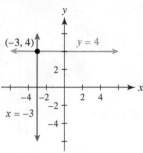

Figure 2.53

Now Try Exercises 75, 77

TECHNOLOGY NOTE: Graphing Vertical Lines

The equation of a vertical line is $x = h$ and cannot be expressed on a graphing calculator in the form "$Y_1 =$". Some graphing calculators graph a vertical line by accessing the DRAW menu. The accompanying figure shows a calculator graph of Figure 2.53.

CALCULATOR HELP

To graph a vertical line, see the Appendix (page AP-6).

$[-6, 6, 1]$ by $[-6, 6, 1]$

Parallel and Perpendicular Lines

Slope is important when we are determining whether two lines are parallel. For example, the lines $y = 2x$ and $y = 2x + 1$ are parallel because they both have slope 2.

> ### PARALLEL LINES
>
> Two lines with the same slope are parallel.
>
> Two nonvertical parallel lines have the same slope.

EXAMPLE 8   Finding parallel lines

Find the slope–intercept form of a line parallel to $y = -2x + 5$, passing through $(-4, 3)$.

Solution

Because the line $y = -2x + 5$ has slope -2, any parallel line also has slope -2. The line passing through $(-4, 3)$ with slope -2 is determined as follows.

$$y = -2(x - (-4)) + 3 \qquad \text{Point–slope form}$$
$$y = -2x - 8 + 3 \qquad \text{Distributive property}$$
$$y = -2x - 5 \qquad \text{Slope–intercept form}$$

Now Try Exercise 55

Figure 2.54 shows three pairs of perpendicular lines with their slopes labeled. Note in Figures 2.54(a) and 2.54(b) that the product m_1m_2 equals -1. That is,

$$m_1m_2 = 1 \cdot (-1) = -1 \quad \text{and} \quad m_1m_2 = 2 \cdot \left(-\frac{1}{2}\right) = -1.$$

A more general situation for two perpendicular lines is shown in Figure 2.54(c), where

$$m_1m_2 = m_1 \cdot \left(-\frac{1}{m_1}\right) = -1.$$

That is, if two nonvertical lines are perpendicular, then the product of their slopes is -1.

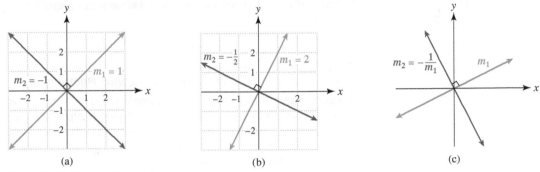

(a)   (b)   (c)

Figure 2.54 Perpendicular Lines

These results are summarized in the following box.

PERPENDICULAR LINES

Two lines with nonzero slopes m_1 and m_2 are perpendicular if $m_1m_2 = -1$.

If two lines have slopes m_1 and m_2 such that $m_1 \cdot m_2 = -1$, then they are perpendicular.

Table 2.14 shows examples of slopes m_1 and m_2 that result in perpendicular lines because $m_1m_2 = -1$. Note that m_1 and m_2 are **negative reciprocals** of each other; that is, $m_2 = -\frac{1}{m_1}$ and $m_1 = -\frac{1}{m_2}$.

TABLE 2.14 Slopes of Perpendicular Lines

m_1	1	$-\frac{1}{2}$	-4	$\frac{2}{3}$	$\frac{3}{4}$	$-\frac{5}{4}$
m_2	-1	2	$\frac{1}{4}$	$-\frac{3}{2}$	$-\frac{4}{3}$	$\frac{4}{5}$
m_1m_2	-1	-1	-1	-1	-1	-1

EXAMPLE 9   Finding perpendicular lines

Find the slope–intercept form of the line perpendicular to $y = -\frac{1}{2}x + 1$, passing through the point $(3, 2)$. Graph the lines.

Solution

The line $y = -\frac{1}{2}x + 1$ has slope $m_1 = -\frac{1}{2}$. From Table 2.14 the slope of a perpendicular line is $m_2 = 2$. The slope–intercept form of a line having slope 2 and passing through $(3, 2)$ can be found as follows.

Figure 2.55

$$y = 2(x - 3) + 2 \qquad \text{Point–slope form}$$
$$y = 2x - 6 + 2 \qquad \text{Distributive property}$$
$$y = 2x - 4 \qquad \text{Slope–intercept form}$$

A graph of these perpendicular lines is shown in Figure 2.55.   Now Try Exercise 65

TECHNOLOGY NOTE: Square Viewing Rectangles

CALCULATOR HELP

To set a square viewing rectangle, see the Appendix (page AP-6).

The accompanying figure shows a square viewing rectangle, in which the perpendicular lines from Example 9 intersect at 90°. Try graphing the two perpendicular lines in Example 9 by using the viewing rectangle $[-6, 6, 1]$ by $[-10, 10, 1]$. Do the lines appear perpendicular? For many graphing calculators a square viewing rectangle results when the distance along the y-axis is about $\frac{2}{3}$ the distance along the x-axis. On some graphing calculators you can create a square viewing rectangle automatically by using the ZOOM menu.

$[-6, 6, 1]$ by $[-4, 4, 1]$

EXAMPLE 10   Equations of perpendicular lines

Find the slope–intercept form of each line shown in Figure 2.56. Verify that the two lines are perpendicular.

Figure 2.56 Perpendicular Lines

Figure 2.57

Solution

In Figure 2.57, the graph of y_1 has slope $m_1 = \frac{2}{3}$ because the line rises 2 units for every 3 units of run. Its y-intercept is -2, and its slope–intercept form is $y_1 = \frac{2}{3}x - 2$. The graph of y_2 has slope $m_2 = -\frac{3}{2}$ because the line falls 3 units for every 2 units of run. Its y-intercept is 1, and its slope–intercept form is $y = -\frac{3}{2}x + 1$. To be perpendicular, the product of their slopes must equal -1; that is,

$$m_1 \cdot m_2 = \frac{2}{3} \cdot \left(-\frac{3}{2}\right) = -1.$$

Now Try Exercise **71**

2.4 PUTTING IT ALL TOGETHER

The following table shows important forms of an equation of a line.

Concept	Comments	Example
Point–Slope Form $y = m(x - x_1) + y_1$ or $y - y_1 = m(x - x_1)$	Used to find an equation of a line, given two points or one point and the slope	Given two points $(1, 2)$ and $(3, 5)$, first compute $$m = \frac{5 - 2}{3 - 1} = \frac{3}{2}.$$ An equation of this line is $$y = \frac{3}{2}(x - 1) + 2.$$
Slope–Intercept Form $y = mx + b$	A unique equation for a line, determined by the slope m and the y-intercept b	An equation of the line with slope $m = 3$ and y-intercept $b = -5$ is $y = 3x - 5$.

The graph of a linear function f is a line. Therefore linear functions can be represented by

$$f(x) = mx + b \quad \text{or} \quad f(x) = m(x - x_1) + y_1.$$

The following table summarizes the important concepts involved with special types of lines.

Concept	Equation(s)	Example
Horizontal Line	$y = b$, where b is a constant	A horizontal line with y-intercept 5 has the equation $y = 5$.
Vertical Line	$x = h$, where h is a constant	A vertical line with x-intercept -3 has the equation $x = -3$.
Parallel Lines	$y = m_1x + b_1$ and $y = m_2x + b_2$, where $m_1 = m_2$	The lines $y = 2x - 1$ and $y = 2x + 5$ are parallel because both have slope 2.
Perpendicular Lines	$y = m_1x + b_1$ and $y = m_2x + b_2$, where $m_1m_2 = -1$	The lines $y = 3x - 5$ and $y = -\frac{1}{3}x + 2$ are perpendicular because $m_1m_2 = 3\left(-\frac{1}{3}\right) = -1$.

2.4 Exercises

CONCEPTS

1. How many lines are determined by two points?

2. How many lines are determined by a point and a slope?

3. Give the slope–intercept form of a line.

4. Give the point–slope form of a line.

5. Give an equation of a horizontal line that has y-intercept b.

6. Give an equation of a vertical line that has x-intercept h.

7. If two parallel lines have slopes m_1 and m_2, what can be said about m_1 and m_2?

8. If two perpendicular lines have slopes m_1 and m_2, then $m_1 \cdot m_2 =$ _____.

9. Give an equation of a line that is parallel to the line $y = -\frac{3}{4}x + 1$.

10. Give an equation of a line that is perpendicular to the line $y = -\frac{3}{4}x$.

11. Give an equation of a line that is perpendicular to the x-axis.

12. Give an equation of a line that is perpendicular to the y-axis.

Exercises 13–16: Determine whether the given point lies on the line.

13. $(-3, 4)$ $y = -\frac{2}{3}x + 2$

14. $(4, 2)$ $y = \frac{1}{4}x - 1$

15. $(-4, 3)$ $y = \frac{1}{2}(x + 4) + 2$

16. $(1, -13)$ $y = 3(x - 5) - 1$

Exercises 17–22: Match the equation with its graph (a.–f.), where m and b are constants.

17. $y = mx + b, m > 0$ and $b \neq 0$

18. $y = mx + b, m < 0$ and $b \neq 0$

19. $y = mx, m < 0$

20. $y = b$

21. $y = mx, m > 0$

22. $x = h$

a.

b.

c.

d.

e.
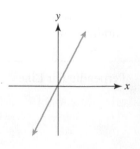

f.

EQUATIONS OF LINES

Exercises 23–26: Use the labeled point and the slope to find the slope–intercept form of the line.

23.

24.

25.

26.
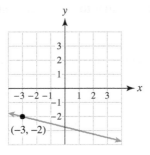

Exercises 27–36: Find a point–slope form of the line satisfying the given conditions.

27. Slope -2, passing through $(2, -3)$

28. Slope $\frac{1}{2}$, passing through $(-4, 1)$

29. Slope 1.3, passing through $(1990, 25)$

30. Slope 45, passing through $(1999, 103)$

31. Passing through $(1, 3)$ and $(-5, -1)$

32. Passing through $(-2, 4)$ and $(3, -1)$

33. Passing through $(1980, 5)$ and $(2000, 45)$

34. Passing through $(1990, 50)$ and $(2000, -10)$

35. Passing through $(6, 0)$ and $(0, 4)$

36. Passing through $(1980, 16)$ and $(2000, 66)$

Exercises 37–42: Write in slope–intercept form.

37. $y = 2(x - 1) - 2$

38. $y = -3(x + 2) + 5$

39. $y = \frac{1}{2}(x + 4) + 1$

40. $y = -\frac{2}{3}(x - 3) - 6$

41. $y = 22(x - 1.5) - 10$

42. $y = -30(x + 3) + 106$

Exercises 43–46: (Refer to Example 3.) Use the slope–intercept form to find the equation of the line passing through the given points.

43. $(-3, 7), (2, -8)$

44. $(-6, -3), (3, 3)$

45. $(-4, 1), (4, -5)$

46. $(-1, 14), (4, -6)$

Exercises 47–64: Find the slope–intercept form of the line satisfying the given conditions.

47. Slope $-\frac{1}{3}$, passing through $(0, -5)$

48. Slope 5, passing through $(-1, 4)$

49. Passing through $(3, -2)$ and $(2, -1)$

50. Passing through $(8, 3)$ and $(-7, 3)$

51. x-intercept 2, y-intercept $-\frac{2}{3}$

52. x-intercept -3, y-intercept 4

53. x-intercept 1, y-intercept 3

54. x-intercept -4, y-intercept -5

55. Parallel to $y = 4x - 2$, passing through $(1, 3)$

56. Parallel to $y = -\frac{2}{3}x$, passing through $(0, -10)$

57. Passing through $(-3, 2)$ and parallel to the line passing through $(-2, 3)$ and $(1, -2)$

58. Passing through $\left(\frac{1}{2}, -1\right)$ and parallel to the line passing through $(1, -4)$ and $(-3, 1)$

59. Perpendicular to $y = -\frac{1}{3}x + 4$, passing through $(-3, 5)$

60. Perpendicular to $y = \frac{3}{4}(x - 2) + 1$, passing through $(-2, -3)$

61. Passing through $\left(-\frac{1}{2}, -2\right)$ and perpendicular to the line passing through $(-1, 6)$ and $(8, -4)$

62. Passing through $(4, -3)$ and perpendicular to the line passing through $(-4, -1)$ and $(2, 7)$

63. Thinking Generally Passing through $(0, b)$ and perpendicular to a line having slope c with $c \neq 0$

64. Thinking Generally Passing through $(a, 0)$ and perpendicular to $y = -mx$ with $m \neq 0$

Exercises 65–70: (Refer to Example 9.) Do the following.

  (a) Find the slope–intercept form of the line perpendicular to the given line, passing through the given point.

  (b) Graph the two lines.

65. $y = \frac{1}{2}x, \quad (0, 2)$

66. $y = -3x, \quad (0, -3)$

67. $y = -2x + 1, \quad (-1, 2)$

68. $y = \frac{2}{3}x + 2, \quad (-1, 0)$

69. $y = -\frac{1}{3}x + 2, \quad (1, 1)$

70. $y = -\frac{4}{3}x + 2, \quad (1, -1)$

Exercises 71–74: (Refer to Example 10.) Do the following.

  (a) Find the slope–intercept form of each line.

  (b) Verify that the two lines are perpendicular.

71.

72.

73.

74.

Exercises 75–82: Find an equation of a line satisfying the given conditions.

75. Vertical, passing through $(-1, 6)$

76. Vertical, passing through $(2, -7)$

77. Horizontal, passing through $\left(\frac{3}{4}, -\frac{5}{6}\right)$

78. Horizontal, passing through $(5.1, 6.2)$

79. Perpendicular to $y = \frac{1}{2}$, passing through $(4, -9)$

80. Perpendicular to $x = 2$, passing through $(3, 4)$

81. Parallel to $x = 4$, passing through $\left(-\frac{2}{3}, \frac{1}{2}\right)$

82. Parallel to $y = -2.1$, passing through $(7.6, 3.5)$

Exercises 83–86: Decide whether the points in the table lie on a line. If they do, find the slope–intercept form of the line.

83.

x	1	2	3	4
y	−4	0	4	8

84.

x	−1	0	1	2
y	8	5	4	1

85.

x	−3	0	3	6
y	4	8	14	18

86.

x	−2	2	4	6
y	−6	0	3	6

GRAPHICAL INTERPRETATION

87. *Distance and Speed* A person is driving a car along a straight road. The graph shows the distance y in miles that the driver is from home after x hours.

  (a) Is the person traveling toward or away from home?

  (b) The graph passes through $(1, 35)$ and $(3, 95)$. Discuss the meaning of these points.

  (c) Find a point-slope form of the line. Interpret the slope as a rate of change.

88. *Water Flow*   The graph shows the amount of water y in an 80-gallon tank after x minutes have elapsed.
  (a) Is water entering or leaving the tank? How much water is in the tank after 3 minutes?
  (b) Find the x- and y-intercepts. Explain each of their meanings.
  (c) Find a slope–intercept form of the line. Interpret the slope as a rate of change.
  (d) Let $y = f(x)$. Find the domain and range.

90. *Cost of Rock*   The graph shows the cost of purchasing landscape rock.
  (a) The graph passes through the points (2, 48) and (5, 120). Discuss the meaning of these points.
  (b) Explain why it is reasonable for the graph to pass through the point (0, 0).
  (c) Find the slope–intercept form of the line.
  (d) Interpret the slope as a rate of change.
  (e) Write the equation of this line as a linear function C that outputs the cost of x tons of landscape rock.

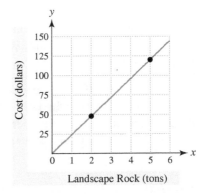

89. *U.S. Population Density*   The graph at the top of the next column illustrates the average number of people living on parcels of land of various sizes in 1960.
  (a) The graph passes through the points (2, 100) and (4, 200). Discuss the meaning of these points.
  (b) Explain why it is reasonable for the graph to pass through the point (0, 0).
  (c) Find the slope–intercept form of the line.
  (d) Interpret the slope as a rate of change.
  (e) Write the equation of this line as a linear function P that outputs the average number of people living on x acres of land.

APPLICATIONS

91. *Projected Cost of College*   The annual cost of the average private college or university is shown in the table. This cost includes tuition, fees, room, and board.

Year	2003	2007
Cost	$25,000	$37,000

Source: Cerulli Associates.

  (a) Find the slope–intercept form of a line that passes through these two data points.
  (b) Interpret the slope as a rate of change.
  (c) Estimate the cost of private college in 2005.

92. *Western Population*   In 1950 the western region of the United States had a population of 20 million, and in 2000 it was 63 million.   (*Source:* U.S. Census Bureau.)
(a) Find a function f defined by $f(x) = mx + b$, which models this population during year x.
(b) Use f to estimate this population in 1960 and 2010.
(c) Estimate this population in 1900 and discuss your result.

Exercises 93–96: Modeling Data   Find $f(x) = mx + b$ so that f models the data, where x is the year. Then use $f(x)$ to make the requested estimate.

93. *Projected Chicken Consumption*   In 2005 the average American ate 57 pounds of chicken and in 2010 this amount will increase to 60 pounds. Estimate chicken consumption in 2008.   (*Source:* Department of Agriculture.)

94. *Internet*   In 2000 the average American spent 9 hours per week on the Internet and in 2002 this time increased to 11 hours per week. Estimate the time spent on the Internet in 2005.   (*Source:* UCLA Center for Communication Policy.)

95. *Life Expectancy*   The life expectancy for a baby born in 1900 was 48 years and in 2000 it was 77 years. Estimate the life expectancy in 1970.
(*Source:* U.S. Census Bureau.)

96. *HIV Infections*   In 1994 about 22,000 Americans became infected with HIV. In 1999 this number was about 15,000. Estimate the number of infections in 1996.   (*Source:* Centers for Disease Control and Prevention.)

Exercises 97–100: Modeling Data   (Refer to Example 6.) Find the slope–intercept form of a line that models the data. Because the data are not exactly linear, answers may vary slightly.

97.

x	1	2	3	4
y	1	4	10	13

98.

x	1	3	5	7
y	3	0	−5	−10

99.

x	1	2	3	4	5
y	8	3	0	−1	−6

100.

x	10	20	30	40	50
y	5	20	30	50	60

Exercises 101–104: Modeling Data   (Refer to Example 6.) Find the slope–intercept form of a line that models the data. Answers may vary.

101. Toyota Vehicles Sold (millions)

x	1998	1999	2000	2001	2002
y	1.4	1.5	1.6	1.7	1.8

Source: Autodata.

102. Basic Cable Costs (dollars)

x	2001	2003	2006
y	9.25	11.25	14.25

Source: Morgan Stanley.

103. Worldwide Cigarette Consumption (trillions)

x	1950	1960	1970	1980	1990
y	1.7	2.2	3.1	4.4	5.4

Source: Department of Agriculture.

104. Online Betting Losses ($ billions)

x	2002	2003	2004	2005	2006
y	4.0	6.1	8.3	10.4	12.6

Source: Christiansen Capital Advisors.

105. *Cost of Driving*   The cost of driving a car includes both fixed costs and mileage costs. Assume that it costs $189.20 per month for insurance and car payments and that it costs $0.30 per mile for gasoline, oil, and routine maintenance.
(a) Find values for a and b so that $f(x) = ax + b$ models the monthly cost of driving x miles.
(b) Interpret the y-intercept on the graph of f.

106. *HIV Infection Rates*   In 1999, there were an estimated 24 million HIV infections worldwide, with an annual infection rate of 5.4 million.   (*Source:* Centers for Disease Control and Prevention.)
(a) Determine values for m, x_1, and y_1 so that $f(x) = m(x - x_1) + y_1$ models the number of HIV infections in year x.
(b) Estimate the number of HIV infections in 2007.

107. *Ring Sizes*   Ring sizes can be modeled by a linear function. If the circumference of a person's finger is 4.9 centimeters, then the ring size is 5 and if the circumference is 5.4 centimeters, then the ring size is 7. (*Source:* Overstock.com.)
 (a) Find $R(c) = mc + b$ so that R calculates the ring size for a finger with circumference c.
 (b) A person's finger has a circumference of 6.16 centimeters. What is the ring size?

108. *Hat Sizes*   Hat sizes can be modeled by a linear function. If the circumference of a person's head is $21\frac{7}{8}$ inches, the hat size is 7 and if the circumference is 25 inches, the hat size is 8.   (*Source:* Brentblack.com.)
 (a) Find $H(c) = mc + b$ so that H calculates the hat size for a head with circumference c.
 (b) A person's head has a circumference of 23 inches. What is the hat size to the nearest eighth?

109. *U.S. Population*   The population for selected years is shown in the table.

Year	1970	1980	1990	2000
Population (millions)	203	227	249	281

Source: U.S. Census Bureau.

 (a) Make a scatterplot of the data.
 (b) Find values for m, x_1, and y_1 so that
$$f(x) = m(x - x_1) + y_1$$
 models the data.
 (c) Use f to estimate the population in 2010.

110. *Women in Politics*   The following table lists percentages of women in state legislatures.

Year	1991	1995	2000
Percent	18.3	20.7	23.5

Source: National Women's Political Caucus.

 (a) Find values for m, x_1, and y_1 so that
$$f(x) = m(x - x_1) + y_1$$
 models these data.
 (b) Assuming that trends continued, estimate the percentage of women in state legislatures in 2005.

WRITING ABOUT MATHEMATICS

111. Explain how you can recognize equations of parallel lines. How can you recognize equations of perpendicular lines?

112. Suppose that some real data can be modeled by a linear function f. Explain what the slope of the graph of f indicates about the data.

CHECKING BASIC CONCEPTS
SECTIONS 2.3 AND 2.4

1. Find the slope and a point on each line.
 (a) $y = -3(x - 5) + 7$
 (b) $y = 10$
 (c) $x = -5$
 (d) $y = 5x + 3$

2. (a) Calculate the slope of the line passing through the points $(2, -4)$ and $(5, 2)$.
 (b) Find a point–slope form and the slope–intercept form of the line.

 (c) Find the x-intercept and the y-intercept of the line.

3. Find the equation of a vertical line and the equation of a horizontal line passing through $(-2, 5)$.

4. Find equations of lines that are perpendicular or parallel to $y = -\frac{1}{2}x + 3$, passing through the point $(2, -4)$.

continued on next page

continued from previous page

5. The graph to the right shows the distance that a car is from home after x hours.
   (a) Is the car moving toward or away from home?
   (b) Find the slope of the line. Interpret the slope as a rate of change.
   (c) Find the x-intercept and the y-intercept. Explain the meaning of each.
   (d) Determine a and b so that $f(x) = ax + b$ models this situation.
   (e) Give the domain and range of f.

CHAPTER 2   SUMMARY

SECTION 2.1 ▪ FUNCTIONS AND THEIR REPRESENTATIONS

Function   A function is a set of ordered pairs (x, y), where each x-value corresponds to exactly one y-value. A function takes a valid input x and computes exactly one output y, forming the ordered pair (x, y).

Domain and Range of a Function   The domain D is the set of all valid inputs, or x-values, and the range R is the set of all outputs, or y-values.

Examples: $f = \{(1, 2), (2, 3), (3, 3)\}$ has $D = \{1, 2, 3\}$ and $R = \{2, 3\}$.

$f(x) = x^2$ has domain all real numbers and range $y \geq 0$. (See the graph below.)

Function Notation $y = f(x)$ and is read "y equals f of x."

Example: $f(x) = \frac{2x}{x-1}$ implies that $f(3) = \frac{2 \cdot 3}{3-1} = \frac{6}{2} = 3$. Thus the point $(3, 3)$ is on the graph of f.

Function Representations   A function can be represented symbolically, numerically, graphically, or verbally.

> *Symbolic Representation (Formula)* $f(x) = x^2$
>
> *Numerical Representation (Table)*   *Graphical Representation (Graph)*

x	y
-2	4
-1	1
0	0
1	1
2	4

> *Verbal Representation (Words)* f computes the square of the input x.

Vertical Line Test   If every vertical line intersects a graph at most once, then the graph represents a function.

Linear Function   A linear function can be represented by $f(x) = ax + b$. Its graph is a (straight) line. For each unit increase in x, $f(x)$ changes by an amount equal to a.

Example: $f(x) = 2x - 1$ represents a linear function with $a = 2$ and $b = -1$.

Numerical Representation		*Graphical Representation*

Each 1-unit increase in x results in a 2-unit increase in $f(x)$.

NOTE: A numerical representation is a table of values of $f(x)$.

Modeling Data with Linear Functions   When data have a constant rate of change, they can be modeled by $f(x) = ax + b$. The constant a represents the *rate of change*, and the constant b represents the *initial amount* or the value when $x = 0$. That is,

$$f(x) = (\text{Rate of change})x + (\text{Initial amount}).$$

Example: In the following table, the y-values decrease by 3 units for each unit increase in x. When $x = 0$, $y = 4$. Thus the data are modeled by $f(x) = -3x + 4$.

x	-2	-1	0	1	2
y	10	7	4	1	-2

Slope   The slope m of the line passing through the points (x_1, y_1) and (x_2, y_2) is

$$m = \frac{\text{rise}}{\text{run}} = \frac{y_2 - y_1}{x_2 - x_1}, \quad \text{where } x_1 \neq x_2.$$

Example: The slope of the line connecting $(-2, 3)$ and $(4, 0)$ is

$$m = \frac{0 - 3}{4 - (-2)} = \frac{-3}{6} = -\frac{1}{2}.$$

Slope–Intercept Form   The equation $y = mx + b$ gives the slope m and y-intercept b of a line.

Example: The graph of $y = -\frac{1}{2}x + 1$ has slope $-\frac{1}{2}$ and y-intercept 1.

x	-2	0	2	4
y	2	1	0	-1

y decreases by 1 unit for each 2-unit increase in x.

Slope as a Rate of Change   The slope of the graph of a linear function indicates how fast the function is increasing or decreasing.

Example: If $V(t) = 10t$ models the volume of water in a tank in gallons after t minutes, water is *entering* the tank at 10 gallons per minute.

SECTION 2.4 ■ EQUATIONS OF LINES AND LINEAR MODELS

Point–Slope Form

$$y = m(x - x_1) + y_1 \quad \text{or} \quad y - y_1 = m(x - x_1),$$

where m is the slope and (x_1, y_1) is a point on the line.

Example: The point–slope form of the line with slope 4 passing through $(2, -3)$ is

$$y = 4(x - 2) - 3.$$

Equations of Horizontal and Vertical Lines

$$y = b \quad \text{(horizontal)}, \quad x = h \quad \text{(vertical)}$$

Example: The equation of the horizontal line passing through $(2, 3)$ is $y = 3$. The equation of the vertical line passing through $(2, 3)$ is $x = 2$.

Parallel Lines

Two lines with the same slope are parallel.

Two nonvertical parallel lines have the same slope.

Example: The lines $y = 2x - 1$ and $y = 2x + 3$ are parallel with slope 2.

Perpendicular Lines   Two lines with nonzero slopes m_1 and m_2 are perpendicular if $m_1 m_2 = -1$. If two lines have slopes m_1 and m_2 such that $m_1 \cdot m_2 = -1$, then they are perpendicular.

Example: The lines $y = 2x - 1$ and $y = -\frac{1}{2}x + 3$ are perpendicular because the product of their slopes equals -1. That is, $2\left(-\frac{1}{2}\right) = -1$.

CHAPTER 2   REVIEW EXERCISES

SECTION 2.1

Exercises 1–4: Evaluate f(x) for the given values of x.

1. $f(x) = 3x - 1$ $x = -2, \frac{1}{3}$

2. $f(x) = 5 - 3x^2$ $x = -3, 1$

3. $f(x) = \sqrt{x} - 2$ $x = 0, 9$

4. $f(x) = 5$ $x = -5, \frac{7}{5}$

Exercises 5 and 6: Do the following.

 (a) *Write a symbolic representation (formula) for the function described.*
 (b) *Evaluate the function for input 5 and interpret the result.*

5. Function P computes the number of pints in q quarts.

6. Function f computes 3 less than 4 times a number x.

7. If $f(3) = -2$, then the point _____ lies on the graph of f.

8. If $(4, -6)$ lies on the graph of f, then $f(\_\_) = \_\_\_$.

Exercises 9–12: Sketch a graph of f.

9. $f(x) = -2x$ 10. $f(x) = \frac{1}{2}x - \frac{3}{2}$

11. $f(x) = x^2 - 1$ 12. $f(x) = \sqrt{x + 1}$

Exercises 13 and 14: Use the graph of f to evaluate the given expressions.

13. $f(0)$ and $f(-3)$ 14. $f(-2)$ and $f(1)$

 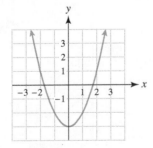

15. Use the table to evaluate $f(-1)$ and $f(3)$.

x	−1	1	3	5
$f(x)$	7	3	−1	−5

16. A function f is represented verbally by "Multiply the input x by 3 and then subtract 2." Give numerical, symbolic, and graphical representations for f. Let $x = -3, -2, -1, \ldots, 3$ in the table of values, and let $-3 \le x \le 3$ for the graph.

Exercises 17 and 18: Use the graph of f to estimate its domain and range.

17.   18.

 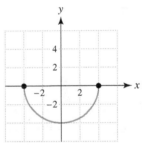

Exercises 19 and 20: Does the graph represent a function?

19.   20.

 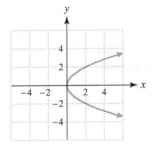

Exercises 21 and 22: Find the domain and range of S. Then state whether S defines a function.

21. $S = \{(-3, 4), (-1, 4), (2, 3), (4, -1)\}$

22. $S = \{(-1, 5), (0, 3), (1, -2), (-1, 2), (2, 4)\}$

Exercises 23–30: Find the domain.

23. $f(x) = -3x + 7$

24. $f(x) = \sqrt{x}$

25. $f(x) = \frac{3}{x}$

26. $f(x) = x^2 + 2$

27. $f(x) = \sqrt{5 - x}$

28. $f(x) = \dfrac{x}{x + 2}$

29. $f(x) = |2x + 1|$

30. $f(x) = x^3$

SECTION 2.2

Exercises 31 and 32: Does the graph represent a linear function?

31.

32.

Exercises 33–36: Determine whether f is a linear function. If f is linear, give values for a and b so that f may be expressed as $f(x) = ax + b$.

33. $f(x) = -4x + 5$

34. $f(x) = 7 - x$

35. $f(x) = \sqrt{x}$

36. $f(x) = 6$

Exercises 37 and 38: Use the table to determine whether $f(x)$ could represent a linear function. If it could, write the formula for f in the form $f(x) = ax + b$.

37.

x	0	2	4	6
$f(x)$	−3	0	3	6

38.

x	−1	0	1	2
$f(x)$	−5	0	10	15

39. Evaluate $f(x) = \frac{1}{2}x + 3$ at $x = -4$.

40. Use the graph to evaluate $f(-2)$ and $f(1)$.

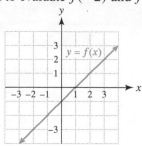

Exercises 41–44: Sketch a graph of $y = f(x)$.

41. $f(x) = x + 1$

42. $f(x) = 1 - 2x$

43. $f(x) = -\frac{1}{3}x$

44. $f(x) = -1$

45. Write a symbolic representation (formula) for a linear function H that calculates the number of hours in x days. Evaluate $H(2)$ and interpret the result.

46. Let $f(x) = \sqrt{x + 2} - x^2$.
   (a) Make a numerical representation (table) for f with $x = 1, 2, 3, \ldots, 7$.
   (b) Graph f in the standard window.   What is the domain of f?

SECTION 2.3

Exercises 47–50: Find the slope of the line.

47.

48.

49.

50.

Exercises 51–54: Calculate the slope of the line passing through the given points.

51. $(-1, 2), (3, 8)$

52. $\left(-3, \frac{5}{2}\right), \left(1, -\frac{1}{2}\right)$

53. $(3, -4), (5, -4)$

54. $(-2, 6), (-2, 8)$

55. Sketch a line passing through $(1, 2)$ with slope $-\frac{1}{2}$.

56. Find the slope and y-intercept of the line $y = -\frac{2}{3}x$. Graph the line.

57. Use the graph to express the line in slope–intercept form.

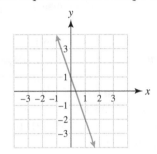

58. Write the slope–intercept form of a line passing through $(0, 2)$ and $(-1, 0)$.

59. Let f be a linear function. Use the table to find the slope and y-intercept of the graph of f.

x	−2	0	3
$f(x)$	3	1	−2

60. The line graph represents the gallons of water in a small swimming pool after x hours.
 (a) Estimate the slope of each line segment.
 (b) Interpret each slope as a rate of change.
 (c) Describe what happens to the amount of water in the pool.

61. *Sketching a Model*   A distance runner starts at home and runs at a constant speed. After 1.5 hours she is 12 miles from home. She then turns around and runs home at the same speed. Sketch a graph that shows the distance that the runner is from home after x hours.

62. Let $f(x) = \frac{1}{2}x - 2$.
 (a) Find the slope and y-intercept of the graph of f.
 (b) Sketch a graph of f.

SECTION 2.4

63. Determine whether the point $(2, 1)$ lies on the graph of $y = \frac{3}{2}x - 2$.

64. Let f be a linear function. Find the slope, x-intercept, and y-intercept of the graph of f.

x	−1	0	1	2
$f(x)$	6	4	2	0

65. Write $y = -3(x - 2) + 1$ in slope–intercept form.

66. Write the point–slope form and the slope–intercept form of the line with slope -3, passing through $(-2, 3)$.

Exercises 67–70: Write the slope–intercept form of a line satisfying the given conditions.

67. x-intercept 2, y-intercept -3

68. Passing through $(-1, 4)$ and $(2, -2)$

69. Parallel to $y = 4x - 3$, passing through $\left(-\frac{3}{5}, \frac{1}{5}\right)$

70. Perpendicular to $y = \frac{1}{2}x$, passing through $(-1, 1)$

Exercises 71 and 72: Find the slope–intercept form of the line.

71.

72.

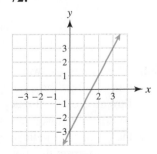

Exercises 73 and 74: Determine whether the given point lies on the line.

73. $(2, -1)$ $y = -2(x - 1) + 3$

74. $\left(4, -\frac{5}{2}\right)$ $y = \frac{1}{4}(x + 2) - 4$

Exercises 75–78: Find an equation of a line satisfying the given conditions.

75. Vertical, passing through $(-4, 14)$

76. Horizontal, passing through $\left(\frac{11}{13}, -\frac{7}{13}\right)$

77. Perpendicular to $x = -3$, passing through $(-2, 1)$

78. Parallel to $y = 5$, passing through $(4, -8)$

Exercises 79 and 80: Decide whether the points in the table lie on a line. If they do, find its slope–intercept form.

79.

x	1	2	3	4
y	6	7	8	7

80.

x	-2	0	2	4
y	1	5	9	13

APPLICATIONS

81. *U.S. Population*   The following line graph shows the population of the United States in millions.
   (a) Find the slope of each line segment.
   (b) Interpret each slope as a rate of change.

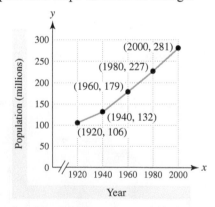

82. *Flow Rates*   A water tank has an inlet pipe with a flow rate of 10 gallons per minute and an outlet pipe with a flow rate of 6 gallons per minute. A pipe can be either completely closed or open. The following graph shows the number of gallons of water in the tank after x minutes. Interpret the graph.

83. *Age at First Marriage*   The median age at the first marriage for men from 1890 to 1960 can be modeled by $f(x) = -0.0492x + 119.1$, where x is the year.
   (*Source:* National Center of Health Statistics.)
   (a) Find the median age in 1910.
   (b) Graph f in [1885, 1965, 10] by [22, 26, 1]. What happened to the median age?
   (c) What is the slope of the graph of f? Interpret the slope as a rate of change.

84. *Marriages*   From 1980 to 2000 the number of U.S. marriages in millions could be modeled by the formula $f(x) = 2.4$, where x is the year.
   (a) Estimate the number of marriages in 1991.
   (b) What information does f give about the number of marriages during this time period?

85. *Fat Grams*   A cup of milk contains 8 grams of fat.
   (a) Give a formula for $f(x)$ that calculates the number of fat grams in x cups of milk.
   (b) What is the slope of the graph of f?
   (c) Interpret the slope as a rate of change.

86. *Birth Rate*   The U.S. birth rate per 1000 people from 1990 through 1997 is shown in the table.

Year	1990	1991	1992	1993
Birth Rate	16.7	16.3	16.0	15.7

Year	1994	1995	1996	1997
Birth Rate	15.3	14.8	14.7	14.5

Source: Bureau of the Census.

   (a) Make a scatterplot of the data.
   (b) Model the data with $f(x) = mx + b$, where x is the year. Answers may vary.
   (c) Use f to estimate the birth rate in 2000.

87. *Unhealthy Air Quality*   The Environmental Protection Agency (EPA) monitors air quality in U.S. cities. The function f gives the annual number of days with unhealthy air quality in Los Angeles, California, for selected years.

x	1995	1997	1999	2000	2003
$f(x)$	113	60	56	87	88

Source: Environmental Protection Agency.

(a) Find $f(1995)$ and interpret your result.
(b) Identify the domain and range of f.
(c) Discuss the trend of air pollution in Los Angeles.

88. *Temperature Scales*   The following table shows equivalent temperatures in degrees Celsius and degrees Fahrenheit.

°C	−40	0	15	35	100
°F	−40	32	59	95	212

 (a) Plot the data. Let the x-axis correspond to the Celsius temperature and the y-axis correspond to the Fahrenheit temperature. What type of relation exists between the data?
(b) Find $f(x) = ax + b$ so that f receives the Celsius temperature x as input and outputs the corresponding Fahrenheit temperature. Interpret the slope of the graph of f.
(c) If the temperature is 20°C, what is this temperature in degrees Fahrenheit?

89. *Graphical Model*   A 500-gallon water tank is initially full and then emptied at a constant rate of 50 gallons per minute. Ten minutes after the tank is empty, it is filled by a pump that outputs 25 gallons per minute. Sketch a graph that depicts the amount of water in the tank after x minutes.

90. *HIV Infections*   In 2000, there were a total of 875,000 AIDS cases in the United States, with an annual infection rate of 25,000.   (*Source:* Centers for Disease Control and Prevention.)
(a) Assuming that this trend continues, determine $f(x) = m(x - x_1) + y_1$ so that f models the number of AIDS cases to date during year x.
(b) Find $f(2007)$ and interpret the result.

Exercises 91–96: Modeling   *Match the situation to the graph (a.–f.) that models it best.*

91. The total federal debt y from 1985 to 1990

92. The distance y from New York City to Seattle, Washington, during year x

93. The amount of money y earned working for x hours at a fixed hourly rate

94. The sales of 8-millimeter movie projectors from 1970 to 1990

95. The average celsius temperature y in a freezer

96. The height above sea level of a rocket launched from a submarine during the first minute of flight

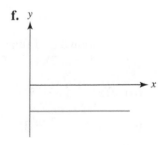

CHAPTER 2   TEST   Pass the Test   Video solutions to all test exercises

1. Evaluate $f(4)$ if $f(x) = 3x^2 - \sqrt{x}$. Give a point on the graph of f.

2. Write a symbolic representation (formula) for a function C that calculates the cost of buying x pounds of candy at \$4 per pound. Evaluate $C(5)$ and interpret your result.

3. Sketch a graph of f.
   (a) $f(x) = -2x + 1$ (b) $f(x) = x^2 + 1$
   (c) $f(x) = \sqrt{x + 3}$ (d) $f(x) = |x + 1|$

4. Use the graph of f to evaluate $f(-3)$ and $f(0)$. Determine the domain and range of f.

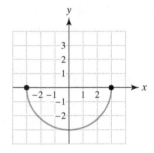

5. A function f is represented verbally by "Square the input x and then subtract 5." Give symbolic, numerical, and graphical representations of f. Let $x = -3, -2, -1, \ldots, 3$ in the numerical representation (table) and let $-3 \leq x \leq 3$ for the graph.

6. Determine whether the graph represents a function. Explain your reasoning.

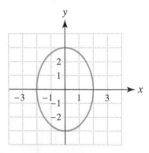

7. Find the domain of function f.
   (a) $f = \{(-2, 3), (-1, 5), (0, 3), (5, 7)\}$

   (b) $f(x) = \frac{3}{4}x - 5$ (c) $f(x) = \sqrt{x + 4}$

   (d) $f(x) = 2x^2 - 1$ (e) $f(x) = \frac{3x}{5 - x}$

8. Determine if $f(x) = 6 - 8x$ is a linear function. If it is, write it in the form $f(x) = ax + b$.

9. Find the slope of the line passing through $(-3, 7)$ and $(6, -2)$.

10. Determine the slope of the line shown in the graph.

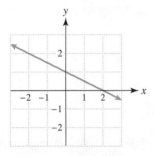

11. Write the slope–intercept form of a line satisfying the conditions.
   (a) x-intercept -2, y-intercept -4
   (b) Passing through $(-5, 2)$ and perpendicular to the line passing through $(-2, 5)$ and $(-1, 3)$
   (c) Passing through $(1, -2)$ and $\left(-5, \frac{3}{2}\right)$.

12. Let f be a linear function. Find the slope, x-intercept, and y-intercept of the graph of f.

x	-2	-1	0	2
$f(x)$	8	6	4	0

13. Give the slope–intercept form of a line parallel to $y = 1 - 3x$, passing through $\left(\frac{1}{3}, 2\right)$.

14. Find the slope–intercept form for the line shown in the graph. Then find the equation of a line that passes through the origin and is perpendicular to the given line.

15. Find equations of the vertical line and the horizontal line passing through the point $\left(\frac{2}{3}, -\frac{1}{7}\right)$.

16. *Modeling* The line graph shows the number of welfare beneficiaries in millions for selected years. (*Source:* Administration for Children and Families.)
 (a) Find the slope of each line segment.
 (b) Interpret each slope as a rate of change.

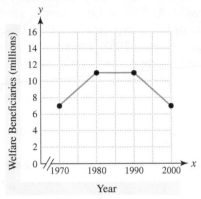

17. *Distance from Home* Starting at home, a driver travels away from home on a straight highway for 2 hours at 60 miles per hour, stops for 1 hour, and then drives home at 40 miles per hour. Sketch a graph that shows the distance between the driver and home.

18. *Memorial Day Travelers* The table shows the number of travelers in millions on Memorial Day for selected years.

Year	1990	1992	1994
Travelers	24.8	27.0	29.2

Year	1996	1998	2000
Travelers	30.3	32.0	34.4

Source: American Automobile Association.

 (a) Make a scatterplot of the data.
 (b) Determine values for m, x_1, and y_1 so that $f(x) = m(x - x_1) + y_1$ models these data.
 (c) Use f to estimate the number of travelers in 2002.

CHAPTER 2   EXTENDED AND DISCOVERY EXERCISES

1. *Developing a Model* Two identical cylindrical tanks, A and B, each contain 100 gallons of water. Tank A has a pump that begins removing water at a constant rate of 8 gallons per minute. Tank B has a plug removed from its bottom and water begins to flow out—faster at first and then more slowly.
 (a) Assuming that the tanks become empty at the same time, sketch a graph that models the amount of water in each tank. Explain your graphs.
 (b) Which tank is half empty first? Explain.

2. *Modeling Real Data* Per capita personal incomes in the United States from 1990 through 2000 are listed in the following table.

Year	1990	1991	1992	1993
Income	$18,666	$19,091	$20,105	$20,800

Year	1994	1995	1996	2000
Income	$21,809	$23,359	$24,436	$29,676

Source: Department of Commerce.

 (a) Make a scatterplot of the data.
 (b) Find a function f that models the data. Explain your reasoning.

 (c) Use f to estimate per capita income in 1998.

3. *Graphing a Rectangle* One side of a rectangle has vertices $(0, 0)$ and $(5, 3)$. If the point $(0, 5)$ lies on one side of this rectangle, as shown in the figure, write the equation of each line.

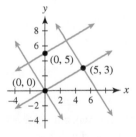

Exercises 4–6: (Refer to Exercise 3.) Graph the rectangle that satisfies the given conditions. Write the equation of each line.

4. Vertices $(0, 0)$, $(2, 2)$, and $(1, 3)$

5. Vertices $(1, 1)$, $(5, 1)$, and $(1, 5)$

6. Vertices $(4, 0)$, $(0, 4)$, $(0, -4)$, and $(-4, 0)$

7. *Remaining Life Expectancy* The table lists the average *remaining* life expectancy E in years for females at age x.

x (year)	0	10	20	30	40
E (year)	72.3	69.9	60.1	50.4	40.9

x (year)	50	60	70	80
E (year)	31.6	23.1	15.5	9.2

Source: Department of Health and Human Services.

(a) Make a line graph of the data.
(b) Assume that the graph represents a function f. Calculate the slopes of each line segment and interpret each slope as a rate of change.
(c) Determine the life expectancy (not the remaining life expectancy) of a 20-year-old woman. What is the life expectancy of a 70-year-old woman? Discuss reasons why these two expectancies are not equal.

8. *Weight of a Small Fish* The graph shows a function f that models the weight in milligrams of a small fish, *Lebistes reticulatus*, during the first 14 weeks of its life. (**Source:** D. Brown and P. Rothery, *Models in Biology*.)

(a) Estimate the weight of the fish when it hatches, at 6 weeks, and at 12 weeks.
(b) If (x_1, y_1) and (x_2, y_2) are points on the graph of a function, the *average rate of change of f from x_1 to x_2* is given by $\frac{y_2 - y_1}{x_2 - x_1}$. Approximate the average rates of change of f from hatching to 6 weeks and from 6 weeks to 12 weeks.
(c) Interpret these rates of change.
(d) During which time period does the fish gain weight the fastest?

9. *Interpreting Carbon Dioxide Levels* Carbon dioxide gas is a greenhouse gas that may cause Earth's climate to warm. Plants absorb carbon dioxide during daylight and release carbon dioxide at night. The burning of fossil fuels, such as gasoline, produces carbon dioxide. At Mauna Loa, Hawaii, atmospheric carbon dioxide levels in parts per million have been measured regularly since 1958. The accompanying figure shows a graph of the carbon dioxide levels between 1960 and 2000. (**Source:** A. Nilsson, *Greenhouse Earth.*)

(a) What is the overall trend in these carbon dioxide levels?
(b) Discuss what happens to these carbon dioxide levels each year.
(c) Give an explanation for the shape of this graph.

10. *Carbon Dioxide in Alaska* (Refer to Exercise 9.) The atmospheric carbon dioxide levels at Barrow, Alaska, in parts per million from 1970 to 2000 are shown in the accompanying figure. (**Source:** M. Zeilik, S. Gregory, and D. Smith, *Introductory Astronomy and Astrophysics.*)

(a) Compare this graph with the graph in Exercise 9.
(b) Discuss possible reasons for their similarities and differences.

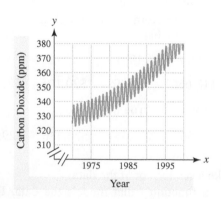

CHAPTERS 1–2   CUMULATIVE REVIEW EXERCISES

Exercises 1 and 2: Classify each real number as one or more of the following: natural number, whole number, integer, rational number, or irrational number.

1. $-3, \frac{3}{4}, \sqrt{7}, -5.8, \sqrt[3]{8}$

2. $0, -5, \frac{1}{2}, -\sqrt{9}, \frac{50}{10}, \sqrt{8}$

Exercises 3 and 4: State whether the equation illustrates an identity, commutative, associative, or distributive property.

3. $6x + 8x = 14x$

4. $a + (b + c) = (b + c) + a$

5. Evaluate $-5^2 + 3 + 4 \cdot 5$ by hand.

6. Write $(x + 1)x + (x + 1)5$ as a product of two factors by using the distributive property.

7. Find the opposite of $a - b$.

8. Find the reciprocal of $\frac{a + b}{c}$.

9. Evaluate $\frac{1}{3} \div \left(\frac{3}{4} \cdot \frac{7}{8}\right) + \frac{5}{6}$ with a calculator.

10. Simplify each expression. Write the result using positive exponents.

(a) $\left(\dfrac{2^{-3}}{3^{-2}}\right)^2$ (b) $\dfrac{(3x^2 y^{-3})^4}{x^3 (y^4)^{-2}}$

(c) $\left(\dfrac{ab^{-2}}{a^{-3} b^4}\right)^{-2}$

11. Write 9540 in scientific notation.

12. Find $f(4)$, if $f(x) = 2x^2 + \sqrt{x}$.

13. Evaluate $B = \frac{1}{2}bh^2$ for $b = 4$ and $h = 3$.

14. Identify the domain of each function f.
(a) $f = \{(-3, 4), (0, 3), (2, -1)\}$
(b) $f(x) = \frac{3}{x + 6}$ (c) $f(x) = \sqrt{x + 4}$

Exercises 15–20: Graph f by hand.

15. $f(x) = -2x + 1$ **16.** $f(x) = -\frac{1}{2}x^2$

17. $f(x) = |x - 2|$ **18.** $f(x) = \sqrt{-x}$

19. $f(x) = -1$ **20.** $f(x) = \frac{1}{3}x$

21. Use the graph of f to do the following.
(a) Determine if the graph represents a function.
(b) Identify the domain and range.
(c) Evaluate $f(-1)$ and $f(0)$.
(d) Identify the x- and y-intercepts.
(e) Find the slope of the line.
(f) Find a formula for $f(x)$.

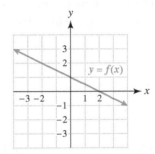

22. Find the slope–intercept form of the line that passes through $(-4, 5)$ and $(2, -4)$.

23. Find the slope–intercept form of the line that passes through $(-1, 2)$ and is perpendicular to the line that passes through $(1, -3)$ and $(2, 0)$.

24. Write an equation of a line that is perpendicular to the x-axis and passes through $(-2, 4)$.

25. Let f be a linear function. Find the slope, x-intercept, and y-intercept of the graph of f.

x	−2	−1	1	2
$f(x)$	9	6	0	−3

26. Write the slope–intercept form of the line.

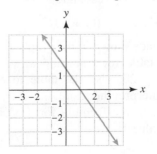

APPLICATIONS

27. *Earnings*   Earning $120 one day and $80 the next day is equivalent to earning $80 the first day and $120 the second day. What property of real numbers is illustrated?

28. *Storage in a Box*   A rectangular box contains 400 cubic inches. If a similar box has the same width but double the length and double the height, how many cubic inches does this box contain?

29. *Injuries at Work*   The table lists the rate of injuries per 100 full-time workers in private industry.

Year	1992	1998	1999	2001
Rate	8.3	6.7	6.3	5.4

Source: Bureau of Labor Statistics.

(a) Estimate the injury rates in 1995 and 2000. Explain how you obtained your estimates.
(b) Which estimate do you think is more accurate? Explain your reasoning.

30. *Calculating Wages*   The amount A that a person makes in dollars after working x hours is given by $A(x) = 9x$. Interpret the slope of the graph of A as a rate of change.

31. *Distance*   A person walks away from home at 4 miles per hour for 30 minutes, rests in a park for 1 hour, and then takes 1 hour to walk back home at a constant speed. Sketch a graph that models the distance y that the person is from home after x hours.

32. *Age in the United States*   The median age of the population for each year x between 1820 and 1995 can be approximated by

$$f(x) = 0.09x - 147.1.$$

(*Source:* U.S. Census Bureau.)

(a) Graph f in the viewing rectangle

   [1820, 1995, 20] by [0, 40, 10].

   Discuss any trends shown in the graph.
(b) Construct the table for f starting at $x = 1820$, incrementing by 20. Use the table to evaluate $f(1900)$ and interpret the result.
(c) The value of a in the formula for $f(x)$ is 0.09. Interpret this value.

33. *Fat Grams*   Some slices of pizza contain 10 grams of fat.
(a) Find a formula $f(x)$ that calculates the number of fat grams in x slices of pizza.
(b) Graph f for $0 \le x \le 6$.
(c) What is the slope of the graph of f?
(d) Interpret the slope as a rate of change.

34. *Two-Cycle Engines*   Two-cycle engines used in snowmobiles, jet skis, chain saws, and outboard motors require a mixture of gas and oil to run properly. For certain engines the amount of oil in pints that should be added to x gallons of gasoline is computed by $f(x) = \frac{4}{25}x$.   (*Source:* Johnson Outboard Motor Company.)
(a) How many pints of oil should be added to 6 gallons of gasoline?
(b) Graph f for $0 \le x \le 25$.
(c) What is the slope of the graph of f?
(d) Interpret the slope as a rate of change.

35. *Municipal Waste*   From 1960 to 1995, municipal solid waste in millions of tons can be modeled by

$$f(x) = 3.4(x - 1960) + 87.8,$$

where x is the year.   (*Source:* EPA.)
(a) Find the tons of waste in 1960.
(b) Graph f in the viewing rectangle [1960, 1995, 5] by [60, 220, 20].
(c) What is the slope of the graph of f? Interpret the slope as a rate of change.

36. *Modeling Distance*   An individual is driving a car along a straight road. The graph shows the distance that the driver is from home after x hours.
(a) Find the slope of each line segment in the graph.
(b) Interpret each slope as a rate of change.
(c) Describe both the motion and location of the car.

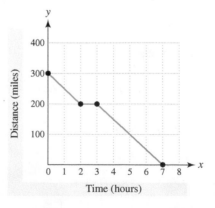

Linear Equations and Inequalities

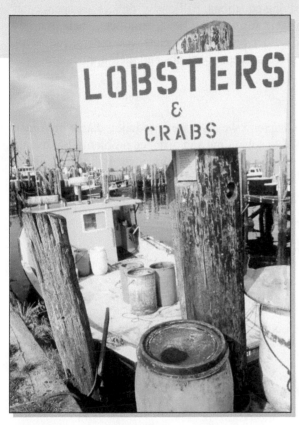

A recent report predicts that 90% of the fish and shellfish species taken from the ocean to feed people may be gone by 2048. As more marine species disappear, the ability of others to survive decreases. This trend is due in part to the increase in people's consumption of fish. The graph shows that the average American's appetite for seafood has increased substantially during past decades.

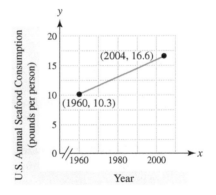

By using the data in the graph and our knowledge of mathematics, we can estimate past consumption of seafood and make predictions about the future. To accomplish this task, we first need to discuss linear equations. An understanding of linear equations is essential to understanding many concepts in mathematics. (See Section 3.1, Exercise 109.)

Say it, I'll forget. Demonstrate it, I may recall. But if I do it, I'll understand.

—OLD CHINESE PROVERB

Source: Science Journal, November 3, 2006.

3.1 LINEAR EQUATIONS

Equations ■ Symbolic Solutions ■ Numerical and Graphical Solutions ■
Identities and Contradictions ■ Intercepts of a Line

A LOOK INTO MATH ▷   A primary objective of mathematics is solving equations. Billions of dollars are spent each year to solve equations that hold the answers for creating better products, such as high-definition televisions, DVD players, iPods, fiber optics, CAT scans, computers, and accurate weather forecasts. In this section we discuss linear equations and their applications.

Equations

▷ REAL-WORLD CONNECTION   In Chapter 2 we discussed modeling data with *linear* functions. Linear functions can also be used to solve time and distance problems. For example, suppose $f(x) = 50x + 100$ models the distance in miles that a car is from the Texas border after x hours. We could use $f(x)$ to determine when the car is **300** miles from the border by solving the equation

$$50x + 100 = 300.$$

This is an example of a *linear equation* in one variable.

LINEAR EQUATION IN ONE VARIABLE

A **linear equation** in one variable is an equation that can be written in the form

$$ax + b = 0,$$

where a and b are constants with $a \neq 0$.

Examples of linear equations include

$$2x - 1 = 0, \quad -5x = 10 + x, \quad \text{and} \quad 3x + 8 = 2.$$

Although the second and third equations do not appear to be in the form $ax + b = 0$, they can be transformed by using properties of algebra, which we discuss later in this section.

To *solve* an equation means to find all values for a variable that make the equation a true statement. Such values are called **solutions**, and the set of all solutions is called the **solution set**. For example, substituting **2** for x in the equation $3x - 1 = 5$ results in $3(2) - 1 = 5$, which is a true statement. The value 2 *satisfies* the equation $3x - 1 = 5$ and is the only solution. The solution set is $\{2\}$. Two equations are *equivalent* if they have the same solution set.

Because every linear equation can be written in the form $ax + b = 0$ with $a \neq 0$, linear equations have *one solution*. To understand this condition visually, consider the graph of $y = ax + b$ shown in Figure 3.1. It is a line that cannot be horizontal. The equation of the x-axis is $y = 0$, so a solution to the linear equation $ax + b = 0$ corresponds to the x-intercept h of the line $y = ax + b$. Because this line intersects the x-axis exactly once, the equation $ax + b = 0$ has one solution.

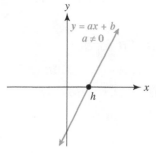

Figure 3.1

Linear Functions and Equations

A linear function can be written as $f(x) = ax + b$.

A linear equation can be written as $ax + b = 0$ with $a \neq 0$.

Symbolic Solutions

Linear equations can be solved symbolically. *One advantage of a symbolic method is that the solution is always exact.* To solve an equation symbolically, we write a sequence of equivalent equations, using algebraic properties. For example, to solve $3x - 5 = 0$, we might add 5 to each side of the equation and then divide each side by 3 to obtain $x = \frac{5}{3}$.

$$3x - 5 = 0 \qquad \text{Given equation}$$
$$3x - 5 + 5 = 0 + 5 \qquad \text{Add 5 to each side.}$$
$$3x = 5 \qquad \text{Simplify.}$$
$$\frac{3x}{3} = \frac{5}{3} \qquad \text{Divide each side by 3.}$$
$$x = \frac{5}{3} \qquad \text{Simplify.}$$

The solution is $\frac{5}{3}$. That is, $3\left(\frac{5}{3}\right) - 5 = 0$ is a true statement.

Adding 5 to each side is an example of the *addition property of equality* and dividing each side by 3 is an example of the *multiplication property of equality*. Note that dividing each side by 3 is equivalent to multiplying each side by $\frac{1}{3}$.

PROPERTIES OF EQUALITY

Addition Property of Equality
If a, b, and c are real numbers, then
$$a = b \quad \text{is equivalent to} \quad a + c = b + c.$$

Multiplication Property of Equality
If a, b, and c are real numbers with $c \neq 0$, then
$$a = b \quad \text{is equivalent to} \quad ac = bc.$$

The addition property states that an equivalent equation results if the same number is added to (or subtracted from) each side of an equation. Similarly, the multiplication property states that an equivalent equation results if each side of an equation is multiplied (or divided) by the same *nonzero* number.

EXAMPLE 1   Applying properties of equality

Solve each equation. Check your answer.
(a) $x - 4 = 5$ **(b)** $5x = 13$

Solution

(a) Isolate x in the equation $x - 4 = 5$ by applying the addition property of equality. To do this, we add 4 to each side of the equation.

$$
\begin{aligned}
x - 4 &= 5 && \text{Given equation} \\
x - 4 + 4 &= 5 + 4 && \text{Add 4 to each side.} \\
x &= 9 && \text{Simplify.}
\end{aligned}
$$

Check: To check that 9 is the solution, we substitute 9 into the *given* equation.

$$
\begin{aligned}
x - 4 &= 5 && \text{Given equation} \\
9 - 4 &\stackrel{?}{=} 5 && \text{Let } x = 9. \\
5 &= 5 && \text{It checks.}
\end{aligned}
$$

(b) Isolate x in the equation $5x = 13$ by applying the multiplication property of equality. To do this, we multiply each side of the equation by $\frac{1}{5}$, the reciprocal of 5. Note that this step is equivalent to dividing each side of the equation by 5.

$$
\begin{aligned}
5x &= 13 && \text{Given equation} \\
\frac{5x}{5} &= \frac{13}{5} && \text{Divide each side by 5.} \\
x &= \frac{13}{5} && \text{Simplify.}
\end{aligned}
$$

Check: To check that $\frac{13}{5}$ is the solution, we substitute $\frac{13}{5}$ into the *given* equation.

$$
\begin{aligned}
5x &= 13 && \text{Given equation} \\
5 \cdot \frac{13}{5} &\stackrel{?}{=} 13 && \text{Let } x = \tfrac{13}{5}. \\
13 &= 13 && \text{It checks.}
\end{aligned}
$$

Now Try Exercises 19, 25

EXAMPLE 2 Solving a linear equation symbolically

Solve $2 - \frac{1}{2}x = 1$.

Solution

To solve, we write a sequence of equivalent equations by using the properties of equality.

$$
\begin{aligned}
2 - \frac{1}{2}x &= 1 && \text{Given equation} \\
-2 + 2 - \frac{1}{2}x &= 1 + (-2) && \text{Add } -2 \text{ to each side.} \\
-\frac{1}{2}x &= -1 && \text{Simplify.} \\
-2\left(-\frac{1}{2}x\right) &= -1(-2) && \text{Multiply each side by } -2, \text{ the reciprocal of } -\tfrac{1}{2}. \\
x &= 2 && \text{Simplify.}
\end{aligned}
$$

The solution is 2.

Now Try Exercise 29

MAKING CONNECTIONS

Expressions and Equations

Expressions and equations are *different* mathematical concepts. An expression does not contain an equals sign, whereas an equation *always* contains an equals sign. *An equation is a statement that two expressions are equal.* For example,

$$2x - 1 \quad \text{and} \quad x + 1$$

are two different expressions, and

$$2x - 1 = x + 1$$

is an equation. We often *solve an equation* for a value of x that makes the equation a true statement, but we *do not solve an expression*. We sometimes *simplify* expressions.

In the next example we use the distributive property to solve a linear equation.

EXAMPLE 3   Solving a linear equation symbolically

Solve $2(x - 1) = 4 - \frac{1}{2}(4 + x)$. Check your answer.

Solution
We begin by applying the distributive property.

$$2(x - 1) = 4 - \frac{1}{2}(4 + x) \qquad \text{Given equation}$$

$$2x - 2 = 4 - 2 - \frac{1}{2}x \qquad \text{Distributive property}$$

$$2x - 2 = 2 - \frac{1}{2}x \qquad \text{Simplify.}$$

Next, we move the constant terms to the right and the x-terms to the left.

$$2x - 2 + 2 = 2 - \frac{1}{2}x + 2 \qquad \text{Add 2 to each side.}$$

$$2x = 4 - \frac{1}{2}x \qquad \text{Simplify.}$$

$$2x + \frac{1}{2}x = 4 - \frac{1}{2}x + \frac{1}{2}x \qquad \text{Add } \frac{1}{2}x \text{ to each side.}$$

$$\frac{5}{2}x = 4 \qquad \text{Simplify.}$$

Finally, we multiply by $\frac{2}{5}$, which is the reciprocal of $\frac{5}{2}$.

$$\frac{2}{5} \cdot \frac{5}{2}x = 4 \cdot \frac{2}{5} \qquad \text{Multiply each side by } \frac{2}{5}.$$

$$x = \frac{8}{5} = 1.6 \qquad \text{Simplify.}$$

The solution is $\frac{8}{5}$.

To check our answer, we substitute $x = \frac{8}{5}$ in the *given* equation.

$$2(x - 1) = 4 - \frac{1}{2}(4 + x) \qquad \text{Given equation}$$

$$2\left(\frac{8}{5} - 1\right) \overset{?}{=} 4 - \frac{1}{2}\left(4 + \frac{8}{5}\right) \qquad \text{Let } x = \frac{8}{5}.$$

$$\frac{16}{5} - 2 \overset{?}{=} 4 - 2 - \frac{4}{5} \qquad \text{Distributive property}$$

$$\frac{6}{5} = \frac{6}{5} \qquad \text{It checks.} \qquad \boxed{\text{Now Try Exercise } 49}$$

CRITICAL THINKING

When you are checking an answer, why is it important to substitute the answer in the *given* equation?

The equation in Example 3 contained a fraction. Sometimes it is easier to avoid working with fractions. To clear fractions we can multiply each side by a common denominator.

EXAMPLE 4   Solving equations involving fractions or decimals

Solve each equation.

(a) $\frac{1}{3}(2z - 3) - \frac{1}{2}z = -2$ (b) $0.4t + 0.3 = 0.75 - 0.05t$

Solution

(a) The least common denominator of $\frac{1}{3}$ and $\frac{1}{2}$ is 6, so multiply each side by 6.

$$\frac{1}{3}(2z - 3) - \frac{1}{2}z = -2 \qquad \text{Given equation}$$

$$6\left(\frac{1}{3}(2z - 3) - \frac{1}{2}z\right) = 6(-2) \qquad \text{Multiply each side by 6.}$$

$$2(2z - 3) - 3z = -12 \qquad \text{Distributive property}$$

$$4z - 6 - 3z = -12 \qquad \text{Distributive property}$$

$$z - 6 = -12 \qquad \text{Combine like terms.}$$

$$z = -6 \qquad \text{Add 6 to each side.}$$

The solution is -6.

(b) The decimals 0.4, 0.75, 0.3, and 0.05 can be written as $\frac{4}{10}, \frac{75}{100}, \frac{3}{10}$, and $\frac{5}{100}$. A common denominator is 100, so multiply each side by 100.

$$0.4t + 0.3 = 0.75 - 0.05t \qquad \text{Given equation}$$

$$100(0.4t + 0.3) = 100(0.75 - 0.05t) \qquad \text{Multiply each side by 100.}$$

$$40t + 30 = 75 - 5t \qquad \text{Distributive property}$$

$$45t + 30 = 75 \qquad \text{Add } 5t \text{ to each side.}$$

$$45t = 45 \qquad \text{Subtract 30 from each side.}$$

$$t = 1 \qquad \text{Divide each side by 45.}$$

The solution is 1. $\boxed{\text{Now Try Exercises } 53, 57}$

▶ **REAL-WORLD CONNECTION**   In the next example, we model some real data with a linear function and then use this function to make an estimate.

EXAMPLE **5** Modeling numbers of LCD screens

Flat screens or LCD (liquid crystal display) screens are becoming increasingly popular. In 2002 about 30 million LCD screens were manufactured and this number increased to 90 million in 2006.
(a) Find a linear function that models these data.
(b) Estimate the year when 105 million LCD screens were manufactured.

Solution
(a) The graph of this linear function must pass through $(2002, 30)$ and $(2006, 90)$. Its slope is

$$m = \frac{90 - 30}{2006 - 2002} = \frac{60}{4} = 15.$$

Using the point $(2002, 30)$ in the point–slope form gives

$$f(x) = 15(x - 2002) + 30.$$

(b) We must solve the equation $f(x) = 105$.

$15(x - 2002) + 30 = 105$	Equation to be solved
$15(x - 2002) = 75$	Subtract 30 from each side.
$x - 2002 = 5$	Divide each side by 15.
$x = 2007$	Add 2002 to each side.

In 2007, 105 million LCD screens might be manufactured. Now Try Exercise **109**

Numerical and Graphical Solutions

Linear equations can also be solved numerically (with a table) and graphically. The disadvantage of using a table or graph is that the solution is often an estimate, rather than exact. In the next example these two methods are applied to the equation in Example 2.

EXAMPLE **6** Solving equations numerically and graphically

Solve $2 - \frac{1}{2}x = 1$ numerically and graphically.

Solution
Numerical Solution Begin by constructing a table for the expression $2 - \frac{1}{2}x$, as shown in Table 3.1. This expression equals 1 when $x = 2$. That is, the solution to $2 - \frac{1}{2}x = 1$ is 2.

X	Y₁
0	2
1	1.5
2	1
3	.5
4	0
5	-.5
6	-1

Y₁■2−(1/2)X

Figure 3.2 A Numerical Solution

TABLE 3.1   A Numerical Solution

x	0	1	2	3	4	5	6
$2 - \frac{1}{2}x$	2	1.5	1	0.5	0	−0.5	−1

In Figure 3.2 a calculator has been used to create the same table.

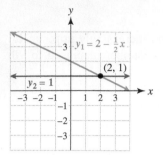

Figure 3.3 Graphical Solution

Graphical Solution   One way to find a graphical solution is to let y_1 equal the left side of the equation, to let y_2 equal the right side of the equation, and then to graph $y_1 = 2 - \frac{1}{2}x$ and $y_2 = 1$, as shown in Figure 3.3. The graphs intersect at the point $(2, 1)$. We are seeking an x-value that satisfies $2 - \frac{1}{2}x = 1$, so 2 is the solution.   Now Try Exercises 69, 77

TECHNOLOGY NOTE: Finding a Numerical Solution

The solution to Example 3 is the decimal number 1.6. It is possible to find it numerically. Let

$$Y_1 = 2(X - 1) \quad \text{and} \quad Y_2 = 4 - (1/2)(4 + X)$$

and start incrementing by 1. There is no value where $y_1 = y_2$, as shown in the left-hand figure. However, note that when $x = 1$, $y_1 < y_2$ and when $x = 2$, $y_1 > y_2$. This change indicates that there is a solution between $x = 1$ and $x = 2$. When x is incremented by 0.1, $y_1 = y_2$ when $x = 1.6$, as shown in the right-hand figure.

X	Y₁	Y₂
-2	-6	3
-1	-4	2.5
0	-2	2
1	0	1.5
2	2	1
3	4	.5
4	6	0

X=1

X	Y₁	Y₂
1.3	.6	1.35
1.4	.8	1.3
1.5	1	1.25
1.6	1.2	1.2
1.7	1.4	1.15
1.8	1.6	1.1
1.9	1.8	1.05

X=1.6

Many times a graphical solution is an *approximate* solution because it depends on how accurately a graph can be read. To verify that a graphical solution is exact, check it by substituting it in the given equation, as is done in the next two examples.

EXAMPLE 7   Solving a linear equation graphically

Figure 3.4 shows graphs of $y_1 = 2x + 1$ and $y_2 = -x + 4$. Use the graph to solve the equation $2x + 1 = -x + 4$. Check your answer.

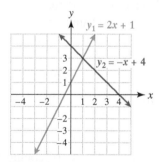

Figure 3.4

Solution
The graphs of y_1 and y_2 intersect at the point $(1, 3)$. Therefore 1 is the solution. We can check this solution by substituting $x = 1$ in the equation.

$$2x + 1 = -x + 4 \qquad \text{Given equation}$$
$$2(1) + 1 \overset{?}{=} -1 + 4 \qquad \text{Let } x = 1.$$
$$3 = 3 \qquad \text{The answer checks.} \quad \text{Now Try Exercise } 73$$

EXAMPLE 8

Solving a linear equation graphically

Solve $3(1 - x) = 2$ graphically.

Solution

$[-6, 6, 1]$ by $[-4, 4, 1]$

Figure 3.5

We begin by graphing $Y_1 = 3(1 - X)$ and $Y_2 = 2$, as shown in Figure 3.5. Their graphs intersect near the point (0.3333, 2). Because $\frac{1}{3} = 0.\overline{3}$, the solution appears to be $\frac{1}{3}$. Note that this graphical solution is *approximate*. We can verify our result as follows.

$$3(1 - x) = 2 \qquad \text{Given equation}$$

$$3\left(1 - \frac{1}{3}\right) \overset{?}{=} 2 \qquad \text{Substitute } x = \frac{1}{3}.$$

$$2 = 2 \qquad \text{It checks.} \qquad \text{Now Try Exercise } 77$$

CALCULATOR HELP

To find a point of intersection, see the Appendix (page AP-7).

Technology can be helpful when we are solving an equation that is complicated. In the next example, we solve an application graphically.

EXAMPLE 9

Solving an application graphically

From 1987 to 2004, the (combined) percentage of music sales from rap and hip hop music can be calculated by $H(x) = \frac{83}{170}x + 3.8$, where x represents the number of years *after* 1987. Similarly, $R(x) = -\frac{22}{17}x + 46$ can calculate the percentage of music sales from rock and roll music. (***Source:*** Recording Industry Association of America.)

(a) Evaluate $R(3)$ and interpret the result.

(b) Estimate graphically the year when rap and hip hop sales might equal rock and roll sales.

Solution

(a) $R(3) = -\frac{22}{17}(3) + 46 = -\frac{66}{17} + 46 \approx 42.1$. Three years after 1987, or in 1990, rock and roll music accounted for about 42.1% of music sales.

(b) Let $Y_1 = (83/170)X + 3.8$ and $Y_2 = -(22/17)X + 46$, as shown in Figure 3.6(a). Their graphs intersect near (23.7, 15.4), as shown in Figure 3.6(b). An x-value of 23.7 corresponds to the year $1987 + 23.7 = 2010.7$, or approximately 2011. Thus, sales of rap and hip hop music could equal rock and roll sales during 2011. At this time each type of music would account for 15.4% of music sales.

```
Plot1  Plot2  Plot3
\Y₁■83/170*X+3.8

\Y₂■-22/17*X+46
\Y₃=
\Y₄=
\Y₅=
\Y₆=
```

$[0, 30, 5]$ by $[0, 50, 10]$

(a)   (b)

Figure 3.6

Now Try Exercise 115

Identities and Contradictions

A linear equation has exactly one solution. However, there are other types of equations, called *identities* and *contradictions*. An **identity** is an equation that is always *true*, regardless of the values of any variables. For example, $x + x = 2x$ is an identity, because it is true for all real numbers x. A **contradiction** is an equation that is always *false*, regardless of the values of any variables. For example, $x = x + 1$ is a contradiction because no real number x can be equal to itself plus 1. If an equation is true for some, but not all, values of any variables, then it is called a **conditional equation**. The equation $x + 1 = 4$ is conditional because 3 is the only solution. Thus far, we have only discussed conditional equations.

EXAMPLE 10   Determining identities and contradictions

Determine whether each equation is an identity, contradiction, or conditional equation.
(a) $0 = 1$ **(b)** $5 = 5$ **(c)** $2x = 6$ **(d)** $2(z - 1) + z = 3z + 2$

Solution
(a) The equation $0 = 1$ is always false. It is a contradiction.
(b) The equation $5 = 5$ is always true. It is an identity.
(c) The equation $2x = 6$ is true only when $x = 3$. It is a conditional equation.
(d) Simplify the equation to obtain the following.

$$2(z - 1) + z = 3z + 2 \qquad \text{Given equation}$$
$$2z - 2 + z = 3z + 2 \qquad \text{Distributive property}$$
$$3z - 2 = 3z + 2 \qquad \text{Combine like terms.}$$
$$-2 = 2 \qquad \text{Subtract } 3z \text{ from each side.}$$

Because $-2 = 2$ is false, the given equation is a contradiction.

Now Try Exercises 91, 93

Intercepts of a Line

Equations of lines can be written in slope–intercept form or point–slope form. A third form for the equation of a line is called *standard form*, which is defined as follows.

STANDARD FORM OF A LINE

An equation for a line is in **standard form** when it is written as

$$ax + by = c,$$

where a, b, and c are constants with a and b not both 0.

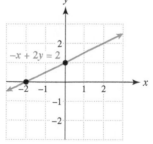
Figure 3.7

Examples of lines in standard form include

$$3x - 7y = -2, \quad -5x - 6y = 0, \quad 2y = 5, \quad \text{and} \quad \tfrac{1}{2}x + y = 4.$$

To graph a line in standard form, we often start by locating the x- and y-intercepts. For example, the graph of $-x + 2y = 2$ is shown in Figure 3.7. All points on the x-axis have a y-coordinate of 0. To find the x-intercept, we let $y = 0$ in the equation $-x + 2y = 2$ and then solve for x.

$$-x + 2(0) = 2 \text{ or } x = -2.$$

The x-intercept is -2. Note that the graph intersects the x-axis at $(-2, 0)$. Similarly, all points on the y-axis have an x-coordinate of 0. To find the y-intercept, we let $x = 0$ in the equation $-x + 2y = 2$ and then solve for y to obtain 1. Note that the graph intersects the y-axis at the point $(0, 1)$. This discussion is summarized by the following.

FINDING INTERCEPTS

To find the x-intercept of a line, let $y = 0$ in its equation and solve for x.

To find the y-intercept of a line, let $x = 0$ in its equation and solve for y.

NOTE: In some texts intercepts are defined to be points rather than real numbers. In this case the x-intercept in Figure 3.7 is $(-2, 0)$ and the y-intercept is $(0, 1)$.

EXAMPLE 11 Finding intercepts of a line in standard form

Let the equation of a line be $3x - 2y = 6$.
(a) Find the x- and y-intercepts.
(b) Graph the line.
(c) Solve the equation for y to obtain the slope–intercept form.

Solution
(a) *x-intercept:* Let $y = 0$ in $3x - 2y = 6$ to obtain $3x - 2(0) = 6$, or $x = 2$. The x-intercept is 2.

   y-intercept: Let $x = 0$ in $3x - 2y = 6$ to obtain $3(0) - 2y = 6$, or $y = -3$. The y-intercept is -3.

(b) Sketch a line passing through $(2, 0)$ and $(0, -3)$, as shown in Figure 3.8.

(c) To solve for y, start by subtracting $3x$ from each side.

$$3x - 2y = 6 \qquad \text{Given equation.}$$
$$-2y = -3x + 6 \qquad \text{Subtract } 3x \text{ from each side.}$$
$$-\frac{1}{2}(-2y) = -\frac{1}{2}(-3x + 6) \qquad \text{Multiply each side by } -\frac{1}{2}.$$
$$y = \frac{3}{2}x - 3 \qquad \text{Distributive property}$$

The slope–intercept form is $y = \frac{3}{2}x - 3$.

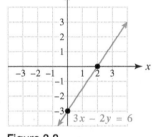

Figure 3.8

Now Try Exercise **101**

3.1 PUTTING IT ALL TOGETHER

The following table summarizes some important topics related to linear equations.

Concept	Explanation	Examples
Linear Equations	Can be written as $ax + b = 0$, where $a \neq 0$; has *one solution*	$3x - 4 = 0$, $2(x + 3) = -2$, and $2x = \frac{2}{3} - 5x$
Solution Set	The set of all solutions	The solution set for $x - 4 = 0$ is $\{4\}$ because 4 is the only solution to the equation.

continued on next page

continued from previous page

Concept	Explanation	Examples
Addition Property of Equality	$a = b$ is equivalent to $a + c = b + c$. "Equals added to equals are equal."	If 2 is added to each side of $x - 2 = 1$, the equation becomes $x = 3$.
Multiplication Property of Equality	$a = b$ is equivalent to $ac = bc$ for $c \neq 0$. "Equals multiplied by equals are equal."	If each side of $\frac{1}{2}x = 3$ is multiplied by 2, the resulting equation is $x = 6$.
Standard Form for a Line	$ax + by = c$, where a, b, and c are constants with a and b not both zero	$3x + 5y = 10$, $-2x + y = 0$, $3y = 18$, and $x = 4$
Finding Intercepts	To find the x-intercept, let $y = 0$ and solve for x. To find the y-intercept, let $x = 0$ and solve for y.	Let $2x + 4y = 8$. x-intercept: $2x + 4(0) = 8$, or $x = 4$ y-intercept: $2(0) + 4y = 8$, or $y = 2$

Linear equations can be solved symbolically, graphically, and numerically. Symbolic solutions are *always exact*, whereas graphical and numerical solutions may be *approximate*. The following illustrates how to solve the equation $2x - 1 = 3$ with each method.

Symbolic Solution

$2x - 1 = 3$

$2x = 4$

$x = 2$

The solution is 2.

Graphical Solution

The solution is 2.

Numerical Solution

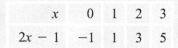

x	0	1	2	3
$2x - 1$	-1	1	3	5

Because $2x - 1$ equals 3 when $x = 2$, the solution is 2.

3.1 Exercises

MyMathLab

 MathXL PRACTICE   WATCH   DOWNLOAD   READ   REVIEW

CONCEPTS

1. Give the general form of a linear equation.

2. How many solutions does a linear equation have?

3. Is 1 the solution for $4x - 1 = 3x$?

4. Are $3x = 6$ and $x = 2$ equivalent equations?

5. The solution to $x + 6 = 10$ is _____.

6. The solution to $7x = -14$ is _____.

7. What symbol must occur in every equation?

8. Name three methods for solving a linear equation.

9. If a graphical solution to a linear equation results in the point of intersection $(3, 4)$, then the solution to the equation is _____.

10. The standard form for the equation of a line is _____.

11. The addition property of equality states that $a = b$ is equivalent to _____.

12. The multiplication property of equality states that $a = b$ is equivalent to _____.

Exercises 13–18: Decide whether the given value for the variable is a solution to the equation.

13. $x - 6 = -2$ $x = 5$

14. $-\frac{1}{2}x + 1 = \frac{1}{3}x - \frac{2}{3}$ $x = 2$

15. $3(2t + 3) = \frac{13}{3} - t$ $t = -\frac{2}{3}$

16. $t - 1 = 2 - (t + 1)$ $t = 2$

17. $-(2z - 3) + 2z = 1 - z$ $z = -2$

18. $-\frac{1}{3}(4 - z) + \frac{2}{5}(z + 1) = -\frac{1}{5}$ $z = 1$

SYMBOLIC SOLUTIONS

Exercises 19–60: Solve the equation symbolically. Check your answer.

19. $x - 4 = 10$ **20.** $x - \frac{1}{2} = \frac{3}{2}$

21. $5 + x = 3$ **22.** $8 + x = -5$

23. $\frac{1}{2} - x = 2$ **24.** $10 - x = -5$

25. $-6x = -18$ **26.** $-5x = 15$

27. $-\frac{1}{3}x = 4$ **28.** $\frac{3}{4}x = 9$

29. $2x + 3 = 13$ **30.** $6x - 4 = -10$

31. $3x - 7 = 8$ **32.** $5 - 2x = -2$

33. $2x = 8 - \frac{1}{2}x$ **34.** $-7 = 3.5x$

35. $3x - 1 = 11(1 - x)$

36. $4 - 3x = -5(1 + 2x)$

37. $x + 4 = 2 - \frac{1}{3}x$

38. $2x - 5 = 6 - \frac{5}{2}x$ **39.** $2(x - 1) = 5 - 2x$

40. $-(x - 4) = 4(x + 1) + 3(x - 2)$

41. $\frac{2x + 1}{3} = \frac{2x - 1}{2}$ **42.** $\frac{3 - 4x}{5} = \frac{3x - 1}{2}$

43. $4.2x - 6.2 = 1 - 1.1x$

44. $8.4 - 2.1x = 1.4x$ **45.** $\frac{1}{2}x - \frac{3}{2} = 4$

46. $5 - \frac{1}{3}x = x - 3$

47. $4(x - 1980) + 6 = 18$

48. $-5(x - 1900) - 55 = 145$

49. $2(y - 3) + 5(1 - 2y) = 4y + 1$

50. $4(y + 1) - (3 - 5y) = -2(y - 2)$

51. $-3(2 - 3z) + 2z = 1 - 3z$

52. $-\left(5 - (z + 1)\right) = 9 - \left(5 - (2z - 3)\right)$

53. $\frac{2}{3}(t - 3) + \frac{1}{2}t = 5$ **54.** $\frac{1}{5}t + \frac{3}{10} = 2 - \frac{1}{2}t$

55. $\dfrac{3k}{4} - \dfrac{2k}{3} = \dfrac{1}{6}$

56. $\dfrac{k + 1}{3} - \dfrac{1}{2} = \dfrac{3k - 3}{6}$

57. $0.2(n - 2) + 0.4n = 0.05$

58. $0.15(n + 1) = 0.1n + 1$

59. $0.7y - 0.8(y - 1) = 2$

60. $0.2y + 0.3(5 - 2y) = -0.2y$

61. Thinking Generally Solve the linear equation $ax + b = 0$ for x if $a \neq 0$.

62. Thinking Generally Solve the linear equation $ax - b = cx$ for x if $a \neq c$.

NUMERICAL SOLUTIONS

Exercises 63–66: Complete the table. Then use the table to solve the equation.

63. $-4x + 8 = 0$

x	1	2	3	4	5
$-4x + 8$	4				

64. $3x + 2 = 5$

x	-2	-1	0	1	2
$3x + 2$	-4				

65. $4 - 2x = x + 7$

x	-2	-1	0	1	2
$4 - 2x$	8				0
$x + 7$	5				9

66. $3(x - 1) = -2(1 - x)$

x	-2	-1	0	1	2
$3(x - 1)$	-9				
$-2(1 - x)$	-6				

Exercises 67–72: Solve the linear equation numerically.

67. $x - 3 = 7$

68. $2x + 1 = 11$

69. $2y - \frac{1}{2} = \frac{3}{2}$

70. $7 - 4y = -5$

 71. $3(z - 1) + 1.5 = 2z$

 72. $-3z - 6 = z + 2$

GRAPHICAL SOLUTIONS

Exercises 73–76: A linear equation is solved graphically by letting y_1 equal the left side of the equation and y_2 equal the right side of the equation. Find the solution. Check your answer.

73.

74.

75.

76.

Exercises 77–86: Solve the equation graphically. Check your answer.

77. $5 - 2x = 7$

78. $-2x + 3 = -7$

79. $2x - (x + 2) = -2$

80. $x + 1 = 3 - x$

81. $3(x + 2) + 1 = x + 1$

82. $x + 5 = 2x + 2$

 83. $5(x - 1990) + 15 = 100$

 84. $10(x - 1985) - 20 = 55$

 85. $\sqrt{2} + 4(x - \pi) = \frac{1}{7}x$

 86. $\pi(x - \sqrt{5}) = \dfrac{7x + 5}{3}$

SOLVING LINEAR EQUATIONS BY MORE THAN ONE METHOD

Exercises 87–90: Solve the equation (a) numerically, (b) graphically, and (c) symbolically.

87. $2x - 1 = 13$

88. $9 - x = 3x + 1$

 89. $3x - 5 - (x + 1) = 0$

 90. $\dfrac{1}{2}x - 1 = \dfrac{5 - x}{2}$

IDENTITIES AND CONTRADICTIONS

Exercises 91–98: Determine whether the equation is an identity, contradiction, or conditional equation.

91. $2x + 3 = 2x$

92. $x + 5 = x - 4$

93. $2x + 3x = 5x$

94. $-3x = 4x - 7x$

95. $2(x - 1) = 2x - 2$

96. $3x - 10 = 2(x - 5) + x$

97. $5 - 7(4 - 3x) = x - 4(2 - 4x)$

98. $7 - 2(x + 3) - x = -4(x - 5) - 22$

99. Thinking Generally Let f and g be linear functions satisfying $f(-4) = 9$, $f(1) = -1$, $g(-3) = 1$, and $g(0) = 13$. Determine the point where their graphs intersect.

100. Thinking Generally Let f and g be linear functions where $f(-2) = -2, f(8) = -7, g(-4) = -11$, and $g(12) = 1$. Determine the point where their graphs intersect.

FINDING INTERCEPTS

Exercises 101–108: Do the following.

  (a) Find the x- and y-intercepts.
  (b) Graph the line.
  (c) Solve the equation for y to obtain the slope–intercept form.

101. $x + y = 4$

102. $x - y = -2$

103. $2x + 5y = 10$

104. $-3x + 4y = -6$

105. $2x - 3y = 9$

106. $\frac{1}{2}x - \frac{1}{4}y = 1$

107. $-\frac{2}{3}x - y = 2$

108. $-x - \frac{2}{5}y = 2$

APPLICATIONS

109. *Seafood Consumption* (Refer to the chapter introduction.) In 1960 the average American consumed 10.3 pounds of seafood and in 2004 this amount increased to 16.6 pounds.
   (a) Determine $S(x) = m(x - x_1) + y_1$, where x is the year, so that S models these data.
   (b) Estimate the amount of seafood that the average American consumed in 2000.
   (c) Assuming this trend continues, estimate the year when the average American will consume 20 pounds of seafood annually.

110. *Centenarians* In 1990 there were 37,306 centenarians, people aged 100 or older, in the United States. The number of centenarians is estimated to increase by 8260 per year. (*Source:* U.S. Census Bureau.)
   (a) Find values for m, x_1, and y_1 so that the formula $f(x) = m(x - x_1) + y_1$ models the number of centenarians during year x.
   (b) Estimate the year when there will be 450,000 centenarians.

111. *State and Federal Inmates* From 1988 to 2000 the number of state and federal prison inmates in thousands can be modeled by $f(x) = 70x - 138,532$ during year x. (*Source:* Department of Justice.)
   (a) Determine symbolically the year when there were 908 thousand inmates.
   (b) Solve part (a) numerically.
   (c) Solve part (a) graphically.

112. *U.S. Government Costs* From 1960 to 1990 the cost (in 1960 dollars) to administer social and economic programs rose from $1.9 billion to $16 billion. This cost in billions of dollars can be modeled by $f(x) = 0.47x - 919.3$, where x is the year. (*Source:* Center for the Study of American Business.)
   (a) Estimate symbolically when the cost was $6.6 billion.

   (b) Solve part (a) numerically.
   (c) Solve part (a) graphically.

113. *Car Sales* In 1998 Toyota sold 1.4 million vehicles. This number increased to 1.8 million in 2002. (*Source:* Autodata.)
   (a) Find a linear function that models the data.
   (b) Determine the year when Toyota sold 1.7 million vehicles by solving a linear equation.
   (c) Determine the year when Toyota sold 2 million vehicles.

114. *Injured at Work* In 1992 private industry reported 8.3 injuries per 100 full-time workers. By 2002 this number decreased to 5.4. (*Source:* Department of Labor.)
   (a) Find a linear function that models the data.
   (b) Estimate the year when the reported injuries equaled 6 per 100 full-time workers.

115. *CD and LP Record Sales* (Refer to Example 9.) From 1985 to 1990, sales of CDs (compact discs) in the United States can be modeled by the equation $y_1 = 51.6(x - 1985) + 9.1$, and sales of LPs (vinyl records) can be modeled by the equation $y_2 = -31.9(x - 1985) + 167.7$. All sales are in millions. Determine the year when sales of CDs and LPs were about equal.

116. *U.S. Population Density* In 1900 there were, on average, 22 people per square mile in the United States. By 2000 the population density had increased to 80 people per square mile. (*Source:* U.S. Census Bureau.)
   (a) Find a linear function that models the data.
   (b) Determine the year when the population density was 51 people per square mile.

WRITING ABOUT MATHEMATICS

117. Explain each of the following terms: linear equation, solution, solution set, and equivalent equations. Give an example of each.

118. Explain how to solve the equation $ax + b = 0$ symbolically and graphically. Use both methods to solve the equation $5x + 10 = 0$.

GROUP ACTIVITY
WORKING WITH REAL DATA

Directions: Form a group of 2 to 4 people. Select someone to record the group's responses for this activity. All members of the group should work cooperatively to answer the questions. If your instructor asks for your results, each member of the group should be prepared to respond.

Private Plane Crashes The number of fatal plane crashes, such as the one involving New York Yankee Cory Lidle, has decreased in past decades. The table lists the number of fatal private plane crashes for selected years.

Year	1982	1987	1993	2004
Fatal Crashes	372	310	265	191

Source: National Transportation Safety Board.

(a) Make a scatterplot of the data.
(b) Find a linear function f given by

$$f(x) = m(x - x_1) + y_1$$

that models the data. Answers may vary.
(c) Interpret m as a rate of change.
(d) Estimate when there were 200 fatal crashes.
(e) If these trends continue, predict the year when fatal crashes might reach 120.

3.2 INTRODUCTION TO PROBLEM SOLVING

Solving a Formula for a Variable ■ Steps for Solving a Problem ■ Percentages

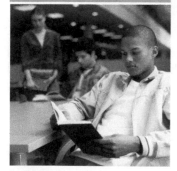

A LOOK INTO MATH ▷ Problem-solving skills are essential because every day we must solve problems—both small and large—for survival. A logical approach to a problem is often helpful, which is especially true in mathematics. In this section we discuss steps that can be used to solve mathematical problems. We begin the section by discussing how to solve a formula for a variable.

Solving a Formula for a Variable

The perimeter P of a rectangle with width W and length L is given by $P = 2W + 2L$, as illustrated in Figure 3.9. Suppose that we know the perimeter P and length L of this rectangle. Even though the formula is written to calculate P, we can still use it to find the width W. This technique is demonstrated in the next example.

Figure 3.9 $P = 2W + 2L$

EXAMPLE 1 Finding the width of a rectangle

A rectangle has a perimeter of 80 inches and a length of 23 inches.
(a) Write a formula to find the width W of a rectangle with known perimeter P and length L.
(b) Use the formula to find W.

Solution

(a) We must solve $P = 2W + 2L$ for W.

$$P = 2W + 2L \qquad \text{Given formula}$$
$$P - 2L = 2W \qquad \text{Subtract } 2L.$$
$$\frac{1}{2}(P - 2L) = \frac{1}{2}(2W) \qquad \text{Multiply by } \tfrac{1}{2}.$$
$$\frac{P}{2} - L = W \qquad \text{Distributive property}$$

The required formula is $W = \frac{P}{2} - L$.

(b) Substitute $P = 80$ and $L = 23$ into this formula. The width is

$$W = \frac{80}{2} - 23 = 17 \text{ inches.} \qquad \boxed{\text{Now Try Exercise } 31}$$

▶ **REAL-WORLD CONNECTION**   In the next example we use a formula that converts degrees Fahrenheit to degrees Celsius to find a formula that converts degrees Celsius to degrees Fahrenheit.

EXAMPLE 2   Converting temperature

The formula $C = \frac{5}{9}(F - 32)$ is used to convert degrees Fahrenheit to degrees Celsius.
(a) Use this formula to convert $212°F$ to an equivalent Celsius temperature.
(b) Solve the formula for F to obtain a formula that can convert degrees Celsius to degrees Fahrenheit. Interpret the slope of the graph of F.
(c) Use this new formula to convert $25°C$ to an equivalent Fahrenheit temperature.

Solution
(a) $C = \frac{5}{9}(212 - 32) = \frac{5}{9}(180) = 100°C$

(b)
$$C = \frac{5}{9}(F - 32) \qquad \text{Given formula}$$
$$\frac{9}{5}C = \frac{9}{5} \cdot \frac{5}{9}(F - 32) \qquad \text{Multiply by } \tfrac{9}{5}.$$
$$\frac{9}{5}C = F - 32 \qquad \text{Simplify.}$$
$$\frac{9}{5}C + 32 = F \qquad \text{Add 32.}$$

Because $F = \frac{9}{5}C + 32$, the slope of the graph of F is $\frac{9}{5}$, which indicates that a $1°$ increase in Celsius temperature is equivalent to a $\frac{9°}{5}$ increase in Fahrenheit temperature.
(c) Substitute 25 for C in this formula to obtain $F = \frac{9}{5}(25) + 32 = 77°F$.

$$\boxed{\text{Now Try Exercise } 35}$$

Sometimes an equation in two variables can be used to determine the formula for a function. To do so, we must let one variable be the dependent variable and the other variable be the independent variable. For example, $2x - 5y = 10$ is the equation of a line written in standard form. Solving for y gives the following result.

$$-5y = -2x + 10 \qquad \text{Subtract } 2x.$$

$$-\frac{1}{5}(-5y) = -\frac{1}{5}(-2x + 10) \qquad \text{Multiply by } -\tfrac{1}{5}.$$

$$y = \frac{2}{5}x - 2 \qquad \text{Distributive property}$$

If y is the dependent variable, x is the independent variable, and $y = f(x)$, then

$$f(x) = \frac{2}{5}x - 2$$

defines a function f whose graph is the line determined by $2x - 5y = 10$.

EXAMPLE 3   Writing a function

Solve each equation for y and write a formula for a function f defined by $y = f(x)$.

(a) $4(x - 2y) = -3x$ **(b)** $\dfrac{x + y}{2} - 5 = 20$

Solution

(a)

$$4(x - 2y) = -3x \qquad \text{Given equation}$$

$$4x - 8y = -3x \qquad \text{Distributive property}$$

$$-8y = -7x \qquad \text{Subtract } 4x.$$

$$y = \frac{7}{8}x \qquad \text{Divide by } -8.$$

Thus $f(x) = \frac{7}{8}x$.

(b)

$$\frac{x + y}{2} - 5 = 20 \qquad \text{Given equation}$$

$$\frac{x + y}{2} = 25 \qquad \text{Add 5.}$$

$$\frac{2(x + y)}{2} = 2(25) \qquad \text{Multiply by 2.}$$

$$x + y = 50 \qquad \text{Simplify.}$$

$$y = 50 - x \qquad \text{Subtract } x.$$

Thus $f(x) = 50 - x$.   Now Try Exercises 15, 19

Steps for Solving a Problem

Solving problems in mathematics can be challenging, especially when formulas and equations are not given to us. In these situations we have to write them, but to do so, we need a strategy. The following steps are often a helpful strategy. They are based on George Polya's (1888–1985) four-step process for problem solving.

STEPS FOR SOLVING A PROBLEM

STEP 1: Read the problem carefully to be sure that you understand it. (You may need to read the problem more than once.) Assign a variable to what you are being asked to find. If necessary, write other quantities in terms of this variable.

STEP 2: Write an equation that relates the quantities described in the problem. You may need to sketch a diagram, make a table, or refer to known formulas.

STEP 3: Solve the equation and determine the solution.

STEP 4: Look back and check your answer. Does it seem reasonable? Did you find the required information?

In the next example we apply these steps to a word problem involving unknown numbers.

EXAMPLE 4   Solving a number problem

The sum of three consecutive *even* integers is 108. Find the three numbers.

Solution

STEP 1: *Start by assigning a variable to an unknown quantity.*

$$n: \text{smallest of the three integers}$$

Next, write the other two numbers in terms of n.

$$n + 2: \text{next consecutive } even \text{ integer}$$
$$n + 4: \text{largest of the three even integers}$$

STEP 2: *Write an equation that relates these unknown quantities.* As the sum of these three even integers is 108, the needed equation is

$$n + (n + 2) + (n + 4) = 108.$$

STEP 3: *Solve the equation in Step 2.*

$n + (n + 2) + (n + 4) = 108$	Equation to be solved
$(n + n + n) + (2 + 4) = 108$	Commutative and associative properties
$3n + 6 = 108$	Combine like terms.
$3n = 102$	Subtract 6 from each side.
$n = 34$	Divide each side by 3.

The smallest of the three numbers is 34, so the three numbers are 34, 36, and 38.

STEP 4: *Check your answer.* The sum of these three even integers is

$$34 + 36 + 38 = 108.$$

The answer checks.   Now Try Exercise **39**

In the next example we apply this procedure to find the dimensions of a room.

EXAMPLE 5   Solving a geometry problem

The length of a rectangular room is 2 feet more than its width. If the perimeter of the room is 80 feet, find the width and length of the room.

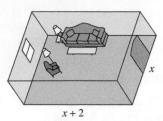

Figure 3.10 Perimeter = 80

Solution

STEP 1: *Start by assigning a variable to an unknown quantity.* See Figure 3.10.

$$x: \text{width of the room}$$
$$x + 2: \text{length of the room}$$

STEP 2: *Write an equation that relates these unknown quantities.* The perimeter is the distance around the room and equals 80 feet. Thus

$$x + (x + 2) + x + (x + 2) = 80,$$

which simplifies to $4x + 4 = 80$.

STEP 3: *Solve the equation in Step 2.*

$4x + 4 = 80$	Equation to be solved
$4x = 76$	Subtract 4 from each side.
$\dfrac{4x}{4} = \dfrac{76}{4}$	Divide each side by 4.
$x = 19$	Simplify.

The width is 19 feet and the length is $19 + 2 = 21$ feet.

STEP 4: *Check your answer.* The perimeter is $19 + 21 + 19 + 21 = 80$ feet. The answer checks.

Now Try Exercise 43

EXAMPLE 6   Solving a geometry problem

A wire, 100 inches long, needs to be cut into two pieces so that it can be bent into a circle and a square. The length of a side of the square must equal the diameter of the circle. Approximate where the 100-inch wire should be cut.

Solution

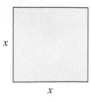

Figure 3.11

STEP 1: *Assign a variable.* Let x be both the diameter of the circle and the length of a side of the square, as shown in Figure 3.11.

STEP 2: *Write an equation.* Because $C = \pi d$, the circumference of the circle is $C = \pi x$, and the perimeter of the square is $P = 4x$. The wire is 100 inches long, so

$$\pi x + 4x = 100.$$

STEP 3: *Solve the equation in Step 2.*

$\pi x + 4x = 100$	Equation to be solved
$(\pi + 4)x = 100$	Distributive property
$x = \dfrac{100}{\pi + 4}$	Divide by $\pi + 4$.
$x \approx 14$	Approximate.

The wire should be cut so that the piece for the square is $4 \times 14 = 56$ inches and the piece for the circle is $100 - 56 = 44$ inches.

STEP 4: *Check the answer.* If the square's perimeter is 56 inches, then each of its sides is $\frac{56}{4} = 14$ inches. If the diameter of the circle is 14 inches, then its circumference is $C = \pi(14) \approx 43.98$, or about 44 inches. Because $56 + 44 = 100$, the answer checks.   Now Try Exercise 45

EXAMPLE 7   Solving a motion problem

Two cars are traveling in opposite lanes on a freeway. Three hours after meeting, they are 420 miles apart. If one car is traveling 10 miles per hour faster than the other car, find the speeds of the two cars.

Solution

STEP 1: *Assign a variable.*

$$x : \text{speed of slower car}$$

$$x + 10 : \text{speed of faster car}$$

STEP 2: *Write an equation.* The information is summarized in Table 3.2.

> **NOTE:** Distance = Rate × Time.

TABLE 3.2

	Rate	Time	Distance
Slower Car	x	3	$3x$
Faster Car	$x + 10$	3	$3(x + 10)$
Total			420

The sum of the distances traveled by the cars is 420 miles. Thus

$$3x + 3(x + 10) = 420.$$

STEP 3: *Solve the equation in Step 2.*

$3x + 3(x + 10) = 420$	Equation to be solved
$3x + 3x + 30 = 420$	Distributive property
$6x + 30 = 420$	Combine like terms.
$6x = 390$	Subtract 30 from each side.
$x = 65$	Divide each side by 6.

The speed of the slower car is 65 miles per hour and the speed of the faster car is 10 miles per hour faster, or 75 miles per hour.

STEP 4: *Check the answer.*

Distance traveled by slower car: $65 \times 3 = 195$ miles

Distance traveled by faster car: $75 \times 3 = 225$ miles

The total distance is $195 + 225 = 420$ miles, so it checks.   Now Try Exercise 47

▶ **REAL-WORLD CONNECTION**   Many times we are called upon to solve a mixture problem. Such problems may involve a mixture of acid solutions or a mixture of loan amounts. In the next example an athlete jogs at two different speeds, and mathematics is used to determine how much time is spent jogging at each speed.

EXAMPLE **8**   Solving a "mixture" problem

An athlete begins jogging at 8 miles per hour and then jogs at 7 miles per hour, traveling 10.9 miles in 1.5 hours. How long did the athlete jog at each speed?

Solution

STEP 1: *Assign a variable.* Let t represent the time spent jogging at 8 miles per hour. Because total time spent jogging is 1.5 hours, the time spent jogging at 7 miles per hour must be $1.5 - t$.

STEP 2: *Write an equation.* A table is often helpful in solving a mixture problem. Because $d = rt$, Table 3.3 shows that the distance the athlete jogs at 8 miles per hour is $8t$. The distance traveled at 7 miles per hour is $7(1.5 - t)$, and the total distance traveled is 10.9 miles. From the third column, we can write the equation

$$8t + 7(1.5 - t) = 10.9.$$

TABLE 3.3

	Speed	Time	Distance
First Part	8	t	$8t$
Second Part	7	$1.5 - t$	$7(1.5 - t)$
Total		1.5	10.9

STEP 3: *Solve the equation in Step 2.*

$$8t + 7(1.5 - t) = 10.9 \qquad \text{Equation to be solved}$$
$$8t + 10.5 - 7t = 10.9 \qquad \text{Distributive property}$$
$$t + 10.5 = 10.9 \qquad \text{Combine like terms.}$$
$$t = 0.4 \qquad \text{Subtract 10.5 from each side.}$$

The athlete jogged 0.4 hour at 8 miles per hour and $1.5 - 0.4 = 1.1$ hours at 7 miles per hour.

STEP 4: *Check your answer.* Start by calculating the distance traveled at each speed.

$$8 \cdot 0.4 = 3.2 \text{ miles} \qquad \text{Distance at 8 mph}$$
$$7 \cdot 1.1 = 7.7 \text{ miles} \qquad \text{Distance at 7 mph}$$

The total distance jogged is $3.2 + 7.7 = 10.9$ miles and the total time is $0.4 + 1.1 = 1.5$ hours. The answer checks.   Now Try Exercise **48**

Percentages

▶ **REAL-WORLD CONNECTION**   Applications involving percentages often make use of linear equations. Taking P percent of x is given by Px, where P is written in decimal form. For example, to calculate 35% of x, we compute $0.35x$. As a result, 35% of $150 is $0.35(150) = 52.5$, or $52.50.

NOTE: The word *of* often indicates multiplication when working with percentages.

EXAMPLE 9   Analyzing smoking data

In 2005 an estimated 20.9% of Americans aged 18 and older, or 45.1 million people, were smokers. Use these data to estimate the number of Americans aged 18 and older in 2005. (*Source:* Department of Health and Human Services.)

Solution

STEP 1: *Assign a variable.* Let x be the number of Americans aged 18 and older.

STEP 2: *Write an equation.* Note that 20.9% of x equals 45.1 million. Thus

$$0.209x = 45.1.$$

STEP 3: *Solve the equation in Step 2.*

$$0.209x = 45.1 \qquad \text{Equation to be solved}$$

$$\frac{0.209x}{0.209} = \frac{45.1}{0.209} \qquad \text{Divide each side by 0.209.}$$

$$x \approx 216 \qquad \text{Approximate with a calculator.}$$

In 2005 there were about 216 million Americans aged 18 and older.

STEP 4: *Check your answer.* If there were 216 million Americans aged 18 and older, then 20.9% of 216 million would equal $0.209 \times 216 \approx 45.1$ million. The answer checks.

Now Try Exercise 59

EXAMPLE 10   Solving a percent problem

In 2004 an estimated $264 billion were spent on advertisement in the United States. This was an increase of 380% over the amount spent in 1980. Determine how much was spent on advertisement in 1980.   (*Source:* Advertising Age.)

Solution

STEP 1: *Assign a variable.* Let x be the amount spent on advertisement in 1980.

STEP 2: *Write an equation.* Note that the increase was 380% of x, or $3.8x$.

$$x \quad + \quad 3.8x \quad = \quad 264$$
$$\text{Amount in 1980} + \text{Increase} = \text{Amount in 2004}$$

STEP 3: *Solve the equation in Step 2.*

$$x + 3.8x = 264 \qquad \text{Equation to be solved}$$

$$4.8x = 264 \qquad \text{Add like terms.}$$

$$x = \frac{264}{4.8} \qquad \text{Divide each side by 4.8.}$$

$$x = 55 \qquad \text{Simplify.}$$

In 1980, $55 billion were spent on advertisement.

STEP 4: *Check your answer.* An increase of 380% of $55 billion is $3.8 \times 55 = \$209$ billion. Thus the amount spent in 2004 would be $55 + 209 = \$264$ billion. The answer checks.

Now Try Exercise 61

EXAMPLE **11**   Solving an interest problem

A college student takes out two unsubsidized loans to pay tuition. The first loan is for 3% annual interest and the second loan is for 7% annual interest. If the total of the two loans is $4000 and the student must pay $170 in interest at the end of the first year, determine the amount borrowed at each interest rate.

Solution
STEP 1: *Assign a variable.*

$$x: \text{the loan amount at 3\%}$$
$$4000 - x: \text{the loan amount at 7\%}$$

STEP 2: *Write an equation.* Note that the total interest is $170.

$$\underbrace{0.03x}_{\text{Interest at 3\%}} + \underbrace{0.07(4000 - x)}_{\text{Interest at 7\%}} = \underbrace{170}_{\text{Total Interest}}$$

STEP 3: *Solve the equation in Step 2.*

$0.03x + 0.07(4000 - x) = 170$	Equation to be solved
$3x + 7(4000 - x) = 17{,}000$	Multiply by 100 to clear decimals.
$3x + 28{,}000 - 7x = 17{,}000$	Distributive property
$-4x + 28{,}000 = 17{,}000$	Combine like terms.
$-4x = -11{,}000$	Subtract 28,000.
$x = 2750$	Divide by -4.

The amount at 3% is $2750 and the amount at 7% is $4000 - 2750 = \$1250$.

STEP 4: *Check the answer.* The sum is $2750 + 1250 = \$4000$. Also, 3% of $2750 is $82.50 and 7% of $1250 is $87.50. The total interest is $82.50 + \$87.50 = \$170$. The answer checks.

Now Try Exercise **51**

▶ **REAL-WORLD CONNECTION**   In chemistry acids are frequently mixed. In the next example, percentages are used to determine how to mix an acid solution with a prescribed concentration.

EXAMPLE **12**   Mixing acid

A chemist mixes 2 liters of 20% sulfuric acid with another sample of 60% sulfuric acid to obtain a sample of 50% sulfuric acid. How much of the 60% sulfuric acid was used? See Figure 3.12.

Figure 3.12 Mixing acid

Solution
STEP 1: *Assign a variable.* Let x be as follows.

$$x: \text{liters of 60\% sulfuric acid}$$
$$x + 2: \text{liters of 50\% sulfuric acid}$$

STEP 2: *Write an equation.* Table 3.4 can be used to organize our calculations. The total amount of pure sulfuric acid in the 20% and 60% samples must equal the amount of pure sulfuric acid in the final 50% acid solution.

TABLE 3.4 **Mixing Acid**

Concentration (as a decimal)	Solution Amount (liters)	Pure Acid (liters)
20% = 0.20	2	0.20(2)
60% = 0.60	x	0.60x
50% = 0.50	$x + 2$	0.50($x + 2$)

From the third column, we can write the equation

$$0.20(2) \quad + \quad 0.60x \quad = \quad 0.50(x + 2).$$
Pure acid in 20% solution + Pure acid in 60% solution = Pure acid in 50% solution

STEP 3: *Solve the equation in Step 2.*

$$0.20(2) + 0.60x = 0.50(x + 2) \qquad \text{Equation to be solved}$$
$$2(2) + 6x = 5(x + 2) \qquad \text{Multiply by 10.}$$
$$4 + 6x = 5x + 10 \qquad \text{Distributive property}$$
$$x = 6 \qquad \text{Subtract } 5x \text{ and 4 from each side.}$$

Six liters of the 60% acid solution was added to the 2 liters of 20% acid solution.

STEP 4: *Check your answer.* If 6 liters of 60% acid solution are added to 2 liters of 20% solution, then there will be 8 liters of acid solution containing

$$0.60(6) + 0.20(2) = 4 \text{ liters}$$

of pure acid. The concentration is $\frac{4}{8} = 0.50$, or 50%. The answer checks.

Now Try Exercise **49**

3.2 PUTTING IT ALL TOGETHER

When solving an application problem, follow the *Steps for Solving a Problem* discussed on page 167. Be sure to read the problem carefully and check your answer. The following table summarizes some other important concepts from this section.

Concept	Explanation	Examples
Writing a Function	If possible, solve an equation for a variable. Express the result in function notation.	$5x + y = 10$ $y = -5x + 10$ If $y = f(x)$, then $f(x) = -5x + 10$.
Changing a Percentage to a Decimal	Move the decimal point two places to the left.	$73\% = 0.73$, $5.3\% = 0.053$, and $125\% = 1.25$
Percent Problems	To find $P\%$ of a quantity Q, change $P\%$ to a decimal and multiply by Q.	To find 45% of $200, calculate $0.45 \times 200 = \$90.$

3.2 Exercises

MyMathLab
PRACTICE   WATCH   DOWNLOAD   READ   REVIEW

CONCEPTS

1. If we solve $2y = x$ for y, we obtain $y =$ _____.

2. If $y = 4x - 7$ and $y = f(x)$, then $f(x) =$ _____.

3. If a rectangle has width W and length L, then its perimeter is $P =$ _____.

4. The first step in solving an application is to _____.

5. Write 43.1% as a decimal.

6. Find 20% of 50.

SOLVING FOR A VARIABLE

Exercises 7–14: Solve the equation for the given variable.

7. $4x + 3y = 12$; y

8. $6x - 3y = 6$; y

9. $5(2x - 3y) = 2x$; x

10. $-2(2x + y) = 3y$; x

11. $S = 6ab$; b

12. $S = 2\pi rh$; r

13. $\dfrac{r + t}{2} = 7$; t

14. $\dfrac{2 + a + b}{3} = 8$; a

Exercises 15–20: Solve the equation for y. Let $y = f(x)$ and write a formula for $f(x)$.

15. $-3x + y = 8$

16. $2x - 5y = 10$

17. $4x = 2\pi y$

18. $\dfrac{x}{2} = \dfrac{y}{3}$

19. $\dfrac{3y}{8} = x$

20. $\dfrac{3x + 2y}{4} = 3$

WRITING AND SOLVING EQUATIONS

Exercises 21–30: Do the following.

   (a) Translate the sentence into an equation, using the variable x.

   (b) Solve the resulting equation.

21. The sum of a number and 2 is 12.

22. Twice a number plus 7 equals 9.

23. A number divided by 5 equals the number plus 1.

24. 25 times a number is 125.

25. If a number is increased by 5 and then divided by 2, the result equals 7.

26. A number subtracted from 8 is 5.

27. The quotient of a number and 2 is 17.

28. The product of 5 and a number equals 95.

29. The sum of three consecutive integers is 30.

30. A rectangle that is 5 inches longer than it is wide has a perimeter of 60 inches.

APPLICATIONS

31. *Perimeter of a Rectangle*   A rectangle has a perimeter of 86 feet and a width of 19 feet.
    (a) Write a formula to find the length L of a rectangle with perimeter P and width W.
    (b) Use the formula to find L.

32. *Perimeter of a Triangle*   The perimeter P of a triangle with sides a, b, and c is $P = a + b + c$.

    (a) Solve this formula for a.
    (b) Find a if $b = 5$, $c = 7$, and $P = 15$.

33. *Area of a Cylinder*   The area A of the side of a cylinder with height h and radius r is $A = 2\pi rh$. Solve this formula for h.

34. *Volume of a Cylinder*   The volume V of a cylinder with height h and radius r is $V = \pi r^2 h$. Solve this formula for h.

35. *Temperature*   (Refer to Example 2.) Solve the formula $F = \frac{9}{5}C + 32$ for C.

36. *Area of a Parallelogram*   The area *A* of a parallelogram with base *b* and height *h* is $A = bh$. Solve this formula for *b*.

37. *Area of a Triangle*   The area *A* of a triangle with base *b* and height *h* is $A = \frac{1}{2}bh$. Solve this formula for *h*.

38. *Volume of a Box*   The volume *V* of a box with length *L*, width *W*, and height *H* is $V = WLH$. Solve this formula for *L*.

39. *Number Problem*   The sum of three consecutive integers is 135. Find the three integers.

40. *Number Problem*   Are there three consecutive *even integers* whose sum is 82? If so, find them.

41. *Number Problem*   Twice the sum of three consecutive *odd integers* is 150. Find the three integers.

42. *Number Problem*   Ten plus twice the sum of two consecutive integers is 196. Find the two integers.

43. *Geometry*   Find the value of *x* in the figure if the perimeter of the room is 48 feet.

44. *Distance and Time*   A train 100 miles west of St. Louis, Missouri, is traveling east at 60 miles per hour. How long will it take for the train to be 410 miles east of St. Louis?

45. *Geometry*   A wire, 41 inches long, needs to be cut into three pieces so that it can be formed into two identical circles and a square. The length of the side of the square must equal the diameter of the circles. Approximate where the wire should be cut.

46. *Fencing*   Three identical pens for dogs are to be enclosed with 120 feet of fence, as illustrated in the figure. If the length of each pen is twice its width plus 2 feet, find the dimensions of each pen.

47. *Distance and Time*   Two cars are traveling in opposite lanes on a freeway. Two and a half hours after they meet they are 355 miles apart. If one car is traveling 6 miles per hour faster than the other car, find the speed of each car.

48. *Distance and Time*   At first an athlete jogs at 6 miles per hour and then jogs at 5 miles per hour, traveling 7 miles in 1.3 hours. How long did the athlete jog at each speed?

49. *Chemical Mixture*   A chemist mixes 3 liters of 30% sulfuric acid with a sample of 80% sulfuric acid to obtain a sample of 60% sulfuric acid. How much of the 80% sulfuric acid was used?

50. *Antifreeze Mixture*   A radiator holds 4 gallons of fluid. If it is full with a 20% solution, how much fluid should be drained and replaced with a 70% antifreeze mixture to result in a 50% mixture of antifreeze?

51. *Loan Interest*   A student takes out two student loans, one at 6% annual interest and the other at 4% annual interest. The total amount of the two loans is $5000, and the total interest after 1 year is $244. Find the amount of each loan.

52. *Investment*   A person invests two amounts of money at 5% and 6% interest. The total amount of money invested is $2400 and the total interest after 1 year is $130.50. Find the amount invested at each rate.

53. *Angles in a Triangle*   The measure of the largest angle in a triangle is twice the measure of the smallest angle. The third angle is 10° less than the largest angle. Find the measure of each angle.

54. *Angles in a Triangle*   The sum of the degree measures of the angles in a triangle equals 180°. Find the measure of x in the triangle shown.

55. *Classroom Ventilation*   Ventilation is effective at removing air pollutants. A classroom should have a ventilation rate of 900 cubic feet of air per hour for each person in the classroom.   (**Source:** ASHRAE.)

   (a) What ventilation rate should a classroom containing 40 people have?

   (b) If a ventilation system moves 60,000 cubic feet of air per hour, find the maximum number of people that should be in the classroom.

56. *Lead Poisoning*   According to the EPA, the maximum amount of lead that can be ingested by a person without becoming ill is 36.5 milligrams per year.

   (a) Write an expression that gives the maximum amount of lead in milligrams that can be "safely" ingested over x years.

   (b) Under these guidelines what is the minimum number of years that the consumption of 500 milligrams should be spread over?

57. *Hybrid Cars*   The 2006 model of the Honda Civic Hybrid averages 50 miles per gallon and has an annual fuel cost of $873. If it was assumed that a person drives 15,000 miles per year, what was the cost of a gallon of gasoline?   (**Source:** Honda Corporation.)

58. *Hybrid Cars*   The 2006 Toyota Camry Hybrid has an annual fuel cost of $1000. If it was assumed that gasoline costs $2.60 per gallon and that a person drives 15,000 miles per year, estimate the average mileage for this vehicle.   (**Source:** Toyota Corporation.)

59. *Solar Energy in Nevada*   The U.S. Department of Energy has estimated that solar power plants covering 9900 square miles, or 9% of Nevada, could generate enough electricity to meet the needs of the entire United States. Find the area of Nevada.

60. *Energy Efficiency Rating*   The Energy Efficiency Rating (EER) of an air conditioner must be at least 8.0. Changing to an air conditioner with an EER of 10.0 can cut electrical bills by 20%. Suppose that a person's monthly electrical bill is $125 and that the more efficient air conditioner costs an extra $275. How many months will it take to recover this added cost? (**Source:** Energy Service Office, Springfield, Illinois.)

61. *Wal-Mart Employees*   In 2007 the number of Wal-Mart employees was 2.2 million, a 57% increase over the number of employees in 2002. How many Wal-Mart employees were there in 2002?

62. *Airline Fares*   In 2002 the average one-way fare paid by American Express clients on domestic routes was $282, an 8.44% decrease from 2001. Find the average one-way fare paid in 2001.

63. *Meeting a Future Mate*   About 32% of adult Americans believe that they will meet their mates on the Internet during this century. In this survey 480 respondents held this belief. Determine the number of people participating in the survey.   (**Source:** Men's Health.)

64. *Union Membership*   In 1998, 6.9 million, or 37.5%, of all government workers were unionized. How many government workers were there in 1998? (**Source:** Department of Labor.)

65. *Cancer and Heart Disease*   About 550,000 people died from cancer in the United States during 2000.

Heart disease accounted for 29.1% more deaths than cancer. What is the total number of people who died from heart disease or cancer during 2000? (*Source: National Center for Health Statistics.*)

66. *Grades* To receive an A in a college course a student must average 90 percent correct on four exams of 100 points each and on a final exam of 200 points. If a student scores 83, 87, 94, and 91 on the 100-point exams, what minimum score on the final exam is necessary for the student to receive an A?

WRITING ABOUT MATHEMATICS

67. A student solves the following equation for y. What is the student's mistake?

$$\frac{x + 2y}{2} = 5$$
$$x + y \stackrel{?}{=} 5$$
$$y \stackrel{?}{=} 5 - x$$

68. Explain how to find $P\%$ of a quantity Q. Give an example.

CHECKING BASIC CONCEPTS
SECTIONS 3.1 AND 3.2

1. How many solutions does a linear equation have?

2. Solve $\frac{1}{2}z - (1 - 2z) = \frac{2}{3}z$.

3. Solve $2(3x + 4) + 3 = -1$

   (a) symbolically,
   (b) graphically, and
   (c) numerically.
   Do your answers agree?

4. At first an athlete jogs at 10 miles per hour and then jogs at 8 miles per hour, traveling 10.2 miles in 1.2 hours. How long did the athlete jog at each speed?

5. Find the x- and y-intercepts for the graph of the equation $5x - 4y = 20$.

6. Classify each equation as either an identity or a contradiction.
   (a) $3(x - 2) = 3x - 6$
   (b) $2x + 3x = 5x - 2$

3.3 LINEAR INEQUALITIES

Basic Concepts ▪ Symbolic Solutions ▪ Numerical and Graphical Solutions ▪ An Application

A LOOK INTO MATH ▷

On a freeway, the speed limit might be 75 miles per hour. A driver traveling x miles per hour is obeying the speed limit if $x \le 75$ and breaking the speed limit if $x > 75$. A speed of $x = 75$ represents the boundary between obeying the speed limit and breaking it. A posted speed limit, or *boundary*, allows drivers to easily determine whether they are speeding.

Solving linear inequalities is closely related to solving linear equations because equality is the boundary between *greater than* and *less than*. In this section we discuss techniques needed to solve linear inequalities.

Basic Concepts

An **inequality** results whenever the equals sign in an equation is replaced with any one of the symbols $<, \le, >,$ or $\ge$. Examples of linear equations include

$$2x + 1 = 0, \quad 1 - x = 6, \quad \text{and} \quad 5x + 1 = 3 - 2x,$$

and, therefore, examples of linear inequalities include

$$2x + 1 < 0, \quad 1 - x \geq 6, \quad \text{and} \quad 5x + 1 \leq 3 - 2x.$$

A **solution** to an inequality is a value of the variable that makes the statement true. The set of all solutions is called the **solution set**. Two inequalities are *equivalent* if they have the same solution set. Inequalities frequently have *infinitely many solutions*. For example, the solution set to the inequality $x - 5 > 0$ includes all real numbers greater than 5, which can be written as $x > 5$. Using **set-builder notation**, we can write the solution set as $\{x \mid x > 5\}$. This expression is read as "the set of all real numbers x such that x is greater than 5." The vertical line | in set-builder notation is read "such that." To summarize, we have the following.

Inequality	*Set-Builder Notation*	*Meaning*
$t \leq 3$	$\{t \mid t \leq 3\}$	The set of all real numbers t such that t is less than or equal to 3
$z > 8$	$\{z \mid z > 8\}$	The set of all real numbers z such that z is greater than 8

Next we more formally define a linear inequality in one variable.

LINEAR INEQUALITY IN ONE VARIABLE

A **linear inequality** in one variable is an inequality that can be written in the form

$$ax + b > 0,$$

where $a \neq 0$. (The symbol $>$ may be replaced with $\geq$, $<$, or $\leq$.)

MAKING CONNECTIONS

Linear Functions, Equations, and Inequalities

A *linear function* is given by $f(x) = ax + b$, a *linear equation* by $ax + b = 0$, and a *linear inequality* by $ax + b > 0$. A linear equation (with $a \neq 0$) has one solution. A linear inequality has infinitely many solutions.

▶ REAL-WORLD CONNECTION   To understand linear inequalities better, suppose that it costs a student $100 to make a large batch of candy. If the student sells bags of this candy for $5 each, then the profit y is $y = 5x - 100$, where x represents the number of bags sold. The graph of y is a line with slope 5 and y-intercept -100, as shown in Figure 3.13.

Figure 3.13 Candy Profit

Because the *x*-intercept is 20, the student will *break even* when $5x - 100 = 0$, or when 20 bags of candy are sold. (The **break-even point** occurs when the *revenue* from selling the candy equals the *cost* of making the candy.) Note that the student incurs a *loss* when the line is below the *x*-axis, or when $5x - 100 < 0$. This situation corresponds to selling less than 20 bags, or $x < 20$. A profit occurs when the graph is above the *x*-axis, or when $5x - 100 > 0$. This situation corresponds to selling more than 20 bags, or $x > 20$. Selling $x = 20$ bags of candy represents the *boundary* between loss and profit.

These concepts for the solution set for a linear inequality are summarized as follows.

SOLUTION SET FOR A LINEAR INEQUALITY

The solution set for $ax + b > 0$ with $a \neq 0$ is either $\{x \mid x < k\}$ or $\{x \mid x > k\}$, where *k* is the solution to $ax + b = 0$ and corresponds to the *x*-intercept for the graph of $y = ax + b$. Similar statements can be made for the symbols $<$, $\leq$, and $\geq$.

Symbolic Solutions

The inequality $3 < 5$ is equivalent to $3 + 1 < 5 + 1$. That is, we can add the same number to each side of an inequality. This is an example of one property of inequalities.

PROPERTIES OF INEQUALITIES

Let *a*, *b*, and *c* be real numbers.

1. $a < b$ and $a + c < b + c$ are equivalent.
    (The same number may be added to or subtracted from each side of an inequality.)
2. If $c > 0$, then $a < b$ and $ac < bc$ are equivalent.
    (Each side of an inequality may be multiplied or divided by the same positive number.)
3. If $c < 0$, then $a < b$ and $ac > bc$ are equivalent.
    (Each side of an inequality may be multiplied or divided by the same negative number provided the inequality symbol is reversed.)

Similar properties exist for the $\leq$ and $\geq$ symbols.

When applying Property 2 or 3, we need to determine whether the inequality symbol should be reversed. For example, if each side of the inequality $3 < 5$ is multiplied by the *positive* number 2, we obtain

$$2 \cdot 3 < 2 \cdot 5 \quad \text{or} \quad 6 < 10,$$

which is a true statement. However, if each side of the inequality $3 < 5$ is multiplied by the *negative* number -2, we obtain

$$-2 \cdot 3 > -2 \cdot 5 \quad \text{or} \quad -6 > -10,$$

$\uparrow$
Reverse inequality symbol.

which is a true statement because the inequality symbol is reversed from $<$ to $>$.

To solve an inequality we apply properties of inequalities to find a simpler, equivalent inequality, as illustrated in the next example.

EXAMPLE 1   Solving linear inequalities

Solve each inequality.

(a) $2x - 1 > 4$ **(b)** $\frac{1}{2}(z - 3) - (2 - z) \le 1$

Solution
(a) Begin by adding 1 to each side of the inequality.

$2x - 1 > 4$	Given inequality
$2x - 1 + 1 > 4 + 1$	Add 1 to each side.
$2x > 5$	Simplify.
$\dfrac{2x}{2} > \dfrac{5}{2}$	Divide by 2; do *not* reverse inequality symbol because $2 > 0$.
$x > \dfrac{5}{2}$	Simplify.

The solution set is $\left\{ x \mid x > \frac{5}{2} \right\}$.

(b) To clear fractions multiply each term by 2.

$\dfrac{1}{2}(z - 3) - (2 - z) \le 1$	Given inequality
$(z - 3) - 2(2 - z) \le 2$	Multiply by 2; do *not* reverse inequality symbol because $2 > 0$.
$z - 3 - 4 + 2z \le 2$	Distributive property
$3z - 7 \le 2$	Combine like terms.
$3z - 7 + 7 \le 2 + 7$	Add 7 to each side.
$3z \le 9$	Simplify.
$z \le 3$	Divide by 3; do *not* reverse inequality symbol because $3 > 0$.

The solution set is $\{ z \mid z \le 3 \}$.   **Now Try Exercises 17, 19**

EXAMPLE 2   Solving linear inequalities

Solve each inequality.

(a) $5 - 3x \le x - 3$ **(b)** $\dfrac{2t - 3}{5} \ge \dfrac{t + 1}{3} + 3t$

Solution
(a) Begin by subtracting 5 from each side of the inequality.

$5 - 3x \le x - 3$	Given inequality
$5 - 3x - 5 \le x - 3 - 5$	Subtract 5 from each side.
$-3x \le x - 8$	Simplify.
$-3x - x \le x - 8 - x$	Subtract x from each side.
$-4x \le -8$	Simplify.

Next divide each side by -4. As we are dividing by a *negative* number, Property 3 requires reversing the inequality by changing $\le$ to $\ge$.

$$\frac{-4x}{-4} \geq \frac{-8}{-4}$$ Divide by -4; reverse the inequality because $-4 < 0$.

$$x \geq 2$$ Simplify.

The solution set is $\{x \mid x \geq 2\}$.

(b) To clear fractions multiply each term by 15.

$$\frac{2t - 3}{5} \geq \frac{t + 1}{3} + 3t$$ Given inequality

$$15 \cdot \left(\frac{2t - 3}{5}\right) \geq 15 \cdot \left(\frac{t + 1}{3}\right) + 15 \cdot 3t$$ Multiply each term by 15; do not reverse the inequality symbol because $15 > 0$.

$$3(2t - 3) \geq 5(t + 1) + 45t$$ Simplify: $\frac{15}{5} = 3$ and $\frac{15}{3} = 5$

$$6t - 9 \geq 5t + 5 + 45t$$ Distributive property

$$6t - 9 + 9 \geq 50t + 5 + 9$$ Add 9; combine like terms.

$$6t \geq 50t + 14$$ Simplify.

$$6t - 50t \geq 50t - 50t + 14$$ Subtract $50t$ from each side.

$$-44t \geq 14$$ Simplify.

$$t \leq \frac{14}{-44}$$ Divide by -44; reverse the inequality symbol because $-44 < 0$.

$$t \leq -\frac{7}{22}$$ Simplify.

The solution set is $\left\{t \mid t \leq -\frac{7}{22}\right\}$.

Now Try Exercises 21, 35

Numerical and Graphical Solutions

In Section 3.1 we solved linear equations with symbolic, numerical, and graphical methods. We can also use these methods to solve linear inequalities.

EXAMPLE 3   Solving linear inequalities numerically

Use Table 3.5 to find the solution set to each equation or inequality.
(a) $-\frac{1}{2}x + 1 = 0$ **(b)** $-\frac{1}{2}x + 1 > 0$ **(c)** $-\frac{1}{2}x + 1 < 0$

TABLE 3.5

x	-1	0	1	2	3	4	5
$-\frac{1}{2}x + 1$	$\frac{3}{2}$	1	$\frac{1}{2}$	0	$-\frac{1}{2}$	-1	$-\frac{3}{2}$

Solution
(a) The expression $-\frac{1}{2}x + 1$ equals 0 when $x = 2$. Thus the solution set is $\{x \mid x = 2\}$.

(b) The expression $-\frac{1}{2}x + 1$ is positive when $x < 2$. Thus the solution set is $\{x \mid x < 2\}$.

(c) The expression $-\frac{1}{2}x + 1$ is negative when $x > 2$. Thus the solution set is $\{x \mid x > 2\}$.

Now Try Exercise 43

EXAMPLE Solving linear inequalities graphically

Use Figure 3.14 to find the solution set to each equation or inequality.

(a) $-\frac{1}{2}x + 1 = 0$ **(b)** $-\frac{1}{2}x + 1 > 0$ **(c)** $-\frac{1}{2}x + 1 < 0$

Solution
(a) The graph of $y = -\frac{1}{2}x + 1$ in Figure 3.14 crosses the x-axis at $x = 2$. Thus the solution set is $\{x \mid x = 2\}$.
(b) The graph is *above* the x-axis when $x < 2$. Thus the solution set is $\{x \mid x < 2\}$.
(c) The graph is *below* the x-axis when $x > 2$. Thus the solution set is $\{x \mid x > 2\}$.

Figure 3.14

Now Try Exercise **49**

NOTE: Numerical and graphical solutions can sometimes be difficult to find if the x-value that determines equality is not an integer. Symbolic methods work well in such situations.

Sometimes linear inequalities are written in the form $y_1 < y_2, y_1 \leq y_2, y_1 > y_2$, or $y_1 \geq y_2$, where both y_1 and y_2 contain variables. These types of inequalities can also be solved graphically or numerically.

▶ **REAL-WORLD CONNECTION**   Figure 3.15 shows the distances that two cars are from Chicago, Illinois, after x hours while traveling in the same direction on a freeway. The distance for Car 1 is denoted y_1, and the distance for Car 2 is denoted y_2.

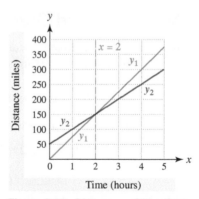

Figure 3.15   Distances of Two Cars

When $x = 2$ hours, $y_1 = y_2$ and both cars are 150 miles from Chicago. To the left of the dashed vertical line $x = 2$, the graph of y_1 is below the graph of y_2, so Car 1 is closer to Chicago than Car 2. Thus

$$y_1 < y_2 \quad \text{when} \quad x < 2.$$

To the right of the dashed vertical line $x = 2$, the graph of y_1 is above the graph of y_2, so Car 1 is farther from Chicago than Car 2. Thus

$$y_1 > y_2 \quad \text{when} \quad x > 2.$$

A linear equation has one solution that can be easily checked. A linear inequality has infinitely many solutions. Discuss ways that the solution set to a linear inequality could be checked.

EXAMPLE 5   Solving an inequality graphically

Solve $5 - 3x \leq x - 3$.

Solution
The graphs of $y_1 = 5 - 3x$ and $y_2 = x - 3$ intersect at the point $(2, -1)$, as shown in Figure 3.16(a). Equality, or $y_1 = y_2$, occurs when $x = 2$ and the graph of y_1 is below the graph of y_2 when $x > 2$. Thus $5 - 3x \leq x - 3$ is satisfied when $x \geq 2$. The solution set is $\{x \mid x \geq 2\}$. Figure 3.16(b) shows the same graph generated with a graphing calculator.

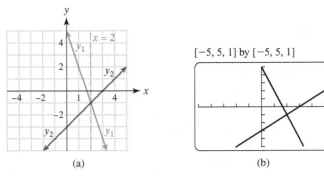

$[-5, 5, 1]$ by $[-5, 5, 1]$

(a)   (b)

Figure 3.16

Now Try Exercise 53

Use the results from Example 5 to write the solution set for $5 - 3x \geq x - 3$.

An Application

▶ REAL-WORLD CONNECTION   In the lower atmosphere, the air generally becomes colder as the altitude increases. See Figure 3.17. One mile above Earth's surface the temperature is about 19°F colder than the ground-level temperature. As the air temperature cools, the chance of clouds forming increases. In the next example we estimate the altitudes at which clouds will not form.

3 miles ⟶ 33°F

2 miles ⟶ 52°F

1 mile ⟶ 71°F

0 miles ⟶ 90°F

Figure 3.17

EXAMPLE 6   Finding the altitude of clouds

If ground-level temperature is 90°F, the temperature T above Earth's surface is modeled by $T(x) = 90 - 19x$, where x is the altitude in miles. Suppose that clouds will form only if the temperature is 53°F or colder. (**Source:** A. Miller and R. Anthes, *Meteorology*.)
(a) Determine symbolically the altitudes at which there are no clouds.
(b) Give graphical support for your answer.
(c) Give numerical support for your answer.

Solution
(a) *Symbolic Solution*   Clouds will not form at altitudes at which the temperature is greater than 53°F. Thus we must solve the inequality $T(x) > 53$.

$$90 - 19x > 53 \qquad \text{Inequality to be solved}$$
$$90 - 19x - 90 > 53 - 90 \qquad \text{Subtract 90 from each side.}$$
$$-19x > -37 \qquad \text{Simplify.}$$
$$\frac{-19x}{-19} < \frac{-37}{-19} \qquad \text{Divide by } -19; \text{ reverse inequality.}$$
$$x < \frac{37}{19} \qquad \text{Simplify.}$$

The result, $\frac{37}{19} \approx 1.95$, indicates that clouds will not form below about 1.95 miles. Note that models are usually not exact, so rounding values is appropriate.
(b) *Graphical Solution*   Graph $Y_1 = 90 - 19X$ and $Y_2 = 53$. In Figure 3.18(a) their graphs intersect near the point $(1.95, 53)$. The graph of y_1 is above the graph of y_2 when $x < 1.95$.
(c) *Numerical Solution*   Make a table of y_1 and y_2, as shown in Figure 3.18(b). When $x = 2$, the air temperature is 52°F. Thus the air temperature would be 53°F when the altitude is slightly less than 2 miles, which supports our symbolic solution of $x \approx 1.95$.

[0, 3, 1] by [0, 100, 20]

CALCULATOR HELP

To find a point of intersection, see the Appendix (page AP-7).

(a)

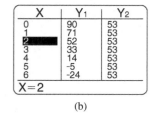

(b)

Figure 3.18

Now Try Exercise 93

3.3 PUTTING IT ALL TOGETHER

The following table summarizes some important topics related to linear inequalities.

Concept	Explanation	Examples
Linear Inequalities in One Variable	Can be written as $$ax + b > 0,$$ where $a \neq 0$ and $>$ may be replaced by $<$, $\leq$, or $\geq$; has infinitely many solutions	$3x - 4 > 0$, $-(x - 5) < 2$, $2x \geq 5 - x$, and $4 - 2(x + 1) \leq 7x - 1$

Concept	Explanation	Examples
Set-Builder Notation	Used to express sets of real numbers	$\{x \mid x > 4\}$ represents the set of real numbers x such that x is greater than 4.
Properties of Inequalities	See the box on page 179. Be sure to note Property 3: When multiplying or dividing by a negative number, *reverse* the inequality symbol.	*Property 1*: $x - 3 \geq 2$ is equivalent to $x \geq 5$. *Property 2*: $2x \leq 6$ is equivalent to $x \leq 3$. *Property 3*: $-3x < 6$ is equivalent to $x > -2$.

Linear inequalities can be solved symbolically, graphically, or numerically. Each method is used as follows to solve the inequality $2x - 4 \geq 0$.

Symbolic Solution

$$2x - 4 \geq 0$$
$$2x \geq 4$$
$$x \geq 2$$

Graphical Solution

The graph of $y = 2x - 4$ is above or intersects the x-axis when $x \geq 2$.

Numerical Solution

x	$2x - 4$
0	-4
1	-2
2	0
3	2
4	4

The values of $2x - 4$ are greater than or equal to 0 when $x \geq 2$.

3.3 Exercises

MyMathLab

CONCEPTS

1. Give an example of a linear inequality.

2. Can a linear inequality have infinitely many solutions? Explain.

3. Are $x + 5 < y + 5$ and $x < y$ equivalent?

4. Are $x - 7 \geq y - 7$ and $x \geq y$ equivalent?

5. Are $2x > 6$ and $x > 3$ equivalent? Explain.

6. Are $-4x < 8$ and $x < -2$ equivalent? Explain.

7. Distinguish between an equation and an inequality.

8. Name three methods for solving a linear inequality.

Exercises 9–12: Decide whether the given value for the variable is a solution to the inequality.

9. $x - 5 \leq 3$ $x = 2$

10. $\frac{3}{2}x - \frac{1}{2} \geq 1 - x$ $x = -2$

11. $2t - 3 > 5t - (2t + 1)$ $t = 5$

12. $2(z - 1) < 3(z + 1)$ $z = \pi$

SYMBOLIC SOLUTIONS

Exercises 13–16: Solve each equation or inequality.

(a) $y_1 = 0$ (b) $y_1 < 0$ (c) $y_1 > 0$

13. $y_1 = x - 2$

14. $y_1 = x + 5$

15. $y_1 = -2x + 6$

16. $y_1 = -6 - 6x$

Exercises 17–42: Solve the inequality symbolically.

17. $x + 3 \le 5$

18. $x - 5 \ge -3$

19. $\frac{1}{4}x > 9$

20. $14 < -3.5x$

21. $4 - 3x \le -\frac{2}{3}$

22. $4x - 2 \ge \frac{5}{2}$

23. $7 - \frac{1}{2}x < x - \frac{3}{2}$

24. $4x - 6 > 12 - 10x$

25. $\frac{5}{2}(2x - 3) < 6 - 2x$

26. $1 - \left(\frac{3}{2}x - 4\right) > \frac{1}{2}(x + 1)$

27. $\frac{3x - 2}{-2} \le \frac{x - 4}{-5}$

28. $\frac{5 - 2x}{2} \ge \frac{2x + 1}{4}$

29. $3(x - 2000) + 15 < 45$

30. $-2(x - 1990) + 75 > 25$

31. $0.4x - 0.7 < 1.3$

32. $-0.3(x - 5) + 0.2 > 2$

33. $\frac{4}{5}x - \frac{1}{5} \ge -5$

34. $\frac{3x}{4} - \frac{1}{2} \le \frac{1}{4}(2x + 1)$

35. $-\frac{1}{3}(z - 3) - \frac{1}{4} \ge \frac{1}{4}(5 - z)$

36. $2(3 - 2z) - (1 - z) \le 4z - (1 + z)$

37. $\frac{3}{4}(2t - 5) \le \frac{1}{2}(4t - 6) + 1$

38. $\frac{5}{6}x + (3 - x) \ge \frac{x - 3}{3}$

39. $\frac{1}{2}\big(4 - (x + 3)\big) + 4 > -\frac{1}{3}\big(2x - (1 - x)\big)$

40. $\frac{x - (2 - 3x)}{2} < \frac{1 - (4 - 5x)}{6}$

41. $0.05 + 0.08x < 0.01x - 0.04(3 - 4x)$

42. $-0.2(5x + 2) \ge 0.4 + 1.5x$

NUMERICAL SOLUTIONS

Exercises 43 and 44: Complete the table. Then use the table to solve the inequality.

43. $-2x + 6 \le 0$

x	1	2	3	4	5
$-2x + 6$	4				-4

44. $3x - 1 < 8$

x	0	1	2	3	4
$3x - 1$					

Exercises 45–48: Solve the inequality numerically.

45. $x - 3 > 0$

46. $2x < 0$

47. $2x - 1 \ge 3$

48. $2 - 3x \le -4$

GRAPHICAL SOLUTIONS

Exercises 49–52: Use the graph of y_1 to solve each equation or inequality.

(a) $y_1 = 0$ (b) $y_1 < 0$ (c) $y_1 > 0$

49.

50.

51.

52.

Exercises 53–56: Use the graph to solve the inequality.

53. $y_1 \leq y_2$

54. $y_2 > y_1$

55. $y_1 > y_2$

56. $y_1 \leq y_2$

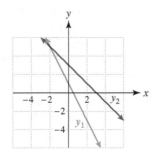

57. *Distance Between Cars* Car 1 and Car 2 are traveling in the same direction. Their distances in miles north of St. Louis, Missouri, after x hours are shown in the following graph, where $x \leq 8$.
   (a) Which car is traveling faster? Explain.
   (b) How many hours elapse before the two cars are the same distance from St. Louis? How far are they from St. Louis when this equality occurs?
   (c) During what time interval is Car 2 farther from St. Louis than Car 1?

58. Use the following graph to solve each inequality.
   (a) $f(x) > g(x)$ **(b)** $f(x) \leq g(x)$

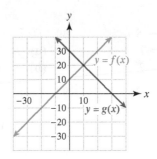

Exercises 59–70: Solve the inequality graphically.

59. $x - 1 < 0$

60. $4 - 2x \leq 0$

61. $2x \geq 0$

62. $3x + 6 > 0$

63. $4 - 2x \leq 8$

64. $-2x + 3 < -3$

65. $x - (2x + 4) > 0$

66. $2x + 1 \geq 3x - 4$

67. $2(x + 2) + 5 < -x$

68. $\dfrac{x + 5}{3} \geq \dfrac{1 - x}{2}$

69. $25(x - 1995) + 100 \leq 0$

70. $5(x - 1980) - 20 > 50$

Exercises 71 and 72: Solve the inequality graphically. Approximate boundary numbers to the nearest thousandth.

71. $\pi(\sqrt{2}x - 1.2) + \sqrt{3}x > \dfrac{\pi + 1}{3}$

72. $3.1x - 0.5(\pi - x) \leq \sqrt{5} - 0.4x$

73. Thinking Generally Let y_1 be a (nonconstant) linear function. If $y_1 < b$ when $x > a$, then solve $y_1 > b$.

74. Thinking Generally Let y_1 be a (nonconstant) linear function and $y_1 = 0$ when $x = a$. What are the possible solution sets to $y_1 \leq 0$?

SOLVING LINEAR INEQUALITIES BY MORE THAN ONE METHOD

*Exercises 75–78: Solve the inequality **(a)** numerically, **(b)** graphically, and **(c)** symbolically.*

75. $5x - 2 < 8$

76. $2x - 4 - 3(x + 3) \leq 0$

77. $2x \geq 3x - 3$

78. $x - 1 > \dfrac{4 - x}{2}$

INEQUALITIES AND FUNCTIONS

Exercises 79–84: Solve each equation or inequality for the given $f(x)$.

79. $f(x) = x - 5$
   (a) $f(x) = 7$
   (b) $f(x) > 7$

80. $f(x) = 4x$
   (a) $f(x) = -2$
   (b) $f(x) < -2$

81. $f(x) = 4 - 3x$
   (a) $f(x) \geq 11$
   (b) $f(x) \leq 11$

82. $f(x) = 9 - 3x$
   (a) $f(x) < 0$
   (b) $f(x) > 0$

83. $f(x) = 3(x + 7) + 1$
   (a) $f(x) \leq -5$
   (b) $f(x) \geq -5$

84. $f(x) = -2(4 - 3x)$
   (a) $f(x) > 16$
   (b) $f(x) < 16$

APPLICATIONS

85. *Federal Debt*   The line graph shows the total federal debt in trillions of dollars from 1940 through 2000. Estimate the years when the deficit was less than $1 trillion dollars.

86. *Interest*   The graph shows the annual interest y on a loan of x dollars with an interest rate of 10%. Find the loan amounts that result in the following.
   (a) An annual interest equal to $100
   (b) An annual interest of more than $100
   (c) An annual interest of $100 or less

87. *Profit*   A band buys 500 blank CDs and records their music on them. They sell the CDs to earn a profit. Refer to the graph to answer the following questions.

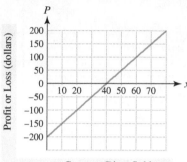

Compact Discs Sold

   (a) How much did the band pay for the blank CDs?
   (b) How much did the band charge for their CDs?
   (c) Write an equation that gives the profit P from selling x CDs.
   (d) Determine the break-even point.
   (e) When will the band make a profit?

88. *Average Temperature*   On March 1 the average high temperature in Minnesota is about 21°F. On March 30 this average increases to about 46°F. Use a linear function to estimate the days in March when the average high temperature is 31°F or less.

89. *Geometry*   Find values for x so that the perimeter of the figure is less than 50 feet.

90. *Geometry*   A rectangle is twice as long as it is wide. If the rectangle is to have a perimeter of 36 inches or less, what values for the width are possible?

91. *Distance and Time*   Two cars are traveling in the same direction along a freeway. After x hours, the first car's distance in miles from a rest stop is given by $y_1 = 70x$ and the second car's distance in miles is given by $y_2 = 60x + 35$.
   (a) What is the speed of each car?
   (b) When are the cars the same distance from the rest stop?
   (c) At what times is the first car farther from the rest stop than the second? Assume that $x \geq 0$.

92. *Sales of CDs and LP Records*   From 1985 to 1990 sales of CDs, in millions, in the United States can be modeled by
$$y_1 = 51.6(x - 1985) + 9.1,$$

and sales of vinyl LP records, in millions, can be modeled by

$$y_2 = -31.9(x - 1985) + 167.7.$$

(a) Graph y_1 and y_2 in the viewing rectangle given by [1984, 1991, 1] by [0, 350, 50].

(b) Estimate the years when CD sales were greater than or equal to LP record sales.

(c) Solve part (b) symbolically.

93. *Altitude and Temperature* (Refer to Example 6.) If the temperature on the ground is 60°F, the air temperature x miles high is given by $T(x) = 60 - 19x$. Determine the altitudes at which the air temperature is greater than 0°F. Support your answer graphically or numerically. (*Source:* A. Miller.)

94. *Altitude and Dew Point* If the dew point on the ground is 70°F, then the dew point x miles high is given by $D(x) = 70 - 5.8x$. (*Source:* A. Miller.)

(a) For each 1-mile increase in altitude, how much does the dew point change?

(b) Determine the altitudes at which the dew point is greater than 30°F.

95. *Body Mass Index* Body mass index, BMI, gives a recommended relationship between a person's height H in inches and weight W in pounds and is given by

$$\text{BMI} = \frac{705W}{H^2}.$$

If a person is 70 inches tall, approximate the range of weights W that result in a BMI between 19 and 25, inclusively.

96. *Grades* A student scores 75, 86, and 72 on three 100-point exams. If the final is worth 150 points, find the range of final exam scores S that gives the student an overall percentage of 80% or higher.

97. *AIDS Research* AIDS research funding in 1994 was $1.3 billion and in 2000 it was $1.8 billion. Use a linear function to estimate the years in which AIDS funding was greater than or equal to $1.55 billion. (*Source:* National Institutes of Health.)

98. *Hepatitis C Research* The hepatitis C virus (HCV) can live in a person for years without any symptoms after the individual was initially infected. An estimated 4 million Americans have HCV, and some 10,000 people die from it each year. From 1994 to 2000 research funding for hepatitis C in millions of dollars may be

modeled by $f(x) = 4.43(x - 1994) + 7$, where x is the year. When was this funding less than or equal to $20.3 million? (*Source:* National Institutes of Health.)

99. *Size and Weight of a Fish* If a bass has a length of x inches, where x is between 20 and 25 inches, its weight W in pounds can be *estimated* by the formula $W(x) = 0.96x - 14.4$.

(a) What length of bass weighs 6.7 pounds?

(b) What lengths of bass weigh less than 6.7 pounds?

100. *Distant Galaxies* In the late 1920s the famous observational astronomer Edwin P. Hubble (1889–1953) determined both the distance to several galaxies and the velocity at which they were receding from Earth. The graph shows four galaxies with their distances x in light-years from Earth and velocities y in miles per second that they are moving away from Earth.

(*Source:* A. Sharov and I. Novikov, *Edwin Hubble, The Discoverer of the Big Bang Universe.*)

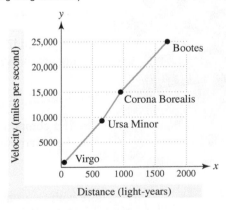

(a) What relationship exists between distance and velocity of a galaxy?

(b) A galaxy is determined to be receding at more than 12,500 miles per second. What can be said about its distance from Earth?

101. Explain the following terms and give examples.
  (a) Linear function   **(b)** Linear equation
  (c) Linear inequality

102. Suppose that a student says that a linear equation and a linear inequality can be solved symbolically in exactly the same way. How would you respond?

GROUP ACTIVITY
WORKING WITH REAL DATA

Directions: Form a group of 2 to 4 people. Select someone to record the group's responses for this activity. All members of the group should work cooperatively to answer the questions. If your instructor asks for your results, each member of the group should be prepared to respond.

1. *Born Outside the United States* The foreign-born portion of the population increased from 4.7% in 1970 to 10.4% in 2000. This increase could be modeled by a linear function. Use these data to estimate the year when this percentage was 7%. (*Source: Bureau of the Census.*)

2. When do you expect the foreign-born population to be 12%?

3. What does your model say about the foreign-born population in 1940 and in 2500? Are your answers reasonable? What do these results say about your model?

3.4 COMPOUND INEQUALITIES

Basic Concepts ■ Symbolic Solutions and Number Lines ■
Numerical and Graphical Solutions ■ Interval Notation

A LOOK INTO MATH ▷

A person weighing 143 pounds and needing to purchase a life vest for white-water rafting is not likely to find one designed exactly for this weight. Life vests are manufactured to support a range of body weights. A vest approved for weights between 100 and 160 pounds might be appropriate for this person. In other words, if a person's weight is w, this life vest is safe if $w \geq 100$ *and* $w \leq 160$. This example illustrates the concept of a *compound inequality*.

Basic Concepts

A **compound inequality** consists of two inequalities joined by the words *and* or *or*. The following are two examples of compound inequalities.

$$2x \geq -3 \quad \text{and} \quad 2x < 5 \qquad (1)$$
$$x + 2 \geq 3 \quad \text{or} \quad x - 1 < -5 \qquad (2)$$

If a compound inequality contains the word *and*, a solution must satisfy *both* inequalities. For example, 1 is a solution to the first compound inequality because

$$2(1) \geq -3 \quad \text{and} \quad 2(1) < 5$$
$$\text{True} \qquad\qquad \text{True}$$

are both true statements.

If a compound inequality contains the word *or*, a solution must satisfy *at least one* of the two inequalities. Thus 5 is a solution to the second compound inequality, because the first statement is true.

$$5 + 2 \geq 3 \quad \text{or} \quad 5 - 1 < -5$$
$$\text{True} \qquad\qquad \text{False}$$

Note that 5 does not need to satisfy both statements for this compound inequality to be true.

EXAMPLE 1 Determining solutions to compound inequalities

Determine whether the given x-values are solutions to the compound inequalities.
(a) $x + 1 < 9$ and $2x - 1 > 8$ $\qquad x = 5, -5$
(b) $5 - 2x \le -4$ or $5 - 2x \ge 4$ $\qquad x = 2, -3$

Solution
(a) Substitute $x = 5$ in the given compound inequality.

$$\underset{\text{True}}{5 + 1 < 9} \quad \text{and} \quad \underset{\text{True}}{2(5) - 1 > 8}$$

Both inequalities are true, so 5 is a solution. Now substitute $x = -5$.

$$\underset{\text{True}}{-5 + 1 < 9} \quad \text{and} \quad \underset{\text{False}}{2(-5) - 1 > 8}$$

To be a solution both inequalities must be true, so -5 is not a solution.
(b) Substitute $x = 2$ into the given compound inequality.

$$\underset{\text{False}}{5 - 2(2) \le -4} \quad \text{or} \quad \underset{\text{False}}{5 - 2(2) \ge 4}$$

Neither inequality is true, so 2 is not a solution. Now substitute $x = -3$.

$$\underset{\text{False}}{5 - 2(-3) \le -4} \quad \text{or} \quad \underset{\text{True}}{5 - 2(-3) \ge 4}$$

At least one of the two inequalities is true, so -3 is a solution.

Now Try Exercises 7, 9

CRITICAL THINKING

Graph the following inequalities and discuss your results.
1. $x < 2$ and $x > 5$
2. $x > 2$ or $x < 5$

Symbolic Solutions and Number Lines

We can use a number line to graph solutions to compound inequalities, such as

$$x \le 6 \quad \text{and} \quad x > -4.$$

The solution set for $x \le 6$ is shaded to the left of 6, with a bracket placed at $x = 6$, as shown in Figure 3.19. The solution set for $x > -4$ can be shown by shading a different number line to the right of -4 and placing a left parenthesis at -4. Because the inequalities are connected by *and*, the solution set consists of all numbers that are shaded on *both* number lines. The final number line represents the *intersection* of the two solution sets. That is, the solution set includes real numbers where the graphs "overlap." For any two sets A and B, the **intersection** of A and B, denoted $A \cap B$, is defined by

$$A \cap B = \{x \mid x \text{ is an element of } A \text{ and an element of } B\}.$$

Figure 3.19

NOTE: A bracket, either [or], is used when an inequality contains $\le$ or $\ge$. A parenthesis, either (or), is used when an inequality contains $<$ or $>$. This notation makes clear whether an endpoint is included in the inequality.

EXAMPLE 2   Solving a compound inequality containing "and"

Solve $2x + 4 > 8$ and $5 - x < 9$. Graph the solution.

Solution
First solve each linear inequality separately.

$$2x + 4 > 8 \quad \text{and} \quad 5 - x < 9$$
$$2x > 4 \quad \text{and} \quad -x < 4$$
$$x > 2 \quad \text{and} \quad x > -4$$

Graph the two inequalities on two different number lines. On a third number line, shade solutions that appear on both of the first two number lines. As shown in Figure 3.20, the solution set is $\{x \mid x > 2\}$.

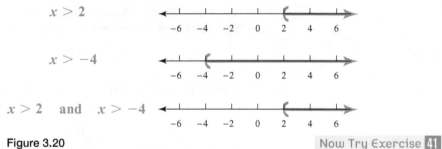

Figure 3.20

Now Try Exercise 41

Sometimes a compound inequality containing the word *and* can be combined into a three-part inequality. For example, rather than writing

$$x > 5 \quad \text{and} \quad x \le 10,$$

we could write the **three-part inequality**

$$5 < x \le 10.$$

This three-part inequality is represented by the number line shown in Figure 3.21.

$5 < x \le 10$

Figure 3.21

EXAMPLE 3   Solving three-part inequalities

Solve each inequality.

(a) $4 < t + 2 \le 8$ **(b)** $-3 \le 3z \le 6$ **(c)** $-\dfrac{5}{2} < \dfrac{1 - m}{2} < 4$

Solution

(a) To solve a three-part inequality, isolate the variable by applying properties of inequalities to each part of the inequality.

$$4 < t + 2 \le 8 \qquad \text{Given three-part inequality}$$
$$4 - 2 < t + 2 - 2 \le 8 - 2 \qquad \text{Subtract 2 from each part.}$$
$$2 < t \le 6 \qquad \text{Simplify each part.}$$

The solution set is $\{t \mid 2 < t \le 6\}$.

(b) To simplify, divide each part by 3.

$$-3 \leq 3z \leq 6 \qquad \text{Given three-part inequality}$$
$$\frac{-3}{3} \leq \frac{3z}{3} \leq \frac{6}{3} \qquad \text{Divide each part by 3.}$$
$$-1 \leq z \leq 2 \qquad \text{Simplify each part.}$$

The solution set is $\{z \mid -1 \leq z \leq 2\}$.

(c) Multiply each part by 2 to clear fractions.

$$-\frac{5}{2} < \frac{1-m}{2} < 4 \qquad \text{Given three-part inequality}$$
$$2 \cdot \left(-\frac{5}{2}\right) < 2 \cdot \left(\frac{1-m}{2}\right) < 2 \cdot 4 \qquad \text{Multiply each part by 2.}$$
$$-5 < 1-m < 8 \qquad \text{Simplify each part.}$$
$$-5 - 1 < 1 - m - 1 < 8 - 1 \qquad \text{Subtract 1 from each part.}$$
$$-6 < -m < 7 \qquad \text{Simplify each part.}$$
$$-1 \cdot (-6) > -1 \cdot (-m) > -1 \cdot 7 \qquad \text{Multiply each part by } -1; \text{ \textit{reverse} inequality symbols.}$$
$$6 > m > -7 \qquad \text{Simplify each part.}$$
$$-7 < m < 6 \qquad \text{Rewrite inequality.}$$

The solution set is $\{m \mid -7 < m < 6\}$.

NOTE: Either $6 > m > -7$ or $-7 < m < 6$ is a correct way to write a three-part inequality. *However*, we usually write the smaller number on the left side and the larger number on the right side. Now Try Exercises **57, 61, 77**

▶ REAL-WORLD CONNECTION Three-part inequalities occur frequently in applications. In the next example we find altitudes at which the air temperature is within a certain range.

EXAMPLE **4** Solving a three-part inequality

If the ground-level temperature is 80°F, the air temperature x miles above Earth's surface is cooler and can be modeled by $T(x) = 80 - 19x$. Find the altitudes at which the air temperature ranges from 42°F down to 23°F. (**Source:** A. Miller and R. Anthes, *Meteorology*.)

Solution
We write and solve the three-part inequality $23 \leq T(x) \leq 42$.

$$23 \leq 80 - 19x \leq 42 \qquad \text{Substitute for } T(x).$$
$$-57 \leq -19x \leq -38 \qquad \text{Subtract 80 from each part.}$$
$$\frac{-57}{-19} \geq x \geq \frac{-38}{-19} \qquad \text{Divide by } -19; \text{ \textit{reverse} inequality symbols.}$$
$$3 \geq x \geq 2 \qquad \text{Simplify.}$$
$$2 \leq x \leq 3 \qquad \text{Rewrite inequality.}$$

The air temperature ranges from 42°F to 23°F for altitudes between 2 and 3 miles.

Now Try Exercise **109**

MAKING CONNECTIONS

Writing Three-Part Inequalities

The inequality $-2 < x < 1$ means that $x > -2$ *and* $x < 1$. A three-part inequality should *not* be used when *or* connects a compound inequality. Writing $x < -2$ or $x > 1$ as $1 < x < -2$ is incorrect because it states that x must be both greater than 1 *and* less than -2. It is impossible for any value of x to satisfy this statement.

We can also solve compound inequalities containing the word *or*. To write the solution to such an inequality we sometimes use *union* notation. For any two sets A and B, the **union** of A and B, denoted $A \cup B$, is defined by

$$A \cup B = \{x \mid x \text{ is an element of } A \text{ or an element of } B\}.$$

If the solution to an inequality is $\{x \mid x < 1\}$ or $\{x \mid x \geq 3\}$, then it can also be written as

$$\{x \mid x < 1\} \cup \{x \mid x \geq 3\}.$$

That is, we can replace the word *or* with the $\cup$ symbol.

EXAMPLE 5   Solving a compound inequality containing "or"

Solve $x + 2 < -1$ or $x + 2 > 1$.

Solution
We first solve each linear inequality.

$$x + 2 < -1 \quad \text{or} \quad x + 2 > 1 \qquad \text{Given compound inequality}$$
$$x < -3 \quad \text{or} \quad x > -1 \qquad \text{Subtract 2.}$$

We can graph the simplified inequalities on different number lines, as shown in Figure 3.22. A solution must satisfy at least one of the two inequalities. Thus the solution set for the compound inequality results from taking the *union* of the first two number lines. We can write the solution, using set-builder notation, as $\{x \mid x < -3\} \cup \{x \mid x > -1\}$ or as $\{x \mid x < -3 \text{ or } x > -1\}$.

$x < -3$

$x > -1$

$x < -3 \quad \text{or} \quad x > -1$

Figure 3.22

Now Try Exercise 45

CRITICAL THINKING

Carbon dioxide is emitted when human beings breathe. In one study of college students, the amount of carbon dioxide exhaled in grams per hour was measured during both lectures and exams. The average amount exhaled during lectures L satisfied $25.33 \le L \le 28.17$, whereas the average amount exhaled during exams E satisfied $36.58 \le E \le 40.92$. What do these results indicate? Explain.   (*Source:* T. Wang, *ASHRAE Trans.*)

Numerical and Graphical Solutions

Compound inequalities can also be solved graphically and numerically, as illustrated in the next example.

EXAMPLE 6   Solving a compound inequality numerically and graphically

Tuition and fees at private colleges and universities from 1980 to 2000 can be modeled by $f(x) = 575(x - 1980) + 3600$. Estimate when the average tuition and fees ranged from $8200 to $10,500.

Solution

Numerical Solution   Let $Y_1 = 575(X - 1980) + 3600$. Make a table of values, as shown in Figure 3.23(a). In 1988, the average tuition and fees were $8200 and in 1992 they were $10,500. Thus from 1988 to 1992 the average tuition and fees ranged from $8200 to $10,500.

Graphical Solution   Graph $Y_1 = 575(X - 1980) + 3600$, $Y_2 = 8200$, and $Y_3 = 10,500$. We must find x-values so that $y_2 \le y_1 \le y_3$. Figures 3.23(b) and (c) show that y_1 is between y_2 and y_3 when $1988 \le x \le 1992$.

[1980, 2000, 1] by [3000, 12000, 3000]   [1980, 2000, 1] by [3000, 12000, 3000]

CALCULATOR HELP

To find a point of intersection, see the Appendix (page AP-7).

(a)

(b)

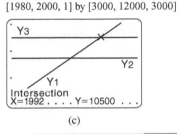

(c)

Figure 3.23

Now Try Exercise 103(b)

Interval Notation

Figure 3.24

The solution set in Example 4 was $\{x \mid 2 \le x \le 3\}$. This solution set can be graphed on a number line, as shown in Figure 3.24.

A convenient notation for number line graphs is called **interval notation**. Instead of drawing the entire number line as in Figure 3.24, the solution set can be expressed as [2, 3] in interval notation. Because the solution set includes the endpoints 2 and 3, brackets are used. A solution set that includes all real numbers satisfying $-2 < x < 3$ can be expressed as $(-2, 3)$. Parentheses indicate that the endpoints are *not* included. The interval $0 \le x < 4$ is represented by $[0, 4)$.

Table 3.6 on the next page provides some examples of interval notation. The symbol ∞ refers to **infinity**, and it does not represent a real number. The interval $(5, \infty)$ represents $x > 5$, which has no maximum x-value, so ∞ is used for the right endpoint. The symbol $-\infty$ may be used similarly and denotes **negative infinity**.

TABLE 3.6   **Interval Notation**

Inequality	Interval Notation	Number Line Graph
$-1 < x < 3$	$(-1, 3)$	
$-3 < x \leq 2$	$(-3, 2]$	
$-2 \leq x \leq 2$	$[-2, 2]$	
$x < -1$ or $x > 2$	$(-\infty, -1) \cup (2, \infty)$ ($\cup$ is the union symbol.)	
$x > -1$	$(-1, \infty)$	
$x \leq 2$	$(-\infty, 2]$	

MAKING CONNECTIONS

Points and Intervals

The expression (1, 2) may represent a point in the xy-plane or the interval $1 < x < 2$. To alleviate confusion, phrases such as "the point (1, 2)" or "the interval (1, 2)" are used.

EXAMPLE 7   Writing inequalities in interval notation

Write each expression in interval notation. `
(a) $-2 \leq x < 5$ (b) $x \geq 3$ (c) $x < -5$ or $x \geq 2$
(d) $\{x \mid x > 0 \text{ and } x \leq 3\}$ (e) $\{x \mid x \leq 1 \text{ or } x \geq 3\}$

Solution
(a) $[-2, 5)$ (b) $[3, \infty)$ (c) $(-\infty, -5) \cup [2, \infty)$
(d) $(0, 3]$ (e) $(-\infty, 1] \cup [3, \infty)$

Now Try Exercises 13, 17, 23, 27, 37

EXAMPLE 8   Solving an inequality

Solve $2x + 1 \leq -1$ or $2x + 1 \geq 3$. Write the solution in interval notation.

Solution
First solve each inequality.

$$2x + 1 \leq -1 \quad \text{or} \quad 2x + 1 \geq 3 \qquad \text{Given compound inequality}$$
$$2x \leq -2 \quad \text{or} \quad 2x \geq 2 \qquad \text{Subtract 1.}$$
$$x \leq -1 \quad \text{or} \quad x \geq 1 \qquad \text{Divide by 2.}$$

The solution set may be written as $(-\infty, -1] \cup [1, \infty)$.

Now Try Exercise 51

3.4 PUTTING IT ALL TOGETHER

The following table summarizes some important topics related to compound inequalities.

Concept	Explanation	Examples
Compound Inequality	Two inequalities joined by *and* or *or*	$x < -1$ or $x > 2$; $2x \geq 10$ and $x + 2 < 6$
Three-Part Inequality	Can be used to write some types of compound inequalities involving *and*	$x > -2$ and $x \leq 3$ is equivalent to $-2 < x \leq 3$.
Interval Notation	Notation used to write sets of real numbers rather than using number lines or inequalities	$-2 \leq z \leq 4$ is equivalent to $[-2, 4]$. $x < 4$ is equivalent to $(-\infty, 4)$. $x \leq -2$ or $x > 0$ is equivalent to $(-\infty, -2] \cup (0, \infty)$.

The following table lists basic strategies for solving compound inequalities.

Type of Inequality	Method to Solve Inequality
Solving a Compound Inequality Containing *and*	**STEP 1:** First solve each inequality individually. **STEP 2:** The solution set includes values that satisfy *both* inequalities from Step 1.
Solving a Compound Inequality Containing *or*	**STEP 1:** First solve each inequality individually. **STEP 2:** The solution set includes values that satisfy *at least one* of the inequalities from Step 1.
Solving a Three-Part Inequality	Work on all three parts at the same time. Be sure to perform the same step on each part. Continue until the variable is isolated in the middle part.

3.4 Exercises

MyMathLab   MathXL PRACTICE   WATCH   DOWNLOAD   READ   REVIEW

CONCEPTS

1. Give an example of a compound inequality containing the word *and*.

2. Give an example of a compound inequality containing the word *or*.

3. Is 1 a solution to $x > 3$ and $x \leq 5$?

4. Is 1 a solution to $x < 3$ or $x \geq 5$?

5. Is the compound inequality $x \geq -5$ and $x \leq 5$ equivalent to $-5 \leq x \leq 5$?

6. Name three ways to solve a compound inequality.

Exercises 7–12: Determine whether the given values of x are solutions to the compound inequality.

7. $x - 1 < 5$ and $2x > 3$ $x = 2, x = 6$

8. $2x + 1 \geq 4$ and $1 - x \leq 3$ $x = -2, x = 3$

9. $3x < -5$ or $2x \geq 3$ $x = 0, x = 3$

10. $x + 1 \leq -4$ or $x + 1 \geq 4$ $x = -5, x = 2$

11. $2 - x > -5$ and $2 - x \leq 4$ $x = -3, x = 0$

12. $x + 5 \geq 6$ or $3x \leq 3$ $x = -1, x = 1$

INTERVAL NOTATION

Exercises 13–38: Write the inequality in interval notation.

13. $2 \leq x \leq 10$ **14.** $-1 < x < 5$

15. $5 < x \leq 8$ **16.** $-\frac{1}{2} \leq x \leq \frac{5}{6}$

17. $x < 4$ **18.** $x \leq -3$

19. $x > -2$ **20.** $x \geq 6$

21. $x \geq -2$ and $x < 5$ **22.** $x \leq 6$ and $x \geq 2$

23. $x \leq 8$ and $x > -8$ **24.** $x \geq -4$ and $x < 3$

25. $x \geq 6$ or $x > 3$ **26.** $x \leq -4$ or $x < -3$

27. $x \leq -2$ or $x \geq 4$ **28.** $x \leq -1$ or $x > 6$

29. $x < 1$ or $x \geq 5$ **30.** $x < -3$ or $x > 3$

31.

32.

33.

34.

35. $\{x \mid x < 4\}$ **36.** $\{x \mid -1 \leq x < 4\}$

37. $\{x \mid x < 1 \text{ or } x > 2\}$ **38.** $\{x \mid -\infty < x < \infty\}$

SYMBOLIC SOLUTIONS

Exercises 39–46: Solve the compound inequality. Graph the solution set on a number line.

39. $x \leq 3$ and $x \geq -1$ **40.** $x \geq 5$ and $x > 6$

41. $2x < 5$ and $2x > -4$

42. $2x + 1 < 3$ and $x - 1 \geq -5$

43. $x \leq -1$ or $x \geq 2$

44. $2x \leq -6$ or $x \geq 6$

45. $5 - x > 1$ or $x + 3 \geq -1$

46. $1 - 2x > 3$ or $2x - 4 \geq 4$

Exercises 47–56: Solve the compound inequality. Write your answer in interval notation.

47. $x - 3 \leq 4$ and $x + 5 \geq -1$

48. $2z \geq -10$ and $z < 8$

49. $3t - 1 > -1$ and $2t - \frac{1}{2} > 6$

50. $2(x + 1) < 8$ and $-2(x - 4) > -2$

51. $x - 4 \geq -3$ or $x - 4 \leq 3$

52. $1 - 3n \geq 6$ or $1 - 3n \leq -4$

53. $-x < 1$ or $5x + 1 < -10$

54. $7x - 6 > 0$ or $-\frac{1}{2}x \leq 6$

55. $1 - 7x < -48$ and $3x + 1 \leq -9$

56. $3x - 4 \leq 8$ or $4x - 1 \leq 13$

Exercises 57–78: Solve the three-part inequality. Write your answer in interval notation.

57. $-2 \leq t + 4 < 5$ **58.** $5 < t - 7 < 10$

59. $-\frac{5}{8} \leq y - \frac{3}{8} < 1$ **60.** $-\frac{1}{2} < y - \frac{3}{2} < \frac{1}{2}$

61. $-27 \leq 3x \leq 9$ **62.** $-4 < 2y < 22$

63. $\frac{1}{2} < -2y \leq 8$ **64.** $-16 \leq -4x \leq 8$

65. $-4 < 5z + 1 \leq 6$ **66.** $-3 \leq 3z + 6 < 9$

67. $3 \leq 4 - n \leq 6$ **68.** $-1 < 3 - n \leq 1$

69. $-1 < 2z - 1 < 3$ **70.** $2 \leq 4z + 5 \leq 6$

71. $-2 \leq 5 - \frac{1}{3}m < 2$ **72.** $-\frac{3}{2} < 4 - 2m < \frac{7}{2}$

73. $100 \leq 10(5x - 2) \leq 200$

74. $-15 < 5(x - 1990) < 30$

75. $-3 < \dfrac{3z + 1}{4} < 1$ **76.** $-3 < \dfrac{z - 1}{2} < 5$

77. $-\dfrac{5}{2} \le \dfrac{2-m}{4} \le \dfrac{1}{2}$ **78.** $\dfrac{4}{5} \le \dfrac{4-2m}{10} \le 2$

NUMERICAL AND GRAPHICAL SOLUTIONS

Exercises 79–82: Use the table to solve the three-part inequality. Write your answer in interval notation.

79. $-3 \le 3x \le 6$ **80.** $-5 \le 2x - 1 \le 1$

81. $-1 < 1 - x < 2$ **82.** $-2 \le -2x < 4$

    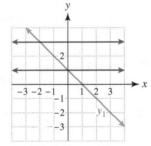

Exercises 83–86: Use the graph to solve the compound inequality. Write your answer in interval notation.

83. $-2 \le y_1 \le 2$ **84.** $1 \le y_1 < 3$

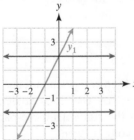

85. $y_1 < -2$ or $y_1 > 2$ **86.** $y_1 \le -2$ or $y_1 \ge 4$

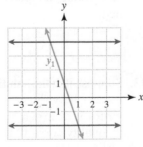

87. *Distance* The function f, shown in the figure, gives the distance y in miles between a car and the city of Omaha, Nebraska, after x hours, where $0 \le x \le 6$.

(a) Is the car moving toward or away from Omaha? Explain.

(b) Determine the times when the car is 100 miles or 200 miles from Omaha.

(c) When is the car from 100 to 200 miles from Omaha?

(d) When is the car's distance from Omaha greater than or equal to 200 miles?

88. Use the figure to solve each equation or inequality. Let the domains of y_1, y_2, and y_3 be $0 \le x \le 5$.

(a) $y_1 = y_2$ **(b)** $y_2 = y_3$

(c) $y_1 \le y_2 \le y_3$ **(d)** $y_2 < y_3$

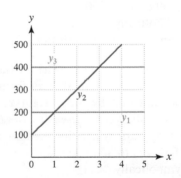

Exercises 89–94: Solve numerically or graphically. Write your answer in interval notation.

89. $-2 \le 2x - 4 \le 4$

90. $-1 \le 1 - x \le 3$

91. $x + 1 < -1$ or $x + 1 > 1$

92. $2x - 1 < -3$ or $2x - 1 > 5$

93. $95 \le 25(x - 2000) + 45 \le 295$

94. $42 \le -13(x - 2005) + 120 \le 94$

USING MORE THAN ONE METHOD

Exercises 95–100: Solve symbolically, graphically, and numerically. Write the solution set in interval notation.

95. $4 \le 5x - 1 \le 14$

96. $-4 < 2x < 4$

97. $4 - x \ge 1$ or $4 - x < 3$

98. $x + 3 \ge -2$ or $x + 3 \le 1$

99. $2x + 1 < 3$ or $2x + 1 \ge 7$

100. $3 - x \le 4$ or $3 - x > 8$

101. Thinking Generally   Solve $c < x + b \le d$ for x.

102. Thinking Generally   Solve $c \le ax + b \le d$ for x, if $a < 0$.

APPLICATIONS

103. *Home Prices*   The average price P of a single-family home in thousands of dollars from 1990 to 2000 can be modeled by $P(x) = 5.7(x - 1990) + 150$, where x is the year.   (**Source:** U.S. Census Bureau.) Determine the years when the average price ranged from $178,500 to $207,000
(**a**) symbolically,
(**b**) graphically or numerically.

104. *Median Family Income*   The median income I of a family in thousands of dollars from 2000 to 2005 can be modeled by $I(x) = 1.4(x - 2000) + 51$, where x is the year. (**Source:** U.S. Census Bureau.) Determine the years when the median income ranged from $52,400 to $56,600
(**a**) symbolically,
(**b**) graphically or numerically.

105. *Altitude and Dew Point*   If the dew point D on the ground is 60°F, then the dew point x miles high is given by $D(x) = 60 - 5.8x$. Find the altitudes where the dew point ranges from 57.1°F to 51.3°F. (**Source:** A. Miller.)

106. *Medicare Costs*   Medicare costs in billions of dollars may be modeled by $f(x) = 18x - 35{,}750$, where $1995 \le x \le 2007$. Estimate the years when Medicare costs were from 250 to 340 billion dollars.
(**Source:** Office of Management and Budget.)

107. *Geometry*   For what values of x is the perimeter of the rectangle from 40 to 60 feet?

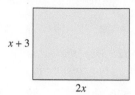

108. *Geometry*   A rectangle is three times as long as it is wide. If the perimeter ranges from 100 to 160 inches, what values for the width are possible?

109. *Altitude and Temperature*   If the air temperature at ground level is 70°F, the air temperature x miles high is given by $T(x) = 70 - 19x$. Determine the altitudes at which the air temperature is from 41.5°F to 22.5°F.   (**Source:** A. Miller and R. Anthes, *Meteorology*.)

110. *Distance*   A car's distance in miles from a rest stop after x hours is given by $f(x) = 70x + 50$.
(**a**) Construct a table for f for $x = 4, 5, 6, \ldots, 10$ and use the table to solve the inequality $470 \le f(x) \le 680$. Explain your result.
(**b**) Solve the inequality in part (a) symbolically.

111. *Temperature*   The formula $F = \frac{9}{5}C + 32$ may be used to convert Celsius temperatures to Fahrenheit temperatures. The greatest temperature ranges on Earth are recorded in Siberia where the temperature has varied from $-90°$F to $98°$F. Find this temperature range in degrees Celsius.

112. *Temperature*   The formula $C = \frac{5}{9}(F - 32)$ may be used to convert Fahrenheit temperatures to Celsius temperatures. If the Celsius temperature ranges from 5°C to 20°C, use this formula to find the corresponding temperature range in degrees Fahrenheit.

WRITING ABOUT MATHEMATICS

113. Suppose that the solution set for a compound inequality can be written as $x < -3$ or $x > 2$. A student writes it as $2 < x < -3$. Is the student's three-part inequality correct? Explain your answer.

114. How can you determine whether an x-value is a solution to a compound inequality containing the word *and*? Give an example. Repeat the question for a compound inequality connected by the word *or*.

CHECKING BASIC CONCEPTS
SECTIONS 3.3 AND 3.4

1. Solve the linear inequality $4 - 3x < \frac{1}{2}x$.

2. Use the graph to solve each equation or inequality.

(a) $\frac{1}{2}x - 1 = 2 - x$

(b) $\frac{1}{2}x - 1 < 2 - x$

(c) $\frac{1}{2}x - 1 \geq 2 - x$

3. (a) Is 3 a solution to the compound inequality $x + 2 < 4$ or $2x - 1 \geq 3$?

(b) Is 3 a solution to the compound inequality $x + 2 < 4$ and $2x - 1 \geq 3$?

4. Solve each compound inequality. Write your answers in interval notation.

(a) $-5 \leq 2x + 1 \leq 3$

(b) $1 - x \leq -2$ or $1 - x > 2$

(c) $-2 < \dfrac{4 - 3x}{2} \leq 6$

3.5 ABSOLUTE VALUE EQUATIONS AND INEQUALITIES

Basic Concepts ▪ Absolute Value Equations ▪ Absolute Value Inequalities

A LOOK INTO MATH ▷

Monthly average temperatures can vary greatly from one month to another, whereas yearly average temperatures remain fairly constant from one year to the next. In Boston, Massachusetts, the yearly average temperature is 50°F, but monthly average temperatures can vary from 28°F to 72°F. Because 50°F − 28°F = 22°F and 72°F − 50°F = 22°F, the monthly average temperatures are always within 22°F of the yearly average temperature. If T represents a monthly average temperature, we can model this situation by using the absolute value inequality

$$|T - 50| \leq 22.$$

The absolute value is necessary because a monthly average temperature T can be either greater than or less than 50°F by as much as 22°F. In this section we discuss absolute value equations and inequalities. (***Source:*** A. Miller and J. Thompson, *Elements of Meteorology*.)

Basic Concepts

In Chapter 1 we discussed the absolute value of a number. We can define the **absolute value function** by $f(x) = |x|$. To graph $y = |x|$, we begin by making a table of values, as shown in Table 3.7. Next we plot these points and then sketch the graph shown in Figure 3.25. Note that the graph is V-shaped.

TABLE 3.7

x	$\|x\|$
-2	2
-1	1
0	0
1	1
2	2

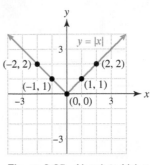

Figure 3.25 Absolute Value

Because the input for $f(x) = |x|$ is any real number, the domain of f is all real numbers, or $(-\infty, \infty)$. The graph of the absolute value function shows that the output y (range) is any real number greater than or equal to 0. That is, the range is $[0, \infty)$.

Absolute Value Equations

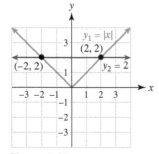

Figure 3.26

An equation that contains an absolute value is an **absolute value equation**. Examples are

$$|x| = 2, \quad |2x - 1| = 5, \quad \text{and} \quad |5 - 3x| - 3 = 1.$$

Consider the absolute value equation $|x| = 2$. This equation has *two* solutions: 2 and -2 because $|2| = 2$ and $|-2| = 2$. We can also demonstrate this result with a table of values or a graph. Refer back to Table 3.7: $|x| = 2$ when $x = -2$ or $x = 2$. In Figure 3.26 the graph of $y_1 = |x|$ intersects the graph of $y_2 = 2$ at the points $(-2, 2)$ and $(2, 2)$. The x-values at these points of intersection correspond to the solutions -2 and 2.

We generalize this discussion in the following manner.

SOLVING $|x| = k$

1. If $k > 0$, then $|x| = k$ is equivalent to $x = k$ or $x = -k$.
2. If $k = 0$, then $|x| = k$ is equivalent to $x = 0$.
3. If $k < 0$, then $|x| = k$ has no solutions.

EXAMPLE 1   Solving absolute value equations

Solve each equation.
(a) $|x| = 20$ **(b)** $|x| = -5$

Solution
(a) The solutions are -20 and 20.
(b) There are no solutions because $|x|$ is never negative.

Now Try Exercises 17, 19

EXAMPLE 2   Solving an absolute value equation

Solve $|2x - 5| = 3$ symbolically.

Solution

If $|2x - 5| = 3$, then either $2x - 5 = 3$ or $2x - 5 = -3$. Solve each equation separately.

$$2x - 5 = 3 \quad \text{or} \quad 2x - 5 = -3 \qquad \text{Equations to be solved}$$
$$2x = 8 \quad \text{or} \qquad 2x = 2 \qquad \text{Add 5.}$$
$$x = 4 \quad \text{or} \qquad x = 1 \qquad \text{Divide by 2.}$$

The solutions are 1 and 4.   Now Try Exercise 25

A table of values can be used to solve the equation $|2x - 5| = 3$ from Example 2. Table 3.8 shows that $|2x - 5| = 3$ when $x = 1$ or $x = 4$.

Numerical Solution

TABLE 3.8

x	0	1	2	3	4	5	6
$|2x - 5|$	5	3	1	1	3	5	7

Graphical Solution

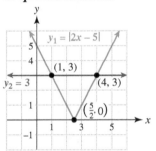

Figure 3.27

This equation can also be solved by graphing $y_1 = |2x - 5|$ and $y_2 = 3$. To graph y_1, first plot some of the points from Table 3.8. Its graph is V-shaped, as shown in Figure 3.27. Note that the x-coordinate of the "point" or vertex of the V can be found by solving the equation $2x - 5 = 0$ to obtain $\frac{5}{2}$. The graph of y_1 intersects the graph of y_2 at the points $(1, 3)$ and $(4, 3)$, giving the solutions 1 and 4, so the graphical solutions agree with the numerical and symbolic solutions.

This discussion leads to the following result.

ABSOLUTE VALUE EQUATIONS

If $k > 0$, then

$$|ax + b| = k$$

is equivalent to

$$ax + b = k \quad \text{or} \quad ax + b = -k.$$

EXAMPLE 3   Solving absolute value equations

Solve.
(a) $|5 - x| - 2 = 8$ (b) $\left|\frac{1}{2}(x - 6)\right| = \frac{3}{4}$

Solution
(a) Start by adding 2 to each side to obtain $|5 - x| = 10$. This new equation is satisfied by the solution from either of the following equations.

$$
\begin{array}{lll}
5 - x = 10 & \text{or} & 5 - x = -10 \qquad \text{Equations to be solved} \\
-x = 5 & \text{or} & -x = -15 \qquad \text{Subtract 5.} \\
x = -5 & \text{or} & x = 15 \qquad \text{Multiply by } -1.
\end{array}
$$

The solutions are -5 and 15.

(b) This equation is satisfied by the solution from either of the following equations.

$$
\begin{array}{lll}
\frac{1}{2}(x - 6) = \frac{3}{4} & \text{or} & \frac{1}{2}(x - 6) = -\frac{3}{4} \qquad \text{Equations to be solved} \\
2(x - 6) = 3 & \text{or} & 2(x - 6) = -3 \qquad \text{Multiply by 4 to clear fractions.} \\
2x - 12 = 3 & \text{or} & 2x - 12 = -3 \qquad \text{Distributive property} \\
2x = 15 & \text{or} & 2x = 9 \qquad \text{Add 12.} \\
x = \frac{15}{2} & \text{or} & x = \frac{9}{2} \qquad \text{Divide by 2.}
\end{array}
$$

The solutions are $\frac{9}{2}$ and $\frac{15}{2}$.   Now Try Exercises 27, 29

The next example illustrates absolute value equations that have either no solutions or one solution.

EXAMPLE 4   Solving absolute value equations

Solve.
(a) $|2x - 1| = -2$ (b) $|4 - 2x| = 0$

Solution
(a) Because an absolute value is never negative, there are no solutions. Figure 3.28 shows that the graph of $y_1 = |2x - 1|$ never intersects the graph of $y_2 = -2$.
(b) If $|y| = 0$, then $y = 0$. Thus $|4 - 2x| = 0$ when $4 - 2x = 0$ or when $x = 2$. The solution is 2.   Now Try Exercises 31, 32

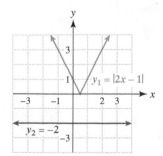

Figure 3.28

Sometimes an equation can have an absolute value on each side. An example would be $|2x| = |x - 3|$. In this situation either $2x = x - 3$ (the two expressions are equal), or $2x = -(x - 3)$ (the two expressions are opposites).

These concepts are summarized as follows.

SOLVING $|ax + b| = |cx + d|$

Let a, b, c, and d be constants. Then $|ax + b| = |cx + d|$ is equivalent to

$$ax + b = cx + d \quad \text{or} \quad ax + b = -(cx + d).$$

EXAMPLE 5   Solving an absolute value equation

Solve $|2x| = |x - 3|$.

Solution
Solve the following compound equality.

$$
\begin{aligned}
2x &= x - 3 &&\text{or} & 2x &= -(x - 3) \\
x &= -3 &&\text{or} & 2x &= -x + 3 \\
& && & 3x &= 3 \\
& && & x &= 1
\end{aligned}
$$

The solutions are -3 and 1.

Now Try Exercise 35

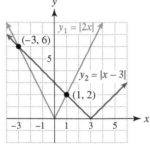

Figure 3.29

Example 5 is solved graphically in Figure 3.29. The graphs of $y_1 = |2x|$ and $y_2 = |x - 3|$ are V-shaped and intersect at $(-3, 6)$ and $(1, 2)$. The solutions are -3 and 1.

Absolute Value Inequalities

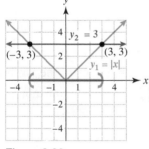

Figure 3.30

We can solve absolute value inequalities graphically. For example, to solve $|x| < 3$, let $y_1 = |x|$ and $y_2 = 3$ (see Figure 3.30). Their graphs intersect at $(-3, 3)$ and $(3, 3)$. The graph of y_1 is *below* the graph of y_2 for x-values *between*, but not including, $x = -3$ and $x = 3$. The solution set is $\{x \mid -3 < x < 3\}$ and is shaded on the x-axis.

Other absolute value inequalities can be solved graphically in a similar way. In Figure 3.31 the solutions to $|2x - 1| = 3$ are -1 and 2. The V-shaped graph of $y_1 = |2x - 1|$ is below the horizontal line $y_2 = 3$ when $-1 < x < 2$. Thus $|2x - 1| < 3$ whenever $-1 < x < 2$. The solution set is shaded on the x-axis.

Figure 3.31 $y_1 < y_2$

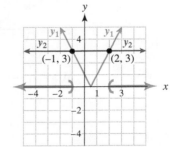

Figure 3.32 $y_1 > y_2$

In Figure 3.32 the V-shaped graph of $y_1 = |2x - 1|$ is above the horizontal line $y_2 = 3$ both to the left of -1 and to the right of 2. That is, $|2x - 1| > 3$ whenever $x < -1$ or $x > 2$. The solution set is shaded on the x-axis.

This discussion is summarized as follows.

ABSOLUTE VALUE INEQUALITIES

Let the solutions to $|ax + b| = k$ be c and d, where $c < d$ and $k > 0$.

1. $|ax + b| < k$ is equivalent to $c < x < d$.
2. $|ax + b| > k$ is equivalent to $x < c$ or $x > d$.

Similar statements can be made for inequalities involving $\leq$ or $\geq$.

EXAMPLE 6   Solving absolute value equations and inequalities

Solve each absolute value equation and inequality.
(a) $|2 - 3x| = 4$ (b) $|2 - 3x| < 4$ (c) $|2 - 3x| > 4$

Solution
(a) The given equation is equivalent to the following equations.

$$2 - 3x = 4 \quad \text{or} \quad 2 - 3x = -4 \qquad \text{Equations to be solved}$$
$$-3x = 2 \quad \text{or} \quad -3x = -6 \qquad \text{Subtract 2.}$$
$$x = -\frac{2}{3} \quad \text{or} \quad x = 2 \qquad \text{Divide by } -3.$$

The solutions are $-\frac{2}{3}$ and 2.

(b) Solutions to $|2 - 3x| < 4$ include x-values **between**, but not including, $-\frac{2}{3}$ and 2. Thus the solution set is $\{x \mid -\frac{2}{3} < x < 2\}$, or in interval notation, $\left(-\frac{2}{3}, 2\right)$.

(c) Solutions to $|2 - 3x| > 4$ include x-values to the **left** of $x = -\frac{2}{3}$ or to the **right** of $x = 2$. Thus the solution set is $\{x \mid x < -\frac{2}{3} \text{ or } x > 2\}$, or in interval notation, $\left(-\infty, -\frac{2}{3}\right) \cup (2, \infty)$.   Now Try Exercise 43

EXAMPLE 7   Solving an absolute value inequality

Solve $\left|\frac{2x - 5}{3}\right| > 3$. Write the solution set in interval notation.

Solution
We can remove the absolute value symbols for $\left|\frac{2x - 5}{3}\right| > 3$ and solve as follows.

$$\frac{2x - 5}{3} > 3 \quad \text{or} \quad \frac{2x - 5}{3} < -3 \qquad \text{Equations to be solved}$$
$$2x - 5 > 9 \quad \text{or} \quad 2x - 5 < -9 \qquad \text{Multiply by 3.}$$
$$2x > 14 \quad \text{or} \quad 2x < -4 \qquad \text{Add 5.}$$
$$x > 7 \quad \text{or} \quad x < -2 \qquad \text{Divide by 2.}$$

The solution in interval notation is $(-\infty, -2) \cup (7, \infty)$.

Now Try Exercise 71

The results from Examples 6 and 7 can be generalized as follows.

INEQUALITIES AND ABSOLUTE VALUES

If $k > 0$ and $y = f(x)$, then

$$|y| < k \text{ is equivalent to } -k < y < k \text{ and}$$

$$|y| > k \text{ is equivalent to } y < -k \text{ or } y > k.$$

Similar statements can be made for inequalities involving $\leq$ and $\geq$.

In the next example, we use the fact that $-k \leq y \leq k$ is equivalent to $|y| \leq k$.

EXAMPLE 8   Analyzing error

An engineer is designing a circular cover for a container. The diameter d of the cover is to be 4.25 inches and must be accurate to within 0.01 inch. Write an absolute value inequality that gives acceptable values for d.

Solution
The diameter d must satisfy $4.24 \leq d \leq 4.26$. Subtracting 4.25 from each part gives

$$-0.01 \leq d - 4.25 \leq 0.01,$$

which is equivalent to $|d - 4.25| \leq 0.01$.   Now Try Exercise 113

EXAMPLE 9   Modeling temperature in Boston

CALCULATOR HELP

To graph an absolute value, see the Appendix (page AP-7).

[0, 100, 10] by [0, 70, 10]

(a)

[0, 100, 10] by [0, 70, 10]

(b)

Figure 3.33

In the introduction to this section we discussed how the inequality $|T - 50| \leq 22$ models the range for the monthly average temperatures T in Boston, Massachusetts.
(a) Solve this inequality and interpret the result.
(b) Give graphical support for part (a).

Solution
(a) *Symbolic Solution*   Start by solving $|T - 50| = 22$.

$$T - 50 = 22 \quad \text{or} \quad T - 50 = -22 \qquad \text{Equations to be solved}$$

$$T = 72 \quad \text{or} \qquad T = 28 \qquad \text{Add 50 to each side.}$$

Thus the solution set to $|T - 50| \leq 22$ is $\{T \mid 28 \leq T \leq 72\}$. Monthly average temperatures in Boston vary from 28°F to 72°F.

(b) *Graphical Solution*   The graphs of $y_1 = |x - 50|$ and $y_2 = 22$ intersect at $(28, 22)$ and $(72, 22)$, as shown in Figures 3.33(a) and (b). The V-shaped graph of y_1 intersects the horizontal graph of y_2, or is below it, when $28 \leq x \leq 72$. Thus the solution set is $\{T \mid 28 \leq T \leq 72\}$. This result agrees with the symbolic result.   Now Try Exercise 105

Sometimes the solution set to an absolute value inequality can be either the empty set or the set of all real numbers. These two situations are illustrated in the next example.

EXAMPLE 10   Solving absolute value inequalities

Solve if possible.
(a) $|2x - 5| > -1$ **(b)** $|5x - 1| + 3 \le 2$

Solution
(a) Because the absolute value of an expression cannot be negative, $|2x - 5|$ is greater than -1 for every x-value. The solution set is all real numbers, or $(-\infty, \infty)$.
(b) Subtracting 3 from each side results in $|5x - 1| \le -1$. Because the absolute value is always greater than or equal to 0, no x-values satisfy this inequality. There are no solutions.

Now Try Exercises 63, 65

3.5 PUTTING IT ALL TOGETHER

The absolute value function is given by $f(x) = |x|$, and its graph is V-shaped. Its domain (set of valid inputs) includes all real numbers, and its range (outputs) includes all nonnegative real numbers. The following table summarizes methods for solving absolute value equations and inequalities involving $<$ and $>$ symbols. Inequalities containing $\le$ and $\ge$ symbols are solved similarly.

Problem	Symbolic Solution	Graphical Solution
$|ax + b| = k, k > 0$	Solve the equations $$ax + b = k$$ and $$ax + b = -k.$$	Graph $y_1 = |ax + b|$ and $y_2 = k$. Find the x-values of the two points of intersection.
$|ax + b| < k, k > 0$	If the solutions to $$|ax + b| = k$$ are c and d, $c < d$, then the solutions to $$|ax + b| < k$$ satisfy $$c < x < d.$$	Graph $y_1 = |ax + b|$ and $y_2 = k$. Find the x-values of the two points of intersection. The solutions are between these x-values on the number line, where the graph of y_1 lies below the graph of y_2.
$|ax + b| > k, k > 0$	If the solutions to $$|ax + b| = k$$ are c and d, $c < d$, then the solutions to $$|ax + b| > k$$ satisfy $$x < c \quad \text{or} \quad x > d.$$	Graph $y_1 = |ax + b|$ and $y_2 = k$. Find the x-values of the two points of intersection. The solutions are outside these x-values on the number line, where the graph of y_1 is above the graph of y_2.

3.5 Exercises

CONCEPTS

1. Give an example of an absolute value equation.

2. Give an example of an absolute value inequality.

3. Is -3 a solution to $|x| = 3$?

4. Is -4 a solution to $|x| > 3$?

5. Is $|x| = 5$ equivalent to $x = -5$ or $x = 5$?

6. Is $|x| < 3$ equivalent to $x < -3$ or $x > 3$? Explain.

7. How many times does the graph of $y = |2x - 1|$ intersect the graph of $y = 5$?

8. How many times does the graph of $y = |2x - 1|$ intersect the graph of $y = -5$?

Exercises 9–14: Determine whether the given values of x are solutions to the absolute value equation or inequality.

9. $|2x - 5| = 1$ $x = -3, x = 3$

10. $|5 - 6x| = 1$ $x = 1, x = 0$

11. $|7 - 4x| \le 5$ $x = -2, x = 2$

12. $|2 + x| < 2$ $x = -4, x = -1$

13. $|7x + 4| > -1$ $x = -\frac{4}{7}, x = 2$

14. $|12x + 3| \ge 3$ $x = -\frac{1}{4}, x = 2$

Exercises 15 and 16: Use the graph to solve the equation.

15. $y_1 = 2$

16. $y_1 = 3$

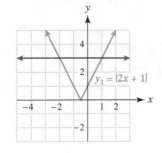

SYMBOLIC SOLUTIONS

Exercises 17–40: Solve the absolute value equation.

17. $|x| = 7$

18. $|x| = 4$

19. $|x| = -6$

20. $|x| = 0$

21. $|4x| = 9$

22. $|-3x| = 7$

23. $|-2x| - 6 = 2$

24. $|5x| + 1 = 5$

25. $|2x + 1| = 11$

26. $|1 - 3x| = 4$

27. $|-2x + 3| + 3 = 4$

28. $|6x + 2| - 2 = 6$

29. $\left|\frac{1}{2}x - 1\right| = 5$

30. $\left|6 - \frac{3}{4}x\right| = 3$

31. $|2x - 6| = -7$

32. $\left|1 - \frac{2}{3}x\right| = 0$

33. $\left|\frac{2}{3}z - 1\right| - 3 = 8$

34. $|1 - 2z| + 5 = 10$

35. $|z - 1| = |2z|$

36. $|2z + 3| = |2 - z|$

37. $|3t + 1| = |2t - 4|$

38. $\left|\frac{1}{2}t - 1\right| = \left|3 - \frac{3}{2}t\right|$

39. $\left|\frac{1}{4}x\right| = \left|3 + \frac{1}{4}x\right|$

40. $|2x - 1| = |2x + 2|$

Exercises 41–44: Solve each equation or inequality.

41. (a) $|2x| = 8$ (b) $|2x| < 8$
    (c) $|2x| > 8$

42. (a) $|3x - 9| = 6$
    (b) $|3x - 9| \le 6$
    (c) $|3x - 9| \ge 6$

43. (a) $|5 - 4x| = 3$ (b) $|5 - 4x| \le 3$
    (c) $|5 - 4x| \ge 3$

44. (a) $\left|\dfrac{x - 5}{2}\right| = 2$ (b) $\left|\dfrac{x - 5}{2}\right| < 2$

    (c) $\left|\dfrac{x - 5}{2}\right| > 2$

Exercises 45–76: Solve the absolute value inequality. Write your answer in interval notation.

45. $|x| \le 3$

46. $|x| < 2$

47. $|k| > 4$

48. $|k| \ge 5$

49. $|t| \leq -3$ **50.** $|t| < -1$

51. $|z| > 0$ **52.** $|2z| \geq 0$

53. $|2x| > 7$ **54.** $|-12x| < 30$

55. $|-4x + 4| < 16$ **56.** $|-5x - 8| > 2$

57. $2|x + 5| \geq 8$ **58.** $-3|x - 1| \geq -9$

59. $|8 - 6x| - 1 \leq 2$ **60.** $4 - \left|\dfrac{2x}{3}\right| < -7$

61. $5 + \left|\dfrac{2 - x}{3}\right| \leq 9$ **62.** $\left|\dfrac{x + 3}{5}\right| \leq 12$

63. $|2x - 1| \leq -3$ **64.** $|x + 6| \geq -5$

65. $|x + 1| - 1 > -3$ **66.** $-2|1 - 7x| \geq 2$

67. $|2z - 4| \leq -1$ **68.** $|4 - z| \leq 0$

69. $|3z - 1| > -3$ **70.** $|2z| \geq -2$

71. $\left|\dfrac{2 - t}{3}\right| \geq 5$ **72.** $\left|\dfrac{2t + 3}{5}\right| \geq 7$

73. $|t - 1| \leq 0.1$ **74.** $|t - 2| \leq 0.01$

75. $|b - 10| > 0.5$ **76.** $|b - 25| \geq 1$

NUMERICAL AND GRAPHICAL SOLUTIONS

Exercises 77 and 78: Use the table of $y = |ax + b|$ to solve each equation or inequality. Write your answers in interval notation for parts (b) and (c).

77. (a) $y = 2$ **(b)** $y < 2$ **(c)** $y > 2$

x	-2	-1	0	1	2	3	4
y	3	2	1	0	1	2	3

78. (a) $y = 6$ **(b)** $y \leq 6$ **(c)** $y \geq 6$

x	-12	-6	0	6	12	18	24
y	9	6	3	0	3	6	9

Exercises 79 and 80: Use the graph of y_1 to solve each equation or inequality. Write your answers in interval notation for parts (b) and (c).

79. (a) $y_1 = 1$ **(b)** $y_1 \leq 1$ **(c)** $y_1 \geq 1$

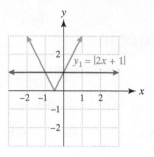

80. (a) $y_1 = 3$ **(b)** $y_1 < 3$ **(c)** $y_1 > 3$

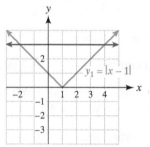

Exercises 81–90: Solve the inequality graphically. Write your answer in interval notation.

81. $|x| \geq 1$ **82.** $|x| < 2$

83. $|x - 1| \leq 3$ **84.** $|x + 5| \geq 2$

85. $|4 - 2x| > 2$ **86.** $|1.5x - 3| \geq 6$

87. $|10 - 3x| < 4$ **88.** $|7 - 4x| \leq 2.5$

89. $|8.1 - x| > -2$ **90.** $\left|\dfrac{5x - 9}{2}\right| \leq -1$

USING MORE THAN ONE METHOD

Exercises 91–94: Solve the absolute value inequality

     (a) symbolically,
     (b) graphically, and
     (c) numerically.

Write your answer in set-builder notation.

91. $|3x| \leq 9$ **92.** $|5 - x| \geq 3$

93. $|2x - 5| > 1$ **94.** $|-8 - 4x| < 6$

WRITING ABSOLUTE VALUE EQUATIONS

Exercises 95–102: Write each compound inequality as an absolute value inequality. Do not simplify Exercises 99–102.

95. $-4 \leq x \leq 4$ **96.** $-0.1 < y < 0.1$

97. $y < -2$ or $y > 2$ **98.** $-0.1 \leq x \leq 0.1$

$|d| \geq 2.502$

99. $-0.3 \leq 2x + 1 \leq 0.3$

100. $4x < -5$ or $4x > 5$

101. $\pi x \leq -7$ or $\pi x \geq 7$

102. $-0.9 \leq x - \sqrt{2} \leq 0.9$

103. **Thinking Generally**   If $a \neq 0$ and $k > 0$, then the graph of $y = |ax + b|$ intersects the graph of $y = k$ at _____ points.

104. **Thinking Generally**   If a and k are positive, then the solution set to $|ax + b| < k$ is _____.

APPLICATIONS

Exercises 105–108: Average Temperatures (Refer to Example 9.) The given inequality models the range for the monthly average temperatures T in degrees Fahrenheit at the location specified.

(a) Solve the inequality.

(b) Give a possible interpretation of the inequality.

105. $|T - 43| \leq 24$, Marquette, Michigan

106. $|T - 62| \leq 19$, Memphis, Tennessee

107. $|T - 10| \leq 36$, Chesterfield, Canada

108. $|T - 61.5| \leq 12.5$, Buenos Aires, Argentina

109. *Highest Elevations*   The table lists the highest elevation in each continent.

Continent	Elevation (feet)
Asia	29,028
S. America	22,834
N. America	20,320
Africa	19,340
Europe	18,510
Antarctica	16,066
Australia	7,310

Source: National Geographic.

(a) Calculate the average A of these elevations.

(b) Which continents have their highest elevations within 1000 feet of A?

(c) Which continents have their highest elevations within 5000 feet of A?

110. *Distance*   Suppose that two cars, both traveling at a constant speed of 60 miles per hour, approach each other on a straight highway.

(a) If they are initially 4 miles apart, sketch a graph of the distance between the cars after x minutes, where $0 \leq x \leq 4$. (*Hint:* 60 miles per hour = 1 mile per minute.)

(b) Write an absolute value equation whose solution gives the times when the cars are 2 miles apart.

(c) Solve your equation from part (b).

111. *Error in Measurements*   Products are often manufactured to be a given size or shape to within a certain tolerance. For instance, if an aluminum can is supposed to have a diameter of 2.5 inches, either 2.501 inches or 2.499 inches might be acceptable. If the maximum error in the diameter of the can is restricted to 0.002 inch, an acceptable diameter d must satisfy the absolute value inequality

$$|d - 2.5| \leq 0.002.$$

Solve this inequality for d and interpret the result.

112. *Error in Measurements*   (Refer to the preceding exercise.) Suppose that a person can operate a stopwatch accurately to within 0.02 second. If a runner's time in the 400-meter dash is recorded as 51.57 seconds, write an absolute value inequality that gives the possible values for the actual time t.

113. *Error in Measurements*   A circular lid is being designed for a container. The diameter d of the lid is to be 3.8 inches and must be accurate to within 0.03 inch. Write an absolute value inequality that gives acceptable values for d.

114. *Manufacturing a Tire*   An engineer is designing a tire for a truck. The diameter d of the tire is to be 36 inches and the circumference must be accurate to within 0.1 inch. Write an absolute value inequality that gives acceptable values for d.

115. *Relative Error*   If a quantity is measured to be x and the true value is t, then the relative error in the measurement is $\left|\frac{x-t}{t}\right|$. If the true measurement is $t = 20$ and you want the relative error to be less than 0.05 (5%), what values for x are possible?

116. *Relative Error*   (Refer to the preceding exercise.) The volume V of a box is 50 cubic inches. How accurately must you measure the volume of the box for the relative error to be less than 3%?

WRITING ABOUT MATHEMATICS

117. If $a \neq 0$, how many solutions are there to the equation $|ax + b| = k$ when
(a) $k > 0$,   **(b)** $k = 0$, and   **(c)** $k < 0$?
Explain each answer.

118. Suppose that you know two solutions to the equation $|ax + b| = k$. How can you use these solutions to solve the inequalities $|ax + b| < k$ and $|ax + b| > k$? Give an example.

CHECKING BASIC CONCEPTS
SECTION 3.5

Write answers in interval notation whenever possible.

1. Solve $\left|\frac{3}{4}x - 1\right| - 3 = 5$.

2. Solve the absolute value equation and inequalities.
   (a) $|3x - 6| = 8$
   (b) $|3x - 6| < 8$
   (c) $|3x - 6| > 8$

3. Solve the inequality $|-2(3 - x)| < 6$. Then solve $|-2(3 - x)| \geq 6$.

4. Use the graph to solve the equation and inequalities.

   (a) $|2x - 4| = 2$ **(b)** $|2x - 4| \leq 2$
   (c) $|2x - 4| \geq 2$

CHAPTER 3   SUMMARY
SECTION 3.1   LINEAR EQUATIONS

Linear Equations in One Variable
Can be written as $ax + b = 0$, where $a \neq 0$. Linear equations have *one* solution.

Examples: $3x - 5 = 0$ and $x + 2 = 1 - 3x$

Symbolic, Graphical, and Numerical Solutions

Example: Solve $3x - 1 = 2$.

Symbolic Solution	Numerical Solution	Graphical Solution

Symbolic Solution

$3x - 1 = 2$

$3x = 3$

$x = 1$

The solution is 1.

Numerical Solution

x	$3x - 1$
0	−1
1	2
2	5
3	8

$3x - 1 = 2$ when $x = 1$.

Graphical Solution

The solution is 1.

Lines

Standard Form $ax + by = c$, where a, b, and c are constants with a and b not both 0.

Finding x-intercepts   Let $y = 0$ and solve for x.

Finding y-intercepts   Let $x = 0$ and solve for y.

Example: $3x - 4y = 24$

$3x - 4(0) = 24$ implies $x = 8$; x-intercept is 8.

$3(0) - 4y = 24$ implies $y = -6$; y-intercept is −6.

Identities and Contradictions

An *identity* is an equation that is always true, regardless of the values of any variables. A *contradiction* is an equation that is always false, regardless of the values of any variables.

Examples: $x + 3x = 4x$ (identity); $4x + 5 = 4x + 1$ (contradiction)

SECTION 3.2 ■ INTRODUCTION TO PROBLEM SOLVING

Solving a Formula for a Variable   Use properties of algebra to solve for a variable.

Example: Solve $N = \frac{a + b}{2}$ for b.

$2N = a + b$ Multiply by 2.

$2N - a = b$ Subtract a.

Steps for Solving a Problem

STEP 1: Read the problem carefully and be sure that you understand it. (You may need to read the problem more than once.) Assign a variable to what you are being asked to find. If necessary, write other quantities in terms of this variable.

STEP 2: Write an equation that relates the quantities described in the problem. You may need to sketch a diagram, make a table, or refer to known formulas.

STEP 3: Solve the equation and determine the solution.

STEP 4: Look back and check your answer. Does it seem reasonable? Did you find the required information?

SECTION 3.3 ▪ LINEAR INEQUALITIES

Linear Inequality in One Variable   Can be written as $ax + b > 0$, where $a \neq 0$. (The symbol $>$ can be replaced with $<$, $\leq$, or $\geq$.) Linear inequalities have *infinitely many* solutions.

Examples: $3x - 5 < 0, x + 2 \geq 1 - 3x$

Symbolic, Numerical, and Graphical Solutions

Example: Solve $4 - 2x \geq 0$.

Symbolic Solution	*Numerical Solution*	*Graphical Solution*

Symbolic Solution

$$4 - 2x \geq 0$$
$$-2x \geq -4$$
$$x \leq 2$$
Reverse inequality.

Numerical Solution

x	$4 - 2x$
0	4
1	2
2	0
3	−2
4	−4

Graphical Solution

$4 - 2x \geq 0$ when $x \leq 2$.   Graph is above or intersects the x-axis for $x \leq 2$.

SECTION 3.4 ▪ COMPOUND INEQUALITIES

Compound Inequality   Two inequalities connected by *and* or *or*.

Examples: For $x + 1 < 3$ *or* $x + 1 > 6$, a solution satisfies *at least* one of the inequalities.
           For $2x + 1 < 3$ *and* $1 - x > 6$, a solution satisfies *both* inequalities.

Three-Part Inequality   A compound inequality in the form $x > a$ *and* $x < b$ can be written as the three-part inequality $a < x < b$.

Example: $1 \leq x < 7$ means $x \geq 1$ *and* $x < 7$.

Interval Notation   Can be used to identify intervals on the real number line.

Examples: $-2 < x \leq 3$ is equivalent to $(-2, 3]$.

           $x < 5$ is equivalent to $(-\infty, 5)$.

           Real numbers are denoted $(-\infty, \infty)$.

SECTION 3.5 ▪ ABSOLUTE VALUE EQUATIONS AND INEQUALITIES

Absolute Value Equations   The graph of $y = |ax + b|$, $a \neq 0$, is V-shaped and intersects the horizontal line $y = k$ twice if $k > 0$. In this case there are two solutions to the equation $|ax + b| = k$ determined by $ax + b = k$ or $ax + b = -k$.

Example: The equation $|2x - 1| = 5$ has two solutions.

Symbolic Solution

$$2x - 1 = 5 \quad \text{or} \quad 2x - 1 = -5$$
$$2x = 6 \quad \text{or} \quad 2x = -4 \qquad \text{Add 1.}$$
$$x = 3 \quad \text{or} \quad x = -2 \qquad \text{Divide by 2.}$$

Graphical Solution

The solutions are -2 and 3.

Numerical Solution

x	-3	-2	-1	0	1	2	3
$|2x - 1|$	7	5	3	1	1	3	5

The solutions are -2 and 3.

Absolute Value Inequalities   If the solutions to $|ax + b| = k$ are c and d with $c < d$, then the solution set for $|ax + b| < k$ is $\{x \mid c < x < d\}$, and the solution set for $|ax + b| > k$ is $\{x \mid x < c \text{ or } x > d\}$.

Example: The solutions to the equation $|2x - 1| = 5$ are -2 and 3, so the solution set for $|2x - 1| < 5$ is $\{x \mid -2 < x < 3\}$, and the solution set for $|2x - 1| > 5$ is $\{x \mid x < -2 \text{ or } x > 3\}$.

If $k > 0$ and $y = f(x)$, then

$$|y| < k \text{ is equivalent to } -k < y < k \text{ and}$$

$$|y| > k \text{ is equivalent to } y < -k \text{ or } y > k.$$

Examples: $|3 - x| < 5$ is equivalent to $-5 < 3 - x < 5$ and

$|3 - x| > 5$ is equivalent to $3 - x < -5$ or $3 - x > 5$.

CHAPTER 3   REVIEW EXERCISES

SECTION 3.1

Exercises 1 and 2: Complete the table and then use the table to solve the equation.

1. $3x - 6 = 0$

x	0	1	2	3	4
$3x - 6$	-6				6

2. $5 - 2x = 3$

x	-1	0	1	2	3
$5 - 2x$					

3. Decide whether $-\frac{2}{3}$ is a solution to the linear equation $\frac{1}{2}z - 2(2z + 3) = 4z - 1$.

4. Use the graph to solve the equation $y_1 = y_2$.

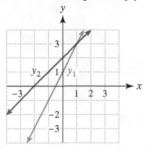

5. Solve $5 - 2x = -1 + x$ graphically.

6. Solve $4x - 3 = 5 + 2x$ graphically or numerically.

Exercises 7–16: Solve the equation.

7. $2x - 7 = 21$　　　　　**8.** $1 - 7x = -\frac{5}{2}$

9. $-2(4x - 1) = 1 - x$

10. $-\frac{3}{4}(x - 1) + 5 = 6$

11. $\dfrac{x - 4}{3} = 2$　　　　**12.** $\dfrac{2x - 3}{2} = \dfrac{x + 3}{5}$

13. $-2(z - 1960) + 32 = 8$

14. $5 - (3 - 2z) + 4 = 5(2z - 3) - (3z - 2)$

15. $\dfrac{2}{3}\left(\dfrac{t - 3}{2}\right) + 4 = \dfrac{1}{3}t - (1 - t)$

16. $0.3r - 0.12(r - 1) = 0.4r + 2.1$

Exercises 17 and 18: Determine whether the equation is an identity or a contradiction.

17. $-4(5 - 3x) = 12x - 20$

18. $4x - (x - 3) = 3x - 3$

Exercises 19 and 20: Find the x- and y-intercepts. Then write the equation in slope–intercept form.

19. $4x - 5y = 20$

20. $2x + \frac{1}{2}y = -6$

SECTION 3.2

Exercises 21–26: Solve the equation for the given variable.

21. $5x - 4y = 20$; y　　　**22.** $-\frac{1}{3}x + \frac{1}{2}y = 1$; y

23. $2a + 3b = a$; a

24. $4m - 5n = 6m + 2n$; n

25. $A = \frac{1}{2}h(a + b)$; b　　　**26.** $V = \frac{1}{3}\pi r^2 h$; h

Exercises 27–30: Solve the equation for y. Let $y = f(x)$ and write a formula for $f(x)$.

27. $\frac{1}{2}x - \frac{3}{4}y = 2$　　　　**28.** $-7(x - 4y) = y + 1$

29. $3x + 4y = 10 - y$　　　**30.** $\dfrac{y}{x} = 3$

Exercises 31 and 32: Translate the sentence into an equation and then solve the equation.

31. The sum of twice x and 25 is 19.

32. If 5 is subtracted from twice x, it equals x plus 1.

SECTION 3.3

33. Use the table to solve $f(x) < 5$, where $f(x)$ represents a linear function.

x	-2	-1	0	1	2
$f(x)$	7	5	3	1	-1

34. Solve $2(3 - x) + 4 < 0$.

35. Solve the inequality $y_1 \geq y_2$, using the graph.

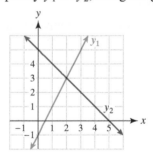

36. Solve each equation or inequality.
   (a) $5 - 4x = -2$　　**(b)** $5 - 4x < -2$
   (c) $5 - 4x > -2$

Exercises 37–44: Solve the inequality.

37. $-2x + 1 \leq 3$　　　　**38.** $x - 5 \geq 2x + 3$

39. $\dfrac{3x - 1}{4} > \dfrac{1}{2}$　　　　**40.** $-3.2(x - 2) < 1.6x$

41. $\dfrac{2}{5}t - (5 - t) + 3 > 2\left(\dfrac{3 - t}{5}\right)$

42. $\dfrac{2(3x-5)}{5} - 3 \geq \dfrac{2-x}{3} + 2$

43. $0.05t - 0.15 \leq 0.03 - 0.75(t-2)$

44. $0.6z - 1.55(z+5) < 1 - 0.35(2z-1)$

 Exercises 45 and 46: Solve the inequality graphically. Approximate boundary numbers to the nearest thousandth.

45. $0.72(\pi - 1.3x) \geq 0.54$

46. $\sqrt{2} - (4 - \pi x) > \sqrt{7}$

SECTION 3.4

Use interval notation whenever possible for the remaining exercises.

Exercises 47–50: Solve the compound inequality. Graph the solution set on a number line.

47. $x + 1 \leq 3$ and $x + 1 \geq -1$

48. $2x + 7 < 5$ and $-2x \geq 6$

49. $5x - 1 \leq 3$ or $1 - x < -1$

50. $3x + 1 > -1$ or $3x + 1 < 10$

51. Use the table to solve $-2 \leq 2x + 2 \leq 4$.

x	-3	-2	-1	0	1	2	3
$2x+2$	-4	-2	0	2	4	6	8

52. Use the following figure to solve each equation and inequality.
(a) $y_1 = y_2$ (b) $y_2 = y_3$
(c) $y_1 \leq y_2 \leq y_3$ (d) $y_2 < y_3$

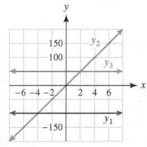

53. The graphs of y_1 and y_2 are shown in the following figure. Solve each equation and inequality.
(a) $y_1 = y_2$ (b) $y_1 < y_2$
(c) $y_1 > y_2$

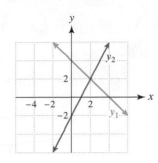

54. The graphs of three linear functions f, g, and h are shown in the following figure. Solve each equation and inequality.
(a) $f(x) = g(x)$ (b) $g(x) = h(x)$
(c) $f(x) < g(x) < h(x)$

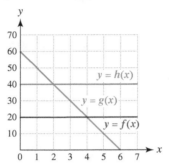

Exercises 55–60: Write the inequality in interval notation.

55. $-3 \leq x \leq \frac{2}{3}$ **56.** $-6 < x \leq 45$

57. $x < \frac{7}{2}$ **58.** $x \geq 1.8$

59. $x > -3$ and $x < 4$ **60.** $x < 4$ or $x > 10$

Exercises 61–66: Solve the three-part inequality. Write the solution set in interval notation.

61. $-4 < x + 1 < 6$ **62.** $20 \leq 2x + 4 \leq 60$

63. $-3 < 4 - \frac{1}{3}x < 7$ **64.** $2 \leq \frac{1}{2}x - 2 \leq 12$

65. $-3 \leq \dfrac{4-5x}{3} - 2 < 3$

66. $30 \leq \dfrac{2x-6}{5} - 4 < 50$

SECTION 3.5

Exercises 67–70: Determine whether the given values of x are solutions to the absolute value equation or inequality.

67. $|12x - 24| = 24$ $x = -3; x = 2$

68. $|5 - 3x| > 3$ $\qquad x = \frac{4}{3}; x = 0$

69. $|3x - 6| \le 6$ $\qquad x = -3; x = 4$

70. $|2 + 3x| + 4 < 11$ $\quad x = -3; x = \frac{2}{3}$

71. Use the accompanying table to solve each equation or inequality.

(a) $y_1 = 2$ (b) $y_1 < 2$ (c) $y_1 > 2$

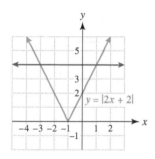

72. Use the graph of $y = |2x + 2|$ to solve each equation or inequality.

(a) $|2x + 2| = 4$ (b) $|2x + 2| \le 4$

(c) $|2x + 2| \ge 4$

Exercises 73–78: Solve the absolute value equation.

73. $|x| = 22$ **74.** $|2x - 9| = 7$

75. $\left|4 - \frac{1}{2}x\right| = 17$ **76.** $\frac{1}{3}|3x - 1| + 1 = 9$

77. $|2x - 5| = |5 - 3x|$

78. $|-3 + 3x| = |-2x + 6|$

Exercises 79 and 80: Solve each absolute value equation or inequality.

79. (a) $|x + 1| = 7$

(b) $|x + 1| \le 7$

(c) $|x + 1| \ge 7$

80. (a) $|1 - 2x| = 6$

(b) $|1 - 2x| \le 6$

(c) $|1 - 2x| \ge 6$

Exercises 81–88: Solve the absolute value inequality.

81. $|x| > 3$ **82.** $|-5x| < 20$

83. $|4x - 2| \le 14$ **84.** $\left|1 - \frac{4}{5}x\right| \ge 3$

85. $|t - 4.5| \le 0.1$ **86.** $-2|13t - 5| \ge -4$

87. $|5 - 4x| > -5$ **88.** $|2t - 3| \le 0$

Exercises 89 and 90: Solve the inequality graphically.

89. $|2x| \ge 3$ **90.** $\left|\frac{1}{2}x - 1\right| \le 2$

Exercises 91 and 92: Write each compound inequality as an absolute value inequality.

91. $-0.05 \le x \le 0.05$

92. $5x - 1 < -4$ or $5x - 1 > 4$

APPLICATIONS

93. *Loan Interest* A student takes out two loans, one at 5% and the other at 7% annual interest. The total amount for both loans is $7700, and the total interest after one year is $469. Find the amount of each loan.

94. *Distance and Time* At first an athlete runs at 8 miles per hour and then runs at 10 miles per hour, traveling 12.8 miles in 1.4 hours. How long did the athlete run at each speed?

95. *Expensive Homes* A typical 2200-square-foot house in Honolulu costs $415,000, which is only 54% of the cost of the same house in San Francisco. (San Francisco has the most expensive housing in the United States.) How much would this Honolulu house cost in San Francisco? (*Source:* Runzheimer International.)

96. *Nightclub Fires* The number of reported nightclub fires has dropped from 1369 in 1980 to 498 in 1999.

(a) Find $f(x) = ax + b$ so that f models these data.

(b) Use $f(x)$ to estimate the number of nightclub fires in 1988.

97. *Distance Between Bicyclists* The following graph shows the distance between two bicyclists traveling toward each other along a straight road after x hours.

(a) After how long did the bicycle riders meet?

(b) When were they 20 miles apart?

(c) Find the times when they were less than 20 miles apart.

(d) Estimate the sum of the speeds of the bicyclists.

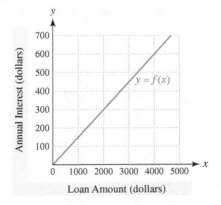

98. *Interest* As shown in the following graph, the function f computes the annual interest y on a loan of x dollars with an interest rate of 15%. Determine the loan amounts that result in the following.
  (a) An annual interest equal to $300
  (b) An annual interest of more than $300
  (c) An annual interest of less than $300

99. *Distance* Two cars, Car 1 and Car 2, are traveling in the same direction on a straight highway. Their

distances in miles north of Austin, Texas, after x hours are shown in the following graph.
  (a) Which car is traveling faster? Explain.
  (b) How many hours elapse before the two cars are the same distance from Austin? How far are they from Austin?
  (c) During what time interval is Car 1 closer to Austin than Car 2?

100. *School Bus Deaths* The line graph shows the number of deaths occurring from school bus crashes. For which years were there more than 10 deaths?
(*Source:* National Center for Statistics and Analysis.)

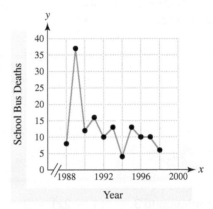

101. *Age in the United States* The median age of the population for each year x between 1820 and 1995 can be approximated by $f(x) = 0.09x - 147.1$.
(*Source:* U.S. Census Bureau.)
  (a) Interpret the slope of the graph of f.
  (b) Estimate when the median age was 23 years.

102. *Women Officers* The number of women officers in the Marine Corps from 1960 to 2000 may be modeled by $f(x) = 17.7x - 34,636$, where x is the year. Estimate the years when this number was between 490 and 670. (*Source:* Department of Defense.)

103. *Weight of a Fish*   If a walleye has a length of x inches, where $30 \le x \le 35$, its weight W in pounds can be *estimated* by $W(x) = 1.11x - 23.3$. (**Source:** Minnesota Department of Natural Resources.)

(a) What length of walleye weighs 12 pounds?

(b) What lengths of walleye weigh less than 12 pounds?

104. *Air Temperature*   Suppose that the air temperature at ground level is $60°F$ and that the air cools $19°F$ for each one-mile increase in altitude.

(a) Write $T(x) = ax + b$ so that T gives the temperature at an altitude of x miles.

(b) Estimate the altitudes at which the air temperature is from $40°F$ to $20°F$.

105. *Distance and Time*   A car is 200 miles west of Rapid City, South Dakota, traveling east at 70 miles per hour. How long will it take for the car to be 395 miles east of Rapid City?

106. *Geometry*   A rectangle is 5 feet longer than twice its width. If the rectangle has a perimeter of 88 feet, what are the dimensions of the rectangle?

107. *Temperature*   The formula $F = \frac{9}{5}C + 32$ may be used to convert Fahrenheit temperature to Celsius temperature. The temperature range at Houghton Lake, Michigan, has varied between $-48°F$ and $107°F$. Find this temperature range in Celsius.

108. *Error in Measurements*   A square garden is being fenced along its 160-foot perimeter. If the length L of the fence must be within 1 foot of the garden's perimeter, write an absolute value inequality that gives acceptable values for L. Solve your inequality.

109. *Average Precipitation*   The average rainfall in Houston, Texas, is 3.9 inches per month. Each month's average A is within 1.7 inches of 3.9 inches. (**Source:** J. Williams, *The Weather Almanac 1995.*)

(a) Write an absolute value inequality that models this situation.

(b) Solve the inequality.

110. *Relative Error*   If a quantity is measured to be T and the actual value is A, then the relative error in this measurement is $\left|\frac{T-A}{A}\right|$. If $A = 35$ and the relative error is to be less than 0.08 (8%), what values for T are possible?

CHAPTER 3   TEST   Pass the Test   Video solutions to all test exercises

1. Is $\frac{1}{6}$ a solution to $3 - 4(1 - 2x) = 2x$?

2. Complete the table and then solve $2 - 3x \le -1$.

x	-2	-1	0	1	2
$2 - 3x$					

3. Solve $3 - 5x = 18$. Check your answer.

4. Use the graph to the right to solve each equation and inequality. Write your answers for parts (b) and (c) in interval notation.

(a) $y_1 = y_2$ (b) $y_1 \ge y_2$ (c) $y_1 \le y_2$

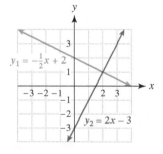

5. Solve $4 - 2x = 1 + x$ graphically.

6. Solve each equation.

(a) $-\frac{2}{3}(3x - 2) + 1 = x$

(b) $\dfrac{2z + 1}{3} = \dfrac{3(1 - z)}{2}$

(c) $0.4(2 - 3x) = 0.5x - 0.2$

7. Find the x- and y-intercepts for the graph of the equation $-6x + 3y = 9$. Then write the equation in slope–intercept form.

8. Translate the sentence into an equation and then solve. "If 2 is added to 5 times x, it equals x minus 4."

9. Solve $3x - 2y = 6$ for y. Let $y = f(x)$ and write a formula for $f(x)$.

Exercises 10 and 11: Solve the inequality. Write your answer in interval notation.

10. $-\frac{5}{2}x + \frac{1}{2} \le 2$ 11. $3.1(3 - x) < 2.9x$

12. Graph the solution set to $2x + 6 < 2$ and $-3x \ge 3$ on a number line.

13. Use the table to solve the compound inequality $-3x < -3$ or $-3x > 6$. Write your answer in interval notation.

x	-3	-2	-1	0	1	2	3
$-3x$	9	6	3	0	-3	-6	-9

14. Use the following figure to solve the equations and inequalities. Write your answers for parts (c) and (d) in interval notation.
    (a) $y_1 = y_2$ (b) $y_2 = y_3$
    (c) $y_1 \le y_2 \le y_3$ (d) $y_2 < y_3$

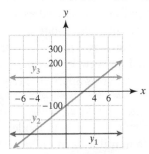

15. Solve $-2 < 2 + \frac{1}{2}x < 2$ and write the solution set in interval notation.

16. Solve the equation $\left| 2 - \frac{1}{3}x \right| = 6$.

17. Solve each inequality. Write your answer in interval notation.
    (a) $|x| \le 5$ (b) $|x| > 0$

(c) $|2x + 7| \le -2$ (d) $|5x| > 10$

(e) $-2|2 - 5x| + 1 \le 5$ (f) $|3 - x| < 5$

18. Solve each equation or inequality. Write your answers for parts (b) and (c) in interval notation.
    (a) $|1 - 5x| = 3$ (b) $|1 - 5x| \le 3$
    (c) $|1 - 5x| \ge 3$

19. *Sport Drinks*   The following graph shows a relationship between the calories in an 8-ounce serving of a sport drink and the corresponding grams of carbohydrates. Estimate the number of calories x in 8 ounces of a sport drink with the following grams of carbohydrates.   (*Source: Runner's World.*)
    (a) 16 grams of carbohydrates
    (b) More than 16 grams of carbohydrates
    (c) Less than 16 grams of carbohydrates
    (d) Interpret the slope of the graph.

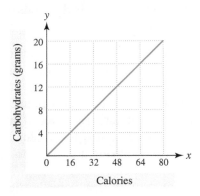

20. *Drinking Fluids and Exercise*   To determine the number of ounces of fluid that a person should drink in a day, divide his or her weight in pounds by 2 and then add 0.4 ounce for every minute of exercise.
    (a) Write a function that gives the fluid requirements for a person weighing 150 pounds and exercising x minutes a day.
    (b) If a 150-pound runner needs 89 ounces of fluid each day, determine the runner's daily minutes of exercise.

21. *Solving a Formula*   Solve the formula $d = \frac{1}{2}gt^2$ for g.

22. *Loan Interest*   A student takes out two loans, one at 4% and the other at 6% annual interest. The total amount for both loans is $5000, and the total interest after one year is $230. Find the amount of each loan.

23. *Angles in a Triangle*   The measure of the largest angle in a triangle is twice the measure of the smallest angle. The third angle is 16° more than the smallest angle. Find the measure of each angle.

24. *Prices*   The sale price of a jacket is $81. If the retail price had been reduced by 25%, find the retail price of the jacket.

CHAPTER 3   EXTENDED AND DISCOVERY EXERCISES

1. *Clouds and Temperature*   If the air temperature is greater than the dew point, clouds do not form. If the air temperature cools to the dew point, fog or clouds may appear. Suppose that the Fahrenheit temperature x miles high is given by $T(x) = 90 - 19x$ and that the dew point x miles high is given by $D(x) = 70 - 5.8x$.   (*Source:* A. Miller.)

(a) Find the temperature and dew point at ground level.

(b) At what altitude are the air temperature and dew point equal?

(c) Find the altitudes at which clouds do not form.

(d) Find the altitudes at which clouds may form.

2. *Critical Thinking*   (Refer to Exercise 1.) For each 1-mile increase in altitude, the air temperature decreases 19°F, whereas the dew point decreases 5.8°F. At ground level the dew point is usually less than the air temperature. However, if the air temperature reaches the dew point, fog or clouds may form.

(a) Discuss why clouds are likely to form at some altitude in the sky.

(b) Suppose that the dew point is slightly less than the air temperature near the ground. How does that affect the altitude at which clouds form?

3. *Recording Music*   A compact disc (CD) can hold approximately 700 million bytes. One *byte* is capable of storing one letter of the alphabet. For example, the word "function" requires 8 bytes to store in computer memory. One million bytes is commonly referred to as a *megabyte* (MB). Recording music requires an enormous amount of memory. The accompanying table lists the megabytes x needed to record y seconds (sec) of music.

x (MB)	0.129	0.231	0.415	0.491
y (sec)	6.010	10.74	19.27	22.83

x (MB)	0.667	1.030	1.160	1.260
y (sec)	31.00	49.00	55.25	60.18

Source: Gateway 2000 System CD.

(a) Make a scatterplot of the data.

(b) What relationship seems to exist between x and y? Why does this relationship seem reasonable?

(c) Find the slope–intercept form of a line that models the data. Interpret the slope of this line as a rate of change. Answers may vary.

(d) Check your answer in part (c) by graphing the line and data in the same graph.

(e) Write a linear equation whose solution gives the megabytes needed to record 120 seconds of music.

(f) Solve the equation in part (e) graphically or symbolically.

4. *Early Cellular Phone Growth*   Cellular phone use has grown dramatically in the United States. When there were 25,000 customers in New York City, the investment cost per cellular site was $12 million. (A cellular site would include such things as a relay tower to transmit signals between cellular phones.) When the number of customers rose to 100,000, the investment cost per cellular site rose to $96 million. Although cost usually decreases with additional customers, such was not the case for early cellular technology. Instead, cost increased as a result of having to purchase expensive real estate and establish communications links among a large number of cellular sites. The relationship between cellular sites and investment cost per site was approximately linear.   (*Source:* M. Paetsch, *Mobile Communications in the US and Europe.*)

(a) Find values for m, x_1, and y_1 so that the formula $f(x) = m(x - x_1) + y_1$ models the cost per cellular site in millions of dollars when there were x customers.

(b) Graph f and the data points (25000, 12) and (100000, 96).

(c) Write an inequality whose solution set gives the numbers of customers when the investment cost per cellular site was between $28.8 million and $51.2 million.

(d) Solve the inequality in part (c) graphically and symbolically.

CHAPTERS 1–3 CUMULATIVE REVIEW EXERCISES

Exercises 1 and 2: Classify each real number as one or more of the following: natural number, whole number, integer, rational number, or irrational number.

1. $-7, -\frac{3}{5}, 0, \sqrt{5}, \frac{8}{2}, 5.\overline{12}$

2. $-\frac{6}{3}, \frac{0}{9}, \sqrt{9}, \pi, 4.\overline{6}$

Exercises 3 and 4: State whether the equation illustrates an identity, commutative, associative, or distributive property.

3. $8x - 2x = 6x$

4. $(6 + z) + 3 = 6 + (z + 3)$

Exercises 5 and 6: Use properties of real numbers to evaluate the expression mentally.

5. $11 + 26 + (-1) + 14$

6. $7 \cdot 98$

7. Plot the numbers $-4, -\frac{5}{2}, 0,$ and 3 on a number line.

8. Find the opposite of $-5y - 4$.

Exercises 9 and 10: Simplify the expression. Write the result using positive exponents.

9. $\dfrac{24x^{-4}y^2}{8xy^{-5}}$

10. $\left(\dfrac{3a^2}{4b^3}\right)^{-3}$

11. Evaluate the expression $15 - 2^3 \div 4$.

12. Write the number 0.000059 in scientific notation.

Exercises 13 and 14: Evaluate the formula for the given value of the variable.

13. $J = \sqrt{38 - t} \quad t = 13$

14. $r = 3 - z^3 \quad z = -3$

15. Select the formula that best models the data in the table.

x	-2	-1	0	1	2
y	7	5	3	1	-1

(i) $y = 2x + 11$ (ii) $y = -2x + 3$
(iii) $y = x - 5$

16. Identify the domain and range of the relation $S = \{(-2, 4), (0, 2), (1, 4), (3, 0)\}$.

Exercises 17 and 18: Evaluate the given formula for $x = -2, -1, 0, 1,$ and 2. Plot these ordered pairs.

17. $y = -2x + 1$

18. $y = \dfrac{x^3 + 4}{2}$

19. Sketch the graph of $f(x) = x^2 - 3$ by hand.

20. Find the domain of $f(x) = \dfrac{4}{x}$.

Exercises 21 and 22: Use the graph or table to evaluate $f(0)$ and $f(-2)$.

21.

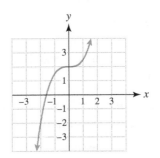

22.

x	-2	-1	0	1	2
$f(x)$	-4	-1	2	5	8

Exercises 23 and 24: Determine whether f is a linear function. If f is linear, give values for a and b so that f may be expressed as $f(x) = ax + b$.

23. $f(x) = 11 - 3x$

24. $f(x) = \sqrt{x} + 2$

25. Use the table to write the formula for $f(x) = ax + b$.

x	-2	-1	0	1	2
$f(x)$	-5	-1	3	7	11

26. Sketch a graph of $f(x) = 3$.

27. Find the slope and the y-intercept of the graph of $f(x) = 5x - 4$.

28. Calculate the slope of the line passing through the points $(3, -2)$ and $(-1, 6)$.

29. Sketch a line passing through the point $(1, 3)$ with slope $m = 2$.

30. Use the graph to express the equation of the line in slope–intercept form.

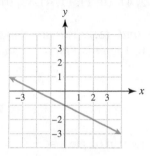

31. Let f be a linear function. Find the slope, x-intercept, and y-intercept of the graph of f.

x	-2	-1	0	1	2
$f(x)$	-3	0	3	6	9

32. Write the equation of the vertical line that passes through the point $(5, 7)$.

Exercises 33 and 34: Write the slope–intercept equation for a line satisfying the given conditions.

33. Parallel to $y = 3x - 4$, passing through $(2, 1)$

34. Perpendicular to $y = -x - 5$, passing through the point $(-3, 0)$

35. Determine whether $\frac{8}{5}$ is a solution to the equation $\frac{1}{2}x - 4(x - 1) = \frac{1}{4}x - 2$.

36. Use the graph to solve the equation $y_1 = y_2$.

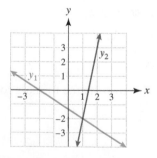

Exercises 37 and 38: Solve the equation.

37. $\frac{3}{4}(x - 2) + 4 = 2$

38. $\frac{2}{3}\left(\dfrac{t - 7}{4}\right) - 2 = \frac{1}{3}t - (2t + 3)$

Exercises 39 and 40: Find the x- and y-intercepts. Write the equation in slope–intercept form.

39. $x - \frac{1}{3}y = 2$

40. $5x - 4y = -10$

41. Use the table to solve $y < 2$, where y represents a linear function. Write the solution set in set-builder notation.

x	-2	-1	0	1	2
y	12	7	2	-3	-8

42. Use the graph to solve the inequality $y_1 \leq y_2$. Write the solution set in interval notation.

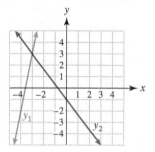

Exercises 43 and 44: Solve the inequality symbolically. Write the solution set in interval notation.

43. $\dfrac{4x - 9}{6} > \dfrac{1}{2}$

44. $\frac{2}{3}z - 2 \leq \frac{1}{4}z - (2z + 2)$

Exercises 45 and 46: Solve the compound inequality. Graph the solution set on a number line.

45. $x + 2 > 1$ and $2x - 1 \leq 9$

46. $4x + 7 < 1$ or $3x + 2 \geq 11$

Exercises 47 and 48: Solve the three-part inequality. Write the solution set in interval notation.

47. $-7 \leq 2x - 3 \leq 5$

48. $-8 \leq -\frac{1}{2}x - 3 \leq 5$

Exercises 49 and 50: Solve the absolute value inequality. Write the solution set in interval notation.

49. $|3x + 5| > 13$ **50.** $-3|2t - 11| \geq -9$

51. Use the graph to solve the equation and inequalities.
  (a) $y_1 = 2$ **(b)** $y_1 \le 2$ **(c)** $y_1 \ge 2$

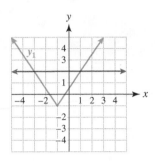

52. Solve the absolute value equation $\left|\frac{2}{3}x - 4\right| = 8$.

APPLICATIONS

53. *Calculating Interest* If P dollars are deposited in a savings account paying 5% annual interest, then the amount A in the account after t years is given by the formula $A = P(1.05)^t$. Find A for the given values of P and t. Round your answer to the nearest cent.
  (a) $P = \$4300$, $t = 10$ years
  (b) $P = \$11,000$, $t = 6$ years

54. *Modeling Motion* The table lists the distance d in miles traveled by a car for various elapsed times t in hours. Find an equation that models these data.

Elapsed Time (hours)	3	5	7	9
Distance (miles)	195	325	455	585

55. *Sodium Content* Some types of diet soda contain 120 milligrams of sodium per 12-ounce can.
  (a) Give a formula for $f(x)$ that calculates the number of milligrams of sodium in x ounces of this type of diet soda.
  (b) What is the slope of the graph of f?
  (c) Interpret the slope as a rate of change.

56. *Graphical Model* A 150-liter aquarium is initially empty. A small hose attached to a faucet begins to fill the aquarium at a constant rate of 5 liters per minute. After 10 minutes, the faucet is turned off for 15 minutes and the small hose is replaced by a larger hose that can fill the aquarium at a rate of 10 liters per minute. The faucet is turned back on until the aquarium is full. Sketch a graph that depicts the amount of water in the aquarium after x minutes.

57. *Distance* A motorcyclist and a bicyclist are traveling toward each other on a straight road. Their distances in miles south of Euclid, Ohio, after x hours are shown in the following graph.
  (a) Is the bicyclist traveling toward or away from Euclid? Explain.
  (b) How many hours will elapse before they are the same distance from Euclid?
  (c) During what time period is the motorcyclist farther away from Euclid than the bicyclist?

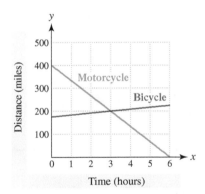

58. *Women Officers* The number of women officers in the Marine Corps from 1960 to 2000 may be modeled by $f(x) = 17.7(x - 1960) + 56$, where x represents the year. Estimate the years in which the number of women officers was between 410 and 605.
  (**Source:** Department of Defense.)

Systems of Linear Equations

I n 1940, a physicist named John Atanasoff at Iowa State University needed to solve 29 equations with 29 variables simultaneously. This task was too difficult to do by hand, so he and a graduate student invented the first fully electronic digital computer. Thus the desire to solve a mathematical problem led to one of the most important inventions of the twentieth century. Today people can solve thousands of equations with thousands of variables. Solutions to such equations have resulted in better airplanes, cars, electronic devices, weather forecasts, and medical equipment.

Equations are also widely used in biology. The following table contains the weight W, neck size N, and chest size C for three black bears. Suppose that park rangers find a bear with a neck size of 22 inches and a chest size of 38 inches. Can they use the data in the table to estimate the bear's weight? Using systems of linear equations, they can answer this question. See Example 7 and Exercise 58 in Section 4.6.

W (pounds)	N (inches)	C (inches)
80	16	26
344	28	45
416	31	54
?	22	38

Education is what survives when what has been learned has been forgotten.

—B. F. SKINNER

Sources: A. Tucker, *Fundamentals of Computing*; M. Triola, *Elementary Statistics*; Minitab, Inc.

4.1 SYSTEMS OF LINEAR EQUATIONS IN TWO VARIABLES

Basic Concepts ■ Graphical and Numerical Solutions ■ Types of Linear Systems

A LOOK INTO MATH ▷

Many formulas involve more than one variable. For example, to calculate the heat index we need to know both the air temperature and the humidity. To calculate monthly car payments we need the loan amount, interest rate, and duration of the loan. Other applications involve large numbers of variables. To design new aircraft it is necessary to solve equations containing thousands of variables. In this section we consider systems of equations containing only two linear equations in two variables. However, the concepts discussed in this section are used to solve larger systems of equations.

Basic Concepts

▶ REAL-WORLD CONNECTION   Each year, more and more people buy music subscriptions through the Internet. These subscriptions provide unlimited access to a large assortment of music through a person's computer. A combined total of $400 million was spent in 2004 and 2005 on music subscriptions, with a $200 million increase from 2004 to 2005. (**Source:** Jupiter Research.)

To determine the amount spent each year, we can let x be the amount spent in 2005 and let y be the amount spent in 2004 where both amounts are in millions of dollars. Then the given information is described by the following *system of equations*.

$$x + y = 400 \qquad \text{The total is \$400 million.}$$
$$x - y = 200 \qquad \text{The difference is \$200 million.}$$

Each equation contains two variables, x and y. These two equations form a **system of two linear equations in two variables**. An ordered pair (x, y) is a **solution** to a system of equations if the values for x and y satisfy *both* equations. Any system of two linear equations in two variables can be written in **standard form** as

$$ax + by = c$$
$$dx + ey = k,$$

where a, b, c, d, e, and k are constants.

EXAMPLE 1   Testing for solutions

Determine which ordered pair is a solution to the system of equations: $(0, 3)$ or $(-1, 2)$.

$$-x + 4y = 9$$
$$3x - 3y = -9$$

Solution

For $(0, 3)$ to be a solution, the values of $x = 0$ and $y = 3$ must satisfy *both* equations.

$$-0 + 4(3) \overset{?}{=} 9 \qquad \text{False}$$
$$3(0) - 3(3) \overset{?}{=} -9 \qquad \text{True}$$

Because $(0, 3)$ does not satisfy *both* equations, $(0, 3)$ is *not* a solution. To test $(-1, 2)$, substitute $x = -1$ and $y = 2$ in each equation.

$$-(-1) + 4(2) \overset{?}{=} 9 \qquad \text{True}$$
$$3(-1) - 3(2) \overset{?}{=} -9 \qquad \text{True}$$

Both equations are true, so $(-1, 2)$ is a solution.

Now Try Exercise 7

Graphical and Numerical Solutions

Graphical, numerical, and symbolic techniques can be used to solve systems of equations. In this section we focus on graphical and numerical techniques and delay discussion of symbolic techniques until the next section.

In the next example we solve a system of linear equations graphically. Note that sometimes it may be difficult to read a graph precisely, so it is important to check our solutions by using the technique described in Example 1.

EXAMPLE 2   Solving a system of equations graphically

Solve the system of equations

$$y = x - 2$$
$$y = 4 - x$$

graphically. Check your answer.

Solution
Both equations are in slope–intercept form, so we can graph

$$y = x - 2 \text{ and } y = 4 - x$$

immediately, as shown in Figure 4.1. Their graphs intersect at the point $(3, 1)$. To check that $(3, 1)$ is the solution, substitute $x = 3$ and $y = 1$ into each equation.

$$1 \overset{?}{=} 3 - 2 \qquad \text{True}$$
$$1 \overset{?}{=} 4 - 3 \qquad \text{True}$$

The answer checks.

Now Try Exercise 11

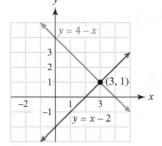

Figure 4.1

In the next example we demonstrate two methods for graphing linear equations that are written in the standard form: $ax + by = c$. The first method uses the slope–intercept form to graph each line and the second method uses the x- and y-intercepts to graph each line.

EXAMPLE 3   Solving a system of equations graphically

Solve the system of equations graphically.

$$x + 2y = 4$$
$$2x - y = 3$$

Figure 4.2

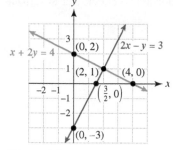

Figure 4.3

Solution

Method I: Finding Slope–Intercept Form   Solve each equation for y and then use the slope–intercept form to graph the line.

$x + 2y = 4$	First equation	$2x - y = 3$	Second equation
$2y = -x + 4$	Subtract x.	$-y = -2x + 3$	Subtract $2x$.
$y = -\frac{1}{2}x + 2$	Multiply by $\frac{1}{2}$.	$y = 2x - 3$	Multiply by -1.

Now graph $y = -\frac{1}{2}x + 2$ and $y = 2x - 3$. See Figure 4.2. Their graphs intersect at $(2, 1)$.

Method II: Finding x- and y-Intercepts   To find the x-intercepts let $y = 0$ in each equation.

$x + 2y = 4$	First equation	$2x - y = 3$	Second equation
$x + 2(0) = 4$	Let $y = 0$.	$2x - 0 = 3$	Let $y = 0$.
$x = 4$	Solve for x.	$x = \frac{3}{2}$	Solve for x.

The x-intercept is 4.   The x-intercept is $\frac{3}{2}$.

To find the y-intercepts let $x = 0$ in each equation.

$x + 2y = 4$	First equation	$2x - y = 3$	Second equation
$0 + 2y = 4$	Let $x = 0$.	$2(0) - y = 3$	Let $x = 0$.
$y = 2$	Solve for y.	$y = -3$	Solve for y.

The y-intercept is 2.   The y-intercept is -3.

Graph $x + 2y = 4$ by drawing a line that passes through $(4, 0)$ and $(0, 2)$. The graph of $2x - y = 3$ passes through $\left(\frac{3}{2}, 0\right)$ and $(0, -3)$. See Figure 4.3. Their graphs intersect at $(2, 1)$.

Now Try Exercises **15, 45**

In the next example we solve the system of equations presented earlier, which models spending on music subscriptions.

EXAMPLE **4**   Solving a system of equations graphically and numerically

Solve the system of equations

$$x + y = 400$$
$$x - y = 200$$

graphically and numerically. Interpret the solution.

Solution

Start by solving each equation for y.

$x + y = 400$	First equation	$x - y = 200$	Second equation
$y = -x + 400$	Subtract x.	$-y = -x + 200$	Subtract x.
		$y = x - 200$	Multiply by -1.

Graphical Solution   The graphs of $y_1 = -x + 400$ and $y_2 = x - 200$ are shown in Figure 4.4. Because x and y represent sales, which are never negative, we graph these lines only in the first quadrant. Their graphs intersect at the point $(300, 100)$. Thus \$300 million was spent in 2005 on music subscriptions, and \$100 million was spent in 2004. Check this solution.

Figure 4.4 Graphical Solution

Numerical Solution Make a table of values for $y_1 = -x + 400$ and $y_2 = x - 200$. Table 4.1 shows that, when $x = 300$, both of the expressions equal 100. Thus the solution is (300, 100). This type of numerical solution is based on trial and error. If the solution is not a "nice" integer, finding the solution numerically may be difficult or even *impossible*. However, the *important mathematical concept* to remember is that you are looking for an x-value where $y_1 = y_2$.

TABLE 4.1   A Numerical Solution

x	100	200	300	400
$y_1 = -x + 400$	300	200	100	0
$y_2 = x - 200$	-100	0	100	200

Figure 4.5

In Figure 4.5 a calculator was used to create a table similar to Table 4.1.

Now Try Exercises 61, 81

EXAMPLE 5   Solving a system of equations graphically

Solve the system of equations

$$2x - 3y = 6$$
$$4x + y = 5$$

graphically. Check your answer.

Solution
Solve the first equation for y.

$2x - 3y = 6$	First equation
$-3y = -2x + 6$	Subtract $2x$ from each side.
$\dfrac{-3y}{-3} = \dfrac{-2x}{-3} + \dfrac{6}{-3}$	Divide each term by -3.
$y = \dfrac{2}{3}x - 2$	Simplify.

$[-6, 6, 1]$ by $[-4, 4, 1]$

(b)

Figure 4.6

Next, solve the second equation for y.

$$4x + y = 5 \qquad \text{Second equation}$$
$$y = -4x + 5 \qquad \text{Subtract } 4x \text{ from each side.}$$

Graph $y_1 = \frac{2}{3}x - 2$ and $y_2 = -4x + 5$, as shown in Figure 4.6(a). (A similar calculator graph is shown in Figure 4.6(b).) Their graphs appear to intersect at $(1.5, -1)$. To be *certain*, check this answer in the *given* equations.

$$2x - 3y = 6 \qquad \text{First equation}$$
$$2(1.5) - 3(-1) \overset{?}{=} 6 \qquad \text{Let } x = 1.5 \text{ and } y = -1.$$
$$6 = 6 \qquad \text{The answer checks.}$$

Now substitute these values in the second equation. (It is essential to check *both* equations.)

$$4x + y = 5 \qquad \text{Second equation}$$
$$4(1.5) + (-1) \overset{?}{=} 5 \qquad \text{Let } x = 1.5 \text{ and } y = -1.$$
$$5 = 5 \qquad \text{The answer checks.}$$

Now Try Exercises 17, 19

Types of Linear Systems

A system of linear equations that has at least one solution is a **consistent system**; otherwise, it is an **inconsistent system**. A system of linear equations in two variables can be represented graphically by two lines in the xy-plane. Three different situations involving two lines are illustrated in Figure 4.7. In Figure 4.7(a) the lines intersect at a single point, which represents a *unique solution*. In this case the equations of the lines are called **independent equations**. In Figure 4.7(b) the two lines are identical, which occurs when the two equations are *equivalent*. For example, the equations $x + y = 1$ and $2x + 2y = 2$ are equivalent. If we divide each side of the second equation by 2 we obtain the first equation. As a result, their graphs are identical and every point on the line represents a solution to the system of linear equations. Thus there are infinitely many solutions, and the equations are called **dependent equations**. Finally, in Figure 4.7(c) the lines are parallel and do not intersect. There are no solutions, so the system is inconsistent.

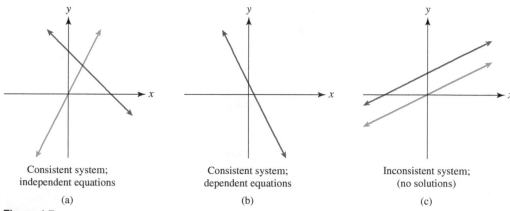

Consistent system; independent equations

(a)

Consistent system; dependent equations

(b)

Inconsistent system; (no solutions)

(c)

Figure 4.7

▶ REAL-WORLD CONNECTION   In the next three examples we illustrate each of these situations with a real-world application.

EXAMPLE 6   Solving a linear system with a unique solution

Suppose that two groups of students go to a football game. The first group buys 3 tickets and 3 soft drinks for \$15, and the second group buys 4 tickets and 2 soft drinks for \$16. Find the price of a ticket and the price of a soft drink graphically.

Solution
Let x be the cost of a ticket and y be the cost of a soft drink. Then $3x + 3y = 15$ represents 3 tickets and 3 soft drinks costing \$15 and $4x + 2y = 16$ represents 4 tickets and 2 soft drinks costing \$16. This information can be written as a system of equations.

$$3x + 3y = 15$$
$$4x + 2y = 16$$

To graph each equation, we will use the x- and y-intercepts (Method II), as discussed in Example 3. The x- and y-intercepts for $3x + 3y = 15$ are both 5. The x- and y-intercepts for $4x + 2y = 16$ are 4 and 8, respectively. Plotting the points $(5, 0)$, $(0, 5)$, $(4, 0)$, and $(0, 8)$ and sketching the corresponding lines in the first quadrant results in Figure 4.8. These graphs intersect at $(3, 2)$. Thus the cost of a ticket is \$3 and the cost of a soft drink is \$2. Note that 3 tickets and 3 soft drinks cost $3(3) + 3(2) = \$15$ and that 4 tickets and 2 soft drinks cost $4(3) + 2(2) = \$16$, so our solution is correct.

Figure 4.8

Now Try Exercise 76

EXAMPLE 7   Solving a dependent linear system

Now suppose that two groups of students go to a different football game. The first group buys 4 tickets and 2 soft drinks for \$16, and the second group buys 2 tickets and 1 soft drink for \$8. If possible, find the price of a ticket and the price of a soft drink graphically.

Solution
Let x be the cost of a ticket and y be the cost of a soft drink. Then this situation can be modeled by the following system of equations.

$$4x + 2y = 16$$
$$2x + \ y = 8$$

Solve each equation for y.

$$4x + 2y = 16 \qquad\qquad 2x + y = 8$$
$$2y = -4x + 16 \qquad\qquad y = -2x + 8$$
$$y = -2x + 8$$

Both equations simplify to the *same* slope–intercept form, $y = -2x + 8$, and thus the lines are identical, as shown in Figure 4.9.

The system is consistent because there is at least one solution. The equations are dependent because not enough information is available to determine a unique solution. Note that the second group bought half what the first group bought and paid half as much. As a result, the two equations contain essentially the *same information* and are *equivalent*. Thus there are infinitely many solutions because every point on the line is a solution. For example, a ticket could cost $3 and a soft drink could cost $2, or a ticket could cost $2 and a soft drink could cost $4. The solution set can be expressed in set-builder notation as $\{(x, y) \mid 2x + y = 8\}$.

Figure 4.9

Now Try Exercise 27

CRITICAL THINKING

Suppose that a system of two linear equations with two variables is dependent. If you try to solve this system numerically by using a table, how could you recognize that the equations are indeed dependent? Explain your answer.

EXAMPLE 8   Recognizing an inconsistent linear system

Now suppose that two groups of students go to a concert. The first group buys 4 tickets and 2 soft drinks for $20, and the second group buys 2 tickets and 1 soft drink for $12. If possible, find the price of a ticket and the price of a soft drink graphically.

Solution
Let x be the cost of a ticket and y be the cost of a soft drink. Then the following system models the data.

$$4x + 2y = 20$$
$$2x + y = 12$$

Solving for y, we can write each equation in slope–intercept form.

$$y = -2x + 10$$
$$y = -2x + 12$$

Their graphs are parallel lines with slope -2 and different y-intercepts. Thus they do not intersect (see Figure 4.10). The linear system is *inconsistent* because there are no solutions. Note that the second group purchased half what the first group purchased. If pricing had been *consistent*, the second group would have paid half, or $10, instead of $12. *Inconsistent pricing* resulted in an *inconsistent linear system*.

Figure 4.10

Now Try Exercise **31**

CRITICAL THINKING

How would a table of values appear when you are solving an inconsistent system of equations?

EXAMPLE **9**   Classifying systems of equations

Classify each system as consistent or inconsistent. If the system is consistent, state whether the equations are dependent or independent.

(a) $x + y = 1$ (b) $x + 2y = 4$ (c) $x + y = 4$
    $x + y = -1$ $2x + 4y = 8$ $x - y = 2$

Solution

(a) The slope–intercept forms for these equations are $y = -x + 1$ and $y = -x - 1$. Their graphs are parallel lines with slope -1 and different y-intercepts, so they do not intersect. See Figure 4.11(a). There are no solutions and the system is inconsistent.

NOTE: The sum of two numbers, x and y, cannot equal both 1 and -1 at the same time, so it is reasonable that there are no solutions.

(b) Because the equations both have slope–intercept form $y = -\frac{1}{2}x + 2$, their graphs are identical. The system is consistent and the equations are dependent. See Figure 4.11(b). There are infinitely many solutions of the form $\{(x, y) \mid x + 2y = 4\}$.

NOTE: The second equation is exactly double the first equation. When one equation is a *nonzero* multiple of the other, the equations are dependent.

(c) The first equation has slope–intercept form $y = -x + 4$ and the second equation has slope–intercept form $y = x - 2$. These lines have different slopes and intersect at one point: (3, 1). The system is consistent and the equations are independent. See Figure 4.11(c).

(a)

(b)

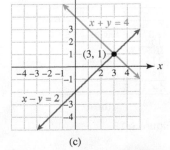

(c)

Figure 4.11

Now Try Exercises **23, 35, 37**

A SYSTEM OF TWO LINEAR EQUATIONS IN TWO VARIABLES

A system involving two linear equations in two variables can have no solutions, one solution, or infinitely many solutions. Its graph consists of two lines.

1. If the lines *are parallel*, the system is inconsistent and there are no solutions.
2. If the lines *intersect at a single point*, there is one solution. The system is consistent and the equations are independent.
3. If the lines *are identical*, the equations are dependent and there are infinitely many solutions. The system is consistent.

EXAMPLE 10   Finding an athlete's running speeds

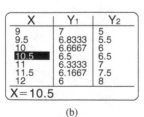

An athlete jogs at a faster pace for 30 minutes and then jogs at a slower pace for 90 minutes. The first pace is 4 miles per hour faster than the second pace, and the athlete covers a total distance of 15 miles.

(a) Write a linear system whose solution gives the athlete's running speeds.
(b) Solve the resulting system graphically and numerically.

Solution

(a) Let x be the faster speed of the runner and y be the slower speed. The athlete runs $\frac{1}{2}$ hour at x miles per hour and $\frac{3}{2}$ hours at y miles per hour. *Rate times time equals distance* and the total distance traveled is 15 miles, so

$$\frac{1}{2}x + \frac{3}{2}y = 15.$$

Because the first pace is 4 miles per hour faster than the second pace,

$$x - y = 4.$$

Thus we need to solve the following linear system of equations.

$$\frac{1}{2}x + \frac{3}{2}y = 15 \qquad \text{First equation}$$

$$x - y = \ 4 \qquad \text{Second equation}$$

[0, 20, 5] by [0, 20, 5]

Intersection
X=10.5   Y=6.5

(a)

X	Y₁	Y₂
9	7	5
9.5	6.8333	5.5
10	6.6667	6
10.5	6.5	6.5
11	6.3333	7
11.5	6.1667	7.5
12	6	8

X=10.5

(b)

Figure 4.12

(b) Multiply the first equation by 2 to clear fractions and then solve for y.

$$x + 3y = 30 \qquad \text{Multiply first equation by 2.}$$

$$3y = -x + 30 \qquad \text{Subtract } x.$$

$$y = -\frac{x}{3} + 10 \qquad \text{Divide by 3.}$$

Solving the second equation for y gives

$$y = x - 4.$$

Graphical Solution We graph $Y_1 = -X/3 + 10$ and $Y_2 = X - 4$, as shown in Figure 4.12(a). The graphs intersect at the point (10.5, 6.5). Thus the athlete ran at 10.5 miles per hour and then slowed to 6.5 miles per hour.

Numerical Solution A numerical solution is shown in Figure 4.12(b). To find this solution, we set the increment for the x-values to 0.5.   Now Try Exercise 71

4.1 PUTTING IT ALL TOGETHER

A system of two linear equations in two variables may be written in standard form as

$$ax + by = c$$
$$dx + ey = k,$$

where a, b, c, d, e, and k are constants (fixed numbers). Linear systems in two variables may be solved graphically or numerically. The following table summarizes the types of systems of equations and the number of solutions that may be encountered.

System	Solution	Graph
Consistent, with a Unique Solution $x + y = 3$ $x - y = 1$ Equations Are Independent	There is one solution: $x = 2$ and $y = 1$. The solution is the ordered pair $(2, 1)$. *Check:* $2 + 1 = 3$ True $2 - 1 = 1$ True	Graph $y_1 = 3 - x$ and $y_2 = x - 1$. Their graphs intersect at $(2, 1)$.
Consistent, with Infinitely Many Solutions $x + \ y = 1$ $3x + 3y = 3$ Equations Are Dependent	There are infinitely many solutions, such as $(2, -1)$ and $(0, 1)$. *Solution Set:* $\{(x, y) \mid x + y = 1\}$ Note that multiplying the first equation by 3 results in the second equation. Also, both equations have the same x- and y-intercepts: 1 and 1.	Graph $y_1 = 1 - x$ and $y_2 = (-3x + 3)/3$. The graphs are identical.
Inconsistent $x + y = 1$ $x + y = 2$	There are no solutions. The sum of two variables, x and y, cannot equal both 1 and 2 at the same time.	Graph $y_1 = 1 - x$ and $y_2 = 2 - x$. The lines are parallel with slope -1 and do not intersect.

Exercises   **MyMathLab**

PRACTICE   WATCH   DOWNLOAD   READ   REVIEW

CONCEPTS

1. Can a system of linear equations have exactly two solutions? Explain.

2. Give an example of a system of linear equations.

3. Name two ways to solve a system of linear equations.

4. If a graphical solution consists of two distinct, intersecting lines, what does this result indicate about the number of solutions?

5. If the graphical solution consists of two parallel lines, what does this result indicate about the number of solutions?

6. How many solutions does a dependent linear system have? How can you recognize a dependent linear system graphically?

Exercises 7–10: (Refer to Example 1.) Decide which of the ordered pairs is a solution for the linear system of equations.

7. $(1, -2), (4, 4)$
   $2x - y = 4$
   $3x + y = 1$

8. $(-3, -1), (3, 1)$
   $x - 3y = 0$
   $3x + y = 10$

9. $(4, 6), \left(-1, \frac{13}{3}\right)$
   $x - 3y = -14$
   $4x + 3y = 9$

10. $(4, 0), (3, 5)$
    $5x - 4y = 20$
    $-x + 4y = -4$

GRAPHICAL SOLUTIONS

Exercises 11–18: Solve the system graphically. Check your answers.

11. $y = 2x - 1$
    $y = 2 - x$

12. $y = -2x$
    $y = x + 3$

13. $y = \frac{1}{2}x + 1$
    $y = 1 - \frac{1}{2}x$

14. $y = -x + 1$
    $y = x + 3$

15. $2x + y = 4$
    $x - y = 5$

16. $2x + y = -1$
    $3x + 2y = -1$

17. $x + y = 3$
    $x - 2y = 6$

18. $3x + 2y = 9$
    $x + 3y = 3$

Exercises 19–22: A system of two linear equations is represented graphically. Use the graph to find any possible solutions.

19.

20.

21.

22.
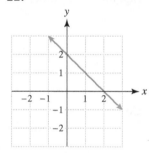

Exercises 23–40: Solve the system of equations. Determine whether the system is consistent or inconsistent. If the system is consistent, state whether the equations are dependent or independent.

23. $-x + y = 1$
    $x + y = 3$

24. $x + y = 2$
    $x - y = 2$

25. $2x + y = 5$
    $-2x + y = -3$

26. $x + 2y = 3$
    $2x - y = 1$

27. $x + y = 3$
    $2x + 2y = 6$

28. $x - y = 1$
    $-x + y = 3$

29. $3x - y = 0$
    $2x + y = 5$

30. $-2x - y = -3$
    $x + y = 2$

31. $-2x + y = 3$
    $4x - 2y = 2$

32. $2x + 4y = 2$
    $-x - 2y = -1$

33. $x + y = 6$
    $x - y = 2$

34. $x + y = 9$
    $x - y = 3$

35. $x - y = 4$
$2x - 2y = 4$

36. $2x + y = 5$
$4x + 2y = 10$

37. $6x - 4y = -2$
$-3x + 2y = 1$

38. $4x - 3y = 3$
$-8x + 6y = 1$

39. $4x + 3y = 2$
$5x + 2y = 6$

40. $-3x + 2y = 4$
$4x - y = 3$

Exercises 41–44: Solve the system of equations. Check your answer.

41. $2x + 2y = 4$
$x - 3y = -2$

42. $6x - y = 3$
$x - 2y = -5$

43. $-\frac{1}{2}x - \frac{1}{2}y = \frac{3}{2}$
$x - \frac{1}{2}y = 3$

44. $\frac{1}{2}x + \frac{1}{8}y = 1$
$-\frac{1}{2}x + \frac{5}{6}y = -1$

Exercises 45–48: Do the following.

(a) *Find the x- and y-intercepts for each equation.*
(b) *Use the intercepts to solve the system graphically.*

45. $x + y = 4$
$x - y = -2$

46. $2x + 3y = 12$
$2x - y = 4$

47. $-2x + 3y = 12$
$-2x + y = 8$

48. $-x + y = 2$
$x + y = 4$

 Exercises 49–56: Use technology to solve the system.

49. $\frac{1}{4}x + \frac{1}{2}y = \frac{3}{20}$
$\frac{1}{8}x - y = -\frac{3}{10}$

50. $\frac{1}{2}x - \frac{3}{8}y = \frac{1}{8}$
$\frac{1}{3}x - \frac{1}{2}y = -\frac{1}{12}$

51. $0.1x + 0.2y = 0.25$
$0.7x - 0.3y = 0.9$

52. $2.3x + 4.3y = 5.63$
$1.1x - 3.6y = 0.43$

53. $0.1x + 0.2y = 50$
$0.3x - 0.1y = 10$

54. $0.5x + 0.2y = 14$
$-0.1x + 0.4y = 6$

55. $x - 2y = 5$
$-2x + 4y = -2$

56. $3x + 4y = 5$
$6x + 8y = 10$

NUMERICAL SOLUTIONS

Exercises 57–60: A system of two linear equations has been solved numerically. Find any possible solutions.

57. $y_1 = 5 - x$
$y_2 = 2x - 1$

X	Y₁	Y₂
0	5	-1
1	4	1
2	3	3
3	2	5
4	1	7
5	0	9
6	-1	11

X=0

58. $y_1 = 1 - 2x$
$y_2 = -1 - 3x$

X	Y₁	Y₂
-6	13	17
-5	11	14
-4	9	11
-3	7	8
-2	5	5
-1	3	2
0	1	-1

X=-6

59. $y_1 = 2 - x$
$y_2 = x$

X	Y₁	Y₂
0	2	0
1	1	1
2	0	2
3	-1	3
4	-2	4
5	-3	5
6	-4	6

X=0

60. $y_1 = 2x - 1$
$y_2 = -3 + 2x$

X	Y₁	Y₂
0	-1	-3
1	1	-1
2	3	1
3	5	3
4	7	5
5	9	7
6	11	9

X=0

Exercises 61–66: Solve the system numerically.

61. $x + y = 3$
$x - y = 7$

62. $2x + y = 3$
$3x - y = 7$

63. $3x + 2y = 5$
$-x - y = -5$

64. $2x + 3y = 3.5$
$3x + 2y = 6.5$

65. $0.5x - 0.1y = 0.1$
$0.1x - 0.3y = -0.4$

66. $\frac{x}{3} + \frac{y}{6} = -\frac{1}{2}$
$\frac{x}{6} + \frac{y}{3} = \frac{5}{2}$

Exercises 67 and 68: Thinking Generally Solve the system of linear equations, if $a \neq 0$.

67. $x + ay = 1$
$2x + 2ay = 4$

68. $-ax + y = 4$
$ax + y = 4$

WRITING AND SOLVING EQUATIONS

Exercises 69–76: Do the following.

(a) *Write a system of linear equations that models the situation.*
(b) *Solve the resulting system.*

69. The sum of two numbers is 18, and their difference is 6. Find the two numbers.

70. Twice a number minus a second number equals 5. The sum of the two numbers is 16. Find the two numbers.

71. An athlete ran for part of an hour at 6 miles per hour and for the rest of the hour at 8 miles per hour. The total distance traveled was 7 miles. How long did the athlete run at each speed?

72. A car was driven for 2 hours, part of the time at 40 miles per hour and the rest of the time at 60 miles per hour. The total distance was 90 miles. How long did the car travel at each speed?

73. The perimeter of a rectangle is 76 inches. The rectangle's length is 4 inches longer than its width. Find the dimensions of this rectangle.

74. An isosceles triangle has a perimeter of 100 inches. The triangle's longest side is 10 inches longer than either of the other two sides. Find the length of each side of the triangle. (*Hint:* An isosceles triangle has two sides with equal measure.)

75. The largest angle in an isosceles triangle is 60° larger than either of the other two angles. Find the measure of each angle. (*Hint:* An isosceles triangle has two angles with equal measure.)

76. If 2 boxes of popcorn and 3 soft drinks cost $7 and 3 boxes of popcorn and 2 soft drinks cost $8, find the price of a box of popcorn and the price of a soft drink.

APPLICATIONS

77. *NCAA Basketball*   Kentucky and UCLA have appeared in the NCAA Division I men's basketball tournament 80 times, with Kentucky appearing 8 more times than UCLA. How many times has each team appeared in this tournament? (*Source:* NCAA.)

78. *Online Consumer Sales*   In 2002, $40 billion were spent on travel and computer hardware online. The amount spent on computer hardware was one-third the amount spent on travel. Find the amount spent on travel and the amount spent on computer hardware. (*Source:* Comscore Networks.)

79. *Home Runs*   In 1998, Mark McGwire and Sammy Sosa hit a total of 136 home runs. McGwire hit 4 more home runs than Sosa. How many home runs did each player hit?

80. *Student Loans*   A student takes out two loans totaling $4000 to help pay for college expenses. One loan is at 10% annual interest, and the other is at 5% annual interest. The first-year interest is $250. Find the amount of each loan.

81. *Investment*   A total of $600 is invested in two accounts at 4% and 5%. One hundred dollars more is invested in the 5% account. Determine the amount invested in each account.

82. *Dimensions*   A small building has a perimeter of 14 yards. Its length is 1 yard more than its width. Find the dimensions of the building.

WRITING ABOUT MATHEMATICS

83. Discuss the types of systems of linear equations having two variables. Explain how you can recognize each type graphically.

84. Given

$$ax + by = c$$
$$dx + ey = k,$$

explain how to solve this linear system graphically. Demonstrate your method with an example.

4.2 THE SUBSTITUTION AND ELIMINATION METHODS

The Substitution Method ▪ The Elimination Method ▪ Models and Applications

The ability to solve systems of equations has resulted in the development of CAT scans, satellites, DVDs, and accurate weather forecasts. In the preceding section we showed how to solve a system of two linear equations in two variables, using graphical and numerical methods. In this section we demonstrate how to solve these systems symbolically.

The Substitution Method

To apply the **substitution method**, we begin by solving an equation for one of its variables. Then we substitute the result into the other equation. For example, consider the following system of equations.

$$2x + y = 5$$
$$3x - 2y = 4$$

It is convenient to solve the first equation for y to obtain $y = 5 - 2x$. Now substitute $(5 - 2x)$ for y in the second equation,

$3x - 2(y) = 4$	Second equation
$3x - 2(5 - 2x) = 4,$	Substitute.

to obtain a linear equation in one variable.

$3x - 2(5 - 2x) = 4$	
$3x - 10 + 4x = 4$	Distributive property
$7x - 10 = 4$	Combine like terms.
$7x = 14$	Add 10 to each side.
$x = 2$	Divide each side by 7.

To determine y substitute 2 for x in $y = 5 - 2x$ to obtain

$$y = 5 - 2(2) = 1.$$

The solution is $(2, 1)$. To check this solution let $x = 2$ and $y = 1$ in each equation.

$2x + y = 5$	First equation	$3x - 2y = 4$	Second equation
$2(2) + 1 \overset{?}{=} 5$	Substitute.	$3(2) - 2(1) \overset{?}{=} 4$	Substitute.
$5 = 5$	It checks.	$4 = 4$	It checks.

Because $(2, 1)$ satisfies *both* equations, it is the solution to the system.

Do not stop after solving for the first variable. You must also solve for the second variable. Remember that a solution to a system of equations in two variables consists of an *ordered pair*, not a single number.

NOTE: When using substitution, you may begin by solving for *either variable in either equation*. The same result is obtained regardless of which equation is used. However, it is often simpler to solve for a variable with a coefficient of 1 because there is less likelihood of encountering fractions.

EXAMPLE 1   Applying the substitution method

Solve each system of equations.

(a) $y = 2x$ (b) $2x + y = -1$ (c) $-3x + 2y = 3$
        $x + y = 21$ $2x - y = -3$ $2x - 4y = -6$

Solution

(a) The first equation is $y = 2x$, so we substitute $(2x)$ for y in the second equation.

$$
\begin{aligned}
x + \quad y &= 21 &&\text{Second equation} \\
x + (2x) &= 21 &&\text{Let } y = 2x. \\
3x &= 21 &&\text{Add like terms.} \\
x &= 7 &&\text{Divide by 3.}
\end{aligned}
$$

Substituting 7 for x in $y = 2x$ gives $y = 14$. The solution is $(7, 14)$.

(b) We start by solving for y in the first equation because its coefficient is 1.

$$
\begin{aligned}
2x + y &= -1 &&\text{First equation} \\
y &= -2x - 1 &&\text{Subtract } 2x.
\end{aligned}
$$

Now we substitute $(-2x - 1)$ for y in the second equation.

$$
\begin{aligned}
2x - y &= -3 &&\text{Second equation} \\
2x - (-2x - 1) &= -3 &&\text{Let } y = (-2x - 1). \\
2x + 2x + 1 &= -3 &&\text{Distributive property} \\
4x &= -4 &&\text{Subtract 1; combine like terms.} \\
x &= -1 &&\text{Divide by 4.}
\end{aligned}
$$

Substituting -1 for x in $y = -2x - 1$ gives $y = 1$. The solution is $(-1, 1)$.

(c) We start by solving for x in the second equation, but we could solve for y.

$$
\begin{aligned}
2x - 4y &= -6 &&\text{Second equation} \\
2x &= 4y - 6 &&\text{Add } 4y. \\
x &= 2y - 3 &&\text{Divide by 2.}
\end{aligned}
$$

Substitute $(2y - 3)$ for x in the first equation.

$$
\begin{aligned}
-3x + 2y &= 3 &&\text{First equation} \\
-3(2y - 3) + 2y &= 3 &&\text{Let } x = (2y - 3). \\
-6y + 9 + 2y &= 3 &&\text{Distributive property} \\
-4y + 9 &= 3 &&\text{Combine like terms.} \\
-4y &= -6 &&\text{Subtract 9.} \\
y &= \tfrac{3}{2} &&\text{Divide by } -4.
\end{aligned}
$$

Substituting $\tfrac{3}{2}$ for y in $x = 2y - 3$ gives $x = 2\left(\tfrac{3}{2}\right) - 3 = 0$. The solution is $\left(0, \tfrac{3}{2}\right)$.

Now Try Exercises **7, 9, 23**

EXAMPLE 2   Finding per capita income

In 2004, the average of the per capita (or per person) incomes for Massachusetts and Maine was \$36,000. The per capita income in Massachusetts exceeded the per capita income in Maine by \$11,000. Find the 2004 per capita income for each state.

Solution

Let x be the per capita income in Massachusetts and y be the per capita income in Maine. The following system of equations models the data.

$$\frac{x + y}{2} = 36{,}000 \qquad \text{Their average is \$36,000.}$$

$$x - y = 11{,}000 \qquad \text{Their difference is \$11,000.}$$

Begin by solving the second equation for x.

$$x = y + 11{,}000$$

Substitute $(y + 11{,}000)$ for x in the first equation and solve for y.

$$\frac{(y + 11{,}000) + y}{2} = 36{,}000$$

$$
\begin{aligned}
(y + 11{,}000) + y &= 72{,}000 & \text{Multiply each side by 2.} \\
2y + 11{,}000 &= 72{,}000 & \text{Combine like terms.} \\
2y &= 61{,}000 & \text{Subtract 11,000 from each side.} \\
y &= 30{,}500 & \text{Divide each side by 2.}
\end{aligned}
$$

Substituting for y in $x = y + 11{,}000$ yields $x = 41{,}500$. In 2004, the per capita income in Massachusetts was \$41,500, and in Maine it was \$30,500.   Now Try Exercise **95**

NOTE: A step-by-step procedure for the substitution method is given in Putting It All Together for this section.

The Elimination Method

The **elimination** (or addition) **method** is a second way to solve linear systems symbolically. This method is based on the property that *equals added to equals are equal*. That is, if

$$a = b \quad \text{and} \quad c = d, \text{then}$$

$$a + c = b + d.$$

The goal of this method is to obtain an equation from which one of the two variables has been eliminated. This task is sometimes accomplished by adding two equations. This method is demonstrated in the next example.

EXAMPLE **3**   Applying the elimination method

Solve each system of equations.

(a) $x + y = 3$ (b) $4x + 3y = \quad 0$
     $x - y = 1$ $4x - 2y = -20$

Solution

(a) If we add the two equations, the y-variable will be eliminated.

$$
\begin{aligned}
x + \ y &= 3 \\
\underline{x - \ y} &= \underline{1} \\
2x + 0y &= 4 \quad \text{or} \quad x = 2 \qquad \text{Add equations and solve.}
\end{aligned}
$$

To find the value of y, we substitute $x = 2$ in either equation.

$$x + y = 3 \qquad \text{First equation}$$
$$2 + y = 3 \qquad \text{Let } x = 2.$$
$$y = 1 \qquad \text{Subtract 2.}$$

The solution is $(2, 1)$.

(b) If we multiply the first equation by -1 and then add the two equations, the x-variable will be eliminated.

$$-4x - 3y = \quad 0 \qquad \text{First equation times } -1$$
$$\underline{4x - 2y = -20} \qquad \text{Second equation}$$
$$0x - 5y = -20 \quad \text{or} \quad y = 4 \qquad \text{Add equations and solve.}$$

To find the value of x, we substitute $y = 4$ in either equation.

$$4x + 3y = \quad 0 \qquad \text{First equation}$$
$$4x + 3(4) = \quad 0 \qquad \text{Let } y = 4.$$
$$4x = -12 \qquad \text{Subtract 12.}$$
$$x = \quad -3 \qquad \text{Divide by 4.}$$

The solution is $(-3, 4)$.   Now Try Exercises **47, 49**

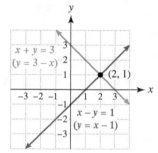

Figure 4.13

Solutions to systems of equations can be *supported graphically*. For example, if we graph the equations in Example 3(a), they intersect at the point $(2, 1)$, as shown in Figure 4.13.

EXAMPLE **4**   Applying the elimination method

Solve the following system by using elimination.

$$2x - y = 4$$
$$x + y = 1$$

Solution
Adding the two equations eliminates the variable y.

$$2x - \quad y = 4$$
$$\underline{x + \quad y = 1}$$
$$3x + 0y = 5 \quad \text{or} \quad x = \frac{5}{3} \qquad \text{Add the two equations and solve for } x.$$

Substituting $x = \frac{5}{3}$ in the second equation gives

$$\frac{5}{3} + y = 1 \quad \text{or} \quad y = -\frac{2}{3}.$$

The solution is $\left(\frac{5}{3}, -\frac{2}{3}\right)$.   Now Try Exercise **51**

NOTE: Example 4 illustrates that the x- and y-values for a solution can be fractions and *not* integers.

In the next example, we use multiplication before we add the two equations.

EXAMPLE 5   Multiplying before applying elimination

Solve the system of equations.

$$x + \frac{1}{2}y = 1$$
$$-3x + 2y = 11$$

Solution
Neither variable can be eliminated by simply adding the given equations. However, if we multiply each side of the first equation by -4, we eliminate fractions and then addition of the two equations eliminates the y-variable.

$$
\begin{array}{ll}
-4x - 2y = -4 & \text{Multiply first equation by } -4. \\
\underline{-3x + 2y = 11} & \\
-7x + 0y = 7 \quad \text{or} \quad x = -1 & \text{Add equations and solve.}
\end{array}
$$

To find the value of y, we substitute $x = -1$ in the second equation.

$$
\begin{array}{ll}
-3x + 2y = 11 & \text{Second equation} \\
-3(-1) + 2y = 11 & \text{Let } x = -1. \\
2y = 8 & \text{Subtract 3 from each side.} \\
y = 4 & \text{Divide each side by 2.}
\end{array}
$$

The solution is $(-1, 4)$.   Now Try Exercise **53**

MAKING CONNECTIONS

Substitution and Elimination

Substitution and elimination are two symbolic methods that accomplish the *same* task: solving a system of linear equations. Be aware that one method may be easier to perform than the other, depending on the system of equations to be solved.

EXAMPLE 6   Multiplying before applying elimination

Solve the following system by using elimination. Support your answer graphically and numerically.

$$3x - 2y = 11$$
$$2x + 3y = 3$$

Solution
Symbolic Solution If we add (or subtract) these equations, neither variable will be eliminated. However, if we multiply the first equation by 3 and multiply the second equation by 2, we can eliminate y.

$$
\begin{array}{ll}
9x - 6y = 33 & \text{Multiply first equation by 3.} \\
\underline{4x + 6y = 6} & \text{Multiply second equation by 2.} \\
13x + 0y = 39 \quad \text{or} \quad x = 3 & \text{Add the equations and solve.}
\end{array}
$$

Substituting $x = 3$ in the first equation, $3x - 2y = 11$, gives

$$3(3) - 2y = 11 \quad \text{or} \quad y = -1.$$

The solution is $(3, -1)$.

$[-5, 5, 1]$ by $[-3, 3, 1]$

(a)

X	Y₁	Y₂
0	-5.5	1
1	-4	.33333
2	-2.5	-.3333
3	-1	-1
4	.5	-1.667
5	2	-2.333
6	3.5	-3

X=3

(b)

Figure 4.14

NOTE: We could have multiplied the first equation by 2 and the second equation by -3. Adding the resulting equations would have eliminated the variable x.

Graphical Solution   If we use a calculator, we solve each equation for y.

$3x - 2y = 11$ First equation $2x + 3y = 3$ Second equation

$-2y = 11 - 3x$ Subtract 3x. $3y = 3 - 2x$ Subtract 2x.

$y = \dfrac{11 - 3x}{-2}$ Divide by -2. $y = \dfrac{3 - 2x}{3}$ Divide by 3.

In Figure 4.14(a), the graphs of $Y_1 = (11 - 3X)/(-2)$ and $Y_2 = (3 - 2X)/3$ intersect at the point $(3, -1)$.

Numerical Solution   In Figure 4.14(b), $y_1 = y_2 = -1$, when $x = 3$.

Now Try Exercises 71, 83

EXAMPLE 7   Recognizing an inconsistent system

Use elimination to solve the following system.

$$3x - 4y = 5$$
$$-6x + 8y = 9$$

Solution

If we multiply the first equation by 2 and add, we obtain the following result.

$6x - 8y = 10$ Multiply first equation by 2.

$\underline{-6x + 8y = 9}$

$ 0 = 19$ Adding the two equations gives a false result.

The statement $0 = 19$ is a *contradiction*, which tells us that the system has no solutions. If we solve each equation for y and graph, we obtain two parallel lines with slope $\frac{3}{4}$ that never intersect. This result is shown in Figure 4.15, where the equations are graphed as $Y_1 = (5 - 3X)/(-4)$ and $Y_2 = (6X + 9)/8$.

$[-6, 6, 1]$ by $[-4, 4, 1]$

Figure 4.15

Now Try Exercise 55

EXAMPLE 8   Recognizing dependent equations

Use elimination to solve the following system.

$$3x - 6y = 3$$
$$x - 2y = 1$$

Solution

If we multiply the second equation by -3 and add, we obtain the following.

$3x - 6y =$	3	First equation
$-3x + 6y =$	-3	Multiply second equation by -3.
$0 =$	0	Adding the two equations gives a true result.

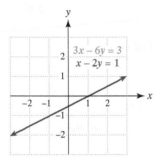

Figure 4.16

The statement $0 = 0$ is an *identity*, so the two equations are equivalent. If an ordered pair (x, y) satisfies the first equation, it also satisfies the second equation. Thus the solution set may be expressed as $\{(x, y) \mid x - 2y = 1\}$. For example, $(1, 0)$ and $(5, 2)$ are both solutions because they both satisfy $x - 2y = 1$.

The graphs of these equations are identical lines, as shown in Figure 4.16.

Now Try Exercise 57

MAKING CONNECTIONS

Graphical Solutions, Substitution, and Elimination

1. ***Unique Solution*** A graphical solution results in two lines intersecting at a unique point. Substitution and elimination give unique values for x and y.
2. ***Inconsistent Linear System*** A graphical solution results in two parallel lines. Substitution and elimination result in a contradiction, such as $0 = 1$.
3. ***Dependent Linear System*** A graphical solution results in two identical lines. Substitution and elimination result in an identity, such as $0 = 0$.

   NOTE: Conditions 2 and 3 occur when *both* variables are eliminated, and the resulting equation is either an identity or a contradiction.

Models and Applications

In Section 3.2, we learned a four-step process for solving problems. We will apply this process to solving applications that involve two variables. A *brief summary* of these four steps is as follows. (See page 167.)

STEPS FOR SOLVING A PROBLEM

STEP 1: Read the problem. Assign two variables to what you are being asked to find.

STEP 2: Write two equations involving these variables.

STEP 3: Solve the systems of equations.

STEP 4: Check your solution.

EXAMPLE 9   Modeling tuition

A student is attempting to graduate on schedule by taking 14 credits of day classes at one college and 4 credits of night classes at a different college. A credit for day classes costs $20 more than a credit for night classes. If the student's total tuition is $2440, how much does each type of credit cost?

Solution
STEP 1: Let x be the cost of a credit for day classes and y be the cost of a credit for night classes.

STEP 2: Then the data can be represented by the following system of equations.

$$\begin{aligned} x - y &= 20 \\ 14x + 4y &= 2440 \end{aligned}$$ Day credits cost $20 more than night credits.
The total cost is $2440 for 14 credits during the day and 4 credits at night.

STEP 3: To solve this system we multiply the first equation by 4 and then add the equations.

$$\begin{aligned} 4x - 4y &= 80 \\ 14x + 4y &= 2440 \\ \hline 18x + 0y &= 2520 \quad \text{or} \quad x = 140 \end{aligned}$$ Multiply by 4.

Add and solve for x.

Because $x = 140$ and $x - y = 20$, $y = 120$. Thus a credit for day classes costs $140 and a credit for night classes costs $120.

STEP 4: Check the solution. The difference is $140 - $120 = $20 and

$$\begin{aligned} 14 \times \$140 &= \$1960 \\ 4 \times \$120 &= \$\ 480 \\ \hline \text{Total cost} &= \$2440. \end{aligned}$$ Cost of day classes
Cost of night classes
The answer checks.

Now Try Exercise 103

In the next example we make use of the formula $d = rt$. (*Distance equals rate times time.*) If we solve this formula for r to obtain $r = \frac{d}{t}$, we can find the average speed (rate) of a boat traveling on a river. This method can also be used to determine the speed of an airplane when there is a wind. See Exercise 97.

EXAMPLE 10   Modeling river travel

A boat travels 150 miles upstream in 10 hours, and the return trip takes 6 hours. Find the speed of the boat in still water and the speed of the current.

Solution
STEP 1: Let x be the speed of the boat and y be the speed of the river current.

STEP 2: The boat travels 150 miles upstream in 10 hours. Thus the speed of the boat *against* the current is $\frac{150}{10} = 15$ miles per hour, or $x - y = 15$. Similarly the boat travels 150 miles downstream in 6 hours. Thus the speed of the boat *with* the current is $\frac{150}{6} = 25$ miles per hour, or $x + y = 25$.

STEP 3: We represent these data with the following equations.

$$x + y = 25$$
$$\underline{x - y = 15}$$
$$2x + 0y = 40 \quad \text{or} \quad x = 20 \qquad \text{Add equations and solve.}$$

Substituting $x = 20$ in $x + y = 25$ gives $y = 5$. The boat can travel 20 miles per hour in still water and the speed of the current is 5 miles per hour.

STEP 4: Check the solution. The speed of the boat *against* the current is $20 - 5 = 15$ miles per hour and the speed of the boat *with* the current is $20 + 5 = 25$ miles per hour.

$$t = \frac{d}{r} = \frac{150}{15} = 10 \text{ hours} \qquad \text{Time to travel upstream}$$

$$t = \frac{d}{r} = \frac{150}{25} = 6 \text{ hours} \qquad \text{Time to travel downstream}$$

The answer checks.   Now Try Exercise 99

EXAMPLE 11   Burning calories while exercising

During strenuous exercise, an athlete can burn 12 calories per minute running and 10 calories per minute on a bicycle. In a 60-minute workout, an athlete burns 644 calories. How long did the athlete spend running and bicycling?

Solution

STEP 1: Let x be the time spent running and y be the time spent bicycling.

STEP 2: Because the workout is 60 minutes long, we write $x + y = 60$. The number of calories burned running equals $12x$, and the number of calories burned bicycling equals $10y$. The total calories burned equals 644 so the system is as follows.

$$x + y = 60 \qquad \text{Total workout is 60 minutes.}$$
$$12x + 10y = 644 \qquad \text{Total calories equal 644.}$$

STEP 3: To solve this system we can multiply the first equation by -10 and add the equations to eliminate the y-variable.

$$-10x - 10y = -600 \qquad \text{Multiply first equation by } -10.$$
$$\underline{12x + 10y = 644}$$
$$2x + 0y = 44 \quad \text{or} \quad x = 22 \qquad \text{Add equations and solve.}$$

Substituting $x = 22$ in $x + y = 60$ gives $y = 38$. The athlete spent 22 minutes running and 38 minutes bicycling.

STEP 4: Check the solution. The total time is $22 + 38 = 60$ minutes and

$$22 \text{ minutes} \times 12 \text{ calories/minute} = 264 \text{ calories} \qquad \text{Calories burned running}$$
$$\underline{38 \text{ minutes} \times 10 \text{ calories/minute} = 380 \text{ calories}} \qquad \text{Calories burned bicycling}$$
$$\text{Total calories burned} = 644 \text{ calories.} \qquad \text{The answer checks.}$$

Now Try Exercise 88

EXAMPLE 12   Mixing antifreeze

A mixture of water and antifreeze in a car is currently 20% antifreeze. If the radiator holds 5 gallons of fluid and this mixture should be 40% antifreeze, how many gallons of radiator fluid should be drained and replaced with a mixture containing 90% antifreeze?

Solution

STEP 1: Let x be the gallons of 20% antifreeze that should remain in the radiator and y be the gallons of 90% antifreeze that should be added to the radiator.

STEP 2: The radiator holds 5 gallons of fluid, so $x + y = 5$. The final solution in the radiator should contain 5 gallons of 40% solution or $5(0.4) = 2$ gallons of (pure) antifreeze. Thus the antifreeze in the 20% solution plus the antifreeze in the 90% solution must equal 2 gallons. That is, $0.2x + 0.9y = 2$. Table 4.2 summarizes this situation.

TABLE 4.2   **Mixing Antifreeze**

	20% Solution	90% Solution	40% Solution
Radiator Fluid (gallons)	x	y	5
Pure Antifreeze (gallons)	$0.2x$	$0.9y$	2

The resulting system to be solved is

$$x + y = 5 \qquad \text{First row in table}$$
$$0.2x + 0.9y = 2. \qquad \text{Second row in table}$$

STEP 3: Multiply the first equation by 2 and the second equation by -10.

$$
\begin{array}{ll}
2x + 2y = 10 & \text{Multiply first equation by 2.} \\
-2x - 9y = -20 & \text{Multiply second equation by } -10. \\
\hline
0x - 7y = -10 \quad \text{or} \quad y = \frac{10}{7} & \text{Add and solve.}
\end{array}
$$

Thus $\frac{10}{7}$ gallons of 90% antifreeze solution should be added.

STEP 4: Check the solution. If $\frac{10}{7}$ gallons are drained from the 5-gallon radiator, then there are $5 - \frac{10}{7} = \frac{35}{7} - \frac{10}{7} = \frac{25}{7}$ gallons of 20% antifreeze remaining and $\frac{10}{7}$ gallons of 90% antifreeze added.

$$20\% \text{ of } \frac{25}{7} = \frac{2}{10} \times \frac{25}{7} = \frac{5}{7} \text{ gallons of pure antifreeze}$$

$$90\% \text{ of } \frac{10}{7} \text{ gallons} = \frac{9}{10} \times \frac{10}{7} = \frac{9}{7} \text{ gallons of pure antifreeze}$$

There are $\frac{5}{7} + \frac{9}{7} = \frac{14}{7} = 2$ gallons of pure antifreeze in the 5-gallon radiator, so the new concentration is $\frac{2}{5} = 0.4$ or 40%. The answer checks.   Now Try Exercise 89

4.2 PUTTING IT ALL TOGETHER

Two symbolic methods for solving a system of linear equations are substitution and elimination. Symbolic methods give exact answers, whereas graphical and numerical methods may give approximate answers. The following table presents a summary.

Concept	Explanation
Substitution Method	**1.** Solve for a convenient variable such as y in the first equation. $$x + y = 3 \quad \text{or} \quad y = 3 - x$$ $$2x - y = 0$$ **2.** Substitute $(3 - x)$ in the second equation for y. Solve the equation for x. $$2x - (3 - x) = 0 \quad \text{or} \quad x = 1$$ **3.** Substitute $x = 1$ in one of the given equations and find y. $$1 + y = 3 \quad \text{or} \quad y = 2$$ **4.** The solution is $(1, 2)$. Check your answer.
Elimination Method	**1.** Multiply the first equation by -2 so that the coefficients of x in the two equations are additive inverses. $$x + 2y = 1 \quad \text{or} \quad -2x - 4y = -2$$ $$2x - 3y = 9 \qquad\qquad 2x - 3y = \;\; 9$$ **2.** Eliminate x by adding the two equations. $$-2x - 4y = -2$$ $$\underline{2x - 3y = \;\; 9}$$ $$0x - 7y = \;\; 7 \quad \text{or} \quad y = -1$$ **3.** Substitute $y = -1$ in one of the given equations and solve for x. $$x + 2(-1) = 1 \quad \text{or} \quad x = 3$$ **4.** The solution is $(3, -1)$. Check your answer.

4.2 Exercises

PRACTICE   WATCH   DOWNLOAD   READ   REVIEW

CONCEPTS

1. Name two symbolic methods for solving a linear system.

2. Are different solutions obtained when the same system of equations is solved symbolically, graphically, and numerically? Explain.

3. When using elimination, how can you recognize an inconsistent system of equations?

4. When using elimination, how can you recognize a dependent system of equations?

5. When you use substitution to solve

$$3x + y = \;\; 4$$
$$5x - 7y = -2,$$

what is a good first step?

6. When you are using elimination to solve

$$2x - 5y = 4$$
$$x + 3y = 11,$$

what is a good first step?

SUBSTITUTION METHOD

Exercises 7–10: Solve the system of linear equations by using substitution.

7. $y = 2x$
$3x + y = 5$

8. $y = x + 1$
$x + 2y = 8$

9. $x = 2y - 1$
$x + 5y = 20$

10. $x = 3y$
$-x + 2y = 4$

Exercises 11 and 12: Use substitution to solve the system of equations. Then use the graph to support your answer.

11. $x - 2y = 0$
$3x + y = 7$

12. $2x + 3y = 8$
$3x - 2y = -14$

 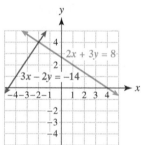

Exercises 13–18: Solve the system of equations by using substitution. Then solve the system graphically.

13. $y = 3x$
$x + y = 4$

14. $x = \frac{1}{2}y$
$2x + y = 4$

15. $x + y = 2$
$2x - y = 1$

16. $x - y = 2$
$x + 2y = -1$

17. $2x + 3y = 6$
$x - 2y = -4$

18. $2x - y = 2$
$3x + 2y = 10$

Exercises 19–34: Solve the system of equations by using substitution.

19. $4x + y = 3$
$2x - 3y = -2$

20. $3x + 4y = 32$
$2x - y = 3$

21. $x - 2y = 0$
$-3x + 2y = -1$

22. $-x + 3y = 3$
$2x + 5y = -\frac{1}{2}$

23. $2x - 5y = -1$
$-x + 3y = 0$

24. $5x + 10y = -5$
$-10x + 5y = 60$

25. $x - y = 1$
$2x + 6y = -2$

26. $4x - y = -4$
$-2x + 5y = 29$

27. $\frac{1}{2}x - \frac{1}{2}y = 1$
$2x - y = 6$

28. $\frac{3}{4}x + \frac{1}{2}y = 5$
$x - 2y = 12$

29. $\frac{1}{6}x - \frac{1}{3}y = -1$
$\frac{1}{3}x + \frac{5}{6}y = 7$

30. $\frac{3}{5}x - \frac{1}{10}y = 4$
$\frac{2}{5}x + \frac{1}{10}y = 6$

31. $\frac{1}{2}x + \frac{2}{3}y = -2$
$\frac{1}{4}x - \frac{1}{3}y = 3$

32. $\frac{1}{5}x - \frac{1}{10}y = \frac{7}{40}$
$\frac{1}{4}x - \frac{1}{5}y = \frac{11}{40}$

33. $0.1x + 0.4y = 1.3$
$0.3x - 0.2y = 1.1$

34. $1.5x - 4.1y = -1.6$
$2.7x - 0.1y = 0.76$

35. The following system is dependent.

$$x - y = 5$$
$$2x - 2y = 10$$

Solve this system by using substitution. Explain how you can recognize a dependent system when you are using substitution.

36. The following system is inconsistent.

$$-x + 2y = 5$$
$$2x - 4y = 10$$

Solve this system by using substitution. Explain how you can recognize an inconsistent system when you are using substitution.

Exercises 37–40: (Refer to Exercises 35 and 36.) Solve the system of equations by using substitution, if possible.

37. $5x + 3y = 6$
$-\frac{5}{3}x - y = 2$

38. $2x - 4y = 5$
$-x + 2y = 1$

39. $x + 3y = -2$
$-\frac{1}{2}x - \frac{3}{2}y = 1$

40. $2x - 4y = 4$
$-3x + 6y = -6$

ELIMINATION METHOD

Exercises 41 and 42: Use elimination to solve the system of equations. Then use the graph at the top of the next page to support your answer.

41. $x - y = 5$
$x + y = 9$

42. $3x - 2y = 9$
$5x + 2y = 7$

Exercises 43–46: Use elimination to solve the system of equations. Then solve the system graphically.

43. $x + y = 3$
$x - y = 1$

44. $2x - y = 3$
$x + 2y = -1$

45. $4x - y = 4$
$x + 2y = 1$

46. $x - y = 1$
$x + 4y = 6$

Exercises 47–62: Use elimination to solve the system.

47. $x + y = 4$
$x - y = 2$

48. $x - 3y = 5$
$-x + 5y = -7$

49. $-3x - y = 5$
$-3x + 2y = -1$

50. $-2x + 3y = 13$
$x + 3y = 7$

51. $2x + y = 4$
$2x - y = -2$

52. $2x + 3y = -6$
$2x - y = 4$

53. $6x - 4y = 12$
$3x + 5y = -6$

54. $-5x - 4y = -8$
$x - 4y = 10$

55. $2x - 4y = 5$
$-x + 2y = 9$

56. $x - 3y = 5$
$2x - 6y = 1$

57. $2x + y = 2$
$4x + 2y = 4$

58. $\frac{1}{2}x + \frac{1}{7}y = 2$
$7x + 2y = 28$

59. $2x + 4y = -22$
$75x + 15y = -120$

60. $-3x + 20y = 67$
$2x + 5y = 47$

61. $0.3x + 0.2y = 0.8$
$0.4x + 0.3y = 1.1$

62. $1.2x + 4.3y = 1.7$
$2.4x - 1.5y = 1.38$

Exercises 63–78: Solve the system of equations.

63. $2x + 3y = 7$
$2x - y = -13$

64. $2x - 3y = -25$
$x + 3y = 10$

65. $3u - 5v = 4$
$5u + v = 2$

66. $4u - 3v = -2$
$-8u + 9v = 5$

67. $2r - 3t = 7$
$-4r + 6t = -14$

68. $r - t = 10$
$-2r + 2t = -20$

69. $m - n = 5$
$m - n = 7$

70. $6m + 9n = 4$
$-4m - 6n = 2$

71. $2x - 3y = 2$
$3x - 5y = 4$

72. $x + 3y = \frac{5}{4}$
$-2x - 7y = -\frac{11}{4}$

73. $0.1x - 0.3y = -5$
$0.5x + 1.1y = 27$

74. $0.6x - 0.2y = 1.8$
$-0.1x - 0.5y = 1.3$

75. $\frac{1}{2}y - \frac{1}{2}z = -1$
$\frac{3}{4}y - \frac{1}{2}z = 1$

76. $\frac{3}{4}y + \frac{1}{4}z = 13$
$-\frac{1}{4}y + \frac{1}{4}z = -3$

77. $\frac{1}{5}x - \frac{2}{5}y = -\frac{3}{5}$
$x - y = 1$

78. $\frac{1}{10}x - \frac{1}{5}y = 2$
$-\frac{1}{5}x + \frac{1}{10}y = -1.9$

USING MORE THAN ONE METHOD

Exercises 79–84: Solve the system of equations graphically, numerically, and symbolically.

79. $x - y = 4$
$x + y = 6$

80. $2x - y = 7$
$3x + y = 3$

81. $5x + 2y = 9$
$3x - y = 1$

82. $-x + 4y = 17$
$3x + 6y = 21$

83. $3x - 2y = 8.5$
$2x + 4y = 3$

84. $-x - 3y = 1.8$
$2x - 5y = 0.8$

Exercises 85 and 86: **Thinking Generally** *Solve the system of equations, where a is a constant and $a \neq 1$.*

85. $ax + y = 4$
$x + y = 4$

86. $2x + y = 1$
$2x + ay = a$

APPLICATIONS

87. *Burning Fat Calories* Two athletes engage in a strenuous 40-minute workout on a stair climber. The heavier athlete burns 58 more fat calories than the lighter athlete. Together they burn a total of 290 fat calories. How many fat calories does each athlete burn? If 1 fat gram equals 9 fat calories, how many fat grams does each athlete burn? (*Source: Runner's World.*)

88. *Burning Calories* During strenuous exercise, an athlete can burn 10 calories per minute on a rowing machine, whereas on a stair climber the athlete can burn 11.5 calories per minute. In a 60-minute workout an athlete burns 633 calories by using both exercise machines. How many minutes does the athlete spend on each type of workout equipment? (*Source: Runner's World.*)

89. *Mixing Antifreeze* A mixture of water and antifreeze in a car is 10% antifreeze. In colder climates this mixture should contain 50% antifreeze. If the radiator contains 4 gallons of fluid, how many gallons of radiator fluid should be drained and replaced with a mixture containing 80% antifreeze?

90. *Mixing Acid* Determine the milliliters of 10% sulfuric acid and the milliliters of 25% sulfuric acid that should be mixed to obtain 20 milliliters of 18% sulfuric acid.

91. *Hotel Rooms* The revenue from renting 50 hotel rooms is $4945. If premium rooms cost $115 and regular rooms cost $80, find the number of each type of room rented.

92. *Coins* A sample of dimes and quarters totals $18. If there are 111 coins in all, how many of each type of coin are there?

93. *Supplementary Angles* The larger of two supplementary angles is 30° more than twice the smaller angle. Find the angles. (*Hint:* Supplementary angles sum to 180°.)

94. *Complementary Angles* The larger of two complementary angles is 6° less than twice the smaller angle. Find the angles. (*Hint:* Complementary angles sum to 90°.)

95. *Population* In 2003, there were 291 million people in the United States and females outnumbered males by 5 million. Determine the number of males and the number of females in 2003. (*Source:* U.S. Census Bureau.)

96. *Per Capita Income* In 2000, the average of the per capita incomes for Alaska and Arizona was $28,000. The per capita income in Alaska exceeded the per capita income in Arizona by $4000. Find the per capita income for each state. (*Source:* Bureau of Economic Analysis.)

97. *Airplane Speed* A plane flies 2400 miles from Orlando, Florida, to Los Angeles, California, against the jet stream in 4 hours and 10 minutes. Then the plane flies back to Orlando with the jet stream in 3 hours and 45 minutes. Find the speed of the plane with no wind and the speed of the jet stream.

98. *Airplane Speed* An airplane flies with the wind and travels 3000 miles in 5 hours. The return trip into the wind requires 6 hours. Find the speed of the wind and of the airplane in no wind.

99. *Boat Speed* A boat travels downstream 150 miles in 5 hours. The return trip takes 7 hours and 30 minutes. Find the speed of the boat without a current and the speed of the current.

100. *River Current* A tugboat can push a barge 165 miles upstream in 33 hours. The same tugboat and barge can make the return trip downstream in 15 hours. Determine the speed of the current and the speed of the tugboat when there is no current.

101. *Student Loans* A student takes out two loans to help pay for college. One loan is at 8% interest, and the other is at 9% interest. The total amount borrowed is $3500, and the interest after 1 year for both loans is $294. Find the amount of each loan.

102. *Student Loans* A student takes out two loans totaling $5000 at 4% and 6% annual interest. The total interest after one year is $254. Find the amount of each loan.

103. *College Tuition* A student takes 12 credits of day classes and 6 credits of night classes. A credit for day classes costs $30 more than a credit for night classes. If the student's total tuition is $1800, how much does each type of credit cost?

104. *Computer Sales* Sales of personal computers are expected to increase in the twenty-first century. In 2000 and 2001, a combined total of 264 million personal computers were sold worldwide, with 12.9% more computers sold in 2001 than in 2000. How many personal computers were sold in 2000, and how many were sold in 2001? Round your answers to the nearest million. (*Source:* International Data Corporation.)

105. *Roof Trusses* Linear systems are used in the design of roof trusses for buildings (see the accompanying figures). One of the simplest types of roof trusses is an equilateral triangle. If a 200-pound force is applied to the peak of the truss, the weights W_1 and W_2 exerted on each rafter are determined by the following system of equations. Solve this system.

$$W_1 - W_2 = 0$$

$$\frac{\sqrt{3}}{2}(W_1 + W_2) = 200$$

200 pounds

W_1 W_2

60°   60°

106. *Roof Trusses*   (Refer to Exercise 105.) The weights W_1 and W_2 exerted on each rafter for the roof truss shown in the accompanying figure are determined by the following system of equations. Solve the system and interpret the result.

150 pounds

W_1 W_2

30°   45°

$$W_1 + \sqrt{2}W_2 = 300$$

$$\sqrt{3}W_1 - \sqrt{2}W_2 = 0$$

107. *Geometry*   A basketball court has a perimeter of 296 feet. Its length is 44 feet greater than its width. Set up a system of two linear equations whose solution gives the length and width of the court. Solve the system
(a) symbolically,   (b) graphically, and
(c) numerically.

x

y

108. *Concert Tickets*   Concert tickets cost $55 and $40. If 2000 tickets were sold for total receipts of $90,500, find how many of each type of ticket were sold
(a) symbolically,   (b) graphically, and
(c) numerically.

WRITING ABOUT MATHEMATICS

109. Explain what it means for a linear system to be inconsistent. Give an example.

110. Describe two possible ways that you could use elimination to solve the following system of linear equations. (Do not actually solve the system.)

$$ax - y = c$$
$$x + dy = e$$

CHECKING BASIC CONCEPTS
SECTIONS 4.1 AND 4.2

1. Solve the system of linear equations

$$2x - y = 5$$
$$-x + 3y = 0$$

(a) graphically and
(b) numerically.
Do your answers agree?

2. Use substitution to solve the system of equations.

$$4x - 3y = -1$$
$$x + 4y = 14$$

3. Use elimination to solve the system of equations. Is the system dependent? Is it inconsistent?

$$4x - 3y = -17$$
$$-6x + 2y = 23$$

4. *Complementary Angles*   The smaller of two complementary angles is 40° less than the larger angle.
(a) Write a system of linear equations whose solution gives the measure of each angle. (*Hint:* Complementary angles sum to 90°.)
(b) Solve the system and interpret the result.

4.3 SYSTEMS OF LINEAR INEQUALITIES

Solving Linear Inequalities in Two Variables ■ Solving Systems of
Linear Inequalities

A LOOK INTO MATH ▷

People often walk or jog in an effort to increase their heart rates and get in better shape. During strenuous exercise, older people should maintain lower heart rates than younger people. A person cannot maintain precisely one heart rate, so a range of heart rates is recommended by health professionals. For aerobic fitness, a 50-year-old's heart rate might be between 120 and 140 beats per minute, whereas a 20-year-old's heart rate might be between 140 and 160. Systems of linear inequalities can be used to model these situations.

Solving Linear Inequalities in Two Variables

▶ **REAL-WORLD CONNECTION**   Suppose that candy costs $2 per pound and that peanuts cost $1 per pound. The total cost C of buying x pounds of candy and y pounds of peanuts is given by

$$C = 2x + y.$$

If we have at most **$5** to spend, the inequality

$$2x + y \leq 5$$

must be satisfied. To determine the different weight combinations of candy and peanuts that could be bought, we could use the graph shown in Figure 4.17. Points located on the line $2x + y = 5$ represent weight combinations resulting in a $5 purchase. For example, the point (2, 1) satisfies the equation $2x + y = 5$ and represents buying 2 pounds of candy and 1 pound of peanuts for $5. Ordered pairs (x, y) located in the shaded region below the line represent purchases of less than $5. The point (1, 2) lies in the shaded region and represents buying 1 pound of candy and 2 pounds of peanuts for $4. Note that if we substitute $x = 1$ and $y = 2$ in the inequality, we obtain

$$2(1) + (2) \leq 5,$$

which is a true statement.

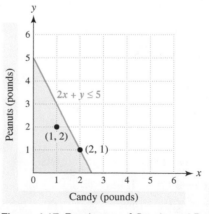

Figure 4.17 Purchases of Candy and Peanuts

When the equals sign in a linear equation in two variables is replaced with one of the symbols $<$, $\leq$, $>$, or $\geq$, a **linear inequality in two variables** results. Examples include

$$2x + y \leq 5, \quad y \geq x - 5, \quad \text{and} \quad \frac{1}{2}x - \frac{3}{5}y < 8.$$

EXAMPLE 1   Solving linear inequalities

Shade the solution set for each inequality.
(a) $x > 1$ **(b)** $y \leq 2x - 1$ **(c)** $x - 2y < 4$

Solution
(a) Begin by graphing the vertical line $x = 1$ with a *dashed* line because equality is *not* included. The solution set includes all points with x-values greater than 1, so shade the region to the right of this line, as shown in Figure 4.18(a).

(a)

(b)

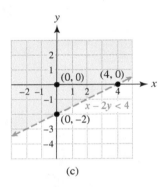
(c)

Figure 4.18

(b) Start by graphing $y = 2x - 1$ with a *solid* line because equality *is* included. The inequality sign is $\leq$, so the solution set includes all points on or below this line, as shown in Figure 4.18(b).

(c) We start by finding the intercepts for the line $x - 2y = 4$.

x-intercept: $y = 0$ implies $x - 2(0) = 4$ or $x = 4$

y-intercept: $x = 0$ implies $0 - 2y = 4$ or $y = -2$

Plot the points $(4, 0)$ and $(0, -2)$ and sketch a dashed line, as shown in Figure 4.18(c). To determine whether to shade above or below this line, substitute a *test point* in the inequality. For example, if we pick the test point $(0, 0)$ and then substitute $x = 0$ and $y = 0$ in the given inequality, we find the following result.

$$x - 2y < 4 \qquad \text{Given inequality}$$
$$0 - 2(0) < 4 \qquad \text{Let } x = 0 \text{ and } y = 0.$$
$$0 < 4 \qquad \text{A true statement}$$

Because this substitution results in a true statement, shade the region *containing* $(0, 0)$, which is located above the dashed line.   Now Try Exercises **7, 11, 19**

The following steps can be used to graph a linear inequality in two variables.

SOLVING A LINEAR INEQUALITY GRAPHICALLY

1. Replace the inequality symbol with an equals sign.
2. Graph the resulting line. Use a solid line if the inequality symbol is $\leq$ or $\geq$ and a dashed line if it is $<$ or $>$.
3. (a) If the inequality is in the form $x \leq k$ or $x < k$ (where k is a constant) shade to the *left* of the vertical line. If the inequality is in the form $x \geq k$ or $x > k$, shade to the *right* of the vertical line.
    (b) If the inequality is in the form $y \leq mx + b$ or $y < mx + b$, shade *below* this line. If the inequality is in the form $y \geq mx + b$ or $y > mx + b$, shade *above* this line.
    (c) If you are uncertain as to which region to shade, choose a **test point** that is *not* on the line. Substitute it in the given inequality. If the test point makes the inequality true, then shade the region containing the test point. Otherwise, shade on the other side of the line.

EXAMPLE 2   Solving a linear inequality graphically

Shade the solution set for the linear inequality $4x - 3y < 12$.

Solution
Start graphing the line $4x - 3y = 12$ by finding its intercepts.

$$x\text{-intercept: } y = 0 \text{ implies } 4x - 3(0) = 12 \text{ or } x = 3.$$

$$y\text{-intercept: } x = 0 \text{ implies } 4(0) - 3y = 12 \text{ or } y = -4.$$

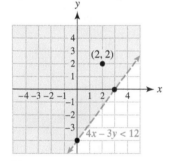

Plot the points $(3, 0)$ and $(0, -4)$ and sketch a dashed line. Any point not on this line can be used for a test point. We use the test point $(2, 2)$.

$$4x - 3y < 12 \qquad \text{Given inequality}$$
$$4(2) - 3(2) < 12 \qquad \text{Let } x = 2 \text{ and } y = 2.$$
$$2 < 12 \qquad \text{A true statement}$$

Figure 4.19

Thus shade the region containing the point $(2, 2)$, as shown in Figure 4.19.

Now Try Exercise 21

Solving Systems of Linear Inequalities

A **system of linear inequalities** results when the equals signs in a system of linear equations are replaced with $<, \leq, >,$ or $\geq$. The system of linear equations

$$x + y = 4$$
$$y = x$$

becomes a system of linear inequalities when it is written as

$$x + y \leq 4$$
$$y \geq x.$$

A solution to a system of inequalities must satisfy *both* inequalities. For example, the ordered pair $(1, 2)$ is a solution to this system because substituting $x = 1$ and $y = 2$ makes both inequalities true.

$$1 + 2 \leq 4 \qquad \text{True}$$
$$2 \geq 1 \qquad \text{True}$$

To see graphically that $(1, 2)$ is a solution, consider the following. The solution set for $x + y \leq 4$ consists of points lying on the line $x + y = 4$ and all points below the line. This region is shaded in Figure 4.20(a). Similarly, the solutions to $y \geq x$ include the line $y = x$ and all points above it. This region is shaded in Figure 4.20(b).

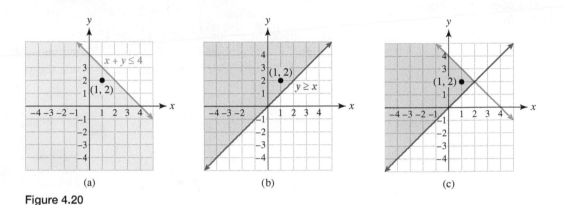

(a)   (b)   (c)

Figure 4.20

For a point (x, y) to be a solution to the *system* of linear inequalities, it must be located in both shaded regions shown in Figures 4.20(a) and 4.20(b). The *intersection* of the shaded regions is shown in Figure 4.20(c). Note that the point $(1, 2)$ is located in each shaded region shown in Figures 4.20(a) and 4.20(b). Therefore the point $(1, 2)$ is located in the shaded region shown in Figure 4.20(c) and is a solution of the system of linear inequalities.

EXAMPLE 3   Solving a system of linear inequalities

Shade the solution set for each system of inequalities.
(a) $x \leq -1$ (b) $y < 2x$ (c) $2x - y < 2$
     $y \geq 2$ $x + y > 3$ $x + 2y \geq 6$

Solution
(a) Graph the vertical line $x = -1$ and the horizontal line $y = 2$ as solid lines. The solution set is to the left of the line $x = -1$ and above the line $y = 2$. See Figure 4.21. The test point $(-2, 3)$ satisfies both inequalities and lies in the shaded region.

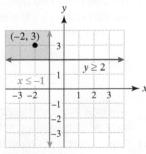

Figure 4.21

CRITICAL THINKING

Is the point where the two lines intersect in Figure 4.20(c) part of the solution set? Why or why not? Repeat this question for Figure 4.22(b).

(b) Graph $y = 2x$ and $x + y = 3$ as dashed lines. These two lines divide the xy-plane into four regions. The test point $(-1, -1)$ does not satisfy the inequalities, so do not shade the region containing it. However, the point $(2, 2)$ does satisfy *both* inequalities. To verify this fact substitute $x = 2$ and $y = 2$ in each inequality.

$$2 < 2(2) \qquad \text{True}$$
$$2 + 2 > 3 \qquad \text{True}$$

Thus shade the region shown in Figure 4.22(a).

(c) Graph $2x - y = 2$ and $x + 2y = 6$ as dashed and solid lines, respectively. The test point $(2, 3)$ satisfies *both* inequalities, so shade the region containing it, as shown in Figure 4.22(b).

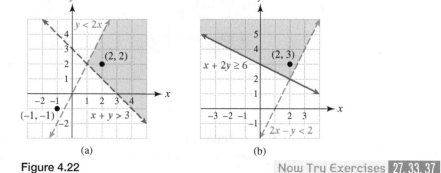

(a)   (b)

Figure 4.22

Now Try Exercises 27, 33, 37

NOTE: Finding a test point that satisfies a system of linear inequalities may require trial and error. You may need to pick one test point from each of the four regions determined by the two lines. One of the four points must satisfy the system of inequalities.

▶ REAL-WORLD CONNECTION   In the next example we demonstrate how systems of inequalities can model the situation discussed in the introduction to this section.

EXAMPLE 4   Modeling target heart rates

When exercising, people often try to maintain target heart rates that are percentages of their maximum heart rates. A person's maximum heart rate (MHR) is MHR $= 220 - A$, where A represents age and the MHR is in beats per minute. The shaded region shown in Figure 4.23 represents target heart rates for aerobic fitness for various ages.   (*Source:* Hebb Industries, Inc.)

(a) Estimate the range R of heart rates that are acceptable for someone 40 years old.

(b) By choosing two points on each line in Figure 4.23 and applying the point–slope form, we can show that the equations for these lines are approximately

$$T = -0.8A + 196 \qquad \text{Upper line}$$

and

$$T = -0.7A + 154, \qquad \text{Lower line}$$

where A represents age and T represents the target heart rate. Write a system of inequalities whose solution set is the shaded region, including the two lines.

(c) Use Figure 4.23 to determine whether $(30, 150)$ is a solution. Then verify your answer by using the system of inequalities.

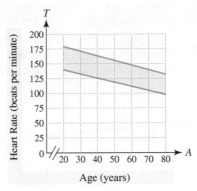

Figure 4.23 Target Heart Rates

Solution

(a) Figure 4.23 reveals that, when the age is 40, $A = 40$, the target heart rates T are *approximately* $125 \leq T \leq 165$ beats per minute.

(b) The region lies **below** the upper line, **above** the lower line, and includes both lines. Therefore this region is modeled by

$$T \leq -0.8A + 196$$

$$T \geq -0.7A + 154.$$

(c) Figure 4.23 shows that the point representing a 30-year-old person with a heart rate of 150 beats per minute lies in the shaded region, so (30, 150) is a solution. This result can be verified by substituting $A = 30$ and $T = \mathbf{150}$ in the system.

$$\mathbf{150} \leq -0.8(\mathbf{30}) + 196 = 172 \qquad \text{True}$$

$$\mathbf{150} \geq -0.7(\mathbf{30}) + 154 = 133 \qquad \text{True} \qquad \text{Now Try Exercise } \boxed{67}$$

EXAMPLE 5   Solving a system of linear inequalities with technology

Shade the solution set for the system of inequalities, using a graphing calculator.

$$2x + y \leq 5$$
$$-2x + y \geq 1$$

Solution

Begin by solving each inequality for y to obtain $y \leq 5 - 2x$ and $y \geq 2x + 1$. The graphs of $Y_1 = 5 - 2X$ and $Y_2 = 2X + 1$ are shown in Figure 4.24(a). The solution set lies below y_1 and above y_2. Figure 4.24(b) shows how to shade this region. The solution set is the region comprised of small squares in Figure 4.24(c).

CALCULATOR HELP

To shade a graph, see the Appendix (page AP-7).

$[-15, 15, 5]$ by $[-10, 10, 5]$

(a)

(b)

$[-15, 15, 5]$ by $[-10, 10, 5]$

(c)

Figure 4.24

Now Try Exercise $\boxed{51}$

TECHNOLOGY NOTE: Shading of Linear Inequalities

When shading the solution set for a linear inequality, graphing calculators often show solid lines even if a line should be dashed. For example, the graphs for $y < 5 - 2x$ and $y \leq 5 - 2x$ are *identical* on some graphing calculators.

CRITICAL THINKING

Graph the solution set to the following system and discuss your results. $3x + y \geq 6$
$3x + y \leq 2$

4.3   PUTTING IT ALL TOGETHER

In this section we presented systems of linear inequalities in two variables. These systems usually have infinitely many solutions and can be represented by a shaded region in the xy-plane. The following table summarizes these concepts.

Concept	Explanation	Examples
Linear Inequality in Two Variables	$ax + by > c$, where a, b, and c are constants. ($>$ may be replaced with $<$, $\leq$, or $\geq$.)	$y \geq 5$, $x - y < -10$, and $6x - 7y \leq 22$
System of Linear Inequalities in Two Variables	Two linear inequalities where a solution must satisfy *both* inequalities	$x + y < 11$ $x - y \geq 4$ $(8, 2)$ is a solution because $x = 8$ and $y = 2$ make *both* inequalities true.
Solution Set to a System of Linear Inequalities	Set of all solutions; typically a region in the xy-plane Two intersecting lines divide the xy-plane into four regions. To determine which region should be shaded, choose one test point from each region. The region that contains the test point satisfying both inequalities should be shaded.	$y \leq 5 - x$ (below $y = 5 - x$) and $y < 2x - 3$ (below $y = 2x - 3$) Use a dashed line for $<$ or $>$. Use a solid line for $\leq$ or $\geq$. The test point $(3, -2)$ satisfies both inequalities.

4.3 Exercises

 MyMathLab
PRACTICE   WATCH   DOWNLOAD   READ   REVIEW

CONCEPTS

1. If a system of inequalities contains two inequalities in two variables, how many of the inequalities does a solution satisfy?

2. Can a system of linear inequalities have infinitely many solutions? Explain.

3. Does $(3, 1)$ satisfy $5x - 2y > 8$? Does $(2, 1)$ satisfy this inequality?

4. Does $(3, 4)$ satisfy the following system of inequalities?
$$x - 2y \geq -8$$
$$2x - y < 1$$
Is $(-2, 0)$ a solution to the system?

5. When you are graphing the solution set to $y \leq x$, the boundary should be a (dashed/solid) line.

6. When you are graphing the solution set to $2x - y > 2$, the boundary should be a (dashed/solid) line.

LINEAR INEQUALITIES

Exercises 7–24: Shade the solution set in the xy-plane.

7. $x > 2$

8. $x \leq -1$

9. $y \leq 1$

10. $y > 0$

11. $y < -2x$

12. $y < 2x$

13. $y \geq x + 1$

14. $y \geq x - 2$

15. $y \geq 3x$

16. $y \leq 1 - x$

17. $y < 3x - 2$

18. $x + y > 3$

19. $2x - y \leq 4$

20. $4x + 2y < 8$

21. $-x + 3y > 3$

22. $-2x + y \leq 0$

23. $5x - 2y \leq -10$

24. $-3x + 2y < 6$

Exercises 25 and 26: **Thinking Generally** *Shade the solution set.*

25. $x > a$ if $a < 0$

26. $x + y \geq a$ if $a > 0$

SYSTEMS OF INEQUALITIES

Exercises 27–48: Shade the solution set in the xy-plane.

27. $x \geq 2$
    $y \leq 1$

28. $x < 3$
    $y > -2$

29. $x \leq 2$
    $y > -x$

30. $y \geq 2$
    $y \geq x$

31. $x \geq y$
    $y \leq 3$

32. $y > x + 1$
    $y < 2$

33. $y \geq x$
    $x \leq -2y$

34. $y > x - 1$
    $x > y - 2$

35. $x + y < 3$
    $x - y < 3$

36. $2x + y > -2$
    $x + y \leq -1$

37. $2x + 3y \geq 6$
    $x + 2y < 3$

38. $-x + y \leq 0$
    $3x + y \leq 3$

39. $\frac{1}{2}x + y \leq 1$
    $x - \frac{1}{3}y < 1$

40. $2x - y > 3$
    $y \leq x + 2$

41. $x \geq 1 + 2y$
    $y \leq 1 - x$

42. $4x + y \leq 4$
    $x - 3y \leq 3$

43. $\frac{1}{2}x - y \geq 1$
    $x - \frac{1}{3}y \geq 1$

44. $2x + y > 4$
    $x - y > 1$

45. $3x < 6 - 2y$
    $2y \geq 2 - 2x$

46. $-4x + 6y > 12$
    $2x - 4y < 8$

47. $\frac{1}{2}x - \frac{1}{2}y > 4$
    $-x - \frac{1}{3}y < 1$

48. $-\frac{2}{3}x + \frac{1}{6}y \geq \frac{4}{3}$
    $-\frac{1}{4}x - \frac{1}{3}y \geq 1$

Exercises 49–54: (Refer to Example 5.) Use a graphing calculator to shade the solution set for the system of inequalities.

49. $y \leq 5$
    $y \geq -3$

50. $y \geq -x$
    $y \leq x + 1$

51. $x + 2y \geq 8$
$6x - 3y \geq 10$

52. $y \geq 2.1x - 3.5$
$y \leq 2.1x - 1.7$

53. $0.9x + 1.7y \leq 3.2$
$1.9x - 0.7y \leq 1.3$

54. $21x \geq 31y - 51$
$5x - 17y \leq 18$

Exercises 55–58: Match the given inequality or system of inequalities with its graph (a.–d.).

55. $x + y \geq 2$

56. $y \leq x + 1$
$y \geq x - 3$

57. $y \leq \frac{1}{2}x$

58. $y \geq x + 1$
$y \leq 5$

a.

b.

c.

d.

Exercises 59–62: Use the graph to write the inequality or system of inequalities.

59.

60.

61.

62.

63. *Sales* Suppose that candy costs $3 per pound and cashews cost $5 per pound. Let x be the number of pounds of candy bought and y be the number of pounds of cashews bought. Graph the region in the *xy*-plane that represents all possible weight combinations that cost *less than* $15.

64. *Tickets and Popcorn* At a movie theater, tickets cost $8 and a bag of popcorn costs $4. Let x be the number of tickets bought and y be the number of bags of popcorn bought. Graph the region in the *xy*-plane that represents all possible combinations of tickets and bags of popcorn that cost $32 or less.

65. *Retail Sales* A small business manufactures compact disc players and radios. Because every CD player contains a radio, the business must make at least as many radios as CD players. The business can make at most a total of 40 compact disc players and radios per day. Let x be the number of compact disc players manufactured and y be the number of radios manufactured. Graph the region that represents all possible combinations of CD players and radios that can be manufactured in one day.

66. *Retail Sales* A small business can manufacture at most 40 large crates and 30 small crates per day. Let x be the number of large crates manufactured per day and y be the number of small crates manufactured per day. Graph the region in the *xy*-plane that represents all possible combinations of large and small crates that can be manufactured.

67. *Target Heart Rate* (Refer to Example 4.) The following graph shows target heart rates for general health and weight loss for a person x years old. These heart rates should be maintained for longer periods of time than the times specified for aerobic fitness.
   (a) What range of heart rates is recommended for someone 30 years old?

(b) The upper line has a slope of -0.6 and passes through the point $(20, 140)$, and the lower line has a slope of -0.5 and passes through the point $(20, 110)$. Write a system of inequalities whose solution set lies in the shaded region in the graph.

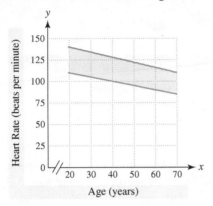

68. *Deserts, Grasslands, and Forests*   Two factors that have a critical effect on plant growth are temperature and precipitation. If a region has too little precipitation, it will be a desert. Forests tend to grow in regions where trees can exist at relatively low temperatures and rainfall is sufficient. At other levels of precipitation and temperature, grasslands may prevail. The following figure illustrates the relationship between forests, grasslands, and deserts as suggested by average annual temperature T in degrees Fahrenheit and precipitation P in inches.   (**Source:** A. Miller and J. Thompson, *Elements of Meteorology.*)

(a) Determine a system of linear inequalities that describes where grasslands are likely to occur.

(b) Bismarck, North Dakota, has an average annual temperature of $40°F$ and precipitation of 15 inches. According to the graph, what type of plant growth would you expect near Bismarck? Do these values satisfy the system of inequalities from part (a)?

Exercises 69–72: Weight and Height   *The following figure shows a weight and height graph. The weight w is listed in pounds, and the height h in inches. The shaded area is the recommended region.*   (**Source:** Department of Agriculture.)

69. What does this graph indicate about an individual weighing 125 pounds with a height of 70 inches?

70. For a person 74 inches tall, use the graph to estimate the recommended weight range.

71. Use the graph to find a system of linear inequalities that describes the recommended region.

72. Explain why inequalities, rather than equalities, are more appropriate for describing recommended weight and height combinations.

Exercises 73 and 74: Graph Sketching   *Suppose that the cost of candy is $3 per pound and the cost of peanuts is $2 per pound. Let x be the number of pounds of candy purchased and let y be the number of pounds of peanuts purchased. Sketch a graph that shows all possible weights of candy and peanuts that could be purchased for each situation.*

73. The amount spent on candy is $6 or less and the amount spent on peanuts is $8 or less.

74. The total amount spent on candy and peanuts is at least $6 but not more than $12.

WRITING ABOUT MATHEMATICS

75. Explain how a system of linear inequalities in two variables can have no solutions. Give an example to illustrate your answer.

76. A student changes the system of linear inequalities

$$2x - y \geq 6 \qquad \text{to} \qquad y \geq 2x - 6$$
$$x - y \leq 4 \qquad \qquad y \leq x - 4.$$

The student tests the point $(-2, -8)$, which satisfies the second system but not the first. Explain the student's errors.

GROUP ACTIVITY
WORKING WITH REAL DATA

Directions: Form a group of 2 to 4 people. Select someone to record the group's responses for this activity. All members of the group should work cooperatively to answer the questions. If your instructor asks for your results, each member of the group should be prepared to respond.

1. *CD Sales*   In 1987, compact disc (CD) sales accounted for 12% of all recorded music sales. By 1997, such sales had increased to 70%. (***Source:*** Recording Industry Association of America.)

   (a) Set up a linear system to find values for a and b so that the graph of $y_1 = ax + b$ passes through the points (1987, 12) and (1997, 70). (*Hint:* To obtain the first equation, let $x = 1987$ and $y_1 = 12$ in $y_1 = ax + b$. To obtain the second equation, let $x = 1997$ and $y_1 = 70$.)

   (b) Have one member of the group solve the system symbolically, a second member solve it graphically, and a third member solve it numerically. If the group consists of only two members, solve it symbolically and graphically. How do your answers compare?

2. *Cassette Sales*   In 1987, cassette tape sales accounted for 63% of all recorded music sales. By 1997, such sales had decreased to 18%. (***Source:*** Recording Industry Association of America.)

   (a) Set up a linear system to find values for c and d so that the graph of $y_2 = cx + d$ passes through the points (1987, 63) and (1997, 18).

   (b) Have one member of the group solve the system symbolically, a second member solve it graphically, and a third member solve it numerically. If the group consists of only two members, solve it symbolically and graphically. How do your answers compare?

3. *Recorded Music Sales*   Estimate the year when CDs and cassette tapes had equal market shares. When were CD sales greater than cassette tape sales?

4.4   INTRODUCTION TO LINEAR PROGRAMMING

Basic Concepts ▪ Region of Feasible Solutions ▪
Solving Linear Programming Problems

A LOOK INTO MATH ▷ During World War II large numbers of troops were at the front. Keeping these soldiers supplied with equipment and food was an essential but complex task. To solve this logistics problem, a new type of mathematics called *linear programming* was invented. Today, linear programming is important to business and the social sciences because it is a procedure that can be used to optimize quantities such as cost and profit. Linear programming applications frequently contain thousands of variables. In this section, we focus on problems involving only two variables. However, the concepts discussed in this section are important to your understanding of larger problems.

Basic Concepts

▶ REAL-WORLD CONNECTION   Suppose that a small business sells candy for $3 per pound and fresh ground coffee for $5 per pound. All inventory is sold by the end of the day. The revenue R collected in dollars is given by

$$R = 3x + 5y,$$

where x is the pounds of candy sold and y is the pounds of coffee sold. For example, if the business sells **80** pounds of candy and **40** pounds of coffee during a day, then its revenue is

$$R = 3(80) + 5(40) = \$440.$$

The function $R = 3x + 5y$ is called an **objective function**.

Suppose also that the company cannot package more than 150 pounds of candy and coffee per day. Then the inequality

$$x + y \leq 150$$

represents a **constraint** on the objective function, which limits the company's revenue for any one day. A goal of this business might be to maximize

$$R = 3x + 5y,$$

subject to the constraints

$$x + y \leq 150$$
$$x \geq 0, \ y \geq 0.$$

Note that the constraints $x \geq 0$ and $y \geq 0$ are included because the number of pounds of candy or coffee cannot be negative. The problem that we have described is called a *linear programming problem*. Before learning how to solve a linear programming problem, we need to discuss the set of *feasible solutions*.

Region of Feasible Solutions

The constraints for a linear programming problem consist of linear inequalities. These inequalities are satisfied by some points in the xy-plane but not by others. The set of solutions to these constraints is called the **feasible solutions**. For example, the region of feasible solutions to the constraints for the business just described is shaded in Figure 4.25.

Figure 4.25 Constraints on Sales

The point (50, 50) lies in the shaded region and represents the business selling 50 pounds of candy and 50 pounds of coffee. In the next example, we shade the region of feasible solutions to a set of constraints.

EXAMPLE Finding the region of feasible solutions

Shade the region of feasible solutions to the following constraints.

$$x + 2y \le 30$$
$$2x + y \le 30$$
$$x \ge 0, \; y \ge 0$$

Figure 4.26

Solution

The feasible solutions are the ordered pairs (x, y) that *satisfy all four* inequalities. They lie below the lines $x + 2y = 30$ and $2x + y = 30$, and above the line $y = 0$ and to the right of $x = 0$, as shown in Figure 4.26. Note that the inequalities $x \ge 0$ and $y \ge 0$ restrict the feasible solutions to quadrant I.   Now Try Exercise 15

Solving Linear Programming Problems

A **linear programming problem** consists of an *objective function* and a system of linear inequalities called *constraints*. The solution set for the system of linear inequalities is called the *region of feasible solutions*. The objective function describes a quantity that is to be optimized. The **optimal value** to a linear programming problem often results in maximum revenue or minimum cost.

When the system of constraints has only two variables, the boundary of the region of feasible solutions often consists of line segments intersecting at points called *vertices* (plural of **vertex**.) To solve a linear programming problem we use the *fundamental theorem of linear programming*.

FUNDAMENTAL THEOREM OF LINEAR PROGRAMMING

If the optimal value for a linear programming problem exists, then it occurs at a vertex of the region of feasible solutions.

The fundamental theorem of linear programming is used to solve the following linear programming problem.

EXAMPLE 2 Maximizing an objective function

Maximize the objective function $R = 2x + 3y$ subject to

$$x + 2y \le 30$$
$$2x + y \le 30$$
$$x \ge 0, \; y \ge 0.$$

Solution

The region of feasible solutions is shaded in Figure 4.26. Note that the vertices on the boundary of feasible solutions are $(0, 0)$, $(15, 0)$, $(10, 10)$, and $(0, 15)$. To find the maximum value of R, substitute each vertex in the formula for R, as shown in Table 4.3. The maximum value of R is 50 when $x = 10$ and $y = 10$.

TABLE 4.3

Vertex	$R = 2x + 3y$	
(0, 0)	$2(0) + 3(0) = 0$	
(15, 0)	$2(15) + 3(0) = 30$	
(10, 10)	$2(10) + 3(10) = 50$	$\leftarrow$ **Maximum** R
(0, 15)	$2(0) + 3(15) = 45$	Now Try Exercise 33

The following steps are helpful in solving linear programming word problems.

STEPS FOR SOLVING A LINEAR PROGRAMMING WORD PROBLEM

STEP 1: Read the problem carefully. Consider making a table.

STEP 2: Write the objective function and all the constraints.

STEP 3: Sketch a graph of the region of feasible solutions. Identify all vertices.

STEP 4: Evaluate the objective function at each vertex. A maximum (or a minimum) occurs at a vertex.

NOTE: If the region is unbounded, a maximum (or minimum) may not exist.

EXAMPLE 3 Minimizing the cost of vitamins

A breeder is mixing two different vitamins, Brand X and Brand Y, into pet food. Each serving of pet food should contain at least 60 units of vitamin A and 30 units of vitamin C. Brand X costs 80 cents per ounce and Brand Y costs 50 cents per ounce. Each ounce of Brand X contains 15 units of vitamin A and 10 units of vitamin C, whereas each ounce of Brand Y contains 20 units of vitamin A and 5 units of vitamin C. Determine how much of each brand of vitamin should be mixed to produce a minimum cost per serving.

Solution
STEP 1: Begin by listing the information, as illustrated in Table 4.4.

TABLE 4.4

Brand	Amount	Vitamin A	Vitamin C	Cost
X	x	15	10	80 cents
Y	y	20	5	50 cents
Minimum		60	30	

STEP 2: If x ounces of Brand X are purchased at 80 cents per ounce and if y ounces of Brand Y are purchased at 50 cents per ounce, then the total cost C is given by $C = 80x + 50y$. Because each ounce of Brand X contains 15 units of vitamin A and each ounce of Brand Y contains 20 units of vitamin A, the total number of units of vitamin A is

$15x + 20y$. If each serving of pet food must contain at least 60 units of vitamin A, the constraint is $15x + 20y \geq 60$. Similarly, because each serving requires at least 30 units of vitamin C, $10x + 5y \geq 30$. The linear programming problem then becomes the following.

Minimize: $C = 80x + 50y$ Cost (in cents)

Subject to: $15x + 20y \geq 60$ Vitamin A

                     $10x + 5y \geq 30$ Vitamin C

                     $x \geq 0, \; y \geq 0$

STEP 3: The region containing the feasible solutions is shown in Figure 4.27.

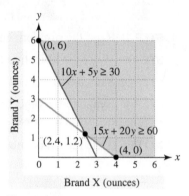

Figure 4.27

NOTE: To determine the vertex (2.4, 1.2) solve the system of equations

$$15x + 20y = 60$$
$$10x + 5y = 30$$

by using elimination.

STEP 4: The vertices for this region are (0, 6), (2.4, 1.2), and (4, 0). Evaluate the objective function C at each vertex, as shown in Table 4.5.

TABLE 4.5

Vertex	$C = 80x + 50y$	
(0, 6)	$80(0) + 50(6) = 300$	
(2.4, 1.2)	$80(2.4) + 50(1.2) = 252$	← **Minimum cost (cents)**
(4, 0)	$80(4) + 50(0) = 320$	

The minimum cost occurs when 2.4 ounces of Brand X and 1.2 ounces of Brand Y are mixed, at a cost of $2.52 per serving.   Now Try Exercise **45**

4.4 PUTTING IT ALL TOGETHER

The following table summarizes the basic concept of linear programming.

Concept	Comments	Example
Linear Programming	In a linear programming problem, the maximum or minimum of an objective function is found, subject to a set of constraints. If a solution exists, it occurs at a vertex in the region of feasible solutions.	Maximize $R = x + 2y$, subject to $3x + 2y \leq 15$, $2x + 3y \leq 15$, $x \geq 0$, and $y \geq 0$. The vertices are $(0, 0)$, $(5, 0)$, $(3, 3)$, and $(0, 5)$. The maximum, $R = 10$, occurs at vertex $(0, 5)$, and the minimum, $R = 0$, occurs at $(0, 0)$.

4.4 Exercises

MyMathLab

CONCEPTS

1. A procedure used in business to optimize quantities such as cost and profit is called _____.

2. In linear programming, the function to be optimized is called the _____ function.

3. The region in the xy-plane that satisfies the constraints is called the region of _____.

4. In linear programming, the constraints typically consist of a system of _____.

5. If the optimal value for a linear programming problem exists, then it occurs at a _____ of the region of feasible solutions.

6. To find the optimal value in a linear programming problem, substitute each vertex in the _____ function.

REGIONS OF FEASIBLE SOLUTIONS

Exercises 7–20: Shade the region of feasible solutions for the following constraints.

7. $x + y \leq 3$
$x \geq 0, y \geq 0$

8. $2x + y \leq 4$
$x \geq 0, y \geq 0$

9. $4x + 3y \leq 12$
$x \geq 0, y \geq 0$

10. $5x + 3y \leq 15$
$x \geq 0, y \geq 0$

11. $x \leq 5$
$y \leq 2$
$x \geq 0, y \geq 0$

12. $x \leq 3$
$y \leq 4$
$x \geq 1, y \geq 1$

13. $x + y \leq 5$
$x + y \geq 2$
$x \geq 0, y \geq 0$

14. $2x + y \leq 6$
$x + y \geq 3$
$x \geq 0, y \geq 0$

15. $3x + 2y \leq 6$
$2x + 3y \leq 6$
$x \geq 0, y \geq 0$

16. $5x + 3y \leq 30$
$3x + 5y \leq 30$
$x \geq 0, y \geq 0$

17. $x + y \leq 3$
$x + 3y \geq 3$
$x \geq 0, y \geq 0$

18. $3x + y \geq 6$
$x + 2y \geq 6$
$x \geq 0, y \geq 0$

19. $x + 2y \geq 4$
$3x + 2y \geq 6$
$x \geq 0, y \geq 0$

20. $4x + 3y \geq 12$
$3x + 4y \geq 12$
$x \geq 0, y \geq 0$

LINEAR PROGRAMMING

Exercises 21–24: Find the maximum of R on the region of feasible solutions shown in the figure.

21. $R = 4x + 5y$

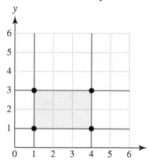

22. $R = 2x + 3y$

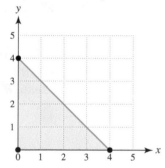

23. $R = x + 3y$

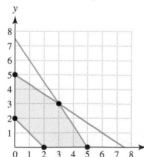

24. $R = 12x + 9y$

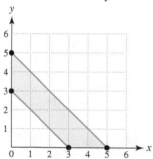

Exercises 25–28: Use the figures in Exercises 21–24 to complete Exercises 25–28, respectively, to minimize C.

25. $C = 2x + 3y$

26. $C = 3x + y$

27. $C = 5x + y$

28. $C = 2x + 7y$

Exercises 29–36: Maximize the objective function R, subject to the given constraints.

29. $R = 3x + 5y$
$x + y \leq 150$
$x \geq 0, y \geq 0$

30. $R = 6x + 5y$
$x + y \leq 8$
$x \geq 0, y \geq 0$

31. $R = 3x + 2y$
$2x + y \leq 6$
$x \geq 0, y \geq 0$

32. $R = x + 3y$
$x + 2y \leq 4$
$x \geq 0, y \geq 0$

33. $R = 12x + 9y$
$3x + y \leq 6$
$x + 3y \leq 6$
$x \geq 0, y \geq 0$

34. $R = 10x + 30y$
$x + 3y \leq 12$
$3x + y \leq 12$
$x \geq 0, y \geq 0$

35. $R = 4x + 5y$
$x + y \geq 2$
$x + 2y \leq 4$
$x \geq 0, y \geq 0$

36. $R = 3x + 7y$
$x + y \geq 1$
$3x + y \leq 3$
$x \geq 0, y \geq 0$

Exercises 37–42: Minimize the objective function C, subject to the given constraints.

37. $C = x + 2y$
$x \leq 3, y \leq 2$
$x \geq 0, y \geq 0$

38. $C = 3x + y$
$x \leq 5, y \leq 3$
$x \geq 1, y \geq 1$

39. $C = 8x + 15y$
$x + y \geq 4$
$x \geq 0, y \geq 0$

40. $C = x + 2y$
$3x + 4y \geq 12$
$x \geq 0, y \geq 0$

41. $C = 30x + 40y$
$2x + y \leq 6$
$x + y \geq 2$
$x \geq 0, y \geq 0$

42. $C = 50x + 70y$
$2x + 3y \leq 6$
$x + y \geq 1$
$x \geq 0, y \geq 0$

APPLICATIONS

Exercises 43–48: Solve the linear programming problem.

43. *Maximizing Revenue*   A small business sells candy for \$4 per pound and coffee for \$6 per pound. The business can package and sell at most a total of 100 pounds of candy and coffee per day, but at least 20 pounds of candy must be sold each day. Determine how many pounds of candy and coffee need to be sold each day to maximize revenue.

44. *Minimizing Cost*   It costs a business $20 to make one compact disc player and $10 to make one radio. Each week the company must make a combined total of at least 50 compact disc players and radios. At least as many compact disc players as radios must be manufactured. Determine how many compact disc players and radios should be made to minimize weekly costs.

45. *Vitamin Cost*   A pet owner is mixing two different vitamins, Brand X and Brand Y, into pet food. Brand X costs 90 cents per ounce and Brand Y costs 60 cents per ounce. Each serving is a mixture of the two brands and should contain at least 40 units of vitamin A and 30 units of vitamin C. Each ounce of Brand X contains 20 units of vitamin A and 10 units of vitamin C, whereas each ounce of Brand Y contains 10 units of vitamin A and 10 units of vitamin C. Determine how much of each brand of vitamin should be mixed to produce a minimum cost per serving.

46. *Pet Food Cost*   A pet owner is buying two brands of food, X and Y, for his animals. Each serving of the mixture of the two foods should contain at least 60 grams of protein and 40 grams of fat. Brand X costs 75 cents per unit and Brand Y costs 50 cents per unit. Each unit of Brand X contains 20 grams of protein and 10 grams of fat, whereas each unit of Brand Y

contains 10 grams of protein and 10 grams of fat. Determine how much of each brand should be bought to obtain a minimum cost per serving.

47. *Raising Animals*   A breeder can raise no more than 50 hamsters and mice but no more than 20 hamsters. If she sells the hamsters for $15 each and the mice for $10 each, find the maximum revenue.

48. *Maximizing Profit*   A business manufactures two parts, X and Y. Machines A and B are needed to make each part. To make part X, machine A is needed 3 hours and machine B is needed 1 hour. To make part Y, machine A is needed 1 hour and machine B is needed 2 hours. Machine A is available 60 hours per week and machine B is available 50 hours per week. The profit from part X is $300 and the profit from part Y is $250. How many parts of each type should be made to maximize weekly profit?

WRITING ABOUT MATHEMATICS

49. Give the steps for solving a linear programming word problem.

50. Is the vertex that gives the optimal solution always unique? Could there be more than one vertex that gives the optimal solution? Explain your reasoning.

CHECKING BASIC CONCEPTS
SECTIONS 4.3 AND 4.4

1. Write an inequality that describes the shaded region in the graph.

2. Graph the solution set for the linear system of inequalities. Use a test point to check your graph.

$$2x + 3y \leq 6$$
$$x + 2y \geq 4$$

3. Use linear programming to find the maximum of $R = 3x + 2y$, subject to the constraints

$$3x + 2y \leq 12$$
$$4x + 4y \leq 20$$
$$x \geq 0, \ y \geq 0.$$

4.5   SYSTEMS OF LINEAR EQUATIONS IN THREE VARIABLES

Basic Concepts ▪ Solving Linear Systems with Substitution and Elimination ▪ Modeling Data ▪ Systems of Equations with No Solutions ▪ Systems of Equations with Infinitely Many Solutions

In Sections 4.1 and 4.2, we described how to solve systems of linear equations in two variables. In applications, systems commonly have many variables. Large linear systems are used in the design of electrical circuits, bridges, and ships. They also are used in business, economics, and psychology. Because of the enormous amount of work needed to solve large systems, technology is usually used to find approximate solutions. In this section we discuss symbolic methods for finding solutions of linear systems in three variables. These methods provide the basis for understanding how technology can solve large linear systems.

Basic Concepts

When we solve a linear system in two variables, we can express a solution as an ordered pair (x, y). A linear equation in two variables can be represented graphically by a line. A system of two linear equations with a unique solution can be represented graphically by two lines intersecting at a point, as shown in Figure 4.28.

When solving linear systems in three variables, we often use the variables x, y, and z. A solution is expressed as an **ordered triple** (x, y, z), rather than an ordered pair (x, y). For example, if the ordered triple $(1, 2, 3)$ is a solution, $x = 1$, $y = 2$, and $z = 3$ satisfy each equation. A linear equation in three variables can be represented by a flat plane in space. If the solution is unique, we can represent a linear system of three equations in three variables graphically by three planes intersecting at a single point, as illustrated in Figure 4.29.

Figure 4.28

Figure 4.29

NOTE: The three planes in Figure 4.29 all intersect at right angles. In general, three planes can intersect at a point even if they are not at right angles to each other.

CRITICAL THINKING

The following figures of three planes in space represent a system of three linear equations in three variables. How many solutions are there in each case? Explain.

(a)   (b)

The next example shows how to check whether an ordered triple is a solution to a system of linear equations in three variables.

EXAMPLE 1   Checking for solutions to a system of three equations

Determine whether $(4, 2, -1)$ or $(-1, 0, 3)$ is a solution to the system.

$$2x - 3y + z = 1$$
$$x - 2y + 2z = 5$$
$$2y + z = 3$$

Solution
To check $(4, 2, -1)$, substitute $x = 4, y = 2,$ and $z = -1$ in each equation.

$$2(4) - 3(2) + (-1) \stackrel{?}{=} 1 \qquad \text{True}$$
$$4 - 2(2) + 2(-1) \stackrel{?}{=} 5 \qquad \text{False}$$
$$2(2) + (-1) \stackrel{?}{=} 3 \qquad \text{True}$$

The ordered triple $(4, 2, -1)$ *does not satisfy all three equations, so it is not a solution.* Next, substitute $x = -1, y = 0,$ and $z = 3$ in each equation.

$$2(-1) - 3(0) + 3 \stackrel{?}{=} 1 \qquad \text{True}$$
$$-1 - 2(0) + 2(3) \stackrel{?}{=} 5 \qquad \text{True}$$
$$2(0) + 3 \stackrel{?}{=} 3 \qquad \text{True}$$

The ordered triple $(-1, 0, 3)$ *satisfies all three equations, so it is a solution.*

Now Try Exercise 9

In the next example we set up a system of three equations in three variables that involves the angles of a triangle. You are asked to solve this system in Exercise 51.

EXAMPLE 2   Setting up a system of equations

The measure of the largest angle in a triangle is 40° greater than the sum of the two smaller angles and 90° more than the smallest angle. Set up a system of three linear equations in three variables whose solution gives the measure of each angle.

Solution
Let $x, y,$ and z be the measures of the three angles from largest to smallest. Because the sum of the measures of the angles in a triangle equals 180°, we have

$$x + y + z = 180.$$

The measure of the largest angle x is 40° greater than the sum of the measures of the two smaller angles $y + z$, so

$$x - (y + z) = 40 \quad \text{or} \quad x - y - z = 40.$$

The measure of the largest angle x is 90° more than the measure of the smallest angle z, so

$$x - z = 90.$$

Thus the required system of equations can be written as follows.

$$x + y + z = 180$$
$$x - y - z = 40$$
$$x \phantom{{} - y} - z = 90$$

Now Try Exercise 49(a)

▶ REAL-WORLD CONNECTION   In the next example we show how a linear system involving three equations and three variables can be used to model a real-world situation. We solve this system of equations in Example 7.

EXAMPLE 3   Modeling real data with a linear system

The Bureau of Land Management studies antelope populations in Wyoming. It monitors the number of adult antelope, the number of fawns each spring, and the severity of the winter. The first two columns of Table 4.6 contain counts of fawns and adults for three representative winters. The third column shows the severity of each winter. The severity of the winter is measured from 1 to 5, with 1 being mild and 5 being severe.

TABLE 4.6

Fawns (F)	Adults (A)	Winter (W)
405	870	3
414	848	2
272	684	5
?	750	4

We want to use the data in the first three rows of the table to estimate the number of fawns F in the fourth row when the number of adults is 750 and the severity of the winter is 4. To do so, we use the formula

$$F = a + bA + cW,$$

where a, b, and c are constants. Write a system of linear equations whose solution gives appropriate values for a, b, and c.

Solution
From the first row in the table, when $F = 405, A = 870$, and $W = 3$, the formula

$$F = a + bA + cW$$

becomes

$$405 = a + b(870) + c(3).$$

Similarly, $F = 414, A = 848$, and $W = 2$ gives

$$414 = a + b(848) + c(2),$$

and $F = 272, A = 684$, and $W = 5$ yields

$$272 = a + b(684) + c(5).$$

To find values for a, b, and c we can solve the following system of linear equations.

$$405 = a + 870b + 3c$$
$$414 = a + 848b + 2c$$
$$272 = a + 684b + 5c$$

We can also write these equations as a linear system in the following form.

$$a + 870b + 3c = 405$$
$$a + 848b + 2c = 414$$
$$a + 684b + 5c = 272$$

Finding values for a, b, and c will allow us to use the formula $F = a + bA + cW$ to predict the number of fawns F when the number of adults A is 750 and the severity of the winter W is 4 (see Example 7).   Now Try Exercise 53(a)

NOTE: Linear systems of two equations can have no solutions, one solution, or infinitely many solutions. The same is true for larger linear systems. In the following subsection we focus on linear systems having one solution.

Solving Linear Systems with Substitution and Elimination

When solving systems of linear equations with more than two variables, we usually use both substitution and elimination. However, in the next example we use only substitution to solve a particular type of linear system in three variables.

EXAMPLE 4   Using substitution to solve a linear system of equations

Solve the following system.

$$2x - y + z = 7$$
$$3y - z = 1$$
$$z = 2$$

Solution
The last equation gives us the value of z immediately. We can substitute $z = 2$ in the second equation and determine y.

$$3y - z = 1 \qquad \text{Second equation}$$
$$3y - 2 = 1 \qquad \text{Substitute } z = 2.$$
$$3y = 3 \qquad \text{Add 2 to each side.}$$
$$y = 1 \qquad \text{Divide each side by 3.}$$

Knowing that $y = 1$ and $z = 2$ allows us to find x by using the first equation.

$$2x - y + z = 7 \qquad \text{First equation}$$
$$2x - 1 + 2 = 7 \qquad \text{Let } y = 1 \text{ and } z = 2.$$
$$2x = 6 \qquad \text{Simplify and subtract 1.}$$
$$x = 3 \qquad \text{Divide each side by 2.}$$

Thus $x = 3$, $y = 1$, and $z = 2$ and the solution is $(3, 1, 2)$.   Now Try Exercise 13

In the next example we use elimination and substitution to solve a system of linear equations. This four-step method is summarized by the following.

SOLVING A LINEAR SYSTEM IN THREE VARIABLES

STEP 1: Eliminate one variable, such as x, from two of the equations.

STEP 2: Use the two resulting equations in two variables to eliminate one of the variables, such as y. Solve for the remaining variable, z.

STEP 3: Substitute z in one of the two equations from Step 2. Solve for the unknown variable y.

STEP 4: Substitute values for y and z in one of the given equations and find x. The solution is (x, y, z).

EXAMPLE 5   Solving a linear system in three variables

Solve the following system.

$$\begin{aligned} x - y + 2z &= 6 \\ 2x + y - 2z &= -3 \\ -x - 2y + 3z &= 7 \end{aligned}$$

Solution

STEP 1: We begin by eliminating the variable x from the second and third equations. To eliminate x from the second equation we multiply the first equation by -2 and then add it to the second equation. To eliminate x from the third equation we add the first and third equations.

$-2x + 2y - 4z = -12$	First equation times -2		$x - y + 2z = 6$	First equation
$2x + y - 2z = -3$	Second equation		$-x - 2y + 3z = 7$	Third equation
$3y - 6z = -15$	Add.		$-3y + 5z = 13$	Add.

STEP 2: Take the two resulting equations from Step 1 and eliminate either variable. Here we add the two equations to eliminate the variable y.

$$\begin{aligned} 3y - 6z &= -15 \\ -3y + 5z &= 13 \\ \hline -z &= -2 \qquad \text{Add the equations.} \\ z &= 2 \qquad \text{Multiply by } -1. \end{aligned}$$

STEP 3: Now we can use substitution to find the values of x and y. We let $z = 2$ in either equation used in Step 2 to find y.

$$\begin{aligned} 3y - 6z &= -15 \\ 3y - 6(2) &= -15 \qquad \text{Substitute } z = 2. \\ 3y - 12 &= -15 \qquad \text{Multiply.} \\ 3y &= -3 \qquad \text{Add 12.} \\ y &= -1 \qquad \text{Divide by 3.} \end{aligned}$$

STEP 4: Finally, we substitute $y = -1$ and $z = 2$ in one of the given equations to find x.

$$x - y + 2z = 6 \qquad \text{First given equation}$$
$$x - (-1) + 2(2) = 6 \qquad \text{Let } y = -1 \text{ and } z = 2.$$
$$x + 1 + 4 = 6 \qquad \text{Simplify.}$$
$$x = 1 \qquad \text{Subtract 5.}$$

The solution is $(1, -1, 2)$. Check this solution.   Now Try Exercise 25

▶ **REAL-WORLD CONNECTION**   In the next example we solve a system of linear equations to determine the number of tickets sold at a play.

EXAMPLE 6   Finding the number of tickets sold

One thousand tickets were sold for a play, which generated $3800 in revenue. The prices of the tickets were $3 for children, $4 for students, and $5 for adults. There were 100 fewer student tickets sold than adult tickets. Find the number of each type of ticket sold.

Solution

Let x be the number of tickets sold to children, y be the number of tickets sold to students, and z be the number of tickets sold to adults. The total number of tickets sold was 1000, so

$$x + y + z = 1000.$$

Each child's ticket cost $3, so the revenue generated from selling x tickets was $3x$. Similarly, the revenue generated from students was $4y$, and the revenue from adults was $5z$. Total ticket sales were $3800, so

$$3x + 4y + 5z = 3800.$$

The equation $z - y = 100$, or $y - z = -100$, must also be satisfied, as 100 fewer tickets were sold to students than adults.

To find the price of a ticket we need to solve the following system of linear equations.

$$x + y + z = 1000$$
$$3x + 4y + 5z = 3800$$
$$y - z = -100$$

STEP 1: We begin by eliminating the variable x from the second equation. To do so, we multiply the first equation by -3 and add the second equation.

$$-3x - 3y - 3z = -3000 \qquad \text{First given equation times } -3$$
$$\underline{3x + 4y + 5z = 3800} \qquad \text{Second equation}$$
$$y + 2z = 800 \qquad \text{Add.}$$

STEP 2: We then multiply the resulting equation from Step 1 by -1 and add the third equation to eliminate y.

$$-y - 2z = -800 \qquad \text{Equation from Step 1 times } -1$$
$$\underline{y - z = -100} \qquad \text{Third equation}$$
$$-3z = -900 \qquad \text{Add the equations.}$$
$$z = 300 \qquad \text{Divide by } -3.$$

STEP 3: To find y we can substitute $z = 300$ in the third equation.

$$y - z = -100 \quad \text{Third equation}$$
$$y - 300 = -100 \quad \text{Let } z = 300.$$
$$y = 200 \quad \text{Add 300.}$$

STEP 4: Finally, we substitute $y = 200$ and $z = 300$ in the first equation.

$$x + y + z = 1000 \quad \text{First equation}$$
$$x + 200 + 300 = 1000 \quad \text{Let } y = 200 \text{ and } z = 300.$$
$$x = 500 \quad \text{Subtract 500.}$$

Thus **500** tickets were sold to children, **200** to students, and **300** to adults.

Now Try Exercise 47

Modeling Data

In the next example we solve the system of equations that we discussed in Example 3.

EXAMPLE 7   Predicting fawns in the spring

Solve the following linear system for a, b, and c.

$$a + 870b + 3c = 405$$
$$a + 848b + 2c = 414$$
$$a + 684b + 5c = 272$$

Then use $F = a + bA + cW$ to predict the number of fawns when there are 750 adults and the severity of the winter is 4.

Solution
STEP 1: We begin by eliminating the variable a from the second and third equations. To do so, we add the second and third equations to the first equation times -1.

$$-a - 870b - 3c = -405 \qquad -a - 870b - 3c = -405 \quad \text{First times } -1$$
$$\underline{a + 848b + 2c = 414} \qquad \underline{a + 684b + 5c = 272} \quad \text{Second/third equation}$$
$$-22b - c = 9 \qquad -186b + 2c = -133 \quad \text{Add.}$$

STEP 2: We use the two resulting equations from Step 1 to eliminate c. To do so we multiply $-22b - c = 9$ by 2 and add it to the other equation.

$$-44b - 2c = 18 \quad (-22b - c = 9) \text{ times 2}$$
$$\underline{-186b + 2c = -133}$$
$$-230b = -115 \quad \text{Add the equations.}$$
$$b = 0.5 \quad \text{Divide by } -230.$$

STEP 3: To find c we substitute $b = 0.5$ in either equation used in Step 2.

$$-44b - 2c = 18$$
$$-44(0.5) - 2c = 18 \quad \text{Let } b = 0.5.$$
$$-22 - 2c = 18 \quad \text{Multiply.}$$
$$-2c = 40 \quad \text{Add 22.}$$
$$c = -20 \quad \text{Divide by } -2.$$

STEP 4: Finally, we substitute $b = 0.5$ and $c = -20$ in one of the given equations to find a.

$$a + 870b + 3c = 405 \qquad \text{First given equation}$$
$$a + 870(0.5) + 3(-20) = 405 \qquad \text{Let } b = 0.5 \text{ and } c = -20.$$
$$a + 435 - 60 = 405 \qquad \text{Multiply.}$$
$$a = 30 \qquad \text{Solve for } a.$$

The solution is $a = 30$, $b = 0.5$, and $c = -20$. Thus we may write

$$F = a + bA + cW$$
$$= 30 + 0.5A - 20W.$$

If there are 750 adults and the winter has a severity of 4, this model predicts

$$F = 30 + 0.5(750) - 20(4)$$
$$= 325 \text{ fawns.} \qquad \text{Now Try Exercise } \boxed{53}$$

CRITICAL THINKING

Give reasons why the coefficient for A is positive and the coefficient for W is negative in the formula

$$F = 30 + 0.5A - 20W.$$

Systems of Equations with No Solutions

It is possible for a system of three linear equations in three variables to be inconsistent and have no solutions. If we apply substitution and elimination to this type of system, we arrive at a contradiction. This case is demonstrated in the next example.

EXAMPLE ▮8▮   Recognizing an inconsistent system

Solve the system, if possible.

$$x + y + z = 4$$
$$-x + y + z = 2$$
$$y + z = 1$$

Solution

STEP 1: If we add the first two equations, we can eliminate x. The variable x is already eliminated from the third equation.

$$\begin{array}{ll} x + y + z = 4 & \text{First equation} \\ \underline{-x + y + z = 2} & \text{Second equation} \\ 2y + 2z = 6 & \text{Add.} \end{array}$$

STEP 2: If we multiply the third *given* equation by -2 and add it to the resulting equation in Step 1, we arrive at a contradiction.

$$\begin{array}{ll} -2y - 2z = -2 & \text{Third equation times } -2 \\ \underline{2y + 2z = 6} & \text{Equation from Step 1} \\ 0 = 4 & \text{Add equations.} \end{array}$$

Because $0 = 4$ is a contradiction, there are no solutions to the given system of equations. Now Try Exercise ▮31▮

Systems of Equations with Infinitely Many Solutions

It is possible for a system of linear equations in three variables to have infinitely many solutions. If we apply substitution and elimination to this type of system, we arrive at an identity. This case is demonstrated in the next example.

EXAMPLE 9   Solving a system with infinitely many solutions

Solve the system.

$$x + y + z = 2$$
$$x - y + z = 4$$
$$3x - y + 3z = 10$$

Solution

STEP 1: To eliminate y from the second equation, add the first equation to the second. To eliminate y from the third equation, add the first equation to the third equation.

$x + y + z = 2$	First equation		$x + y + z = 2$	First equation
$x - y + z = 4$	Second equation		$3x - y + 3z = 10$	Third equation
$2x + 2z = 6$	Add.		$4x + 4z = 12$	Add.

STEP 2: If we multiply the first resulting equation in Step 1 by -2 and add it to the second resulting equation in Step 1, we arrive at an identity.

$-4x - 4z = -12$	$(2x + 2z = 6)$ times -2
$4x + 4z = 12$	Second equation from Step 1
$0 = 0$	Add. (Identity)

The variable x can be written in terms of z by solving $2x + 2z = 6$ for x.

$2x + 2z = 6$	Equation from Step 1
$2x = 6 - 2z$	Subtract $2z$.
$x = 3 - z$	Divide by 2.

STEP 3: To find y in terms of z, substitute $3 - z$ for x in the first *given* equation.

$x + y + z = 2$	First equation
$(3 - z) + y + z = 2$	Let $x = 3 - z$.
$y = -1$	Solve for y.

All solutions have the form $(3 - z, -1, z)$, where z can be any real number. For example, if $z = 1$, then $(2, -1, 1)$ is one of infinitely many solutions to the system of equations.

Now Try Exercise 33

4.5   PUTTING IT ALL TOGETHER

In this section we discussed how to solve a system of three linear equations in three variables. Systems of linear equations can have no solutions, one solution, or infinitely many solutions. The following table summarizes some of the important concepts presented in this section.

Concept	Explanation
System of Linear Equations in Three Variables	The following is a system of three linear equations in three variables. $$x - 2y + z = 0$$ $$-x + y + z = 4$$ $$-y + 4z = 10$$
Solution to a Linear System in Three Variables	The solution to a linear system in three variables is an ordered triple, expressed as (x, y, z). The solution to the preceding system is $(1, 2, 3)$ because substituting $x = 1, y = 2$, and $z = 3$ in each equation results in a true statement. We can check solutions this way. $(1) - 2(2) + (3) = 0$ True $-(1) + (2) + (3) = 4$ True $- (2) + 4(3) = 10$ True
Solving a Linear System with Substitution and Elimination	**STEP 1:** Eliminate one variable, such as x, from two of the equations. **STEP 2:** Use the two resulting equations in two variables to eliminate one of the variables, such as y. Solve for the remaining variable z. **STEP 3:** Substitute z in one of the two equations from Step 2. Solve for the unknown variable y. **STEP 4:** Substitute values for y and z in one of the given equations and find x. The solution is (x, y, z).

4.5 Exercises

MyMathLab   Math XL   PRACTICE   WATCH   DOWNLOAD   READ   REVIEW

CONCEPTS

1. Can a system of three linear equations and three variables have exactly two solutions? Explain.

2. Give an example of a system of three linear equations in three variables.

3. Does the ordered triple $(1, 2, 3)$ satisfy the equation $x + y + z = 6$?

4. Does $(3, 4)$ represent a solution to the equation $x + y + z = 7$? Explain.

5. To solve uniquely for two variables, how many equations do you usually need?

6. To solve uniquely for three variables, how many equations do you usually need?

7. If a contradiction occurs while solving a system of linear equations, then there are _____ solution(s).

8. If an identity occurs while solving a linear system, how many solutions are there?

SOLVING LINEAR SYSTEMS

Exercises 9–12: Determine which ordered triple is a solution to the linear system.

9. $(1, 2, 3), (0, 2, 4)$
$$x + y + z = 6$$
$$x - y - z = -4$$
$$-x - y + z = 0$$

10. $(-1, 0, 2), (0, 4, 4)$
$$2x + y - 3z = -8$$
$$x - 3y + 2z = -4$$
$$3x - 2y + z = -4$$

11. $(1, 0, 3), (-1, 1, 2)$
$$3x - 2y + z = -3$$
$$-x + 3y - 2z = 0$$
$$x + 4y + 2z = 7$$

12. $\left(\frac{1}{2}, \frac{3}{2}, -\frac{1}{2}\right), (-1, 0, -2)$
$$x + 3y - 4z = 7$$
$$-x + 5y + 3z = \frac{11}{2}$$
$$3x - 2y - 7z = 2$$

Exercises 13–18: (Refer to Example 4.) Use substitution to solve the system of linear equations. Check your solution.

13. $x + y - z = 1$
$$2y + z = -1$$
$$z = 1$$

14. $2x + y - 3z = 1$
$$y + 4z = 0$$
$$z = -1$$

15. $-x - 3y + z = -2$
$$2y + 3z = 3$$
$$z = 2$$

16. $3x + 2y - 3z = -4$
$$-y + 2z = 4$$
$$z = 0$$

17. $a - b + 2c = 3$
$$-3b + c = 4$$
$$c = -2$$

18. $5a + 2b - 3c = 10$
$$5b - 2c = -4$$
$$c = 3$$

Exercises 19–44: Solve the system, if possible.

19. $x + y - z = 11$
$$-x + 2y + 3z = -1$$
$$2z = 4$$

20. $x + 2y - 3z = -7$
$$-2x + y + z = -1$$
$$3z = 9$$

21. $x + y - z = -2$
$$-x + z = 1$$
$$y + 2z = 3$$

22. $x + y - 3z = 11$
$$-2x + y + 2z = 1$$
$$-3y + 3z = -21$$

23. $x + y - 2z = -7$
$$y + z = -1$$
$$-y + 3z = 9$$

24. $2x + 3y + z = 5$
$$y + 2z = 4$$
$$-2y + z = 2$$

25. $x + 2y + 2z = 1$
$$x + y + z = 0$$
$$-x - 2y + 3z = -11$$

26. $x + y - z = 0$
$$x - 3y + z = -2$$
$$x - y + 3z = 8$$

27. $x + y + z = 5$
$$y + z = 6$$
$$x + z = 3$$

28. $x + y + z = 0$
$$x - y - z = 6$$
$$-x + y - z = 4$$

29. $x + 2y + 3z = 24$
$$-x + y + 2z = 1$$
$$x + y - 2z = 9$$

30. $5x - 15y + z = 22$
$$-10x + 12y - 2z = -8$$
$$4x - 2y - 3z = 9$$

31. $x + y + z = 2$
$$x - y + z = 1$$
$$x + z = 3$$

32. $4x - y + 3z = 3$
$$2x + y + z = 2$$
$$x - y + z = 1$$

33. $x + y + z = 6$
$$x - y + z = 2$$
$$-x + 5y - z = 6$$

34. $x - y + z = 3$
$$2x - y + z = 2$$
$$-x - y + z = 5$$

35. $2x + y + z = 3$
$$2x - y - z = 9$$
$$x + y - z = 0$$

36. $x + 3y + z = -8$
$$x - 2y = 11$$
$$2y - z = -16$$

37. $2x + 6y - 2z = 47$
$$2x + y + 3z = -28$$
$$-x + y + z = -\frac{7}{2}$$

38. $x + y + 2z = 23$
$$3x - y + 3z = 8$$
$$2x + 2y + z = 13$$

39. $x + 3y - 4z = \frac{13}{2}$
$$-2x + 3y - z = \frac{1}{2}$$
$$3x + z = 4$$

40. $x - 2y + z = \frac{9}{2}$
$$4x - y + 3z = 9$$
$$x + 2y = -\frac{3}{2}$$

41. $2x - 2y + z = 4$
$$x - y + z = 1$$
$$x - y + z = 3$$

42. $x - 2y + 3z = 1$
$$x + 3y + z = 2$$
$$3x + 4y + 5z = 7$$

43. $x + y + z = 5$
$$x - y + z = 3$$
$$2x + y + 2z = 9$$

44. $x + y - 2z = 0$
$$x + 2y - 4z = -1$$
$$y - 2z = -1$$

Exercises 45 and 46: **Thinking Generally** *Solve the system of linear equations, if $a \neq 0$.*

45. $x + y + z = a$
$$x + y + z = 2a$$
$$-x + y + z = 0$$

46. $x + y + z = a$
$$-x - y - z = -a$$
$$y - z = 0$$

APPLICATIONS

47. *Finding Costs*   The accompanying table shows the costs of purchasing different combinations of hamburgers, fries, and soft drinks.

Hamburgers	Fries	Soft Drinks	Total Cost
1	2	4	$10
1	4	6	$15
0	3	2	$6

(a) Let x be the cost of a hamburger, y the cost of fries, and z be the cost of a soft drink. Write a system of three linear equations that represents the data in the table.

(b) Solve the system and interpret your answer.

48. *Cost of CDs*   The accompanying table shows the total cost of purchasing combinations of differently priced CDs. The types of CDs are labeled A, B, and C.

A	B	C	Total Cost
1	1	1	$37
3	2	1	$69
1	1	4	$82

(a) Let x be the cost of a CD of type A, y be the cost of a CD of type B, and z be the cost of a CD of type C. Write a system of three linear equations that represents the data in the table.

(b) Solve the system and interpret your answer.

49. *Geometry*   The largest angle in a triangle is 55° more than the smallest angle. The sum of the measures of the two smaller angles is 10° more than the measure of the largest angle.

(a) Let x, y, and z be the measures of the three angles from largest to smallest. Write a system of three linear equations whose solution gives the measure of each angle.

(b) Solve the system.

(c) Check your solution.

50. *Geometry*   The perimeter of a triangle is 90 inches. The longest side is 20 inches longer than the shortest side and 10 inches longer than the remaining side.

(a) Let x, y, and z be the lengths of the three sides from largest to smallest. Write a system of three linear equations whose solution gives the lengths of each side.

(b) Solve the system.

(c) Check your solution.

51. *Geometry*   (Refer to Example 2.) Solve the system to find the measure of each angle.

$$x + y + z = 180$$
$$x - y - z = 40$$
$$x \quad\ - z = 90$$

52. *Loan Mixture*   A student takes out a total of $5000 in three loans: one subsidized, one unsubsidized, and

one from the parents of the student. The subsidized loan is $200 more than the combined total of the unsubsidized and parent loans. The unsubsidized loan is twice the amount of the parent loan. Find the amount of each loan.

53. *Predicting Fawns*   (Refer to Examples 3 and 7.) The accompanying table shows counts for fawns and adult deer and the severity of the winter. These data may be modeled by the equation $F = a + bA + cW$.

Fawns (F)	Adults (A)	Winter (W)
525	600	4
365	400	2
805	900	5
?	500	3

(a) Use the first three rows to write a system of three linear equations in three variables whose solution gives values for a, b, and c.

(b) Solve the system.

(c) Predict the number of fawns when there are 500 adults and the winter has severity 3.

54. *Business Production*   A business has three machines that manufacture containers. Together they make 100 containers per day, whereas the two fastest machines can make 80 containers per day. The fastest machine makes 34 more containers per day than the slowest machine.

(a) Let x, y, and z be the number of containers that the machines make from fastest to slowest. Write a system of three equations whose solution gives the number of containers that each machine can make.

(b) Solve the system.

55. *Mixture Problem*   One type of lawn fertilizer consists of a mixture of nitrogen, N, phosphorus, P, and potassium, K. An 80-pound sample contains 8 more pounds of nitrogen and phosphorus than potassium. There is 9 times as much potassium as phosphorus.
   (a) Write a system of three equations whose solution gives the amount of nitrogen, phosphorus, and potassium in this sample.
   (b) Solve the system.

56. *Predicting Home Prices*   Selling prices of homes can depend on several factors such as size and age. The accompanying table shows the selling price for three homes. In this table, price P is given in thousands of dollars, age A in years, and home size S in thousands of square feet. These data may be modeled by the equation $P = a + bA + cS$.

Price (P)	Age (A)	Size (S)
190	20	2
320	5	3
50	40	1

   (a) Write a system of linear equations whose solution gives a, b, and c.
   (b) Solve the system.
   (c) Predict the price of a home that is 10 years old and has 2500 square feet.

57. *Investment Mixture*   A sum of $30,000 was invested in three mutual funds. In one year the first fund grew by 8%, the second by 10%, and the third by 15%. Total earnings were $3550. The amount invested in the third fund was $2000 less than the combined amount invested in the other two funds. Use a linear system of equations to determine the amount invested in each fund.

58. *Football Tickets*   A total of 2500 tickets were sold at a football game. Prices were $2 for children, $3 for students, and $5 for adults. Twice as many tickets were sold to students as children and ticket revenues were $7250. Use a system of linear equations to determine how many of each type of ticket were sold.

WRITING ABOUT MATHEMATICS

59. In the previous section we solved problems with two variables; to obtain a unique solution we needed two linear equations. In this section we solved problems with three variables; to obtain a unique solution we needed three equations. Try to generalize these results. In the design of aircraft, problems commonly involve 100,000 variables. How many equations are required to solve such problems? Can such problems be solved by hand? If not, how are such problems solved? Explain your answers.

60. In Exercise 56 the price of a home was estimated by its age and size. What other factors might affect the price of a home? Explain how these factors might affect the number of variables and equations in the linear system.

Directions: Form a group of 2 to 4 people. Select someone to record the group's responses for this activity. All of the members of the group should work cooperatively to answer the questions. If your instructor asks for your results, each member of the group should be prepared to respond.

CEO Salaries   In 2002, hourly wages for the top three CEOs (chief executive officers) of U.S. corporations were calculated based on their working 14 hours per day for 365 days. Together the three CEOs made $44,000 per hour. The top CEO earned $2,000 more per hour than the combined hourly wages of the next two top CEOs, and the top CEO earned $7,000 more per hour than the next top CEO. (*Source: USA Today*, March 31, 2003.)

   (a) Let x, y, and z be the hourly wages in *thousands* of dollars for the top CEOs from greatest to least. Write a system of equations whose solution gives these hourly wages.
   (b) Solve the system. Interpret the answer.
   (c) The average American worker earned $16.23 per hour in 2002. How many hours did the average American work to earn an amount equal to one hour of work by the top CEO in 2002?

4.6 MATRIX SOLUTIONS OF LINEAR SYSTEMS

Representing Systems of Linear Equations with Matrices ▪ Gauss–Jordan Elimination ▪ Using Technology to Solve Systems of Linear Equations (Optional)

A LOOK INTO MATH ▷ Suppose that the size of a bear's head and its overall length are known. Can its weight be estimated from these variables? Can a bear's weight be estimated if its neck size and chest size are known? In this section we show that systems of linear equations can be used to make such estimates.

In the previous section we solved systems of three linear equations in three variables by using elimination and substitution. In real life, systems of equations often contain thousands of variables. To solve a large system of equations, we need an efficient method. Long before the invention of the computer, Carl Fredrich Gauss (1777–1855) developed a method called *Gaussian elimination* to solve systems of linear equations. Even though it was developed more than 150 years ago, it is still used today in modern computers and calculators. In this section we introduce the Gauss–Jordan method, which is based on Gaussian elimination.

Representing Systems of Linear Equations with Matrices

Arrays of numbers are used frequently in many different real-world situations. Spreadsheets often make use of arrays. A **matrix** is a rectangular array of numbers. Each number in a matrix is called an **element**. The following are examples of *matrices* (plural of matrix), with their dimensions written below them.

$$\begin{bmatrix} 2 & 0 \\ 3 & 1 \end{bmatrix} \quad \begin{bmatrix} -1.2 & 5 & 0 \\ 1 & 0 & 1 \\ 4 & -5 & 7 \end{bmatrix} \quad \begin{bmatrix} 3 & -6 & 0 & \sqrt{3} \\ 1 & 4 & 0 & 9 \\ -3 & 1 & 1 & 18 \\ -10 & -4 & 5 & -1 \end{bmatrix} \quad \begin{bmatrix} 4 & 2 \\ 0 & 1 \\ 1 & 0 \end{bmatrix} \quad \begin{bmatrix} 1 & 5 & -1 \\ 3 & 4 & 2 \end{bmatrix}$$

2×2 3×3 4×4 3×2 2×3

rows × columns

▶ **REAL-WORLD CONNECTION**   The dimension of a matrix is stated much like the dimensions of a rectangular room. We might say that a room is m feet long and n feet wide. Similarly, the **dimension of a matrix** is $m \times n$ (m by n), if it has m rows and n columns. For example, the last matrix in the preceding group has a dimension of 2×3 because it has 2 rows and 3 columns. If the number of rows equals the number of columns, the matrix is a **square matrix**. The first three matrices in that group are square matrices.

Matrices can be used to represent a system of linear equations. For example, if we have the system of equations

$$3x - y + 2z = 7$$
$$x - 2y + z = 0$$
$$2x + 5y - 7z = -9,$$

we can represent the system with the following **augmented matrix**. Note how the coefficients of the variables were placed in the matrix. A vertical line is positioned in the matrix where the equals signs occur in the system. The rows and columns are labeled, and the elements of the **main diagonal** of the augmented matrix are circled. The matrix has dimension 3×4.

Main diagonal

$$\begin{bmatrix} 3 & -1 & 2 & | & 7 \\ 1 & -2 & 1 & | & 0 \\ 2 & 5 & -7 & | & -9 \end{bmatrix}$$ ← Row 1
← Row 2
← Row 3

Column 1   Column 2   Column 3   Column 4

EXAMPLE 1   Representing a linear system

Represent each linear system with an augmented matrix. State the dimension of the matrix.

(a) $x - 2y = 9$
$6x + 7y = 16$

(b) $x - 3y + 7z = 4$
$2x + 5y - z = 15$
$2x + y = 8$

Solution

(a) This system can be represented by the following 2×3 augmented matrix.

$$\begin{bmatrix} 1 & -2 & | & 9 \\ 6 & 7 & | & 16 \end{bmatrix}$$

(b) This system can be represented by the following 3×4 augmented matrix.

$$\begin{bmatrix} 1 & -3 & 7 & | & 4 \\ 2 & 5 & -1 & | & 15 \\ 2 & 1 & 0 & | & 8 \end{bmatrix}$$

Now Try Exercises 11, 13

Gauss–Jordan Elimination

A convenient matrix form for representing a system of linear equations is **reduced row–echelon form**. The following matrices are examples of reduced row–echelon form. Note that there are 1s on the main diagonal with 0s above and below the 1s.

$$\begin{bmatrix} 1 & 0 & | & 3 \\ 0 & 1 & | & -2 \end{bmatrix} \quad \begin{bmatrix} 1 & 0 & 0 & | & 3 \\ 0 & 1 & 0 & | & 1 \\ 0 & 0 & 1 & | & -1 \end{bmatrix} \quad \begin{bmatrix} 1 & 0 & 0 & | & 8 \\ 0 & 1 & 0 & | & 2 \\ 0 & 0 & 1 & | & 3 \end{bmatrix}$$

If an augmented matrix representing a linear system is in reduced row–echelon form, we can usually determine the solution easily.

EXAMPLE 2   Determining a solution from reduced row–echelon form

Each matrix represents a system of linear equations. Find the solution.

(a) $\begin{bmatrix} 1 & 0 & 0 & | & 2 \\ 0 & 1 & 0 & | & -3 \\ 0 & 0 & 1 & | & 5 \end{bmatrix}$ **(b)** $\begin{bmatrix} 1 & 0 & | & 10 \\ 0 & 1 & | & -4 \end{bmatrix}$

Solution

(a) The top row represents $1x + 0y + 0z = 2$ or $x = 2$. The second and third rows tell us that $y = -3$ and $z = 5$. The solution is $(2, -3, 5)$.

(b) The system involves two equations in two variables. The solution is $(10, -4)$.

Now Try Exercise 19

We can use a numerical method called **Gauss–Jordan elimination** to solve a linear system. It makes use of the following matrix row transformations.

MATRIX ROW TRANSFORMATIONS

For any augmented matrix representing a system of linear equations, the following row transformations result in an equivalent system of linear equations.

1. Any two rows may be interchanged.
2. The elements of any row may be multiplied by a nonzero constant.
3. Any row may be changed by adding to (or subtracting from) its elements a nonzero multiple of the corresponding elements of another row.

Gauss–Jordan elimination can be used to transform an augmented matrix into reduced row–echelon form. Its objective is to use these matrix row transformations to obtain a matrix that has the following reduced row–echelon form, where (a, b) represents the solution.

$$\begin{bmatrix} 1 & 0 & a \\ 0 & 1 & b \end{bmatrix}$$

This method is illustrated in the next example.

EXAMPLE 3   Transforming a matrix into reduced row–echelon form

Use Gauss–Jordan elimination to transform the augmented matrix of the linear system into reduced row–echelon form. Find the solution.

$$x + y = 5$$
$$-x + y = 1$$

Solution

Both the linear system and the augmented matrix are shown.

Linear System   **Augmented Matrix**

$$x + y = 5$$
$$-x + y = 1$$

$$\begin{bmatrix} 1 & 1 & 5 \\ -1 & 1 & 1 \end{bmatrix}$$

First, we want to obtain a 0 in the second row, where the -1 is highlighted. To do so, we add row 1 to row 2 and place the result in row 2. This step is denoted $R_2 + R_1$ and eliminates the x-variable from the second equation.

$$x + y = 5$$
$$2y = 6 \qquad R_2 + R_1 \rightarrow \begin{bmatrix} 1 & 1 & 5 \\ 0 & 2 & 6 \end{bmatrix}$$

To obtain a 1 where the 2 in the second row is located, we multiply the second row by $\frac{1}{2}$, denoted $\frac{1}{2}R_2$.

$$\begin{array}{r} x + y = 5 \\ y = 3 \end{array} \qquad \frac{1}{2}R_2 \to \quad \left[\begin{array}{cc|c} 1 & 1 & 5 \\ 0 & 1 & 3 \end{array}\right]$$

Next, we need to obtain a 0 where the 1 is highlighted. We do so by subtracting row 2 from row 1 and placing the result in row 1, denoted $R_1 - R_2$.

$$\begin{array}{r} x = 2 \\ y = 3 \end{array} \qquad R_1 - R_2 \to \quad \left[\begin{array}{cc|c} 1 & 0 & 2 \\ 0 & 1 & 3 \end{array}\right]$$

This matrix is in reduced row–echelon form. The solution is (2, 3).   Now Try Exercise 21

In the next example, we use Gauss–Jordan elimination to solve a system with three linear equations and three variables. To do so we transform the matrix into the following reduced row–echelon form, where (a, b, c) represents the solution.

$$\left[\begin{array}{ccc|c} 1 & 0 & 0 & a \\ 0 & 1 & 0 & b \\ 0 & 0 & 1 & c \end{array}\right]$$

EXAMPLE 4   Transforming a matrix to reduced row–echelon form

Use Gauss–Jordan elimination to transform the augmented matrix of the linear system into reduced row–echelon form. Find the solution.

$$\begin{array}{rcr} x + y + 2z &=& 1 \\ -x + z &=& -2 \\ 2x + y + 5z &=& -1 \end{array}$$

Solution
The linear system and the augmented matrix are both shown.

Linear System   **Augmented Matrix**

$$\begin{array}{rcr} x + y + 2z &=& 1 \\ -x + z &=& -2 \\ 2x + y + 5z &=& -1 \end{array} \qquad \left[\begin{array}{ccc|c} 1 & 1 & 2 & 1 \\ -1 & 0 & 1 & -2 \\ 2 & 1 & 5 & -1 \end{array}\right]$$

First, we want to put 0s in the second and third rows, where the -1 and 2 are highlighted. To obtain a 0 in the first position of the second row we add row 1 to row 2 and place the result in row 2, denoted $R_2 + R_1$. To obtain a 0 in the first position of the third row we subtract 2 times row 1 from row 3 and place the result in row 3, denoted $R_3 - 2R_1$. Row 1 does not change. These steps eliminate the x-variable from the second and third equations.

$$\begin{array}{rcr} x + y + 2z &=& 1 \\ y + 3z &=& -1 \\ -y + z &=& -3 \end{array} \qquad \begin{array}{l} \\ R_2 + R_1 \to \\ R_3 - 2R_1 \to \end{array} \left[\begin{array}{ccc|c} 1 & 1 & 2 & 1 \\ 0 & 1 & 3 & -1 \\ 0 & -1 & 1 & -3 \end{array}\right]$$

To eliminate the y-variable in row 1, we subtract row 2 from row 1. To eliminate the y-variable from row 3, we add row 2 to row 3.

$$
\begin{aligned}
x \quad\;\; - z &= 2 \\
y + 3z &= -1 \\
4z &= -4
\end{aligned}
\qquad
\begin{matrix}
R_1 - R_2 \rightarrow \\
\\
R_3 + R_2 \rightarrow
\end{matrix}
\left[\begin{array}{ccc|c}
1 & 0 & -1 & 2 \\
0 & 1 & 3 & -1 \\
0 & 0 & 4 & -4
\end{array}\right]
$$

To obtain a 1 in row 3, where the highlighted 4 is located, we multiply row 3 by $\frac{1}{4}$.

$$
\begin{aligned}
x \quad\;\; - z &= 2 \\
y + 3z &= -1 \\
z &= -1
\end{aligned}
\qquad
\begin{matrix}
\\
\\
\frac{1}{4}R_3 \rightarrow
\end{matrix}
\left[\begin{array}{ccc|c}
1 & 0 & -1 & 2 \\
0 & 1 & 3 & -1 \\
0 & 0 & 1 & -1
\end{array}\right]
$$

For the matrix to be in reduced row–echelon form, we need 0s in the highlighted locations. We first add row 3 to row 1 and then subtract 3 times row 3 from row 2.

$$
\begin{aligned}
x &= 1 \\
y &= 2 \\
z &= -1
\end{aligned}
\qquad
\begin{matrix}
R_1 + R_3 \rightarrow \\
R_2 - 3R_3 \rightarrow \\
\\
\end{matrix}
\left[\begin{array}{ccc|c}
1 & 0 & 0 & 1 \\
0 & 1 & 0 & 2 \\
0 & 0 & 1 & -1
\end{array}\right]
$$

This matrix is now in reduced row–echelon form. The solution is $(1, 2, -1)$.

Now Try Exercise 31

CRITICAL THINKING

An *inconsistent* system of linear equations has no solutions, and a system of *dependent* linear equations has infinitely many solutions. Suppose that an augmented matrix row reduces to either of the following matrices. Explain what each matrix indicates about the given system of linear equations.

$$
\left[\begin{array}{ccc|c}
1 & 0 & 0 & 2 \\
0 & 1 & 0 & 3 \\
0 & 0 & 0 & 1
\end{array}\right]
\qquad
\left[\begin{array}{ccc|c}
1 & 0 & 1 & 2 \\
0 & 1 & 2 & 3 \\
0 & 0 & 0 & 0
\end{array}\right]
$$

In the next example we find the amounts invested in three mutual funds.

EXAMPLE 5 Determining investment amounts in mutual funds

A total of $8000 was invested in three funds that grew at a rate of 5%, 10%, and 20% over 1 year. After 1 year, the combined value of the three funds had grown by $1200. Five times as much money was invested at 20% as at 10%. Find the amount invested in each fund.

Solution
Let x be the amount invested at 5%, y be the amount invested at 10%, and z be the amount invested at 20%. The total amount invested was $8000, so

$$x + y + z = 8000.$$

The growth in the first mutual fund, paying 5% of x, is given by $0.05x$. Similarly, the growths in the other mutual funds are given by $0.10y$ and $0.20z$. As the total growth was $1200, we can write

$$0.05x + 0.10y + 0.20z = 1200.$$

Multiplying each side of this equation by 20 to eliminate decimals results in

$$x + 2y + 4z = 24{,}000.$$

Five times as much was invested at 20% as at 10%, so $z = 5y$, or $5y - z = 0$.

These three equations can be written as a system of linear equations and as an augmented matrix.

Linear System   **Augmented Matrix**

$$\begin{aligned} x + y + z &= 8{,}000 \\ x + 2y + 4z &= 24{,}000 \\ 5y - z &= 0 \end{aligned} \qquad \left[\begin{array}{ccc|c} 1 & 1 & 1 & 8{,}000 \\ 1 & 2 & 4 & 24{,}000 \\ 0 & 5 & -1 & 0 \end{array}\right]$$

A 0 can be obtained in the highlighted position by subtracting row 1 from row 2.

$$\begin{aligned} x + y + z &= 8{,}000 \\ y + 3z &= 16{,}000 \\ 5y - z &= 0 \end{aligned} \qquad R_2 - R_1 \rightarrow \left[\begin{array}{ccc|c} 1 & 1 & 1 & 8{,}000 \\ 0 & 1 & 3 & 16{,}000 \\ 0 & 5 & -1 & 0 \end{array}\right]$$

Zeros can be obtained in the highlighted positions by subtracting row 2 from row 1 and by subtracting 5 times row 2 from row 3.

$$\begin{aligned} x - 2z &= -8{,}000 \\ y + 3z &= 16{,}000 \\ -16z &= -80{,}000 \end{aligned} \qquad \begin{aligned} R_1 - R_2 \rightarrow \\ \\ R_3 - 5R_2 \rightarrow \end{aligned} \left[\begin{array}{ccc|c} 1 & 0 & -2 & -8{,}000 \\ 0 & 1 & 3 & 16{,}000 \\ 0 & 0 & -16 & -80{,}000 \end{array}\right]$$

To obtain a 1 in the highlighted position, multiply row 3 by $-\frac{1}{16}$.

$$\begin{aligned} x - 2z &= -8{,}000 \\ y + 3z &= 16{,}000 \\ z &= 5{,}000 \end{aligned} \qquad -\frac{1}{16}R_3 \rightarrow \left[\begin{array}{ccc|c} 1 & 0 & -2 & -8{,}000 \\ 0 & 1 & 3 & 16{,}000 \\ 0 & 0 & 1 & 5{,}000 \end{array}\right]$$

To obtain a 0 in each of the highlighted positions, add twice row 3 to row 1 and subtract three times row 3 from row 2.

$$\begin{aligned} x &= 2{,}000 \\ y &= 1{,}000 \\ z &= 5{,}000 \end{aligned} \qquad \begin{aligned} R_1 + 2R_3 \rightarrow \\ R_2 - 3R_3 \rightarrow \\ \end{aligned} \left[\begin{array}{ccc|c} 1 & 0 & 0 & 2{,}000 \\ 0 & 1 & 0 & 1{,}000 \\ 0 & 0 & 1 & 5{,}000 \end{array}\right]$$

Thus $2000 was invested at 5%, $1000 at 10%, and $5000 at 20%.   Now Try Exercise 63

Using Technology to Solve Systems of Linear Equations (Optional)

▶ REAL-WORLD CONNECTION   Examples 4 and 5 involve a lot of arithmetic. Trying to solve a large system of equations by hand is an enormous—if not impossible—task. In the real world, people use technology to solve large systems. In the next example we solve the linear systems from Examples 3 and 4 with a graphing calculator.

EXAMPLE 6   Using technology

Use a graphing calculator to solve the following systems of equations.

(a) $x + y = 5$
$-x + y = 1$

(b) $x + y + 2z = 1$
$-x + \quad z = -2$
$2x + y + 5z = -1$

Solution

(a) Enter the 2×3 augmented matrix from Example 3 in a graphing calculator, as shown in Figure 4.30(a). Then transform the matrix into reduced row–echelon form (rref), as shown in Figure 4.30(b). The solution is $(2, 3)$.

(a)

(b)

Figure 4.30

(b) Enter the 3×4 augmented matrix from Example 4, as shown in Figure 4.31(a). (The fourth column of A can be seen by scrolling right.) Then transform the matrix into reduced row–echelon form (rref), as shown in Figure 4.31(b). The solution is $(1, 2, -1)$.

CALCULATOR HELP

To enter a matrix and put it in reduced row–echelon form, see the Appendix (pages AP-8 and AP-9).

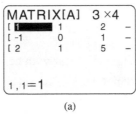
(a)

rref([A])
[[1 0 0 1]
[0 1 0 2]
[0 0 1 -1]]
(b)

Figure 4.31

Now Try Exercises 39, 41

▶ **REAL-WORLD CONNECTION** In the next example we use technology to solve an application.

EXAMPLE 7   Modeling the weight of male bears

The data shown in Table 4.7 give the weight W, head length H, and overall length L of three bears. These data can be modeled with the equation $W = a + bH + cL$, where a, b, and c are constants that we need to determine. (**Sources:** M. Triola, *Elementary Statistics*; Minitab, Inc.)

TABLE 4.7

W (pound)	H (inches)	L (inches)
362	16	72
300	14	68
147	11	52

(a) Set up a system of equations whose solution gives values for constants a, b, and c.
(b) Solve the system.
(c) Predict the weight of a bear with $H = 13$ inches and $L = 65$ inches.

Solution
(a) Substitute each row of Table 4.7 in the equation $W = a + bH + cL$.

$$362 = a + b(16) + c(72)$$
$$300 = a + b(14) + c(68)$$
$$147 = a + b(11) + c(52)$$

Rewrite this system as

$$a + 16b + 72c = 362$$
$$a + 14b + 68c = 300$$
$$a + 11b + 52c = 147$$

and represent it as the augmented matrix

(a)

$$A = \begin{bmatrix} 1 & 16 & 72 & \big| & 362 \\ 1 & 14 & 68 & \big| & 300 \\ 1 & 11 & 52 & \big| & 147 \end{bmatrix}.$$

(b)

Figure 4.32

(b) Enter A and put it in reduced row–echelon form, as shown in Figures 4.32(a) and (b), respectively. The solution is $a = -374$, $b = 19$, and $c = 6$.
(c) For $W = a + bH + cL$, use

$$W = -374 + 19H + 6L$$

to predict the weight of a bear with head length $H = 13$ and overall length $L = 65$.

$$W = -374 + 19(13) + 6(65) = 263 \text{ pounds}$$

Now Try Exercise 58

4.6 PUTTING IT ALL TOGETHER

A matrix is a rectangular array of numbers. An augmented matrix may be used to represent any system of linear equations. One common method for solving a system of linear equations is Gauss–Jordan elimination. Matrix row operations may be used to transform an augmented matrix to reduced row–echelon form. Technology can be used to solve systems of linear equations efficiently. The following table summarizes augmented matrices and reduced row–echelon form.

Concept	Explanation
Augmented Matrix	A linear system can be represented by an augmented matrix. The following matrix has dimension 3×4. *Linear System* *Augmented Matrix* $\begin{aligned} x + 2y - z &= 6 \\ -2x + y - z &= 7 \\ 2x + 3z &= -11 \end{aligned}$ $\left[\begin{array}{ccc|c} 1 & 2 & -1 & 6 \\ -2 & 1 & -1 & 7 \\ 2 & 0 & 3 & -11 \end{array}\right]$
Reduced Row–Echelon Form	The following augmented matrix is in reduced row–echelon form, which results from transforming the preceding system to reduced row–echelon form. There are 1s along the main diagonal and 0s elsewhere in the first three columns. The solution to the linear system is $(-1, 2, -3)$. $\left[\begin{array}{ccc|c} 1 & 0 & 0 & -1 \\ 0 & 1 & 0 & 2 \\ 0 & 0 & 1 & -3 \end{array}\right]$

4.6 Exercises

CONCEPTS

1. What is a matrix?

2. Give an example of a matrix and state its dimension.

3. Give an example of an augmented matrix and state its dimension.

4. If an augmented matrix is used to solve a system of three linear equations in three variables, what will be its dimension?

5. Give an example of a matrix that is in reduced row–echelon form.

6. Identify the elements on the main diagonal in the augmented matrix.

$$\left[\begin{array}{ccc|c} 4 & -6 & -1 & 3 \\ 6 & 2 & -2 & 9 \\ 7 & 5 & -3 & 1 \end{array}\right]$$

DIMENSIONS OF MATRICES AND AUGMENTED MATRICES

Exercises 7–10: State the dimension of the matrix.

7. $\begin{bmatrix} 3 & -3 & 7 \\ 2 & 6 & -2 \\ 4 & 2 & 5 \end{bmatrix}$ **8.** $\begin{bmatrix} -2 & 3 & 0 \\ 1 & -8 & 4 \end{bmatrix}$

9. $\begin{bmatrix} 1 & 7 \\ 0 & 2 \\ 2 & -5 \end{bmatrix}$ **10.** $\begin{bmatrix} 4 & 2 & -3 & -1 \\ 4 & -3 & 2 & -7 \\ 14 & 6 & 4 & 0 \end{bmatrix}$

Exercises 11–14: Represent the linear system as an augmented matrix.

11. $\begin{aligned} x - 3y &= 1 \\ -x + 3y &= -1 \end{aligned}$ **12.** $\begin{aligned} 4x + 2y &= -5 \\ 5x + 8y &= 2 \end{aligned}$

13. $\begin{aligned} 2x - y + 2z &= -4 \\ x - 2y &= 2 \\ -x + y - 2z &= -6 \end{aligned}$ **14.** $\begin{aligned} 3x - 2y + z &= 5 \\ -x + 2z &= -4 \\ x - 2y + z &= -1 \end{aligned}$

Exercises 15–20: Write the system of linear equations that the augmented matrix represents. Use the variables x, y, and z.

15. $\begin{bmatrix} 1 & 2 & | & -6 \\ 5 & -1 & | & 4 \end{bmatrix}$

16. $\begin{bmatrix} 1 & -5 & | & 7 \\ 0 & -3 & | & 6 \end{bmatrix}$

17. $\begin{bmatrix} 1 & -1 & 2 & | & 6 \\ 2 & 1 & -2 & | & 1 \\ -1 & 2 & -1 & | & 3 \end{bmatrix}$

18. $\begin{bmatrix} 3 & -1 & 2 & | & -1 \\ 2 & -2 & 2 & | & 4 \\ 1 & 7 & -2 & | & 2 \end{bmatrix}$

19. $\begin{bmatrix} 1 & 0 & 0 & | & 4 \\ 0 & 1 & 0 & | & -2 \\ 0 & 0 & 1 & | & 7 \end{bmatrix}$

20. $\begin{bmatrix} 1 & 0 & 0 & | & 6 \\ 0 & 1 & 0 & | & -2 \\ 0 & 0 & 1 & | & 4 \end{bmatrix}$

GAUSSIAN ELIMINATION

Exercises 21–38: Use Gauss–Jordan elimination to find the solution. Write the solution as an ordered pair or ordered triple and check the solution.

21. $x + y = 4$
$x + 3y = 10$

22. $x - 3y = -7$
$2x + y = 0$

23. $2x + 3y = 3$
$-2x + 2y = 7$

24. $x + 3y = -14$
$2x + 5y = -24$

25. $x - y = 5$
$x + 3y = -1$

26. $x + 4y = 1$
$3x - 2y = 10$

27. $4x - 8y = -10$
$x + y = 2$

28. $x - 7y = -16$
$4x + 10y = 50$

29. $x + y + z = 6$
$2y - z = 1$
$y + z = 5$

30. $x + y + z = 3$
$x + y - z = 2$
$y + z = 2$

31. $x + 2y + 3z = 6$
$-x + 3y + 4z = 0$
$x + y - 2z = -6$

32. $2x - 4y + 2z = 10$
$-x + 3y - 4z = -19$
$2x - y - 6z = -28$

33. $x + y + z = 0$
$2x + y + 2z = -1$
$x + y = 0$

34. $x + y - 2z = 5$
$x + 2y - 2z = 4$
$-x - y + z = -4$

35. $x + y + z = 3$
$-x - z = -2$
$x + y + 2z = 4$

36. $x + 2y - z = 3$
$-x - y + z = 0$
$x + 2y = 5$

37. $x + 2y + z = 3$
$2x + y - z = -6$
$-x - y + 2z = 5$

38. $x + y + z = -3$
$x - y - z = -1$
$-2x + y + 4z = 4$

Exercises 39–48: Technology   Use a graphing calculator to solve the system of linear equations.

39. $x + 4y = 13$
$5x - 3y = -50$

40. $9x - 11y = 7$
$5x + 6y = 16$

41. $2x - y + 3z = 9$
$-4x + 5y + 2z = 12$
$2x + 7z = 23$

42. $3x - 2y + 4z = 29$
$2x + 3y - 7z = -14$
$5x - y + 11z = 59$

43. $6x + 2y + z = 4$
$-2x + 4y + z = -3$
$2x - 8y = -2$

44. $-x - 9y + 2z = -28.5$
$2x - y + 4z = -17$
$x - y + 8z = -9$

45. $4x + 3y + 12z = -9.25$
$15y + 8z = -4.75 + x$
$7z = -5.5 - 6y$

46. $5x + 4y = 13.3 + z$
$7y + 9z = 16.9 - x$
$x - 3y + 4z = -4.1$

47. $1.2x - 0.9y + 2.7z = 5.37$
$3.1x - 5.1y + 7.2z = 14.81$
$1.8y + 6.38 = 3.6z - 0.2x$

48. $11x + 13y - 17z = 380$
$5x - 14y - 19z = 24$
$-21y + 46z = -676 + 7x$

Exercises 49–54: (Refer to the Critical Thinking box in this section.) Row-reduce the matrix associated with the given system to determine whether the system of linear equations is inconsistent or dependent.

49. $x + 2y = 4$
$-2x - 4y = -8$

50. $x - 5y = 4$
$-2x + 10y = 8$

51. $x + y + z = 3$
$x + y - z = 1$
$x + y = 3$

52. $x + y + z = 5$
$x - y - z = 8$
$2x + 2y + 2z = 6$

53.
$$x + 2y + 3z = 14$$
$$2x - 3y - 2z = -10$$
$$3x - y + z = 4$$

54.
$$x + 2y + 3z = 6$$
$$-x + 3y + 4z = 6$$
$$5y + 7z = 12$$

Exercises 55 and 56: **Thinking Generally**   *The matrix represents a linear system of equations. Solve the system, if a and b are nonzero constants.*

55.
$$\left[\begin{array}{ccc|c} a & 0 & 0 & 1 \\ 0 & b & 0 & 1 \\ 0 & 0 & ab & 2 \end{array} \right]$$

56.
$$\left[\begin{array}{ccc|c} a & 0 & 0 & 1 \\ 0 & b & 0 & 2 \\ 0 & 0 & 0 & a \end{array} \right]$$

APPLICATIONS

57. *Weight of a Bear*   Use the results of Example 7 to estimate the weight of a bear with a head length of 12 inches and an overall length of 60 inches.

58. *Weight of a Bear*   (Refer to Example 7.) Head length and overall length are not the only variables that can be used to estimate the weight of a bear. The data in the accompanying table list the weight W, neck size N, and chest size C of three bears. These data can be modeled by $W = a + bN + cC$.   (*Sources:* M. Triola, *Elementary Statistics*; Minitab, Inc.)

W (pounds)	N (inches)	C (inches)
80	16	26
344	28	45
416	31	54

(a) Set up a system of equations whose solution gives values for the constants a, b, and c.
(b) Solve this system. Round each value to the nearest tenth.
(c) Predict the weight of a bear with neck size $N = 22$ inches and chest size $C = 38$ inches.

59. *Garbage and Household Size*   A larger household produces more garbage, on average, than a smaller household. If we know the amount of metal M and plastic P waste produced each week, we can estimate the household size H from $H = a + bM + cP$. The table contains representative data for three households.   (*Source:* M. Triola, *Elementary Statistics*.)

H (people)	M (pounds)	P (pounds)
3	2.00	1.40
2	1.50	0.65
6	4.00	3.40

(a) Set up a system of equations whose solution gives values for the constants a, b, and c.
(b) Solve this system with a graphing calculator.
(c) Predict the size of a household that produces 3 pounds of metal waste and 2 pounds of plastic waste each week.

60. *Old Faithful Geyser*   In Yellowstone National Park, Old Faithful Geyser has been a favorite attraction for decades. Although this geyser erupts about every 80 minutes, this time interval varies, as do the duration and height of the eruptions. The accompanying table shows the height H, duration D, and time interval T for three eruptions.   (*Source:* National Park Service.)

H (feet)	D (seconds)	T (minutes)
160	276	94
125	203	84
140	245	79

(a) Assume that these data can be modeled by $H = a + bD + cT$. Set up a system of equations whose solution gives values for the constants a, b, and c.
(b) Solve this system by using a graphing calculator. Round each value to the nearest thousandth.
(c) Use this equation to estimate H when $D = 220$ and $T = 81$.

61. *Jogging Speeds*   A runner in preparation for a marathon jogs at 5, 6, and 8 miles per hour. The runner travels a total distance of 12.5 miles in 2 hours and jogs the same length of time at 5 miles per hour and at 8 miles per hour. How long does the runner jog at each speed?

62. *Mixture Problem*   Three types of candy that cost $2, $3, and $4 per pound are to be mixed to produce a 5-pound bag of candy that costs $14.50. If there are to be equal amounts of the $3-per-pound candy and the $4-per-pound candy, how much of each type of candy should be included in the mixture?

63. *Interest and Investments*   (Refer to Example 5.) A total of $3000 is invested at 5%, 8%, and 12% annual interest. The interest earned after 1 year equals $285. The amount invested at 12% is triple the amount invested at 5%. Find the amount invested at each rate.

64. *Geometry*   The measure of the largest angle in a triangle is twice the measure of the smallest angle. The remaining angle is 10° less than the largest angle. Find the measure of each angle.

WRITING ABOUT MATHEMATICS

65. Explain what the dimension of a matrix means. What is the difference between a matrix that has dimension 3×4 and one that has dimension 4×3?

66. Discuss the advantages of using technology to transform an augmented matrix to reduced row–echelon form. Are there any disadvantages? Explain.

CHECKING BASIC CONCEPTS

SECTIONS **4.5** AND **4.6**

1. Determine which ordered triple is the solution to the system of equations: $(5, -4, 0)$, $(1, 3, -1)$.

$$x - y + 7z = -9$$
$$2x - 2y + 5z = -9$$
$$-x + 3y - 2z = 10$$

2. Solve the system of equations by using elimination and substitution.

$$x - y + z = 2$$
$$2x - 3y + z = -1$$
$$-x + y + z = 4$$

3. Use an augmented matrix to represent the system of equations. Solve the system by using
  (a) Gauss–Jordan elimination
   (b) technology.

$$x + 2y + z = 1$$
$$x + y + z = -1$$
$$y + z = 1$$

4.7 DETERMINANTS

Calculation of Determinants   ■   Area of Regions   ■   Cramer's Rule

A LOOK INTO MATH ▷   Surveyors commonly calculate the areas of parcels of land. To do so, they frequently divide the land into triangular regions. When the coordinates of the vertices of a triangle are known, determinants may be used to find the area of the triangle. *A determinant is a real number that can be calculated for any square matrix.* In this section we use determinants to find areas and to solve systems of linear equations.

Calculation of Determinants

▶ **REAL-WORLD CONNECTION**   The concept of determinants originated with the Japanese mathematician Seki Kowa (1642–1708), who used them to solve systems of linear equations. Later, Gottfried Leibniz (1646–1716) formally described determinants and also used them to solve systems of linear equations.   (**Source:** *Historical Topics for the Mathematical Classroom*, NCTM.)

We begin by defining a determinant of a 2×2 matrix.

DETERMINANT OF A 2 × 2 MATRIX

The **determinant** of

$$A = \begin{bmatrix} a & b \\ c & d \end{bmatrix}$$

is a *real number* defined by

$$\det A = ad - cb.$$

EXAMPLE 1   Calculating determinants

Find $\det A$ for each 2×2 matrix.

(a) $A = \begin{bmatrix} 1 & 2 \\ 3 & 4 \end{bmatrix}$ **(b)** $A = \begin{bmatrix} -1 & -3 \\ 2 & -8 \end{bmatrix}$

Solution

(a) The determinant is calculated as follows.

$$\det A = \det \begin{bmatrix} 1 & 2 \\ 3 & 4 \end{bmatrix} = (1)(4) - (3)(2) = -2$$

(b) Similarly,

$$\det A = \det \begin{bmatrix} -1 & -3 \\ 2 & -8 \end{bmatrix} = (-1)(-8) - (2)(-3) = 14.$$

Now Try Exercise **5**

We can use determinants of 2×2 matrices to find determinants of 3×3 matrices. This method is called **expansion of a determinant by minors**.

DETERMINANT OF A 3 × 3 MATRIX

$$\det A = \det \begin{bmatrix} a_1 & b_1 & c_1 \\ a_2 & b_2 & c_2 \\ a_3 & b_3 & c_3 \end{bmatrix}$$

$$= a_1 \cdot \det \begin{bmatrix} b_2 & c_2 \\ b_3 & c_3 \end{bmatrix} - a_2 \cdot \det \begin{bmatrix} b_1 & c_1 \\ b_3 & c_3 \end{bmatrix} + a_3 \cdot \det \begin{bmatrix} b_1 & c_1 \\ b_2 & c_2 \end{bmatrix}$$

The 2×2 matrices in this equation are called **minors**.

EXAMPLE 2   Calculating 3 × 3 determinants

Evaluate det A.

(a) $A = \begin{bmatrix} 2 & 1 & -1 \\ -1 & 3 & 2 \\ 4 & -3 & -5 \end{bmatrix}$ (b) $A = \begin{bmatrix} 5 & -2 & 4 \\ 0 & 2 & 1 \\ -1 & 4 & -4 \end{bmatrix}$

Solution

(a) We evaluate the determinant as follows.

$$\det \begin{bmatrix} 2 & 1 & -1 \\ -1 & 3 & 2 \\ 4 & -3 & -5 \end{bmatrix} = 2 \cdot \det \begin{bmatrix} 3 & 2 \\ -3 & -5 \end{bmatrix} - (-1) \cdot \det \begin{bmatrix} 1 & -1 \\ -3 & -5 \end{bmatrix}$$

$$+ 4 \cdot \det \begin{bmatrix} 1 & -1 \\ 3 & 2 \end{bmatrix}$$

$$= 2(-9) + 1(-8) + 4(5)$$

$$= -6$$

(b) We evaluate the determinant as follows.

$$\det \begin{bmatrix} 5 & -2 & 4 \\ 0 & 2 & 1 \\ -1 & 4 & -4 \end{bmatrix} = 5 \cdot \det \begin{bmatrix} 2 & 1 \\ 4 & -4 \end{bmatrix} - (0) \cdot \det \begin{bmatrix} -2 & 4 \\ 4 & -4 \end{bmatrix}$$

$$+ (-1) \cdot \det \begin{bmatrix} -2 & 4 \\ 2 & 1 \end{bmatrix}$$

$$= 5(-12) - 0(-8) + (-1)(-10)$$

$$= -50$$

Now Try Exercise 13

Many graphing calculators can evaluate the determinant of a matrix, as illustrated in the next example, where we evaluate the determinants from Example 2.

EXAMPLE 3   Using technology to find determinants

Find each determinant of A, using a graphing calculator.

(a) $A = \begin{bmatrix} 2 & 1 & -1 \\ -1 & 3 & 2 \\ 4 & -3 & -5 \end{bmatrix}$ (b) $A = \begin{bmatrix} 5 & -2 & 4 \\ 0 & 2 & 1 \\ -1 & 4 & -4 \end{bmatrix}$

Solution

(a) Begin by entering the matrix and then evaluate the determinant, as shown in Figure 4.33. The result is det $A = -6$, which agrees with our earlier calculation.

CALCULATOR HELP

To find a determinant, see the Appendix (page AP-9).

```
MATRIX[A]  3×3
[  2        1        -1     ]
[ -1        3         2     ]
[  4       -3        -5     ]
```
(a)

```
[A]
       [[2    1   -1]
        [-1   3    2 ]
        [4   -3   -5]]
det([A])
                   -6
```
(b)

Figure 4.33

(b) The determinant of A evaluates to -50 (see Figure 4.34).

(a)

(b)

Figure 4.34

Now Try Exercise **21**

Area of Regions

▶ REAL-WORLD CONNECTION   A determinant may be used to find the area of a triangle. For example, if a triangle has vertices (a_1, a_2), (b_1, b_2), and (c_1, c_2), its area equals the absolute value of D, where

$$D = \frac{1}{2}\det \begin{bmatrix} a_1 & b_1 & c_1 \\ a_2 & b_2 & c_2 \\ 1 & 1 & 1 \end{bmatrix}.$$

If the vertices are entered in the columns of D counterclockwise as they appear in the xy-plane, D will be positive.   (**Source:** W. Taylor, *The Geometry of Computer Graphics*.)

EXAMPLE **4**   Computing the area of a triangular parcel of land

A triangular parcel of land is shown in Figure 4.35. If all units are miles, find the area of the parcel of land by using a determinant.

Solution
The vertices of the triangular parcel of land are $(2, 2)$, $(5, 4)$, and $(3, 8)$. The area of the triangle is

$$D = \frac{1}{2}\det \begin{bmatrix} 2 & 5 & 3 \\ 2 & 4 & 8 \\ 1 & 1 & 1 \end{bmatrix} = \frac{1}{2} \cdot 16 = 8.$$

The area of the triangle is 8 square miles.

Now Try Exercise **27**

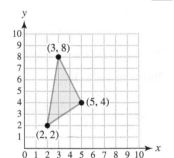

Figure 4.35

CRITICAL THINKING

Suppose that you are given three distinct points in the xy-plane and $D = 0$. What must be true about the three points?

Cramer's Rule

▶ REAL-WORLD CONNECTION   Determinants were developed independently by Gabriel Cramer (1704–1752). His work, published in 1750, provided a method called **Cramer's rule** for solving systems of linear equations.

CRAMER'S RULE FOR LINEAR SYSTEMS IN TWO VARIABLES

The solution to the system of linear equations

$$a_1 x + b_1 y = c_1$$

$$a_2 x + b_2 y = c_2$$

is given by $x = \frac{E}{D}$ and $y = \frac{F}{D}$, where

$$E = \det\begin{bmatrix} c_1 & b_1 \\ c_2 & b_2 \end{bmatrix}, \quad F = \det\begin{bmatrix} a_1 & c_1 \\ a_2 & c_2 \end{bmatrix}, \quad \text{and} \quad D = \det\begin{bmatrix} a_1 & b_1 \\ a_2 & b_2 \end{bmatrix} \neq 0.$$

NOTE: If $D = 0$, the system has either no solutions or infinitely many solutions.

EXAMPLE **5**   Using Cramer's rule

Use Cramer's rule to solve the following linear systems.
(a) $3x - 4y = 18$ **(b)** $-4x + 9y = -24$
    $7x + 5y = -1$ $6x + 17y = -25$

Solution

(a) $E = \det\begin{bmatrix} c_1 & b_1 \\ c_2 & b_2 \end{bmatrix} = \det\begin{bmatrix} 18 & -4 \\ -1 & 5 \end{bmatrix} = (18)(5) - (-1)(-4) = 86$

$F = \det\begin{bmatrix} a_1 & c_1 \\ a_2 & c_2 \end{bmatrix} = \det\begin{bmatrix} 3 & 18 \\ 7 & -1 \end{bmatrix} = (3)(-1) - (7)(18) = -129$

$D = \det\begin{bmatrix} a_1 & b_1 \\ a_2 & b_2 \end{bmatrix} = \det\begin{bmatrix} 3 & -4 \\ 7 & 5 \end{bmatrix} = (3)(5) - (7)(-4) = 43$

Because $x = \frac{E}{D} = \frac{86}{43} = 2$ and $y = \frac{F}{D} = \frac{-129}{43} = -3$, the solution is $(2, -3)$.

(b) $E = \det\begin{bmatrix} c_1 & b_1 \\ c_2 & b_2 \end{bmatrix} = \det\begin{bmatrix} -24 & 9 \\ -25 & 17 \end{bmatrix} = (-24)(17) - (-25)(9) = -183$

$F = \det\begin{bmatrix} a_1 & c_1 \\ a_2 & c_2 \end{bmatrix} = \det\begin{bmatrix} -4 & -24 \\ 6 & -25 \end{bmatrix} = (-4)(-25) - (6)(-24) = 244$

$D = \det\begin{bmatrix} a_1 & b_1 \\ a_2 & b_2 \end{bmatrix} = \det\begin{bmatrix} -4 & 9 \\ 6 & 17 \end{bmatrix} = (-4)(17) - (6)(9) = -122$

Because $x = \frac{E}{D} = \frac{-183}{-122} = 1.5$ and $y = \frac{F}{D} = \frac{244}{-122} = -2$, the solution is $(1.5, -2)$.

Now Try Exercise **33**

Cramer's rule can be applied to systems that have any number of linear equations. Cramer's rule for three linear equations is discussed in the Extended and Discovery Exercises at the end of this chapter.

▶ **REAL-WORLD CONNECTION**   In applications, equations with hundreds of variables are routinely solved. Such systems of equations could be solved with Cramer's rule.

However, using Cramer's rule and the expansion of a determinant with minors to solve a linear system of equations with n variables requires at least

$$1 \cdot 2 \cdot 3 \cdot 4 \cdot \cdots \cdot n \cdot (n + 1)$$

multiplication operations. To solve a linear system involving only 25 variables would require about

$$1 \cdot 2 \cdot 3 \cdot 4 \cdot \cdots \cdot 25 \cdot 26 \approx 4 \times 10^{26}$$

multiplication operations. Supercomputers can perform about 1 trillion (1×10^{12}) multiplication operations per second. This would take about

$$\frac{4 \times 10^{26}}{1 \times 10^{12}} = 4 \times 10^{14} \text{ seconds.}$$

With $60 \times 60 \times 24 \times 365 = 31{,}536{,}000$ seconds in a year, 4×10^{14} seconds equals

$$\frac{4 \times 10^{14}}{31{,}536{,}000} \approx 12{,}700{,}000 \text{ years!}$$

Modern software packages do *not* use Cramer's rule for three or more variables.

4.7 PUTTING IT ALL TOGETHER

The determinant of a square matrix A is a real number, denoted det A. Cramer's rule is a method that uses determinants to solve systems of linear equations. The following table summarizes important topics from this section.

Concept	Explanation
Determinant of a 2×2 Matrix	The determinant of a 2×2 matrix A is given by $$\det A = \det \begin{bmatrix} a & b \\ c & d \end{bmatrix} = ad - cb.$$
Determinant of a 3×3 Matrix	The determinant of a 3×3 matrix A is given by $$\det A = \det \begin{bmatrix} a_1 & b_1 & c_1 \\ a_2 & b_2 & c_2 \\ a_3 & b_3 & c_3 \end{bmatrix}$$ $$= a_1 \cdot \det \begin{bmatrix} b_2 & c_2 \\ b_3 & c_3 \end{bmatrix} - a_2 \cdot \det \begin{bmatrix} b_1 & c_1 \\ b_3 & c_3 \end{bmatrix}$$ $$+ a_3 \cdot \det \begin{bmatrix} b_1 & c_1 \\ b_2 & c_2 \end{bmatrix}$$

continued on next page

continued from previous page

Concept	Explanation
Area of a Triangle	If a triangle has vertices (a_1, a_2), (b_1, b_2), and (c_1, c_2), its area equals the absolute value of D, where $$D = \frac{1}{2}\det\begin{bmatrix} a_1 & b_1 & c_1 \\ a_2 & b_2 & c_2 \\ 1 & 1 & 1 \end{bmatrix}.$$
Cramer's Rule for Linear Systems in Two Variables	The solution to the linear system $$a_1 x + b_1 y = c_1$$ $$a_2 x + b_2 y = c_2$$ is given by $x = \frac{E}{D}$ and $y = \frac{F}{D}$, where $$E = \det\begin{bmatrix} c_1 & b_1 \\ c_2 & b_2 \end{bmatrix}, \quad F = \det\begin{bmatrix} a_1 & c_1 \\ a_2 & c_2 \end{bmatrix}, \quad \text{and}$$ $$D = \det\begin{bmatrix} a_1 & b_1 \\ a_2 & b_2 \end{bmatrix} \neq 0.$$ **NOTE:** If $D = 0$, then the system has either no solutions or infinitely many solutions.

4.7 Exercises

MyMathLab   Math XL PRACTICE   WATCH   DOWNLOAD   READ   REVIEW

CONCEPTS

1. We can find the determinant of a _____ matrix.

2. If we find a determinant, the answer is a _____.

3. Cramer's rule can be used to solve a _____ .

4. If the first column of a matrix is all 0s, then its determinant equals _____.

CALCULATING DETERMINANTS

Exercises 5–20: Evaluate det A by hand where A is the given matrix.

5. $\begin{bmatrix} 1 & -2 \\ 3 & -8 \end{bmatrix}$

6. $\begin{bmatrix} 5 & -1 \\ 3 & 7 \end{bmatrix}$

7. $\begin{bmatrix} -3 & 7 \\ 8 & -1 \end{bmatrix}$

8. $\begin{bmatrix} 0 & -7 \\ -3 & 1 \end{bmatrix}$

9. $\begin{bmatrix} 23 & 4 \\ 6 & -13 \end{bmatrix}$

10. $\begin{bmatrix} 44 & -51 \\ -9 & 32 \end{bmatrix}$

11. $\begin{bmatrix} 1 & -1 & 2 \\ 0 & 1 & -3 \\ 0 & -4 & 7 \end{bmatrix}$

12. $\begin{bmatrix} 2 & -1 & -5 \\ -1 & 4 & -2 \\ 0 & 1 & 4 \end{bmatrix}$

13. $\begin{bmatrix} 2 & -1 & 0 \\ 1 & -2 & 6 \\ 0 & 1 & 8 \end{bmatrix}$

14. $\begin{bmatrix} 0 & 1 & -4 \\ 3 & -6 & 10 \\ 4 & -2 & 7 \end{bmatrix}$

15. $\begin{bmatrix} -1 & 3 & 5 \\ 3 & -3 & 5 \\ 2 & -3 & 7 \end{bmatrix}$ **16.** $\begin{bmatrix} 6 & -1 & 9 \\ 7 & 0 & -3 \\ 2 & 5 & -1 \end{bmatrix}$

17. $\begin{bmatrix} 5 & 0 & 0 \\ 0 & -2 & 0 \\ 0 & 0 & 5 \end{bmatrix}$ **18.** $\begin{bmatrix} 1 & 2 & 3 \\ 2 & 4 & 6 \\ 3 & 6 & 9 \end{bmatrix}$

19. $\begin{bmatrix} 0 & 2 & -3 \\ 0 & 3 & -9 \\ 0 & 5 & 9 \end{bmatrix}$ **20.** $\begin{bmatrix} 3 & -1 & 2 \\ 0 & 5 & 7 \\ 0 & 0 & -1 \end{bmatrix}$

 Exercises 21–24: Use technology to calculate det A, where A is the given matrix.

21. $\begin{bmatrix} 2 & -5 & 13 \\ 10 & 15 & -10 \\ 17 & -19 & 22 \end{bmatrix}$ **22.** $\begin{bmatrix} 1.6 & 3.1 & 5.7 \\ 2.1 & 6.7 & 8.1 \\ -0.4 & -0.8 & -3.1 \end{bmatrix}$

23. $\begin{bmatrix} 17 & 0 & 4 \\ -9 & 14 & 1.5 \\ 13 & 67 & -11 \end{bmatrix}$ **24.** $\begin{bmatrix} 121 & 45 & -56 \\ -45 & 87 & 32 \\ -14 & -34 & 67 \end{bmatrix}$

Exercises 25 and 26: **Thinking Generally** *Find det A, if a, b, and c are nonzero constants.*

25. $A = \begin{bmatrix} a & 0 & 0 \\ 0 & b & 0 \\ 0 & 0 & c \end{bmatrix}$ **26.** $A = \begin{bmatrix} 0 & 0 & 0 \\ a & b & 0 \\ 0 & 0 & c \end{bmatrix}$

CALCULATING AREA

Exercises 27–32: Find the area of the figure by using a determinant. Assume that units are feet.

27.

28.

29.

30.

31.

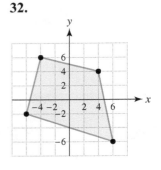

32.

CRAMER'S RULE

Exercises 33–38: Solve the system of equations by using Cramer's rule.

33. $5x + 3y = 4$
$6x - 4y = 20$

34. $-5x + 4y = -5$
$4x + 4y = -32$

35. $7x - 5y = -3$
$-4x + 6y = -8$

36. $-4x - 9y = -17$
$8x + 4y = 9$

37. $8x = 3y - 61$
$-x = 4y - 23$

38. $15y = -188 - 22x$
$23y = -173 - 16x$

WRITING ABOUT MATHEMATICS

39. Suppose that one row of a 3×3 matrix A is all 0s. What is the value of det A? Give an example and explain your answer.

40. Estimate how long it might take a supercomputer to solve a linear system of equations with 15 variables, using Cramer's rule and expansion of a determinant by minors. Explain your calculations. (*Hint:* See the discussion at the end of this section.)

CHECKING BASIC CONCEPTS
SECTION 4.7

1. Evaluate det A.

(a) $A = \begin{bmatrix} -3 & 4 \\ -2 & 3 \end{bmatrix}$

(b) $A = \begin{bmatrix} 1 & -2 & 3 \\ 5 & 1 & 1 \\ 0 & 2 & -1 \end{bmatrix}$

2. Use Cramer's rule to solve the system of linear equations.

$$2x - y = -14$$
$$3x - 4y = -36$$

3. Find the area of a triangle that has the vertices $(-1, 2)$, $(5, 6)$, and $(2, -3)$.

CHAPTER 4   SUMMARY

SECTION 4.1 ■ SYSTEMS OF LINEAR EQUATIONS IN TWO VARIABLES

Systems of Linear Equations in Two Variables

$$ax + by = c$$
$$dx + ey = k$$

Systems of linear equations in two variables can have no solutions, one solution, or infinitely many solutions. A solution is an ordered pair (x, y).

| Inconsistent System; (No Solutions) | Consistent System; Independent Equations | Consistent System; Dependent Equations |

Examples:

$x + y = 4$ $x + y = 4$ $x + y = 1$
$x + y = 2$ $x - y = 2$ $2x + 2y = 2$

No solutions   The solution is (3, 1). $\{(x, y) \mid x + y = 1\}$

Graphical and Numerical Solutions   These methods use graphs and tables to solve systems.

Example: $2x + y = 4$
$\qquad\qquad x + y = 3$

Graph and make a table for $y_1 = 4 - 2x$ and $y_2 = 3 - x$. The solution is $(1, 2)$.

Graphical Solution

Numerical Solution

x	$4 - 2x$	$3 - x$
0	4	3
1	2	2
2	0	1
3	−2	0

SECTION 4.2 ■ THE SUBSTITUTION AND ELIMINATION METHODS

Two symbolic methods for solving systems of linear equations are *substitution* and *elimination*.

Substitution

$$x + y = 5 \quad \text{or} \quad y = 5 - x$$
$$x - y = -3$$

Substituting in the second equation, $x - (5 - x) = -3$, yields $x = 1$ and $y = 4$. Solution is $(1, 4)$.

Elimination

$$x + y = 5$$
$$\underline{x - y = -3}$$
$$2x + 0y = 2 \quad \text{Add the equations.}$$

Thus $x = 1$ and $y = 4$. Solution is $(1, 4)$.

SECTION 4.3 ■ SYSTEMS OF LINEAR INEQUALITIES

Linear Inequalities in Two Variables

$$ax + by > c,$$

where $>$ can be replaced by $<$, $\leq$, or $\geq$. The solution set is typically a region in the xy-plane.

Example: $x + y \leq 4$

Any point in the shaded region must satisfy the given inequality. The *test point*, $(0, 0)$, lies in the shaded region and satisfies the inequality $x + y \leq 4$ because $0 + 0 \leq 4$.

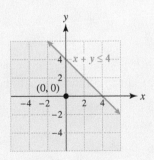

Systems of Linear Inequalities in Two Variables

$$ax + by > c$$
$$dx + ey > k,$$

where $>$ can be replaced by $<$, $\leq$, or $\geq$.

Example: $x + y \leq 2$

$\qquad\qquad y \geq x$

The test point $(-2, 1)$ satisfies both inequalities so shade the region containing $(-2, 1)$.

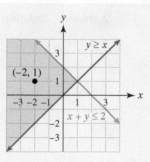

SECTION 4.4 ■ INTRODUCTION TO LINEAR PROGRAMMING

Linear Programming Problem   A linear programming problem consists of an *objective function* to be minimized or maximized (optimized) and a system of linear inequalities called *constraints*. The solution set to the constraints is called the *region of feasible solutions*.

Fundamental Theorem of Linear Programming   If the optimal value for a linear programming problem exists, then it occurs at a *vertex* of the region of feasible solutions.

Example: The maximum of $R = 2x + 3y$ must occur at one of the vertices $(0, 0)$, $(0, 4.5)$, $(3, 3)$, and $(4.5, 0)$.

Vertex	$R = 2x + 3y$
$(0, 0)$	$2(0) + 3(0) = 0$
$(0, 4.5)$	$2(0) + 3(4.5) = 13.5$
$(3, 3)$	$2(3) + 3(3) = 15$ ⟵
$(4.5, 0)$	$2(4.5) + 3(0) = 9$

Maximum of $R = 15$ occurs at vertex $(3, 3)$.

SECTION 4.5 ■ SYSTEMS OF LINEAR EQUATIONS IN THREE VARIABLES

Solution to a System of Linear Equations in Three Variables   An ordered triple (x, y, z) that satisfies *every* equation

Example: $x - y + 2z = 3$

$\qquad\qquad 2x - y + z = 5$

$\qquad\qquad x + y + z = 6$

The solution is $(3, 2, 1)$ because these values for (x, y, z) satisfy all three equations.

$$3 - 2 + 2(1) = 3 \qquad \text{True}$$
$$2(3) - 2 + 1 = 5 \qquad \text{True}$$
$$3 + 2 + 1 = 6 \qquad \text{True}$$

Elimination and Substitution   Systems of linear equations in *three* variables can be solved by elimination and substitution, using the following steps.

STEP 1: Eliminate one variable, such as x, from two of the given equations.

STEP 2: Use the two resulting equations in two variables to eliminate one of the variables, such as y. Solve for the remaining variable z.

STEP 3: Substitute z in one of the two equations from Step 2. Solve for the unknown variable y.

STEP 4: Substitute values for y and z in one of the given equations. Then find x.
The solution is (x, y, z).

SECTION 4.6 ■ MATRIX SOLUTIONS OF LINEAR SYSTEMS

Matrix A rectangular array of numbers is a matrix. If a matrix has m rows and n columns, it has dimension $m \times n$.

Example: Matrix $A = \begin{bmatrix} 3 & -1 & 7 \\ 0 & 6 & -2 \end{bmatrix}$ has dimension 2×3.

Augmented Matrix Any linear system can be represented with an augmented matrix.

Linear System

$4x - 3y = 5$
$x + 2y = 4$

Augmented Matrix

$\begin{bmatrix} 4 & -3 & | & 5 \\ 1 & 2 & | & 4 \end{bmatrix}$

Gauss–Jordan Elimination A numerical method that uses matrix row transformations to tranform a matrix into reduced row–echelon form

Example: The matrix $\begin{bmatrix} 4 & -3 & | & 5 \\ 1 & 2 & | & 4 \end{bmatrix}$ reduces to $\begin{bmatrix} 1 & 0 & | & 2 \\ 0 & 1 & | & 1 \end{bmatrix}$.

The solution to the system is $(2, 1)$.

SECTION 4.7 ■ DETERMINANTS

Determinant for a 2 × 2 Matrix A determinant is a *real number*. The determinant of a 2×2 matrix is

$$\det A = \det \begin{bmatrix} a & b \\ c & d \end{bmatrix} = ad - cb.$$

Example: $\det \begin{bmatrix} 2 & 3 \\ 4 & 5 \end{bmatrix} = (2)(5) - (4)(3) = -2$

Determinant for a 3 × 3 Matrix

$$\det A = \det \begin{bmatrix} a_1 & b_1 & c_1 \\ a_2 & b_2 & c_2 \\ a_3 & b_3 & c_3 \end{bmatrix}$$

$$= a_1 \cdot \det \begin{bmatrix} b_2 & c_2 \\ b_3 & c_3 \end{bmatrix} - a_2 \cdot \det \begin{bmatrix} b_1 & c_1 \\ b_3 & c_3 \end{bmatrix} + a_3 \cdot \det \begin{bmatrix} b_1 & c_1 \\ b_2 & c_2 \end{bmatrix}$$

Example: $\det \begin{bmatrix} 2 & 3 & 2 \\ 3 & 7 & -3 \\ 0 & 0 & -1 \end{bmatrix} = 2 \det \begin{bmatrix} 7 & -3 \\ 0 & -1 \end{bmatrix} - 3 \det \begin{bmatrix} 3 & 2 \\ 0 & -1 \end{bmatrix} + 0$

$$= 2(-7) - 3(-3) = -5$$

Cramer's rule uses determinants to solve linear systems of equations. Determinants can also be used to find areas of triangles. See Putting It All Together for Section 4.7.

CHAPTER 4   REVIEW EXERCISES

SECTION 4.1

Exercises 1 and 2: Which ordered pair is a solution?

1. $(2, -1)$, $(3, 2)$

$3x - 2y = 5$
$-2x + 4y = 2$

2. $(4, -3)$, $(-1, 2)$

$x - 5y = 19$
$4x + 3y = 7$

3. A system of linear equations is represented graphically. Find any solutions. Check your answer.

4. Use the accompanying table to solve

$$3x - y = 2$$
$$-x + y = 5.$$

Check your answer.

x	2	2.5	3	3.5	4
$3x - 2$	4	5.5	7	8.5	10
$x + 5$	7	7.5	8	8.5	9

Exercises 5–8: Solve the system of equations graphically. Determine whether the system is consistent or inconsistent. If the system is consistent, state whether the equations are dependent or independent.

5. $x + y = 6$
$x - y = -4$

6. $x - y = -2$
$-2x + 2y = 4$

7. $4x + 2y = 1$
$2x + y = 5$

8. $x - 3y = 5$
$x + 5y = -3$

Exercises 9 and 10: Solve the system numerically.

9. $3x + y = 7$
$6x + y = 16$

10. $4x + 2y = -6$
$3x - y = -7$

Exercises 11 and 12: Complete the following.

   (a) *Write a system that models the situation.*

   (b) *Solve the resulting system graphically.*

11. The sum of two numbers is 25 and their difference is 10. Find the two numbers.

12. Three times a number minus two times another number equals 19. The sum of the two numbers is 18. Find the two numbers.

Exercises 13 and 14: Solve the system graphically. Estimate values to the nearest thousandth.

13. $\pi x - 2.1y = \sqrt{2}$
$\sqrt{3}x + y = \frac{5}{6}$

14. $\sqrt{5}x - \pi y = \frac{2}{7}$
$x + 0.3y = \pi$

SECTION 4.2

Exercises 15–18: Use substitution to solve the system.

15. $2x + 5y = -1$
$x + 2y = -1$

16. $3x + y = 6$
$4x + 5y = 8$

17. $2x - 3y = -8$
$4x + 2y = 0$

18. $5x + 3y = -1$
$3x - 5y = -21$

Exercises 19–22: Use elimination to solve the system of equations, if possible.

19. $3x + y = 4$
$2x - y = -2$

20. $2x + 3y = -13$
$3x - 2y = 0$

21. $3x - y = 5$
$-6x + 2y = -10$

22. $8x - 6y = 7$
$-4x + 3y = 11$

SECTION 4.3

Exercises 23–30: Shade the solution set in the xy-plane.

23. $y \geq 2$

24. $y < 2x - 3$

25. $2x - y \leq 4$

26. $-x + 3y > 3$

27. $y - x \geq 1$
$y \leq 2$

28. $-x + y \leq 3$
$3x + 2y \geq 6$

29. $y > x - 1$
$y < 4 - 3x$

30. $x + y \geq 5$
$2x - 3 < 6$

Exercises 31 and 32: Use the graph to write the system of inequalities.

31.

32.

33. Find the maximum of $R = 7x + 8y$ in the shaded region of feasible solutions.

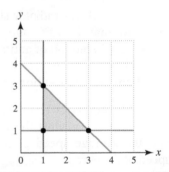

34. Use the figure from Exercise 33 to find the minimum of $C = x + 2y$.

Exercises 35 and 36: Maximize the objective function R subject to the given constraints.

35. $R = 2x + y$

$x + y \le 3$

$x + y \ge 1$

$x \ge 0, y \ge 0$

36. $R = 6x + 9y$

$3x + y \le 12$

$x + 3y \le 12$

$x \ge 0, y \ge 0$

37. Is $(3, -4, 5)$ a solution for $x + y + z = 4$?

38. Decide whether either ordered triple is a solution: $(1, -1, 2)$ or $(1, 0, 5)$.

$2x - 3y + z = 7$

$-x - y + 3z = 6$

$3x - 2y + z = 7$

Exercises 39–44: Use elimination and substitution to solve the system of linear equations, if possible.

39. $x - y - 2z = -11$

$-x + 2y + 3z = 16$

$3z = 6$

40. $x + y = 4$

$-2x + y + 3z = -2$

$x - 2y + 5z = -26$

41. $2x - y = -5$

$x + 2y + z = 7$

$-2x + y + z = 7$

42. $2x + 3y + z = 6$

$-x + 2y + 2z = 3$

$x + y + 2z = 4$

43. $x - y + 3z = 2$

$2x + y + 4z = 3$

$x + 2y + z = 5$

44. $x - y + 3z = 3$

$x + y - z = 1$

$x + z = 2$

Exercises 45–48: Write the system of linear equations as an augmented matrix. Then use Gauss–Jordan elimination to solve the system, writing the solution as an ordered triple. Check your solution.

45. $x + y + z = -6$

$x + 2y + z = -8$

$y + z = -5$

46. $x + y + z = -3$

$-x + y = 5$

$y + z = -1$

47. $x + 2y - z = 1$

$-x + y - 2z = 5$

$2y + z = 10$

48. $2x + 2y - 2z = -14$

$-2x - 3y + 2z = 12$

$x + y - 4z = -22$

Exercises 49 and 50: Technology   Use a graphing calculator to solve the system of linear equations.

49. $3x - 2y + 6z = -17$

$-2x - y + 5z = 20$

$4y + 7z = 30$

50. $19x - 13y - 7z = 7.4$

$22x + 33y - 8z = 110.5$

$10x - 56y + 9z = 23.7$

Exercises 51–54: Evaluate det A, if A is the given matrix.

51. $\begin{bmatrix} 6 & -5 \\ -4 & 2 \end{bmatrix}$

52. $\begin{bmatrix} 0 & -6 \\ 5 & 9 \end{bmatrix}$

53. $\begin{bmatrix} 3 & -5 & -3 \\ 1 & 4 & 7 \\ 0 & -3 & 1 \end{bmatrix}$ **54.** $\begin{bmatrix} -2 & -1 & -7 \\ 2 & 1 & -3 \\ 3 & -5 & 8 \end{bmatrix}$

Exercises 55 and 56: Use technology to calculate det A, where A is the given matrix.

55. $\begin{bmatrix} 22 & -45 & 3 \\ 15 & -12 & -93 \\ 5 & 81 & -21 \end{bmatrix}$ **56.** $\begin{bmatrix} 0.5 & -7.3 & 9.6 \\ 0.1 & 3.1 & 9.2 \\ -0.5 & -1.9 & 5.4 \end{bmatrix}$

Exercises 57 and 58: Use a determinant to find the area of the triangle. Assume that the units are feet.

57.

58.

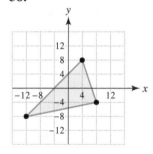

Exercises 59–62: Use Cramer's rule to solve the system.

59. $7x + 6y = 8$
$\quad\;\; 5x - 8y = 18$

60. $-2x + 5y = 25$
$\quad\;\;\; 3x + 4y = -3$

61. $3x - 6y = 1.5$
$\quad\;\; 7x - 5y = 8$

62. $-5x + 4y = -47$
$\quad\;\;\;\, 6x - 7y = 63$

APPLICATIONS

63. *Pedestrian Fatalities*   Forty-seven percent of pedestrian fatalities occur on Friday and Saturday nights. The combined total of pedestrian fatalities in 1994 and 2004 was 10,130. There were 848 more fatalities in 1994 than in 2004. Find the number of pedestrian fatalities during each year. (**Source:** National Highway Traffic Safety Administration.)

64. *Burning Calories*   During strenuous exercise, an athlete burns 11.5 calories per minute on a stair climber and 9 calories per minute on a stationary bicycle. In a 30-minute workout the athlete burns 290 calories. How many minutes are spent on each type of workout equipment? (**Source:** Runner's World.)

65. *Candy Sales*   Suppose that candy costs $4 per pound and cashews cost $5 per pound. Let x be the number of pounds of candy bought and y be the number of pounds of cashews bought. Graph the region in the xy-plane that represents all possible weight combinations of candy and cashews that cost less than or equal to $20.

66. *Loan Mixture*   A student takes out two loans for a total of $4000. The unsubsidized loan is $500 less than the subsidized loan. Find the amount of each loan.

67. *Linear Programming*   A business makes shirts and pants, which require both cutting and sewing. A shirt requires 20 minutes of cutting and 10 minutes of sewing, whereas a pair of pants requires 10 minutes of cutting and 20 minutes of sewing. The machine that sews is available for 480 minutes per day, and the machine that cuts is available 360 minutes per day. The profit from a shirt is $20 and the profit from a pair of pants is $25. How many shirts and how many pairs of pants should be made to maximize daily profit? What is the maximum profit?

68. *Mixing Antifreeze*   A car radiator should contain 4 gallons of fluid that is 40% antifreeze. An auto mechanic has a 30% solution of antifreeze and a 55% solution of antifreeze. If the car radiator is empty, how many gallons of each solution should be added?

69. *Boat Speed*   A boat travels 18 miles down a river in 1 hour. The return trip against the current takes 1.5 hours. Find the average speed of the boat and the average speed of the current.

70. *Tickets*   Tickets for a football game cost $8 and $12. If 480 tickets were sold for total receipts of $4620, how many of each type of ticket were sold?

71. *Determining Costs*   The accompanying table shows the costs for purchasing different combinations of malts, cones, and ice cream bars.

Malts	Cones	Bars	Total Cost
1	3	5	$14
1	2	4	$11
0	1	3	$5

(a) Let m be the cost of a malt, c the cost of a cone, and b the cost of an ice cream bar. Write a system of equations that represents the data in the table.

(b) Solve this system.

72. *Geometry* The largest angle in a triangle is 20° more than the sum of the two smaller angles. The measure of the largest angle is 85° more than the smallest angle. Find the measure of each angle in the triangle.

73. *Mixture Problem* Three types of candy that cost $1.50, $2.00, and $2.50 per pound are to be mixed to produce 12 pounds of candy worth $26.00. If there is to be 2 pounds more of the $2.50 candy than the $2.00 candy, how much of each type of candy should be used in the mixture?

74. *Estimating the Chest Size of a Bear* The accompanying table shows the chest size C, weight W, and overall length L of three bears. These data can be modeled with the formula $C = a + bW + cL$.

(*Sources:* M. Triola, *Elementary Statistics*; Minitab, Inc.)

C (inches)	W (pounds)	L (inches)
40	202	63
50	365	70
55	446	77

(a) Set up a system of linear equations whose solution gives values for the constants a, b, and c.

(b) Solve this system. Round each value to the nearest thousandth.

(c) Predict the chest size of a bear weighing 300 pounds and having a length of 68 inches.

CHAPTER 4 TEST Pass the Test Video solutions to all test exercises

Exercises 1–4: Solve the system of equations graphically. Determine whether the system is consistent or inconsistent. If the system is consistent, state whether the equations are dependent or independent.

1. $2x + y = 7$
$3x - 2y = 7$

2. $8x - 4y = 3$
$-4x + 2y = 6$

3. $2x - 6y = 2$
$-3x + 9y = -3$

4. $2x - 5y = 36$
$-4x + 3y = -23$

5. Solve the system of equations using substitution.
$$2x + 5y = -1$$
$$3x + 2y = -7$$

6. The difference of two numbers is 34. The first number is twice the second number.
(a) Write a system of linear equations that models the situation.
(b) Solve the system using elimination.

7. Solve the system graphically. Estimate values to the nearest thousandth.
$$-\pi x + \sqrt{3}y = 3.3$$
$$\sqrt{5}x + (1 + \sqrt{2})y = 2.1$$

8. Solve the system numerically.
$$3x + y = 17$$
$$2x - 3y = 37$$

9. Shade the solution set for $y \leq 2$ in the xy-plane.

10. Shade the solution set for $x - 2y > 3$ in the xy-plane.

11. Shade the solution set in the xy-plane. Use a test point to check your graph.
$$-2x + y \geq 3$$
$$x - 2y < -3$$

Exercises 12 and 13: Use substitution and elimination to solve the system, if possible.

12. $x + 3y = 2$
$-2x + y + z = 5$
$y + z = -3$

13. $x + y - z = 1$
$2x - 3y + z = 0$
$x - 4y + 2z = 2$

14. Use the graph to write the system of inequalities.

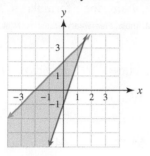

15. Consider the system of linear equations.

$$x + y + z = 2$$
$$x - y - z = 3$$
$$2x + 2y + z = 6$$

(a) Write the system as an augmented matrix.
(b) Use Gauss–Jordan elimination to solve the system, writing the solution as an ordered triple.

16. Evaluate det A if $A = \begin{bmatrix} 3 & 2 & -1 \\ 6 & 2 & -6 \\ 0 & 8 & -3 \end{bmatrix}$.

17. Solve the system of equations with Cramer's rule.

$$5x - 3y = 7$$
$$-4x + 2y = 11$$

18. *College Tuition*   In 2000, the average cost of private tuition, including room and board, was $12,636 more than public tuition. Private tuition was 4.6 times higher than public tuition.   (***Source:*** Department of Education.)

(a) Write a system that models the situation.
(b) Solve the system and interpret the solution.

19. *Burning Calories*   An athlete burns 12 calories per minute while running and 9 calories per minute on a rowing machine. During a one-hour workout, the athlete burns 669 calories. How many minutes are spent on each type of exercise?

20. *Airplane Speed*   An airplane travels 600 miles into the wind in 2.5 hours. The return trip with the wind takes 2 hours. Find the average speed of the airplane with no wind and the average wind speed.

21. *Geometry*   The largest angle in a triangle is 50° more than the smallest angle. The sum of the measures of the smaller two angles is 10° more than the largest angle. Find the measure of each angle.

22. *Linear Programming*   Maximize $R = x + 2y$ subject to the constraints

$$x \geq 0, y \geq 0$$
$$2x + 3y \leq 6.$$

23. *Candy Sales*   Suppose that candy costs $3 per pound and cashews cost $5 per pound. Let x be the number of pounds of candy bought and y be the number of pounds of cashews bought. Graph the region in the xy-plane that represents all possible weight combinations of candy and cashews that cost less than $30.

24. *Loan Mixture*   A student takes out two loans for a total of $4400. The unsubsidized loan is $700 more than the subsidized loan. Find the amount of each loan.

CHAPTER 4   EXTENDED AND DISCOVERY EXERCISES

CRAMER'S RULE

Exercises 1–6: Cramer's rule can be applied to systems of three equations in three variables. For the system of equations

$$a_1 x + b_1 y + c_1 z = d_1$$
$$a_2 x + b_2 y + c_2 z = d_2$$
$$a_3 x + b_3 y + c_3 z = d_3,$$

the solution can be written as follows.

$$D = \det \begin{bmatrix} a_1 & b_1 & c_1 \\ a_2 & b_2 & c_2 \\ a_3 & b_3 & c_3 \end{bmatrix}, \quad E = \det \begin{bmatrix} d_1 & b_1 & c_1 \\ d_2 & b_2 & c_2 \\ d_3 & b_3 & c_3 \end{bmatrix}$$

$$F = \det \begin{bmatrix} a_1 & d_1 & c_1 \\ a_2 & d_2 & c_2 \\ a_3 & d_3 & c_3 \end{bmatrix}, \quad G = \det \begin{bmatrix} a_1 & b_1 & d_1 \\ a_2 & b_2 & d_2 \\ a_3 & b_3 & d_3 \end{bmatrix}$$

If $D \neq 0$, a unique solution exists and is given by

$$x = \frac{E}{D}, \quad y = \frac{F}{D}, \quad z = \frac{G}{D}.$$

Use Cramer's rule to solve the equations.

1. $x + y + z = 6$
$2x + y + 2z = 9$
$y + 3z = 9$

2. $y + z = 1$
$2x - y - z = -1$
$x + y - z = 3$

3. $x + z = 2$
$x + y = 0$
$y + 2z = 1$

4. $x + y + 2z = 1$
$-x - 2y - 3z = -2$
$y - 3z = 5$

5. $x + 2z = 7$
$-x + y + z = 5$
$2x - y + 2z = 6$

6. $x + 2y + 3z = -1$
$2x - 3y - z = 12$
$x + 4y - 2z = -12$

MATRICES AND ROAD MAPS

*Exercises 7–12: Adjacency Matrix   A matrix A can be used to represent a map showing distances between cities. Let a_{ij} denote the number in row i and column j of a matrix A. Now consider the following map illustrating freeway distances in miles between four cities. Each city has been assigned a number. For example, there is a direct route from Denver, Colorado (city 1), to Colorado Springs, Colorado (city 2), of approximately 60 miles. Therefore $a_{12} = 60$ in the accompanying matrix A at the top of the next column. (Note that a_{12} is the number in row 1 and column 2.) The distance from Colorado Springs to Denver is also 60 miles, so $a_{21} = 60$. As there is no direct freeway connection between Las Vegas, Nevada (city 4), and Colorado Springs (city 2), we let $a_{24} = a_{42} = *$. The matrix A is called an **adjacency matrix**.*   (Source: S. Baase, *Computer Algorithms: Introduction to Design and Analysis.*)

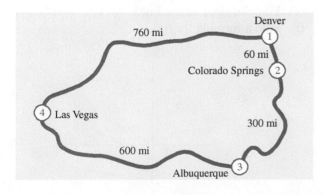

$$A = \begin{bmatrix} 0 & 60 & * & 760 \\ 60 & 0 & 300 & * \\ * & 300 & 0 & 600 \\ 760 & * & 600 & 0 \end{bmatrix}$$

7. Explain how to use A to find the freeway distance from Denver to Las Vegas.

8. Explain how to use A to find the freeway distance from Denver to Albuquerque.

9. If a map shows 20 cities, what would be the dimension of the adjacency matrix? How many elements would there be in this matrix?

10. Why are there only zeros on the main diagonal of A?

11. What does $a_{14} + a_{41}$ equal?

12. What does $a_{11} + a_{44}$ equal?

Exercises 13 and 14: (Refer to Exercises 7–12.) Determine an adjacency matrix A for the road map.

13.

14.

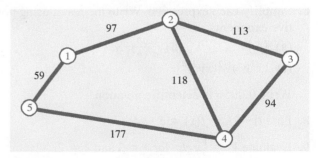

Exercises 15 and 16: (Refer to Exercises 7–12.) Sketch a road map represented by the adjacency matrix A. Is your answer unique?

15. $A = \begin{bmatrix} 0 & 30 & 20 & 5 \\ 30 & 0 & 15 & * \\ 20 & 15 & 0 & 25 \\ 5 & * & 25 & 0 \end{bmatrix}$

16. $A = \begin{bmatrix} 0 & 5 & * & 13 & 20 \\ 5 & 0 & 5 & * & * \\ * & 5 & 0 & 13 & * \\ 13 & * & 13 & 0 & 10 \\ 20 & * & * & 10 & 0 \end{bmatrix}$

SOLVING AN EQUATION IN FOUR VARIABLES

17. *Weight of a Bear* In Section 4.6 we estimated the weight of a bear by using two variables. We may be able to make more accurate estimates by using three variables. The accompanying table shows the weight W, neck size N, overall length L, and chest size C for four bears. (**Sources:** M. Triola, *Elementary Statistics*; Minitab, Inc.)

W (pounds)	N (inches)	L (inches)	C (inches)
125	19	57.5	32
316	26	65	42
436	30	72	48
514	30.5	75	54

(a) We can model the data in the table with the equation $W = a + bN + cL + dC$, where a, b, c, and d are constants. To do so, represent a system of linear equations by a 4×5 augmented matrix whose solution gives values for a, b, c, and d.

(b) Solve the system with a graphing calculator. Round each value to the nearest thousandth.

(c) Predict the weight of a bear with $N = 24$, $L = 63$, and $C = 39$. Interpret the result.

CHAPTERS 1–4 CUMULATIVE REVIEW EXERCISES

Exercises 1 and 2: State whether the equation illustrates an identity, commutative, associative, or distributive property.

1. $x + 0 = x$

2. $1 + (b + 3) = (1 + b) + 3$

3. Evaluate $\frac{1 + 2}{3 - 1} - 2^2 \cdot 4$ by hand.

4. Evaluate $-1 + 8 - 19 + 12$ mentally.

5. Find the opposite of $\frac{a}{b}$.

6. Simplify each expression. Write the result using positive exponents.
   (a) $\left(\frac{4^2}{3}\right)^{-2}$ (b) $\frac{(2ab^{-4})^2}{a^7(b^2)^{-3}}$
   (c) $(x^2 y^3)^{-2}(xy^2)^4$

7. Write 0.0056 in scientific notation.

8. Find $f(-2)$, if $f(x) = 5 - 4x$.

9. Evaluate $V = \frac{1}{3}\pi r h^2$ for $r = 3$ and $h = 2$.

10. Identify the domain of $f(x) = \frac{x}{2x + 1}$.

Exercises 11 and 12: Graph f by hand.

11. $f(x) = 2 - 4x$ 12. $f(x) = 2x^2$

13. Use the graph to answer the following.
    (a) Does the graph represent a function?
    (b) Identify the domain and range.
    (c) Evaluate $f(-1)$ and $f(2)$.
    (d) Identify the x- and y-intercepts.
    (e) Find the slope of the line.
    (f) Find a formula for $f(x)$.

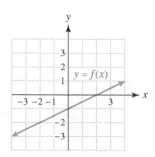

14. Find slope–intercept form of the line that passes through $(-6, 3)$ and is perpendicular to $y = -\frac{3}{4}x$.

15. Let f be a linear function. Find the slope, x-intercept, and y-intercept of the graph of f.

x	-2	-1	0	2
$f(x)$	-6	-2	2	10

16. Solve $\frac{1}{2}(1 - x) + 2x = 3x + 1$.

17. Solve $2(1 - x) > 4x - (2 + x)$.

18. Solve $x + 1 < 2$ or $x + 1 > 4$.

19. Solve $-3 \le 2 - 4x < 5$.

20. Solve each equation or inequality.
   (a) $|3x - 2| = 4$
   (b) $|3x - 2| < 4$
   (c) $|3x - 2| > 4$

21. Solve each system graphically or numerically.
   (a) $2x + y = 3$ **(b)** $4x + 3y = 8$
         $x - 2y = -1$ $2x + 7y = 4$

22. Solve each system, if possible.
   (a) $x + 2y = 4$ **(b)** $-x + y = 2$
         $3x - 2y = -2$ $2x - 2y = 5$

23. Shade the solution set in the xy-plane.
   (a) $x + 2y < 3$ **(b)** $x + y \le 2$
                                     $3x - y > 6$

24. Solve the system.
$$-x + 2y + z = 2$$
$$3x + y + z = 12$$
$$x - y - 2z = -1$$

25. Use Gauss–Jordan elimination to solve the system.
$$x + y + z = -3$$
$$2x - y + z = -11$$
$$-x - y + z = -5$$

26. Calculate $\det \begin{bmatrix} 1 & 2 & 0 \\ -1 & 0 & 4 \\ 2 & 4 & 3 \end{bmatrix}$.

APPLICATIONS

27. *Investment*   Suppose x dollars are deposited in an account paying 7% annual interest.
   (a) Write a formula that calculates the interest I after 1 year.
   (b) Calculate $I(500)$ and interpret the result.

28. *Tuition and Fees*   Average tuition and fees in dollars at private colleges from 1980 to 2000 are modeled by $T(x) = 572.3(x - 1980) + 3617$.
   (a) Evaluate $T(1990)$ and interpret the result.
   (b) Interpret the slope of the graph of T.

29. *Geometry*   A rectangle is 7 inches longer than it is wide. If the perimeter is 74 inches, find the dimensions of the rectangle.

30. *Error in Measurements*   The perimeter of a square is measured to be 12.4 feet. If the measurement of the perimeter P is accurate to within 0.2 foot, write an absolute value inequality that describes this situation.

31. *Investment*   Five thousand dollars are invested in three accounts paying 5%, 6%, and 8% interest. The amount invested at 8% is $500 more than the amount invested at 6% and the amount invested at 6% is $1000 less than the total amount invested at 5% and 8%. Find the amount invested at each interest rate.

32. *Population*   In 2002, the combined population of Florida and Texas was 38.5 million. The population of Texas was 5.1 million greater than the population of Florida. Solve a linear system to determine the population of each state.

Polynomial Expressions and Functions

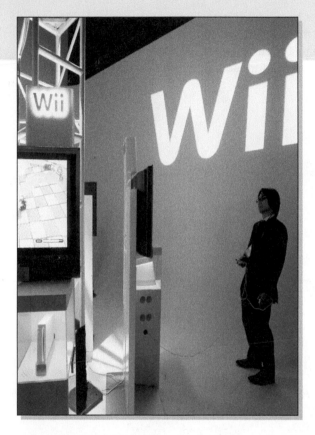

V ideo games have been available to consumers for many years. However, most of these older games lacked the graphic capability to make the action appear real on a screen. During the past three decades the computing power of processors has *doubled every 2 years*. Now video games systems, such as the PlayStation 3, Wii, and Xbox 360, are taking advantage of the new generation of powerful processors to make action scenes look incredibly realistic. Thousands of objects can be tracked and manipulated simultaneously, making the experience more lifelike to the user.

Video games are mathematically intensive because separate equations must be formed and solved in real time to determine the position of each person and object on the screen. Whether it is an athlete, a football, or an exploding object, *mathematics is essential* to making the movements look real.

Because flying objects do not follow straight-line paths, we cannot use linear functions and equations to model their paths. Instead we need functions whose graphs are curves. Polynomial functions are frequently used in modeling *nonlinear motion* of objects and are excellent at describing flying objects. In this chapter you will begin to learn about polynomials and how they can be used to model the motion of objects like golf balls in flight.

The struggle is what teaches us.

—SUE GRAFTON

Source: Microsoft.

5.1 POLYNOMIAL FUNCTIONS

Monomials and Polynomials ▪ Addition and Subtraction of Polynomials ▪ Polynomial Functions ▪ Evaluating Polynomials ▪ Operations on Functions ▪ Applications and Models

A LOOK INTO MATH ▷ Many quantities in applications cannot be modeled with linear functions and equations. If data points do not lie on a line, we say that the data are *nonlinear*. For example, a scatterplot of the *cumulative* number of AIDS deaths from 1981 through 2004 is shown in Figure 5.1. Monomials and polynomials are often used to model nonlinear data such as these. (*Source:* U.S. Department of Health and Human Services.)

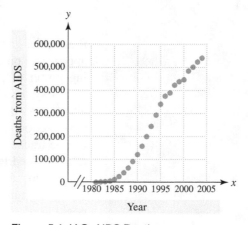

Figure 5.1 U.S. AIDS Deaths

Monomials and Polynomials

A **term** is a number, a variable, or a *product* of numbers and variables raised to powers. Examples of terms include

$$-15, \quad y, \quad x^4, \quad 3x^3z, \quad x^{-1/2}y^{-2}, \quad \text{and} \quad 6x^{-1}y^3.$$

If the variables in a term have only *nonnegative integer* exponents, the term is called a **monomial**. Examples of monomials include

$$-4, \quad 5y, \quad x^2, \quad 5x^2z^6, \quad -xy^7, \quad \text{and} \quad 6xy^3.$$

NOTE: Although a monomial can have a negative sign, it cannot contain any addition or subtraction signs. Also, a monomial cannot have division by a variable.

EXAMPLE 1   Identifying monomials

Determine whether the expression is a monomial.

(a) $-8x^3y^5$ **(b)** xy^{-1} **(c)** $9 + x^2$ **(d)** $\dfrac{2}{x}$

Solution

(a) The expression $-8x^3y^5$ represents a monomial because it is a product of the number -8 and the variables x and y, which have the nonnegative integer exponents 3 and 5.

(b) The expression xy^{-1} is not a monomial because y has a negative exponent.

(c) The expression $9 + x^2$ is not a monomial; it is the sum of two monomials, 9 and x^2.

(d) This expression is not a monomial because it involves division by a variable. Note also that $\frac{2}{x} = 2x^{-1}$, which has a negative exponent. Now Try Exercises **13, 15, 17, 19**

Monomials occur in applications involving geometry, as illustrated in the next example.

EXAMPLE **2** Writing monomials

Write a monomial that represents the volume of a cube with sides of length x.

Solution

The volume of a rectangular box equals the product of its length, width, and height. For a cube with sides of length x, its volume is given by $x \cdot x \cdot x = x^3$. See Figure 5.2.

Now Try Exercise **21**

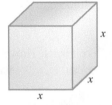

Figure 5.2 Volume: x^3

The **degree of a monomial** equals the sum of the exponents of the variables. A constant term has degree 0, unless the term is 0 (which has an undefined degree). The numeric constant in a monomial is called its **coefficient**. Table 5.1 shows the degree and coefficient of several monomials.

TABLE 5.1

Monomial	64	$4x^2y^3$	$-5x^2$	xy^3
Degree	0	5	2	4
Coefficient	64	4	-5	1

A **polynomial** is either a monomial or a sum of monomials. Examples include

$$5x^4z^2, \quad 9x^4 - 5, \quad 4x^2 + 5xy - y^2, \quad \text{and} \quad 4 - y^2 + 5y^4 + y^5.$$

1 term   2 terms   3 terms   4 terms

Polynomials containing one variable are called **polynomials of one variable**. The second and fourth polynomials shown are examples of polynomials of one variable. The **leading coefficient** of a polynomial of one variable is the coefficient of the monomial with highest degree. The **degree of a polynomial** equals the degree of the monomial with highest degree. Table 5.2 shows several polynomials of one variable along with their degrees and leading coefficients. A polynomial of degree 1 is a **linear polynomial**, a polynomial of degree 2 is a **quadratic polynomial**, and a polynomial of degree 3 is a **cubic polynomial**.

TABLE 5.2

Polynomial	Degree	Leading Coefficient	Type
-98	0	-98	Constant
$2x - 7$	1	2	Linear
$-5z + 9z^2 + 7$	2	9	Quadratic
$-2x^3 + 4x^2 + x - 1$	3	-2	Cubic
$7 - x + 4x^2 + x^5$	5	1	Fifth degree

Addition and Subtraction of Polynomials

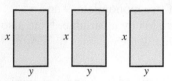

Figure 5.3 Total Area: $3xy$

Suppose that we have 3 rectangles of the same dimension having length x and width y, as shown in Figure 5.3. The total area is given by

$$xy + xy + xy.$$

This area is equivalent to 3 times xy, which can be expressed as $3xy$. In symbols we write

$$xy + xy + xy = 3xy.$$

We can add these three terms because they are *like terms*. If two terms contain the *same variables raised to the same powers*, we call them **like terms**. We can add or subtract *like* terms but not *unlike* terms. For example, if one cube has sides of length x and another cube has sides of length y, their respective volumes are x^3 and y^3. The total volume equals

$$x^3 + y^3,$$

but we cannot combine these terms into one term because they are unlike terms. However, the distributive property can be used to simplify the expression $2x^3 + 3x^3$ as

$$2x^3 + 3x^3 = (2 + 3)x^3 = 5x^3$$

because $2x^3$ and $3x^3$ are like terms. Table 5.3 lists examples of like terms and unlike terms.

TABLE 5.3

Like terms	$-x^4, 2x^4$	$-2x^2y, 4x^2y$	$a^2b^4, \frac{1}{2}a^2b^4$
Unlike terms	$-x^3, 2x^4$	$-2xy^2, 4x^2y$	$ab^5, \frac{1}{2}a^2b^4$

To add or subtract monomials we simply apply the distributive property.

EXAMPLE **3**   Adding and subtracting monomials

Simplify each expression by combining like terms.
(a) $8x^2 - 4x^2 + x^3$ **(b)** $9x - 6xy^2 + 2xy^2 + 4x$ **(c)** $5ab^2 - 4a^2 - ab^2 + a^2$

Solution
(a) The terms $8x^2$ and $-4x^2$ are like terms, so they can be combined.

$$8x^2 - 4x^2 + x^3 = (8 - 4)x^2 + x^3 \qquad \text{Combine like terms.}$$
$$= 4x^2 + x^3 \qquad \text{Simplify.}$$

However, $4x^2$ and x^3 are unlike terms and cannot be combined.
(b) The terms $9x$ and $4x$ can be combined, as can $-6xy^2$ and $2xy^2$.

$$9x - 6xy^2 + 2xy^2 + 4x = 9x + 4x - 6xy^2 + 2xy^2 \qquad \text{Commutative property}$$
$$= (9 + 4)x + (-6 + 2)xy^2 \qquad \text{Combine like terms.}$$
$$= 13x - 4xy^2 \qquad \text{Simplify.}$$

(c) The terms $5ab^2$ and $-ab^2$ are like terms, as are $-4a^2$ and a^2, so they can be combined.

$$5ab^2 - 4a^2 - ab^2 + a^2 = 5ab^2 - 1ab^2 - 4a^2 + 1a^2 \qquad \text{Commutative property}$$
$$= (5 - 1)ab^2 + (-4 + 1)a^2 \qquad \text{Combine like terms.}$$
$$= 4ab^2 - 3a^2 \qquad \text{Simplify.}$$

Now Try Exercises **39, 47**

To add two polynomials we combine like terms, as in the next example.

EXAMPLE 4   Adding polynomials

Simplify each expression.
(a) $(2x^2 - 3x + 7) + (3x^2 + 4x - 2)$ (b) $(z^3 + 4z + 8) + (4z^2 - z + 6)$

Solution
(a) $(2x^2 - 3x + 7) + (3x^2 + 4x - 2) = 2x^2 + 3x^2 - 3x + 4x + 7 - 2$
$$= (2 + 3)x^2 + (-3 + 4)x + (7 - 2)$$
$$= 5x^2 + x + 5$$

(b) $(z^3 + 4z + 8) + (4z^2 - z + 6) = z^3 + 4z^2 + 4z - z + 8 + 6$
$$= z^3 + 4z^2 + (4 - 1)z + (8 + 6)$$
$$= z^3 + 4z^2 + 3z + 14 \quad \text{Now Try Exercises } 53, 55$$

We can also add polynomials vertically, as in the next example.

EXAMPLE 5   Adding polynomials vertically

Find the sum.
(a) $(3x^2 - 5xy - 7y^2) + (xy + 4y^2 - x^2)$ (b) $(3x^3 - 2x + 7) + (x^3 + 5x^2 - 9)$

Solution
(a) Polynomials can be added vertically by placing like terms in the same columns and then adding each column.

$$
\begin{array}{l}
3x^2 - 5xy - 7y^2 \\
\underline{-x^2 + xy + 4y^2} \\
2x^2 - 4xy - 3y^2 \quad \text{Add each column.}
\end{array}
$$

(b) Note that the first polynomial does not contain an x^2-term and that the second polynomial does not contain an x-term. When you are adding vertically, leave a blank for a missing term.

$$
\begin{array}{l}
3x^3 - 2x + 7 \\
\underline{x^3 + 5x^2 - 9} \\
4x^3 + 5x^2 - 2x - 2 \quad \text{Add each column.}
\end{array}
$$

Now Try Exercises 57, 61

Recall that to subtract integers we add the first integer and the *additive inverse* or *opposite* of the second integer. For example, to evaluate $3 - 5$ we perform the following operations.

$$3 - 5 = 3 + (-5) \quad \text{Add the opposite.}$$
$$= -2 \quad \text{Simplify.}$$

Similarly, to subtract two polynomials we add the first polynomial and the opposite of the second polynomial. To find the **opposite of a polynomial**, we negate each term. Table 5.4 shows three polynomials and their opposites.

TABLE 5.4

Polynomial	Opposite
$9 - x$	$-9 + x$
$5x^2 + 4x - 1$	$-5x^2 - 4x + 1$
$-x^4 + 5x^3 - x^2 + 5x - 1$	$x^4 - 5x^3 + x^2 - 5x + 1$

EXAMPLE 6   Subtracting polynomials

Simplify.
(a) $(y^5 + 3y^3) - (-y^4 + 2y^3)$ **(b)** $(5x^3 + 9x^2 - 6) - (5x^3 - 4x^2 - 7)$

Solution
(a) The opposite of $(-y^4 + 2y^3)$ is $(y^4 - 2y^3)$.

$$(y^5 + 3y^3) - (-y^4 + 2y^3) = (y^5 + 3y^3) + (y^4 - 2y^3)$$
$$= y^5 + y^4 + (3 - 2)y^3$$
$$= y^5 + y^4 + y^3$$

(b) The opposite of $(5x^3 - 4x^2 - 7)$ is $(-5x^3 + 4x^2 + 7)$.

$$(5x^3 + 9x^2 - 6) - (5x^3 - 4x^2 - 7) = (5x^3 + 9x^2 - 6) + (-5x^3 + 4x^2 + 7)$$
$$= (5 - 5)x^3 + (9 + 4)x^2 + (-6 + 7)$$
$$= 0x^3 + 13x^2 + 1$$
$$= 13x^2 + 1$$

Now Try Exercises 69, 71

The following summarizes addition and subtraction of polynomials.

CRITICAL THINKING

Is the sum of two quadratic polynomials always a quadratic polynomial? Explain.

ADDITION AND SUBTRACTION OF POLYNOMIALS

1. To *add* two polynomials, combine like terms.
2. To *subtract* two polynomials, add the first polynomial and the opposite of the second polynomial.

NOTE: The *opposite* of a polynomial is found by changing the sign of every term.

Polynomial Functions

The following expressions are examples of polynomials of one variable.

$$1 - 5x, \quad 3x^2 - 5x + 1, \quad \text{and} \quad x^3 + 5$$

As a result, we say that the following are *symbolic representations* of polynomial functions of one variable.

$$f(x) = 1 - 5x, \quad g(x) = 3x^2 - 5x + 1, \quad \text{and} \quad h(x) = x^3 + 5$$

Function f is a **linear function** because it has degree 1, function g is a **quadratic function** because it has degree 2, and function h is a **cubic function** because it has degree 3.

EXAMPLE 7 Identifying polynomial functions

Determine whether $f(x)$ represents a polynomial function. If possible, identify the type of polynomial function and its degree.

(a) $f(x) = 5x^3 - x + 10$ (b) $f(x) = x^{-2.5} + 1$

(c) $f(x) = 1 - 2x$ (d) $f(x) = \dfrac{3}{x-1}$

Solution

(a) The expression $5x^3 - x + 10$ is a cubic polynomial, so $f(x)$ represents a cubic polynomial function. It has degree 3.

(b) $f(x)$ does not represent a polynomial function because the variables in a polynomial must have *nonnegative integer* exponents.

(c) $f(x) = 1 - 2x$ represents a polynomial function that is linear. It has degree 1.

(d) $f(x)$ does not represent a polynomial function because $\dfrac{3}{x-1}$ is not a polynomial.

Now Try Exercises 77, 79

Evaluating Polynomials

▶ REAL-WORLD CONNECTION   Frequently, monomials and polynomials represent formulas that can be evaluated. This situation is illustrated in the next three examples.

EXAMPLE 8 Evaluating a polynomial function graphically and symbolically

A graph of $f(x) = 4x - x^3$ is shown in Figure 5.4. Evaluate $f(-1)$ graphically and check your result symbolically.

Figure 5.4

Solution

Graphical Evaluation   To calculate $f(-1)$ graphically find -1 on the x-axis and move down until the graph of f is reached. Then move horizontally to the y-axis, as shown in Figure 5.5. Thus, when $x = -1, y = -3$ and $f(-1) = -3$.

Symbolic Evaluation   Evaluation of $f(x) = 4x - x^3$ is performed as follows.

$$f(-1) = 4(-1) - (-1)^3 = -4 - (-1) = -3$$

Figure 5.5 $f(-1) = -3$

Now Try Exercises 91, 95

EXAMPLE **9**   Writing and evaluating a polynomial

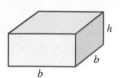

Write a polynomial that represents the total volume of two identical boxes having square bases. Make a sketch to illustrate your formula. Find the total volume of the boxes if each base is 11 inches on a side and the height of each box is 5 inches.

Solution

Figure 5.6 Volume: b^2h

Let b be the length (width) of the square base and h be the height of a side. The volume of one box is length times width times height, or b^2h, as illustrated in Figure 5.6, and the volume of two boxes is $2b^2h$. To calculate their total volumes let $b = 11$ and $h = 5$ in the expression $2b^2h$. Then

$$2 \cdot 11^2 \cdot 5 = 1210 \text{ cubic inches.} \qquad \text{Now Try Exercise } \boxed{123}$$

EXAMPLE **10**   Evaluating a polynomial function symbolically

Evaluate $f(x)$ at the given value of x.
(a) $f(x) = -3x^4 - 2, \quad x = 2$ **(b)** $f(x) = -2x^3 - 4x^2 + 5, \quad x = -3$

Solution
(a) Be sure to evaluate exponents before multiplying.
$$f(2) = -3(2)^4 - 2 = -3 \cdot 16 - 2 = -50$$
(b) $f(-3) = -2(-3)^3 - 4(-3)^2 + 5 = -2(-27) - 4(9) + 5 = 23$

Now Try Exercises $\boxed{99, 103}$

Operations on Functions

▶ REAL-WORLD CONNECTION   Frequently, we have found it necessary to add numbers or variables. Similarly, there may be a need to add two functions. For example, suppose that a student works road construction during summer break. On the taxable portion of this income, there might be a 6% state income tax and a 15% federal income tax. If x is the student's taxable income, then $S(x) = 0.06x$ calculates the state income tax and $F(x) = 0.15x$ calculates the federal income tax. Thus if $x = \$5000$, then the *total income tax T* is

$$T(5000) = S(5000) + F(5000)$$
$$= 0.06(5000) + 0.15(5000)$$
$$= \$300 + \$750$$
$$= \$1050.$$

That is, to find the total tax, we add state and federal taxes. This statement can be written in *function notation* for a taxable income x as
$$T(x) = S(x) + F(x).$$
Given two functions, f and g, we define the sum, $f + g$, and difference, $f - g$, as follows.

SUM AND DIFFERENCE OF TWO FUNCTIONS

The sum and difference of two functions f and g are defined as follows.
$$(f + g)(x) = f(x) + g(x)$$
$$(f - g)(x) = f(x) - g(x)$$
provided both $f(x)$ and $g(x)$ are defined.

EXAMPLE 11 Calculating sums and differences of functions

Let $f(x) = 2x^2 + 1$ and $g(x) = 5 - x^2$. Find each sum or difference.
(a) $(f + g)(1)$ **(b)** $(f - g)(-2)$
(c) $(f + g)(x)$ **(d)** $(f - g)(x)$

Solution
(a) Because $f(1) = 2 \cdot 1^2 + 1 = 3$ and $g(1) = 5 - 1^2 = 4$, it follows that

$$(f + g)(1) = f(1) + g(1) = 3 + 4 = 7.$$

(b) Because $f(-2) = 2 \cdot (-2)^2 + 1 = 9$ and $g(-2) = 5 - (-2)^2 = 1$, it follows that

$$(f - g)(-2) = f(-2) - g(-2) = 9 - 1 = 8.$$

(c) $(f + g)(x) = f(x) + g(x)$ Addition of functions

$\qquad = (2x^2 + 1) + (5 - x^2)$ Substitute for $f(x)$ and $g(x)$.

$\qquad = x^2 + 6$ Combine like terms.

(d) $(f - g)(x) = f(x) - g(x)$ Subtraction of functions

$\qquad = (2x^2 + 1) - (5 - x^2)$ Substitute for $f(x)$ and $g(x)$.

$\qquad = (2x^2 + 1) + (-5 + x^2)$ Add the opposite.

$\qquad = 3x^2 - 4$ Combine like terms.

Now Try Exercise 113

Applications and Models

▶ REAL-WORLD CONNECTION Polynomials are used to model a wide variety of data. A scatterplot of the cumulative number of reported AIDS cases in thousands from 1984 to 1994 is shown in Figure 5.7. In this graph $x = 4$ corresponds to 1984, $x = 5$ to 1985, and so on until $x = 14$ represents 1994. These data can be modeled with a quadratic function, as shown in Figure 5.8, where $f(x) = 4.1x^2 - 25x + 46$ is graphed with the data. Note that $f(x)$ was found by using a graphing calculator.   (*Source:* U.S. Department of Health and Human Services.)

Figure 5.7 AIDS Cases (1984–1994)

Figure 5.8 Modeling AIDS Cases

EXAMPLE 12 Modeling AIDS cases in the United States

Use $f(x) = 4.1x^2 - 25x + 46$ to model the number of AIDS cases.
(a) Estimate the number of AIDS cases reported by 1987. Compare it to the actual value of 71.4 thousand.

(b) By 1997, the total number of AIDS cases reported was 631 thousand. What estimate does $f(x)$ give? Discuss your result.

Solution

(a) The value $x = 7$ corresponds to 1987. Let $f(x) = 4.1x^2 - 25x + 46$ and evaluate $f(7)$, which gives

$$f(7) = 4.1(7)^2 - 25(7) + 46 = \mathbf{71.9}.$$

This model estimates that a cumulative total of 71.9 thousand AIDS cases were reported by 1987. This result compares favorably to the actual value of 71.4 thousand cases.

(b) To estimate the number in 1997, we evaluate $f(17)$ because $x = 17$ corresponds to 1997, obtaining

$$f(17) = 4.1(17)^2 - 25(17) + 46 = 805.9.$$

This result is considerably more than the actual value of 631 thousand. The reason is that f models data only from 1984 through 1994. After 1994, f gives estimates that are too large because the growth in AIDS cases has slowed more in recent years.

Now Try Exercise **122**

▶ **REAL-WORLD CONNECTION**   A well-conditioned athlete's heart rate can reach 200 beats per minute during strenuous physical activity. Upon quitting, a typical heart rate decreases rapidly at first and then more gradually after a few minutes, as illustrated in the next example.

EXAMPLE **13**   Modeling heart rate of an athlete

Let $P(t) = 1.875t^2 - 30t + 200$ model an athlete's heart rate (or pulse P) in beats per minute (bpm) t minutes after strenuous exercise has stopped, where $0 \le t \le 8$.   (*Source:* V. Thomas, *Science and Sport.*)

(a) What is the initial heart rate when the athlete stops exercising?
(b) What is the heart rate after 8 minutes?
(c) A graph of P is shown in Figure 5.9. Interpret this graph.

Figure 5.9

Solution

(a) To find the initial heart rate evaluate $P(t)$ at $t = 0$, or

$$P(0) = 1.875(0)^2 - 30(0) + 200 = 200.$$

When the athlete stops exercising, the heart rate is 200 beats per minute. (This result agrees with the graph.)

(b) $P(8) = 1.875(8)^2 - 30(8) + 200 = 80$ beats per minute.

(c) The heart rate does not drop at a constant rate; rather, it drops rapidly at first and then gradually begins to level off.

Now Try Exercise **119**

5.1 PUTTING IT ALL TOGETHER

In this section we introduced monomials, polynomials, and polynomial functions. A monomial is a number or a product of numbers and variables, where each variable has a *nonnegative integer* exponent. A polynomial is a monomial or a sum of monomials. Examples are given in the following table.

Concept	Examples
Addition of Polynomials	$\begin{aligned}(-3x^2 + 2x - 7) + (4x^2 - x + 1) &= -3x^2 + 4x^2 + 2x - x - 7 + 1 \\ &= (-3 + 4)x^2 + (2 - 1)x + (-7 + 1) \\ &= x^2 + x - 6\end{aligned}$ $\begin{aligned}(x^4 + 8x^3 - 7x) + (5x^4 - 3x) &= x^4 + 5x^4 + 8x^3 - 7x - 3x \\ &= (1 + 5)x^4 + 8x^3 + (-7 - 3)x \\ &= 6x^4 + 8x^3 - 10x\end{aligned}$
Opposite of a Polynomial	The opposite of $-5x^2 + 3x - 5$ is $5x^2 - 3x + 5$. The opposite of $-6x^6 + 4x^4 - 8x^2 - 17$ is $6x^6 - 4x^4 + 8x^2 + 17$.
Subtraction of Polynomials (Add the Opposite.)	$\begin{aligned}(5x^2 - 6x + 1) - (-5x^2 + 3x - 5) &= (5x^2 - 6x + 1) + (5x^2 - 3x + 5) \\ &= (5 + 5)x^2 + (-6 - 3)x + (1 + 5) \\ &= 10x^2 - 9x + 6\end{aligned}$ $\begin{aligned}(x^4 - 6x^2 + 5x) - (x^4 - 5x + 7) &= (x^4 - 6x^2 + 5x) + (-x^4 + 5x - 7) \\ &= (1 - 1)x^4 - 6x^2 + (5 + 5)x - 7 \\ &= -6x^2 + 10x - 7\end{aligned}$
Polynomial Functions	The following represent polynomial functions. $\begin{array}{lll} f(x) = 3 & \text{Degree} = 0 & \text{Constant} \\ f(x) = 5x - 3 & \text{Degree} = 1 & \text{Linear} \\ f(x) = x^2 - 2x - 1 & \text{Degree} = 2 & \text{Quadratic} \\ f(x) = 3x^3 + 2x^2 - 6 & \text{Degree} = 3 & \text{Cubic} \end{array}$
Evaluating a Polynomial Function	To evaluate $f(x) = -4x^2 + 3x - 1$ at $x = 2$, substitute 2 for x. $$f(2) = -4(2)^2 + 3(2) - 1 = -16 + 6 - 1 = -11$$
Sums and Differences of Functions	Let $f(x) = 2x + 3$ and $g(x) = x + 2$. $(f + g)(x) = (2x + 3) + (x + 2) = 3x + 5$ $(f - g)(x) = (2x + 3) - (x + 2) = x + 1$

5.1 Exercises

MyMathLab

 Math XL
PRACTICE

WATCH

DOWNLOAD

READ

REVIEW

CONCEPTS

1. Give an example of a monomial.

2. What are the degree and leading coefficient of the polynomial $3x^2 - x^3 + 1$?

3. Are $-5x^3y$ and $6xy^3$ like terms? Explain.

4. Give an example of a polynomial that has 3 terms and is degree 4.

5. Does the opposite of $x^2 + 1$ equal $-x^2 + 1$? Explain.

6. Evaluate $4x^3y$ when $x = 2$ and $y = 3$.

7. When you evaluate a polynomial function at one value of x, can you calculate two answers? Explain.

8. Could the graph of a polynomial function be a line? Explain.

9. If $f(x) = x^2 + x$, then $f(2) = $ _____.

10. If $f(x) = x^2$ and $g(x) = 2x^2$, then it follows that $(f + g)(x) = $ _____.

MONOMIALS AND POLYNOMIALS

Exercises 11–20: Determine whether the expression is a monomial.

11. x^4

12. x^{-4}

13. $2x^2y + y^2$

14. $5 - \sqrt{x}$

15. $-4x^3y^3$

16. xy

17. $\dfrac{3}{x - 2}$

18. $\pi x^4 y^2 z$

19. $x^{-3}y$

20. x^{-2}

Exercises 21–26: Write a monomial that represents the described quantity.

21. The area of a square with sides equal to x

22. The circumference of a circle with diameter d

23. The area of a circle with radius r

24. The area of three congruent triangles with base b and height h

25. The number of members in a marching band that has x rows with y people in each row

26. The revenue from selling w items for z dollars each

Exercises 27–32: Identify the degree and coefficient.

27. $3x^7$

28. $-5y^3$

29. $-3x^2y^5$

30. xy^5

31. $-x^3y^3$

32. $\sqrt{2}xy$

Exercises 33–38: Identify the degree and leading coefficient of the polynomial.

33. $5x^2 - 4x + \frac{3}{4}$

34. $-9y^4 + y^2 + 5$

35. $5 - x + 3x^2 - \frac{2}{5}x^3$

36. $7x + 4x^4 - \frac{4}{3}x^3$

37. $8x^4 + 3x^3 - 4x + x^5$

38. $5x^2 - x^3 + 7x^4 + 10$

Exercises 39–50: Combine like terms whenever possible.

39. $x^2 + 4x^2$

40. $-3z + 5z$

41. $6y^4 - 3y^4$

42. $9xy - 7xy$

43. $5x^2y + 8xy^2$

44. $5x + 4y$

45. $9x^2 - x + 4x - 6x^2$

46. $-xy^2 - \frac{1}{2}xy^2$

47. $x^2 + 9xy - y^2 + 4x^2 + y^2$

48. $6xy + 4x - 6xy$

49. $4x + 7x^3y^7 - \frac{1}{2}x^3y^7 + 9x - \frac{3}{2}x^3y^7$

50. $19x^3 + x^2 - 3x^3 + x - 4x^2 + 1$

Exercises 51–62: Add the polynomials.

51. $(3x + 1) + (-x + 1)$

52. $(5y^3 + y) + (12y^3 - 5y)$

53. $(x^2 - 2x + 15) + (-3x^2 + 5x - 7)$

54. $(4x) + (1 - 4.5x)$

55. $(3x^3 - 4x + 3) + (5x^2 + 4x + 12)$

56. $(y^5 + y) + \left(5 - y + \frac{1}{3}y^2\right)$

57. $(x^4 - 3x^2 - 4) + \left(-8x^4 + x - \frac{1}{2}\right)$

58. $(3z + z^4 + 2) + (-3z^4 - 5 + z^2)$

59. $(4r^4 - r + 2) + (r^3 - 5r)$

60. $(5t^3 + 3t) + (4t^4 - 3t^3 + 1)$

61. $(4xy - x^2 + y^2) + (4y^2 - 8xy - x^2)$

62. $(3x^2 + 6xy - y^2) + (8y^2 - xy - 2x^2)$

Exercises 63–68: Find the opposite of the polynomial.

63. $6x^5$

64. $-5y^7$

65. $19x^5 - 5x^3 + 3x$

66. $-x^2 - x - 5$

67. $-7z^4 + z^2 - 8$

68. $6 - 4x + 5x^2 - \frac{1}{10}x^3$

Exercises 69–76: Subtract the polynomials.

69. $(5x - 3) - (2x + 4)$

70. $(10x + 5) - (-6x - 4)$

71. $(x^2 - 3x + 1) - (-5x^2 + 2x - 4)$

72. $(-x^2 + x - 5) - (x^2 - x + 5)$

73. $3(4x^4 + 2x^2 - 9) - 4(x^4 - 2x^2 - 5)$

74. $2(8x^3 + 5x^2 - 3x + 1) - 5(-5x^3 + 6x - 11)$

75. $4(x^4 - 1) - (4x^4 + 3x + 7)$

76. $(5x^4 - 6x^3 + x^2 + 5) - (x^3 + 11x^2 + 9x - 3)$

Exercises 77–84: Determine whether $f(x)$ represents a polynomial function. If possible, identify the degree and type of polynomial function.

77. $f(x) = x^4 + 5x^2$

78. $f(x) = 5x^3 + 1$

79. $f(x) = x^{-2}$

80. $f(x) = |x|$

81. $f(x) = \dfrac{1}{x^2 + 1}$

82. $f(x) = 5x - 7$

83. $f(x) = 3x - x^2$

84. $f(x) = x + 3x^{-2}$

EVALUATING POLYNOMIALS

Exercises 85–90: Evaluate the polynomial at the given value(s) of the variable(s).

85. $-4x^2$ $x = 2$

86. $-2y^3$ $y = -3$

87. $2x^2y$ $x = 2, y = 3$

88. $-xy^3$ $x = 4, y = -1$

89. $a^2b - ab^2$ $a = -3, b = 4$

90. $3a^3 + 2b^3$ $a = -2, b = 3$

Exercises 91–94: Evaluate the expressions graphically.

91. $f(1)$ and $f(-2)$

92. $f(0)$ and $f(2)$

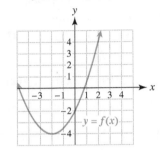

93. $f(-1)$ and $f(2)$

94. $f(-1)$ and $f(0)$

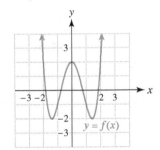

Exercises 95–108: Evaluate $f(x)$ at the given x-value.

95. $f(x) = 3x^2$ $x = -2$

96. $f(x) = x^2 - 2x$ $x = 3$

97. $f(x) = 5 - 4x$ $x = -\frac{1}{2}$

98. $f(x) = x^2 + 4x - 5$ $x = -3$

99. $f(x) = 0.5x^4 - 0.3x^3 + 5$ $x = -1$

100. $f(x) = 6 - 2x + x^3$ $x = 0$

101. $f(x) = -x^3$ $x = -1$

102. $f(x) = 3 - 2x$ $x = \frac{3}{10}$

103. $f(x) = -x^2 - 3x$ $x = -3$

104. $f(x) = 2x^3 - 4x + 1$ $x = 1$

105. $f(x) = 1 - 2x + x^2$ $x = 2.4$

106. $f(x) = 4x^2 - 20x + 25$ $\qquad x = 1.8$

107. $f(x) = x^5 - 5$ $\qquad x = -1$

108. $f(x) = 1.2x^4 - 5.7x + 3$ $\qquad x = \frac{3}{2}$

109. Thinking Generally If $f(x) = x^2 - 2x$, then it follows that $f(a) = $ _____.

110. Thinking Generally If $f(x) = 2x - 1$, then it follows that $f(a + 2) = $ _____.

Exercises 111–118: For the given f(x) and g(x), find the following and simplify.
  (a) $(f + g)(2)$ $\qquad$ **(b)** $(f - g)(-1)$
  (c) $(f + g)(x)$ $\qquad$ **(d)** $(f - g)(x)$

111. $f(x) = 3x - 1, g(x) = 5 - x$

112. $f(x) = -4x + 3, g(x) = 5x$

113. $f(x) = -3x^2, g(x) = x^2 + 1$

114. $f(x) = 2x^2 - 2, g(x) = 3 - x^2$

115. $f(x) = -x^3, g(x) = 3x^3$

116. $f(x) = x^3 + x, g(x) = 2x - 3x^3$

117. $f(x) = x^2 - 2x + 1, g(x) = 4x^2 + 3x$

118. $f(x) = 3 + x - 2x^2, g(x) = 5x + 8$

APPLICATIONS

119. *Women on the Run* The number of women participating in the New York marathon has increased dramatically in recent years. The polynomial function $f(x) = 8.87x^2 + 232x + 769$ models the number of women running each year from 1978 through 2000, where $x = 0$ corresponds to 1978, $x = 10$ to 1988, and $x = 22$ to 2000. See the accompanying figure. (*Source: Runner's World.*)

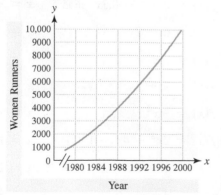

Year

(a) Use the graph to estimate the number of women running in 1980 and in 1995.

(b) Answer part (a), using the polynomial. How do your answers compare with your answers in part (a)?

(c) Use the polynomial to find the increase in women runners from 1978 to 1998.

120. *A PC for All?* Worldwide sales of computers have climbed as prices have continued to drop. The function $f(x) = 0.7868x^2 + 12x + 79.5$ models the number of personal computers sold in millions during year x, where $x = 0$ corresponds to 1997, $x = 1$ to 1998, and so on. Estimate the number of personal computers sold in 2003, using both the graph and the polynomial. (*Source:* International Data Corporation.)

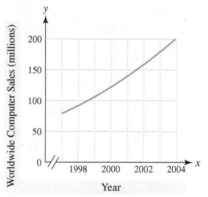

Year

121. *Geometry* A house has 8-foot-high ceilings. Three rooms are x feet by y feet and two rooms are x feet by z feet. Write a polynomial that gives the total volume of the five rooms. Find their total volume if $x = 10$ feet, $y = 12$ feet, and $z = 7$ feet.

122. *U.S. AIDS Deaths* The scatterplot shows the cumulative number of reported AIDS deaths. In this graph $x = 4$ corresponds to 1984, $x = 5$ to 1985, and so on until $x = 14$ corresponds to 1994. The data may be modeled by $f(x) = 2.4x^2 - 14x + 23$, where the output is in thousands of deaths.

Year (1984 ⟷ 4)

(a) Use $f(x)$ to estimate the cumulative total of AIDS deaths in 1990. Compare it with the actual value of 121.6 thousand.

(b) In 1997 the cumulative number of AIDS deaths was 390 thousand. What estimate does $f(x)$ give? Discuss your result.

123. Write a monomial that represents the volume of five identical cubes with sides having length s.

124. Write a monomial that represents the area of six identical rectangles with length L and width W.

125. *Squares and Circles* Write a polynomial that gives the sum of the areas of a square with sides of length x and a circle with radius x. Find the combined area when $x = 10$ inches.

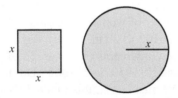

126. *Spheres* Write a monomial that gives the volume of 9 spheres with radius y. Find the combined volumes when $y = 3$ feet. (*Hint:* $V = \frac{4}{3}\pi r^3$.)

127. *Heart Rate* (Refer to Example 13.) Make a table of $f(t) = 1.875t^2 - 30t + 200$, starting at $t = 3$ and incrementing by 1. When was the athlete's heart rate between 80 and 110, inclusive?

128. *SUV Sales* Sales of sport utility vehicles (SUVs) increased dramatically between 1991 and 1999. In 1991 about 1 million SUVs were sold, and in 1999 3.2 million were sold. Growth in sales could be modeled by a linear function f.
(*Source:* Autodata Corporation.)
(a) Find values for a and b so that $f(x) = ax + b$ models the data. (*Hint:* The graph of f should pass through the points (1991, 1) and (1999, 3.2).)
(b) Estimate the number of SUVs sold in 1995.

129. *Microsoft Stocks* If a person had bought $2500 of Microsoft stock in 1986, it would have been worth about $1.2 million in 1999. The following table shows the cost of this stock (adjusted for splits) in various years.

Year	1986	1994	1999
Cost ($)	0.19	20	90

Source: USA Today.

Which of the following polynomials models the data best, where $x = 6$ corresponds to 1986, $x = 14$ to 1994, and $x = 19$ to 1999? Explain how you made your decision.
(i) $f(x) = 0.886x^2 - 15.25x + 59.79$
(ii) $g(x) = 0.882x^2 - 15.4x + 60.15$

130. *Ocean Temperatures* The polynomial function
$$f(x) = -0.064x^3 + 0.56x^2 + 2.9x + 61$$
models the ocean temperature in degrees Fahrenheit at Naples, Florida. In this formula $x = 1$ corresponds to January, $x = 2$ to February, and so on. (*Source:* J. Williams.)
(a) What is the average ocean temperature in April?
(b) Use the graph of f to estimate when the maximum ocean temperature occurs. What is this maximum?

131. *Profit from CDs* Suppose the cost in dollars for a band to produce x compact discs is given by $C(x) = 4x + 2000$. If the band sells CDs for $16 each, complete the following.
(a) Write a function R that gives the revenue for selling x compact discs.
(b) If profit equals revenue minus cost, write a formula $P(x)$ for the profit.
(c) Evaluate $P(3000)$ and interpret the answer.

132. *Income Tax* Let the state tax be 7% and the federal tax be 15%.
   (a) Find a function T that calculates the total tax on a taxable income of x dollars.
   (b) Evaluate $T(4000)$ and interpret the result.

WRITING ABOUT MATHEMATICS

133. Discuss how to subtract two polynomials. Demonstrate your method with an example.

134. Explain the difference between a monomial and a polynomial. Give examples of each and an example that is neither a monomial nor a polynomial.

135. If a polynomial function has degree 1, what can be said about its graph? If a polynomial function has degree greater than 1, what can be said about its graph?

136. Explain how to evaluate a function graphically. Use your method to evaluate $f(x) = x^2$ at $x = -2$.

GROUP ACTIVITY
WORKING WITH REAL DATA

Directions: Form a group of 2 to 4 people. Select someone to record the group's responses for this activity. All members of the group should work cooperatively to answer the questions. If your instructor asks for the results, each member of the group should be prepared to respond.

 Women in College The table shows the number of women attending 4-year institutions of higher education.

Year	1983	1993	2003
Women (millions)	3.8	4.7	5.2

Source: National Center for Education Statistics.

(a) Verify that these data are modeled by
$$f(x) = -0.002x^2 + 8.042x - 8078.908,$$
where x is the year.

(b) Make a table of $f(x)$, starting at $x = 2004$ and incrementing by 1. What does this model predict will happen in 2010? Is this model accurate that far into the future? Explain.

(c) Would $f(x)$ be more accurate predicting the number of women attending college in 2001 than in 2010? Explain.

(d) The x-intercepts on the graph of $f(x)$ are approximately 1959 and 2062. Do these x-intercepts have meaning in this model? Explain.

5.2 MULTIPLICATION OF POLYNOMIALS

Review of Basic Properties ■ Multiplying Polynomials ■ Some Special Products ■ Multiplying Functions

A LOOK INTO MATH ▷

The study of polynomials dates back to Babylonian civilization in about 1800–1600 B.C. Much later, Gottfried Leibniz (1646–1716) was the first to generalize polynomial functions of degree n. Many eighteenth-century mathematicians devoted their entire careers to the study of polynomials. Their studies included multiplying and factoring polynomials. Both skills are used to solve equations. In this section we discuss the basics of polynomial multiplication. (**Sources:** *Historical Topics for the Mathematics Classroom, Thirty-first Yearbook*, NCTM; L. Motz and J. Weaver, *The Story of Mathematics*.)

Review of Basic Properties

Distributive properties are used frequently in the multiplication of polynomials. For all real numbers a, b, and c

$$a(b + c) = ab + ac \quad \text{and}$$
$$a(b - c) = ab - ac.$$

In the next example we use these distributive properties to multiply expressions.

EXAMPLE 1   Using distributive properties

Multiply.
(a) $4(5 + x)$ **(b)** $-3(x - 4y)$ **(c)** $(2x - 5)(6)$

Solution

(a) $4(5 + x) = 4 \cdot 5 + 4 \cdot x = 20 + 4x$

(b) $-3(x - 4y) = -3 \cdot x - (-3) \cdot (4y) = -3x + 12y$

(c) $(2x - 5)(6) = 2x \cdot 6 - 5 \cdot 6 = 12x - 30$ Now Try Exercises 19, 23

You can visualize the solution to part (a) of Example 1 by using areas of rectangles. If a rectangle has width 4 and length $5 + x$, its area is $20 + 4x$, as shown in Figure 5.10.

In Section 1.3 we discussed several properties of exponents. The following three properties of exponents are frequently used in the multiplication of polynomials.

Figure 5.10 Area: $20 + 4x$

PROPERTIES OF EXPONENTS

For any numbers a and b and integers m and n,

$$a^m \cdot a^n = a^{m+n}, \quad (a^m)^n = a^{mn}, \quad \text{and} \quad (ab)^n = a^n b^n.$$

We use these three properties to simplify expressions in the next two examples.

EXAMPLE 2   Multiplying powers of variables

Multiply each expression.
(a) $-2x^3 \cdot 4x^5$ **(b)** $(3xy^3)(4x^2y^2)$ **(c)** $6y^3(2y - y^2)$ **(d)** $-mn(m^2 - n)$

Solution
(a) $-2x^3 \cdot 4x^5 = (-2)(4)x^3 x^5 = -8x^{3+5} = -8x^8$
(b) $(3xy^3)(4x^2y^2) = (3)(4)xx^2y^3y^2 = 12x^{1+2}y^{3+2} = 12x^3y^5$

NOTE: We cannot simplify $12x^3y^5$ further because x^3 and y^5 have different bases.

(c) $6y^3(2y - y^2) = 6y^3 \cdot 2y - 6y^3 \cdot y^2 = 12y^4 - 6y^5$

(d) $-mn(m^2 - n) = -mn \cdot m^2 + mn \cdot n = -m^3n + mn^2$

Now Try Exercises 9, 13, 25, 27

EXAMPLE 3   Using properties of exponents

Simplify.
(a) $(x^2)^5$ **(b)** $(2x)^3$ **(c)** $(5x^3)^2$ **(d)** $(-mn^3)^2$

Solution
(a) $(x^2)^5 = x^{2 \cdot 5} = x^{10}$ **(b)** $(2x)^3 = 2^3 x^3 = 8x^3$
(c) $(5x^3)^2 = 5^2 (x^3)^2 = 25x^6$ **(d)** $(-mn^3)^2 = (-m)^2 (n^3)^2 = m^2 n^6$

Now Try Exercises 79, 81, 83

Multiplying Polynomials

A polynomial with one term is a **monomial**, with two terms a **binomial**, and with three terms a **trinomial**. Examples are shown in Table 5.5.

TABLE 5.5

Monomials	$2x^2$	$-3x^4y$	9
Binomials	$3x - 1$	$2x^3 - x$	$x^2 + 5$
Trinomials	$x^2 - 3x + 5$	$5x^4 - 2x + 10$	$2x^3 - x^2 - 2$

In the next example we multiply binomials, using geometric and symbolic techniques.

EXAMPLE 4   Multiplying binomials

Multiply $(x + 1)(x + 3)$
(a) geometrically and   **(b)** symbolically.

Solution
(a) To multiply $(x + 1)(x + 3)$ geometrically, draw a rectangle $x + 1$ wide and $x + 3$ long, as shown in Figure 5.11(a). The area of the rectangle equals the product $(x + 1)(x + 3)$. This large rectangle can be divided into four smaller rectangles as shown in Figure 5.11(b). The sum of the areas of these four smaller rectangles equals the area of the large rectangle. The smaller rectangles have areas of $x^2, x, 3x$, and 3. Thus

$$(x + 1)(x + 3) = x^2 + x + 3x + 3$$
$$= x^2 + 4x + 3.$$

(a) Area: $(x + 1)(x + 3)$

(b) Area: $x^2 + 4x + 3$

Figure 5.11

(b) To multiply $(x + 1)(x + 3)$ symbolically we apply the distributive property.

$$(x + 1)(x + 3) = (x + 1)(x) + (x + 1)(3)$$
$$= x \cdot x + 1 \cdot x + x \cdot 3 + 1 \cdot 3$$
$$= x^2 + x + 3x + 3$$
$$= x^2 + 4x + 3$$

Now Try Exercises 29, 33

GRAPHICAL AND NUMERICAL SUPPORT   We can give graphical and numerical support to our result in Example 4 by letting $Y_1 = (X + 1)(X + 3)$ and by letting $Y_2 = X^2 + 4X + 3$. The graphs of y_1 and y_2 appear to be identical in Figures 5.12(a) and 5.12(b). Figure 5.12(c) shows that $y_1 = y_2$ for each value of x in the table.

[−6, 6, 1] by [−4, 4, 1]

[−6, 6, 1] by [−4, 4, 1]

(a)

(b)

(c)

Figure 5.12

FOIL   One way to multiply $(x + 1)$ by $(x + 3)$ is to multiply every term in $x + 1$ by every term in $x + 3$. That is,

$$(x + 1)(x + 3) = x^2 + 3x + x + 3$$
$$= x^2 + 4x + 3.$$

NOTE: This process of multiplying binomials is called *FOIL*. You may use it to remind yourself to multiply the first terms (F), outside terms (O), inside terms (I), and last terms (L).

Multiply the *First terms* to obtain x^2. $(x + 1)(x + 3)$

Multiply the *Outside terms* to obtain $3x$. $(x + 1)(x + 3)$

Multiply the *Inside terms* to obtain x. $(x + 1)(x + 3)$

Multiply the *Last terms* to obtain 3. $(x + 1)(x + 3)$

The following method summarizes how to multiply two polynomials in general.

MULTIPLICATION OF POLYNOMIALS

The product of two polynomials may be found by multiplying every term in the first polynomial by every term in the second polynomial.

EXAMPLE 5   Multiplying polynomials

Multiply each binomial.
(a) $(2x - 1)(x + 2)$ **(b)** $(1 - 3x)(2 - 4x)$ **(c)** $(x^2 + 1)(5x - 3)$

Solution

(a) $(2x - 1)(x + 2) = 2x \cdot x + 2x \cdot 2 - 1 \cdot x - 1 \cdot 2$
$$= 2x^2 + 4x - x - 2$$
$$= 2x^2 + 3x - 2$$

(b) $(1 - 3x)(2 - 4x) = 1 \cdot 2 - 1 \cdot 4x - 3x \cdot 2 + 3x \cdot 4x$
$= 2 - 4x - 6x + 12x^2$
$= 2 - 10x + 12x^2$
(c) $(x^2 + 1)(5x - 3) = x^2 \cdot 5x - x^2 \cdot 3 + 1 \cdot 5x - 1 \cdot 3$
$= 5x^3 - 3x^2 + 5x - 3$ Now Try Exercises 49, 53, 59

EXAMPLE 6   Multiplying polynomials

Multiply each expression.
(a) $3x(x^2 + 5x - 4)$ **(b)** $-x^2(x^4 - 2x + 5)$ **(c)** $(x + 2)(x^2 + 4x - 3)$

Solution

(a) Multiply each term in the second polynomial by $3x$.

$3x(x^2 + 5x - 4) = 3x \cdot x^2 + 3x \cdot 5x - 3x \cdot 4$
$= 3x^3 + 15x^2 - 12x$
(b) $-x^2(x^4 - 2x + 5) = -x^2 \cdot x^4 + x^2 \cdot 2x - x^2 \cdot 5$
$= -x^6 + 2x^3 - 5x^2$
(c) $(x + 2)(x^2 + 4x - 3) = x \cdot x^2 + x \cdot 4x - x \cdot 3 + 2 \cdot x^2 + 2 \cdot 4x - 2 \cdot 3$
$= x^3 + 4x^2 - 3x + 2x^2 + 8x - 6$
$= x^3 + 6x^2 + 5x - 6$ Now Try Exercises 63, 69

EXAMPLE 7   Multiplying polynomials

Multiply each expression.
(a) $2ab^3(a^2 - 2ab + 3b^2)$ **(b)** $4m(mn^2 + 3m)(m^2n - 4n)$

Solution
(a) Multiply each term in the second polynomial by $2ab^3$.

$2ab^3(a^2 - 2ab + 3b^2) = 2ab^3 \cdot a^2 - 2ab^3 \cdot 2ab + 2ab^3 \cdot 3b^2$
$= 2a^3b^3 - 4a^2b^4 + 6ab^5$

(b) Start by multiplying every term in $(mn^2 + 3m)$ by $4m$.

$4m(mn^2 + 3m)(m^2n - 4n) = (4m \cdot mn^2 + 4m \cdot 3m)(m^2n - 4n)$

$= (4m^2n^2 + 12m^2)(m^2n - 4n)$

$= 4m^2n^2 \cdot m^2n - 4m^2n^2 \cdot 4n + 12m^2 \cdot m^2n - 12m^2 \cdot 4n$
$= 4m^4n^3 - 16m^2n^3 + 12m^4n - 48m^2n$

Now Try Exercises 73, 75

Sometimes it is convenient to multiply polynomials vertically. After multiplying, always place like terms in their respective columns. Leave blanks for missing terms.

EXAMPLE 8   Multiplying polynomials vertically

Multiply $(3x - 4y)(2x^2 + xy - 4y^2)$.

Solution
Start by stacking the polynomials as follows. Note that unlike terms can be multiplied but not added.

$$
\begin{array}{r}
2x^2 + xy - 4y^2 \\
3x - 4y \\
\hline
-8x^2y - 4xy^2 + 16y^3 \\
6x^3 + 3x^2y - 12xy^2 \\
\hline
6x^3 - 5x^2y - 16xy^2 + 16y^3
\end{array}
$$

Multiply first row by $-4y$.

Multiply first row by $3x$.

Add columns.   **Now Try Exercise** 69

▶ **REAL-WORLD CONNECTION**   Polynomials frequently occur in business applications. For example, the **demand** D for buying a new video game might vary with its price. If the price is high, fewer games are sold and if the price is low, more games are sold. The revenue R from selling D games at price p is given by $R = pD$. This concept is used in the next example.

EXAMPLE 9   Using polynomials in a business application

Let the demand D, or number of games sold in thousands, be given by $D = 30 - \frac{1}{5}p$, where $p \geq 10$ is the price of the game in dollars.
(a) Find the demand when $p = \$30$ and when $p = \$60$.
(b) Write an expression for the revenue R. Multiply your expression.
(c) Find the revenue when $p = \$40$.

Solution
(a) When $p = 30$, $D = 30 - \frac{1}{5}(30) = 24$ thousand games.
    When $p = 60$, $D = 30 - \frac{1}{5}(60) = 18$ thousand games.
(b) $R = pD = p(30 - \frac{1}{5}p) = 30p - \frac{1}{5}p^2$
(c) When $p = 40$, $R = 30(40) - \frac{1}{5}(40)^2 = \$880$ thousand.   **Now Try Exercise** 127

Some Special Products

The following special product often occurs in mathematics.

$$
\begin{aligned}
(a + b)(a - b) &= a \cdot a - a \cdot b + b \cdot a - b \cdot b \\
&= a^2 - ab + ba - b^2 \\
&= a^2 - b^2
\end{aligned}
$$

That is, the product of a sum and difference equals the difference of their squares.

PRODUCT OF A SUM AND DIFFERENCE

For any real numbers a and b,
$$(a + b)(a - b) = a^2 - b^2.$$

EXAMPLE 10 Finding the product of a sum and difference

Multiply.
(a) $(x + 3)(x - 3)$ **(b)** $(5 - 4x^2)(5 + 4x^2)$

Solution
(a) If we let $a = x$ and $b = 3$, we can apply the rule

$$(a + b)(a - b) = a^2 - b^2.$$

Thus

$$(x + 3)(x - 3) = (x)^2 - (3)^2$$
$$= x^2 - 9.$$

(b) Because $(a - b)(a + b) = a^2 - b^2$, we can multiply as follows.

$$(5 - 4x^2)(5 + 4x^2) = (5)^2 - (4x^2)^2$$
$$= 25 - 16x^4$$

Now Try Exercises 87, 105

EXAMPLE 11 Finding the product of sums and differences

Multiply each expression.
(a) $4rt(r - 4t)(r + 4t)$ **(b)** $(2z + 5k^4)(2z - 5k^4)$

Solution
(a) Start by finding the product of the difference and sum and then simplify.

$$4rt(r - 4t)(r + 4t) = 4rt(r^2 - 16t^2)$$
$$= 4rt \cdot r^2 - 4rt \cdot 16t^2$$
$$= 4r^3t - 64rt^3$$

(b) $(2z + 5k^4)(2z - 5k^4) = (2z)^2 - (5k^4)^2$
$$= 4z^2 - 25k^8$$

Now Try Exercises 103, 106

Two other special products involve *squaring a binomial:*

$$(a + b)^2 = (a + b)(a + b) \qquad\qquad (a - b)^2 = (a - b)(a - b)$$
$$= a^2 + ab + ba + b^2 \quad \text{and} \quad = a^2 - ab - ba + b^2$$
$$= a^2 + 2ab + b^2 \qquad\qquad\qquad = a^2 - 2ab + b^2.$$

The first product is illustrated geometrically in Figure 5.13, where each side of a square has length $(a + b)$. The area of the square is

$$(a + b)(a + b) = (a + b)^2.$$

This area can also be computed by adding the areas of the four small rectangles.

$$a^2 + ab + ba + b^2 = a^2 + 2ab + b^2$$

Thus $(a + b)^2 = a^2 + 2ab + b^2$. *To obtain the middle term, multiply the two terms in the binomial and double the result.*

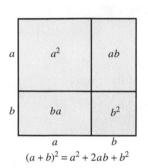

$(a + b)^2 = a^2 + 2ab + b^2$

Figure 5.13

SQUARE OF A BINOMIAL

For any real numbers a and b,

$$(a + b)^2 = a^2 + 2ab + b^2 \quad \text{and} \quad (a - b)^2 = a^2 - 2ab + b^2.$$

EXAMPLE 12   Squaring a binomial

Multiply.
(a) $(x + 5)^2$ (b) $(3 - 2x)^2$ (c) $(2m^3 + 4n)^2$ (d) $\big((2z - 3) + k\big)\big((2z - 3) - k\big)$

Solution
(a) If we let $a = x$ and $b = 5$, we can apply $(a + b)^2 = a^2 + 2ab + b^2$. Thus

$$(x + 5)^2 = (x)^2 + 2(x)(5) + (5)^2 \qquad \text{To find the middle term, multiply}$$
$$= x^2 + 10x + 25. \qquad \qquad x \text{ and } 5 \text{ and double the result.}$$

(b) Applying the formula $(a - b)^2 = a^2 - 2ab + b^2$, we find

$$(3 - 2x)^2 = (3)^2 - 2(3)(2x) + (2x)^2$$
$$= 9 - 12x + 4x^2.$$

(c) $(2m^3 + 4n)^2 = (2m^3)^2 + 2(2m^3)(4n) + (4n)^2$
$$= 4m^6 + 16m^3n + 16n^2$$

(d) If $a = 2z - 3$ and $b = k$, we can use $(a + b)(a - b) = a^2 - b^2$.

$$\big((2z - 3) + k\big)\big((2z - 3) - k\big) = (2z - 3)^2 - k^2$$
$$= (2z)^2 - 2(2z)(3) + (3)^2 - k^2$$
$$= 4z^2 - 12z + 9 - k^2$$

Now Try Exercises 95, 107, 113

Now Try Exercises 95, 107, 113

CRITICAL THINKING

Suppose that a friend is convinced that the expressions

$(x + 3)^2$ and $x^2 + 9$

are equivalent. How could you convince your friend that $(x + 3)^2 \neq x^2 + 9$?

NOTE: If you forget these special products, you can still use techniques learned earlier to multiply the polynomials in Examples 10–12. For example,

$$(3 - 2x)^2 = (3 - 2x)(3 - 2x)$$
$$= 3 \cdot 3 - 3 \cdot 2x - 2x \cdot 3 + 2x \cdot 2x$$
$$= 9 - 6x - 6x + 4x^2$$
$$= 9 - 12x + 4x^2.$$

Multiplying Functions

In Section 5.1 we discussed how to add and subtract functions. These concepts can be extended to include multiplication of two functions, f and g, by using the following definition.

$$(fg)(x) = f(x)g(x)$$

NOTE: There is no operation symbol written between f and g in $(fg)(x)$, and so the operation is assumed to be multiplication, just as in the expression xy.

EXAMPLE 13   Multiplying polynomial functions

Let $f(x) = x^2 - x$ and $g(x) = 2x^2 + 4$. Find $(fg)(3)$ and $(fg)(x)$.

Solution

To find $(fg)(3)$, evaluate $f(3)$ and $g(3)$. Then multiply the results.

$$(fg)(3) = f(3)g(3) = (3^2 - 3)(2 \cdot 3^2 + 4) = (6)(22) = 132$$

To find $(fg)(x)$, multiply the formulas for $f(x)$ and $g(x)$.

$$(fg)(x) = f(x)g(x) = (x^2 - x)(2x^2 + 4) = 2x^4 - 2x^3 + 4x^2 - 4x$$

Now Try Exercise 117

5.2 PUTTING IT ALL TOGETHER

The following table summarizes some important concepts in this section.

Concept	Explanation	Examples
Distributive Properties	For all real numbers a, b, and c, $$a(b + c) = ab + ac \quad \text{and}$$ $$a(b - c) = ab - ac.$$	$4(3 + a) = 12 + 4a, \quad 5(x - 1) = 5x - 5,$ and $-(b - 5) = -1(b - 5) = -b + 5$
Multiplying Polynomials	The product of two polynomials may be found by multiplying every term in the first polynomial by every term in the second polynomial.	$(2x + 3)(x - 7) = 2x \cdot x - 2x \cdot 7 + 3 \cdot x - 3 \cdot 7$ $\quad = 2x^2 - 14x + 3x - 21$ $\quad = 2x^2 - 11x - 21$
Properties of Exponents	For numbers a and b and integers m and n, $$a^m \cdot a^n = a^{m+n},$$ $$(a^m)^n = a^{mn}, \quad \text{and}$$ $$(ab)^n = a^n b^n.$$	$5^2 \cdot 5^6 = 5^8,$ $(2^3)^2 = 2^6,$ $(5y^4)^2 = 25y^8,$ $(a^2 b^3)^4 = a^8 b^{12},$ and $(-4rt^3)^2 = 16r^2 t^6$
Special Products of Binomials	Product of a sum and difference $$(a + b)(a - b) = a^2 - b^2$$ Squares of binomials $$(a + b)^2 = a^2 + 2ab + b^2$$ $$(a - b)^2 = a^2 - 2ab + b^2$$	$(x + 2)(x - 2) = x^2 - 4,$ $(7y - 6z^2)(7y + 6z^2) = 49y^2 - 36z^4,$ $(x + 4)^2 = x^2 + 8x + 16,$ $(x - 4)^2 = x^2 - 8x + 16,$ and $(2m - 3n^2)^2 = 4m^2 - 12mn^2 + 9n^4$
Multiplication of Functions	$(fg)(x) = f(x)g(x)$	If $f(x) = x^2$ and $g(x) = x + 2$, then $(fg)(x) = x^2(x + 2) = x^3 + 2x^2.$

5.2 Exercises

CONCEPTS

1. $5(x - 4) = 5x - 20$ illustrates what property?

2. Give an example of a monomial, a binomial, and a trinomial.

3. Simplify the expression $x^3 \cdot x^5$.

4. Simplify $(2x)^3$ and $(x^2)^3$.

5. $(a + b)(a - b) =$ _____

6. $(a + b)^2 =$ _____

7. $x(x - 1) =$ _____

8. Does $(x + 1)^2$ equal $x^2 + 1$? Explain.

MULTIPLYING POLYNOMIALS

Exercises 9–16: Multiply the monomials.

9. $x^4 \cdot x^8$

10. $2x \cdot 4x^3$

11. $-5y^7 \cdot 4y$

12. $3xy^2 \cdot 6x^3y^2$

13. $(-xy)(4x^3y^5)$

14. $(4z^3)(-5z^2)$

15. $(5y^2z)(4x^2yz^5)$

16. $x^2(-xy^2)$

Exercises 17–28: Multiply.

17. $5(y + 2)$

18. $4(y - 7)$

19. $-2(5x + 9)$

20. $-3x(5 + x)$

21. $-6y(y - 3)$

22. $(2y - 5)8y^3$

23. $(9 - 4x)3x$

24. $-(5 - x^2)$

25. $-ab(a^2 - b^2)$

26. $a^2b^2(1 - 4ab)$

27. $-5m(n^3 + m)$

28. $7n(3n - 2m^2)$

Exercises 29–32: Use the figure to write the product. Find the area of the rectangle if $x = 5$ inches.

29. $(x + 1)(x + 2)$

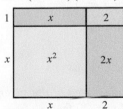

30. $(x + 3)(x + 4)$

31. $(2x + 1)(x + 1)$

32. $(2x + 4)(3x + 2)$

Exercises 33–36: (Refer to Example 4.) Multiply geometrically and symbolically. Support your answer graphically or numerically.

33. $(x + 5)(x + 6)$

34. $(x + 1)(x + 4)$

35. $(2x + 1)(2x + 1)$

36. $(x + 3)(2x + 4)$

Exercises 37 and 38: The pair of graphing calculator screens show graphs of y_1 and y_2. Does $y_1 = y_2$? Interpret this result in general.

37. $y_1 = (x + 1)^2, y_2 = x^2 + 1$

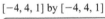
$[-4, 4, 1]$ by $[-4, 4, 1]$ $[-4, 4, 1]$ by $[-4, 4, 1]$

38. $y_1 = (x - 2)^2, y_2 = x^2 - 4$

$[-4, 4, 1]$ by $[-4, 4, 1]$ $[-4, 4, 1]$ by $[-4, 4, 1]$

Exercises 39–44: Determine whether the equation is an identity. (Hint: If it is an identity, the equation must be true for all x-values.)

39. $(x - 2)^2 = x^2 - 4$

40. $(x + 4)^2 = x^2 + 16$

41. $(x + 3)(x - 2) = x^2 + x - 6$

42. $(5x - 1)^2 = 25x^2 - 10x + 1$

43. $2z(3z + 1) = 6z^2 + 1$

44. $-(z^2 + 4z) = -z^2 + 4z$

Exercises 45–62: Multiply the binomials.

45. $(x + 5)(x + 10)$ **46.** $(x - 5)(x - 10)$

47. $(x - 3)(x - 4)$ **48.** $(x + 3)(x + 4)$

49. $(2z - 1)(z + 2)$ **50.** $(2z + 1)(z - 2)$

51. $(y + 3)(y - 4)$ **52.** $(2y + 1)(5y + 1)$

53. $(4x - 3)(4 - 9x)$ **54.** $(1 - x)(1 + 2x)$

55. $(-2z + 3)(z - 2)$ **56.** $(z - 2)(4z + 3)$

57. $\left(z - \frac{1}{2}\right)\left(z + \frac{1}{4}\right)$ **58.** $\left(z - \frac{1}{3}\right)\left(z - \frac{1}{6}\right)$

59. $(x^2 + 1)(2x^2 - 1)$ **60.** $(x^2 - 2)(x^2 + 4)$

61. $(x + y)(x - 2y)$ **62.** $(x^2 + y^2)(x - y)$

Exercises 63–76: Multiply the polynomials.

63. $4x(x^2 - 2x - 3)$ **64.** $2x(3 - x + x^2)$

65. $-x(x^4 - 3x^2 + 1)$

66. $-3m^2(4m^3 + m^2 - 2m)$

67. $(2n^2 - 4n + 1)(3n^2)$

68. $(x - y + 5)(xy)$

69. $(x + 1)(x^2 + 2x - 3)$

70. $(2x - 1)(3x^2 - x + 6)$

71. $z(2 + z)(1 - z - z^2)$

72. $z^2(1 - z)(2 + z)$

73. $2ab^2(2a^2 - ab + 3b^2)$

74. $2n(mn^2 + 2n)(3m^2n - 3n)$

75. $(2r - 4t)(3r^2 + rt - t^2)$

76. $-2(x - y)(x^2 + xy + y^2)$

Exercises 77–86: Simplify the expression.

77. $(2^3)^2$ **78.** $(x^3)^5$

79. $2(z^3)^6$ **80.** $(5y)^3$

81. $(-5x)^2$ **82.** $(2y)^4$

83. $(-2xy^2)^3$ **84.** $(3x^2y^3)^4$

85. $(-4a^2b^3)^2$ **86.** $-(5r^3t)^2$

Exercises 87–114: Multiply the expression.

87. $(x - 3)(x + 3)$ **88.** $(x + 5)(x - 5)$

89. $(3 - 2x)(3 + 2x)$ **90.** $(4 - 5x)(4 + 5x)$

91. $(x - y)(x + y)$ **92.** $(2x + 2y)(2x - 2y)$

93. $(x + 2)^2$ **94.** $(y + 5)^2$

95. $(2x + 1)^2$ **96.** $(3x + 5)^2$

97. $(x - 1)^2$ **98.** $(x - 7)^2$

99. $(3x - 2)^2$ **100.** $(6x - 5)^2$

101. $3x(x + 1)(x - 1)$ **102.** $-4x(3x - 5)^2$

103. $3rt(t - 2r)(t + 2r)$

104. $5r^2t^2(t - 4)(t + 4)$

105. $(a^2 + 2b^2)(a^2 - 2b^2)$

106. $(2a + 5b^4)(2a - 5b^4)$

107. $(3m^3 + 5n^2)^2$ **108.** $(6m + 4n^2)^2$

109. $(x^3 - 2y^3)^2$ **110.** $(6m - n^4)^2$

111. $\big((x - 3) + y\big)\big((x - 3) - y\big)$

112. $\big((2m - 1) + n\big)\big((2m - 1) - n\big)$

113. $\big(r - (t + 2)\big)\big(r + (t + 2)\big)$

114. $\big(y - (z + 1)\big)\big(y + (z + 1)\big)$

Exercises 115 and 116: Thinking Generally *Use*
$$(a + b)(a - b) = a^2 - b^2$$
to multiply the pair of integers mentally.

115. $102, 98$ **116.** $51, 49$

Exercises 117–122: Find $(fg)(2)$ and $(fg)(x)$.

117. $f(x) = x + 1, g(x) = x - 2$

118. $f(x) = 2x + 3, g(x) = 4 - x$

119. $f(x) = x^2, g(x) = 3 - 5x$

120. $f(x) = x^2 - 4x, g(x) = x^2 - 5$

121. $f(x) = 2x^2 + 1, g(x) = x^2 + x - 3$

122. $f(x) = x^3 - 3x^2, g(x) = 2x^2 + 4x$

AREA

Exercises 123–126: Express the shaded area of the given figure in terms of x. Find the area if $x = 20$ feet.

123.

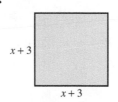

x

$x + 4$

124.

$x - 1$

$x + 1$

125.

$x + 3$

$x + 3$

126.

$2x + 1$

(a) Multiply this expression.

(b) Let $x = 25$. Use both the given expression and the expression you obtained in part (a) to find the likelihood that two consecutive serves are in bounds.

APPLICATIONS

Exercises 127 and 128: Price and Demand (Refer to Example 9.) Let D be the demand in thousands of units and p be the price in dollars of one unit.
   (a) *Find D when p = 20.*
   (b) *Write an expression for the revenue R. Multiply your expression.*
   (c) *Find the revenue when p = 30.*

127. $D = 40 - \frac{1}{2}p$ **128.** $D = 20 - \frac{1}{10}p$

129. *Interest*   If the annual interest rate r is expressed as a decimal and N dollars are deposited into an account, then the amount in the account after two years is $N(1 + r)^2$.
   (a) Multiply this expression.
   (b) Let $r = 0.10$ and $N = 200$. Use both the given expression and the expression you obtained in part (a) to find the amount of money in the account after 2 years. Do your answers agree?

130. *Probability*   Suppose that the likelihood, or chance, that a volleyball player's serve will be *out* of bounds is x percent. Then the likelihood as a percentage that two consecutive serves are *in* bounds is given by the expression $100(1 - \frac{x}{100})^2$.

131. *Numbers*   Write a polynomial that represents the product of two consecutive integers, where x is the smaller integer.

132. *Revenue*   Write a polynomial that represents the revenue received from selling $2y + 1$ items at a price of x dollars each.

133. *Rectangular Pen*   A rectangular pen has a perimeter of 100 feet. If x represents its width, write a polynomial that gives the area of the pen in terms of x.

134. *Numbers*   Find an expression that represents the product of the sum and difference of two numbers. Let the two numbers be x and y.

WRITING ABOUT MATHEMATICS

135. Suppose that a student insists that
$$(x + 5)(x + 5)$$
equals $x^2 + 25$. Explain how you could convince the student otherwise.

136. Explain how to multiply two polynomials. Give an example of how your method works. Does your method give the correct result for any two polynomials?

CHECKING BASIC CONCEPTS
SECTIONS 5.1 AND 5.2

1. Combine like terms.
   (a) $8x^2 + 4x - 5x^2 + 3x$
   (b) $(5x^2 - 3x + 2) - (3x^2 - 5x^3 + 1)$

2. Write a polynomial that represents the revenue from ticket sales if $x + 120$ tickets are sold for x dollars each. Evaluate the polynomial for $x = 10$ and interpret the result.

continued on next page

continued from previous page

3. An athlete's heart rate t minutes after exercise is stopped is modeled by
$$f(t) = 2t^2 - 25t + 160,$$
where $0 \le t \le 6$.
(a) What was the initial heart rate?
(b) What was the heart rate after 4 minutes?

4. Multiply the expressions.
(a) $-5(x - 6)$
(b) $4x^3(3x^2 - 5x)$
(c) $(2x - 1)(x + 3)$

5. Multiply the following special products.
(a) $(5x - 6)(5x + 6)$
(b) $(3x - 4)^2$

6. Make a sketch of a rectangle whose area illustrates that $(x + 2)(x + 4) = x^2 + 6x + 8$.

5.3 FACTORING POLYNOMIALS

Common Factors ▪ Factoring and Equations ▪ Factoring by Grouping

A LOOK INTO MATH ▷

Video games involving sports frequently have to show a ball traveling through the air. To make the motion look realistic, the game must solve an equation in real time to determine when the ball hits the ground. For example, suppose that a golf ball is hit with an *upward* velocity of 88 feet per second, or 60 miles per hour. Then its height h in feet above the ground after t seconds is modeled by $h(t) = 88t - 16t^2$. To estimate when the ball strikes the ground, we can solve the *polynomial equation*

$$88t - 16t^2 = 0. \qquad \text{At ground level, } h = 0.$$

One method for solving this equation is factoring (see Example 6). In this section we discuss factoring and how it is used to solve equations.

Common Factors

When factoring a polynomial, we first look for factors that are common to each term. By applying a distributive property, we can write a polynomial as two factors. For example, each term in $2x^2 + 4x$ contains a factor of $2x$.

$$2x^2 = 2x \cdot x$$

$$4x = 2x \cdot 2$$

Thus the polynomial $2x^2 + 4x$ can be factored as follows.

$$2x^2 + 4x = 2x(x + 2)$$

EXAMPLE 1   Finding common factors

Factor.
(a) $4x^2 + 5x$ **(b)** $12x^3 - 4x^2$ **(c)** $6z^3 - 2z^2 + 4z$ **(d)** $4x^3y^2 + x^2y^3$

Solution
(a) Both $4x^2$ and $5x$ contain a common factor of x. That is,

$$4x^2 = x \cdot 4x \quad \text{and} \quad 5x = x \cdot 5.$$

Thus $4x^2 + 5x = x(4x + 5)$.
(b) Both $12x^3$ and $4x^2$ contain a common factor of $4x^2$. That is,

$$12x^3 = 4x^2 \cdot 3x \quad \text{and} \quad 4x^2 = 4x^2 \cdot 1.$$

Thus $12x^3 - 4x^2 = 4x^2(3x - 1)$.
(c) Each of the terms $6z^3$, $2z^2$, and $4z$ contains a common factor of $2z$. That is,

$$6z^3 = 2z \cdot 3z^2, \quad 2z^2 = 2z \cdot z, \quad \text{and} \quad 4z = 2z \cdot 2.$$

Thus $6z^3 - 2z^2 + 4z = 2z(3z^2 - z + 2)$.
(d) Both $4x^3y^2$ and x^2y^3 contain a common factor of x^2y^2. That is,

$$4x^3y^2 = x^2y^2 \cdot 4x \quad \text{and} \quad x^2y^3 = x^2y^2 \cdot y.$$

Thus $4x^3y^2 + x^2y^3 = x^2y^2(4x + y)$.   Now Try Exercises 7, 15, 19, 25

Many times we factor out the *greatest common factor*. For example, the polynomial $15x^4 - 5x^2$ has a common factor of $5x$. We could write this polynomial as

$$15x^4 - 5x^2 = 5x(3x^3 - x).$$

However, we can also factor out $5x^2$ to obtain

$$15x^4 - 5x^2 = 5x^2(3x^2 - 1).$$

Because $5x^2$ is the common factor with the highest degree and largest (integer) coefficient, we say that $5x^2$ is the **greatest common factor** (GCF) of $15x^4 - 5x^2$. In Example 1, we factored out the GCF in each case.

EXAMPLE 2   Factoring greatest common factors

Factor.
(a) $24x^5 + 12x^3 - 6x^2$ **(b)** $6m^3n^2 - 3mn^2 + 9m$ **(c)** $-9x^3 + 6x^2 - 3x$

Solution
(a) The GCF of $24x^5$, $12x^3$, and $6x^2$ is $6x^2$.

$$24x^5 = 6x^2 \cdot 4x^3, \quad 12x^3 = 6x^2 \cdot 2x, \quad \text{and} \quad 6x^2 = 6x^2 \cdot 1$$

Thus $24x^5 + 12x^3 - 6x^2 = 6x^2(4x^3 + 2x - 1)$.
(b) The GCF of $6m^3n^2$, $3mn^2$, and $9m$ is $3m$.

$$6m^3n^2 = 3m \cdot 2m^2n^2, \quad 3mn^2 = 3m \cdot n^2, \quad \text{and} \quad 9m = 3m \cdot 3$$

Thus $6m^3n^2 - 3mn^2 + 9m = 3m(2m^2n^2 - n^2 + 3)$.
(c) Rather than factoring out $3x$, we can also factor out $-3x$ and make the leading coefficient of the remaining expression positive.

$$-9x^3 = -3x \cdot 3x^2, \quad 6x^2 = -3x \cdot -2x, \quad \text{and} \quad -3x = -3x \cdot 1$$

Thus $-9x^3 + 6x^2 - 3x = -3x(3x^2 - 2x + 1)$.   Now Try Exercises 23, 31, 37

Factoring and Equations

To solve equations by using factoring, we use the **zero-product property**. It states that, if the product of two numbers is 0, then at least one of the numbers must equal 0.

ZERO-PRODUCT PROPERTY

For all real numbers a and b, if $ab = 0$, then $a = 0$ or $b = 0$ (or both).

NOTE: The zero-product property works only for 0. If $ab = 1$, then it does *not* follow that $a = 1$ or $b = 1$. For example, $a = \frac{1}{3}$ and $b = 3$ also satisfy the equation $ab = 1$.

Sometimes factoring needs to be performed on an equation before the zero-product property can be applied. For example, the left side of the equation

$$2x^2 + 4x = 0$$

may be factored to obtain

$$2x(x + 2) = 0.$$

Note that $2x$ times $(x + 2)$ equals 0. By the zero-product property, we must have either

$$2x = 0 \quad \text{or} \quad x + 2 = 0.$$

Solving each equation for x gives

$$x = 0 \quad \text{or} \quad x = -2.$$

The x-values of 0 and -2 are called **zeros** of the polynomial $2x^2 + 4x$ because, when they are substituted in $2x^2 + 4x$, the result is 0. That is, $2(0)^2 + 4(0) = 0$ and $2(-2)^2 + 4(-2) = 0$.

MAKING CONNECTIONS

Expressions and Equations

There are important distinctions between expressions and equations. We often *factor expressions* and *solve equations*. For example, when we solved the *equation* $2x^2 + 4x = 0$, we started by factoring the *expression* $2x^2 + 4x$, as $2x(x + 2)$. The equivalent equation, $2x(x + 2) = 0$, resulted. Then the zero-product property was used to obtain the *solutions to the equation*: 0 and -2.

An equation is a statement that two expressions are equal. Equations always have an equals sign. We often solve equations, but we do *not* solve expressions.

EXAMPLE **3**   Applying the zero-product property

Solve.
(a) $x(x - 1) = 0$ **(b)** $2x(x + 3) = 0$ **(c)** $(2x - 1)(3x + 2) = 0$

Solution

(a) The expression $x(x - 1)$ is the product of x and $(x - 1)$. By the zero-product property, either $x = 0$ or $x - 1 = 0$. The solutions are 0 and 1.

(b)

$$2x(x + 3) = 0 \qquad \text{Given equation}$$

$$2x = 0 \quad \text{or} \quad x + 3 = 0 \qquad \text{Zero-product property}$$

$$x = 0 \quad \text{or} \quad x = -3 \qquad \text{Solve each equation.}$$

The solutions are 0 and -3.

(c)

$$(2x - 1)(3x + 2) = 0 \qquad \text{Given equation}$$

$$2x - 1 = 0 \quad \text{or} \quad 3x + 2 = 0 \qquad \text{Zero-product property}$$

$$2x = 1 \quad \text{or} \quad 3x = -2 \qquad \text{Add 1; Subtract 2.}$$

$$x = \frac{1}{2} \quad \text{or} \quad x = -\frac{2}{3} \qquad \text{Divide by 2; divide by 3.}$$

The solutions are $\frac{1}{2}$ and $-\frac{2}{3}$.

Now Try Exercises **43, 47**

EXAMPLE **4**   Solving polynomial equations with factoring

Solve each polynomial equation.
(a) $x^2 + 3x = 0$ **(b)** $4x^2 = 16x$ **(c)** $2x^3 + 2x = 0$

Solution

(a) We begin by factoring out the greatest common factor x.

$$x^2 + 3x = 0 \qquad \text{Given equation}$$

$$x(x + 3) = 0 \qquad \text{Factor out } x.$$

$$x = 0 \quad \text{or} \quad x + 3 = 0 \qquad \text{Zero-product property}$$

$$x = 0 \quad \text{or} \quad x = -3 \qquad \text{Solve.}$$

The solutions are 0 and -3.

(b) Write the equation so that there is a 0 on its right side before applying the zero-product property.

$$4x^2 = 16x \qquad \text{Given equation}$$

$$4x^2 - 16x = 0 \qquad \text{Subtract } 16x \text{ from each side.}$$

$$4x(x - 4) = 0 \qquad \text{Factor out } 4x.$$

$$4x = 0 \quad \text{or} \quad x - 4 = 0 \qquad \text{Zero-product property}$$

$$x = 0 \quad \text{or} \quad x = 4 \qquad \text{Solve.}$$

The solutions are 0 and 4.

(c) Start by factoring out the GCF of $2x$.

$$2x^3 + 2x = 0 \qquad \text{Given equation}$$

$$2x(x^2 + 1) = 0 \qquad \text{Factor out } 2x.$$

$$2x = 0 \quad \text{or} \quad x^2 + 1 = 0 \qquad \text{Zero-product property}$$

$$x = 0 \quad \text{or} \quad x^2 = -1 \qquad \text{Solve.}$$

Because $x^2 \geq 0$ for any x, it follows that no real number can satisfy $x^2 = -1$. The only solution is 0.

Now Try Exercises **65, 69, 73**

Polynomial equations can also be solved numerically and graphically. For example, to find a graphical solution to $x^2 - 2x = 0$, graph $y = x^2 - 2x$ by making a table of values, as shown in Table 5.6. When the points are plotted and connected a ∪-shaped curve results, with x-intercepts 0 and 2. This curve shown in Figure 5.14 is called a *parabola*.

NOTE: The zeros, 0 and 2, of $x^2 - 2x$ in Table 5.6, the x-intercepts, 0 and 2, in Figure 5.14, and the solutions, 0 and 2, to the equation $x^2 - 2x = 0$ are *identical*.

Numerical Solution	*Graphical Solution*	*Symbolic Solution*

Numerical Solution

TABLE 5.6

$y = x^2 - 2x$

x	y
-1	3
0	**0**
1	-1
2	**0**
3	3

Graphical Solution

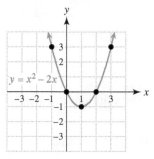

Figure 5.14 x-intercepts: 0 and 2

Symbolic Solution

$$x^2 - 2x = 0$$
$$x(x - 2) = 0$$
$$x = 0 \quad \text{or} \quad x - 2 = 0$$
$$x = 0 \quad \text{or} \quad x = 2$$

These concepts are generalized in the following.

MAKING CONNECTIONS

Zeros, x-Intercepts, and Solutions

The following statements are *equivalent*, where k is a real number and $P(x)$ is a polynomial.

1. A *zero* of a polynomial $P(x)$ is k.
2. An *x-intercept* on the graph of $y = P(x)$ is k.
3. A *solution* to the equation $P(x) = 0$ is k.

In the next example we solve an equation numerically, graphically, and symbolically.

EXAMPLE 5   Solving an equation

Solve the equation $4x - x^2 = 0$ numerically, graphically, and symbolically.

Solution
Numerical Solution   Make a table of values for $y = 4x - x^2$, as shown in Table 5.7. Note that 0 and 4 are solutions to $4x - x^2 = 0$, because $4(0) - 0^2 = 0$ and $4(4) - 4^2 = 0$.

Graphical Solution   Plot the points given in Table 5.7 and sketch a curve through them, as shown in Figure 5.15. The curve is a ∩-shaped graph, or parabola, with x-intercepts 0 and 4, which are the solutions to the given equation.

Numerical Solution		*Graphical Solution*

TABLE 5.7

x	y
-1	-5
0	**0**
1	3
2	4
3	3
4	**0**
5	-5

Figure 5.15

Symbolic Solution   Start by factoring the left side of the equation.

$$4x - x^2 = 0 \qquad \text{Given equation}$$
$$x(4 - x) = 0 \qquad \text{Factor out } x.$$
$$x = 0 \quad \text{or} \quad 4 - x = 0 \qquad \text{Zero-product property}$$
$$x = 0 \quad \text{or} \quad x = 4 \qquad \text{Solve each equation.}$$

Note that the numerical and graphical solutions agree with the symbolic solutions.

Now Try Exercise **75**

GRAPH OF $y = ax^2 + bx + c$

The graph of $y = ax^2 + bx + c$ is a **parabola**. It is a U-shaped graph if $a > 0$ and a ∩-shaped graph if $a < 0$. This graph can have zero, one, or two x-intercepts.

TECHNOLOGY NOTE: Locating *x*-intercepts

CALCULATOR HELP

To find an x-intercept or zero, see the Appendix (page AP-10).

Many calculators have the capability to locate an x-intercept or zero. This method is illustrated in the accompanying figures, where the solution 2 to the equation $x^2 - 4 = 0$ is found.

$[-9, 9, 1]$ by $[-6, 6, 1]$

In the next example we use factoring to estimate when a golf ball strikes the ground.

EXAMPLE **6**   Modeling the flight of a golf ball

If a golf ball is hit upward at 88 feet per second, or 60 miles per hour, its height h in feet after t seconds is modeled by $h(t) = 88t - 16t^2$.
(a) Use factoring to determine when the golf ball strikes the ground.
(b) Solve part (a) graphically and numerically.

Solution

(a) *Symbolic Solution*   The golf ball strikes the ground when its height is 0.

$$88t - 16t^2 = 0 \qquad h(t) = 0$$

$$8t(11 - 2t) = 0 \qquad \text{Factor out } 8t.$$

$$8t = 0 \quad \text{or} \quad 11 - 2t = 0 \qquad \text{Zero-product property}$$

$$t = 0 \quad \text{or} \quad t = \frac{11}{2} \qquad \text{Solve for } t.$$

The ball strikes the ground after $\frac{11}{2}$, or 5.5 seconds. The solution of $t = 0$ is not used in this problem because it corresponds to when the ball is initially hit on the ground.

(b) *Graphical and Numerical Solutions*   Graph $Y_1 = 88X - 16X^2$. Using a graphing calculator to find an x-intercept (or zero) yields the solution, 5.5. See Figure 5.16(a). Numerical support is shown in Figure 5.16(b), where $y_1 = 0$ when $x = 5.5$.

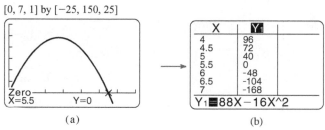

(a)   (b)

Figure 5.16

Now Try Exercise 99

Factoring by Grouping

Factoring by grouping is a technique that makes use of the associative and distributive properties. The next example illustrates the first step in this factoring technique.

EXAMPLE 7   Factoring out binomials

Factor.
(a) $2x(x + 1) + 3(x + 1)$ **(b)** $2x^2(3x - 2) - x(3x - 2)$

Solution
(a) Both terms in the expression $2x(x + 1) + 3(x + 1)$ contain the binomial $(x + 1)$. Therefore the distributive property can be used to factor out this expression.

$$2x(x + 1) + 3(x + 1) = (2x + 3)(x + 1)$$

(b) Both terms in the expression $2x^2(3x - 2) - x(3x - 2)$ contain the binomial $(3x - 2)$. Therefore the distributive property can be used to factor this expression.

$$2x^2(3x - 2) - x(3x - 2) = (2x^2 - x)(3x - 2)$$

Now Try Exercises 79, 81

Now consider the polynomial

$$3t^3 + 6t^2 + 2t + 4.$$

We can factor this polynomial by first grouping it into two binomials.

$$(3t^3 + 6t^2) + (2t + 4) \qquad \text{Associative property}$$
$$3t^2(t + 2) + 2(t + 2) \qquad \text{Factor out common factors.}$$
$$(3t^2 + 2)(t + 2) \qquad \text{Factor out } (t + 2).$$

The following steps summarize factoring a polynomial with four terms by grouping.

FACTORING BY GROUPING

STEP 1: Use parentheses to group the terms into binomials with common factors. Begin by writing the expression with a plus sign between the binomials.

STEP 2: Factor out the common factor in each binomial.

STEP 3: Factor out the common binomial. If there is no common binomial, try a different grouping.

These steps are used in Example 8.

EXAMPLE **8** Factoring by grouping

Factor each polynomial.
(a) $x^3 - 2x^2 + 3x - 6$ **(b)** $12x^3 - 9x^2 - 8x + 6$ **(c)** $2x - 2y + ax - ay$

CRITICAL THINKING

Solve
$xy - 4x - 3y + 12 = 0.$

Solution

(a) $x^3 - 2x^2 + 3x - 6 = (x^3 - 2x^2) + (3x - 6)$ Group terms.

$$= x^2(x - 2) + 3(x - 2) \qquad \text{Factor out } x^2 \text{ and 3.}$$
$$= (x^2 + 3)(x - 2) \qquad \text{Factor out } x - 2.$$

(b) $12x^3 - 9x^2 - 8x + 6 = (12x^3 - 9x^2) + (-8x + 6)$ Write with a plus sign between binomials.

$$= 3x^2(4x - 3) - 2(4x - 3) \qquad \text{Factor out } 3x^2 \text{ and } -2.$$
$$= (3x^2 - 2)(4x - 3) \qquad \text{Factor out } 4x - 3.$$

(c) $2x - 2y + ax - ay = (2x - 2y) + (ax - ay)$ Group terms.

$$= 2(x - y) + a(x - y) \qquad \text{Factor out 2 and } a.$$
$$= (2 + a)(x - y) \qquad \text{Factor out } x - y.$$

Now Try Exercises 83, 89, 93

5.3 PUTTING IT ALL TOGETHER

The following table summarizes topics covered in this section.

Concept	Explanation	Examples
Greatest Common Factor (GCF)	We can sometimes factor the greatest common factor out of a polynomial. The GCF has the largest (integer) coefficient and greatest degree possible.	$3x^4 - 9x^3 + 12x^2 = 3x^2(x^2 - 3x + 4)$ The terms in $(x^2 - 3x + 4)$ have no obvious common factor, so $3x^2$ is called the *greatest common factor* of $3x^4 - 9x^3 + 12x^2$.

continued on next page

continued from previous page

Concept	Explanation	Examples
Zero-Product Property	If the product of two numbers is 0, then at least one of the numbers equals 0.	$xy = 0$ implies that $x = 0$ or $y = 0$. $x(2x + 1) = 0$ implies that $x = 0$ or $2x + 1 = 0$.
Factoring and Equations	Factoring may be used to solve equations.	$6x^2 - 9x = 0$ $3x(2x - 3) = 0$ Common factor, $3x$ $3x = 0$ or $2x - 3 = 0$ Zero-product property $x = 0$ or $x = \frac{3}{2}$ Solve for x.
Factoring by Grouping	Factoring by grouping is a method that can be used to factor four terms into a product of two binomials. It involves the associative and distributive properties.	$4x^3 + 6x^2 + 10x + 15 = (4x^3 + 6x^2) + (10x + 15)$ $= 2x^2(2x + 3) + 5(2x + 3)$ $= (2x^2 + 5)(2x + 3)$
Zeros, x-Intercepts, and Solutions	An x-intercept on the graph of $y = P(x)$ corresponds to a zero of $P(x)$ and to a solution to $P(x) = 0$. These three concepts are closely connected.	x-Intercepts: 0, 1 Zeros of $x^2 - x$: 0, 1 Solutions to $x^2 - x = 0$: 0, 1

5.3 Exercises

MyMathLab   Math XL PRACTICE   WATCH   DOWNLOAD   READ   REVIEW

CONCEPTS

1. Give one reason for factoring expressions.

2. If $x(x - 3) = 0$, what can be said about x or $(x - 3)$? What property did you use?

3. Is $2x$ a common factor of $(4x^3 - 12x^2)$? Explain.

4. Is $2x$ the GCF of $(4x^3 - 12x^2)$? Explain.

5. If $ab = 2$, must either $a = 2$ or $b = 2$? Explain.

6. If $xy = 0$, must either $x = 0$ or $y = 0$? Explain.

FACTORING AND EQUATIONS

Exercises 7–34: Factor out the greatest common factor.

7. $10x - 15$

8. $32 - 16x$

9. $4x + 6y$

10. $50a + 20b$

11. $9r - 15t$

12. $16m - 24n$

13. $2x^3 - 5x$

14. $3y - 9y^2$

15. $8a^3 + 10a$

16. $20b^3 + 25b^2$

17. $6r^3 - 18r^5$

18. $7n^2 - 21n^4$

19. $8x^3 - 4x^2 + 16x$

20. $5x^3 - x^2 + 4x$

21. $9n^4 - 6n^2 + 3n$

22. $5n^4 + 10n^2 - 25n$

23. $6t^6 - 4t^4 + 2t^2$

24. $15t^6 + 25t^4 - 20t^2$

25. $5x^2y^2 - 15x^2y^3$

26. $21xy + 14x^3y^3$

27. $6a^3b^2 - 15a^2b^3$

28. $45a^2b + 30a^3b^2$

29. $18mn^2 + 12m^2n^3$

30. $24m^2n^3 - 36m^3n^2$

31. $15x^2y + 10xy - 25x^2y^2$

32. $14a^3b^2 - 21a^2b^2 + 35a^2b$

33. $4a^2 - 2ab + 6ab^2$

34. $5a^2 + 10a^2b^2 - 15ab$

Exercises 35–40: (Refer to Example 2(c).) Factor out the negative of the greatest common factor.

35. $-2x^2 + 4x - 6$

36. $-7x^5 - 21x^3 - 14x^2$

37. $-8z^4 - 16z^3$

38. $-8z^5 - 24z^4$

39. $-4m^2n^3 - 6mn^2 - 8mn$

40. $-13m^4n^4 - 13m^3n^3 + 26m^2n^2$

Exercises 41–50: Use the zero-product property to solve the equation.

41. $mn = 0$

42. $xyz = 0$

43. $3z(z + 4) = 0$

44. $2z(z - 1) = 0$

45. $(r - 1)(r + 3) = 0$

46. $(2r + 3)(r - 5) = 0$

47. $(x + 2)(3x - 1) = 0$

48. $(4y - 3)(2y + 1) = 0$

49. $3x(y - 6) = 0$

50. $7m(3n + 1) = 0$

Exercises 51–56: Use the graph of $y = P(x)$ to do the following.
  (a) Find the x-intercepts.
  (b) Solve the equation $P(x) = 0$.
  (c) Find the zeros of $P(x)$.

51.

52.

53.

54.

55.

56.

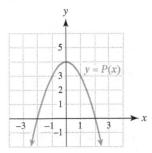

Exercises 57–62: Solve the equation graphically. Check your answer.

57. $x^2 - 2x = 0$

58. $x^2 + x = 0$

59. $x - x^2 = 0$

60. $3x - x^2 = 0$

61. $x^2 + 4x = 0$

62. $x^2 - 4x = 0$

Exercises 63–74: Solve the equation.

63. $x^2 - x = 0$

64. $4x - 2x^2 = 0$

65. $5x^2 - x = 0$

66. $4x^2 + 3x = 0$

67. $10x^2 + 5x = 0$

68. $6x - 12x^2 = 0$

69. $15x^2 = 10x$

70. $4x = 8x^2$

71. $25x = 10x^2$

72. $34x^2 = 51x$

73. $32x^4 - 16x^3 = 0$

74. $45x^4 - 30x^3 = 0$

 Exercises 75–78: Solve the equation numerically, graphically, and symbolically.

75. $x^2 + 2x = 0$

76. $x^2 + 3x = 0$

77. $2x^2 - 3x = 0$

78. $2x - 3x^2 = 0$

FACTORING BY GROUPING

Exercises 79–96: Factor the polynomial.

79. $2x(x + 2) + 3(x + 2)$

80. $5(x - 1) - 2x(x - 1)$

81. $(x - 5)x^2 - (x - 5)2$

82. $7x(x - 1) - 3(x - 1)$

83. $x^3 + 3x^2 + 2x + 6$

84. $4x^3 + 3x^2 + 8x + 6$

85. $6x^3 - 4x^2 + 9x - 6$

86. $x^3 - 3x^2 - 5x + 15$

87. $2x^3 - 3x^2 + 2x - 3$

88. $8x^3 - 2x^2 + 12x - 3$

89. $x^3 - 7x^2 - 3x + 21$

90. $6x^3 - 15x^2 - 4x + 10$

91. $3x^3 - 15x^2 + 5x - 25$

92. $2x^4 - x^3 + 4x - 2$

93. $xy + x + 3y + 3$

94. $ax + bx - ay - by$

95. $ab - 3a + 2b - 6$

96. $2ax - 6bx - ay + 3by$

97. *Graphical Interpretation*   Which graph might represent the height h of a golf ball in flight after t seconds? Which graph might represent the height h of a yo-yo above the ground after t seconds?

a. h

b. h

98. **Thinking Generally**   The zero-product property states $ab = 0$ implies that either $a = 0$ or $b = 0$.
(a) Why isn't there a "five-product" property?
(b) Solve $ax^2 - bx = 0$, where $a \neq 0$.

APPLICATIONS

99. *Flight of a Golf Ball*   (Refer to Example 6.) If a golf ball is hit upward at a velocity of 128 feet per second (about 87 mph), its height h in feet above the ground can be modeled by

$$h(t) = -16t^2 + 128t,$$

where t is in seconds.
(a) Use factoring to determine when the golf ball strikes the ground.
(b) Use the graph of $y = h(t)$ to estimate when the golf ball strikes the ground.

(c) Make a table of h, starting at $t = 3$ and incrementing by 1. Does the table support your answer in part (a)?
(d) Use the table and graph of h to determine the maximum height of the golf ball. At what value of t does this occur?

100. *Flight of a Golf Ball*   The height h in feet reached by a golf ball after t seconds is given by

$$h(t) = -16t^2 + 96t.$$

After how many seconds does the golf ball strike the ground?

Exercises 101 and 102: Global Warming Atmospheric carbon dioxide (CO_2) in parts per million (ppm) from 1958 to 2005 is modeled by $f(x) = 0.0148x^2 + 0.686x + 315$, where x represents years after 1958. Do the following.
(**Source:** The Honolulu Advertiser.)

101. Evaluate $f(47)$ and interpret the result.

102. Solve $f(x) = 340$ numerically or graphically. Interpret the result.

103. *Geometry* The area of a rectangle with width y and length 8 is $A = 8y$. A circle with radius y has area $A = \pi y^2$. For what positive value of y are these two areas equal?

104. *U.S. AIDS Cases* The cumulative number of AIDS cases in thousands can be modeled by the function $f(x) = 4.1x^2 - 25x + 46$, where $x = 4$ corresponds to 1984, $x = 5$ to 1985, and so on. Estimate graphically or numerically when the cumulative number of AIDS cases first reached 500 thousand.

105. *Space Shuttle* Approximate altitudes y in feet reached by the space shuttle *Endeavour*, t seconds after liftoff, are shown in the table.

t (seconds)	20	30	40
y (feet)	4500	10,000	18,000

t (seconds)	50	60
y (feet)	28,000	40,000

Source: NASA.

(a) The function $f(t) = 11t^2 + 6t$ models the data, where $y = f(t)$. Make a table of f, starting at $t = 20$ and incrementing by 10. Comment on how well f models the data.

(b) Predict the altitude reached by the shuttle 70 seconds after liftoff. Round your answer to the nearest thousand feet.

(c) Solve the equation $11t^2 + 6t = 0$. Do your results have any physical meaning? Explain.

106. *Average Temperature* Suppose that the monthly average temperatures T in degrees Fahrenheit for a city are given by $T(x) = 24x - 2x^2$, where $x = 1$ corresponds to January, $x = 2$ to February, and so on.
(a) What is the average temperature in October?
(b) Use factoring to solve the quadratic equation $24x - 2x^2 = 0$. Do your results have any physical meaning?
(c) Support your results in part (b) either graphically or numerically.

107. *Area* Suppose that the area of a rectangular room is 216 square feet. Can you find the dimensions of the room from this information? Explain.

108. *Area* Suppose that the area of a rectangular room is $4x^2 + 8x$ square feet. If the length of the room is $4x$, is it possible to determine the width of the room in terms of x? Explain.

WRITING ABOUT MATHEMATICS

109. A student solves the following equation *incorrectly*.

$$x^2 - 5x \stackrel{?}{=} 1$$
$$x(x - 5) \stackrel{?}{=} 1$$
$$x \stackrel{?}{=} 1 \quad \text{or} \quad x - 5 \stackrel{?}{=} 1$$
$$x \stackrel{?}{=} 1 \quad \text{or} \quad x \stackrel{?}{=} 6$$

What is the student's mistake? Explain.

110. Explain how you would solve $ax^2 + bx = 0$ symbolically and graphically.

5.4 FACTORING TRINOMIALS

Factoring $x^2 + bx + c$ ■ Factoring Trinomials by Grouping ■
Factoring Trinomials with FOIL ■ Factoring with Graphs and Tables

A LOOK INTO MATH ▷

Items usually sell better at a lower price. At a higher price fewer items are sold, but more money is made on each item. For example, suppose that if concert tickets are priced at $100 no one will buy a ticket, but for each $1 reduction in price 100 additional tickets will be sold. If the promoters of the concert need to gross $240,000 from ticket sales, what ticket price accomplishes this goal? To solve this problem we need to set up and solve a polynomial equation. In this section we describe how to solve polynomial equations by factoring trinomials in the form $x^2 + bx + c$ and $ax^2 + bx + c$.

Factoring $x^2 + bx + c$

The product $(x + 3)(x + 4)$ can be found as follows.

$$(x + 3)(x + 4) = x^2 + 4x + 3x + 12$$
$$= x^2 + 7x + 12$$

The middle term $7x$ is found by calculating the sum $4x + 3x$, and the last term is found by calculating the product $3 \cdot 4 = 12$.

When we factor polynomials, we are *reversing* the process of multiplication. To factor $x^2 + 7x + 12$ we must find m and n that satisfy

$$x^2 + 7x + 12 = (x + m)(x + n).$$

Because

$$(x + m)(x + n) = x^2 + (m + n)x + mn,$$

it follows that $mn = 12$ and $m + n = 7$. To determine m and n we list factors of 12 and their sum, as shown in Table 5.8.

Because $3 \cdot 4 = 12$ and $3 + 4 = 7$, we can write the factored form as

$$x^2 + 7x + 12 = (x + 3)(x + 4).$$

This result can always be checked by multiplying the two binomials.

$$(x + 3)(x + 4) = x^2 + 7x + 12$$

$3x$
$+4x$
$7x$ ⟵ The middle term checks.

TABLE 5.8
Factor Pairs for 12

Factors	Sum
1, 12	13
2, 6	8
3, 4	7

FACTORING $x^2 + bx + c$

To factor the trinomial $x^2 + bx + c$, find numbers m and n that satisfy

$$m \cdot n = c \quad \text{and} \quad m + n = b.$$

Then $x^2 + bx + c = (x + m)(x + n)$.

EXAMPLE 1 Factoring the form $x^2 + bx + c$

Factor each trinomial.
(a) $x^2 + 10x + 16$ (b) $x^2 - 5x - 24$ (c) $x^2 + 7x - 30$

Solution
(a) We need to find a factor pair for 16 whose sum is 10. From Table 5.9 the required factor pair is $m = 2$ and $n = 8$. Thus

$$x^2 + 10x + 16 = (x + 2)(x + 8).$$

(b) Factors of -24 whose sum equals -5 are 3 and -8. Thus

$$x^2 - 5x - 24 = (x + 3)(x - 8).$$

(c) Factors of -30 whose sum equals 7 are -3 and 10. Thus

$$x^2 + 7x - 30 = (x - 3)(x + 10).$$

Now Try Exercises 15, 21, 23

TABLE 5.9
Factor Pairs for 16

Factors	Sum
1, 16	17
2, 8	10
4, 4	8

EXAMPLE 2 Removing common factors first

Factor completely.
(a) $3x^2 + 15x + 18$ (b) $5x^3 + 5x^2 - 60x$

Solution
(a) If we first factor out the common factor of 3, the resulting trinomial is easier to factor.

$$3x^2 + 15x + 18 = 3(x^2 + 5x + 6)$$

Now we find m and n such that $mn = 6$ and $m + n = 5$. These numbers are 2 and 3.

$$3x^2 + 15x + 18 = 3(x^2 + 5x + 6)$$
$$= 3(x + 2)(x + 3)$$

(b) First, we factor out the common factor of $5x$. Then we factor the resulting trinomial.

$$5x^3 + 5x^2 - 60x = 5x(x^2 + x - 12)$$
$$= 5x(x - 3)(x + 4) \qquad \text{Now Try Exercises 53, 65}$$

▶ **REAL-WORLD CONNECTION**   Factoring may be used to solve the problem presented in the introduction to this section. To do so we let x be the number of dollars that the price of a ticket is reduced below $100. Then $100 - x$ represents the price of a ticket. For each $1 reduction in price, 100 additional tickets will be sold, so the number of tickets sold is given by $100x$. Because the number of tickets sold times the price of each ticket equals the total sales, we need to solve

$$100x(100 - x) = 240{,}000$$

to determine when gross sales will reach $240,000. We cannot immediately apply the zero-product property because the product of $100x$ and $(100 - x)$ does not equal 0.

EXAMPLE 3 Determining ticket price

Solve the equation $100x(100 - x) = 240{,}000$ symbolically. What should be the price of the tickets and how many tickets will be sold? Support your answer graphically.

CRITICAL THINKING

In Example 3 what price will maximize the revenue from ticket sales? (*Hint:* See Figure 5.17.)

Solution

Symbolic Solution   Begin by applying the distributive property.

$$100x(100 - x) = 240,000 \qquad \text{Given equation}$$
$$10,000x - 100x^2 = 240,000 \qquad \text{Distributive property}$$
$$-100x^2 + 10,000x - 240,000 = 0 \qquad \text{Subtract 240,000.}$$
$$-100(x^2 - 100x + 2400) = 0 \qquad \text{Factor out } -100.$$
$$-100(x - 40)(x - 60) = 0 \qquad \text{Factor.}$$
$$x = 40 \quad \text{or} \quad x = 60 \qquad \text{Solve.}$$

If $x = 40$, the price is $100 - 40 = \$60$ per ticket and $100 \cdot 40 = 4000$ tickets are sold at \$60 each. If $x = 60$, the price is $100 - 60 = \$40$ and $100 \cdot 60 = 6000$ tickets are sold at \$40 each. In either case, ticket sales are \$240,000.

Graphical Solution   The graphs of $Y_1 = 100X(100 - X)$ and $Y_2 = 240000$ intersect in Figure 5.17 at $x = 40$ and $x = 60$, which agrees with the symbolic solution.

NOTE: These graphs also illustrate how revenue increases to a maximum value and then decreases as the price of the tickets decreases from \$100 to \$0.

CALCULATOR HELP

To find a point of intersection, see the Appendix (page AP-7).

[0, 100, 20] by [0, 300000, 100000]   [0, 100, 20] by [0, 300000, 100000]

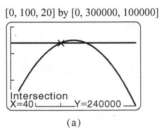

Intersection
X=40   Y=240000   Intersection
X=60   Y=240000

(a)   (b)

Figure 5.17   Now Try Exercise 101

Factoring Trinomials by Grouping

In this subsection we use grouping to factor trinomials in the form $ax^2 + bx + c$ with $a \neq 1$. For example, one way to factor $3x^2 + 14x + 8$ is to find two numbers m and n such that $mn = 3 \cdot 8 = 24$ and $m + n = 14$. Because $2 \cdot 12 = 24$ and $2 + 12 = 14$, $m = 2$ and $n = 12$. Using grouping, we can now factor this trinomial.

$$3x^2 + 14x + 8 = 3x^2 + 2x + 12x + 8 \qquad \text{Write } 14x \text{ as } 2x + 12x.$$
$$= (3x^2 + 2x) + (12x + 8) \qquad \text{Associative property}$$
$$= x(3x + 2) + 4(3x + 2) \qquad \text{Factor out } x \text{ and } 4.$$
$$= (x + 4)(3x + 2) \qquad \text{Factor out } 3x + 2.$$

FACTORING $ax^2 + bx + c$ BY GROUPING

To factor $ax^2 + bx + c$ perform the following steps. (Assume that a, b, and c have no factor in common.)

1. Find numbers m and n such that $mn = ac$ and $m + n = b$. (This step may require trial and error.)
2. Write the trinomial as $ax^2 + mx + nx + c$.
3. Use grouping to factor this expression as two binomials.

EXAMPLE 4   **Factoring** $ax^2 + bx + c$ **by grouping**

Factor each trinomial.

(a) $3x^2 + 17x + 10$ **(b)** $12y^2 + 5y - 3$ **(c)** $6r^2 - 19r + 10$

Solution

(a) In this trinomial $a = 3$, $b = 17$, and $c = 10$. Because $mn = ac$ and $m + n = b$, the numbers m and n satisfy $mn = 30$ and $m + n = 17$. Thus $m = 2$ and $n = 15$.

$$
\begin{aligned}
3x^2 + 17x + 10 &= 3x^2 + 2x + 15x + 10 &&\text{Write } 17x \text{ as } 2x + 15x. \\
&= (3x^2 + 2x) + (15x + 10) &&\text{Associative property} \\
&= x(3x + 2) + 5(3x + 2) &&\text{Factor out } x \text{ and } 5. \\
&= (x + 5)(3x + 2) &&\text{Distributive property}
\end{aligned}
$$

(b) In this trinomial $a = 12$, $b = 5$, and $c = -3$. Because $mn = ac$ and $m + n = b$, the numbers m and n satisfy $mn = -36$ and $m + n = 5$. Thus $m = 9$ and $n = -4$.

$$
\begin{aligned}
12y^2 + 5y - 3 &= 12y^2 + 9y - 4y - 3 &&\text{Write } 5y \text{ as } 9y - 4y. \\
&= (12y^2 + 9y) + (-4y - 3) &&\text{Associative property} \\
&= 3y(4y + 3) - 1(4y + 3) &&\text{Factor out } 3y \text{ and } -1. \\
&= (3y - 1)(4y + 3) &&\text{Distributive property}
\end{aligned}
$$

(c) In this trinomial $a = 6$, $b = -19$, and $c = 10$. Because $mn = ac$ and $m + n = b$, the numbers m and n satisfy $mn = 60$ and $m + n = -19$. Thus $m = -4$ and $n = -15$.

$$
\begin{aligned}
6r^2 - 19r + 10 &= 6r^2 - 4r - 15r + 10 &&\text{Write } -19r \text{ as } -4r - 15r. \\
&= (6r^2 - 4r) + (-15r + 10) &&\text{Associative property} \\
&= 2r(3r - 2) - 5(3r - 2) &&\text{Factor out } 2r \text{ and } -5. \\
&= (2r - 5)(3r - 2) &&\text{Distributive property}
\end{aligned}
$$

Now Try Exercises 33, 39, 41

Factoring Trinomials with FOIL

An alternative to factoring trinomials by grouping is to use FOIL in reverse. For example, the factors of $3x^2 + 7x + 2$ are two binomials.

$$3x^2 + 7x + 2 \stackrel{?}{=} (\underline{\quad} + \underline{\quad})(\underline{\quad} + \underline{\quad})$$

The expressions to be placed in the four blanks are yet to be found. By the FOIL method, we know that the product of the first terms is $3x^2$. Because $3x^2 = 3x \cdot x$, we can write

$$3x^2 + 7x + 2 \stackrel{?}{=} (\underline{\ 3x\ } + \underline{\quad})(\underline{\ x\ } + \underline{\quad}).$$

The product of the last terms in each binomial must equal 2. Because $2 = 1 \cdot 2$, we can put the 1 and 2 in the blanks, but we must be sure to place them correctly so that the product of the *outside terms* plus the product of the *inside terms* equals $7x$.

$$(3x + 1)(x + 2) = 3x^2 + 7x + 2$$

$$\underset{7x}{\underline{\overset{\displaystyle \lfloor 1x \rfloor}{\lfloor\ +6x\ \rfloor}}} \qquad \longleftarrow \text{ Middle term checks.}$$

If we had interchanged the 1 and 2, we would have obtained an incorrect result.

$$(3x + 2)(x + 1) = 3x^2 + 5x + 2$$

$$\overline{5x} \quad \longleftarrow \text{ Middle term is } not \text{ } 7x.$$

In the next example we factor expressions of the form $ax^2 + bx + c$, where $a \neq 1$. In this situation, we may need to *guess and check* or use *trial and error* a few times before finding the correct factors.

EXAMPLE **5**   Factoring the form $ax^2 + bx + c$

Factor each trinomial.
(a) $2x^2 + 9x + 4$ **(b)** $6x^2 - x - 2$ **(c)** $4x^3 - 14x^2 + 6x$

Solution
(a) The factors of $2x^2$ are $2x$ and x, so we begin by writing

$$2x^2 + 9x + 4 \stackrel{?}{=} (2x + \_\_)(x + \_\_).$$

The factors of the last term, 4, are either 1 and 4 or 2 and 2. Selecting the factors 2 and 2 results in a middle term of $6x$ rather than $9x$.

$$(2x + 2)(x + 2) = 2x^2 + 6x + 4$$

$$\overline{6x} \quad \longleftarrow \text{ Middle term is } not \text{ } 9x.$$

Next we try the factors 1 and 4.

$$(2x + 4)(x + 1) = 2x^2 + 6x + 4$$

$$\overline{6x} \quad \longleftarrow \text{ Middle term is } not \text{ } 9x.$$

Again we obtain the wrong middle term. By interchanging the 1 and 4, we find the correct factorization.

$$(2x + 1)(x + 4) = 2x^2 + 9x + 4$$

$$\overline{9x} \quad \longleftarrow \text{ Middle term is } 9x.$$

NOTE: If a trinomial does not have any common factors, then its binomial factors will not have any common factors either. Thus $(2x + 2)$ and $(2x + 4)$ cannot be factors of $2x^2 + 9x + 4$. These factors can be eliminated without checking.

(b) The factors of $6x^2$ are either $2x$ and $3x$ or $6x$ and x. The factors of -2 are either -1 and 2 or 1 and -2. To obtain a middle term of $-x$ we use the following factors.

$$(3x - 2)(2x + 1) = 6x^2 - x - 2$$

$$\overline{-x} \quad \longleftarrow \text{ It checks.}$$

To find the correct factorization we may need to guess and check a few times.

(c) Each term contains a common factor of $2x$, so we do the following step first.

$$4x^3 - 14x^2 + 6x = 2x(2x^2 - 7x + 3)$$

Next we factor $2x^2 - 7x + 3$. The factors of $2x^2$ are $2x$ and x. Because the middle term is negative, we use -1 and -3 for factors of 3.

$$4x^3 - 14x^2 + 6x = 2x(2x^2 - 7x + 3)$$
$$= 2x(2x - 1)(x - 3)$$

Now Try Exercises 35, 37, 67

EXAMPLE 6

Estimating passing distance

A car traveling 48 miles per hour accelerates at a constant rate to pass a car in front of it. A no-passing zone begins 2000 feet away. The distance d traveled in feet by the car after t seconds is $d(t) = 3t^2 + 70t$. How long does it take the car to reach the no-passing zone?

Solution
We must determine the time when $d(t) = 2000$.

$3t^2 + 70t = 2000$	Equation to be solved
$3t^2 + 70t - 2000 = 0$	Subtract 2000.
$(3t - 50)(t + 40) = 0$	Factor.
$3t - 50 = 0 \quad \text{or} \quad t + 40 = 0$	Zero-product property
$t = \dfrac{50}{3} \quad \text{or} \quad t = -40$	Solve.

The car reaches the no-passing zone after $\frac{50}{3} \approx 16.7$ seconds. (The solution $t = -40$ has no physical meaning in this problem.)

Now Try Exercise 105

CRITICAL THINKING

Can every trinomial be factored with the methods discussed in this section? Try to factor the following trinomials and then make a conjecture.

$$x^2 + 2x + 2, \quad x^2 - x + 1, \quad \text{and} \quad 2x^2 + x + 2.$$

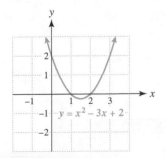

Figure 5.18

Factoring with Graphs and Tables

Polynomials can also be factored graphically. One way to do so is to use a graph of the polynomial to find its zeros. A number p is a *zero* if a value of 0 results when p is substituted in the polynomial. For example, both -2 and 2 are zeros of $x^2 - 4$ because

$$(-2)^2 - 4 = 0 \quad \text{and} \quad (2)^2 - 4 = 0.$$

Now consider the trinomial $x^2 - 3x + 2$, whose graph is shown in Figure 5.18. Its x-intercepts or zeros are 1 and 2, and this trinomial factors as

$$x^2 - 3x + 2 = (x - 1)(x - 2).$$

We generalize these concepts as follows.

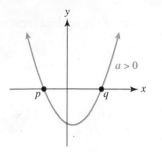

Figure 5.19

FACTORING WITH A GRAPH OR A TABLE OF VALUES

To factor the trinomial $x^2 + bx + c$, either graph or make a table of $y = x^2 + bx + c$. If the zeros of the trinomial are p and q, then the trinomial can be factored as

$$x^2 + bx + c = (x - p)(x - q).$$

If the trinomial $ax^2 + bx + c$ has zeros p and q, then it may be factored as

$$ax^2 + bx + c = a(x - p)(x - q).$$

See Figure 5.19.

EXAMPLE **7**   Factoring with technology

Factor each trinomial graphically or numerically.
(a) $x^2 - 2x - 24$ **(b)** $2x^2 - 51x + 220$

Solution
(a) Graph $Y_1 = X^2 - 2X - 24$. When the trace feature is used, the zeros of the trinomial are -4 and **6**, as shown in Figure 5.20. Thus the trinomial factors as follows.

$$x^2 - 2x - 24 = \left(x - (-4)\right)(x - 6)$$
$$= (x + 4)(x - 6)$$

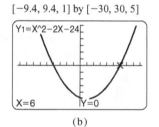

Figure 5.20

(b) Construct a table for $Y_1 = 2X^2 - 51X + 220$. Figure 5.21 reveals that the zeros are **5.5** and **20**. The leading coefficient of $2x^2 - 51x + 220$ is 2, so we factor this expression as follows.

$$2x^2 - 51x + 220 = 2(x - 5.5)(x - 20)$$
$$= (2x - 11)(x - 20)$$

Figure 5.21

Now Try Exercises 93, 97

5.4 PUTTING IT ALL TOGETHER

Equations of the form $ax^2 + bx + c = 0$ occur in applications. One way to solve such equations is to factor the trinomial $ax^2 + bx + c$. This factorization may be done symbolically, graphically, or numerically. The following table includes an explanation and examples of each technique. To factor by grouping, see the box on page 360.

Technique	Explanation	Example
Symbolic Factoring	To factor $x^2 + bx + c$ find two factors of c whose sum is b.	To factor $x^2 - 3x - 4$ find two factors of -4 whose sum is -3. These factors are 1 and -4. $$x^2 - 3x - 4 = (x + 1)(x - 4)$$ It checks. $-3x$
	To factor $ax^2 + bx + c$ find factors of ax^2 and c so that the middle term is bx. Grouping can also be used.	To factor $2x^2 + 3x - 2$ find factors of $2x^2$ and -2 so that the middle term is $3x$. $$2x^2 + 3x - 2 = (2x - 1)(x + 2)$$ It checks. $3x$
Graphical Factoring	If p and q are zeros of $x^2 + bx + c$, then the expression factors as $$(x - p)(x - q).$$ If p and q are zeros of $ax^2 + bx + c$, then the expression factors as $$a(x - p)(x - q).$$	To factor $x^2 - 3x - 4$ ($a = 1$), graph $y = x^2 - 3x - 4$. The zeros (x-intercepts) are -1 and 4, and it follows that $$x^2 - 3x - 4 = (x + 1)(x - 4).$$
Numerical Factoring	If p and q are zeros of $x^2 + bx + c$, then the expression factors as $$(x - p)(x - q).$$ If p and q are zeros of $ax^2 + bx + c$, then the expression factors as $$a(x - p)(x - q).$$	To factor $2x^2 + 3x - 2$ make a table for $Y_1 = 2X^2 + 3X - 2$. The zeros are 0.5 and -2. $$2x^2 + 3x - 2 = 2(x - 0.5)(x + 2)$$ $$= (2x - 1)(x + 2)$$

5.4 Exercises

MyMathLab   Math XL PRACTICE   WATCH   DOWNLOAD   READ   REVIEW

CONCEPTS

1. What is a trinomial? Give an example.

2. Name two methods for factoring $ax^2 + bx + c$.

3. The trinomial $3x^2 - x - 3$ is written in the form $ax^2 + bx + c$. Identify a, b, and c.

4. If you factor the trinomial $x^2 + 3x + 2$, do you obtain $(x + 1)(x + 2)$? Explain.

5. Suppose that the graph of $y = x^2 + bx + c$ has x-intercepts -3 and 1. Factor $x^2 + bx + c$.

6. The graph of $y = 6x^2 - 15x + 6$ has x-intercepts $\frac{1}{2}$ and 2. Factor $6x^2 - 15x + 6$.

FACTORING TRINOMIALS

Exercises 7–14: Determine whether the factors of the trinomial are the given binomials.

7. $x^2 + 5x + 6$ $(x + 2)(x + 3)$

8. $x^2 - 13x + 30$ $(x - 10)(x - 3)$

9. $x^2 - x - 20$ $(x + 5)(x - 4)$

10. $x^2 + 3x - 28$ $(x + 4)(x - 7)$

11. $6z^2 - 11z + 4$ $(2z - 1)(3z - 4)$

12. $4z^2 - 19z + 12$ $(2z - 4)(2z - 3)$

13. $10m^2 - 21m + 10$ $(5m + 2)(2m - 5)$

14. $12n^2 + 5n - 2$ $(3n + 2)(4n - 1)$

Exercises 15–70: Factor completely.

15. $x^2 + 7x + 10$ 16. $x^2 + 3x - 10$

17. $x^2 + 8x + 12$ 18. $x^2 - 8x + 12$

19. $x^2 - 13x + 36$ 20. $x^2 + 11x + 24$

21. $x^2 - 7x - 8$ 22. $x^2 - 21x - 100$

23. $z^2 + z - 72$ 24. $z^2 + 6z - 55$

25. $t^2 - 15t + 56$ 26. $t^2 - 14t + 40$

27. $y^2 - 18y + 72$ 28. $y^2 - 15y + 54$

29. $m^2 - 18m - 40$ 30. $m^2 - 22m - 75$

31. $n^2 - 20n - 300$ 32. $n^2 - 13n - 30$

33. $2x^2 + 7x + 3$ 34. $2x^2 - 5x - 3$

35. $6x^2 - x - 2$ 36. $10x^2 + 3x - 1$

37. $4z^2 + 19z + 12$ 38. $4z^2 + 17z + 4$

39. $6t^2 - 17t + 12$ 40. $6t^2 - 13t + 6$

41. $10y^2 + 13y - 3$ 42. $10y^2 + 23y - 5$

43. $6m^2 - m - 12$ 44. $20m^2 - m - 12$

45. $42n^2 + 5n - 25$ 46. $42n^2 + 65n + 25$

47. $1 + x - 2x^2$ 48. $3 - 5x - 2x^2$

49. $20 + 7x - 6x^2$ 50. $4 + 13x - 12x^2$

51. $5y^2 + 5y - 30$ 52. $3y^2 - 27y + 24$

53. $2z^2 + 12z + 16$ 54. $4z^2 + 32z + 60$

55. $z^3 + 9z^2 + 14z$ 56. $z^3 + 7z^2 + 12z$

57. $t^3 - 10t^2 + 21t$ 58. $t^3 - 11t^2 + 24t$

59. $m^4 + 6m^3 + 5m^2$ 60. $m^4 - m^3 - 2m^2$

61. $5x^3 + x^2 - 6x$ 62. $2x^3 + 8x^2 - 24x$

63. $6x^3 + 21x^2 + 9x$ 64. $12x^3 - 8x^2 - 20x$

65. $2x^3 - 14x^2 + 20x$ 66. $7x^3 + 35x^2 + 42x$

67. $60z^3 + 230z^2 - 40z$ 68. $24z^3 + 8z^2 - 80z$

69. $4x^4 + 10x^3 - 6x^2$ 70. $30x^4 + 3x^3 - 9x^2$

Exercises 71–74: **Thinking Generally** *Factor the given expression completely.*

71. $x^2 + (2 + 3)x + 2 \cdot 3$

72. $x^2 - (3 + 4)x + 3 \cdot 4$

73. $x^2 + (a + b)x + ab$

74. $x^2 - (a + b)x + ab$

75. Thinking Generally If $x^2 + bx + c = 0$ for $x = 1$ and $x = 2$, find b and c.

76. Thinking Generally If $x^2 + bx = 0$ for $x = -4$, find b.

Exercises 77–80: Multiplying Functions Use factoring to find $f(x)$ and $g(x)$ so that $h(x) = f(x) \, g(x)$.

77. $h(x) = x^2 + 3x + 2$ **78.** $h(x) = x^2 - 4x + 3$

79. $h(x) = x^2 - 2x - 8$ **80.** $h(x) = x^2 + 3x - 10$

FACTORING WITH GRAPHS AND TABLES

Exercises 81–86: Factor the expression by using the graph of $y = f(x)$, where $f(x)$ is the given expression. Check your answer by multiplying.

81. $x^2 - 6x + 8$

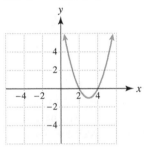

82. $x^2 - x - 6$

83. $2x^2 - 2x - 4$

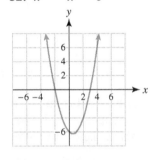

84. $3x^2 + 3x - 18$

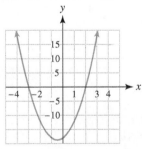

85. $2 + x - x^2$

86. $3 - 2x - x^2$

Exercises 87–90: Use the table to factor the expression. Check your answer by multiplying.

87. $x^2 - 3x - 4$

X	Y1
-2	6
-1	0
0	-4
1	-6
2	-6
3	-4
4	0

Y1■X^2-3X-4

88. $x^2 - 40x + 300$

X	Y1
-10	800
0	300
10	0
20	-100
30	0
40	300
50	800

Y1■X^2-40X+300

89. $2x^2 - 2x - 4$

X	Y1
-3	20
-2	8
-1	0
0	-4
1	-4
2	0
3	8

Y1■2X^2-2X-4

90. $3x^2 - 18x + 24$

X	Y1
0	24
1	9
2	0
3	-3
4	0
5	9
6	24

Y1■3X^2-18X+24

Exercises 91–100: Factor graphically or numerically.

91. $x^2 + 3x - 10$ **92.** $x^2 + 7x + 12$

93. $x^2 - 3x - 28$ **94.** $x^2 - 25x + 100$

95. $2x^2 - 14x + 20$ **96.** $12x^2 - 6x - 6$

97. $5x^2 - 30x - 200$ **98.** $12x^2 - 30x + 12$

99. $8x^2 - 44x + 20$ **100.** $20x^2 + 3x - 9$

APPLICATIONS

101. *Ticket Prices*   (Refer to Example 3.) If tickets are sold for $35, 1200 tickets are expected to be sold. For each $1 reduction in ticket price, an additional 100 tickets will be sold.
  (a) Find the revenue from ticket sales when ticket prices are reduced by x dollars.
  (b) Find the ticket prices that give sales of $54,000.

102. *Ticket Prices*   One airline ticket costs $295. For each additional ticket sold to a group of up to 30 people, the price of all the tickets is reduced by $5. For example, 2 tickets cost $2 \cdot \$290 = \$580$ and 3 tickets cost $3 \cdot \$285 = \$855$.
  (a) Find the cost of x tickets.
  (b) What is the cost of 20 tickets?
  (c) How many tickets are sold if the total cost is $2500?

103. *Area of a Rectangle*   A rectangle has an area of 91 square feet. Its length is 6 feet more than its width. Find the dimensions of the rectangle.

x

$x + 6$

104. *Area of a Triangle*   The base of a triangle is 2 inches less than its height. If the area of the triangle is 60 square inches, find its height.

105. *Passing Distances*   (Refer to Example 6.) The distance traveled in feet by a car passing another car after t seconds is given by $2t^2 + 88t$.
  (a) Use factoring to determine how long it takes for the car to travel 600 feet.

(b) Solve part (a) either graphically or numerically.

106. *Numbers*   Find two consecutive positive integers whose product is 132.

WRITING ABOUT MATHEMATICS

107. A student factors each trinomial into the given pair of binomials.
  (i) $x^2 - 5x - 6$ $(x - 1)(x + 6)$
  (ii) $10x^2 - 11x - 6$ $(5x - 3)(2x + 2)$
  (iii) $12x^2 + 13x + 3$ $(6x + 1)(2x + 3)$
  Explain the error that the student is making.

108. Suppose that a graph of $y = x^2 + bx + c$ intersects the x-axis at p and at q. Explain how you could use the graph to factor $x^2 + bx + c$.

CHECKING BASIC CONCEPTS
SECTIONS 5.3 AND 5.4

1. Factor out the greatest common factor.
  (a) $3x^2 - 6x$ **(b)** $16x^3 - 8x^2 + 4x$

2. Use factoring to solve each equation.
  (a) $x^2 - 2x = 0$ **(b)** $9x^2 = 81x$

3. Factor each trinomial.
  (a) $x^2 + 3x - 10$ **(b)** $x^2 - 3x - 10$
  (c) $8x^2 + 14x + 3$

4. Solve $x^2 + 3x + 2 = 0$.

5. A baseball is thrown upward at 64 feet per second or approximately 44 miles per hour. Its height above the ground after t seconds is given by

$$h(t) = -16t^2 + 64t + 8.$$

Determine when the baseball is 56 feet above the ground.

5.5   SPECIAL TYPES OF FACTORING

Difference of Two Squares ■ Perfect Square Trinomials ■ Sum and Difference of Two Cubes

A LOOK INTO MATH ▷   Some polynomials can be factored with special methods. These factoring techniques are used in other mathematics courses to solve equations and simplify expressions. In this section we discuss these methods.

Difference of Two Squares

When we factor polynomials, we are *reversing* the process of multiplying polynomials. In Section 5.2 we discussed the equation

$$(a - b)(a + b) = a^2 - b^2.$$

We can use this equation to factor a difference of two squares. For example, if we want to factor $x^2 - 25$, we can substitute x for a and 5 for b in

$$a^2 - b^2 = (a - b)(a + b)$$

to get

$$x^2 - 5^2 = (x - 5)(x + 5).$$

DIFFERENCE OF TWO SQUARES

For any real numbers a and b,
$$a^2 - b^2 = (a - b)(a + b).$$

NOTE: The sum of two squares *cannot* be factored (using real numbers). For example, $x^2 + y^2$ cannot be factored, whereas $x^2 - y^2$ can be factored. *It is important to remember that* $x^2 + y^2 \neq (x + y)^2$.

EXAMPLE 1 Factoring the difference of two squares

Factor each polynomial, if possible.
(a) $9x^2 - 64$ **(b)** $4x^2 + 9y^2$ **(c)** $9x^4 - y^6$ **(d)** $4a^3 - 4a$

Solution
(a) Note that $9x^2 = (3x)^2$ and $64 = 8^2$.
$$9x^2 - 64 = (3x)^2 - (8)^2$$
$$= (3x - 8)(3x + 8)$$

(b) Because $4x^2 + 9y^2$ is the *sum* of two squares, it *cannot* be factored.

(c) If we let $a^2 = 9x^4$ and $b^2 = y^6$, then $a = 3x^2$ and $b = y^3$. Thus
$$9x^4 - y^6 = (3x^2)^2 - (y^3)^2$$
$$= (3x^2 - y^3)(3x^2 + y^3).$$

(d) Start by factoring out the common factor of $4a$.
$$4a^3 - 4a = 4a(a^2 - 1)$$
$$= 4a(a - 1)(a + 1)$$

Now Try Exercises 15, 17, 23, 27

EXAMPLE 2 Applying the difference of two squares

Factor each expression.
(a) $(n + 1)^2 - 9$ **(b)** $x^4 - y^4$ **(c)** $6r^2 - 24t^4$ **(d)** $x^3 + 3x^2 - 4x - 12$

Solution
(a) Use $a^2 - b^2 = (a - b)(a + b)$, with $a = n + 1$ and $b = 3$.

$(n + 1)^2 - 9 = (n + 1)^2 - 3^2$ $9 = 3^2$
$= ((n + 1) - 3)((n + 1) + 3)$ Difference of squares
$= (n - 2)(n + 4)$ Combine terms.

(b) Use $a^2 - b^2 = (a - b)(a + b)$, with $a = x^2$ and $b = y^2$.

$$
\begin{aligned}
x^4 - y^4 &= (x^2)^2 - (y^2)^2 & &\text{Write as squares.} \\
&= (x^2 - y^2)(x^2 + y^2) & &\text{Difference of squares} \\
&= (x - y)(x + y)(x^2 + y^2) & &\text{Difference of squares again}
\end{aligned}
$$

(c) Start by factoring out the common factor of 6.

$$
\begin{aligned}
6r^2 - 24t^4 &= 6(r^2 - 4t^4) & &\text{Factor out 6.} \\
&= 6\left(r^2 - (2t^2)^2\right) & &\text{Write as squares.} \\
&= 6(r - 2t^2)(r + 2t^2) & &\text{Difference of squares}
\end{aligned}
$$

(d) Start factoring by using *grouping* and then factor the difference of squares.

$$
\begin{aligned}
x^3 + 3x^2 - 4x - 12 &= (x^3 + 3x^2) + (-4x - 12) & &\text{Associative property} \\
&= x^2(x + 3) - 4(x + 3) & &\text{Factor out } x^2 \text{ and } -4. \\
&= (x^2 - 4)(x + 3) & &\text{Distributive property} \\
&= (x - 2)(x + 2)(x + 3) & &\text{Difference of squares}
\end{aligned}
$$

Now Try Exercises 21, 29, 35, 37

Perfect Square Trinomials

In Section 5.2 we also showed how to multiply $(a + b)^2$ and $(a - b)^2$.

$$(a + b)^2 = a^2 + 2ab + b^2 \quad \text{and} \quad (a - b)^2 = a^2 - 2ab + b^2$$

The expressions $a^2 + 2ab + b^2$ and $a^2 - 2ab + b^2$ are **perfect square trinomials**. If we can recognize a perfect square trinomial, we can use these formulas to factor it.

PERFECT SQUARE TRINOMIALS

For any real numbers a and b,

$$
\begin{aligned}
a^2 + 2ab + b^2 &= (a + b)^2 \quad \text{and} \\
a^2 - 2ab + b^2 &= (a - b)^2.
\end{aligned}
$$

EXAMPLE 3   Factoring perfect square trinomials

Factor.
(a) $x^2 + 6x + 9$ **(b)** $81x^2 - 72x + 16$

Solution
(a) Let $a^2 = x^2$ and $b^2 = 3^2$. For a *perfect square trinomial*, the middle term must be $2ab$.

$$2ab = 2(x)(3) = 6x,$$

which equals the given middle term. Thus $a^2 + 2ab + b^2 = (a + b)^2$ implies

$$x^2 + 6x + 9 = (x + 3)^2.$$

(b) Let $a^2 = (9x)^2$ and $b^2 = 4^2$. Again, the middle term must be $2ab$.

$$2ab = 2(9x)(4) = 72x,$$

which equals the given middle term. Thus $a^2 - 2ab + b^2 = (a - b)^2$ implies

$$81x^2 - 72x + 16 = (9x - 4)^2. \quad \text{Now Try Exercises } \boxed{49, 56}$$

EXAMPLE 4   Factoring perfect square trinomials

Factor each expression.
(a) $4x^2 + 4xy + y^2$ **(b)** $9r^2 - 12rt + 4t^2$ **(c)** $25a^3 + 10a^2b + ab^2$

Solution
(a) Let $a^2 = (2x)^2$ and $b^2 = y^2$. The middle term must be $2ab$.

$$2ab = 2(2x)(y) = 4xy,$$

which equals the given middle term. Thus $a^2 + 2ab + b^2 = (a + b)^2$ implies

$$4x^2 + 4xy + y^2 = (2x + y)^2.$$

(b) Let $a^2 = (3r)^2$ and $b^2 = (2t)^2$. The middle term must be $2ab$.

$$2ab = 2(3r)(2t) = 12rt,$$

which equals the given middle term. Thus $a^2 - 2ab + b^2 = (a - b)^2$ implies

$$9r^2 - 12rt + 4t^2 = (3r - 2t)^2.$$

(c) Factor out the common factor of a. Then factor the resulting perfect square trinomial.

$$25a^3 + 10a^2b + ab^2 = a(25a^2 + 10ab + b^2)$$
$$= a(5a + b)^2 \quad \text{Now Try Exercises } \boxed{61, 63, 65}$$

MAKING CONNECTIONS

Special Factoring and General Techniques

If you do *not* recognize a polynomial as being either the difference of two squares or a perfect square trinomial, then you can factor the polynomial by using the methods discussed in earlier sections.

Sum and Difference of Two Cubes

The sum or difference of two cubes may be factored. This fact is justified by the following two equations.

$$(a + b)(a^2 - ab + b^2) = a^3 + b^3 \quad \text{and}$$
$$(a - b)(a^2 + ab + b^2) = a^3 - b^3$$

These equations can be verified by multiplying the left side to obtain the right side. For example,

$$(a + b)(a^2 - ab + b^2) = a \cdot a^2 - a \cdot ab + a \cdot b^2 + b \cdot a^2 - b \cdot ab + b \cdot b^2$$
$$= a^3 - a^2b + ab^2 + a^2b - ab^2 + b^3$$
$$= a^3 + b^3.$$

SUM AND DIFFERENCE OF TWO CUBES

For any real numbers a and b,

$$a^3 + b^3 = (a + b)(a^2 - ab + b^2) \quad \text{and}$$
$$a^3 - b^3 = (a - b)(a^2 + ab + b^2).$$

EXAMPLE 5   Factoring the sum and difference of two cubes

Factor each polynomial.
(a) $x^3 + 8$ **(b)** $27x^3 - 64y^3$

Solution
(a) Because $x^3 = (x)^3$ and $8 = 2^3$, we let $a = x$, $b = 2$, and factor. Substituting in

$$a^3 + b^3 = (a + b)(a^2 - ab + b^2)$$

gives

$$x^3 + 2^3 = (x + 2)(x^2 - x \cdot 2 + 2^2)$$
$$= (x + 2)(x^2 - 2x + 4).$$

Note that the quadratic factor does not factor further.
(b) Here, $27x^3 = (3x)^3$ and $64y^3 = (4y)^3$, so

$$27x^3 - 64y^3 = (3x)^3 - (4y)^3.$$

Substituting $a = 3x$ and $b = 4y$ in

$$a^3 - b^3 = (a - b)(a^2 + ab + b^2)$$

gives

$$(3x)^3 - (4y)^3 = (3x - 4y)\big((3x)^2 + 3x \cdot 4y + (4y)^2\big)$$
$$= (3x - 4y)(9x^2 + 12xy + 16y^2).$$

Now Try Exercises 67, 73

EXAMPLE 6   Factoring the sum and difference of two cubes

Factor each expression.
(a) $x^6 + 8y^3$ **(b)** $27p^9 - 8q^6$

Solution
(a) Let $a^3 = (x^2)^3$ and $b^3 = (2y)^3$. Then $a^3 + b^3 = (a + b)(a^2 - ab + b^2)$ implies

$$x^6 + 8y^3 = (x^2 + 2y)(x^4 - 2x^2y + 4y^2).$$

(b) Let $a^3 = (3p^3)^3$ and $b^3 = (2q^2)^3$. Then $a^3 - b^3 = (a - b)(a^2 + ab + b^2)$ implies

$$27p^9 - 8q^6 = (3p^3 - 2q^2)(9p^6 + 6p^3q^2 + 4q^4).$$

Now Try Exercises 79, 81

5.5 PUTTING IT ALL TOGETHER

In this section we presented three special types of factoring, which are summarized in the following table.

Type of Factoring	Description	Example
The Difference of Two Squares	To factor the difference of two squares use $a^2 - b^2 = (a - b)(a + b)$. **Note:** $a^2 + b^2$ cannot be factored.	$25x^2 - 16 = (5x - 4)(5x + 4)$ $a = 5x, b = 4$ $4x^2 + y^2$ cannot be factored.
A Perfect Square Trinomial	To factor a perfect square trinomial use $a^2 + 2ab + b^2 = (a + b)^2$ or $a^2 - 2ab + b^2 = (a - b)^2$.	$x^2 + 4x + 4 = (x + 2)^2$ $a = x, b = 2$ $16x^2 - 24x + 9 = (4x - 3)^2$ $a = 4x, b = 3$ Be sure to check the middle term.
The Sum and Difference of Two Cubes	The sum and difference of two cubes can be factored as $a^3 + b^3 = (a + b)$ $\cdot (a^2 - ab + b^2)$ or $a^3 - b^3 = (a - b)$ $\cdot (a^2 + ab + b^2)$.	$x^3 + 8y^3 = (x + 2y)(x^2 - x \cdot 2y + (2y)^2)$ $\qquad = (x + 2y)(x^2 - 2xy + 4y^2)$ $a = x, b = 2y$ $125x^3 - 64 = (5x - 4)((5x)^2 + 5x \cdot 4 + 4^2)$ $\qquad = (5x - 4)(25x^2 + 20x + 16)$ $a = 5x, b = 4$

5.5 Exercises

PRACTICE   WATCH   DOWNLOAD   READ   REVIEW

CONCEPTS

1. Give an example of a difference of two squares.

2. Give an example of a perfect square trinomial.

3. Give an example of the sum of two cubes.

4. Factor $a^2 - b^2$.

5. Factor $a^2 + 2ab + b^2$.

6. Factor $a^3 - b^3$.

DIFFERENCE OF TWO SQUARES

Exercises 7–10: Determine whether the expression represents a difference of two squares. Factor the expression.

7. $x^2 - 25$

8. $16x^2 - 100$

9. $x^3 + y^3$

10. $9x^2 + 36y^2$

Exercises 11–36: Factor the expression, if possible.

11. $x^2 - 36$ **12.** $y^2 - 144$

13. $25 - z^2$ **14.** $36 - y^2$

15. $4z^2 + 25$ **16.** $9z^2 + 64$

17. $36x^2 - 100$ **18.** $4y^2 - 64$

19. $49a^2 - 64b^2$ **20.** $9x^2 - 4y^2$

21. $64z^2 - 25z^4$ **22.** $64z^4 - 49z^2$

23. $5x^3 - 125x$ **24.** $100x^3 - x$

25. $4r^4 + t^6$ **26.** $9t^4 - 25r^6$

27. $16t^4 - r^2$ **28.** $t^4 + 9r^2$

29. $(x + 1)^2 - 25$ **30.** $(x - 2)^2 - 9$

31. $100 - (n - 4)^2$ **32.** $81 - (n + 3)^2$

33. $y^4 - 16$ **34.** $16z^4 - 1$

35. $16x^4 - y^4$ **36.** $r^4 - 81t^4$

Exercises 37–40: Use grouping to help factor the expression.

37. $x^3 + x^2 - x - 1$ **38.** $x^3 + x^2 - 9x - 9$

39. $4x^3 - 8x^2 - x + 2$

40. $9x^3 - 18x^2 - 16x + 32$

PERFECT SQUARE TRINOMIALS

Exercises 41–48: Determine whether the trinomial is a perfect square. If it is, factor it.

41. $x^2 + x + 16$ **42.** $4x^2 - 2x + 25$

43. $x^2 + 8x + 16$ **44.** $x^2 - 4x + 4$

45. $4z^2 - 4z + 1$ **46.** $9z^2 + 6z + 4$

47. $16t^2 - 12t + 9$ **48.** $4t^2 + 12t + 9$

Exercises 49–66: Factor the expression.

49. $x^2 + 2x + 1$ **50.** $x^2 - 6x + 9$

51. $4x^2 + 20x + 25$ **52.** $x^2 + 10x + 25$

53. $x^2 - 12x + 36$ **54.** $x^2 + 20x + 100$

55. $36z^2 + 12z + 1$ **56.** $9z^2 - 24z + 16$

57. $4y^4 + 4y^3 + y^2$ **58.** $16z^4 - 24z^3 + 9z^2$

59. $9z^3 - 6z^2 + z$ **60.** $49y^2 + 42y + 9$

61. $9x^2 + 6xy + y^2$ **62.** $25x^2 + 30xy + 9y^2$

63. $49a^2 - 28ab + 4b^2$ **64.** $64a^2 - 16ab + b^2$

65. $4x^4 - 4x^3y + x^2y^2$

66. $4x^3y + 12x^2y^2 + 9xy^3$

SUM AND DIFFERENCE OF TWO CUBES

Exercises 67–84: Factor the expression.

67. $x^3 - 8$ **68.** $x^3 + 8$

69. $y^3 + z^3$ **70.** $y^3 - z^3$

71. $27x^3 - 8$ **72.** $64 - y^3$

73. $64z^3 + 27t^3$ **74.** $125t^3 - 64r^3$

75. $8x^4 + 125x$ **76.** $x^3y^2 + 8y^5$

77. $27y - 8x^3y$ **78.** $x^3y^3 + 1$

79. $z^6 - 27y^3$ **80.** $z^6 + 27y^3$

81. $125z^6 + 8y^9$ **82.** $125z^6 - 8y^9$

83. $5m^6 + 40n^3$ **84.** $10m^9 - 270n^6$

GENERAL FACTORING

Exercises 85–118: Factor the expression completely.

85. $25x^2 - 64$ **86.** $25x^2 - 30x + 9$

87. $x^3 + 27$ **88.** $4 - 16y^2$

89. $64x^2 + 16x + 1$ **90.** $2x^2 - 5x + 3$

91. $3x^2 + 14x + 8$ **92.** $125x^3 - 1$

93. $x^4 + 8x$ **94.** $2x^3 - 12x^2 + 18x$

95. $64x^3 + 8y^3$ **96.** $54 - 16x^3$

97. $2r^2 - 8t^2$ **98.** $a^3 - ab^2$

99. $a^3 + 4a^2b + 4ab^2$ **100.** $8r^4 + rt^3$

101. $x^2 - 3x + 2$ **102.** $x^2 + 4x - 5$

103. $4z^2 - 25$ **104.** $(z + 1)^2 - 49$

105. $x^4 + 16x^3 + 64x^2$ **106.** $4x^2 - 12xy + 9y^2$

107. $z^3 - 1$ **108.** $8z^3 + 1$

109. $3t^2 - 5t - 8$ **110.** $15t^2 - 11t + 2$

111. $7a^3 + 20a^2 - 3a$

112. $b^3 - b^2 - 2b$

113. $x^6 - y^6$

114. $a^8 - b^8$

115. $100x^2 - 1$

116. $4x^2 + 28x + 49$

117. $p^3q^3 - 27$

118. $a^2b^2 - c^2d^2$

119. Explain how factoring $x^3 + y^3$ and $x^3 - y^3$ are similar.

120. Can $x^2 - y^2$ be factored? Can $x^2 + y^2$ be factored? Explain your answers.

GROUP ACTIVITY
WORKING WITH REAL DATA

Directions: Form a group of 2 to 4 people. Select someone to record the group's responses for this activity. All members of the group should work cooperatively to answer the questions. If your instructor asks for your results, each member of the group should be prepared to respond.

Exercises 1–6: *Geometric Factoring*   The polynomial $x^2 + 4x + 3$ can be factored by grouping.

$$x^2 + 4x + 3 = x^2 + x + 3x + 3$$
$$= (x^2 + x) + (3x + 3)$$
$$= x(x + 1) + 3(x + 1)$$
$$= (x + 3)(x + 1)$$

This factorization is represented geometrically in the accompanying figure. Note that the outside dimensions of the large rectangle are $x + 3$ by $x + 1$ and therefore its area is $(x + 3)(x + 1)$. This area equals the sum of the four smaller rectangles inside the large rectangle. Thus

$$(x + 3)(x + 1) = x^2 + x + 3x + 3 = x^2 + 4x + 3.$$

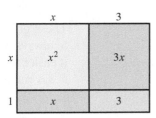

Factor the following expressions geometrically. If the rectangle turns out to be a square, what can you say about the trinomial?

1. $x^2 + 3x + 2$

2. $x^2 + 6x + 5$

3. $4x^2 + 4x + 1$

4. $x^2 + 6x + 9$

5. $6x^2 + 29x + 20$

6. $8x^2 + 59x + 21$

5.6 SUMMARY OF FACTORING

Guidelines for Factoring Polynomials ▪ Factoring Polynomials

A LOOK INTO MATH ▷

Mathematics is being used more and more to model all types of phenomena. Modeling is not only used in science; it is also used to describe consumer behavior and to search the Internet. To model the world around us, mathematical equations need to be solved. One important technique for solving equations is to set an expression equal to 0 and then factor. Factoring is an important method for solving equations and for simplifying complicated expressions. In this section, we discuss general guidelines that can be used to factor polynomials.

Guidelines for Factoring Polynomials

The following guidelines can be used to factor polynomials in general.

FACTORING POLYNOMIALS

STEP 1: Factor out the greatest common factor, if possible.

STEP 2: A. If the polynomial has *four terms*, try factoring by grouping.

        B. If the polynomial is a *binomial*, try one of the following.

           1. $a^2 - b^2 = (a - b)(a + b)$ Difference of two squares

           2. $a^3 - b^3 = (a - b)(a^2 + ab + b^2)$ Difference of two cubes

           3. $a^3 + b^3 = (a + b)(a^2 - ab + b^2)$ Sum of two cubes

        C. If the polynomial is a *trinomial*, check for a perfect square.

           1. $a^2 + 2ab + b^2 = (a + b)^2$ Perfect square trinomial

           2. $a^2 - 2ab + b^2 = (a - b)^2$ Perfect square trinomial

        Otherwise, apply FOIL or grouping, as described in Section 5.4.

STEP 3: Check to make sure that the polynomial is *completely* factored.

These guidelines give a general strategy for factoring a polynomial by hand. It is important to always perform Step 1 first. Factoring out the greatest common factor first usually makes it easier to factor the resulting polynomial. In the next subsection we apply these guidelines to several polynomials.

Factoring Polynomials

In the first example, we apply Step 1 to a polynomial with a common factor.

EXAMPLE 1 Factoring out a common factor

Factor $3x^3 - 9x^2$.

Solution

STEP 1: The greatest common factor is $3x^2$.

$$3x^3 - 9x^2 = 3x^2(x - 3)$$

STEP 2B: The binomial, $x - 3$, cannot be factored further.

STEP 3: The completely factored polynomial is $3x^2(x - 3)$.   Now Try Exercise 19

In several of the next examples we apply more than one factoring technique.

EXAMPLE 2 Factoring a difference of squares

Factor $5x^3 - 20x$.

Solution

STEP 1: The greatest common factor is $5x$.

$$5x^3 - 20x = 5x(x^2 - 4)$$

STEP 2B: We can factor the binomial $x^2 - 4$ as a difference of squares.

$$5x(x^2 - 4) = 5x(x - 2)(x + 2)$$

STEP 3: The completely factored polynomial is $5x(x - 2)(x + 2)$.   Now Try Exercise 21

EXAMPLE 3   Factoring a difference of squares

Factor $5x^4 - 80$.

Solution

STEP 1: The greatest common factor is 5.

$$5x^4 - 80 = 5(x^4 - 16)$$

STEP 2B: We can factor $x^4 - 16$ as a difference of squares *twice*.

$$5(x^4 - 16) = 5(x^2 - 4)(x^2 + 4) = 5(x - 2)(x + 2)(x^2 + 4)$$

The sum of squares, $x^2 + 4$, cannot be factored further.

STEP 3: The completely factored polynomial is $5(x - 2)(x + 2)(x^2 + 4)$.

Now Try Exercise **23**

EXAMPLE 4   Factoring a perfect square trinomial

Factor $12x^3 + 36x^2 + 27x$.

Solution

STEP 1: The greatest common factor is $3x$.

$$12x^3 + 36x^2 + 27x = 3x(4x^2 + 12x + 9)$$

STEP 2C: The trinomial $4x^2 + 12x + 9$ is a perfect square trinomial.

$$3x(4x^2 + 12x + 9) = 3x(2x + 3)(2x + 3)$$

STEP 3: The completely factored polynomial is $3x(2x + 3)^2$.   Now Try Exercise **37**

EXAMPLE 5   Factoring a sum of cubes

Factor $-8x^4 - 27x$.

Solution

STEP 1: The negative of the greatest common factor is $-x$.

$$-8x^4 - 27x = -x(8x^3 + 27)$$

STEP 2B: The binomial $8x^3 + 27$ can be factored as a sum of cubes.

$$-x(8x^3 + 27) = -x(2x + 3)(4x^2 - 6x + 9)$$

The trinomial, $4x^2 - 6x + 9$, cannot be factored further.

STEP 3: The completely factored polynomial is $-x(2x + 3)(4x^2 - 6x + 9)$.

Now Try Exercise **43**

EXAMPLE 6   Factoring by grouping

Factor $x^3 - 2x^2 + x - 2$.

Solution

STEP 1: There are no common factors.

STEP 2A: Because there are four terms, we apply grouping.

$$x^3 - 2x^2 + x - 2 = (x^3 - 2x^2) + (x - 2) \qquad \text{Associative property}$$
$$= x^2(x - 2) + 1(x - 2) \qquad \text{Distributive property}$$
$$= (x^2 + 1)(x - 2) \qquad \text{Distributive property}$$

The sum of squares, $x^2 + 1$, cannot be factored further.

STEP 3: The completely factored polynomial is $(x^2 + 1)(x - 2)$.   Now Try Exercise **31**

EXAMPLE 7   Factoring a trinomial

Factor $2x^4 - 7x^3 + 6x^2$.

Solution

STEP 1: The greatest common factor is x^2.

$$2x^4 - 7x^3 + 6x^2 = x^2(2x^2 - 7x + 6)$$

STEP 2C: We can factor the resulting trinomial by using FOIL.

$$x^2(2x^2 - 7x + 6) = x^2(x - 2)(2x - 3)$$

STEP 3: The completely factored polynomial is $x^2(x - 2)(2x - 3)$.   Now Try Exercise **27**

EXAMPLE 8   Factoring with two variables

Factor $12x^2 - 27a^2$.

Solution

STEP 1: The greatest common factor is 3.

$$12x^2 - 27a^2 = 3(4x^2 - 9a^2)$$

STEP 2B: We can factor the binomial as the difference of squares.

$$3(4x^2 - 9a^2) = 3(2x - 3a)(2x + 3a)$$

STEP 3: The completely factored polynomial is $3(2x - 3a)(2x + 3a)$.

Now Try Exercise **49**

In the next example, we use common factors, grouping, the difference of two cubes, and the difference of two squares to factor a polynomial.

EXAMPLE 9   Applying several techniques

Factor $2x^5 - 8x^3 - 2x^2 + 8$.

Solution

STEP 1: The expression has a greatest common factor of 2.

$$2x^5 - 8x^3 - 2x^2 + 8 = 2(x^5 - 4x^3 - x^2 + 4)$$

STEP 2A: The resulting four terms can be factored by grouping.

$$2(x^5 - 4x^3 - x^2 + 4) = 2((x^5 - 4x^3) + (-x^2 + 4)) \qquad \text{Associative property}$$
$$= 2(x^3(x^2 - 4) - 1(x^2 - 4)) \qquad \text{Distributive property}$$
$$= 2(x^3 - 1)(x^2 - 4) \qquad \text{Distributive property}$$

STEP 2B: Both of the resulting binomials can be factored further as the difference of two cubes and the difference of two squares.

$$2(x^3 - 1)(x^2 - 4) = 2(x - 1)(x^2 + x + 1)(x - 2)(x + 2)$$

The trinomial, $x^2 + x + 1$, cannot be factored further.

STEP 3: The completely factored polynomial is $2(x - 1)(x^2 + x + 1)(x - 2)(x + 2)$.

Now Try Exercise 57

5.6 PUTTING IT ALL TOGETHER

When using the guidelines presented in this section for general factoring strategy, the following rules can be helpful.

Concept	Explanation	Examples
Greatest Common Factor	Factor out the greatest common factor, or monomial, that occurs in each term.	$4x^2 - 8x = 4x(x - 2)$ $2x^2 - 4x + 8 = 2(x^2 - 2x + 4)$ $x^5 + x^3 = x^3(x^2 + 1)$
Factoring by Grouping	Use the associative and distributive properties to factor a polynomial with four terms.	$x^3 - 2x^2 + 3x - 6$ $= (x^3 - 2x^2) + (3x - 6)$ $= x^2(x - 2) + 3(x - 2)$ $= (x^2 + 3)(x - 2)$
Factoring Binomials	Use the difference of squares, the difference of cubes, or the sum of cubes.	$4x^2 - 9 = (2x - 3)(2x + 3)$ $x^3 - 8 = (x - 2)(x^2 + 2x + 4)$ $x^3 + 8 = (x + 2)(x^2 - 2x + 4)$
Factoring Trinomials	Use FOIL or grouping to factor a trinomial, after factoring out the greatest common factor.	$x^2 - 3x + 2 = (x - 1)(x - 2)$ $6x^2 + 13x + 5$ $= (6x^2 + 3x) + (10x + 5)$ $= 3x(2x + 1) + 5(2x + 1)$ $= (3x + 5)(2x + 1)$

5.6 Exercises

MyMathLab   MathXL PRACTICE   WATCH   DOWNLOAD   READ   REVIEW

CONCEPTS

1. When factoring a polynomial, what is a good first step?

2. What is the greatest common factor for $4x^2 + 2x$?

3. Can you factor $x^2 + 4$? Explain.

4. What method might you use to factor a polynomial with four terms?

WARM UP

Exercises 5–18: Factor completely, if possible.

5. $a^2 - a$ 6. $2x - 4$

7. $a^2 - 9$

8. $4b^2 - 1$

9. $x^2 - 2x + 1$

10. $a^2 + 2ab + b^2$

11. $x^3 - a^3$

12. $x^3 + a^3$

13. $a^2 + 4$

14. $36x^2 + y^2$

15. $x(x + 2) - 3(x + 2)$

16. $2x(x - 3) + (x - 3)$

17. $x^3 + 2x^2 + x + 2$

18. $x^3 - x^2 + 2x - 2$

FACTORING

Exercises 19–58: Factor completely.

19. $6x^2 - 14x$

20. $-27x^3 - 15x$

21. $2x^3 - 18x$

22. $8x^2 - 18$

23. $4a^4 - 64$

24. $b^4 - 81$

25. $6x^3 - 13x^2 - 15x$

26. $10x^4 + 13x^3 - 3x^2$

27. $2x^4 - 5x^3 - 25x^2$

28. $10x^3 + 28x^2 - 6x$

29. $2x^4 + 5x^2 + 3$

30. $2x^4 + 2x^2 - 4$

31. $x^3 + 3x^2 + x + 3$

32. $x^3 + 5x^2 + 4x + 20$

33. $5x^3 - 5x^2 + 10x - 10$

34. $5x^4 - 20x^3 + 10x - 40$

35. $ax + bx - ay - by$

36. $ax - bx - ay + by$

37. $18x^2 + 12x + 2$

38. $-3x^2 + 30x - 75$

39. $-4x^3 + 24x^2 - 36x$

40. $18x^3 - 60x^2 + 50x$

41. $8x^3 - 27$

42. $27x^3 + 8$

43. $-x^4 - 8x$

44. $x^5 - 27x^2$

45. $x^4 - 2x^3 - x + 2$

46. $x^4 + 3x^3 + x + 3$

47. $r^4 - 16$

48. $r^4 - 81$

49. $25x^2 - 4a^2$

50. $9y^2 - 16z^2$

51. $2x^4 - 2y^4$

52. $a^4 - b^4$

53. $9x^3 + 6x^2 - 3x$

54. $8x^3 + 28x^2 - 16x$

55. $(z - 2)^2 - 9$

56. $(y + 2)^2 - 4$

57. $3x^5 - 27x^3 + 3x^2 - 27$

58. $2x^5 - 8x^3 - 16x^2 + 64$

APPLICATIONS

59. *Greenhouse Gas Puzzle* Atmospheric carbon dioxide levels continue to increase and are suspected to contribute to global warming. The solution to the polynomial equation

$$x^3 - 380x^2 + 2x - 760 = 0$$

gives the record high amount of carbon dioxide in parts per million (ppm) in 2005, as measured at Mauna Loa Observatory. (*Source: The Honolulu Advertiser.*)
  (a) Factor the expression on the left side of the equation.
  (b) Solve the equation and determine this record amount.

60. *Greenhouse Gas Puzzle* (Refer to the preceding exercise.) The solution to the polynomial equation

$$2x^3 - 620x^2 + x - 310 = 0$$

gives the amount of carbon dioxide in parts per million (ppm) in 1958, as measured at Mauna Loa Observatory. (*Source: The Honolulu Advertiser.*)
  (a) Factor the expression on the left side of the equation.
  (b) Solve the equation and determine this amount.

61. *Dimensions of a Box* A box has a volume of 6 cubic feet. The height of a box is 1 foot more than its length, and its length is 1 foot more than its width. Let x be the height.
  (a) Write a polynomial that gives the volume of the box in terms of x.
  (b) Write an equation whose solution gives the height of the box.
  (c) Solve the equation by using factoring.

62. *Dimensions of a Rectangle*   The length of a rectangle is 2 inches more than its width and the area is 24 square inches. Let x be the width.
   (a) Write a polynomial that gives the area of the rectangle in terms of x.
   (b) Write an equation whose solution gives the width of the rectangle.
   (c) Solve the equation by using factoring.

WRITING ABOUT MATHEMATICS

63. Give the basic guidelines for factoring a polynomial.

64. What are some ways to recognize that a polynomial is completely factored?

CHECKING BASIC CONCEPTS
SECTIONS 5.5 AND 5.6

1. Factor each special type of polynomial.
   (a) $25x^2 - 16$
   (b) $x^2 + 12x + 36$
   (c) $9x^2 - 30x + 25$
   (d) $x^3 - 27$
   (e) $81x^4 - 16$

2. Factor each expression.
   (a) $x^3 - 2x^2 + 3x - 6$
   (b) $x^2 - 4x - 21$
   (c) $12x^3 + 2x^2 - 4x$

5.7 POLYNOMIAL EQUATIONS

Quadratic Equations ■ Higher Degree Equations ■ Equations in Quadratic Form ■ Applications

A LOOK INTO MATH ▷

Figure 5.22

Polynomials are used to solve important problems. One example is found in highway construction where the elevations of hills and valleys are modeled by quadratic polynomials. (**Source:** F. Mannering and W. Kilareski, *Principles of Highway Engineering and Traffic Analysis.*)

The quadratic polynomial

$$h(x) = -0.0001x^2 + 100$$

could model the height of a hill, where $x = 0$ corresponds to the peak or crest of the hill, as illustrated in Figure 5.22. To determine any locations where the height of the hill is 75 feet, we can solve the *quadratic equation*

$$-0.0001x^2 + 100 = 75.$$

Quadratic Equations

Any **quadratic equation** can be written as $ax^2 + bx + c = 0$, where a, b, and c are constants, with $a \neq 0$. Quadratic equations can sometimes be solved by factoring and then applying the zero-product property. They can also be solved graphically. These techniques are demonstrated in the next two examples.

EXAMPLE 1   Solving a quadratic equation

Solve $x^2 - 4 = 0$ symbolically and graphically.

Solution

Symbolic Solution   Start by factoring the left side of the equation.

$$x^2 - 4 = 0 \qquad \text{Given equation}$$
$$(x - 2)(x + 2) = 0 \qquad \text{Difference of squares}$$
$$x - 2 = 0 \quad \text{or} \quad x + 2 = 0 \qquad \text{Zero-product property}$$
$$x = 2 \quad \text{or} \quad x = -2 \qquad \text{Solve each equation.}$$

The solutions are -2 and 2.

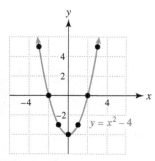

Figure 5.23

Graphical Solution   Start by making Table 5.10. Plot these points and connect them with a smooth curve called a parabola, as shown in Figure 5.23. The x-intercepts, or zeros, are -2 and 2, which are also the solutions to the equation.

TABLE 5.10 $y = x^2 - 4$

x	-3	-2	-1	0	1	2	3
y	5	0	-3	-4	-3	0	5

Now Try Exercise 7

EXAMPLE 2   Solving quadratic equations

Solve each equation.
(a) $4x^2 - 20x + 25 = 0$ **(b)** $3x^2 + 11x = 20$ **(c)** $x^2 + 25 = 0$

Solution
(a) Start by factoring the left side, which is a perfect square trinomial.

$$4x^2 - 20x + 25 = 0 \qquad \text{Given equation}$$
$$(2x - 5)(2x - 5) = 0 \qquad \text{Factor.}$$
$$2x - 5 = 0 \qquad \text{Zero-product property}$$
$$x = \tfrac{5}{2} \qquad \text{Solve.}$$

The only solution is $\frac{5}{2}$.

(b) Start by subtracting 20 from each side to obtain a 0 on the right side.

$$3x^2 + 11x = 20 \qquad \text{Given equation}$$
$$3x^2 + 11x - 20 = 0 \qquad \text{Subtract 20.}$$
$$(x + 5)(3x - 4) = 0 \qquad \text{Factor.}$$
$$x + 5 = 0 \quad \text{or} \quad 3x - 4 = 0 \qquad \text{Zero-product property}$$
$$x = -5 \quad \text{or} \quad x = \tfrac{4}{3} \qquad \text{Solve.}$$

The solutions are -5 and $\frac{4}{3}$.

(c) $x^2 + 25 = 0$ implies that $x^2 = -25$, which has no solutions because $x^2 \geq 0$ for all real numbers.

Now Try Exercises 25, 29, 33

MAKING CONNECTIONS

Quadratic Equations and Solutions

Example 2 demonstrates that a quadratic equation can have no solutions, one solution, or two solutions. The following graphs illustrate this concept.

| $x^2 + 25 = 0$ | $4x^2 - 20x + 25 = 0$ | $3x^2 + 11x = 20$ |
| No solutions | One solution | Two solutions |

EXAMPLE 3 Determining highway elevations

Solve the equation $-0.0001x^2 + 100 = 75$, which is discussed in the introduction to this section. See Figure 5.22 on page 381.

Solution
Start by subtracting 75 from each side. Then multiply each side by $-10,000$ to clear decimals.

$$-0.0001x^2 + 100 = 75 \qquad \text{Given equation}$$
$$-0.0001x^2 + 25 = 0 \qquad \text{Subtract 75.}$$
$$-10,000(-0.0001x^2 + 25) = -10,000(0) \qquad \text{Multiply by } -10,000.$$
$$x^2 - 250,000 = 0 \qquad \text{Distributive property}$$
$$(x - 500)(x + 500) = 0 \qquad \sqrt{250,000} = 500$$
$$x - 500 = 0 \quad \text{or} \quad x + 500 = 0 \qquad \text{Zero-product property}$$
$$x = 500 \quad \text{or} \quad x = -500 \qquad \text{Solve each equation.}$$

Thus the highway elevation is 75 feet high a distance of 500 feet on either side of the crest of the hill.   Now Try Exercise 75

Higher Degree Equations

Using the techniques of factoring that we discussed in earlier sections, we can solve equations that involve higher degree polynomials. They can have more than two solutions.

EXAMPLE 4 Solving higher degree equations

Solve each equation.
(a) $x^3 = 4x$ **(b)** $2x^3 + 2x^2 - 12x = 0$ **(c)** $x^3 - 5x^2 - x + 5 = 0$

Solution

(a) Start by subtracting $4x$ from each side of $x^3 = 4x$ to obtain a 0 on the right side. (Do *not* divide each side by x because the solution $x = 0$ will be lost.)

$$x^3 = 4x \qquad \text{Given equation}$$
$$x^3 - 4x = 0 \qquad \text{Subtract } 4x.$$
$$x(x^2 - 4) = 0 \qquad \text{Factor out } x.$$
$$x(x - 2)(x + 2) = 0 \qquad \text{Difference of squares}$$
$$x = 0 \quad \text{or} \quad x - 2 = 0 \quad \text{or} \quad x + 2 = 0 \qquad \text{Zero-product property}$$
$$x = 0 \quad \text{or} \quad x = 2 \quad \text{or} \quad x = -2 \qquad \text{Solve each equation.}$$

The solutions are $-2, 0$, and 2.

(b) Start by factoring out the common factor $2x$.

$$2x^3 + 2x^2 - 12x = 0 \qquad \text{Given equation}$$
$$2x(x^2 + x - 6) = 0 \qquad \text{Factor out } 2x.$$
$$2x(x + 3)(x - 2) = 0 \qquad \text{Factor the trinomial.}$$
$$2x = 0 \quad \text{or} \quad x + 3 = 0 \quad \text{or} \quad x - 2 = 0 \qquad \text{Zero-product property}$$
$$x = 0 \quad \text{or} \quad x = -3 \quad \text{or} \quad x = 2 \qquad \text{Solve each equation.}$$

The solutions are $-3, 0$, and 2.

(c) To solve this equation use *grouping* to factor the left side.

$$x^3 - 5x^2 - x + 5 = 0 \qquad \text{Given equation}$$
$$(x^3 - 5x^2) + (-x + 5) = 0 \qquad \text{Associative property}$$
$$x^2(x - 5) - 1(x - 5) = 0 \qquad \text{Factor out } x^2 \text{ and } -1.$$
$$(x^2 - 1)(x - 5) = 0 \qquad \text{Distributive property}$$
$$(x - 1)(x + 1)(x - 5) = 0 \qquad \text{Difference of squares}$$
$$x - 1 = 0 \quad \text{or} \quad x + 1 = 0 \quad \text{or} \quad x - 5 = 0 \qquad \text{Zero-product property}$$
$$x = 1 \quad \text{or} \quad x = -1 \quad \text{or} \quad x = 5 \qquad \text{Solve each equation.}$$

The solutions are $-1, 1$, and 5.   Now Try Exercises 43, 47, 51

In the next example, we demonstrate how an equation can be solved symbolically, graphically, and numerically with the aid of a graphing calculator.

EXAMPLE **5** Solving a polynomial equation

Solve $16x^4 - 64x^3 + 64x^2 = 0$ symbolically, graphically, and numerically.

Solution

Symbolic Solution   Begin by factoring out the common factor $16x^2$.

$$16x^4 - 64x^3 + 64x^2 = 0 \qquad \text{Given equation}$$
$$16x^2(x^2 - 4x + 4) = 0 \qquad \text{Factor out } 16x^2.$$
$$16x^2(x - 2)^2 = 0 \qquad \text{Perfect square trinomial}$$

Solving results in

$$16x^2 = 0 \quad \text{or} \quad (x - 2)^2 = 0 \qquad \text{Zero-product property}$$
$$x = 0 \quad \text{or} \quad x = 2. \qquad \text{Solve.}$$

Graphical Solution   Graph $Y_1 = 16X^4 - 64X^3 + 64X^2$, as shown in Figures 5.24(a) and 5.24(b). When the trace feature is used, solutions to $y_1 = 0$ occur when $x = 0$ and $x = 2$.

Numerical Solution   Construct the table for $Y_1 = 16X^4 - 64X^3 + 64X^2$, as shown in Figure 5.24(c). Solutions occur at $x = 0$ and $x = 2$.

$[-4.7, 4.7, 1]$ by $[-100, 100, 25]$ $[-4.7, 4.7, 1]$ by $[-100, 100, 25]$

(a)

(b)   (c)

Figure 5.24

Now Try Exercise **61**

Equations in Quadratic Form

Sometimes equations do not appear to be quadratic, but they can be solved by using factoring techniques that we have already applied to quadratic equations. In these situations we often factor more than once, as demonstrated in the next example.

EXAMPLE **6**   Solving equations in quadratic form

Solve each equation.
(a) $x^4 - 81 = 0$ **(b)** $x^4 - 5x^2 + 4 = 0$

Solution
(a) To solve this equation use the difference of squares twice.

$$
\begin{aligned}
(x^2)^2 - 9^2 &= 0 && \text{Rewrite given equation.} \\
(x^2 - 9)(x^2 + 9) &= 0 && \text{Difference of squares} \\
(x - 3)(x + 3)(x^2 + 9) &= 0 && \text{Difference of squares again}
\end{aligned}
$$

$x - 3 = 0$ or $x + 3 = 0$ or $x^2 + 9 = 0$ Zero-product property

$x = 3$ or $x = -3$ or $x^2 = -9$ Solve each equation.

The solutions are -3 and 3 because $x^2 = -9$ has no real number solutions.
(b) To solve this equation start by factoring the trinomial.

$$
\begin{aligned}
x^4 - 5x^2 + 4 &= 0 && \text{Given equation} \\
(x^2 - 4)(x^2 - 1) &= 0 && \text{Factor.} \\
(x - 2)(x + 2)(x - 1)(x + 1) &= 0 && \text{Difference of squares twice}
\end{aligned}
$$

$x = 2$ or $x = -2$ or $x = 1$ or $x = -1$ Solve.

The solutions are $-2, -1, 1,$ and 2.

Now Try Exercises **65, 69**

NOTE: To factor the equation in Example 6(a), it may be helpful to let $z = x^2$ and $z^2 = x^4$. Then the given equation becomes $z^2 - 81 = 0$, or $(z - 9)(z + 9) = 0$ after factoring. Substituting $z = x^2$ gives the factored equation $(x^2 - 9)(x^2 + 9) = 0$. Similar comments can be made for Example 6(b).

MAKING CONNECTIONS

Symbolic, Graphical, and Numerical Solutions

The following illustrates how to solve $x^3 - 4x = 0$ with each method. Note that the solutions to $x^3 - 4x = 0$, the x-intercepts of the graph of $y = x^3 - 4x$, and the zeros of $x^3 - 4x$ are *all identical*.

Symbolic Solution	Graphical Solution	Numerical Solution

Symbolic Solution

$$x^3 - 4x = 0$$
$$x(x^2 - 4) = 0$$
$$x(x - 2)(x + 2) = 0$$
$$x = 0, x = 2, x = -2$$

Graphical Solution

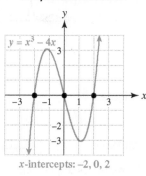

x-intercepts: $-2, 0, 2$

Numerical Solution

x	$x^3 - 4x$
-3	-15
-2	0
-1	3
0	0
1	-3
2	0
3	15

Applications

▶ REAL-WORLD CONNECTION   Many times applications involving geometry make use of quadratic equations. In the next example we solve a quadratic equation to find the dimensions of a picture.

EXAMPLE **7**   Finding the dimensions of a picture

A frame surrounding a picture is 3 inches wide. The picture inside the frame is 5 inches wider than it is high. If the overall area of the picture and frame is 336 square inches, find the dimensions of the picture inside the frame.

Solution

Let x be the height of the picture and $x + 5$ be its width. The dimensions of the picture and frame, in inches, are illustrated in Figure 5.25.

The overall area is given by $(x + 6)(x + 11)$, which equals 336 square inches.

$$(x + 6)(x + 11) = 336 \qquad \text{Equation to solve}$$
$$x^2 + 17x + 66 = 336 \qquad \text{Multiply binomials.}$$
$$x^2 + 17x - 270 = 0 \qquad \text{Subtract 336.}$$
$$(x - 10)(x + 27) = 0 \qquad \text{Factor.}$$
$$x = 10 \quad \text{or} \quad x = -27 \qquad \text{Zero-product property; solve.}$$

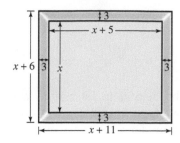

Figure 5.25

The only valid solution for x is 10 inches. Because the width is 5 inches more than the height, the dimensions are 10 inches by 15 inches.   Now Try Exercise **73**

▶ REAL-WORLD CONNECTION   Highway engineers often use quadratic functions to calculate stopping distances for cars. The faster a car is traveling, the farther it takes for the car to stop. The stopping distance for a car can be used to estimate its speed, as demonstrated in the next example.   (*Source:* F. Mannering.)

EXAMPLE 8   Finding the speed of a car

On wet, level pavement highway engineers sometimes estimate stopping distance d in feet for a car traveling at x miles per hour by

$$d(x) = \frac{1}{9}x^2 + \frac{11}{3}x.$$

Use this formula to approximate the speed of a car that takes 180 feet to stop.

Solution
We need to solve the equation $d(x) = 180$. Start by multiplying by **9** to clear fractions.

$$\frac{1}{9}x^2 + \frac{11}{3}x = 180 \qquad \text{Equation to be solved}$$

$$9\left(\frac{1}{9}x^2 + \frac{11}{3}x\right) = 9 \cdot 180 \qquad \text{Multiply by 9.}$$

$$x^2 + 33x = 1620 \qquad \text{Distributive property}$$

$$x^2 + 33x - 1620 = 0 \qquad \text{Subtract 1620.}$$

$$(x - 27)(x + 60) = 0 \qquad \text{Factor.}$$

$$x = 27 \quad \text{or} \quad x = -60 \qquad \text{Zero-product property; solve.}$$

The speed of the car is 27 miles per hour.

Now Try Exercise 81

NOTE: To factor $x^2 + 33x - 1620$ we find values for m and n such that $mn = -1620$ and $m + n = 33$, which may require some trial and error.

EXAMPLE 9   Finding the dimensions of an iPod Mini

The width of an iPod Mini is 1.5 inches more than its thickness, and its length is 3 inches more than its thickness. If the volume of an iPod Mini is 3.5 cubic inches, find its dimensions graphically.

$[-6, 6, 1]$ by $[-2, 6, 1]$

Intersection
X=.5   Y=3.5

Figure 5.26

Solution
Let x be its thickness, $x + 1.5$ be its width, and $x + 3$ be its length. Because volume equals thickness times width times length, we have

$$x(x + 1.5)(x + 3) = 3.5.$$

The graphs of $Y_1 = X(X + 1.5)(X + 3)$ and $Y_2 = 3.5$ intersect at $(0.5, 3.5)$, as shown in Figure 5.26. Thus the iPod Mini is 0.5 inch thick, 2 inches wide, and 3.5 inches long.

Now Try Exercise 83

5.7 PUTTING IT ALL TOGETHER

The following is a typical strategy for solving a polynomial equation. When you have finished, *be sure to check your answers*.

STEP 1: If necessary, rewrite the equation so that a 0 appears on one side of the equation.
STEP 2: Factor out common factors.
STEP 3: Factor the remaining polynomial, using the techniques presented in this chapter.
STEP 4: Apply the *zero-product* property.
STEP 5: Solve each resulting equation.

The following table summarizes how to solve three types of higher degree polynomial equations.

Concept	Explanation	Example
Higher Degree Equations	Factor out common factors; then use the techniques for factoring.	$2x^3 - 32x = 0$ $2x(x^2 - 16) = 0$ $2x(x - 4)(x + 4) = 0$ $x = 0$ or $x = 4$ or $x = -4$
Equations in Quadratic Form	Factor these forms as $ax^2 + bx + c$.	$x^4 - 13x^2 + 36 = 0$ $(x^2 - 4)(x^2 - 9) = 0$ $(x - 2)(x + 2)(x - 3)(x + 3) = 0$ $x = 2$ or $x = -2$ or $x = 3$ or $x = -3$
Solving by Grouping	Use grouping to help factor a cubic expression having four terms. Apply the distributive property.	$x^3 - 7x^2 - 16x + 112 = 0$ $(x^3 - 7x^2) + (-16x + 112) = 0$ $x^2(x - 7) - 16(x - 7) = 0$ $(x^2 - 16)(x - 7) = 0$ $(x - 4)(x + 4)(x - 7) = 0$ $x = 4$ or $x = -4$ or $x = 7$

5.7 Exercises

MyMathLab | Math XL PRACTICE   WATCH   DOWNLOAD   READ   REVIEW

CONCEPTS

1. Explain why factoring is important in mathematics.

2. Factoring a polynomial is the *reverse* of _____ polynomials.

3. When you are solving $x^2 = 16$ by factoring, what is a good first step?

4. To solve $x^2 - 3x - 3 = 1$ could you start by factoring the left side of the equation? Explain.

5. What is the solution to $(x - 1)^2 = 0$?

6. Does the equation $x^2 + 4 = 0$ have any real number solutions? Explain.

SOLVING QUADRATIC EQUATIONS

Exercises 7–12: Solve the equation graphically. Then solve the equation symbolically.

7. $x^2 - 1 = 0$

8. $x^2 - 9 = 0$

9. $\frac{1}{4}x^2 - 1 = 0$

10. $\frac{1}{16}x^2 - 1 = 0$

11. $x^2 - x - 2 = 0$

12. $x^2 - x - 6 = 0$

Exercises 13–34: Solve the given quadratic equation, if possible.

13. $z^2 - 64 = 0$

14. $z^2 - 100 = 0$

15. $4y^2 - 1 = 0$ - -

16. $9y^2 - 36 = 0$

17. $x^2 - 3x - 4 = 0$

18. $x^2 - 8x + 7 = 0$

19. $x^2 + 4x - 12 = 0$

20. $x^2 - 3x - 28 = 0$

21. $2x^2 + 5x - 3 = 0$

22. $3x^2 + 8x + 4 = 0$

23. $2x^2 = 32$

24. $4x^2 = 64$

25. $z^2 + 14z + 49 = 0$

26. $z^2 + 64 = 16z$

27. $9t^2 + 1 = 6t$

28. $49t^2 + 28t + 4 = 0$

29. $15n^2 = 7n + 2$

30. $7n^2 + 57n + 8 = 0$

31. $24m^2 + 23m = 12$

32. $11m^2 = 31m + 6$

33. $x^2 + 12 = 0$

34. $2x^2 + 3 = 0$

Exercises 35–38: Use the graph to solve the equation. Then solve the equation by factoring.

35. $x^2 + x - 6 = 0$

36. $x^2 - 2x - 3 = 0$

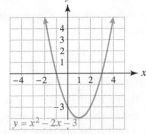

37. $2x^2 - 4x - 16 = 0$

38. $2x^2 + 3x - 2 = 0$

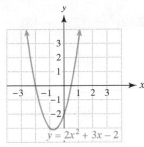

Exercises 39–42: The graph of the quadratic expression $y = ax^2 + bx + c$ is $\cap$-shaped when $a < 0$. If possible, sketch a graph of a quadratic expression with $a < 0$ that satisfies the condition.

39. No x-intercepts

40. One x-intercept

41. Two x-intercepts

42. Three x-intercepts

HIGHER DEGREE EQUATIONS

Exercises 43–54: Solve the equation.

43. $z^3 = 9z$

44. $2z^3 + 8z = 0$

45. $x^3 + x = 0$

46. $x^3 = x$

47. $2x^3 - 6x^2 = 20x$

48. $3x^3 + 15x^2 + 12x = 0$

49. $t^4 - 4t^3 - 5t^2 = 0$

50. $2t^4 - 8t^3 + 6t^2 = 0$

51. $x^3 + 7x^2 - 4x - 28 = 0$

52. $x^3 + 5x^2 = 9x + 45$

53. $n^3 - 2n^2 - 36n + 72 = 0$

54. $n^3 - 10n^2 - 4n + 40 = 0$

Exercises 55–62: (Refer to Example 5.) Solve the equation
  (a) symbolically,
  (b) graphically, and
  (c) numerically.

55. $x^2 - 2x - 15 = 0$

56. $x^2 + 7x + 10 = 0$

57. $2x^2 - 3x = 2$

58. $4t^2 + 25 = 20t$

59. $3t^2 + 18t + 15 = 0$

60. $4z^2 = 16$

61. $4x^4 + 16x^2 = 16x^3$

62. $2x^3 + 12x^2 + 18x = 0$

EQUATIONS IN QUADRATIC FORM

Exercises 63–72: Solve the equation.

63. $x^4 - 2x^2 - 8 = 0$ **64.** $x^4 - 8x^2 - 9 = 0$

65. $x^4 - 26x^2 + 25 = 0$

66. $x^4 - 21x^2 - 100 = 0$

67. $x^4 - 13x^2 + 36 = 0$

68. $x^4 - 18x^2 + 81 = 0$

69. $x^4 - 16 = 0$ **70.** $4x^4 = x^2 + 18$

71. $9x^4 - 13x^2 + 4 = 0$

72. $64x^4 - 180x^2 + 81 = 0$

APPLICATIONS

73. *Picture Frame*   (Refer to Example 7.) A rectangular frame surrounding a picture is made from boards that are 2 inches wide. The picture inside the frame is 4 inches wider than it is high. If the overall area of the picture and frame is 525 square inches, find the dimensions of the picture.

74. *Picture Frame*   The outside measurements of a rectangular frame for a picture are 30 inches by 40 inches. The area of the rectangular picture inside the frame is 936 square inches. Find the width of the frame that surrounds the picture.

75. *Modeling a Hill*   (Refer to Example 3.) The elevation E in feet of a highway x feet along a hill is modeled by

$$E(x) = -0.0001x^2 + 500,$$

where $-2000 \leq x \leq 2000$. Determine the x-values where the elevation is 400 feet.

76. *Numbers*   If a positive number n is increased by 3, its square equals 121. Find n.

77. *Sidewalk Around a Pool*   A 5-foot-wide sidewalk around a rectangular swimming pool has a total area of 900 square feet. Find the dimensions of the swimming pool if the pool is 20 feet longer than it is wide.

78. *Height Reached by a Baseball*   The height in feet reached by a batted baseball after t seconds is given by

$$h(t) = -16t^2 + 88t + 4.$$

Determine when the baseball is 100 feet in the air.

79. *Height Reached by a Baseball*   The height in feet reached by a batted baseball after t seconds is given by

$$h(t) = -16t^2 + 66t + 2.$$

Determine when the baseball is 70 feet in the air.

80. *Geometry*   A rectangle is 2 inches longer than it is wide. If each side is increased by 3 inches, the area increases by 183 square inches. Find the dimensions of the rectangle.

Exercises 81 and 82: (Refer to Example 8.) On dry, level pavement the stopping distance d in feet for a car traveling at x miles per hour can be estimated by

$$d(x) = \frac{1}{11}x^2 + \frac{11}{3}x.$$

Use this formula to approximate the speed of a car that takes d feet to stop.

81. $d = 220$ feet   **82.** $d = 638$ feet

83. *iPod Dimensions*   The width of an iPod is 1.8 inches more than its thickness, and its length is 3.5 inches more than its thickness. If the volume of an iPod is 5.904 cubic inches, find its dimensions graphically.

84. *Box Dimensions* The width of a rectangular mailing box is 9 inches more than its thickness, and its length is 11 inches more than its thickness. If the volume of the box is 286 cubic inches, find its dimensions graphically.

85. *Modeling a Highway* In highway design quadratic polynomials are used not only to model hills but also to model valleys. Valleys or sags in the road are sometimes referred to as *sag curves*. Suppose that the elevation E in feet of the sag curve x (horizontal) feet along a proposed route is modeled by

$$E(x) = 0.0002x^2 - 0.3x + 500,$$

where $0 \le x \le 1500$. See the accompanying figure. (**Source:** F. Mannering.)

(a) Make a table of the elevations for $x = 0, 300, 600, \ldots, 1500$ and interpret these values.

(b) Determine where the elevation is 400 feet.

86. *Biology* Some types of worms have a remarkable ability to live without moisture. The following table from one study shows the number of worms y surviving after x days without moisture.

x (days)	0	20	40
y (worms)	50	48	45

x (days)	80	120	160
y (worms)	36	20	3

Source: D. Brown and P. Rothery, *Models in Biology*.

(a) Plot the data and graph

$$y = -0.00138x^2 - 0.076x + 50.1$$

in the same viewing rectangle.

(b) Discuss how well the equation models the data.

(c) Estimate the day x when 10 worms remained.

WRITING ABOUT MATHEMATICS

87. Explain why the graph of $y = ax^2 + bx + c$ is used to model a dip or valley in a highway rather than the graph of $y = |ax + b|$. Make a sketch to support your reasoning. Assume that $a > 0$.

88. Explain the basic steps that you would use to solve the equation $ax^2 + bx + c = 0$ graphically and numerically. Assume that the equation has two solutions.

CHECKING BASIC CONCEPTS
SECTION 5.7

1. Use the graph to solve $x^2 + 4x + 3 = 0$. Then solve the equation symbolically.

2. Solve $x^2 - 9 = 0$ graphically. Then solve the equation by factoring.

3. If possible, solve each equation.
(a) $x^2 + 9 = 6x$
(b) $x^2 + 9 = 0$
(c) $12x^2 + 7x - 10 = 0$

4. Solve each equation.
(a) $x^3 + 5x = 0$
(b) $x^4 - 81 = 0$
(c) $z^4 + z^2 = 20$
(d) $x^3 + 2x^2 - 49x = 98$

CHAPTER 5 SUMMARY

Monomials and Polynomials   A monomial is a term with only *nonnegative integer* exponents. A polynomial is either a monomial or a sum of monomials.

Examples: Monomial: $-4x^3y^2$ has degree 5 and coefficient -4

Polynomial: $3x^2 - 4x + 2$ has degree 2 and leading coefficient 3

Addition and Subtraction of Polynomials   To add two polynomials, combine like terms. When subtracting two polynomials, add the first polynomial and the opposite of the second polynomial. Combine like terms.

Examples: $(3x^3 - 4x) + (-5x^3 + 7x) = (3 - 5)x^3 + (-4 + 7)x$
$$= -2x^3 + 3x$$

$(3xy^2 + 4x^2) - (4xy^2 - 6x) = (3xy^2 + 4x^2) + (-4xy^2 + 6x)$
$$= 3xy^2 - 4xy^2 + 4x^2 + 6x$$
$$= -xy^2 + 4x^2 + 6x$$

Polynomial Functions   If the formula for a function f is a polynomial, then f is a polynomial function. The following are examples of polynomial functions.

$f(x) = 2x - 7$ Linear   Degree 1
$f(x) = 4x^2 - 5x + 1$ Quadratic   Degree 2
$f(x) = 9x^3 + 6x$ Cubic   Degree 3

Example: $f(x) = 4x^3 - 2x^2 + 4$ represents a polynomial function of one variable.

$f(2) = 4(2)^3 - 2(2)^2 + 4 = 32 - 8 + 4 = 28$

Product of Two Polynomials   The product of two polynomials may be found by multiplying every term in the first polynomial by every term in the second polynomial.

Example: $(2x + 3)(3x - 4) = 6x^2 - 8x + 9x - 12 = 6x^2 + x - 12$

Special Products

Product of a Sum and Difference $(a + b)(a - b) = a^2 - b^2$

Example: $(x + 3)(x - 3) = x^2 - 9$

Square of a Binomial $(a + b)^2 = a^2 + 2ab + b^2$
$(a - b)^2 = a^2 - 2ab + b^2$

Examples: $(x + 3)^2 = x^2 + 6x + 9$
$(x - 3)^2 = x^2 - 6x + 9$

SECTION 5.3 ■ FACTORING POLYNOMIALS

Common Factors   When factoring a polynomial, start by factoring out the greatest common factor (GCF).

Examples: $8z^3 - 12z^2 + 16z = 4z(2z^2 - 3z + 4)$

$18x^2y^3 - 12x^3y^2 = 6x^2y^2(3y - 2x)$

Zero-Product Property   For all real numbers a and b, if $ab = 0$, then $a = 0$ or $b = 0$ (or both).

Example: $(x - 3)(x + 2) = 0$ implies that either $x - 3 = 0$ or $x + 2 = 0$.

Solving Polynomial Equations by Factoring   Obtain a zero on one side of the equation. Factor the other side of the equation and apply the zero-product property.

Example:

$$x^2 - 7x = 0$$

$$x(x - 7) = 0 \qquad \text{Factor out common factor.}$$

$$x = 0 \quad \text{or} \quad x = 7 \qquad \text{Zero-product property; solve.}$$

Factoring by Grouping   Grouping can be used to factor some polynomial expressions with four terms by applying the distributive and associative properties.

Example: $x^3 + x^2 + 5x + 5 = (x^3 + x^2) + (5x + 5) \qquad \text{Associative property}$

$$= x^2(x + 1) + 5(x + 1) \qquad \text{Distributive property}$$

$$= (x^2 + 5)(x + 1) \qquad \text{Distributive property}$$

SECTION 5.4 ■ FACTORING TRINOMIALS

Factoring $x^2 + bx + c$ Find integers m and n that satisfy $mn = c$ and $m + n = b$. Then $x^2 + bx + c = (x + m)(x + n)$.

Example: $x^2 + 3x + 2 = (x + 1)(x + 2) \quad m = 1, n = 2$

Factoring $ax^2 + bx + c$ Either grouping or FOIL (in reverse) can be used to factor $ax^2 + bx + c$. Trinomials can also be factored graphically or numerically.

Examples: *Grouping*   Find m and n so that $mn = ac = 30$ and $m + n = b = 17$.

$$6x^2 + 17x + 5 = (6x^2 + 2x) + (15x + 5) \qquad m = 2, n = 15$$

$$= 2x(3x + 1) + 5(3x + 1)$$

$$= (2x + 5)(3x + 1)$$

FOIL   Correctly factoring a trinomial requires checking the middle term.

$$2x^2 + 3x - 14 = (2x + 7)(x - 2)$$

It checks. $\qquad \dfrac{\begin{array}{r} 7x \\ -4x \end{array}}{3x}$

Graphically or Numerically   The x-intercepts on the graph of $f(x) = 2x^2 + x - 1$ are $x = 0.5$ and $x = -1$. The zeros of f are 0.5 and -1. Thus $f(x)$ can be factored as

$$2x^2 + x - 1 = 2(x - 0.5)(x + 1)$$

$$= (2x - 1)(x + 1).$$

SECTION 5.5 ▪ SPECIAL TYPES OF FACTORING

Difference of Two Squares $a^2 - b^2 = (a - b)(a + b)$

Example: $49x^2 - 36y^2 = (7x)^2 - (6y)^2 = (7x - 6y)(7x + 6y)$ $a = 7x, b = 6y$

Perfect Square Trinomials

$$a^2 + 2ab + b^2 = (a + b)^2 \quad \text{and} \quad a^2 - 2ab + b^2 = (a - b)^2$$

Examples: $x^2 + 2xy + y^2 = (x + y)^2$ and $9r^2 - 12r + 4 = (3r - 2)^2$

Sum and Difference of Two Cubes

$$a^3 + b^3 = (a + b)(a^2 - ab + b^2) \quad \text{and}$$
$$a^3 - b^3 = (a - b)(a^2 + ab + b^2)$$

Examples: $x^3 + y^3 = (x + y)(x^2 - xy + y^2)$ $\qquad a = x, b = y$
$\qquad\qquad\quad 8t^3 - 27r^6 = (2t - 3r^2)(4t^2 + 6tr^2 + 9r^4)$ $\qquad a = 2t, b = 3r^2$

SECTION 5.6 ▪ SUMMARY OF FACTORING

Factoring Polynomials   The following steps can be used as general guidelines for factoring a polynomial.

STEP 1: Factor out the greatest common factor, if possible.

STEP 2: **A.** If the polynomial has four terms, try factoring by grouping.

B. If the polynomial is a binomial, consider the difference of two squares, difference of two cubes, or sum of two cubes.

C. If the polynomial is a trinomial, check for a perfect square. Otherwise, apply FOIL or grouping, as described in Section 5.4.

STEP 3: Check to make sure that the polynomial is *completely* factored.

SECTION 5.7 ▪ POLYNOMIAL EQUATIONS

Solving Polynomial Equations   Follow the strategy presented in Putting It All Together for Section 5.7.

Example:

$$x^4 = 2x^2 + 8 \qquad \text{Given equation}$$
$$x^4 - 2x^2 - 8 = 0 \qquad \text{Subtract } 2x^2 + 8 \text{ from each side.}$$
$$(x^2 - 4)(x^2 + 2) = 0 \qquad \text{Factor trinomial.}$$
$$(x - 2)(x + 2)(x^2 + 2) = 0 \qquad \text{Difference of squares}$$
$$x = 2 \quad \text{or} \quad x = -2 \qquad \text{Zero-product property; solve.}$$

CHAPTER 5 REVIEW EXERCISES

SECTION 5.1

1. Give an example of a binomial and of a trinomial.

2. Write a monomial that represents the volume of 10 identical boxes x inches tall with square bases y inches on a side. What is the total volume of the boxes if $x = 5$ and $y = 8$?

Exercises 3–6: Identify the degree and coefficient.

3. $-4x^5$

4. y^3

5. $5xy^6$

6. $-9y^{10}$

Exercises 7–9: Combine like terms.

7. $5x - 4x + 10x$

8. $9x^3 - 5x^3 + x^2$

9. $6x^3y - 4x^3 + 8x^3y + 5x^3$

10. Evaluate $2x^3y^2 - 3y$ when $x = 2$ and $y = -1$.

Exercises 11 and 12: Identify the degree and leading coefficient of the polynomial.

11. $5x^2 - 3x + 5$

12. $x^3 - 5x + 5 + 2x^4$

Exercises 13–16: Combine the polynomials.

13. $(3x^2 - x + 7) + (5x^2 + 4x - 8)$

14. $(6z^3 + z) + (17z^3 - 4z^2)$

15. $(-4x^2 - 6x + 1) - (-3x^2 - 7x + 1)$

16. $(3x^3 - 5x + 7) - (8x^3 + x^2 - 2x + 1)$

Exercises 17 and 18: Evaluate $f(x)$ at the value of x.

17. $f(x) = 2x^2 - 3x + 2 \quad x = -1$

18. $f(x) = 1 - x - 4x^3 \quad x = 4$

19. Use the graph to evaluate $f(2)$.

20. If $f(x) = x^2 - 1$ and $g(x) = x - 3x^2$, then find $(f + g)(-2)$ and $(f - g)(x)$.

SECTION 5.2

Exercises 21 and 22: Multiply.

21. $5(3x - 4)$

22. $-2x(1 + x - 4x^2)$

Exercises 23–26: Multiply the monomials.

23. $x^3 \cdot x^5$

24. $-2x^3 \cdot 3x$

25. $(-7xy^7)(6xy)$

26. $(12xy^4)(5x^2y)$

Exercises 27–38: Multiply the expressions.

27. $(x + 4)(x + 5)$

28. $(x - 7)(x - 8)$

29. $(6x + 3)(2x - 9)$

30. $\left(y - \frac{1}{3}\right)\left(y + \frac{1}{3}\right)$

31. $4x^2(2x^2 - 3x - 1)$

32. $-x(4 + 5x - 7x^2)$

33. $(4x + y)(4x - y)$

34. $(x + 3)^2$

35. $(2y - 5)^2$

36. $(a - b)(a^2 + ab + b^2)$

37. $(5m - 2n^4)^2$

38. $\big((r - 1) + t\big)\big((r - 1) - t\big)$

SECTION 5.3

Exercises 39 and 40: Factor out the greatest common factor.

39. $25x^2 - 30x$

40. $12x^4 + 8x^3 - 16x^2$

Exercises 41–44: Use factoring to solve the equation.

41. $x^2 + 3x = 0$

42. $7x^4 = 28x^2$

43. $2t^2 - 3t + 1 = 0$

44. $4z(z - 3) + 4(z - 3) = 0$

Exercises 45–47: Use grouping to factor the polynomial.

45. $2x^3 + 2x^2 - 3x - 3$

46. $z^3 + z^2 + z + 1$

47. $ax - bx + ay - by$

48. If $f(x) = x + 1$ and $g(x) = x - 3$, find $(fg)(4)$ and $(fg)(x)$.

Exercises 49 and 50: Use the graph to do the following.

   (a) *Find the x-intercepts.*
   (b) *Solve the equation* $P(x) = 0$.
   (c) *Find the zeros of* $P(x)$.

49.

50.

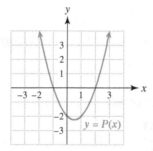

SECTION 5.4

Exercises 51–58: Factor completely.

51. $x^2 + 8x + 12$ **52.** $x^2 - 5x - 50$

53. $9x^2 + 25x - 6$ **54.** $4x^2 - 22x + 10$

55. $x^3 - 4x^2 + 3x$ **56.** $2x^4 + 14x^3 + 20x^2$

57. $5x^4 + 15x^3 - 90x^2$ **58.** $10x^3 - 90x^2 + 200x$

Exercises 59 and 60: Use the table to factor the expression. Check your answer by multiplying.

59. $x^2 - 2x - 15$

X	Y₁
-5	20
-3	0
-1	-12
1	-16
3	-12
5	0
7	20
Y₁■X^2−2X−15	

60. $x^2 - 24x + 143$

X	Y₁
9	8
10	3
11	0
12	-1
13	0
14	3
15	8
Y₁■X^2−24X+143	

61. Use the graph to factor $x^2 + 3x - 28$. Check your answer by multiplying.

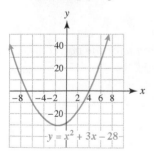

62. Use the graph to solve $x^2 - 21x + 104 = 0$. Check your solutions.

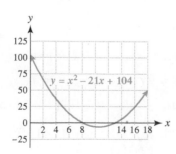

SECTION 5.5

Exercises 63–76: Factor completely.

63. $t^2 - 49$ **64.** $4y^2 - 9x^2$

65. $x^2 + 4x + 4$ **66.** $16x^2 - 8x + 1$

67. $x^3 - 27$ **68.** $64x^3 + 27y^3$

69. $10y^3 - 10y$ **70.** $4r^4 - t^6$

71. $m^4 - 16n^4$ **72.** $n^3 - 2n^2 - n + 2$

73. $25a^2 - 30ab + 9b^2$ **74.** $2r^3 - 12r^2t + 18rt^2$

75. $a^6 + 27b^3$ **76.** $8p^6 - q^3$

SECTION 5.6

Exercises 77–86: Factor completely.

77. $5x^3 - 10x^2$ **78.** $-2x^3 + 32x$

79. $x^4 - 16y^4$ **80.** $4x^3 + 8x^2 - 12x$

81. $-2x^3 + 11x^2 - 12x$ **82.** $x^4 - 8x^2 - 9$

83. $64a^3 + b^3$ **84.** $8 - y^3$

85. $(z + 3)^2 - 16$

86. $x^4 - 5x^3 - 4x^2 + 20x$

SECTION 5.7

Exercises 87 and 88: Solve the equation symbolically and graphically.

87. $x^2 - 16 = 0$ **88.** $x^2 - 2x - 3 = 0$

Exercises 89–98: Solve the equation.

89. $4x^2 - 28x + 49 = 0$

90. $x^2 + 8 = 0$

91. $3x^2 = 2x + 5$

92. $4x^2 + 5x = 6$

93. $x^3 = x$

94. $x^3 - 6x^2 + 11x = 6$

95. $x^3 + x^2 - 72x = 0$

96. $x^4 - 15x^3 + 56x^2 = 0$

97. $x^4 = 16$

98. $x^4 + 5x^2 = 36$

APPLICATIONS

99. *Profit from DVDs*   Suppose a band produces x music videos with cost C in dollars of $C(x) = 3x + 9000$. If they sell each DVD for $15, do the following.
 (a) Write a revenue function R that gives the amount the band makes for selling x compact discs.
 (b) If profit equals revenue minus cost, write a formula $P(x)$ for the profit function.
 (c) Evaluate $P(4000)$ and interpret the answer.

100. *Dimensions of a Box*   The length of a box is 5 inches more than its width, its width is 5 inches more than its height, and its volume is 168 cubic inches. Let x be the height.
 (a) Write an expression that gives the volume of the box in terms of x.
 (b) Write an equation whose solution gives the height of the rectangle.
 (c) Find the dimensions of the box.

101. *Picture Frame*   A rectangular frame surrounding a picture is made from boards that are 3 inches wide. The picture inside the frame is 2 inches wider than it is high. If the overall area of the picture and frame is 224 square inches, find the dimensions of the picture.

102. *Geometry*   Suppose that a triangle has base $x + 2$ and height $x - 3$. Find a polynomial that gives the area of the triangle.

103. *High Temperatures*   The formula

$$f(x) = -1.466x^2 + 20.25x + 9$$

models the monthly average high temperatures in degrees Fahrenheit at Columbus, Ohio. In this formula, let $x = 1$ be January, $x = 2$ be February, and so on.   (**Source:** J. Williams, *The Weather Almanac.*)
 (a) What is the average high temperature in May?
 (b) Make a table of $f(x)$, starting at $x = 1$ and incrementing by 1. During what month is the average temperature the greatest?
 (c) Graph f in $[1, 12, 1]$ by $[30, 90, 10]$ and interpret the graph.

104. *Probability*   Suppose that the likelihood, or chance, that a pitch in softball will be a strike is x percent. Then the likelihood, as a percentage, that two consecutive pitches will not be strikes is given by $100\left(1 - \frac{x}{100}\right)^2$.
 (a) Multiply this expression.

(b) Let $x = 70$. Use both the given expression and the expression you found in part (a) to obtain the likelihood that two consecutive pitches are not strikes.

105. *Numbers*   Write a polynomial that represents the product of three consecutive integers, where x corresponds to the largest integer.

106. *Area*   Use the area of a rectangle to illustrate that $(x + 2)(x + 7) = x^2 + 9x + 14$.

107. *Area*   Suppose that the area of a small building is 144 square feet and its length is 7 feet longer than its width. Find the dimensions of the building
 (a) graphically,
 (b) numerically, and
 (c) symbolically.

108. *Rectangular Pen*   A rectangular pen has a perimeter of 50 feet. If x represents its width, write a polynomial that gives the area of the pen in terms of x.

109. *Flight of a Golf Ball*   If a golf ball is hit upward with a velocity of 66 feet per second (45 mph), its height h in feet above the ground after t seconds can be modeled by

$$h(t) = -16t^2 + 66t.$$

 (a) Determine when the ball strikes the ground.
 (b) When is the height of the ball 50 feet?

110. *Ticket Prices*   If tickets are sold for $50, then 600 tickets are expected to be sold. For each $1 reduction in price, an additional 20 tickets will be sold.
 (a) Write an expression that gives the revenue from ticket sales when ticket prices are reduced by x dollars.
 (b) Determine the ticket price that results in sales of $32,000.

111. *Modeling a Hill*   The elevation E of a hill x feet along a highway can be modeled by

$$E(x) = -0.0001x^2 + 500,$$

where E is in feet. The crest of the hill corresponds to $x = 0$. Find values of x where E is 400 feet.

CHAPTER 5   TEST   Pass the Test   Video solutions to all test exercises

Exercises 1 and 2: Simplify by combining like terms.

1. $x^2y^2 - 4x + 9x - 5x^2y^2$

2. $(-2x^3 - 6x + 1) - (5x^3 - x^2 + x - 10)$

3. Evaluate $f(x) = 2x^3 - x^2 - 5x + 2$ at $x = -2$.

4. Use the graph to evaluate $f(2)$.

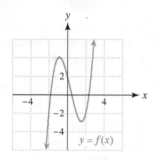

5. Give the degree and coefficient of $3x^3y$.

6. Write a monomial that gives the volume of 8 identical boxes with width x, length y, and height z.

7. Evaluate $-x^2y + 3xy^2$ when $x = -2$ and $y = 3$.

8. If $f(x) = 2x - 5$ and $g(x) = 1 - x^3$, then find $(f - g)(4)$ and $(f + g)(x)$.

Exercises 9–16: Multiply and simplify.

9. $-\frac{2}{5}x^2(10x - 5)$ **10.** $2xy^7 \cdot 7xy$

11. $(2x + 1)(5x - 7)$ **12.** $(5 - 3x)^2$

13. $(5x - 4y)(5x + 4y)$ **14.** $-2x^2(x^2 - 3x + 2)$

15. $(x - 2y)(x^2 + 2xy + 4y^2)$

16. $2x^2(x - 1)(x + 1)$

Exercises 17–25: Factor completely.

17. $x^2 - 3x - 10$ **18.** $2x^3 + 6x$

19. $3x^2 + 7x - 20$ **20.** $5x^4 - 5x^2$

21. $2x^3 + x^2 - 10x - 5$

22. $49x^2 - 14x + 1$ **23.** $x^3 + 8$

24. $4x^2y^4 + 8x^4y^2$ **25.** $a^2 - 3ab + 2b^2$

26. Identify the degree and leading coefficient of the polynomial $5 - 4x + x^3$.

27. Multiply $(2m^3 - 4n^2)^2$.

28. Use the graph to factor $x^2 + 2x - 48$.

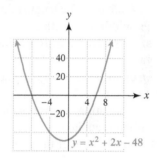

29. *Numbers* Write a polynomial that represents the product of two consecutive even integers, where x is the smaller integer.

Exercises 30–34: Use factoring to solve the polynomial equation.

30. $5x^2 = 15x$ **31.** $4t^2 + 19t - 5 = 0$

32. $2z^4 - 8z^2 = 0$ **33.** $x^4 - 2x^2 + 1 = 0$

34. $x(x - 3) + (x - 3) = 0$

35. *Area* A rectangular picture frame is 4 inches wider than it is high and has an area of 221 square inches.
 (a) Write an equation whose solution gives the height of the picture frame.
 (b) Solve the equation in part (a).
 (c) Find the perimeter of the picture frame.

36. *Dew Point* The formula

$$f(x) = -0.091x^3 + 0.66x^2 + 5.78x + 23.5$$

models the monthly average dew point in degrees Fahrenheit in Birmingham, Alabama. In this formula $x = 1$ corresponds to January, $x = 2$ to February, and so on. (**Source:** J. Williams, *The Weather Almanac.*)
 (a) What is the average dew point in May?
 (b) Use the graph of f at the top of the next page to discuss how the dew point changes during the year.

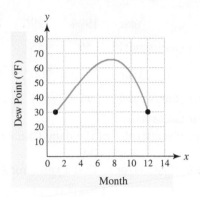

Month

37. *Geometry* Multiply $(x + 2)(x + 3)$ geometrically by drawing a rectangle.

38. *Height Reached by a Baseball* The height h in feet reached by a batted baseball after t seconds is given by

$$h(t) = -16t^2 + 96t + 3.$$

Determine when the baseball is 131 feet in the air.

CHAPTER 5 | EXTENDED AND DISCOVERY EXERCISES

INTERPRETING GRAPHS OF REAL-WORLD DATA

1. *Lynx and Hares* During the years from 1875 through 1905, the Hudson Bay Company in Canada logged trap records of both lynx and snowshoe hares. Line graphs representing these records are shown in the accompanying figures. (*Source:* C. S. Elton and M. Nicholson, "The ten year cycle in numbers of lynx in Canada.")

Year

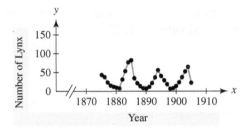

Year

(a) Describe how the numbers of lynx varied during this period.
(b) Describe how the numbers of snowshoe hares varied during this period.
(c) What is the relationship between these graphs? Explain your answer completely.

MODELING NONLINEAR DATA

Exercises 2–4: Real-world data often do not lie on a line when they are plotted. Such data are called nonlinear

data, and nonlinear functions are used to model this type of data. In the next three exercises you will be asked to find your own functions that model real-world data.

 2. *Planetary Orbits* Johannes Kepler (1571–1630) was the first person to find a formula that models the relationship between a planet's average distance from the sun and the time it takes to orbit the sun. The following table lists a planet's average distance x from the sun and the number of years y it takes to orbit the sun. In this table distances have been normalized so that Earth's distance is exactly 1. For example, Saturn is 9.54 times farther from the sun than Earth is and requires 29.5 years to orbit the sun.

Planet	x (distance)	y (period)
Mercury	0.387	0.241
Venus	0.723	0.615
Earth	1.00	1.00
Mars	1.52	1.88
Jupiter	5.20	11.9
Saturn	9.54	29.5

Source: C. Ronan, *The Natural History of the Universe.*

(a) Make a scatterplot of the data. Are the data linear or nonlinear?
(b) Kepler discovered a formula having the form $y = x^k$, which models the data in the table. Graph $y = x^{2.5}$ and the data in the same viewing rectangle. Does y model the data accurately? Explain.
(c) Try to discover a value for k so that $y = x^k$ models the data. (Continued on the next page)

(d) The average distances of Neptune and Pluto from the sun are 30.1 and 39.4, respectively. Estimate how long it takes for each of them to orbit the sun. Check a reference to see whether your answers are accurate.

3. *Women in the Work Force* The number of women gainfully employed in the work force has changed significantly since 1900. The table lists these numbers in millions at 10-year intervals.

Year	1900	1910	1920	1930	1940
Work Force	5.3	7.4	8.6	10.8	12.8

Year	1950	1960	1970	1980	1990
Work Force	18.4	23.2	31.5	45.5	56.6

Source: Department of Labor.

(a) Make a scatterplot of the data in [1890, 2000, 20] by [0, 60, 10]. Are the data linear or nonlinear? Explain your answer.
(b) Use trial and error to find a value for k so that $y = k(x - 1900)^2 + 5.3$ models the data.
(c) Use y to predict the number of women that will be in the work force in 2005.

4. *Aging of America* Americans are living longer. The table at the top of the next column shows the number of Americans expected to be more than 100 years old for various years.

Year	1994	1996	1998
Number (thousands)	50	56	65

Year	2000	2002	2004
Number (thousands)	75	94	110

Source: U.S. Census Bureau.

(a) Make a scatterplot of the data. Choose an appropriate viewing rectangle.
(b) Use trial and error to find a value for k so that
$$y = k(x - 1994)^2 + 50$$
models the data.
(c) Use y to predict the number of Americans that were more than 100 years old in 2006.

5. *Charitable Giving* Average charitable giving varies according to income. The average amount given for three different incomes is listed in the table.

Income	$10,000	$40,000	$100,000
Giving	$412	$843	$2550

Source: Gallup for Independent Sector (1999).

(a) Let x be income and y be charitable giving. Set up an augmented matrix whose solution gives values for a, b, and c so that the graph of $y = ax^2 + bx + c$ passes through the points (10000, 412), (40000, 843), and (100000, 2550).
(b) Use a graphing calculator to solve this system of linear equations.
(c) Estimate the average charitable giving for someone earning $20,000. Compare your answer to the actual value of $525.

CHAPTERS 1–5   CUMULATIVE REVIEW EXERCISES

1. Evaluate $A = \frac{1}{2}ab$ when $a = 5$ and $b = \frac{3}{2}$.

2. Find the reciprocal of $\frac{a}{b-a}$.

3. Simplify each expression. Write the result using positive exponents.
  (a) $\left(\frac{x^{-3}}{y}\right)^2$ **(b)** $\frac{(3r^{-1}t)^{-4}}{r^2(t^2)^{-2}}$ **(c)** $(ab^{-2})^4(ab^3)^{-1}$

4. Write 5.859×10^4 in standard (decimal) form.

5. Find $f(-3)$, if $f(x) = -2x^2 + 3x$.

6. Find the domain of $f(x) = \sqrt{x - 4}$.

Exercises 7 and 8: Graph f by hand.

7. $f(x) = 3 - 2x$ **8.** $f(x) = x^2 - x - 2$

9. Use the graph to answer the following.
  (a) Does the graph represent a function?
  (b) Identify the domain and range.

(c) Evaluate $f(1)$ and $f(2)$.
(d) Identify the x-intercepts.
(e) Solve the equation $f(x) = 0$.
(f) Write $f(x)$ completely factored, if $f(x)$ is quadratic with leading coefficient 1.

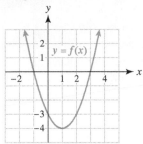

10. Find the slope–intercept form of the line that passes through $(-2, 5)$ and is parallel to $2x - y = 4$.

11. Let f be a linear function. Find a formula for $f(x)$.

x	-2	-1	1	2
$f(x)$	12	7	-3	-8

12. Solve $-2(5x - 1) = 1 - (5 - x)$.

13. Solve $3x + 4 \le x - 1$.

14. Solve $|5x - 10| > 5$.

15. Solve $-2 < 2 - 7x \le 2$.

16. Solve the system graphically or numerically.
$$4x + 2y = 10$$
$$-x + 5y = 3$$

17. Solve each system symbolically.
(a) $-x - 2y = 5$
    $2x + 4y = -10$
(b) $3x + 2y = 7$
    $2x - 2y = 3$

18. Shade the solution set in the xy-plane.
$$2x + y \le 4$$
$$x - 2y < -2$$

19. Solve the system.
$$x + y - z = -2$$
$$x - y + z = -6$$
$$x - y - 2z = 3$$

20. Use Gauss–Jordan elimination to solve the system.
$$x - y - z = -2$$
$$2x + y + z = 8$$
$$-x - y + 2z = 0$$

21. Calculate $\det \begin{bmatrix} 0 & 1 & -3 \\ 1 & 0 & -1 \\ 3 & 1 & 0 \end{bmatrix}$

22. Solve $x^2 + 4 = 0$, if possible.

Exercises 23–28: Multiply the expression.

23. $-2x(x^2 - 2x + 5)$ **24.** $(2a + b)(2a - b)$

25. $(x - 1)(x + 1)(x + 3)$ **26.** $(4x + 9)(2x - 1)$

27. $(x^2 + 3y^3)^2$ **28.** $-2x(1 - x^2)$

Exercises 29–34: Factor the expression.

29. $x^2 - 8x - 33$ **30.** $10x^3 + 65x^2 - 35x$

31. $4x^2 - 100$ **32.** $49x^2 - 70x + 25$

33. $r^4 - r$ **34.** $x^3 + 2x^2 + x + 2$

Exercises 35–38: Solve the equation.

35. $4x^2 - 1 = 0$ **36.** $3x^2 + 14x - 5 = 0$

37. $x^3 + 4x = 4x^2$ **38.** $x^4 = x^2$

Exercises 39 and 40: Solve each equation graphically or numerically to the nearest tenth.

39. $\sqrt{2}x - 1.1(x - \pi) = 1 - 2x$

40. $(\pi - 1)x^2 - \sqrt{3} = 5 - 1.3x$

APPLICATIONS

41. *Investment* Suppose $4000 are deposited in two accounts paying 6% and 7% annual interest. If the interest after 1 year is $257, how much is invested at each rate?

42. *Cost of Car* Suppose the cost C of an antique car from 1990 to 2005 is modeled by
$$C(x) = 750(x - 1990) + 6800.$$
(a) Evaluate $C(1995)$ and interpret the result.
(b) Interpret the slope of the graph of C.

43. *Geometry* A rectangular box with a square base has a volume of 1008 cubic inches. If its height is 5 inches less than the length of an edge of the base, find the dimensions of the box.

44. *Angles in a Triangle* The measure of the largest angle in a triangle is 20° less than the sum of the measures of the two smaller angles. The sum of the measures of the two larger angles is 100° greater than the measure of the smaller angle. Find the measure of each angle.

Rational Expressions and Functions

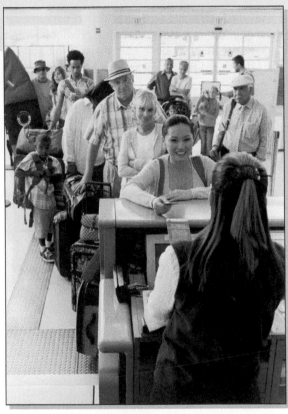

On average, a person spends an estimated 45 to 60 minutes waiting each day. This waiting could be at the doctor's office, at the grocery store, in airports, or stuck in traffic. In a 70-year life span, a person might spend as much as 3 years waiting!

Motorists in the nation's top 68 urban areas spend about 50 percent more time stuck in traffic than they did 10 years ago. Traffic congestion delays travelers 3.7 billion hours and wastes 2.3 billion gallons of fuel at a cost of $63 billion each year. Many urban areas are not adding enough capacity to keep traffic moving.

The time spent waiting in lines is subject to a *nonlinear effect*. For example, you can put more cars on the road up to a point. Then, if the traffic intensity increases even slightly, congestions and long lines increase dramatically. This phenomenon cannot be modeled by linear or polynomial functions. Instead we need a new function, called a rational function, to describe this type of behavior. (See Example 5 in Section 6.4.) Rational functions can also be used to describe railroad track design, gravity, population growth, electricity, and aerial photography.

The future belongs to those who believe in the beauty of their dreams.
—Eleanor Roosevelt

Sources: Phillip J. Longman, "American Gridlock," *U.S. News & World Report*, May 28, 2001; answers.google.com; CBS/AP, 2007.

6.1 INTRODUCTION TO RATIONAL FUNCTIONS AND EQUATIONS

Recognizing and Using Rational Functions ▪ Solving Rational Equations ▪ Operations on Functions

A LOOK INTO MATH ▷ Suppose that a parking lot attendant can wait on 5 cars per minute and that cars are randomly leaving the parking lot at a rate of 4 cars per minute. Is it possible to predict how long the average driver will wait in line? Using rational functions, we can answer this question (see Exercise 103). In this section we introduce rational functions and equations.

Recognizing and Using Rational Functions

In Chapter 5 we discussed polynomials. Examples of polynomials include

$$4, \quad x, \quad x^2, \quad 2x - 5, \quad 3x^2 - 6x + 1, \quad \text{and} \quad 3x^4 - 7.$$

Rational expressions result when a polynomial is divided by a nonzero polynomial. Three examples of rational expressions are

$$\frac{4}{x}, \quad \frac{x^2}{2x - 5}, \quad \text{and} \quad \frac{3x^2 - 6x + 1}{3x^4 - 7}.$$

EXAMPLE 1   Recognizing a rational expression

Determine whether each expression is rational.

(a) $\dfrac{4 - x}{5x^2 + 3}$ **(b)** $\dfrac{x^2 - 1}{\sqrt{x} + 2x}$ **(c)** $\dfrac{6}{x - 1}$

Solution
(a) This expression is rational because both $4 - x$ and $5x^2 + 3$ are polynomials.
(b) This expression is not rational because $\sqrt{x} + 2x$ is not a polynomial.
(c) This expression is rational because both 6 and $x - 1$ are polynomials.

Now Try Exercises 11,13

Rational expressions are used to define *rational functions*. For example, $\frac{4}{x + 1}$ is a rational expression and so $f(x) = \frac{4}{x + 1}$ represents a rational function.

RATIONAL FUNCTION

Let $p(x)$ and $q(x)$ be polynomials. Then a **rational function** is given by

$$f(x) = \frac{p(x)}{q(x)}.$$

The domain of f includes all x-values such that $q(x) \neq 0$.

EXAMPLE 2   Identifying the domain of rational functions

Identify the domain of each function.

(a) $f(x) = \dfrac{1}{x + 2}$ **(b)** $g(x) = \dfrac{2x}{x^2 - 3x + 2}$ **(c)** $h(t) = \dfrac{4}{t^3 - t}$

Solution
(a) The domain of f includes all x-values for which the expression $f(x) = \frac{1}{x+2}$ is defined. Thus we must *exclude* values of x for which the denominator equals 0.

$$x + 2 = 0 \qquad \text{Set denominator equal to 0.}$$
$$x = -2 \qquad \text{Subtract 2.}$$

In set-builder notation, $D = \{x \mid x \neq -2\}$.

(b) The domain of g includes all values of x except where the denominator equals 0.

$$x^2 - 3x + 2 = 0 \qquad \text{Set denominator equal to 0.}$$
$$(x - 1)(x - 2) = 0 \qquad \text{Factor.}$$
$$x = 1 \quad \text{or} \quad x = 2 \qquad \text{Zero-product property; solve.}$$

Thus $D = \{x \mid x \neq 1, x \neq 2\}$.

(c) The domain of h includes all values of t except where the denominator equals 0.

$$t^3 - t = 0 \qquad \text{Set denominator equal to 0.}$$
$$t(t^2 - 1) = 0 \qquad \text{Factor out } t.$$
$$t(t - 1)(t + 1) = 0 \qquad \text{Difference of squares}$$
$$t = 0 \quad \text{or} \quad t = 1 \quad \text{or} \quad t = -1 \qquad \text{Zero-product property; solve.}$$

Thus $D = \{t \mid t \neq 0, t \neq 1, t \neq -1\}$.

Now Try Exercises 19, 25, 27

Like other functions, rational functions have graphs. To graph a rational function by hand, we usually start by making a table of values, as demonstrated in the next example. Because the graphs of rational functions are typically nonlinear, it is a good idea to plot at least 3 points on each side of an x-value where the formula is undefined.

EXAMPLE 3   Graphing a rational function

Graph $f(x) = \frac{1}{x}$. State the domain of f.

Solution
Make a table of values for $f(x) = \frac{1}{x}$, as shown in Table 6.1. Notice that $x = 0$ is not in the domain of f, and a dash can be used to denote this undefined value. The domain of f is all real numbers such that $x \neq 0$. Start by picking three x-values on each side of 0.

TABLE 6.1

x	-2	-1	$-\frac{1}{2}$	0	$\frac{1}{2}$	1	2
$\frac{1}{x}$	$-\frac{1}{2}$	-1	-2	—	2	1	$\frac{1}{2}$

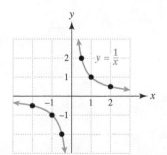

Figure 6.1

Plot the points shown in Table 6.1 and then connect the points with a smooth curve, as shown in Figure 6.1. Because $f(0)$ is undefined, the graph of $f(x) = \frac{1}{x}$ does not cross the line $x = 0$, the y-axis.

Now Try Exercise 29

In the next example we evaluate a rational function in three ways.

EXAMPLE 4   Evaluating a rational function

Use Table 6.2, the formula for $f(x)$, and Figure 6.2 to evaluate $f(-1), f(1)$, and $f(2)$.

(a) TABLE 6.2

x	$f(x)$
-3	$\frac{3}{2}$
-2	$\frac{4}{3}$
-1	1
0	0
1	—
2	4
3	3

(b) $f(x) = \dfrac{2x}{x - 1}$

(c)

Figure 6.2

Solution
(a) *Numerical Evaluation*   Table 6.2 shows that

$$f(-1) = 1, \quad f(1) \text{ is undefined}, \quad \text{and} \quad f(2) = 4.$$

(b) *Symbolic Evaluation*

$$f(-1) = \frac{2(-1)}{-1 - 1} = 1$$

$$f(1) = \frac{2(1)}{1 - 1} = \frac{2}{0}, \text{ which is undefined. Input 1 is not in the domain of } f.$$

$$f(2) = \frac{2(2)}{2 - 1} = 4$$

(c) *Graphical Evaluation*   To evaluate $f(-1)$ graphically, find $x = -1$ on the x-axis and move upward to the graph of f. The y-value is 1 at the point of intersection, so $f(-1) = 1$, as shown in Figure 6.3(a). In Figure 6.3(b) the vertical line $x = 1$ is called a *vertical asymptote*. Because the graph of f does not intersect this line, $f(1)$ is undefined. Figure 6.3(c) reveals that $f(2) = 4$.

(a)

(b)

(c)

Figure 6.3

Now Try Exercises 41, 47, 51

A **vertical asymptote** is a vertical line that typically occurs in (but is not part of) the graph of a rational function when the denominator of the rational expression is 0 but the numerator is *not* 0. The graph of a rational function *never* crosses a vertical asymptote. In Figure 6.1, the vertical asymptote is the *y*-axis or $x = 0$.

NOTE: In Figures 6.1 and 6.2 the *y*-values on the graph of *f* become very large (approach ∞) or become very small (approach $-\infty$) for *x*-values near the vertical asymptote. This characteristic is true in general for vertical asymptotes.

TECHNOLOGY NOTE: Asymptotes, Dot Mode, and Decimal Windows

When rational functions are graphed on graphing calculators, pseudo-asymptotes often occur because the calculator is simply connecting dots to draw a graph. The accompanying figures show the graph of $y = \frac{2}{x-2}$ in connected mode, dot mode, and with a *decimal*, or *friendly*, *window*. In dot mode, pixels in the calculator screen are not connected. With dot mode (and sometimes with a decimal window) pseudo-asymptotes do not appear. To learn more about these features consult your owner's manual.

CALCULATOR HELP

To set a calculator in dot mode or to set a decimal window, see the Appendix (page AP-10).

$[-6, 6, 1]$ by $[-4, 4, 1]$ $[-6, 6, 1]$ by $[-4, 4, 1]$ $[-4.7, 4.7, 1]$ by $[-3.1, 3.1, 1]$

Connected Mode   Dot Mode   Decimal Window

▶ REAL-WORLD CONNECTION   Applications involving rational functions are numerous. One instance is in the design of curves for train tracks, which we discuss in the next example.

EXAMPLE 5   Modeling a train track curve

When curves are designed for train tracks, sometimes the outer rail is elevated, or banked, so that a locomotive and its cars can safely negotiate the curve at a higher speed than if the tracks were level. Suppose that a circular curve with a radius of *r* feet is being designed for a train traveling 60 miles per hour. Then $f(r) = \frac{2540}{r}$ calculates the proper elevation *y* in inches for the outer rail, where $y = f(r)$. See Figure 6.4. (*Source:* L. Haefner, *Introduction to Transportation Systems.*)

(a) Evaluate $f(300)$ and interpret the result.
(b) A graph of *f* is shown in Figure 6.5. Discuss how the elevation of the outer rail changes as the radius *r* increases.

Figure 6.4

$f(r) = \frac{2540}{r}$

Elevation (inches)

Radius (feet)

Figure 6.5

Solution

(a) $f(300) = \frac{2540}{300} \approx 8.5$. Thus the outer rail on a curve with a radius of 300 feet should be elevated about 8.5 inches for a train to safely travel through it at 60 miles per hour.

(b) As the radius increases (and the curve becomes less sharp), the outer rail needs less elevation.   Now Try Exercise 99(a)

Solving Rational Equations

▶ REAL-WORLD CONNECTION   When working with rational functions, we commonly encounter rational equations. In Example 5, we used $f(r) = \frac{2540}{r}$ to calculate the elevation of the outer rail in a train track curve. Now suppose that the outer rail for a curve is elevated 6 inches. What should be the radius of the curve? To answer this question, we need to solve the **rational equation**

$$\frac{2540}{r} = 6.$$

We solve this equation in the next example.

EXAMPLE 6   Determining the proper radius for a train track curve

Solve the rational equation $\frac{2540}{r} = 6$ and interpret the result.

Solution
We begin by multiplying each side of the equation by r.

$$r \cdot \frac{2540}{r} = 6 \cdot r \qquad \text{Multiply by } r.$$
$$2540 = 6r \qquad \text{Simplify.}$$
$$\frac{2540}{6} = r \qquad \text{Divide by 6.}$$
$$r = 423.\overline{3} \qquad \text{Rewrite.}$$

A train track curve designed for 60 miles per hour and banked 6 inches should have a radius of about 423 feet.   Now Try Exercise 99(d)

Multiplication is often used as a first step when solving rational equations. To do so we apply the following property of rational expressions, with $D \neq 0$.

$$D \cdot \frac{C}{D} = C$$

Examples of this property include

$$5 \cdot \frac{7}{5} = 7 \quad \text{and} \quad (x - 1) \cdot \frac{4x}{x - 1} = 4x.$$

EXAMPLE 7   Solving rational equations

Solve each rational equation and check your answer.

(a) $\dfrac{3x}{2x - 1} = 3$ (b) $\dfrac{x + 1}{x - 2} = \dfrac{3}{x - 2}$ (c) $\dfrac{6}{x + 1} = x$

Solution

(a) First note that $\frac{1}{2}$ cannot be a solution to this equation because $x = \frac{1}{2}$ results in the left side of the equation being undefined; division by 0 is not possible. Multiply each side of the equation by the denominator, $2x - 1$.

$$(2x - 1) \cdot \frac{3x}{2x - 1} = 3 \cdot (2x - 1) \qquad \text{Multiply by } (2x - 1).$$

$$3x = 6x - 3 \qquad \text{Simplify.}$$

$$-3x = -3 \qquad \text{Subtract } 6x.$$

$$x = 1 \qquad \text{Divide by } -3.$$

To check your answer substitute 1 in the given equation for x.

$$\frac{3(1)}{2(1) - 1} = 3 \qquad \text{The answer checks.}$$

(b) Each side of the equation is undefined when $x = 2$. Thus 2 cannot be a solution. Begin by multiplying each side of the equation by the denominator, $x - 2$.

$$(x - 2) \cdot \frac{x + 1}{x - 2} = \frac{3}{x - 2} \cdot (x - 2) \qquad \text{Multiply by } x - 2.$$

$$x + 1 = 3 \qquad \text{Simplify.}$$

$$x = 2 \qquad \text{Subtract } 1.$$

In this case 2 is not a valid solution. There are no solutions. Instead, 2 is called an **extraneous solution**, which cannot be used. It is *important* to check your answers.

(c) The left side of the equation is undefined when $x = -1$. Thus -1 cannot be a solution. To solve this equation start by multiplying each side by the denominator, $x + 1$.

$$(x + 1) \cdot \frac{6}{x + 1} = x \cdot (x + 1) \qquad \text{Multiply by } x + 1.$$

$$6 = x^2 + x \qquad \text{Simplify.}$$

$$x^2 + x - 6 = 0 \qquad \text{Rewrite the equation.}$$

$$(x + 3)(x - 2) = 0 \qquad \text{Factor.}$$

$$x = -3 \quad \text{or} \quad x = 2 \qquad \text{Zero-product property}$$

Checking these results confirms that both -3 and 2 are solutions.

Now Try Exercises 55, 63, 67

▶ **REAL-WORLD CONNECTION**   The *grade x* of a hill is a measure of its steepness and corresponds to the slope of the road. For example, if a road rises 10 feet for every 100 feet of horizontal distance, it has an uphill grade of $x = \frac{10}{100}$, or 10%, as illustrated in Figure 6.6. The braking distance D in feet for a car traveling 60 miles per hour on a wet, uphill grade is given by

$$D(x) = \frac{3600}{30x + 9}.$$

In the next example we use this formula to determine the grade associated with a given braking distance.   (**Source:** N. Garber and L. Hoel, *Traffic and Highway Engineering*.)

‡10 feet

100 feet

Figure 6.6

EXAMPLE 8

Solving a rational equation

The braking distance for a car traveling at 60 miles per hour on a wet, uphill grade is 250 feet. Use the formula $D(x) = \frac{3600}{30x + 9}$ to find the grade of the hill

(a) symbolically,   **(b)** graphically, and   **(c)** numerically.

Solution

(a) Symbolic Solution   To solve the equation $\frac{3600}{30x + 9} = 250$ symbolically, we begin by multiplying each side by the denominator, $30x + 9$.

$$(30x + 9) \cdot \frac{3600}{30x + 9} = 250 \cdot (30x + 9) \qquad \text{Multiply by } (30x + 9).$$

$$3600 = 250(30x + 9) \qquad \text{Simplify.}$$

$$3600 = 7500x + 2250 \qquad \text{Distributive property}$$

$$1350 = 7500x \qquad \text{Subtract 2250.}$$

$$x = \frac{1350}{7500} \qquad \text{Divide by 7500; rewrite.}$$

$$x = 0.18 \qquad \text{Write } x \text{ in decimal form.}$$

Thus the grade is 0.18, or 18%.

(b) Graphical Solution   To solve this equation graphically, we let $Y_1 = 3600/(30X + 9)$ and $Y_2 = 250$. Their graphs intersect at $(0.18, 250)$, as shown in Figure 6.7(a).

[0, 0.3, 0.1] by [0, 500, 100]

CALCULATOR HELP

To find a point of intersection, see the Appendix (page AP-7).

Intersection
X=.18   Y=250

(a)

(b)

Figure 6.7

(c) Numerical Solution   Figure 6.7(b) indicates that $y_1 = 250$ when $x = 0.18$.

Now Try Exercise 101

MAKING CONNECTIONS

Symbolic, Numerical, and Graphical Solutions to a Rational Equation

Symbolic Solution

$$\frac{x + 3}{2x} = 2$$

$$2x \cdot \frac{x + 3}{2x} = 2 \cdot 2x$$

$$x + 3 = 4x$$

$$3 = 3x$$

$$x = 1$$

The solution is **1**.

Numerical Solution

x	$(x + 3)/(2x)$
-2	-0.25
-1	-1
0	—
1	**2**
2	1.25

When $x = 1$, $\frac{x + 3}{2x} = 2$.

Graphical Solution

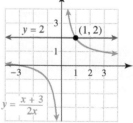

The graphs intersect at $(\mathbf{1}, 2)$.

Graphing calculators are helpful for making tables or graphs of rational functions.

Operations on Functions

We have performed addition, subtraction, multiplication, and division on numbers and variables. In Chapter 5, we performed addition, subtraction, and multiplication on functions. In this subsection we will review these operations and also perform division on functions.

OPERATIONS ON FUNCTIONS

If $f(x)$ and $g(x)$ are both defined, then the sum, difference, product, and quotient of two functions f and g are defined by

$$(f + g)(x) = f(x) + g(x) \qquad \text{Sum}$$
$$(f - g)(x) = f(x) - g(x) \qquad \text{Difference}$$
$$(fg)(x) = f(x) \cdot g(x) \qquad \text{Product}$$
$$\left(\frac{f}{g}\right)(x) = \frac{f(x)}{g(x)}, \text{ where } g(x) \neq 0. \qquad \text{Quotient}$$

EXAMPLE 9 Performing arithmetic on functions

Use $f(x) = x^2$ and $g(x) = 2x - 4$ to evaluate each of the following.

(a) $(f + g)(3)$ **(b)** $(fg)(-1)$ **(c)** $\left(\dfrac{f}{g}\right)(0)$ **(d)** $(f/g)(2)$

Solution

(a) $(f + g)(3) = f(3) + g(3) = 3^2 + (2 \cdot 3 - 4) = 9 + 2 = 11$

(b) $(fg)(-1) = f(-1) \cdot g(-1) = (-1)^2 \cdot (2 \cdot (-1) - 4) = 1 \cdot (-6) = -6$

(c) $\left(\dfrac{f}{g}\right)(0) = \dfrac{f(0)}{g(0)} = \dfrac{0^2}{2 \cdot 0 - 4} = \dfrac{0}{-4} = 0$

(d) Note that $(f/g)(2)$ is equivalent to $\left(\dfrac{f}{g}\right)(2)$.

$$(f/g)(2) = \frac{f(2)}{g(2)} = \frac{2^2}{2 \cdot 2 - 4} = \frac{4}{0},$$

which is not possible. Thus $(f/g)(2)$ is undefined.   Now Try Exercise **87**

In the next example, we find the sum, difference, product, and quotient of two functions for a general x.

EXAMPLE 10 Performing arithmetic on functions

Use $f(x) = 4x - 5$ and $g(x) = 3x + 1$ to evaluate each of the following.

(a) $(f + g)(x)$ **(b)** $(f - g)(x)$ **(c)** $(fg)(x)$ **(d)** $\left(\dfrac{f}{g}\right)(x)$

Solution

(a) $(f + g)(x) = f(x) + g(x) = (4x - 5) + (3x + 1) = 7x - 4$

(b) $(f - g)(x) = f(x) - g(x) = (4x - 5) - (3x + 1) = x - 6$

(c) $(fg)(x) = f(x) \cdot g(x) = (4x - 5)(3x + 1) = 12x^2 - 11x - 5$

(d) $\left(\dfrac{f}{g}\right)(x) = \dfrac{f(x)}{g(x)} = \dfrac{4x - 5}{3x + 1}$

Now Try Exercise **91**

6.1 PUTTING IT ALL TOGETHER

The following table summarizes basic concepts about rational functions and equations.

Term	Explanation	Example
Rational Function	Let $p(x)$ and $q(x)$ be polynomials with $q(x) \neq 0$. Then a *rational function* is given by $$f(x) = \frac{p(x)}{q(x)}.$$	$$f(x) = \frac{3x}{x + 2}$$ The domain of f includes all real numbers except $x = -2$. A vertical asymptote occurs at $x = -2$ in the graph of f.
Rational Equation	An equation that contains rational expressions is a *rational equation*. When you are solving a rational equation, multiplication is often a good first step. *Be sure to check your results.*	To solve $\frac{3x}{x + 1} = 6$ begin by multiplying each side by $x + 1$. $$(x + 1) \cdot \frac{3x}{x + 1} = 6 \cdot (x + 1)$$ $$3x = 6x + 6$$ $$-3x = 6$$ $$x = -2$$
Division of Functions	$$(f/g)(x) = \frac{f(x)}{g(x)}, \ g(x) \neq 0$$	If $f(x) = x^2$ and $g(x) = x + 1$, then $(f/g)(x) = \dfrac{x^2}{x + 1}$.

6.1 Exercises

CONCEPTS

1. What is a rational expression? Give an example.

2. If $f(x) = \frac{6}{x - 4}$, for what input x is $f(x)$ undefined?

3. What would be a good first step in solving the rational equation $\frac{3}{x + 7} = x$?

4. Is 5 a solution to the equation $\frac{x + 5}{x - 5} = \frac{10}{x - 5}$? Explain.

5. Does $x \cdot \frac{5 + x}{x}$ simplify to $5x$? Explain.

6. If $x \neq 3$, then $\frac{x - 3}{x - 3} = $ _____.

7. If $b \neq 0$, then $b \cdot \dfrac{a}{b} = $ _____

8. The domain of $f(x) = \dfrac{p(x)}{q(x)}$ includes all x-values such that $q(x) \neq$ _____.

Exercises 9–14: Determine if the expression is rational.

9. $\dfrac{2}{x}$

10. $\dfrac{5 - 2x}{x^2}$

11. $\dfrac{3x - 5}{2x + 1}$

12. $|x| + \dfrac{4}{|x|}$

13. $\dfrac{\sqrt{x}}{x^2 - 1}$

14. $\dfrac{4x^2 - 3x + 1}{x^3 - 4x}$

RATIONAL FUNCTIONS

Exercises 15–18: Write a symbolic representation (or formula) for the rational function f described.

15. Divide x by the quantity x plus 1.

16. Add 2 to x and then divide the result by the quantity x plus 5.

17. Divide x squared by the quantity x minus 2.

18. Compute the reciprocal of twice x.

Exercises 19–28: Identify the domain of f. Write your answer in set-builder notation.

19. $f(x) = \dfrac{x + 1}{x + 2}$

20. $f(x) = \dfrac{2x}{x - 4}$

21. $f(x) = \dfrac{1 - x}{3x - 1}$

22. $f(x) = \dfrac{x}{5x + 4}$

23. $f(t) = \dfrac{2}{t^2 - 4}$

24. $f(t) = \dfrac{5t}{9 - t^2}$

25. $f(x) = \dfrac{x^2 + 1}{x^2 - 3x + 2}$

26. $f(x) = \dfrac{2x^2 + x + 5}{2x^2 - x - 15}$

27. $f(x) = \dfrac{5}{x^3 - 4x}$

28. $f(x) = \dfrac{x^2 + 4}{9x - x^3}$

Exercises 29–40: Graph $y = f(x)$. Be sure to include any vertical asymptotes as dashed lines. State the domain of f in set-builder notation.

29. $f(x) = \dfrac{1}{x - 1}$

30. $f(x) = \dfrac{1}{x + 3}$

31. $f(x) = \dfrac{1}{2x}$

32. $f(x) = \dfrac{2}{x}$

33. $f(x) = \dfrac{1}{x + 2}$

34. $f(x) = \dfrac{1}{x - 2}$

35. $f(x) = \dfrac{4}{x^2 + 1}$

36. $f(x) = \dfrac{6}{x^2 + 2}$

37. $f(x) = \dfrac{3}{2x - 3}$

38. $f(x) = \dfrac{1}{3x + 2}$

39. $f(x) = \dfrac{1}{x^2 - 1}$

40. $f(x) = \dfrac{4}{4 - x^2}$

Exercises 41–46: Evaluate $f(x)$ at the given value of x.

41. $f(x) = \dfrac{1}{x - 1}$ $x = -2$

42. $f(x) = \dfrac{3x}{x^2 - 1}$ $x = 2$

43. $f(x) = \dfrac{x + 1}{x - 1}$ $x = -3$

44. $f(x) = \dfrac{2x + 1}{3x - 1}$ $x = 0$

45. $f(x) = \dfrac{x^2 - 3x + 5}{x^2 + 1}$ $x = -2$

46. $f(x) = \dfrac{5}{x^2 - x}$ $x = -1$

Exercises 47–50: Use the graph to evaluate each expression. Give the equation of any vertical asymptotes.

47. $f(-3)$ and $f(1)$

48. $f(-3)$ and $f(2)$

49. $f(-1)$ and $f(2)$ **50.** $f(-1)$ and $f(1)$

          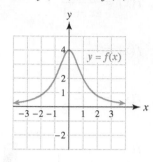

Exercises 51 and 52: Complete the table. Then evaluate $f(1)$.

51.

x	-2	-1	0	1	2
$f(x) = \dfrac{1}{x-1}$					

52.

x	-2	-1	0	1	2
$f(x) = \dfrac{2x}{x+2}$					

RATIONAL EQUATIONS

Exercises 53–72: Solve. Check your result.

53. $\dfrac{3}{x} = 5$ **54.** $\dfrac{5}{x} = 7$

55. $\dfrac{1}{x-2} = -1$ **56.** $\dfrac{-5}{x+4} = -5$

57. $\dfrac{x}{x+1} = 2$ **58.** $\dfrac{3x}{x+3} = -6$

59. $\dfrac{2x+1}{3x-2} = 1$ **60.** $\dfrac{x+3}{4x+1} = \dfrac{3}{5}$

61. $\dfrac{3}{x+2} = x$ **62.** $\dfrac{6}{2x+1} = x$

63. $\dfrac{6}{x+1} = 3x$ **64.** $\dfrac{4}{x-3} = x$

65. $\dfrac{1}{x^2-1} = -1$ **66.** $\dfrac{5x}{x^2-5} = \dfrac{x+2}{x^2-5}$

67. $\dfrac{x}{x-5} = \dfrac{2x-5}{x-5}$ **68.** $\dfrac{x}{x+1} = \dfrac{2x+1}{x+1}$

69. $\dfrac{4x}{x+2} = \dfrac{-8}{2x+4}$ **70.** $\dfrac{6x}{3x-2} = \dfrac{4}{4-6x}$

71. $\dfrac{2x}{x+2} = \dfrac{x-4}{x+2}$ **72.** $\dfrac{x+3}{x+1} = \dfrac{3x+4}{x+1}$

Exercises 73–78: Solve the rational equation either graphically or numerically. Check your answer.

73. $\dfrac{4+x}{2x} = -0.5$ **74.** $\dfrac{2x-1}{x-5} = -\dfrac{5}{2}$

75. $\dfrac{2x}{x^2-4} = -\dfrac{2}{3}$ **76.** $\dfrac{x-1}{x+2} = x$

77. $\dfrac{1}{x-1} = x-1$ **78.** $\dfrac{2}{x+2} = x+1$

USING MORE THAN ONE METHOD

Exercises 79–82: Solve the equation (a) symbolically, (b) graphically, and (c) numerically.

79. $\dfrac{1}{x+2} = 1$ **80.** $\dfrac{3}{x-1} = 2$

81. $\dfrac{x}{2x+1} = \dfrac{2}{5}$ **82.** $\dfrac{4x-2}{x+1} = \dfrac{3}{2}$

Exercises 83 and 84: Solve to the nearest hundredth.

83. $\dfrac{x^3}{x-1} = \dfrac{-1}{x+1}$ **84.** $\dfrac{x^2-1}{2x^2} = \dfrac{x+2}{1-x}$

85. Thinking Generally   If $a = \frac{x}{b}$, then $x = $ _____.

86. Thinking Generally   If $\frac{a}{b} = \frac{c}{d}$, then $ad = $ _____.

OPERATIONS ON FUNCTIONS

Exercises 87–90: Use $f(x)$ and $g(x)$ to evaluate each of the following.
(a) $(f+g)(3)$ (b) $(f-g)(-2)$
(c) $(fg)(5)$ (d) $(f/g)(0)$

87. $f(x) = 5x, g(x) = x+1$

88. $f(x) = x^2+2, g(x) = -2x$

89. $f(x) = 2x-1, g(x) = 4x^2$

90. $f(x) = x^2-1, g(x) = x+2$

Exercises 91–94: Use $f(x)$ and $g(x)$ to find each of the following.
(a) $(f+g)(x)$ (b) $(f-g)(x)$
(c) $(fg)(x)$ (d) $(f/g)(x)$

91. $f(x) = x+1, g(x) = x+2$

92. $f(x) = -3x, g(x) = x-1$

93. $f(x) = 1-x, g(x) = x^2$

94. $f(x) = x^2+4, g(x) = 6x$

APPLICATIONS

Exercises 95–98: Graphical Interpretation   Match the physical situation with the graph of the rational function that models it best.

95. A population of fish that increases and then levels off

96. An insect population that dies out

97. The length of a ticket line as the rate at which people arrive in line increases

98. The wind speed during a day that is initially calm, becomes windy, and then is calm again

99. *Train Track Curves*   (Refer to Example 5.) Let $f(r) = \frac{2540}{r}$ compute the elevation of the outer rail in inches for a curve designed for 60 miles per hour with a radius of r feet.   (*Source:* L. Haefner.)
(a) Evaluate $f(400)$ and interpret the result.
(b) Construct a table of f, starting at $r = 100$ and incrementing by 50.
(c) From the table, if the radius of the curve doubles, what happens to the elevation of the outer rail?
(d) If the outer rail is elevated 5 inches, what should be the radius of the curve?

100. *Highway Curves*   Engineers need to calculate a minimum safe radius for highway curves. To make a sharp curve safer, the road can be banked, or elevated, as illustrated in the figure. If a curve is designed for a speed of 40 miles per hour and is banked with slope m, then a minimum radius R is computed by

$$R(m) = \frac{1600}{15m + 2}.$$

(*Source:* N. Garber.)

(a) Evaluate $R(0.1)$ and interpret the result.
(b) A graph of R is shown in the figure. Describe what happens to the radius of the curve as the slope of the banking increases.

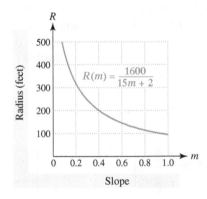

(c) If the curve has a radius of 320 feet, what is m?

101. *Uphill Highway Grade*   (Refer to Example 8.) The braking distance for a car traveling 30 miles per hour on a wet *uphill* grade x is given by

$$D(x) = \frac{900}{10.5 + 30x}.$$

(*Source:* N. Garber.)
(a) Evaluate $D(0.05)$ and interpret the result.
(b) If the braking distance for this car is 60 feet, find the uphill grade x.

102. *Downhill Highway Grade*   (See Exercise 101.) The braking distance for a car traveling 30 miles per hour on a wet, *downhill* grade x is given by

$$S(x) = \frac{900}{10.5 - 30x}.$$

(a) Evaluate $S(0.05)$ and interpret the result.

(b) Construct a table for $D(x)$ from Exercise 101 and $S(x)$, starting at $x = 0$ and incrementing by 0.05.

(c) How do the braking distances for uphill and downhill grades compare? Does this result agree with your driving experience?

103. *Time Spent in Line*   If a parking lot attendant can wait on 5 vehicles per minute and vehicles are leaving the lot randomly at an average rate of x vehicles per minute, then the average time T in minutes spent waiting in line *and* paying the attendant is given by

$$T(x) = \frac{1}{5 - x},$$

where $x < 5$.   **(Source:** N. Garber.)

(a) Evaluate $T(4)$ and interpret the result.

(b) A graph of T is shown in the figure. Interpret the graph as x increases from 0 to 5. Does this result agree with your intuition?

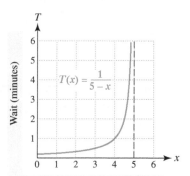

Traffic Rate (vehicles per minute)

(c) Find x if the waiting time is 3 minutes.

104. *People Waiting in Line*   At a post office, workers can wait on 50 people per hour. If people arrive randomly at an average rate of x per hour, then the average number of people N waiting in line is given by

$$N(x) = \frac{x^2}{2500 - 50x},$$

where $x < 50$.   **(Source:** N. Garber.)

(a) Evaluate $N(30)$ and interpret the result.

(b) A graph of N is shown in the figure. Interpret the graph as x increases from 0 to 50. Does this result agree with your intuition?

(c) Find x if $N = 8$.

105. *Probability*   A jar contains x balls. Each ball has a unique number written on it and only one ball has the winning number. The likelihood, or probability P, of *not* drawing the winning ball is given by

$$P(x) = \frac{x - 1}{x},$$

where $x > 0$. For example, if $P = 0.99$, then there is a 99% chance of not drawing the winning ball.

(a) Evaluate $P(1)$ and $P(50)$ and interpret the result.

(b) Graph P in $[0, 100, 10]$ by $[0, 1, 0.1]$.

(c) What happens to the probability of not winning as the number of balls increases? Does this result agree with your intuition? Explain.

(d) How many balls are in the jar if the probability of not winning is 0.975?

106. *Insect Population*   Suppose that an insect population in thousands per acre is modeled by

$$P(x) = \frac{5x + 2}{x + 1},$$

where $x \geq 0$ is time in months.

(a) Evaluate $P(10)$ and interpret the result.

(b) Graph P in $[0, 50, 10]$ by $[0, 6, 1]$.

(c) What happens to the insect population after several years?

(d) After how many months is the insect population 4.8 thousand per acre?

WRITING ABOUT MATHEMATICS

107. Is every polynomial function a rational function? Explain your answer.

108. The domain of a polynomial function includes all real numbers. Does the domain of a rational function include all real numbers? Explain your answer and give an example.

GROUP ACTIVITY
WORKING WITH REAL DATA

Directions: Form a group of 2 to 4 people. Select someone to record the group's responses for this activity. All members of the group should work cooperatively to answer the questions. If your instructor asks for your results, each member of the group should be prepared to respond.

Slippery Roads If a car is moving on a level highway, its stopping distance depends on road conditions. If the road is slippery, stopping may take longer. A measure of the slipperiness of a road is the coefficient of friction x between the tire and the road, where x satisfies $0 < x \le 1$. A smaller value for x indicates that the road is slipperier. The stopping distance D in feet for a car traveling at 50 miles per hour on a road with a coefficient of friction x is given by

$$D(x) = \frac{250}{3x}.$$

 (a) Graph D. Identify any vertical asymptotes.

(b) What happens to the stopping distance as x increases to 1? Explain.

(c) What happens to the stopping distance as x decreases to 0? Explain.

(d) In reality, could $x = 0$? Explain. What would happen if a road could have $x = 0$ and a car tried to stop?

6.2 MULTIPLICATION AND DIVISION OF RATIONAL EXPRESSIONS

Simplifying Rational Expressions ■ Review of Multiplication and Division of Fractions ■ Multiplication of Rational Expressions ■ Division of Rational Expressions

A LOOK INTO MATH ▷ In previous chapters we demonstrated how to add, subtract, and multiply polynomials. In this section we show you how to multiply and divide rational expressions, and in the next section we discuss addition and subtraction of rational expressions. We start this section by discussing how to simplify rational expressions.

Simplifying Rational Expressions

When simplifying fractions, we often use the **basic principle of fractions**, which states that

$$\frac{a \cdot c}{b \cdot c} = \frac{a}{b}.$$

This principle holds because $\frac{c}{c} = 1$ and $\frac{a}{b} \cdot 1 = \frac{a}{b}$. That is,

$$\frac{a \cdot c}{b \cdot c} = \frac{a}{b} \cdot \frac{c}{c} = \frac{a}{b} \cdot 1 = \frac{a}{b}.$$

For example, this principle can be used to simplify a fraction.

$$\frac{6}{44} = \frac{3 \cdot 2}{22 \cdot 2} = \frac{3}{22}$$

This same principle can also be used to simplify rational expressions. For example,

$$\frac{(z + 1)(z + 3)}{z(z + 3)} = \frac{z + 1}{z}, \quad \text{provided } z \ne -3.$$

SIMPLIFYING RATIONAL EXPRESSIONS

The following principle can be used to simplify rational expressions, where A, B, and C are polynomials.

$$\frac{A \cdot C}{B \cdot C} = \frac{A}{B} \qquad B \text{ and } C \text{ not zero}$$

To *simplify* a rational expression, we *completely factor* the numerator and the denominator and then apply the principle for simplifying rational expressions. These concepts are illustrated in the next example.

EXAMPLE 1   Simplifying rational expressions

Simplify each expression.

(a) $\dfrac{9x}{3x^2}$ **(b)** $\dfrac{5y - 10}{10y - 20}$ **(c)** $\dfrac{2z^2 - 3z - 9}{z^2 + 2z - 15}$ **(d)** $\dfrac{a^2 - b^2}{a + b}$

Solution

(a) First factor out the greatest common factor, $3x$, in the numerator and denominator.

$$\frac{9x}{3x^2} = \frac{3 \cdot 3x}{x \cdot 3x} = \frac{3}{x}$$

(b) Use the distributive property and then apply the basic principle of fractions.

$$\frac{5y - 10}{10y - 20} = \frac{5(y - 2)}{10(y - 2)} = \frac{5}{10} = \frac{1}{2}$$

(c) Start by factoring the numerator and denominator.

$$\frac{2z^2 - 3z - 9}{z^2 + 2z - 15} = \frac{(2z + 3)(z - 3)}{(z + 5)(z - 3)} = \frac{2z + 3}{z + 5}$$

(d) Start by factoring the numerator as the difference of squares.

$$\frac{a^2 - b^2}{a + b} = \frac{(a - b)(a + b)}{a + b} = a - b$$

Now Try Exercises   21, 23, 37, 41

There are a number of ways that a negative sign can be placed in a fraction. For example,

$$-\frac{2}{3} = \frac{-2}{3} = \frac{2}{-3}$$

illustrates three fractions that are equal. This property can also be applied to rational expressions, as demonstrated in the next example.

EXAMPLE 2   Distributing a negative sign

Simplify each expression.

(a) $-\dfrac{1 - z}{z - 1}$ **(b)** $\dfrac{-y - 2}{4y + 8}$ **(c)** $\dfrac{5 - x}{x - 5}$

Solution

(a) Start by distributing the negative sign over the numerator.

$$-\frac{1-z}{z-1} = \frac{-(1-z)}{z-1} = \frac{-1+z}{z-1} = \frac{z-1}{z-1} = 1$$

Note that the negative sign could also be distributed over the denominator.

(b) Factor -1 out of the numerator and 4 out of the denominator.

$$\frac{-y-2}{4y+8} = \frac{-1(y+2)}{4(y+2)} = -\frac{1}{4}$$

(c) Start by factoring -1 out of the numerator.

$$\frac{5-x}{x-5} = \frac{-1(-5+x)}{x-5} = \frac{-1(x-5)}{x-5} = -1$$

Now Try Exercises 45, 47, 49

MAKING CONNECTIONS

Negative Signs and Rational Expressions

In general, $(b-a)$ equals $-1(a-b)$. As a result, if $a \neq b$, then

$$\frac{b-a}{a-b} = -1.$$

See Example 2(c).

Review of Multiplication and Division of Fractions

Recall that to multiply two fractions we use the property

$$\frac{a}{b} \cdot \frac{c}{d} = \frac{ac}{bd}.$$

For example, $\frac{2}{5} \cdot \frac{3}{7} = \frac{2 \cdot 3}{5 \cdot 7} = \frac{6}{35}$.

EXAMPLE 3 Multiplying fractions

Multiply and simplify the product.

(a) $\dfrac{4}{9} \cdot \dfrac{3}{8}$ **(b)** $\dfrac{2}{3} \cdot \dfrac{3}{4} \cdot \dfrac{5}{6}$

Solution

(a) $\dfrac{4}{9} \cdot \dfrac{3}{8} = \dfrac{4 \cdot 3}{9 \cdot 8} = \dfrac{12}{72} = \dfrac{1 \cdot 12}{6 \cdot 12} = \dfrac{1}{6}$ **(b)** $\dfrac{2}{3} \cdot \dfrac{3}{4} \cdot \dfrac{5}{6} = \dfrac{6 \cdot 5}{12 \cdot 6} = \dfrac{5}{12}$

Now Try Exercises 9, 11

Recall that to divide two fractions we "invert and multiply." That is, we change a division problem to a multiplication problem, using the property

$$\frac{a}{b} \div \frac{c}{d} = \frac{a}{b} \cdot \frac{d}{c}.$$

For example, $\frac{3}{4} \div \frac{5}{4} = \frac{3}{4} \cdot \frac{4}{5} = \frac{3 \cdot 4}{5 \cdot 4} = \frac{3}{5}$.

Multiplication of Rational Expressions

Multiplying rational expressions is similar to multiplying fractions.

> ### PRODUCTS OF RATIONAL EXPRESSIONS
>
> To multiply two rational expressions, multiply numerators and multiply denominators.
>
> $$\frac{A}{B} \cdot \frac{C}{D} = \frac{AC}{BD}$$ B and D not zero

EXAMPLE 4   Multiplying rational expressions

Multiply.

(a) $\dfrac{1}{x} \cdot \dfrac{x+1}{2x}$ (b) $\dfrac{x-1}{x} \cdot \dfrac{x-1}{x+2}$

Solution

(a) $\dfrac{1}{x} \cdot \dfrac{x+1}{2x} = \dfrac{1 \cdot (x+1)}{x \cdot 2x} = \dfrac{x+1}{2x^2}$

(b) $\dfrac{x-1}{x} \cdot \dfrac{x-1}{x+2} = \dfrac{(x-1)(x-1)}{x(x+2)}$

Now Try Exercises 59, 61

Many times the product of two rational expressions can be simplified. This process is demonstrated in the next two examples.

EXAMPLE 5   Multiplying rational expressions

Multiply and simplify.

(a) $\dfrac{5x}{8} \cdot \dfrac{4}{10x^2}$ (b) $\dfrac{x-2}{2x-1} \cdot \dfrac{x+1}{2x-4}$ (c) $\dfrac{x^2-1}{x^2-4} \cdot \dfrac{x+2}{x-1}$

Solution

(a) $\dfrac{5x}{8} \cdot \dfrac{4}{10x^2} = \dfrac{20x}{80x^2}$ Multiply rational expressions.

$= \dfrac{1}{4x}$ Simplify.

(b) $\dfrac{x-2}{2x-1} \cdot \dfrac{x+1}{2x-4} = \dfrac{(x-2)(x+1)}{(2x-1)(2x-4)}$ Multiply rational expressions.

$= \dfrac{(x-2)(x+1)}{(2x-1)2(x-2)}$ Factor $2x-4$.

$= \dfrac{(x+1)(x-2)}{2(2x-1)(x-2)}$ Commutative property

$= \dfrac{x+1}{2(2x-1)}$ Simplify.

(c) $\dfrac{x^2 - 1}{x^2 - 4} \cdot \dfrac{x + 2}{x - 1} = \dfrac{(x^2 - 1)(x + 2)}{(x^2 - 4)(x - 1)}$ Multiply rational expressions.

$= \dfrac{(x - 1)(x + 1)(x + 2)}{(x - 2)(x + 2)(x - 1)}$ Difference of squares

$= \dfrac{(x + 1)(x - 1)(x + 2)}{(x - 2)(x - 1)(x + 2)}$ Commutative property

$= \dfrac{x + 1}{x - 2}$ Simplify.

Now Try Exercises 63, 69, 71

EXAMPLE 6   Multiplying rational expressions

Multiply and simplify.

(a) $\dfrac{2x^2y^3}{3xy^2} \cdot \dfrac{(2x^3y)^2}{2(xy)^3}$ (b) $\dfrac{x^3 - x}{x - 1} \cdot \dfrac{x + 1}{x}$ (c) $\dfrac{a}{b} \cdot \dfrac{a^2 - b^2}{2} \cdot \dfrac{b}{a + b}$

Solution

(a) $\dfrac{2x^2y^3}{3xy^2} \cdot \dfrac{(2x^3y)^2}{2(xy)^3} = \dfrac{2x^2y^3 \cdot 4x^6y^2}{3xy^2 \cdot 2x^3y^3}$ Multiply; properties of exponents.

$= \dfrac{8x^8y^5}{6x^4y^5}$ Multiply; properties of exponents.

$= \dfrac{4}{3}x^4$ Simplify.

(b) $\dfrac{x^3 - x}{x - 1} \cdot \dfrac{x + 1}{x} = \dfrac{(x^3 - x)(x + 1)}{x(x - 1)}$ Multiply.

$= \dfrac{x(x^2 - 1)(x + 1)}{x(x - 1)}$ Factor out x.

$= \dfrac{x(x - 1)(x + 1)(x + 1)}{x(x - 1)}$ Difference of squares

$= (x + 1)(x + 1)$ Simplify.

$= (x + 1)^2$ Rewrite.

(c) $\dfrac{a}{b} \cdot \dfrac{a^2 - b^2}{2} \cdot \dfrac{b}{a + b} = \dfrac{a(a^2 - b^2)b}{b(2)(a + b)}$ Multiply fractions.

$= \dfrac{a(a - b)(a + b)\boldsymbol{b}}{2(a + b)\boldsymbol{b}}$ Difference of squares

$= \dfrac{a(a - b)}{2}$ Simplify.

Now Try Exercises 67, 73, 81

Division of Rational Expressions

When dividing two rational expressions, *multiply* the first expression by the reciprocal of the second expression. This technique is similar to the division of fractions.

QUOTIENTS OF RATIONAL EXPRESSIONS

To divide two rational expressions, multiply by the reciprocal of the divisor.

$$\frac{A}{B} \div \frac{C}{D} = \frac{A}{B} \cdot \frac{D}{C} \qquad B, C, \text{ and } D \text{ not zero}$$

NOTE: This technique of multiplying the first rational expression and the reciprocal of the second rational expression is sometimes summarized as "Invert and multiply."

The **reciprocal of a polynomial** $p(x)$ is $\frac{1}{p(x)}$, and the **reciprocal of a rational expression** $\frac{p(x)}{q(x)}$ is $\frac{q(x)}{p(x)}$. The next example demonstrates how to find reciprocals.

EXAMPLE 7 Finding reciprocals

Write the reciprocal of each expression.

(a) $3x + 4$ **(b)** $\dfrac{5}{x^2 + 1}$ **(c)** $\dfrac{x - 7}{x + 7}$

Solution
(a) The reciprocal of $3x + 4$ is $\frac{1}{3x + 4}$.

(b) The reciprocal of $\frac{5}{x^2 + 1}$ is $\frac{x^2 + 1}{5}$.

(c) The reciprocal of $\frac{x - 7}{x + 7}$ is $\frac{x + 7}{x - 7}$.

Now Try Exercises **51, 55, 57**

EXAMPLE 8 Dividing two rational expressions

Divide and simplify.

(a) $\dfrac{2}{x} \div \dfrac{2x - 1}{4x}$ **(b)** $\dfrac{x^2 - 1}{x^2 + x - 6} \div \dfrac{x - 1}{x + 3}$

Solution

(a)
$$\frac{2}{x} \div \frac{2x - 1}{4x} = \frac{2}{x} \cdot \frac{4x}{2x - 1} \qquad \text{"Invert and multiply."}$$
$$= \frac{8x}{x(2x - 1)} \qquad \text{Multiply.}$$
$$= \frac{8}{2x - 1} \qquad \text{Simplify.}$$

(b)
$$\frac{x^2 - 1}{x^2 + x - 6} \div \frac{x - 1}{x + 3} = \frac{x^2 - 1}{x^2 + x - 6} \cdot \frac{x + 3}{x - 1} \qquad \text{"Invert and multiply."}$$
$$= \frac{(x + 1)(x - 1)}{(x - 2)(x + 3)} \cdot \frac{x + 3}{x - 1} \qquad \text{Factor completely.}$$
$$= \frac{(x + 1)(x - 1)(x + 3)}{(x - 2)(x - 1)(x + 3)} \qquad \text{Commutative property}$$
$$= \frac{x + 1}{x - 2} \qquad \text{Simplify.}$$

Now Try Exercises **83, 97**

EXAMPLE 9   Dividing rational expressions

Divide and simplify.

(a) $\dfrac{7a^2}{4b^3} \div \dfrac{21a}{8b^4}$ (b) $\dfrac{2x+2}{x-1} \div (x+1)$ (c) $\dfrac{x^2-25}{x^2+5x+4} \div \dfrac{x^2-10x+25}{2x^2+8x}$

Solution

(a)
$$\dfrac{7a^2}{4b^3} \div \dfrac{21a}{8b^4} = \dfrac{7a^2}{4b^3} \cdot \dfrac{8b^4}{21a}$$ "Invert and multiply."
$$= \dfrac{56a^2b^4}{84ab^3}$$ Multiply rational expressions.
$$= \dfrac{56}{84}a^{2-1}b^{4-3}$$ Properties of exponents
$$= \dfrac{2}{3}ab$$ Simplify.

(b)
$$\dfrac{2x+2}{x-1} \div (x+1) = \dfrac{2x+2}{x-1} \cdot \dfrac{1}{x+1}$$ "Invert and multiply."
$$= \dfrac{2(x+1)}{x-1} \cdot \dfrac{1}{x+1}$$ Factor.
$$= \dfrac{2(x+1)}{(x-1)(x+1)}$$ Multiply rational expressions.
$$= \dfrac{2}{x-1}$$ Simplify.

(c)
$$\dfrac{x^2-25}{x^2+5x+4} \div \dfrac{x^2-10x+25}{2x^2+8x} = \dfrac{x^2-25}{x^2+5x+4} \cdot \dfrac{2x^2+8x}{x^2-10x+25}$$
$$= \dfrac{(x-5)(x+5)}{(x+1)(x+4)} \cdot \dfrac{2x(x+4)}{(x-5)^2}$$
$$= \dfrac{2x(x+5)(x-5)(x+4)}{(x+1)(x-5)(x-5)(x+4)}$$
$$= \dfrac{2x(x+5)}{(x+1)(x-5)}$$

Now Try Exercises 85, 87, 95

In the next example, we divide three rational expressions. It is important to realize that *the associative property does not apply to division*. For example,

$$(24 \div 6) \div 2 = 4 \div 2 = 2 \quad \text{but} \quad 24 \div (6 \div 2) = 24 \div 3 = 8.$$

The order in which we do division *does matter*. As a result, we perform division from *left to right* and

$$24 \div 6 \div 2 = 4 \div 2 = 2.$$

EXAMPLE 10   Dividing three fractions

Divide and simplify $\dfrac{4x}{y} \div \dfrac{x^2}{y} \div \dfrac{3y}{2x}$.

Solution

$$\frac{4x}{y} \div \frac{x^2}{y} \div \frac{3y}{2x} = \left(\frac{4x}{y} \div \frac{x^2}{y}\right) \div \frac{3y}{2x} \qquad \text{Divide left to right.}$$

$$= \left(\frac{4x}{y} \cdot \frac{y}{x^2}\right) \div \frac{3y}{2x} \qquad \text{``Invert and multiply.''}$$

$$= \frac{4xy}{x^2y} \div \frac{3y}{2x} \qquad \text{Multiply fractions.}$$

$$= \frac{4xy}{x^2y} \cdot \frac{2x}{3y} \qquad \text{``Invert and multiply.''}$$

$$= \frac{8x^2y}{3x^2y^2} \qquad \text{Multiply fractions.}$$

$$= \frac{8}{3y} \qquad \text{Simplify.}$$

Now Try Exercise 99

In the next example, we find the length of a rectangle when its area and width are expressed as polynomials.

EXAMPLE 11 Finding the dimensions of a rectangle

The area A of a rectangle is $3x^2 + 14x + 15$ and its width W is $x + 3$. See Figure 6.8.
(a) Find the length L of the rectangle.
(b) Find the length if the width is 12 inches.

$x + 3$ | $A = 3x^2 + 14x + 15$
L

Figure 6.8

Solution

(a) Because the area equals length times width, $A = LW$, length equals area divided by width, or $L = \frac{A}{W}$. To determine L, factor the expression for A and then simplify.

$$L = \frac{3x^2 + 14x + 15}{x + 3} = \frac{(3x + 5)(x + 3)}{x + 3} = 3x + 5.$$

The length of the rectangle is $3x + 5$.

(b) If the width is 12 inches, then $x + 3 = 12$ or $x = 9$. The length is

$$L = 3x + 5 = 3(9) + 5 = 32 \text{ inches.}$$

Now Try Exercise 107

6.2 PUTTING IT ALL TOGETHER

The following table summarizes some important concepts found in this section.

Concept	Explanation	Examples
Simplifying Rational Expressions	Use the principle $$\frac{A \cdot C}{B \cdot C} = \frac{A}{B}.$$ B and C not zero	$\dfrac{5a(a + b)}{7b(a + b)} = \dfrac{5a}{7b}$ and $\dfrac{x^2 - 1}{x - 1} = \dfrac{(x + 1)(x - 1)}{x - 1} = x + 1$

Concept	Explanation	Examples
Multiplying Rational Expressions	To multiply two rational expressions, multiply numerators and multiply denominators. $$\frac{A}{B} \cdot \frac{C}{D} = \frac{AC}{BD}$$ B and D not zero	$$\frac{5a}{4b^2} \cdot \frac{2b^3}{10a^3} = \frac{10ab^3}{40a^3b^2} = \frac{b}{4a^2}$$
Dividing Rational Expressions	To divide two rational expressions, multiply by the reciprocal of the divisor. ("Invert and multiply.") $$\frac{A}{B} \div \frac{C}{D} = \frac{A}{B} \cdot \frac{D}{C}$$ B, C, and D not zero	$$\frac{x}{x+1} \div \frac{x+2}{x+1} = \frac{x}{x+1} \cdot \frac{x+1}{x+2}$$ $$= \frac{x(x+1)}{(x+2)(x+1)}$$ $$= \frac{x}{x+2}$$

6.2 Exercises

CONCEPTS

1. Simplify $\frac{2x+3}{2x+3}$.

2. Simplify $\frac{x-3}{3-x}$.

3. Is $\frac{x^2-1}{x-1}$ equal to x? Explain.

4. Is $\frac{3}{3+x}$ equal to $\frac{1}{x}$? Is it equal to $1 + \frac{3}{x}$?

5. To divide $\frac{2}{3}$ by $\frac{5}{7}$ multiply _____ by _____.

6. $\frac{a}{b} \cdot \frac{c}{d} = $ _____.

7. $\frac{a}{b} \div \frac{c}{d} = $ _____.

8. $\frac{ac}{bc} = $ _____.

REVIEW OF FRACTIONS

Exercises 9–20: Simplify.

9. $\frac{1}{2} \cdot \frac{4}{5}$

10. $\frac{5}{6} \cdot \frac{3}{10}$

11. $\frac{7}{8} \cdot \frac{4}{3} \cdot (-3)$

12. $4 \cdot \frac{7}{4} \cdot \frac{1}{2}$

13. $\frac{3}{8} \cdot 2$

14. $-5 \cdot \frac{2}{7}$

15. $-\frac{7}{11} \div 14$

16. $6 \div \frac{6}{5}$

17. $\frac{5}{7} \div \frac{15}{14}$

18. $-\frac{2}{3} \div 2$

19. $6 \div \left(-\frac{1}{3}\right)$

20. $\frac{10}{9} \div \frac{5}{3}$

SIMPLIFYING RATIONAL EXPRESSIONS

Exercises 21–50: Simplify the rational expression.

21. $\frac{5x}{x^2}$

22. $\frac{18t^3}{6t}$

23. $\frac{3z+6}{z+2}$

24. $\frac{6}{12x+6}$

25. $\frac{2z+2}{3z+3}$

26. $\frac{4x-12}{2x-6}$

27. $\frac{(x-1)(x+1)}{x-1}$

28. $(x+2) \cdot \frac{x-6}{x+2}$

29. $\frac{x^2-4}{x+2}$

30. $\frac{(x+2)(x-5)}{(x+10)(x+2)}$

31. $\frac{x(x-1)}{(x+1)(x-1)}$

32. $\frac{(2x-1)(x-3)}{(x-3)(2x+5)}$

33. $\frac{(3x+1)(x+2)}{(x+2)(5x-2)}$

34. $\frac{(3x+2)(x-7)}{x(x-7)}$

35. $\dfrac{x + 5}{x^2 + 2x - 15}$

36. $\dfrac{x^2 - 9}{x^2 + 6x + 9} \cdot (x + 3)$

37. $\dfrac{x^2 + 2x}{x^2 + 3x + 2}$

38. $\dfrac{x^2 - 3x - 10}{x^2 - 6x + 5}$

39. $\dfrac{6x^2 + 7x - 5}{2x^2 - 11x + 5}$

40. $\dfrac{30x^2 - 7x - 15}{6x^2 + 7x - 10}$

41. $\dfrac{a^2 - b^2}{a - b}$

42. $\dfrac{a^2 + 2ab + b^2}{a + b}$

43. $\dfrac{m^3 + n^3}{m + n}$

44. $\dfrac{m^3 - n^3}{m - n}$

45. $-\dfrac{4 - t}{t - 4}$

46. $-\dfrac{t - r}{r - t}$

47. $\dfrac{4m - n}{-4m + n}$

48. $\dfrac{2n + 10m}{-n - 5m}$

49. $\dfrac{5 - y}{y - 5}$

50. $\dfrac{a - b}{b - a}$

RECIPROCALS

Exercises 51–58: Write the reciprocal of the expression.

51. $4x$

52. $5x - 2$

53. $\dfrac{2a}{5b}$

54. $\dfrac{5b^3}{7a^2}$

55. $\dfrac{3 - x}{5 - x}$

56. $\dfrac{x^2 - 4}{3x + 1}$

57. $\dfrac{1}{x^2 + 1}$

58. $\dfrac{-1}{5 - x}$

MULTIPLICATION AND DIVISION OF RATIONAL EXPRESSIONS

Exercises 59–102: Simplify the expression.

59. $\dfrac{2}{x} \cdot \dfrac{x - 1}{3x}$

60. $\dfrac{2}{x - 3} \cdot \dfrac{x}{x + 1}$

61. $\dfrac{x - 2}{x} \cdot \dfrac{x - 3}{x + 4}$

62. $\dfrac{x}{x + 5} \cdot \dfrac{x - 6}{x + 4}$

63. $\dfrac{1}{2x} \cdot \dfrac{4x}{2}$

64. $\dfrac{5a^2}{7} \cdot \dfrac{7}{10a}$

65. $\dfrac{5a}{4} \cdot \dfrac{12}{5a}$

66. $\dfrac{a^2 b}{4c} \cdot \dfrac{8c^2}{3ab^2}$

67. $\dfrac{9x^2 y^4}{8xy^6} \cdot \dfrac{(2xy^2)^3}{3(xy)^4}$

68. $\dfrac{(7rt)^2}{8} \cdot \dfrac{8r}{49(rt^2)^3}$

69. $\dfrac{x + 1}{2x - 5} \cdot \dfrac{2x - 5}{x}$

70. $\dfrac{x + 1}{x} \cdot \dfrac{x}{x + 2}$

71. $\dfrac{b^2 + 1}{b^2 - 1} \cdot \dfrac{b - 1}{b + 1}$

72. $\dfrac{(x - 5)(x + 3)}{3x - 1} \cdot \dfrac{x(3x - 1)}{(x - 5)}$

73. $\dfrac{x^2 - 2x - 35}{2x^3 - 3x^2} \cdot \dfrac{x^3 - x^2}{2x - 14}$

74. $\dfrac{2x + 4}{x + 1} \cdot \dfrac{x^2 + 3x + 2}{4x + 2}$

75. $\dfrac{3n - 9}{n^2 - 9} \cdot (n^3 + 27)$

76. $(10n + 15) \cdot \dfrac{n + 1}{6n + 9}$

77. $\dfrac{3n - 9}{n^2 - 9} \cdot \dfrac{n^3 + 27}{12}$

78. $\dfrac{10n + 15}{n^2 - 1} \cdot \dfrac{n + 1}{6n + 9}$

79. $\dfrac{x}{y} \cdot \dfrac{2y}{x} \cdot \dfrac{2}{xy}$

80. $\dfrac{4z^2}{r^3} \cdot \dfrac{5r}{2z} \cdot \dfrac{r}{z}$

81. $\dfrac{x - 1}{y} \cdot \dfrac{y(x + y)}{2} \cdot \dfrac{y}{x + y}$

82. $\dfrac{x}{y^2} \cdot \dfrac{y^3 - y^2}{x + y} \cdot \dfrac{x^2 + xy}{5x^2}$

83. $\dfrac{3x}{2} \div \dfrac{2x}{5}$

84. $\dfrac{x^2 + x}{2x + 6} \div \dfrac{x}{x + 3}$

85. $\dfrac{8a^4}{3b} \div \dfrac{a^5}{9b^2}$

86. $\dfrac{5m^4}{n^2} \div 5m$

87. $(2n + 4) \div \dfrac{n + 2}{n - 1}$

88. $\dfrac{n + 1}{n + 3} \div \dfrac{n + 1}{n + 3}$

89. $\dfrac{6b}{b + 2} \div \dfrac{3b^4}{2b + 4}$

90. $\dfrac{5x^5}{x - 2} \div \dfrac{10x^3}{5x - 10}$

91. $\dfrac{3a + 1}{a^7} \div \dfrac{a + 1}{3a^8}$

92. $\dfrac{16 - x^2}{x + 3} \div \dfrac{x + 4}{9 - x^2}$

93. $\dfrac{x + 5}{x - x^3} \div \dfrac{25 - x^2}{x^3}$

94. $\dfrac{x^2 + x - 12}{2x^2 - 9x - 5} \div \dfrac{x^2 + 7x + 12}{2x^2 - 7x - 4}$

95. $\dfrac{x^2 - 3x + 2}{x^2 + 5x + 6} \div \dfrac{x^2 + x - 2}{x^2 + 2x - 3}$

96. $\dfrac{2x^2 + x - 1}{6x^2 + x - 2} \div \dfrac{2x^2 + 5x + 3}{6x^2 + 13x + 6}$

97. $\dfrac{x^2 - 4}{x^2 + x - 2} \div \dfrac{x - 2}{x - 1}$

98. $\dfrac{x^2 + 2x + 1}{x - 2} \div \dfrac{x + 1}{2x - 4}$

99. $\dfrac{3y}{x^2} \div \dfrac{y^2}{x} \div \dfrac{y}{5x}$

100. $\dfrac{x + 1}{y - 2} \div \dfrac{2x + 2}{y - 2} \div \dfrac{x}{y}$

101. $\dfrac{x - 3}{x - 1} \div \dfrac{x^2}{x - 1} \div \dfrac{x - 3}{x}$

102. $\dfrac{2x}{x - 2} \div \dfrac{x + 2}{x} \div \dfrac{7x}{x^2 - 4}$

OPERATIONS ON FUNCTIONS

103. If $f(x) = \dfrac{x + 2}{x^2 - 3x + 2}$ and $g(x) = \dfrac{x - 1}{x + 2}$, then find $(fg)(x)$.

104. If $f(x) = \dfrac{2}{x^2 - 5x + 4}$ and $g(x) = \dfrac{x - 4}{x + 1}$, then find $(fg)(x)$.

105. Find $(f/g)(x)$ if $f(x) = x^2 - 1$ and $g(x) = x + 1$.

106. Find $(f/g)(x)$ if $f(x) = \dfrac{2x - 4}{5}$ and $g(x) = \dfrac{4 - 2x}{15}$.

GEOMETRY

107. *Area of a Rectangle*   The area A of a rectangle is $5x^2 + 12x + 4$ and its width W is $x + 2$, as shown in the figure.
(a) Find the length L of the rectangle.
(b) Find the length if the width is 8 feet.

108. *Area of a Rectangle*   The area A of a rectangle is given by $x^2 - 1$.
(a) Find its length if its width is $x - 1$.
(b) Find the dimensions and area of the rectangle when $x = 15$.

109. *Volume of a Box*   The volume V of a box with a square bottom is $4x^3 + 4x^2 + x$.
(a) If its height is x, find the area of the bottom.
(b) Find the dimensions of the box when $x = 10$.

110. *Area of a Triangle*   The area A of a triangle is $6x^2 - x - 15$. Find its height if the base of the triangle is $2x + 3$.

WRITING ABOUT MATHEMATICS

111. A student does the following to simplify a rational expression. Is the work correct? Explain any errors and how you would correct them.

$$\dfrac{3x + x^2}{3x} \overset{?}{=} 1 + x^2$$

112. Explain how to multiply two rational expressions and how to divide two rational expressions.

CHECKING BASIC CONCEPTS
SECTIONS 6.1 AND 6.2

1. Let $f(x) = \frac{x}{x-1}$.
   (a) Evaluate $f(2)$.
   (b) Find the domain of f.
   (c) Graph f. Identify any vertical asymptotes.

2. Solve each equation. Check your answers.
   (a) $\frac{6}{2x+3} = 3$ **(b)** $\frac{2}{x-1} = x$

3. Simplify $\frac{x^2 - 6x - 7}{x^2 - 1}$.

4. Simplify each expression.
   (a) $\frac{2x^2}{x^2 - 1} \cdot \frac{x+1}{4x}$
   (b) $\frac{1}{x-2} \div \frac{3}{(x-2)(x+3)}$

6.3 ADDITION AND SUBTRACTION OF RATIONAL EXPRESSIONS

Least Common Multiples ▪ Review of Addition and Subtraction of Fractions ▪ Addition of Rational Expressions ▪ Subtraction of Rational Expressions

A LOOK INTO MATH ▷ Rational expressions occur in many real-world applications. For example, addition of rational expressions is used in the design of electrical circuits. (See Example 8.) In this section we demonstrate how to add and subtract rational expressions. These techniques are similar to techniques used to add and subtract fractions. We begin by discussing least common multiples, which are used to find least common denominators.

Least Common Multiples

▶ **REAL-WORLD CONNECTION**   Two friends work part-time at a store. The first person works every fourth day and the second person works every sixth day. If they are both working today, how many days pass before they both work on the same day again?
   We can answer this question by listing the days that each person works.

First person: 4,   8,   **12**,   16,   20,   **24**,   28,   32,   **36**,   40
Second person: 6,   **12**,   18,   **24**,   30,   **36**,   42

After 12 days, the two friends work on the same day. The next time is after 24 days. The numbers 12 and 24 are *common multiples* of 4 and 6. (Find two more.) However, 12 is the **least common multiple** (LCM) of 4 and 6. Note that 12 is the smallest positive number that has both 4 and 6 as factors.
   Another way to find the least common multiple for 4 and 6 is first to factor each number into prime numbers:

$$4 = 2 \cdot 2 \quad \text{and} \quad 6 = 2 \cdot 3.$$

To find the least common multiple, list each factor the *greatest* number of times that it occurs in either factorization. Then find the product of these numbers. For our example, the factor 2 occurs two times in the factorization of 4 and only once in the factorization of 6, so list 2 two times. The factor 3 appears only once in the factorization of 6 and not at all in the factorization of 4, so list it once:

$$2, 2, 3.$$

The least common multiple is their product: $2 \cdot 2 \cdot 3 = 12$. This same procedure can also be used to find the least common multiple for two (or more) polynomials.

FINDING THE LEAST COMMON MULTIPLE

The least common multiple (LCM) of two polynomials can be found as follows.

STEP 1: Factor each polynomial completely.

STEP 2: List each factor the greatest number of times that it occurs in either factorization.

STEP 3: Find the product of this list of factors. The result is the LCM.

The next example illustrates how to use this procedure.

EXAMPLE 1 Finding least common multiples

Find the least common multiple for each pair of expressions.
(a) $4x, 5x^3$ **(b)** $x^2 - 2x, (x - 2)^2$
(c) $x + 2, x - 1$ **(d)** $x^2 + 4x + 4, x^2 + 3x + 2$

Solution
(a) STEP 1: Factor each polynomial completely.

$$4x = 2 \cdot 2 \cdot x \quad \text{and} \quad 5x^3 = 5 \cdot x \cdot x \cdot x$$

STEP 2: The factor 2 occurs twice, the factor 5 occurs once, and the factor x occurs at most three times. The list is $2, 2, 5, x, x$, and x.

STEP 3: The LCM is the product $2 \cdot 2 \cdot 5 \cdot x \cdot x \cdot x$, or $20x^3$.

(b) STEP 1: Factor each polynomial completely.

$$x^2 - 2x = x(x - 2) \quad \text{and} \quad (x - 2)^2 = (x - 2)(x - 2)$$

STEP 2: The factor x occurs once, and the factor $(x - 2)$ occurs at most twice. The list of factors is x, $(x - 2)$, and $(x - 2)$.

STEP 3: The LCM is the product: $x(x - 2)^2$, which is left in factored form.

(c) STEP 1: Neither polynomial can be factored.

STEP 2: The list of factors is $(x + 2)$ and $(x - 1)$.

STEP 3: The LCM is the product $(x + 2)(x - 1)$, or $x^2 + x - 2$.

(d) **STEP 1:** Factor each polynomial as follows.

$$x^2 + 4x + 4 = (x + 2)(x + 2) \quad \text{and} \quad x^2 + 3x + 2 = (x + 1)(x + 2)$$

STEP 2: The factor $(x + 1)$ occurs once and $(x + 2)$ occurs at most twice.

STEP 3: The LCM is the product $(x + 1)(x + 2)^2$, which is left in factored form.

Now Try Exercises 13, 15, 17

Review of Addition and Subtraction of Fractions

Recall that to add two fractions we use the property

$$\frac{a}{c} + \frac{b}{c} = \frac{a + b}{c}.$$

This property requires that the fractions have like denominators. For example,

$$\frac{1}{5} + \frac{3}{5} = \frac{1 + 3}{5} = \frac{4}{5}.$$

When the denominators are not alike, we must find a common denominator. Before adding two fractions, such as $\frac{2}{3}$ and $\frac{1}{4}$, we write them with 12 as their common denominator. That is, we multiply each fraction by 1 written in an appropriate form. For example, to write $\frac{2}{3}$ with a denominator of 12 we multiply $\frac{2}{3}$ by 1, written as $\frac{4}{4}$.

$$\frac{2}{3} = \frac{2}{3} \cdot \frac{4}{4} = \frac{8}{12} \quad \text{and} \quad \frac{1}{4} = \frac{1}{4} \cdot \frac{3}{3} = \frac{3}{12}$$

Once the fractions have a common denominator, we can add them, as in

$$\frac{2}{3} + \frac{1}{4} = \frac{8}{12} + \frac{3}{12} = \frac{11}{12}.$$

Note that a **common denominator** for $\frac{2}{3}$ and $\frac{1}{4}$ is also a *common multiple* of 3 and 4. The **least common denominator** (LCD) for $\frac{2}{3}$ and $\frac{1}{4}$ is equal to the *least common multiple* (LCM) of 3 and 4. Thus the least common denominator is 12.

EXAMPLE 2   Adding fractions

Find the sum.

(a) $\dfrac{3}{4} + \dfrac{1}{8}$ **(b)** $\dfrac{3}{5} + \dfrac{2}{7}$

Solution
(a) The LCD is 8.

$$\frac{3}{4} + \frac{1}{8} = \frac{3}{4} \cdot \frac{2}{2} + \frac{1}{8} = \frac{6}{8} + \frac{1}{8} = \frac{7}{8}$$

(b) The LCD is 35.

$$\frac{3}{5} + \frac{2}{7} = \frac{3}{5} \cdot \frac{7}{7} + \frac{2}{7} \cdot \frac{5}{5} = \frac{21}{35} + \frac{10}{35} = \frac{31}{35}$$

Now Try Exercises 21, 22

Recall that subtraction is similar to addition. To subtract two fractions with like denominators we use the property

$$\frac{a}{c} - \frac{b}{c} = \frac{a - b}{c}.$$

For example, $\frac{3}{11} - \frac{7}{11} = \frac{3 - 7}{11} = -\frac{4}{11}$.

EXAMPLE 3   Subtracting fractions

Find the difference.
(a) $\dfrac{3}{10} - \dfrac{2}{15}$ (b) $\dfrac{3}{8} - \dfrac{5}{6}$

Solution
(a) The LCD is 30.

$$\frac{3}{10} - \frac{2}{15} = \frac{3}{10} \cdot \frac{3}{3} - \frac{2}{15} \cdot \frac{2}{2} = \frac{9}{30} - \frac{4}{30} = \frac{5}{30} = \frac{1}{6}$$

(b) The LCD is 24.

$$\frac{3}{8} - \frac{5}{6} = \frac{3}{8} \cdot \frac{3}{3} - \frac{5}{6} \cdot \frac{4}{4} = \frac{9}{24} - \frac{20}{24} = -\frac{11}{24}$$ Now Try Exercise **27**

Addition of Rational Expressions

Addition of rational expressions is similar to addition of fractions.

> **SUMS OF RATIONAL EXPRESSIONS**
>
> To add two rational expressions with like denominators, add their numerators. The denominator does not change.
>
> $$\frac{A}{C} + \frac{B}{C} = \frac{A + B}{C} \qquad C \text{ not zero}$$

EXAMPLE 4   Adding rational expressions with like denominators

Add and simplify.
(a) $\dfrac{x}{x + 2} + \dfrac{3x - 1}{x + 2}$ (b) $\dfrac{x}{3x^2 + 4x - 4} + \dfrac{2}{3x^2 + 4x - 4}$

Solution
(a) The expressions have like denominators, so add the numerators.

$$\frac{x}{x + 2} + \frac{3x - 1}{x + 2} = \frac{x + 3x - 1}{x + 2} \qquad \text{Add numerators.}$$

$$= \frac{4x - 1}{x + 2} \qquad \text{Combine like terms.}$$

(b) The expressions have like denominators, so add the numerators. However, the resulting sum can be simplified by factoring the denominator.

$$\frac{x}{3x^2 + 4x - 4} + \frac{2}{3x^2 + 4x - 4} = \frac{x + 2}{3x^2 + 4x - 4} \qquad \text{Add numerators.}$$

$$= \frac{x + 2}{(3x - 2)(x + 2)} \qquad \text{Factor denominator.}$$

$$= \frac{1}{3x - 2} \qquad \text{Simplify.}$$

Now Try Exercises 29, 43

To add rational expressions with unlike denominators, we must first write each expression so that it has the same common denominator. For example, the least common denominator for $\frac{1}{x + 2}$ and $\frac{2}{x - 1}$ equals the least common multiple of $x + 2$ and $x - 1$, which was shown to be their product $(x + 2)(x - 1)$ in Example 1(c). To rewrite $\frac{1}{x + 2}$ with the new denominator we multiply it by 1, expressed as $\frac{x - 1}{x - 1}$.

$$\frac{1}{x + 2} \cdot 1 = \frac{1}{x + 2} \cdot \frac{x - 1}{x - 1} = \frac{x - 1}{(x + 2)(x - 1)}$$

Similarly, we multiply $\frac{2}{x - 1}$ by 1, expressed as $\frac{x + 2}{x + 2}$.

$$\frac{2}{x - 1} \cdot 1 = \frac{2}{x - 1} \cdot \frac{x + 2}{x + 2} = \frac{2x + 4}{(x - 1)(x + 2)}$$

Now the two rational expressions have like denominators and can be added.

$$\frac{1}{x + 2} + \frac{2}{x - 1} = \frac{x - 1}{(x + 2)(x - 1)} + \frac{2x + 4}{(x - 1)(x + 2)} \qquad \text{Write with LCD.}$$

$$= \frac{x - 1 + 2x + 4}{(x + 2)(x - 1)} \qquad \text{Add numerators.}$$

$$= \frac{3x + 3}{(x + 2)(x - 1)} \qquad \text{Combine like terms.}$$

EXAMPLE 5 Adding rational expressions with unlike denominators

Add and simplify.

(a) $\dfrac{1}{x} + \dfrac{2}{x^2}$ **(b)** $\dfrac{1}{x^2 - 9} + \dfrac{2}{x + 3}$ **(c)** $\dfrac{a}{a - b} + \dfrac{b}{a + b}$ **(d)** $\dfrac{1}{x - 1} + \dfrac{1}{1 - x}$

Solution
(a) The LCD is x^2.

$$\frac{1}{x} \cdot \frac{x}{x} + \frac{2}{x^2} = \frac{x}{x^2} + \frac{2}{x^2} \qquad \text{Write with LCD.}$$

$$= \frac{x + 2}{x^2} \qquad \text{Add numerators.}$$

(b) The LCD is $x^2 - 9 = (x - 3)(x + 3)$.

$$\frac{1}{x^2 - 9} + \frac{2}{x + 3} \cdot \frac{x - 3}{x - 3} = \frac{1}{(x + 3)(x - 3)} + \frac{2x - 6}{(x + 3)(x - 3)} \qquad \text{Write with LCD.}$$

$$= \frac{2x - 5}{(x + 3)(x - 3)} \qquad \text{Add numerators.}$$

(c) The LCD is $(a - b)(a + b)$.

$$\frac{a}{a - b} \cdot \frac{a + b}{a + b} + \frac{b}{a + b} \cdot \frac{a - b}{a - b} = \frac{a^2 + ab}{(a - b)(a + b)} + \frac{ab - b^2}{(a - b)(a + b)} \qquad \text{Write with LCD.}$$

$$= \frac{a^2 + 2ab - b^2}{(a - b)(a + b)} \qquad \text{Add numerators.}$$

(d) By multiplying the second expression by $\frac{-1}{-1}$, the LCD can be found.

$$\frac{1}{x - 1} + \frac{1}{1 - x} \cdot \frac{-1}{-1} = \frac{1}{x - 1} + \frac{-1}{(1 - x)(-1)} \qquad \text{Write with LCD.}$$

$$= \frac{1}{x - 1} + \frac{-1}{x - 1} \qquad \text{Distributive property}$$

$$= \frac{0}{x - 1} \qquad \text{Add numerators.}$$

$$= 0 \qquad \text{Simplify.}$$

NOTE: When one denominator is the opposite of the other, try multiplying one expression by 1 in the form $\frac{-1}{-1}$.   Now Try Exercises 47, 53, 57

Subtraction of Rational Expressions

Subtraction of rational expressions is similar to subtraction of fractions.

DIFFERENCES OF RATIONAL EXPRESSIONS

To subtract two rational expressions with like denominators, subtract their numerators. The denominator does not change.

$$\frac{A}{C} - \frac{B}{C} = \frac{A - B}{C} \qquad C \text{ not zero}$$

When you are subtracting numerators of rational expressions, it is *essential* to apply the distributive property correctly: Subtract every term in the numerator of the second rational expression. For example,

$$\frac{1}{x + 1} - \frac{2x - 1}{x + 1} = \frac{1 - (2x - 1)}{x + 1} = \frac{1 - 2x + 1}{x + 1} = \frac{2 - 2x}{x + 1}.$$

Be sure to place parentheses around the second numerator before subtracting.

EXAMPLE 6   Subtracting rational expressions with like denominators

Subtract and simplify.

(a) $\dfrac{3}{x^2} - \dfrac{x+3}{x^2}$ (b) $\dfrac{2x}{x^2-1} - \dfrac{x+1}{x^2-1}$

Solution

(a) The expressions have like denominators, so subtract the numerators.

$$\dfrac{3}{x^2} - \dfrac{x+3}{x^2} = \dfrac{3-(x+3)}{x^2}$$ Subtract numerators.

$$= \dfrac{3-x-3}{x^2}$$ Distributive property

$$= \dfrac{-x}{x^2}$$ Subtract.

$$= -\dfrac{1}{x}$$ Simplify.

(b) The expressions have like denominators, so subtract the numerators.

$$\dfrac{2x}{x^2-1} - \dfrac{x+1}{x^2-1} = \dfrac{2x-(x+1)}{x^2-1}$$ Subtract numerators.

$$= \dfrac{2x-x-1}{x^2-1}$$ Distributive property

$$= \dfrac{x-1}{(x+1)(x-1)}$$ Combine like terms; factor.

$$= \dfrac{1}{x+1}$$ Simplify.

Now Try Exercises 31, 39

TECHNOLOGY NOTE: Graphical and Numerical Support

We can give support to our work in Example 6(a) by letting $Y_1 = 3/X^2 - (X+3)/X^2$, the given expression, and $Y_2 = -1/X$, the simplified expression. In Figures 6.9(a) and 6.9(b) the graphs of y_1 and y_2 appear to be identical. In Figure 6.9(c) numerical support is given, where $y_1 = y_2$ for each value of x.

$[-4.7, 4.7, 1]$ by $[-3.1, 3.1, 1]$ $[-4.7, 4.7, 1]$ by $[-3.1, 3.1, 1]$

(a)   (b)   (c)

Figure 6.9

EXAMPLE 7   Subtracting rational expressions with unlike denominators

Subtract and simplify.

(a) $\dfrac{5a}{b^2} - \dfrac{4b}{a^2}$ (b) $\dfrac{x-1}{x} - \dfrac{5}{x+5}$ (c) $\dfrac{1}{x^2-3x+2} - \dfrac{1}{x^2-x-2}$

Solution

(a) The LCD is a^2b^2.

$$\frac{5a}{b^2} \cdot \frac{a^2}{a^2} - \frac{4b}{a^2} \cdot \frac{b^2}{b^2} = \frac{5a^3}{b^2a^2} - \frac{4b^3}{a^2b^2} \qquad \text{Write with LCD.}$$

$$= \frac{5a^3 - 4b^3}{a^2b^2} \qquad \text{Subtract numerators.}$$

(b) The LCD is $x(x + 5)$.

$$\frac{x - 1}{x} \cdot \frac{x + 5}{x + 5} - \frac{5}{x + 5} \cdot \frac{x}{x} \qquad \text{Write with LCD.}$$

$$= \frac{(x - 1)(x + 5)}{x(x + 5)} - \frac{5x}{x(x + 5)} \qquad \text{Multiply.}$$

$$= \frac{(x - 1)(x + 5) - 5x}{x(x + 5)} \qquad \text{Subtract numerators.}$$

$$= \frac{x^2 + 4x - 5 - 5x}{x(x + 5)} \qquad \text{Multiply binomials.}$$

$$= \frac{x^2 - x - 5}{x(x + 5)} \qquad \text{Combine like terms.}$$

(c) Because $x^2 - 3x + 2 = (x - 2)(x - 1)$ and $x^2 - x - 2 = (x - 2)(x + 1)$, the LCD is $(x - 1)(x + 1)(x - 2)$.

$$\frac{1}{(x - 2)(x - 1)} \cdot \frac{(x + 1)}{(x + 1)} - \frac{1}{(x - 2)(x + 1)} \cdot \frac{(x - 1)}{(x - 1)} \qquad \text{Write with LCD.}$$

$$= \frac{(x + 1)}{(x - 2)(x - 1)(x + 1)} - \frac{(x - 1)}{(x - 2)(x + 1)(x - 1)} \qquad \text{Multiply.}$$

$$= \frac{(x + 1) - (x - 1)}{(x - 2)(x - 1)(x + 1)} \qquad \text{Subtract numerators.}$$

$$= \frac{x + 1 - x + 1}{(x - 2)(x - 1)(x + 1)} \qquad \text{Distributive property}$$

$$= \frac{2}{(x - 2)(x - 1)(x + 1)} \qquad \text{Simplify numerator.}$$

Now Try Exercises 45, 49, 67

The following procedure summarizes how to add or subtract rational expressions.

STEPS FOR FINDING SUMS AND DIFFERENCES OF RATIONAL EXPRESSIONS

STEP 1: If the denominators are not common, multiply each expression by 1 written in the appropriate form to obtain the LCD.

STEP 2: Add or subtract the numerators. Combine like terms.

STEP 3: If possible, simplify the final expression.

▶ REAL-WORLD CONNECTION Sums of rational expressions occur in applications such as electrical circuits. The flow of electricity through a wire can be compared to the flow of water through a hose. Voltage is the force "pushing" the electricity and corresponds to water pressure

Figure 6.10

in a hose. Resistance is the opposition to the flow of electricity, and more resistance results in less flow of electricity. Resistance corresponds to the diameter of a hose; if the diameter is smaller, less water flows. An ordinary light bulb is an example of a resistor in an electrical circuit.

Suppose that two light bulbs are wired in parallel so that electricity can flow through either light bulb, as depicted in Figure 6.10. If their resistances are R_1 and R_2, their combined resistance R can be computed by the equation

$$\frac{1}{R} = \frac{1}{R_1} + \frac{1}{R_2}.$$

Resistance is often measured in a unit called *ohms*. A standard 60-watt light bulb might have a resistance of about 200 ohms. (**Source:** R. Weidner and R. Sells, *Elementary Classical Physics, Vol. 2.*)

EXAMPLE 8　Modeling electrical resistance

A 100-watt light bulb with a resistance of $R_1 = 120$ ohms and a 75-watt light bulb with a resistance of $R_2 = 160$ ohms are placed in an electrical circuit, as shown in Figure 6.10. Find their combined resistance.

Solution
Let $R_1 = 120$ and $R_2 = 160$ in the given equation and solve for R.

CRITICAL THINKING

If $\frac{1}{R} = \frac{1}{R_1} + \frac{1}{R_2}$, does it follow that $R = R_1 + R_2$? Explain your answer.

$$\frac{1}{R} = \frac{1}{R_1} + \frac{1}{R_2} \qquad \text{Given equation}$$

$$= \frac{1}{120} + \frac{1}{160} \qquad \text{Substitute for } R_1 \text{ and } R_2.$$

$$= \frac{1}{120} \cdot \frac{4}{4} + \frac{1}{160} \cdot \frac{3}{3} \qquad \text{LCD is 480.}$$

$$= \frac{4}{480} + \frac{3}{480} \qquad \text{Multiply.}$$

$$= \frac{7}{480} \qquad \text{Add.}$$

Because $\frac{1}{R} = \frac{7}{480}$, $R = \frac{480}{7} \approx 69$ ohms.

Now Try Exercise 91

6.3 PUTTING IT ALL TOGETHER

The following table summarizes some important concepts from this section.

Concept	Explanation	Example
Least Common Multiple (LCM)	To find the LCM, follow the three-step procedure presented on page 429.	To find the LCM of $2x^2 - 2x$ and $8x^2$, factor each expression: $$2x^2 - 2x = 2 \cdot x \cdot (x - 1) \quad \text{and}$$ $$8x^2 = 2 \cdot 2 \cdot 2 \cdot x \cdot x.$$ The LCM is $$2 \cdot 2 \cdot 2 \cdot x \cdot x \cdot (x - 1) = 8x^2(x - 1).$$

Concept	Explanation	Example
Least Common Denominator (LCD)	*The* LCD *equals the* LCM *of the denominators.*	The LCD for $\dfrac{3x}{2x^2 - 2x}$ and $\dfrac{5}{8x^2}$ is $8x^2(x - 1)$.
Addition and Subtraction of Rational Expressions	To add (or subtract) two rational expressions with like denominators, add (or subtract) their numerators. The denominator does not change. $$\frac{A}{C} + \frac{B}{C} = \frac{A + B}{C}$$ $$\frac{A}{C} - \frac{B}{C} = \frac{A - B}{C} \quad C \text{ not zero}$$ If the denominators are *not alike*, write each term with the LCD first.	Like denominators $$\frac{x}{x + 1} + \frac{3x}{x + 1} = \frac{4x}{x + 1}$$ Unlike denominators $$\frac{1}{x} - \frac{2x}{x + 1} = \frac{1}{x} \cdot \frac{x + 1}{x + 1} - \frac{2x}{x + 1} \cdot \frac{x}{x}$$ $$= \frac{x + 1}{x(x + 1)} - \frac{2x^2}{x(x + 1)}$$ $$= \frac{-2x^2 + x + 1}{x(x + 1)}$$

6.3 Exercises

MyMathLab
PRACTICE   WATCH   DOWNLOAD   READ   REVIEW

CONCEPTS

1. What is the LCM for 6 and 9?

2. What is the LCD for $\frac{1}{6}$ and $\frac{1}{9}$?

3. What is the LCM for $x^2 - 25$ and $x + 5$?

4. What is the LCD for $\frac{1}{x^2 - 25}$ and $\frac{1}{x + 5}$?

5. What do you need to find before you can add $\frac{1}{4}$ and $\frac{1}{3}$?

6. What do you need to find before you can add the expressions $\frac{2}{x}$ and $\frac{1}{2x - 1}$?

7. $\dfrac{a}{c} + \dfrac{b}{c} =$ _____.

8. $\dfrac{a}{c} - \dfrac{b}{c} =$ _____.

LEAST COMMON MULTIPLES

Exercises 9–20: Find the least common multiple.

9. 10, 15

10. 9, 12

11. 34, 51

12. 24, 36

13. $6a, 9a^2$

14. $12ab, 6a^2$

15. $10x^2, 25(x^2 - x)$

16. $x^2 - 4, x^2 + 2x$

17. $x^2 + 2x + 1, x^2 - 4x - 5$

18. $4x^2 + 20x + 25, 2x^2 + 5x$

19. $x + y, x - y$

20. $(x - y)^2, x^2 - y^2$

REVIEW OF FRACTIONS

Exercises 21–28: Simplify.

21. $\frac{1}{7} + \frac{4}{7}$

22. $\frac{2}{5} + \frac{1}{2}$

23. $\frac{2}{3} + \frac{5}{6} + \frac{1}{4}$

24. $\frac{3}{11} + \frac{1}{2} + \frac{1}{6}$

25. $\frac{1}{10} - \frac{3}{10}$

26. $\frac{2}{9} - \frac{1}{11}$

27. $\frac{3}{2} - \frac{1}{8}$

28. $\frac{3}{12} - \frac{5}{16}$

ADDITION AND SUBTRACTION OF RATIONAL EXPRESSIONS

Exercises 29–82: Simplify.

29. $\dfrac{1}{x} + \dfrac{3}{x}$

30. $\dfrac{2}{x - 1} + \dfrac{x}{x - 1}$

31. $\dfrac{2}{x^2 - 4} - \dfrac{x + 1}{x^2 - 4}$

32. $\dfrac{2x - 1}{x^2 + 6} - \dfrac{2x + 1}{x^2 + 6}$

33. $\dfrac{4}{x^2} + \dfrac{5}{x^2}$

34. $\dfrac{8}{b^3} - \dfrac{5}{b^3}$

35. $\dfrac{4}{xy} - \dfrac{7}{xy}$

36. $\dfrac{9}{a^2b} + \dfrac{1}{a^2b}$

37. $\dfrac{x}{x+1} + \dfrac{1}{x+1}$

38. $\dfrac{1}{2x-1} - \dfrac{2x}{2x-1}$

39. $\dfrac{2z}{4-z} - \dfrac{3z-4}{4-z}$

40. $\dfrac{z}{z^2-9} - \dfrac{3}{z^2-9}$

41. $\dfrac{4r}{5t^2} + \dfrac{r}{5t^2}$

42. $\dfrac{1}{2ab} + \dfrac{1}{2ab}$

43. $\dfrac{3t}{t^2-t-6} + \dfrac{2-2t}{t^2-t-6}$

44. $\dfrac{t}{t^2+5t} + \dfrac{5}{t^2+5t}$

45. $\dfrac{5b}{3a} - \dfrac{7b}{5a}$

46. $\dfrac{a}{ab^2} - \dfrac{b}{a^2b}$

47. $\dfrac{4}{n-4} + \dfrac{3}{2-n}$

48. $\dfrac{3}{2n-1} - \dfrac{3}{1-2n}$

49. $\dfrac{x}{x+4} - \dfrac{x+1}{x}$

50. $\dfrac{4x}{x+2} + \dfrac{x-5}{x-2}$

51. $\dfrac{2}{x^2} - \dfrac{4x-1}{x}$

52. $\dfrac{2x}{x-5} - \dfrac{x}{x+5}$

53. $\dfrac{x+3}{x-5} + \dfrac{5}{x-3}$

54. $\dfrac{x}{2x-1} + \dfrac{1-x}{3x}$

55. $\dfrac{4n}{n^2-9} - \dfrac{8}{n-3}$

56. $\dfrac{3n}{(4n-3)^2} - \dfrac{1}{4n-3}$

57. $\dfrac{x}{x^2-9} + \dfrac{5x}{x-3}$

58. $\dfrac{a^2+1}{a^2-1} + \dfrac{a}{1-a^2}$

59. $\dfrac{b}{2b-4} - \dfrac{b-1}{b-2}$

60. $\dfrac{y^2}{2-y} - \dfrac{y}{y^2-4}$

61. $\dfrac{2x}{x-5} + \dfrac{2x-1}{3x^2-16x+5}$

62. $\dfrac{x+3}{2x-1} + \dfrac{3}{10x^2-5x}$

63. $\dfrac{4x}{x-y} - \dfrac{9}{x+y}$

64. $\dfrac{1}{a-b} - \dfrac{3a}{a^2-b^2}$

65. $\dfrac{3}{(x-1)(x-2)} + \dfrac{4x}{(x+1)(x-2)}$

66. $\dfrac{x}{(x-1)^2} - \dfrac{1}{(x-1)(x+3)}$

67. $\dfrac{3}{x^2-x-6} - \dfrac{2}{x^2+5x+6}$

68. $\dfrac{x}{x^2-5x+4} + \dfrac{2}{x^2-2x-8}$

69. $\dfrac{3}{x^2-2x+1} + \dfrac{1}{x^2-3x+2}$

70. $\dfrac{x}{x^2-4} - \dfrac{1}{x^2+4x+4}$

71. $\dfrac{3x}{x^2+2x-3} + \dfrac{1}{x^2-2x+1}$

72. $\dfrac{3x}{x-y} - \dfrac{3y}{x^2-2xy+y^2}$

73. $\dfrac{4c}{ab} + \dfrac{3b}{ac} - \dfrac{2a}{bc}$

74. $x + \dfrac{1}{x-1} - \dfrac{1}{x+1}$

75. $5 - \dfrac{6}{n^2-36} + \dfrac{3}{n-6}$

76. $\dfrac{6}{t-1} + \dfrac{2}{t-2} + \dfrac{1}{t}$

77. $\dfrac{3}{x-5} - \dfrac{1}{x-3} - \dfrac{2x}{x-5}$

78. $\dfrac{2x+1}{x-1} - \dfrac{3}{x+1} + \dfrac{x}{x-1}$

79. $\dfrac{5}{2x-3} + \dfrac{x}{x+1} - \dfrac{x}{2x-3}$

80. $\dfrac{1}{x-3} - \dfrac{2}{x+3} + \dfrac{x}{x^2-9}$

81. $\dfrac{1}{x-1} - \dfrac{2}{x+1} + \dfrac{x}{x^2-1}$

82. $\dfrac{2}{x-2} + \dfrac{1}{x+3} - \dfrac{1}{x-1}$

Exercises 83 and 84: **Thinking Generally**　*Simplify.*

83. $\dfrac{a-b}{a+b} + \dfrac{a+b}{a-b}$

84. $\dfrac{1}{a^2-b^2} - \dfrac{1}{a^2+b^2}$

ADDITION AND SUBTRACTION OF FUNCTIONS

Exercises 85–88: Find $(f + g)(x)$ and $(f - g)(x)$.

85. $f(x) = \dfrac{1}{x + 1}, g(x) = \dfrac{x}{x + 1}$

86. $f(x) = \dfrac{1}{2x}, g(x) = \dfrac{3}{4x}$

87. $f(x) = \dfrac{1}{x + 2}, g(x) = \dfrac{1}{x - 2}$

88. $f(x) = \dfrac{1}{x + 1}, g(x) = \dfrac{1}{x}$

APPLICATIONS

89. *Planet Alignment*   Suppose that Saturn and Jupiter are in alignment with respect to the sun. If Jupiter orbits the sun every 12 years and Saturn orbits the sun every 30 years, how many years will it be before these two planets are back in the same location with the same alignment again?

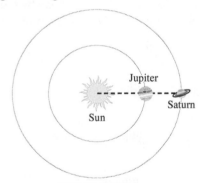

NOT TO SCALE

90. *Working Shifts*   Two friends work part-time at a store. The first person works every sixth day and the second person works every tenth day. If they are both working today, how many days pass before they both work on the same day again?

91. *Electrical Resistance*   (Refer to Example 8.) A 150-watt light bulb with a resistance of 80 ohms and a 40-watt light bulb with a resistance of 300 ohms are wired in parallel. Find the combined resistance.

92. *Electrical Resistance*   Solve the formula
$$\frac{1}{R} = \frac{1}{R_1} + \frac{1}{R_2}$$
for R. Use your formula to solve Exercise 91.

93. *Photography*   A lens in a camera has a focal length, which is important in focusing the camera. If an object is at distance D from a lens that has a focal length F, then to be in focus the distance S between the lens and the film should satisfy the equation

$$\frac{1}{S} = \frac{1}{F} - \frac{1}{D}.$$

(See the accompanying figure.) If the focal length is $F = 0.1$ foot and the object is $D = 10$ feet from the camera, find S.

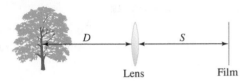

94. *Photography*   (Continuation of Exercise 93.) Suppose that the object is closer to the lens than the focal length of the lens. That is, suppose $D < F$. According to the formula, is it possible to focus the image on the film? Explain your reasoning.

95. *Intensity of a Light Bulb*   The intensity of a light bulb at a point varies according to its distance from the light bulb. The expression $\frac{8}{d^2}$ approximates the intensity of a 100-watt light bulb in watts per square meter (W/m^2) at a distance of d meters. Calculate the combined intensity at a point d meters from two 100-watt light bulbs.

96. *Intensity of a Light Bulb*   (Refer to the preceding exercise.) Suppose that one 100-watt light bulb is at a distance d and another 100-watt light bulb is at a distance $\frac{1}{2}d$ from a point. Write an expression for the combined intensity of the two light bulbs.

WRITING ABOUT MATHEMATICS

97. A student does the following to add two rational expressions. Explain the error that the student is making and how it can be corrected.

$$\frac{x}{x + 1} + \frac{6x}{x} \overset{?}{=} \frac{7x}{2x + 1}$$

98. Explain in words how to subtract two rational expressions with like denominators.

6.4 RATIONAL EQUATIONS

Solving Rational Equations ▪ Solving an Equation for a Variable

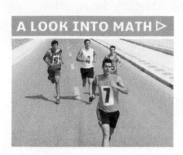

A LOOK INTO MATH ▷

In Section 6.1 we introduced rational equations. If an equation contains one or more rational expressions, it is often called a *rational equation*. Rational equations occur in applications involving distance and time. For example, if one athlete runs 2 miles per hour faster and finishes 3 minutes sooner than another athlete in a 3-mile race, then the speed of the slower athlete x can be found by solving the rational equation

$$\frac{3}{x+2} + \frac{1}{20} = \frac{3}{x}.$$

(To better understand why, refer to Example 7.) In this section we discuss how to solve different types of rational equations.

Solving Rational Equations

A rational expression is a ratio of two polynomials. In Sections 6.2 and 6.3, we *simplified* and *evaluated* rational expressions. Unlike a rational expression, a rational equation always contains an equals sign, and we *solve* this equation for any x-values that make the equation a true statement. One way to solve a rational equation is to *clear fractions* by multiplying each side of the equation by the least common denominator (LCD). For example, to solve

$$\frac{1}{2x} + \frac{2}{3} = \frac{5}{2x}$$

multiply each side by the LCD (LCM of 3 and $2x$), which is $6x$.

$$6x\left(\frac{1}{2x} + \frac{2}{3}\right) = 6x\left(\frac{5}{2x}\right) \qquad \text{Multiply each side by } 6x.$$

$$\frac{6x}{2x} + \frac{12x}{3} = \frac{30x}{2x} \qquad \text{Distributive property}$$

$$3 + 4x = 15 \qquad \text{Simplify.}$$

$$4x = 12 \qquad \text{Subtract 3 from each side.}$$

$$x = 3 \qquad \text{Divide each side by 4.}$$

Check this answer to verify that 3 is indeed a solution. *When solving a rational equation, always check your answer.* If one of your *possible answers* makes the denominator of an expression in the given equation equal to 0, it cannot be a solution.

EXAMPLE **1**   Solving rational equations

Solve each equation and check your answer.

(a) $\dfrac{x+1}{2x} - \dfrac{x-1}{4x} = \dfrac{1}{3}$ **(b)** $\dfrac{3}{x-2} + \dfrac{5}{x+2} = \dfrac{12}{x^2-4}$

Solution

(a) Note that the left side of the equation is undefined when $x = 0$. Thus 0 cannot be a solution. Start by determining the LCD, which is **$12x$**.

$$12x\left(\frac{x+1}{2x} - \frac{x-1}{4x}\right) = 12x\left(\frac{1}{3}\right) \qquad \text{Multiply each side by } 12x.$$

$$\frac{12x(x+1)}{2x} - \frac{12x(x-1)}{4x} = \frac{12x}{3} \qquad \text{Distributive property}$$

$$6(x+1) - 3(x-1) = 4x \qquad \text{Simplify.}$$

$$6x + 6 - 3x + 3 = 4x \qquad \text{Distributive property}$$

$$3x + 9 = 4x \qquad \text{Combine like terms.}$$

$$x = 9 \qquad \text{Solve for } x.$$

Check:

$$\frac{9+1}{2(9)} - \frac{9-1}{4(9)} \stackrel{?}{=} \frac{1}{3} \qquad \text{Let } x = 9 \text{ in given equation.}$$

$$\frac{10}{18} - \frac{8}{36} \stackrel{?}{=} \frac{1}{3} \qquad \text{Simplify.}$$

$$\frac{1}{3} = \frac{1}{3} \qquad \text{It checks.}$$

(b) Note that both sides of the equation are undefined when $x = 2$ or $x = -2$. Thus neither 2 nor -2 can be a solution. The LCD is $x^2 - 4 = (x-2)(x+2)$.

$$\frac{3(x-2)(x+2)}{x-2} + \frac{5(x-2)(x+2)}{x+2} = \frac{12(x^2-4)}{x^2-4} \qquad \text{Multiply each term by the LCD.}$$

$$3(x+2) + 5(x-2) = 12 \qquad \text{Simplify.}$$

$$3x + 6 + 5x - 10 = 12 \qquad \text{Distributive property}$$

$$8x - 4 = 12 \qquad \text{Combine like terms.}$$

$$8x = 16 \qquad \text{Add 4.}$$

$$x = 2 \qquad \text{Divide by 8.}$$

Check: We already noted that 2 cannot be a solution. However, checking this answer gives the following result.

$$\frac{3}{2-2} + \frac{5}{2+2} \stackrel{?}{=} \frac{12}{2^2-4} \qquad \text{Let } x = 2.$$

$$\frac{3}{0} + \frac{5}{4} \stackrel{?}{=} \frac{12}{0} \qquad \text{Simplify fractions.}$$

Both sides are undefined because division by 0 is not possible. There are no solutions.

Now Try Exercises 29, 37

The next example illustrates how to solve a rational equation graphically. Because graphical solutions are only estimates, be sure to check them by substituting observed values in the given equation.

EXAMPLE **2**   Solving a rational equation graphically

Solve the equation $\frac{4}{x-1} = 2x$ graphically. Check your results.

Solution
Start by graphing $y_1 = \frac{4}{x-1}$ and $y_2 = 2x$. The graph of y_2 is a line with slope 2 passing through the origin. To help graph y_1 make a table of values or use a graphing calculator. The two graphs intersect when $x = -1$ and $x = 2$, as shown in Figure 6.11.

Figure 6.11

Check: $\frac{4}{-1-1} \overset{?}{=} 2(-1)$ Let $x = -1$. $\frac{4}{2-1} \overset{?}{=} 2(2)$ Let $x = 2$.

$-2 = -2$ It checks. $4 = 4$ It checks.

Now Try Exercise **55**

The next example illustrates how to solve two rational equations and support the results with a graphing calculator.

EXAMPLE **3**   Solving rational equations

Solve each equation. Support your results either graphically or numerically.

(a) $\frac{1}{2} + \frac{x}{3} = \frac{x}{5}$ **(b)** $\frac{3}{x+3} - 2 = \frac{x}{x+3}$ **(c)** $\frac{3}{x-2} = \frac{5}{x+2}$

Solution
(a) The LCD is the product of 2, 3, and 5, which is **30**.

$$30 \cdot \left(\frac{1}{2} + \frac{x}{3}\right) = \frac{x}{5} \cdot 30$$ Multiply by the LCD.

$$\frac{30}{2} + \frac{30x}{3} = \frac{30x}{5}$$ Distributive property

$$15 + 10x = 6x$$ Simplify.

$$4x = -15$$ Subtract $6x$ and 15.

$$x = -\frac{15}{4}$$ Solve.

[−9, 9, 1] by [−6, 6, 1]

Intersection
X=-3.75   Y=-.75

Figure 6.12

This result can be supported graphically by letting $Y_1 = 1/2 + X/3$ and $Y_2 = X/5$. Their graphs intersect at the point $(-3.75, -0.75)$, as shown in Figure 6.12. Therefore the solution to this equation is -3.75, or $-\frac{15}{4}$.

(b) Multiply each side by the LCD, which is $x + 3$.

$$(x + 3) \cdot \left(\frac{3}{x+3} - 2\right) = \frac{x}{x+3} \cdot (x + 3)$$ Multiply by the LCD.

$$3 - 2(x + 3) = x$$ Distributive property

$$3 - 2x - 6 = x$$ Distributive property

$$-3 = 3x$$ Add $2x$ to each side.

$$x = -1$$ Divide by 3; rewrite.

[−9.4, 9.4, 1] by [−6.2, 6.2, 1]

Intersection
X=-1   \ | Y=-.5

Figure 6.13

Figure 6.13 supports that -1 is a solution by showing that the graphs of the equations $Y_1 = 3/(X + 3) - 2$ and $Y_2 = X/(X + 3)$ intersect at $(-1, -0.5)$.

NOTE: Because graphs of rational expressions are often nonlinear, it may be difficult to locate graphical solutions.

(c) Multiply each side by the LCD, which is $(x - 2)(x + 2)$.

$$(x - 2)(x + 2) \cdot \frac{3}{x - 2} = \frac{5}{x + 2} \cdot (x - 2)(x + 2) \qquad \text{Multiply by the LCD.}$$

$$\frac{3(x - 2)(x + 2)}{x - 2} = \frac{5(x - 2)(x + 2)}{x + 2} \qquad \text{Multiply expressions.}$$

$$3(x + 2) = 5(x - 2) \qquad \text{Simplify.}$$

$$3x + 6 = 5x - 10 \qquad \text{Distributive property}$$

$$16 = 2x \qquad \text{Add 10 and subtract } 3x.$$

$$x = 8 \qquad \text{Divide by 2; rewrite.}$$

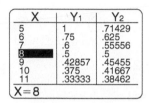

Figure 6.14

To support this result numerically, let $Y_1 = 3/(X - 2)$ and $Y_2 = 5/(X + 2)$. The table in Figure 6.14 shows that $y_1 = y_2 = 0.5$ when $x = 8$. The solution is 8.

Now Try Exercises 65, 67

TECHNOLOGY NOTE: Entering Rational Expressions

When entering a rational expression, use parentheses around the numerator and denominator, as in the following example. Enter

$$y = \frac{x + 1}{2x - 1} \quad \text{as} \quad Y_1 = (X + 1)/(2X - 1).$$

Sometimes solving a rational equation results in the need to solve a quadratic equation, which is demonstrated in the next example.

EXAMPLE 4   Solving rational equations

Solve the equation.

(a) $\dfrac{1}{x} + \dfrac{1}{x^2} = \dfrac{3}{4}$ **(b)** $\dfrac{2x}{x + 2} + \dfrac{3x}{x - 1} = 7$

Solution
(a) The LCD is $4x^2$. Note that 0 cannot be a solution.

$$4x^2 \cdot \left(\frac{1}{x} + \frac{1}{x^2} \right) = \frac{3}{4} \cdot 4x^2 \qquad \text{Multiply by } 4x^2.$$

$$\frac{4x^2}{x} + \frac{4x^2}{x^2} = \frac{12x^2}{4} \qquad \text{Distributive property}$$

$$4x + 4 = 3x^2 \qquad \text{Simplify.}$$

$$0 = 3x^2 - 4x - 4 \qquad \text{Subtract } 4x \text{ and 4.}$$

$$0 = (3x + 2)(x - 2) \qquad \text{Factor.}$$

$$x = -\frac{2}{3} \quad \text{or} \quad x = 2 \qquad \text{Solve.}$$

Both solutions check.

(b) The LCD is $(x + 2)(x - 1)$. Note that -2 and 1 cannot be solutions.

$$(x + 2)(x - 1)\left(\frac{2x}{x + 2} + \frac{3x}{x - 1}\right) = 7(x + 2)(x - 1) \qquad \text{Multiply by the LCD.}$$

$$\frac{2x(x + 2)(x - 1)}{x + 2} + \frac{3x(x + 2)(x - 1)}{x - 1} = 7(x + 2)(x - 1) \qquad \text{Distributive property.}$$

$$2x(x - 1) + 3x(x + 2) = 7(x + 2)(x - 1) \qquad \text{Simplify.}$$

$$2x^2 - 2x + 3x^2 + 6x = 7(x^2 + x - 2) \qquad \text{Multiply.}$$

$$5x^2 + 4x = 7x^2 + 7x - 14 \qquad \text{Simplify.}$$

$$0 = 2x^2 + 3x - 14 \qquad \text{Subtract } 5x^2 \text{ and } 4x.$$

$$0 = (2x + 7)(x - 2) \qquad \text{Factor.}$$

$$x = -\frac{7}{2} \quad \text{or} \quad x = 2 \qquad \text{Solve.}$$

Both solutions check.   Now Try Exercises 33, 39

▶ **REAL-WORLD CONNECTION**   Rational equations are frequently used to estimate the time spent waiting in line whenever arrivals are random. This concept is illustrated in the next example.

EXAMPLE 5   Modeling waiting time

Suppose that cars are arriving randomly at a construction zone and that the flag person can instruct x drivers per minute. If cars arrive at an average rate of 7 cars per minute, the average time T in minutes for each driver to wait and talk to the flag person is

$$T(x) = \frac{1}{x - 7},$$

where $x > 7$. How many drivers per minute should the flag person be able to instruct to keep the average wait to 1 minute?   (*Source:* N. Garber.)

Solution
We must determine x such that $T(x) = 1$.

$$\frac{1}{x - 7} = 1 \qquad \text{Equation to be solved.}$$

$$(x - 7) \cdot \frac{1}{x - 7} = 1 \cdot (x - 7) \qquad \text{Multiply by the LCD.}$$

$$1 = x - 7 \qquad \text{Simplify.}$$

$$8 = x \qquad \text{Add 7 to each side.}$$

The flag person should be able to instruct 8 drivers per minute to limit the average wait to 1 minute.   Now Try Exercise 86

▶ **REAL-WORLD CONNECTION**   Rational equations occur in applications involving time and rate, as demonstrated in the next example.

EXAMPLE 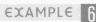 6 Determining the time required to empty a pool

A pump can empty a swimming pool in 50 hours. To speed up the process a second pump is used that can empty the pool in 80 hours. How long will it take for both pumps working together to empty the pool?

Solution

Because the first pump can empty the entire pool in 50 hours, it can empty $\frac{1}{50}$ of the pool in 1 hour, $\frac{2}{50}$ of the pool in 2 hours, $\frac{3}{50}$ of the pool in 3 hours, and in general, it can empty $\frac{t}{50}$ of the pool in t hours. The second pump can empty the pool in 80 hours, so (using similar reasoning) it can empty $\frac{t}{80}$ of the pool in t hours.

   Together the pumps can empty

$$\frac{t}{50} + \frac{t}{80}$$

of the pool in t hours. The job will be complete when the fraction of the pool that is empty equals 1. Thus we must solve the equation

$$\frac{t}{50} + \frac{t}{80} = 1.$$

To clear fractions we can multiply each side by $(50)(80)$. (We could also use the LCD of 400.)

$$(50)(80)\left(\frac{t}{50} + \frac{t}{80}\right) = 1(50)(80)$$

$$\frac{50 \cdot 80 \cdot t}{50} + \frac{50 \cdot 80 \cdot t}{80} = 4000 \qquad \text{Distributive property}$$

$$80t + 50t = 4000 \qquad \text{Simplify.}$$

$$130t = 4000 \qquad \text{Combine like terms.}$$

$$t = \frac{4000}{130} \approx 30.8 \text{ hours} \qquad \text{Solve.}$$

The two pumps can empty the pool in about 30.8 hours.   Now Try Exercise 88

▶ REAL-WORLD CONNECTION   If a person drives a car 60 miles per hour for 4 hours, the total distance d traveled is

$$d = 60 \cdot 4 = 240 \text{ miles.}$$

That is, distance equals the product of the rate (speed) and the elapsed time. This may be written as $d = rt$ and expressed verbally as "distance equals rate times time." This formula is used in Example 7.

CRITICAL THINKING

A bicyclist rides uphill at 6 miles per hour for 1 mile and then rides downhill at 12 miles per hour for 1 mile. What is the average speed of the bicyclist?

EXAMPLE 7   Solving an application

The winner of a 3-mile race finishes 3 minutes ahead of another runner. If the winner runs 2 miles per hour faster than the slower runner, find the average speed of each runner.

Figure 6.15

Solution
Let x be the speed of the slower runner. Then $x + 2$ represents the speed of the winner. See Figure 6.15. To determine the time for each runner to finish the race divide each side of $d = rt$ by r to obtain

$$t = \frac{d}{r}.$$

The slower runner runs 3 miles at x miles per hour, so the time is $\frac{3}{x}$; the winner runs 3 miles at $x + 2$ miles per hour, so the winning time is $\frac{3}{x + 2}$. We summarize this in Table 6.3.

TABLE 6.3

	Distance (mi)	Rate (mi/hr)	Time (hr)
Winning Runner	3	$x + 2$	$\frac{3}{x + 2}$
Other Runner	3	x	$\frac{3}{x}$

If you add 3 minutes (or equivalently $\frac{3}{60} = \frac{1}{20}$ hour) to the winner's time, it equals the slower runner's time, or

$$\frac{3}{x + 2} + \frac{1}{20} = \frac{3}{x}.$$

NOTE: The runners' speeds are in miles per *hour*, so you need to keep time in hours.

Multiply each side by the LCD, which is $20x(x + 2)$.

$$20x(x + 2)\left(\frac{3}{x + 2} + \frac{1}{20}\right) = 20x(x + 2)\left(\frac{3}{x}\right) \qquad \text{Multiply by the LCD.}$$
$$60x + x(x + 2) = 60(x + 2) \qquad \text{Distributive property}$$
$$60x + x^2 + 2x = 60x + 120 \qquad \text{Distributive property}$$
$$x^2 + 2x - 120 = 0 \qquad \text{Rewrite the equation.}$$
$$(x + 12)(x - 10) = 0 \qquad \text{Factor.}$$
$$x = -12 \quad \text{or} \quad x = 10 \qquad \text{Solve.}$$

The only valid solution is 10 because a running speed cannot be negative. Thus the slower runner is running at 10 miles per hour, and the faster runner is running at 12 miles per hour.

Now Try Exercise 89

Solving an Equation for a Variable

▶ REAL-WORLD CONNECTION   Sometimes in science and other disciplines, it is necessary to solve a formula for a variable. These formulas are often rational equations. This technique is demonstrated in the next two examples.

EXAMPLE 8   Solving an equation for a variable

Solve the equation $P = \frac{nrT}{V}$ for V. (This formula is used to calculate the pressure of a gas.)

Solution
Start by multiplying each side of the equation by V.

$$V \cdot P = V\left(\frac{nrT}{V}\right)$$ Multiply by V.

$$PV = nrT$$ Simplify.

$$\frac{PV}{P} = \frac{nrT}{P}$$ Divide each side by P.

$$V = \frac{nrT}{P}$$ Simplify.   Now Try Exercise 71

EXAMPLE 9   Solving an equation from electricity

Solve the equation $\frac{1}{R} = \frac{1}{R_1} + \frac{1}{R_2}$ for R_2.

Solution
Start by multiplying each side of the equation by the LCD: RR_1R_2.

$$(RR_1R_2)\frac{1}{R} = (RR_1R_2)\left(\frac{1}{R_1} + \frac{1}{R_2}\right)$$ Multiply by the LCD.

$$R_1R_2 = RR_2 + RR_1$$ Distributive property

$$R_1R_2 - RR_2 = RR_1$$ Subtract RR_2.

$$R_2(R_1 - R) = RR_1$$ Factor out R_2.

$$R_2 = \frac{RR_1}{R_1 - R}$$ Divide each side by $R_1 - R$.

Now Try Exercise 77

6.4   PUTTING IT ALL TOGETHER

The following table summarizes the basic steps for solving a rational equation.

Concept	Explanation	Example
Rational Equations	To solve a rational equation, first multiply each side of the equation by the LCD. Then solve the resulting polynomial equation. Be sure to check your answer(s). *The LCD is the LCM of the denominators.*	Multiply each term by $4x^2$. $$\frac{1}{4x} + \frac{2}{x^2} = \frac{1}{x}$$ $$\frac{4x^2}{4x} + \frac{8x^2}{x^2} = \frac{4x^2}{x}$$ $$x + 8 = 4x$$ $$8 = 3x$$ $$x = \frac{8}{3}$$

continued on next page

continued from previous page

The following example illustrates how to solve the rational equation $\frac{2}{x} + 2 = 3$ symbolically, graphically, and numerically with the aid of a graphing calculator, where we let $Y_1 = 2/X + 2$ and $Y_2 = 3$.

Symbolic Solution

$$\frac{2}{x} + 2 = 3$$

$$\frac{2}{x} = 1$$

$$2 = x$$

The solution is **2**.

Numerical Solution

$y_1 = 3$ when $x = $ **2**.

Graphical Solution

$[-4.7, 4.7, 1]$ by $[-1, 5, 1]$

The graphs intersect at (**2**, 3).

6.4 Exercises

MyMathLab   Math XL PRACTICE   WATCH   DOWNLOAD   READ   REVIEW

CONCEPTS

1. When solving the equation $\frac{4}{x+2} = 2$, what is a good first step?

2. In general, what is a good first step when solving a rational equation?

3. If $\frac{1}{x} = 2$, then $x = $ _____.

4. If $\frac{a}{b} = c$, then $a = $ _____.

5. To clear an equation of fractions, multiply each side of the equation by the _____.

6. To solve a rational equation graphically, graph each side of the equation and determine x-coordinates of the point(s) where the graphs _____.

SOLVING RATIONAL EQUATIONS

Exercises 7–12: Find the LCD.

7. $\frac{1}{x}, \frac{1}{5}$

8. $\frac{1}{x-1}, \frac{1}{x+5}$

9. $\frac{1}{x-1}, \frac{1}{x^2-1}$

10. $\frac{1}{x^2-x}, \frac{1}{2x}$

11. $\frac{3}{2}, \frac{x}{2x+1}, \frac{x}{2x-4}$

12. $\frac{1}{x}, \frac{1}{x^2-4x}, \frac{1}{2x}$

Exercises 13–46: Solve. Check your result.

13. $\frac{x}{3} + \frac{1}{2} = \frac{5}{6}$

14. $\frac{7}{8} - \frac{x}{4} = -\frac{11}{8}$

15. $\frac{2}{x} - \frac{7}{3} = -\frac{29}{15}$

16. $\frac{1}{3x} + \frac{1}{x} = \frac{4}{15}$

17. $\frac{x}{x-1} = \frac{4}{3}$

18. $\frac{4}{5x} = -\frac{1}{x+1}$

19. $\frac{1}{2x} - \frac{5}{3x} = 1$

20. $\frac{3}{4x} + \frac{5}{6x} = -\frac{19}{12}$

21. $\frac{1}{x+1} - 1 = \frac{3}{x+1}$

22. $\frac{2}{x-2} + 2 = \frac{4}{x-2}$

23. $\frac{1}{x-3} + \frac{x}{x-3} = \frac{2x}{x-3}$

24. $\frac{6}{x+2} + \frac{3x}{x+2} = \frac{3}{x+2}$

25. $\frac{3}{x-1} = \frac{6}{x+4}$

26. $\frac{1}{x+5} = \frac{2}{2x+1}$

27. $\dfrac{6}{3z + 4} = \dfrac{4}{2z - 5}$

28. $\dfrac{2}{z - 1} - \dfrac{5}{z + 1} = \dfrac{4}{z^2 - 1}$

29. $\dfrac{5}{t - 1} + \dfrac{2}{t + 2} = \dfrac{15}{t^2 + t - 2}$

30. $\dfrac{3}{5t} - \dfrac{1}{t + 1} = \dfrac{6}{5t^2 + 5t}$

31. $\dfrac{1}{3n} - 2 = \dfrac{1}{2n}$

32. $\dfrac{4}{n} - 3 = \dfrac{1}{3n}$

33. $\dfrac{1}{x} + \dfrac{1}{x^2} = 2$

34. $\dfrac{1}{x} - \dfrac{1}{x + 1} = \dfrac{1}{56}$

35. $\dfrac{x}{x + 2} = \dfrac{4}{x - 3}$

36. $\dfrac{2x}{1 - x} - \dfrac{1}{x} = 0$

37. $\dfrac{2w + 1}{3w} - \dfrac{4w - 3}{w} = 0$

38. $\dfrac{1}{2w} - \dfrac{2}{1 - w} = -\dfrac{3}{2}$

39. $\dfrac{3}{2y} + \dfrac{2y}{y - 4} = -\dfrac{11}{2}$

40. $\dfrac{3}{y - 2} + \dfrac{6y}{y + 1} = 2$

41. $\dfrac{1}{(x - 1)^2} + \dfrac{3}{x^2 - 1} = \dfrac{5}{x^2 - 1}$

42. $\dfrac{1}{x^2 - 4} + \dfrac{1}{(x - 2)^2} = \dfrac{2}{(x + 2)^2}$

43. $\dfrac{x^2 + x - 2}{x - 2} - \dfrac{4}{x - 2} = 0$

44. $\dfrac{x^2 - 4x - 5}{x - 1} + \dfrac{8}{x - 1} = 0$

45. $\dfrac{4}{x + 3} - \dfrac{x}{3 - x} = \dfrac{18}{x^2 - 9}$

46. $\dfrac{12}{x^2 - 9} + \dfrac{2}{x + 3} = \dfrac{x}{3 - x}$

Exercises 47 and 48: Solve $f(x) = 0$ for the given $f(x)$.

47. $f(x) = \dfrac{1}{x} - 4x$

48. $f(x) = \dfrac{2 - x}{x} + 2$

Exercises 49 and 50: **Thinking Generally** *Solve for x.*

49. $\dfrac{a}{x} - \dfrac{b}{x} = c$

50. $\dfrac{ab}{x} - c = \dfrac{1}{x}$

Exercises 51–54: Use the graph to solve the rational equation. Then check your answer.

51. $\dfrac{2}{x} + 1 = 3$

52. $\dfrac{1}{x - 1} = \dfrac{2}{x}$

53. $\dfrac{3}{x^2 - 1} = \dfrac{1}{2}x$

54. $\dfrac{1}{x^2} = -x$

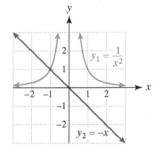

Exercises 55–64: Solve the rational equation graphically. Approximate your answer(s) to the nearest hundredth when appropriate.

55. $\dfrac{1}{x - 1} = \dfrac{1}{2}$

56. $\dfrac{1}{x + 1} = 2$

57. $\dfrac{3}{x + 2} = x$

58. $\dfrac{3}{x - 2} = x$

59. $\dfrac{1}{x - 2} = 2$

60. $\dfrac{2x}{x + 1} = 3$

 61. $\dfrac{1}{x} + \dfrac{1}{x^2} = \dfrac{15}{4}$

62. $\dfrac{1}{x} + \dfrac{1}{2x} = 2x$

63. $\dfrac{1}{x + 2} - \dfrac{1}{x - 2} = \dfrac{4}{3}$

64. $\dfrac{x}{2x + 4} - \dfrac{2x}{x^2 - 4} = 2.7$

USING MORE THAN ONE METHOD

Exercises 65–68: Solve the equation (a) symbolically, (b) graphically, and (c) numerically.

65. $\dfrac{1}{x} + \dfrac{2}{3} = 1$

66. $\dfrac{1}{x} - \dfrac{1}{x^2} = -2$

67. $\dfrac{1}{x} + \dfrac{1}{x+2} = \dfrac{4}{3}$

68. $\dfrac{1}{x-2} + \dfrac{1}{x+2} = -\dfrac{2}{3}$

Exercises 69 and 70: Solve the equation graphically to the nearest hundredth.

69. $\dfrac{x}{x^2-1} - \dfrac{3}{x+2} = 2$

70. $\dfrac{2.2}{x-0.1} + \dfrac{x}{0.4x-1} = 1$

SOLVING AN EQUATION FOR A VARIABLE

Exercises 71–84: Solve for the specified variable.

71. $t = \dfrac{d}{r}$ for r

72. $r = \dfrac{C}{2\pi}$ for C

73. $h = \dfrac{2A}{b}$ for b

74. $P = VT$ for T

75. $\dfrac{1}{2a} = \dfrac{1}{b}$ for a

76. $\dfrac{a}{b} = \dfrac{c}{d}$ for d

77. $\dfrac{1}{R} = \dfrac{1}{R_1} + \dfrac{1}{R_2}$ for R_1

78. $S = \dfrac{5}{8H}$ for H

79. $T = \dfrac{1}{15-x}$ for x

80. $h = \dfrac{V}{\pi r^2}$ for V

81. $\dfrac{1}{r} = \dfrac{1}{t+1}$ for t

82. $R = \dfrac{R_1 R_2}{R_1 + R_2}$ for R_2

83. $\dfrac{1}{r} = \dfrac{a}{a+b}$ for b

84. $\dfrac{1}{t+1} = \dfrac{a}{a-b}$ for b

APPLICATIONS

85. *Waiting in Line* At a parking lot, the attendant can wait on 60 people per hour. If people arrive randomly at an average rate of x cars per hour, the average number of cars N waiting to exit the lot is given by

$$N(x) = \frac{x^2}{3600 - 60x},$$

where $x < 60$. (*Source:* N. Garber.)
(a) Approximate x when $N(x) = 8$.
(b) Interpret your answer.

86. *Waiting in Traffic* Suppose that cars are arriving randomly at a construction zone and the flag person can instruct x drivers per hour. If cars arrive at an average rate of 80 cars per hour, the average time T in minutes for each driver to wait and talk to the flag person is given by the formula

$$T(x) = \frac{1}{x - 80},$$

where $x > 80$. (*Source:* N. Garber.)
(a) How many drivers per hour should the flag person be able to instruct to keep the average wait to 0.5 minute?
(b) What happens to T if x is only slightly more than 80?

87. *Mowing the Lawn* Suppose that a person with a push mower can mow a large lawn in 5 hours, whereas the same lawn can be mowed with a riding mower in 2 hours.
(a) Write an equation whose solution gives the time needed to mow the lawn if both mowers are used at the same time.
(b) Solve the equation in part (a) symbolically.
(c) Solve the equation in part (a) either graphically or numerically.

88. *Pumping Water* (Refer to Example 6.) Suppose that a large pump can empty a swimming pool in 40 hours and that a small pump can empty the same pool in 70 hours.
(a) Write an equation whose solution gives the time needed for both pumps to empty the pool.
(b) Solve the equation in part (a) symbolically.
(c) Solve the equation in part (a) either graphically or numerically.

89. *Running a Race*   (Refer to Example 7.) The winner of a 5-mile race finishes 7.5 minutes ahead of the second-place runner. On average, the winner ran 2 miles per hour faster than the second-place runner. Find the average running speed for each runner.

90. *Filling a Water Tank*   A large pump can fill a 10,000-gallon tank 5 hours faster than a small pump. The large pump outputs water 100 gallons per hour faster than the small pump. Find the number of gallons pumped in 1 hour by each pump.

91. *Aerial Photographs*   An aerial photograph is being taken of an area of land. The scale S for the photograph is planned to be $S = \frac{1}{10,000}$. (This value for S means that a distance of 10,000 feet on land will be represented by 1 foot in the photograph.) If H represents the height of the airplane above the ground (see the accompanying figure), these quantities are related by the rational equation

$$S = \frac{0.625}{H}.$$

Determine the height at which the plane must fly for the photograph to have the correct scale.   (*Source:* N. Garber and L. Hoel, *Traffic and Highway Engineering*.)

92. *Aerial Photographs*   (Continuation of Exercise 91.) Suppose that the scale for the photograph is changed from $\frac{1}{10,000}$ to $\frac{1}{5000}$.
   (a) Should the plane fly higher or lower for this new scale? Explain your reasoning.
   (b) Test your conjecture in part (a) by letting S equal $\frac{1}{5000}$ in the equation and finding H.

93. *Speed of a Current*   In still water a tugboat can travel 15 miles per hour. It travels 36 miles upstream and then 36 miles downstream in a total time of 5 hours. Find the speed of the current.

94. *Wind Speed*   Without any wind an airplane flies at 200 miles per hour. The plane travels 800 miles into the wind and then returns with the wind in a total time of 8 hours and 20 minutes. Find the average speed of the wind.

95. *Speed of an Airplane*   When there is a 50-mile per hour wind, an airplane can fly 675 miles with the wind in the same time that it can fly 450 miles against the wind. Find the speed of the plane when there is no wind.

96. *Waiting in Line*   If a ticket agent can wait on 25 people per hour and people are arriving randomly at an average rate of x people per hour, the average time T in hours for people waiting in line *and* paying the agent is

$$T(x) = \frac{1}{25 - x},$$

where $x < 25$.   (*Source:* N. Garber.)
   (a) Solve the equation $T(x) = 5$ symbolically and interpret the result.
   (b) Solve part (a) either graphically or numerically.

97. *Working Alone*   It takes one employee 3 hours longer to mow a football field than it does a more experienced employee. Together they can mow the grass in 2 hours. How long does it take for each person to mow the football field working alone?

98. *Painting a House*   It takes one painter 20 hours longer to paint a house than it does a more experienced painter. Together they can paint the house in 24 hours. How long does it take for each painter to paint the house working alone?

99. *Walking Speed*   One person can walk 1 mile per hour faster than another person. The faster person can walk 12 miles in the time it takes the slower person to walk 9 miles. What is the walking speed of each person?

100. *Freeway Speed*   A car passes another car on a freeway traveling 5 miles per hour faster than the slower car. The faster car travels 340 miles in the time it takes the slower car to travel 315 miles. What is the speed of each car?

101. *Emptying a Pool*   An inlet pipe can fill a pool in 60 hours whereas an outlet pipe can empty the pool in 40 hours. If both pipes are left open, how long will it take to empty the pool if the pool is full initially?

102. *Emptying a Boat*   A small leak will fill an empty boat in 5 hours. The boat's bilge pump will empty a full boat in 3 hours. If the boat were half full and leaking, how long would it take the pump to empty the boat?

Exercises 103 and 104: Graphical Interpretation Use the graph of the rational function f to decide if there is a solution to the given equation. If there is a solution, discuss its value.

103. $f(x) = 100$ **104.** $f(x) = -100$

WRITING ABOUT MATHEMATICS

105. A student does the following to solve a rational equation. Is the work correct? Explain any errors and how you might correct them.

$$\frac{1}{x+1} + \frac{2}{x-1} = -1$$
$$(x-1) + 2(x+1) \overset{?}{=} -1$$
$$3x + 1 \overset{?}{=} -1$$
$$x \overset{?}{=} -\frac{2}{3}$$

106. Explain the difference between simplifying the rational expression $\frac{x+1}{x^2-1}$ and solving the rational equation $\frac{x+1}{x^2-1} = \frac{1}{2}$.

CHECKING BASIC CONCEPTS
SECTIONS 6.3 AND 6.4

1. Simplify each expression.

(a) $\dfrac{x}{x^2-1} + \dfrac{1}{x^2-1}$

(b) $\dfrac{1}{x-2} - \dfrac{3}{x}$

(c) $\dfrac{1}{x(x-1)} + \dfrac{1}{x^2-1} - \dfrac{2}{x(x+1)}$

2. Solve each equation.

(a) $\dfrac{6}{x} - \dfrac{1}{2} = 1$ **(b)** $\dfrac{3}{2x-1} = \dfrac{2}{x+1}$

(c) $\dfrac{2}{x-1} + \dfrac{3}{x+2} = \dfrac{x}{x^2+x-2}$

3. If a gas pump can fill a 200-gallon tank in 12 minutes and a smaller gas pump can fill the same tank in 28 minutes, how long will it take for the pumps to fill the tank together?

4. Solve $\frac{1}{S} = \frac{1}{F} - \frac{1}{D}$ for S.

6.5   COMPLEX FRACTIONS

Basic Concepts ■ Simplifying Complex Fractions

A LOOK INTO MATH ▷

If two and a half pizzas are cut into fourths, then there are 10 pieces of pizza. This problem can be written as

$$\frac{2 + \dfrac{1}{2}}{\dfrac{1}{4}} = 10.$$

The expression on the left side of the equation is called a *complex fraction*. Typically, we want to simplify a complex fraction to a fraction with the standard form $\frac{a}{b}$. In this section we discuss how to simplify complex fractions.

Basic Concepts

A **complex fraction** is a rational expression that contains fractions in its numerator, denominator, or both. Examples of complex fractions include

$$\frac{1 + \dfrac{1}{x}}{1 - \dfrac{1}{x}}, \quad \frac{2x}{\dfrac{4}{x} + \dfrac{3}{y}}, \quad \text{and} \quad \frac{\dfrac{a}{3} + \dfrac{a}{4}}{a - \dfrac{1}{a - 1}}.$$

Complex fractions involve division of fractions. When dividing two fractions, we can multiply the first fraction by the reciprocal of the second fraction.

SIMPLIFYING COMPLEX FRACTIONS

For any real numbers a, b, c, and d,

$$\frac{\dfrac{a}{b}}{\dfrac{c}{d}} = \frac{a}{b} \cdot \frac{d}{c},$$

where b, c, and d are not zero.

EXAMPLE 1   Simplifying basic types of complex fractions

Simplify.

(a) $\dfrac{\dfrac{7}{8}}{\dfrac{3}{4}}$ **(b)** $\dfrac{\dfrac{a}{4b}}{\dfrac{a}{6b^2}}$ **(c)** $\dfrac{2 + \dfrac{1}{2}}{\dfrac{1}{4}}$

Solution
(a) Rather than dividing $\frac{7}{8}$ by $\frac{3}{4}$, multiply $\frac{7}{8}$ by $\frac{4}{3}$.

$$\frac{\dfrac{7}{8}}{\dfrac{3}{4}} = \frac{7}{8} \cdot \frac{4}{3} \qquad \text{"Invert and multiply."}$$

$$= \frac{7}{6} \qquad \text{Multiply and simplify.}$$

(b) Rather than dividing $\frac{a}{4b}$ by $\frac{a}{6b^2}$, multiply $\frac{a}{4b}$ by $\frac{6b^2}{a}$.

$$\frac{\dfrac{a}{4b}}{\dfrac{a}{6b^2}} = \frac{a}{4b} \cdot \frac{6b^2}{a} \qquad \text{"Invert and multiply."}$$

$$= \frac{6ab^2}{4ab} \qquad \text{Multiply fractions.}$$

$$= \frac{3b}{2} \qquad \text{Simplify.}$$

(c) Start by writing $2 + \frac{1}{2}$ as one fraction.

$$\frac{2 + \dfrac{1}{2}}{\dfrac{1}{4}} = \frac{\dfrac{5}{2}}{\dfrac{1}{4}} \qquad \text{Write as an improper fraction.}$$

$$= \frac{5}{2} \cdot \frac{4}{1} \qquad \text{"Invert and multiply."}$$

$$= 10 \qquad \text{Simplify.} \qquad \boxed{\text{Now Try Exercises } \; 7, 11, 13}$$

Simplifying Complex Fractions

There are two basic strategies for simplifying a complex fraction. The first is to simplify both the numerator and the denominator and then divide the resulting fractions as was done in Example 1(c). The second is to multiply the numerator and denominator by the least common denominator of the fractions in the numerator and denominator.

SIMPLIFYING THE NUMERATOR AND DENOMINATOR   The next example illustrates the method whereby the numerator and denominator are simplified first.

EXAMPLE 2   Simplifying complex fractions

Simplify.

(a) $\dfrac{1 + \dfrac{1}{x}}{1 - \dfrac{1}{x}}$ (b) $\dfrac{2t - \dfrac{1}{2t}}{2t + \dfrac{1}{2t}}$ (c) $\dfrac{\dfrac{1}{z+1} - \dfrac{1}{z-1}}{\dfrac{2}{z+2} - \dfrac{2}{z-2}}$

Solution

(a) First, simplify the numerator by writing it as one term. The LCD is x.

$$1 + \frac{1}{x} = \frac{x}{x} + \frac{1}{x} = \frac{x+1}{x}$$

Second, simplify the denominator by writing it as one term.

$$1 - \frac{1}{x} = \frac{x}{x} - \frac{1}{x} = \frac{x-1}{x}$$

Finally, simplify the complex fraction.

$$\frac{1 + \dfrac{1}{x}}{1 - \dfrac{1}{x}} = \frac{\dfrac{x+1}{x}}{\dfrac{x-1}{x}} \qquad \text{Simplify.}$$

$$= \frac{x+1}{x} \cdot \frac{x}{x-1} \qquad \text{"Invert and multiply."}$$

$$= \frac{x+1}{x-1} \qquad \text{Multiply and simplify.}$$

(b) Combine the terms in the numerator and in the denominator. The LCD is $2t$.

$$\frac{2t - \dfrac{1}{2t}}{2t + \dfrac{1}{2t}} = \frac{\dfrac{4t^2}{2t} - \dfrac{1}{2t}}{\dfrac{4t^2}{2t} + \dfrac{1}{2t}} \qquad \text{Write with the LCD.}$$

$$= \frac{\dfrac{4t^2 - 1}{2t}}{\dfrac{4t^2 + 1}{2t}} \qquad \text{Combine terms.}$$

$$= \frac{4t^2 - 1}{2t} \cdot \frac{2t}{4t^2 + 1} \qquad \text{“Invert and multiply.”}$$

$$= \frac{4t^2 - 1}{4t^2 + 1} \qquad \text{Multiply and simplify.}$$

(c) For the numerator the LCD is $(z + 1)(z - 1)$, and for the denominator the LCD is $(z + 2)(z - 2)$.

$$\frac{\dfrac{1}{z + 1} - \dfrac{1}{z - 1}}{\dfrac{2}{z + 2} - \dfrac{2}{z - 2}} = \frac{\dfrac{z - 1}{(z + 1)(z - 1)} - \dfrac{z + 1}{(z + 1)(z - 1)}}{\dfrac{2(z - 2)}{(z + 2)(z - 2)} - \dfrac{2(z + 2)}{(z + 2)(z - 2)}}$$

$$= \frac{\dfrac{-2}{(z + 1)(z - 1)}}{\dfrac{-8}{(z + 2)(z - 2)}}$$

$$= \frac{-2}{(z + 1)(z - 1)} \cdot \frac{(z + 2)(z - 2)}{-8}$$

$$= \frac{(z + 2)(z - 2)}{4(z + 1)(z - 1)}$$

Now Try Exercises 27, 29, 31

MULTIPLYING BY THE LEAST COMMON DENOMINATOR   A second strategy for simplifying a complex fraction is to multiply by 1 in the form $\frac{\text{LCD}}{\text{LCD}}$. To do this, we multiply the numerator and denominator by the LCD of the fractions in the numerator *and* denominator. For example, the LCD for the complex fraction

$$\frac{1 - \dfrac{1}{x}}{1 + \dfrac{1}{2x}}$$

is $2x$. To simplify, multiply the complex fraction by 1, expressed in the form $\frac{2x}{2x}$.

$$\frac{\left(1 - \dfrac{1}{x}\right) \cdot 2x}{\left(1 + \dfrac{1}{2x}\right) \cdot 2x} = \frac{2x - \dfrac{2x}{x}}{2x + \dfrac{2x}{2x}} \qquad \text{Distributive property}$$

$$= \frac{2x - 2}{2x + 1} \qquad \text{Simplify fractions.}$$

In the next example we use this method to simplify other complex fractions.

EXAMPLE 3   Simplifying complex fractions

Simplify.

$$\textbf{(a)} \ \ \frac{1 + \dfrac{1}{x}}{1 + \dfrac{1}{y}} \qquad \textbf{(b)} \ \ \frac{\dfrac{1}{x} - \dfrac{1}{y}}{x - y} \qquad \textbf{(c)} \ \ \frac{\dfrac{3}{x - 1} - \dfrac{2}{x}}{\dfrac{1}{x - 1} + \dfrac{3}{x}} \qquad \textbf{(d)} \ \ \frac{n^{-2} + m^{-2}}{1 + (nm)^{-2}}$$

Solution

(a) The LCD for the numerator *and* the denominator is xy.

$$\frac{1 + \dfrac{1}{x}}{1 + \dfrac{1}{y}} = \frac{\left(1 + \dfrac{1}{x}\right) \cdot xy}{\left(1 + \dfrac{1}{y}\right) \cdot xy} \qquad \text{Multiply by the LCD.}$$

$$= \frac{xy + y}{xy + x} \qquad \text{Distributive property}$$

(b) The LCD is xy. Multiply the expression by $\frac{xy}{xy}$.

$$\frac{\left(\dfrac{1}{x} - \dfrac{1}{y}\right) \cdot xy}{(x - y) \cdot xy} = \frac{\dfrac{xy}{x} - \dfrac{xy}{y}}{xy(x - y)} \qquad \text{Distributive and commutative properties}$$

$$= \frac{y - x}{xy(x - y)} \qquad \text{Simplify fractions in numerator.}$$

$$= \frac{-1(x - y)}{xy(x - y)} \qquad \text{Factor out } -1; \text{ rewrite numerator.}$$

$$= -\frac{1}{xy} \qquad \text{Simplify.}$$

(c) The LCD is $x(x - 1)$. Multiply the expression by $\frac{x(x - 1)}{x(x - 1)}$.

$$\frac{\left(\dfrac{3}{x - 1} - \dfrac{2}{x}\right) \cdot x(x - 1)}{\left(\dfrac{1}{x - 1} + \dfrac{3}{x}\right) \cdot x(x - 1)} = \frac{\dfrac{3x(x - 1)}{x - 1} - \dfrac{2x(x - 1)}{x}}{\dfrac{x(x - 1)}{x - 1} + \dfrac{3x(x - 1)}{x}} \qquad \text{Distributive property}$$

$$= \frac{3x - 2(x - 1)}{x + 3(x - 1)} \qquad \text{Simplify.}$$

$$= \frac{3x - 2x + 2}{x + 3x - 3} \qquad \text{Distributive property}$$

$$= \frac{x + 2}{4x - 3} \qquad \text{Combine like terms.}$$

CRITICAL THINKING

Does the expression

$$\frac{\frac{x}{y}}{2 + \frac{x}{y}}$$ equal $\frac{1}{2}$? Explain.

Does the expression

$$\frac{2 + \frac{x}{y}}{\frac{x}{y}}$$ equal 3? Explain.

(d) Start by rewriting the ratio with positive exponents.

$$\frac{n^{-2} + m^{-2}}{1 + (nm)^{-2}} = \frac{\frac{1}{n^2} + \frac{1}{m^2}}{1 + \frac{1}{n^2 m^2}}$$

The LCD for the numerator *and* the denominator is $n^2 m^2$.

$$\frac{\frac{1}{n^2} + \frac{1}{m^2}}{1 + \frac{1}{n^2 m^2}} = \frac{\left(\frac{1}{n^2} + \frac{1}{m^2}\right) \cdot n^2 m^2}{\left(1 + \frac{1}{n^2 m^2}\right) \cdot n^2 m^2}$$ Multiply by LCD.

$$= \frac{m^2 + n^2}{n^2 m^2 + 1}$$ Distributive property

Now Try Exercises 25, 37, 39, 43

6.5 PUTTING IT ALL TOGETHER

Important concepts from this section are summarized in the following table.

Concept	Explanation	Examples
Complex Fraction	A rational expression that contains fractions in its numerator, denominator, or both	$\dfrac{\frac{1}{x} + \frac{1}{2x+1}}{1 - \frac{1}{2x+1}}$ and $\dfrac{\frac{a}{2b} - \frac{b}{2a}}{\frac{a}{2b} + \frac{b}{2a}}$
Simplifying Basic Complex Fractions	$\dfrac{\frac{a}{b}}{\frac{c}{d}} = \dfrac{a}{b} \cdot \dfrac{d}{c}$	$\dfrac{\frac{2y}{z}}{\frac{y}{z-1}} = \dfrac{2y}{z} \cdot \dfrac{z-1}{y} = \dfrac{2(z-1)}{z}$
Method I: Simplifying the Numerator and Denominator First and Then Dividing	Combine the terms in the numerator, combine the terms in the denominator, and then invert and multiply.	$\dfrac{\frac{1}{2b} + \frac{1}{2a}}{\frac{1}{2b} - \frac{1}{2a}} = \dfrac{\frac{a+b}{2ab}}{\frac{a-b}{2ab}}$ $= \dfrac{a+b}{2ab} \cdot \dfrac{2ab}{a-b}$ $= \dfrac{a+b}{a-b}$

continued on next page

continued from previous page

Concept	Explanation	Examples
Method II: Multiplying the Numerator and Denominator by the LCD	Start by multiplying the numerator and denominator by the LCD of the numerator *and* the denominator.	$\dfrac{\dfrac{1}{2b} + \dfrac{1}{2a}}{\dfrac{1}{2b} - \dfrac{1}{2a}} = \dfrac{\left(\dfrac{1}{2b} + \dfrac{1}{2a}\right) \cdot 2ab}{\left(\dfrac{1}{2b} - \dfrac{1}{2a}\right) \cdot 2ab}$ $= \dfrac{a + b}{a - b}$ Note that the LCD is $2ab$.

6.5 Exercises

MyMathLab
PRACTICE   WATCH   DOWNLOAD   READ   REVIEW

CONCEPTS

1. $\dfrac{\dfrac{5}{7}}{\dfrac{3}{11}} = $ _____ .

2. $\dfrac{\dfrac{a}{b}}{\dfrac{c}{d}} = $ _____ .

3. What is a good first step when simplifying

$$\dfrac{2 + \dfrac{1}{x - 1}}{2 - \dfrac{1}{x - 1}}?$$

4. Explain what a complex fraction is.

5. Write the phrase "the quantity z plus three-fourths divided by the quantity z minus three-fourths" as a complex fraction.

6. Write the expression $\dfrac{a}{b} \div \dfrac{a - b}{a + b}$ as a complex fraction.

SIMPLIFYING COMPLEX FRACTIONS

Exercises 7–48: Simplify the complex fraction.

7. $\dfrac{\dfrac{1}{5}}{\dfrac{4}{7}}$

8. $\dfrac{\dfrac{3}{7}}{\dfrac{2}{9}}$

9. $\dfrac{1 + \dfrac{1}{3}}{1 - \dfrac{1}{3}}$

10. $\dfrac{\dfrac{1}{2} - 3}{\dfrac{1}{2} + 3}$

11. $\dfrac{2 + \dfrac{2}{3}}{2 - \dfrac{1}{4}}$

12. $\dfrac{\dfrac{1}{2} + \dfrac{3}{4}}{\dfrac{1}{2} - \dfrac{3}{4}}$

13. $\dfrac{\dfrac{a}{b}}{\dfrac{3a}{2b^2}}$

14. $\dfrac{\dfrac{7}{y}}{\dfrac{14}{y}}$

15. $\dfrac{\dfrac{x}{2y}}{\dfrac{2x}{3y}}$

16. $\dfrac{\dfrac{ab^2}{2c}}{\dfrac{a}{4bc}}$

17. $\dfrac{\dfrac{8}{n + 1}}{\dfrac{4}{n - 1}}$

18. $\dfrac{\dfrac{n}{m - 2}}{\dfrac{3n}{m - 2}}$

19. $\dfrac{\dfrac{2k + 3}{k}}{\dfrac{k - 4}{k}}$

20. $\dfrac{\dfrac{2k}{k - 7}}{\dfrac{1}{(k - 7)^2}}$

21. $\dfrac{\dfrac{3}{z^2 - 4}}{\dfrac{z}{z^2 - 4}}$

22. $\dfrac{\dfrac{z}{(z - 2)^2}}{\dfrac{2z}{z^2 - 4}}$

23. $\dfrac{\dfrac{x}{x^2 - 16}}{\dfrac{1}{x - 4}}$

24. $\dfrac{\dfrac{4y}{x - y}}{\dfrac{1}{x^2 - y^2}}$

25. $\dfrac{1 + \dfrac{1}{x}}{x + 1}$

26. $\dfrac{2 - x}{\dfrac{1}{x} - \dfrac{1}{2}}$

27. $\dfrac{\dfrac{1}{x - 3}}{\dfrac{1}{x} - \dfrac{3}{x - 3}}$

28. $\dfrac{5 + \dfrac{1}{x - 1}}{\dfrac{1}{x - 1} - \dfrac{1}{4}}$

29. $\dfrac{\dfrac{1}{x} + \dfrac{2}{x^2}}{\dfrac{3}{x} - \dfrac{1}{x^2}}$

30. $\dfrac{\dfrac{1}{x - 1} + \dfrac{2}{x}}{2 - \dfrac{1}{x}}$

31. $\dfrac{\dfrac{1}{x + 3} + \dfrac{2}{x - 3}}{2 - \dfrac{1}{x - 3}}$

32. $\dfrac{\dfrac{1}{x} + \dfrac{2}{x}}{\dfrac{1}{x - 1} + \dfrac{x}{2}}$

33. $\dfrac{\dfrac{4}{x - 5}}{\dfrac{1}{x + 5} + \dfrac{1}{x}}$

34. $\dfrac{\dfrac{1}{x - 4} + \dfrac{1}{x - 4}}{1 - \dfrac{1}{x + 4}}$

35. $\dfrac{\dfrac{1}{p^2 q} + \dfrac{1}{pq^2}}{\dfrac{1}{p^2 q} - \dfrac{1}{pq^2}}$

36. $\dfrac{\dfrac{1}{p - 1}}{\dfrac{1}{p - 1} + 2}$

37. $\dfrac{\dfrac{1}{a} + \dfrac{1}{b}}{\dfrac{1}{b} - \dfrac{1}{a}}$

38. $\dfrac{\dfrac{1}{a} + \dfrac{1}{b} + \dfrac{1}{c}}{\dfrac{1}{ab} + \dfrac{1}{bc}}$

39. $\dfrac{\dfrac{1}{x} + \dfrac{1}{x + 1}}{\dfrac{2}{x + 1} - \dfrac{1}{x + 1}}$

40. $\dfrac{\dfrac{2}{x - 1} - 4}{\dfrac{1}{x - 1} + \dfrac{1}{x - 2}}$

41. $\dfrac{3^{-1} - 4^{-1}}{5^{-1} + 4^{-1}}$

42. $\dfrac{1 + 2^{-3}}{2^{-3} - 1}$

43. $\dfrac{m^{-1} - 2n^{-2}}{1 + (mn)^{-2}}$

44. $\dfrac{1 + p^{-2}}{1 - p^{-2}}$

45. $\dfrac{1 - (2n + 1)^{-1}}{1 + (2n + 1)^{-1}}$

46. $\dfrac{(a + b)^{-1} - (a - b)^{-1}}{1 + (a - b)^{-1}}$

47. $\dfrac{\dfrac{x}{x^2 - 4} - \dfrac{1}{x^2 - 4}}{\dfrac{1}{x + 4}}$

48. $\dfrac{\dfrac{1}{x^2 + 2x + 1} - \dfrac{1}{x^2 - 2x + 1}}{(x + 1)(x - 1)}$

APPLICATIONS

49. *Annuity*   If P dollars are deposited every month in an account paying an annual interest rate r expressed as a decimal, then the amount A in the account after 2 years can be approximated by

$$\left(P \left(1 + \frac{r}{12} \right)^{24} - P \right) \div \frac{r}{12}.$$

Write this expression as a complex fraction.

50. *Annuity*   (Continuation of the preceding exercise.) Use a calculator to evaluate the expression when $r = 0.06$ (6%) and $P = \$250$. Interpret the result.

51. *Resistance in Electricity*   Light bulbs are often wired so that electricity can flow through either bulb as illustrated in the accompanying figure.

In this way, if one bulb burns out, the other bulb still works. If two light bulbs have resistances R_1 and R_2, then their combined resistance R is given by the complex fraction

$$R = \frac{1}{\dfrac{1}{R_1} + \dfrac{1}{R_2}}.$$

Simplify this formula.

52. *Resistance in Electricity* (Refer to the preceding exercise.) Evaluate the formula

$$R = \dfrac{1}{\dfrac{1}{R_1} + \dfrac{1}{R_2}}$$

when $R_1 = 75$ ohms and $R_2 = 100$ ohms.

53. Describe a method to simplify a complex fraction.

54. A student simplifies a complex fraction as follows. Explain what the student's mistake is and how to work it correctly.

$$\dfrac{\dfrac{1}{x} + \dfrac{1}{y}}{\dfrac{1}{x} + \dfrac{1}{y}} \overset{?}{=} \dfrac{\dfrac{1}{x}}{\dfrac{1}{x}} + \dfrac{\dfrac{1}{y}}{\dfrac{1}{y}} \overset{?}{=} 1 + 1 = 2$$

6.6 MODELING WITH PROPORTIONS AND VARIATION

Proportions ▪ Direct Variation ▪ Inverse Variation ▪ Joint Variation

A LOOK INTO MATH ▷

Proportions are used frequently to solve problems. The following are examples.

- If someone earns $100 per day, that person can earn $500 in 5 days.
- If a car goes 210 miles on 10 gallons of gasoline, the car can go 420 miles on 20 gallons of gasoline.
- If a person walks a mile in 16 minutes, that person can walk a half mile in 8 minutes.

Many applications involve proportions or variation. In this section we discuss some of them.

Proportions

▶ **REAL-WORLD CONNECTION** A 650-megabyte compact disc (CD) can store about 74 minutes of music. (*Source:* Maxell Corporation.) Suppose that we have already selected some music to record on the CD and 256 megabytes are still available. Using proportions we can determine how many more minutes of music could be recorded. A **proportion** is a statement (equation) that two ratios (fractions) are equal.

Let x be the number of minutes available on the CD. Then 74 minutes *are to* 650 megabytes *as* x minutes *are to* 256 megabytes, which can be written as the proportion

$$\frac{74}{650} = \frac{x}{256}. \qquad \frac{\text{Minutes}}{\text{Megabytes}} = \frac{\text{Minutes}}{\text{Megabytes}}$$

Solving this equation for x gives

$$x = \frac{74 \cdot 256}{650} \approx 29.1 \text{ minutes.}$$

About 29 minutes are still available on the CD.

MAKING CONNECTIONS

Proportions and Fractional Parts

We could have solved the preceding problem by noting that the fraction of the CD still available for recording music is $\frac{256}{650}$. So $\frac{256}{650}$ of 74 minutes equals

$$\frac{256}{650} \cdot 74 \approx 29.1 \text{ minutes.}$$

The following property is a convenient way to solve proportions:

$$\frac{a}{b} = \frac{c}{d} \quad \text{is equivalent to} \quad ad = bc,$$

provided $b \neq 0$ and $d \neq 0$. This is a result of multiplying each side of the equation by a common denominator bd, and is sometimes referred to as *clearing fractions*.

$$bd \cdot \frac{a}{b} = \frac{c}{d} \cdot bd \qquad \text{Multiply by } bd.$$

$$\frac{bda}{b} = \frac{cbd}{d} \qquad \text{Property of multiplying fractions}$$

$$ad = bc \qquad \text{Simplify.}$$

For example, the proportion

is equivalent to

$$6x = 5 \cdot 8 \quad \text{or} \quad x = \frac{40}{6} = \frac{20}{3}.$$

EXAMPLE 1   Calculating the water content in snow

Six inches of light, fluffy snow is equivalent to about half an inch of rain in terms of water content. If 21 inches of snow fall, use proportions to estimate the water content.

Solution
Let x be the equivalent amount of rain. Then 6 inches of snow is to $\frac{1}{2}$ inch of rain as 21 inches of snow is to x inches of rain, which can be written as the proportion

$$\frac{6}{\frac{1}{2}} = \frac{21}{x}. \qquad \frac{\text{Snow}}{\text{Rain}} = \frac{\text{Snow}}{\text{Rain}}$$

Solving this equation gives

$$6x = \frac{21}{2} \quad \text{or} \quad x = \frac{21}{12} = 1.75.$$

Thus 21 inches of light, fluffy snow is equivalent to about 1.75 inches of rain.

Now Try Exercise 65

▶ REAL-WORLD CONNECTION   Proportions frequently occur in geometry when we work with similar figures. Two triangles are similar if the measures of their corresponding

Figure 6.16

angles are equal. Corresponding sides of similar triangles are proportional. Figure 6.16 shows two right triangles that are similar because each has angles of 30°, 60°, and 90°.

We can find the length of side x by using proportions. Side x *is to* 12 *as* 4.5 *is to* 6, which can be written as the proportion

$$\frac{x}{12} = \frac{4.5}{6}.$$ $\frac{\text{Hypotenuse}}{\text{Hypotenuse}} = \frac{\text{Shorter leg}}{\text{Shorter leg}}$

Solving yields the equation

$$6x = 4.5(12) \qquad \text{Clear fractions.}$$
$$x = 9. \qquad \text{Divide by 6.}$$

EXAMPLE 2   Calculating the height of a tree

A 6–foot tall person casts a 4–foot long shadow. If a nearby tree casts a 44–foot long shadow, estimate the height of the tree. See Figure 6.17.

6 feet

4 feet   44 feet

NOT TO SCALE

Figure 6.17

Solution

The triangles in Figure 6.18 are similar because the measures of corresponding angles are equal. Therefore corresponding sides are proportional. Let h be the height of the tree.

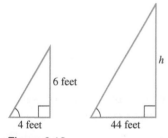

6 feet h

4 feet   44 feet

Figure 6.18

$$\frac{h}{6} = \frac{44}{4} \qquad \frac{\text{Height}}{\text{Height}} = \frac{\text{Shadow length}}{\text{Shadow length}}$$
$$4h = 6(44) \qquad \text{Clear fractions.}$$
$$h = \frac{6(44)}{4} \qquad \text{Divide by 4.}$$
$$h = 66 \qquad \text{Simplify.}$$

The tree is 66 feet tall.   Now Try Exercise **63**

▶ **REAL-WORLD CONNECTION**   Biologists sometimes use proportions to determine fish populations. They tag a small number of a particular species of fish and then release them. It is assumed that over time these tagged fish will distribute themselves evenly throughout the lake. Later, a sample of fish is taken and the number of tagged fish is compared to the total number of fish in the sample. These numbers can be used to estimate the population of a particular species of fish in the lake.   (*Source:* Minnesota Department of Natural Resources.)

EXAMPLE 3   Estimating fish population

In May, 500 tagged largemouth bass are released into a lake. Later in the summer, a sample of 194 largemouth bass from the lake contains 28 tagged fish. Estimate the population of largemouth bass in the lake to the nearest hundred.

Solution

The sample contains 28 tagged bass out of a total of 194 bass. The ratio of tagged bass to the total number of bass in this sample is $\frac{28}{194}$. Let B be the total number of largemouth bass in the lake. Then the ratio of tagged bass to the total number of bass in the lake is $\frac{500}{B}$. If the bass are evenly distributed throughout the lake, then these two ratios are equal and form the following proportion.

Tagged bass in sample   Total number of tagged bass

$$\frac{28}{194} = \frac{500}{B}$$

Total number of bass in sample   Total number of bass in the lake

To solve this proportion we clear fractions to obtain the following equation.

$$28B = 194 \cdot 500 \qquad \text{Clear fractions.}$$

$$B = \frac{194 \cdot 500}{28} \approx 3464 \qquad \text{Divide by 28 and approximate.}$$

To the nearest hundred there are approximately 3500 largemouth bass in the lake.

Now Try Exercise 67

Direct Variation

▶ REAL-WORLD CONNECTION   If your wage is \$9 per hour, the amount you earn is proportional to the number of hours that you work. If you worked H hours, your total pay P satisfies the equation

$$\frac{P}{H} = \frac{9}{1}, \qquad \frac{\text{Pay}}{\text{Hours}}$$

or, equivalently,

$$P = 9H.$$

We say that your pay P is *directly proportional* to the number of hours H worked, and the *constant of proportionality* is 9.

DIRECT VARIATION

Let x and y denote two quantities. Then y is **directly proportional** to x, or y **varies directly** with x, if there is a nonzero number k such that

$$y = kx.$$

The number k is called the **constant of proportionality**, or the **constant of variation**.

The graph of $y = kx$ is a line passing through the origin, as illustrated in Figure 6.19. Sometimes data in a scatterplot indicate that two quantities are directly proportional. The constant of proportionality k corresponds to the slope of the graph.

$y = kx, k > 0$

Figure 6.19 Direct Variation

EXAMPLE 4   Modeling college tuition

Table 6.4 lists the tuition for taking various numbers of credits.

TABLE 6.4

Credits	3	5	8	11	17
Tuition	\$189	\$315	\$504	\$693	\$1071

(a) A scatterplot of the data is shown in Figure 6.20. Could the data be modeled using a line?

TABLE 6.4   (Repeated)

Credits	Tuition
3	$189
5	$315
8	$504
11	$693
17	$1071

Figure 6.20

(b) Explain why tuition is directly proportional to the number of credits taken.
(c) Find the constant of proportionality. Interpret your result.
(d) Predict the cost of taking 15 credits.

Solution

(a) The data are linear and suggest a line passing through the origin.
(b) Because the data can be modeled by a line passing through the origin, tuition is directly proportional to the number of credits taken. Hence doubling the credits will double the tuition and tripling the credits will triple the tuition.
(c) The slope of the line equals the constant of proportionality k. If we use the first and last data points $(3, 189)$ and $(17, 1071)$, the slope is

$$k = \frac{1071 - 189}{17 - 3} = 63.$$

That is, tuition is $63 per credit. If we graph the line $y = 63x$, it models the data as shown in Figure 6.21. This graph can also be created with a graphing calculator.

(d) If y represents tuition and x represents the credits taken, 15 credits would cost

$$y = 63(15) = \$945.$$

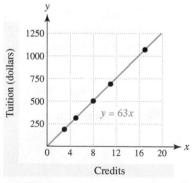

Figure 6.21

Now Try Exercise 76

MAKING CONNECTIONS

Ratios and the Constant of Proportionality

The constant of proportionality in Example 4 can also be found by calculating the ratios $\frac{y}{x}$, where y is the tuition and x is the credits taken. Note that each ratio in the table equals 63 because the equation $y = 63x$ is equivalent to the equation $\frac{y}{x} = 63$.

x	3	5	8	11	17
y	189	315	504	693	1071
$\frac{y}{x}$	63	63	63	63	63

Inverse Variation

▶ **REAL-WORLD CONNECTION**   When two quantities vary inversely, an increase in one quantity results in a decrease in the second quantity. For example, at 25 miles per hour a car travels 100 miles in 4 hours, whereas at 50 miles per hour the car travels 100 miles in 2 hours. Doubling the speed (or rate) decreases the travel time by half. Distance equals rate times time, so $d = rt$. Thus

$$100 = rt, \quad \text{or equivalently,} \quad t = \frac{100}{r}.$$

We say that the time t to travel 100 miles is *inversely proportional* to the speed or rate r. The constant of proportionality or constant of variation is 100.

INVERSE VARIATION

Let x and y denote two quantities. Then y is **inversely proportional** to x, or y **varies inversely** with x, if there is a nonzero number k such that

$$y = \frac{k}{x}.$$

NOTE: We assume that the constant k is positive.

The data shown in Figure 6.22 represent inverse variation and are modeled by $y = \frac{k}{x}$. Note that as x increases, y decreases.

$y = \frac{k}{x}, k > 0$

Figure 6.22 Inverse Variation

▶ **REAL-WORLD CONNECTION**   A wrench is commonly used to loosen a nut on a bolt. See Figure 6.23. If the nut is difficult to loosen, a wrench with a longer handle is often helpful because a longer wrench requires less force. The length of the wrench and the force needed to loosen a nut on a bolt are inversely proportional, as illustrated in the next example.

L

F

Figure 6.23

EXAMPLE 5   Loosening a nut on a bolt

Table 6.5 lists the force F necessary to loosen a particular nut using wrenches of different lengths L.
(a) Make a scatterplot of the data and discuss the graph. Are the data linear?
(b) Explain why the force F is inversely proportional to the handle length L. Find k so that $F = \frac{k}{L}$ models the data.
(c) Predict the force needed to loosen the nut using an 8-inch wrench.

TABLE 6.5

L (inches)	6	10	12	15	20
F (pounds)	10	6	5	4	3

TECHNOLOGY NOTE:

Scatterplots and Graphs

A scatterplot of the data in Table 6.5 is shown in the first figure. In the second figure the data and the equation $y = \frac{60}{x}$ are graphed.

[0, 24, 4] by [0, 12, 4]

[0, 24, 4] by [0, 12, 4]

CALCULATOR HELP

To make a scatterplot, see the Appendix (page AP-4).

Solution
(a) The scatterplot shown in Figure 6.24 reveals that the data are nonlinear. As the length L of the wrench increases, the force F necessary to loosen the nut decreases.

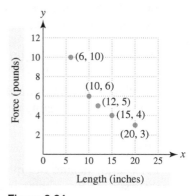

Figure 6.24

(b) If F is inversely proportional to L, then $F = \frac{k}{L}$, or $FL = k$. That is, the product of F and L equals the constant of proportionality k. In Table 6.5, the product of F and L always equals 60 for each data point. Thus F is inversely proportional to L with constant of proportionality $k = 60$.
(c) If $L = 8$, then $F = \frac{60}{8} = 7.5$. A wrench with an 8-inch handle requires a force of 7.5 pounds to loosen the nut.   Now Try Exercise 75

EXAMPLE 6   Analyzing data

Determine whether the data in each table represent direct variation, inverse variation, or neither. For direct and inverse variation, find an equation. Graph the data and equation.

(a)

x	4	5	10	20
y	50	40	20	10

(b)

x	2	5	9	11
y	14	35	63	77

(c)

x	2	4	6	8
y	10	16	24	48

Solution

(a) As x increases, y decreases. Because $xy = 200$ for each data point, the equation $y = \frac{200}{x}$ models the data. The data represent inverse variation. The data and equation are graphed in Figure 6.25(a).

(b) As $\frac{y}{x} = 7$ for each data point in the table, the equation $y = 7x$ models the data. These data represent direct variation. The data and equation are graphed in Figure 6.25(b).

(c) Neither the product xy nor the ratio $\frac{y}{x}$ are constant for the data in the table. Therefore these data represent neither direct variation nor inverse variation. The data are plotted in Figure 6.25(c). Note that the data values increase and are nonlinear.

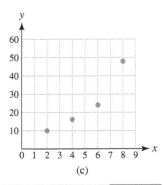

(a) (b) (c)

Figure 6.25

Now Try Exercises 49, 50, 51

Joint Variation

▶ REAL-WORLD CONNECTION In many applications a quantity depends on more than one variable. In *joint variation* a quantity varies with the product of more than one variable. For example, the formula for the area A of a rectangle is given by

$$A = WL,$$

where W and L are the width and length, respectively. Thus the area of a rectangle varies jointly with the width and length.

JOINT VARIATION

Let x, y, and z denote three quantities. Then z **varies jointly** with x and y if there is a nonzero number k such that

$$z = kxy.$$

Figure 6.26

Sometimes joint variation can involve a power of a variable. For example, the volume V of a cylinder is given by $V = \pi r^2 h$, where r is its radius and h is its height, as illustrated in Figure 6.26. In this case we say that the volume varies jointly with the height and the *square* of the radius. The constant of variation is $k = \pi$.

EXAMPLE 7   Finding the strength of a rectangular beam

The strength S of a rectangular beam varies jointly as its width w and the square of its thickness t. See Figure 6.27. If a beam 3 inches wide and 5 inches thick supports 750 pounds, how much can a similar beam 2 inches wide and 6 inches thick support?

Figure 6.27

Solution

The strength of a beam is modeled by $S = kwt^2$, where k is a constant of variation. We can find k by substituting $S = 750$, $w = 3$, and $t = 5$ in the formula.

$$750 = k \cdot 3 \cdot 5^2 \qquad \text{Substitute in } S = kwt^2.$$

$$k = \frac{750}{3 \cdot 5^2} \qquad \text{Solve for } k; \text{ rewrite.}$$

$$= 10 \qquad \text{Simplify.}$$

Thus $S = 10wt^2$ models the strength of this type of beam. When $w = 2$ and $t = 6$, the beam can support

$$S = 10 \cdot 2 \cdot 6^2 = 720 \text{ pounds.} \qquad \text{Now Try Exercise } 83$$

CRITICAL THINKING

Compare the increased strength of a beam if the width doubles and if the thickness doubles. What happens to the strength of a beam if both the width and thickness triple?

6.6 PUTTING IT ALL TOGETHER

In this section we introduced some basic concepts of proportion and variation. They are summarized in the following table.

Concept	Explanation	Examples
Proportion	A statement (equation) that two ratios (fractions) are equal The proportion $\frac{a}{b} = \frac{c}{d}$ can be expressed verbally as "a is to b as c is to d."	10 is to 13 as 32 is to x. $\frac{10}{13} = \frac{32}{x}$ x is to 7 as 2 is to 5. $\frac{x}{7} = \frac{2}{5}$
Direct Variation	Two quantities x and y vary according to the equation $y = kx$, where k is a nonzero constant. The constant of proportionality (or variation) is k.	$y = 3x$ or $\frac{y}{x} = 3$ <table><tr><td>x</td><td>1</td><td>2</td><td>4</td></tr><tr><td>y</td><td>3</td><td>6</td><td>12</td></tr></table> If x doubles, then y also doubles.

Concept	Explanation	Examples
Inverse Variation	Two quantities x and y vary according to the equation $y = \frac{k}{x}$, where k is a nonzero constant. The constant of proportionality (or variation) is k.	$y = \dfrac{2}{x}$ or $xy = 2$ $\begin{array}{c\|ccc} x & 1 & 2 & 4 \\ \hline y & 2 & 1 & \frac{1}{2} \end{array}$ If x doubles, then y decreases by half.
Joint Variation	Three quantities x, y, and z vary according to the equation $z = kxy$, where k is a constant.	The area A of a triangle varies jointly as b and h according to the equation $A = \frac{1}{2}bh$, where b is its base and h is its height. The constant of variation is $k = \frac{1}{2}$.

6.6 Exercises

CONCEPTS

1. What is a proportion?

2. If 5 is to 6 as x is to 7, write a proportion that allows you to find x.

3. Suppose that y is directly proportional to x. If x doubles, what happens to y?

4. Suppose that y is inversely proportional to x. If x doubles, what happens to y?

5. If y varies inversely with x, then xy equals a _____.

6. If y varies directly with x, then $\frac{y}{x}$ equals a _____.

7. If z varies jointly with x and y, then $z = $ _____.

8. If z varies jointly with the square of x and the cube of y, then $z = $ _____.

9. Would a food bill B generally vary directly or inversely with the number of people N being fed? Explain your reasoning.

10. Would the time T needed to paint a building vary directly or inversely with the number of painters N working on the job? Explain your reasoning.

PROPORTIONS

Exercises 11–22: Solve the proportion.

11. $\dfrac{x}{14} = \dfrac{5}{7}$

12. $\dfrac{x}{5} = \dfrac{4}{9}$

13. $\dfrac{8}{x} = \dfrac{2}{3}$

14. $\dfrac{5}{11} = \dfrac{9}{x}$

15. $\dfrac{6}{13} = \dfrac{h}{156}$

16. $\dfrac{25}{a} = \dfrac{15}{8}$

17. $\dfrac{7}{4z} = \dfrac{5}{3}$

18. $\dfrac{3}{2} = \dfrac{2x}{9}$

19. $\dfrac{2}{3x + 1} = \dfrac{5}{x}$

20. $\dfrac{7}{x - 1} = -\dfrac{5}{3x}$

21. $\dfrac{4}{x} = \dfrac{x}{9}$

22. $\dfrac{2x}{5} = \dfrac{40}{x}$

Exercises 23–30: Complete the following.
  (a) Write a proportion that models the situation.
  (b) Solve the proportion for x.

23. 7 is to 9, as 10 is to x

24. x is to 11, as 9 is to 2

25. A triangle has sides of 3, 4, and 6. In a similar triangle the shortest side is 5 and the longest side is x.

26. A rectangle has sides of 9 and 14. In a similar rectangle the longer side is 8 and the shorter side is x.

27. If you earn $78 in 6 hours, you earn x dollars in 8 hours.

28. If 12 gallons of gas contain 1.2 gallons of ethanol, 18 gallons of gas contain x gallons of ethanol.

29. If 2 cassette tapes can record 90 minutes of music, 5 cassette tapes can record x minutes.

30. If a gas pump fills a 30-gallon tank in 8 minutes, it can fill a 17-gallon tank in x minutes.

VARIATION

Exercises 31–36: Let y be directly proportional to x.
  (a) Find the constant of proportionality k.
  (b) Use y = kx to find y when x = 7.

31. $y = 6$ when $x = 3$ **32.** $y = 7$ when $x = 14$

33. $y = 5$ when $x = 2$ **34.** $y = 11$ when $x = 22$

35. $y = -120$ when $x = 16$

36. $y = -34$ when $x = 17$

Exercises 37–42: Let y be inversely proportional to x.
  (a) Find the constant of proportionality k.
  (b) Use $y = \frac{k}{x}$ to find y when x = 10.

37. $y = 5$ when $x = 4$ **38.** $y = 2$ when $x = 30$

39. $y = 100$ when $x = \frac{1}{2}$ **40.** $y = \frac{1}{4}$ when $x = 40$

41. $y = 20$ when $x = 20$ **42.** $y = \frac{45}{4}$ when $x = 8$

Exercises 43–48: Let z vary jointly with x and y.
  (a) Find the constant of variation k.
  (b) Use z = kxy to find z when x = 5 and y = 7.

43. $z = 6$ when $x = 3$ and $y = 8$

44. $z = 135$ when $x = 2.5$ and $y = 9$

45. $z = 5775$ when $x = 25$ and $y = 21$

46. $z = 1530$ when $x = 22.5$ and $y = 4$

47. $z = 25$ when $x = \frac{1}{2}$ and $y = 5$

48. $z = 12$ when $x = \frac{1}{4}$ and $y = 12$

Exercises 49–56: (Refer to Example 6.)
  (a) Determine whether the data represent direct variation, inverse variation, or neither.
  (b) If the data represent either direct or inverse variation, find an equation that models the data.
  (c) Graph the equation and the data.

49.

x	2	3	4	5
y	3	4.5	6	7.5

50.

x	3	6	9	12
y	12	6	4	3

51.

x	10	20	30	40
y	12	6	5	4

52.

x	2	6	10	14
y	105	35	21	15

53.

x	4	6	12	20
y	10	20	30	40

54.

x	1	5	9	15
y	6	30	54	90

55. Thinking Generally   (Do not graph.)

x	-2	-1	1	2
y	$4b$	$2b$	$-2b$	$-4b$

56. Thinking Generally   (Do not graph.)

x	$-2a$	$-a$	a	$2a$
y	$-b$	$-2b$	$2b$	b

Exercises 57–62: Use the graph to determine whether the data represent direct variation, inverse variation, or neither. Find the constant of variation whenever possible.

57.

58.

59.

60.

61.

62.

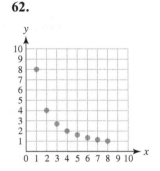

APPLICATIONS

63. *Height of a Tree*   (Refer to Example 2.) A 6-foot person casts a 7-foot shadow, and a nearby tree casts a 27-foot shadow. Estimate the height of the tree.

64. *Recording Music*   A 600-megabyte CD can record 68 minutes of music. How many minutes can be recorded on 360 megabytes?

65. *Water Content in Snow*   (Refer to Example 1.) Eight inches of heavy, wet snow are equivalent to an inch of rain. Estimate the water content in 11 inches of heavy, wet snow.

66. *Wages*   If a person working for an hourly wage earns $143 in 11 hours, how much will that person earn in 17 hours?

67. *Largemouth Bass Population*   (Refer to Example 3.) Three hundred largemouth bass are tagged and released into a lake. Later, a sample of 112 largemouth bass contains 17 tagged bass. Estimate the largemouth bass population to the nearest hundred.

68. *Eagle Population*   Twenty-two bald eagles are tagged and released into the wilderness. Later, an observed sample of 56 bald eagles contains 7 eagles that are tagged. Estimate the bald eagle population in this wilderness area.

69. *Braking Distance*   The distance d required for a car to stop after the brakes have been applied is directly proportional to the square of the car's speed x. If a car moving at 60 miles per hour requires 300 feet to stop on dry, level pavement, how many feet would be required to stop the car at 30 miles per hour?

70. *Points in Basketball*   If a player scores 132 points in 11 games, use proportions to estimate the number of points the player might score in a 20-game season.

71. *Rolling Resistance of Cars*   If you were to try to push a car, you would experience *rolling resistance*. This resistance equals the force necessary to keep the car moving slowly in neutral gear. The following table shows the rolling resistance R for passenger cars of different gross weights W. (**Source:** N. Garber and L. Hoel, *Traffic and Highway Engineering*.)

W (pounds)	2000	2500	3000	3500
R (pounds)	24	30	36	42

(a) Do the data represent direct or inverse variation? Explain.

(b) Find an equation that models the data. Graph the equation with the data.

(c) Find the rolling resistance of a 3200-pound car.

72. *Transportation Costs*   The use of a toll bridge varies inversely according to the toll. When the toll is $0.75, 6000 vehicles use the bridge. Estimate the number of users if the toll is $0.40.   (*Source:* N. Garber.)

73. *Flow of Water*   The gallons of water G flowing in 1 minute through a hose with a cross-sectional area A are shown in the table.

A (square inch)	0.2	0.3	0.4	0.5
G (gallons)	5.4	8.1	10.8	13.5

(a) Do the data represent direct or inverse variation? Explain.

(b) Find an equation that models the data. Graph the equation with the data.

(c) Interpret the constant of variation k.

74. *Hooke's Law*   The table shows the distance D that a spring stretches when a weight W is hung on it.

W (pounds)	2	6	9	15
D (inches)	1.5	4.5	6.75	11.25

(a) Do the data represent direct or inverse variation? Explain.

(b) Find an equation that models the data.

(c) How far will the spring stretch if an 11-pound weight is hung on it, as depicted in the figure?

75. *Tightening Lug Nuts*   (Refer to Example 5.) When a tire is mounted on a car, the lug nuts should not be over-tightened. The following table shows the maximum force used with wrenches of different lengths.

L (inches)	8	10	16
F (pounds)	150	120	75

Source: Tires Plus.

(a) Model the data, using the equation $F = \frac{k}{L}$.

(b) How much force should be used with a wrench 20 inches long?

76. *Cost of Tuition*   (Refer to Example 4.) The cost of tuition is directly proportional to the number of credits taken. If 6 credits cost $435, find the cost of 11 credits. What does the constant of proportionality represent?

77. *Air Temperature and Altitude*   In the first 6 miles of Earth's atmosphere, air cools as the altitude increases. The following graph shows the temperature change y in degrees Fahrenheit at an altitude of x miles. (*Source:* A. Miller and R. Anthes, *Meteorology*.)

(a) Does this graph represent direct variation or inverse variation?

(b) Find an equation for the line in the graph.

(c) Is the constant of proportionality k positive or negative? Interpret k.

(d) Estimate the temperature change 3.5 miles high.

78. *Ozone and UV Radiation*   Depletion of the ozone layer has caused an increase in the amount of UV radiation reaching Earth's surface. An increase in UV radiation is associated with skin cancer. The following graph shows the percentage increase y in UV radiation for a decrease in the ozone layer of x percent.   (*Source:* R. Turner, D. Pearce, and I. Bateman, *Environmental Economics*.)

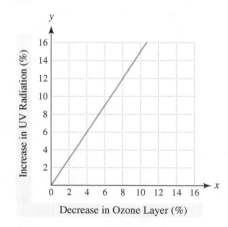

(a) Does this graph represent direct variation or inverse variation?

(b) Find an equation for the line in the graph.

(c) Estimate the percentage increase in UV radiation if the ozone layer decreases by 7%.

79. *Electrical Resistance*   The electrical resistance of a wire is directly proportional to its length. If a 35-foot-long wire has a resistance of 2 ohms, find the resistance of a 25-foot-long wire.

80. *Resistance and Current*   The current that flows through an electrical circuit is inversely proportional to the resistance. When the resistance R is 150 ohms, the current I is 0.8 amp. Find the current when the resistance is 40 ohms.

81. *Joint Variation*   The variable z varies jointly as the second power of x and the third power of y. Write a formula for z if $z = 31.9$ when $x = 2$ and $y = 2.5$.

82. *Wind Power*   The electrical power generated by a windmill varies jointly with the square of the diameter of the area swept out by the blades and the cube of the wind velocity. If a windmill with a 10-foot diameter and a 16-mile-per-hour wind generates 15,392 watts, how much power would be generated if the blades swept out an area 12 feet in diameter and the wind speed was 15 miles per hour?

83. *Strength of a Beam*   (Refer to Example 7.) If a wood beam 5 inches wide and 3 inches thick sup-

ports 300 pounds, how much can a similar beam 5 inches wide and 2 inches thick support?

84. *Carpeting*   The cost of carpet for a rectangular room varies jointly as its width and length. If a room 11 feet wide and 14 feet long costs $539 to carpet, find the cost to carpet a room 17 feet by 19 feet. Interpret the constant of variation k.

85. *Weight on the Moon*   The weight of a person on the moon is directly proportional to the weight of the person on Earth. If a 175-pound person weighs 28 pounds on the moon, how much will a 220-pound person weigh on the moon?

86. *Weight Near Earth*   The weight W of a person near Earth is inversely proportional to the square of the person's distance d from the *center* of Earth. If a person weighs 200 pounds when $d = 4000$ miles, how much does the same person weigh when $d = 7000$ miles? (*Note:* The radius of Earth is about 4000 miles.)

87. *Ohm's Law*   The voltage V in an electrical circuit varies jointly with the amperage I and resistance R. If $V = 220$ when $I = 10$ and $R = 22$, find V when $I = 15$ and $R = 50$.

88. *Revenue*   The revenue R from selling x items at price p varies jointly with x and p. If $R = \$24,000$ when $x = 3000$ and $p = \$8$, find the number of items sold x when $R = \$30,000$ and $p = \$6$.

WRITING ABOUT MATHEMATICS

89. Explain in words what it means for a quantity y to be directly proportional to a quantity x.

90. Explain in words what it means for a quantity y to be inversely proportional to a quantity x.

CHECKING BASIC CONCEPTS
SECTIONS 6.5 AND 6.6

1. Simplify each complex fraction.

(a) $\dfrac{3 - \dfrac{1}{x^2}}{3 + \dfrac{1}{x^2}}$ (b) $\dfrac{\dfrac{2}{x - 1} - \dfrac{2}{x + 1}}{\dfrac{4}{x^2 - 1}}$

2. Suppose that y is directly proportional to x and that $y = 6$ when $x = 8$.
   (a) Find the constant of proportionality k.
   (b) Use $y = kx$ to find y when $x = 11$.

3. Determine whether the data represent direct variation or inverse variation. Find an equation that models the data.

(a)

x	10	15	25	40
y	4	6	10	16

(b)

x	5	10	15	20
y	24	12	8	6

6.7 DIVISION OF POLYNOMIALS

Division by a Monomial ▪ Division by a Polynomial ▪ Synthetic Division

Girolamo Cardano (1501–1576)

A LOOK INTO MATH ▷ The study of polynomials has occupied the minds of mathematicians for centuries. During the sixteenth century, Italian mathematicians, such as Cardano, discovered how to solve higher degree polynomial equations. In this section we demonstrate symbolic methods for dividing polynomials. Division is often needed to factor higher degree polynomials and to solve polynomial equations. (***Source:*** H. Eves, *An Introduction to the History of Mathematics.*)

Division by a Monomial

To divide a polynomial by a monomial we use the two properties

$$\frac{a + b}{c} = \frac{a}{c} + \frac{b}{c} \quad \text{and} \quad \frac{a - b}{c} = \frac{a}{c} - \frac{b}{c}.$$

For example,

$$\frac{3x^2 + x}{x} = \frac{3x^2}{x} + \frac{x}{x} = 3x + 1. \qquad \text{Divide each term by } x.$$

When dividing natural numbers, we can check our work by using multiplication. Because

$$\frac{6}{2} = 3,$$

$2 \cdot 3 = 6$. Similarly, to check whether

$$\frac{3x^2 + x}{x} = 3x + 1,$$

we multiply x and $3x + 1$.

$$x(3x + 1) = x \cdot 3x + x \cdot 1 \qquad \text{Distributive property}$$
$$= 3x^2 + x \qquad \text{It checks.}$$

Graphical support is shown in Figures 6.28(a) and 6.28(b), where the graphs of $Y_1 = (3X^2 + X)/X$ and $Y_2 = 3X + 1$ appear to be identical. In Figure 6.28(c) numerical support is given, where $y_1 = y_2$ for all x-values except 0. Note that we assumed that $x \neq 0$ in $\frac{3x^2 + x}{x}$ because 0 would result in this expression being undefined.

[−4.7, 4.7, 1] by [−3.1, 3.1, 1]   [−4.7, 4.7, 1] by [−3.1, 3.1, 1]

(a)

(b)

(c)

Figure 6.28

EXAMPLE **1**   Dividing by a monomial

Divide and check.

(a) $\dfrac{5x^3 - 15x^2}{15x}$ (b) $\dfrac{4x^2 + 8x - 12}{4x^2}$ (c) $\dfrac{5x^2y + 10xy^2}{5xy}$

Solution

(a) $\dfrac{5x^3 - 15x^2}{15x} = \dfrac{5x^3}{15x} - \dfrac{15x^2}{15x} = \dfrac{x^2}{3} - x$

     Check: $15x\left(\dfrac{x^2}{3} - x\right) = \dfrac{15x \cdot x^2}{3} - 15x \cdot x$

                                $= 5x^3 - 15x^2$

(b) $\dfrac{4x^2 + 8x - 12}{4x^2} = \dfrac{4x^2}{4x^2} + \dfrac{8x}{4x^2} - \dfrac{12}{4x^2} = 1 + \dfrac{2}{x} - \dfrac{3}{x^2}$

     Check: $4x^2\left(1 + \dfrac{2}{x} - \dfrac{3}{x^2}\right) = 4x^2 \cdot 1 + \dfrac{4x^2 \cdot 2}{x} - \dfrac{4x^2 \cdot 3}{x^2}$

                                $= 4x^2 + 8x - 12$

(c) $\dfrac{5x^2y + 10xy^2}{5xy} = \dfrac{5x^2y}{5xy} + \dfrac{10xy^2}{5xy} = x + 2y$

     Check: $5xy(x + 2y) = 5xy \cdot x + 5xy \cdot 2y$

                             $= 5x^2y + 10xy^2$

Now Try Exercises **9, 11, 19**

MAKING CONNECTIONS

Division and "Canceling" Incorrectly

When dividing expressions, students commonly "cancel" incorrectly. For example,

$$\dfrac{x - 3x^3}{x} \neq 1 - 3x^3 \quad \text{and} \quad \dfrac{x - 3x^3}{x} \neq -3x^2.$$

Rather, $\dfrac{x - 3x^3}{x} = \dfrac{x}{x} - \dfrac{3x^3}{x} = 1 - 3x^2.$

Divide the monomial into *every* term in the numerator.

Division by a Polynomial

First, we briefly review division of natural numbers.

$$
\begin{array}{r}
\text{Quotient} \longrightarrow 58 \text{ R } 1 \longleftarrow \text{Remainder} \\
\text{Divisor} \longrightarrow 3\overline{)175} \longleftarrow \text{Dividend} \\
\underline{15} \\
25 \\
\underline{24} \\
1
\end{array}
$$

Because $3 \cdot 58 + 1 = 175$, the answer checks. The quotient and remainder also can be expressed as $58\frac{1}{3}$. Division of polynomials is similar to long division of natural numbers.

EXAMPLE **2**   Dividing polynomials

Divide $4x^2 - 2x + 1$ by $2x + 1$ and check.

Solution
Begin by dividing $2x$ into $4x^2$.

$$
\begin{array}{r}
2x \\
2x + 1\overline{)4x^2 - 2x + 1} \\
\underline{4x^2 + 2x} \\
-4x + 1
\end{array}
$$

$\dfrac{4x^2}{2x} = 2x$

$2x(2x + 1) = 4x^2 + 2x$

Subtract $-2x - 2x = -4x$.

Bring down the 1.

Next, divide $2x$ into $-4x$.

$$
\begin{array}{r}
2x - 2 \\
2x + 1\overline{)4x^2 - 2x + 1} \\
\underline{4x^2 + 2x} \\
-4x + 1 \\
\underline{-4x - 2} \\
3
\end{array}
$$

$\dfrac{-4x}{2x} = -2$

$-2(2x + 1) = -4x - 2$

Subtract $1 - (-2) = 3$.

Remainder is 3.

The quotient is $2x - 2$ with remainder 3, which can also be written as

$$
2x - 2 + \frac{3}{2x + 1}, \qquad \text{Quotient} + \frac{\text{Remainder}}{\text{Divisor}}
$$

in the same manner as 58 R 1 was expressed as $58\frac{1}{3}$. Polynomial division is checked by multiplying the divisor and the quotient and adding the remainder.

$$
\underbrace{(2x + 1)}\underbrace{(2x - 2)} + \underbrace{3} = 4x^2 - 4x + 2x - 2 + 3
$$
$$
 = 4x^2 - 2x + 1 \quad \leftarrow \text{Dividend}
$$

Divisor   Quotient   Remainder

Now Try Exercise **23**

EXAMPLE **3**   Dividing polynomials

Divide $2x^3 - 5x^2 + 4x - 1$ by $x - 1$.

Solution
Begin by dividing x into $2x^3$.

$$
\begin{array}{r}
2x^2 \\
x - 1\overline{)2x^3 - 5x^2 + 4x - 1} \\
\underline{2x^3 - 2x^2} \\
-3x^2 + 4x
\end{array}
$$

$\dfrac{2x^3}{x} = 2x^2$

$2x^2(x - 1) = 2x^3 - 2x^2$

Subtract $-5x^2 - (-2x^2) = -3x^2$.

Bring down $4x$.

Next, divide x into $-3x^2$.

$$
\begin{array}{r}
2x^2 - 3x \\
x - 1\overline{)2x^3 - 5x^2 + 4x - 1} \\
\underline{2x^3 - 2x^2} \\
-3x^2 + 4x \\
\underline{-3x^2 + 3x} \\
x - 1
\end{array}
$$

$\dfrac{-3x^2}{x} = -3x$

$-3x(x - 1) = -3x^2 + 3x$

Subtract $4x - 3x = x$.

Bring down -1.

Finally, divide x into x.

$$
\begin{array}{r}
2x^2 - 3x + 1 \\
x - 1 \overline{)2x^3 - 5x^2 + 4x - 1} \\
\underline{2x^3 - 2x^2} \\
-3x^2 + 4x \\
\underline{-3x^2 + 3x} \\
x - 1 \\
\underline{x - 1} \\
0
\end{array}
$$

$\dfrac{x}{x} = 1$

$1(x - 1) = x - 1$

Subtract. Remainder is 0.

The quotient is $2x^2 - 3x + 1$, and the remainder is 0.

Now Try Exercise **29**

EXAMPLE **4** Dividing by a quadratic divisor

Divide $3x^3 - 2x^2 - 4x + 4$ by $x^2 - 1$.

Solution
Begin by writing $x^2 - 1$ as $x^2 + 0x - 1$.

$$
\begin{array}{r}
3x - 2 \\
x^2 + 0x - 1 \overline{)3x^3 - 2x^2 - 4x + 4} \\
\underline{3x^3 + 0x^2 - 3x} \\
-2x^2 - x + 4 \\
\underline{-2x^2 - 0x + 2} \\
-x + 2
\end{array}
$$

The quotient is $3x - 2$ with remainder $-x + 2$, or $2 - x$, which can be written as

$$
3x - 2 + \frac{2 - x}{x^2 - 1}.
$$

Now Try Exercise **37**

EXAMPLE **5** Dividing into a polynomial with missing terms

Divide $2x^3 - 3$ by $x + 1$.

Solution
Begin by writing $2x^3 - 3$ as $2x^3 + 0x^2 + 0x - 3$.

$$
\begin{array}{r}
2x^2 - 2x + 2 \\
x + 1 \overline{)2x^3 + 0x^2 + 0x - 3} \\
\underline{2x^3 + 2x^2} \\
-2x^2 + 0x \\
\underline{-2x^2 - 2x} \\
2x - 3 \\
\underline{2x + 2} \\
-5
\end{array}
$$

The quotient is $2x^2 - 2x + 2$ with remainder -5, which can be written as

$$
2x^2 - 2x + 2 - \frac{5}{x + 1}.
$$

Now Try Exercise **31**

Synthetic Division

A shortcut called **synthetic division** can be used to divide $x - k$, where k is a constant, into a polynomial. For example, to divide $x - 2$ into $3x^3 - 8x^2 + 7x - 6$, we do the following (with the equivalent long division shown at the right).

Synthetic Division	Long Division of Polynomials

$$\underline{2|}\ \ \ 3\ \ \ -8\ \ \ \ \ 7\ \ \ -6$$
$$\phantom{\underline{2|}\ \ 3\ \ \ }\ 6\ \ \ -4\ \ \ \ \ 6$$
$$\overline{\phantom{\underline{2|}\ \ }\ 3\ \ \ -2\ \ \ \ \ 3\ \ \ \ \ 0.}$$

$$\begin{array}{r} 3x^2 - 2x + 3 \\ x - 2\overline{)\,3x^3 - 8x^2 + 7x - 6} \\ \underline{3x^3 - 6x^2} \\ -2x^2 + 7x \\ \underline{-2x^2 + 4x} \\ 3x - 6 \\ \underline{3x - 6} \\ 0 \end{array}$$

Note that the blue numbers in the expression for long division correspond to the third row in synthetic division. The remainder is 0, which is the last number in the third row. The quotient is $3x^2 - 2x + 3$. Its coefficients are 3, -2, and 3 and are located in the third row. To divide $x - 2$ into $3x^3 - 8x^2 + 7x - 6$ with synthetic division use the following.

STEP 1: In the top row write 2 (the value of k) on the left and then write the coefficients of the dividend $3x^3 - 8x^2 + 7x - 6$.

STEP 2: (a) Copy the leading coefficient 3 of $3x^3 - 8x^2 + 7x - 6$ in the third row and multiply it by 2 (the value of k). Write the result 6 in the second row below -8. Add -8 and 6 in the second column to obtain the -2 in the third row.

(b) Repeat the process by multiplying -2 by 2 and place the result -4 below 7. Then add 7 and -4 to obtain 3.

(c) Multiply 3 by 2 and place the result 6 below the -6. Adding 6 and -6 gives 0.

STEP 3: The last number in the third row is 0, which is the remainder. The other numbers in the third row are the coefficients of the quotient, which is $3x^2 - 2x + 3$.

EXAMPLE 6   Performing synthetic division

Use synthetic division to divide $x^4 - 5x^3 + 9x^2 - 10x + 3$ by $x - 3$.

Solution
Because the divisor is $x - 3$, the value of k is 3.

$$\underline{3|}\ \ \ 1\ \ \ -5\ \ \ \ \ 9\ \ \ -10\ \ \ \ \ 3$$
$$\phantom{\underline{3|}\ \ \ 1\ \ }\ \ \ 3\ \ \ -6\ \ \ \ \ \ 9\ \ \ -3$$
$$\overline{\phantom{\underline{3|}\ }\ \ 1\ \ \ -2\ \ \ \ \ 3\ \ \ -1\ \ \ \ \ \ 0}$$

The quotient is $x^3 - 2x^2 + 3x - 1$ and the remainder is 0. This result is expressed by

$$\frac{x^4 - 5x^3 + 9x^2 - 10x + 3}{x - 3} = x^3 - 2x^2 + 3x - 1 + \frac{0}{x - 3},\quad \text{or}$$

$$\frac{x^4 - 5x^3 + 9x^2 - 10x + 3}{x - 3} = x^3 - 2x^2 + 3x - 1.$$

Now Try Exercise **49**

MAKING CONNECTIONS

Factors and Remainders

Multiplying the last equation in the solution to Example 6 by $x - 3$ gives

$$x^4 - 5x^3 + 9x^2 - 10x + 3 = (x - 3)(x^3 - 2x^2 + 3x - 1).$$

That is, $x - 3$ is a *factor* of $x^4 - 5x^3 + 9x^2 - 10x + 3$ because the remainder is 0.

  This concept is true in general: If a polynomial $p(x)$ is divided by $x - k$ and the remainder is 0, then $x - k$ is a factor of $p(x)$. See Exercises 61 and 62.

EXAMPLE **7**   Performing synthetic division

Use synthetic division to divide $2x^3 - x + 5$ by $x + 1$.

Solution
Write $2x^3 - x + 5$ as $2x^3 + 0x^2 - x + 5$. The divisor $x + 1$ can be written as

$$x + 1 = x - (-1),$$

so we let $k = -1$.

CRITICAL THINKING

Suppose that $p(x)$ is a polynomial and that $(x - k)$ divides into $p(x)$ with remainder 0.

1. Evaluate $p(k)$.
2. Give one x-intercept on the graph of $p(x)$.

$$
\begin{array}{r|rrrr}
-1 & 2 & 0 & -1 & 5 \\
   &   & -2 & 2 & -1 \\
\hline
   & 2 & -2 & 1 & 4
\end{array}
$$

The remainder is 4, and the quotient is $2x^2 - 2x + 1$. This result can also be expressed as

$$\frac{2x^3 - x + 5}{x + 1} = 2x^2 - 2x + 1 + \frac{4}{x + 1}.$$

Now Try Exercise **53**

6.7 PUTTING IT ALL TOGETHER

The following table summarizes division of polynomials.

Type of Division	Explanation	Example
By a Monomial	Use the property $\frac{a \pm b}{c} = \frac{a}{c} \pm \frac{b}{c}$ to divide a polynomial by a monomial. Be sure to divide the denominator into every term of the numerator.	$\dfrac{8a^3 - 4a^2}{2a} = \dfrac{8a^3}{2a} - \dfrac{4a^2}{2a} = 4a^2 - 2a$
By a Polynomial	Division by a polynomial may be done in a manner similar to long division of natural numbers. See Examples 2–5.	When $2x^2 - 7x + 4$ is divided by $2x - 1$, the quotient is $x - 3$ and the remainder is 1. This result may be expressed as $$\dfrac{2x^2 - 7x + 4}{2x - 1} = x - 3 + \dfrac{1}{2x - 1}.$$

continued on next page

continued from previous page

Type of Division	Explanation	Example
Synthetic	Synthetic division is a fast way to divide a polynomial by a divisor in the form $x - k$.	Divide $4x^2 + 7x - 14$ by $x + 3$. $\begin{array}{r\|rrr} -3 & 4 & 7 & -14 \\ & & -12 & 15 \\ \hline & 4 & -5 & 1 \end{array}$ The quotient is $4x - 5$ with remainder 1.

6.7 Exercises

MathXL PRACTICE   WATCH   DOWNLOAD   READ   REVIEW

CONCEPTS

1. To divide a monomial into a polynomial, divide the monomial into every _____ in the numerator.

2. $\dfrac{a + b}{c} = $ _____.

3. Because $\frac{21}{5} = 4$ with remainder 1, it follows that $21 = $ _____ $\cdot$ _____ $+$ _____.

4. Because $\frac{3x^2 - 11x + 8}{3x - 5} = x - 2$ with remainder -2, $3x^2 - 11x + 8 = ($_____$) \cdot ($_____$) + ($_____$)$.

5. Is it possible to use synthetic division to divide $3x^3 - 2x^2 + x - 3$ by $x^2 - 2x$? Explain.

6. Where is the remainder located when you finish with synthetic division?

DIVISION BY A MONOMIAL

Exercises 7–12: Divide and check. Give graphical or numerical support for your result.

7. $\dfrac{4x - 6}{2}$

8. $\dfrac{4x^2 - 8x + 12}{4}$

9. $\dfrac{6x^3 - 9x}{3x}$

10. $\dfrac{3x^4 + x^2}{6x^2}$

11. $(4x^2 - x + 1) \div 2x^2$

12. $(5x^3 - 4x + 2) \div 20x$

Exercises 13–22: Divide.

13. $\dfrac{9x^2 - 12x - 3}{3}$

14. $\dfrac{10x^3 - 15x^2 + 5x}{5}$

15. $\dfrac{12a^3 - 18a}{6a}$

16. $\dfrac{50x^4 + 25x^2 + 100x}{25x}$

17. $(16x^3 - 24x) \div (12x)$

18. $(2y^4 - 4y^2 + 16) \div (2y^2)$

19. $(a^2b^2 - 4ab + ab^2) \div (ab)$

20. $(10x^3y^2 + 5x^2y^3) \div (5x^2y^2)$

21. $\dfrac{6m^4n^4 + 3m^2n^2 - 12}{3m^2n^2}$

22. $\dfrac{6p^2q^4 - 9p^6q^2}{-3pq}$

DIVISION BY A POLYNOMIAL

Exercises 23–28: Divide and check.

23. $\dfrac{3x^2 - 16x + 21}{x - 3}$

24. $\dfrac{4x^2 - x - 18}{x + 2}$

25. $\dfrac{2x^3 + 3x^2 - 2x - 2}{2x + 3}$

26. $\dfrac{2x^3 - 7x^2 + 8}{x - 2}$

27. $(10x^2 - 5) \div (x - 1)$

28. $(6x^2 - 11x + 4) \div (2x - 3)$

Exercises 29–42: Divide.

29. $\dfrac{4x^3 + 8x^2 - x - 2}{x + 2}$ **30.** $\dfrac{3x^3 - 4x^2 + 3x - 2}{x - 1}$

31. $\dfrac{x^3 + 3x - 4}{x + 4}$ **32.** $\dfrac{2x^3 - x^2 + 5}{x - 2}$

33. $(3x^3 + 8x^2 - 21x + 7) \div (3x - 1)$

34. $(14x^3 + 3x^2 - 9x + 3) \div (7x - 2)$

35. $(2a^4 + 5a^3 - 2a^2 - 5a) \div (2a + 5)$

36. $(4b^4 + 10b^3 - 2b^2 - 3b + 5) \div (2b + 1)$

37. $\dfrac{3x^3 + 4x^2 - 12x - 16}{x^2 - 4}$

38. $\dfrac{2x^4 - x^3 - 5x^2 + 4x - 12}{2x^2 - x + 3}$

39. $\dfrac{x^3 + x^2 - x}{x^2 - 1}$ **40.** $\dfrac{x^3 + x^2 - 6x}{x^2 - 2x}$

41. $(2a^4 - 3a^3 + 14a^2 - 8a + 10) \div (a^2 - a + 5)$

42. $(2z^3 + 3z^2 - 9z - 12) \div (z^2 - 1)$

43. Thinking Generally If the divisor is $a - b$, the quotient is $a^2 + ab + b^2$, and the remainder is 1, find the dividend.

44. Thinking Generally If the dividend is given by $x^3 + x^2 - 3x - 2$, the quotient is $x^2 - 3$, and the remainder is 1, find the divisor.

SYNTHETIC DIVISION

Exercises 45–56: Use synthetic division to divide.

45. $\dfrac{x^2 + 3x - 1}{x - 1}$ **46.** $\dfrac{2x^2 + x - 1}{x - 3}$

47. $(3x^2 - 22x + 7) \div (x - 7)$

48. $(5x^2 + 29x - 6) \div (x + 6)$

49. $\dfrac{x^3 + 7x^2 + 14x + 8}{x + 4}$ **50.** $\dfrac{2x^3 + 3x^2 + 2x + 4}{x + 1}$

51. $\dfrac{2x^3 + x^2 - 1}{x - 2}$ **52.** $\dfrac{x^3 + x - 2}{x + 3}$

53. $(2x^4 + 3x^2 - 4) \div (x + 2)$

54. $(x^3 - 2x^2 - 2x + 4) \div (x - 4)$

55. $(b^4 - 1) \div (b - 1)$

56. $(a^2 + a) \div (a + 2.5)$

GEOMETRY

57. *Area of a Rectangle* Use the figure to find the length L of the rectangle from its width and area A. Determine the length when $x = 8$ feet.

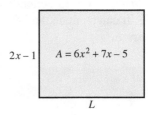

58. *Area of a Rectangle* Use the figure to find the width W of the rectangle from its length and area A. Determine the width when $x = 20$ inches.

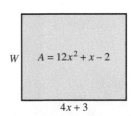

59. *Volume of a Box* The volume of a rectangular box is $x^3 + 7x^2 + 14x + 8$. If the width of the box is $x + 1$ and its length is $x + 4$, find the height of the box.

60. *Area of a Triangle* The area A of a triangle is $12x^2 - 5x - 3$. If the height of the triangle is $3x + 1$, find the length of its base.

THEOREMS ABOUT POLYNOMIALS

61. *Remainder Theorem* Divide $p(x)$ by $x - k$ and determine the remainder. Then evaluate $p(k)$.
(a) $p(x) = x^2 - 3x + 2$ $k = 1$
(b) $p(x) = 3x^2 + 5x - 2$ $k = -2$
(c) $p(x) = 3x^3 - 4x^2 - 5x + 3$ $k = 2$
(d) $p(x) = x^3 - 2x^2 - x + 2$ $k = -1$
(e) $p(x) = x^4 - 5x^2 - 1$ $k = 3$

62. *Remainder Theorem* Try to generalize the results from Exercise 61. It can be done, and the result is called the **remainder theorem**.

63. *Factor Theorem*   Evaluate $p(k)$. Then determine whether $x - k$ is a factor of $p(x)$.

(a) $p(x) = x^2 + x - 6$ $k = 2$

(b) $p(x) = x^2 + 4x - 5$ $k = 1$

(c) $p(x) = x^2 + 8x + 11$ $k = -2$

(d) $p(x) = x^3 + x^2 + x + 1$ $k = -1$

(e) $p(x) = x^3 - 3x^2 - x - 3$ $k = 2$

64. *Factor Theorem*   Try to generalize the results from Exercise 63. It can be done, and the result is called the **factor theorem**.

WRITING ABOUT MATHEMATICS

65. A student dividing $2x^3 + 5x^2 - 13x + 5$ by $2x - 1$ does the following.

$$\begin{array}{r|rrrr} 1 & 2 & 5 & -13 & 5 \\ & & 2 & 7 & -6 \\ \hline & 2 & 7 & -6 & -1 \end{array}$$

What would you tell the student?

66. If you add, subtract, or multiply two polynomials, is the result a polynomial? If you divide two polynomials, is the result always a polynomial? Explain.

CHECKING BASIC CONCEPTS
SECTION 6.7

1. Divide and simplify.

(a) $\dfrac{2x - x^2}{x^2}$ (b) $\dfrac{6a^2 - 9a + 15}{3a}$

2. Divide $\dfrac{10x^2 - x + 4}{2x + 1}$.

3. Use synthetic division to divide $2x^3 - 5x^2 - 1$ by each expression.

(a) $x - 1$ (b) $x + 2$

CHAPTER 6 | SUMMARY

SECTION 6.1 ■ INTRODUCTION TO RATIONAL FUNCTIONS AND EQUATIONS

Rational Functions   A rational function is given by $f(x) = \dfrac{p(x)}{q(x)}$, where $p(x)$ and $q(x)$ are polynomials. The domain of f includes all x-values such that $q(x) \neq 0$.

Example: $f(x) = \dfrac{4}{x - 2}$ defines a rational function with domain $\{x \mid x \neq 2\}$.

Graphs of Rational Functions   Graphs of rational functions are usually curves. A vertical asymptote typically occurs at x-values where the denominator equals zero, but the numerator does not. The graph of a rational function never crosses a vertical asymptote. Graphing a rational function by hand may require plotting several points on each side of a vertical asymptote.

Example: $f(x) = \dfrac{2x}{x - 2}$

A vertical asymptote occurs at $x = 2$. The graph does not cross this vertical asymptote.

Rational Equations A rational equation contains one or more rational expressions. To solve a rational equation in the form $\frac{A}{B} = C$, start by multiplying each side of the equation by B to obtain $A = BC$. This step clears fractions from the equation.

Example: To solve $\frac{2x}{x-3} = 8$, start by multiplying each side by $x - 3$.

$$(x-3)\frac{2x}{x-3} = (x-3)8$$

$$2x = 8x - 24$$

$$x = 4 \qquad \text{Check your answer.}$$

Operations on Functions If $f(x)$ and $g(x)$ are both defined, then the sum, difference, product, and quotient of two functions f and g are defined by

$$(f+g)(x) = f(x) + g(x) \qquad \text{Sum}$$

$$(f-g)(x) = f(x) - g(x) \qquad \text{Difference}$$

$$(fg)(x) = f(x) \cdot g(x) \qquad \text{Product}$$

$$\left(\frac{f}{g}\right)(x) = \frac{f(x)}{g(x)}, \text{ where } g(x) \neq 0. \qquad \text{Quotient}$$

Example: Let $f(x) = x^2 - 1$ and $g(x) = x^2 + 1$.

$$(f+g)(x) = f(x) + g(x) = (x^2 - 1) + (x^2 + 1) = 2x^2$$

$$(f-g)(x) = f(x) - g(x) = (x^2 - 1) - (x^2 + 1) = -2$$

$$(fg)(x) = f(x) \cdot g(x) = (x^2 - 1)(x^2 + 1) = x^4 - 1$$

$$\left(\frac{f}{g}\right)(x) = \frac{f(x)}{g(x)} = \frac{x^2 - 1}{x^2 + 1}$$

SECTION 6.2 ■ MULTIPLICATION AND DIVISION OF RATIONAL EXPRESSIONS

Simplifying a Rational Expression To simplify a rational expression, factor the numerator and the denominator. Then apply the following principle.

$$\frac{PR}{QR} = \frac{P}{Q}$$

Example: $\dfrac{x^2 - 1}{x^2 + 2x + 1} = \dfrac{(x-1)(x+1)}{(x+1)(x+1)} = \dfrac{x-1}{x+1}$

Multiplying Rational Expressions To multiply two rational expressions, multiply numerators and multiply denominators. Simplify the result, if possible.

$$\frac{A}{B} \cdot \frac{C}{D} = \frac{AC}{BD} \qquad B \text{ and } D \text{ not zero}$$

Example: $\dfrac{3}{x-1} \cdot \dfrac{x-1}{x+1} = \dfrac{3(x-1)}{(x-1)(x+1)} = \dfrac{3}{x+1}$

Dividing Rational Expressions To divide two rational expressions, multiply by the reciprocal of the divisor. Simplify the result, if possible.

$$\frac{A}{B} \div \frac{C}{D} = \frac{A}{B} \cdot \frac{D}{C} = \frac{AD}{BC} \qquad B, C, \text{ and } D \text{ not zero}$$

Example: $\dfrac{x+1}{x^2-4} \div \dfrac{x+1}{x-2} = \dfrac{x+1}{(x-2)(x+2)} \cdot \dfrac{x-2}{x+1}$

$$= \frac{(x+1)(x-2)}{(x-2)(x+2)(x+1)} = \frac{1}{x+2}$$

SECTION 6.3 ADDITION AND SUBTRACTION OF RATIONAL EXPRESSIONS

Addition and Subtraction of Rational Expressions with Like Denominators To add (subtract) two rational expressions with like denominators, add (subtract) their numerators. The denominator does not change.

$$\frac{A}{C} + \frac{B}{C} = \frac{A+B}{C} \quad \text{and} \quad \frac{A}{C} - \frac{B}{C} = \frac{A-B}{C}$$

Examples: $\dfrac{2x}{2x+1} + \dfrac{3x}{2x+1} = \dfrac{5x}{2x+1}$ and

$$\frac{x}{x^2-1} - \frac{1}{x^2-1} = \frac{x-1}{x^2-1} = \frac{x-1}{(x-1)(x+1)} = \frac{1}{x+1}$$

Finding the Least Common Denominator The least common denominator (LCD) is the least common multiple (LCM) of the denominators.

Example: The LCD for $\dfrac{1}{x(x+1)}$ and $\dfrac{1}{x^2}$ is $x^2(x+1)$.

Addition and Subtraction of Rational Expressions with Unlike Denominators First write each rational expression with the LCD. Then add or subtract the numerators.

Examples: $\dfrac{2}{x+1} - \dfrac{1}{x} = \dfrac{2x}{x(x+1)} - \dfrac{x+1}{x(x+1)} = \dfrac{2x-(x+1)}{x(x+1)} = \dfrac{x-1}{x(x+1)}$

$$\frac{1}{x+1} + \frac{2}{x-1} = \frac{1(x-1)}{(x+1)(x-1)} + \frac{2(x+1)}{(x-1)(x+1)} = \frac{3x+1}{(x-1)(x+1)}$$

SECTION 6.4 RATIONAL EQUATIONS

Solving Rational Equations A first step in solving a rational equation is to multiply each side by the LCD of the rational expressions to clear fractions from the equation. *Be sure to check all answers.*

Example: The LCD for the equation $\frac{2}{x} + 1 = \frac{4-x}{x}$ is x.

$$\frac{2}{x} + 1 = \frac{4-x}{x} \qquad \text{Given equation}$$

$$x\left(\frac{2}{x} + 1\right) = \left(\frac{4-x}{x}\right)x \qquad \text{Multiply by } x.$$

$$2 + x = 4 - x \qquad \text{Clear fractions.}$$

$$2x = 2 \qquad \text{Add } x \text{ and subtract 2.}$$

$$x = 1 \qquad \text{Divide by 2. Check your answer.}$$

SECTION 6.5 ■ COMPLEX FRACTIONS

Complex Fractions   A complex fraction is a rational expression that contains fractions in its numerator, denominator, or both. The following equation can be used to help simplify basic complex fractions.

$$\frac{\dfrac{a}{b}}{\dfrac{c}{d}} = \frac{a}{b} \cdot \frac{d}{c} \qquad \text{Invert and multiply.}$$

Example: $\dfrac{\dfrac{1-x}{2}}{\dfrac{4}{1+x}} = \dfrac{1-x}{2} \cdot \dfrac{1+x}{4} = \dfrac{(1-x)(1+x)}{(2)(4)} = \dfrac{1-x^2}{8}$

Simplifying Complex Fractions

Method I: Combine terms in the numerator, combine terms in the denominator, and simplify the resulting expression.

Method II: Multiply the numerator and the denominator by the LCD and simplify the resulting expression.

Example: *Method I:*

$$\frac{2 - \dfrac{1}{b}}{2 + \dfrac{1}{b}} = \frac{\dfrac{2b-1}{b}}{\dfrac{2b+1}{b}} = \frac{2b-1}{b} \cdot \frac{b}{2b+1} = \frac{2b-1}{2b+1}$$

Method II: The LCD is b.

$$\frac{\left(2 - \dfrac{1}{b}\right)b}{\left(2 + \dfrac{1}{b}\right)b} = \frac{2b - \dfrac{b}{b}}{2b + \dfrac{b}{b}} = \frac{2b-1}{2b+1}$$

SECTION 6.6 ■ MODELING WITH PROPORTIONS AND VARIATION

Proportions   A proportion is a statement (equation) that two ratios (fractions) are equal.

Example: $\frac{5}{x} = \frac{4}{7}$ (in words, 5 *is to x as* 4 *is to* 7.)

Similar Triangles   Two triangles are similar if the measures of their corresponding angles are equal. Corresponding sides of similar triangles are proportional.

Example: A right triangle has legs with lengths 3 and 4. A similar right triangle has a shorter leg with length 6. Its longer leg can be found by solving the proportion $\frac{3}{6} = \frac{4}{x}$, or $x = 8$.

Direct Variation   A quantity y is *directly proportional* to a quantity x, or y *varies directly* with x, if there is a nonzero constant k such that $y = kx$. The number k is called the *constant of proportionality* or the *constant of variation*.

Example: If y varies directly with x, then the ratio $\frac{y}{x}$ always equals k. The following data satisfy $\frac{y}{x} = 4$, so the constant of variation is 4.

x	1	2	3	4
y	4	8	12	16

Inverse Variation   A quantity y is *inversely proportional* to a quantity x, or y *varies inversely* with x, if there is a nonzero constant k such that $y = \frac{k}{x}$. (We assume that $k > 0$.)

Example: If y varies inversely with x, then $xy = k$. The following data satisfy $xy = 12$, so the constant of variation is 12.

x	1	2	4	6
y	12	6	3	2

Joint Variation   The quantity z *varies jointly* with x and y if $z = kxy$, $k \neq 0$.

Example: The area A of a rectangle varies jointly, with the width W and length L because $A = LW$. Note that $k = 1$ in this example.

SECTION 6.7 ■ DIVISION OF POLYNOMIALS

Division of a Polynomial by a Monomial   Divide the monomial in the denominator into *every* term of the numerator.

Example: $\dfrac{4x^4 - 8x^3 + 16x^2}{8x^2} = \dfrac{4x^4}{8x^2} - \dfrac{8x^3}{8x^2} + \dfrac{16x^2}{8x^2} = \dfrac{x^2}{2} - x + 2$

Division of a Polynomial by a Polynomial   Division of polynomials is similar to long division of natural numbers.

Example: Divide $2x^3 - 3x + 3$ by $x - 1$. (Be sure to include $0x^2$.)

$$\begin{array}{r}
2x^2 + 2x - 1 \\
x - 1\overline{)2x^3 + 0x^2 - 3x + 3} \\
\underline{2x^3 - 2x^2} \\
2x^2 - 3x \\
\underline{2x^2 - 2x} \\
-x + 3 \\
\underline{-x + 1} \\
2
\end{array}$$

The quotient is $2x^2 + 2x - 1$ with remainder 2, which can be written as

$$2x^2 + 2x - 1 + \frac{2}{x - 1}.$$

Synthetic Division   Synthetic division is a fast way to divide a polynomial by an expression in the form $x - k$, where k is a constant.

Example: Divide $3x^3 + 4x^2 - 7x - 1$ by $x + 2$.

$$\begin{array}{r}
-2\,\underline{|\ \ 3\quad\ \ 4\quad -7\quad -1} \\
-6\quad\ \ 4\quad\ \ \ 6 \\
\overline{\ \ 3\ \ -2\quad -3\quad\ \ \ 5}
\end{array}$$

The quotient is $3x^2 - 2x - 3$ with remainder 5.

CHAPTER 6   REVIEW EXERCISES

SECTION 6.1

Exercises 1 and 2: Write a symbolic representation (or formula) for the rational function f described.

1. Divide 1 by the quantity x minus 1.

2. Subtract 3 from x and then divide the result by x.

3. Sketch a graph of $f(x) = \frac{1}{2x + 4}$. Show any vertical asymptotes as dashed lines. State the domain of f in set-builder notation.

4. Evaluate $f(x) = \frac{1}{x^2 - 1}$ at $x = 3$. Find any x-values that are not in the domain of f.

Exercises 5 and 6: If possible, evaluate f(x) for each x.

5. $f(x) = \dfrac{3}{x + 2}$ $x = -3, x = 2$

6. $f(x) = \dfrac{2x}{x^2 - 4}$ $x = -2, x = 3$

Exercises 7 and 8: Use the graph of f to evaluate the expressions. Give the equation of any vertical asymptotes.

7. $f(0)$ and $f(2)$

8. $f(-3)$ and $f(-2)$

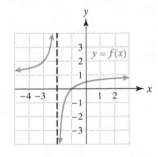

Exercises 9–12: Solve. Check your answer.

9. $\dfrac{3 - x}{x} = 2$

10. $\dfrac{1}{x + 3} = \dfrac{1}{5}$

11. $\dfrac{x}{x-2} = \dfrac{2x-2}{x-2}$ **12.** $\dfrac{4}{2-3x} = -1$

13. Use $f(x) = 2x^2 - 3x$ and $g(x) = 2x - 3$ to find each of the following.
  (a) $(f+g)(3)$ **(b)** $(fg)(3)$

14. Use $f(x) = x^2 - 1$ and $g(x) = x - 1$ to find each of the following.
  (a) $(f-g)(x)$ **(b)** $(f/g)(x)$

SECTION 6.2

Exercises 15–20: Simplify the expression.

15. $\dfrac{4a}{6a^4}$ **16.** $\dfrac{(x-3)(x+2)}{(x+1)(x-3)}$

17. $\dfrac{x^2-4}{x-2}$ **18.** $\dfrac{x^2-6x-7}{2x^2-x-3}$

19. $\dfrac{8-x}{x-8}$ **20.** $-\dfrac{3-2x}{2x-3}$

Exercises 21–30: Simplify the expression.

21. $\dfrac{1}{2y} \cdot \dfrac{4y^2}{8}$ **22.** $\dfrac{x+2}{x-5} \cdot \dfrac{x-5}{x+1}$

23. $\dfrac{x^2+1}{x^2-1} \cdot \dfrac{x-1}{x+1}$ **24.** $\dfrac{x^2+2x+1}{x^2-9} \cdot \dfrac{x+3}{x+1}$

25. $\dfrac{1}{3y} \div \dfrac{1}{9y^4}$ **26.** $\dfrac{2x+2}{3x-3} \div \dfrac{x+1}{x-1}$

27. $\dfrac{x^2+2x}{x^2-25} \div \dfrac{x+2}{x+5}$

28. $\dfrac{x^2+2x-15}{x^2+4x+3} \div \dfrac{x-3}{x+1}$

29. $\dfrac{x^2+x-2}{2x^2-7x+3} \cdot \dfrac{x^2-3x}{x^2+2x-3}$

30. $\dfrac{x^2+3x+2}{x^2+7x+12} \div \dfrac{x^2+4x+4}{x^2+4x+3}$

SECTION 6.3

Exercises 31–36: Find the least common multiple.

31. 36, 24, 16   **32.** $4ab, a^2b$

33. $9x^2y, 6xy^3$ **34.** $(x-1), (x+2)$

35. $x^2 - 9, x(x+3)$

36. $x^2, x-3, x^2-6x+9$

Exercises 37–50: Simplify.

37. $\dfrac{1}{x+4} + \dfrac{3}{x+4}$ **38.** $\dfrac{2}{x} + \dfrac{x-3}{x}$

39. $\dfrac{1}{x+1} - \dfrac{x}{x+1}$ **40.** $\dfrac{2x}{x-2} - \dfrac{2}{x-2}$

41. $\dfrac{4}{1-t} + \dfrac{t}{t-1}$

42. $\dfrac{2}{y-2} - \dfrac{2}{y+2}$

43. $\dfrac{4b}{a^2c} - \dfrac{3a}{b^2c}$ **44.** $\dfrac{r}{5t^2} + \dfrac{t}{5r^2}$

45. $\dfrac{4}{a^2-b^2} - \dfrac{2}{a+b}$ **46.** $\dfrac{a}{a-b} + \dfrac{b}{a+b}$

47. $\dfrac{1}{x^2-3x+2} + \dfrac{1}{x^2+x-2}$

48. $\dfrac{1}{x^2-5x+6} - \dfrac{1}{x^2+x-6}$

49. $\dfrac{1}{x-2} + \dfrac{2}{x+2} - \dfrac{x}{x-2}$

50. $\dfrac{2x}{2x-1} - \dfrac{3}{2x+1} - \dfrac{1}{2x-1}$

SECTION 6.4

Exercises 51–60: Solve. Check your result.

51. $\dfrac{4}{x} - \dfrac{5}{2x} = \dfrac{1}{2}$ **52.** $\dfrac{1}{x-4} = \dfrac{3}{2x-1}$

53. $\dfrac{2}{x^2} - \dfrac{1}{x} = 1$ **54.** $\dfrac{1}{x+4} - \dfrac{1}{x} = 1$

55. $\dfrac{1}{x^2-1} - \dfrac{1}{x-1} = \dfrac{2}{3}$

56. $\dfrac{1}{x-3} + \dfrac{1}{x+3} = \dfrac{-5}{x^2-9}$

57. $\dfrac{1}{(x-2)^2} - \dfrac{1}{x^2-4} = \dfrac{2}{(x-2)^2}$

58. $\dfrac{1}{x^2+3x+2} + \dfrac{x}{x+2} = \dfrac{1}{2}$

59. $\dfrac{-3x-3}{x-3} + \dfrac{x^2+x}{x-3} = 7x+7$

60. $\dfrac{1}{x-4} + \dfrac{x}{x+4} = \dfrac{8}{x^2-16}$

Exercises 61 and 62: Use the graph to solve the rational equation. Then check your answer.

61. $\dfrac{1}{x} = \dfrac{2}{x+2}$

62. $\dfrac{3}{x-1} = \dfrac{1}{2}x$

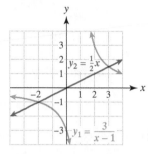

Exercises 63–66: Solve for the specified variable.

63. $m = \dfrac{y_2 - y_1}{x_2 - x_1}$ for y_2

64. $T = \dfrac{a}{b+2}$ for a

65. $\dfrac{1}{f} = \dfrac{1}{p} + \dfrac{1}{q}$ for p

66. $I = \dfrac{2a+3b}{ab}$ for b

SECTION 6.5

Exercises 67–74: Simplify the complex fraction.

67. $\dfrac{\frac{3}{5}}{\frac{10}{13}}$

68. $\dfrac{\frac{4}{ab}}{\frac{2}{bc}}$

69. $\dfrac{\frac{2n-1}{n}}{\frac{3n}{2n+1}}$

70. $\dfrac{\frac{1}{x-y}}{\frac{1}{x^2-y^2}}$

71. $\dfrac{2+\frac{3}{x}}{2-\frac{3}{x}}$

72. $\dfrac{\frac{1}{x}+\frac{1}{2}}{\frac{1}{4}-\frac{2}{x}}$

73. $\dfrac{\frac{4}{x}+\frac{1}{x-1}}{\frac{1}{x}-\frac{2}{x-1}}$

74. $\dfrac{\frac{1}{x+3}-\frac{1}{x-3}}{\frac{4}{x+3}-\frac{2}{x-3}}$

SECTION 6.6

Exercises 75–78: Solve the proportion.

75. $\dfrac{x}{6} = \dfrac{6}{20}$

76. $\dfrac{11}{x} = \dfrac{5}{7}$

77. $\dfrac{x+1}{5} = \dfrac{x}{3}$

78. $\dfrac{3}{7} = \dfrac{4}{x-1}$

79. If $x + 1$ is to 5 as 10 is to 15, use a proportion to find the value of x.

80. A rectangle has sides with lengths 7 and 8. Find the longer side of a similar rectangle whose shorter side has length 11.

81. Suppose that y varies directly with x. If $y = 8$ when $x = 2$, find y when $x = 7$.

82. Suppose that y varies inversely with x. If $y = 5$ when $x = 10$, find y when $x = 25$.

83. Suppose that z varies jointly with x and y. If $z = 483$ when $x = 23$ and $y = 7$, find the constant of variation k.

84. Suppose that z varies jointly with x and the square of y. If $z = 891$ when $x = 22$ and $y = 3$, find z when $x = 10$ and $y = 4$.

Exercises 85 and 86: Use the table to determine whether the data represent direct or inverse variation. Find an equation that models the data.

85.

x	2	4	5	8
y	100	50	40	25

86.

x	3	7	8	11
y	9	21	24	33

Exercises 87 and 88: Decide if the graph represents direct or inverse variation. Find the constant of variation k.

87.

88.

SECTION 6.7

Exercises 89–96: Divide.

89. $\dfrac{10x+15}{5}$

90. $\dfrac{2x^2+x}{x}$

91. $(4x^3 - x^2 + 2x) \div (2x^2)$

92. $(4a^3b - 6ab^2) \div (2a^2b^2)$

93. $\dfrac{2x^2 - x - 2}{x + 1}$

94. $(x^3 + x - 1) \div (x + 1)$

95. $(6x^3 - 7x^2 + 5x - 1) \div (3x - 2)$

96. $\dfrac{2x^3 - 9x^2 + 21x - 21}{x^2 - 2}$

Exercises 97 and 98: Use synthetic division to divide.

97. $\dfrac{2x^2 - 11x + 13}{x - 3}$

98. $(3x^3 + 10x^2 - 4x + 19) \div (x + 4)$

APPLICATIONS

99. *Downhill Highway Grade*　The braking distance D in feet for a car traveling downhill at 40 miles per hour on a wet grade x is given by

$$D(x) = \dfrac{1600}{9.6 - 30x}.$$

(*Source:* N. Garber.)

(a) In this formula a level road is represented by $x = 0$ and a 10% downhill grade is represented by $x = 0.1$. Evaluate $D(0)$ and $D(0.1)$. How much does the downhill grade add to the braking distance compared to a level road?

(b) If the braking distance is 200 feet, estimate the downhill grade x.

100. *Time Spent in Line*　Suppose that amusement park attendants can wait on 10 vehicles per minute and vehicles are arriving at the park randomly at an average rate of x vehicles per minute. Then the average time T in minutes spent waiting in line *and* paying the attendant is given by

$$T(x) = \dfrac{1}{10 - x},$$

where $x < 10$.　(*Source:* N. Garber.)

(a) Construct a table of T, starting at $x = 9$ and incrementing by 0.1.

(b) What happens to the waiting time as the value of x approaches 10? Interpret this result.

101. *Number of Cars Waiting*　A car wash can clean 15 cars per hour. If cars are arriving randomly at an average rate of x per hour, the average number N of cars waiting in line is given by

$$N(x) = \dfrac{x^2}{225 - 15x},$$

where $x < 15$.　(*Source:* N. Garber.)

(a) Estimate the average length of a line when 14 cars per hour are arriving.

(b) A graph of $y = N(x)$ is shown in the figure. Interpret the graph as x increases. Does it agree with your intuition?

102. *Fish Population*　Suppose that a fish population P in thousands in a lake after x years is modeled by

$$P(x) = \dfrac{5}{x^2 + 1}.$$

(a) Evaluate $P(0)$ and interpret the result.

(b) Graph P in $[0, 6, 1]$ by $[0, 6, 1]$.

(c) What happens to the population over this 6-year period?

(d) When was the population 1000?

103. *Working Together*   Suppose that two students are working collaboratively to solve a large number of quadratic equations. The first student can solve all the problems in 2 hours, whereas the second student can solve them in 3 hours.

(a) Write an equation whose solution gives the time needed to solve all the problems if the two students split the problems up and share answers.

(b) Solve the equation in part (a) symbolically.

(c) Solve the equation in part (a) either graphically or numerically.

104. *Speed of a Boat*   In still water a riverboat can travel 12 miles per hour. It travels 48 miles upstream and then 48 miles downstream in a total time of 9 hours. Find the speed of the current.

105. *Recording Music*   A 650-megabyte CD can record 74 minutes of music. Estimate the number of minutes that can be recorded on 387 megabytes.

106. *Height of a Building*   A 5-foot-tall person casts a 3-foot-long shadow, while a nearby building casts a 26-foot-long shadow, as illustrated in the accompanying figure. Find the height of the building.

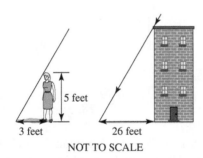

5 feet

3 feet   26 feet

NOT TO SCALE

107. *Light Bulbs*   The approximate resistances R for light bulbs of wattage W are measured and recorded in the following table.   (*Source:* D. Horn, *Basic Electronics Theory.*)

W (watts)	50	100	200	250
R (ohms)	242	121	60.5	48.4

(a) Make a scatterplot of the data. Do the data represent direct or inverse variation?

(b) Find an equation that models the data. What is the constant of proportionality k?

(c) Find R for a 55-watt light bulb.

108. *Scales*   The distance D that the spring in a produce scale stretches is directly proportional to the weight W of the fruits and vegetables placed in the pan.

(a) If 5 pounds of apples stretch the spring 0.3 inch, find an equation that relates D and W. What is the constant of proportionality k?

(b) How far will 7 pounds of oranges stretch the spring?

109. *Air Temperature and Altitude*   In the first 30,000 feet of Earth's atmosphere the *change* in air temperature is directly proportional to the altitude. If the temperature is $80°F$ on the ground and $62°F$ 4000 feet above the ground, find the air temperature at 6000 feet.   (*Source:* L. Battan, *Weather in Your Life.*)

110. *Skin Cancer and UV Radiation*   Depletion of the ozone layer has caused an increase in the amount of UV radiation reaching Earth's surface. The following table shows the estimated percent increase in skin cancer y for an x percent increase in the amount of UV radiation reaching Earth's surface.   (*Source:* R. Turner, D. Pearce, and I. Bateman, *Environmental Economics.*)

x (%)	0	1	2	3	4
y (%)	0	3.5	7	10.5	14

(a) Do these data represent direct variation, inverse variation, or neither?

(b) Find an equation that models the data.

(c) Estimate the percent increase in skin cancer if UV radiation increases by 2.3%.

CHAPTER 6   TEST ✏️Pass the Test   Pass the Test CD: Video solutions to all test exercises

1. Write a symbolic representation (formula) for $f(x)$ that divides x by the quantity x plus 2.

2. Let $f(x) = \frac{1}{4x^2 - 1}$.

   (a) Evaluate $f(-2)$.
   (b) Write the domain of f in set-builder notation.

3. Graph $y = \frac{x}{x + 1}$. Show any vertical asymptotes as dashed lines.

Exercises 4–6: Simplify the expression.

4. $\dfrac{2a^3}{4a^2}$

5. $\dfrac{1 - 2t}{2t - 1}$

6. $\dfrac{x^2 - 2x - 15}{2x^2 - x - 21}$

Exercises 7–15: Simplify.

7. $\dfrac{x^2 + 4}{x^2 - 4} \cdot \dfrac{x - 2}{x + 2}$

8. $\dfrac{1}{4y^2} \div \dfrac{1}{8y^4}$

9. $\dfrac{x}{x + 5} + \dfrac{1 - x}{x + 5}$

10. $\dfrac{2x}{x - 2} - \dfrac{1}{x + 2}$

11. $\dfrac{a^2}{3b} - \dfrac{2b^3}{5a}$

12. $\dfrac{x}{x - 2} - \dfrac{4}{x^2} - \dfrac{2}{x}$

13. $\dfrac{3 + \frac{3}{x}}{3 - \frac{3}{x}}$

14. $\dfrac{1}{z + 4} - \dfrac{z}{(z + 4)^2}$

15. $\dfrac{\frac{1}{x - 2} + \frac{x}{x - 2}}{\frac{1}{3} - \frac{5}{x - 2}}$

Exercises 16–19: Solve. Check your result.

16. $\dfrac{t}{5t + 1} = \dfrac{2}{7}$

17. $\dfrac{x}{2x - 1} = \dfrac{x + 2}{x + 4}$

18. $\dfrac{x + 4}{2 - x} - \dfrac{2x - 1}{2 - x} = 0$

19. $\dfrac{1}{x^2 - 4} - \dfrac{1}{x - 2} = \dfrac{1}{x + 2}$

20. Solve $F = \dfrac{Gm}{r^2}$ for m.

21. Solve the equation $\dfrac{\sqrt{2}}{x^2 + 2} - \dfrac{1.7x}{x - 1.2} = \sqrt{3}$ to the nearest hundredth.

22. Let $f(x) = x - 1$ and $g(x) = x^2 - 2x + 1$. Find $(f - g)(2)$ and $(f/g)(x)$.

23. A triangle has sides with lengths 12, 15, and 20. Find the longest side of a similar triangle with a shortest side of length 7.

24. Suppose that y varies directly with x. If $y = 8$ when $x = 23$, find y when $x = 10$.

25. Use the table to determine whether the data represent direct or inverse variation. Find an equation that models the data.

x	2	4	5	10
y	50	25	20	10

26. Determine whether the data represent direct or inverse variation. Find an equation that models the data.

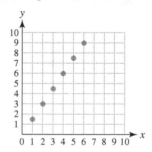

Exercises 27 and 28: Divide.

27. $\dfrac{4a^3 + 10a}{2a}$

28. $\dfrac{3x^3 + 5x^2 - 2}{x + 2}$

29. *Height of a Building* A person 73 inches tall casts a shadow 50 inches long while a nearby building casts a shadow 15 feet long. Find the height of the building.

30. *Time Spent in Line* Suppose that parking lot attendants can wait on 25 vehicles per minute and vehicles are arriving at the lot randomly at an average rate of x vehicles per minute. Then the average time T in minutes spent waiting in line *and* paying the attendant is given by

$$T(x) = \dfrac{1}{25 - x},$$

where $x < 25$. (*Source:* N. Garber.)

(a) Graph T in $[0, 25, 5]$ by $[0, 2, 0.5]$. Identify any vertical asymptotes.

(b) If the wait is 1 minute, how many vehicles are arriving on average?

31. *Working Together*   Suppose that one pump can empty a pool in 24 hours, and a second pump can empty the pool in 30 hours.
   (a) Write an equation whose solution gives the time needed for the pumps working together to empty the pool.
   (b) Solve the equation in part (a).

32. *Dew Point and Altitude*   In the first 30,000 feet of Earth's atmosphere the change in the dew point is directly proportional to the altitude. If the dew point is 50°F on the ground and 39°F 10,000 feet above the ground, find the dew point at 7500 feet.   (*Source:* L. Battan, *Weather in Your Life.*)

CHAPTER 6   EXTENDED AND DISCOVERY EXERCISES

RATIONAL APPROXIMATIONS

1. Rational expressions are used to approximate other types of expressions in computer software. Graph each expression on the left for $1 \le x \le 15$ and try to match it with the graph of the rational expression on the right that approximates it best.

(a) $\sqrt{x}$

   i. $\dfrac{2 - 2x^2}{3x^2 + 10x + 3}$

(b) $\sqrt{4x + 1}$

   ii. $\dfrac{15x^2 + 75x + 33}{x^2 + 23x + 31}$

(c) $\sqrt[3]{x}$

   iii. $\dfrac{10x^2 + 80x + 32}{x^2 + 40x + 80}$

(d) $\dfrac{1 - \sqrt{x}}{1 + \sqrt{x}}$

   iv. $\dfrac{7x^3 + 42x^2 + 30x + 2}{2x^3 + 30x^2 + 42x + 7}$

OTHER TYPES OF DIRECT VARIATION

Exercises 2–5: Sometimes a quantity y varies directly as a power of x. For example, the area A of a circle varies directly as the second power of the radius r, since $A = \pi r^2$ and π is a constant. Let x and y denote two quantities and n be a positive number. Then y is directly proportional to the nth power of x, or y varies directly with the nth power of x, if there exists a nonzero number k such that

$$y = kx^n.$$

2. Let y be directly proportional to the second power of x. If x doubles, what happens to y?

3. Let y be directly proportional to the $\frac{1}{2}$ power of x. If x quadruples, what happens to y?

4. *Allometric Growth*   If x is the weight of a fiddler crab and y is the weight of its claws, then y is directly proportional to the 1.25 power of x; that is, $y = kx^{1.25}$. Suppose that a typical crab with a body weight of 2.1 grams has claws weighing 1.125 grams.   (*Source:* D. Brown and P. Rothery, *Models in Biology: Mathematics, Statistics, and Computing.*)
   (a) Find the constant of proportionality k. Round your answer to the nearest thousandth.
   (b) Estimate the weight of a fiddler crab with claws weighing 0.8 gram.

5. *Volume*   The volume V of a cylinder is directly proportional to the square of its radius r. If a cylinder with a radius of 5 inches has a volume of 150 cubic inches, what is the volume of a cylinder with the same height and a radius of 7 inches?

OTHER TYPES OF INVERSE VARIATION

Exercises 6–9: Sometimes a quantity varies inversely to a power of x. Let x and y denote two quantities and n be a positive number. Then y is inversely proportional to the nth power of x, or y varies inversely with the nth power of x, if there exists a nonzero number k such that

$$y = \frac{k}{x^n}.$$

6. Let y be inversely proportional to the second power of x. If x doubles, what happens to y?

7. Let y be inversely proportional to the third power of x. If x doubles, what happens to y?

8. *Earth's Gravity*   The weight W of an object can be modeled by $W = \frac{k}{d^2}$, where d is the distance that the object is from Earth's center and k is a constant. Earth's radius is about 4000 miles.

(a) Find k for a person who weighs 200 pounds on Earth's surface.

 (b) Graph W in a convenient viewing rectangle. At what distance from Earth's center is this person's weight 50 pounds?

(c) How far from the center of Earth would an object be if its weight were 1% of its weight on the surface of Earth?

9. *Modeling Brightness*   Inverse variation occurs when the intensity of a light is measured. If you increase your distance from a light bulb, the intensity of the light decreases. Intensity I is inversely proportional to the second power of the distance d. The equation $I = \frac{k}{d^2}$ mod-

els this phenomenon. The following table gives the intensity of a 100-watt light bulb at various distances. (*Source:* R. Weidner and R. Sells, *Elementary Classical Physics, Vol. 2.*)

d (meters)	0.5	2	3	4
I (watts/square meter)	31.68	1.98	0.88	0.495

(a) Find the constant of proportionality k.

(b) Graph I in [0, 5, 1] by [0, 30, 5]. What happens to the intensity as the distances increase?

(c) If the distance from the light bulb doubles, what happens to the intensity?

(d) Determine d when $I = 1$ watt per square meter.

CHAPTERS 1–6 CUMULATIVE REVIEW EXERCISES

Exercises 1 and 2: Evaluate the formula for the given value of the variable.

1. $y = \sqrt{74 + t}$ $t = 7$

2. $r = 16 - w^2$ $w = -4$

3. Classify each number as one or more of the following: natural number, whole number, integer, rational number, or irrational number.

$$-\frac{12}{4}, 0, \sqrt{3}, 1, 2.\overline{11}, \frac{13}{2}$$

4. Select the formula that best models the data.
   (i) $y = 2x - 5$ (ii) $y = x - 7$ (iii) $y = 2x + 3$

x	−2	−1	0	1	2
y	−9	−7	−5	−3	−1

Exercises 5 and 6: Simplify the expression. Write the result using positive exponents.

5. $\dfrac{18x^{-2}y^3}{3x^2y^{-3}}$

6. $\left(\dfrac{2c^2}{3d^3}\right)^{-2}$

7. Write 67,300,000,000 in scientific notation.

8. Identify the domain and range of the relation given by $S = \{(-3, 5), (0, 1), (-1, -2), (4, 0)\}$.

Exercises 9 and 10: Evaluate the given formula for $x = -2, -1, 0, 1,$ and 2. Plot the resulting ordered pairs.

9. $y = 3x - 1$

10. $y = \dfrac{4 - x^2}{2}$

11. Sketch the graph of $f(x) = x^2 + 2$ by hand.

12. Find the domain of $f(x) = \frac{5}{x - 1}$.

13. Use the table to write the formula for $f(x) = ax + b$.

x	−2	−1	0	1	2
$f(x)$	−5	−3	−1	1	3

14. Sketch a graph of $f(x) = -2$.

15. Find the slope and the y-intercept of the graph of $f(x) = -3x + 2$.

16. Calculate the slope of the line passing through the points $(6, -3)$ and $(2, 9)$.

17. Sketch the graph of a line passing through the point $(3, -1)$ with slope $m = -2$.

18. Use the graph to express the equation of the line in slope–intercept form.

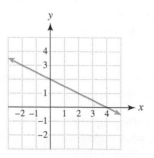

Exercises 19 and 20: Write the slope–intercept form for a line satisfying the given conditions.

19. Parallel to $y = 2x + 3$, passing through $(1, 4)$

20. Perpendicular to $y = \frac{2}{3}x - 2$, passing through $(2, 1)$

Exercises 21 and 22: Solve the equation.

21. $\frac{2}{5}(x + 1) - 6 = -4$

22. $\frac{1}{4}\left(\frac{t - 5}{3}\right) - 6 = \frac{2}{3}t - (3t + 7)$

23. Use the graph to solve the equation $y_1 = y_2$.

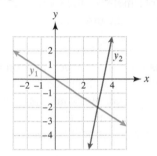

Exercises 24 and 25: Solve the inequality symbolically. Write the solution set in interval notation.

24. $\frac{2x + 3}{4} \leq \frac{1}{3}$

25. $\frac{1}{2}z - 5 > \frac{3}{4}z - (2z + 5)$

Exercises 26 and 27: Solve the compound inequality. Graph the solution set on a number line.

26. $-6 \leq -\frac{2}{3}x - 4 < -2$

27. $3x - 1 \leq 5$ or $2x + 5 > 13$

28. Solve the absolute value equation $\left|\frac{1}{3}x + 6\right| = 4$.

Exercises 29 and 30: Solve the absolute value inequality. Write the solution set in interval notation.

29. $|2x - 3| < 11$ **30.** $-3|t - 5| \leq -18$

31. Determine which pair is a solution to the system of equations: $(2, -6), (-8, -1)$.
$$x + 2y = -10$$
$$3x - 10y = -14$$

32. Shade the solution set in the xy-plane.
$$x + y < 4$$
$$x - 2y \geq 1$$

Exercises 33 and 34: Solve the system of equations.

33. $2x - 8y = 5$ **34.** $2x - 3y = 12$
$\quad\;\; 4x + 2y = 1$ $\qquad\;\; -x + 2y = -6$

35. Maximize the objective function R subject to the given constraints.
$$R = 2x + 3y$$
$$2x + y \leq 6$$
$$x + 2y \leq 6$$
$$x \geq 0, y \geq 0$$

36. Use elimination and substitution to solve the system of linear equations.
$$2x + 3y - z = 3$$
$$3x - y + 4z = 10$$
$$2x + y - 2z = -1$$

37. Write the system of linear equations as an augmented matrix. Then use Gauss–Jordan elimination to solve the system. Write the solution as an ordered triple.
$$x + y - z = 4$$
$$-x - y - z = 0$$
$$x - 2y + z = -9$$

38. Evaluate $\det A$ if $A = \begin{bmatrix} 4 & -2 \\ 1 & 3 \end{bmatrix}$.

39. Find the area of the triangle by using a determinant. Assume that the units are inches.

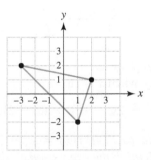

40. Use Cramer's rule to solve the system of equations.
$$6x + 7y = 8$$
$$-8x + 5y = 18$$

Exercises 41 and 42: Multiply the expressions.

41. $3x^2(x^3 + 5x - 2)$ **42.** $(2x - 5)(x + 3)$

43. Use factoring to solve $6x + 3x^2 = 0$.

44. Use grouping to factor $3a^3 - a^2 + 15a - 5$.

Exercises 45–48: Factor completely.

45. $4x^2 + 5x - 6$

46. $6x^3 - 9x^2 - 6x$

47. $9a^2 - 4b^2$

48. $64t^3 + 27$

Exercises 49 and 50: Solve the equation.

49. $3x^2 - 11x = 4$

50. $x^4 - x^3 - 30x^2 = 0$

Exercises 51–54: Simplify the expressions.

51. $\dfrac{x^2 + 3x - 10}{x^2 - 4} \cdot \dfrac{x - 2}{x + 5}$

52. $\dfrac{x^2 + 2x - 24}{x^2 + 3x - 18} \div \dfrac{x + 3}{x^2 - 9}$

53. $\dfrac{2}{t + 2} - \dfrac{t}{t^2 - 4}$

54. $\dfrac{4a}{3ab^2} + \dfrac{b}{a^2c}$

Exercises 55 and 56: Solve. Check your result.

55. $\dfrac{1}{x + 4} + \dfrac{1}{x - 4} = \dfrac{-7}{x^2 - 16}$

56. $\dfrac{1}{y^2 + 3y - 4} - \dfrac{y}{y - 1} = -1$

57. Solve $J = \dfrac{y + z}{z}$ for z.

58. Simplify the complex fraction.

$$\dfrac{\dfrac{4}{x^2} + \dfrac{1}{x}}{\dfrac{4}{x^2} - \dfrac{1}{x}}$$

59. Suppose that y varies inversely as x. If $y = 2$ when $x = 4$, find y when x is 16.

60. Simplify $(x^3 + 2x + 11) \div (x + 2)$.

Exercises 61 and 62: Let $f(x) = x^2 - 3x + 2$ and let $g(x) = x - 2$. Simplify the expression.

61. $(f + g)(3)$

62. $(f/g)(x)$

APPLICATIONS

63. *Temperature Scales* The accompanying table shows equivalent temperatures in degrees Fahrenheit and degrees Celsius.

°F	−40	32	59	95	212
°C	−40	0	15	35	100

(a) Plot the data. Let the x-axis correspond to the Fahrenheit temperature and the y-axis correspond to the Celsius temperature. What type of relation exists between the data?

(b) Find $f(x) = m(x - h) + k$ so that f receives the Fahrenheit temperature as input and outputs the corresponding Celsius temperature.

(c) If the temperature is 104° F, what is the equivalent temperature in degrees Celsius?

64. *Geometry* An isosceles triangle has two shorter sides of the same length and a longer side that is 7 inches longer than half of the length of either of the shorter sides. If the perimeter of the triangle is 22 inches, what are the lengths of the three sides?

65. *Burning Calories* During strenuous exercise, an athlete burns 690 calories per hour on a stair climber and 540 calories per hour on a stationary bicycle. During a 90-minute workout the athlete burns 885 calories. How much time (in hours) is spent on each type of exercise equipment? (**Source:** *Runner's World.*)

66. *Tickets* The price of admission to a county fair is $2 for children and $5 for adults. If a group of 30 people pays $78 to enter the fairgrounds, find the number of children and the number of adults in the group.

67. *Area of a Rectangle* A rectangle has an area of 165 square feet. Its length is 4 feet more than its width. Find the dimensions of the rectangle.

68. *Flight of a Ball* If a ball is thrown upward with a velocity of 44 feet per second (30 miles per hour), its height h in feet above the ground after t seconds can be modeled by

$$h(t) = -16t^2 + 44t.$$

(a) Determine when the ball strikes the ground.

(b) When does the ball reach a height of 18 feet?

69. *Working Together* An amateur painter can paint a room in 15 hours. A professional painter can paint the same room in 10 hours.

(a) Write an equation whose solution gives the time to paint the room if the painters work together.

(b) Solve the equation in part (a).

70. *Height of a Tree* A 6-foot-tall person casts a 4-foot-long shadow while a nearby tree casts a 32-foot-long shadow. Find the height of the tree.

Radical Expressions and Functions

Throughout history, people have created new numbers. Often these new numbers were met with resistance and regarded as being imaginary or unreal. The number 0 was not invented at the same time as the natural numbers. There was no Roman numeral for 0, which is one reason why our calendar started with A.D. 1 and, as a result, the twenty-first century began in 2001. No doubt there were skeptics during the time of the Roman Empire who questioned why anyone needed a number to represent nothing. Negative numbers also met strong resistance. After all, how could anyone possibly have −6 apples?

In this chapter we describe a new number system called *complex numbers*, which involve square roots of negative numbers. The Italian mathematician Cardano (1501–1576) was one of the first mathematicians to work with complex numbers and called them useless. René Descartes (1596–1650) originated the term *imaginary number*, which is associated with complex numbers. However, today complex numbers are used in many applications, such as electricity, fiber optics, and the design of airplanes. We are privileged to study in a period of days what took people centuries to discover.

Bear in mind that the wonderful things you learn in schools are the work of many generations, produced by enthusiastic effort and infinite labor in every country.

—ALBERT EINSTEIN

Source: Historical Topics for the Mathematics Classroom, Thirty-first Yearbook, NCTM.

7.1 RADICAL EXPRESSIONS AND RATIONAL EXPONENTS

Radical Notation ▪ Rational Exponents ▪ Properties of Rational Exponents

A LOOK INTO MATH ▷ Cellular phone technology has become a part of everyday life. In order to have cellular phone coverage, transmission towers, or cellular sites, are spread throughout a region. To estimate the minimum broadcasting distance for each cellular site, *radical expressions* are needed. (See Example 4.) In this section we discuss radical expressions and rational exponents and show how to manipulate them symbolically.   (**Source:** C. Smith, *Practical Cellular & PCS Design*.)

Radical Notation

Recall the definition of the square root of a number a.

SQUARE ROOT

The number b is a *square root* of a if $b^2 = a$.

EXAMPLE 1   Finding square roots

Find the square roots of 100.

Solution
The square roots of 100 are 10 *and* -10 because $10^2 = 100$ and $(-10)^2 = 100$.

Now Try Exercise **1**

Every positive number a has two square roots, one positive and one negative. Recall that the *positive* square root is called the *principal square root* and is denoted $\sqrt{a}$. The *negative square root* is denoted $-\sqrt{a}$. To identify both square roots we write $\pm\sqrt{a}$. The symbol $\pm$ is read "plus or minus." The symbol $\sqrt{}$ is called the **radical sign**. The expression under the radical sign is called the **radicand**, and an expression containing a radical sign is called a **radical expression**. Examples of radical expressions include

$$\sqrt{6}, \quad 5 + \sqrt{x + 1}, \quad \text{and} \quad \sqrt{\frac{3x}{2x - 1}}.$$

MAKING CONNECTIONS

Expressions and Equations

Expressions and equations are *different* mathematical concepts. An expression does not contain an equals sign, whereas an equation *always* contains an equals sign. *An equation is a statement that two expressions are equal.* For example,

$$\sqrt{x + 1} \quad \text{and} \quad \sqrt{5 - x}$$

are two different expressions, and

$$\sqrt{x + 1} = \sqrt{5 - x}$$

is an equation. We often *solve an equation*, but we *do not solve an expression*. Instead, we simplify and evaluate expressions.

In the next example we show how to find the principal square root of an expression.

EXAMPLE 2   Finding principal square roots

Evaluate each square root.

(a) $\sqrt{25}$ (b) $\sqrt{0.49}$ (c) $\sqrt{\frac{4}{9}}$ (d) $\sqrt{c^2}, c > 0$

Solution

(a) Because $5 \cdot 5 = 25$, the principal, or *positive*, square root of 25 is $\sqrt{25} = 5$.

(b) Because $(0.7)(0.7) = 0.49$, the principal square root of 0.49 is $\sqrt{0.49} = 0.7$.

(c) Because $\frac{2}{3} \cdot \frac{2}{3} = \frac{4}{9}$, the principal square root of $\frac{4}{9}$ is $\sqrt{\frac{4}{9}} = \frac{2}{3}$.

(d) The principal square root of c^2 is $\sqrt{c^2} = c$, as c is positive.

Now Try Exercises   **11, 13, 15, 17**

EXAMPLE 3   Approximating a square root

Approximate $\sqrt{17}$ to the nearest thousandth.

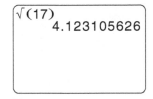

√(17)
     4.123105626

Solution

Figure 7.1 shows that $\sqrt{17} \approx 4.123$, rounded to the nearest thousandth. This result means that $4.123 \times 4.123 \approx 17$.

NOTE: Calculators often give decimal approximations rather than exact answers when evaluating radical expressions.

Now Try Exercise **35**

Figure 7.1

▶ REAL-WORLD CONNECTION   In the next example we use the principal square root to estimate the minimum transmission distance for a cellular site.

EXAMPLE 4   Estimating cellular phone transmission distance

If the ground is level, a cellular transmission tower will broadcast its signal in roughly a circular pattern, whose radius can be altered by changing the strength of its signal. See Figure 7.2. Suppose that a city has an area of 50 square miles and that there are 10 identical transmission towers spread evenly throughout the city. Estimate a *minimum* transmission radius R for each tower. (Note that a larger radius would probably be necessary to adequately cover the city.)   (*Source:* C. Smith.)

Figure 7.2

Solution

The circular area A covered by one transmission tower is $A = \pi R^2$. The total area covered by 10 towers is $10\pi R^2$, which must equal *at least* 50 square miles.

$$10\pi R^2 = 50$$

$$R^2 = \frac{50}{10\pi} \qquad \text{Divide by } 10\pi.$$

$$R^2 = \frac{5}{\pi} \qquad \text{Simplify.}$$

$$R = \sqrt{\frac{5}{\pi}} \approx 1.26 \qquad \text{Take principal square root.}$$

Each transmission tower must broadcast with a minimum radius of about 1.26 miles.

Now Try Exercise **117**

Another common radical expression is the cube root of a number a, denoted $\sqrt[3]{a}$.

CUBE ROOT

The number b is a *cube root* of a if $b^3 = a$.

Although the square root of a negative number is *not* a real number, the cube root of a negative number is a negative real number. *Every real number has one real cube root.*

EXAMPLE 5   Finding cube roots

Evaluate the cube root. Approximate your answer to the nearest hundredth when appropriate.

(a) $\sqrt[3]{8}$ **(b)** $\sqrt[3]{-27}$ **(c)** $\sqrt[3]{\frac{1}{64}}$ **(d)** $\sqrt[3]{d^6}$ **(e)** $\sqrt[3]{16}$

Solution

(a) $\sqrt[3]{8} = 2$ because $2^3 = 2 \cdot 2 \cdot 2 = 8$.

(b) $\sqrt[3]{-27} = -3$ because $(-3)^3 = (-3)(-3)(-3) = -27$.

(c) $\sqrt[3]{\frac{1}{64}} = \frac{1}{4}$ because $\left(\frac{1}{4}\right)^3 = \frac{1}{4} \cdot \frac{1}{4} \cdot \frac{1}{4} = \frac{1}{64}$.

(d) $\sqrt[3]{d^6} = d^2$ because $(d^2)^3 = d^2 \cdot d^2 \cdot d^2 = d^{2+2+2} = d^6$.

(e) $\sqrt[3]{16}$ is not an integer. Figure 7.3 shows that $\sqrt[3]{16} \approx 2.52$.

Now Try Exercises 19, 21, 23, 27, 37

```
3√(16)
              2.5198421
```

Figure 7.3

CALCULATOR HELP

To calculate a cube root, see the Appendix (page AP-1).

NOTE: $\sqrt[3]{-b} = -\sqrt[3]{b}$ for any real number b. That is, the cube root of a negative is the negative of the cube root. For example, $\sqrt[3]{-8} = -\sqrt[3]{8} = -2$.

We can generalize square roots and cube roots to include nth roots of a number a. The number b is an ***n*th root** of a if $b^n = a$, where n is a positive integer. For example, $2^5 = 32$ and so the 5th root of 32 is 2 and can be written as $\sqrt[5]{32} = 2$.

THE NOTATION $\sqrt[n]{a}$

The equation $\sqrt[n]{a} = b$ means that $b^n = a$, where n is a natural number called the **index**. If n is odd, we are finding an **odd root** and if n is even, we are finding an **even root**.

1. If $a > 0$, then $\sqrt[n]{a}$ is a positive number.
2. If $a < 0$ and
    (a) n is odd, then $\sqrt[n]{a}$ is a negative number.
    (b) n is even, then $\sqrt[n]{a}$ is *not* a real number.

If $a > 0$ and n is even, then a has two real nth roots: one positive and one negative. In this case, the positive root is denoted $\sqrt[n]{a}$ and called the **principal *n*th root of *a*.** For example, $(-3)^4 = 81$ *and* $3^4 = 81$, but $\sqrt[4]{81} = 3$ in the same way *principal square roots* are calculated.

EXAMPLE 6 Finding nth roots

Find each root, if possible.

(a) $\sqrt[4]{16}$ (b) $\sqrt[5]{-32}$ (c) $\sqrt[4]{-81}$

Solution

(a) $\sqrt[4]{16} = 2$ because $2^4 = 2 \cdot 2 \cdot 2 \cdot 2 = 16$.

(b) $\sqrt[5]{-32} = -2$ because $(-2)^5 = (-2)(-2)(-2)(-2)(-2) = -32$.

(c) An *even* root of a *negative* number is *not* a real number.

Now Try Exercises 29, 31, 33

Consider the calculations

$$\sqrt{3^2} = \sqrt{9} = 3, \quad \sqrt{(-4)^2} = \sqrt{16} = 4, \quad \text{and} \quad \sqrt{(-6)^2} = \sqrt{36} = 6.$$

In general, the expression $\sqrt{x^2}$ equals $|x|$. Graphical support is shown in Figure 7.4, where the graphs of $Y_1 = \sqrt{(X\^2)}$ and $Y_2 = \text{abs}(X)$ appear to be identical.

CRITICAL THINKING

Evaluate $\sqrt[6]{(-2)^6}$ and $\sqrt[3]{(-2)^3}$. Now simplify $\sqrt[n]{x^n}$ when n is even and when n is odd.

$[-6, 6, 1]$ by $[-4, 4, 1]$ $[-6, 6, 1]$ by $[-4, 4, 1]$

(a) $y_1 = \sqrt{x^2}$ (b) $y_2 = |x|$

Figure 7.4

THE EXPRESSION $\sqrt{x^2}$

For every real number x, $\sqrt{x^2} = |x|$.

EXAMPLE 7 Simplifying expressions

Write each expression in terms of an absolute value.

(a) $\sqrt{(-3)^2}$ (b) $\sqrt{(x + 1)^2}$ (c) $\sqrt{z^2 - 4z + 4}$

Solution

(a) $\sqrt{x^2} = |x|$, so $\sqrt{(-3)^2} = |-3| = 3$

(b) $\sqrt{(x + 1)^2} = |x + 1|$

(c) $\sqrt{z^2 - 4z + 4} = \sqrt{(z - 2)^2} = |z - 2|$

Now Try Exercises 103, 107, 109

Rational Exponents

When m and n are integers, the product rule states that $a^m a^n = a^{m+n}$. This rule can be extended to include exponents that are fractions. For example,

$$4^{1/2} \cdot 4^{1/2} = 4^{1/2+1/2} = 4^1 = 4.$$

That is, if we multiply the expression $4^{1/2}$ by itself, the result is 4. Because we also know that $\sqrt{4} \cdot \sqrt{4} = 4$, this discussion suggests that $4^{1/2} = \sqrt{4}$ and motivates the following definition.

THE EXPRESSION $a^{1/n}$

If n is an integer greater than 1 and a is a real number, then

$$a^{1/n} = \sqrt[n]{a}.$$

NOTE: If $a < 0$ and n is an even positive integer, then $a^{1/n}$ is not a real number.

In the next two examples, we show how to interpret rational exponents.

EXAMPLE 8   Interpreting rational exponents

Write each expression in radical notation. Then evaluate the expression and round to the nearest hundredth when appropriate.

(a) $36^{1/2}$ (b) $23^{1/5}$ (c) $x^{1/3}$ (d) $(5x)^{1/2}$

Solution
(a) The exponent $\frac{1}{2}$ indicates a square root. Thus $36^{1/2} = \sqrt{36}$, which evaluates to 6.
(b) The exponent $\frac{1}{5}$ indicates a fifth root. Thus $23^{1/5} = \sqrt[5]{23}$, which is not an integer. Figure 7.5 shows this expression approximated in both exponential and radical notation. In either case $23^{1/5} \approx 1.87$.
(c) The exponent $\frac{1}{3}$ indicates a cube root, so $x^{1/3} = \sqrt[3]{x}$.
(d) The exponent $\frac{1}{2}$ indicates a square root, so $(5x)^{1/2} = \sqrt{5x}$.

Now Try Exercises 41, 49, 63, 67

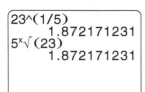

```
23^(1/5)
          1.872171231
5ˣ√(23)
          1.872171231
```

Figure 7.5

CALCULATOR HELP

To calculate other roots, see the Appendix (page AP-1).

Suppose that we want to define the expression $8^{2/3}$. On the one hand, using properties of exponents we have

$$8^{1/3} \cdot 8^{1/3} = 8^{1/3+1/3} = 8^{2/3}.$$

On the other hand, we have

$$8^{1/3} \cdot 8^{1/3} = \sqrt[3]{8} \cdot \sqrt[3]{8} = 2 \cdot 2 = 4.$$

Thus $8^{2/3} = 4$, and that value is obtained whether we interpret $8^{2/3}$ as either

$$8^{2/3} = (8^{1/3})^2 = (\sqrt[3]{8})^2 = 2^2 = 4$$

or

$$8^{2/3} = (8^2)^{1/3} = \sqrt[3]{8^2} = \sqrt[3]{64} = 4.$$

This result suggests the following definition.

THE EXPRESSION $a^{m/n}$

If m and n are positive integers with $\frac{m}{n}$ in lowest terms, then

$$a^{m/n} = \sqrt[n]{a^m} = (\sqrt[n]{a})^m.$$

NOTE: If $a < 0$ and n is an even integer, then $a^{m/n}$ is *not* a real number.

The exponent $\frac{m}{n}$ indicates that we either take the nth root and then calculate the mth power of the result or calculate the mth power and then take the nth root. For example, $4^{3/2}$ means that we can either take the square root of 4 and then cube the result or we cube 4 and then take the square root of the result. In either case the result is the same: $4^{3/2} = 8$. This concept is illustrated in the next example.

EXAMPLE 9   Interpreting rational exponents

Write each expression in radical notation. Evaluate the expression by hand when possible.

(a) $(-27)^{2/3}$ **(b)** $12^{3/5}$

Solution

(a) The exponent $\frac{2}{3}$ indicates that we either take the cube root of -27 and then square it or that we square -27 and then take the cube root. Thus

$$(-27)^{2/3} = (\sqrt[3]{-27})^2 = (-3)^2 = 9$$

or

$$(-27)^{2/3} = \sqrt[3]{(-27)^2} = \sqrt[3]{729} = 9.$$

Same result

(b) The exponent $\frac{3}{5}$ indicates that we either take the fifth root of 12 and then cube it or that we cube 12 and then take the fifth root. Thus

$$12^{3/5} = (\sqrt[5]{12})^3 \quad \text{or} \quad 12^{3/5} = \sqrt[5]{12^3}.$$

This result cannot be evaluated by hand.   Now Try Exercises 45, 55

TECHNOLOGY NOTE: Rational Exponents

When evaluating expressions with rational (fractional) exponents, be sure to put parentheses around the fraction. For example, most calculators will evaluate 8^(2/3) and 8^2/3 differently. The accompanying figure shows evaluation of $8^{2/3}$ input correctly, 8^(2/3), as 4 but shows evaluation of $8^{2/3}$ input incorrectly, 8^2/3, as $\frac{8^2}{3} = 21.\overline{3}$.

Correct → | 8^(2/3)
          | 4
Incorrect → | 8^2/3
            | 21.33333333

From properties of exponents we know that $a^{-n} = \frac{1}{a^n}$, where n is a positive integer. We now define this property for negative rational exponents.

THE EXPRESSION $a^{-m/n}$

If m and n are positive integers with $\frac{m}{n}$ in lowest terms, then

$$a^{-m/n} = \frac{1}{a^{m/n}}, \qquad a \neq 0.$$

EXAMPLE 10   Interpreting negative rational exponents

Write each expression in radical notation and then evaluate.

(a) $64^{-1/3}$ **(b)** $81^{-3/4}$

Solution

(a) $64^{-1/3} = \dfrac{1}{64^{1/3}} = \dfrac{1}{\sqrt[3]{64}} = \dfrac{1}{4}.$

(b) $81^{-3/4} = \dfrac{1}{81^{3/4}} = \dfrac{1}{(\sqrt[4]{81})^3} = \dfrac{1}{3^3} = \dfrac{1}{27}.$

Now Try Exercises 57, 59

▶ **REAL-WORLD CONNECTION**   In the next example, we use a formula from biology that involves a rational exponent.

EXAMPLE 11   Analyzing stepping frequency

When smaller (four-legged) animals walk, they tend to take faster, shorter steps, whereas larger animals tend to take slower, longer steps. If an animal is h feet high at the shoulder, then the number N of steps per second that the animal takes *while walking* can be estimated by $N(h) = 1.6h^{-1/2}$. Use a calculator to estimate N for an elephant that is 10 feet high at the shoulder.   (*Source: C. Pennycuick, Newton Rules Biology.*)

Solution

$$N(10) = 1.6(10)^{-1/2} = \dfrac{1.6}{\sqrt{10}} \approx 0.51$$

The elephant takes about $\frac{1}{2}$ step per second while walking or about 1 step every 2 seconds.

Now Try Exercise 119

Properties of Rational Exponents

Any rational number can be written as a ratio of two integers. That is, if p is a rational number, then $p = \frac{m}{n}$, where m and n are integers. Properties for integer exponents also apply to rational exponents, with one exception. If n is even in the expression $a^{m/n}$ and $\frac{m}{n}$ is written in lowest terms, then a must be nonnegative (not negative) for the result to be a real number.

PROPERTIES OF EXPONENTS

Let p and q be rational numbers written in lowest terms. For all real numbers a and b for which the expressions are real numbers the following properties hold.

1. $a^p \cdot a^q = a^{p+q}$ Product rule for exponents

2. $a^{-p} = \dfrac{1}{a^p}, \quad \dfrac{1}{a^{-p}} = a^p$ Negative exponents

3. $\left(\dfrac{a}{b}\right)^{-p} = \left(\dfrac{b}{a}\right)^p$ Negative exponents for quotients

4. $\dfrac{a^p}{a^q} = a^{p-q}$ Quotient rule for exponents

5. $(a^p)^q = a^{pq}$ Power rule for exponents

6. $(ab)^p = a^p b^p$ Power rule for products

7. $\left(\dfrac{a}{b}\right)^p = \dfrac{a^p}{b^p}$ Power rule for quotients

In the next two examples, we apply these properties.

EXAMPLE 12   Applying properties of exponents

Write each expression using rational exponents and simplify. Write the answer with a positive exponent. Assume that all variables are positive numbers.

(a) $\sqrt{x} \cdot \sqrt[3]{x}$ (b) $\sqrt[3]{27x^2}$ (c) $\dfrac{\sqrt[4]{16x}}{\sqrt[3]{x}}$ (d) $\left(\dfrac{x^2}{81}\right)^{-1/2}$

Solution

(a) $\sqrt{x} \cdot \sqrt[3]{x} = x^{1/2} \cdot x^{1/3}$ Use rational exponents.

$= x^{1/2 + 1/3}$ Product rule for exponents

$= x^{5/6}$ Simplify: $\frac{1}{2} + \frac{1}{3} = \frac{3}{6} + \frac{2}{6} = \frac{5}{6}$.

(b) $\sqrt[3]{27x^2} = (27x^2)^{1/3}$ Use rational exponents.

$= 27^{1/3}(x^2)^{1/3}$ Power rule for products

$= 3x^{2/3}$ Simplify; power rule for exponents

(c) $\dfrac{\sqrt[4]{16x}}{\sqrt[3]{x}} = \dfrac{(16x)^{1/4}}{x^{1/3}}$ Use rational exponents.

$= \dfrac{16^{1/4}x^{1/4}}{x^{1/3}}$ Power rule for products

$= 16^{1/4}x^{1/4 - 1/3}$ Quotient rule for exponents

$= 2x^{-1/12}$ Simplify: $\frac{1}{4} - \frac{1}{3} = \frac{3}{12} - \frac{4}{12} = -\frac{1}{12}$.

$= \dfrac{2}{x^{1/12}}$ Negative exponents

(d) $\left(\dfrac{x^2}{81}\right)^{-1/2} = \left(\dfrac{81}{x^2}\right)^{1/2}$ Negative exponents for quotients

$= \dfrac{(81)^{1/2}}{(x^2)^{1/2}}$ Power rule for quotients

$= \dfrac{9}{x}$ Simplify; power rule for exponents

Now Try Exercises 81, 89, 90, 97

EXAMPLE **13**   Applying properties of exponents

Write each expression with positive rational exponents and simplify, if possible.

(a) $\sqrt[3]{\sqrt{x+1}}$ **(b)** $\sqrt[5]{c^{15}}$ **(c)** $\dfrac{y^{-1/2}}{x^{-1/3}}$ **(d)** $\sqrt{x}(\sqrt{x}-1)$

Solution

(a) $\sqrt[3]{\sqrt{x+1}} = \left((x+1)^{1/2}\right)^{1/3} = (x+1)^{1/6}$

(b) $\sqrt[5]{c^{15}} = c^{15/5} = c^{3}$

(c) $\dfrac{y^{-1/2}}{x^{-1/3}} = \dfrac{x^{1/3}}{y^{1/2}}$

(d) $\sqrt{x}(\sqrt{x}-1) = x^{1/2}(x^{1/2}-1) = x^{1/2}x^{1/2} - x^{1/2} = x - x^{1/2}$

Now Try Exercises 91, 95, 101, 115

7.1   PUTTING IT ALL TOGETHER

Properties of radicals and rational exponents are summarized in the following table.

Concept	Explanation	Examples
nth Root of a Real Number	An nth root of a real number a is b if $b^{n} = a$ and the (principal) nth root is denoted $\sqrt[n]{a}$. If $a < 0$ and n is even, $\sqrt[n]{a}$ is not a real number.	The square roots of 25 are 5 and -5. The principal square root is $\sqrt{25} = 5$. $\sqrt[3]{-125} = -5$ because $(-5)^{3} = -125$.
Rational Exponents	If m and n are positive integers with $\frac{m}{n}$ in lowest terms, $$a^{m/n} = \sqrt[n]{a^{m}} = \left(\sqrt[n]{a}\right)^{m}.$$ If $a < 0$ and n is even, $a^{m/n}$ is not a real number.	$8^{4/3} = \left(\sqrt[3]{8}\right)^{4} = 2^{4} = 16$ $(-27)^{3/4} = (\sqrt[4]{-27})^{3}$ is *not* a real number.
Properties of Exponents	Let p and q be rational numbers. **1.** $a^{p} \cdot a^{q} = a^{p+q}$ **2.** $a^{-p} = \dfrac{1}{a^{p}}, \ \dfrac{1}{a^{-p}} = a^{p}$ **3.** $\left(\dfrac{a}{b}\right)^{-p} = \left(\dfrac{b}{a}\right)^{p}$ **4.** $\dfrac{a^{p}}{a^{q}} = a^{p-q}$ **5.** $(a^{p})^{q} = a^{pq}$ **6.** $(ab)^{p} = a^{p}b^{p}$ **7.** $\left(\dfrac{a}{b}\right)^{p} = \dfrac{a^{p}}{b^{p}}$	**1.** $2^{1/3} \cdot 2^{2/3} = 2^{1/3+2/3} = 2^{1} = 2$ **2.** $2^{-1/2} = \dfrac{1}{2^{1/2}}, \ \dfrac{1}{3^{-1/4}} = 3^{1/4}$ **3.** $\left(\dfrac{3}{4}\right)^{-4/5} = \left(\dfrac{4}{3}\right)^{4/5}$ **4.** $\dfrac{7^{2/3}}{7^{1/3}} = 7^{2/3-1/3} = 7^{1/3}$ **5.** $(8^{2/3})^{1/2} = 8^{(2/3)\cdot(1/2)} = 8^{1/3} = 2$ **6.** $(2x)^{1/3} = 2^{1/3}x^{1/3}$ **7.** $\left(\dfrac{x}{y}\right)^{1/6} = \dfrac{x^{1/6}}{y^{1/6}}$

7.1 Exercises

MyMathLab

PRACTICE   WATCH   DOWNLOAD   READ   REVIEW

CONCEPTS

1. What are the square roots of 9?

2. What is the principal square root of 9?

3. What is the cube root of 8?

4. Does every real number have a cube root?

5. If $b^n = a$ and $b > 0$, then $\sqrt[n]{a} =$ _____.

6. Use a rational exponent to write $\sqrt{x}$.

7. Use a rational exponent to write $\sqrt[3]{a^4}$.

8. Write $a^{1/n}$ in radical notation.

9. Write $a^{m/n}$ in radical notation.

10. Does $(a^{1/3})^2 = a^{2/3}$?

RADICAL EXPRESSIONS AND RATIONAL EXPONENTS

Exercises 11–34: Evaluate the expression by hand, if possible. Variables represent any real number.

11. $\sqrt{9}$
12. $\sqrt{121}$

13. $\sqrt{0.36}$
14. $\sqrt{0.64}$

15. $\sqrt{\frac{16}{25}}$
16. $\sqrt{\frac{9}{49}}$

17. $\sqrt{x^2}, x > 0$
18. $\sqrt{(x-1)^2}, x > 1$

19. $\sqrt[3]{27}$
20. $\sqrt[3]{64}$

21. $\sqrt[3]{-64}$
22. $-\sqrt[3]{-1}$

23. $\sqrt[3]{\frac{8}{27}}$
24. $\sqrt[3]{-\frac{1}{125}}$

25. $-\sqrt[3]{x^9}$
26. $\sqrt[3]{(x+1)^6}$

27. $\sqrt[3]{(2x)^6}$
28. $\sqrt[3]{27x^3}$

29. $\sqrt[4]{81}$
30. $\sqrt[5]{-1}$

31. $\sqrt[5]{-243}$
32. $\sqrt[4]{625}$

33. $\sqrt[4]{-16}$
34. $\sqrt[6]{-64}$

Exercises 35–48: Approximate to the nearest hundredth.

35. $-\sqrt{5}$
36. $\sqrt{11}$

37. $\sqrt[3]{5}$
38. $\sqrt[3]{-13}$

39. $\sqrt[5]{-7}$
40. $\sqrt[4]{6}$

41. $16^{1/5}$
42. $7^{1/4}$

43. $5^{1/3}$
44. $11^{1/2}$

45. $9^{3/5}$
46. $13^{5/4}$

47. $4^{-3/7}$
48. $2^{-3/4}$

Exercises 49–68: Write each expression in radical notation. Evaluate the expression by hand when possible.

49. $9^{1/2}$
50. $100^{1/2}$

51. $8^{1/3}$
52. $(-8)^{1/3}$

53. $\left(\frac{4}{9}\right)^{1/2}$
54. $\left(\frac{64}{27}\right)^{1/3}$

55. $(-8)^{2/3}$
56. $(16)^{3/2}$

57. $\left(\frac{1}{8}\right)^{-1/3}$
58. $\left(\frac{1}{81}\right)^{-1/4}$

59. $16^{-3/4}$
60. $(32)^{-2/5}$

61. $(4^{1/2})^{-3}$
62. $(8^{1/3})^{-2}$

63. $z^{1/4}$
64. $b^{1/3}$

65. $y^{-2/5}$
66. $z^{-3/4}$

67. $(3x)^{1/3}$
68. $(5x)^{1/2}$

Exercises 69–76: Use a positive rational exponent to write the expression.

69. $\sqrt{y}$
70. $\sqrt{z+1}$

71. $\sqrt{x} \cdot \sqrt{x}$
72. $\sqrt[3]{x} \cdot \sqrt[3]{x}$

73. $\sqrt[3]{8x^2}$
74. $\sqrt[3]{27z}$

75. $\dfrac{\sqrt{49x}}{\sqrt[3]{x^2}}$
76. $\dfrac{\sqrt[3]{8x}}{\sqrt[4]{x^3}}$

Exercises 77 and 78: Thinking Generally Simplify the expression. Assume that a and b are positive integers.

77. $(b^{1/a}b^{2/a})^a$
78. $b^{(b-1)/b} \cdot \sqrt[b]{b}$

Exercises 79–102: Simplify the expression. Assume that all variables are positive.

79. $(x^2)^{3/2}$ **80.** $(y^4)^{1/2}$

81. $\sqrt[3]{x^3 y^6}$ **82.** $\sqrt{16x^4}$

83. $\sqrt{\dfrac{y^4}{x^2}}$ **84.** $\sqrt[3]{\dfrac{x^{12}}{z^6}}$

85. $\sqrt{y^3} \cdot \sqrt[3]{y^2}$ **86.** $\left(\dfrac{x^6}{81}\right)^{1/4}$

87. $\left(\dfrac{x^6}{27}\right)^{2/3}$ **88.** $\left(\dfrac{1}{x^8}\right)^{-1/4}$

89. $\left(\dfrac{x^2}{y^6}\right)^{-1/2}$ **90.** $\dfrac{\sqrt{x}}{\sqrt[3]{27x^6}}$

91. $\sqrt{\sqrt{y}}$ **92.** $\sqrt{\sqrt[3]{(3x)^2}}$

93. $(a^{-1/2})^{4/3}$ **94.** $(x^{-3/2})^{2/3}$

95. $\dfrac{(k^{1/2})^{-3}}{(k^2)^{1/4}}$ **96.** $\dfrac{(b^{3/4})^4}{(b^{4/5})^{-5}}$

97. $\sqrt{b} \cdot \sqrt[4]{b}$ **98.** $\sqrt[3]{t} \cdot \sqrt[5]{t}$

99. $p^{1/2}\left(p^{3/2} + p^{1/2}\right)$ **100.** $d^{3/4}(d^{1/4} - d^{-1/4})$

101. $\sqrt[3]{x}\left(\sqrt{x} - \sqrt[3]{x^2}\right)$ **102.** $\tfrac{1}{2}\sqrt{x}\left(\sqrt{x} + \sqrt[4]{x^2}\right)$

Exercises 103–116: Simplify the expression. Assume that all variables are real numbers.

103. $\sqrt{(-4)^2}$ **104.** $\sqrt{9^2}$

105. $\sqrt{y^2}$ **106.** $\sqrt{z^4}$

107. $\sqrt{(x-5)^2}$ **108.** $\sqrt{(2x-1)^2}$

109. $\sqrt{x^2 - 2x + 1}$ **110.** $\sqrt{4x^2 + 4x + 1}$

111. $\sqrt[4]{y^4}$ **112.** $\sqrt[4]{x^8 z^4}$

113. $\sqrt[4]{x^{12}}$ **114.** $\sqrt[6]{x^6}$

115. $\sqrt[5]{x^5}$ **116.** $\sqrt[5]{32(x+4)^5}$

APPLICATIONS

117. *Cellular Phone Technology*   (Refer to Example 4.) Suppose that a city has an area of 65 square miles and 15 cellular transmission towers spread evenly throughout it. Estimate a minimum radius R for each tower.

118. *Musical Tones*   One octave on a piano contains 12 keys (including both the black and white keys). The frequency of each successive key increases by a factor of $2^{1/12}$. For example, middle C is two keys below the first D above it. Therefore the frequency of this D is

$$2^{1/12} \cdot 2^{1/12} = 2^{1/6} \approx 1.12$$

times the frequency of middle C.
(a) If two tones are one octave apart, how do their frequencies compare?
(b) The A tone below middle C has a frequency of 220 cycles per second. Middle C is 3 keys above this A note. Estimate the frequency of middle C.

one octave

119. *Animal Stepping Frequency*   (Refer to Example 11.) Use the formula $N(h) = 1.6h^{-1/2}$ to estimate the stepping frequency of a dog that is 2.5 feet high at the shoulders.   (*Source:* C. Pennycuick.)

120. *Animal Pulse Rate*   According to one model, an animal's heart rate varies according to its weight. The formula $N(w) = 885w^{-1/2}$ gives an estimate for the average number N of beats per minute for an animal that weighs w pounds. Use the formula to estimate the heart rate for a horse that weighs 800 pounds. (*Source:* C. Pennycuick.)

Exercises 121 and 122: Heron's Formula   Suppose the lengths of the sides of a triangle are a, b, and c as illustrated in the figure.

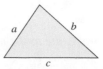

If the **semiperimeter** of the triangle is $s = \frac{1}{2}(a + b + c)$, then the area of the triangle is

$$A = \sqrt{s(s - a)(s - b)(s - c)}.$$

Find the area of the triangle with the given sides.

121. $a = 3, b = 4, c = 5$

122. $a = 5, b = 9, c = 10$

WRITING ABOUT MATHEMATICS

123. Try to calculate $\sqrt{-7}$, $\sqrt[4]{-56}$, and $\sqrt[6]{-10}$ with a calculator. Describe what happens when you evaluate an even root of a negative number. Does the same difficulty occur when you evaluate an odd root of a negative number? Try to evaluate $\sqrt[3]{-7}$, $\sqrt[5]{-56}$, and $\sqrt[7]{-10}$. Explain.

124. Explain the difference between a root and a positive integer power of a number. Give examples.

7.2 SIMPLIFYING RADICAL EXPRESSIONS

Product Rule for Radical Expressions ▪ Quotient Rule for Radical Expressions

A LOOK INTO MATH ▷

Radical expressions often occur in biology. For example, heavier birds tend to have larger wings. The relationship between the weight of a bird and the surface area of its wings can be modeled by a radical expression. (See Exercise 111.) In this section we discuss performing arithmetic operations with radical expressions.

Product Rule for Radical Expressions

Consider the following examples of multiplying radical expressions. The equations

$$\sqrt{4} \cdot \sqrt{25} = 2 \cdot 5 = 10 \quad \text{and} \quad \sqrt{4 \cdot 25} = \sqrt{100} = 10$$

imply that

$$\sqrt{4} \cdot \sqrt{25} = \sqrt{4 \cdot 25} \quad \text{(see Figure 7.6(a))}.$$

Similarly, the equations

$$\sqrt[3]{8} \cdot \sqrt[3]{27} = 2 \cdot 3 = 6 \quad \text{and} \quad \sqrt[3]{8 \cdot 27} = \sqrt[3]{216} = 6$$

imply that

$$\sqrt[3]{8} \cdot \sqrt[3]{27} = \sqrt[3]{8 \cdot 27} \quad \text{(see Figure 7.6(b))}.$$

These examples suggest that *the product of the roots is equal to the root of the product.*

(a)

(b)

Figure 7.6

PRODUCT RULE FOR RADICAL EXPRESSIONS

Let a and b be real numbers, where $\sqrt[n]{a}$ and $\sqrt[n]{b}$ are both defined. Then

$$\sqrt[n]{a} \cdot \sqrt[n]{b} = \sqrt[n]{a \cdot b}.$$

NOTE: The product rule only works when the radicals have the *same index*. For example, the product $\sqrt{2} \cdot \sqrt[3]{4}$ cannot be simplified because the indexes are 2 and 3. (However, by using rational exponents, we can simplify this product. See Example 5(b).)

We apply the product rule in the next two examples.

EXAMPLE 1 Multiplying radical expressions

Multiply each radical expression.

(a) $\sqrt{5} \cdot \sqrt{20}$ **(b)** $\sqrt[3]{-3} \cdot \sqrt[3]{9}$ **(c)** $\sqrt[4]{\frac{1}{3}} \cdot \sqrt[4]{\frac{1}{9}} \cdot \sqrt[4]{\frac{1}{3}}$

Solution
(a) $\sqrt{5} \cdot \sqrt{20} = \sqrt{5 \cdot 20} = \sqrt{100} = 10$
(b) $\sqrt[3]{-3} \cdot \sqrt[3]{9} = \sqrt[3]{-3 \cdot 9} = \sqrt[3]{-27} = -3$
(c) The product rule can also be applied to three or more factors. Thus

$$\sqrt[4]{\frac{1}{3}} \cdot \sqrt[4]{\frac{1}{9}} \cdot \sqrt[4]{\frac{1}{3}} = \sqrt[4]{\frac{1}{3} \cdot \frac{1}{9} \cdot \frac{1}{3}} = \sqrt[4]{\frac{1}{81}} = \frac{1}{3}$$

because $\frac{1}{3} \cdot \frac{1}{3} \cdot \frac{1}{3} \cdot \frac{1}{3} = \frac{1}{81}$.   Now Try Exercises **13, 15, 21**

EXAMPLE 2 Multiplying radical expressions containing variables

Multiply each radical expression. Assume that all variables are positive.

(a) $\sqrt{x} \cdot \sqrt{x^3}$ **(b)** $\sqrt[3]{2a} \cdot \sqrt[3]{5a}$ **(c)** $\sqrt{11} \cdot \sqrt{xy}$ **(d)** $\sqrt[5]{\frac{2x}{y}} \cdot \sqrt[5]{\frac{16y}{x}}$

Solution
(a) $\sqrt{x} \cdot \sqrt{x^3} = \sqrt{x \cdot x^3} = \sqrt{x^4} = x^2$
(b) $\sqrt[3]{2a} \cdot \sqrt[3]{5a} = \sqrt[3]{2a \cdot 5a} = \sqrt[3]{10a^2}$
(c) $\sqrt{11} \cdot \sqrt{xy} = \sqrt{11xy}$

(d) $\sqrt[5]{\frac{2x}{y}} \cdot \sqrt[5]{\frac{16y}{x}} = \sqrt[5]{\frac{2x}{y} \cdot \frac{16y}{x}}$ Product rule

$= \sqrt[5]{\frac{32xy}{xy}}$ Multiply fractions.

$= \sqrt[5]{32}$ Simplify.

$= 2$ $2^5 = 32$ Now Try Exercises **23, 51, 57, 61**

An integer a is a **perfect nth power** if there exists an integer b such that $b^n = a$. Thus 36 is a **perfect square** because $6^2 = 36$. Similarly, 8 is a **perfect cube** because $2^3 = 8$, and 81 is a *perfect fourth power* because $3^4 = 81$.

The product rule for radicals can be used to simplify radical expressions. For example, because the largest perfect square factor of 50 is 25, the expression $\sqrt{50}$ can be simplified as

$$\sqrt{50} = \sqrt{25 \cdot 2} = \sqrt{25} \cdot \sqrt{2} = 5\sqrt{2}.$$

This procedure is generalized as follows.

SIMPLIFYING RADICALS (nth ROOTS)

STEP 1: Determine the largest perfect nth power factor of the radicand.

STEP 2: Use the product rule to factor out and simplify this perfect nth power.

EXAMPLE 3   Simplifying radical expressions

Simplify each expression.

(a) $\sqrt{300}$ **(b)** $\sqrt[3]{16}$ **(c)** $\sqrt{54}$ **(d)** $\sqrt[4]{512}$

Solution

(a) First note that $300 = 100 \cdot 3$ and that 100 is the largest perfect square factor of 300.
$$\sqrt{300} = \sqrt{100} \cdot \sqrt{3} = 10\sqrt{3}$$

(b) The largest perfect cube factor of 16 is 8. Thus $\sqrt[3]{16} = \sqrt[3]{8} \cdot \sqrt[3]{2} = 2\sqrt[3]{2}$.

(c) $\sqrt{54} = \sqrt{9} \cdot \sqrt{6} = 3\sqrt{6}$

(d) $\sqrt[4]{512} = \sqrt[4]{256} \cdot \sqrt[4]{2} = 4\sqrt[4]{2}$ because $4^4 = 256$.   Now Try Exercises 73, 75, 77, 79

NOTE: To simplify a cube root of a negative number we factor out the negative of the largest perfect cube factor. For example, $-16 = -8 \cdot 2$, so $\sqrt[3]{-16} = \sqrt[3]{-8} \cdot \sqrt[3]{2} = -2\sqrt[3]{2}$. This procedure can be used with any odd root of a negative number.

EXAMPLE 4   Simplifying radical expressions

Simplify each expression. Assume that all variables are positive.

(a) $\sqrt{25x^4}$ **(b)** $\sqrt{32n^3}$ **(c)** $\sqrt[3]{-16x^3y^5}$ **(d)** $\sqrt[3]{2a} \cdot \sqrt[3]{4a^2b}$

Solution

(a) $\sqrt{25x^4} = 5x^2$ Perfect square: $(5x^2)^2 = 25x^4$

(b) $\sqrt{32n^3} = \sqrt{(16n^2)2n}$ $16n^2$ is the largest perfect square factor.

$\qquad\qquad = \sqrt{16n^2} \cdot \sqrt{2n}$ Product rule

$\qquad\qquad = 4n\sqrt{2n}$ $(4n)^2 = 16n^2$

(c) $\sqrt[3]{-16x^3y^5} = \sqrt[3]{(-8x^3y^3)2y^2}$ $8x^3y^3$ is the largest perfect cube factor.

$\qquad\qquad = \sqrt[3]{-8x^3y^3} \cdot \sqrt[3]{2y^2}$ Product rule

$\qquad\qquad = -2xy\sqrt[3]{2y^2}$ $(-2xy)^3 = -8x^3y^3$

(d) $\sqrt[3]{2a} \cdot \sqrt[3]{4a^2b} = \sqrt[3]{(2a)(4a^2b)}$ Product rule

$\qquad\qquad = \sqrt[3]{(8a^3)b}$ $8a^3$ is the largest perfect cube factor.

$\qquad\qquad = \sqrt[3]{8a^3} \cdot \sqrt[3]{b}$ Product rule

$\qquad\qquad = 2a\sqrt[3]{b}$ $(2a)^3 = 8a^3$

Now Try Exercises 45, 85, 89, 91

The product rule for radical expressions cannot be used if the radicals do not have the same indexes. In this case we use rational exponents, as illustrated in the next example.

EXAMPLE 5   Multiplying radicals with different indexes

Simplify each expression. Write your answer in radical notation.

(a) $\sqrt{5} \cdot \sqrt[4]{5}$ **(b)** $\sqrt{2} \cdot \sqrt[4]{4}$ **(c)** $\sqrt[3]{x} \cdot \sqrt[4]{x}$

Solution

(a) The given expression is $\sqrt{5} \cdot \sqrt[4]{5}$. Because $\sqrt{5} = 5^{1/2}$ and $\sqrt[4]{5} = 5^{1/4}$,

$$\sqrt{5} \cdot \sqrt[4]{5} = 5^{1/2} \cdot 5^{1/4} = 5^{1/2+1/4} = 5^{3/4}.$$

In radical notation, $5^{3/4} = \sqrt[4]{5^3} = \sqrt[4]{125}$.

(b) The given expression is $\sqrt{2} \cdot \sqrt[3]{4}$. Because $\sqrt[3]{4} = \sqrt[3]{2^2} = 2^{2/3}$,

$$\sqrt{2} \cdot \sqrt[3]{4} = 2^{1/2} \cdot 2^{2/3} = 2^{1/2+2/3} = 2^{7/6}.$$

In radical notation, $2^{7/6} = \sqrt[6]{2^7} = \sqrt[6]{2^6 \cdot 2^1} = \sqrt[6]{2^6} \cdot \sqrt[6]{2} = 2\sqrt[6]{2}$.

(c) $\sqrt[3]{x} \cdot \sqrt[4]{x} = x^{1/3} \cdot x^{1/4} = x^{7/12} = \sqrt[12]{x^7}$ Now Try Exercises 101, 103, 107

Quotient Rule for Radical Expressions

Consider the following examples of dividing radical expressions. The equations

$$\sqrt{\frac{4}{9}} = \sqrt{\frac{2}{3} \cdot \frac{2}{3}} = \frac{2}{3} \quad \text{and} \quad \frac{\sqrt{4}}{\sqrt{9}} = \frac{2}{3}$$

imply that

$$\sqrt{\frac{4}{9}} = \frac{\sqrt{4}}{\sqrt{9}} \quad \text{(see Figure 7.7)}.$$

These examples suggest that *the root of a quotient is equal to the quotient of the roots.*

Figure 7.7

CALCULATOR HELP

To use the Frac feature, see the Appendix (page AP-2).

> ### QUOTIENT RULE FOR RADICAL EXPRESSIONS
>
> Let a and b be real numbers, where $\sqrt[n]{a}$ and $\sqrt[n]{b}$ are both defined and $b \neq 0$. Then
>
> $$\sqrt[n]{\frac{a}{b}} = \frac{\sqrt[n]{a}}{\sqrt[n]{b}}.$$

EXAMPLE 6   **Simplifying quotients**

Simplify each radical expression. Assume that all variables are positive.

(a) $\sqrt[3]{\frac{5}{8}}$ **(b)** $\sqrt[4]{\frac{x}{16}}$ **(c)** $\sqrt{\frac{16}{y^2}}$

Solution

(a) $\sqrt[3]{\frac{5}{8}} = \frac{\sqrt[3]{5}}{\sqrt[3]{8}} = \frac{\sqrt[3]{5}}{2}$ **(b)** $\sqrt[4]{\frac{x}{16}} = \frac{\sqrt[4]{x}}{\sqrt[4]{16}} = \frac{\sqrt[4]{x}}{2}$

(c) $\sqrt{\frac{16}{y^2}} = \frac{\sqrt{16}}{\sqrt{y^2}} = \frac{4}{y}$ because $y > 0$.

Now Try Exercises 25, 27, 29

EXAMPLE 7   Simplifying quotients

Simplify each radical expression. Assume that all variables are positive.

(a) $\dfrac{\sqrt{40}}{\sqrt{10}}$ (b) $\dfrac{\sqrt[3]{2}}{\sqrt[3]{16}}$ (c) $\dfrac{\sqrt{x^2y}}{\sqrt{y}}$

Solution

(a) $\dfrac{\sqrt{40}}{\sqrt{10}} = \sqrt{\dfrac{40}{10}} = \sqrt{4} = 2$

(b) $\dfrac{\sqrt[3]{2}}{\sqrt[3]{16}} = \sqrt[3]{\dfrac{2}{16}} = \sqrt[3]{\dfrac{1}{8}} = \dfrac{1}{2}$ because $\dfrac{1}{2} \cdot \dfrac{1}{2} \cdot \dfrac{1}{2} = \dfrac{1}{8}$.

(c) $\dfrac{\sqrt{x^2y}}{\sqrt{y}} = \sqrt{\dfrac{x^2y}{y}} = \sqrt{x^2} = x$ because $x > 0$.

Now Try Exercises **33, 39, 41**

NOTE: When we simplify a radical *expression* we do *not* set the expression equal to 0 and solve the equation. Instead we write a sequence of equivalent expressions.

MAKING CONNECTIONS

Rules for Radical Expressions and Rational Exponents

The rules for radical expressions are a result of the properties of rational exponents.

$$\sqrt[n]{a \cdot b} = \sqrt[n]{a} \cdot \sqrt[n]{b} \quad \text{is equivalent to} \quad (a \cdot b)^{1/n} = a^{1/n} \cdot b^{1/n}.$$

$$\sqrt[n]{\dfrac{a}{b}} = \dfrac{\sqrt[n]{a}}{\sqrt[n]{b}} \quad \text{is equivalent to} \quad \left(\dfrac{a}{b}\right)^{1/n} = \dfrac{a^{1/n}}{b^{1/n}}.$$

EXAMPLE 8   Simplifying radical expressions

Simplify each radical expression. Assume that all variables are positive.

(a) $\sqrt[4]{\dfrac{16x^3}{y^4}}$ (b) $\sqrt{\dfrac{5a^2}{8}} \cdot \sqrt{\dfrac{5a^3}{2}}$

Solution

(a) To simplify this expression we first use the quotient rule for radical expressions and then apply the product rule for radical expressions.

$$\sqrt[4]{\dfrac{16x^3}{y^4}} = \dfrac{\sqrt[4]{16x^3}}{\sqrt[4]{y^4}} \qquad \text{Quotient rule}$$

$$= \dfrac{\sqrt[4]{16}\,\sqrt[4]{x^3}}{\sqrt[4]{y^4}} \qquad \text{Product rule}$$

$$= \dfrac{2\,\sqrt[4]{x^3}}{y} \qquad \text{Evaluate 4th roots.}$$

(b) To simplify this expression, we use both the product and quotient rules.

$$\sqrt{\frac{5a^2}{8}} \cdot \sqrt{\frac{5a^3}{2}} = \sqrt{\frac{25a^5}{16}} \qquad \text{Product rule}$$

$$= \frac{\sqrt{25a^5}}{\sqrt{16}} \qquad \text{Quotient rule}$$

$$= \frac{\sqrt{25a^4 \cdot a}}{\sqrt{16}} \qquad \text{Factor out largest perfect square.}$$

$$= \frac{\sqrt{25a^4} \cdot \sqrt{a}}{\sqrt{16}} \qquad \text{Product rule}$$

$$= \frac{5a^2 \sqrt{a}}{4} \qquad (5a^2)^2 = 25a^4$$

Now Try Exercises 95, 97

EXAMPLE 9 Simplifying products and quotients of roots

Simplify each expression. Assume all radicands are positive.

(a) $\sqrt{x-3} \cdot \sqrt{x+3}$ **(b)** $\dfrac{\sqrt[3]{x^2+3x+2}}{\sqrt[3]{x+1}}$

Solution

(a) Start by applying the product rule for radical expressions.

$$\sqrt{x-3} \cdot \sqrt{x+3} = \sqrt{(x-3)(x+3)} \qquad \text{Product rule}$$

$$= \sqrt{x^2-9} \qquad \text{Multiply binomials.}$$

NOTE: The expression $\sqrt{x^2-9}$ is *not* simplified further. It is important to realize that

$$\sqrt{x^2-9} \neq \sqrt{x^2} - \sqrt{9} = x-3.$$

For example, $\sqrt{5^2-3^2} = \sqrt{16} = 4$, but $\sqrt{5^2} - \sqrt{3^2} = 5-3 = 2$.

(b) Start by applying the quotient rule for radical expressions.

$$\frac{\sqrt[3]{x^2+3x+2}}{\sqrt[3]{x+1}} = \sqrt[3]{\frac{x^2+3x+2}{x+1}} \qquad \text{Quotient rule}$$

$$= \sqrt[3]{\frac{(x+1)(x+2)}{x+1}} \qquad \text{Factor trinomial.}$$

$$= \sqrt[3]{x+2} \qquad \text{Simplify quotient.}$$

Now Try Exercises 63, 67

7.2 PUTTING IT ALL TOGETHER

In this section we discussed how to simplify radical expressions. Results are summarized in the following table.

Procedure	Explanation	Examples
Product Rule for Radical Expressions	Let a and b be real numbers, where $\sqrt[n]{a}$ and $\sqrt[n]{b}$ are both defined. Then $$\sqrt[n]{a} \cdot \sqrt[n]{b} = \sqrt[n]{a \cdot b}.$$	$$\sqrt{2} \cdot \sqrt{32} = \sqrt{64} = 8$$ $$\sqrt{500} = \sqrt{100} \cdot \sqrt{5} = 10\sqrt{5}$$
Quotient Rule for Radical Expressions	Let a and b be real numbers, where $\sqrt[n]{a}$ and $\sqrt[n]{b}$ are both defined and $b \neq 0$. Then $$\sqrt[n]{\dfrac{a}{b}} = \dfrac{\sqrt[n]{a}}{\sqrt[n]{b}}.$$	$$\dfrac{\sqrt{60}}{\sqrt{15}} = \sqrt{\dfrac{60}{15}} = \sqrt{4} = 2 \quad \text{and}$$ $$\sqrt[3]{\dfrac{x^2}{-27}} = \dfrac{\sqrt[3]{x^2}}{\sqrt[3]{-27}} = \dfrac{\sqrt[3]{x^2}}{-3} = -\dfrac{\sqrt[3]{x^2}}{3}$$
Simplifying Radicals (nth roots)	**STEP 1:** Find the largest nth power factor of the radicand. **STEP 2:** Factor out and simplify this perfect nth power.	$$\sqrt{12} = \sqrt{4 \cdot 3} = \sqrt{4} \cdot \sqrt{3} = 2\sqrt{3}$$ $$\sqrt[3]{81} = \sqrt[3]{27 \cdot 3} = \sqrt[3]{27} \cdot \sqrt[3]{3} = 3\sqrt[3]{3}$$ $$\sqrt[4]{x^5} = \sqrt[4]{x^4 \cdot x} = \sqrt[4]{x^4} \cdot \sqrt[4]{x} = x\sqrt[4]{x},$$ provided $x \geq 0$.

7.2 Exercises

MyMathLab | Math XL PRACTICE | WATCH | DOWNLOAD | READ | REVIEW

CONCEPTS

1. Does $\sqrt{2} \cdot \sqrt{3}$ equal $\sqrt{6}$?

2. Does $\sqrt{5} \cdot \sqrt[3]{5}$ equal 5?

3. $\sqrt[3]{a} \cdot \sqrt[3]{b} = $ _____

4. $\dfrac{\sqrt{a}}{\sqrt{b}} = \sqrt{?}$ 5. $\dfrac{\sqrt[n]{a}}{\sqrt[n]{b}} = \sqrt[n]{?}$

6. $\dfrac{\sqrt{3}}{\sqrt{27}} = $ _____

7. Does $\sqrt{50} = \sqrt{25} + \sqrt{25}$?

8. Does $\sqrt{50} = 5\sqrt{2}$?

9. Is $\sqrt[3]{3}$ equal to 1? Explain.

10. Is 64 a perfect cube? Explain.

MULTIPLYING AND DIVIDING

Exercises 11–62: Simplify the expression. Assume that all variables are positive.

11. $\sqrt{3} \cdot \sqrt{3}$ 12. $\sqrt{2} \cdot \sqrt{18}$

13. $\sqrt{2} \cdot \sqrt{50}$ 14. $\sqrt[3]{-2} \cdot \sqrt[3]{-4}$

15. $\sqrt[3]{4} \cdot \sqrt[3]{16}$ 16. $\sqrt[3]{x} \cdot \sqrt[3]{x^2}$

17. $\sqrt{\dfrac{9}{25}}$ 18. $\sqrt[3]{\dfrac{x}{8}}$

19. $\sqrt{\dfrac{1}{2}} \cdot \sqrt{\dfrac{1}{8}}$ 20. $\sqrt{\dfrac{5}{3}} \cdot \sqrt{\dfrac{1}{3}}$

21. $\sqrt[3]{\dfrac{2}{3}} \cdot \sqrt[3]{\dfrac{4}{3}} \cdot \sqrt[3]{\dfrac{1}{3}}$ 22. $\sqrt[4]{\dfrac{8}{3}} \cdot \sqrt[4]{\dfrac{4}{9}} \cdot \sqrt[4]{\dfrac{8}{3}}$

23. $\sqrt{x^3} \cdot \sqrt{x^3}$ 24. $\sqrt{z} \cdot \sqrt{z^7}$

25. $\sqrt[3]{\dfrac{7}{27}}$

26. $\sqrt[3]{\dfrac{9}{64}}$

27. $\sqrt[4]{\dfrac{x}{81}}$

28. $\sqrt[4]{\dfrac{16x}{81}}$

29. $\sqrt{\dfrac{9}{z^2}}$

30. $\sqrt{\dfrac{x^2}{81}}$

31. $\sqrt{\dfrac{x}{2}} \cdot \sqrt{\dfrac{x}{8}}$

32. $\sqrt{\dfrac{4}{y}} \cdot \sqrt{\dfrac{y}{5}}$

33. $\dfrac{\sqrt{45}}{\sqrt{5}}$

34. $\dfrac{\sqrt{7}}{\sqrt{28}}$

35. $\sqrt[3]{-4} \cdot \sqrt[3]{-16}$

36. $\sqrt[3]{9} \cdot \sqrt[3]{3}$

37. $\sqrt[4]{9} \cdot \sqrt[4]{9}$

38. $\sqrt[5]{16} \cdot \sqrt[5]{-2}$

39. $\dfrac{\sqrt[5]{64}}{\sqrt[5]{-2}}$

40. $\dfrac{\sqrt[4]{324}}{\sqrt[4]{4}}$

41. $\dfrac{\sqrt{a^2 b}}{\sqrt{b}}$

42. $\dfrac{\sqrt{4xy^2}}{\sqrt{x}}$

43. $\dfrac{\sqrt[3]{54}}{\sqrt[3]{2}}$

44. $\dfrac{\sqrt[3]{x^3 y^7}}{\sqrt[3]{y^4}}$

45. $\sqrt{4x^4}$

46. $\sqrt[3]{-8y^3}$

47. $\sqrt[3]{-5a^6}$

48. $\sqrt{9x^2 y}$

49. $\sqrt[4]{16x^4 y}$

50. $\sqrt[3]{8xy^3}$

51. $\sqrt{3x} \cdot \sqrt{12x}$

52. $\sqrt{6x^5} \cdot \sqrt{6x}$

53. $\sqrt[3]{8x^6 y^3 z^9}$

54. $\sqrt{16x^4 y^6}$

55. $\sqrt[4]{\dfrac{3}{4}} \cdot \sqrt[4]{\dfrac{27}{4}}$

56. $\sqrt[5]{\dfrac{4}{-9}} \cdot \sqrt[5]{\dfrac{8}{-27}}$

57. $\sqrt[3]{12} \cdot \sqrt[3]{ab}$

58. $\sqrt{5x} \cdot \sqrt{5z}$

59. $\sqrt[4]{25z} \cdot \sqrt[4]{25z}$

60. $\sqrt[5]{3z^2} \cdot \sqrt[5]{7z}$

61. $\sqrt[5]{\dfrac{7a}{b^2}} \cdot \sqrt[5]{\dfrac{b^2}{7a^6}}$

62. $\sqrt[3]{\dfrac{8m}{n}} \cdot \sqrt[3]{\dfrac{n^4}{m^2}}$

Exercises 63–68: Use properties of polynomials to simplify the expression. Assume all radicands are positive.

63. $\sqrt{x + 4} \cdot \sqrt{x - 4}$

64. $\sqrt[3]{x - 1} \cdot \sqrt[3]{x^2 + x + 1}$

65. $\sqrt[3]{a + 1} \cdot \sqrt[3]{a^2 - a + 1}$

66. $\sqrt{b - 1} \cdot \sqrt{b + 1}$

67. $\dfrac{\sqrt{x^2 + 2x + 1}}{\sqrt{x + 1}}$

68. $\dfrac{\sqrt{x^2 - 4x + 4}}{\sqrt{x - 2}}$

Exercises 69–74: Complete the equation.

69. $\sqrt{500} = \underline{\quad} \sqrt{5}$ **70.** $\sqrt{28} = \underline{\quad} \sqrt{7}$

71. $\sqrt{8} = \underline{\quad} \sqrt{2}$ **72.** $\sqrt{99} = \underline{\quad} \sqrt{11}$

73. $\sqrt{45} = \underline{\quad} \sqrt{5}$ **74.** $\sqrt{243} = \underline{\quad} \sqrt{3}$

Exercises 75–98: Simplify the radical expression by factoring out the largest perfect nth power. Assume that all variables are positive.

75. $\sqrt{200}$

76. $\sqrt{72}$

77. $\sqrt[3]{81}$

78. $\sqrt[3]{256}$

79. $\sqrt[4]{64}$

80. $\sqrt[5]{27 \cdot 81}$

81. $\sqrt[5]{-64}$

82. $\sqrt[3]{-81}$

83. $\sqrt{b^5}$

84. $\sqrt{t^3}$

85. $\sqrt{8n^3}$

86. $\sqrt{32a^2}$

87. $\sqrt{12a^2 b^5}$

88. $\sqrt{20a^3 b^2}$

89. $\sqrt[3]{-125x^4 y^5}$

90. $\sqrt[3]{-81a^5 b^2}$

91. $\sqrt[3]{5t} \cdot \sqrt[3]{125t}$

92. $\sqrt[4]{4bc^3} \cdot \sqrt[4]{64ab^3 c^2}$

93. $\sqrt[4]{\dfrac{9t^5}{r^8}} \cdot \sqrt[4]{\dfrac{9r}{5t}}$

94. $\sqrt[5]{\dfrac{4t^6}{r}} \cdot \sqrt[5]{\dfrac{8t}{r^6}}$

95. $\sqrt[3]{\dfrac{27x^2}{y^3}}$

96. $\sqrt[4]{\dfrac{32x^8}{z^4}}$

97. $\sqrt{\dfrac{7a^2}{27}} \cdot \sqrt{\dfrac{7a}{3}}$

98. $\sqrt{\dfrac{8a}{125}} \cdot \sqrt{\dfrac{2a}{5}}$

Exercises 99 and 100: **Thinking Generally**   *Assume that m and n are positive integers and that each expression exists.*

99. Simplify $\left(\sqrt[mn]{a^m b^m} \right)^n$ so that it equals ab.

100. Simplify $\left(\sqrt[mn]{a^n b^m} \right) \cdot \left(\sqrt[mn]{a^m b^n} \right)$ so that it equals $\sqrt[m]{ab} \cdot \sqrt[n]{ab}$.

Exercises 101–110: Simplify the expression. Assume that all variables are positive and write your answer in radical notation.

101. $\sqrt{3} \cdot \sqrt[3]{3}$　　　**102.** $\sqrt{5} \cdot \sqrt[3]{5}$

103. $\sqrt[4]{8} \cdot \sqrt[3]{4}$　　　**104.** $\sqrt[5]{16} \cdot \sqrt{2}$

105. $\sqrt[4]{27} \cdot \sqrt[3]{9} \cdot \sqrt{3}$　　　**106.** $\sqrt[5]{16} \cdot \sqrt[3]{16}$

107. $\sqrt[4]{x^3} \cdot \sqrt[3]{x}$　　　**108.** $\sqrt[4]{x^3} \cdot \sqrt{x}$

109. $\sqrt[4]{rt} \cdot \sqrt[3]{r^2 t}$　　　**110.** $\sqrt[3]{a^3 b^2} \cdot \sqrt{a^2 b}$

APPLICATIONS

111. *Bird Wings* Heavier birds tend to have larger wings than lighter birds do. For some birds the relationship between the surface area A of the bird's wings in square inches and its weight W in pounds can be modeled by $A = 100 \sqrt[3]{W^2}$. (*Source:* C. Pennycuick, *Newton Rules Biology.*)

(a) Find the area of the wings when the weight is 8 pounds.

(b) Write this formula with rational exponents.

112. *Orbits and Distance* Johannes Kepler (1571–1630) discovered a relationship between a planet's distance D from the sun and the time T it takes to orbit the sun. This formula is $T = \sqrt{D^3}$, where T is in Earth years and $D = 1$ corresponds to the distance between Earth and the sun, or 93,000,000 miles.

(a) Neptune is 30 times farther from the sun than Earth ($D = 30$). Estimate the number of years required for Neptune to orbit the sun.

(b) Write this formula with rational exponents.

WRITING ABOUT MATHEMATICS

113. Explain what it means for a positive integer to be a *perfect square* or a *perfect cube*. List the positive integers that are perfect squares and less than 101. List the positive integers that are perfect cubes and less than 220.

114. Explain how the product and quotient rules for radical expressions are the result of properties of rational exponents.

CHECKING BASIC CONCEPTS
SECTIONS 7.1 AND 7.2

1. Find the following.
   (a) The square roots of 49
   (b) The principal square root of 49

2. Evaluate.
   (a) $\sqrt[3]{-8}$　　　(b) $-\sqrt[4]{81}$

3. Write the expression in radical notation.
   (a) $x^{3/2}$　　(b) $x^{2/3}$　　(c) $x^{-2/5}$

4. Simplify $\sqrt{(x-1)^2}$ for any real number x.

5. Simplify each expression. Assume that all variables are positive.
   (a) $(64^{-3/2})^{1/3}$　　　(b) $\sqrt{5} \cdot \sqrt{20}$
   (c) $\sqrt[3]{-8x^4 y}$　　　(d) $\sqrt{\dfrac{4b}{5}} \cdot \sqrt{\dfrac{4b^3}{5}}$

6. Simplify $\sqrt[3]{7} \cdot \sqrt{7}$.

7.3 OPERATIONS ON RADICAL EXPRESSIONS

Addition and Subtraction ■ Multiplication ■ Rationalizing the Denominator

A LOOK INTO MATH ▷ So far we have discussed how to add, subtract, multiply, and divide numbers and variables. In this section we extend these operations to radical expressions. In doing so, we use many of the techniques discussed in Sections 7.1 and 7.2.

Addition and Subtraction

We can add $2x^2$ and $5x^2$ to obtain $7x^2$ because they are *like* terms. That is,

$$2x^2 + 5x^2 = (2 + 5)x^2 = 7x^2.$$

We can also add and subtract *like radicals*. **Like radicals** *have the same index and the same radicand.* For example, we can add $3\sqrt{2}$ and $5\sqrt{2}$ because they are like radicals.

$$3\sqrt{2} + 5\sqrt{2} = (3 + 5)\sqrt{2} = 8\sqrt{2}$$

EXAMPLE 1   Adding like radicals

If possible, add the expressions and simplify.
(a) $10\sqrt{11} + 4\sqrt{11}$ **(b)** $5\sqrt[3]{6} + \sqrt[3]{6}$
(c) $4 + 5\sqrt{3}$ **(d)** $\sqrt{7} + \sqrt{11}$

Solution
(a) These terms are like radicals because they have the same index, 2, and the same radicand, 11.

$$10\sqrt{11} + 4\sqrt{11} = (10 + 4)\sqrt{11} = 14\sqrt{11}$$

(b) These terms are like radicals because they have the same index, 3, and the same radicand, 6. Note that the coefficient on the second term is understood to be 1.

$$5\sqrt[3]{6} + 1\sqrt[3]{6} = (5 + 1)\sqrt[3]{6} = 6\sqrt[3]{6}$$

(c) The expression $4 + 5\sqrt{3}$ can be written as $4\sqrt{1} + 5\sqrt{3}$. These terms cannot be added because they are not like radicals.

NOTE: $4 + 5\sqrt{3} \neq 9\sqrt{3}$

(d) The expression $\sqrt{7} + \sqrt{11}$ contains unlike radicals that *cannot* be added.

Now Try Exercises 19, 21, 23, 25

Sometimes two radical expressions that are not alike can be added by changing them to like radicals. For example, $\sqrt{20}$ and $\sqrt{5}$ are unlike radicals. However,

$$\sqrt{20} = \sqrt{4 \cdot 5} = \sqrt{4} \cdot \sqrt{5} = 2\sqrt{5},$$

so

$$\sqrt{20} + \sqrt{5} = 2\sqrt{5} + 1\sqrt{5} = 3\sqrt{5}.$$

We cannot combine $x + x^2$ because they are unlike terms. Similarly, we cannot combine $\sqrt{2} + \sqrt{5}$ because they are unlike radicals. When combining radicals, the first step is to see if we can write pairs of terms as like radicals, as demonstrated in the next example.

EXAMPLE 2   Finding like radicals

Write each pair of terms as like radicals, if possible.
(a) $\sqrt{45}, \sqrt{20}$ **(b)** $\sqrt{27}, \sqrt{5}$ **(c)** $5\sqrt[3]{16}, 4\sqrt[3]{54}$

Solution

(a) The expressions $\sqrt{45}$ and $\sqrt{20}$ are unlike radicals. However, they can be changed to like radicals as follows.

$$\sqrt{45} = \sqrt{9 \cdot 5} = \sqrt{9} \cdot \sqrt{5} = 3\sqrt{5} \quad \text{and}$$
$$\sqrt{20} = \sqrt{4 \cdot 5} = \sqrt{4} \cdot \sqrt{5} = 2\sqrt{5}$$

The expressions $3\sqrt{5}$ and $2\sqrt{5}$ are like radicals.

(b) Because $\sqrt{27} = \sqrt{9 \cdot 3} = \sqrt{9} \cdot \sqrt{3} = 3\sqrt{3}$, the given expressions $\sqrt{27}$ and $\sqrt{5}$ are unlike radicals and cannot be written as like radicals.

(c) $5\sqrt[3]{16} = 5\sqrt[3]{8 \cdot 2} = 5\sqrt[3]{8} \cdot \sqrt[3]{2} = 5 \cdot 2 \cdot \sqrt[3]{2} = 10\sqrt[3]{2}$ and
$4\sqrt[3]{54} = 4\sqrt[3]{27 \cdot 2} = 4\sqrt[3]{27} \cdot \sqrt[3]{2} = 4 \cdot 3 \cdot \sqrt[3]{2} = 12\sqrt[3]{2}$

The expressions $10\sqrt[3]{2}$ and $12\sqrt[3]{2}$ are like radicals.

Now Try Exercises 9, 11, 13

We use these techniques to add radical expressions in the next two examples.

EXAMPLE 3 Adding radical expressions

Add the expressions and simplify.

(a) $\sqrt{12} + 7\sqrt{3}$ **(b)** $\sqrt[3]{16} + \sqrt[3]{2}$ **(c)** $3\sqrt{2} + \sqrt{8} + \sqrt{18}$

Solution

(a)
$$\sqrt{12} + 7\sqrt{3} = \sqrt{4 \cdot 3} + 7\sqrt{3}$$
$$= \sqrt{4} \cdot \sqrt{3} + 7\sqrt{3}$$
$$= 2\sqrt{3} + 7\sqrt{3}$$
$$= 9\sqrt{3}$$

(b)
$$\sqrt[3]{16} + \sqrt[3]{2} = \sqrt[3]{8 \cdot 2} + \sqrt[3]{2}$$
$$= \sqrt[3]{8} \cdot \sqrt[3]{2} + \sqrt[3]{2}$$
$$= 2\sqrt[3]{2} + 1\sqrt[3]{2}$$
$$= (2 + 1)\sqrt[3]{2}$$
$$= 3\sqrt[3]{2}$$

(c) $3\sqrt{2} + \sqrt{8} + \sqrt{18} = 3\sqrt{2} + \sqrt{4 \cdot 2} + \sqrt{9 \cdot 2}$
$$= 3\sqrt{2} + \sqrt{4} \cdot \sqrt{2} + \sqrt{9} \cdot \sqrt{2}$$
$$= 3\sqrt{2} + 2\sqrt{2} + 3\sqrt{2}$$
$$= 8\sqrt{2}$$

Now Try Exercises 29, 31, 43

EXAMPLE 4 Adding radical expressions

Add the expressions and simplify. Assume that all variables are positive.

(a) $\sqrt[4]{32} + 3\sqrt[4]{2}$ **(b)** $-2\sqrt{4x} + \sqrt{x}$ **(c)** $3\sqrt{3k} + 5\sqrt{12k} + 9\sqrt{48k}$

Solution

(a) Because $\sqrt[4]{32} = \sqrt[4]{16 \cdot 2} = \sqrt[4]{16} \cdot \sqrt[4]{2} = 2\sqrt[4]{2}$, we can add and simplify as follows.

$$\sqrt[4]{32} + 3\sqrt[4]{2} = 2\sqrt[4]{2} + 3\sqrt[4]{2} = 5\sqrt[4]{2}$$

(b) Note that $\sqrt{4x} = \sqrt{4} \cdot \sqrt{x} = 2\sqrt{x}$.

$$-2\sqrt{4x} + \sqrt{x} = -2(2\sqrt{x}) + \sqrt{x} = -4\sqrt{x} + 1\sqrt{x} = -3\sqrt{x}$$

(c) Note that $\sqrt{12k} = \sqrt{4} \cdot \sqrt{3k} = 2\sqrt{3k}$ and that $\sqrt{48k} = \sqrt{16} \cdot \sqrt{3k} = 4\sqrt{3k}$.

$$3\sqrt{3k} + 5\sqrt{12k} + 9\sqrt{48k} = 3\sqrt{3k} + 5(2\sqrt{3k}) + 9(4\sqrt{3k})$$
$$= (3 + 10 + 36)\sqrt{3k}$$
$$= 49\sqrt{3k} \qquad \text{Now Try Exercises } 45, 47, 49$$

Subtraction of radical expressions is similar to addition, as illustrated in the next three examples.

EXAMPLE 5   Subtracting like radicals

Simplify the expressions.

(a) $5\sqrt{7} - 3\sqrt{7}$ (b) $8\sqrt[3]{5} - 3\sqrt[3]{5} + \sqrt[3]{11}$ (c) $5\sqrt{z} + \sqrt[3]{z} - 2\sqrt{z}$

Solution

(a) $\qquad 5\sqrt{7} - 3\sqrt{7} = (5 - 3)\sqrt{7} = 2\sqrt{7}$

(b) $8\sqrt[3]{5} - 3\sqrt[3]{5} + \sqrt[3]{11} = (8 - 3)\sqrt[3]{5} + \sqrt[3]{11} = 5\sqrt[3]{5} + \sqrt[3]{11}$

(c) $\quad 5\sqrt{z} + \sqrt[3]{z} - 2\sqrt{z} = 5\sqrt{z} - 2\sqrt{z} + \sqrt[3]{z}$ $\qquad$ Commutative property

$\qquad\qquad\qquad\qquad = (5 - 2)\sqrt{z} + \sqrt[3]{z}$ $\qquad$ Distributive property

$\qquad\qquad\qquad\qquad = 3\sqrt{z} + \sqrt[3]{z}$ $\qquad$ Subtract.

NOTE: We cannot combine $3\sqrt{z} + \sqrt[3]{z}$ because their indexes are different. That is, one term is a square root and the other is a cube root. $\qquad$ Now Try Exercises 33, 35, 39

EXAMPLE 6   Subtracting radical expressions

Subtract and simplify. Assume that all variables are positive.

(a) $3\sqrt[3]{xy^2} - 2\sqrt[3]{xy^2}$ (b) $\sqrt{16x^3} - \sqrt{x^3}$ (c) $\sqrt[3]{\dfrac{5x}{27}} - \dfrac{\sqrt[3]{5x}}{6}$

Solution

(a) $\qquad 3\sqrt[3]{xy^2} - 2\sqrt[3]{xy^2} = (3 - 2)\sqrt[3]{xy^2} = \sqrt[3]{xy^2}$

(b) $\qquad \sqrt{16x^3} - \sqrt{x^3} = \sqrt{16x^2} \cdot \sqrt{x} - \sqrt{x^2} \cdot \sqrt{x}$ $\qquad$ Factor out perfect squares.

$\qquad\qquad\qquad\qquad = 4x\sqrt{x} - x\sqrt{x}$ $\qquad$ Simplify.

$\qquad\qquad\qquad\qquad = (4x - x)\sqrt{x}$ $\qquad$ Distributive property

$\qquad\qquad\qquad\qquad = 3x\sqrt{x}$ $\qquad$ Subtract.

(c)

$$\sqrt[3]{\dfrac{5x}{27}} - \dfrac{\sqrt[3]{5x}}{6} = \dfrac{\sqrt[3]{5x}}{\sqrt[3]{27}} - \dfrac{\sqrt[3]{5x}}{6}$$ Quotient rule for radical expressions

$$= \dfrac{\sqrt[3]{5x}}{3} - \dfrac{\sqrt[3]{5x}}{6}$$ Evaluate $\sqrt[3]{27} = 3$.

$$= \dfrac{2\sqrt[3]{5x}}{6} - \dfrac{\sqrt[3]{5x}}{6}$$ Find a common denominator.

$$= \dfrac{2\sqrt[3]{5x} - \sqrt[3]{5x}}{6}$$ Subtract numerators.

$$= \dfrac{\sqrt[3]{5x}}{6}$$ Simplify.

Now Try Exercises 55, 59, 61

EXAMPLE 7   Subtracting radical expressions

Subtract and simplify. Assume that all variables are positive.

(a) $\dfrac{5\sqrt{2}}{3} - \dfrac{2\sqrt{2}}{4}$ (b) $\sqrt[4]{81a^5b^6} - \sqrt[4]{16ab^2}$ (c) $3\sqrt[3]{\dfrac{n^5}{27}} - 2\sqrt[3]{n^2}$

Solution

(a)

$$\dfrac{5\sqrt{2}}{3} - \dfrac{2\sqrt{2}}{4} = \dfrac{5\sqrt{2}}{3} \cdot \dfrac{4}{4} - \dfrac{2\sqrt{2}}{4} \cdot \dfrac{3}{3}$$ LCD is 12.

$$= \dfrac{20\sqrt{2}}{12} - \dfrac{6\sqrt{2}}{12}$$ Multiply fractions.

$$= \dfrac{14\sqrt{2}}{12}$$ Subtract numerators.

$$= \dfrac{7\sqrt{2}}{6}$$ Simplify.

(b) $\sqrt[4]{81a^5b^6} - \sqrt[4]{16ab^2} = \sqrt[4]{81a^4b^4} \cdot \sqrt[4]{ab^2} - \sqrt[4]{16} \cdot \sqrt[4]{ab^2}$ Factor out perfect powers.

$$= 3ab\sqrt[4]{ab^2} - 2\sqrt[4]{ab^2}$$ Simplify.

$$= (3ab - 2)\sqrt[4]{ab^2}$$ Distributive property

(c) $3\sqrt[3]{\dfrac{n^5}{27}} - 2\sqrt[3]{n^2} = 3\sqrt[3]{\dfrac{n^3}{27}} \cdot \sqrt[3]{n^2} - 2\sqrt[3]{n^2}$ Factor out perfect cube.

$$= \dfrac{3\sqrt[3]{n^3}}{\sqrt[3]{27}} \cdot \sqrt[3]{n^2} - 2\sqrt[3]{n^2}$$ Quotient rule

$$= n\sqrt[3]{n^2} - 2\sqrt[3]{n^2}$$ Simplify.

$$= (n - 2)\sqrt[3]{n^2}$$ Distributive property

Now Try Exercises 65, 73, 75

Radicals often occur in geometry. In the next example, we find the perimeter of a triangle by adding radical expressions.

Figure 7.8

EXAMPLE 8   Finding the perimeter of a triangle

Find the *exact* perimeter of the right triangle shown in Figure 7.8. Then approximate your answer to the nearest hundredth of a foot.

Solution
The sum of the lengths of the sides of the triangle is

$$\sqrt{18} + \sqrt{32} + \sqrt{50} = 3\sqrt{2} + 4\sqrt{2} + 5\sqrt{2} = 12\sqrt{2}.$$

The perimeter is $12\sqrt{2} \approx 16.97$ feet.   Now Try Exercise 117

Multiplication

Some types of radical expressions can be multiplied like binomials. For example, because

$$(x + 1)(x + 2) = x^2 + 3x + 2,$$

we have $(\sqrt{x} + 1)(\sqrt{x} + 2) = (\sqrt{x})^2 + 2\sqrt{x} + 1\sqrt{x} + 2 = x + 3\sqrt{x} + 2,$

provided that $x \geq 0$. The next example demonstrates this technique.

EXAMPLE 9   Multiplying radical expressions

Multiply and simplify.
(a) $(\sqrt{b} - 4)(\sqrt{b} + 5)$ **(b)** $(4 + \sqrt{3})(4 - \sqrt{3})$

Solution
(a) This expression can be multiplied and then simplified.

$$(\sqrt{b} - 4)(\sqrt{b} + 5) = \sqrt{b} \cdot \sqrt{b} + 5\sqrt{b} - 4\sqrt{b} - 4 \cdot 5$$
$$= b + \sqrt{b} - 20$$

Compare this product with $(b - 4)(b + 5) = b^2 + b - 20$.
(b) This expression is in the form $(a + b)(a - b)$, which equals $a^2 - b^2$.

$$(4 + \sqrt{3})(4 - \sqrt{3}) = (4)^2 - (\sqrt{3})^2$$
$$= 16 - 3$$
$$= 13$$ Now Try Exercises 77, 79

NOTE: Example 9(b) illustrates a special case for multiplying radicals. In general,

$$(\sqrt{a} + \sqrt{b})(\sqrt{a} - \sqrt{b}) = (\sqrt{a})^2 - (\sqrt{b})^2 = a - b,$$

provided a and b are nonnegative.

Rationalizing the Denominator

In mathematics it is common to write expressions without radicals in the denominator. Quotients containing radical expressions in the numerator or denominator can appear to be different but actually be equal. For example, $\frac{1}{\sqrt{3}}$ and $\frac{\sqrt{3}}{3}$ represent the same real number even though they look like they are unequal. To show that they are equal, we multiply the first quotient by 1 in the form $\frac{\sqrt{3}}{\sqrt{3}}$:

$$\frac{1}{\sqrt{3}} \cdot \frac{\sqrt{3}}{\sqrt{3}} = \frac{1 \cdot \sqrt{3}}{\sqrt{3} \cdot \sqrt{3}} = \frac{\sqrt{3}}{3}.$$

If the denominator of a quotient contains only one term with one square root, then we can rationalize the denominator by multiplying the numerator and denominator by this square root. For example, the denominator of $\frac{1}{\sqrt{3}}$ contains one term, which is $\sqrt{3}$. Therefore, we multiplied the $\frac{1}{\sqrt{3}}$ by $\frac{\sqrt{3}}{\sqrt{3}}$ to rationalize the denominator.

NOTE: $\sqrt{b} \cdot \sqrt{b} = \sqrt{b^2} = b$ for any *positive* number b.

One way to *standardize* radical expressions is to remove any radical expressions from the denominator. This process is called **rationalizing the denominator**. Exercise 119 suggests one reason why people rationalized denominators before calculators were invented. The next example demonstrates how to rationalize the denominator of several quotients.

EXAMPLE 10   Rationalizing the denominator

Rationalize each denominator. Assume that all variables are positive.

(a) $\dfrac{1}{\sqrt{2}}$ (b) $\dfrac{3}{5\sqrt{3}}$ (c) $\sqrt{\dfrac{x}{24}}$ (d) $\dfrac{xy}{\sqrt{y^3}}$

Solution

(a) We start by multiplying this expression by 1 in the form $\frac{\sqrt{2}}{\sqrt{2}}$:

$$\frac{1}{\sqrt{2}} \cdot \frac{\sqrt{2}}{\sqrt{2}} = \frac{\sqrt{2}}{\sqrt{4}} = \frac{\sqrt{2}}{2}.$$

Note that the expression $\frac{\sqrt{2}}{2}$ does not have a radical in the denominator.

(b) We multiply this expression by 1 in the form $\frac{\sqrt{3}}{\sqrt{3}}$:

$$\frac{3}{5\sqrt{3}} \cdot \frac{\sqrt{3}}{\sqrt{3}} = \frac{3\sqrt{3}}{5\sqrt{9}} = \frac{3\sqrt{3}}{5 \cdot 3} = \frac{\sqrt{3}}{5}.$$

(c) Because $\sqrt{24} = \sqrt{4} \cdot \sqrt{6} = 2\sqrt{6}$, we start by simplifying the expression.

$$\sqrt{\frac{x}{24}} = \frac{\sqrt{x}}{\sqrt{24}} = \frac{\sqrt{x}}{2\sqrt{6}}$$

To rationalize the denominator we multiply this expression by 1 in the form $\frac{\sqrt{6}}{\sqrt{6}}$:

$$\frac{\sqrt{x}}{2\sqrt{6}} = \frac{\sqrt{x}}{2\sqrt{6}} \cdot \frac{\sqrt{6}}{\sqrt{6}} = \frac{\sqrt{6x}}{12}.$$

(d) Because $\sqrt{y^3} = \sqrt{y^2} \cdot \sqrt{y} = y\sqrt{y}$, we start by simplifying the expression.

$$\frac{xy}{\sqrt{y^3}} = \frac{xy}{y\sqrt{y}} = \frac{x}{\sqrt{y}}$$

To rationalize the denominator we multiply by 1 in the form $\frac{\sqrt{y}}{\sqrt{y}}$:

$$\frac{x}{\sqrt{y}} \cdot \frac{\sqrt{y}}{\sqrt{y}} = \frac{x\sqrt{y}}{y}.$$

Now Try Exercises 89, 93, 95, 97

When the denominator is either a sum or difference containing a square root, we multiply the numerator and denominator by the *conjugate* of the denominator. In this case, the **conjugate** of the denominator is found by changing a + sign to a − sign or vice versa. Table 7.1 lists examples of conjugates.

TABLE 7.1

Expression	$1 + \sqrt{2}$	$\sqrt{3} - 2$	$\sqrt{x} + 7$	$\sqrt{a} - \sqrt{b}$
Conjugate	$1 - \sqrt{2}$	$\sqrt{3} + 2$	$\sqrt{x} - 7$	$\sqrt{a} + \sqrt{b}$

In the next two examples we illustrate this method to rationalize a denominator.

EXAMPLE 11   Using a conjugate to rationalize the denominator

Rationalize the denominator of $\frac{1}{1 + \sqrt{2}}$.

Solution
From Table 7.1, the conjugate of $1 + \sqrt{2}$ is $1 - \sqrt{2}$.

$$\frac{1}{1 + \sqrt{2}} = \frac{1}{1 + \sqrt{2}} \cdot \frac{(1 - \sqrt{2})}{(1 - \sqrt{2})} \qquad \text{Multiply numerator and denominator by the conjugate.}$$

$$= \frac{1 - \sqrt{2}}{(1)^2 - (\sqrt{2})^2} \qquad (a + b)(a - b) = a^2 - b^2$$

$$= \frac{1 - \sqrt{2}}{1 - 2} \qquad \text{Simplify.}$$

$$= \frac{1 - \sqrt{2}}{-1} \qquad \text{Subtract.}$$

$$= \frac{1}{-1} - \frac{\sqrt{2}}{-1} \qquad \frac{a - b}{c} = \frac{a}{c} - \frac{b}{c}$$

$$= -1 + \sqrt{2} \qquad \text{Simplify.} \qquad \text{Now Try Exercise 99}$$

EXAMPLE 12   Rationalizing the denominator

Rationalize the denominator.

(a) $\dfrac{3 + \sqrt{5}}{2 - \sqrt{5}}$ (b) $\dfrac{\sqrt{x}}{\sqrt{x} - 2}$

Solution

(a) The conjugate of the denominator is $2 + \sqrt{5}$.

$$\frac{3 + \sqrt{5}}{2 - \sqrt{5}} = \frac{(3 + \sqrt{5})}{(2 - \sqrt{5})} \cdot \frac{(2 + \sqrt{5})}{(2 + \sqrt{5})} \qquad \text{Multiply by 1.}$$

$$= \frac{6 + 3\sqrt{5} + 2\sqrt{5} + (\sqrt{5})^2}{(2)^2 - (\sqrt{5})^2} \qquad \text{Multiply.}$$

$$= \frac{11 + 5\sqrt{5}}{4 - 5} \qquad \text{Combine terms.}$$

$$= -11 - 5\sqrt{5} \qquad \text{Simplify.}$$

(b) The conjugate of the denominator is $\sqrt{x} + 2$.

$$\frac{\sqrt{x}}{\sqrt{x} - 2} = \frac{\sqrt{x}}{(\sqrt{x} - 2)} \cdot \frac{(\sqrt{x} + 2)}{(\sqrt{x} + 2)} \qquad \text{Multiply by 1.}$$

$$= \frac{x + 2\sqrt{x}}{x - 4} \qquad \text{Multiply.}$$

Now Try Exercises 103, 107

EXAMPLE 13   Rationalizing a denominator having a cube root

Rationalize the denominator of $\dfrac{5}{\sqrt[3]{x}}$.

Solution

The expression $\dfrac{5}{\sqrt[3]{x}}$ is equal to $\dfrac{5}{x^{1/3}}$. To rationalize the denominator, $x^{1/3}$, we can multiply it by $x^{2/3}$ because $x^{1/3} \cdot x^{2/3} = x^{1/3+2/3} = x^1$.

$$\frac{5}{x^{1/3}} = \frac{5}{x^{1/3}} \cdot \frac{x^{2/3}}{x^{2/3}} \qquad \text{Multiply by 1.}$$

$$= \frac{5x^{2/3}}{x^{1/3+2/3}} \qquad \text{Product rule}$$

$$= \frac{5\sqrt[3]{x^2}}{x} \qquad \text{Add; write in radical notation.}$$

Now Try Exercise 113

7.3 PUTTING IT ALL TOGETHER

In this section we discussed how to add, subtract, and multiply radical expressions. Rationalization of the denominator is a technique that can sometimes be helpful when dividing rational expressions. The following table summarizes important topics in this section.

Concept	Explanation	Examples
Like Radicals	Like radicals have the same index and the same radicand.	$7\sqrt{5}$ and $3\sqrt{5}$ are like radicals. $5\sqrt[3]{ab}$ and $\sqrt[3]{ab}$ are like radicals. $\sqrt[3]{5}$ and $\sqrt[3]{4}$ are unlike radicals. $\sqrt[3]{7}$ and $\sqrt{7}$ are unlike radicals.
Adding and Subtracting Radical Expressions	Combine like radicals when adding or subtracting. We cannot combine unlike radicals such as $\sqrt{2}$ and $\sqrt{5}$. But sometimes we can rewrite radicals and then combine.	$6\sqrt{13} + \sqrt{13} = (6+1)\sqrt{13} = 7\sqrt{13}$ $\sqrt{40} - \sqrt{10} = \sqrt{4} \cdot \sqrt{10} - \sqrt{10}$ $= 2\sqrt{10} - \sqrt{10}$ $= \sqrt{10}$
Multiplying Radical Expressions	Radical expressions can sometimes be multiplied like binomials.	$(\sqrt{a} - 5)(\sqrt{a} + 5) = a - 25$ and $(\sqrt{x} - 3)(\sqrt{x} + 1) = x - 2\sqrt{x} - 3$
Conjugate	The conjugate is found by changing a $+$ sign to a $-$ sign or vice versa.	*Expression* *Conjugate* $\sqrt{x} + 7$ $\sqrt{x} - 7$ $\sqrt{a} - 2\sqrt{b}$ $\sqrt{a} + 2\sqrt{b}$
Rationalizing a Denominator Having One Term	Write the quotient without a radical expression in the denominator.	To rationalize $\frac{5}{\sqrt{7}}$, multiply the expression by 1 in the form $\frac{\sqrt{7}}{\sqrt{7}}$: $\frac{5}{\sqrt{7}} \cdot \frac{\sqrt{7}}{\sqrt{7}} = \frac{5\sqrt{7}}{\sqrt{49}} = \frac{5\sqrt{7}}{7}.$
Rationalizing a Denominator Having Two Terms Containing Square Roots	Multiply the numerator and denominator by the conjugate of the denominator.	$\frac{1}{2 - \sqrt{3}} = \frac{1}{2 - \sqrt{3}} \cdot \frac{(2 + \sqrt{3})}{(2 + \sqrt{3})}$ $= \frac{2 + \sqrt{3}}{4 - 3} = 2 + \sqrt{3}$

7.3 Exercises

CONCEPTS

1. $\sqrt{a} + \sqrt{a} =$ _____

2. $\sqrt[3]{b} + \sqrt[3]{b} + \sqrt[3]{b} =$ _____

3. You cannot simplify $\sqrt[3]{4} + \sqrt[3]{7}$ because they are not _____ radicals.

4. Can you simplify $4\sqrt{15} - 3\sqrt{15}$? Explain.

5. Does $6 + 3\sqrt{5}$ equal $9\sqrt{5}$?

6. To rationalize the denominator of $\frac{2}{\sqrt{7}}$, multiply this expression by _____.

7. What is the conjugate of $\sqrt{t} - 5$?

8. To rationalize the denominator of $\frac{1}{5 - \sqrt{2}}$, multiply this expression by _____.

LIKE RADICALS

Exercises 9–18: (Refer to Example 2.) Write the terms as like radicals, if possible. Assume that all variables are positive.

9. $\sqrt{12}, \sqrt{24}$

10. $\sqrt{18}, \sqrt{27}$

11. $\sqrt{7}, \sqrt{28}, \sqrt{63}$

12. $\sqrt{200}, \sqrt{300}, \sqrt{500}$

13. $\sqrt[3]{16}, \sqrt[3]{-54}$

14. $\sqrt[3]{80}, \sqrt[3]{10}$

15. $\sqrt{x^2 y}, \sqrt{4y^2}$

16. $\sqrt{x^5 y^3}, \sqrt{9xy}$

17. $\sqrt[3]{8xy}, \sqrt[3]{x^4 y^4}$

18. $\sqrt[3]{64x^4}, \sqrt[3]{-8x}$

ADDITION AND SUBTRACTION OF RADICALS

Exercises 19–76: If possible, simplify the expression. Assume that all variables are positive.

19. $2\sqrt{3} + 7\sqrt{3}$

20. $8\sqrt{7} + 2\sqrt{7}$

21. $4\sqrt[3]{5} + 2\sqrt[3]{5}$

22. $\sqrt[3]{13} + 3\sqrt[3]{13}$

23. $7 + 4\sqrt{7}$

24. $8 - 4\sqrt{3}$

25. $2\sqrt{3} + 3\sqrt{2}$

26. $\sqrt{6} + \sqrt{17}$

27. $\sqrt{3} + \sqrt[3]{3}$

28. $\sqrt{6} + \sqrt[4]{6}$

29. $\sqrt[3]{16} + 3\sqrt[3]{2}$

30. $\sqrt[3]{24} + \sqrt[3]{81}$

31. $\sqrt{2} + \sqrt{18} + \sqrt{32}$

32. $2\sqrt{3} + \sqrt{12} + \sqrt{27}$

33. $11\sqrt{11} - 5\sqrt{11}$

34. $9\sqrt{5} + \sqrt{2} - \sqrt{5}$

35. $\sqrt{x} + \sqrt{x} - \sqrt{y}$

36. $\sqrt{xy^2} - \sqrt{x}$

37. $\sqrt[3]{z} + \sqrt[3]{z}$

38. $\sqrt[3]{y} - \sqrt[3]{y}$

39. $2\sqrt[3]{6} - 7\sqrt[3]{6}$

40. $18\sqrt[3]{3} + 3\sqrt[3]{3}$

41. $\sqrt[3]{y^6} - \sqrt[3]{y^3}$

42. $2\sqrt{20} + 7\sqrt{5} + 3\sqrt{2}$

43. $3\sqrt{28} + 3\sqrt{7}$

44. $9\sqrt{18} - 2\sqrt{8}$

45. $\sqrt[4]{48} + 4\sqrt[4]{3}$

46. $\sqrt[4]{32} + \sqrt[4]{16}$

47. $\sqrt{9x} + \sqrt{16x}$

48. $-3\sqrt{x} + 5\sqrt{x}$

49. $3\sqrt{2k} + \sqrt{8k} + \sqrt{18k}$

50. $3\sqrt{k} + 2\sqrt{4k} + \sqrt{9k}$

51. $\sqrt{44} - 4\sqrt{11}$

52. $\sqrt[4]{5} + 2\sqrt[4]{5}$

53. $2\sqrt[3]{16} + \sqrt[3]{2} - \sqrt{2}$

54. $5\sqrt[3]{x} - 3\sqrt[3]{x}$

55. $\sqrt[3]{xy} - 2\sqrt[3]{xy}$

56. $3\sqrt{x^3} - \sqrt{x}$

57. $\sqrt{4x + 8} + \sqrt{x + 2}$

58. $\sqrt{2a + 1} + \sqrt{8a + 4}$

59. $\sqrt{25x^3} - \sqrt{x^3}$

60. $\sqrt{36x^5} - \sqrt{25x^5}$

61. $\sqrt[3]{\dfrac{7x}{8}} - \dfrac{\sqrt[3]{7x}}{3}$

62. $\sqrt[3]{\dfrac{8x^2}{27}} - \sqrt[3]{\dfrac{x^2}{8}}$

63. $\dfrac{4\sqrt{3}}{3} + \dfrac{\sqrt{3}}{6}$

64. $\dfrac{8\sqrt{5}}{7} + \dfrac{4\sqrt{5}}{2}$

65. $\dfrac{15\sqrt{8}}{4} - \dfrac{2\sqrt{2}}{5}$

66. $\dfrac{23\sqrt{11}}{2} - \dfrac{\sqrt{44}}{8}$

67. $2\sqrt[4]{64} - \sqrt[4]{324} + \sqrt[4]{4}$

68. $2\sqrt[3]{16} - 5\sqrt[3]{54} + 10\sqrt[3]{2}$

69. $5\sqrt[4]{x^5} - \sqrt[4]{x}$

70. $20\sqrt[3]{b^4} - 4\sqrt[3]{b}$

71. $\sqrt{64x^3} - \sqrt{x} + 3\sqrt{x}$

72. $2\sqrt{3z} + 3\sqrt{12z} + 3\sqrt{48z}$

73. $\sqrt[4]{81a^5b^5} - \sqrt[4]{ab}$ **74.** $\sqrt[4]{xy^5} - \sqrt[4]{x^5y}$

75. $5\sqrt[3]{\dfrac{n^4}{125}} - 2\sqrt[3]{n}$ **76.** $\sqrt[3]{\dfrac{8x}{27}} - \dfrac{2\sqrt[3]{x}}{3}$

MULTIPLYING BINOMIALS CONTAINING RADICALS

Exercises 77–88: Multiply and simplify.

77. $(\sqrt{x} - 3)(\sqrt{x} + 2)$

78. $(2\sqrt{x} + 1)(\sqrt{x} + 4)$

79. $(3 + \sqrt{7})(3 - \sqrt{7})$

80. $(5 - \sqrt{5})(5 + \sqrt{5})$

81. $(11 - \sqrt{2})(11 + \sqrt{2})$

82. $(6 + \sqrt{3})(6 - \sqrt{3})$

83. $(\sqrt{x} + 8)(\sqrt{x} - 8)$

84. $(\sqrt{ab} - 3)(\sqrt{ab} + 3)$

85. $(\sqrt{ab} - \sqrt{c})(\sqrt{ab} + \sqrt{c})$

86. $(\sqrt{2x} + \sqrt{3y})(\sqrt{2x} - \sqrt{3y})$

87. $(\sqrt{x} - 7)(\sqrt{x} + 8)$

88. $(\sqrt{ab} - 1)(\sqrt{ab} - 2)$

RATIONALIZING THE DENOMINATOR

Exercises 89–116: Rationalize the denominator.

89. $\dfrac{1}{\sqrt{7}}$ **90.** $\dfrac{1}{\sqrt{23}}$

91. $\dfrac{4}{\sqrt{3}}$ **92.** $\dfrac{8}{\sqrt{2}}$

93. $\dfrac{5}{3\sqrt{5}}$ **94.** $\dfrac{6}{11\sqrt{3}}$

95. $\sqrt{\dfrac{b}{12}}$ **96.** $\sqrt{\dfrac{5b}{72}}$

97. $\dfrac{rt}{2\sqrt{r^3}}$ **98.** $\dfrac{m^2n}{2\sqrt{m^5}}$

99. $\dfrac{1}{3 - \sqrt{2}}$ **100.** $\dfrac{1}{\sqrt{3} - 2}$

101. $\dfrac{\sqrt{2}}{\sqrt{5} + 2}$ **102.** $\dfrac{\sqrt{3}}{\sqrt{3} + 2}$

103. $\dfrac{\sqrt{7} - 2}{\sqrt{7} + 2}$ **104.** $\dfrac{\sqrt{3} - 1}{\sqrt{3} + 1}$

105. $\dfrac{1}{\sqrt{7} - \sqrt{6}}$ **106.** $\dfrac{1}{\sqrt{8} - \sqrt{7}}$

107. $\dfrac{\sqrt{z}}{\sqrt{z} - 3}$ **108.** $\dfrac{2\sqrt{z}}{2 - \sqrt{z}}$

109. $\dfrac{\sqrt{a} + \sqrt{b}}{\sqrt{a} - \sqrt{b}}$ **110.** $\dfrac{\sqrt{x} - 2\sqrt{y}}{\sqrt{x} + 2\sqrt{y}}$

111. $\dfrac{1}{\sqrt{x + 1} - \sqrt{x}}$ **112.** $\dfrac{1}{\sqrt{a + 1} + \sqrt{a}}$

113. $\dfrac{3}{\sqrt[3]{x}}$ **114.** $\dfrac{6}{5\sqrt[3]{x}}$

115. $\dfrac{1}{\sqrt[3]{x^2}}$ **116.** $\dfrac{2}{\sqrt[3]{(x - 2)^2}}$

GEOMETRY

117. *Perimeter*   (Refer to Example 8.) Find the exact perimeter of the right triangle. Then approximate your answer.

118. *Perimeter*   Find the exact perimeter of the rectangle. Then approximate your answer.

WRITING ABOUT MATHEMATICS

119. Suppose that a student knows that $\sqrt{3} \approx 1.73205$ and does not have a calculator. Which of the following expressions would be easier to evaluate by hand? Why?

$$\frac{1}{\sqrt{3}} \quad \text{or} \quad \frac{\sqrt{3}}{3}$$

120. A student simplifies an expression *incorrectly*:

$$\sqrt{8} + \sqrt[3]{16} \overset{?}{=} \sqrt{4 \cdot 2} + \sqrt[3]{8 \cdot 2}$$
$$\overset{?}{=} \sqrt{4} \cdot \sqrt{2} + \sqrt[3]{8} \cdot \sqrt[3]{2}$$
$$\overset{?}{=} 2\sqrt{2} + 2\sqrt[3]{2}$$
$$\overset{?}{=} 4\sqrt{4}$$
$$\overset{?}{=} 8.$$

Explain any errors that the student made. What would you do differently?

Directions: Form a group of 2 to 4 people. Select someone to record the group's responses for this activity. All members of the group should work cooperatively to answer the questions. If your instructor asks for your results, each member of the group should be prepared to respond.

Designing a Paper Cup   A paper drinking cup is being designed in the shape shown in the accompanying figure. The amount of paper needed to manufacture the cup is determined by the surface area S of the cup, which is given by

$$S = \pi r \sqrt{r^2 + h^2},$$

where r is the radius and h is the height.

(a) Approximate S to the nearest hundredth when $r = 1.5$ inches and $h = 4$ inches.

(b) Could the formula for S be simplified as follows?

$$\pi r \sqrt{r^2 + h^2} \stackrel{?}{=} \pi r \left(\sqrt{r^2} + \sqrt{h^2}\right)$$
$$\stackrel{?}{=} \pi r (r + h)$$

Try evaluating this second formula with $r = 1.5$ inches and $h = 4$ inches. Is your answer the same as in part (a)? Explain.

(c) Discuss why evaluating real-world formulas correctly is important.

(d) In general, does $\sqrt{a + b}$ equal $\sqrt{a} + \sqrt{b}$? Justify your answer by completing the following table. Approximate answers to the nearest hundredth when appropriate.

a	b	$\sqrt{a + b}$	$\sqrt{a} + \sqrt{b}$
0	4		
4	0		
5	4		
9	7		
4	16		
25	100		

7.4 RADICAL FUNCTIONS

The Square Root Function ▪ The Cube Root Function ▪ Power Functions ▪ Modeling with Power Functions (Optional)

A LOOK INTO MATH ▷   A good punter can kick a football so that it has a long *hang time*. Hang time is the length of time that the football is in the air. Long hang time gives the kicking team time to run down the field and stop the punt return. Using square roots, we can derive a function that calculates hang time. (See the discussion before Example 3.) First, we discuss the square root function.

The Square Root Function

The square root function is given by $f(x) = \sqrt{x}$. The domain of the square root function is all nonnegative real numbers because we have not defined the square root of a negative number. Table 7.2 lists three points that lie on the graph of $f(x) = \sqrt{x}$. In Figure 7.9 these points are plotted and the graph of $y = \sqrt{x}$ has been sketched. The graph does not appear to the left of the origin because $f(x) = \sqrt{x}$ is undefined for negative inputs.

TABLE 7.2

x	$\sqrt{x}$
0	0
1	1
4	2

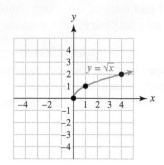

Figure 7.9 Square Root Function

TECHNOLOGY NOTE: Square Roots of Negative Numbers

If a table of values for $y_1 = \sqrt{x}$ includes both negative and positive values for x, then many calculators give error messages when x is negative, as shown in the accompanying figure.

EXAMPLE **1**   Evaluating functions involving square roots

If possible, evaluate $f(1)$ and $f(-2)$ for each $f(x)$.
(a) $f(x) = \sqrt{2x - 1}$ **(b)** $f(x) = \sqrt{4 - x^2}$

Solution
(a) $f(1) = \sqrt{2(1) - 1} = \sqrt{1} = 1$
    $f(-2) = \sqrt{2(-2) - 1} = \sqrt{-5}$, which does not equal a real number.
(b) $f(1) = \sqrt{4 - (1)^2} = \sqrt{3}$; $f(-2) = \sqrt{4 - (-2)^2} = \sqrt{0} = 0$

Now Try Exercises **11, 13**

In the next example we find a formula, a table of values, and a graph for a function.

EXAMPLE **2**   Finding symbolic, numerical, and graphical representations

A function f takes the square root of x and then multiplies the result by 2. Give symbolic, numerical, and graphical representations of f.

Solution
First find a formula for f. The square root of x multiplied by 2 equals $2\sqrt{x}$, so $f(x) = 2\sqrt{x}$. A table of values is shown in Table 7.3. A curve is sketched through these points to obtain the graph of f in Figure 7.10. The domain of f includes all nonnegative numbers.

Symbolic Representation	Numerical Representation	Graphical Representation

$$f(x) = 2\sqrt{x}$$

TABLE 7.3

x	$2\sqrt{x}$
0	0
1	2
4	4
9	6

Figure 7.10

Now Try Exercise 25

▶ REAL-WORLD CONNECTION   To derive a function that calculates the hang time of a football we need two facts from physics. First, when a ball is kicked into the air, half the hang time of the ball is spent going up and the other half is spent coming down. Second, the time t in seconds required for a ball to fall from a height of h feet is modeled by the equation $16t^2 = h$. Solving this equation for t gives half the hang time.

$$16t^2 = h \qquad \text{Given equation}$$

$$t^2 = \frac{h}{16} \qquad \text{Divide by 16.}$$

$$t = \sqrt{\frac{h}{16}} \qquad \text{Take the principal square root.}$$

$$t = \frac{\sqrt{h}}{4} \qquad \text{Simplify.}$$

Half the hang time is $\frac{\sqrt{h}}{4}$, so the total hang time T in seconds is given by

$$T(h) = 2 \cdot \frac{\sqrt{h}}{4} = \frac{\sqrt{h}}{2},$$

where h is the maximum height of the ball.

In the next example, we use this formula to calculate hang time.

EXAMPLE 3   Calculating hang time

If a football is kicked 50 feet into the air, estimate the hang time. Does the hang time double for a football kicked 100 feet into the air?

50 feet

Solution

A football kicked 50 feet into the air has a hang time of $T(50) = \frac{\sqrt{50}}{2} \approx 3.5$ seconds. For 100 feet, the hang time is $T(100) = \frac{\sqrt{100}}{2} = 5$ seconds. The hang time does not double.

Now Try Exercise 79

CRITICAL THINKING

How high would a football have to be kicked to have twice the hang time of a football kicked 50 feet into the air?

EXAMPLE **4**   Finding the domain of a function

Let $f(x) = \sqrt{x - 1}$.

(a) Find the domain of f. Write your answer in interval notation.
(b) Graph $y = f(x)$ and compare it to the graph of $y = \sqrt{x}$.

Solution

(a) For $f(x)$ to be defined, $x - 1$ cannot be negative. Thus valid inputs for x must satisfy

$$x - 1 \geq 0 \quad \text{or} \quad x \geq 1.$$

The domain is $[1, \infty)$.

(b) Table 7.4 lists points that lie on the graph of $y = \sqrt{x - 1}$. Note in Figure 7.11 that the graph appears only when $x \geq 1$. This graph is similar to $y = \sqrt{x}$ (see Figure 7.9) except that it is shifted one unit to the right.

TABLE 7.4

x	$\sqrt{x - 1}$
1	0
2	1
5	2

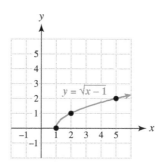

Figure 7.11   Now Try Exercises 33, 47

EXAMPLE **5**   Finding the domains of functions

Find the domain of each function. Write your answer in interval notation.
(a) $f(x) = \sqrt{4 - 2x}$ (b) $g(x) = \sqrt{x^2 + 1}$

Solution

(a) To determine when $f(x)$ is defined, we must solve the inequality $4 - 2x \geq 0$.

$$4 - 2x \geq 0 \qquad \text{Inequality to be solved}$$
$$4 \geq 2x \qquad \text{Add } 2x \text{ to each side.}$$
$$2 \geq x \qquad \text{Divide each side by 2.}$$

The domain is $(-\infty, 2]$.

(b) Regardless of the value of x, the expression $x^2 + 1$ is always positive because $x^2 \geq 0$. Thus $g(x)$ is defined for all real numbers, and its domain is $(-\infty, \infty)$.

Now Try Exercises 41, 43

Domains of Functions and Their Graphs

In Example 5, the domains of f and g were found *symbolically*. Notice that the graph of f does not appear to the right of $x = 2$ because the domain of f is $(-\infty, 2]$, whereas the graph of g appears for all values of x because the domain of g is $(-\infty, \infty)$.

  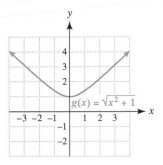

The Cube Root Function

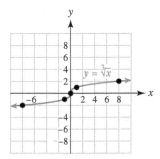

Figure 7.12 Cube Root Function

In Section 7.1, we discussed the cube root of a number. We can define the **cube root function** by $f(x) = \sqrt[3]{x}$. Cube roots are defined for both positive and negative numbers, so *the domain of the cube root function includes all real numbers*. Table 7.5 lists points that lie on the graph of the cube root function. Figure 7.12 shows a graph of $y = \sqrt[3]{x}$.

TABLE 7.5 **Cube Root Function**

x	-27	-8	-1	0	1	8	27
$\sqrt[3]{x}$	-3	-2	-1	0	1	2	3

Domains of the Square Root and Cube Root Functions

$f(x) = \sqrt{x}$ equals a real number for any nonnegative x. Thus $D = [0, \infty)$.

$f(x) = \sqrt[3]{x}$ equals a real number for any x. Thus $D = (-\infty, \infty)$.

Examples: $\sqrt{4} = 2$ but $\sqrt{-4}$ is *not* a real number. $\sqrt[3]{8} = 2$ and $\sqrt[3]{-8} = -2$.

EXAMPLE 6   Evaluating functions involving cube roots

Evaluate $f(1)$ and $f(-3)$ for each $f(x)$.
(a) $f(x) = \sqrt[3]{x^2 - 1}$ (b) $f(x) = \sqrt[3]{2 - x^2}$

Solution
(a) $f(1) = \sqrt[3]{1^2 - 1} = \sqrt[3]{0} = 0$; $f(-3) = \sqrt[3]{(-3)^2 - 1} = \sqrt[3]{8} = 2$
(b) $f(1) = \sqrt[3]{2 - 1^2} = \sqrt[3]{1} = 1$; $f(-3) = \sqrt[3]{2 - (-3)^2} = \sqrt[3]{-7}$ or $-\sqrt[3]{7}$

Now Try Exercises 15, 19

EXAMPLE 7   Finding symbolic, numerical, and graphical representations

A function f takes the cube root of twice x. Give symbolic, numerical, and graphical representations of f.

Solution

First find a formula for f. Twice x is $2x$, so $f(x) = \sqrt[3]{2x}$. A table of values is shown in Table 7.6. A curve is sketched through these points to obtain the graph of f in Figure 7.13.

Symbolic Representation	*Numerical Representation*	*Graphical Representation*
$f(x) = \sqrt[3]{2x}$	TABLE 7.6	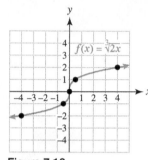

x	$\sqrt[3]{2x}$
-4	-2
$-\frac{1}{2}$	-1
0	0
$\frac{1}{2}$	1
4	2

Figure 7.13

Now Try Exercise 29

Power Functions

Power functions are a generalization of root functions. Examples of power functions include

$$f(x) = x^{1/2}, \quad g(x) = x^{2/3}, \quad \text{and} \quad h(x) = x^{-3/5}.$$

The exponents for power functions can be rational numbers. Any rational number can be written in lowest terms as $\frac{m}{n}$, where m and n are integers. When n is an odd integer, then $f(x) = x^{m/n}$ is defined for all real numbers. When n is even, $f(x) = x^{m/n}$ is defined only for nonnegative real numbers.

> ### POWER FUNCTION
>
> If a function f can be represented by
>
> $$f(x) = x^p,$$
>
> where p is a rational number, then f is a **power function**. If $p = \frac{1}{n}$, where $n \geq 2$ is an integer, then f is also a **root function**, which is given by
>
> $$f(x) = \sqrt[n]{x}.$$

EXAMPLE 8   Evaluating power functions

If possible, evaluate $f(x)$ at the given value of x.

(a) $f(x) = x^{0.75}$ at $x = 16$ (b) $f(x) = x^{1/4}$ at $x = -81$

Solution

(a) $0.75 = \frac{3}{4}$, so $f(x) = x^{3/4}$. Thus $f(16) = 16^{3/4} = (16^{1/4})^3 = 2^3 = 8$.

   NOTE: $16^{1/4} = \sqrt[4]{16} = 2$.

(b) $f(-81) = (-81)^{1/4} = \sqrt[4]{-81}$, which is undefined. There is no real number a such that $a^4 = -81$ because a^4 is never negative.   Now Try Exercises 59, 63

▶ REAL-WORLD CONNECTION   The surface area of the skin covering the human body is influenced by both the height and weight of a person. A taller person tends to have a larger surface area, as does a heavier person. In the next example, we use a power function from biology to model this situation.

EXAMPLE 9   Modeling surface area of the human body

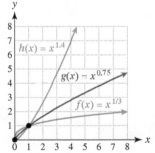

The surface area of a person who is 66 inches tall and weighs w pounds can be estimated by $S(w) = 327w^{0.425}$, where S is in square inches.   (*Source:* H. Lancaster, Quantitative *Methods in Biological and Medical Sciences.*)

(a) Find S if this person weighs 130 pounds.

(b) If the person gains 20 pounds, by how much does the person's surface area increase?

Solution

(a) $S(130) = 327(130)^{0.425} \approx 2588$ square inches

(b) Because $S(150) = 327(150)^{0.425} \approx 2750$ square inches, the surface area of the person increases by about $2750 - 2588 = 162$ square inches.   Now Try Exercise 87

In the next example, we investigate the graph of $y = x^p$ for different values of p.

EXAMPLE 10   Graphing power functions

The graphs of three power functions,

$$f(x) = x^{1/3}, \quad g(x) = x^{0.75}, \quad \text{and} \quad h(x) = x^{1.4},$$

are shown in Figure 7.14. Discuss how the value of p affects the graph of $y = x^p$ when $x > 1$ and when $0 < x < 1$.

Figure 7.14 Power Functions

Solution

First note that $g(x)$ and $h(x)$ can be written as $g(x) = x^{3/4}$ and $h(x) = x^{7/5}$. When $x > 1$, $h(x) > g(x) > f(x)$ and the graphs increase (rise) faster for larger values of p. When $0 < x < 1$, $h(x) < g(x) < f(x)$. Thus smaller values of p result in larger y-values when $0 < x < 1$. All three graphs appear to intersect at the points $(0, 0)$ and $(1, 1)$.
     Now Try Exercise 67

Modeling with Power Functions (Optional)

▶ REAL-WORLD CONNECTION   Allometry is the study of the relative sizes of different characteristics of an organism. For example, the weight of a bird is related to the surface area of its wings: Heavier birds tend to have larger wings. Allometric relations are often modeled with $f(x) = kx^p$, where k and p are constants.   (*Source:* C. Pennycuick, *Newton Rules Biology.*)

EXAMPLE 11   Modeling surface area of wings

The surface area A of a bird's wings with weight w is shown in Table 7.7.

TABLE 7.7   **Weight and Wing Size**

w (kilograms)	0.5	2.0	3.5	5.0
A (square meters)	0.069	0.175	0.254	0.325

CALCULATOR HELP

To make a scatterplot, see the Appendix (page AP-4).

[0, 6, 1] by [0, 0.4, 0.1]

(a)

[0, 6, 1] by [0, 0.4, 0.1]

(b)

Figure 7.15

(a) Make a scatterplot of the data. Discuss any trends in the data.
(b) Biologists modeled the data with $A(w) = kw^{2/3}$, where k is a constant. Find k.
(c) Graph A and the data in the same viewing rectangle.
(d) Estimate the area of the wings of a 3-kilogram bird.

Solution
(a) A scatterplot of the data is shown in Figure 7.15(a). As the weight of a bird increases so does the surface area of its wings.
(b) To determine k, substitute one of the data points into $A(w)$. We use $(2.0, 0.175)$.

$$A(w) = kw^{2/3} \qquad \text{Given formula}$$

$$0.175 = k(2)^{2/3} \qquad \begin{array}{l}\text{Let } w = 2 \text{ and } A(w) = 0.175 \\ \text{(any data point could be used).}\end{array}$$

$$k = \frac{0.175}{2^{2/3}} \qquad \text{Solve for } k; \text{ rewrite equation.}$$

$$k \approx 0.11 \qquad \text{Approximate } k.$$

Thus $A(w) = 0.11w^{2/3}$.
(c) The data and graph of $Y_1 = 0.11X^\wedge(2/3)$ are shown in Figure 7.15(b). Note that the graph appears to pass through each data point.
(d) $A(3) = 0.11(3)^{2/3} \approx 0.23$ square meter

Now Try Exercise 83

7.4   PUTTING IT ALL TOGETHER

In this section we discussed some new functions involving radicals and rational exponents. Properties of these functions are summarized in the following table.

Function	Explanation
Square Root and Cube Root	$f(x) = \sqrt{x}$ and $g(x) = \sqrt[3]{x}$ The cube root function g is defined for all inputs, whereas the square root function f is defined only for nonnegative inputs.

Function	Explanation
Square Root and Cube Root (*continued*)	 Square Root Function Cube Root Function
Power and Root	$f(x) = x^p$, where p is a rational number, is a power function. If $p = \frac{1}{n}$, where $n \geq 2$ is an integer, f is also a root function, given by $f(x) = \sqrt[n]{x}$. ***Examples:*** $f(x) = x^{5/3}$ Power function $g(x) = x^{1/4} = \sqrt[4]{x}$ Root and power function

7.4 Exercises

MyMathLab   Math XL PRACTICE   WATCH   DOWNLOAD   READ   REVIEW

CONCEPTS

1. Sketch a graph of the square root function.

2. Sketch a graph of the cube root function.

3. What is the domain of the square root function?

4. What is the domain of the cube root function?

5. Give a symbolic representation for a power function.

6. Give a symbolic representation for a root function.

7. What is the domain of $f(x) = \sqrt[4]{x}$?

8. What is the domain of $f(x) = \sqrt[5]{x}$?

ROOT FUNCTIONS

Exercises 9–24: If possible, evaluate the function at the given value(s) of the variable.

9. $f(x) = \sqrt{x-1}$ $x = 10, 0$

10. $f(x) = \sqrt{4-3x}$ $x = -4, 1$

11. $f(x) = \sqrt{3-3x}$ $x = -1, 5$

12. $f(x) = \sqrt{x-5}$ $x = -1, 5$

13. $f(x) = \sqrt{x^2-x}$ $x = -4, 3$

14. $f(x) = \sqrt{2x^2-3}$ $x = -1, 2$

15. $f(x) = \sqrt[3]{x^2-8}$ $x = -3, 4$

16. $f(x) = \sqrt[3]{2x^2}$ $x = -2, 2$

17. $f(x) = \sqrt[3]{x-9}$ $x = 1, 10$

18. $f(x) = \sqrt[3]{5x-2}$ $x = -5, 2$

19. $f(x) = \sqrt[3]{3-x^2}$ $x = -2, 3$

20. $f(x) = \sqrt[3]{-1-x^2}$ $x = 0, 3$

21. $T(h) = \frac{1}{2}\sqrt{h}$ $h = 64$

22. $L(k) = 2\sqrt{k+2}$ $k = 23$

23. $f(x) = \sqrt{x+5} + \sqrt{x}$ $x = 4$

24. $f(x) = \dfrac{\sqrt{x-5} - \sqrt{x}}{2}$ $x = 9$

Exercises 25–32: Give symbolic, numerical, and graphical representations for the function f.

25. Function f takes the square root of x and then adds 1 to the result.

26. Function f takes the square root of x and then subtracts 2 from the result.

27. Function f takes the square root of three times x.

28. Function f takes the square root of the quantity x plus 1.

29. Function f takes the cube root of x and then multiplies the result by 2.

30. Function f takes the cube root of 4 times x.

31. Function f takes the cube root of the quantity x minus 1.

32. Function f takes the cube root of x and then adds 1.

Exercises 33–46: Find the domain of f. Write your answer in interval notation.

33. $f(x) = \sqrt{x + 2}$ **34.** $f(x) = \sqrt{x - 1}$

35. $f(x) = \sqrt{x - 2}$ **36.** $f(x) = \sqrt{x + 1}$

37. $f(x) = \sqrt{2x - 4}$ **38.** $f(x) = \sqrt{4x + 2}$

39. $f(x) = \sqrt{1 - x}$ **40.** $f(x) = \sqrt{6 - 3x}$

41. $f(x) = \sqrt{8 - 5x}$ **42.** $f(x) = \sqrt{3 - 2x}$

43. $f(x) = \sqrt{3x^2 + 4}$ **44.** $f(x) = \sqrt{1 + 2x^2}$

45. $f(x) = \dfrac{1}{\sqrt{2x + 1}}$ **46.** $f(x) = \dfrac{1}{\sqrt{x - 1}}$

Exercises 47–52: Graph the equation. Compare the graph to either $y = \sqrt{x}$ or $y = \sqrt[3]{x}$.

47. $y = \sqrt{x} + 2$ **48.** $y = \sqrt{x} - 1$

49. $y = \sqrt{x + 2}$ **50.** $y = \sqrt[3]{x} + 2$

51. $y = \sqrt[3]{x + 2}$ **52.** $y = \sqrt[3]{x} - 1$

POWER FUNCTIONS

Exercises 53–58: Use a radical to write f(x).

53. $f(x) = x^{1/2}$ **54.** $f(x) = x^{1/3}$

55. $f(x) = x^{2/3}$ **56.** $f(x) = x^{3/4}$

57. $f(x) = x^{-1/5}$ **58.** $f(x) = x^{-2/5}$

Exercises 59–66: If possible, evaluate f(x) at the given values of x. When appropriate, approximate the answer to the nearest hundredth.

59. $f(x) = x^{5/2}$ $x = 4, x = 5$

60. $f(x) = x^{-3/4}$ $x = 1, x = 3$

61. $f(x) = x^{-7/5}$ $x = -32, x = 10$

62. $f(x) = x^{4/3}$ $x = -8, x = 27$

63. $f(x) = x^{1/4}$ $x = 256, x = -10$

64. $f(x) = x^{3/4}$ $x = 16, x = -1$

65. $f(x) = x^{2/5}$ $x = 32, x = -32$

66. $f(x) = x^{5/6}$ $x = -5, x = 64$

Exercises 67–70: Graph f and g in the window [0, 6, 1] by [0, 6, 1]. Which function is greater when x > 1?

67. $f(x) = x^{1/5}, g(x) = x^{1/3}$

68. $f(x) = x^{4/5}, g(x) = x^{5/4}$

69. $f(x) = x^{1.2}, g(x) = x^{0.45}$

70. $f(x) = x^{-1.4}, g(x) = x^{1.4}$

Exercises 71 and 72: **Thinking Generally**   *Let $0 < q < p$, where p and q are rational numbers.*

71. For $x > 1$, is $x^p > x^q$ or $x^p < x^q$?

72. For $0 < x < 1$, is $x^p > x^q$ or $x^p < x^q$?

Exercises 73 and 74: *Operations on Functions*   *For the given f(x) and g(x), evaluate each expression.*

  (a) $(f + g)(2)$ **(b)** $(f - g)(x)$
  (c) $(fg)(x)$ **(d)** $(f/g)(x)$

73. $f(x) = \sqrt{8x}, g(x) = \sqrt{2x}$

74. $f(x) = \sqrt{9x + 18}, g(x) = \sqrt{4x + 8}$

Exercises 75–78: *Graphical Interpretation*   *Match the situation with the graph of the power function (a.–d.) on the next page that models it best.*

75. Amount of water in a barrel that is initially full and has a hole near the bottom

76. The average weight of a type of bird as its wing span increases (*Hint:* The exponent is greater than 1.)

77. Money made after x hours by a person who works for a fixed hourly wage

78. Rapid growth of an insect population that eventually slows down

a.

b.

c.

d.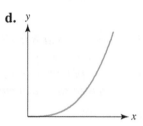

APPLICATIONS

79. *Jumping* (Refer to Example 3.) If a person jumps 4 feet off the ground, estimate how long the person is in the air.

80. *Hang Time* (Refer to Example 3.) Find the hang time for a golf ball hit 80 feet into the air.

81. *Aging More Slowly* Albert Einstein in his theory of relativity showed that if a person travels at nearly the speed of light, then time slows down significantly. Suppose that there are twins; one remains on Earth and the other leaves in a very fast spaceship having velocity v. If the twin on Earth ages T_0 years, then according to Einstein the twin in the spaceship ages T years, where

$$T(v) = T_0 \sqrt{1 - (v/c)^2}.$$

In this formula c represents the speed of light, which is 186,000 miles per second.

(a) Evaluate T when $v = 0.8c$ (eight-tenths the speed of light) and $T_0 = 10$ years. (*Hint:* Simplify $\frac{v}{c}$ without using 186,000 miles per second.)

(b) Interpret your result.

82. *Increasing Your Weight* (Refer to Exercise 81.) Albert Einstein also showed that the weight (mass) of an object increases when traveling near the speed of light. If a person's weight on Earth is W_0, then the same person's weight W in a spaceship traveling at velocity v is

$$W(v) = \frac{W_0}{\sqrt{1 - (v/c)^2}}.$$

(a) Evaluate W when $v = 0.6c$ (six-tenths the speed of light) and $W_0 = 220$ pounds (100 kilograms).

(b) Interpret your result.

83. *Modeling Wing Size* (Refer to Example 11.) The surface area of wings for a species of bird with weight w is shown in the table.

w (kilograms)	2	3	4
A (square meters)	0.254	0.333	0.403

(a) Make a scatterplot of the data.

(b) The data can be modeled with $A(w) = kw^{2/3}$. Find k.

(c) Graph A and the data in the same viewing rectangle. Does the graph of A pass through the data points?

(d) Estimate the area of the wings of a 2.5-kilogram bird.

84. *Pulse Rate in Animals* The following table lists typical pulse rates R in beats per minute (bpm) for animals with various weights W in pounds.
(*Source:* C. Pennycuick.)

W (pounds)	20	150	500	1500
R (beats per minute)	198	72	40	23

(a) Describe what happens to the pulse rate as the size of the animal increases.

(b) Plot the data in [0, 1600, 400] by [0, 220, 20].

(c) If $R = kW^{-1/2}$, find k.

(d) Find R when $W = 700$, and interpret the result.

85. *Modeling Wing Span*   (Refer to Example 11.) Biologists have found that the weight W of a bird and the length L of its wing span are related by $L = kW^{1/3}$, where k is a constant. The following table lists L and W for one species of bird.   (*Source:* C. Pennycuick.)

W (kilograms)	0.1	0.4	0.8	1.1
L (meters)	0.422	0.670	0.844	0.938

(a) Use the data to approximate the value of k.
(b) Graph L and the data in the same viewing rectangle. What happens to L as W increases?
(c) Find the wing span of a 0.7-kilogram bird.
(d) Find L when $W = 0.65$, and interpret the result.

86. *Design of Open Channels*   To protect cities from flooding during heavy rains, open channels are sometimes constructed to handle runoff. The rate R at which water flows through the channel is modeled by $R = k\sqrt{m}$, where m is the slope of the channel and k is a constant determined by the shape of the channel. (*Source:* N. Garber and L. Hoel, *Traffic and Highway Design.*)

(a) Suppose that a channel has a slope of $m = 0.01$ (or 1%) and a runoff rate of $R = 340$ cubic feet per second (cfs). Find k.
(b) If the slope of the channel increases to $m = 0.04$ (or 4%), what happens to R? Be specific.

Exercises 87 and 88: (Refer to Example 9.) The surface area of the skin of a person who is 70 inches tall and weighs w pounds can be estimated by $S(w) = 342w^{0.425}$, where S is in square inches. Evaluate each of the following.

87. $S(150)$ **88.** $S(200)$

89. Explain why a root function is an example of a power function.

90. Discuss the shape of the graph of $y = x^p$ as p increases. Assume that p is a positive rational number and that x is a positive real number.

CHECKING BASIC CONCEPTS
SECTIONS 7.3 AND 7.4

1. Simplify each expression.
(a) $\sqrt{3} \cdot \sqrt{12}$ (b) $\dfrac{\sqrt[3]{81}}{\sqrt[3]{3}}$
(c) $\sqrt{36x^6}, x > 0$

2. Simplify each expression.
(a) $5\sqrt{6} + 2\sqrt{6} + \sqrt{7}$
(b) $8\sqrt[3]{x} - 3\sqrt[3]{x}$ (c) $\sqrt{9x} - \sqrt{4x}$

3. Simplify each expression.
(a) $\sqrt[3]{xy^4} - \sqrt[3]{x^4y}$
(b) $(4 - \sqrt{2})(4 + \sqrt{2})$

4. Rationalize the denominator of $\dfrac{6}{2\sqrt{6}}$.

5. Rationalize the denominator of $\dfrac{2}{\sqrt{5} - 1}$.

6. Sketch a graph of each function and then evaluate $f(-1)$, if possible.
(a) $f(x) = \sqrt{x}$
(b) $f(x) = \sqrt[3]{x}$
(c) $f(x) = \sqrt{x^2}$

7. Evaluate $f(x) = 0.2x^{2/3}$ when $x = 64$.

8. Find the domain of $f(x) = \sqrt{x - 4}$. Write your answer in interval notation.

7.5 EQUATIONS INVOLVING RADICAL EXPRESSIONS

Solving Radical Equations ■ The Distance Formula ■ Solving the Equation $x^n = k$

A LOOK INTO MATH ▷

In Section 7.4 we showed that for some types of birds there is a relationship between weight and the size of the wings—heavier birds tend to have larger wings. This relationship can sometimes be modeled by $A = 100\sqrt[3]{W^2}$, where W is weight in pounds and A is area in square inches. Suppose that we want to estimate the weight of a bird whose wings have an area of 600 square inches. To do so, we would need to solve the equation

$$600 = 100\sqrt[3]{W^2}$$

for W. This equation contains a radical expression. In this section we explain how to solve this type of equation.   (**Source:** C. Pennycuick, *Newton Rules Biology.*)

Solving Radical Equations

Many times, equations contain either radical expressions or rational exponents. Examples include

$$\sqrt{x} = 6, \quad 5x^{1/2} = 1, \quad \text{and} \quad \sqrt[3]{x-1} = 3.$$

One strategy for solving an equation containing a square root is to isolate the square root (if necessary) and then square each side of the equation. This technique is an example of the *power rule for solving equations.*

POWER RULE FOR SOLVING EQUATIONS

If each side of an equation is raised to the same positive integer power, then any solutions to the given equation are among the solutions to the new equation. That is, the solutions to the equation $a = b$ are among the solutions to $a^n = b^n$.

We must check our solutions when applying the power rule. For example, consider the equation $2x = 6$. If we square each side, we obtain $4x^2 = 36$. Solving this second equation gives $x^2 = 9$, or $x = \pm 3$. Here, 3 is a solution to both equations, but -3 is an **extraneous solution** that satisfies the second equation but not the given equation. That is, $4(-3)^2 = 36$ is a *true* statement, but $2(-3) = 6$ is a *false* statement. Thus -3 is *not* a solution to the given equation.

We illustrate the power rule in the next example.

EXAMPLE 1   Solving a radical equation symbolically

Solve $\sqrt{2x - 1} = 3$. Check your solution.

Solution
Begin by squaring each side of the equation.

$$\sqrt{2x - 1} = 3 \qquad \text{Given equation}$$
$$(\sqrt{2x - 1})^2 = 3^2 \qquad \text{Square each side.}$$
$$2x - 1 = 9 \qquad \text{Simplify.}$$
$$2x = 10 \qquad \text{Add 1.}$$
$$x = 5 \qquad \text{Divide by 2.}$$

To check this answer we substitute $x = 5$ in the given equation.

$$\sqrt{2(5) - 1} \overset{?}{=} 3$$

$$3 = 3 \qquad \text{It checks.} \qquad \boxed{\text{Now Try Exercise } 21}$$

NOTE: To simplify $(\sqrt{2x - 1})^2$ in Example 1, we used the fact that

$$\left(\sqrt{a}\right)^2 = \sqrt{a} \cdot \sqrt{a} = a.$$

The following steps can be used to solve a radical equation.

SOLVING A RADICAL EQUATION

STEP 1: Isolate a radical term on one side of the equation.

STEP 2: Apply the power rule by raising each side of the equation to the power equal to the index of the isolated radical term.

STEP 3: Solve the equation. If it still contains a radical, repeat Steps 1 and 2.

STEP 4: Check your answers by substituting each result in the *given* equation.

NOTE: In Sections 7.1–7.3, we *simplified expressions*. In this section we *solve equations*. Equations contain equals signs and when we solve an equation, we try to find values of the variable that make the equation a true statement.

In the next example, we apply these steps to a radical equation.

EXAMPLE 2   Isolating the radical term

Solve $\sqrt{4 - x} + 5 = 8$.

Solution
STEP 1: To isolate the radical term, we subtract 5 from each side of the equation.

$$\sqrt{4 - x} + 5 = 8 \qquad \text{Given equation}$$

$$\sqrt{4 - x} = 3 \qquad \text{Subtract 5.}$$

STEP 2: The isolated term involves a square root, so we must square each side.

$$(\sqrt{4 - x})^2 = (3)^2 \qquad \text{Square each side.}$$

STEP 3: Next we solve the resulting equation. (It is not necessary to repeat Steps 1 and 2 because the resulting equation does not contain any radical expressions.)

$$4 - x = 9 \qquad \text{Simplify.}$$

$$-x = 5 \qquad \text{Subtract 4.}$$

$$x = -5 \qquad \text{Multiply by } -1.$$

STEP 4: To check this answer we substitute $x = -5$ in the given equation.

$$\sqrt{4 - (-5)} + 5 \overset{?}{=} 8$$

$$\sqrt{9} + 5 \overset{?}{=} 8$$

$$8 = 8 \qquad \text{It checks.} \qquad \boxed{\text{Now Try Exercise } 23}$$

Example 3 shows that we must check our answers when squaring each side of an equation to identify extraneous solutions.

EXAMPLE 3 Solving a radical equation

Solve $\sqrt{3x + 3} = 2x - 1$. Check your results and then solve the equation graphically.

Solution

Symbolic Solution Begin by squaring each side of the equation.

$$\sqrt{3x + 3} = 2x - 1 \qquad \text{Given equation}$$
$$(\sqrt{3x + 3})^2 = (2x - 1)^2 \qquad \text{Square each side.}$$
$$3x + 3 = 4x^2 - 4x + 1 \qquad \text{Multiply.}$$
$$0 = 4x^2 - 7x - 2 \qquad \text{Subtract } 3x + 3.$$
$$0 = (4x + 1)(x - 2) \qquad \text{Factor.}$$
$$x = -\frac{1}{4} \quad \text{or} \quad x = 2 \qquad \text{Solve for } x.$$

To check these values substitute $x = -\frac{1}{4}$ and $x = 2$ in the given equation.

$$\sqrt{3\left(-\tfrac{1}{4}\right) + 3} \overset{?}{=} 2\left(-\tfrac{1}{4}\right) - 1$$
$$\sqrt{2.25} \overset{?}{=} -1.5$$
$$1.5 \neq -1.5 \qquad \text{It does not check.}$$

Thus $-\frac{1}{4}$ is an *extraneous solution*. Next substitute $x = 2$ in the given equation.

$$\sqrt{3 \cdot 2 + 3} \overset{?}{=} 2 \cdot 2 - 1$$
$$\sqrt{9} \overset{?}{=} 3$$
$$3 = 3 \qquad \text{It checks.}$$

The only solution is 2.

Graphical Solution The solution 2 is supported graphically in Figure 7.16, where the graphs of $Y_1 = \sqrt{(3X + 3)}$ and $Y_2 = 2X - 1$ intersect at the point (2, 3). *Note that the graphical solution does not give an extraneous solution.* Now Try Exercises 27, 79(a), (b)

Example 3 demonstrates that *checking a solution is essential when you are squaring each side of an equation*. Squaring may introduce extraneous solutions, which are solutions to the resulting equation but are not solutions to the given equation.

CRITICAL THINKING

Will a numerical solution give extraneous solutions?

When an equation contains two or more terms with square roots, it may be necessary to square each side of the equation more than once. In these situations, isolate one of the square roots and then square each side of the equation. If a radical term remains after simplifying, repeat these steps. We apply this technique in the next example.

$[-5, 5, 1]$ by $[-5, 5, 1]$

Intersection
X=2   Y=3

Figure 7.16

CALCULATOR HELP

To find a point of intersection, see the Appendix (page AP-7).

EXAMPLE 4 Squaring twice

Solve $\sqrt{2x} - 1 = \sqrt{x + 1}$.

Solution

Begin by squaring each side of the equation.

$$\sqrt{2x} - 1 = \sqrt{x + 1} \qquad \text{Given equation}$$

$$(\sqrt{2x} - 1)^2 = (\sqrt{x + 1})^2 \qquad \text{Square each side.}$$

$$(\sqrt{2x})^2 - 2(\sqrt{2x})(1) + 1^2 = x + 1 \qquad (a - b)^2 = a^2 - 2ab + b^2$$

$$2x - 2\sqrt{2x} + 1 = x + 1 \qquad \text{Simplify.}$$

$$2x - 2\sqrt{2x} = x \qquad \text{Subtract 1.}$$

$$x = 2\sqrt{2x} \qquad \text{Subtract } x \text{ and add } 2\sqrt{2x}.$$

$$x^2 = 4(2x) \qquad \text{Square each side again.}$$

$$x^2 - 8x = 0 \qquad \text{Subtract } 8x.$$

$$x(x - 8) = 0 \qquad \text{Factor.}$$

$$x = 0 \quad \text{or} \quad x = 8 \qquad \text{Solve.}$$

To check these answers substitute $x = 0$ and $x = 8$ in the given equation.

$$\sqrt{2 \cdot 0} - 1 \overset{?}{=} \sqrt{0 + 1} \qquad\qquad \sqrt{2 \cdot 8} - 1 \overset{?}{=} \sqrt{8 + 1}$$

$$-1 \neq 1 \quad \text{It does not check.} \qquad\qquad 3 = 3 \quad \text{It checks.}$$

The only solution is 8. Now Try Exercise 43

In the next example we apply the power rule to an equation that contains a cube root.

EXAMPLE 5 Solving an equation containing a cube root

Solve $\sqrt[3]{4x - 7} = 4$.

Solution

STEP 1: The cube root term is already isolated, so we proceed to Step 2.

STEP 2: Because the index is 3, we cube each side of the equation.

$$\sqrt[3]{4x - 7} = 4 \qquad \text{Given equation}$$

$$(\sqrt[3]{4x - 7})^3 = (4)^3 \qquad \text{Cube each side.}$$

STEP 3: We solve the resulting equation.

$$4x - 7 = 64 \qquad \text{Simplify.}$$

$$4x = 71 \qquad \text{Add 7 to each side.}$$

$$x = \frac{71}{4} \qquad \text{Divide each side by 4.}$$

STEP 4: To check this answer we substitute $x = \frac{71}{4}$ in the given equation.

$$\sqrt[3]{4\left(\frac{71}{4}\right) - 7} \overset{?}{=} 4$$

$$\sqrt[3]{64} \overset{?}{=} 4$$

$$4 = 4 \qquad \text{It checks.} \quad \text{Now Try Exercise 31}$$

▶ REAL-WORLD CONNECTION   In the next example we solve the equation presented in the introduction to this section that relates a bird's weight and wing surface area.

EXAMPLE 6   Finding the weight of a bird

Solve the equation $600 = 100\sqrt[3]{W^2}$ to determine the weight in pounds of a bird having wings with an area of 600 square inches.

Solution
Begin by dividing each side of the equation by 100 to isolate the radical term.

$$\frac{600}{100} = \sqrt[3]{W^2} \qquad \text{Divide each side by 100.}$$

$$(6)^3 = (\sqrt[3]{W^2})^3 \qquad \text{Cube each side.}$$

$$216 = W^2 \qquad \text{Simplify.}$$

$$\sqrt{216} = W \qquad \text{Take principal square root, } W > 0.$$

$$W \approx 14.7 \qquad \text{Approximate.}$$

The weight of the bird is approximately 14.7 pounds.   Now Try Exercise 117

TECHNOLOGY NOTE: Graphing Radical Expressions

The equation in Example 6 can be solved graphically. Sometimes it is more convenient to use rational exponents than radical notation. Thus $y = 100\sqrt[3]{W^2}$ can be entered as $Y_1 = 100X^{\wedge}(2/3)$. (Be sure to include parentheses around the 2/3.) The accompanying figure shows y_1 intersecting the line $y_2 = 600$ near the point $(14.7, 600)$, which supports our symbolic result.

[0, 20, 5] by [0, 800, 100]

In the next example we solve an equation that would be difficult to solve symbolically, but an *approximate* solution can be found graphically.

EXAMPLE 7   Solving an equation with rational exponents

Solve $x^{2/3} = 3 - x^2$ graphically.

Solution
Graph $Y_1 = X^{\wedge}(2/3)$ and $Y_2 = 3 - X^{\wedge}2$. Their graphs intersect near $(-1.34, 1.21)$ and $(1.34, 1.21)$, as shown in Figure 7.17. Thus the solutions are given by $x \approx \pm 1.34$.

$[-6, 6, 1]$ by $[-4, 4, 1]$ $[-6, 6, 1]$ by $[-4, 4, 1]$

(a)   (b)

Figure 7.17   Now Try Exercise 73

The Distance Formula

Figure 7.18
$a^2 + b^2 = c^2$

▶ REAL-WORLD CONNECTION   One of the most famous theorems in mathematics is the **Pythagorean theorem**. It states that if a right triangle has legs a and b with hypotenuse c (see Figure 7.18), then

$$a^2 + b^2 = c^2.$$

For example, if the legs of a right triangle are $a = 3$ and $b = 4$, the hypotenuse is $c = 5$ because $3^2 + 4^2 = 5^2$. Also, if the sides of a triangle satisfy $a^2 + b^2 = c^2$, it is a right triangle.

EXAMPLE 8   Applying the Pythagorean theorem

A rectangular television screen has a width of 20 inches and a height of 15 inches. Find the diagonal of the television. Why is it called a 25-inch television?

Figure 7.19

Solution
In Figure 7.19, let $a = 20$ and $b = 15$. Then the diagonal of the television corresponds to the hypotenuse of a right triangle with legs of 20 inches and 15 inches.

$$c^2 = a^2 + b^2 \qquad \text{Pythagorean theorem}$$
$$c = \sqrt{a^2 + b^2} \qquad \text{Take the principal square root, } c > 0.$$
$$c = \sqrt{20^2 + 15^2} \qquad \text{Substitute } a = 20 \text{ and } b = 15.$$
$$c = 25 \qquad \text{Simplify.}$$

A 25-inch television has a diagonal of 25 inches.   Now Try Exercise 123

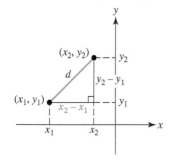

Figure 7.20

The Pythagorean theorem can be used to determine the distance between two points. Suppose that a line segment has endpoints (x_1, y_1) and (x_2, y_2), as illustrated in Figure 7.20. The lengths of the legs of the right triangle are $x_2 - x_1$ and $y_2 - y_1$. The distance d is the hypotenuse of a right triangle. Applying the Pythagorean theorem, we have

$$d^2 = (x_2 - x_1)^2 + (y_2 - y_1)^2.$$

Distance is nonnegative, so we let d be the principal square root and obtain

$$d = \sqrt{(x_2 - x_1)^2 + (y_2 - y_1)^2}.$$

DISTANCE FORMULA

The **distance** d between the points (x_1, y_1) and (x_2, y_2) in the xy-plane is
$$d = \sqrt{(x_2 - x_1)^2 + (y_2 - y_1)^2}.$$

EXAMPLE 9   Finding distance between points

Find the distance between the points $(-2, 3)$ and $(1, -4)$.

Figure 7.21

Solution
Start by letting $(x_1, y_1) = (-2, 3)$ and $(x_2, y_2) = (1, -4)$. Then substitute these values into the distance formula.

$$
\begin{aligned}
d &= \sqrt{(x_2 - x_1)^2 + (y_2 - y_1)^2} && \text{Distance formula} \\
&= \sqrt{(1 - (-2))^2 + (-4 - 3)^2} && \text{Substitute.} \\
&= \sqrt{9 + 49} && \text{Simplify.} \\
&= \sqrt{58} && \text{Add.} \\
&\approx 7.62 && \text{Approximate.}
\end{aligned}
$$

The distance between the points, as shown in Figure 7.21, is exactly $\sqrt{58}$ units, or about 7.62 units. Note that we would obtain the same result if we let $(x_1, y_1) = (1, -4)$ and $(x_2, y_2) = (-2, 3)$. ▸ Now Try Exercise **109**

NOTE: In Example 9, $\sqrt{9 + 49} \neq \sqrt{9} + \sqrt{49} = 3 + 7 = 10$. In general, for any a and b, $\sqrt{a^2 + b^2} \neq a + b$.

▶ **REAL-WORLD CONNECTION**   In the next example the distance formula is applied to road construction.

EXAMPLE 10 Designing a highway curve

Figure 7.22 shows a circular highway curve joining a straight section of road. A surveyor is trying to locate the x-coordinate of the *point of curvature PC* where the two sections of the highway meet. The distance between the surveyor and *PC* should be 400 feet. Estimate the x-coordinate of *PC* if x is positive.

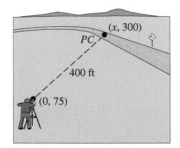

Figure 7.22

Solution
In Figure 7.22, the distance between the points $(0, 75)$ and $(x, 300)$ is 400 feet. We can apply the distance formula and solve for x.

$$
\begin{aligned}
d &= \sqrt{(x_2 - x_1)^2 + (y_2 - y_1)^2} && \text{Distance formula} \\
400 &= \sqrt{(x - 0)^2 + (300 - 75)^2} && \text{Substitute.} \\
400^2 &= (x - 0)^2 + (300 - 75)^2 && \text{Square each side.} \\
160{,}000 &= x^2 + 50{,}625 && \text{Simplify.} \\
x^2 &= 109{,}375 && \text{Solve for } x^2. \\
x &= \sqrt{109{,}375} && \text{Take the principal square root, } x > 0. \\
x &\approx 330.7 && \text{Approximate.}
\end{aligned}
$$

The x-coordinate is about 330.7.   ▸ Now Try Exercise **113**

Solving the Equation $x^n = k$

The equation $x^n = k$, where n is a *positive integer*, can be solved by taking the nth root of each side of the equation. The following technique allows us to find all *real* solutions to this equation.

SOLVING THE EQUATION $x^n = k$

Take the nth root of each side of $x^n = k$ to obtain $\sqrt[n]{x^n} = \sqrt[n]{k}$.

1. If n is odd, then $\sqrt[n]{x^n} = x$ and the equation becomes $x = \sqrt[n]{k}$.
2. If n is *even* and $k > 0$, then $\sqrt[n]{x^n} = |x|$ and the equation becomes $|x| = \sqrt[n]{k}$.
   (If $k < 0$, there are no real solutions.)

To understand this technique better, consider the following examples. First let $x^3 = 8$, so that n is odd. Taking the cube root of each side gives

$$\sqrt[3]{x^3} = \sqrt[3]{8}, \quad \text{which is equivalent to} \quad x = \sqrt[3]{8}, \quad \text{or} \quad x = 2.$$

Next let $x^2 = 4$, so that n is even. Taking the square root of each side gives

$$\sqrt{x^2} = \sqrt{4}, \quad \text{which is equivalent to} \quad |x| = \sqrt{4}, \quad \text{or} \quad |x| = 2.$$

The solutions to $|x| = 2$ are -2 or 2, which can be written ± 2.

EXAMPLE 11   Solving the equation $x^n = k$

Solve each equation.
(a) $x^3 = -64$ **(b)** $x^2 = 12$ **(c)** $2(x - 1)^4 = 32$

Solution
(a) Taking the cube root of each side of $x^3 = -64$ gives
$$\sqrt[3]{x^3} = \sqrt[3]{-64} \quad \text{or} \quad x = -4.$$

(b) Taking the square root of each side of $x^2 = 12$ gives
$$\sqrt{x^2} = \sqrt{12} \quad \text{or} \quad |x| = \sqrt{12}.$$
The equation $|x| = \sqrt{12}$ is equivalent to $x = \pm\sqrt{12}$.

(c) First divide each side of $2(x - 1)^4 = 32$ by 2 to isolate the power of $x - 1$.

$(x - 1)^4 = 16$	Divide each side by 2.
$\sqrt[4]{(x - 1)^4} = \sqrt[4]{16}$	Take the 4th root of each side.
$\|x - 1\| = 2$	Simplify: $\sqrt[4]{y^4} = \|y\|$.
$x - 1 = -2$ or $x - 1 = 2$	Solve the absolute value equation.
$x = -1$ or $x = 3$	Add 1 to each side.

Now Try Exercises **47, 55, 67**

▶ **REAL-WORLD CONNECTION**   In some parts of the United States, wind power is used to generate electricity. Suppose that the diameter of the circular path created by the blades of a wind-powered generator is 8 feet. Then the wattage W generated by a wind velocity of v miles per hour is modeled by

$$W(v) = 2.4v^3.$$

If the wind blows at 10 miles per hour, the generator can produce about

$$W(10) = 2.4 \cdot 10^3 = 2400 \text{ watts.}$$

(**Source:** *Conquering the Sciences*, Sharp Electronics.)

EXAMPLE 12   Modeling a wind generator

The formula $W(v) = 2.4v^3$ is used to calculate the watts generated when there is a wind velocity of v miles per hour.

(a) Find a function f that calculates the wind velocity when W watts are being produced.

(b) If the wattage doubles, has the wind velocity also doubled? Explain.

Solution

(a) Given W we need a formula to find v, so solve $W = 2.4v^3$ for v.

$$W = 2.4v^3 \qquad \text{Given formula}$$

$$\frac{W}{2.4} = v^3 \qquad \text{Divide by 2.4.}$$

$$\sqrt[3]{\frac{W}{2.4}} = \sqrt[3]{v^3} \qquad \text{Take the cube root of each side.}$$

$$v = \sqrt[3]{\frac{W}{2.4}} \qquad \text{Simplify and rewrite equation.}$$

Thus $f(W) = \sqrt[3]{\frac{W}{2.4}}$.

(b) Suppose that the power generated is 1000 watts. Then the wind speed is

$$f(1000) = \sqrt[3]{\frac{1000}{2.4}} \approx 7.5 \text{ miles per hour.}$$

If the power doubles to 2000 watts, then the wind speed is

$$f(2000) = \sqrt[3]{\frac{2000}{2.4}} \approx 9.4 \text{ miles per hour.}$$

Thus for the wattage to double, the wind speed does not need to double.

Now Try Exercise 131

7.5 PUTTING IT ALL TOGETHER

In this section we focused on equations that contain either radical expressions or rational exponents. A good strategy for solving an equation containing radical expressions *symbolically* is to raise each side of the equation to the same positive integer power. However, checking answers is important to eliminate extraneous solutions. Note that these extraneous solutions do not occur when an equation is being solved graphically or numerically.

Concept	Description	Example
Power Rule for Solving Equations	If each side of an equation is raised to the same positive integer power, any solutions to the given equation are among the solutions to the new equation.	$\sqrt{2x} = x$ $2x = x^2$ Square each side. $x^2 - 2x = 0$ Rewrite equation. $x = 0$ or $x = 2$ Factor and solve. Be sure to check any solutions.

continued on next page

continued from previous page

Concept	Description	Example
Pythagorean Theorem	If c is the hypotenuse of a right triangle and a and b are its legs, then $a^2 + b^2 = c^2$.	If the sides of the right triangle are $a = 5$, $b = 12$, and $c = 13$, then they satisfy $a^2 + b^2 = c^2$ or $5^2 + 12^2 = 13^2$. ![right triangle with sides 13, 5, 12]
Distance Formula	The distance d between the points (x_1, y_1) and (x_2, y_2) is $$d = \sqrt{(x_2 - x_1)^2 + (y_2 - y_1)^2}.$$	The distance between the points $(2, 3)$ and $(-3, 4)$ is $$d = \sqrt{(-3 - 2)^2 + (4 - 3)^2}$$ $$= \sqrt{(-5)^2 + (1)^2} = \sqrt{26}.$$
Solving the Equation $x^n = k$, Where n Is a Positive Integer	Take the nth root of each side to obtain $\sqrt[n]{x^n} = \sqrt[n]{k}$. Then, **1.** $x = \sqrt[n]{k}$, if n is odd. **2.** $x = \pm \sqrt[n]{k}$, if n is even and $k \geq 0$.	**1.** n odd: If $x^5 = 32$, then $x = \sqrt[5]{32} = 2$. **2.** n even: If $x^4 = 81$, then $x = \pm \sqrt[4]{81} = \pm 3$.

Equations involving radical expressions can be solved symbolically, numerically, and graphically. All symbolic solutions must be checked; *numerical and graphical methods do not give extraneous solutions*. These concepts are illustrated for the equation $\sqrt{x + 2} = x$, where $Y_1 = \sqrt{(X + 2)}$ and $Y_2 = X$.

Symbolic Solution

$$\sqrt{x + 2} = x$$
$$x + 2 = x^2$$
$$x^2 - x - 2 = 0$$
$$(x - 2)(x + 1) = 0$$
$$x = 2 \text{ or } x = -1$$

Check: $\sqrt{2 + 2} = 2$
$$\sqrt{-1 + 2} \neq -1$$

The only solution is 2.

Numerical Solution

X	Y₁	Y₂
-2	0	-2
-1	1	-1
0	1.4142	0
1	1.7321	1
2	2	2
3	2.2361	3
4	2.4495	4

X=2

$y_1 = y_2$ when $x = 2$, so 2 is a solution. Note that -1 is *not* a solution.

Graphical Solution

$[-4.7, 4.7, 1]$ by $[-3.1, 3.1, 1]$

Intersection
X=2   Y=2

The graphs intersect at $(2, 2)$. Note that there is no point of intersection when $x = -1$.

7.5 Exercises

MyMathLab   PRACTICE WATCH DOWNLOAD READ REVIEW

CONCEPTS

1. What is a good first step for solving $\sqrt{4x - 1} = 5$?

2. What is a good first step for solving $\sqrt[3]{x + 1} = 6$?

3. Can an equation involving rational exponents have more than one solution?

4. When you square each side of an equation to solve for an unknown, what must you do with any answers?

5. What is the Pythagorean theorem used for?

6. If the legs of a right triangle are 3 and 4, what is the length of the hypotenuse?

7. What formula can you use to find the distance d between two points?

8. Write the equation $\sqrt{x} + \sqrt[4]{x^3} = 2$ with rational exponents.

SIMPLIFYING RADICALS

Exercises 9–16: Simplify. Assume radicands of square roots are positive.

9. $\sqrt{2} \cdot \sqrt{2}$

10. $\sqrt{5} \cdot \sqrt{5}$

11. $\sqrt{x} \cdot \sqrt{x}$

12. $\sqrt{2x} \cdot \sqrt{2x}$

13. $(\sqrt{2x + 1})^2$

14. $(\sqrt{7x})^2$

15. $(\sqrt[3]{5x^2})^3$

16. $(\sqrt[3]{2x - 5})^3$

SYMBOLIC SOLUTIONS

Exercises 17–46: Solve the equation symbolically. Check your results.

17. $\sqrt{x} = 8$

18. $\sqrt{3z} = 6$

19. $\sqrt[4]{x} = 3$

20. $\sqrt[3]{x - 4} = 2$

21. $\sqrt{2t + 4} = 4$

22. $\sqrt{y + 4} = 3$

23. $\sqrt{x + 1} - 3 = 4$

24. $\sqrt{2x + 5} + 2 = 5$

25. $2\sqrt{x - 2} + 1 = 5$

26. $-\sqrt{x + 7} - 1 = -7$

27. $\sqrt{x + 6} = x$

28. $\sqrt{z + 6} = z$

29. $\sqrt[3]{x} = 3$

30. $\sqrt[3]{x + 10} = 4$

31. $\sqrt[3]{2z - 4} = -2$

32. $\sqrt[3]{z - 1} = -3$

33. $\sqrt[4]{t + 1} = 2$

34. $\sqrt[4]{5t} = 5$

35. $\sqrt{5z - 1} = \sqrt{z + 1}$

36. $y = \sqrt{y + 1} + 1$

37. $\sqrt{1 - x} = 1 - x$

38. $\sqrt[3]{4x} = x$

39. $\sqrt{b^2 - 4} = b - 2$

40. $\sqrt{b^2 - 2b + 1} = b$

41. $\sqrt{1 - 2x} = x + 7$

42. $\sqrt{4 - y} = y - 2$

43. $\sqrt{x} = \sqrt{x - 5} + 1$

44. $\sqrt{x - 1} = \sqrt{x + 4} - 1$

45. $\sqrt{2t - 2} + \sqrt{t} = 7$

46. $\sqrt{x + 1} - \sqrt{x - 6} = 1$

SOLVING THE EQUATION $x^n = k$

Exercises 47–68: (Refer to Example 11.) Solve.

47. $x^2 = 49$

48. $x^2 = 9$

49. $2z^2 = 200$

50. $3z^2 = 48$

51. $(t + 1)^2 = 16$

52. $(t - 5)^2 = 81$

53. $(4 - 2x)^2 = 100$

54. $(3x - 6)^2 = 25$

55. $b^3 = 64$

56. $a^3 = 1000$

57. $2t^3 = -128$

58. $3t^3 = -81$

59. $(x + 1)^3 = 8$

60. $(4 - x)^3 = -1$

61. $(2 - 5z)^3 = -125$

62. $(2x + 4)^3 = 125$

63. $x^4 = 16$

64. $x^4 = 7$

65. $x^5 = 12$

66. $x^5 = -32$

67. $2(x + 2)^4 = 162$

68. $\frac{1}{2}(x - 1)^5 = 16$

GRAPHICAL SOLUTIONS

Exercises 69–78: Solve graphically. Approximate solutions to the nearest hundredth when appropriate.

69. $\sqrt[3]{x + 5} = 2$

70. $\sqrt[3]{x} + \sqrt{x} = 3.43$

71. $\sqrt{2x - 3} = \sqrt{x} - \frac{1}{2}$

72. $x^{4/3} - 1 = 2$

73. $x^{5/3} = 2 - 3x^2$ **74.** $x^{3/2} = \sqrt{x + 2} - 2$

75. $z^{1/3} - 1 = 2 - z$ **76.** $z^{3/2} - 2z^{1/2} - 1 = 0$

77. $\sqrt{y + 2} + \sqrt{3y + 2} = 2$

78. $\sqrt{x + 1} - \sqrt{x - 1} = 4$

USING MORE THAN ONE METHOD

Exercises 79–82: Solve the equation
   (a) symbolically,
   (b) graphically, and
   (c) numerically.

79. $2\sqrt{x} = 8$ **80.** $\sqrt[3]{5 - x} = 2$

81. $\sqrt{6z - 2} = 8$ **82.** $\sqrt{y + 4} = \dfrac{y}{3}$

SOLVING AN EQUATION FOR A VARIABLE

Exercises 83–86: Solve for the indicated variable.

83. $T = 2\pi\sqrt{\dfrac{L}{32}}$ for L

84. $Z = \sqrt{L^2 + R^2}$ for R

85. $r = \sqrt{\dfrac{A}{\pi}}$ for A

86. $F = \dfrac{1}{2\pi\sqrt{LC}}$ for C

PYTHAGOREAN THEOREM

Exercises 87–94: If the sides of a triangle are a, b, and c and they satisfy $a^2 + b^2 = c^2$, the triangle is a right triangle. Determine whether the triangle with the given sides is a right triangle.

87. $a = 6$ $b = 8$ $c = 10$

88. $a = 5$ $b = 12$ $c = 13$

89. $a = \sqrt{5}$ $b = \sqrt{9}$ $c = \sqrt{14}$

90. $a = 4$ $b = 5$ $c = 7$

91. $a = 7$ $b = 24$ $c = 25$

92. $a = 1$ $b = \sqrt{3}$ $c = 2$

93. $a = 8$ $b = 8$ $c = 16$

94. $a = 11$ $b = 60$ $c = 61$

Exercises 95–98: Find the length of the missing side in the right triangle.

95.

96.

97.

98.

Exercises 99–104: A right triangle has legs a and b with hypotenuse c. Find the length of the missing side.

99. $a = 3, b = 4$ **100.** $a = 4, b = 7$

101. $a = \sqrt{3}, c = 8$ **102.** $a = \sqrt{6}, c = \sqrt{10}$

103. $b = 48, c = 50$ **104.** $b = 10, c = 26$

DISTANCE FORMULA

Exercises 105–108: Find the length of the line segment.

105.

106.

107.

108.

Exercises 109–112: Find the distance between the points.

109. $(-1, 2), (4, 10)$ **110.** $(5, -40), (-6, 20)$

111. $(0, -3), (4, 0)$ **112.** $(3, 9), (-4, 2)$

Exercises 113–116: (Refer to Example 10.) Find x if the distance between the points is d. Assume that $x \geq 0$.

113. $(x, 3), (0, 6)$ $d = 5$

114. $(x, -1), (6, 11)$ $d = 13$

115. $(x, -5), (62, 6)$ $d = 61$

116. $(x, 3), (12, -4)$ $d = 25$

APPLICATIONS

Exercises 117 and 118: **Weight of a Bird** *(Refer to Example 6.) Estimate the weight W of a bird having wings of area A. Let $A = 100\sqrt[3]{W^2}$.*

117. $A = 400$ square inches

118. $A = 1000$ square inches

Exercises 119–122: **Distance to the Horizon** *Because of Earth's curvature, a person can see a limited distance to the horizon. The higher the location of the person, the farther that person can see. The distance D in miles to the horizon can be estimated by $D(h) = 1.22\sqrt{h}$, where h is the height of the person above the ground in feet.*

119. Find D for a 6-foot-tall person standing on level ground.

120. Find D for a person on top of Mount Everest with a height of 29,028 feet.

121. How high does a person need to be to see 20 miles?

122. How high does a plane need to fly for the pilot to be able to see 100 miles?

123. *Diagonal of a Television*   (Refer to Example 8.) A rectangular television screen is 11.4 inches by 15.2 inches. Find the diagonal of the television set.

124. *Dimensions of a Television*   The height of a television with a 13-inch diagonal is $\frac{3}{4}$ of its width. Find the width and height of the television set.

125. *DVD and Picture Dimensions*   If the picture shown on a television set is h units high and w units wide, the *aspect ratio* of the picture is $\frac{w}{h}$ (see the accompanying figure). Digital video discs support the newer aspect ratio of $\frac{16}{9}$ rather than the older ratio of $\frac{4}{3}$. If the width of a picture with an aspect ratio of $\frac{16}{9}$ is 29 inches, approximate the height and diagonal of the rectangular picture. (*Source:* J. Taylor, *DVD Demystified.*)

126. *Flood Control*   The spillway capacity of a dam is important in flood control. Spillway capacity Q in cubic feet of water per second flowing over the spillway depends on the width W and the depth D of the spillway, as illustrated in the accompanying figure. If W and D are measured in feet, capacity can be modeled by $Q = 3.32WD^{3/2}$.   (*Source:* D. Callas, Project Director, *Snapshots of Applications in Mathematics.*)

    (a) Find the capacity of a spillway with $W = 20$ feet and $D = 5$ feet.

    (b) A spillway with a width of 30 feet is to have a capacity of $Q = 2690$ cubic feet per second. Estimate to the nearest foot the appropriate depth of the spillway.

127. *Sky Diving*   When sky divers initially fall from an airplane, their velocity v in miles per hour after free falling d feet can be approximated by $v = \frac{60}{11}\sqrt{d}$. (Because of air resistance, they will eventually reach a terminal velocity.) How far do sky divers need to fall to attain the following velocities? (These values for d represent minimum distances.)

   (a) 60 miles per hour   **(b)** 100 miles per hour

128. *Guy Wire*   A guy wire attached to the top of a 30-foot-long pole is anchored 10 feet from the base of the pole, as illustrated in the figure. Find the length of the guy wire to the nearest tenth of a foot.

129. *Skid Marks*   Vehicles involved in accidents often leave skid marks, which can be used to determine how fast a vehicle was traveling. To determine this speed, officials often use a test vehicle to compare skid marks on the same section of road. Suppose that a vehicle in a crash left skid marks D feet long and that a test vehicle traveling at v miles per hour leaves skid marks d feet long. Then the speed V of the vehicle involved in the crash is given by

$$V = v\sqrt{\frac{D}{d}}.$$

(*Source:* N. Garber and L. Hoel, *Traffic and Highway Engineering.*)

   (a) Find V if $v = 30$ mph, $D = 285$ feet, and $d = 178$ feet. Interpret your result.

   (b) A test vehicle traveling at 45 mph leaves skid marks 255 feet long. How long would the skid marks be for a vehicle traveling 60 miles per hour?

130. *Highway Curves*   If a circular curve without any banking has a radius of R feet, the speed limit L in miles per hour for the curve is $L = 1.5\sqrt{R}$. (*Source:* N. Garber.)

   (a) Find the speed limit for a curve having a radius of 400 feet.

   (b) If the radius of a curve doubles, what happens to the speed limit?

   (c) A curve with a 40-mile-per-hour speed limit is being designed. What should be its radius?

131. *Wind Power*   (Refer to Example 12.) If a wind-powered generator has blades that create a circular path with a diameter of 10 feet, then the wattage W generated by a wind velocity of v miles per hour is modeled by $W(v) = 3.8v^3$.

   (a) If the wind velocity doubles, what happens to the wattage generated?

   (b) Solve $W = 3.8v^3$ for v.

   (c) If the wind generator is producing 30,400 watts, find the wind speed.

132. *Height and Weight*   Suppose that the weight of a person is directly proportional to the cube of the person's height. If one person weighs twice as much as a (similarly proportioned) second person, by what factor is the heavier person's height greater than the shorter person's height?

133. *45°–45° Right Triangle*   Suppose that the legs of a right triangle with angles of 45° and 45° both have length a, as depicted in the accompanying figure. Find the length of the hypotenuse.

134. *30°–60° Right Triangle*   In a right triangle with angles of 30° and 60°, the shortest side is half the length of the hypotenuse (see the accompanying figure). If the hypotenuse has length c, find the length of the other two sides, a and b, in terms of c.

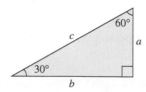

WRITING ABOUT MATHEMATICS

135. A student solves an equation *incorrectly* as follows.

$$\sqrt{3 - x} = \sqrt{x} - 1$$
$$(\sqrt{3 - x})^2 \overset{?}{=} (\sqrt{x})^2 - (1)^2$$
$$3 - x \overset{?}{=} x - 1$$
$$-2x \overset{?}{=} -4$$
$$x \overset{?}{=} 2$$

(a) How could you convince the student that the answer is wrong?

(b) Discuss where any errors were made.

136. When each side of an equation is squared, you must check your results. Explain why.

GROUP ACTIVITY
WORKING WITH REAL DATA

Directions: Form a group of 2 to 4 people. Select someone to record the group's responses for this activity. All members of the group should work cooperatively to answer the questions. If your instructor asks for your results, each member of the group should be prepared to respond.

Simple Pendulum Gravity is responsible for an object falling toward Earth. The farther the object falls, the faster it is moving when it hits the ground. For each second that an object falls, its speed increases by a constant amount, called the *acceleration due to gravity*, denoted g. One way to calculate the value of g is to use a simple pendulum. See the accompanying figure.

The time T for a pendulum to swing back and forth once is called its *period* and is given by

$$T = 2\pi\sqrt{\frac{L}{g}},$$

where L equals the length of the pendulum. The table lists the periods of pendulums with different lengths.

L (feet)	0.5	1.0	1.5
T (seconds)	0.78	1.11	1.36

(a) Solve the formula for g.
(b) Use the table to determine the value of g. (*Note:* The units for g are feet per second per second.)
(c) Interpret your result.

7.6 COMPLEX NUMBERS

Basic Concepts ▪ Addition, Subtraction, and Multiplication ▪ Powers of i ▪ Complex Conjugates and Division

A LOOK INTO MATH ▷

Mathematics is both applied and theoretical. A common misconception is that abstract or theoretical mathematics is unimportant in today's world. Many new ideas with great practical importance were first developed as abstract concepts with no particular application in mind. For example, complex numbers, which are related to square roots of negative numbers, started as an abstract concept to solve equations. Today complex numbers are used in many sophisticated applications, such as the design of electrical circuits, ships, and airplanes. Even the *fractal image* shown to the left would not have been discovered without complex numbers.

Basic Concepts

Figure 7.23

A graph of $y = x^2 + 1$ is shown in Figure 7.23. There are no x-intercepts, so the equation $x^2 + 1 = 0$ has no real number solutions.

If we try to solve $x^2 + 1 = 0$ by subtracting 1 from each side, the result is $x^2 = -1$. Because $x^2 \geq 0$ for any real number x, there are no real solutions. However, mathematicians have invented solutions.

$$x^2 = -1$$
$$x = \pm\sqrt{-1} \quad \text{Solve for } x.$$

We now define a number called the **imaginary unit**, denoted i.

PROPERTIES OF THE IMAGINARY UNIT i

$$i = \sqrt{-1} \quad \text{and} \quad i^2 = -1$$

By creating the number i, the solutions to the equation $x^2 + 1 = 0$ are i and $-i$. Using the real numbers and the imaginary unit i, we can define a new set of numbers called the *complex numbers*. A **complex number** can be written in **standard form**, as $a + bi$, where a and b are real numbers. The **real part** is a and the **imaginary part** is b. Every real number a is also a complex number because it can be written $a + 0i$. A complex number $a + bi$ with $b \neq 0$ is an **imaginary number**. A complex number $a + bi$ with $a = 0$ and $b \neq 0$ is sometimes called a **pure imaginary number**. Examples include $4i$ and $-2i$. Table 7.8 lists several complex numbers with their real and imaginary parts.

TABLE 7.8

Complex Number: $a + bi$	$-3 + 2i$	5	$-3i$	$-1 + 7i$	$-5 - 2i$	$4 + 6i$
Real Part: a	-3	5	0	-1	-5	4
Imaginary Part: b	2	0	-3	7	-2	6

Figure 7.24 shows how different sets of numbers are related. Note that *the set of complex numbers contains the set of real numbers.*

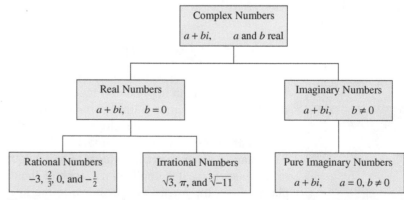

Figure 7.24

Using the imaginary unit i, we may write the square root of a negative number as a complex number. For example, $\sqrt{-2} = i\sqrt{2}$, and $\sqrt{-4} = i\sqrt{4} = 2i$. This method is summarized as follows.

THE EXPRESSION $\sqrt{-a}$

If $a > 0$, then $\sqrt{-a} = i\sqrt{a}$.

NOTE: Although it is standard for a complex number to be expressed as $a + bi$, we often write $\sqrt{2}i$ as $i\sqrt{2}$ so that it is clear that i is *not under the square root*. Similarly $\frac{1}{2}\sqrt{2}i$ is sometimes written $\frac{1}{2}i\sqrt{2}$ or $\frac{i\sqrt{2}}{2}$.

EXAMPLE 1 Writing the square root of a negative number

Write each square root using the imaginary unit i.

(a) $\sqrt{-25}$ **(b)** $\sqrt{-7}$ **(c)** $\sqrt{-20}$

Solution
(a) $\sqrt{-25} = i\sqrt{25} = 5i$ **(b)** $\sqrt{-7} = i\sqrt{7}$
(c) $\sqrt{-20} = i\sqrt{20} = i\sqrt{4}\sqrt{5} = 2i\sqrt{5}$

Now Try Exercises 13, 15, 19

Addition, Subtraction, and Multiplication

Addition can be defined for complex numbers in a similar manner to how we add binomials. For example,

$$(-3 + 2x) + (2 - x) = (-3 + 2) + (2x - x) = -1 + x.$$

ADDITION AND SUBTRACTION To add the complex numbers $(-3 + 2i)$ and $(2 - i)$ add the real parts and then add the imaginary parts.

$$(-3 + 2i) + (2 - i) = (-3 + 2) + (2i - i)$$
$$= (-3 + 2) + (2 - 1)i$$
$$= -1 + i$$

This same process works for subtraction.

$$(6 - 3i) - (2 + 5i) = (6 - 2) + (-3i - 5i)$$
$$= (6 - 2) + (-3 - 5)i$$
$$= 4 - 8i$$

This method is summarized as follows.

SUM OR DIFFERENCE OF COMPLEX NUMBERS

Let $a + bi$ and $c + di$ be two complex numbers. Then

$$(a + bi) + (c + di) = (a + c) + (b + d)i \quad \text{Sum}$$

and $\qquad (a + bi) - (c + di) = (a - c) + (b - d)i.$ Difference

EXAMPLE **2**   Adding and subtracting complex numbers

Write each sum or difference in standard form.
(a) $(-7 + 2i) + (3 - 4i)$ **(b)** $3i - (5 - i)$

Solution
(a) $(-7 + 2i) + (3 - 4i) = (-7 + 3) + (2 - 4)i = -4 - 2i$
(b) $3i - (5 - i) = 3i - 5 + i = -5 + (3 + 1)i = -5 + 4i$

Now Try Exercises 23, 29

TECHNOLOGY NOTE: Complex Numbers

Many calculators can perform arithmetic with complex numbers. The figure shows a calculator display for the results in Example 2.

CALCULATOR HELP

To access the imaginary unit i, see the Appendix (page AP-11).

```
(-7+2i)+(3-4i)
                -4-2i
3i-(5-i)
                -5+4i
```

MULTIPLICATION   We multiply two complex numbers in the same way that we multiply binomials and then we apply the property $i^2 = -1$. For example,

$$(2 - 3x)(1 + 4x) = 2 + 8x - 3x - 12x^2 = 2 + 5x - 12x^2.$$

In the next example we find the product of $2 - 3i$ and $1 + 4i$ in a similar manner.

EXAMPLE **3**   Multiplying complex numbers

Write each product in standard form.
(a) $(2 - 3i)(1 + 4i)$ **(b)** $(5 - 2i)(5 + 2i)$

Solution
(a) Multiply the complex numbers like binomials.

$$(2 - 3i)(1 + 4i) = (2)(1) + (2)(4i) - (3i)(1) - (3i)(4i)$$
$$= 2 + 8i - 3i - 12i^2$$
$$= 2 + 5i - 12(-1)$$
$$= 14 + 5i$$

```
(2-3i)(1+4i)
              14+5i
(5-2i)(5+2i)
                 29
```

(b) $$(5 - 2i)(5 + 2i) = (5)(5) + (5)(2i) - (2i)(5) - (2i)(2i)$$
$$= 25 + 10i - 10i - 4i^2$$
$$= 25 - 4(-1)$$
$$= 29$$

Figure 7.25

These results are supported in Figure 7.25.

Now Try Exercises 31, 35

Powers of i

An interesting pattern appears when powers of i are calculated.

$$i^1 = i$$
$$i^2 = -1$$
$$i^3 = i^2 \cdot i = -1 \cdot i = -i$$
$$i^4 = i^2 \cdot i^2 = (-1)(-1) = 1$$
$$i^5 = i^4 \cdot i = (1)i = i$$
$$i^6 = i^4 \cdot i^2 = (1)(-1) = -1$$
$$i^7 = i^4 \cdot i^3 = (1)(-i) = -i$$
$$i^8 = i^4 \cdot i^4 = (1)(1) = 1$$

The powers of i cycle with the pattern i, -1, $-i$, and 1. These examples suggest the following method for calculating powers of i.

POWERS OF i

The value of i^n can be found by dividing n (a positive integer) by 4. If the remainder is r, then

$$i^n = i^r.$$

Note that $i^0 = 1$, $i^1 = i$, $i^2 = -1$, and $i^3 = -i$.

EXAMPLE 4 Calculating powers of i

Evaluate each expression.
(a) i^9 **(b)** i^{19} **(c)** i^{40}

Solution
(a) When 9 is divided by 4, the result is 2 with remainder 1. Thus $i^9 = i^1 = i$.
(b) When 19 is divided by 4, the result is 4 with remainder 3. Thus $i^{19} = i^3 = -i$.
(c) When 40 is divided by 4, the result is 10 with remainder 0. Thus $i^{40} = i^0 = 1$.

Now Try Exercises 49, 51, 55

Complex Conjugates and Division

The **complex conjugate** of $a + bi$ is $a - bi$. To find the conjugate, we change the sign of the imaginary part b. Table 7.9 contains some complex numbers and their conjugates.

TABLE 7.9 **Complex Conjugates**

Number	$2 + 5i$	$6 - 3i$	$-2 + 7i$	$-1 - i$	5	$-4i$
Conjugate	$2 - 5i$	$6 + 3i$	$-2 - 7i$	$-1 + i$	5	$4i$

NOTE: The product of a complex number and its conjugate is a real number. That is,

$$(a + bi)(a - bi) = a^2 + b^2.$$

For example, $(3 + 4i)(3 - 4i) = 3^2 + 4^2 = 25$, which is a real number.

This property of complex conjugates is used to divide two complex numbers. To convert the quotient $\frac{2 + 3i}{3 - i}$ into standard form $a + bi$, we multiply the numerator and the denominator by the complex conjugate of the *denominator*, which is $3 + i$. The next example illustrates this method.

EXAMPLE 5   Dividing complex numbers

Write each quotient in standard form.

(a) $\dfrac{2 + 3i}{3 - i}$ (b) $\dfrac{4}{2i}$

Solution
(a) Multiply the numerator and denominator by $3 + i$.

$$\dfrac{2 + 3i}{3 - i} = \dfrac{(2 + 3i)(3 + i)}{(3 - i)(3 + i)} \qquad \text{Multiply by 1.}$$

$$= \dfrac{2(3) + (2)(i) + (3i)(3) + (3i)(i)}{(3)(3) + (3)(i) - (i)(3) - (i)(i)} \qquad \text{Multiply.}$$

$$= \dfrac{6 + 2i + 9i + 3i^2}{9 + 3i - 3i - i^2} \qquad \text{Simplify.}$$

$$= \dfrac{6 + 11i + 3(-1)}{9 - (-1)} \qquad i^2 = -1$$

$$= \dfrac{3 + 11i}{10} \qquad \text{Simplify.}$$

$$= \dfrac{3}{10} + \dfrac{11}{10}i \qquad \frac{a + bi}{c} = \frac{a}{c} + \frac{b}{c}i$$

(b) Multiply the numerator and denominator by $-2i$.

$$\dfrac{4}{2i} = \dfrac{(4)(-2i)}{(2i)(-2i)} \qquad \text{Multiply by 1.}$$

$$= \dfrac{-8i}{-4i^2} \qquad \text{Simplify.}$$

$$= \dfrac{-8i}{-4(-1)} \qquad i^2 = -1$$

$$= \dfrac{-8i}{4} \qquad \text{Simplify.}$$

$$= -2i \qquad \text{Divide.}$$

```
(2+3i)/(3-i)▶Fra
c
         3/10+11/10i
4/(2i)
              -2i
```

Figure 7.26

These results are supported in Figure 7.26.

Now Try Exercises 71, 73

7.6 PUTTING IT ALL TOGETHER

In this section we discussed complex numbers and how to perform arithmetic operations with them. Complex numbers allow us to solve equations that could not be solved only with real numbers. The following table summarizes the important concepts in the section.

Concept	Explanation	Examples
Complex Numbers	A complex number can be expressed as $a + bi$, where a and b are real numbers. The imaginary unit i satisfies $i = \sqrt{-1}$ and $i^2 = -1$. As a result, we can write $\sqrt{-a} = i\sqrt{a}$ if $a > 0$.	The real part of $5 - 3i$ is 5 and the imaginary part is -3. $$\sqrt{-13} = i\sqrt{13} \quad \text{and} \quad \sqrt{-9} = 3i$$
Addition, Subtraction, and Multiplication	To add (subtract) complex numbers, add (subtract) the real parts and then add (subtract) the imaginary parts. Multiply complex numbers in a similar manner to how *FOIL* is used to multiply binomials. Then apply the property $i^2 = -1$.	$(3 + 6i) + (-1 + 2i)$ Sum $\quad = (3 + -1) + (6 + 2)i$ $\quad = 2 + 8i$ $(2 - 5i) - (1 + 4i)$ Difference $\quad = (2 - 1) + (-5 - 4)i$ $\quad = 1 - 9i$ $(-1 + 2i)(3 + i)$ Product $\quad = (-1)(3) + (-1)(i) + (2i)(3) + (2i)(i)$ $\quad = -3 - i + 6i + 2i^2$ $\quad = -3 + 5i + 2(-1)$ $\quad = -5 + 5i$
Complex Conjugates	The conjugate of $a + bi$ is $a - bi$.	The conjugate of $3 - 5i$ is $3 + 5i$. The conjugate of $2i$ is $-2i$.
Division	To simplify a quotient, multiply the numerator and denominator by the complex conjugate of the *denominator*. Then simplify the expression and write it in standard form as $a + bi$.	$\dfrac{10}{1 + 2i} = \dfrac{10(1 - 2i)}{(1 + 2i)(1 - 2i)}$ Quotient $\quad = \dfrac{10 - 20i}{5}$ $\quad = 2 - 4i$

7.6 Exercises

MyMathLab | Math XL PRACTICE WATCH DOWNLOAD READ REVIEW

CONCEPTS

1. Give an example of a complex number that is not a real number.

2. Can you give an example of a real number that is not a complex number? Explain.

3. $\sqrt{-1} =$ _____

4. $i^2 =$ _____

5. $\sqrt{-a} =$ _____, if $a > 0$.

6. The complex conjugate of $10 + 7i$ is _____.

7. The standard form for a complex number is _____.

8. Write $\frac{2 + 4i}{2}$ in standard form.

9. The real part of $4 - 5i$ is _____.

10. The imaginary part of $4 - 5i$ is _____.

11. The imaginary part of -7 is _____.

12. The number $7i$ is called a(n) _____ imaginary number.

COMPLEX NUMBERS

Exercises 13–22: Use i to write the expression.

13. $\sqrt{-5}$

14. $\sqrt{-21}$

15. $\sqrt{-100}$

16. $\sqrt{-49}$

17. $\sqrt{-144}$

18. $\sqrt{-64}$

19. $\sqrt{-12}$

20. $\sqrt{-8}$

21. $\sqrt{-18}$

22. $\sqrt{-48}$

Exercises 23–46: Write the expression in standard form.

23. $(5 + 3i) + (-2 - 3i)$

24. $(1 - i) + (5 - 7i)$

25. $2i + (-8 + 5i)$

26. $-3i + 5i$

27. $(2 - 7i) - (1 + 2i)$

28. $(1 + 8i) - (3 + 9i)$

29. $5i - (10 - 2i)$

30. $-3(4 - 3i)$

31. $(3 + 2i)(-1 + 5i)$

32. $(1 + i) - (1 - i)$

33. $4(5 - 3i)$

34. $(1 + 2i)(-6 - i)$

35. $(5 + 4i)(5 - 4i)$

36. $(3 + 5i)(3 - 5i)$

37. $(-4i)(5i)$

38. $(-6i)(-4i)$

39. $3i + (2 - 3i) - (1 - 5i)$

40. $4 - (5 - 7i) + (3 + 7i)$

41. $(2 + i)^2$

42. $(-1 + 2i)^2$

43. $2i(-3 + i)$

44. $5i(1 - 9i)$

45. $i(1 + i)^2$

46. $2i(1 - i)^2$

Exercises 47 and 48: **Thinking Generally**   *Write in standard form.*

47. $(a + 3bi)(a - 3bi)$

48. $(a + bi) - (a - bi)$

Exercises 49–56: (Refer to Example 4.) Simplify.

49. i^{11}

50. i^{50}

51. i^{21}

52. i^{103}

53. i^{58}

54. i^{61}

55. i^{64}

56. i^{28}

Exercises 57–64: Write the complex conjugate.

57. $3 + 4i$

58. $1 - 4i$

59. $-6i$

60. -10

61. $5 - 4i$

62. $7 + 2i$

63. -1

64. $19i$

Exercises 65–78: Write the expression in standard form.

65. $\dfrac{2}{1 + i}$

66. $\dfrac{-6}{2 - i}$

67. $\dfrac{3i}{5 - 2i}$

68. $\dfrac{-8}{2i}$

69. $\dfrac{8 + 9i}{5 + 2i}$

70. $\dfrac{3 - 2i}{1 + 4i}$

71. $\dfrac{5 + 7i}{1 - i}$

72. $\dfrac{-7 + 4i}{3 - 2i}$

73. $\dfrac{2 - i}{i}$ **74.** $\dfrac{3 + 2i}{-i}$

75. $\dfrac{1}{i} + \dfrac{1}{2i}$ **76.** $\dfrac{3}{4i} + \dfrac{2}{i}$

77. $\dfrac{1}{-1 + i} - \dfrac{2}{i}$ **78.** $-\dfrac{3}{2i} - \dfrac{2}{1 + i}$

APPLICATIONS

Exercises 79 and 80: Corrosion in Airplanes Corrosion in the metal surface of an airplane can be difficult to detect visually. One test used to locate it involves passing an alternating current through a small area on the plane's surface. If the current varies from one region to another, it may indicate that corrosion is occurring. The impedance Z (or opposition to the flow of electricity) of the metal is related to the voltage V and current I by the equation $Z = \dfrac{V}{I}$, where Z, V, and I are complex numbers. Calculate Z for the given values of V and I. (*Source:* Society for Industrial and Applied Mathematics.)

79. $V = 40 + 70i, I = 2 + 3i$

80. $V = 10 + 20i, I = 3 + 7i$

WRITING ABOUT MATHEMATICS

81. A student multiplies $(2 + 3i)(4 - 5i)$ *incorrectly* to obtain $8 - 15i$. What is the student's mistake?

82. A student divides $\dfrac{6 - 10i}{3 + 2i}$ *incorrectly* to obtain $2 - 5i$. What is the student's mistake?

CHECKING BASIC CONCEPTS
SECTIONS 7.5 AND 7.6

1. Solve each equation. Check your answers.
  (a) $\sqrt{2x - 4} = 2$ **(b)** $\sqrt[3]{x - 1} = 3$
  (c) $\sqrt{3x} = 1 + \sqrt{x + 1}$

2. Find the distance between $(-3, 5)$ and $(2, -7)$.

3. A 16-inch diagonal television set has a rectangular picture with a width of 12.8 inches. Find the height of the picture.

4. Solve $(x + 1)^4 = 16$.

5. Use i to write each expression.
  (a) $\sqrt{-64}$ **(b)** $\sqrt{-17}$

6. Simplify each expression.
  (a) $(2 - 3i) + (1 - i)$
  (b) $4i - (2 + i)$
  (c) $(3 - 2i)(1 + i)$
  (d) $\dfrac{3}{2 - 2i}$

CHAPTER 7 SUMMARY

SECTION 7.1 ▪ RADICAL EXPRESSIONS AND RATIONAL EXPONENTS

Radicals and Radical Notation

Square Root	b is a square root of a if $b^2 = a$.
Principal Square Root	$\sqrt{a} = b$ if $b^2 = a$ and $b \geq 0$.
	Examples: $\sqrt{16} = 4$, $-\sqrt{9} = -3$,
	and $\pm\sqrt{36} = \pm 6$

Cube Root	b is a cube root of a if $b^3 = a$.
	Examples: $\sqrt[3]{27} = 3$, $\sqrt[3]{-8} = -2$
nth Root	b is an nth root of a if $b^n = a$.
	Example: $\sqrt[4]{16} = 2$ because $2^4 = 16$.
	NOTE: An *even* root of a *negative* number is not a real number. Also, $\sqrt[n]{a}$ denotes the *principal* nth root.
Absolute Value	The expressions $|x|$ and $\sqrt{x^2}$ are equivalent.
	Example: $\sqrt{(x + y)^2} = |x + y|$
The Expression $a^{1/n}$	$a^{1/n} = \sqrt[n]{a}$ if n is an integer greater than 1.
	Examples: $5^{1/2} = \sqrt{5}$ and $64^{1/3} = \sqrt[3]{64} = 4$
The Expression $a^{m/n}$	$a^{m/n} = \sqrt[n]{a^m}$ or $a^{m/n} = (\sqrt[n]{a})^m$
	Examples: $8^{2/3} = \sqrt[3]{8^2} = \sqrt[3]{64} = 4$ and
	$\qquad\qquad 8^{2/3} = (\sqrt[3]{8})^2 = (2)^2 = 4$

Properties of Exponents

Product Rule	$a^p a^q = a^{p+q}$
Negative Exponents	$a^{-p} = \dfrac{1}{a^p}, \ \dfrac{1}{a^{-p}} = a^p$
Negative Exponents for Quotients	$\left(\dfrac{a}{b}\right)^{-p} = \left(\dfrac{b}{a}\right)^{p}$
Quotient Rule for Exponents	$\dfrac{a^p}{a^q} = a^{p-q}$
Power Rule for Exponents	$(a^p)^q = a^{pq}$
Power Rule for Products	$(ab)^p = a^p b^p$
Power Rule for Quotients	$\left(\dfrac{a}{b}\right)^{p} = \dfrac{a^p}{b^p}$

SECTION 7.2 ■ SIMPLIFYING RADICAL EXPRESSIONS

Product Rule for Radical Expressions   Provided each expression is defined,

$$\sqrt[n]{a} \cdot \sqrt[n]{b} = \sqrt[n]{a \cdot b}.$$

Example: $\sqrt[3]{3} \cdot \sqrt[3]{9} = \sqrt[3]{27} = 3$

Perfect nth Power   An integer a is a perfect nth power if $b^n = a$ for some integer b.

Examples: 25 is a perfect square, 8 is a perfect cube, and 16 is a perfect fourth power.

Quotient Rule for Radical Expressions   Provided each expression is defined,

$$\sqrt[n]{\frac{a}{b}} = \frac{\sqrt[n]{a}}{\sqrt[n]{b}}.$$

Example: $\dfrac{\sqrt[3]{24}}{\sqrt[3]{3}} = \sqrt[3]{\dfrac{24}{3}} = \sqrt[3]{8} = 2$

SECTION 7.3 ▪ OPERATIONS ON RADICAL EXPRESSIONS

Addition and Subtraction   Combine like radicals.

Examples: $2\sqrt[3]{4} + 3\sqrt[3]{4} = 5\sqrt[3]{4}$ and $\sqrt{5} - 2\sqrt{5} = -\sqrt{5}$

Multiplication   Sometimes radical expressions can be multiplied like binomials.

Examples: $(4 - \sqrt{2})(2 + \sqrt{2}) = 8 + 4\sqrt{2} - 2\sqrt{2} - 2 = 6 + 2\sqrt{2}$

$(5 - \sqrt{3})(5 + \sqrt{3}) = (5)^2 - (\sqrt{3})^2 = 25 - 3 = 22$ because

$(a - b)(a + b) = a^2 - b^2.$

Rationalizing the Denominator   One technique is to multiply the numerator and denominator by the conjugate of the denominator if the denominator is a binomial containing square roots.

Examples: $\dfrac{1}{4 + \sqrt{2}} = \dfrac{1}{(4 + \sqrt{2})} \cdot \dfrac{(4 - \sqrt{2})}{(4 - \sqrt{2})} = \dfrac{4 - \sqrt{2}}{(4)^2 - (\sqrt{2})^2} = \dfrac{4 - \sqrt{2}}{14}$

$\dfrac{4}{\sqrt{7}} = \dfrac{4}{\sqrt{7}} \cdot \dfrac{\sqrt{7}}{\sqrt{7}} = \dfrac{4\sqrt{7}}{7}$

SECTION 7.4 ▪ RADICAL FUNCTIONS

The Square Root Function   The square root function is denoted $f(x) = \sqrt{x}$. Its domain is $\{x \mid x \ge 0\}$ and its graph is shown in the figure.

The Cube Root Function

The cube root function is denoted $f(x) = \sqrt[3]{x}$. Its domain is all real numbers and its graph is shown in the figure.

Power Functions

If a function can be defined by $f(x) = x^p$, where p is a rational number, then it is a power function.

Examples: $f(x) = x^{4/5}$ and $g(x) = x^{2.3}$

SECTION 7.5 ■ EQUATIONS INVOLVING RADICAL EXPRESSIONS

Power Rule for Solving Radical Equations   The solutions to $a = b$ are among the solutions to $a^n = b^n$, where n is a positive integer.

Example: The solutions to the equation $\sqrt{3x + 3} = 2x - 1$ are among the solutions to $3x + 3 = (2x - 1)^2$.

Solving Radical Equations

STEP 1: Isolate a radical term on one side of the equation.

STEP 2: Apply the power rule by raising each side of the equation to the power equal to the index of the isolated radical term.

STEP 3: Solve the equation. If it still contains a radical, repeat Steps 1 and 2.

STEP 4: Check your answers by substituting each result in the *given* equation.

Example: To isolate the radical in $\sqrt{x + 1} + 4 = 6$ subtract 4 from each side to obtain $\sqrt{x + 1} = 2$. Next square each side, which gives $x + 1 = 4$ or $x = 3$. Checking verifies that 3 is a solution.

Pythagorean Theorem

If a right triangle has legs a and b with hypotenuse c, then
$$a^2 + b^2 = c^2.$$

Example: If a right triangle has legs 8 and 15, then the hypotenuse equals
$$c = \sqrt{8^2 + 15^2} = \sqrt{289} = 17.$$

The Distance Formula

The distance d between (x_1, y_1) and (x_2, y_2) is
$$d = \sqrt{(x_2 - x_1)^2 + (y_2 - y_1)^2}.$$

Example: The distance between $(-1, 3)$ and $(4, 5)$ is
$$d = \sqrt{\left(4 - (-1)\right)^2 + (5 - 3)^2} = \sqrt{25 + 4} = \sqrt{29}.$$

Solving the Equation $x^n = k$ Let n be a positive integer.

Take the nth root of each side of $x^n = k$ to obtain $\sqrt[n]{x^n} = \sqrt[n]{k}$.

1. If n is *odd*, then $\sqrt[n]{x^n} = x$ and the equation becomes $x = \sqrt[n]{k}$.
2. If n is *even* and $k \geq 0$, then $\sqrt[n]{x^n} = |x|$ and the equation becomes $|x| = \sqrt[n]{k}$.

Examples: $x^3 = -27$ implies that $x = \sqrt[3]{-27} = -3$.
$x^4 = 81$ implies that $|x| = \sqrt[4]{81} = 3$ or $x = \pm 3$.

SECTION 7.6 ■ COMPLEX NUMBERS

Complex Numbers

Imaginary Unit	$i = \sqrt{-1}$ and $i^2 = -1$
Standard Form	$a + bi$, where a and b are real numbers
	Examples: $4 + 3i$, $5 - 6i$, 8, and $-2i$
Real Part	The real part of $a + bi$ is a.
	Example: The real part of $3 - 2i$ is 3.
Imaginary Part	The imaginary part of $a + bi$ is b.
	Example: The imaginary part of $2 - i$ is -1.
Arithmetic Operations	Arithmetic operations are similar to arithmetic operations on binomials.

Examples: $(2 + 2i) + (3 - i) = 5 + i,$

$(1 - i) - (1 - 2i) = i,$

$(1 - i)(1 + i) = 1^2 - i^2 = 1 - (-1) = 2,$ and

$$\frac{2}{1 - i} = \frac{2}{1 - i} \cdot \frac{1 + i}{1 + i} = \frac{2 + 2i}{2} = 1 + i$$

Powers of i   The value of i^n equals i^r, where r is the remainder when n is divided by 4. Note that $i^0 = 1$, $i^1 = i$, $i^2 = -1$, and $i^3 = -i$.

Example: $i^{21} = i^1 = i$ because when 21 is divided by 4 the remainder is 1.

CHAPTER 7   REVIEW EXERCISES

SECTION 7.1

Exercises 1–12: Simplify the expression.

1. $\sqrt{4}$

2. $\sqrt{36}$

3. $\sqrt{9x^2}$

4. $\sqrt{(x - 1)^2}$

5. $\sqrt[3]{-64}$

6. $\sqrt[3]{-125}$

7. $\sqrt[3]{x^6}$

8. $\sqrt[3]{27x^3}$

9. $\sqrt[4]{16}$

10. $\sqrt[5]{-1}$

11. $\sqrt[4]{x^8}$

12. $\sqrt[5]{(x + 1)^5}$

Exercises 13–16: Write the expression in radical notation.

13. $14^{1/2}$

14. $(-5)^{1/3}$

15. $\left(\dfrac{x}{y}\right)^{3/2}$

16. $(xy)^{-2/3}$

Exercises 17–20: Evaluate the expression.

17. $(-27)^{2/3}$ **18.** $16^{1/4}$

19. $16^{3/2}$ **20.** $81^{3/4}$

Exercises 21–24: Simplify the expression. Assume that all variables are positive.

21. $(z^3)^{2/3}$ **22.** $(x^2y^4)^{1/2}$

23. $\left(\dfrac{x^2}{y^6}\right)^{3/2}$ **24.** $\left(\dfrac{x^3}{y^6}\right)^{-1/3}$

SECTION 7.2

Exercises 25–40: Simplify the expression. Assume that all variables are positive.

25. $\sqrt{2} \cdot \sqrt{32}$ **26.** $\sqrt[3]{-4} \cdot \sqrt[3]{2}$

27. $\sqrt[3]{x^4} \cdot \sqrt[3]{x^2}$ **28.** $\dfrac{\sqrt{80}}{\sqrt{20}}$

29. $\sqrt[3]{-\dfrac{x}{8}}$ **30.** $\sqrt{\dfrac{1}{3}} \cdot \sqrt{\dfrac{1}{3}}$

31. $\sqrt{48}$ **32.** $\sqrt{54}$

33. $\sqrt[3]{\dfrac{3}{x}} \cdot \sqrt[3]{\dfrac{9}{x^2}}$ **34.** $\sqrt{32a^3b^2}$

35. $\sqrt{3xy} \cdot \sqrt{27xy}$ **36.** $\sqrt[3]{-25z^2} \cdot \sqrt[3]{-5z^2}$

37. $\sqrt{x^2 + 2x + 1}$ **38.** $\sqrt[4]{\dfrac{2a^2}{b}} \cdot \sqrt[4]{\dfrac{8a^3}{b^3}}$

39. $2\sqrt{x} \cdot \sqrt[3]{x}$ **40.** $\sqrt[3]{rt} \cdot \sqrt[4]{r^2t^4}$

SECTION 7.3

Exercises 41–50: Simplify the expression. Assume that all variables are positive.

41. $3\sqrt{3} + \sqrt{3}$ **42.** $\sqrt[3]{x} + 2\sqrt[3]{x}$

43. $3\sqrt[3]{5} - 6\sqrt[3]{5}$ **44.** $\sqrt[4]{y} - 2\sqrt[4]{y}$

45. $2\sqrt{12} + 7\sqrt{3}$ **46.** $3\sqrt{18} - 2\sqrt{2}$

47. $7\sqrt[3]{16} - \sqrt[3]{2}$ **48.** $\sqrt{4x + 4} + \sqrt{x + 1}$

49. $\sqrt{4x^3} - \sqrt{x}$ **50.** $\sqrt[3]{ab^4} + 2\sqrt[3]{a^4b}$

Exercises 51–56: Multiply and simplify.

51. $(1 + \sqrt{2})(3 + \sqrt{2})$

52. $(7 - \sqrt{5})(1 + \sqrt{3})$

53. $(3 + \sqrt{6})(3 - \sqrt{6})$

54. $(10 - \sqrt{5})(10 + \sqrt{5})$

55. $(\sqrt{a} + \sqrt{2b})(\sqrt{a} - \sqrt{2b})$

56. $(\sqrt{xy} - 1)(\sqrt{xy} + 2)$

Exercises 57–62: Rationalize the denominator.

57. $\dfrac{4}{\sqrt{5}}$ **58.** $\dfrac{r}{2\sqrt{t}}$

59. $\dfrac{1}{\sqrt{2} + 3}$ **60.** $\dfrac{2}{5 - \sqrt{7}}$

61. $\dfrac{1}{\sqrt{8} - \sqrt{7}}$ **62.** $\dfrac{\sqrt{a} - \sqrt{b}}{\sqrt{a} + \sqrt{b}}$

SECTION 7.4

Exercises 63 and 64: Graph the equation.

63. $y = \sqrt{x}$ **64.** $y = \sqrt[3]{x}$

Exercises 65 and 66: Write $f(x)$ in radical notation and evaluate $f(4)$.

65. $f(x) = x^{1/2}$ **66.** $f(x) = x^{2/7}$

Exercises 67 and 68: Graph the equation. Compare the graph to either $y = \sqrt{x}$ or $y = \sqrt[3]{x}$.

67. $y = \sqrt{x} - 2$ **68.** $y = \sqrt[3]{x - 1}$

Exercises 69–72: Find the domain of f. Write your answer in interval notation.

69. $f(x) = \sqrt{x - 1}$ **70.** $f(x) = \sqrt{6 - 2x}$

71. $f(x) = \sqrt{x^2 + 1}$ **72.** $f(x) = \dfrac{1}{\sqrt{x + 2}}$

SECTION 7.5

Exercises 73–78: Solve. Check your answer.

73. $\sqrt{x + 2} = x$ **74.** $\sqrt{2x - 1} = \sqrt{x + 3}$

75. $\sqrt[3]{x - 1} = 2$ **76.** $\sqrt[3]{3x} = 3$

77. $\sqrt{2x} = x - 4$ **78.** $\sqrt{x + 1} = \sqrt{x + 2}$

Exercises 79 and 80: Solve graphically. Approximate solutions to the nearest hundredth when appropriate.

79. $\sqrt[3]{2x - 1} = 2$ **80.** $x^{2/3} = 3 - x$

Exercises 81 and 82: A right triangle has legs a and b with hypotenuse c. Find the length of the missing side.

81. $a = 4, b = 7$

82. $a = 5, c = 8$

Exercises 83 and 84: Find the exact distance between the given points.

83. $(-2, 3), (2, -2)$

84. $(2, -3), (-4, 1)$

Exercises 85–94: Solve.

85. $x^2 = 121$

86. $2z^2 = 32$

87. $(x - 1)^2 = 16$

88. $x^3 = 64$

89. $(x - 1)^3 = 8$

90. $(2x - 1)^3 = 27$

91. $x^4 = 256$

92. $x^5 = -1$

93. $(x - 3)^5 = -32$

94. $3(x + 1)^4 = 3$

SECTION 7.6

Exercises 95–100: Write the complex expression in standard form.

95. $(1 - 2i) + (-3 + 2i)$

96. $(1 + 3i) - (3 - i)$

97. $(1 - i)(2 + 3i)$

98. $\dfrac{3 + i}{1 - i}$

99. $\dfrac{i(4 + i)}{2 - 3i}$

100. $(1 - i)^2(1 + i)$

APPLICATIONS

101. *Hang Time* (Refer to Example 3, Section 7.4.) A football is punted and has a hang time T of 4.6 seconds. Use the formula $T(h) = \frac{1}{2}\sqrt{h}$ to estimate the height h that it was kicked to the nearest foot.

102. *Baseball Diamond* The four bases of a baseball diamond form a square that is 90 feet on a side. Find the distance from home plate to second base.

103. *Falling Time* The time T in seconds for an object to fall from a height of h feet is given by $T = \frac{1}{4}\sqrt{h}$. If a person steps off a 10-foot-high board into a swimming pool, how long is the person in the air?

104. *Geometry* A cube has sides of length $\sqrt{5}$.
  (a) Find the area of one side of the cube.
  (b) Find the volume of the cube.
  (c) Find the length of the diagonal of one of the sides.
  (d) Find the distance from A to B in the figure.

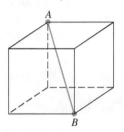

105. *Pendulum* The time required for a pendulum to swing back and forth is called its *period* (see the figure). The period T of a pendulum does not depend on its weight, only on its length L and gravity. It is given by $T = 2\pi\sqrt{\frac{L}{32.2}}$, where T is in seconds and L is in feet. Estimate the length of a pendulum with a period of 1 second.

106. *Pendulum* (Refer to Exercise 105.) If a pendulum were on the moon, its period could be calculated by $T = 2\pi\sqrt{\frac{L}{5.1}}$. Estimate the length of a pendulum with a period of 1 second on the moon. Compare your answer to that for Exercise 105.

107. *Population Growth* In 1790 the population of the United States was 4 million, and by 2000 it had grown to 281 million. The *average* annual percentage growth in the population r (expressed as a decimal) can be determined by the polynomial equation $281 = 4(1 + r)^{210}$. Solve this equation for r and interpret the result.

108. *Highway Curves* If a circular highway curve is banked with a slope of $m = \frac{1}{10}$ (see the accompanying figure) and has a radius of R feet, then the speed limit L in miles per hour for the curve is given by

$$L = \sqrt{3.75R}.$$

(*Source:* N. Garber and L. Hoel, *Traffic and Highway Engineering.*)

(a) Find the speed limit if R is 500 feet.

(b) With no banking, the speed limit is given by $L = 1.5\sqrt{R}$. Find the speed limit for a curve with no banking and a radius of 500 feet. How does banking affect the speed limit? Does this result agree with your intuition?

109. *Geometry* Find the length of a side of a square if the square has an area of 7 square feet.

110. *Surface Area of a Cone* The surface area of a cone having radius r and height h is given by the formula $S = \pi r \sqrt{r^2 + h^2}$. See the accompanying figure. Estimate the surface area if $r = 11$ inches and $h = 60$ inches.

111. *Radioactive Carbon Dating* Living plants and animals have a constant amount of radioactive carbon in their cells, which comes from the carbon dioxide they breathe. When a plant or animal dies, the exchange of oxygen and carbon dioxide halts and the amount of radioactive carbon starts to decrease. The fraction of radioactive carbon remaining t years after death is given by $2^{-t/5700}$. Find the fraction left after each time period.

(a) 5700 years   **(b)** 20,000 years

CHAPTER 7   TEST   Video solutions to all test exercises

Exercises 1–6: Simplify the expression.

1. $\sqrt[3]{-27}$

2. $\sqrt{(z + 1)^2}$

3. $\sqrt{25x^4}$

4. $\sqrt[3]{8z^6}$

5. $\sqrt[4]{16x^4y^5}; x > 0, y > 0$

6. $(\sqrt{3} - \sqrt{2})(\sqrt{3} + \sqrt{2})$

Exercises 7 and 8: Write the expression in radical notation.

7. $7^{2/5}$

8. $\left(\dfrac{x}{y}\right)^{-2/3}$

Exercises 9 and 10: Evaluate the expression by hand.

9. $(-8)^{4/3}$

10. $36^{-3/2}$

Exercises 11 and 12: Use rational exponents to write the expression.

11. $\sqrt[3]{x^4}$

12. $\sqrt{x} \cdot \sqrt[5]{x}$

13. Find the domain of $f(x) = \sqrt{4 - x}$. Write your answer in interval notation.

14. Sketch a graph of $y = \sqrt{x} + 3$.

Exercises 15–22: Simplify the expression. Assume that all variables are positive.

15. $(2z^{1/2})^3$

16. $\left(\dfrac{y^2}{z^3}\right)^{-1/3}$

17. $\sqrt{3} \cdot \sqrt{27}$

18. $\dfrac{\sqrt{y^3}}{\sqrt{4y}}$

19. $7\sqrt{7} - 3\sqrt{7} + \sqrt{5}$

20. $7\sqrt[3]{x} - \sqrt[3]{x}$

21. $4\sqrt{18} + \sqrt{8}$

22. $\dfrac{\sqrt[3]{32}}{\sqrt[3]{4}}$

23. Solve each equation.

(a) $\sqrt{x} - 2 = 5$ **(b)** $\sqrt[3]{x} + 1 = 2$

(c) $(x - 1)^3 = 8$ **(d)** $\sqrt{2x + 2} = x - 11$

24. Rationalize the denominator.

(a) $\dfrac{2}{3\sqrt{7}}$ **(b)** $\dfrac{1}{1 + \sqrt{5}}$

25. Solve $\sqrt{3x} - x + 1 = \sqrt[3]{x-1}$ graphically. Round solutions to the nearest hundredth.

26. One leg of a right triangle has length 7 and the hypotenuse has length 13. Find the length of the third side.

27. Find the distance between $(-3, 5)$ and $(-1, 7)$.

Exercises 28–31: Write the complex expression in standard form.

28. $(-5 + i) + (7 - 20i)$

29. $(3i) - (6 - 5i)$

30. $\left(\frac{1}{2} - i\right)\left(\frac{1}{2} + i\right)$

31. $\dfrac{2i}{5 + 2i}$

32. *Volume of a Sphere*   The volume V of a sphere is given by $V = \frac{4}{3}\pi r^3$, where r is its radius.
   (a) Solve the equation for r.
   (b) Find r if $V = 50$ cubic inches.

33. *Wing Span of a Bird*   The wing span L of a bird with weight W can sometimes be modeled by $L = 27.4W^{1/3}$, where L is in inches and W is in pounds. Use this formula to estimate the weight of a bird that has a wing span of 30 inches.   (*Source:* C. Pennycuick, *Newton Rules Biology.*)

CHAPTER 7   EXTENDED AND DISCOVERY EXERCISES

 1. *Moons of Jupiter*   The accompanying table lists the orbital distances and periods of several moons of Jupiter. Let x be the distance and y be the period. These data can be modeled by a power function of the form $f(x) = 0.0002x^{m/n}$. Use trial and error to find the value of the fraction $\frac{m}{n}$. Graph f and the data in the same viewing rectangle.

Moon	Distance $(10^3$ kilometers$)$	Period (days)
Metis	128	0.29
Almathea	181	0.50
Thebe	222	0.67
Io	422	1.77
Europa	671	3.55
Ganymede	1070	7.16
Callisto	1883	16.69

Source: M. Zeilik, *Introductory Astronomy and Astrophysics.*

2. *Modeling Wood in a Tree*   In forestry the volume of timber in a given area of forest is often estimated. To make such estimates, scientists have developed formulas to find the amount of wood contained in a tree with height h in feet and diameter d in inches. One study concluded that the volume V of wood in cubic feet in a tree is given by $V = kh^{1.12}d^{1.98}$,

where k is a constant. Note that the diameter is measured 4.5 feet above the ground.   (*Source:* B. Ryan, B. Joiner, and T. Ryan, *Minitab Handbook.*)
   (a) A tree with an 11-inch diameter and a 47-foot height has a volume of 11.4 cubic feet. Approximate the constant k.
   (b) Estimate the volume of wood in the same type of tree with $d = 20$ inches and $h = 105$ feet.

3. *Area of Skin*   The surface area of the skin covering the human body is a function of more than one variable. Both height and weight influence the surface area of a person's body. Hence a taller person tends to have a larger surface area, as does a heavier person. A formula to determine the area of a person's skin in square inches is $S = 15.7w^{0.425}h^{0.725}$, where w is weight in pounds and h is height in inches.   (*Source:* H. Lancaster, *Quantitative Methods in Biological and Medical Sciences.*)
   (a) Use S to estimate the area of a person's skin who is 65 inches tall and weighs 154 pounds.
   (b) If a person's weight doubles, what happens to the area of the person's skin? Explain.
   (c) If a person's height doubles, what happens to the area of the person's skin? Explain.

4. *Minimizing Cost*   A natural gas line running along a river is to be connected from point A to a cabin on the other bank located at point D, as illustrated in the figure on the next page. The width of the river is 500 feet, and the distance from point A to point C is 1000 feet.

The cost of running the pipe along the shoreline is $30 per foot, and the cost of running it underwater is $50 per foot. The cost of connecting the gas line from A to D is to be minimized.

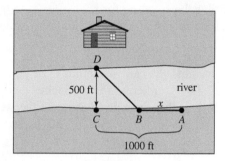

(a) Write an expression that gives the cost of running the line from A to B if the distance between these points is x feet.
(b) Find the distance from B to D in terms of x.
(c) Write an expression that gives the cost of running the line from B to D.
(d) Use your answer from parts (a) and (c) to write an expression that gives the cost of running the line from A to B to D.
 (e) Graph your expression from part (d) in the window [0, 1000, 100] by [40000, 60000, 5000] to determine the value of x that minimizes the cost of the line going from A to D. What is the minimum cost?

CHAPTERS 1–7   CUMULATIVE REVIEW EXERCISES

1. Evaluate $S = 4\pi r^2$ when $r = 3$.

2. Identify the domain and range of the relation given by $S = \{(-1, 2), (0, 4), (1, 2)\}$.

3. Simplify each expression. Write the result using positive exponents.

   (a) $\left(\dfrac{ab^2}{b^{-1}}\right)^{-3}$ (b) $\dfrac{(x^2y)^3}{x^2(y^2)^{-3}}$ (c) $(rt)^2(r^2t)^3$

4. Write 0.00043 in scientific notation.

5. Find $f(3)$ if $f(x) = \dfrac{x}{x - 2}$. What is the domain of f?

6. Find the domain of $f(x) = \sqrt[3]{2x}$.

Exercises 7 and 8: Graph f by hand.

7. $f(x) = 1 - 2x$ 8. $f(x) = \sqrt{x + 1}$

9. Sketch a graph of $f(x) = x^2 - 4$.
   (a) Identify the domain and range.
   (b) Evaluate $f(-2)$.
   (c) Identify the x-intercepts.
   (d) Solve the equation $f(x) = 0$.

10. Find slope–intercept form of the line that passes through $(-1, 2)$ and is perpendicular to $y = -2x$.

11. Let f be a linear function. Find a formula for $f(x)$.

x	-2	-1	1	2
$f(x)$	7	4	-2	-5

12. Sketch a graph of a line passing through $(-1, 1)$ with slope $-\frac{1}{2}$.

13. Solve $5x - (3 - x) = \frac{1}{2}x$.

14. Solve $2x - 5 \le 4 - x$.

15. Solve $|x - 2| \le 3$.

16. Solve $-1 \le 1 - 2x \le 6$.

17. Solve each system symbolically if possible.
    (a) $2x - y = 4$ (b) $3x - 4y = 2$
        $x + y = 8$ $x - \frac{4}{3}y = 1$

18. Shade the solution set in the xy-plane.
$$x + 2y \le 2$$
$$-x + 3y \ge 3$$

19. Solve the system.
$$x + 2y - z = 6$$
$$x - 3y + z = -2$$
$$x + y + z = 6$$

20. Calculate $\det \begin{bmatrix} 4 & 2 & -1 \\ 2 & 1 & 0 \\ 0 & -2 & 1 \end{bmatrix}$.

Exercises 21–24: Multiply the expression.

21. $4x(4 - x^3)$ 22. $(x - 4)(x + 4)$

23. $(5x + 3)(x - 2)$ 24. $(4x + 9)^2$

Exercises 25–30: Factor the expression.

25. $9x^2 - 16$

26. $x^2 - 4x + 4$

27. $15x^3 - 9x^2$

28. $12x^2 - 5x - 3$

29. $r^3 - 1$

30. $x^3 - 3x^2 + 5x - 15$

Exercises 31 and 32: Solve each equation.

31. $x^2 - 3x + 2 = 0$

32. $x^3 = 4x$

Exercises 33 and 34: Simplify the expression.

33. $\dfrac{x^2 + 3x + 2}{x - 3} \div \dfrac{x + 1}{2x - 6}$

34. $\dfrac{2}{x - 1} + \dfrac{5}{x}$

Exercises 35–42: Simplify the expression. Assume all variables are positive.

35. $\sqrt{36x^2}$

36. $\sqrt[3]{64}$

37. $16^{-3/2}$

38. $\sqrt[4]{625}$

39. $\sqrt{2x} \cdot \sqrt{8x}$

40. $\sqrt{x} \cdot \sqrt[4]{x}$

41. $\dfrac{\sqrt[3]{16x^4}}{\sqrt[3]{2x}}$

42. $4\sqrt{12x} - 2\sqrt{3x}$

43. Multiply $(2x + \sqrt{3})(x - \sqrt{3})$.

44. Find the domain of $f(x) = \sqrt{1 - x}$.

45. Graph $f(x) = 3\sqrt[3]{x}$.

46. Find the distance between $(-2, 3)$ and $(1, 2)$.

47. Write $(1 - i)(2 + 3i)$ in standard form.

48. The lengths of the legs of a right triangle are 5 and 12. What is the length of the hypotenuse?

Exercises 49–52: Solve symbolically.

49. $2\sqrt{x + 3} = x$

50. $\sqrt[3]{x - 1} = 3$

51. $\sqrt{x + 4} = 2\sqrt{x + 5}$

52. $\frac{1}{3}x^4 = 27$

Exercises 53 and 54: Solve graphically and approximate your answer to the nearest hundredth.

53. $\sqrt[3]{x^2 - 2} + x = \sqrt{x}$

54. $x - \sqrt[3]{x} = \sqrt{x + 2}$

APPLICATIONS

55. *Calculating Water Flow*   The gallons G of water in a tank after t minutes are given by $G(t) = 300 - 15t$. Interpret the slope of the graph of G as a rate of change.

56. *Distance*   A person jogs away from home at 8 miles per hour for 1 hour, rests in a park for 2 hours, and then walks back home at 4 miles per hour. Sketch a graph that models the distance y that the person is from home after x hours.

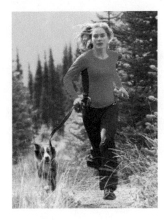

57. *Investment*   Suppose $2000 are deposited in two accounts paying 5% and 4% annual interest. If the total interest after 1 year is $93, how much is invested at each rate?

58. *Geometry*   A rectangular box with a square base has a volume of 256 cubic inches. If its height is 4 inches less than the length of an edge of the base, find the dimensions of the box.

59. *Height of a Building*   A 5-foot 3-inch person casts a shadow that is 7.5 feet while a nearby building casts a 32-foot shadow. Find the height of the building.

60. *Angles in a Triangle*   The measure of the largest angle in a triangle is 20° less than the sum of the measures of the two smaller angles. The sum of the measures of the two larger angles is 90° greater than the measure of the smaller angle. Find the measure of each angle.

CHAPTER 8

Quadratic Functions and Equations

W hat size television should you buy? Should you buy a 32-inch screen or a 50-inch screen? According to a home entertainment article in *Money* magazine, the answer depends on how far you sit from your television. The farther you sit from your television, the larger the television that is recommended. For example, if you sit only 6 feet from the screen, then a 32-inch television would be adequate; if you sit 10 feet from the screen, then a 50-inch television is more appropriate.

We can use a *quadratic function* to calculate the size S of the television screen needed for a person who sits x feet from the screen, where $6 \leq x \leq 15$. This function is given by

$$S(x) = -0.227x^2 + 8.155x - 8.8.$$

You might want to use S to determine the size of screen recommended when you sit 8 feet from a television. (See Exercises 89 and 90 in Section 8.1.) Quadratic functions are a special type of polynomial function that occur frequently in applications involving economics, road construction, falling objects, geometry, and modeling real-world data. In this chapter we discuss quadratic functions and equations.

> *There is no branch of mathematics, however abstract, which may not some day be applied to the real world.*
>
> —NIKOLAI LOBACHEVSKY

Source: *Money*, January 2007, p. 107; hdguru.com.

8.1 QUADRATIC FUNCTIONS AND THEIR GRAPHS

Graphs of Quadratic Functions ▪ Basic Transformations of Graphs ▪
More About Graphing Quadratic Functions (Optional) ▪ Min–Max Applications

A LOOK INTO MATH ▷ Suppose that a hotel is considering giving a group discount on room rates. The regular price is $80, but for each room rented the price decreases by $2. On the one hand, if the hotel rents one room, it makes only $78. On the other hand, if the hotel rents 40 rooms, the rooms are all free and the hotel makes nothing. Is there an optimal number of rooms between 1 and 40 that should be rented to maximize the revenue? In this section we use quadratic functions and their graphs to answer this question.

Graphs of Quadratic Functions

In Chapter 5 we discussed how a quadratic function could be represented by a polynomial of degree 2. We now give an alternative definition of a quadratic function.

> **QUADRATIC FUNCTION**
>
> A **quadratic function** can be written in the form
>
> $$f(x) = ax^2 + bx + c,$$
>
> where a, b, and c are constants with $a \neq 0$.

The graph of *any* quadratic function is a *parabola*. Recall that a parabola is a ∪-shaped graph that either opens upward or downward. The graph of the simple quadratic function $y = x^2$ is a parabola that opens upward, with its *vertex* located at the origin, as shown in Figure 8.1(a). The **vertex** is the *lowest* point on the graph of a parabola that opens upward and the *highest* point on the graph of a parabola that opens downward. A parabola opening downward is shown in Figure 8.1(b). Its vertex is the point $(0, 2)$ and is the highest point on the graph. If we were to fold the xy-plane along the y-axis, the left and right sides of the graph would match. That is, the graph is symmetric with respect to the y-axis. In this case the y-axis is the **axis of symmetry** for the graph. Figure 8.1(c) shows a parabola that opens upward with vertex $(2, -1)$ and axis of symmetry $x = 2$.

(a)

(b)

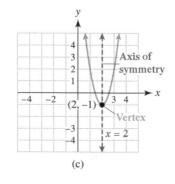
(c)

Figure 8.1

INCREASING AND DECREASING Suppose that the graph of the equation $y = x^2$ shown in Figure 8.2 represents a valley. If we walk from *left to right*, the valley "goes down" and then "goes up." Mathematically, we say that the graph of $y = x^2$ is *decreasing* when $x \leq 0$ and *increasing* when $x \geq 0$. The vertex represents the point at which the graph switches from decreasing to increasing. In Figure 8.1(b), the graph increases when $x \leq 0$ and decreases when $x \geq 0$, and in Figure 8.1(c) the graph decreases when $x \leq 2$ and increases when $x \geq 2$.

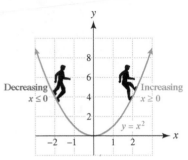

Figure 8.2

NOTE: When determining where a graph is increasing and where it is decreasing, we must "walk" along the graph *from left to right*. (We read English from left to right, which might help you remember.)

EXAMPLE **1**   Graphing quadratic functions

Graph each quadratic function. Identify the vertex and the axis of symmetry. Then state where the graph is increasing and where it is decreasing.
(a) $f(x) = x^2 - 1$ **(b)** $f(x) = -(x + 1)^2$ **(c)** $f(x) = x^2 + 4x + 3$

Solution
(a) Begin by making a convenient table of values (see Table 8.1). Then plot the points and sketch a smooth ∪-shaped curve that opens upward, as shown in Figure 8.3. The lowest point on this graph is $(0, -1)$, which is the vertex. The axis of symmetry is the vertical line $x = 0$, which passes through the vertex and coincides with the y-axis. Note also the symmetry of the y-values in Table 8.1 about the point $(0, -1)$. This graph is decreasing when $x \leq 0$ and increasing when $x \geq 0$.

TABLE 8.1

x	$y = x^2 - 1$
-2	3
-1	0
0	-1
1	0
2	3

Vertex → (row $x = 0$)

Equal

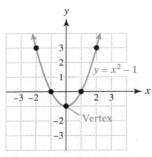

Figure 8.3

(b) Make a table of values (see Table 8.2). Plot the points and sketch a smooth ∩-shaped curve opening downward, as shown in Figure 8.4. The highest point on this graph is $(-1, 0)$, which is the vertex. The axis of symmetry is the vertical line $x = -1$, which passes through the vertex. This graph is increasing when $x \le -1$ and decreasing when $x \ge -1$.

TABLE 8.2

x	$y = -(x + 1)^2$	
-3	-4	
-2	-1	
Vertex → -1	0	Equal
0	-1	
1	-4	

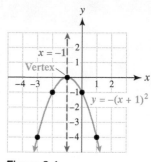

Figure 8.4

(c) Table 8.3 lists points on the graph of f, which is shown in Figure 8.5. The vertex is $(-2, -1)$ and the axis of symmetry is $x = -2$. The graph is decreasing when $x \le -2$ and increasing when $x \ge -2$.

TABLE 8.3

x	$y = x^2 + 4x + 3$	
-5	8	
-4	3	
-3	0	
Vertex → -2	-1	Equal
-1	0	
0	3	
1	8	

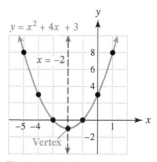

Figure 8.5

Now Try Exercises 15, 17, 21, 23

THE VERTEX FORMULA   Rather than finding a vertex by graphing, we can use the following formula. This formula can be derived by completing the square, a technique discussed in the next section.

VERTEX FORMULA

The x-coordinate of the vertex of the graph of $y = ax^2 + bx + c, a \ne 0$, is given by

$$x = -\frac{b}{2a}.$$

To find the y-coordinate of the vertex, substitute this x-value in the equation.

NOTE: The equation of the axis of symmetry for $f(x) = ax^2 + bx + c$ is $x = -\frac{b}{2a}$, and the vertex is the point $\left(-\frac{b}{2a}, f\left(-\frac{b}{2a}\right)\right)$.

We apply the vertex formula in the next example.

EXAMPLE 2   Finding the vertex of a parabola

Find the vertex for the graph of $f(x) = 2x^2 - 4x + 1$. Support your answer graphically.

Solution

For $f(x) = 2x^2 - 4x + 1$, $a = 2$ and $b = -4$. The x-coordinate of the vertex is

$$x = -\frac{b}{2a} = -\frac{(-4)}{2(2)} = 1.$$

To find the y-coordinate of the vertex, substitute $x = 1$ in the given formula.

$$f(1) = 2(1)^2 - 4(1) + 1 = -1.$$

Thus the vertex is located at $(1, -1)$, which is supported by Figure 8.6.

Now Try Exercise 39

[−4.7, 4.7, 1] by [−3.1, 3.1, 1]

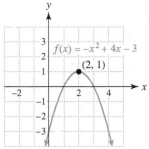

Y1=2X^2−4X+1

X=1   Y=-1

Figure 8.6

The vertex formula can help us find maximum y-values on a graph.

EXAMPLE 3   Finding a maximum y-value

Find the maximum y-value on the graph of $f(x) = -x^2 + 4x - 3$. Then state where the graph of f is increasing and where it is decreasing.

Solution

For $f(x) = -x^2 + 4x - 3$, $a = -1$ and $b = 4$. The graph of $f(x) = -x^2 + 4x - 3$ is a parabola that *opens downward* because $a < 0$. The highest point on the graph of f is the vertex and the y-coordinate of the vertex corresponds to the maximum y-coordinate. (A graph of f is shown in Figure 8.7, but it is not necessary to graph f.) The x-coordinate of the vertex is

$$x = -\frac{b}{2a} = -\frac{4}{2(-1)} = 2.$$

The corresponding y-coordinate of the vertex is $f(2) = -(2)^2 + 4(2) - 3 = 1$. The maximum y-value is 1. Because the graph opens downward, f is increasing when $x \leq 2$ and decreasing when $x \geq 2$.

Now Try Exercise 61

$f(x) = -x^2 + 4x - 3$

(2, 1)

Figure 8.7 Maximum y-value: 1

Basic Transformations of Graphs

THE GRAPH OF $y = ax^2, a > 0$ First, graph $y_1 = \frac{1}{2}x^2$, $y_2 = x^2$, and $y_3 = 2x^2$, as shown in Figure 8.8(a) on the next page. Note that $a = \frac{1}{2}$, $a = 1$, and $a = 2$, respectively, and that as a increases, the resulting parabola becomes steeper. The graph of $y_1 = \frac{1}{2}x^2$ is less steep than the graph of $y_2 = x^2$, and the graph of $y_3 = 2x^2$ is steeper than the graph of $y_2 = x^2$. In general, the graph of $y = ax^2$ is less steep than the graph of $y = x^2$ when $0 < a < 1$ and steeper than the graph of $y = x^2$ when $a > 1$. When $a > 0$, the graph of $y = ax^2$ never lies *below* the x-axis.

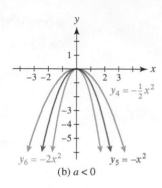

(a) $a > 0$ (b) $a < 0$

Figure 8.8 $y = ax^2$

THE GRAPH OF $y = ax^2$, $a < 0$ When $a < 0$, the graph of $y = ax^2$ never lies *above* the x-axis because, for any input x, the product $ax^2 \leq 0$. The graphs of $y_4 = -\frac{1}{2}x^2$, $y_5 = -x^2$, and $y_6 = -2x^2$ are shown in Figure 8.8(b). The graph of $y_4 = -\frac{1}{2}x^2$ is less steep than the graph of $y_5 = -x^2$ and the graph of $y_6 = -2x^2$ is steeper than the graph of $y_5 = -x^2$.

> ### THE GRAPH OF $y = ax^2$
>
> The graph of $y = ax^2$ is a parabola with the following characteristics.
>
> 1. The vertex is $(0, 0)$, and the axis of symmetry is given by $x = 0$.
> 2. It opens upward if $a > 0$ and opens downward if $a < 0$.
> 3. It is less steep than the graph of $y = x^2$, if $0 < |a| < 1$. It is steeper than the graph of $y = x^2$, if $|a| > 1$.

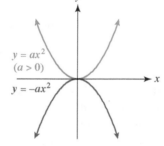

Figure 8.9 Reflection Across the x-Axis

REFLECTIONS OF $y = ax^2$ In Figure 8.8 the graph of $y_1 = \frac{1}{2}x^2$ can be *transformed* into the graph of $y_4 = -\frac{1}{2}x^2$ by *reflecting* it across the x-axis. The graph of y_4 is a **reflection** of the graph of y_1 across the x-axis. In general, *the graph of* $y = -ax^2$ *is a reflection of the graph of* $y = ax^2$ *across the x-axis*, as shown in Figure 8.9. That is, if we folded the xy-plane along the x-axis the two graphs would match.

EXAMPLE 4   Graphing $y = ax^2$

Compare the graph of $g(x) = -3x^2$ to the graph of $f(x) = x^2$. Then graph both functions on the same coordinate axes.

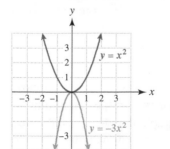

Figure 8.10

Solution
Both graphs are parabolas. However, the graph of g opens downward and is steeper than the graph of f. Their graphs are shown in Figure 8.10.   Now Try Exercise **47**

More About Graphing Quadratic Functions (Optional)

The graph of a quadratic function is a parabola, and any quadratic function f can be written as $f(x) = ax^2 + bx + c$, where a, b, and c are constants. As a result, the values of a, b, and c

determine both the shape and position of the parabola in the xy-plane. In this subsection, we summarize some of the effects that these constants have on the graph of f.

THE EFFECTS OF a   The effects of a on the graph of $y = ax^2$ were discussed extensively in the previous subsection, and these effects can be generalized to include the graph of $y = ax^2 + bx + c$.

1. **Width:** The graph of $f(x) = ax^2 + bx + c$ is wider than the graph of $y = x^2$ if $0 < |a| < 1$ and narrower if $|a| > 1$. See Figures 8.11(a) and (b).
2. **Opening:** The graph of $f(x) = ax^2 + bx + c$ opens upward if $a > 0$ and downward if $a < 0$. See Figure 8.11(c).

(a)

(b)

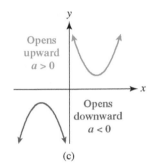
(c)

Figure 8.11 The Effects of a

THE EFFECTS OF c   The value of c affects the vertical placement of the parabola in the xy-plane.

1. **y-intercept:** Because $f(0) = a(0)^2 + b(0) + c = c$, it follows that the y-intercept for the graph of f is c. See Figure 8.12(a).
2. **Vertical Shifts:** The graph of $f(x) = ax^2 + bx + c$ is shifted vertically c units compared to the graph of $y = ax^2 + bx$. If $c < 0$, the shift is downward; if $c > 0$, the shift is upward. See Figures 8.12(b) and (c). The parabolas in both figures have identical shapes.

(a) y-intercept: c

(b) Shifted downward: $c < 0$

(c) Shifted upward: $c > 0$

Figure 8.12 The Effects of c

Figure 8.13 The Combined Effects of a and b

THE COMBINED EFFECTS OF a AND b   The combined values of a and b determine the x-coordinate of the vertex and the equation of the axis of symmetry.

1. **Vertex:** The x-coordinate of the vertex is $-\frac{b}{2a}$.
2. **Axis of Symmetry:** The axis of symmetry is given by $x = -\frac{b}{2a}$.

Figure 8.13 illustrates these concepts.

EXAMPLE **5**   Analyzing the graph of $y = ax^2 + bx + c$

Let $f(x) = -\frac{1}{2}x^2 + x + \frac{3}{2}$.

(a) Does the graph of f open upward or downward? Is this graph wider or narrower than the graph of $y = x^2$?
(b) Find the axis of symmetry and the vertex.
(c) Find the y-intercept and any x-intercepts.
(d) Sketch a graph of f.

Solution
(a) If $f(x) = -\frac{1}{2}x^2 + x + \frac{3}{2}$, then $a = -\frac{1}{2}$, $b = 1$, and $c = \frac{3}{2}$. Because $a = -\frac{1}{2} < 0$, the parabola opens downward. Also, because $0 < |a| < 1$, the graph is wider than the graph of $y = x^2$.

(b) The axis of symmetry is $x = -\frac{b}{2a} = -\dfrac{1}{2\left(-\frac{1}{2}\right)} = 1$, or $x = 1$. Because

$$f(1) = -\frac{1}{2}(1)^2 + (1) + \frac{3}{2} = -\frac{1}{2} + 1 + \frac{3}{2} = 2,$$

the vertex is $(1, 2)$.

(c) The y-intercept equals c, or $\frac{3}{2}$. To find x-intercepts we let $y = 0$ and solve for x.

$$-\frac{1}{2}x^2 + x + \frac{3}{2} = 0 \qquad \text{Equation to be solved}$$

$$x^2 - 2x - 3 = 0 \qquad \text{Multiply by } -2; \text{ clear fractions.}$$

$$(x + 1)(x - 3) = 0 \qquad \text{Factor.}$$

$$x + 1 = 0 \text{ or } x - 3 = 0 \qquad \text{Zero-product property}$$

$$x = -1 \quad \text{or} \quad x = 3 \qquad \text{Solve.}$$

The x-intercepts are -1 and 3.

(d) Start by plotting the vertex and intercepts, as shown in Figure 8.14. Then sketch a smooth, $\cap$-shaped graph that connects these points.

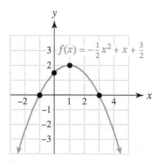

Figure 8.14   Now Try Exercise **67**

Min–Max Applications

Sometimes when a quadratic function f is used to model real-world data, the vertex provides important information. The reason is that the y-coordinate of the vertex gives either the maximum value of $f(x)$ or the minimum value of $f(x)$. For example, Figure 8.15(a) shows a parabola that opens upward. The minimum y-value on this graph is 1 and occurs at the vertex $(2, 1)$. Similarly, Figure 8.15(b) shows a parabola that opens downward. The maximum y-value on this graph is 3 and occurs at the vertex $(-1, 3)$.

(a)   (b)

Figure 8.15

▶ **REAL-WORLD CONNECTION**   In the next example, we demonstrate finding a maximum height reached by a baseball.

EXAMPLE 6   Finding maximum height

A baseball is hit into the air and its height h in feet after t seconds can be calculated by $h(t) = -16t^2 + 96t + 3$.
(a) What is the height of the baseball when it is hit?
(b) Determine the maximum height of the baseball.

Solution
(a) The baseball is hit when $t = 0$, so $h(0) = -16(0)^2 + 96(0) + 3 = 3$ feet.
(b) The graph of h opens downward because $a = -16 < 0$. Thus the maximum height of the baseball occurs at the vertex. To find the vertex, we apply the vertex formula with $a = -16$ and $b = 96$ because $h(t) = -16t^2 + 96t + 3$.

$$t = -\frac{b}{2a} = -\frac{96}{2(-16)} = 3 \text{ seconds}$$

The maximum height of the baseball occurs at $t = 3$ seconds and is

$$h(3) = -16(3)^2 + 96(3) + 3 = 147 \text{ feet.}$$ Now Try Exercise 79

▶ **REAL-WORLD CONNECTION**   In the next example, we answer the question presented in the introduction to this section.

EXAMPLE 7   Maximizing revenue

A hotel is considering giving the following group discount on room rates. The regular price for a room is $80, but for each room rented the price decreases by $2. A graph of the revenue received from renting x rooms is shown in Figure 8.16 on the next page.

Figure 8.16

(a) Interpret the graph.
(b) What is the maximum revenue? How many rooms should be rented to receive the maximum revenue?
(c) Write a formula for $y = f(x)$ whose graph is shown in Figure 8.16.
(d) Use $f(x)$ to determine symbolically the maximum revenue and the number of rooms that should be rented.

Solution

(a) The revenue increases at first, reaches a maximum, which corresponds to the vertex, and then decreases.
(b) In Figure 8.16 the vertex is (20, 800). Thus the maximum revenue of $800 occurs when 20 rooms are rented.
(c) If x rooms are rented, the price for each room is $80 - 2x$. The revenue equals the number of rooms rented times the price of each room. Thus $f(x) = x(80 - 2x)$.
(d) First, multiply $x(80 - 2x)$ to obtain $80x - 2x^2$ and then let $f(x) = -2x^2 + 80x$. The x-coordinate of the vertex is

$$x = -\frac{b}{2a} = -\frac{80}{2(-2)} = 20.$$

The y-coordinate is $f(20) = -2(20)^2 + 80(20) = 800$. These calculations verify our results in part (b).   Now Try Exercise 83

TECHNOLOGY NOTE: Locating a Vertex

Some graphing calculators can locate a vertex on a parabola with either the MAXIMUM or MINIMUM utility. The maximum for the graph in Example 7 is found in the accompanying figure. This utility is typically more accurate than the TRACE utility.

CALCULATOR HELP

To find a minimum or maximum, see the Appendix (page AP-12).

[0, 50, 10] by [0, 1000, 100]

▶ REAL-WORLD CONNECTION   In the next example, we minimize a quadratic function that models percentages of births by cesarean section (C-section).

EXAMPLE 8   Analyzing percentage of births by cesarean section

The percentage P of births performed by cesarean section between 1991 and 2001 is modeled by the formula $P(t) = 0.105t^2 - 1.08t + 23.6$, where $t = 1$ corresponds to 1991, $t = 2$ to 1992, and so on.   (**Source:** The National Center for Health Statistics.)
(a) Estimate the year when the percentage of births by cesarean section was minimum.
(b) What is this minimum percentage?

Solution
(a) The graph of P is a parabola that opens upward because $a = 0.105 > 0$. Therefore the t-coordinate of the vertex represents the year when the percentage of births done by cesarean section was minimum, or

$$t = -\frac{b}{2a} = -\frac{-1.08}{2(0.105)} \approx 5.1.$$

Because $t = 5$ corresponds to 1995, the minimum percentage occurred during 1995.
(b) In 1995, this percentage was about $P(5) = 0.105(5)^2 - 1.08(5) + 23.6 \approx 20.8\%$.

Now Try Exercise 88

8.1 PUTTING IT ALL TOGETHER

The following table summarizes some of the important topics in this section.

Concept	Explanation	Examples
Quadratic Function	Can be written as $f(x) = ax^2 + bx + c, a \neq 0$	$f(x) = x^2 + x - 2$ and $g(x) = -2x^2 + 4$ $(b = 0)$
Graph of a Quadratic Function	Its graph is a parabola that opens upward if $a > 0$ and downward if $a < 0$. The value of $|a|$ affects the width of the parabola. The vertex can be used to determine the maximum or minimum output of a quadratic function.	The graph of $y = -\frac{1}{4}x^2$ opens downward, and is wider than the graph of $y = x^2$ as shown in the figure. Each graph has its vertex at $(0, 0)$.

continued on next page

continued from previous page

Concept	Explanation	Examples
Vertex of a Parabola	The x-coordinate of the vertex for the function $f(x) = ax^2 + bx + c$ with $a \neq 0$ is given by $$x = -\frac{b}{2a}.$$ The y-coordinate of the vertex is found by substituting this x-value in the equation. Hence the vertex is $\left(-\frac{b}{2a}, f\left(-\frac{b}{2a}\right)\right)$.	If $f(x) = -2x^2 + 8x - 7$, then $$x = -\frac{8}{2(-2)} = 2$$ and $$f(2) = -2(2)^2 + 8(2) - 7 = 1.$$ The vertex is $(2, 1)$. The graph of f opens downward because $a < 0$.

Like other functions that we have studied, quadratic functions also have symbolic, numerical, and graphical representations. The following gives these representations for the quadratic function f that *squares the input x and then subtracts 1.*

Symbolic Representation

$f(x) = x^2 - 1$

Numerical Representation

Graphical Representation

8.1 Exercises

MyMathLab   Math XL PRACTICE   WATCH   DOWNLOAD   READ   REVIEW

CONCEPTS

1. The graph of a quadratic function is called a _____.

2. If a parabola opens upward, what is the lowest point on the parabola called?

3. If a parabola is symmetric with respect to the y-axis, the y-axis is called the _____.

4. The vertex of $y = x^2$ is _____.

5. Sketch a parabola that opens downward with a vertex of $(1, 2)$.

6. If $y = ax^2 + bx + c$, the x-coordinate of the vertex is given by $x = $ _____.

7. Compared to the graph of $y = x^2$, the graph of $y = 2x^2$ is (wider/narrower).

8. The graph of $y = -x^2$ is similar to the graph of $y = x^2$ except that it is _____ across the x-axis.

9. Any quadratic function can be written in the form $f(x) = $ _____.

10. If a parabola opens downward, the point with the largest y-value is called the _____.

GRAPHS OF QUADRATIC FUNCTIONS

Exercises 11–14: Use the given graph of f to evaluate the expressions.

11. $f(-2)$ and $f(0)$

12. $f(-2)$ and $f(2)$

13. $f(-3)$ and $f(1)$

14. $f(-1)$ and $f(2)$

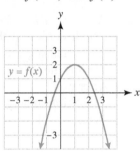

Exercises 15–18: Identify the vertex, axis of symmetry, and whether the parabola opens upward or downward. State where the graph is increasing and where it is decreasing.

15.

16.

17.

18.

Exercises 19–38: Do the following for the given f(x).
    (a) Graph $y = f(x)$.
    (b) Identify the vertex and axis of symmetry.
    (c) Evaluate $f(-2)$ and $f(3)$.

19. $f(x) = \frac{1}{2}x^2$ **20.** $f(x) = -3x^2$

21. $f(x) = x^2 - 2$ **22.** $f(x) = x^2 - 1$

23. $f(x) = -3x^2 + 1$ **24.** $f(x) = \frac{1}{2}x^2 + 2$

25. $f(x) = (x - 1)^2$ **26.** $f(x) = (x + 2)^2$

27. $f(x) = -(x + 2)^2$ **28.** $f(x) = -(x - 1)^2$

29. $f(x) = x^2 + x - 2$ **30.** $f(x) = x^2 - 2x + 2$

31. $f(x) = 2x^2 - 3$ **32.** $f(x) = 1 - 2x^2$

33. $f(x) = 2x - x^2$ **34.** $f(x) = x^2 + 2x - 8$

35. $f(x) = -2x^2 + 4x - 1$

36. $f(x) = -\frac{1}{2}x^2 + 2x - 3$

37. $f(x) = \frac{1}{4}x^2 - x + 5$ **38.** $f(x) = 3 - 6x - 4x^2$

Exercises 39–46: Find the vertex of the parabola.

39. $f(x) = x^2 - 4x - 2$

40. $f(x) = 2x^2 + 6x - 3$

41. $f(x) = -\frac{1}{3}x^2 - 2x + 1$

42. $f(x) = 5 - 4x + x^2$ **43.** $f(x) = 3 - 2x^2$

44. $f(x) = \frac{1}{4}x^2 - 3x - 2$

45. $f(x) = -0.3x^2 + 0.6x + 1.1$

46. $f(x) = 25 - 10x + 20x^2$

Exercises 47–54: Graph f(x). Compare the graph to $y = x^2$.

47. $f(x) = -x^2$ **48.** $f(x) = -2x^2$

49. $f(x) = 2x^2$ **50.** $f(x) = 3x^2$

51. $f(x) = \frac{1}{4}x^2$ **52.** $f(x) = \frac{1}{2}x^2$

53. $f(x) = -\frac{1}{2}x^2$ **54.** $f(x) = -\frac{3}{2}x^2$

Exercises 55–60: Find the minimum y-value on the graph of $y = f(x)$. Then state where the graph of f is increasing and where it is decreasing.

55. $f(x) = x^2 + 2x - 1$ **56.** $f(x) = x^2 + 6x + 2$

57. $f(x) = x^2 - 5x$ **58.** $f(x) = x^2 - 3x$

59. $f(x) = 2x^2 + 2x - 3$ **60.** $f(x) = 3x^2 - 3x + 7$

Exercises 61–66: Find the maximum y-value on the graph of $y = f(x)$. Then state where the graph of f is increasing and where it is decreasing.

61. $f(x) = -x^2 + 2x + 5$

62. $f(x) = -x^2 + 4x - 3$

63. $f(x) = 4x - x^2$ **64.** $f(x) = 6x - x^2$

65. $f(x) = -2x^2 + x - 5$

66. $f(x) = -5x^2 + 15x - 2$

Exercises 67–72: (Refer to Example 5.) Use the given $f(x)$ to complete the following.
  (a) *Does the graph of f open upward or downward? Is this graph wider, narrower, or the same as the graph of $y = x^2$?*
  (b) *Find the axis of symmetry and the vertex.*
  (c) *Find the y-intercept and any x-intercepts.*
  (d) *Sketch a graph of f.*

67. $f(x) = \frac{1}{2}x^2 + x - \frac{3}{2}$ **68.** $f(x) = -x^2 + 4x + 5$

69. $f(x) = 2x - x^2$ **70.** $f(x) = x - 2x^2$

71. $f(x) = 2x^2 + 2x - 4$ **72.** $f(x) = \frac{1}{2}x^2 - \frac{1}{2}x - 1$

73. *Numbers*   Find two positive numbers whose sum is 20 and whose product is maximum.

74. Thinking Generally   Find two positive numbers whose sum is k and whose product is maximum.

APPLICATIONS

Exercises 75–78: Quadratic Models   Match the physical situation with the graph (a.–d.) that models it best.

75. The height y of a stone thrown from ground level after x seconds.

76. The number of people attending a popular movie x weeks after its opening.

77. The temperature after x hours in a house when the furnace quits and a repair person fixes it.

78. U.S. population from 1800 to the present.

a.

b.

c.

d.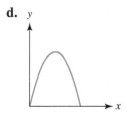

79. *Height Reached by a Baseball*   (Refer to Example 6.) A baseball is hit into the air, and its height h in feet after t seconds is given by $h(t) = -16t^2 + 64t + 2$.
  (a) What is the height of the baseball when it is hit?
  (b) After how many seconds does the baseball reach its maximum height?
  (c) Determine the maximum height of the baseball.

80. *Height Reached by a Golf Ball*   A golf ball is hit into the air, and its height h in feet after t seconds is given by $h(t) = -16t^2 + 128t$.
  (a) What is the height of the golf ball when it is hit?
  (b) After how many seconds does the golf ball reach its maximum height?
  (c) Determine the maximum height of the golf ball.

81. *Height Reached by a Baseball*   Suppose that a baseball is thrown upward with an initial velocity of 66 feet per second (45 miles per hour) and it is released 6 feet above the ground. Its height h after t seconds is given by $h(t) = -16t^2 + 66t + 6$. After how many seconds does the baseball reach a maximum height? Estimate this height.

82. *Throwing a Baseball on the Moon*   (Refer to Exercise 81.) If the same baseball were thrown the same way on the moon, its height h above the moon's surface after t seconds would be

$$h(t) = -2.55t^2 + 66t + 6.$$

Does the baseball go higher on the moon or on Earth? What is the difference in these two heights?

83. *Concert Tickets*   (Refer to Example 7.) An agency is promoting concert tickets by offering a group-discount rate. The regular price is $100 and for each ticket bought the price decreases by $1. (One ticket costs $99, two tickets cost $98 *each*, and so on.)

(a) A graph of the revenue received from selling x tickets is shown in the figure. When is revenue increasing and when is it decreasing?

Tickets Sold

(b) What is the maximum revenue? How many tickets should be sold to maximize revenue?

(c) Write a formula for $y = f(x)$ whose graph is shown in the figure.

(d) Use $f(x)$ to determine symbolically the maximum revenue and the number of tickets that should be sold to maximize revenue.

84. *Maximizing Revenue* The regular price for a round-trip ticket to Las Vegas, Nevada, charged by an airline charter company is $300. For a group rate the company will reduce the price of each ticket by $1.50 for every passenger on the flight.

(a) Write a formula $f(x)$ that gives the revenue from selling x tickets.

(b) Determine how many tickets should be sold to maximize the revenue. What is the maximum revenue?

85. *Maximizing Area* A farmer is fencing a rectangular area for cattle using a straight portion of a river as one side of the rectangle as illustrated in the figure. Note that there is no fence along the river. If the farmer has 1200 feet of fence, find the dimensions for the rectangular area that gives a maximum area for the cattle.

86. *Maximizing Area* A rectangular pen being constructed for a pet requires 60 feet of fence.

(a) Write a formula $f(x)$ that gives the area of the pen if one side of the pen has length x.

(b) Find the dimensions of the pen that give the largest area. What is the largest area?

87. *Seedling Growth* The effect of temperature on the growth of melon seedlings was studied, where the seedlings were grown at different temperatures, and their heights were measured after a fixed period of time. The findings of this study can be modeled by

$$f(x) = -0.095x^2 + 5.4x - 52.2,$$

where x is the temperature in degrees Celsius and the output $f(x)$ gives the resulting average height in centimeters. (*Source:* R. Pearl, "The growth of *Cucumis melo* seedlings at different temperatures.")

(a) Graph f in [20, 40, 5] by [0, 30, 5].

(b) Estimate graphically the temperature that resulted in the greatest height for the melon seedlings.

(c) Solve part (b) symbolically.

88. *Game Length* The quadratic function defined by

$$L(x) = -2x^2 + 8000x - 7,999,820$$

approximates the length of the average major league baseball game in minutes during year x, where $1998 \le x \le 2002$. (*Source:* Elias Sports Bureau.)

(a) Determine the year when games were the longest.

(b) How long did the average game last?

Exercises 89 and 90: Large Screen Televisions (Refer to the introduction to this chapter.) Use the formula

$$S(x) = -0.227x^2 + 8.155x - 8.8$$

to estimate the recommended screen size in inches when viewers sit x feet from the screen.

89. $x = 8$ feet   **90.** $x = 12$ feet

91. If $f(x) = ax^2 + bx + c$, explain how the values of a and c affect the graph of f.

92. Suppose that a quantity Q is modeled by the formula $Q(x) = ax^2 + bx + c$ with $a < 0$. Explain how to find the x-value that maximizes $Q(x)$. How do you find the maximum value of $Q(x)$?

8.2   PARABOLAS AND MODELING

Vertical and Horizontal Translations ▪ Vertex Form ▪ Modeling with Quadratic Functions (Optional)

A LOOK INTO MATH ▷

A taxiway used by an airplane to exit a runway often contains curves. A curve that is too sharp for the speed of the plane is a safety hazard. The scatterplot shown in Figure 8.17 gives an appropriate radius R of a curve designed for an airplane taxiing x miles per hour. The data are nonlinear because they do not lie on a line. In this section we explain how a quadratic function may be used to model such data. First, we discuss translations of parabolas.

Figure 8.17

Vertical and Horizontal Translations

The graph of $y = x^2$ is a parabola opening upward with vertex $(0, 0)$. Suppose that we graph $y_1 = x^2, y_2 = x^2 + 1$, and $y_3 = x^2 - 2$ in the same xy-plane, as calculated for Table 8.4 and shown in Figure 8.18. All three graphs have the same shape. However, compared to the graph of $y_1 = x^2$, the graph of $y_2 = x^2 + 1$ is shifted *upward* 1 unit and the graph of $y_3 = x^2 - 2$ is shifted *downward* 2 units. Such shifts are called **translations** because they do not change the shape of a graph—only its position.

TABLE 8.4

x	$y_1 = x^2$	$y_2 = x^2 + 1$	$y_3 = x^2 - 2$
-2	4	5	2
-1	1	2	-1
0	0	1	-2
1	1	2	-1
2	4	5	2

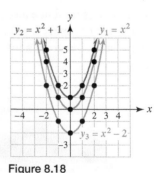

Figure 8.18

Next, suppose that we graph $y_1 = x^2$ and $y_2 = (x - 1)^2$ in the same xy-plane. Compare Tables 8.5 and 8.6. Note that the y-values are equal when the x-value for y_2 is 1 unit *larger* than the x-value for y_1. For example, $y_1 = 4$ when $x = -2$ and $y_2 = 4$ when $x = -1$. Thus the graph of $y_2 = (x - 1)^2$ has the same shape as the graph of $y_1 = x^2$, except that it is translated *horizontally to the right* 1 unit, as illustrated in Figure 8.19.

TABLE 8.5

x	$y_1 = x^2$
-2	4
-1	1
0	0
1	1
2	4

TABLE 8.6

x	$y_2 = (x - 1)^2$
-1	4
0	1
1	0
2	1
3	4

Figure 8.19

The graphs $y_1 = x^2$ and $y_2 = (x + 2)^2$ are shown in Figure 8.20. Note that Tables 8.7 and 8.8 show their y-values to be equal when the x-value for y_2 is 2 units *smaller* than the x-value for y_1. As a result, the graph of $y_2 = (x + 2)^2$ has the same shape as the graph of $y_1 = x^2$ except that it is translated *horizontally to the left* 2 units.

TABLE 8.7

x	$y_1 = x^2$
-2	4
-1	1
0	0
1	1
2	4

TABLE 8.8

x	$y_2 = (x + 2)^2$
-4	4
-3	1
-2	0
-1	1
0	4

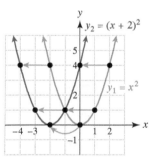

Figure 8.20

These results are summarized as follows.

VERTICAL AND HORIZONTAL TRANSLATIONS OF PARABOLAS

Let h and k be positive numbers.

To graph	shift the graph of $y = x^2$ by k units
$y = x^2 + k$	upward.
$y = x^2 - k$	downward.

To graph	shift the graph of $y = x^2$ by h units
$y = (x - h)^2$	right.
$y = (x + h)^2$	left.

The next example demonstrates this method.

EXAMPLE **1**   Translating the graph $y = x^2$

Sketch the graph of the equation and identify the vertex.
(a) $y = x^2 + 2$ **(b)** $y = (x + 3)^2$ **(c)** $y = (x - 2)^2 - 3$

Solution
(a) The graph of $y = x^2 + 2$ is similar to the graph of $y = x^2$ except that it has been translated upward 2 units, as shown in Figure 8.21(a). The vertex is $(0, 2)$.
(b) The graph of $y = (x + 3)^2$ is similar to the graph of $y = x^2$ except that it has been translated *left* 3 units, as shown in Figure 8.21(b). The vertex is $(-3, 0)$.

> **NOTE:** If you are thinking that the graph should be shifted right (instead of left) 3 units, try graphing $y = (x + 3)^2$ on a graphing calculator.

(c) The graph of $y = (x - 2)^2 - 3$ is similar to the graph of $y = x^2$ except that it has been translated downward 3 units *and* right 2 units, as shown in Figure 8.21(c). The vertex is $(2, -3)$.

(a)

(b)

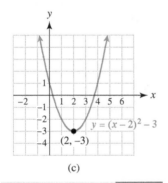
(c)

Figure 8.21

Now Try Exercises 9, 13, 21

Vertex Form

Suppose that a parabola has the equation $y = ax^2 + bx + c$ with vertex (h, k). We can write this equation in a different form called the *vertex form* by transforming the graph of $y = x^2$. The vertex for $y = x^2$ is $(0, 0)$ so we need to translate it h units horizontally and k units vertically. Thus $y = (x - h)^2 + k$ has vertex (h, k). For the graph of our new equation to open correctly and have the same shape as $y = ax^2 + bx + c$, we must be sure that their leading coefficients are identical. That is, the graph of $y = a(x - h)^2 + k$ is identical to $y = ax^2 + bx + c$, provided that the vertex for the second equation is (h, k). This discussion is summarized as follows.

> **VERTEX FORM**
>
> The **vertex form** of the equation of a parabola with vertex (h, k) is
> $$y = a(x - h)^2 + k,$$
> where $a \neq 0$ is a constant. If $a > 0$, the parabola opens upward; if $a < 0$, the parabola opens downward.

NOTE: Vertex form is sometimes called **standard form for a parabola with a vertical axis**.

In the next three examples, we demonstrate the graphing of parabolas in vertex form, finding their equations, and writing vertex forms of equations.

EXAMPLE 2   Graphing parabolas in vertex form

Compare the graph of $y = f(x)$ to the graph of $y = x^2$. Then sketch a graph of $y = f(x)$ and $y = x^2$ in the same xy-plane.

(a) $f(x) = \frac{1}{2}(x - 5)^2 + 2$ **(b)** $f(x) = -3(x + 5)^2 - 3$

Solution

(a) Compared to the graph of $y = x^2$, the graph of $y = f(x)$ is translated 5 units right and 2 units upward. The vertex for $f(x)$ is $(5, 2)$, whereas the vertex of $y = x^2$ is $(0, 0)$. Because $a = \frac{1}{2}$, the graph of $y = f(x)$ opens upward and is wider than the graph of $y = x^2$. These graphs are shown in Figure 8.22(a).

(b) Compared to the graph of $y = x^2$, the graph of $y = f(x)$ is translated 5 units left and 3 units downward. The vertex for $f(x)$ is $(-5, -3)$. Because $a = -3$, the graph of $y = f(x)$ opens downward and is narrower than the graph of $y = x^2$. These graphs are shown in Figure 8.22(b).

 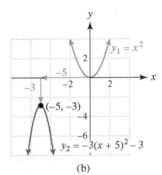

(a)   (b)

Figure 8.22

Now Try Exercises 29, 31

EXAMPLE 3   Finding equations of parabolas

Write the vertex form of a parabola with $a = 2$ and vertex $(-2, 1)$. Then express this equation in the form $y = ax^2 + bx + c$.

Solution

The vertex form of a parabola is $y = a(x - h)^2 + k$, where the vertex is (h, k). For $a = 2, h = -2$, and $k = 1$, the equation becomes

$$y = 2(x - (-2))^2 + 1 \quad \text{or} \quad y = 2(x + 2)^2 + 1.$$

To write this equation in the form $y = ax^2 + bx + c$, do the following.

$$y = 2(x^2 + 4x + 4) + 1 \qquad \text{Multiply } (x + 2)^2.$$
$$= (2x^2 + 8x + 8) + 1 \qquad \text{Distributive property}$$
$$= 2x^2 + 8x + 9 \qquad \text{Add.}$$

The equivalent equation is $y = 2x^2 + 8x + 9$.

Now Try Exercise 35

COMPLETING THE SQUARE TO FIND THE VERTEX   If we are given the equation $y = x^2 + 4x + 2$, can we write it in an equivalent vertex form? The answer is *yes*, and in this process we use the **completing the square method**. In Chapter 5 we learned that $(a + b)^2 = a^2 + 2ab + b^2$. If we apply this result to $\left(x + \frac{b}{2}\right)^2$, we obtain the following.

$$\left(x + \frac{b}{2}\right)^2 = x^2 + 2x\left(\frac{b}{2}\right) + \left(\frac{b}{2}\right)^2$$

$$= x^2 + bx + \left(\frac{b}{2}\right)^2$$

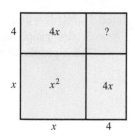

Thus we can always complete the square for $x^2 + bx$ by adding $\left(\frac{b}{2}\right)^2$. For example, if $y = x^2 + 8x + 2$, then $b = 8$ and so $\left(\frac{b}{2}\right)^2 = \left(\frac{8}{2}\right)^2 = 16$. If we simply add 16 to the right side of this equation to complete the square, the resulting equation will *not be equivalent* to the given equation. To avoid this situation, we *add and subtract* 16 on the right side of the equation. Adding 16 and then subtracting 16 is equivalent to adding 0, which does not change the equation.

$$y = x^2 + 8x + 2 \qquad \text{Given equation}$$

$$= (x^2 + 8x + 16) - 16 + 2 \qquad \text{Add and subtract 16.}$$

$$= (x + 4)^2 - 14 \qquad \text{Perfect square trinomial}$$

Thus $y = x^2 + 8x + 2$ and $y = (x + 4)^2 - 14$ are equivalent equations. The vertex for this parabola is $(-4, -14)$. Note that we added *and* subtracted 16, so the right side of the equation did not change in value.

EXAMPLE 4   Writing vertex form

Write each equation in vertex form. Identify the vertex.
(a) $y = x^2 - 6x - 1$ **(b)** $y = x^2 + 3x + 4$ **(c)** $y = 2x^2 + 4x - 1$

Solution
(a) Because $\left(\frac{b}{2}\right)^2 = \left(\frac{-6}{2}\right)^2 = 9$, add and subtract 9 on the right side.

$$y = x^2 - 6x - 1 \qquad \text{Given equation}$$

$$= (x^2 - 6x + 9) - 9 - 1 \qquad \text{Add and subtract 9.}$$

$$= (x - 3)^2 - 10 \qquad \text{Perfect square trinomial}$$

The vertex is $(3, -10)$.
(b) Because $\left(\frac{b}{2}\right)^2 = \left(\frac{3}{2}\right)^2 = \frac{9}{4}$, add and subtract $\frac{9}{4}$ on the right side.

$$y = x^2 + 3x + 4 \qquad \text{Given equation}$$

$$= \left(x^2 + 3x + \frac{9}{4}\right) - \frac{9}{4} + 4 \qquad \text{Add and subtract } \frac{9}{4}.$$

$$= \left(x + \frac{3}{2}\right)^2 + \frac{7}{4} \qquad \text{Perfect square trinomial}$$

The vertex is $\left(-\frac{3}{2}, \frac{7}{4}\right)$.

(c) This equation is slightly different because the leading coefficient is 2 rather than 1. Start by factoring 2 from the first two terms on the right side.

$$y = 2x^2 + 4x - 1 \qquad \text{Given equation}$$
$$= 2(x^2 + 2x) - 1 \qquad \text{Factor out 2.}$$
$$= 2(x^2 + 2x + 1 - 1) - 1 \qquad \left(\tfrac{b}{2}\right)^2 = \left(\tfrac{2}{2}\right)^2 = 1$$
$$= 2(x^2 + 2x + 1) - 2 - 1 \qquad \text{Distributive property } (2 \cdot -1)$$
$$= 2(x + 1)^2 - 3 \qquad \text{Perfect square trinomial; add.}$$

The vertex is $(-1, -3)$.

Now Try Exercises ▐47, 51, 55▐

Modeling with Quadratic Functions (Optional)

▶ REAL-WORLD CONNECTION   In the introduction to this section we discussed airport taxiway curves designed for airplanes. The data previously shown in Figure 8.17 are listed in Table 8.9.

TABLE 8.9

x (mph)	10	20	30	40	50	60
R (ft)	50	200	450	800	1250	1800

Source: Federal Aviation Administration.

A second scatterplot of the data is shown in Figure 8.23. The data may be modeled by $R(x) = ax^2$ for some value a. To illustrate this relation, graph R for different values of a. In Figures 8.24–8.26, R has been graphed for $a = 2, -1$, and $\tfrac{1}{2}$, respectively. When $a > 0$ the parabola opens upward and when $a < 0$ the parabola opens downward. Larger values of $|a|$ make a parabola narrower, whereas smaller values of $|a|$ make the parabola wider. Through trial and error, $a = \tfrac{1}{2}$ gives a good fit to the data, so $R(x) = \tfrac{1}{2}x^2$ models the data.

CALCULATOR HELP

To make a scatterplot, see the Appendix (page AP-4).

$[-70, 70, 10]$ by $[-2000, 2000, 500]$

Figure 8.23

$[-70, 70, 10]$ by $[-2000, 2000, 500]$

Figure 8.24 $a = 2$

$[-70, 70, 10]$ by $[-2000, 2000, 500]$

Figure 8.25 $a = -1$

$[-70, 70, 10]$ by $[-2000, 2000, 500]$

Figure 8.26 $a = \tfrac{1}{2}$

This value of a can also be found *symbolically*, as demonstrated in the next example.

EXAMPLE **5**   Modeling safe taxiway speed

Find a value for the constant a symbolically so that $R(x) = ax^2$ models the data in Table 8.9 on the previous page. Check your result by making a table of values for $R(x)$.

Solution
When $x = 10$ miles per hour, the curve radius is $R(x) = 50$ feet. Therefore

$$R(10) = 50 \quad \text{or} \quad a(10)^2 = 50.$$

Solving for a gives

$$a = \frac{50}{10^2} = \frac{1}{2}.$$

To be sure that $R(x) = \frac{1}{2}x^2$ is correct, construct a table, as shown in Figure 8.27. Its values agree with those in Table 8.9.

Now Try Exercise **69**

X	Y₁
0	0
10	50
20	200
30	450
40	800
50	1250
60	1800

Y₁ ▪ .5X²

Figure 8.27

▶ **REAL-WORLD CONNECTION**   In 1981, the first cases of AIDS were reported in the United States. Since then, AIDS has become one of the most devastating diseases of recent times. Table 8.10 lists the *cumulative* number of AIDS cases in the United States for various years. For example, between 1981 and 1990, a total of 199,608 AIDS cases were reported.

A scatterplot of these data is shown in Figure 8.28. To model these nonlinear data, we want to find (the right half of) a parabola with the shape illustrated in Figure 8.29. We do so in the next example.

TABLE 8.10

Year	AIDS Cases
1981	425
1984	11,106
1987	71,414
1990	199,608
1993	417,835
1996	609,933

Source: Department of Health and Human Services.

Figure 8.28 AIDS Cases

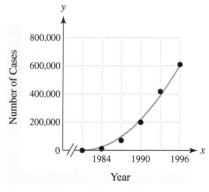

Figure 8.29 Modeling AIDS Cases

EXAMPLE **6**   Modeling AIDS cases

Use the data in Table 8.10 to complete the following.
(a) Make a scatterplot of the data in [1980, 1997, 2] by [−10000, 800000, 100000].
(b) The lowest data point in Table 8.10 is (1981, 425). Let this point be the vertex of a parabola that opens upward. Graph $y = a(x - 1981)^2 + 425$ together with the data by first letting $a = 1000$.
(c) Use trial and error to adjust the value of a until the graph models the data.
(d) Use your final equation to estimate the number of AIDS cases in 1992. Compare it to the known value of 338,786.

Solution

(a) A scatterplot of the data is shown in Figure 8.30.

[1980, 1997, 2] by
[−10000, 800000, 100000]

[1980, 1997, 2] by
[−10000, 800000, 100000]

[1980, 1997, 2] by
[−10000, 800000, 100000]

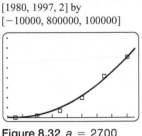

Figure 8.30

Figure 8.31 $a = 1000$

Figure 8.32 $a = 2700$

(b) A graph of $y = 1000(x − 1981)^2 + 425$ is shown in Figure 8.31. To have a better fit of the data, a larger value for a is needed.

(c) Figure 8.32 shows the effect of adjusting the value of a to 2700. This value provides a reasonably good fit. (Note that you may decide on a slightly different value for a.)

(d) If $a = 2700$, the modeling equation becomes

$$y = 2700(x − 1981)^2 + 425.$$

To estimate the number of AIDS cases in 1992, substitute $x = 1992$ to obtain

$$y = 2700(1992 − 1981)^2 + 425 = 327{,}125.$$

This number is about 12,000 less than the known value of 338,786.

Now Try Exercise **71**

8.2 PUTTING IT ALL TOGETHER

The following table summarizes some of the important topics in this section.

Concept	Explanation	Examples
Translations of Parabolas	Compared to the graph $y = x^2$, the graph of $y = x^2 + k$ is shifted vertically k units and the graph of $y = (x − h)^2$ is shifted horizontally h units.	Compared to the graph of $y = x^2$, the graph of $y = x^2 − 4$ is shifted downward 4 units. Compared to the graph of $y = x^2$, the graph of $y = (x − 4)^2$ is shifted right 4 units and the graph of $y = (x + 4)^2$ is shifted left 4 units.
Vertex Form	The vertex form of the equation of a parabola with vertex (h, k) is $$y = a(x − h)^2 + k,$$ where $a \neq 0$ is a constant. If $a > 0$, the parabola opens upward; if $a < 0$, the parabola opens downward.	The graph of $y = 3(x + 2)^2 − 7$ has a vertex of $(−2, −7)$ and opens upward because $3 > 0$.

continued on next page

continued from previous page

Concept	Explanation	Examples
Completing the Square Method	To complete the square to obtain the vertex form, add and subtract $\left(\frac{b}{2}\right)^2$ on the right side of $y = x^2 + bx + c$. Then factor the perfect square trinomial.	If $y = x^2 + 10x - 3$, then add and subtract $\left(\frac{b}{2}\right)^2 = \left(\frac{10}{2}\right)^2 = 25$ on the right side of this equation. $y = (x^2 + 10x + 25) - 25 - 3$ $= (x + 5)^2 - 28$ The vertex is $(-5, -28)$.

8.2 Exercises

 MyMathLab

 Math XL PRACTICE   WATCH   DOWNLOAD   READ   REVIEW

CONCEPTS

1. Compared to the graph of $y = x^2$, the graph of $y =$ _____ is shifted upward 2 units.

2. Compared to the graph of $y = x^2$, the graph of $y =$ _____ is shifted to the right 2 units.

3. The vertex of $y = (x - 1)^2 + 2$ is _____.

4. The vertex of $y = (x + 1)^2 - 2$ is _____.

5. A quadratic function f may be written either in the form _____ or _____.

6. The vertex form of a parabola is given by _____ and its vertex is _____.

7. The graph of $y = -x^2$ is a parabola that opens _____.

8. The x-coordinate of the vertex of $y = ax^2 + bx + c$ is $x =$ _____.

GRAPHS OF PARABOLAS

Exercises 9–28: Do the following.
  (a) Sketch a graph of the equation.
  (b) Identify the vertex.
  (c) Compare the graph to the graph of $y = x^2$. (State any transformations used.)

9. $f(x) = x^2 - 4$ 10. $f(x) = x^2 - 1$

11. $f(x) = 2x^2 + 1$ 12. $f(x) = \frac{1}{2}x^2 + 1$

13. $f(x) = (x - 3)^2$ 14. $f(x) = (x + 1)^2$

15. $f(x) = -x^2$ 16. $f(x) = -(x + 2)^2$

17. $f(x) = 2 - x^2$ 18. $f(x) = (x - 1)^2$

19. $f(x) = (x + 2)^2$ 20. $f(x) = (x - 2)^2 - 3$

21. $f(x) = (x + 1)^2 - 2$

22. $f(x) = (x - 3)^2 + 1$

23. $f(x) = (x - 1)^2 + 2$

24. $f(x) = \frac{1}{2}(x + 3)^2 - 3$

25. $f(x) = 2(x - 5)^2 - 4$

26. $f(x) = -3(x + 4)^2 + 5$

27. $f(x) = -\frac{1}{2}(x + 3)^2 + 1$

28. $f(x) = 2(x - 5)^2 + 10$

Exercises 29–32: Compare the graph of $y = f(x)$ to the graph of $y = x^2$. Then sketch a graph of $y = f(x)$ and $y = x^2$ in the same xy-plane.

29. $f(x) = \frac{1}{2}(x - 1)^2 - 2$

30. $f(x) = 2(x + 2)^2 - 1$

31. $f(x) = -2(x + 1)^2 + 3$

32. $f(x) = -\frac{1}{2}(x - 2)^2 + 2$

Exercises 33 and 34: *Graph the equation in a window that shows the vertex and all intercepts.*

33. $f(x) = -0.4x^2 + 6x - 10$

34. $f(x) = 3x^2 - 40x + 50$

VERTEX FORM

Exercises 35–38: *(Refer to Example 3.) Write the vertex form of a parabola that satisfies the conditions given. Then write the equation in the form $y = ax^2 + bx + c$.*

35. Vertex $(3, 4)$ and $a = 3$

36. Vertex $(-1, 3)$ and $a = -5$

37. Vertex $(5, -2)$ and $a = -\frac{1}{2}$

38. Vertex $(-2, -6)$ and $a = \frac{3}{4}$

Exercises 39–42: *Write the vertex form of a parabola that satisfies the conditions given. Assume that $a = \pm 1$.*

39. Opens upward, vertex $(1, 2)$

40. Opens downward, vertex $(-1, -2)$

41. Opens downward, vertex $(0, -3)$

42. Opens upward, vertex $(5, -4)$

Exercises 43–46: *Write the vertex form of the parabola shown in the graph. Assume that $a = \pm 1$.*

43.

44.

45.

46.

Exercises 47–60: *(Refer to Example 4.) Write the equation in vertex form. Identify the vertex.*

47. $y = x^2 + 2x - 3$

48. $y = x^2 + 4x + 1$

49. $y = x^2 - 4x + 5$

50. $y = x^2 - 8x + 10$

51. $y = x^2 + 3x - 2$

52. $y = x^2 + 5x - 4$

53. $y = x^2 - 7x + 1$

54. $y = x^2 - 3x + 5$

55. $y = 3x^2 + 6x - 1$

56. $y = 2x^2 + 4x - 9$

57. $y = 2x^2 - 3x$

58. $y = 3x^2 - 7x$

59. $y = -2x^2 - 8x + 5$

60. $y = -3x^2 + 6x + 1$

MODELING DATA

Exercises 61–64: *Find a value for the constant a so that $f(x) = ax^2$ models the data. If you are uncertain about your value for a, check it by making a table of values.*

61.

x	1	2	3
y	2	8	18

62.

x	-2	0	2
y	6	0	6

63.

x	2	4	6	8
y	1.2	4.8	10.8	19.2

64.

x	5	10	15	20
y	17.5	70	157.5	280

Exercises 65–68: *Modeling Quadratic Data (Refer to Example 6.) Find a quadratic function expressed in vertex form that models the data in the given table.*

65.

x	1	2	3	4
y	-3	-1	5	15

66.

x	-2	-1	0	1	2
y	5	2	-7	-22	-43

67.

x	1980	1990	2000	2010
y	6	55	210	450

68.

x	1990	1995	2000	2005
y	10	60	205	470

69. *Braking Distance*   The table lists approximate braking distances D in feet for cars traveling at x miles per hour on dry, level pavement.

x	12	24	36	48
D	12	48	108	192

(a) Make a scatterplot of the data.
(b) Find a function given by $D(x) = ax^2$ that models these data.

70. *Health Care Costs*   The table lists approximate *annual* percentage increases in the cost of health insurance premiums between 1992 and 2000.

Year	1992	1994	1996	1998	2000
Increase	11%	4%	1%	4%	11%

Source: Kaiser Family Foundation.

(a) Make a scatterplot of the data.
(b) Find a function given by $C(x) = a(x - h)^2 + k$ that models these data. (Answers may vary.)

71. *U.S. AIDS Deaths*   (Refer to Example 6.) The table at the top of the next column lists cumulative numbers of AIDS deaths in *thousands* for selected years.

Year	1982	1986	1990	1994
Deaths (thousands)	1	25	123	300

(*Source:* Department of Health and Human Services.)

(a) Determine $f(x) = a(x - h)^2 + k$, so that f models these data.
(b) Estimate the number of AIDS deaths in 1992 and compare it to the actual value of 202 thousand.

72. *Head Start Enrollment*   The table lists numbers of students *in thousands* enrolled in Head Start for selected years.

Year	1966	1980	1995
Students (thousands)	733	376	750

(a) Determine $f(x) = a(x - h)^2 + k$, so that f models these data.
(b) Estimate Head Start enrollment in 1990 and compare it to the actual value of 541 thousand.

WRITING ABOUT MATHEMATICS

73. Explain how to find the vertex of $y = x^2 + bx + c$ by completing the square.

74. If $f(x) = a(x - h)^2 + k$, explain how the values of a, h, and k affect the graph of $y = f(x)$.

CHECKING BASIC CONCEPTS
SECTIONS 8.1 AND 8.2

1. Graph each quadratic function. Identify the vertex and axis of symmetry.
   (a) $f(x) = x^2 - 2$
   (b) $f(x) = x^2 - 2x - 2$

2. Compare the graph of $y_1 = 2x^2$ to the graph of $y_2 = -\frac{1}{2}x^2$.

3. Find the maximum y-value on the graph of $y = -3x^2 + 12x - 5$. State where the graph is increasing and where it is decreasing.

4. Sketch a graph of $y = f(x)$. Compare the graph of f to the graph of $y = x^2$.
   (a) $f(x) = (x - 1)^2 + 2$
   (b) $f(x) = -(x + 3)^2$

5. Write the vertex form for each equation.
   (a) $y = x^2 + 14x - 7$
   (b) $y = 4x^2 + 8x - 2$

8.3 QUADRATIC EQUATIONS

Basics of Quadratic Equations ▪ The Square Root Property ▪ Completing the Square ▪ Solving an Equation for a Variable ▪ Applications of Quadratic Equations

A LOOK INTO MATH ▷

In Section 8.2 we modeled curves on airport taxiways by using $R(x) = \frac{1}{2}x^2$. In this formula x represented the airplane's speed in miles per hour, and R represented the radius of the curve in feet. This formula may be used to determine the speed limit for a curve with a radius of **650** feet by solving the *quadratic equation*

$$\frac{1}{2}x^2 = 650.$$

In this section we demonstrate techniques for solving this and other quadratic equations.

Basics of Quadratic Equations

Any quadratic function f can be represented by $f(x) = ax^2 + bx + c$ with $a \neq 0$. Examples of quadratic functions include

$$f(x) = 2x^2 - 1, \quad g(x) = -\frac{1}{3}x^2 + 2x, \quad \text{and} \quad h(x) = x^2 + 2x - 1.$$

Quadratic functions can be used to write quadratic equations. Examples of quadratic equations include

$$2x^2 - 1 = 0, \quad -\frac{1}{3}x^2 + 2x = 0, \quad \text{and} \quad x^2 + 2x - 1 = 0.$$

QUADRATIC EQUATION

A **quadratic equation** is an equation that can be written as

$$ax^2 + bx + c = 0,$$

where a, b, and c are constants with $a \neq 0$.

Solutions to the quadratic equation $ax^2 + bx + c = 0$ correspond to x-intercepts of the graph of $y = ax^2 + bx + c$. Because the graph of a quadratic function is either $\cup$-shaped or $\cap$-shaped, it can intersect the x-axis zero, one, or two times, as illustrated in Figure 8.33. Hence a quadratic equation can have zero, one, or two real solutions.

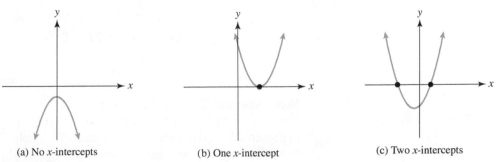

(a) No x-intercepts   (b) One x-intercept   (c) Two x-intercepts

Figure 8.33

We have already solved quadratic equations by factoring, graphing, and constructing tables. In the next example we apply these three techniques to quadratic equations that have no real solutions, one real solution, and two real solutions.

EXAMPLE 1   Solving quadratic equations

Solve each quadratic equation. Support your results numerically and graphically.

(a) $2x^2 + 1 = 0$ (No real solutions)

(b) $x^2 + 4 = 4x$ (One real solution)

(c) $x^2 - 6x + 8 = 0$ (Two real solutions)

Solution

(a) *Symbolic Solution*

$$
\begin{aligned}
2x^2 + 1 &= 0 && \text{Given equation} \\
2x^2 &= -1 && \text{Subtract 1.} \\
x^2 &= -\frac{1}{2} && \text{Divide by 2.}
\end{aligned}
$$

This equation has no real-number solutions because $x^2 \geq 0$ for all real numbers x.

Numerical and Graphical Solution   The points in Table 8.11 for $y = 2x^2 + 1$ are plotted in Figure 8.34 and connected with a parabolic graph. The graph of $y = 2x^2 + 1$ has no x-intercepts, indicating that there are no real solutions.

TABLE 8.11

x	y
-2	9
-1	3
0	1
1	3
2	9

For all x, $y \neq 0$.

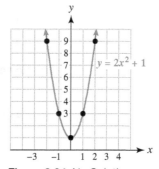

Figure 8.34 No Solutions

(b) *Symbolic Solution*

$$
\begin{aligned}
x^2 + 4 &= 4x && \text{Given equation} \\
x^2 - 4x + 4 &= 0 && \text{Subtract } 4x \text{ from each side.} \\
(x - 2)(x - 2) &= 0 && \text{Factor.} \\
x - 2 = 0 \quad \text{or} \quad x - 2 &= 0 && \text{Zero-product property} \\
x &= 2 && \text{There is one solution.}
\end{aligned}
$$

Numerical and Graphical Solution   Because the given quadratic equation is equivalent to $x^2 - 4x + 4 = 0$, we let $y = x^2 - 4x + 4$. The points in Table 8.12 are plotted in Figure 8.35 and connected with a parabolic graph. The graph of $y = x^2 - 4x + 4$ has one x-intercept, 2. Note that in Table 8.12, $y = 0$ when $x = 2$, indicating that the equation has one solution.

TABLE 8.12

x	y
0	4
1	1
2	**0**
3	1
4	4

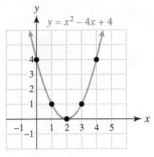

Figure 8.35 One Solution

(c) Symbolic Solution

$$
\begin{array}{ll}
x^2 - 6x + 8 = 0 & \text{Given equation} \\
(x - 2)(x - 4) = 0 & \text{Factor.} \\
x - 2 = 0 \quad \text{or} \quad x - 4 = 0 & \text{Zero-product property} \\
x = 2 \quad \text{or} \quad x = 4 & \text{There are two solutions.}
\end{array}
$$

Numerical and Graphical Solution   The points in Table 8.13 for $y = x^2 - 6x + 8$ are plotted in Figure 8.36 and connected with a parabolic graph. The graph of $y = x^2 - 6x + 8$ has two x-intercepts, 2 and 4, indicating two solutions. Note that in Table 8.13 $y = 0$ when $x = 2$ or $x = 4$.

TABLE 8.13

x	y
0	8
1	3
2	**0**
3	−1
4	**0**
5	3
6	8

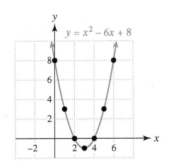

Figure 8.36 Two Solutions

Now Try Exercises 29, 37, 39

The Square Root Property

The **square root property** is used to solve quadratic equations that have no x-terms. The following is an example of the square root property.

$$x^2 = 25 \quad \text{is equivalent to} \quad x = \pm 5.$$

The equation $x = \pm 5$ (read "x equals plus or minus 5") indicates that either $x = 5$ or $x = -5$. Each value is a solution because $(5)^2 = 25$ and $(-5)^2 = 25$.

We can derive this result in general for $k \geq 0$.

$$
\begin{array}{ll}
x^2 = k & \text{Given quadratic equation} \\
\sqrt{x^2} = \sqrt{k} & \text{Take the square root of each side.} \\
|x| = \sqrt{k} & \sqrt{x^2} = |x| \text{ for all } x. \\
x = \pm\sqrt{k} & |x| = b \text{ implies } x = \pm b, b \geq 0.
\end{array}
$$

This result is summarized by the *square root property*.

SQUARE ROOT PROPERTY

Let k be a nonnegative number. Then the solutions to the equation

$$x^2 = k$$

are given by $x = \pm \sqrt{k}$. If $k < 0$, then this equation has no real solutions.

Before applying the square root property in the next two examples, we review a quotient property of square roots. If a and b are positive numbers, then

$$\sqrt{\frac{a}{b}} = \frac{\sqrt{a}}{\sqrt{b}}.$$

For example, $\sqrt{\frac{25}{36}} = \frac{\sqrt{25}}{\sqrt{36}} = \frac{5}{6}$.

EXAMPLE 2   Using the square root property

Solve each equation.
(a) $x^2 = 7$ **(b)** $16x^2 - 9 = 0$ **(c)** $(x - 4)^2 = 25$

Solution
(a) $x^2 = 7$ is equivalent to $x = \pm \sqrt{7}$ by the square root property. The solutions are $\sqrt{7}$ and $-\sqrt{7}$.

(b)

$$16x^2 - 9 = 0 \qquad \text{Given equation}$$

$$16x^2 = 9 \qquad \text{Add 9.}$$

$$x^2 = \frac{9}{16} \qquad \text{Divide by 16.}$$

$$x = \pm\sqrt{\frac{9}{16}} \qquad \text{Square root property}$$

$$x = \pm\frac{3}{4} \qquad \text{Simplify.}$$

The solutions are $\frac{3}{4}$ and $-\frac{3}{4}$.

(c)

$$(x - 4)^2 = 25 \qquad \text{Given equation}$$

$$(x - 4) = \pm\sqrt{25} \qquad \text{Square root property}$$

$$x - 4 = \pm 5 \qquad \text{Simplify.}$$

$$x = 4 \pm 5 \qquad \text{Add 4.}$$

$$x = 9 \quad \text{or} \quad x = -1 \qquad \text{Evaluate } 4 + 5 \text{ and } 4 - 5.$$

The solutions are 9 and -1.

Now Try Exercises 51, 53, 57

▶ **REAL-WORLD CONNECTION**   If an object is dropped from a height of h feet, its distance d above the ground after t seconds is given by

$$d(t) = h - 16t^2.$$

This formula can be used to estimate the time it takes for a falling object to hit the ground.

EXAMPLE 3 Modeling a falling object

A toy falls 30 feet from a window. How long does the toy take to hit the ground?

Solution

The height of the window above the ground is 30 feet so let $d(t) = 30 - 16t^2$. The toy strikes the ground when the distance d above the ground equals 0.

$$
\begin{array}{ll}
30 - 16t^2 = 0 & \text{Equation to solve for } t \\[4pt]
-16t^2 = -30 & \text{Subtract 30.} \\[4pt]
t^2 = \dfrac{30}{16} & \text{Divide by } -16. \\[8pt]
t = \pm\sqrt{\dfrac{30}{16}} & \text{Square root property} \\[8pt]
t = \pm\dfrac{\sqrt{30}}{4} & \text{Simplify.}
\end{array}
$$

Time cannot be negative in this problem, so the appropriate solution is $t = \frac{\sqrt{30}}{4} \approx 1.4$. The toy hits the ground after about 1.4 seconds.   Now Try Exercise 115

Completing the Square

In Section 8.2 we used the *method of completing the square* to find the vertex of a parabola. This method can also be used to solve quadratic equations. Because

$$x^2 + bx + \left(\frac{b}{2}\right)^2 = \left(x + \frac{b}{2}\right)^2,$$

CRITICAL THINKING

Use the figure to *complete the square* for $x^2 + 6x$.

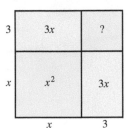

we can solve a quadratic equation in the form $x^2 + bx = d$, where b and d are constants, by adding $\left(\frac{b}{2}\right)^2$ to each side and then factoring the resulting perfect square trinomial.

In the equation $x^2 + 6x = 7$ we have $b = 6$, so we add $\left(\frac{6}{2}\right)^2 = 9$ to each side.

$$
\begin{array}{ll}
x^2 + 6x = 7 & \text{Given equation} \\[4pt]
x^2 + 6x + 9 = 7 + 9 & \text{Add 9 to each side.} \\[4pt]
(x + 3)^2 = 16 & \text{Perfect square trinomial} \\[4pt]
x + 3 = \pm 4 & \text{Square root property} \\[4pt]
x = -3 \pm 4 & \text{Add } -3 \text{ to each side.} \\[4pt]
x = 1 \quad \text{or} \quad x = -7 & \text{Simplify } -3 + 4 \text{ and } -3 - 4.
\end{array}
$$

The solutions are 1 and -7. Note that the left side of the equation becomes a perfect square trinomial. We show how to create one in the next example.

EXAMPLE 4 Creating a perfect square trinomial

Find the term that should be added to $x^2 - 10x$ to form a perfect square trinomial.

Solution

The coefficient of the x-term is -10, so we let $b = -10$. To complete the square we divide b by 2 and then square the result.

$$\left(\frac{b}{2}\right)^2 = \left(\frac{-10}{2}\right)^2 = 25$$

If we add **25** to $x^2 - 10x$, a perfect square trinomial is formed.

$$x^2 - 10x + 25 = (x - 5)^2$$ Now Try Exercise **67**

Completing the square can be used to solve quadratic equations when a trinomial does not factor easily, as illustrated in the next two examples.

EXAMPLE **5**   Completing the square when the leading coefficient is 1

Solve the equation $x^2 - 4x + 2 = 0$.

Solution
Start by writing the equation in the form $x^2 + bx = d$.

$x^2 - 4x + 2 = 0$	Given equation
$x^2 - 4x = -2$	Subtract 2.
$x^2 - 4x + 4 = -2 + 4$	Add $\left(\frac{b}{2}\right)^2 = \left(\frac{-4}{2}\right)^2 = 4$.
$(x - 2)^2 = 2$	Perfect square trinomial; add.
$x - 2 = \pm\sqrt{2}$	Square root property
$x = 2 \pm \sqrt{2}$	Add 2.

The solutions are $2 + \sqrt{2} \approx 3.41$ and $2 - \sqrt{2} \approx 0.59$.   Now Try Exercise **73**

EXAMPLE **6**   Completing the square when the leading coefficient is not 1

Solve the equation $2x^2 + 7x - 5 = 0$.

Solution
Start by writing the equation in the form $x^2 + bx = d$. That is, add 5 to each side and then divide the equation by 2 so that the leading coefficient of the x^2-term becomes 1.

$2x^2 + 7x - 5 = 0$	Given equation
$2x^2 + 7x = 5$	Add 5.
$x^2 + \frac{7}{2}x = \frac{5}{2}$	Divide by 2.
$x^2 + \frac{7}{2}x + \frac{49}{16} = \frac{5}{2} + \frac{49}{16}$	Add $\left(\frac{b}{2}\right)^2 = \left(\frac{7}{4}\right)^2 = \frac{49}{16}$.
$\left(x + \frac{7}{4}\right)^2 = \frac{89}{16}$	Perfect square trinomial; add.
$x + \frac{7}{4} = \pm\frac{\sqrt{89}}{4}$	Square root property
$x = -\frac{7}{4} \pm \frac{\sqrt{89}}{4}$	Add $-\frac{7}{4}$.
$x = \frac{-7 \pm \sqrt{89}}{4}$	Combine fractions.

CRITICAL THINKING

What happens if you try to solve
$$2x^2 - 13 = 1$$
by completing the square? What method could you use to solve this problem?

The solutions are $\frac{-7 + \sqrt{89}}{4} \approx 0.61$ and $\frac{-7 - \sqrt{89}}{4} \approx -4.1$.   Now Try Exercise **81**

Figure 8.37

Solving an Equation for a Variable

We often need to solve an equation or formula for a variable. For example, the formula $V = \frac{1}{3}\pi r^2 h$ calculates the volume of the cone shown in Figure 8.37. Let's say that we know the volume V is 120 cubic inches and the height h is 15 inches. We can then find the radius of the cone by solving the equation for r.

$$V = \frac{1}{3}\pi r^2 h \qquad \text{Solve the equation for } r.$$

$$3V = \pi r^2 h \qquad \text{Multiply by 3.}$$

$$\frac{3V}{\pi} = r^2 h \qquad \text{Divide by } \pi.$$

$$\frac{3V}{\pi h} = r^2 \qquad \text{Divide by } h.$$

$$r = \pm\sqrt{\frac{3V}{\pi h}} \qquad \text{Square root property; rewrite.}$$

Because $r \geq 0$, we use the positive or *principal square root*. Thus for $V = 120$ cubic inches and $h = 15$ inches,

$$r = \sqrt{\frac{3(120)}{\pi(15)}} = \sqrt{\frac{24}{\pi}} \approx 2.8 \text{ inches.}$$

EXAMPLE 7   Solving equations for variables

Solve each equation for the specified variable.
(a) $s = -\frac{1}{2}gt^2 + h$, for t **(b)** $d^2 = x^2 + y^2$, for y

Solution
(a) Begin by subtracting h from each side of the equation.

$$s = -\tfrac{1}{2}gt^2 + h \qquad \text{Solve the equation for } t.$$

$$s - h = -\tfrac{1}{2}gt^2 \qquad \text{Subtract } h.$$

$$-2(s - h) = gt^2 \qquad \text{Multiply by } -2.$$

$$\frac{2h - 2s}{g} = t^2 \qquad \text{Divide by } g; \text{ simplify.}$$

$$t = \pm\sqrt{\frac{2h - 2s}{g}} \qquad \text{Square root property; rewrite.}$$

(b) Begin by subtracting x^2 from each side of the equation.

$$d^2 = x^2 + y^2 \qquad \text{Solve the equation for } y.$$

$$d^2 - x^2 = y^2 \qquad \text{Subtract } x^2.$$

$$y = \pm\sqrt{d^2 - x^2} \qquad \text{Square root property; rewrite.}$$

Now Try Exercises 107, 108

Applications of Quadratic Equations

▶ REAL-WORLD CONNECTION   In the introduction to this section we discussed how the solution to $\frac{1}{2}x^2 = 650$ would give a safe speed limit for a curve with a radius of 650 feet on an airport taxiway. We solve this problem in the next example.   (*Source:* FAA.)

EXAMPLE 8   Finding a safe speed limit

Solve $\frac{1}{2}x^2 = 650$ and interpret any solutions.

Solution
Use the square root property to solve this problem.

$$\frac{1}{2}x^2 = 650 \qquad \text{Given equation}$$

$$x^2 = 1300 \qquad \text{Multiply by 2.}$$

$$x = \pm \sqrt{1300} \qquad \text{Square root property}$$

The solutions are $\sqrt{1300} \approx 36$ and $-\sqrt{1300} \approx -36$. The solution of $x \approx 36$ indicates that a safe speed limit for a curve with a radius of 650 feet should be 36 miles per hour. (The negative solution has no physical meaning in this problem.)   Now Try Exercise 113

▶ REAL-WORLD CONNECTION   In applications, solving a quadratic equation either graphically or numerically is often easier than solving it symbolically. We do so in the next example.

EXAMPLE 9   Modeling numbers of Internet users

Use of the Internet in Western Europe has increased dramatically. Figure 8.38 shows a scatterplot of online users in Western Europe, together with a graph of a function f that models the data. The function f is given by

$$f(x) = 0.976x^2 - 4.643x + 0.238,$$

where the output is in millions of users. In this formula $x = 6$ corresponds to 1996, $x = 7$ to 1997, and so on, until $x = 12$ represents 2002.   (*Source:* Nortel Networks.)

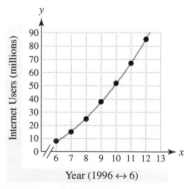

Figure 8.38 Internet Usage in Western Europe

(a) Evaluate $f(10)$ and interpret the result.
(b) Graph f and estimate the year when the number of Internet users reached 85 million. Compare your result with Figure 8.38.
(c) Solve part (b) numerically.

Solution
(a) Substituting $x = 10$ in the formula gives

$$f(10) = 0.976(10)^2 - 4.643(10) + 0.238 \approx 51.4.$$

Because $x = 10$ corresponds to 2000, there were about 51.4 million Internet users in Western Europe in 2000.
(b) Graph $Y_1 = .976X^2 - 4.643X + .238$ and $Y_2 = 85$, as shown in Figure 8.39. Their graphs intersect near $x = 12$, which corresponds to 2002 and agrees with Figure 8.38.
(c) The table for y_1, shown in Figure 8.40, reveals $y_1 \approx 85$ when $x = 12$.

CALCULATOR HELP

To find a point of intersection, see the Appendix (page AP-7).

[5, 13, 1] by [0, 100, 10]

Intersection
X=11.996485 Y=85

Figure 8.39

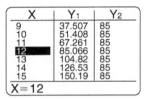

X	Y₁	Y₂
9	37.507	85
10	51.408	85
11	67.261	85
12	85.066	85
13	104.82	85
14	126.53	85
15	150.19	85

X=12

Figure 8.40

Now Try Exercise 124

8.3 PUTTING IT ALL TOGETHER

Quadratic equations can be expressed in the form $ax^2 + bx + c = 0$, $a \neq 0$. They can have no real solutions, one real solution, or two real solutions and may be solved symbolically, graphically, and numerically. Symbolic techniques for solving quadratic equations include factoring, the square root property, and completing the square. We discussed factoring extensively in Chapter 5, so the following table summarizes only the square root property and the method of completing the square.

Technique	Description	Examples
Square Root Property	If $k \geq 0$, the solutions to the equation $x^2 = k$ are $\pm \sqrt{k}$.	$x^2 = 100$ is equivalent to $x = \pm 10$ and $x^2 = 13$ is equivalent to $x = \pm \sqrt{13}$. $x^2 = -2$ has no real solutions.

continued on next page

continued from previous page

Technique	Description	Examples
Method of Completing the Square	To solve an equation in the form $x^2 + bx = d$, add $\left(\frac{b}{2}\right)^2$ to each side of the equation. Factor the resulting perfect square trinomial and solve for x by applying the square root property.	To solve $x^2 + 8x = 3$, add $\left(\frac{8}{2}\right)^2 = 16$ to each side. $x^2 + 8x + 16 = 3 + 16$ Add 16 to each side. $(x + 4)^2 = 19$ Perfect square trinomial $x + 4 = \pm\sqrt{19}$ Square root property $x = -4 \pm \sqrt{19}$ Add -4.

8.3 Exercises

MyMathLab   Math XL PRACTICE   WATCH   DOWNLOAD   READ   REVIEW

CONCEPTS

1. Give an example of a quadratic equation. How many real solutions can a quadratic equation have?

2. Is a quadratic equation a linear equation or a nonlinear equation?

3. Name three symbolic methods that can be used to solve a quadratic equation.

4. Sketch a graph of a quadratic function that has two x-intercepts and opens downward.

5. Sketch a graph of a quadratic function that has no x-intercepts and opens upward.

6. If the graph of $y = ax^2 + bx + c$ intersects the x-axis twice, how many solutions does the equation $ax^2 + bx + c = 0$ have? Explain.

7. Solve $x^2 = 64$. What property did you use?

8. To solve $x^2 + bx = 6$ by completing the square, what value should be added to each side of the equation?

Exercises 9–16: Is the given equation quadratic?

9. $x^2 - 3x + 1 = 0$ 10. $2x^2 - 3 = 0$

11. $3x + 1 = 0$ 12. $x^3 - 3x^2 + x = 0$

13. $-3x^2 + x = 16$ 14. $x^2 - 1 = 4x$

15. $x^2 = \sqrt{x} + 1$ 16. $\frac{1}{x - 1} = 5$

Exercises 17–20: Approximate to the nearest hundredth.

17. (a) $1 \pm \sqrt{7}$ (b) $-2 \pm \sqrt{11}$

18. (a) $\pm\frac{\sqrt{3}}{2}$ (b) $\pm\frac{2\sqrt{5}}{7}$

19. (a) $\frac{3 \pm \sqrt{13}}{5}$ (b) $\frac{-5 \pm \sqrt{6}}{9}$

20. (a) $\frac{2}{5} \pm \frac{\sqrt{5}}{5}$ (b) $-\frac{3}{7} \pm \frac{\sqrt{3}}{7}$

SOLVING QUADRATIC EQUATIONS

Exercises 21–24: A graph of $y = ax^2 + bx + c$ is given. Use this graph to solve $ax^2 + bx + c = 0$, if possible.

21.

22.

23.

24.

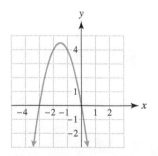

Exercises 25–28: A table of $y = ax^2 + bx + c$ is given. Use this table to solve $ax^2 + bx + c = 0$.

25.

X	Y₁	
-3	6	
-2	0	
-1	-4	
0	-6	
1	-6	
2	-4	
3	0	

Y₁≡X^2−X−6

26.

X	Y₁	
-6	0	
-4	-16	
-2	-24	
0	-24	
2	-16	
4	0	
6	24	

Y₁≡X^2+2X−24

27.

X	Y₁	
-2	9	
-1.5	4	
-1	1	
-.5	0	
0	1	
.5	4	
1	9	

Y₁≡4X^2+4X+1

28.

X	Y₁	
-4	-2.5	
-3	0	
-2	1.5	
-1	2	
0	1.5	
1	0	
2	-2.5	

Y₁≡−X^2/2−X+3/2

Exercises 29–40: Solve the quadratic equation. Support your results numerically and graphically.

29. $x^2 - 4x - 5 = 0$

30. $x^2 - x - 6 = 0$

31. $x^2 + 2x = 3$

32. $x^2 + 4x = 5$

33. $x^2 = 9$

34. $x^2 = 4$

35. $4x^2 - 4x - 3 = 0$

36. $2x^2 + x = 1$

37. $x^2 + 2x = -1$

38. $4x^2 - 4x + 1 = 0$

39. $x^2 + 2 = 0$

40. $-4x^2 - 1 = 2$

Exercises 41–50: Solve by factoring.

41. $x^2 + 2x - 35 = 0$

42. $2x^2 - 7x + 3 = 0$

43. $6x^2 - x - 1 = 0$

44. $x^2 + 4x + 6 = -3x$

45. $2x^2 + x + 3 = 6x$

46. $6x^2 - x = 15$

47. $25x^2 - 350 = 125x$

48. $20x^2 + 150 = 130x$

49. $2(5x^2 + 9) = 27x$

50. $15(3x^2 + x) = 10$

Exercises 51–62: Use the square root property to solve.

51. $x^2 = 144$

52. $4x^2 - 5 = 0$

53. $5x^2 - 64 = 0$

54. $3x^2 = 7$

55. $(x + 1)^2 = 25$

56. $(x + 4)^2 = 9$

57. $(x - 1)^2 = 64$

58. $(x - 3)^2 = 0$

59. $(2x - 1)^2 = 5$

60. $(5x + 3)^2 = 7$

61. $10(x - 5)^2 = 50$

62. $7(3x + 1)^2 = 14$

COMPLETING THE SQUARE

Exercises 63–66: To solve by completing the square, what value should you add to each side of the equation?

63. $x^2 + 4x = -3$

64. $x^2 - 6x = 4$

65. $x^2 - 5x = 4$

66. $x^2 + 3x = 1$

Exercises 67–70: (Refer to Example 4.) Find the term that should be added to the expression to form a perfect square trinomial. Write the resulting perfect square trinomial in factored form.

67. $x^2 - 8x$

68. $x^2 - 5x$

69. $x^2 + 9x$

70. $x^2 + x$

Exercises 71–86: Solve by completing the square.

71. $x^2 - 2x = 24$

72. $x^2 - 2x + \frac{1}{2} = 0$

73. $x^2 + 6x - 2 = 0$

74. $x^2 - 16x = 5$

75. $x^2 - 3x = 5$

76. $x^2 + 5x = 2$

77. $x^2 - 5x + 1 = 0$

78. $x^2 - 9x + 7 = 0$

79. $x^2 - 4 = 2x$

80. $x^2 + 1 = 7x$

81. $2x^2 - 3x = 4$

82. $3x^2 + 6x - 5 = 0$

83. $4x^2 - 8x - 7 = 0$

84. $25x^2 - 20x - 1 = 0$

85. $36x^2 + 18x + 1 = 0$

86. $12x^2 + 8x - 2 = 0$

Exercises 87–96: Solve by any method.

87. $3x^2 + 12x = 36$

88. $6x^2 + 9x = 27$

89. $x^2 + 4x = -2$

90. $x^2 + 6x + 3 = 0$

91. $3x^2 - 4 = 2$

92. $-2x^2 + 3 = 1$

93. $-6x^2 + 70 = 16x$

94. $-15x^2 + 25x + 10 = 0$

95. $-3x(x - 8) = 6$

96. $-2x(4 - x) = 8$

Exercises 97 and 98: **Thinking Generally** *Solve for x. Assume a and c are positive.*

97. $ax^2 - c = 0$

98. $ax^2 + bx = 0$

SOLVING EQUATIONS BY MORE THAN ONE METHOD

Exercises 99–104: Solve the quadratic equation
   (a) symbolically,
   (b) graphically, and
   (c) numerically.

99. $x^2 - 3x - 18 = 0$ **100.** $\frac{1}{2}x^2 + 2x - 6 = 0$

101. $x^2 - 8x + 15 = 0$ **102.** $2x^2 + 3 = 7x$

103. $4(x^2 + 35) = 48x$ **104.** $4x(2 - x) = -5$

SOLVING AN EQUATION FOR A VARIABLE

Exercises 105–112: Solve for the specified variable.

105. $x = y^2 - 1$ for y **106.** $x = 9y^2$ for y

107. $K = \frac{1}{2}mv^2$ for v **108.** $c^2 = a^2 + b^2$ for b

109. $E = \frac{k}{r^2}$ for r **110.** $W = I^2R$ for I

111. $LC = \dfrac{1}{(2\pi f)^2}$ for f **112.** $F = \dfrac{KmM}{r^2}$ for r

APPLICATIONS

113. *Safe Curve Speed*   (Refer to Example 8.) Find a safe speed limit x for an airport taxiway curve with the given radius R by using $R = \frac{1}{2}x^2$.
   (a) $R = 450$ feet   **(b)** $R = 800$ feet

114. *Braking Distance*   The braking distance y in feet that it takes for a car to stop on wet, level pavement can be estimated by $y = \frac{1}{9}x^2$, where x is the speed of the car in miles per hour. Find the speed associated with each braking distance.   (*Source:* L. Haefner, *Introduction to Transportation Systems.*)
   (a) 25 feet   **(b)** 361 feet   **(c)** 784 feet

115. *Falling Object*   (Refer to Example 3.) How long does it take for a toy to hit the ground if it is dropped out of a window 60 feet above the ground? Does it take twice as long as it takes to fall from a window 30 feet above the ground?

116. *Falling Object*   If a metal ball is thrown *downward* with an initial velocity of 22 feet per second (15 mph)

from a 100-foot water tower, its height h in feet above the ground after t seconds is modeled by

$$h(t) = -16t^2 - 22t + 100.$$

(a) Determine symbolically when the height of the ball is 62 feet.

(b) Support your result in part (a) either graphically or numerically.

(c) If the ball is thrown *upward* at 22 feet per second, then its height is given by

$$h(t) = -16t^2 + 22t + 100.$$

Determine when the height of the ball is 80 feet.

Exercises 117 and 118: Television Size (Refer to the introduction of this chapter.) The size S of the television screen recommended for a person who sits x feet from the screen ($6 \leq x \leq 15$) is given by

$$S(x) = -0.227x^2 + 8.155x - 8.8.$$

If a person buys a television set with a size S screen, how far from the screen should the person sit?

117. $S = 42$ inches   **118.** $S = 50$ inches

119. *Distance*   Two athletes start jogging at the same time. One jogs north at 6 miles per hour while the second jogs east at 8 miles per hour. After how long are the two athletes 20 miles apart?

120. *Geometry* A triangle has an area of 35 square inches, and its base is 3 inches more than its height. Find the base and height of the triangle.

121. *Construction* A rectangular plot of land has an area of 520 square feet and is 6 feet longer than it is wide.
(a) Write a quadratic equation in the form $ax^2 + bx + c = 0$, whose solution gives the width of the plot of land.
(b) Solve the equation.

122. *Modeling Motion* The height y in feet of a tennis ball after x seconds is shown in the graph. Estimate when the ball was 25 feet above the ground.

123. *Seedling Growth* (Refer to Exercise 87, Section 8.1.) The heights of melon seedlings grown at different temperatures are shown in the following graph. At what temperatures were the heights of the seedlings about 22 centimeters? (*Source:* R. Pearl, "The growth of *Cucumis melo* seedlings at different temperatures.")

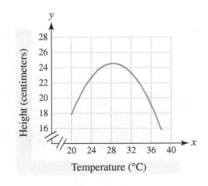

124. *Internet Users* (Refer to Example 9.) Estimate either graphically or numerically when the number of Internet users in Western Europe reached 150 million.

125. *U.S. Population* The table shows the population of the United States in millions from 1800 through 2000 at 20-year intervals.

Year	1800	1820	1840	1860
Population	5	10	17	31

Year	1880	1900	1920	1940
Population	50	76	106	132

Year	1960	1980	2000
Population	179	226	269

Source: U.S. Census Bureau.

(a) Without plotting the data, how do you know that the data are nonlinear?
(b) These data are modeled by

$$f(x) = 0.0066(x - 1800)^2 + 5.$$

Find the vertex of the graph of f and interpret it.
(c) Estimate when the U.S. population reached 85 million.

126. *Trade Deficit* The U.S. trade deficit in billions of dollars for the years 1997, 1998, and 1999 can be computed by

$$f(x) = 16x^2 - 63,861x + 63,722,378,$$

where x is the year. In which year was the trade deficit \$164 billion? (*Source:* Department of Commerce.)

WRITING ABOUT MATHEMATICS

127. Suppose that you are asked to solve

$$ax^2 + bx + c = 0.$$

Explain how the graph of $y = ax^2 + bx + c$ can be used to find any real solutions to the equation.

128. Explain why a quadratic equation could not have more than two solutions. (*Hint:* Consider the graph of $y = ax^2 + bx + c$.)

GROUP ACTIVITY
WORKING WITH REAL DATA

Directions: Form a group of 2 to 4 people. Select someone to record the group's responses for this activity. All members of the group should work cooperatively to answer the questions. If your instructor asks for the results, each member of the group should be prepared to respond.

Minimum Wage   The table shows the minimum wage for three different years.

Year	1940	1968	1997
Wage ($)	0.25	1.60	5.15

Source: Bureau of Labor Statistics.

 (a) Make a scatterplot of the data in the viewing rectangle [1930, 2010, 10] by [0, 6, 1].

(b) Find a quadratic function given by
$$f(x) = a(x - h)^2 + k$$
that models the data.

(c) Estimate the minimum wage in 1976 and compare it to the actual value of $2.30.

(d) Estimate when the minimum wage was $1.00.

(e) If current trends continue, predict the minimum wage in 2009. Compare it to the projected value of $7.25.

8.4   THE QUADRATIC FORMULA

Solving Quadratic Equations ■ The Discriminant ■ Quadratic Equations Having Complex Solutions

A LOOK INTO MATH ▷   To model the stopping distance of a car, highway engineers compute two quantities. The first quantity is the *reaction distance*, which is the distance a car travels from the time a driver first recognizes a hazard until the brakes are applied. The second quantity is *braking distance*, which is the distance a car travels after a driver applies the brakes. *Stopping distance* equals the sum of the reaction distance and the braking distance. If a car is traveling x miles per hour, highway engineers estimate the reaction distance in feet as $\frac{11}{3}x$ and the braking distance in feet as $\frac{1}{9}x^2$. See Figure 8.41. (*Source:* L. Haefner, *Introduction to Transportation Systems.*)

Figure 8.41 Stopping Distance

To estimate the total stopping distance d in feet, add the two expressions to obtain
$$d(x) = \frac{1}{9}x^2 + \frac{11}{3}x.$$

If a car's headlights don't illuminate the road beyond 500 feet, a safe nighttime speed limit x for the car can be determined by solving the quadratic equation

$$\frac{1}{9}x^2 \quad + \quad \frac{11}{3}x \quad = \quad 500.$$

Braking Distance $+$ Reaction Distance $=$ Stopping Distance

In this section we learn how to solve this equation with the quadratic formula.

Solving Quadratic Equations

Recall that any quadratic equation can be written in the form

$$ax^2 + bx + c = 0.$$

If we solve this equation for x in terms of a, b, and c by completing the square, we obtain the **quadratic formula**. We assume that $a > 0$ and derive it as follows.

$ax^2 + bx + c = 0$	Quadratic equation
$ax^2 + bx = -c$	Subtract c.
$x^2 + \dfrac{b}{a}x = -\dfrac{c}{a}$	Divide by a.
$x^2 + \dfrac{b}{a}x + \dfrac{b^2}{4a^2} = -\dfrac{c}{a} + \dfrac{b^2}{4a^2}$	Add $\left(\frac{b/a}{2}\right)^2 = \frac{b^2}{4a^2}$.
$\left(x + \dfrac{b}{2a}\right)^2 = -\dfrac{c}{a} + \dfrac{b^2}{4a^2}$	Perfect square trinomial
$\left(x + \dfrac{b}{2a}\right)^2 = -\dfrac{c \cdot 4a}{a \cdot 4a} + \dfrac{b^2}{4a^2}$	Multiply $-\frac{c}{a}$ by $\frac{4a}{4a}$.
$\left(x + \dfrac{b}{2a}\right)^2 = -\dfrac{4ac}{4a^2} + \dfrac{b^2}{4a^2}$	Simplify.
$\left(x + \dfrac{b}{2a}\right)^2 = \dfrac{-4ac + b^2}{4a^2}$	Add fractions.
$\left(x + \dfrac{b}{2a}\right)^2 = \dfrac{b^2 - 4ac}{4a^2}$	Rewrite.
$x + \dfrac{b}{2a} = \pm\sqrt{\dfrac{b^2 - 4ac}{4a^2}}$	Square root property
$x = -\dfrac{b}{2a} \pm \sqrt{\dfrac{b^2 - 4ac}{4a^2}}$	Add $-\frac{b}{2a}$.
$x = -\dfrac{b}{2a} \pm \dfrac{\sqrt{b^2 - 4ac}}{2a}$	Property of square roots
$x = \dfrac{-b \pm \sqrt{b^2 - 4ac}}{2a}$	Combine fractions.

QUADRATIC FORMULA

The solutions to $ax^2 + bx + c = 0$ with $a \neq 0$ are given by

$$x = \frac{-b \pm \sqrt{b^2 - 4ac}}{2a}.$$

NOTE: The quadratic formula can be used to solve *any* quadratic equation. It always "works."

MAKING CONNECTIONS

Completing the Square and the Quadratic Formula

The quadratic formula results from completing the square for the equation $ax^2 + bx + c = 0$. When you use the quadratic formula, the work of completing the square has already been done for you. However, you can always complete the square rather than use the quadratic formula. See Example 10.

The next three examples show symbolic and graphical solutions to quadratic equations.

EXAMPLE 1 Solving a quadratic equation having two solutions

Solve the equation $2x^2 - 3x - 1 = 0$. Support your results graphically.

Solution
Symbolic Solution Let $a = 2$, $b = -3$, and $c = -1$.

$$x = \frac{-b \pm \sqrt{b^2 - 4ac}}{2a} \qquad \text{Quadratic formula}$$

$$x = \frac{-(-3) \pm \sqrt{(-3)^2 - 4(2)(-1)}}{2(2)} \qquad \text{Substitute for } a, b, \text{ and } c.$$

$$x = \frac{3 \pm \sqrt{17}}{4} \qquad \text{Simplify.}$$

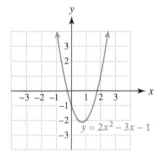

The solutions are $\frac{3 + \sqrt{17}}{4} \approx 1.78$ and $\frac{3 - \sqrt{17}}{4} \approx -0.28$.

Figure 8.42 Two *x*-intercepts

Graphical Solution The graph of $y = 2x^2 - 3x - 1$ is shown in Figure 8.42. Note that the two *x*-intercepts correspond to the two solutions to $2x^2 - 3x - 1 = 0$. Estimating from this graph, we see that the solutions are approximately -0.25 and 1.75, which supports our symbolic solution. (You could also use a graphing calculator to find the *x*-intercepts.)

Now Try Exercise 9

CRITICAL THINKING

Use the results of Example 1 to evaluate each expression mentally.

$$2\left(\frac{3 + \sqrt{17}}{4}\right)^2 - 3\left(\frac{3 + \sqrt{17}}{4}\right) - 1 \quad \text{and} \quad 2\left(\frac{3 - \sqrt{17}}{4}\right)^2 - 3\left(\frac{3 - \sqrt{17}}{4}\right) - 1$$

EXAMPLE 2 Solving a quadratic equation having one solution

Solve the equation $25x^2 + 20x + 4 = 0$. Support your result graphically.

Solution
Symbolic Solution   Let $a = 25$, $b = 20$, and $c = 4$.

$$x = \frac{-b \pm \sqrt{b^2 - 4ac}}{2a} \qquad \text{Quadratic formula}$$

$$= \frac{-20 \pm \sqrt{20^2 - 4(25)(4)}}{2(25)} \qquad \text{Substitute for } a, b, \text{ and } c.$$

$$= \frac{-20 \pm \sqrt{0}}{50} \qquad \text{Simplify.}$$

$$= \frac{-20}{50} = -0.4 \qquad \sqrt{0} = 0$$

There is one solution, -0.4.

Figure 8.43 One x-intercept

Graphical Solution   The graph of $y = 25x^2 + 20x + 4$ is shown in Figure 8.43. Note that the one x-intercept, -0.4, corresponds to the solution to $25x^2 + 20x + 4 = 0$.

Now Try Exercise 11

EXAMPLE 3 Recognizing a quadratic equation having no real solutions

Solve the equation $5x^2 - x + 3 = 0$. Support your result graphically.

Solution
Symbolic Solution   Let $a = 5$, $b = -1$, and $c = 3$.

$$x = \frac{-b \pm \sqrt{b^2 - 4ac}}{2a} \qquad \text{Quadratic formula}$$

$$= \frac{-(-1) \pm \sqrt{(-1)^2 - 4(5)(3)}}{2(5)} \qquad \text{Substitute for } a, b, \text{ and } c.$$

$$= \frac{1 \pm \sqrt{-59}}{10} \qquad \text{Simplify.}$$

There are no real solutions to this equation because $\sqrt{-59}$ *is not a real number.* (Later in this section we discuss how to find complex solutions to quadratic equations like this one.)

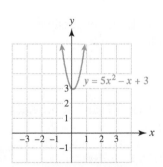

Figure 8.44 No x-intercepts

Graphical Solution   The graph of $y = 5x^2 - x + 3$ is shown in Figure 8.44. There are no x-intercepts, indicating that the equation $5x^2 - x + 3 = 0$ has no real solutions.

Now Try Exercise 12

▶ REAL-WORLD CONNECTION   Earlier in this section we discussed how engineers estimate safe stopping distances for automobiles. In the next example we solve the equation presented in the introduction.

EXAMPLE **4**   Modeling stopping distance

If a car's headlights do not illuminate the road beyond 500 feet, estimate a safe nighttime speed limit x for the car by solving $\frac{1}{9}x^2 + \frac{11}{3}x = 500$.

500 feet

Solution

Begin by subtracting 500 from each side of the given equation.

$$\frac{1}{9}x^2 + \frac{11}{3}x - 500 = 0. \qquad \text{Subtract 500.}$$

To eliminate fractions multiply each side by the LCD, which is 9. (This step is not necessary, but it makes the problem easier to work.)

$$x^2 + 33x - 4500 = 0. \qquad \text{Multiply by 9.}$$

Now let $a = 1$, $b = 33$, and $c = -4500$ in the quadratic formula.

$$x = \frac{-b \pm \sqrt{b^2 - 4ac}}{2a} \qquad \text{Quadratic formula}$$

$$= \frac{-33 \pm \sqrt{33^2 - 4(1)(-4500)}}{2(1)} \qquad \text{Substitute for } a, b, \text{ and } c.$$

$$= \frac{-33 \pm \sqrt{19{,}089}}{2} \qquad \text{Simplify.}$$

The solutions are

$$\frac{-33 + \sqrt{19{,}089}}{2} \approx 52.6 \quad \text{and} \quad \frac{-33 - \sqrt{19{,}089}}{2} \approx -85.6.$$

The negative solution has no physical meaning because negative speeds are not possible. The other solution is 52.6, so an appropriate speed limit might be 50 miles per hour.

Now Try Exercise **101**

The Discriminant

The expression $b^2 - 4ac$ in the quadratic formula is called the **discriminant**. It provides information about the number of solutions to a quadratic equation.

THE DISCRIMINANT AND QUADRATIC EQUATIONS

To determine the number of solutions to the quadratic equation $ax^2 + bx + c = 0$, evaluate the discriminant $b^2 - 4ac$.

1. If $b^2 - 4ac > 0$, there are two real solutions.
2. If $b^2 - 4ac = 0$, there is one real solution.
3. If $b^2 - 4ac < 0$, there are no real solutions; there are two complex solutions.

EXAMPLE 5   Using the discriminant

Use the discriminant to determine the number of solutions to $4x^2 + 25 = 20x$. Then solve the equation, using the quadratic formula.

Solution
Write the equation as $4x^2 - 20x + 25 = 0$ so that $a = 4$, $b = -20$, and $c = 25$. The discriminant evaluates to

$$b^2 - 4ac = (-20)^2 - 4(4)(25) = 0.$$

Thus there is one real solution.

$$x = \frac{-b \pm \sqrt{b^2 - 4ac}}{2a} \qquad \text{Quadratic formula}$$

$$= \frac{-(-20) \pm \sqrt{0}}{2(4)} \qquad \text{Substitute.}$$

$$= \frac{20}{8} = 2.5 \qquad \text{Simplify.}$$

The only solution is 2.5.   Now Try Exercise 37(a), (b)

We also need to be able to analyze graphs of quadratic functions, which we demonstrate in the next example.

EXAMPLE 6   Analyzing graphs of quadratic functions

Figure 8.45

A graph of $f(x) = ax^2 + bx + c$ is shown in Figure 8.45.
(a) State whether $a > 0$ or $a < 0$.
(b) Solve the equation $ax^2 + bx + c = 0$.
(c) Determine whether the discriminant is positive, negative, or zero.

Solution
(a) The parabola opens downward, so $a < 0$.
(b) The graph of $f(x) = ax^2 + bx + c$ intersects the x-axis at -3 and 2. Therefore $f(-3) = 0$ and $f(2) = 0$. The solutions to $ax^2 + bx + c = 0$ are -3 and 2.
(c) There are two solutions, so the discriminant is positive.   Now Try Exercise 31

Quadratic Equations Having Complex Solutions

The quadratic equation written as $ax^2 + bx + c = 0$ has no real solutions if the discriminant, $b^2 - 4ac$, is negative. For example, the quadratic equation $x^2 + 4 = 0$ has $a = 1$, $b = 0$, and $c = 4$. Its discriminant is

$$b^2 - 4ac = 0^2 - 4(1)(4) = -16 < 0,$$

so this equation has no real solutions. However, if we use complex numbers, we can solve this equation as follows.

$$x^2 + 4 = 0 \qquad \text{Given equation}$$

$$x^2 = -4 \qquad \text{Subtract 4.}$$

$$x = \pm\sqrt{-4} \qquad \text{Square root property}$$

$$x = \sqrt{-4} \quad \text{or} \quad x = -\sqrt{-4} \qquad \text{Meaning of } \pm$$

$$x = 2i \quad \text{or} \quad x = -2i \qquad \text{The expression } \sqrt{-a}$$

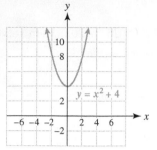

Figure 8.46 No *x*-intercepts

The solutions are $\pm 2i$. We check each solution to $x^2 + 4 = 0$ as follows.

$$(2i)^2 + 4 = (2)^2 i^2 + 4 = 4(-1) + 4 = 0 \qquad \text{It checks.}$$
$$(-2i)^2 + 4 = (-2)^2 i^2 + 4 = 4(-1) + 4 = 0 \qquad \text{It checks.}$$

The fact that the equation $x^2 + 4 = 0$ has only imaginary solutions can be seen visually from the graph of $y = x^2 + 4$, shown in Figure 8.46. This parabola does not intersect the *x*-axis, and so the equation $x^2 + 4 = 0$ has no real solutions.

These results can be generalized as follows.

THE EQUATION $x^2 + k = 0$

If $k > 0$, the solutions to $x^2 + k = 0$ are given by $x = \pm i\sqrt{k}$.

NOTE: This result is a form of the *square root property* that includes complex solutions.

EXAMPLE 7 Solving a quadratic equation having complex solutions

Solve $x^2 + 5 = 0$.

Solution
The solutions are $\pm i\sqrt{5}$. That is, $x = i\sqrt{5}$ or $x = -i\sqrt{5}$.   Now Try Exercise **55**

When $b \neq 0$, the preceding method cannot be used. Consider the quadratic equation $2x^2 + x + 3 = 0$, which has $a = 2$, $b = 1$, and $c = 3$. Its discriminant is

$$b^2 - 4ac = 1^2 - 4(2)(3) = -23 < 0.$$

This equation has two complex solutions as demonstrated in the next example.

EXAMPLE 8 Solving a quadratic equation having complex solutions

Solve $2x^2 + x + 3 = 0$. Write your answer in standard form: $a + bi$.

Solution
Let $a = 2$, $b = 1$, and $c = 3$.

$$x = \frac{-b \pm \sqrt{b^2 - 4ac}}{2a} \qquad \text{Quadratic formula}$$

$$= \frac{-1 \pm \sqrt{1^2 - 4(2)(3)}}{2(2)} \qquad \text{Substitute for } a, b, \text{ and } c.$$

$$= \frac{-1 \pm \sqrt{-23}}{4} \qquad \text{Simplify.}$$

$$= \frac{-1 \pm i\sqrt{23}}{4} \qquad \sqrt{-23} = i\sqrt{23}$$

$$= -\frac{1}{4} \pm i\frac{\sqrt{23}}{4} \qquad \text{Divide each term by 4.}$$

The solutions are $-\frac{1}{4} + i\frac{\sqrt{23}}{4}$ and $-\frac{1}{4} - i\frac{\sqrt{23}}{4}$.

Now Try Exercise 71

CRITICAL THINKING

Use the results of Example 8 to evaluate each expression mentally.

$$2\left(-\frac{1}{4} + i\frac{\sqrt{23}}{4}\right)^2 + \left(-\frac{1}{4} + i\frac{\sqrt{23}}{4}\right) + 3 \quad \text{and} \quad 2\left(-\frac{1}{4} - i\frac{\sqrt{23}}{4}\right)^2 + \left(-\frac{1}{4} - i\frac{\sqrt{23}}{4}\right) + 3$$

Sometimes we can use properties of radicals to simplify a solution to a quadratic equation, as demonstrated in the next example.

EXAMPLE 9   Solving a quadratic equation having complex solutions

Solve $\frac{3}{4}x^2 + 1 = x$. Write your answer in standard form: $a + bi$.

Solution
Begin by subtracting x from each side of the equation and then multiply by 4 to clear fractions. The resulting equation is $3x^2 - 4x + 4 = 0$. Substitute $a = 3$, $b = -4$, and $c = 4$ in the quadratic formula.

$$x = \frac{-b \pm \sqrt{b^2 - 4ac}}{2a} \qquad \text{Quadratic formula}$$

$$= \frac{-(-4) \pm \sqrt{(-4)^2 - 4(3)(4)}}{2(3)} \qquad \text{Substitute.}$$

$$= \frac{4 \pm \sqrt{-32}}{6} \qquad \text{Simplify.}$$

$$= \frac{4 \pm 4i\sqrt{2}}{6} \qquad \sqrt{-32} = i\sqrt{32} = i\sqrt{16}\sqrt{2} = 4i\sqrt{2}$$

$$= \frac{2}{3} \pm \frac{2}{3}i\sqrt{2} \qquad \text{Divide 6 into each term and simplify.}$$

Now Try Exercise 77

In the next example, we use completing the square to obtain complex solutions to a quadratic equation.

EXAMPLE **10**   Completing the square to find complex solutions

Solve $x(x + 2) = -2$ by completing the square.

Solution

After applying the distributive property, the equation becomes $x^2 + 2x = -2$. Because $b = 2$, add $\left(\frac{b}{2}\right)^2 = \left(\frac{2}{2}\right)^2 = 1$ to each side of the equation.

$$x^2 + 2x = -2 \qquad \text{Equation to be solved}$$
$$x^2 + 2x + 1 = -2 + 1 \qquad \text{Add 1 to each side.}$$
$$(x + 1)^2 = -1 \qquad \text{Perfect square trinomial; add.}$$
$$x + 1 = \pm\sqrt{-1} \qquad \text{Square root property}$$
$$x + 1 = \pm i \qquad \sqrt{-1} = i, \text{ the imaginary unit}$$
$$x = -1 \pm i \qquad \text{Add } -1 \text{ to each side.}$$

The solutions are $-1 + i$ and $-1 - i$.

Now Try Exercise **75**

8.4 PUTTING IT ALL TOGETHER

Quadratic equations can be solved symbolically by using factoring, the square root property, completing the square, and the quadratic formula. Graphical and numerical methods can also be used to solve quadratic equations. In this section we discussed the quadratic formula and its discriminant, which we summarize in the following table.

Concept	Explanation	Examples
Quadratic Formula	The quadratic formula can be used to solve *any* quadratic equation written as $ax^2 + bx + c = 0$. The solutions are given by $$x = \frac{-b \pm \sqrt{b^2 - 4ac}}{2a}.$$	For the equation $$2x^2 - 3x + 1 = 0$$ with $a = 2$, $b = -3$, and $c = 1$, the solutions are $$\frac{-(-3) \pm \sqrt{(-3)^2 - 4(2)(1)}}{2(2)} = \frac{3 \pm \sqrt{1}}{4} = 1, \frac{1}{2}.$$
The Discriminant	The expression $b^2 - 4ac$ is called the discriminant. 1. $b^2 - 4ac > 0$ indicates two real solutions. 2. $b^2 - 4ac = 0$ indicates one real solution. 3. $b^2 - 4ac < 0$ indicates no real solutions; rather, there are two complex solutions.	For the equation $$x^2 + 4x - 1 = 0$$ with $a = 1$, $b = 4$, and $c = -1$, the discriminant is $$b^2 - 4ac = 4^2 - 4(1)(-1) = 20 > 0,$$ indicating two real solutions.

Concept	Explanation	Examples
Quadratic Formula and Complex Solutions	If the discriminant is negative $(b^2 - 4ac < 0)$, the solutions to a quadratic equation are complex numbers. If $k > 0$, the solutions to $x^2 + k = 0$ are given by $x = \pm i\sqrt{k}$.	$2x^2 - x + 3 = 0$ $x = \dfrac{1 \pm \sqrt{(-1)^2 - 4(2)(3)}}{2(2)}$ $= \dfrac{1 \pm \sqrt{-23}}{4} = \dfrac{1}{4} \pm i\dfrac{\sqrt{23}}{4}$ $x^2 + 7 = 0$ is equivalent to $x = \pm i\sqrt{7}$.

Like other equations that we have studied, quadratic equations can be solved symbolically, numerically, and graphically. The equation $x(x - 1) = 2$ is solved by these three methods.

NOTE: Symbolic solutions are *exact*. Numerical and graphical solutions are often *approximate*, particularly when solutions contain fractions or square roots.

Symbolic Solution

$$x(x - 1) = 2$$
$$x^2 - x = 2$$
$$x^2 - x - 2 = 0$$
$$(x + 1)(x - 2) = 0$$
$$x = -1 \text{ or } x = 2$$

Solutions are -1 and 2.

Numerical Solution

$x(x - 1) = 2$ when
$x = -1$ or 2.

Graphical Solution

Points of intersectios are $(-1, 2)$ and $(2, 2)$, where $y_1 = x(x - 1)$ and $y_2 = 2$.

8.4 Exercises

MyMathLab Math XL PRACTICE   WATCH   DOWNLOAD   READ   REVIEW

CONCEPTS

1. What is the quadratic formula used for?

2. What basic algebraic technique is used to derive the quadratic formula?

3. Write the discriminant.

4. If the discriminant evaluates to 0, what does that indicate about the quadratic equation?

5. Name four symbolic techniques for solving a quadratic equation.

6. Does every quadratic equation have at least one real solution? Explain.

7. Solve $x^2 - 4 = 0$.   8. Solve $x^2 + 4 = 0$.

THE QUADRATIC FORMULA

Exercises 9–12: Use the quadratic formula to solve the equation. Support your result graphically or numerically. If there are no real solutions, say so.

9. $2x^2 + 11x - 6 = 0$ 10. $x^2 + 2x - 24 = 0$

11. $-x^2 + 2x - 1 = 0$ 12. $3x^2 - x + 1 = 0$

Exercises 13–30: Solve by using the quadratic formula. If there are no real solutions, say so.

13. $x^2 - 6x - 16 = 0$ 14. $2x^2 - 9x + 7 = 0$

15. $4x^2 - x - 1 = 0$ 16. $-x^2 + 2x + 1 = 0$

17. $-3x^2 + 2x - 1 = 0$ 18. $x^2 + x + 3 = 0$

19. $36x^2 - 36x + 9 = 0$

20. $4x^2 - 5.6x + 1.96 = 0$

21. $2x(x - 3) = 2$ **22.** $x(x + 1) + x = 5$

23. $(x - 1)(x + 1) + 2 = 4x$

24. $\frac{1}{2}(x - 6) = x^2 + 1$ **25.** $\frac{1}{2}x(x + 1) = 2x^2 - \frac{3}{2}$

26. $\frac{1}{2}x^2 - \frac{1}{4}x + \frac{1}{2} = x$ **27.** $2x(x - 1) = 7$

28. $3x(x - 4) = 4$ **29.** $-3x^2 + 10x - 5 = 0$

30. $-2x^2 + 4x - 1 = 0$

THE DISCRIMINANT

Exercises 31–36: A graph of $y = ax^2 + bx + c$ is shown.
(a) State whether $a > 0$ or $a < 0$.
(b) Solve $ax^2 + bx + c = 0$, if possible.
(c) Determine whether the discriminant is positive, negative, or zero.

31.

32.

33.

34.

35.

36.

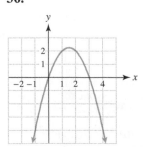

Exercises 37–44: Do the following for the given equation.
(a) Evaluate the discriminant.
(b) How many real solutions are there?
(c) Support your answer for part (b) by using graphing.

37. $3x^2 + x - 2 = 0$ **38.** $5x^2 - 13x + 6 = 0$

39. $x^2 - 4x + 4 = 0$ **40.** $\frac{1}{4}x^2 + 4 = 2x$

41. $\frac{1}{2}x^2 + \frac{3}{2}x + 2 = 0$ **42.** $x - 3 = 2x^2$

43. $x(x + 3) = 3$

44. $(4x - 1)(x - 3) = -25$

Exercises 45–54: Use the quadratic formula to find any x-intercepts on the graph of the equation.

45. $y = x^2 - 2x - 1$ **46.** $y = x^2 + 3x + 1$

47. $y = -2x^2 - x + 3$ **48.** $y = -3x^2 - x + 4$

49. $y = x^2 + x + 5$ **50.** $y = 3x^2 - 2x + 5$

51. $y = x^2 + 9$ **52.** $y = x^2 + 11$

53. $y = 3x^2 + 4x - 2$ **54.** $y = 4x^2 - 2x - 3$

COMPLEX SOLUTIONS

Exercises 55–86: Solve the equation. Write complex solutions in standard form.

55. $x^2 + 9 = 0$ **56.** $x^2 + 16 = 0$

57. $x^2 + 80 = 0$ **58.** $x^2 + 20 = 0$

59. $x^2 + \frac{1}{4} = 0$ **60.** $x^2 + \frac{9}{4} = 0$

61. $16x^2 + 9 = 0$ **62.** $25x^2 + 36 = 0$

63. $x^2 = -6$ **64.** $x^2 = -75$

65. $x^2 - 3 = 0$ **66.** $x^2 - 8 = 0$

67. $x^2 + 2 = 0$ **68.** $x^2 + 4 = 0$

69. $x^2 - x + 2 = 0$ **70.** $x^2 + 2x + 3 = 0$

71. $2x^2 + 3x + 4 = 0$ **72.** $3x^2 - x = 1$

73. $x^2 + 1 = 4x$ **74.** $3x^2 + 2 = x$

75. $x^2 + x = -2$ **76.** $x(x - 4) = -8$

77. $5x^2 + 2x + 4 = 0$ **78.** $7x^2 - 2x + 4 = 0$

79. $\frac{1}{2}x^2 + \frac{3}{4}x + 1 = 0$ **80.** $-\frac{1}{3}x^2 + x - 2 = 0$

81. $x(x + 2) = x - 4$ **82.** $x - 5 = 2x(2x + 1)$

83. $x(2x - 1) = 1 + x$ **84.** $2x = x(3 - 4x)$

85. $x^2 = x(1 - x) - 2$ **86.** $2x^2 = 2x(5 - x) - 8$

YOU DECIDE THE METHOD

Exercises 87–100: Find exact solutions to the quadratic equation, using a method of your choice. Explain why you chose the method you did. Answers may vary.

87. $x^2 - 3x + 2 = 0$ **88.** $x^2 + 2x + 1 = 0$

89. $0.5x^2 - 1.75x - 1 = 0$ **90.** $\frac{3}{5}x^2 + \frac{9}{10}x - \frac{3}{5} = 0$

91. $x^2 - 5x + 2 = 0$ **92.** $2x^2 - x - 4 = 0$

93. $2x^2 + x = -8$ **94.** $4x^2 = 2x - 3$

95. $4x^2 - 1 = 0$ **96.** $3x^2 = 9$

97. $3x^2 + 6 = 0$ **98.** $4x^2 + 7 = 0$

99. $9x^2 + 1 = 6x$ **100.** $10x^2 + 15x = 25$

APPLICATIONS

Exercises 101–104: Modeling Stopping Distance   (Refer to Example 4.) Use $d = \frac{1}{9}x^2 + \frac{11}{3}x$ to find a safe speed x for the following stopping distances d.

101. 42 feet   **102.** 152 feet

103. 390 feet   **104.** 726 feet

105. *U.S. AIDS Deaths*   The cumulative numbers in thousands of AIDS deaths from 1984 through 1994 may be modeled by

$$f(x) = 2.39x^2 + 5.04x + 5.1,$$

where $x = 0$ corresponds to 1984, $x = 1$ to 1985, and so on until $x = 10$ corresponds to 1994. See the accompanying graph. Use the formula for $f(x)$ to estimate the year when the total number of AIDS

deaths reached 200 thousand. Compare your result with that shown in the graph.

106. *Canoeing*   A camper paddles a canoe 2 miles downstream in a river that has a 2-mile-per-hour current. To return to camp, the canoeist travels upstream on a different branch of the river. It is 4 miles long and has a 1-mile-per-hour current. The total trip (both ways) takes 3 hours. Find the average speed of the canoe in still water. (*Hint:* Time equals distance divided by rate.)

107. *Distance*   Two cars leave an intersection, one traveling south and one traveling east, as shown in the figure. After 1 hour the two cars are 50 miles apart and the car traveling east has traveled 10 miles farther than the car traveling south. How far did each car travel?

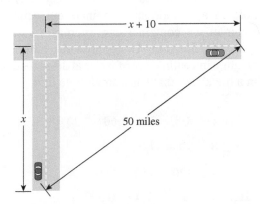

108. *Airplane Speed*   A pilot flies 500 miles against a 20-mile-per-hour wind. On the next day, the pilot flies back home with a 10-mile-per-hour tail wind. The total trip (both ways) takes 4 hours. Find the speed of the airplane without a wind.

109. *Screen Dimensions* The width of a rectangular computer screen is 3 inches more than its height. If the area of the screen is 154 square inches, find its dimensions

(a) graphically,
(b) numerically, and
(c) symbolically.

110. *Sidewalk Dimension* A rectangular flower garden in a park is 30 feet wide and 40 feet long. A sidewalk around the perimeter of the garden is being planned, as shown in the figure. The gardener has enough money to pour 624 square feet of cement sidewalk. Find the width of the sidewalk.

30 ft

40 ft

111. *Modeling Water Flow* When water runs out of a hole in a cylindrical container, the height of the water in the container can often be modeled by a quadratic function. The data in the table show the height y in centimeters of water at 30-second intervals in a metal can that has a small hole in it.

Time	0	30	60	90
Height	16	11.9	8.4	5.3

Time	120	150	180
Height	3.1	1.4	0.5

These data are modeled by

$$f(x) = 0.0004x^2 - 0.15x + 16.$$

(a) Explain why a linear function would not be appropriate for modeling these data.

(b) Use the table to estimate the time at which the height was 7 centimeters.
(c) Use $f(x)$ and the quadratic formula to solve part (b).

112. *Hospitals* The general trend in the number of hospitals in the United States from 1945 through 2000 is modeled by

$$f(x) = -1.38x^2 + 84x + 5865,$$

where $x = 5$ corresponds to 1945, $x = 10$ to 1950, and so on until $x = 60$ represents 2000. See the scatterplot and accompanying graph.

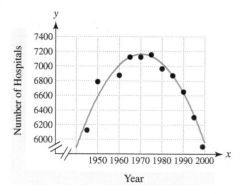

Year

(a) Describe any trends in the numbers of hospitals from 1945 to 2000.
(b) What information does the vertex give?
(c) Use the formula for $f(x)$ to estimate the number of hospitals in 1970. Compare your result with that shown in the graph.
(d) Use the formula for $f(x)$ to estimate the year (or years) when there were 6300 hospitals. Compare your result with that shown in the graph.

WRITING ABOUT MATHEMATICS

113. Explain how the discriminant $b^2 - 4ac$ can be used to determine the number of solutions to a quadratic equation.

114. Let $f(x) = ax^2 + bx + c$. If you know the value of $b^2 - 4ac$, what information does this give you about the graph of f? Explain your answer.

1. Solve the quadratic equation $2x^2 - 7x + 3 = 0$ symbolically and graphically.

2. Use the square root property to solve $x^2 = 5$.

3. Complete the square to solve $x^2 - 4x + 1 = 0$.

4. Solve the equation $x^2 + y^2 = 1$ for y.

5. Use the quadratic formula to solve each equation.
   (a) $2x^2 = 3x + 1$

   (b) $9x^2 - 24x + 16 = 0$
   (c) $x^2 + x + 2 = 0$

6. Calculate the discriminant for each equation and give the number of *real* solutions.
   (a) $x^2 - 5x + 5 = 0$
   (b) $2x^2 - 5x + 4 = 0$
   (c) $49x^2 - 56x + 16 = 0$

8.5 QUADRATIC INEQUALITIES

Basic Concepts ▪ Graphical and Numerical Solutions ▪ Symbolic Solutions

A LOOK INTO MATH ▷ Parabolas are frequently used in highway design. Sometimes it is necessary for engineers to determine where a highway is below a particular elevation. To do this, they may need to solve a *quadratic inequality*. Quadratic inequalities are nonlinear inequalities. These inequalities are often simple enough to be solved by hand. In this section we discuss how to solve them graphically, numerically, and symbolically.

Basic Concepts

If the equals sign in a quadratic equation is replaced with $>, \geq, <,$ or $\leq$, a **quadratic inequality** results. Examples of quadratic inequalities include

$$x^2 + 4x - 3 < 0, \quad 5x^2 \geq 5, \quad \text{and} \quad 1 - z \leq z^2.$$

Any quadratic equation can be written as

$$ax^2 + bx + c = 0, \quad a \neq 0,$$

so any quadratic inequality can be written as

$$ax^2 + bx + c > 0, \quad a \neq 0,$$

where $>$ may be replaced with $\geq, <,$ or $\leq$.

EXAMPLE 1   Identifying a quadratic inequality

Determine whether the inequality is quadratic.
(a) $5x + x^2 - x^3 \leq 0$ (b) $4 + 5x^2 > 4x^2 + x$

Solution

(a) The inequality $5x + x^2 - x^3 \le 0$ is not quadratic because it has an x^3-term.

(b) Write the inequality as follows.

$$4 + 5x^2 > 4x^2 + x \qquad \text{Given inequality}$$

$$4 + 5x^2 - 4x^2 - x > 0 \qquad \text{Subtract } 4x^2 \text{ and } x.$$

$$4 + x^2 - x > 0 \qquad \text{Combine like terms.}$$

$$x^2 - x + 4 > 0 \qquad \text{Rewrite.}$$

Because the inequality can be written in the form $ax^2 + bx + c > 0$ with $a = 1$, $b = -1$, and $c = 4$, it is a quadratic inequality.   Now Try Exercises **7, 11**

Graphical and Numerical Solutions

Figure 8.47

Equality often is the boundary between *greater than* and *less than*, so a first step in solving an inequality is to determine the x-values where equality occurs. We begin by using this concept with graphical and numerical techniques.

A graph of $y = x^2 - x - 2$ with x-intercepts -1 and 2 is shown in Figure 8.47. The solutions to $x^2 - x - 2 = 0$ are given by $x = -1$ or $x = 2$. Between the x-intercepts the graph dips below the x-axis and the y-values are negative. Thus the solutions to $x^2 - x - 2 < 0$ satisfy $-1 < x < 2$. To check this result we select a **test value**. For example, 0 lies between -1 and 2. If we substitute $x = 0$ in $x^2 - x - 2 < 0$, it results in a true statement.

$$0^2 - 0 - 2 < 0 \qquad \text{True}$$

When $x < -1$ or $x > 2$, the graph lies above the x-axis and the y-values are positive. Thus the solutions to $x^2 - x - 2 > 0$ satisfy $x < -1$ or $x > 2$. For example, 3 is greater than 2 and -3 is less than -1. Therefore both 3 and -3 are solutions. We can verify this result by substituting 3 and -3 as test values in $x^2 - x - 2 > 0$.

$$3^2 - 3 - 2 > 0 \qquad \text{True}$$

$$(-3)^2 - (-3) - 2 > 0 \qquad \text{True}$$

In the next three examples, we use these concepts to solve quadratic inequalities.

EXAMPLE 2   Solving a quadratic inequality

Make a table of values for $y = x^2 - 3x - 4$ and then sketch the graph. Use the table and graph to solve $x^2 - 3x - 4 \le 0$. Write your answer in interval notation.

Solution

The points calculated for Table 8.14 are plotted in Figure 8.48 and connected with a smooth $\cup$-shaped graph.

Numerical Solution   Table 8.14 shows that $x^2 - 3x - 4$ equals 0 when $x = -1$ or $x = 4$. Between these values, $x^2 - 3x - 4$ is negative so the solution set to $x^2 - 3x - 4 \le 0$ is given by $-1 \le x \le 4$ or in interval notation, $[-1, 4]$.

Graphical Solution   In Figure 8.48 the graph of $y = x^2 - 3x - 4$ shows that the x-intercepts are -1 and 4. Between these values, the graph dips *below* the x-axis. Thus the solution set is $[-1, 4]$.

TABLE 8.14

x	$y = x^2 - 3x - 4$
-2	6
-1	**0**
0	-4
1	-6
2	-6
3	-4
4	**0**
5	6

Figure 8.48

Now Try Exercises 19, 25

EXAMPLE 3   Solving a quadratic inequality

Solve $x^2 > 1$. Write your answer in interval notation.

Solution
First, rewrite $x^2 > 1$ as $x^2 - 1 > 0$. The graph $y = x^2 - 1$ is shown in Figure 8.49 with x-intercepts -1 and 1. The graph lies *above* the x-axis and is shaded green to the left of $x = -1$ and to the right of $x = 1$. Thus the solution set is given by $x < -1$ or $x > 1$, which can be written in interval notation as $(-\infty, -1) \cup (1, \infty)$.

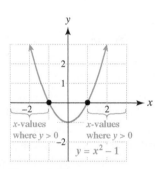

Figure 8.49

Now Try Exercise 33

EXAMPLE 4   Solving some special cases

Solve each of the inequalities graphically.
(a) $x^2 + 1 > 0$ **(b)** $x^2 + 1 < 0$ **(c)** $(x - 1)^2 \leq 0$

Solution
(a) Because the graph of $y = x^2 + 1$, shown in Figure 8.50, is always above the x-axis, $x^2 + 1$ is always greater than 0. The solution set includes all real numbers, or $(-\infty, \infty)$.
(b) Because the graph of $y = x^2 + 1$, shown in Figure 8.50, never goes below the x-axis, $x^2 + 1$ is never less than 0. Thus there are no real solutions.
(c) Because the graph of $y = (x - 1)^2$, shown in Figure 8.51 on the next page, never goes below the x-axis, $(x - 1)^2$ is never less than 0. When $x = 1$, $y = 0$, so 1 is the only solution to the inequality $(x - 1)^2 \leq 0$.

Figure 8.50

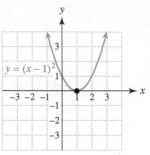

Figure 8.51

Now Try Exercises 35, 39, 41

▶ REAL-WORLD CONNECTION   In the next example we show how quadratic inequalities are used in highway design.

EXAMPLE 5   Determining elevations on a sag curve

Parabolas are frequently used in highway design to model hills and sags (valleys) along a proposed route. Suppose that the elevation E in feet of a sag, or *sag curve*, is given by

$$E(x) = 0.00004x^2 - 0.4x + 2000,$$

where x is the horizontal distance in feet along the sag curve and $0 \le x \le 10{,}000$. See Figure 8.52. Estimate graphically the x-values where the elevation is 1500 feet or less.

(**Source:** F. Mannering and W. Kilareski, *Principles of Highway Engineering and Traffic Analysis.*)

Figure 8.52

Solution

Graphical Solution   We must solve the quadratic inequality

$$0.00004x^2 - 0.4x + 2000 \le 1500.$$

To do so, we let $Y_1 = .00004X\verb^2 - .4X + 2000$ represent the sag or valley in the road and $Y_2 = 1500$ represent a horizontal line with an elevation of 1500 feet. Their graphs intersect at $x \approx 1464$ and $x \approx 8536$, as shown in Figure 8.53. The elevation of the proposed route is less than 1500 feet between these x-values. Therefore the elevation of the road is 1500 feet or less when $1464 \le x \le 8536$ (approximately).

CALCULATOR HELP

To find a point of intersection, see the Appendix (page AP-7).

[0, 10000, 1000] by [0, 2500, 500]   [0, 10000, 1000] by [0, 2500, 500]

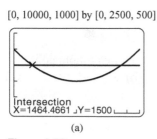

(a)   (b)

Figure 8.53

Now Try Exercise 63

Symbolic Solutions

To solve a quadratic inequality symbolically we first solve the corresponding equality. We can then write the solution to the inequality, using the following method.

SOLUTIONS TO QUADRATIC INEQUALITIES

Let $ax^2 + bx + c = 0, a > 0$, have two real solutions p and q, where $p < q$.

$ax^2 + bx + c < 0$ is equivalent to $p < x < q$ (see left-hand figure).

$ax^2 + bx + c > 0$ is equivalent to $x < p$ or $x > q$ (see right-hand figure).

Quadratic inequalities involving $\leq$ or $\geq$ can be solved similarly.

Solutions lie between p and q.

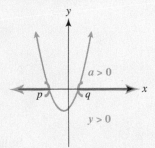

Solutions lie "outside" p and q.

One way to handle the situation, where $a < 0$, is to multiply each side of the inequality by -1, in which case we must be sure to *reverse* the inequality symbol. For example, the inequality $-2x^2 + 8 \leq 0$ has $a = -2$, which is negative. If we multiply each side of this inequality by -1, we obtain $2x^2 - 8 \geq 0$ and now $a = 2$, which is positive. Another way to solve this inequality is to graph $y = -2x^2 + 8$, which is a parabola that opens downward. The following Critical Thinking addresses this situation. However, when $a < 0$ we will usually rewrite the quadratic inequality so that $a > 0$.

CRITICAL THINKING

The graph of $y = -x^2 + x + 12$ is a parabola opening downward with x-intercepts -3 and 4. Solve each inequality.

i. $-x^2 + x + 12 > 0$ **ii.** $-x^2 + x + 12 < 0$

EXAMPLE **6**   Solving quadratic inequalities

Solve each inequality symbolically. Write your answer in interval notation.
(a) $6x^2 - 7x - 5 \geq 0$ **(b)** $x(3 - x) > -18$

Solution
(a) Begin by solving $6x^2 - 7x - 5 = 0$.

$$6x^2 - 7x - 5 = 0 \qquad \text{Quadratic equation}$$
$$(2x + 1)(3x - 5) = 0 \qquad \text{Factor.}$$
$$2x + 1 = 0 \quad \text{or} \quad 3x - 5 = 0 \qquad \text{Zero-product property}$$
$$x = -\frac{1}{2} \quad \text{or} \quad x = \frac{5}{3} \qquad \text{Solve.}$$

Therefore the solutions to $6x^2 - 7x - 5 \geq 0$ lie "outside" these two values and satisfy $x \leq -\frac{1}{2}$ or $x \geq \frac{5}{3}$. In interval notation the solution set is $\left(-\infty, -\frac{1}{2}\right] \cup \left[\frac{5}{3}, \infty\right)$.

(b) First, rewrite the inequality as follows.

$$x(3 - x) > -18 \qquad \text{Given inequality}$$
$$3x - x^2 > -18 \qquad \text{Distributive property}$$
$$3x - x^2 + 18 > 0 \qquad \text{Add 18.}$$
$$-x^2 + 3x + 18 > 0 \qquad \text{Rewrite.}$$
$$x^2 - 3x - 18 < 0 \qquad \begin{array}{l}\text{Multiply by } -1 \text{ because } a < 0; \\ \text{reverse the inequality symbol.}\end{array}$$

Next, solve $x^2 - 3x - 18 = 0$.

$$(x + 3)(x - 6) = 0 \qquad \text{Factor.}$$
$$x = -3 \quad \text{or} \quad x = 6 \qquad \text{Solve.}$$

Solutions to $x^2 - 3x - 18 < 0$ lie between these two values and satisfy $-3 < x < 6$. In interval notation the solution set is $(-3, 6)$.   **Now Try Exercises** 29, 31

Figure 8.54

EXAMPLE 7   Finding the dimensions of a building

A rectangular building needs to be 7 feet longer than it is wide, as illustrated in Figure 8.54. The area of the building must be at least 450 square feet. What widths x are possible for this building? Support your results with a table of values.

Solution

Symbolic Solution   If x is the width of the building, $x + 7$ is the length of the building and its area is $x(x + 7)$. The area must be at least 450 square feet, so the inequality $x(x + 7) \geq 450$ must be satisfied. First solve the following quadratic equation.

$$x(x + 7) = 450 \qquad \text{Quadratic equation}$$
$$x^2 + 7x = 450 \qquad \text{Distributive property}$$
$$x^2 + 7x - 450 = 0 \qquad \text{Subtract 450.}$$
$$x = \frac{-7 \pm \sqrt{7^2 - 4(1)(-450)}}{2(1)} \qquad \begin{array}{l}\text{Quadratic formula; } a = 1, \\ b = 7, \text{ and } c = -450\end{array}$$
$$= \frac{-7 \pm \sqrt{1849}}{2} \qquad \text{Simplify.}$$
$$= \frac{-7 \pm 43}{2} \qquad \sqrt{1849} = 43$$
$$= 18, -25 \qquad \text{Evaluate.}$$

X	Y₁
15	330
16	368
17	408
18	450
19	494
20	540
21	588

$Y_1 = X(X+7)$

Figure 8.55

Thus the solutions to $x(x + 7) \geq 450$ are $x \leq -25$ or $x \geq 18$. The width is positive, so the building width must be 18 feet or more.

Numerical Solution   A table of values is shown in Figure 8.55, where $Y_1 = X(X + 7)$ equals 450 when $x = 18$. For $x \geq 18$ the area is *at least* 450 square feet.

Now Try Exercise 67

8.5 PUTTING IT ALL TOGETHER

The following table summarizes solutions of quadratic inequalities containing the symbols $<$ or $>$. Cases involving $\leq$ or $\geq$ are solved similarly.

Method	Explanation
Solving a Quadratic Inequality Symbolically	Let $ax^2 + bx + c = 0$, $a > 0$, have two real solutions p and q, where $p < q$. $ax^2 + bx + c < 0$ is equivalent to $p < x < q$. $ax^2 + bx + c > 0$ is equivalent to $x < p$ or $x > q$. *Examples:* The solutions to $x^2 - 3x + 2 = 0$ are given by $x = 1$ or $x = 2$. The solutions to $x^2 - 3x + 2 < 0$ are given by $1 < x < 2$. The solutions to $x^2 - 3x + 2 > 0$ are given by $x < 1$ or $x > 2$.
Solving a Quadratic Inequality Graphically	Given $ax^2 + bx + c < 0$ with $a > 0$, graph $y = ax^2 + bx + c$ and locate any x-intercepts. If there are two x-intercepts, then solutions correspond to x-values between the x-intercepts. Solutions to $ax^2 + bx + c > 0$ correspond to x-values "outside" the x-intercepts. See the box on page 631.
Solving a Quadratic Inequality Numerically	If a quadratic inequality is expressed as $ax^2 + bx + c < 0$ with $a > 0$, then we can solve $y = ax^2 + bx + c = 0$ with a table. If there are two solutions, then the solutions to the given inequality lie between these values. Solutions to $ax^2 + bx + c > 0$ lie "outside" these values.

8.5 Exercises

 MyMathLab Math XL PRACTICE WATCH DOWNLOAD READ REVIEW

CONCEPTS

1. How is a quadratic inequality different from a quadratic equation?

2. Do quadratic inequalities typically have two solutions? Explain.

3. Is 3 a solution to $x^2 < 7$?

4. Is 5 a solution to $x^2 \geq 25$?

5. The solutions to $x^2 - 2x - 8 = 0$ are -2 and 4. What are the solutions to $x^2 - 2x - 8 < 0$? Write your answer as an inequality.

6. The solutions to $x^2 + 2x - 3 = 0$ are -3 and 1. What are the solutions to $x^2 + 2x - 3 > 0$? Write your answer as an inequality.

QUADRATIC INEQUALITIES

Exercises 7–12: Is the inequality quadratic?

7. $x^2 + 4x + 5 < 0$ 8. $x > x^3 - 5$

9. $x^2 > 19$ 10. $x(x - 1) - 2 \geq 0$

11. $4x > 1 - x$ 12. $2x(x^2 + 3) < 0$

Exercises 13–18: Is the given value of x a solution?

13. $2x^2 + x - 1 > 0$ $x = 3$

14. $x^2 - 3x + 2 \leq 0$ $x = 2$

15. $x^2 + 2 \leq 0$ $x = 0$

16. $2x(x - 3) \geq 0$ $x = 1$

17. $x^2 - 3x \leq 1$ $x = -3$

18. $4x^2 - 5x + 1 > 30$ $x = -2$

SOLVING QUADRATIC INEQUALITIES

Exercises 19–24: The graph of $y = ax^2 + bx + c$ *is given. Solve each equation or inequality.*

   (a) $ax^2 + bx + c = 0$
   (b) $ax^2 + bx + c < 0$
   (c) $ax^2 + bx + c > 0$

19.

20.

21.

22.

23.

24.

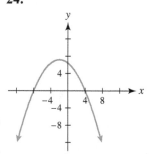

Exercises 25–28: A table for $y = ax^2 + bx + c$ *is given. Solve each equation or inequality.*

   (a) $ax^2 + bx + c = 0$
   (b) $ax^2 + bx + c < 0$
   (c) $ax^2 + bx + c > 0$

25. $y = x^2 - 4$

x	-3	-2	-1	0	1	2	3
y	5	0	-3	-4	-3	0	5

26. $y = x^2 - x - 2$

x	-3	-2	-1	0	1	2	3
y	10	4	0	-2	-2	0	4

27. $y = x^2 + 4x$

x	-5	-4	-3	-2	-1	0	1
y	5	0	-3	-4	-3	0	5

28. $y = -2x^2 - 2x + 1.5$

x	-2	-1.5	-1	-0.5	0	0.5	1
y	-2.5	0	1.5	2	1.5	0	-2.5

Exercises 29–46: Solve the inequality by any method. Write your answer in interval notation when appropriate.

29. $x^2 + 4x + 3 < 0$ **30.** $x^2 + x - 2 \leq 0$

31. $2x^2 - x - 15 \geq 0$ **32.** $3x^2 - 3x - 6 > 0$

33. $2x^2 \leq 8$ **34.** $x^2 < 9$

35. $x^2 > -5$ **36.** $-x^2 \geq 1$

37. $-x^2 + 3x > 0$ **38.** $-8x^2 - 2x + 1 \leq 0$

39. $x^2 + 2 \leq 0$ **40.** $x^2 + 3 \geq -5$

41. $(x - 2)^2 \leq 0$ **42.** $(x + 2)^2 \leq 0$

43. $(x + 1)^2 > 0$ **44.** $(x - 3)^2 > 0$

45. $x(1 - x) \geq -2$ **46.** $x(x - 2) < 3$

Exercises 47–50: Solve the equation in part (a). Use the results to solve the inequalities in parts (b) and (c).

47. **(a)** $x^2 - 4 = 0$ **48.** **(a)** $x^2 - 5 = 0$
    (b) $x^2 - 4 < 0$ **(b)** $x^2 - 5 \leq 0$
    (c) $x^2 - 4 > 0$ **(c)** $x^2 - 5 \geq 0$

49. **(a)** $x^2 + x - 1 = 0$
    (b) $x^2 + x - 1 < 0$
    (c) $x^2 + x - 1 > 0$

50. **(a)** $x^2 + 4x - 5 = 0$
    (b) $x^2 + 4x - 5 \leq 0$
    (c) $x^2 + 4x - 5 \geq 0$

Exercises 51–60: Solve the quadratic inequality symbolically. Write your answer in interval notation.

51. $x^2 + 10x + 21 \leq 0$ **52.** $x^2 - 7x - 18 < 0$

53. $3x^2 - 9x + 6 > 0$

54. $7x^2 + 34x - 5 \geq 0$

55. $x^2 < 10$

56. $x^2 \geq 64$

57. $x(x - 6) > 0$

58. $1 - x^2 \leq 0$

59. $x(4 - x) \leq 2$

60. $2x(1 - x) \geq 2$

 Exercises 61 and 62: Solve the inequality graphically to the nearest thousandth.

61. $\pi x^2 - \sqrt{3}x \leq \frac{3}{11}$

62. $\sqrt{5}x^2 - \pi^2 x \geq 10.3$

APPLICATIONS

 63. *Highway Design* (Refer to Example 5.) The elevation E of a sag curve in feet is given by

$$E(x) = 0.0000375x^2 - 0.175x + 1000,$$

where $0 \leq x \leq 4000$.

(a) Estimate graphically the x-values for which the elevation is 850 feet or less. (*Hint:* Use [0, 4000, 1000] by [500, 1200, 100] as a viewing rectangle.)

(b) For what x-values is the elevation 850 feet or more?

64. *Early Cellular Phone Use* Our society is in transition from an industrial to an informational society. Cellular communication has played an increasingly large role in this transition. The number of cellular subscribers in the United States in thousands from 1985 to 1991 can be modeled by

$$f(x) = 163x^2 - 146x + 205,$$

where x is the year and $x = 0$ corresponds to 1985, $x = 1$ to 1986, and so on. (*Source:* M. Paetsch, *Mobile Communication in the U.S. and Europe.*)

(a) Write a quadratic inequality whose solution set represents the years when there were 2 million subscribers or more.

(b) Solve this inequality.

65. *Heart Disease Death Rates* From 1960 to 2000, age-adjusted heart disease rates decreased dramatically. The number of deaths per 100,000 people can be modeled by

$$f(x) = -0.05107x^2 + 194.74x - 184{,}949,$$

where x is the year, as illustrated in the accompanying figure. (*Source:* Department of Health and Human Services.)

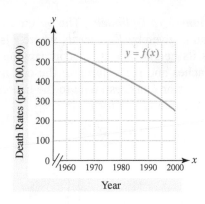

Year

(a) Evaluate $f(1985)$, using both the formula and the graph. How do your results compare?

(b) Use the graph to estimate the years when this death rate was 500 or less.

(c) Solve part (b) by using the quadratic formula.

66. *Accidental Deaths* From 1910 to 2000 the number of accidental deaths per 100,000 people generally decreased and can be modeled by

$$f(x) = -0.001918x^2 + 6.93x - 6156,$$

where x is the year, as shown in the accompanying figure. (*Source:* Department of Health and Human Services.)

Year

(a) Evaluate $f(1955)$, using both the formula and the graph. How do your results compare?

(b) Use the graph to estimate when this death rate was 60 or more.

(c) Solve part (b) by using the quadratic formula.

67. *Dimensions of a Pen* A rectangular pen for a pet is 5 feet longer than it is wide. Give possible values for the width w of the pen if its area must be between 176 and 500 square feet, inclusively.

68. *Dimensions of a Cylinder*   The volume of a cylindrical can is given by $V = \pi r^2 h$, where r is its radius and h is its height. See the accompanying figure. If $h = 6$ inches and the volume of the can must be 50 cubic inches or more, estimate to the nearest tenth of an inch possible values for r.

69. Consider the inequality $x^2 < 0$. Discuss the solutions to this inequality and explain your reasoning.

70. Explain how the graph of $y = ax^2 + bx + c$ can be used to solve the inequality

$$ax^2 + bx + c > 0$$

when $a < 0$. Assume that the x-intercepts of the graph are p and q with $p < q$.

8.6   EQUATIONS IN QUADRATIC FORM

Higher Degree Polynomial Equations ▪ Equations Having Rational Exponents ▪ Equations Having Complex Solutions

A LOOK INTO MATH ▷   Although many equations are *not* quadratic equations, they can sometimes be written in quadratic form. These equations are *reducible to quadratic form*. To express such an equation in quadratic form we often use substitution. In this section we discuss this process.

Higher Degree Polynomial Equations

Sometimes a fourth degree polynomial can be factored like a quadratic trinomial, provided it does not have an x-term or an x^3-term. Let's consider the equation $x^4 - 5x^2 + 4 = 0$.

$$x^4 - 5x^2 + 4 = 0 \qquad \text{Given equation}$$
$$(x^2)^2 - 5(x^2) + 4 = 0 \qquad \text{Properties of exponents}$$

We use the substitution $u = x^2$.

$$u^2 - 5u + 4 = 0 \qquad \text{Let } u = x^2.$$
$$(u - 4)(u - 1) = 0 \qquad \text{Factor.}$$
$$u - 4 = 0 \quad \text{or} \quad u - 1 = 0 \qquad \text{Zero-product property}$$
$$u = 4 \quad \text{or} \quad u = 1 \qquad \text{Solve each equation.}$$

Because the given equation uses the variable x, we must give the solutions in terms of x. We substitute x^2 for u and then solve to obtain the following four solutions.

$$x^2 = 4 \quad \text{or} \quad x^2 = 1 \qquad \text{Substitute } x^2 \text{ for } u.$$
$$x = \pm 2 \quad \text{or} \quad x = \pm 1 \qquad \text{Square root property}$$

The solutions are $-2, -1, 1$, and 2.

In the next example we solve a sixth degree polynomial equation.

EXAMPLE 1   Solving equations by substitution

Solve $2x^6 + x^3 = 1$.

Solution
Start by subtracting 1 from each side.

$$2x^6 + x^3 - 1 = 0 \qquad \text{Subtract 1.}$$
$$2(x^3)^2 + (x^3) - 1 = 0 \qquad \text{Properties of exponents}$$
$$2u^2 + u - 1 = 0 \qquad \text{Let } u = x^3.$$
$$(2u - 1)(u + 1) = 0 \qquad \text{Factor.}$$
$$2u - 1 = 0 \quad \text{or} \quad u + 1 = 0 \qquad \text{Zero-product property}$$
$$u = \tfrac{1}{2} \quad \text{or} \quad u = -1 \qquad \text{Solve.}$$

Now substitute x^3 for u, and solve for x to obtain the following two solutions.

$$x^3 = \tfrac{1}{2} \quad \text{or} \quad x^3 = -1 \qquad \text{Substitute } x^3 \text{ for } u.$$
$$x = \sqrt[3]{\tfrac{1}{2}} \quad \text{or} \quad x = -1 \qquad \text{Take cube root of each side.}$$

Now Try Exercise **3**

Equations Having Rational Exponents

Equations that have negative exponents are sometimes reducible to quadratic form. Consider the following example, in which two methods are presented.

EXAMPLE 2   Solving an equation having negative exponents

Solve $-6m^{-2} + 13m^{-1} + 5 = 0$.

Solution
Method I   Use the substitution $u = m^{-1} = \tfrac{1}{m}$ and $u^2 = m^{-2} = \tfrac{1}{m^2}$.

$$-6m^{-2} + 13m^{-1} + 5 = 0 \qquad \text{Given equation}$$
$$-6u^2 + 13u + 5 = 0 \qquad \text{Let } u = m^{-1} \text{ and } u^2 = m^{-2}.$$
$$6u^2 - 13u - 5 = 0 \qquad \text{Multiply by } -1.$$
$$(2u - 5)(3u + 1) = 0 \qquad \text{Factor.}$$
$$2u - 5 = 0 \quad \text{or} \quad 3u + 1 = 0 \qquad \text{Zero-product property}$$
$$u = \tfrac{5}{2} \quad \text{or} \quad u = -\tfrac{1}{3} \qquad \text{Solve for } u.$$

Because $u = \tfrac{1}{m}$, $m = \tfrac{1}{u}$. Thus the solutions are given by $m = \tfrac{2}{5}$ or $m = -3$.

Method II   Another way to solve this equation is to multiply each side by the LCD, m^2.

$$-6m^{-2} + 13m^{-1} + 5 = 0 \qquad \text{Given equation}$$
$$m^2(-6m^{-2} + 13m^{-1} + 5) = m^2 \cdot 0 \qquad \text{Multiply by } m^2.$$
$$-6m^2m^{-2} + 13m^2m^{-1} + 5m^2 = 0 \qquad \text{Distributive property}$$
$$-6 + 13m + 5m^2 = 0 \qquad \text{Add exponents.}$$
$$5m^2 + 13m - 6 = 0 \qquad \text{Rewrite the equation.}$$
$$(5m - 2)(m + 3) = 0 \qquad \text{Factor.}$$
$$5m - 2 = 0 \quad \text{or} \quad m + 3 = 0 \qquad \text{Zero-product property}$$
$$m = \tfrac{2}{5} \quad \text{or} \quad m = -3 \qquad \text{Solve.}$$

Now Try Exercise **5**

In the next example we solve an equation having fractional exponents.

EXAMPLE 3   Solving an equation having fractional exponents

Solve $x^{2/3} - 2x^{1/3} - 8 = 0$.

Solution

Use the substitution $u = x^{1/3}$.

$$
\begin{array}{ll}
x^{2/3} - 2x^{1/3} - 8 = 0 & \text{Given equation} \\
(x^{1/3})^2 - 2(x^{1/3}) - 8 = 0 & \text{Properties of exponents} \\
u^2 - 2u - 8 = 0 & \text{Let } u = x^{1/3}. \\
(u - 4)(u + 2) = 0 & \text{Factor.} \\
u - 4 = 0 \quad \text{or} \quad u + 2 = 0 & \text{Zero-product property} \\
u = 4 \quad \text{or} \quad u = -2 & \text{Solve.}
\end{array}
$$

Because $u = x^{1/3}$, $u^3 = (x^{1/3})^3 = x$. Thus $x = 4^3 = 64$ or $x = (-2)^3 = -8$. The solutions are -8 and 64.

Now Try Exercise 13

Equations Having Complex Solutions

Sometimes an equation that is reducible to quadratic form also has complex solutions. This situation is discussed in the next two examples.

EXAMPLE 4   Solving the fourth degree equation

Find all complex solutions to $x^4 - 1 = 0$.

Solution

$$
\begin{array}{ll}
x^4 - 1 = 0 & \text{Given equation} \\
(x^2)^2 - 1 = 0 & \text{Properties of exponents} \\
u^2 - 1 = 0 & \text{Let } u = x^2. \\
(u - 1)(u + 1) = 0 & \text{Factor difference of squares.} \\
u - 1 = 0 \quad \text{or} \quad u + 1 = 0 & \text{Zero-product property} \\
u = 1 \quad \text{or} \quad u = -1 & \text{Solve for } u.
\end{array}
$$

Now substitute x^2 for u, and solve for x.

$$
\begin{array}{ll}
x^2 = 1 \quad \text{or} \quad x^2 = -1 & \text{Let } x^2 = u. \\
x = \pm 1 \quad \text{or} \quad x = \pm i & \text{Square root property}
\end{array}
$$

There are four complex solutions: $-1, 1, -i$, and i.

Now Try Exercise 25

EXAMPLE 5   Solving a rational equation

Find all complex solutions to $\frac{1}{x} + \frac{1}{x^2} = -1$.

Solution

This equation is a rational equation. However, if we multiply through by the LCD, x^2, we clear fractions and obtain a quadratic equation with complex solutions.

$$\frac{1}{x} + \frac{1}{x^2} = -1 \qquad\qquad \text{Given equation}$$

$$\frac{x^2}{x} + \frac{x^2}{x^2} = -1x^2 \qquad\qquad \text{Multiply each term by } x^2.$$

$$x + 1 = -x^2 \qquad\qquad \text{Simplify.}$$

$$x^2 + x + 1 = 0 \qquad\qquad \text{Add } x^2.$$

$$x = \frac{-1 \pm \sqrt{1^2 - 4(1)(1)}}{2(1)} \qquad\qquad \text{Quadratic formula}$$

$$x = \frac{-1 \pm i\sqrt{3}}{2} \qquad\qquad \sqrt{-3} = i\sqrt{3}$$

$$x = -\frac{1}{2} \pm \frac{i\sqrt{3}}{2} \qquad\qquad \frac{a \pm b}{c} = \frac{a}{c} \pm \frac{b}{c}$$

Now Try Exercise **31**

8.6 PUTTING IT ALL TOGETHER

The following table demonstrates how to reduce some types of equations to quadratic form.

Equation	Substitution	Examples
Higher Degree Polynomial	Let $u = x^n$ for some integer n.	To solve $x^4 - 3x^2 - 4 = 0$, let $u = x^2$. This equation becomes $$u^2 - 3u - 4 = 0.$$
Rational Exponents	Pick a substitution that reduces the equation to quadratic form.	To solve $n^{-2} + 6n^{-1} + 9 = 0$, let $u = n^{-1}$. This equation becomes $$u^2 + 6u + 9 = 0.$$ To solve $6x^{2/5} - 5x^{1/5} - 4 = 0$, let $u = x^{1/5}$. This equation becomes $$6u^2 - 5u - 4 = 0.$$
Equations Having Complex Solutions	Both polynomial and rational equations can have complex solutions. Use the fact that if $a > 0$, then $\sqrt{-a} = i\sqrt{a}$.	$$1 + \frac{1}{x^2} = 0$$ $$x^2 \cdot \left(1 + \frac{1}{x^2}\right) = 0 \cdot x^2$$ $$x^2 + 1 = 0$$ $$x^2 = -1$$ $$x = \pm i$$

8.6 Exercises

PRACTICE   WATCH   DOWNLOAD   READ   REVIEW

EQUATIONS REDUCIBLE TO QUADRATIC FORM

Exercises 1–6: Use the given substitution to solve the equation.

1. $x^4 - 7x^2 + 6 = 0$ $\qquad u = x^2$

2. $2k^4 - 7k^2 + 6 = 0$ $\qquad u = k^2$

3. $3z^6 + z^3 - 10 = 0$ $\qquad u = z^3$

4. $2x^6 + 17x^3 + 8 = 0$ $\qquad u = x^3$

5. $4n^{-2} + 17n^{-1} + 15 = 0$ $\quad u = n^{-1}$

6. $m^{-2} + 24 = 10m^{-1}$ $\qquad u = m^{-1}$

Exercises 7–24: Solve. Find all real solutions.

7. $x^4 = 8x^2 + 9$ $\qquad$ 8. $3x^4 = 10x^2 + 8$

9. $3x^6 - 5x^3 - 2 = 0$ $\quad$ 10. $6x^6 + 11x^3 + 4 = 0$

11. $2z^{-2} + 11z^{-1} = 40$ $\quad$ 12. $z^{-2} - 10z^{-1} + 25 = 0$

13. $x^{2/3} - 2x^{1/3} + 1 = 0$ $\quad$ 14. $3x^{2/3} + 18x^{1/3} = 48$

15. $x^{2/5} - 33x^{1/5} + 32 = 0$

16. $x^{2/5} - 80x^{1/5} - 81 = 0$

17. $x - 13\sqrt{x} + 36 = 0$

18. $x - 17\sqrt{x} + 16 = 0$

19. $z^{1/2} - 2z^{1/4} + 1 = 0$

20. $z^{1/2} - 4z^{1/4} + 4 = 0$

21. $(x + 1)^2 - 5(x + 1) - 14 = 0$

22. $2(x - 5)^2 + 5(x - 5) + 3 = 0$

23. $(x^2 - 1)^2 - 4 = 0$

24. $(x^2 - 9)^2 - 8(x^2 - 9) + 16 = 0$

EQUATIONS HAVING COMPLEX SOLUTIONS

Exercises 25–34: Find all complex solutions.

25. $x^4 - 16 = 0$ $\qquad$ 26. $\frac{1}{3}x^4 - 27 = 0$

27. $x^3 + x = 0$ $\qquad$ 28. $4x^3 + x = 0$

29. $x^4 - 2 = x^2$ $\qquad$ 30. $x^4 - 3 = 2x^2$

31. $\dfrac{1}{x} + \dfrac{1}{x^2} = -\dfrac{1}{2}$ $\qquad$ 32. $\dfrac{2}{x - 1} - \dfrac{1}{x} = -1$

33. $\dfrac{2}{x - 2} - \dfrac{1}{x} = -\dfrac{1}{2}$ $\qquad$ 34. $\dfrac{1}{x} - \dfrac{1}{x^2} = \dfrac{1}{2}$

WRITING ABOUT MATHEMATICS

35. Explain how to solve $ax^4 - bx^2 + c = 0$. Assume that the left side of the equation factors.

36. Explain what it means for an equation to be reducible to quadratic form.

CHECKING BASIC CONCEPTS
SECTIONS 8.5 AND 8.6

1. Solve the inequality $x^2 - x - 6 > 0$. Write your answer in interval notation.

2. Solve the inequality $3x^2 + 5x + 2 \le 0$. Write your answer in interval notation.

3. Solve $x^6 + 6x^3 - 16 = 0$.

4. Solve $x^{2/3} - 7x^{1/3} - 8 = 0$.

5. Find all complex solutions to
$$x^4 + 2x^2 + 1 = 0.$$

CHAPTER 8 | SUMMARY

SECTION 8.1 ■ QUADRATIC FUNCTIONS AND THEIR GRAPHS

Quadratic Function   Any quadratic function f can be written as

$$f(x) = ax^2 + bx + c \quad (a \neq 0).$$

Graph of a Quadratic Function   Its graph is a parabola that is wider than the graph of $y = x^2$, if $0 < |a| < 1$ and narrower, if $|a| > 1$. The y-intercept is c.

Axis of Symmetry   The parabola is symmetric with respect to this vertical line. The axis of symmetry passes through the vertex.

Vertex Formula   The x-coordinate of the vertex is $-\frac{b}{2a}$.

Example: Let $y = x^2 - 4x + 1$.

$$x = -\frac{-4}{2(1)} = 2 \quad \text{and} \quad y = 2^2 - 4(2) + 1 = -3. \text{ The vertex is } (2, -3).$$

SECTION 8.2 ■ PARABOLAS AND MODELING

Vertical and Horizontal Translations   Let h and k be positive numbers.

To graph	*shift the graph of $y = x^2$ by k units*
$y = x^2 + k$	upward.
$y = x^2 - k$	downward.

To graph	*shift the graph of $y = x^2$ by h units*
$y = (x - h)^2$	right.
$y = (x + h)^2$	left.

Example: Compared to $y = x^2$, the graph of $y = (x - 1)^2 + 2$ is translated right 1 unit and upward 2 units.

Vertex Form   Any quadratic function can be expressed as $f(x) = a(x - h)^2 + k$. In this form the point (h, k) is the vertex. A quadratic function can be put in this form by completing the square.

Example:
$$y = x^2 + 10x - 4 \qquad \text{Given equation}$$
$$= (x^2 + 10x + 25) - 25 - 4 \qquad \left(\tfrac{b}{2}\right)^2 = \left(\tfrac{10}{2}\right)^2 = 25$$
$$= (x + 5)^2 - 29 \qquad \text{Perfect square trinomial; add.}$$

The vertex is $(-5, -29)$.

SECTION 8.3 ▪ QUADRATIC EQUATIONS

Quadratic Equations Any quadratic equation can be written as $ax^2 + bx + c = 0$ and can have no real solutions, one real solution, or two real solutions. These solutions correspond to the x-intercepts on the graph of $y = ax^2 + bx + c$.

Example: $x^2 + x - 2 = 0$

$(x + 2)(x - 1) = 0$

$x = -2$ or $x = 1$

The x-intercepts for $y = x^2 + x - 2$ are -2 and 1.

Completing the Square   Write the equation in the form $x^2 + bx = d$. Complete the square by adding $\left(\frac{b}{2}\right)^2$ to each side of the equation.

SECTION 8.4 ▪ THE QUADRATIC FORMULA

The Quadratic Formula   The solutions to $ax^2 + bx + c = 0$ $(a \neq 0)$ are given by

$$x = \frac{-b \pm \sqrt{b^2 - 4ac}}{2a}.$$

Example: Solve $2x^2 + 3x - 1 = 0$ by letting $a = 2, b = 3$, and $c = -1$.

$$x = \frac{-3 \pm \sqrt{3^2 - 4(2)(-1)}}{2(2)} = \frac{-3 \pm \sqrt{17}}{4} \approx 0.28, -1.78$$

The Discriminant   The expression $b^2 - 4ac$ is called the discriminant. If $b^2 - 4ac > 0$, there are two real solutions; if $b^2 - 4ac = 0$, there is one real solution; and if $b^2 - 4ac < 0$, there are no real solutions, rather there are two complex solutions.

Example: For $2x^2 + 3x - 1 = 0$, the discriminant is

$$b^2 - 4ac = 3^2 - 4(2)(-1) = 17 > 0.$$

There are two real solutions to this quadratic equation.

SECTION 8.5 ▪ QUADRATIC INEQUALITIES

Quadratic Inequalities   When the equals sign in a quadratic equation is replaced with $<, >, \leq$, or $\geq$, a quadratic inequality results. For example,

$$3x^2 - x + 1 = 0$$

is a quadratic equation and

$$3x^2 - x + 1 > 0$$

is a quadratic inequality. Like quadratic equations, quadratic inequalities can be solved symbolically, graphically, and numerically. An important first step in solving a quadratic inequality is to solve the corresponding quadratic equation.

Examples: The solutions to $x^2 - 5x - 6 = 0$ are given by $x = -1, 6$.

The solutions to $x^2 - 5x - 6 < 0$ satisfy $-1 < x < 6$.

The solutions to $x^2 - 5x - 6 > 0$ satisfy $x < -1$ or $x > 6$.

SECTION 8.6 ■ EQUATIONS IN QUADRATIC FORM

Equations Reducible to Quadratic Form An equation that is not quadratic, but can be put into quadratic form by using a substitution is reducible to quadratic form.

Example: To solve $x^{2/3} - 2x^{1/3} - 15 = 0$ let $u = x^{1/3}$. This equation becomes

$$u^2 - 2u - 15 = 0.$$

Factoring results in $(u + 3)(u - 5) = 0$, or $u = -3$ or 5. Because $u = x^{1/3}$, $x = u^3$ and $x = (-3)^3 = -27$ or $x = (5)^3 = 125$.

CHAPTER 8 | REVIEW EXERCISES

SECTION 8.1

Exercises 1 and 2: Identify the vertex, axis of symmetry, and whether the parabola opens upward or downward. State where the graph is increasing and where it is decreasing.

1.

2.

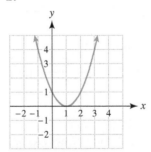

Exercises 3–6: Do the following.
  (a) *Graph f.*
  (b) *Identify the vertex and axis of symmetry.*
  (c) *Evaluate $f(x)$ at the given value of x.*

3. $f(x) = x^2 - 2$, $x = -1$

4. $f(x) = -x^2 + 4x - 3$, $x = 3$

5. $f(x) = -\frac{1}{2}x^2 + x + \frac{3}{2}$, $x = -2$

6. $f(x) = 2x^2 + 8x + 5$, $x = -3$

7. Find the minimum y-value located on the graph of $y = 2x^2 - 6x + 1$.

8. Find the maximum y-value located on the graph of $y = -3x^2 + 2x - 5$.

Exercises 9–12: Find the vertex of the parabola.

9. $f(x) = x^2 - 4x - 2$ **10.** $f(x) = 5 - x^2$

11. $f(x) = -\frac{1}{4}x^2 + x + 1$ **12.** $f(x) = 2 + 2x + x^2$

SECTION 8.2

Exercises 13–18: Do the following.
  (a) *Graph f.*
  (b) *Compare the graph of f with the graph of $y = x^2$.*

13. $f(x) = x^2 + 2$ **14.** $f(x) = 3x^2$

15. $f(x) = (x - 2)^2$ **16.** $f(x) = (x + 1)^2 - 3$

17. $f(x) = \frac{1}{2}(x + 1)^2 + 2$

18. $f(x) = 2(x - 1)^2 - 3$

19. Write the vertex form of a parabola with $a = -4$ and vertex $(2, -5)$.

20. Write the vertex form of a parabola that opens downward with vertex $(-4, 6)$. Assume that $a = \pm 1$.

Exercises 21–24: Write the equation in vertex form. Identify the vertex.

21. $y = x^2 + 4x - 7$ **22.** $y = x^2 - 7x + 1$

23. $y = 2x^2 - 3x - 8$ **24.** $y = 3x^2 + 6x - 2$

Exercises 25 and 26: Find a value for the constant a so that $f(x) = ax^2 - 1$ models the data.

25.

x	1	2	3
$f(x)$	2	11	26

26.

x	-1	0	1
$f(x)$	$-\frac{3}{4}$	-1	$-\frac{3}{4}$

Exercises 27 and 28: Write $f(x)$ in the form given by $f(x) = ax^2 + bx + c$. Identify the y-intercept on the graph of f.

27. $f(x) = -5(x - 3)^2 + 4$

28. $f(x) = 3(x + 2)^2 - 4$

SECTION 8.3

Exercises 29–32: Use the graph of $y = ax^2 + bx + c$ to solve $ax^2 + bx + c = 0$.

29.

30.

31.

32.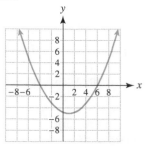

Exercises 33 and 34: A table of $y = ax^2 + bx + c$ is given. Solve $ax^2 + bx + c = 0$.

33.

X	Y1	
-20	250	
-15	100	
-10	0	
-5	-50	
0	-50	
5	0	
10	100	

Y1■X^2+5X−50

34.

X	Y1	
-.75	2	
-.5	0	
-.25	-1	
0	-1	
.25	0	
.5	2	
.75	5	

Y1■8X^2+2X−1

Exercises 35–38: Solve the quadratic equation (a) graphically and (b) numerically.

35. $x^2 - 5x - 50 = 0$ **36.** $\frac{1}{2}x^2 + x - \frac{3}{2} = 0$

37. $\frac{1}{4}x^2 + \frac{1}{2}x = 2$ **38.** $\frac{1}{2}x + \frac{3}{4} = \frac{1}{4}x^2$

Exercises 39–42: Solve by factoring.

39. $x^2 + x - 20 = 0$ **40.** $x^2 + 11x + 24 = 0$

41. $15x^2 - 4x - 4 = 0$ **42.** $7x^2 - 25x + 12 = 0$

Exercises 43–46: Use the square root property to solve.

43. $x^2 = 100$ **44.** $3x^2 = \frac{1}{3}$

45. $4x^2 - 6 = 0$ **46.** $5x^2 = x^2 - 4$

Exercises 47–50: Solve by completing the square.

47. $x^2 + 6x = -2$ **48.** $x^2 - 4x = 6$

49. $x^2 - 2x - 5 = 0$ **50.** $2x^2 + 6x - 1 = 0$

Exercises 51 and 52: Solve for the specified variable.

51. $F = \dfrac{k}{(R + r)^2}$ for R **52.** $2x^2 + 3y^2 = 12$ for y

SECTION 8.4

Exercises 53–58: Use the quadratic formula to solve.

53. $x^2 - 9x + 18 = 0$ **54.** $x^2 - 24x + 143 = 0$

55. $6x^2 + x = 1$ **56.** $5x^2 + 1 = 5x$

57. $x(x - 8) = 5$ **58.** $2x(2 - x) = 3 - 2x$

Exercises 59–64: Solve by any method.

59. $x^2 - 4 = 0$ **60.** $4x^2 - 1 = 0$

61. $2x^2 + 15 = 11x$ **62.** $2x^2 + 15 = 13x$

63. $x(5 - x) = 2x + 1$ **64.** $-2x(x - 1) = x - \frac{1}{2}$

Exercises 65–68: *A graph of* $y = ax^2 + bx + c$ *is shown.*
- (a) *State whether* $a > 0$ *or* $a < 0$.
- (b) *Solve* $ax^2 + bx + c = 0$.
- (c) *Determine whether the discriminant is positive, negative, or zero.*

65.

66.

67.

68.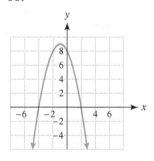

Exercises 69–72: *Do the following for the given equation.*
- (a) *Evaluate the discriminant.*
- (b) *How many real solutions are there?*
- (c) *Support your answer for part (b) graphically.*

69. $2x^2 - 3x + 1 = 0$ **70.** $7x^2 + 2x - 5 = 0$

71. $3x^2 + x + 2 = 0$

72. $4.41x^2 - 12.6x + 9 = 0$

Exercises 73–76: *Solve. Write any complex solutions in standard form.*

73. $x^2 + x + 5 = 0$ **74.** $2x^2 + 8 = 0$

75. $2x^2 = x - 1$ **76.** $7x^2 = 2x - 5$

SECTION 8.5

Exercises 77 and 78: *The graph of* $y = ax^2 + bx + c$ *is shown. Solve each equation or inequality.*

- (a) $ax^2 + bx + c = 0$
- (b) $ax^2 + bx + c < 0$
- (c) $ax^2 + bx + c > 0$

77.   **78.**

    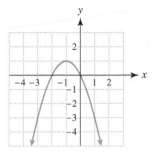

Exercises 79 and 80: *A table of* $y = ax^2 + bx + c$ *is shown. Solve each equation or inequality.*
- (a) $ax^2 + bx + c = 0$
- (b) $ax^2 + bx + c < 0$
- (c) $ax^2 + bx + c > 0$

79. $y = x^2 - 16$

x	-6	-4	-2	0	2	4	6
y	20	0	-12	-16	-12	0	20

80. $y = x^2 + x - 2$

x	-3	-2	-1	0	1	2	3
y	4	0	-2	-2	0	4	10

Exercises 81 and 82: *Solve the quadratic equation in part (a). Use the results to solve the inequalities in parts (b) and (c).*

81. (a) $x^2 - 2x - 3 = 0$
(b) $x^2 - 2x - 3 < 0$
(c) $x^2 - 2x - 3 > 0$

82. (a) $2x^2 - 7x - 15 = 0$
(b) $2x^2 - 7x - 15 \leq 0$
(c) $2x^2 - 7x - 15 \geq 0$

Exercises 83–88: *Solve the quadratic inequality. Write your answer in interval notation.*

83. $x^2 + 4x + 3 \leq 0$ **84.** $5x^2 - 16x + 3 < 0$

85. $6x^2 - 13x + 2 > 0$ **86.** $x^2 \geq 5$

87. $(x - 1)^2 \geq 0$ **88.** $x^2 + 3 < 2$

SECTION 8.6

Exercises 89–92: Solve the equation.

89. $x^4 - 14x^2 + 45 = 0$

90. $2z^{-2} + z^{-1} - 28 = 0$

91. $x^{2/3} - 9x^{1/3} + 8 = 0$

92. $(x - 1)^2 + 2(x - 1) + 1 = 0$

Exercises 93 and 94: Find all complex solutions.

93. $4x^4 + 4x^2 + 1 = 0$　　**94.** $\dfrac{1}{x - 2} - \dfrac{3}{x} = -1$

APPLICATIONS

95. *Construction*　A rain gutter is being fabricated from a flat sheet of metal so that the cross section of the gutter is a rectangle, as shown in the accompanying figure. The width of the metal sheet is 12 inches.

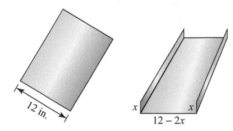

    $12 - 2x$

(a) Write a formula $f(x)$ that gives the area of the cross section.

(b) To hold the greatest amount of rainwater, the cross section should have maximum area. Find the dimensions that result in this maximum.

96. *Height of a Stone*　Suppose that a stone is thrown upward with an initial velocity of 44 feet per second (30 miles per hour) and is released 4 feet above the ground. Its height h in feet after t seconds is given by

$$h(t) = -16t^2 + 44t + 4.$$

(a) When does the stone reach a height of 32 feet?

(b) After how many seconds does the stone reach maximum height? Estimate this height.

97. *Maximizing Revenue*　Hotel rooms normally cost $90 per night. However, for a group rate the management is considering reducing the cost of a room by $3 for every room rented.

(a) Write a formula $f(x)$ that gives the revenue from renting x rooms at the group rate.

(b) Graph f in [0, 30, 5] by [0, 800, 100].

(c) How many rooms should be rented to receive revenue of $600?

(d) How many rooms should be rented to maximize revenue?

98. *Airline Complaints*　In 2000, major U.S. airlines promised better customer service. From 1997 through 1999, the number of complaints per 100,000 passengers can be modeled by

$$f(x) = 0.4(x - 1997)^2 + 0.8,$$

where x represents the year.　(*Source:* Department of Transportation.)

(a) Evaluate $f(1999)$. Interpret the result.

(b) Graph f in [1997, 1999, 1] by [0.5, 3, 0.5]. Discuss how complaints changed over this period.

99. *Braking Distance*　On dry pavement a safe braking distance d in feet for a car traveling x miles per hour is $d = \frac{x^2}{12}$. For each distance d, find x.　(*Source:* F. Mannering, *Principles of Highway Engineering and Traffic Control.*)

(a) $d = 144$ feet　　　**(b)** $d = 300$ feet

100. *Numbers*　The product of two numbers is 143. One number is 2 more than the other.

(a) Write an equation whose solution gives the smaller number x.

(b) Solve the equation.

101. *Educational Attainment*　From 1940 through 1991, the percentage of people with a high school diploma increased dramatically, as shown in the table.

Year	1940	1950	1960
H.S. Diploma (%)	25	34	44

Year	1970	1980	1991
H.S. Diploma (%)	55	69	78

Source: U.S. Census Bureau.

(a) Plot the data.

(b) Would it be reasonable to model these data with a linear function rather than a quadratic function? Explain your reasoning.

(c) Find a function that models the data.

(d) Use your answer from part (c) to estimate the percentage of people with a high school diploma in 1995 and 2005. Compare your answer to the actual values of 82% and 85%, respectively.

102. *U.S. Energy Consumption* From 1950 to 1970 per capita consumption of energy in millions of Btu can be modeled by $f(x) = \frac{1}{4}(x - 1950)^2 + 220$, where x is the year. (*Source:* Department of Energy.)
   (a) Find and interpret the vertex.
   (b) Graph f in [1950, 1970, 5] by [200, 350, 25]. What happened to energy consumption during this time period?
   (c) Use f to predict the consumption in 1996. Actual consumption was 354 million Btu. Did f provide a good model for 1996? Explain.

103. *Screens* A square computer screen has an area of 123 square inches. Approximate its dimensions to the nearest tenth of an inch.

104. *Flying a Kite* A kite is being flown, as illustrated in the accompanying figure. If 130 feet of string have been let out, find the value of x.

105. *Area* A uniform strip of grass is to be planted around a rectangular swimming pool, as illustrated in the accompanying figure. The swimming pool is 30 feet wide and 50 feet long. If there is only enough grass seed to cover 250 square feet, estimate the width x that the strip of grass should be.

106. *Dimensions of a Cone* The volume V of a cone is given by $V = \frac{1}{3}\pi r^2 h$, where r is its base radius and h is its height. See the accompanying figure. If $h = 20$ inches and the volume of the cone must be between 750 and 1700 cubic inches, inclusively, estimate to the nearest tenth of an inch possible values for r.

CHAPTER 8   TEST   Pass the Test Video solutions to all test exercises

1. Find the vertex and axis of symmetry for the graph of $f(x) = -\frac{1}{2}x^2 + x + 1$. Evaluate $f(-2)$.

2. Find the minimum y-value located on the graph of $y = x^2 + 3x - 5$.

3. Find the exact value for the constant a so that $f(x) = ax^2 + 2$ models the data in the table.

x	−2	0	2	4
$f(x)$	0	2	0	−6

4. Graph $f(x) = \frac{1}{2}(x - 3)^2 + 2$ and compare the graph of f to the graph of $y = x^2$.

5. Write $y = x^2 - 6x + 2$ in vertex form. Identify the vertex and axis of symmetry.

6. Use the graph of $f(x) = ax^2 + bx + c$ to solve $ax^2 + bx + c = 0$. Then evaluate $f(1)$.

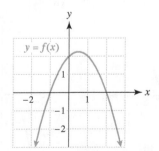

Exercises 7 and 8: Solve the quadratic equation.

7. $3x^2 + 11x - 4 = 0$ **8.** $2x^2 = 2 - 6x^2$

9. Solve $x^2 - 8x = 1$ by completing the square.

10. Solve $x(-2x + 3) = -1$ by using the quadratic formula.

11. Solve $9x^2 - 16 = 0$.

12. Solve $F = \dfrac{Gm^2}{r^2}$ for m.

13. A graph of $y = ax^2 + bx + c$ is shown.
   (a) State whether $a > 0$ or $a < 0$.
   (b) Solve $ax^2 + bx + c = 0$.
   (c) Determine whether the discriminant is positive, negative, or zero.

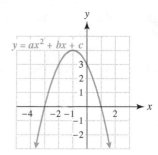

14. Complete the following for $-3x^2 + 4x - 5 = 0$.
   (a) Evaluate the discriminant.
   (b) How many real solutions are there?
   (c) Support your answer for part (b) graphically.

Exercises 15 and 16: The graph of $y = ax^2 + bx + c$ is shown. Solve each equation or inequality.
   (a) $ax^2 + bx + c = 0$
   (b) $ax^2 + bx + c < 0$
   (c) $ax^2 + bx + c > 0$

15.

16.

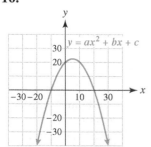

17. Solve the quadratic equation in part (a). Use the result to solve the inequalities in parts (b) and (c) and write your answer in interval notation.
   (a) $8x^2 - 2x - 3 = 0$
   (b) $8x^2 - 2x - 3 \le 0$
   (c) $8x^2 - 2x - 3 \ge 0$

18. Solve $x^2 + 2x \le 0$.

19. Solve $x^6 - 3x^3 + 2 = 0$. Find all real solutions.

20. Solve $2x^2 + 4x + 3 = 0$. Find all complex solutions.

21. Solve $\sqrt{2} - \pi x^2 = 2.12x - 0.5\pi$ graphically. Round your answers to the nearest hundredth.

22. *Braking Distance*   On wet pavement a safe braking distance d in feet for a car traveling x miles per hour is $d = \frac{x^2}{9}$. What speed corresponds to a braking distance of 250 feet?   (*Source:* F. Mannering, *Principles of Highway Engineering and Traffic Control.*)

23. *Construction*   A fence is being constructed along a 20-foot building, as shown in the accompanying figure. No fencing is used along the building.
   (a) If 200 feet of fence are available, find a formula $f(x)$ (in terms of x) that gives the area enclosed.
   (b) What value of x gives the greatest area?

24. *Height of a Stone*   Suppose that a stone is thrown upward with an initial velocity of 88 feet per second (60 miles per hour) and is released 8 feet above the ground. Its height h in feet after t seconds is given by

$$h(t) = -16t^2 + 88t + 8.$$

   (a) Graph h in [0, 6, 1] by [0, 150, 50].
   (b) When does the stone strike the ground?
   (c) After how many seconds does the stone reach maximum height? Estimate this height.

CHAPTER 8 EXTENDED AND DISCOVERY EXERCISES

MODELING DATA WITH A QUADRATIC FUNCTION

1. *Survival Rate of Birds*   The survival rate of sparrowhawks varies according to their age. The following table summarizes the results of one study by listing the age in years and the percentage of birds that survived the previous year. For example, 52% of sparrowhawks that reached age 6 lived to be 7 years old. (*Source:* D. Brown and P. Rothery, *Models in Biology.*)

Age	1	2	3	4	5
Percent (%)	45	60	71	67	67

Age	6	7	8	9
Percent (%)	61	52	30	25

(a) Try to explain the relationship between age and the likelihood of surviving the next year.
(b) Make a scatterplot of the data. What type of function might model the data? Explain.
(c) Graph each function. Which of the following functions models the data better?

$$f_1(x) = -3.57x + 71.1$$
$$f_2(x) = -2.07x^2 + 17.1x + 33$$

(d) Use one of these functions to estimate the likelihood of a 5.5-year-old sparrowhawk surviving for 1 more year.

2. *Photosynthesis and Temperature*   Photosynthesis is the process by which plants turn sunlight into energy. At very cold temperatures photosynthesis may halt even though the sun is shining. In one study the efficiency of photosynthesis for an Antarctic species of grass was investigated. The following table lists results for various temperatures. The temperature x is in degrees Celsius, and the efficiency y is given as a percent. The purpose of the research was to determine the temperature at which photosynthesis is most efficient. (*Source:* D. Brown.)

x (°C)	−1.5	0	2.5	5	7	10	12
y (%)	33	46	55	80	87	93	95

x (°C)	15	17	20	22	25	27	30
y (%)	91	89	77	72	54	46	34

(a) Plot the data.
(b) What type of function might model these data? Explain your reasoning.
(c) Find a function f that models the data.
(d) Use f to estimate the temperature at which photosynthesis is most efficient in this type of grass.

TRANSLATIONS OF PARABOLAS IN COMPUTER GRAPHICS

Exercises 3 and 4: In older video games with two-dimensional graphics, the background is often translated to give the illusion that a character in the game is moving. The simple scene on the left shows a mountain and an airplane. To make it appear that the airplane is flying, the mountain can be translated to the left, as shown in the figure on the right.   (*Reference:* C. Pokorny and C. Gerald, *Computer Graphics.*)

3. *Video Games*   Suppose that the mountain in the figure on the left is modeled by $f(x) = -0.4x^2 + 4$ and that the airplane is located at the point $(1, 5)$.
(a) Graph f in $[-4, 4, 1]$ by $[0, 6, 1]$, where the units are kilometers. Plot the point $(1, 5)$ to show the location of the airplane.
(b) Assume that the airplane is moving horizontally to the right at 0.2 kilometer per second. To give a video game player the illusion that the airplane is moving, graph the image of the mountain and the position of the airplane after 10 seconds.

4. *Video Games*   (Refer to Exercise 3.) Discuss how you could create the illusion of the airplane moving to the left and gaining altitude as it passes over the mountain. Try to perform a translation of this type. Explain your reasoning.

Exercises 5–8:   Factoring and the Discriminant   If the discriminant of the trinomial $ax^2 + bx + c$ with integer coefficients is a perfect square, then it can be factored. For example, on the one hand, the discriminant of $6x^2 + x - 2$ is

$$1^2 - 4(6)(-2) = 49,$$

which is a perfect square ($7^2 = 49$), so we can factor the trinomial as

$$6x^2 + x - 2 = (2x - 1)(3x + 2).$$

On the other hand, the discriminant for $x^2 + x - 1$ is

$$1^2 - 4(1)(-1) = 5,$$

which is not a perfect square, so we cannot factor this trinomial by using integers as coefficients. Similarly, if the discriminant is negative, the trinomial cannot be factored by using integer coefficients. Use the discriminant to predict whether the trinomial can be factored. Then test your prediction.

5. $10x^2 - x - 3$ **6.** $4x^2 - 3x - 6$

7. $3x^2 + 2x - 2$ **8.** $2x^2 + x + 3$

Exercises 9–14:   Polynomial Inequalities   The solution set for a polynomial inequality can be found by first determining the boundary numbers. For example, to solve $f(x) = x^3 - 4x > 0$ begin by solving $x^3 - 4x = 0$. The solutions (boundary numbers) are $-2, 0,$ and 2. The function $f(x) = x^3 - 4x$ is either only positive or only negative on intervals between consecutive zeros. To determine the solution set, we can evaluate test values for each interval as shown on the left below.

Interval	Test Value	$f(x) = x^3 - 4x$
$(-\infty, -2)$	$x = -3$	$f(-3) = -15 < 0$
$(-2, 0)$	$x = -1$	$f(-1) = 3 > 0$
$(0, 2)$	$x = 1$	$f(1) = -3 < 0$
$(2, \infty)$	$x = 3$	$f(3) = 15 > 0$

$$[-6, 6, 1] \text{ by } [-4, 4, 1]$$

We can see that $f(x) > 0$ for $(-2, 0) \cup (2, \infty)$. These results also are supported graphically in the figure on the right above, where the graph of f is above the x-axis when $-2 < x < 0$ or when $x > 2$.

Use these concepts to solve the polynomial inequality.

9. $x^3 - x^2 - 6x > 0$

10. $x^3 - 3x^2 + 2x < 0$

11. $x^3 - 7x^2 + 14x \leq 8$

12. $9x - x^3 \geq 0$

13. $x^4 - 5x^2 + 4 > 0$

14. $1 < x^4$

Exercises   15–20:   Rational   Inequalities   Rational inequalities can be solved using many of the same techniques that are used to solve other types of inequalities. However, there is one important difference. For a rational inequality, the boundary between greater than and less than can either be an x-value where equality occurs or an x-value where a rational expression is undefined. For example, consider the inequality $f(x) = \frac{2 - x}{2x} > 0$. The solution to the equation $\frac{2 - x}{2x} = 0$ is 2. The rational expression $\frac{2 - x}{2x}$ is undefined when $x = 0$. Therefore we select test values on the intervals $(-\infty, 0), (0, 2),$ and $(2, \infty)$. The table reveals that $f(x) > 0$ for $(0, 2)$.

Interval	Test Value	$f(x) = \dfrac{2 - x}{2x}$
$(-\infty, 0)$	$x = -0.5$	$f(-0.5) = -2.5 < 0$
$(0, 2)$	$x = 1$	$f(1) = 0.5 > 0$
$(2, \infty)$	$x = 2.5$	$f(2.5) = -0.1 < 0$

$$[-4.7, 4.7, 1] \text{ by } [-3.1, 3.1, 1]$$

Note that $f(x)$ changes from negative to positive at $x = 0$, where $f(x)$ is undefined. These results are supported graphically in the figure on the right above.

Solve the rational inequality.

15. $\frac{3 - x}{3x} \geq 0$ **16.** $\frac{x - 2}{x + 2} > 0$

17. $\frac{3 - 2x}{1 + x} < 3$ **18.** $\frac{x + 1}{4 - 2x} \geq 1$

19. $\frac{5}{x^2 - 4} < 0$ **20.** $\frac{x}{x^2 - 1} \geq 0$

1. Evaluate $F = \dfrac{5}{z^2 + 1}$ when $z = -2$.

2. Classify each number as one or more of the following: natural number, whole number, integer, rational number, or irrational number: $0.\overline{4}$, $\sqrt{7}$, 0, -5, $\sqrt[3]{8}$, $-\frac{4}{3}$.

3. Simplify each expression. Write the result using positive exponents.

   (a) $\left(\dfrac{x^2y^6}{x^{-3}}\right)^2$ (b) $\dfrac{(xy^{-3})^2}{x(y^{-2})^{-1}}$

   (c) $(a^2b)^2\,(ab^3)^{-4}$

4. Write 9,290,000 in scientific notation.

5. Find $f(-2)$, if $f(x) = \sqrt{2 - x}$. What is the domain of f?

6. If $f(2) = 5$, then what point lies on the graph of f?

Exercises 7 and 8: Graph f by hand.

7. $f(x) = x^2 + 2x$ 8. $f(x) = |2x - 4|$

9. Find the slope–intercept form of the line that passes through $(4, -1)$ and is parallel to the line passing through $(0, 1)$ and $(-2, 4)$.

10. Find the equation of a vertical line that passes through $(-3, 4)$.

11. Solve $2x - 3(x + 2) = 6$.

Exercises 12–14: Solve the inequality. Write your answer in interval notation.

12. $7 - x > 3x$ 13. $|3x - 2| \le 1$

14. $-4 \le 1 - x < 2$

15. Solve the system.
$$-x - 4y = -3$$
$$5x + y = -4$$

16. Shade the solution set in the xy-plane.
$$3x + y \le 3$$
$$x - 3y \le 3$$

17. Solve the system.
$$x + y - z = 3$$
$$x - y + z = 1$$
$$2x - y - z = 1$$

Exercises 18–20: Multiply the expression.

18. $(3x - 2)(2x + 7)$ 19. $3xy(x^2 + y^2)$

20. $(\sqrt{x} + 3)(\sqrt{x} - 3)$

Exercises 21 and 22: Factor the expression.

21. $x^3 - x^2 - 2x$ 22. $4x^2 - 25$

Exercises 23 and 24: Solve each equation.

23. $x^2 - 3 = 0$ 24. $x^2 + 1 = 2x$

Exercises 25 and 26: Simplify the expression.

25. $\dfrac{(x + 3)^2}{x + 2} \cdot \dfrac{x + 2}{2x + 6}$ 26. $\dfrac{1}{x + 2} - \dfrac{1}{x}$

Exercises 27–30: Simplify the expression. Assume all variables are positive.

27. $\sqrt{16x^6}$ 28. $16^{-3/2}$

29. $\dfrac{\sqrt[3]{81x}}{\sqrt[3]{3x}}$ 30. $\sqrt{8x} + \sqrt{2x}$

31. Graph $f(x) = \sqrt{4x}$.

32. Find the distance between $(-1, 2)$ and $(4, 3)$.

33. Write $\frac{3 - i}{2 + i}$ in standard form.

34. Solve $3\sqrt{x + 1} = 2x$.

35. Solve the equation $2x = \sqrt{2.1 - x} + \sqrt[3]{0.1x}$ to the nearest hundredth.

36. Sketch a graph of $f(x) = x^2 - 2x + 3$.
    (a) Find the vertex.
    (b) Evaluate $f(-1)$.
    (c) What is the axis of symmetry?
    (d) Where is f increasing?

37. Write $f(x) = 2x^2 - 4x - 1$ in vertex form.

38. Compare the graph of $f(x) = 4(x + 1)^2 - 2$ to the graph of $y = x^2$.

39. Solve $x^2 + 6x = 2$ by completing the square.

40. Solve $2x^2 - 3x = 1$ by using the quadratic formula.

41. Solve $x(4 - x) = 3$.

42. The graph of $y = ax^2 + bx + c$ is shown. Solve each equation or inequality.
   (a) $ax^2 + bx + c = 0$ **(b)** $ax^2 + bx + c \le 0$

43. Solve $x^2 - 3x + 2 > 0$.

44. Solve $x^4 - 256 = 0$. Find all complex solutions.

Exercises 45–52: **Thinking Generally** *Match the graph (a.–h.) with its equation. Assume that a, b, and c are positive constants.*

45. $y = ax - b$ **46.** $y = b$

47. $y = -ax^2 + c$ **48.** $y = \dfrac{a}{x}$

49. $y = ax^3$ **50.** $y = |ax + b|$

51. $y = a\sqrt{x}$ **52.** $y = a\sqrt[3]{x}$

a.

b.

c.

d.

e.

f.

g.

h.

APPLICATIONS

53. *Calculating Water Flow* Water is being pumped out of a tank. The gallons G of water in the tank after t minutes is shown in the figure, where $y = G(t)$.
   (a) Evaluate $G(0)$. Interpret your answer.
   (b) What is the t-intercept? Interpret your answer.
   (c) What is the slope of the graph of G? Interpret your answer.
   (d) Find a formula for $G(t)$.

54. *Investment* Suppose $4000 are deposited in three accounts paying 4%, 5%, and 6% annual interest. The amount invested at 6% is $1000 more than the amount invested at 5%. The interest after 1 year is $216. How much is invested at each rate?

55. *Maximizing Area* There are 490 feet of fence available to surround the perimeter of a rectangular garden. On one side, there is a 10-foot gate that requires no fencing. What dimensions for the garden give the largest area?

56. *Height of a Tree* A 6-foot person casts a shadow that is 10 feet while a nearby tree casts a 55-foot shadow. Find the height of the tree.

Appendix Using the Graphing Calculator

Overview of the Appendix

This appendix provides instruction for the TI-83, TI-83 Plus, and TI-84 Plus graphing calculators that may be used in conjunction with this textbook. It includes specific keystrokes needed to work several examples from the text. Students are advised to consult the *Graphing Calculator Guidebook* provided by the manufacturer.

Entering Mathematical Expressions

```
π
      3.141592654
√(200)
       14.14213562
10^4
             10000
```

Figure A.1

EVALUATING π To evaluate π, use the following keystrokes, as shown in the first and second lines of Figure A.1. (Do *not* use 3.14 or $\frac{22}{7}$ for π.)

(2nd) (^[π]) (ENTER)

EVALUATING A SQUARE ROOT   To evaluate a square root, such as $\sqrt{200}$, use the following keystrokes, as shown in the third and fourth lines of Figure A.1.

(2nd) (x²[√]) (2) (0) (0) ( )) (ENTER)

```
³√(64)
                 4
5ˣ√23
        1.872171231
```

Figure A.2

EVALUATING AN EXPONENTIAL EXPRESSION   To evaluate an exponential expression, such as 10^4, use the following keystrokes, as shown in the last two lines of Figure A.1.

(1) (0) (^) (4) (ENTER)

EVALUATING A CUBE ROOT   To evaluate a cube root, such as $\sqrt[3]{64}$, use the following keystrokes, as shown in the first and second lines of Figure A.2.

(MATH) (4) (6) (4) ( )) (ENTER)

EVALUATING OTHER ROOTS   To evaluate a fifth root, such as $\sqrt[5]{23}$, use the following keystrokes, as shown in the third and fourth lines of Figure A.2.

(5) (MATH) (5) (2) (3) (ENTER)

```
14e^(.0153*8)
       15.82288531
log(100)
                 2
ln(10)
        2.302585093
```

Figure A.3

EVALUATING THE NATURAL EXPONENTIAL FUNCTION   To evaluate $14e^{0.0153(8)}$, use the following keystrokes, as shown in the first and second lines of Figure A.3.

(1) (4) (2nd) (LN [eˣ]) (.) (0) (1) (5) (3) (×) (8) ( )) (ENTER)

EVALUATING THE COMMON LOGARITHMIC FUNCTION   To evaluate $\log(100)$, use the following keystrokes, as shown in the third and fourth lines of Figure A.3.

(LOG) (1) (0) (0) ( )) (ENTER)

EVALUATING THE NATURAL LOGARITHMIC FUNCTION   To evaluate $\ln(10)$, use the following keystrokes, as shown in the last two lines of Figure A.3.

(LN) (1) (0) ( )) (ENTER)

To access the *number* π, use (2nd) (^[π]).

To evaluate a *square root*, use (2nd) (x²[√]).

To evaluate an *exponential expression*, use the (^) key. To square a number, the (x²) key can also be used.

To evaluate a *cube root*, use (MATH) (4).

To evaluate a *kth root*, use (k) (MATH) (5).

To access the *natural exponential function*, use (2nd) (LN [eˣ]).

To access the *common logarithmic function*, use (LOG).

To access the *natural logarithmic function*, use (LN).

Expressing Answers as Fractions

To evaluate $\frac{1}{3} + \frac{2}{5} - \frac{4}{9}$ in fraction form, use the following keystrokes, as shown in the last three lines of Figure 1.8 on page 17.

Enter the arithmetic expression. To access the "Frac" feature, use the keystrokes (MATH) (1). Then press (ENTER).

Displaying Numbers in Scientific Notation

Figure A.4

To display numbers in scientific notation, set the graphing calculator in scientific mode (Sci), by using the following keystrokes. See Figure A.4. (These keystrokes assume that the calculator is in normal mode.)

(MODE) (▷) (ENTER) (2nd) (MODE [QUIT])

In scientific mode we can display the numbers 5432 and 0.00001234 in scientific notation, as shown in Figure A.5.

```
5432
          5.432ε3
.00001234
          1.234ε-5
```

Figure A.5

If your calculator is in normal mode, it can be set in scientific mode by pressing

(MODE) (▷) (ENTER) (2nd) (MODE [QUIT]).

These keystrokes return the graphing calculator to the home screen.

Entering Numbers in Scientific Notation

```
4.2E-3
                    .0042
4.2*10^(-3)
                    .0042
```

Figure A.6

Numbers can be entered in scientific notation. For example, to enter 4.2×10^{-3} in scientific notation, use the following keystrokes. (Be sure to use the negation key $(-)$ rather than the subtraction key.)

$$\boxed{4}\ \boxed{.}\ \boxed{2}\ \boxed{\text{2nd}}\ \boxed{,\text{[EE]}}\ \boxed{(-)}\ \boxed{3}$$

This number can also be entered using the following keystrokes. See Figure A.6.

$$\boxed{4}\ \boxed{.}\ \boxed{2}\ \boxed{\times}\ \boxed{1}\ \boxed{0}\ \boxed{\wedge}\ \boxed{(}\ \boxed{(-)}\ \boxed{3}\ \boxed{)}$$

SUMMARY: ENTERING NUMBERS IN SCIENTIFIC NOTATION

One way to enter a number in scientific notation is to use the keystrokes

$$\boxed{\text{2nd}}\ \boxed{,\text{[EE]}}$$

to access an exponent (EE) of 10.

Making a Table

```
Plot1  Plot2  Plot3
\Y1■3X+1
\Y2=
\Y3=
\Y4=
\Y5=
\Y6=
\Y7=
```

Figure A.7

To make a table of values for $y = 3x + 1$ starting at $x = 4$ and incrementing by 2, begin by pressing $\boxed{\text{Y=}}$ and then entering the formula $Y_1 = 3X + 1$, as shown in Figure A.7. To set the table parameters, press the following keys. See Figure A.8.

$$\boxed{\text{2nd}}\ \boxed{\text{WINDOW [TBLSET]}}\ \boxed{4}\ \boxed{\text{ENTER}}\ \boxed{2}$$

These keystrokes specify a table that starts at $x = 4$ and increments the x-values by 2. Therefore, the values of Y_1 at $x = 4, 6, 8, \ldots$ appear in the table. To create this table, press the following keys.

$$\boxed{\text{2nd}}\ \boxed{\text{GRAPH [TABLE]}}$$

```
TABLE SETUP
 TblStart=4
 △Tbl=2
Indpnt:  Auto  Ask
Depend:  Auto  Ask
```

Figure A.8

We can scroll through x- and y-values by using the arrow keys. See Figure A.9. Note that there is no first or last x-value in the table.

```
  X  |  Y1
  4  |  13
  6  |  19
  8  |  25
 10  |  31
 12  |  37
 14  |  43
 16  |  49
Y1■3X+1
```

Figure A.9

SUMMARY: MAKING A TABLE

1. Enter the formula for the equation using $\boxed{\text{Y=}}$.
2. Press $\boxed{\text{2nd}}\ \boxed{\text{WINDOW [TBLSET]}}$ to set the starting x-value and the increment between x-values appearing in the table.
3. Create the table by pressing $\boxed{\text{2nd}}\ \boxed{\text{GRAPH [TABLE]}}$.

ZOOM MEMORY
1:ZBox
2:Zoom In
3:Zoom Out
4:ZDecimal
5:ZSquare
6:ZStandard
7↓ZTrig

Figure A.10

WINDOW
 Xmin=-10
 Xmax=10
 Xscl=1
 Ymin=-10
 Ymax=10
 Yscl=1
 Xres=1

Figure A.11

Setting the Viewing Rectangle (Window)

There are at least two ways to set the standard viewing rectangle of $[-10, 10, 1]$ by $[-10, 10, 1]$. The first involves pressing (ZOOM) followed by (6). See Figure A.10. The second method for setting the standard viewing rectangle is to press (WINDOW) and enter the following keystrokes. See Figure A.11.

$$\boxed{(-)}\ \boxed{1}\ \boxed{0}\ \boxed{\text{ENTER}}\ \boxed{1}\ \boxed{0}\ \boxed{\text{ENTER}}\ \boxed{1}\ \boxed{\text{ENTER}}$$
$$\boxed{(-)}\ \boxed{1}\ \boxed{0}\ \boxed{\text{ENTER}}\ \boxed{1}\ \boxed{0}\ \boxed{\text{ENTER}}\ \boxed{1}\ \boxed{\text{ENTER}}$$

(Be sure to use the negation key $(-)$ rather than the subtraction key.) Other viewing rectangles can be set in a similar manner by pressing (WINDOW) and entering the appropriate values. To see the viewing rectangle, press (GRAPH). An example is shown in Figure 1.33 on page 57.

> ### SUMMARY: SETTING THE VIEWING RECTANGLE
>
> To set the standard viewing rectangle, press (ZOOM)(6). To set any viewing rectangle, press (WINDOW) and enter the necessary values. To see the viewing rectangle, press (GRAPH).
>
> **NOTE:** You do not need to change "Xres" from 1.

Making a Scatterplot or a Line Graph

L1	L2	L3	1
1	4	------	
2	5		
3	6		
------	------		

L1={1, 2, 3}

Figure A.12

L1	L2	L3	1
-5	-5	------	
-2	3		
1	-7		
4	8		
------	------		

L1(5) =

Figure A.13

STAT PLOTS
1:Plot1...Off
   ⨽ L1 L2 □
2:Plot2...Off
   ⨽ L1 L2 □
3:Plot3...Off
   ⨽ L1 L2 □
4↓PlotsOff

Figure A.14

To make a scatterplot with the points $(-5, -5)$, $(-2, 3)$, $(1, -7)$, and $(4, 8)$, begin by following these steps.

1. Press (STAT) followed by (1).
2. If list L1 is not empty, use the arrow keys to place the cursor on L1, as shown in Figure A.12. Then press (CLEAR) followed by (ENTER). This deletes all elements in the list. Similarly, if L2 is not empty, clear the list.
3. Input each x-value into list L1 followed by (ENTER). Input each y-value into list L2 followed by (ENTER). See Figure A.13.

It is essential that both lists have the same number of values—otherwise an error message appears when a scatterplot is attempted. Before these four points can be plotted, "STATPLOT" must be turned on. It is accessed by pressing

$$\boxed{\text{2nd}}\ \boxed{\text{Y} = \text{[STAT PLOT]}},$$

as shown in Figure A.14.

There are three possible "STATPLOTS," numbered 1, 2, and 3. Any one of the three can be selected. The first plot can be selected by pressing (1). Next, place the cursor over "On" and press (ENTER) to turn "Plot1" on. There are six types of plots that can be selected. The first type is a *scatterplot* and the second type is a *line graph*, so place the cursor over the first type of plot and press (ENTER) to select a scatterplot. (To make the line graph, place the cursor over the second type of plot and press (ENTER).) The x-values are stored in list L1, so select L1 for "Xlist" by pressing (2nd)(1). Similarly, press (2nd)(2) for the "Ylist," since the y-values are stored in list L2. Finally, there are three styles of marks that can be used to show data points in the graph. We will usually use the first because it is largest and shows up the best.

Figure A.15

$[-10, 10, 1]$ by $[-10, 10, 1]$

Figure A.16

Make the screen appear as in Figure A.15. Before plotting the four data points, be sure to set an appropriate viewing rectangle. Then press (GRAPH). The data points appear as in Figure A.16.

REMARK 1:   A fast way to set the viewing rectangle for any scatterplot is to select the "ZOOMSTAT" feature by pressing (ZOOM)(9). This feature automatically scales the viewing rectangle so that all data points are shown.

REMARK 2:   If an equation has been entered into the (Y=) menu and selected, it will be graphed with the data. This feature is used frequently to model data.

SUMMARY: MAKING A SCATTERPLOT OR A LINE GRAPH

The following are basic steps necessary to make either a scatterplot or a line graph.

1. Use (STAT)(1) to access lists L1 and L2.
2. If list L1 is not empty, place the cursor on L1 and press (CLEAR)(ENTER). Repeat for list L2, if it is not empty.
3. Enter the x-values into list L1 and the y-values into list L2.
4. Use (2nd)(Y = [STAT PLOT]) to select appropriate parameters for the scatterplot or line graph.
5. Set an appropriate viewing rectangle. Press (GRAPH). Otherwise, press (ZOOM)(9). This feature automatically sets the viewing rectangle and plots the data.

NOTE: (ZOOM)(9) *cannot* be used to set a viewing rectangle for the graph of a function.

Figure A.17

Entering a Formula

To enter a formula, press (Y=). For example, use the following keystrokes after "$Y_1 =$ " to enter $y = x^2 - 4$. See Figure A.17.

(Y =)(CLEAR)(X, T, θ, n)(^)(2)(−)(4)

Note that there is a built-in key to enter the variable X. If "$Y_1 =$ " does not appear after pressing (Y=), press (MODE) and make sure the calculator is set in *function mode,* denoted "Func". See Figure A.18.

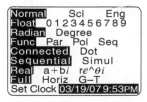

Figure A.18

SUMMARY: ENTERING A FORMULA

To enter a formula, press (Y =). To delete formula, press (CLEAR).

$[-10, 10, 1]$ by $[-10, 10, 1]$

Figure A.19

Graphing a Function

To graph a function, such as $y = x^2 - 4$, start by pressing (Y=) and enter $Y_1 = X^2 - 4$. If there is an equation already entered, remove it by pressing (CLEAR). The equals signs in "$Y_1 =$ " should be in reverse video (a dark rectangle surrounding a white equals sign), which indicates that the equation will be graphed. If the equals sign is not in reverse video, place the cursor over it and press (ENTER). Set an appropriate viewing rectangle and then press (GRAPH). The graph of f will appear in the specified viewing rectangle. See Figures A.17 and A.19.

1. Use the $\boxed{Y=}$ menu to enter the formula for the function.
2. Use the $\boxed{\text{WINDOW}}$ menu to set an appropriate viewing rectangle.
3. Press $\boxed{\text{GRAPH}}$.

Graphing a Vertical Line

Set an appropriate window (or viewing rectangle). Then return to the home screen by pressing

$$\boxed{\text{2nd}}\ \boxed{\text{MODE [QUIT]}}.$$

To graph a vertical line, such as $x = -4$, press

$$\boxed{\text{2nd}}\ \boxed{\text{PRGM [DRAW]}}\ \boxed{4}\ \boxed{(-)}\ \boxed{4}.$$

See Figure A.20. Pressing $\boxed{\text{ENTER}}$ will make the vertical line appear, as shown in Figure A.21.

Figure A.20

$[-6, 6, 1]$ by $[-6, 6, 1]$

Figure A.21

SUMMARY: GRAPHING THE VERTICAL LINE $x = h$

1. Set an appropriate window by pressing $\boxed{\text{WINDOW}}$.
2. Return to the home screen by pressing $\boxed{\text{2nd}}\boxed{\text{MODE [QUIT]}}$.
3. Draw a vertical line by pressing $\boxed{\text{2nd}}\boxed{\text{PRGM [DRAW]}}\boxed{4}\boxed{h}\boxed{\text{ENTER}}$.

Squaring a Viewing Rectangle

In a square viewing rectangle the graph of $y = x$ is a line that makes a 45° angle with the positive x-axis, a circle appears circular, and all sides of a square have the same length. An approximate square viewing rectangle can be set if the distance along the x-axis is 1.5 times the distance along the y-axis. Examples of viewing rectangles that are (approximately) square include

$$[-6, 6, 1] \text{ by } [-4, 4, 1] \quad \text{and} \quad [-9, 9, 1] \text{ by } [-6, 6, 1].$$

Square viewing rectangles can be set automatically by pressing either

$$\boxed{\text{ZOOM}}\boxed{4} \quad \text{or} \quad \boxed{\text{ZOOM}}\boxed{5}.$$

ZOOM 4 provides a *decimal window*, which is discussed later. See Figure A.22.

Figure A.22

SUMMARY: SQUARING A VIEWING RECTANGLE

Either $\boxed{\text{ZOOM}}\boxed{4}$ or $\boxed{\text{ZOOM}}\boxed{5}$ may be used to produce a square viewing rectangle. An (approximately) square viewing rectangle has the form

$$[-1.5k, 1.5k, 1] \text{ by } [-k, k, 1],$$

where k is a positive number.

Locating a Point of Intersection

Figure A.23

In Example 8, Section 3.1 on page 157, we find the point of intersection for two lines. To find the point of intersection for the graphs of

$$y_1 = 3(1 - x) \quad \text{and} \quad y_2 = 2,$$

start by entering Y_1 and Y_2, as shown in Figure A.23. Set the window, and graph both equations. Then press the following keys to find the intersection point.

(2nd) (TRACE [CALC]) (5)

Figure A.24

See Figure A.24, where the "intersect" utility is being selected. The calculator prompts for the first curve, as shown in Figure A.25. Use the arrow keys to locate the cursor near the point of intersection and press (ENTER). Repeat these steps for the second curve. Finally we are prompted for a guess. For each of the three prompts, place the free-moving cursor near the point of intersection and press (ENTER). The approximate coordinates of the point of intersection are shown in Figure 3.5 on page 157.

$[-6, 6, 1]$ by $[-4, 4, 1]$

Figure A.25

SUMMARY: FINDING A POINT OF INTERSECTION

1. Graph the two equations in an appropriate viewing rectangle.
2. Press (2nd) (TRACE [CALC]) (5).
3. Use the arrow keys to select an approximate location for the point of intersection. Press (ENTER) to make the three selections for "First curve?", "Second curve?", and "Guess?". (Note that if the cursor is near the point of intersection, you usually do not need to move the cursor for each selection. Just press (ENTER) three times.)

Accessing the Absolute Value

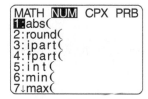

Figure A.26

In Example 9, Section 3.5 on page 207, the absolute value is used to graph $y_1 = |x - 50|$. To graph y_1, begin by entering $Y_1 = \text{abs}(X - 50)$. The absolute value (abs) is accessed by pressing

(MATH) (▷) (1).

See Figure A.26.

SUMMARY: ACCESSING THE ABSOLUTE VALUE

1. Press (MATH).
2. Position the cursor over "NUM".
3. Press (1) to select the absolute value.

Shading a System of Inequalities

In Example 5, Section 4.3 on page 261, we are asked to shade the solution set for the system of linear inequalities $2x + y \le 5$, $-2x + y \ge 1$. Begin by solving each inequality for y to obtain $y \le 5 - 2x$ and $y \ge 2x + 1$. Then let $Y_1 = 5 - 2X$ and $Y_2 = 2X + 1$, as shown in

Figure 4.24(b). Position the cursor to the left of Y_1 and press (ENTER) three times. The triangle that appears indicates that the calculator will shade the region below the graph of Y_1. Next locate the cursor to the left of Y_2 and press (ENTER) twice. This triangle indicates that the calculator will shade the region above the graph of Y_2. After setting the viewing rectangle to $[-15, 15, 5]$ by $[-10, 10, 5]$, press (GRAPH). The result is shown in Figure 4.24(c).

SUMMARY: SHADING A SYSTEM OF INEQUALITIES

1. Solve each inequality for y.
2. Enter each formula as Y_1 and Y_2 in the (Y =) menu.
3. Locate the cursor to the left of Y_1 and press (ENTER) two or three times to shade either above or below the graph of Y_1. Repeat for Y_2.
4. Set an appropriate viewing rectangle.
5. Press (GRAPH).

NOTE: The "Shade" utility in the DRAW menu can also be used to shade the region *between* two graphs.

Entering the Elements of a Matrix

In Example 6(b), Section 4.6 on page 293, the elements of a matrix are entered. The augmented matrix A is given by

$$A = \left[\begin{array}{ccc|c} 1 & 1 & 2 & 1 \\ -1 & 0 & 1 & -2 \\ 2 & 1 & 5 & -1 \end{array}\right].$$

Use the following keystrokes on the TI-83 Plus or TI-84 Plus to define a matrix A with dimension 3×4. (*Note:* On the TI-83 the matrix menu is found by pressing (MATRX).)

(2nd) (x^{-1} [MATRIX]) (▷) (▷) (1) (3) (ENTER) (4) (ENTER)

See Figure 4.31(a).

Then input the 12 elements of the matrix A, row by row. Finish each entry by pressing (ENTER). After these elements have been entered, press

(2nd) (MODE [QUIT])

to return to the home screen. To display the matrix A, press

(2nd) (x^{-1} [MATRIX]) (1) (ENTER).

See Figure A.27.

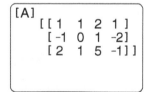

Figure A.27

SUMMARY: ENTERING THE ELEMENTS OF A MATRIX A

1. Begin by accessing the matrix A by pressing (2nd) (x^{-1} [MATRIX]) (▷) (▷) (1).
2. Enter the dimension of A by pressing (m) (ENTER) (n) (ENTER), where the dimension of the matrix is $m \times n$.
3. Input each element of the matrix, row by row. Finish each entry by pressing (ENTER). Use (2nd) (MODE [QUIT]) to return to the home screen.

NOTE: On the TI-83, replace the keystrokes (2nd) (x^{-1} [MATRIX]) with (MATRX).

Reduced Row–Echelon Form

In Example 6(b), Section 4.6 on page 293, the reduced row–echelon form of a matrix is found. To find this reduced row–echelon form, use the following keystrokes from the home screen on the TI-83 Plus or TI-84 Plus.

(2nd) (x⁻¹ [MATRIX]) (▷) (ALPHA) (APPS [B]) (2nd) (x⁻¹ [MATRIX]) (1) ( )) (ENTER)

The resulting matrix is shown in Figure 4.31(b). On the TI-83 graphing calculator, use the following keystrokes to find the reduced row–echelon form.

(MATRX) (▷) (ALPHA) (MATRX [B]) (MATRX) (1) ( )) (ENTER)

SUMMARY: FINDING REDUCED ROW–ECHELON FORM OF A MATRIX

1. To make rref([A]) appear on the home screen, use the following keystrokes for the TI-83 Plus or TI-84 Plus graphing calculator.

(2nd) (x⁻¹ [MATRIX]) (▷) (ALPHA) (APPS [B]) (2nd) (x⁻¹ [MATRIX]) (1) ( ))

2. Press (ENTER) to calculate the reduced row–echelon form.
3. Use arrow keys to access elements that do not appear on the screen.

NOTE: On the TI-83, replace the keystrokes (2nd)(x⁻¹ [MATRIX]) with (MATRX) and (APPS [B]) with (MATRX [B]).

Evaluating a Determinant

In Example 3(a), Section 4.7 on page 300, a graphing calculator is used to evaluate a determinant of a matrix. Start by entering the 9 elements of the 3 × 3 matrix A, as shown in Figure 4.33(a). To compute det A, perform the following keystrokes from the home screen.

(2nd) (x⁻¹ [MATRIX]) (▷) (1) (2nd) (x⁻¹ [MATRIX]) (1) ( )) (ENTER)

The results are shown in the last two lines of Figure 4.33(b).

SUMMARY: EVALUATING A DETERMINANT OF A MATRIX

1. Enter the dimension and elements of the matrix A.
2. Return to the home screen by pressing

(2nd) (MODE [QUIT]).

3. On the TI-83 Plus or TI-84 Plus, perform the following keystrokes.

(2nd) (x⁻¹ [MATRIX]) (▷) (1) (2nd) (x⁻¹ [MATRIX]) (1) ( )) (ENTER)

NOTE: On the TI-83, replace the keystrokes (2nd) (x⁻¹ [MATRIX]) with (MATRX).

Figure A.28

Locating an x-Intercept or Zero

In Section 5.3 on page 351, we locate an x-intercept or *zero* of $f(x) = x^2 - 4$. Start by entering $Y_1 = X^\wedge 2 - 4$ into the $\boxed{Y =}$ menu. Set the viewing rectangle to $[-9, 9, 1]$ by $[-6, 6, 1]$ and graph Y_1. Afterwards, press the following keys to invoke the zero finder. See Figure A.28.

$$\boxed{2nd}\ \boxed{TRACE\ [CALC]}\ \boxed{2}$$

The graphing calculator prompts for a left bound. Use the arrow keys to set the cursor to the left of the x-intercept and press $\boxed{ENTER}$. The graphing calculator then prompts for a right bound. Set the cursor to the right of the x-intercept and press $\boxed{ENTER}$. Finally, the graphing calculator prompts for a guess. Set the cursor roughly at the x-intercept and press $\boxed{ENTER}$. See Figures A.29–A.31. The calculator then approximates the x-intercept or zero automatically, as shown in the Technology Note on page 351. The zero of -2 can be found similarly.

$[-9, 9, 1]$ by $[-6, 6, 1]$

Figure A.29

$[-9, 9, 1]$ by $[-6, 6, 1]$

Figure A.30

$[-9, 9, 1]$ by $[-6, 6, 1]$

Figure A.31

SUMMARY: LOCATING AN x-INTERCEPT OR ZERO

1. Graph the function in an appropriate viewing rectangle.
2. Press $\boxed{2nd}\ \boxed{TRACE\ [CALC]}\ \boxed{2}$.
3. Select the left and right bounds, followed by a guess. Press $\boxed{ENTER}$ after each selection. The calculator then approximates the x-intercept or zero.

Setting Connected and Dot Mode

Figure A.32

To set your graphing calculator in dot mode, press $\boxed{MODE}$, position the cursor over "Dot", and press $\boxed{ENTER}$. See Figure A.32. Graphs will now appear in dot mode rather than connected mode.

SUMMARY: SETTING CONNECTED OR DOT MODE

1. Press $\boxed{MODE}$.
2. Position the cursor over "Connected" or "Dot". Press $\boxed{ENTER}$.

Setting a Decimal Window

With a decimal window, the cursor stops on convenient x-values. In the decimal window $[-9.4, 9.4, 1]$ by $[-6.2, 6.2, 1]$ the cursor stops on x-values that are multiples of 0.2. If we reduce the viewing rectangle to $[-4.7, 4.7, 1]$ by $[-3.1, 3.1, 1]$, the cursor stops on x-values

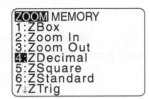

Figure A.33

that are multiples of 0.1. To set this smaller window automatically, press $\boxed{\text{ZOOM}}\boxed{4}$. See Figure A.33. Decimal windows are also useful when graphing rational functions with asymptotes in connected mode.

SUMMARY: SETTING A DECIMAL WINDOW

1. Press $\boxed{\text{ZOOM}}\boxed{4}$ to set the viewing rectangle $[-4.7, 4.7, 1]$ by $[-3.1, 3.1, 1]$.
2. A larger decimal window is $[-9.4, 9.4, 1]$ by $[-6.2, 6.2, 1]$.

Figure A.34

Setting $a + bi$ Mode

In Example 1(a), Section 7.6 on page 557, the expression $\sqrt{-25}$ is evaluated. To evaluate expressions containing square roots of negative numbers, set your calculator in $a + bi$ mode by using the following keystrokes.

See Figures A.34 and A.35.

Figure A.35

SUMMARY: SETTING $a + bi$ MODE

1. Press $\boxed{\text{MODE}}$.
2. Move the cursor to the seventh line, highlight $a + bi$, and press $\boxed{\text{ENTER}}$.
3. Press $\boxed{\text{2nd}}\boxed{\text{MODE [QUIT]}}$ and return to the home screen.

Evaluating Complex Arithmetic

Complex arithmetic can be performed much like other arithmetic expressions. This is done by entering

$$\boxed{\text{2nd}}\boxed{.\,[i]}$$

Figure A.36

to obtain the imaginary unit i from the home screen. For example, to find the sum $(-2 + 3i) + (4 - 6i)$, perform the following keystrokes on the home screen.

The result is shown in Figure A.36. Other complex arithmetic operations are done similarly.

SUMMARY: EVALUATING COMPLEX ARITHMETIC

Enter a complex expression in the same way as you would any arithmetic expression. To obtain the complex number i, use $\boxed{\text{2nd}}\boxed{.\,[i]}$.

Finding Maximum and Minimum Values

To find a minimum y-value (or vertex) on the graph of $f(x) = 1.5x^2 - 6x + 4$, start by entering $Y_1 = 1.5X^2 - 6X + 4$ from the $\boxed{Y =}$ menu. Set the viewing rectangle and then perform the following keystrokes to find the minimum y-value.

$$\boxed{\text{2nd}}\ \boxed{\text{TRACE [CALC]}}\ \boxed{3}$$

See Figure A.37.

The calculator prompts for a left bound. Use the arrow keys to position the cursor left of the vertex and press $\boxed{\text{ENTER}}$. Similarly, position the cursor to the right of the vertex for the right bound and press $\boxed{\text{ENTER}}$. Finally, the graphing calculator asks for a guess between the left and right bounds. Place the cursor near the vertex and press $\boxed{\text{ENTER}}$. See Figures A.38–A.40. The minimum value is shown in Figure A.41.

CALCULATE
1:value
2:zero
3:minimum
4:maximum
5:intersect
6:dy/dx
7:∫f(x)dx

Figure A.37

$[-4.7, 4.7, 1]$ by $[-3.1, 3.1, 1]$

Figure A.38

$[-4.7, 4.7, 1]$ by $[-3.1, 3.1, 1]$

Figure A.39

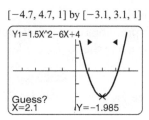

$[-4.7, 4.7, 1]$ by $[-3.1, 3.1, 1]$

Figure A.40

$[-4.7, 4.7, 1]$ by $[-3.1, 3.1, 1]$

Figure A.41

A maximum of the function f on an interval can be found in a similar manner, except enter

$$\boxed{\text{2nd}}\ \boxed{\text{TRACE [CALC]}}\ \boxed{4}.$$

The calculator prompts for left and right bounds, followed by a guess. Press $\boxed{\text{ENTER}}$ after the cursor has been located appropriately for each prompt. The graphing calculator will display the maximum y-value. For example, see the Technology Note on page 584.

SUMMARY: FINDING MAXIMUM AND MINIMUM VALUES

1. Graph the function in an appropriate viewing rectangle.
2. Press $\boxed{\text{2nd}}\ \boxed{\text{TRACE [CALC]}}\ \boxed{3}$ to find a minimum y-value.
3. Press $\boxed{\text{2nd}}\ \boxed{\text{TRACE [CALC]}}\ \boxed{4}$ to find a maximum y-value.
4. Use the arrow keys to locate the left and right x-bounds, followed by a guess. Press $\boxed{\text{ENTER}}$ to select each position of the cursor.

Answers to Selected Exercises

SECTION 1.1 (pp. 9–12)

1. $N = \{1, 2, 3, \dots\}$; $W = \{0, 1, 2, 3, \dots\}$
2. $I = \{\dots, -2, -1, 0, 1, 2, \dots\}$; -5
3. $\frac{p}{q}$, where p and q are integers and $q \neq 0$; $\frac{3}{4}$ (answers may vary)   **4.** Any number that can be expressed as a decimal; irrational; $\sqrt{2}$ (answers may vary)   **5.** $3 + 2 = 2 + 3$ (answers may vary)   **6.** $4 \cdot 3 = 3 \cdot 4$ (answers may vary)
7. $a \cdot 1 = a$, for any real number a
8. $0 + a = a$, for any real number a
9. $2 \cdot (3 \cdot 4) = (2 \cdot 3) \cdot 4$ (answers may vary)
10. $2(3 + 4) = 2 \cdot 3 + 2 \cdot 4$ (answers may vary)
11. Commutative property for addition
12. Commutative property for multiplication
13. Natural, integer, rational, and real
15. Rational and real   **17.** Rational and real   **19.** Real
21. Natural numbers: 6; whole numbers: 6; integers: -5, 6; rational numbers: $-5, 6, \frac{1}{7}, 0.2$; irrational numbers: $\sqrt{7}$
23. Natural numbers: $\frac{3}{1} = 3$; whole numbers: $\frac{3}{1} = 3$; integers: $\frac{3}{1} = 3$; rational numbers: $\frac{3}{1} = 3, -\frac{5}{8}, 0.\overline{45}$; irrational numbers: $\sqrt{5}, \pi$ **25.** Natural: $\sqrt{9}$; whole: $\sqrt{9}$; integer: $-2, \sqrt{9}$; rational: $-2, \frac{1}{2}, \sqrt{9}, 0.\overline{26}$; irrational: none   **27.** Rational   **29.** Rational
31. Integers   **33.** Identity   **35.** Commutative
37. Distributive   **39.** Associative   **41.** Commutative
43. Commutative   **45.** Distributive   **47.** $a + 4$ **49.** $\frac{1}{3}a$
51. $x + 1$ **53.** xy **55.** $(4 + 5) + b$ or $9 + b$
57. $(5 \cdot 10)x$ or $50x$ **59.** $x + (y + z)$
61. $x \cdot (3 \cdot 4)$ or $x \cdot 12$ **63.** $4x + 4y$ **65.** $5x - 35$
67. $-x - 1$ **69.** $a(x - y)$ **71.** $3(4 + x)$
73. $(3 + 7)x$ or $10x$ **75.** $(8 - 2)t$ or $6t$
77. $\left(1 - \frac{3}{4}\right)x$ or $\frac{1}{4}x$ **79.** $3 - 1 + 2z$ or $2 + 2z$ **81.** $8z$
83. $5t$ **85.** 56   **87.** 507   **89.** 60   **91.** 5, natural, integer, and rational   **93.** $43.\overline{3}$, rational   **95.** 78.1, rational
97. 20   **99.** 6   **101.** 40   **103.** 9   **105.** Identity property of 1 (answers may vary)   **107.** No; the commutative property for multiplication   **109.** (a) 16.3 million
(b) About 15.7 million   **(c)** 15.675 million; yes
111. (a) Valid   (b) Valid   (c) Not valid

SECTION 1.2 (pp. 19–22)

1. right   **2.** left   **3.** positive   **4.** negative   **5.** negative
6. negative   **7.** $-a$ **8.** $\frac{b}{a}$ **9** positive   **10.** $-a - b$

11.
13.
15.

17. 6.1   **19.** 3   **21.** x **23.** $x - y$ **25.** Positive
27. Both   **29.** Positive   **31.** -56 **33.** 6.9
35. $\pi - 2$ **37.** $-a + b$ **39.** $x - y$ **41.** $-2z + 2$
43. $\frac{1}{3}$ **45.** $-\frac{3}{2}$ **47.** $\frac{1}{\pi}$ **49.** $\frac{1}{a + 3}$ **51.** $-\frac{b}{2a}$
53. $x - 7$ **55.** -2 **57.** -16.6 **59.** $-\frac{2}{4} = -\frac{1}{2}$
61. -5 **63.** 72   **65.** $-\frac{5}{42}$ **67.** $\frac{4}{6} = \frac{2}{3}$ **69.** $-\frac{3}{8}$
71. -4 **73.** 5   **75.** Undefined   **77.** 140   **79.** -2
81. $-5x$ **83.** $-z$ **85.** 57.2   **87.** $\frac{19}{42}$ **89.** $-\frac{9}{25}$ **91.** $\frac{21}{55}$
93. 5   **95.** 0   **97.** 60   **99.** $\frac{a + b}{2}$ **101.** 0   **103.** 100
105. 1   **107.** $\frac{2}{6} = \frac{1}{3}$ **109.** 1   **111.** 1200   **113.** 16 days
115. $2600; answers may vary; $2577.76
117. (a) No   (b) 34,020.2   (c) 120,000; answers may vary.
119. (a) They are increasing.   (b) About 26.1 million; answers may vary.

CHECKING BASIC CONCEPTS 1.1 & 1.2 (p. 22)

1. (a) Integer, rational, and real   (b) Natural, integer, rational, and real   (c) Real   (d) Rational and real
2. (a) Commutative; $a + b = b + a$ (b) Associative; $a \cdot (b \cdot c) = (a \cdot b) \cdot c$ (c) Distributive; $a(b + c) = ab + ac$ (d) Distributive; $a(b - c) = ab - ac$ with $a = -1$ **3.** (a) -4 (b) -40.8 (c) $-\frac{5}{12}$
4. About 12 billion gallons

SECTION 1.3 (pp. 34–38)

1. Base: 8; exponent: 3   **2.** $1; \frac{1}{2}$ **3.** 7^3 **4.** 5^2
5. No, $2^3 = 8$ and $3^2 = 9$.
6. No, $-4^2 = -16$ and $(-4)^2 = 16$ **7.** $\frac{1}{7^n}$ **8.** 6^{m+n}
9. 5^{m-n} **10.** $3^k x^k$ **11.** 2^{mk} **12.** $\frac{x^m}{y^m}$ **13.** x^n **14.** $\frac{b^m}{a^n}$
15. $\left(\frac{z}{y}\right)^n$ or $\frac{z^n}{y^n}$ **16.** 500   **17.** 2^3 **19.** 4^4 **21.** 6^0
23. (a) 64   (b) 81   **25.** (a) 16   (b) 27
27. (a) $\frac{8}{27}$ (b) $-\frac{27}{8}$ **29.** (a) $\frac{16}{9}$ (b) $\frac{25}{64}$
31. (a) $\frac{x^3}{2}$ (b) ab **33.** (a) 3^2 or 9   (b) x^7
35. (a) $-15x^3$ (b) $\frac{a^3}{b^2}$ **37.** (a) $\frac{5}{2}$ (b) $\frac{8}{ab^3}$
39. (a) 4   (b) 10^2 or 100   **41.** (a) $\frac{1}{b^5}$ (b) $4x^2$
43. (a) $\frac{2b}{3a^2}$ (b) $\frac{3y^6}{x^7}$ **45.** (a) 3^8 or 6561   (b) $\frac{1}{x^6}$

47. (a) $64y^6$ **(b)** $\frac{1}{16x^4y^{12}}$ **49. (a)** $\frac{64}{x^3}$ **(b)** $\frac{z^{20}}{32x^5}$

51. $\frac{3m}{2n^3}$ **53.** $\frac{y^4}{4x^6}$ **55.** b^8 **57.** $-\frac{27b^4}{a}$ **59.** $\frac{n^3}{m^3}$

61. $\frac{a^{12}}{81b^4}$ **63.** t^2 **65.** $\frac{2y^2}{x}$ **67.** $-\frac{r^6}{8t^3}$ **69.** $\frac{1}{rt^3}$

71. y **73.** $-\frac{125r^{15}}{t^9}$ **75.** 34   **77.** -8 **79.** 40

81. $-\frac{11}{2}$ **83.** -155 **85.** 5   **87.** -2 **89.** 1   **91.** 5

93. 5   **95.** 2.447×10^6 **97.** 2.69×10^{10}

99. 5.1×10^{-2} **101.** 1.0×10^{-6} **103.** 500,000

105. 9,300,000   **107.** -0.006 **109.** 0.00005876

111. 6×10^6; 6,000,000   **113.** 8×10^{-6}; 0.000008

115. 2×10^5; 200,000   **117. (a)** $k = 10$

(b) $\frac{1024}{52} \approx 20$ years   **119.** $V = (2a)^3 = 8a^3$

121. $A = (3ab)^2 = 9a^2b^2$ **123. (a)** $551.25

(b) $1215.51   **125.** About $8795 per person

127. $256 \times 2^{20} = 268,435,456$ bytes

129.

Country	1996	2025
China	1.2551×10^9	1.48×10^9
Germany	8.24×10^7	8.09×10^7
India	9.758×10^8	1.3302×10^9
Mexico	9.58×10^7	1.302×10^8
U.S.	2.65×10^8	3.325×10^8

SECTION 1.4 (pp. 44–49)

1. variable   **2.** equation   **3.** equals   **4.** formula
5. x and y **6.** $3 + 7 = 10$ (answers may vary)   **7.** $3x = 15$
(answers may vary)   **8.** $3y + x = 5$ (answers may vary)
9. 3   **10.** -2 **11.** b **12.** b **13.** 6   **14.** 4
15. $y = 5280x$ **17.** $A = s^2$ **19.** $y = 3600x$
21. $A = \frac{1}{2}bh$ **23.** $A = \frac{1}{4}\pi d^2$ **25.** $y = 30$
27. $y = 1.9$ **29.** $d = 10$ **31.** $z = 6$ **33.** $y = -\frac{1}{4}$
35. $N = -\frac{8}{9}$ **37.** $P = 0.3$ **39.** $A = 9$ **41.** $V = \frac{5}{4}\pi$
43. (ii)   **45.** (iii)   **47.** -3 **49.** 2

51.

x	0	2	4	6	8
y	-0.5	4.5	9.5	14.5	19.5

53.

x	-3	-1	1	3
y	15	5	5	15

55.

x	-1	0	1	8
y	-3	-2	-1	0

57.

x	a	$a-1$	a^2-1
y	$\sqrt{a+1}$	$\sqrt{a}$	a

59.   **61.**

63. $y = 60t$

65. (a)

Speed (mph)	10	20	30	40	50	60	70
Braking Distance (ft)	$8.\overline{3}$	$33.\overline{3}$	75	$133.\overline{3}$	$208.\overline{3}$	300	$408.\overline{3}$

(b) $133.\overline{3}$ ft   **(c)** It quadruples.   **(d)** 100 ft   **67.** 152.25 mph
69. (a) About 0.464 kilograms   **(b)** About 3.7125 kilograms   **(c)** It increases by 8 times.
71. The taller animal has half the stepping frequency of the other.   **73.** Venus: $E \approx 22{,}995$ miles per hour; Earth: $C \approx 17{,}706$ miles per hour; Moon: $C \approx 3790$ miles per hour; Mars: $E \approx 11{,}384$ miles per hour
75. About 80,610 miles per hour
77. (a) About 177 beats per minute   **(b)** About 22 beats per minute   **79. (a)** $\sqrt{3} \approx 1.73$ ft^2 **(b)** $4\sqrt{3} \approx 6.93$ m^2
81. (a) $28\pi \approx 88$ in.   **(b)** $2.6\pi \approx 8.2$ mi   **83.** 9 in.
85. 3 m   **87. (a)** $C = 336x$ **(b)** 10,080 calories

CHECKING BASIC CONCEPTS 1.3 & 1.4 (p. 49)

1. (a) 16   **(b)** $\frac{1}{9}$ **(c)** 32   **(d)** x **(e)** $4x^6y^8$
2. (a) -6 **(b)** -4 **(c)** 58
3. (a) 1.03×10^5 **(b)** 5.23×10^{-4} **(c)** 6.7×10^0
4. (a) 5,430,000   **(b)** 0.0098
5. 900 cubic feet per person

People	10	20	30	40
Ventilation (ft^3/hr)	9000	18,000	27,000	36,000

SECTION 1.5 (pp. 60–62)

1. A set of ordered pairs (x, y)
2. Domain: set of all x-values; Range: set of all y-values
3.

Q. II   Q. I   y-axis   Origin   x-axis   Q. III   Q. IV

4. Scatterplot (answers may vary)   Line Graph (answers may vary)

5. No   **6.** Quadrant III

7. $D = \{1, 3, 5\}; R = \{-4, 2, 6\}$

9. $D = \{-2, -1, 0, 1, 2\}; R = \{0, 1, 2, 3\}$

11. $D = \{41, 87, 96\}; R = \{24, 53, 67, 88\}$

13. $S = \{(1, 3), (3, 7), (5, 11), (7, 15), (9, 19)\}$

$D = \{1, 3, 5, 7, 9\}; R = \{3, 7, 11, 15, 19\}$

15. $S = \{(2000, 4.0), (2001, 4.2), (2002, 5.8),$

$(2003, 6.0), (2004, 5.5)\};$

$D = \{2000, 2001, 2002, 2003, 2004\};$

$R = \{4.0, 4.2, 5.5, 5.8, 6.0\}$

17. $(1, 2)$ is in QI; $(-1, 3)$ is in QII; $(-3, 0)$ is on the x-axis; $(0, -2)$ is on the y-axis.

19. $(10, 50)$ is in QI; $(-30, 20)$ is in QII; $(-20, -25)$ is in QIII; $(50, -25)$ is in QIV.

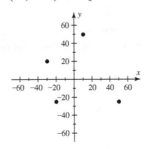

21. $(0, 0), (1, 4), (2, 8), (3, 12)$

23. $(0, 4), (1, 3), (2, 0), (3, -5)$

25. $(0, 1), \left(1, \frac{1}{2}\right), \left(2, \frac{1}{5}\right), \left(3, \frac{1}{10}\right)$

27. $S = \{(-3, 2), (-2, 1), (2, -3), (3, 3)\}$

$D = \{-3, -2, 2, 3\}; R = \{-3, 1, 2, 3\}$

29. $S = \{(-4, 4), (-3, 2), (-2, 0), (0, -3), (2, 4),$

$(4, 4)\}; D = \{-4, -3, -2, 0, 2, 4\}; R = \{-3, 0, 2, 4\}$

31. $S = \{(1970, 29), (1980, 41), (1990, 79), (2000, 64)\}$

$D = \{1970, 1980, 1990, 2000\}; R = \{29, 41, 64, 79\}$

33. $a = b$

35. (a)

$D = \{-3, -2, 0, 1\};$

$R = \{-4, -3, 0, 2, 4\}$

(b) Xmin: -3, Xmax: 1, Ymin: -4, Ymax: 4

(c) and **(d)** See the graph.

37. (a)

$D = \{-30, 10, 20, 30\};$

$R = \{-50, 20, 40, 50\}$

(b) Xmin: -30, Xmax: 30, Ymin: -50, Ymax: 50

(c) and **(d)** See the graph.

39.

41.

43.

45.

47. $(-2, -6), (-1, -3),$ $(0, 0), (1, 3), (2, 6)$

49. $(-2, 4), (-1, 3),$ $(0, 2), (1, 1), (2, 0)$

51. $(-2, 1), \left(-1, \frac{1}{2}\right),$ $(0, 0), \left(1, -\frac{1}{2}\right), (2, -1)$

53. $(-2, 3), (-1, 0),$ $(0, -1), (1, 0), (2, 3)$

55. $(-2, -4), (-1, -1),$ $(0, 0), (1, -1), (2, -4)$

57. $(-2, 2), (-1, 1),$ $(0, 0), (1, 1), (2, 2)$

59. 10; 10
[−10, 10, 1] by [−10, 10, 1]

61. 10; 5
[0, 100, 10] by [−50, 50, 10]

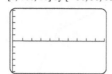

63. 16; 5
[1980, 1995, 1] by [12000, 16000, 1000]

65. $S = \{(-2, 1), (-1, 0), (1, -1), (2, 1)\}$

67. $S = \{(-4, -2), (-2, -2), (0, 2), (2, 1), (4, -1)\}$

69. [−6, 6, 1] by [−6, 6, 1]

71. [−30, 30, 5] by [−50, 50, 5]

73. [−200, 200, 50] by [−250, 250, 50]

75. (a) See the graph.
(b) Participation decreased and then increased.

77. (a) See the graph.
(b) The number of welfare beneficiaries decreased.

79. (a) See the graph.
(b) Asian-American population increased.

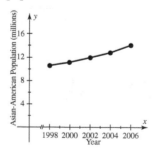

CHECKING BASIC CONCEPTS 1.5 (p. 63)

1. $D = \{-5, 1, 2\}$; $R = \{-1, 3, 4\}$

2. (1, 4) is in QI;
(−2, 3) is in QII;
(2, −2) is in QIV;
(0, −3) is on the y-axis.

3. (−2, −2), (−1, 1), (0, 2), (1, 1), (2, −2)

4. The number of people below the poverty level decreased, started to increase, then decreased again.

CHAPTER 1 REVIEW (pp. 66–69)

1. Natural numbers: 9; whole numbers: 9; integers: −2, 9; rational numbers: $-2, 9, \frac{2}{5}, 2.68$; irrational numbers: $\sqrt{11}, \pi$

2. Natural numbers: $\frac{6}{2} = 3$; whole numbers: $\frac{6}{2} = 3, \frac{0}{4} = 0$; integers: $\frac{6}{2} = 3, \frac{0}{4} = 0$; rational numbers: $\frac{6}{2} = 3, -\frac{2}{7}, 0.\overline{3} = \frac{1}{3}, \frac{0}{4} = 0$; irrational numbers: $\sqrt{6}$ **3.** Identity

4. Commutative **5.** Associative **6.** Distributive

7. Distributive **8.** Distributive **9.** a **10.** $\frac{1}{4}x$

11. $(8 \cdot 10)x$ or $80x$ **12.** $(5 - 3)z$ or $2z$ **13.** 95 **14.** 12

15. 9 **16.** 5.72 **17.** 40 **18.** 1 **19.** 150 **20.** 0

21.

22. 3.2 **23.** $\frac{2}{3}$ **24.** $\frac{5}{4}$ **25.** $2x - 3$

26. $-(a + b) = -a - b$ **27.** −4 **28.** 2 **29.** −4

30. $-\frac{3}{4}$ **31.** $-\frac{1}{2}$ **32.** $\frac{29}{110}$ **33.** 4 **34.** $\frac{10}{7}$ **35.** $9x$

36. $7z$ **37.** $-\frac{33}{910}$ **38.** 30; 5 **39.** Base: 4; exponent: −2

40. $3^{\pi} \approx 31.54$; $\pi^3 \approx 31.01$; not equal **41.** −16 **42.** 16

43. 1 **44.** $\frac{27}{8}$ **45.** $\frac{1}{64}$ **46.** 25 **47.** $\frac{9}{125}$ **48.** 8

49. $\frac{1}{4^2}$ or $\frac{1}{16}$ **50.** 10^2 or 100 **51.** x^5 **52.** 3^{11} **53.** $\frac{1}{2a^6}$

54. $\frac{5a^2}{b^3}$ **55.** 2^8 **56.** $\frac{1}{x^{15}}$ **57.** $\frac{16y^6}{x^4}$ **58.** 4^5a^5 or $1024a^5$

59. $\frac{125x^9}{27z^{12}}$ **60.** $\frac{z^2}{9x^8y^6}$ **61.** $\frac{9b^{14}}{16a^8}$ **62.** $3mn^5$ **63.** $\frac{8r^6}{t^6}$

64. $\frac{9r^4t^6}{16}$ **65.** 29 **66.** -3 **67.** 40 **68.** $\frac{11}{3}$ **69.** $\frac{5}{2}$

70. 11 **71.** 1.86×10^5 **72.** 3.4×10^{-4} **73.** 45,000

74. 0.00923 **75.** $y = 12x$ **76.** $A = 6\pi r^2$ **77.** $y = 36$

78. $d = 8$ **79.** $N = \frac{3}{2}$ **80.** $P = -10$ **81.** $A = 10$

82. $V = 27$ **83.** (iii) **84.** $a = \frac{3}{2}$

85.

x	-2	-1	0	1	2
y	-7	0	1	2	9

86.

87. $D = \{-1, 2, 3\}; R = \{-6, 1, 3, 7\}$

88. $S = \{(-8, 4), (-4, -4), (4, 0), (8, 4)\}$

$D = \{-8, -4, 4, 8\}, R = \{-4, 0, 4\}$

89. $(-2, 6), (-1, 3),$
$(0, 0), (1, -3), (2, -6)$

90. $(-2, -2), (-1, -1.5),$
$(0, -1)(1, -0.5), (2, 0)$

91. $(-2, 4), (-1, 1),$
$(0, 0), (1, 1), (2, 4)$

92. $(-2, 1), (-1, 2.5),$
$(0, 5), (1, 2.5), (2, 1)$

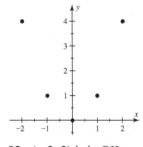

93. $(-2, 2)$ is in QII;
$(-1, -3)$ is in QIII;
$(2, -1)$ is in QIV;
$(0, 1)$ is on the y-axis.

94. $(10, 20)$ is in QI;
$(-15, -5)$ is in QIII;
$(20, -10)$ is in QIV;
$(-5, 0)$ is on the x-axis.

95. 9; 2

[−9, 9, 1] by [−6, 6, 3]

96. 4; 3

[−20, 20, 5] by [−12, 12, 4]

97.
$D = \{-1, 0, 2, 3, 4\};$
$R = \{-1, 0, 2, 3, 4\}$

98.
$D = \{-20, -10, 45, 50\};$
$R = \{-30, -25, 10, 20\}$

99. (a) $163,200 **(b)** $163,200

100. (a) $2525 **(b)** $816.08

101. (a) 5.8×10^8 miles **(b)** 66,700 miles per hour

102. $d = 40t$ **103.** 221 bpm; 74 bpm

104. The threshold has increased.

105. $A = (4ab)^2 = 16a^2b^2$ **106.** $V = (5z)^3 = 125z^3$

CHAPTER 1 TEST (pp. 69–70)

1. Natural numbers: $\sqrt{9}$; whole numbers: $\sqrt{9}$; integers: $-5, \sqrt{9}$; rational numbers: $-5, \frac{2}{3}, \sqrt{9}, -1.83$; irrational numbers: $-\frac{1}{\sqrt{5}}, \pi$ **2. (a)** Identity **(b)** Associative **(c)** Commutative **(d)** Distributive **3. (a)** a **(b)** x **(c)** $8x$ **(d)** a^2 **4.** 31.2

5.

6. (a) $\frac{3}{2}$ **(b)** 20 **(c)** $\frac{3}{4}$ **(d)** 0 **7. (a)** $-\frac{4}{5}$ **(b)** $\frac{b+1}{2}$

8. (a) $-\frac{5}{18}$ **(b)** $-\frac{20}{3}$ **(c)** -5 **(d)** 2

9. (a) $\frac{1}{25}$ **(b)** 1 **(c)** $\frac{16}{625}$ **(d)** $\frac{4}{9}$ **(e)** 125 **(f)** $\frac{1}{4}$

10. (a) x^2y^3 **(b)** $\frac{8y^{15}}{3x^3}$ **(c)** $\frac{8y^3}{z^6}$ **(d)** $\frac{4}{9x^6y^4}$

11. 0.00052 **12.** 3.4×10^6 **13.** $H = \frac{x}{60}$ **14.** 5; -1

15. $D = \{-3, -1, 2\}; R = \{-4, 2, 3\}$

16. $(2, 1)$ is in QI; $(-2, 3)$ is in QII; $(-1, -2)$ is in QIII; $(1, -1)$ is in QIV; $(0, 2)$ is on the y-axis.

17. $S = \{(-30, 20), (-20, 20),(-10, 10), (10, 30),$ $(20, 10), (30, -20)\}$; $D = \{-30, -20, -10, 10, 20, 30\}$; $R = \{-20, 10, 20, 30\}$

18. $y = 1.25x$

19. Window sizes may vary.
$[-20, 20, 5]$ by $[-5, 40, 5]$

20. $-15°C$ **21.** 4.6631×10^8 gallons

22. $\sqrt{\frac{25}{\pi}} \approx 2.82$ feet   **23.** $M = 61t$

41.

43.

45.

47.

49.

51. $3; -1$ **53.** $0; 2$ **55.** $-4; -3$ **57.** $5.5; 3.7$
59. 26.9; in 1990 average fuel efficiency was 26.9 mpg.
61. Numerical:

x	-3	-2	-1	0	1	2	3
$y = f(x)$	2	3	4	5	6	7	8

Graphical:

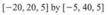

Symbolic: $y = x + 5$

63. Numerical:

x	-3	-2	-1	0	1	2	3
$y = f(x)$	-17	-12	-7	-2	3	8	13

CHAPTER 2: LINEAR FUNCTIONS AND MODELS

SECTION 2.1 (pp. 86–91)

1. function   **2.** y equals f of x **3.** symbolic   **4.** numerical
5. domain   **6.** range   **7.** one   **8.** To identify graphs
of functions   **9.** Verbal, numerical, symbolic, and graphical
or diagrammatic   **10.** $(3, 4)$; 3; 6   **11.** (a, b) **12.** d
13. 1   **14.** equal   **15.** Yes   **17.** No   **19.** $-6; -2$
21. $0; \frac{3}{2}$ **23.** $25; \frac{9}{4}$ **25.** 3; 3   **27.** $13; -22$ **29.** $-\frac{1}{2}; \frac{2}{5}$
31. (a) $I(x) = 36x$ (b) $I(10) = 360$
33. (a) $A(r) = \pi r^2$ (b) $A(10) = 100\pi \approx 314.2$
35. (a) $A(x) = 43,560x$ (b) $A(10) = 435,600$
37. $f = \{(1, 3), (2, -4), (3, 0)\};$
$D = \{1, 2, 3\}; R = \{-4, 0, 3\}$
39. $f = \{(a, b), (c, d), (e, a), (d, b)\};$
$D = \{a, c, d, e\}; R = \{a, b, d\}$

Graphical:

Symbolic: $y = 5x - 2$

65. Numerical   Graphical

$[-10, 10, 1]$ by $[-10, 10, 1]$

67. Numerical   Graphical (Dot Mode)

$[-10, 10, 1]$ by $[-10, 10, 1]$

69. Subtract $\frac{1}{2}$ from the input x to obtain the output y.
71. Divide the input x by 3 to obtain the output y.
73. Subtract 1 from the input x and then take the square root to obtain the output y.
75. $f(x) = 0.50x$

Miles	10	20	30	40	50	60	70
Cost	$5	$10	$15	$20	$25	$30	$35

77. 178.5; in 1995 the average price was $178,500.
79. D: $-2 \le x \le 2$; R: $0 \le y \le 2$
81. D: $-2 \le x \le 4$; R: $-2 \le y \le 2$
83. D: All real numbers; R: $y \ge -1$
85. D: $-3 \le x \le 3$; R: $-3 \le y \le 2$
87. $D = \{1, 2, 3, 4\}$; $R = \{5, 6, 7\}$ **89.** All real numbers
91. All real numbers   **93.** $x \ne 5$ **95.** All real numbers
97. $x \ge 1$ **99.** All real numbers   **101.** $x \ne 0$
103. **(a)** 60.3   **(b)** $D = \{1910, 1930, 1950, 1970, 1990, 2000\}$; $R = \{35.5, 36.9, 56.2, 60.3, 80.5, 84.4\}$ **(c)** Decreased

105. No   **107.** Yes   **109.** **(a)** 0.2   **(b)** Yes. Each month has one average amount of precipitation.   **(c)** 2, 3, 7, 11
111. Yes. D: All real numbers; R: All real numbers   **113.** No
115. Yes. D: $-4 \le x \le 4$; R: $0 \le y \le 4$ **117.** Yes. D: All real numbers; R: $y = 3$ **119.** No   **121.** Yes   **123.** No
125. The person walks away from home, then turns around and walks back a little slower.

SECTION 2.2 (pp. 100–104)

1. $ax + b$ **2.** b **3.** line   **4.** horizontal   **5.** 7   **6.** 0
7. Carpet costs $2 per square foot. Ten square feet of carpet costs $20.   **8.** The rate at which water is leaving the tank is 4 gallons per minute. After 5 minutes the tank contains 80 gallons of water.   **9.** Yes; $a = \frac{1}{2}, b = -6$ **11.** No
13. Yes; $a = 0, b = -9$ **15.** Yes; $a = -9, b = 0$
17. Yes   **19.** No   **21.** Yes; $f(x) = 3x - 6$
23. Yes; $f(x) = -\frac{3}{2}x + 3$ **25.** No
27. Yes; $f(x) = 2x - 2$ **29.** -16; 20   **31.** $\frac{17}{3}$; 2
33. -22; -22 **35.** -2; 0   **37.** -1; -4 **39.** 1; 1
41. $f(x) = 6x$; 18   **43.** $f(x) = \frac{x}{6} - \frac{1}{2}$; 0   **45.** d.   **47.** b.
49.   **51.**

53.   **55.**

57.

59. $f(x) = \frac{1}{16}x$ **61.** $f(t) = 65t$ **63.** $f(x) = 24$ **65.** a

67. (a) f multiplies the input x by -2 and then adds 1 to obtain the output y.
(b)

x	-2	0	2
$y = f(x)$	5	1	-3

(c)

69. (a) f multiplies the input x by $\frac{1}{2}$ and then subtracts 1 to obtain the output y.
(b)

x	-2	0	2
$y = f(x)$	-2	-1	0

(c)

71. (a)

(b) $[-6, 6, 1]$ by $[-4, 4, 1]$

73. (a)

(b) $[-6, 6, 1]$ by $[-4, 4, 1]$

75. b.   **77.** c.
79. (a) Symbolic: $f(x) = 70$
Graphical:

(b)

Hours	0	4	8	12	16	20	24
Temp. (°F)	70	70	70	70	70	70	70

(c) Constant
81. $D(t) = 60t + 50$ **83. (a)** $f(x) = 2.7x$; 162
(b) $g(x) = 4.3x$; 258
85. (a) $[1, 7, 1]$ by $[0, 300, 100]$

(b) Malware increased.   **(c)** 184; in March there were 184 malware viruses.   **(d)** The number of malware viruses increased, on average, at a rate of 16 per month.
87. (a) $V(T) = 0.5T + 137$ **(b)** 162 cm³
89. $f(x) = 40x$; about 2.92 pounds
91. (a) 180 minutes   **(b)** Decreased by 4 minutes
(c) $f(x) = -4x + 180$ **(d)** 164 minutes

CHECKING BASIC CONCEPTS 2.1 & 2.2 (pp. 104–105)

1. Symbolic: $f(x) = x^2 - 1$
Graphical:

2. (a) D: $-3 \leq x \leq 3$; R: $-4 \leq y \leq 4$ **(b)** 0; 4
(c) No. The graph is not a line.   **3. (a)** Yes   **(b)** No
(c) Yes   **(d)** Yes
4. $f(-2) = 10$

5. $f(x) = \frac{1}{2}x - 1$ **6. (a)** 32.98; in 1990 the median age was about 33 years.   **(b)** 0.264: the median age is increasing by 0.264 years each year. 27.7: in 1970 the median age was 27.7 years.

SECTION 2.3 (pp. 113–118)

1. y; x **2.** 0   **3.** rises   **4.** horizontal   **5.** vertical
6. slope–intercept   **7.** 2   **9.** $-\frac{2}{3}$ **11.** 0   **13.** 2
15. $-\frac{2}{3}$ **17.** 0   **19.** Undefined   **21.** -10 **23.** $\frac{3}{5}$
25. $-0.\overline{21}$ **27.** $\frac{3b}{a}$ **29.** -1

31. (a) $-\frac{3}{4}$
(b)

33. (a) $\frac{2}{3}$
(b)

47. (a) $\frac{1}{3}$; 0
(b)

49. (a) 0; 2
(b)

(c) The graph falls 3 units for every 4-unit increase in x

(c) The graph rises 2 units for every 3-unit increase in x

51. (a) -1; 3
(b)

35.

37.

39.

41.

53. $y = -x + 4$ **55.** $y = 2$ **57.** $y = x - 2$
59. $y = 3x - 5$ **61.** $y = \frac{3}{2}x - \frac{3}{2}$ **63.** 2; -2
65. -7; 4   **67. (a)** 3   **(b)** $f(x) = 2x - 1$
69. (a) 5   **(b)** $f(x) = \frac{3}{2}x + 5$ **71.** c.   **73.** b.
75. (a) $m_1 = 50, m_2 = 0, m_3 = 150$ **(b)** m_1: Water is being added at the rate of 50 gallons per hour. m_2: The pump is neither adding nor removing water. m_3: Water is being added at the rate of 150 gallons per hour.   **(c)** The pool initially contained 100 gallons of water. Water was added at the rate of 50 gallons per hour for the first 4 hours. Then the pump was turned off for 2 hours. Finally, water was added at the rate of 150 gallons per hour for 2 hours. The pool contains 600 gallons after 8 hours.
77. (a) $m_1 = 100, m_2 = 25, m_3 = -100$ **(b)** m_1: Water is being added at the rate of 100 gallons per hour. m_2: Water is being added at the rate of 25 gallons per hour. m_3: Water is being removed at the rate of 100 gallons per hour.
(c) The pool initially contained 100 gallons of water. Water was added at the rate of 100 gallons per hour for the first 2 hours. Then water was added at the rate of 25 gallons per hour for 4 hours. Finally, water was removed at the rate of 100 gallons per hour for 2 hours. The pool contains 200 gallons after 8 hours.
79. (a) $m_1 = 50, m_2 = 0, m_3 = -20, m_4 = 0$ **(b)** m_1: The car is moving away from home at the rate of 50 miles per hour. m_2: The car is not moving. m_3: The car is moving toward home at the rate of 20 miles per hour. m_4: The car is not moving.   **(c)** The car starts at home and moves away from home at 50 miles per hour for 1 hour. Then the car does not move for 1 hour. The car then moves toward home at the

43. (a) 1; 2
(b)

45. (a) -3; 2
(b)

rate of 20 miles per hour for 2 hours. Finally, the car stops and does not move for 1 hour. The car is 10 miles from home at the end of the trip.

81.

83.

85. (a) 62 thousand
(b) Increasing

(c) 4   **(d)** The number of children born to older mothers increased by about 4000 each year.   **87. (a)** 8347
(b) -358.4; the number of federally insured banks decreased on average by 358.4 per year.   **(c)** 13,723; initially, there were 13,723 federally insured banks in 1987.
89. $m = 10$; the carpet costs \$10 per square yard.
91. 1500 gallons per hour   **93. (a)** $a = \frac{83}{170}, b = 3.8$
(b) 10.1%; this estimate is 0.4% too high.
95. (a) $a \approx 1533.3; b = 37,000$ **(b)** \$52,333

SECTION 2.4 (pp. 130–135)

1. 1   **2.** 1.   **3.** $y = mx + b$
4. $y = m(x - x_1) + y_1$ or $y - y_1 = m(x - x_1)$
5. $y = b$ **6.** $x = h$ **7.** $m_1 = m_2$ **8.** -1
9. $y = -\frac{3}{4}x - 3$ (answers may vary)   **10.** $y = \frac{4}{3}x + 2$
(answers may vary)   **11.** $x = 1$ (answers may vary)
12. $y = -5$ (answers may vary)   **13.** Yes   **15.** No
17. d.   **19.** a.   **21.** f.   **23.** $y = -\frac{3}{4}x - \frac{1}{4}$
25. $y = \frac{1}{3}x + \frac{8}{3}$ **27.** $y = -2(x - 2) - 3$
29. $y = 1.3(x - 1990) + 25$
31. $y = \frac{2}{3}(x - 1) + 3$ or $y = \frac{2}{3}(x + 5) - 1$
33. $y = 2(x - 1980) + 5$ or $y = 2(x - 2000) + 45$
35. $y = -\frac{2}{3}(x - 6) + 0$ or $y = -\frac{2}{3}(x - 0) + 4$

37. $y = 2x - 4$ **39.** $y = \frac{1}{2}x + 3$ **41.** $y = 22x - 43$
43. $y = -3x - 2$ **45.** $y = -\frac{3}{4}x - 2$
47. $y = -\frac{1}{3}x - 5$ **49.** $y = -x + 1$ **51.** $y = \frac{1}{3}x - \frac{2}{3}$
53. $y = -3x + 3$ **55.** $y = 4x - 1$ **57.** $y = -\frac{5}{3}x - 3$
59. $y = 3x + 14$ **61.** $y = \frac{9}{10}x - \frac{31}{20}$
63. $y = -\frac{1}{c}x + b$
65. (a) $y = -2x + 2$ **67. (a)** $y = \frac{1}{2}x + \frac{5}{2}$
(b)   **(b)**

69. (a) $y = 3x - 2$

(b)

71. (a) $y_1 = 2x; y_2 = -\frac{1}{2}x$ **(b)** $m_1 m_2 = 2\left(-\frac{1}{2}\right) = -1$
73. (a) $y_1 = -\frac{3}{2}x - 1; y_2 = \frac{2}{3}x - 1$
(b) $m_1 m_2 = -\frac{3}{2} \cdot \frac{2}{3} = -1$ **75.** $x = -1$ **77.** $y = -\frac{5}{6}$
79. $x = 4$ **81.** $x = -\frac{2}{3}$ **83.** Yes; $y = 4x - 8$ **85.** No
87. (a) Away   **(b)** After 1 hour the person is 35 miles from home. After 3 hours the person is 95 miles from home.
(c) $y = 30(x - 1) + 35$; the person is traveling at 30 mph.
89. (a) Two acres have 100 people and 4 acres have 200 people.   **(b)** A zero-acre parcel has no people.
(c) $y = 50x$ **(d)** The land has 50 people per acre, on average.   **(e)** $P(x) = 50x$
91. (a) $y = 3000x - 5,984,000$ **(b)** The cost is increasing by \$3000 per year.   **(c)** \$31,000
93. $f(x) = 0.6x - 1146$; 58.8 lb
95. $f(x) = 0.29x - 503$; 68.3 yr   **97.** $y = 4x - 3$
99. $y = -3.5x + 11.5$ **101.** $y = 0.1x - 198.4$
103. $y = 0.09x - 173.8$ **105. (a)** $a = 0.30, b = 189.20$
(b) The fixed cost of owning the car for one month
107. (a) $R(c) = 4c - 14.6$ **(b)** About 10

109. (a)

(b) $m = 2.6, x_1 = 1970, y_1 = 203$ (answers may vary)
(c) 307 million (answers may vary)

CHECKING BASIC CONCEPTS 2.3 & 2.4
(pp. 135–136)

1. (a) $m = -3; (5, 7)$ (answers may vary)   **(b)** $m = 0$;
$(1, 10)$ (answers may vary)   **(c)** m is undefined; $(-5, 0)$
(answers may vary)   **(d)** $m = 5; (0, 3)$ (answers may vary)
2. (a) 2   **(b)** $y = 2(x - 2) - 4$ or
$y = 2(x - 5) + 2; y = 2x - 8$ **(c)** x-int: 4; y-int: -8
3. $x = -2; y = 5$ **4.** $y = 2x - 8; y = -\frac{1}{2}x - 3$
5. (a) Toward home   **(b)** -50; the car is moving toward
home at 50 mph.   **(c)** x-int: 5, after 5 hours the driver is
home; y-int: 250, the driver is initially 250 miles from home.
(d) $a = -50, b = 250$ **(e)** $D: 0 \le x \le 5$;
$R: 0 \le y \le 250$

CHAPTER 2 REVIEW (pp. 139–143)

1. $-7; 0$ **2.** $-22; 2$ **3.** $-2; 1$ **4.** $5; 5$

5. (a) $P(q) = 2q$ **(b)** $P(5) = 10$; there are 10 pints in
5 quarts.   **6. (a)** $f(x) = 4x - 3$ **(b)** $f(5) = 17$; three
less than four times 5 is 17.   **7.** $(3, -2)$ **8.** $4; -6$
9.

10.

11.

12.

13. $1; 4$ **14.** $1; -2$ **15.** $7; -1$
16. Numerical:

x	-3	-2	-1	0	1	2	3
$y = f(x)$	-11	-8	-5	-2	1	4	7

Symbolic: $f(x) = 3x - 2$
Graphical:

17. D: All real numbers; $R: y \le 4$ **18.** $D: -4 \le x \le 4$;
$R: -4 \le y \le 0$ **19.** Yes   **20.** No
21. $D = \{-3, -1, 2, 4\}; R = \{-1, 3, 4\}$; yes
22. $D = \{-1, 0, 1, 2\}; R = \{-2, 2, 3, 4, 5\}$; no
23. All real numbers   **24.** $x \ge 0$ **25.** $x \ne 0$
26. All real numbers   **27.** $x \le 5$ **28.** $x \ne 2$
29. All real numbers   **30.** All real numbers
31. No   **32.** Yes   **33.** Yes; $a = -4, b = 5$
34. Yes; $a = -1, b = 7$ **35.** No   **36.** Yes; $a = 0, b = 6$
37. Yes; $f(x) = \frac{3}{2}x - 3$ **38.** No   **39.** 1
40. $f(-2) = -3; f(1) = 0$
41.   **42.**

43.   **44.**

45. $H(x) = 24x; H(2) = 48$; there are 48 hours in 2 days.

46. (a)

(b) Domain: $x \geq 2$

$[-10, 10, 1]$ by $[-10, 10, 1]$

47. -2 **48.** 0 **49.** $\frac{1}{3}$ **50.** Undefined   **51.** $\frac{3}{2}$

52. $-\frac{3}{4}$ **53.** 0 **54.** Undefined

55.

56. $-\frac{2}{3}; 0$

57. $y = -3x + 1$ **58.** $y = 2x + 2$ **59.** $-1; 1$
60. (a) $m_1 = 250, m_2 = 500, m_3 = 0, m_4 = -750$
(b) m_1: Water is being added to the pool at a rate of
250 gallons per hour. m_2: Water is being added to the pool
at a rate of 500 gallons per hour. m_3: No water is being
added or removed. m_4: Water is being removed from the
pool at a rate of 750 gallons per hour.   **(c)** Initially the
pool contains 500 gallons of water. For the first 2 hours
water is added to the pool at a rate of 250 gallons per hour
until there are 1000 gallons in the pool. Then water is added
at a rate of 500 gallons per hour for 1 hour until there are
1500 gallons in the pool. For the next hour, no water is added
or removed. Finally, water is removed from the pool at a rate
of 750 gallons per hour for 1 hour until it contains 750 gallons.

61.

62. (a) $\frac{1}{2}; -2$
(b)

63. Yes   **64.** $-2; 2; 4$ **65.** $y = -3x + 7$
66. $y = -3(x + 2) + 3; y = -3x - 3$ **67.** $y = \frac{3}{2}x - 3$
68. $y = -2x + 2$ **69.** $y = 4x + \frac{13}{5}$ **70.** $y = -2x - 1$
71. $y = -x + 2$ **72.** $y = 2x - 3$ **73.** No   **74.** Yes
75. $x = -4$ **76.** $y = -\frac{7}{13}$ **77.** $y = 1$ **78.** $y = -8$

79. No   **80.** Yes; $y = 2x + 5$
81. (a) $m_1 = 1.3, m_2 = 2.35, m_3 = 2.4, m_4 = 2.7$
(b) m_1: From 1920 to 1940 the population increased on
average by 1.3 million per year. The other slopes may be
interpreted similarly.
82. For the first 2 minutes the inlet pipe is open. For the
next 3 minutes both pipes are open. For the next 2 minutes
only the outlet pipe is open. Finally, for the last 3 minutes
both pipes are closed.
83. (a) About 25.1
(b) Decreased
$[1885, 1965, 10]$ by $[22, 26, 1]$

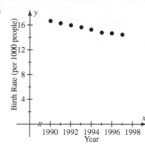

(c) -0.0492; the median age decreased by about 0.0492
year per year.
84. (a) 2.4 million   **(b)** The number of marriages each
year did not change.   **85. (a)** $f(x) = 8x$ **(b)** 8
(c) The total fat increases at the rate of 8 grams per cup.
86. (a)

(b) $f(x) = -0.31x + 633.6$ **(c)** About 13.6 per 1000
people (answers may vary)
87. (a) 113; in 1995 there were 113 unhealthy days.
(b) $D = \{1995, 1997, 1999, 2000, 2003\}$
$R = \{56, 60, 87, 88, 113\}$
(c) It decreased and then increased.
88. (a) Linear

(b) $f(x) = \frac{9}{5}x + 32$; a 1°C change equals $\frac{9}{5}$°F change.
(c) 68°F

89.

90. (a) $f(x) = 25,000(x - 2000) + 875,000$
(b) 1,050,000; total (cumulative) number of U.S. AIDS cases reported in 2007   **91.** b.   **92.** e.   **93.** a.   **94.** d.
95. f.   **96.** c.

CHAPTER 2 TEST (pp. 144–145)

1. 46, (4, 46)   **2.** $C(x) = 4x$; $C(5) = 20$, 5 pounds of candy costs $20.

3. (a)

(b)

(c)

(d)

4. 0, -3; D: $-3 \le x \le 3$, R: $-3 \le y \le 0$
5. Symbolic: $f(x) = x^2 - 5$
Numerical:

x	-3	-2	-1	0	1	2	3
$y = f(x)$	4	-1	-4	-5	-4	-1	4

Graphical:

6. No, it fails the vertical line test.
7. (a) $D = \{-2, -1, 0, 5\}$ **(b)** All real numbers
(c) $x \ge -4$ **(d)** All real numbers   **(e)** $x \ne 5$
8. It is.; $f(x) = -8x + 6$ **9.** -1 **10.** $-\frac{1}{2}$
11. (a) $y = -2x - 4$ **(b)** $y = \frac{1}{2}x + \frac{9}{2}$
(c) $y = -\frac{7}{12}x - \frac{17}{12}$ **12.** -2; 2; 4   **13.** $y = -3x + 3$
14. $y = \frac{2}{3}x - 2$; $y = -\frac{3}{2}x$ **15.** $x = \frac{2}{3}$; $y = -\frac{1}{7}$
16. (a) $m_1 = 0.4$, $m_2 = 0$, $m_3 = -0.4$ **(b)** From 1970 to 1980, beneficiaries increased by 0.4 million per year. From 1980 to 1990, there was no change. From 1990 to 2000, beneficiaries decreased by 0.4 million per year; answers may vary slightly.

17.

18. (a)

(b) $m = 0.96$, $x_1 = 1990$, $y_1 = 24.8$ (answers may vary)
(c) About 36.3 million

CHAPTERS 1 AND 2 CUMULATIVE REVIEW (pp. 147–148)

1. Natural number: $\sqrt[3]{8}$; whole number: $\sqrt[3]{8}$; integer: -3, $\sqrt[3]{8}$; rational number: $-3, \frac{3}{4}, -5.8, \sqrt[3]{8}$; irrational number: $\sqrt{7}$
2. Natural number: $\frac{50}{10}$; whole number: $0, \frac{50}{10}$; integer: $0, -5, -\sqrt{9}, \frac{50}{10}$; rational number: $0, -5, \frac{1}{2}, -\sqrt{9}, \frac{50}{10}$; irrational number: $\sqrt{8}$
3. Distributive property   **4.** Commutative property
5. -2 **6.** $(x + 1)(x + 5)$ **7.** $-a + b$ **8.** $\frac{c}{a + b}$
9. $\frac{169}{126}$ **10. (a)** $\frac{81}{64}$ **(b)** $\frac{81x^5}{y^4}$ **(c)** $\frac{b^{12}}{a^8}$ **11.** 9.54×10^3
12. 34   **13.** $B = 18$
14. (a) $\{-3, 0, 2\}$ **(b)** $x \ne -6$ **(c)** $x \ge -4$

15.

16.

17.

18.

19.

20.

21. (a) Yes   **(b)** Both include all real numbers.
(c) $f(-1) = 1.5; f(0) = 1$ **(d)** x-intercept: 2;
y-intercept: 1   **(e)** $-\frac{1}{2}$ **(f)** $f(x) = -\frac{1}{2}x + 1$
22. $y = -\frac{3}{2}x - 1$ **23.** $y = -\frac{1}{3}x + \frac{5}{3}$ **24.** $x = -2$
25. $m = -3$; x-int: 1; y-int: 3   **26.** $y = -\frac{3}{2}x + \frac{3}{2}$
27. Commutative property for addition   **28.** 1600 cubic
inches   **29. (a)** 7.5; average of 1992 and 1998 rates. 5.85;
average of 1999 and 2001 rates   **(b)** 5.85 (answers may
vary); answers may vary.   **30.** The person earns $9 per hour.

31.

32. (a) Median age is increasing.

[1820, 1995, 20] by [0, 40, 10]

(b)

Year (x)	1820	1840	1860	1880	1900	1920	1940
Median Age	16.7	18.5	20.3	22.1	23.9	25.7	27.5

(c) Each year the median age increased by 0.09 year, on
average.
33. (a) $f(x) = 10x$ **34. (a)** $\frac{24}{25} = 0.96$ pint
(b)   **(b)**

(c) 10   **(c)** $\frac{4}{25} = 0.16$
(d) The total amount of fat   **(d)** 0.16 pint of oil should
increases at a rate of 10 g of   be added per gallon
fat per slice of pizza.   of gasoline.
35. (a) 87.8 million tons
(b) [1960, 1995, 5] by [60, 220, 20]

(c) 3.4; solid waste increased by about 3.4 million tons per year.
36. (a) $m_1 = -50, m_2 = 0, m_3 = -50$
(b) m_1: The driver is traveling toward home at a rate of
50 miles per hour. m_2: The car is not moving. m_3: The driver
is traveling toward home at a rate of 50 miles per hour.
(c) The car started 300 miles from home and moved toward
home at 50 mph for 2 hours to a location 200 miles from home.
The car was then parked for 1 hour. Finally, the car moved toward
home at 50 mph for 4 hours, at which point it was home.

CHAPTER 3: LINEAR EQUATIONS AND
INEQUALITIES

SECTION 3.1 (pp. 160–163)

1. $ax + b = 0, a \neq 0$ **2.** One   **3.** Yes   **4.** Yes   **5.** 4
6. -2 **7.** An equals sign ($=$)   **8.** Numerical, graphical,
symbolic   **9.** 3   **10.** $ax + by = c$, a and b not both 0
11. $a + c = b + c$ **12.** $ac = bc$, for $c \neq 0$ **13.** No

15. Yes **17.** Yes **19.** 14 **21.** -2 **23.** $-\frac{3}{2}$ **25.** 3
27. -12 **29.** 5 **31.** 5 **33.** $\frac{16}{5}$ **35.** $\frac{6}{7}$ **37.** $-\frac{3}{2}$ **39.** $\frac{7}{4}$
41. $\frac{5}{2}$ **43.** $\frac{72}{53} \approx 1.36$ **45.** 11 **47.** 1983 **49.** $-\frac{1}{6}$ **51.** $\frac{1}{2}$
53. 6 **55.** 2 **57.** 0.75 **59.** -12 **61.** $x = -\frac{b}{a}$
63. 2

x	1	2	3	4	5
$-4x + 8$	4	0	-4	-8	-12

65. -1

x	-2	-1	0	1	2
$4 - 2x$	8	6	4	2	0
$x + 7$	5	6	7	8	9

67. 10 **69.** 1 **71.** 1.5 **73.** -2 **75.** -1 **77.** -1
79. 0 **81.** -3 **83.** 2007 **85.** 2.89 **87.** 7 **89.** 3
91. Contradiction **93.** Identity **95.** Identity
97. Conditional **99.** $(-2, 5)$
101. (a) x-int: 4; y-int: 4   **103. (a)** x-int: 5; y-int: 2
(b)   **(b)**

(c) $y = -x + 4$ **(c)** $y = -\frac{2}{5}x + 2$
105. (a) x-int: $\frac{9}{2}$; y-int: -3 **107. (a)** x-int: -3; y-int: -2
(b)   **(b)**

(c) $y = \frac{2}{3}x - 3$ **(c)** $y = -\frac{2}{3}x - 2$
109. (a) $S(x) = \frac{63}{440}(x - 1960) + 10.3$
(b) About 16 pounds **(c)** 2028 **111. (a)** 1992
(b) 1992 **(c)** 1992 **113. (a)** $f(x) = 0.1x - 198.4$
(b) 2001 **(c)** 2004 **115.** About 1987

SECTION 3.2 (pp. 174–177)

1. $\frac{x}{2}$ **2.** $4x - 7$ **3.** $2W + 2L$ **4.** Read the problem
carefully. **5.** 0.431 **6.** 10 **7.** $y = -\frac{4}{3}x + 4$

9. $x = \frac{15}{8}y$ **11.** $b = \frac{S}{6a}$ **13.** $t = 14 - r$
15. $f(x) = 3x + 8$ **17.** $f(x) = \frac{2x}{\pi}$ **19.** $f(x) = \frac{8x}{3}$
21. (a) $x + 2 = 12$ **(b)** 10 **23. (a)** $\frac{x}{5} = x + 1$
(b) $-\frac{5}{4}$ **25. (a)** $\frac{x + 5}{2} = 7$ **(b)** 9 **27. (a)** $\frac{x}{2} = 17$
(b) 34 **29. (a)** $x + (x + 1) + (x + 2) = 30$ **(b)** 9
31. (a) $L = \frac{P}{2} - W$ **(b)** 24 feet **33.** $h = \frac{A}{2\pi r}$
35. $C = \frac{5}{9}(F - 32)$ **37.** $h = \frac{2A}{b}$ **39.** 44, 45, 46
41. 23, 25, 27 **43.** 8 feet **45.** About 16 in. for the square;
12.5 in. for each circle **47.** 68 mph; 74 mph **49.** 4.5 liters
51. $2200 at 6%; $2800 at 4% **53.** 38°, 66°, 76°
55. (a) 36,000 cubic feet per hour **(b)** 66 people
57. $2.91 **59.** 110,000 sq mi **61.** About 1.4 million
63. 1500 people **65.** About 1,260,000

CHECKING BASIC CONCEPTS 3.1 & 3.2 (p. 177)

1. 1 **2.** $\frac{6}{11}$ **3. (a)** -2 **(b)** -2 **(c)** -2 Yes
4. 0.3 hour at 10 miles per hour; 0.9 hour at 8 miles per hour
5. x-int: 4; y-int: -5 **6. (a)** Identity **(b)** Contradiction

SECTION 3.3 (pp. 185–190)

1. $3x + 2 < 5$ (answers may vary)
2. Yes; consider $x + 2 > 2$. **3.** Yes **4.** Yes
5. Yes; they have the same solution set.
6. No; $-4x < 8$ is equivalent to $x > -2$.
7. An equation has an equals sign, whereas an inequality
has an inequality symbol.
8. Numerical, graphical, symbolic **9.** Yes **11.** No
13. (a) $\{x \mid x = 2\}$ **(b)** $\{x \mid x < 2\}$ **(c)** $\{x \mid x > 2\}$
15. (a) $\{x \mid x = 3\}$ **(b)** $\{x \mid x > 3\}$ **(c)** $\{x \mid x < 3\}$
17. $\{x \mid x \le 2\}$ **19.** $\{x \mid x > 36\}$ **21.** $\{x \mid x \ge \frac{14}{9}\}$
23. $\{x \mid x > \frac{17}{3}\}$ **25.** $\{x \mid x < \frac{27}{14}\}$ **27.** $\{x \mid x \ge \frac{2}{13}\}$
29. $\{x \mid x < 2010\}$ **31.** $\{x \mid x < 5\}$ **33.** $\{x \mid x \ge -6\}$
35. $\{z \mid z \le -6\}$ **37.** $\{t \mid t \ge -\frac{7}{2}\}$ **39.** $\{x \mid x > -\frac{25}{3}\}$
41. $\{x \mid x > \frac{17}{9}\}$
43. $\{x \mid x \ge 3\}$

x	1	2	3	4	5
$-2x + 6$	4	2	0	-2	-4

45. $\{x \mid x > 3\}$ **47.** $\{x \mid x \ge 2\}$ **49. (a)** $\{x \mid x = -1\}$
(b) $\{x \mid x < -1\}$ **(c)** $\{x \mid x > -1\}$ **51. (a)** $\{x \mid x = \frac{1}{2}\}$
(b) $\{x \mid x > \frac{1}{2}\}$ **(c)** $\{x \mid x < \frac{1}{2}\}$ **53.** $\{x \mid x \ge 1\}$
55. $\{x \mid x > 2\}$ **57. (a)** Car 1; the slope of the line for
Car 1 is greater than the slope of the line for Car 2.
(b) 5 hours; 400 miles **(c)** $x < 5$ **59.** $\{x \mid x < 1\}$
61. $\{x \mid x \ge 0\}$ **63.** $\{x \mid x \ge -2\}$ **65.** $\{x \mid x < -4\}$
67. $\{x \mid x < -3\}$ **69.** $\{x \mid x \le 1991\}$ **71.** $\{x \mid x > 0.834\}$

73. $\{x \mid x < a\}$ **75.** $\{x \mid x < 2\}$ **77.** $\{x \mid x \le 3\}$
79. (a) $\{x \mid x = 12\}$ **(b)** $\{x \mid x > 12\}$
81. (a) $\{x \mid x \le -\frac{7}{3}\}$ **(b)** $\{x \mid x \ge -\frac{7}{3}\}$
83. (a) $\{x \mid x \le -9\}$ **(b)** $\{x \mid x \ge -9\}$
85. 1980 or before   **87. (a)** $200   **(b)** $5.00 each
(c) $P = 5x - 200$ **(d)** $x = 40$ CDs   **(e)** $x > 40$ CDs
89. $x < 10$ feet   **91. (a)** First car: 70 miles per hour;
second car: 60 miles per hour   **(b)** When $x = 3.5$ hours
(c) Elapsed times after 3.5 hours   **93.** Below about 3.16 miles
95. Between 132 and 174 lb   **97.** 1997 or after
99. (a) About 22 inches   **(b)** Less than 22 inches

SECTION 3.4 (pp. 197–200)

1. $x > 1$ and $x \le 7$ (answers may vary)
2. $x \le 3$ or $x > 5$ (answers may vary)   **3.** No   **4.** Yes
5. Yes   **6.** Numerically, graphically, symbolically
7. Yes, no **9.** No, yes   **11.** No, yes   **13.** [2, 10]
15. (5, 8]   **17.** $(-\infty, 4)$ **19.** $(-2, \infty)$ **21.** $[-2, 5)$
23. $(-8, 8]$ **25.** $(3, \infty)$ **27.** $(-\infty, -2] \cup [4, \infty)$
29. $(-\infty, 1) \cup [5, \infty)$ **31.** $(-3, 5]$ **33.** $(-\infty, -2)$
35. $(-\infty, 4)$ **37.** $(-\infty, 1) \cup (2, \infty)$
39. $\{x \mid -1 \le x \le 3\}$

41. $\{x \mid -2 < x < 2.5\}$

43. $\{x \mid x \le -1 \text{ or } x \ge 2\}$

45. All real numbers

47. $[-6, 7]$ **49.** $\left(\frac{13}{4}, \infty\right)$ **51.** $(-\infty, \infty)$
53. $\left(-\infty, -\frac{11}{5}\right) \cup (-1, \infty)$ **55.** No solutions
57. $[-6, 1)$ **59.** $\left[-\frac{1}{4}, \frac{11}{8}\right)$ **61.** $[-9, 3]$ **63.** $\left[-4, -\frac{1}{4}\right)$
65. $(-1, 1]$ **67.** $[-2, 1]$ **69.** $(0, 2)$ **71.** $(9, 21]$
73. $\left[\frac{12}{5}, \frac{22}{5}\right]$ **75.** $\left(-\frac{13}{3}, 1\right)$ **77.** $[0, 12]$ **79.** $[-1, 2]$
81. $(-1, 2)$ **83.** $[-3, 1]$ **85.** $(-\infty, -2) \cup (0, \infty)$
87. (a) Toward, because distance is decreasing
(b) 4 hours, 2 hours   **(c)** From 2 to 4 hours   **(d)** During
the first 2 hours   **89.** $[1, 4]$ **91.** $(-\infty, -2) \cup (0, \infty)$
93. $[2002, 2010]$ **95.** $[1, 3]$ **97.** $(-\infty, \infty)$
99. $(-\infty, 1) \cup [3, \infty)$ **101.** $(c - b, d - b]$
103. From 1995 to 2000   **105.** From 0.5 to 1.5 miles
107. From $5.\overline{6}$ to 9 feet   **109.** From 1.5 to 2.5 miles
111. $-67.\overline{7}°C$ to $36.\overline{6}°C$

CHECKING BASIC CONCEPTS 3.3 & 3.4 (p. 201)

1. $\left\{x \mid x > \frac{8}{7}\right\}$ **2. (a)** $\{x \mid x = 2\}$ **(b)** $\{x \mid x < 2\}$
(c) $\{x \mid x \ge 2\}$ **3. (a)** Yes   **(b)** No   **4. (a)** $[-3, 1]$
(b) $(-\infty, -1) \cup [3, \infty)$ **(c)** $\left[-\frac{8}{3}, \frac{8}{3}\right]$

SECTION 3.5 (pp. 209–212)

1. $|3x + 2| = 6$ (answers may vary)
2. $|2x - 1| \le 17$ (answers may vary)   **3.** Yes   **4.** Yes
5. Yes   **6.** No, it is equivalent to $-3 < x < 3$.   **7.** 2
8. 0   **9.** No, yes   **11.** No, yes   **13.** Yes, yes   **15.** 0, 4
17. $-7, 7$.   **19.** No solutions   **21.** $-\frac{9}{4}, \frac{9}{4}$ **23.** $-4, 4$
25. $-6, 5$ **27.** 1, 2   **29.** $-8, 12$ **31.** No solutions
33. $-15, 18$ **35.** $-1, \frac{1}{3}$ **37.** $-5, \frac{3}{5}$ **39.** -6
41. (a) $-4, 4$ **(b)** $\{x \mid -4 < x < 4\}$
(c) $\{x \mid x < -4 \text{ or } x > 4\}$ **43. (a)** $\frac{1}{2}, 2$
(b) $\{x \mid \frac{1}{2} \le x \le 2\}$ **(c)** $\{x \mid x \le \frac{1}{2} \text{ or } x \ge 2\}$
45. $[-3, 3]$ **47.** $(-\infty, -4) \cup (4, \infty)$ **49.** No solutions
51. $(-\infty, 0) \cup (0, \infty)$ **53.** $\left(-\infty, -\frac{7}{2}\right) \cup \left(\frac{7}{2}, \infty\right)$
55. $(-3, 5)$ **57.** $(-\infty, -9] \cup [-1, \infty)$ **59.** $\left[\frac{5}{6}, \frac{11}{6}\right]$
61. $[-10, 14]$ **63.** No solutions   **65.** $(-\infty, \infty)$
67. No solutions   **69.** $(-\infty, \infty)$ **71.** $(-\infty, -13] \cup [17, \infty)$
73. $[0.9, 1.1]$ **75.** $(-\infty, 9.5) \cup (10.5, \infty)$ **77. (a)** $-1, 3$
(b) $(-1, 3)$ **(c)** $(-\infty, -1) \cup (3, \infty)$ **79. (a)** $-1, 0$
(b) $[-1, 0]$ **(c)** $(-\infty, -1] \cup [0, \infty)$
81. $(-\infty, -1] \cup [1, \infty)$ **83.** $[-2, 4]$
85. $(-\infty, 1) \cup (3, \infty)$ **87.** $(2, 4.\overline{6})$ **89.** $(-\infty, \infty)$
91. $\{x \mid -3 \le x \le 3\}$ **93.** $\{x \mid x < 2 \text{ or } x > 3\}$
95. $|x| \le 4$ **97.** $|y| > 2$ **99.** $|2x + 1| \le 0.3$
101. $|\pi x| \ge 7$ **103.** two   **105. (a)** $\{T \mid 19 \le T \le 67\}$
(b) Monthly average temperatures vary from 19°F to 67°F.
107. (a) $\{T \mid -26 \le T \le 46\}$ **(b)** Monthly average
temperatures vary from $-26°F$ to 46°F.   **109. (a)** About
19,058 feet   **(b)** Africa and Europe   **(c)** South America,
North America, Africa, Europe, and Antarctica
111. $\{d \mid 2.498 \le d \le 2.502\}$; the diameter can vary from
2.498 to 2.502 inches.   **113.** $|d - 3.8| \le 0.03$
115. Values between 19 and 21, exclusively

CHECKING BASIC CONCEPTS 3.5 (p. 212)

1. $-\frac{28}{3}, 12$ **2. (a)** $-\frac{2}{3}, \frac{14}{3}$ **(b)** $\left(-\frac{2}{3}, \frac{14}{3}\right)$
(c) $\left(-\infty, -\frac{2}{3}\right) \cup \left(\frac{14}{3}, \infty\right)$ **3.** $(0, 6)$; $(-\infty, 0] \cup [6, \infty)$
4. (a) 1, 3   **(b)** $[1, 3]$ **(c)** $(-\infty, 1] \cup [3, \infty)$

CHAPTER 3 REVIEW (pp. 215–220)

1. 2

x	0	1	2	3	4
$3x - 6$	-6	-3	0	3	6

2. 1

x	-1	0	1	2	3
$5-2x$	7	5	3	1	-1

3. Yes **4.** 1 **5.** 2 **6.** 4 **7.** 14 **8.** $\frac{1}{2}$ **9.** $\frac{1}{7}$
10. $-\frac{1}{3}$ **11.** 10 **12.** $\frac{21}{8}$ **13.** 1972 **14.** $\frac{19}{5}$ **15.** 4
16. -9 **17.** Identity **18.** Contradiction
19. x-int: 5, y-int: -4; $y = \frac{4}{5}x - 4$
20. x-int: -3, y-int: -12; $y = -4x - 12$
21. $y = \frac{5}{4}x - 5$ **22.** $y = \frac{2}{3}x + 2$ **23.** $a = -3b$
24. $n = -\frac{2}{7}m$ **25.** $b = \frac{2A}{h} - a$ **26.** $h = \frac{3V}{\pi r^2}$
27. $f(x) = \frac{2}{3}x - \frac{8}{3}$ **28.** $f(x) = \frac{7}{27}x + \frac{1}{27}$
29. $f(x) = -\frac{3}{5}x + 2$ **30.** $f(x) = 3x$
31. $2x + 25 = 19; -3$ **32.** $2x - 5 = x + 1; 6$
33. $\{x \mid x > -1\}$ **34.** $\{x \mid x > 5\}$ **35.** $\{x \mid x \geq 2\}$
36. (a) $\frac{7}{4}$ (b) $\{x \mid x > \frac{7}{4}\}$ (c) $\{x \mid x < \frac{7}{4}\}$
37. $\{x \mid x \geq -1\}$ **38.** $\{x \mid x \leq -8\}$ **39.** $\{x \mid x > 1\}$
40. $\{x \mid x > \frac{4}{3}\}$ **41.** $\{t \mid t > \frac{16}{9}\}$ **42.** $\{x \mid x \geq 5\}$
43. $\{t \mid t \leq 2.1\}$ **44.** $\{z \mid z > -36.4\}$
45. $\{x \mid x \leq 1.840\}$ **46.** $\{x \mid x > 1.665\}$
47. $[-2, 2]$

48. $(-\infty, -3]$

49. $\left(-\infty, \frac{4}{5}\right] \cup (2, \infty)$

50. $(-\infty, \infty)$

51. $[-2, 1]$ **52.** (a) -4 (b) 2 (c) $[-4, 2]$
(d) $(-\infty, 2)$ **53.** (a) 2 (b) $(2, \infty)$ (c) $(-\infty, 2)$
54. (a) 4 (b) 2 (c) $(2, 4)$ **55.** $\left[-3, \frac{2}{3}\right]$ **56.** $(-6, 45]$
57. $\left(-\infty, \frac{7}{2}\right)$ **58.** $[1.8, \infty)$ **59.** $(-3, 4)$
60. $(-\infty, 4) \cup (10, \infty)$ **61.** $(-5, 5)$ **62.** $[8, 28]$
63. $(-9, 21)$ **64.** $[8, 28]$ **65.** $\left(-\frac{11}{5}, \frac{7}{5}\right)$ **66.** $[88, 138]$
67. No, no **68.** No, yes **69.** No, yes **70.** No, yes
71. (a) 0, 4 (b) $(0, 4)$ (c) $(-\infty, 0) \cup (4, \infty)$
72. (a) $-3, 1$ (b) $[-3, 1]$ (c) $(-\infty, -3] \cup [1, \infty)$
73. $-22, 22$ **74.** 1, 8 **75.** $-26, 42$ **76.** $-\frac{23}{3}, \frac{25}{3}$
77. 0, 2 **78.** $-3, \frac{9}{5}$ **79.** (a) $-8, 6$ (b) $[-8, 6]$
(c) $(-\infty, -8] \cup [6, \infty)$ **80.** (a) $-\frac{5}{2}, \frac{7}{2}$ (b) $\left[-\frac{5}{2}, \frac{7}{2}\right]$
(c) $\left(-\infty, -\frac{5}{2}\right] \cup \left[\frac{7}{2}, \infty\right)$ **81.** $(-\infty, -3) \cup (3, \infty)$

82. $(-4, 4)$ **83.** $[-3, 4]$ **84.** $\left(-\infty, -\frac{5}{2}\right] \cup [5, \infty)$
85. $[4.4, 4.6]$ **86.** $\left[\frac{3}{13}, \frac{7}{13}\right]$ **87.** $(-\infty, \infty)$ **88.** $\frac{3}{2}$
89. $(-\infty, -1.5] \cup [1.5, \infty)$ **90.** $[-2, 6]$
91. $|x| \leq 0.05$ **92.** $|5x - 1| > 4$ **93.** \$3500 at 5%;
\$4200 at 7% **94.** 0.6 hour at 8 miles per hour; 0.8 hour
at 10 miles per hour **95.** About \$769,000
96. (a) $f(x) = -45.84x + 92{,}136$ (approx.)
(b) About 1006 **97.** (a) 3 hours (b) 2 hours and 4 hours
(c) Between 2 and 4 hours, exclusively (d) 20 miles per hour
98. (a) \$2000 (b) More than \$2000 (c) Less than \$2000
99. (a) Car 1; its graph has the steeper slope. (b) 3 hours;
200 miles (c) Before 3 hours **100.** 1989, 1990, 1991,
1993, and 1995 **101.** (a) Median age is increasing at 0.09
year per year. (b) 1890 **102.** Approximately from 1985
to 1995 **103.** (a) About 31.8 inches (b) Lengths less than
31.8 inches **104.** (a) $T(x) = -19x + 60$
(b) Approximately from 1.05 to 2.11 miles **105.** 8.5 hours
106. 13 feet by 31 feet **107.** $-44.\overline{4}°C$ to $41.\overline{6}°C$
108. $|L - 160| \leq 1; 159 \leq L \leq 161$
109. (a) $|A - 3.9| \leq 1.7$ (b) $2.2 \leq A \leq 5.6$
110. Values between 32.2 and 37.8

CHAPTER 3 TEST (pp. 220–222)

1. Yes

2.
x	-2	-1	0	1	2
$2 - 3x$	8	5	2	-1	-4

; $\{x \mid x \geq 1\}$

3. -3 **4.** (a) 2 (b) $(-\infty, 2]$ (c) $[2, \infty)$ **5.** 1
6. (a) $\frac{7}{9}$ (b) $\frac{7}{13}$ (c) $\frac{10}{17}$ **7.** x-int: $-\frac{3}{2}$, y-int: 3; $y = 2x + 3$
8. $2 + 5x = x - 4; -\frac{3}{2}$ **9.** $f(x) = \frac{3}{2}x - 3$
10. $\left[-\frac{3}{5}, \infty\right)$ **11.** $(1.55, \infty)$
12.

13. $(-\infty, -2) \cup (1, \infty)$ **14.** (a) -5 (b) 5
(c) $[-5, 5]$ (d) $(-\infty, 5)$ **15.** $(-8, 0)$ **16.** $-12, 24$
17. (a) $[-5, 5]$ (b) $(-\infty, 0) \cup (0, \infty)$
(c) No solutions (d) $(-\infty, -2) \cup (2, \infty)$
(e) $(-\infty, \infty)$ (f) $(-2, 8)$ **18.** (a) $-\frac{2}{5}, \frac{4}{5}$ (b) $\left[-\frac{2}{5}, \frac{4}{5}\right]$
(c) $\left(-\infty, -\frac{2}{5}\right] \cup \left[\frac{4}{5}, \infty\right)$ **19.** (a) 64 calories
(b) More than 64 calories (c) Less than 64 calories
(d) Each gram of carbohydrates corresponds to 4 calories.
20. (a) $f(x) = 0.4x + 75$ (b) 35 minutes **21.** $g = \frac{2d}{t^2}$
22. \$3500 at 4%; \$1500 at 6% **23.** $41°, 57°, 82°$ **24.** \$108

CHAPTERS 1–3 CUMULATIVE REVIEW (pp. 223–225)

1. Natural: $\frac{8}{2}$; whole: 0, $\frac{8}{2}$; integer: $-7, 0, \frac{8}{2}$;
rational: $-7, -\frac{3}{5}, 0, \frac{8}{2}, 5.\overline{12}$; irrational: $\sqrt{5}$

2. Natural: $\sqrt{9}$; whole: $\frac{0}{9}$, $\sqrt{9}$; integer: $-\frac{6}{3}$, $\frac{0}{9}$, $\sqrt{9}$; rational: $-\frac{6}{3}$, $\frac{0}{9}$, $\sqrt{9}$, $4.\overline{6}$; irrational: π **3.** Distributive
4. Associative   **5.** 50   **6.** 686
7.

8. $5y + 4$ **9.** $\frac{3y^7}{x^5}$ **10.** $\frac{64b^9}{27a^6}$ **11.** 13
12. 5.9×10^{-5} **13.** 5   **14.** 30   **15.** (ii)
16. $D = \{-2, 0, 1, 3\}$; $R = \{0, 2, 4\}$
17. $(-2, 5), (-1, 3), (0, 1),$ **18.** $(-2, -2), \left(-1, \frac{3}{2}\right),$
$(1, -1), (2, -3)$ $(0, 2), \left(1, \frac{5}{2}\right), (2, 6)$

19.

20. $x \neq 0$ **21.** $2, -2$ **22.** $2, -4$
23. Yes; $a = -3, b = 11$ **24.** No   **25.** $f(x) = 4x + 3$
26.

27. $5; -4$ **28.** -2
29.

30. $y = -\frac{1}{2}x - 1$ **31.** $3; -1; 3$ **32.** $x = 5$
33. $y = 3x - 5$ **34.** $y = x + 3$ **35.** Yes   **36.** 1
37. $x = -\frac{2}{3}$ **38.** $\frac{1}{11}$ **39.** x-int: 2, y-int: -6; $y = 3x - 6$
40. x-int: -2, y-int: $\frac{5}{2}$; $y = \frac{5}{4}x + \frac{5}{2}$ **41.** $\{x \mid x > 0\}$
42. $(-\infty, -3]$ **43.** $(3, \infty)$ **44.** $(-\infty, 0]$
45. $(-1, 5]$

46. $\left(-\infty, -\frac{3}{2}\right) \cup [3, \infty)$

47. $[-2, 4]$ **48.** $[-16, 10]$
49. $(-\infty, -6) \cup \left(\frac{8}{3}, \infty\right)$ **50.** $[4, 7]$ **51.** (a) $-3, 1$
(b) $[-3, 1]$ **(c)** $(-\infty, -3] \cup [1, \infty)$ **52.** $-6, 18$
53. **(a)** $\$7004.25$ **(b)** $\$14,741.05$ **54.** $d = 65t$
55. **(a)** $f(x) = 10x$ **(b)** 10   **(c)** The soda contains 10 mg of sodium per ounce.
56.

57. **(a)** Away; the slope of the line is positive.   **(b)** 3 hours
(c) From 0 to 3 hours   **58.** From 1980 to 1991

CHAPTER 4: SYSTEMS OF LINEAR EQUATIONS

SECTION 4.1 (pp. 238–240)

1. No. Two straight lines cannot have exactly two points of intersection.   **2.** $3x + 2y = 5, 2x - y = 0$ (answers may vary)   **3.** Numerically and graphically   **4.** There is one solution.   **5.** There are no solutions.   **6.** There are infinitely many solutions because the two lines are identical.
7. $(1, -2)$ **9.** $\left(-1, \frac{13}{3}\right)$ **11.** $(1, 1)$ **13.** $(0, 1)$
15. $(3, -2)$ **17.** $(4, -1)$ **19.** $(3, 1)$ **21.** No solutions
23. $(1, 2)$; consistent; independent   **25.** $(2, 1)$; consistent; independent   **27.** $\{(x, y) \mid x + y = 3\}$; consistent; dependent
29. $(1, 3)$; consistent; independent   **31.** No solutions; inconsistent   **33.** $(4, 2)$; consistent; independent
35. No solutions; inconsistent   **37.** $\{(x, y) \mid -3x + 2y = 1\}$; consistent; dependent   **39.** $(2, -2)$; consistent; independent
41. $(1, 1)$ **43.** $(1, -4)$
45. **(a)** x-intercepts: 4, -2; y-intercepts: 4, 2   **(b)** $(1, 3)$
47. **(a)** x-intercepts: $-6, -4$; y-intercepts: 4, 8   **(b)** $(-3, 2)$
49. $(0, 0.3)$ **51.** $(1.5, 0.5)$ **53.** $(100, 200)$

55. No solutions   **57.** $(2, 3)$ **59.** $(1, 1)$ **61.** $(5, -2)$
63. $(-5, 10)$ **65.** $(0.5, 1.5)$ **67.** No solutions
69. (a) $x + y = 18, x - y = 6$ (b) $x = 12, y = 6$
71. (a) $x + y = 1, 6x + 8y = 7$ (b) $\frac{1}{2}$ hour at 6 miles
per hour; $\frac{1}{2}$ hour at 8 miles per hour
73. (a) $2x + 2y = 76, x - y = 4$ (b) 21 by 17 inches
75. (a) $x + 2y = 180, x - y = 60$ (b) $100°, 40°, 40°$
77. UCLA: 36 times; Kentucky: 44 times
79. McGwire: 70; Sosa: 66   **81.** $350 at 5%; $250 at 4%

SECTION 4.2 (pp. 251–255)

1. Substitution and elimination   **2.** No; all methods produce the same solution. However, graphical and numerical
answers are sometimes rounded.   **3.** Elimination yields a
contradiction.   **4.** Elimination yields an identity.
5. Solve the first equation for y.   **6.** Multiply the second
equation by -2.   **7.** $(1, 2)$ **9.** $(5, 3)$ **11.** $(2, 1)$
13. $(1, 3)$ **15.** $(1, 1)$ **17.** $(0, 2)$ **19.** $\left(\frac{1}{2}, 1\right)$ **21.** $\left(\frac{1}{2}, \frac{1}{4}\right)$
23. $(-3, -1)$ **25.** $\left(\frac{1}{2}, -\frac{1}{2}\right)$ **27.** $(4, 2)$ **29.** $(6, 6)$
31. $(4, -6)$ **33.** $(5, 2)$ **35.** For $x = y + 5$ the result is
$10 = 10$, which is an identity.   **37.** Inconsistent; no solutions
39. Dependent; $\{(x, y) \mid x + 3y = -2\}$ **41.** $(7, 2)$
43. $(2, 1)$ **45.** $(1, 0)$ **47.** $(3, 1)$ **49.** $(-1, -2)$
51. $\left(\frac{1}{2}, 3\right)$ **53.** $\left(\frac{6}{7}, -\frac{12}{7}\right)$ **55.** Inconsistent; no solutions
57. Dependent; $\{(x, y) \mid 2x + y = 2\}$ **59.** $\left(-\frac{5}{9}, -\frac{47}{9}\right)$
61. $(2, 1)$ **63.** $(-4, 5)$ **65.** $\left(\frac{1}{2}, -\frac{1}{2}\right)$
67. Dependent; $\{(r, t) \mid 2r - 3t = 7\}$
69. Inconsistent; no solutions   **71.** $(-2, -2)$
73. $(10, 20)$ **75.** $(8, 10)$ **77.** $(5, 4)$ **79.** $(5, 1)$
81. $(1, 2)$ **83.** $(2.5, -0.5)$ **85.** $(0, 4)$
87. The heavier athlete burned 174 fat calories or about 19.3
fat grams; the lighter athlete burned 116 fat calories or about
12.9 fat grams.   **89.** $\frac{16}{7}$ gallons   **91.** 27 premium rooms; 23
regular rooms   **93.** $50°$ and $130°$ **95.** 148 million females,
143 million males   **97.** Plane: 608 miles per hour; jet
stream: 32 miles per hour   **99.** Boat: 25 mph, current: 5 mph
101. $2100 at 8% and $1400 at 9%   **103.** Day: $110,
night: $80   **105.** Approximately 115.5 pounds on each rafter
107. $2x + 2y = 296, x - y = 44$; (a)–(c) Length = 96 feet,
width = 52 feet

CHECKING BASIC CONCEPTS 4.1 & 4.2 (p. 255)

1. $(3, 1)$; yes   **2.** $(2, 3)$ **3.** $\left(-\frac{7}{2}, 1\right)$; no; no
4. (a) $x + y = 90, x - y = 40$ (b) $(65, 25)$; the smaller
angle is $25°$ and the larger angle is $65°$.

SECTION 4.3 (pp. 263–266)

1. Two   **2.** Yes; many points may satisfy a system of
inequalities.   **3.** Yes; no   **4.** No; yes   **5.** Solid   **6.** dashed
7.

9.

11.

13.

15.

17.

19.

21.

23.

25.

27.

29.

31.

33.

35.

37.

39.

41.

43.

45.

47.

49. [−10, 10, 1] by [−10, 10, 1]

51. [−10, 10, 1] by [−10, 10, 1]

53. [−10, 10, 1] by [−10, 10, 1]

55. b.   **57.** a.   **59.** $y \geq 2$ **61.** $y \geq x; x \geq -2$

63.

65.

67. (a) About 105 to 134 beats per minute

(b) $y \leq -0.6x + 152, y \geq -0.5x + 120$

69. The person weighs less than recommended.

71. $25h - 7w \leq 800; 5h - w \geq 170$

73.

SECTION 4.4 (pp. 271–273)

1. linear programming   **2.** objective   **3.** feasible solutions
4. linear inequalities   **5.** vertex   **6.** objective
7.

9.

11.

13.

15.

17.

19.

21. $R = 31$ **23.** $R = 15$ **25.** $C = 5$ **27.** $C = 2$
29. $R = 750$ **31.** $R = 12$ **33.** $R = 31.5$
35. $R = 16$ **37.** $C = 0$ **39.** $C = 32$ **41.** $C = 60$
43. 20 pounds of candy, 80 pounds of coffee
45. 1 ounce Brand X, 2 ounces Brand Y   **47.** \$600

CHECKING BASIC CONCEPTS 4.3 & 4.4 (p. 273)

1. $y \le -2x + 3$
2.

3. $R = 12$

SECTION 4.5 (pp. 283–286)

1. No; three planes cannot intersect at exactly 2 points.
2. $x + y + z = 5, 2x - 3y + z = 7, x + 2y - 4z = 2$
(answers may vary)   **3.** Yes

4. No; a solution must be an ordered triple.   **5.** Two
6. Three   **7.** no   **8.** Infinitely many   **9.** $(1, 2, 3)$
11. $(-1, 1, 2)$ **13.** $(3, -1, 1)$ **15.** $\left(\frac{17}{2}, -\frac{3}{2}, 2\right)$
17. $(5, -2, -2)$ **19.** $(11, 2, 2)$ **21.** $(1, -1, 2)$
23. $(0, -3, 2)$ **25.** $(-1, 3, -2)$ **27.** $(-1, 2, 4)$
29. $(8, 5, 2)$ **31.** No solutions   **33.** $(4 - z, 2, z)$
35. $(3, -3, 0)$ **37.** $\left(-\frac{3}{2}, 5, -10\right)$ **39.** $\left(\frac{3}{2}, 1, -\frac{1}{2}\right)$
41. No solutions   **43.** $(4 - z, 1, z)$ **45.** No solutions
47. (a) $x + 2y + 4z = 10, x + 4y + 6z = 15,$
$3y + 2z = 6$ **(b)** $(2, 1, 1.5)$; a hamburger costs \$2,
fries \$1, and a soft drink \$1.50.   **49. (a)** $x + y + z = 180,$
$x - z = 55, x - y - z = -10$ **(b)** $x = 85°, y = 65°,$
and $z = 30°$ **(c)** These values check.   **51.** $110°, 50°, 20°$
53. (a) $a + 600b + 4c = 525, a + 400b + 2c = 365,$
$a + 900b + 5c = 805$ **(b)** $a = 5, b = 1, c = -20,$
$F = 5 + A - 20W$ **(c)** 445 fawns
55. (a) $N + P + K = 80, N + P - K = 8, 9P - K = 0$
(b) $(40, 4, 36)$; 40 pounds nitrogen, 4 pounds phosphorus,
36 pounds potassium   **57.** \$7500 at 8%, \$8500 at 10%, and
\$14,000 at 15%

SECTION 4.6 (pp. 295–298)

1. A rectangular array of numbers
2. $\begin{bmatrix} 2 & 1 & 3 \\ 0 & -4 & 2 \end{bmatrix}$ is 2 × 3 (answers may vary).

3. $\left[\begin{array}{cc|c} 1 & 3 & 10 \\ 2 & -6 & 4 \end{array}\right]$ is 2 × 3 (answers may vary).

4. 3 × 4   **5.** $\left[\begin{array}{cc|c} 1 & 0 & -3 \\ 0 & 1 & 5 \end{array}\right]$ (answers may vary)

6. $4, 2, -3$ **7.** 3 × 3   **9.** 3 × 2
11. $\left[\begin{array}{cc|c} 1 & -3 & 1 \\ -1 & 3 & -1 \end{array}\right]$ **13.** $\left[\begin{array}{ccc|c} 2 & -1 & 2 & -4 \\ 1 & -2 & 0 & 2 \\ -1 & 1 & -2 & -6 \end{array}\right]$
15. $x + 2y = -6, 5x - y = 4$ **17.** $x - y + 2z = 6,$
$2x + y - 2z = 1, -x + 2y - z = 3$
19. $x = 4, y = -2, z = 7$ **21.** $(1, 3)$ **23.** $\left(-\frac{3}{2}, 2\right)$
25. $\left(\frac{7}{2}, -\frac{3}{2}\right)$ **27.** $\left(\frac{1}{2}, \frac{3}{2}\right)$ **29.** $(1, 2, 3)$ **31.** $(3, -3, 3)$
33. $(-1, 1, 0)$ **35.** $(1, 1, 1)$ **37.** $(-3, 2, 2)$
39. $(-7, 5)$ **41.** $(1, 2, 3)$ **43.** $(1, 0.5, -3)$
45. $(0.5, 0.25, -1)$ **47.** $(0.5, -0.2, 1.7)$
49. Dependent   **51.** Inconsistent   **53.** Dependent
55. $\left(\frac{1}{a}, \frac{1}{b}, \frac{2}{ab}\right)$ **57.** 214 pounds
59. (a) $a + 2b + 1.4c = 3, a + 1.5b + 0.65c = 2,$
$a + 4b + 3.4c = 6$ **(b)** $a = 0.6, b = 0.5,$ and $c = 1$
(c) $4.1 \approx 4$ people   **61.** $\frac{1}{2}$ hour at 5 miles per hour, 1 hour
at 6 miles per hour, and $\frac{1}{2}$ hour at 8 miles per hour
63. \$500 at 5%, \$1000 at 8%, and \$1500 at 12%

CHECKING BASIC CONCEPTS 4.5 & 4.6 (p. 298)

1. $(1, 3, -1)$ **2.** $(1, 2, 3)$ **3.** $(-2, 2, -1)$

SECTION 4.7 (pp. 304–305)

1. square   **2.** number   **3.** system of linear equations
4. 0   **5.** -2 **7.** -53 **9.** -323 **11.** -5 **13.** -36
15. -42 **17.** -50 **19.** 0   **21.** -3555 **23.** -7466.5
25. abc **27.** 15 square feet   **29.** 52 square feet
31. 25.5 square feet   **33.** $(2, -2)$
35. $\left(-\frac{29}{11}, -\frac{34}{11}\right)$ **37.** $(-5, 7)$

CHECKING BASIC CONCEPTS 4.7 (p. 306)

1. (a) -1 **(b)** 17   **2.** $x = -4, y = 6$
3. 21 square units

CHAPTER 4 REVIEW (pp. 310–313)

1. $(3, 2)$ **2.** $(4, -3)$ **3.** $(-1, -3)$ **4.** $(3.5, 8.5)$
5. $(1, 5)$; consistent; independent
6. $\{(x, y) \mid x - y = -2\}$; consistent; dependent
7. No solutions; inconsistent   **8.** $(2, -1)$; consistent;
independent   **9.** $(3, -2)$ **10.** $(-2, 1)$
11. (a) $x + y = 25, x - y = 10$ **(b)** $(17.5, 7.5)$
12. (a) $3x - 2y = 19, x + y = 18$ **(b)** $(11, 7)$
13. $(0.467, 0.025)$ **14.** $(2.611, 1.768)$ **15.** $(-3, 1)$
16. $(2, 0)$ **17.** $(-1, 2)$ **18.** $(-2, 3)$ **19.** $\left(\frac{2}{5}, \frac{14}{5}\right)$
20. $(-2, -3)$ **21.** $\{(x, y) \mid 3x - y = 5\}$
22. No solutions
23.

24.

25.

26.

27.

28.

29.

30.

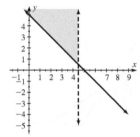

31. $x > 1, y < -1$ **32.** $y \leq -x + 4, y \geq 2x + 1$
33. $R = 31$ **34.** $C = 3$ **35.** $R = 6$ **36.** $R = 45$
37. Yes   **38.** $(1, -1, 2)$ **39.** $(-4, 3, 2)$
40. $(-1, 5, -3)$ **41.** $(-1, 3, 2)$ **42.** $(1, 1, 1)$
43. No solutions   **44.** $(2 - z, 2z - 1, z)$

45. $\begin{bmatrix} 1 & 1 & 1 & | & -6 \\ 1 & 2 & 1 & | & -8 \\ 0 & 1 & 1 & | & -5 \end{bmatrix}$; $(-1, -2, -3)$

46. $\begin{bmatrix} 1 & 1 & 1 & | & -3 \\ -1 & 1 & 0 & | & 5 \\ 0 & 1 & 1 & | & -1 \end{bmatrix}$; $(-2, 3, -4)$

47. $\begin{bmatrix} 1 & 2 & -1 & | & 1 \\ -1 & 1 & -2 & | & 5 \\ 0 & 2 & 1 & | & 10 \end{bmatrix}$; $(-5, 4, 2)$

48. $\begin{bmatrix} 2 & 2 & -2 & | & -14 \\ -2 & -3 & 2 & | & 12 \\ 1 & 1 & -4 & | & -22 \end{bmatrix}$; $(-4, 2, 5)$

49. $(-7, 4, 2)$ **50.** $(5.4, 2.1, 9.7)$ **51.** -8 **52.** 30
53. 89   **54.** 130   **55.** 181,845   **56.** 67.688
57. 46 square feet   **58.** 128 square feet   **59.** $(2, -1)$
60. $(-5, 3)$ **61.** $\left(\frac{3}{2}, \frac{1}{2}\right)$ **62.** $(7, -3)$ **63.** 5489 in 1994;
4641 in 2004   **64.** Stair climber: 8 minutes; bicycle: 22 minutes
65.

66. Unsubsidized: $1750; subsidized: $2250   **67.** 8 shirts, 20 pants; $660   **68.** 30% solution: 2.4 gallons; 55% solution: 1.6 gallons   **69.** Boat: 15 miles per hour; current: 3 miles per hour   **70.** $8 tickets: 285; $12 tickets: 195
71. (a) $m + 3c + 5b = 14$, $m + 2c + 4b = 11$, $c + 3b = 5$ **(b)** Malts: $3; cones: $2; bars: $1
72. $100°$, $65°$, and $15°$ **73.** 2 pounds of $1.50 candy, 4 pounds of $2 candy, 6 pounds of $2.50 candy
74. (a) $a + 202b + 63c = 40$, $a + 365b + 70c = 50$, $a + 446b + 77c = 55$ **(b)** $a \approx 27.134$; $b \approx 0.061$, $c \approx 0.009$ **(c)** About 46 inches

CHAPTER 4 TEST (pp. 313–314)

1. $(3, 1)$; consistent; independent   **2.** No solutions; inconsistent   **3.** $\{(x, y) \mid x - 3y = 1\}$; consistent; dependent
4. $\left(\frac{1}{2}, -7\right)$; consistent; independent   **5.** $(-3, 1)$
6. (a) $x - y = 34$, $x - 2y = 0$ **(b)** $(68, 34)$
7. $(-0.378, 1.220)$ **8.** $(8, -7)$
9.   **10.**

11.

12. $(-4, 2, -5)$ **13.** No solutions
14. $y \le x + 2$, $y \ge 3x - 1$
15. (a) $\begin{bmatrix} 1 & 1 & 1 & 2 \\ 1 & -1 & -1 & 3 \\ 2 & 2 & 1 & 6 \end{bmatrix}$ **(b)** $\left(\frac{5}{2}, \frac{3}{2}, -2\right)$
16. 114   **17.** $\left(-\frac{47}{2}, -\frac{83}{2}\right)$
18. (a) $x - y = 12{,}636$, $x - 4.6y = 0$ **(b)** Approximately $(16{,}146, 3510)$; private tuition was $16,146, and public tuition was $3510.   **19.** Running: 43 minutes; rowing: 17 minutes   **20.** Airplane: 270 miles per hour; wind: 30 miles per hour   **21.** $85°$, $60°$, and $35°$ **22.** $R = 4$

23.

24. Unsubsidized: $2550; subsidized: $1850

CHAPTERS 1–4 CUMULATIVE REVIEW (pp. 316–317)

1. Identity   **2.** Associative   **3.** -14.5 **4.** 0
5. $-\frac{a}{b}$ **6. (a)** $\frac{9}{256}$ **(b)** $\frac{4}{a^5 b^2}$ **(c)** y^2 **7.** 5.6×10^{-3}
8. 13   **9.** $V = 4\pi$ **10.** $x \ne -\frac{1}{2}$
11.   **12.**

13. (a) Yes   **(b)** D and R: all real numbers   **(c)** -1.5; 0
(d) 2; -1 **(e)** $\frac{1}{2}$ **(f)** $f(x) = \frac{1}{2}x - 1$
14. $y = \frac{4}{3}x + 11$ **15.** 4; $-\frac{1}{2}$; 2   **16.** $-\frac{1}{3}$ **17.** $\left(-\infty, \frac{4}{5}\right)$
18. $(-\infty, 1) \cup (3, \infty)$ **19.** $\left(-\frac{3}{4}, \frac{5}{4}\right]$ **20. (a)** $-\frac{2}{3}, 2$
(b) $\left(-\frac{2}{3}, 2\right)$ **(c)** $\left(-\infty, -\frac{2}{3}\right) \cup (2, \infty)$ **21. (a)** $(1, 1)$
(b) $(2, 0)$ **22. (a)** $\left(\frac{1}{2}, \frac{7}{4}\right)$ **(b)** No solutions
23. (a)   **(b)**

24. $(3, 2, 1)$ **25.** $(-2, 3, -4)$ **26.** 6
27. (a) $I(x) = 0.07x$ **(b)** $35; the interest after 1 year for $500 at 7% is $35.   **28. (a)** 9340; average tuition and fees in 1990 were $9340.   **(b)** Tuition and fees increased, on average, by $572.30 per year from 1980 to 2000.
29. 15 in. by 22 in.   **30.** $|P - 12.4| \le 0.2$
31. $500 at 5%; $2000 at 6%; $2500 at 8%
32. Texas: 21.8 million; Florida: 16.7 million

CHAPTER 5: POLYNOMIAL EXPRESSIONS AND FUNCTIONS

SECTION 5.1 (pp. 330–334)

1. $3x^2$ (answers may vary)   **2.** $3; -1$ **3.** No; the powers must match for each variable.   **4.** $x^4 - 3x + 5$ (answers may vary)   **5.** No; the opposite is $-x^2 - 1$.   **6.** 96
7. No; a function has only one output for each input.
8. Yes, if the polynomial is linear.   **9.** 6   **10.** $3x^2$
11. Yes   **13.** No   **15.** Yes   **17.** No   **19.** No   **21.** x^2
23. πr^2 **25.** xy **27.** $7; 3$ **29.** $7; -3$ **31.** $6; -1$
33. $2; 5$ **35.** $3; -\frac{2}{5}$ **37.** $5; 1$ **39.** $5x^2$ **41.** $3y^4$
43. Not possible   **45.** $3x^2 + 3x$ **47.** $5x^2 + 9xy$
49. $5x^3y^7 + 13x$ **51.** $2x + 2$ **53.** $-2x^2 + 3x + 8$
55. $3x^3 + 5x + 15$ **57.** $-7x^4 - 3x^2 + x - \frac{9}{2}$
59. $4r^4 + r^3 - 6r + 2$ **61.** $5y^2 - 4xy - 2x^2$
63. $-6x^5$ **65.** $-19x^5 + 5x^3 - 3x$ **67.** $7z^4 - z^2 + 8$
69. $3x - 7$ **71.** $6x^2 - 5x + 5$ **73.** $8x^4 + 14x^2 - 7$
75. $-3x - 11$ **77.** Yes; 4; fourth degree   **79.** No
81. No   **83.** Yes; 2; quadratic   **85.** -16 **87.** 24   **89.** 84
91. $-1; 2$ **93.** $-4; 2$ **95.** 12   **97.** 7   **99.** 5.8   **101.** 1
103. 0   **105.** 1.96   **107.** -6 **109.** $a^2 - 2a$
111. (a) 8   (b) -10 (c) $2x + 4$ (d) $4x - 6$
113. (a) -7 (b) -5 (c) $-2x^2 + 1$ (d) $-4x^2 - 1$
115. (a) 16   (b) 4   (c) $2x^3$ (d) $-4x^3$ **117.** (a) 23
(b) 3   (c) $5x^2 + x + 1$ (d) $-3x^2 - 5x + 1$
119. (a) 1250; 7250   (b) 1268; 7276; they are similar.
(c) 8188   **121.** $24xy + 16xz$; 4000 ft^3 **123.** $5s^3$
125. $x^2 + \pi x^2$; $100 + 100\pi \approx 414.2$ square inches
127. From 4 to 8 minutes

t	3	4	5	6	7	8	9
$y = f(t)$	126.875	110	96.875	87.5	81.875	80	81.875

129. $f(x)$ is the best, which can be determined from a table of values.   **131.** (a) $R(x) = 16x$ (b) $P(x) = 12x - 2000$
(c) 34,000; profit is $34,000 for selling 3000 CDs.

SECTION 5.2 (pp. 343–345)

1. Distributive   **2.** $3x, 2x - 7, x^2 - 3x + 1$ (answers may vary)   **3.** x^8 **4.** $8x^3; x^6$ **5.** $a^2 - b^2$
6. $a^2 + 2ab + b^2$ **7.** $x^2 - x$ **8.** No, it equals $x^2 + 2x + 1$.   **9.** x^{12} **11.** $-20y^8$ **13.** $-4x^4y^6$
15. $20x^2y^3z^6$ **17.** $5y + 10$ **19.** $-10x - 18$
21. $-6y^2 + 18y$ **23.** $27x - 12x^2$ **25.** $-a^3b + ab^3$
27. $-5mn^3 - 5m^2$ **29.** $x^2 + 3x + 2$; 42 square inches
31. $2x^2 + 3x + 1$; 66 square inches   **33.** $x^2 + 11x + 30$
35. $4x^2 + 4x + 1$ **37.** No, a square of a sum does not equal the sum of the squares.   **39.** No   **41.** Yes   **43.** No
45. $x^2 + 15x + 50$ **47.** $x^2 - 7x + 12$
49. $2z^2 + 3z - 2$ **51.** $y^2 - y - 12$
53. $-36x^2 + 43x - 12$ **55.** $-2z^2 + 7z - 6$

57. $z^2 - \frac{1}{4}z - \frac{1}{8}$ **59.** $2x^4 + x^2 - 1$ **61.** $x^2 - xy - 2y^2$
63. $4x^3 - 8x^2 - 12x$ **65.** $-x^5 + 3x^3 - x$
67. $6n^4 - 12n^3 + 3n^2$ **69.** $x^3 + 3x^2 - x - 3$
71. $-z^4 - 3z^3 - z^2 + 2z$ **73.** $4a^3b^2 - 2a^2b^3 + 6ab^4$
75. $6r^3 - 10r^2t - 6rt^2 + 4t^3$ **77.** $2^6 = 64$ **79.** $2z^{18}$
81. $25x^2$ **83.** $-8x^3y^6$ **85.** $16a^4b^6$ **87.** $x^2 - 9$
89. $9 - 4x^2$ **91.** $x^2 - y^2$ **93.** $x^2 + 4x + 4$
95. $4x^2 + 4x + 1$ **97.** $x^2 - 2x + 1$
99. $9x^2 - 12x + 4$ **101.** $3x^3 - 3x$ **103.** $3rt^3 - 12r^3t$
105. $a^4 - 4b^4$ **107.** $9m^6 + 30m^3n^2 + 25n^4$
109. $x^6 - 4x^3y^3 + 4y^6$ **111.** $x^2 - 6x - y^2 + 9$
113. $r^2 - t^2 - 4t - 4$ **115.** 9996
117. $0; x^2 - x - 2$ **119.** $-28; -5x^3 + 3x^2$
121. $27; 2x^4 + 2x^3 - 5x^2 + x - 3$
123. $x(x + 4)$; 480 square feet
125. $(x + 3)^2$; 529 square feet
127. (a) 30 thousand   (b) $40p - \frac{1}{2}p^2$ (c) $750 thousand
129. (a) $Nr^2 + 2Nr + N$ (b) $242; the answers agree.
131. $x(x + 1)$ or $x^2 + x$ **133.** $x(50 - x)$ or $50x - x^2$

CHECKING BASIC CONCEPTS 5.1 & 5.2 (pp. 345–346)

1. (a) $3x^2 + 7x$ (b) $5x^3 + 2x^2 - 3x + 1$
2. $x(x + 120)$; 1300, when tickets cost $10 each, the revenue will be $1300.   **3.** (a) 160 bpm   (b) 92 bpm
4. (a) $-5x + 30$ (b) $12x^5 - 20x^4$ (c) $2x^2 + 5x - 3$
5. (a) $25x^2 - 36$ (b) $9x^2 - 24x + 16$
6.

2	$2x$	8
x	x^2	$4x$
	x	4

SECTION 5.3 (pp. 354–357)

1. To solve equations   **2.** Either $x = 0$ or $x - 3 = 0$; zero-product property   **3.** Yes; because $2x$ is a factor of each term.
4. No, because $4x^2$ is the greatest common factor.
5. No; because $\frac{1}{2}(4) = 2$, and $\frac{1}{2} \neq 2$ and $4 \neq 2$.
6. Yes; by the zero-product property   **7.** $5(2x - 3)$
9. $2(2x + 3y)$ **11.** $3(3r - 5t)$ **13.** $x(2x^2 - 5)$
15. $2a(4a^2 + 5)$ **17.** $6r^3(1 - 3r^2)$
19. $4x(2x^2 - x + 4)$ **21.** $3n(3n^3 - 2n + 1)$
23. $2t^2(3t^4 - 2t^2 + 1)$ **25.** $5x^2y^2(1 - 3y)$
27. $3a^2b^2(2a - 5b)$ **29.** $6mn^2(3 + 2mn)$
31. $5xy(3x + 2 - 5xy)$ **33.** $2a(2a - b + 3b^2)$
35. $-2(x^2 - 2x + 3)$ **37.** $-8z^3(z + 2)$
39. $-2mn(2mn^2 + 3n + 4)$ **41.** $m = 0$ or $n = 0$
43. $z = 0$ or $z = -4$ **45.** $r = 1$ or $r = -3$
47. $x = -2$ or $x = \frac{1}{3}$ **49.** $x = 0$ or $y = 6$

51. (a) $-3, 0$ (b) $-3, 0$ (c) $-3, 0$ **53.** (a) $0, 2$
(b) $0, 2$ (c) $0, 2$ **55.** (a) $-1, 1$ (b) $-1, 1$ (c) $-1, 1$
57. $0, 2$ **59.** $0, 1$ **61.** $-4, 0$ **63.** $0, 1$ **65.** $0, \frac{1}{5}$
67. $-\frac{1}{2}, 0$ **69.** $0, \frac{2}{3}$ **71.** $0, \frac{5}{2}$ **73.** $0, \frac{1}{2}$ **75.** $-2, 0$
77. $0, \frac{3}{2}$ **79.** $(2x + 3)(x + 2)$ **81.** $(x - 5)(x^2 - 2)$
83. $(x + 3)(x^2 + 2)$ **85.** $(3x - 2)(2x^2 + 3)$
87. $(x^2 + 1)(2x - 3)$ **89.** $(x^2 - 3)(x - 7)$
91. $(x - 5)(3x^2 + 5)$ **93.** $(y + 1)(x + 3)$
95. $(a + 2)(b - 3)$ **97.** b.; a.
99. (a) After 8 seconds (b) After 8 seconds (c) Yes

t	3	4	5	6	7	8
$y = h(t)$	240	256	240	192	112	0

(d) 256 ft; 4 seconds
101. 380; CO_2 concentration in 2005 was 380 ppm. **103.** $\frac{8}{\pi}$
105. (a) The function models the data quite well.

t	20	30	40	50	60	70	80
$y = f(t)$	4520	10,080	17,840	27,800	39,960	54,320	70,880

(b) About 54,000 feet (c) $-\frac{6}{11}, 0$; the shuttle is on the
ground at time $t = 0$; the value $t = -\frac{6}{11}$ has no physical
meaning. **107.** No; there are many possibilities, such as
9×24 and 8×27.

SECTION 5.4 (pp. 366–368)

1. A polynomial with three terms; $x^2 - x + 1$ (answers
may vary) **2.** Symbolic and graphical, grouping and FOIL
(answers may vary) **3.** $a = 3, b = -1, c = -3$ **4.** Yes;
it checks, using FOIL. **5.** $(x + 3)(x - 1)$
6. $(6x - 3)(x - 2)$ or $3(2x - 1)(x - 2)$
or $6\left(x - \frac{1}{2}\right)(x - 2)$ **7.** Yes **9.** No **11.** Yes **13.** No
15. $(x + 2)(x + 5)$ **17.** $(x + 2)(x + 6)$
19. $(x - 9)(x - 4)$ **21.** $(x - 8)(x + 1)$
23. $(z - 8)(z + 9)$ **25.** $(t - 8)(t - 7)$
27. $(y - 12)(y - 6)$ **29.** $(m - 20)(m + 2)$
31. $(n - 30)(n + 10)$ **33.** $(x + 3)(2x + 1)$
35. $(2x + 1)(3x - 2)$ **37.** $(z + 4)(4z + 3)$
39. $(2t - 3)(3t - 4)$ **41.** $(2y + 3)(5y - 1)$
43. $(2m - 3)(3m + 4)$ **45.** $(6n + 5)(7n - 5)$
47. $(1 - x)(1 + 2x)$ **49.** $(5 - 2x)(4 + 3x)$
51. $5(y - 2)(y + 3)$ **53.** $2(z + 2)(z + 4)$
55. $z(z + 2)(z + 7)$ **57.** $t(t - 7)(t - 3)$
59. $m^2(m + 1)(m + 5)$ **61.** $x(x - 1)(5x + 6)$
63. $3x(x + 3)(2x + 1)$ **65.** $2x(x - 5)(x - 2)$
67. $10z(z + 4)(6z - 1)$ **69.** $2x^2(x + 3)(2x - 1)$
71. $(x + 2)(x + 3)$ **73.** $(x + a)(x + b)$ **75.** $-3; 2$
77. $f(x) = x + 1, g(x) = x + 2$
79. $f(x) = x + 2, g(x) = x - 4$ **81.** $(x - 2)(x - 4)$
83. $2(x + 1)(x - 2)$ **85.** $-(x - 2)(x + 1)$
87. $(x + 1)(x - 4)$ **89.** $2(x + 1)(x - 2)$

91. $(x - 2)(x + 5)$ **93.** $(x - 7)(x + 4)$
95. $2(x - 5)(x - 2)$ **97.** $5(x - 10)(x + 4)$
99. $4(x - 5)(2x - 1)$ **101.** (a) $(35 - x)(1200 + 100x)$
(b) $20 or $27 **103.** 7 by 13 feet **105.** (a) 6 sec (b) 6 sec

CHECKING BASIC CONCEPTS 5.3 & 5.4 (p. 368)

1. (a) $3x(x - 2)$ (b) $4x(4x^2 - 2x + 1)$
2. (a) $0, 2$ (b) $0, 9$ **3.** (a) $(x - 2)(x + 5)$
(b) $(x - 5)(x + 2)$ (c) $(2x + 3)(4x + 1)$
4. $-1, -2$ **5.** After 1 and 3 seconds

SECTION 5.5 (pp. 373–375)

1. $x^2 - 9$ (answers may vary) **2.** $x^2 - 8x + 16$
(answers may vary) **3.** $x^3 + 8$ (answers may vary)
4. $(a - b)(a + b)$ **5.** $(a + b)^2$
6. $(a - b)(a^2 + ab + b^2)$ **7.** Yes; $(x - 5)(x + 5)$
9. No; $(x + y)(x^2 - xy + y^2)$ **11.** $(x - 6)(x + 6)$
13. $(5 - z)(5 + z)$ **15.** Cannot be factored
17. $4(3x - 5)(3x + 5)$ **19.** $(7a - 8b)(7a + 8b)$
21. $z^2(8 - 5z)(8 + 5z)$ **23.** $5x(x - 5)(x + 5)$
25. Cannot be factored **27.** $(4t^2 - r)(4t^2 + r)$
29. $(x - 4)(x + 6)$ **31.** $(14 - n)(6 + n)$
33. $(y - 2)(y + 2)(y^2 + 4)$
35. $(2x - y)(2x + y)(4x^2 + y^2)$ **37.** $(x - 1)(x + 1)^2$
39. $(2x - 1)(2x + 1)(x - 2)$ **41.** No
43. Yes; $(x + 4)^2$ **45.** Yes; $(2z - 1)^2$ **47.** No
49. $(x + 1)^2$ **51.** $(2x + 5)^2$ **53.** $(x - 6)^2$
55. $(6z + 1)^2$ **57.** $y^2(2y + 1)^2$ **59.** $z(3z - 1)^2$
61. $(3x + y)^2$ **63.** $(7a - 2b)^2$ **65.** $x^2(2x - y)^2$
67. $(x - 2)(x^2 + 2x + 4)$ **69.** $(y + z)(y^2 - yz + z^2)$
71. $(3x - 2)(9x^2 + 6x + 4)$
73. $(4z + 3t)(16z^2 - 12zt + 9t^2)$
75. $x(2x + 5)(4x^2 - 10x + 25)$
77. $y(3 - 2x)(9 + 6x + 4x^2)$
79. $(z^2 - 3y)(z^4 + 3z^2y + 9y^2)$
81. $(5z^2 + 2y^3)(25z^4 - 10z^2y^3 + 4y^6)$
83. $5(m^2 + 2n)(m^4 - 2m^2n + 4n^2)$
85. $(5x - 8)(5x + 8)$ **87.** $(x + 3)(x^2 - 3x + 9)$
89. $(8x + 1)^2$ **91.** $(x + 4)(3x + 2)$
93. $x(x + 2)(x^2 - 2x + 4)$
95. $8(2x + y)(4x^2 - 2xy + y^2)$
97. $2(r - 2t)(r + 2t)$ **99.** $a(a + 2b)^2$
101. $(x - 2)(x - 1)$ **103.** $(2z - 5)(2z + 5)$
105. $x^2(x + 8)^2$ **107.** $(z - 1)(z^2 + z + 1)$

109. $(t + 1)(3t - 8)$ **111.** $a(a + 3)(7a - 1)$
113. $(x + y)(x - y)(x^2 + xy + y^2)(x^2 - xy + y^2)$
115. $(10x - 1)(10x + 1)$
117. $(pq - 3)(p^2q^2 + 3pq + 9)$

SECTION 5.6 (pp. 379–381)

1. Factor out the GCF.   **2.** $2x$ **3.** No; the sum of two squares cannot be factored.   **4.** Grouping   **5.** $a(a - 1)$
7. $(a - 3)(a + 3)$ **9.** $(x - 1)^2$
11. $(x - a)(x^2 + ax + a^2)$ **13.** Not possible
15. $(x - 3)(x + 2)$ **17.** $(x + 2)(x^2 + 1)$
19. $2x(3x - 7)$ **21.** $2x(x - 3)(x + 3)$
23. $4(a - 2)(a + 2)(a^2 + 4)$ **25.** $x(x - 3)(6x + 5)$
27. $x^2(x - 5)(2x + 5)$ **29.** $(x^2 + 1)(2x^2 + 3)$
31. $(x^2 + 1)(x + 3)$ **33.** $5(x^2 + 2)(x - 1)$
35. $(a + b)(x - y)$ **37.** $2(3x + 1)^2$
39. $-4x(x - 3)^2$ **41.** $(2x - 3)(4x^2 + 6x + 9)$
43. $-x(x + 2)(x^2 - 2x + 4)$
45. $(x - 1)(x - 2)(x^2 + x + 1)$
47. $(r - 2)(r + 2)(r^2 + 4)$ **49.** $(5x - 2a)(5x + 2a)$
51. $2(x - y)(x + y)(x^2 + y^2)$ **53.** $3x(3x - 1)(x + 1)$
55. $(z - 5)(z + 1)$
57. $3(x + 1)(x^2 - x + 1)(x - 3)(x + 3)$
59. (a) $(x^2 + 2)(x - 380)$ **(b)** 380 ppm
61. (a) $x^3 - 3x^2 + 2x$ **(b)** $x^3 - 3x^2 + 2x = 6$ **(c)** 3 ft

CHECKING BASIC CONCEPTS 5.5 & 5.6 (p. 381)

1. (a) $(5x - 4)(5x + 4)$ **(b)** $(x + 6)^2$
(c) $(3x - 5)^2$ **(d)** $(x - 3)(x^2 + 3x + 9)$
(e) $(3x - 2)(3x + 2)(9x^2 + 4)$
2. (a) $(x^2 + 3)(x - 2)$ **(b)** $(x + 3)(x - 7)$
(c) $2x(2x - 1)(3x + 2)$

SECTION 5.7 (pp. 388–391)

1. It is used in solving polynomial equations (answers may vary).   **2.** multiplying   **3.** Subtract 16 from each side.
4. No; the right side is not 0.   **5.** 1   **6.** No; it implies that $x^2 = -4$.   **7.** $-1, 1$ **9.** $-2, 2$ **11.** $-1, 2$ **13.** $-8, 8$
15. $-\frac{1}{2}, \frac{1}{2}$ **17.** $-1, 4$ **19.** $-6, 2$ **21.** $-3, \frac{1}{2}$ **23.** $-4, 4$
25. -7 **27.** $\frac{1}{3}$ **29.** $-\frac{1}{5}, \frac{2}{3}$ **31.** $-\frac{4}{3}, \frac{3}{8}$ **33.** No solutions
35. $-3, 2$ **37.** $-2, 4$

39.   **41.**

43. $-3, 0, 3$ **45.** 0   **47.** $-2, 0, 5$ **49.** $-1, 0, 5$
51. $-7, -2, 2$ **53.** $-6, 2, 6$ **55.** $-3, 5$ **57.** $-\frac{1}{2}, 2$
59. $-5, -1$ **61.** $0, 2$ **63.** $-2, 2$ **65.** $-5, -1, 1, 5$
67. $-3, -2, 2, 3$ **69.** $-2, 2$ **71.** $-1, -\frac{2}{3}, \frac{2}{3}, 1$
73. 17 by 21 inches   **75.** $-1000, 1000$ **77.** 30 by 50 feet
79. After 2 and $\frac{17}{8}$ seconds   **81.** 33 mph   **83.** 0.6 by 2.4 by 4.1 in.   **85. (a)** The elevation begins at 500 feet, decreases, and then increases back to 500 feet.

x	0	300	600	900	1200	1500
$y = E(x)$	500	428	392	392	428	500

(b) 500 feet and 1000 feet

CHECKING BASIC CONCEPTS 5.7 (p. 391)

1. $-3, -1$ **2.** $-3, 3$
3. (a) 3   **(b)** No solutions   **(c)** $-\frac{5}{4}, \frac{2}{3}$
4. (a) 0   **(b)** $-3, 3$ **(c)** $-2, 2$ **(d)** $-7, -2, 7$

CHAPTER 5 REVIEW (pp. 395–397)

1. $x + 5, x^2 - 3x + 1$ (answers may vary)
2. $10xy^2$; 3200 cubic inches   **3.** $5; -4$ **4.** $3; 1$
5. $7; 5$ **6.** $10; -9$ **7.** $11x$ **8.** $4x^3 + x^2$
9. $14x^3y + x^3$ **10.** 19   **11.** $2; 5$ **12.** $4; 2$
13. $8x^2 + 3x - 1$ **14.** $23z^3 - 4z^2 + z$ **15.** $-x^2 + x$
16. $-5x^3 - x^2 - 3x + 6$ **17.** 7   **18.** -259 **19.** -4
20. $-11; 4x^2 - x - 1$ **21.** $15x - 20$
22. $-2x - 2x^2 + 8x^3$ **23.** x^8 **24.** $-6x^4$ **25.** $-42x^2y^8$
26. $60x^3y^5$ **27.** $x^2 + 9x + 20$ **28.** $x^2 - 15x + 56$
29. $12x^2 - 48x - 27$ **30.** $y^2 - \frac{1}{9}$
31. $8x^4 - 12x^3 - 4x^2$ **32.** $-4x - 5x^2 + 7x^3$
33. $16x^2 - y^2$ **34.** $x^2 + 6x + 9$ **35.** $4y^2 - 20y + 25$
36. $a^3 - b^3$ **37.** $25m^2 - 20mn^4 + 4n^8$
38. $r^2 - 2r + 1 - t^2$ **39.** $5x(5x - 6)$
40. $4x^2(3x^2 + 2x - 4)$ **41.** $-3, 0$ **42.** $-2, 0, 2$
43. $\frac{1}{2}, 1$ **44.** $-1, 3$ **45.** $(x + 1)(2x^2 - 3)$
46. $(z + 1)(z^2 + 1)$ **47.** $(a - b)(x + y)$
48. $5; x^2 - 2x - 3$ **49. (a)** $0, 3$ **(b)** $0, 3$ **(c)** $0, 3$
50. (a) $-1, 2$ **(b)** $-1, 2$ **(c)** $-1, 2$

51. $(x + 2)(x + 6)$ **52.** $(x - 10)(x + 5)$
53. $(x + 3)(9x - 2)$ **54.** $2(x - 5)(2x - 1)$
55. $x(x - 3)(x - 1)$ **56.** $2x^2(x + 2)(x + 5)$
57. $5x^2(x - 3)(x + 6)$ **58.** $10x(x - 5)(x - 4)$
59. $(x + 3)(x - 5)$ **60.** $(x - 11)(x - 13)$
61. $(x + 7)(x - 4)$ **62.** $8, 13$ **63.** $(t - 7)(t + 7)$
64. $(2y - 3x)(2y + 3x)$ **65.** $(x + 2)^2$
66. $(4x - 1)^2$ **67.** $(x - 3)(x^2 + 3x + 9)$
68. $(4x + 3y)(16x^2 - 12xy + 9y^2)$
69. $10y(y - 1)(y + 1)$ **70.** $(2r^2 - t^3)(2r^2 + t^3)$
71. $(m - 2n)(m + 2n)(m^2 + 4n^2)$
72. $(n - 2)(n - 1)(n + 1)$ **73.** $(5a - 3b)^2$
74. $2r(r - 3t)^2$ **75.** $(a^2 + 3b)(a^4 - 3a^2b + 9b^2)$
76. $(2p^2 - q)(4p^4 + 2p^2q + q^2)$ **77.** $5x^2(x - 2)$
78. $-2x(x - 4)(x + 4)$
79. $(x - 2y)(x + 2y)(x^2 + 4y^2)$
80. $4x(x - 1)(x + 3)$ **81.** $-x(2x - 3)(x - 4)$
82. $(x^2 + 1)(x - 3)(x + 3)$
83. $(4a + b)(16a^2 - 4ab + b^2)$
84. $(2 - y)(y^2 + 2y + 4)$ **85.** $(z - 1)(z + 7)$
86. $x(x - 2)(x + 2)(x - 5)$ **87.** $-4, 4$
88. $-1, 3$ **89.** $\frac{7}{2}$ **90.** No solutions   **91.** $-1, \frac{5}{3}$
92. $-2, \frac{3}{4}$ **93.** $-1, 0, 1$ **94.** $1, 2, 3$ **95.** $-9, 0, 8$
96. $0, 7, 8$ **97.** $-2, 2$ **98.** $-2, 2$
99. **(a)** $R(x) = 15x$ **(b)** $P(x) = 12x - 9000$
(c) 39,000; profit is $39,000 for selling 4000 DVDs.
100. **(a)** $x(x + 5)(x + 10)$
(b) $x(x + 5)(x + 10) = 168$ **(c)** 2 by 7 by 12 in.
101. 8 by 10 in.   **102.** $\frac{1}{2}x^2 - \frac{1}{2}x - 3$
103. **(a)** $73.6°F$ **(b)** July

(c) Temperatures increase from January through July and then decrease from July through December.
[1, 12, 1] by [30, 90, 10]

104. **(a)** $100 - 2x + \frac{x^2}{100}$ **(b)** 9%
105. $(x - 2)(x - 1)(x) = x^3 - 3x^2 + 2x$
106.

	2x	14
x	x^2	$7x$
	x	7

107. 9 feet by 16 feet   **108.** $25x - x^2$

109. **(a)** After $\frac{33}{8} = 4.125$ seconds   **(b)** After 1 second and after $\frac{25}{8} = 3.125$ seconds
110. **(a)** $R(x) = (50 - x)(600 + 20x)$ **(b)** $40
111. $-1000, 1000$

CHAPTER 5 TEST (pp. 398–399)

1. $5x - 4x^2y^2$ **2.** $-7x^3 + x^2 - 7x + 11$ **3.** -8
4. -2 **5.** $4; 3$ **6.** $8xyz$ **7.** -66
8. $66; -x^3 + 2x - 4$ **9.** $-4x^3 + 2x^2$ **10.** $14x^2y^8$
11. $10x^2 - 9x - 7$ **12.** $9x^2 - 30x + 25$
13. $25x^2 - 16y^2$ **14.** $-2x^4 + 6x^3 - 4x^2$ **15.** $x^3 - 8y^3$
16. $2x^4 - 2x^2$ **17.** $(x - 5)(x + 2)$ **18.** $2x(x^2 + 3)$
19. $(x + 4)(3x - 5)$ **20.** $5x^2(x - 1)(x + 1)$
21. $(2x + 1)(x^2 - 5)$ **22.** $(7x - 1)^2$
23. $(x + 2)(x^2 - 2x + 4)$ **24.** $4x^2y^2(y^2 + 2x^2)$
25. $(a - b)(a - 2b)$ **26.** $3; 1$
27. $4m^6 - 16m^3n^2 + 16n^4$ **28.** $(x + 8)(x - 6)$
29. $x(x + 2)$ or $x^2 + 2x$ **30.** $0, 3$ **31.** $-5, \frac{1}{4}$
32. $-2, 0, 2$ **33.** $-1, 1$ **34.** $-1, 3$
35. **(a)** $x(x + 4) = 221$ **(b)** $13, -17$; height is 13 inches.
(c) 60 inches   **36.** **(a)** About $57.5°F$ **(b)** The dew point starts at about $30°F$ in January and increases to a maximum of about $65°F$ in July. Then it decreases to $30°F$ by the end of December.
37. $x^2 + 5x + 6$

	2x	6
2		
x	x^2	$3x$
	x	3

38. After 2 and 4 sec

1. $\frac{15}{4}$ **2.** $\frac{b - a}{a}$ **3.** **(a)** $\frac{1}{x^6y^2}$ **(b)** $\frac{r^2}{81}$ **(c)** $\frac{a^3}{b^{11}}$
4. 58,590   **5.** -27 **6.** $D: x \geq 4$
7.   **8.**

9. **(a)** Yes   **(b)** D: all real numbers; $R: y \geq -4$
(c) $-4, -3$ **(d)** $-1, 3$ **(e)** $-1, 3$
(f) $f(x) = (x + 1)(x - 3)$

10. $y = 2x + 9$ **11.** $f(x) = 2 - 5x$ **12.** $\frac{6}{11}$
13. $\left(-\infty, -\frac{5}{2}\right]$ **14.** $(-\infty, 1) \cup (3, \infty)$ **15.** $\left[0, \frac{4}{7}\right)$
16. $(2, 1)$ **17.** (a) $\{(x, y) \mid x + 2y = -5\}$ (b) $\left(2, \frac{1}{2}\right)$
18.

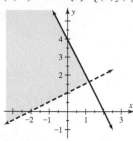

19. $(-4, -1, -3)$ **20.** $(2, 2, 2)$ **21.** -6
22. No solutions   **23.** $-2x^3 + 4x^2 - 10x$
24. $4a^2 - b^2$ **25.** $x^3 + 3x^2 - x - 3$
26. $8x^2 + 14x - 9$ **27.** $x^4 + 6x^2y^3 + 9y^6$
28. $2x^3 - 2x$ **29.** $(x + 3)(x - 11)$
30. $5x(2x - 1)(x + 7)$ **31.** $4(x - 5)(x + 5)$
32. $(7x - 5)^2$ **33.** $r(r - 1)(r^2 + r + 1)$
34. $(x + 2)(x^2 + 1)$ **35.** $-\frac{1}{2}, \frac{1}{2}$ **36.** $-5, \frac{1}{3}$ **37.** $0, 2$
38. $-1, 0, 1$ **39.** -1.1 **40.** $-2.1, 1.5$
41. $2300 at 6%, $1700 at 7%   **42.** (a) 10,550; in 1995
the car cost $10,550   (b) The cost increased, on average,
by $750 per year from 1990 to 2005.   **43.** 12 in. by 12 in.
by 7 in.   **44.** 80°, 60°, 40°

CHAPTER 6: RATIONAL EXPRESSIONS
AND FUNCTIONS

SECTION 6.1 (pp. 412–416)

1. A polynomial divided by a nonzero polynomial; $\frac{x^2 + 1}{3x}$
(answers may vary)   **2.** $x = 4$ **3.** Multiply each side by
$x + 7$.   **4.** No; the equation is undefined when $x = 5$.
5. No, it simplifies to $5 + x$.   **6.** 1   **7.** a **8.** 0
9. Yes   **11.** Yes   **13.** No   **15.** $f(x) = \frac{x}{x + 1}$
17. $f(x) = \frac{x^2}{x - 2}$ **19.** $\{x \mid x \neq -2\}$ **21.** $\{x \mid x \neq \frac{1}{3}\}$
23. $\{t \mid t \neq -2, t \neq 2\}$ **25.** $\{x \mid x \neq 1, x \neq 2\}$
27. $\{x \mid x \neq -2, x \neq 0, x \neq 2\}$
29. $\{x \mid x \neq 1\}$ **31.** $\{x \mid x \neq 0\}$

   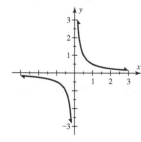

33. $\{x \mid x \neq -2\}$ **35.** $\{x \mid -\infty < x < \infty\}$

37. $\{x \mid x \neq \frac{3}{2}\}$ **39.** $\{x \mid x \neq -1, x \neq 1\}$

41. $-\frac{1}{3}$ **43.** $\frac{1}{2}$ **45.** 3   **47.** $2, 0; x = -1$
49. $0,$ undefined; $x = -2, x = 2$
51.

x	-2	-1	0	1	2
$f(x) = \frac{1}{x - 1}$	$-\frac{1}{3}$	$-\frac{1}{2}$	-1	—	1

; undefined

53. $\frac{3}{5}$ **55.** 1   **57.** -2 **59.** 3   **61.** $-3, 1$ **63.** $-2, 1$
65. 0   **67.** No solutions   **69.** -1 **71.** -4 **73.** -2
75. $-4, 1$ **77.** $0, 2$ **79.** -1 **81.** 2   **83.** $-1.62, 0.62$
85. ab **87.** (a) 19   (b) -9 (c) 150   (d) 0
89. (a) 41   (b) -21 (c) 900   (d) Undefined
91. (a) $2x + 3$ (b) -1 (c) $x^2 + 3x + 2$ (d) $\frac{x + 1}{x + 2}$
93. (a) $x^2 - x + 1$ (b) $1 - x - x^2$ (c) $x^2 - x^3$
(d) $\frac{1 - x}{x^2}$ **95.** c.   **97.** d.   **99.** (a) 6.35; a curve with radius
of 400 feet will have an outer rail elevation of 6.35 inches.
(b)   (c) It is halved.   (d) 508 ft

101. (a) 75; the braking distance is 75 feet when the uphill
grade is 0.05.   (b) 0.15   **103.** (a) 1; when cars are leaving the ramp at a rate of 4 vehicles per minute, the average
wait is 1 minute.   (b) As more cars try to exit, the waiting
time increases; yes.   (c) $4.\overline{6}$ vehicles per minute
105. (a) $P(1) = 0, P(50) = 0.98$; when there is only 1
ball, there is no chance of losing. With 50 balls there is a
98% chance of losing.
(b) $[0, 100, 10]$ by $[0, 1, 0.1]$

(c) It increases; yes, there are more balls without winning numbers.   **(d)** 40 balls

SECTION 6.2 (pp. 425–427)

1. 1   **2.** -1 **3.** No, it is equal to $x + 1$.   **4.** No; no
5. $\frac{2}{3}; \frac{7}{5}$ **6.** $\frac{ac}{bd}$ **7.** $\frac{ad}{bc}$ **8.** $\frac{a}{b}$ **9.** $\frac{2}{5}$ **11.** $-\frac{7}{2}$ **13.** $\frac{3}{4}$
15. $-\frac{1}{22}$ **17.** $\frac{2}{3}$ **19.** -18 **21.** $\frac{5}{x}$ **23.** 3   **25.** $\frac{2}{3}$
27. $x + 1$ **29.** $x - 2$ **31.** $\frac{x}{x + 1}$ **33.** $\frac{3x + 1}{5x - 2}$
35. $\frac{1}{x - 3}$ **37.** $\frac{x}{x + 1}$ **39.** $\frac{3x + 5}{x - 5}$ **41.** $a + b$
43. $m^2 - mn + n^2$ **45.** 1   **47.** -1 **49.** -1 **51.** $\frac{1}{4x}$
53. $\frac{5b}{2a}$ **55.** $\frac{5 - x}{3 - x}$ **57.** $x^2 + 1$ **59.** $\frac{2(x - 1)}{3x^2}$
61. $\frac{(x - 2)(x - 3)}{x(x + 4)}$ **63.** 1   **65.** 3   **67.** 3   **69.** $\frac{x + 1}{x}$
71. $\frac{b^2 + 1}{(b + 1)^2}$ **73.** $\frac{(x - 1)(x + 5)}{2(2x - 3)}$ **75.** $3(n^2 - 3n + 9)$
77. $\frac{(n^2 - 3n + 9)}{4}$ **79.** $\frac{4}{xy}$ **81.** $\frac{y(x - 1)}{2}$ **83.** $\frac{15}{4}$
85. $\frac{24b}{a}$ **87.** $2(n - 1)$ **89.** $\frac{4}{b^3}$ **91.** $\frac{3a(3a + 1)}{a + 1}$
93. $\frac{x^2}{(x - 5)(x^2 - 1)}$ **95.** $\frac{(x - 2)(x - 1)}{(x + 2)^2}$ **97.** 1   **99.** $\frac{15}{y^2}$
101. $\frac{1}{x}$ **103.** $\frac{1}{x - 2}$ **105.** $x - 1$ **107. (a)** $5x + 2$
(b) 32 ft   **109. (a)** $4x^2 + 4x + 1$ **(b)** 21 by 21 by 10

CHECKING BASIC CONCEPTS 6.1 & 6.2 (p. 428)

1. (a) 2   **(b)** $\{x \mid x \ne 1\}$
(c)

$x = 1$

2. (a) $-\frac{1}{2}$ **(b)** $-1, 2$ **3.** $\frac{x - 7}{x - 1}$
4. (a) $\frac{x}{2(x - 1)}$ **(b)** $\frac{x + 3}{3}$

SECTION 6.3 (pp. 437–439)

1. 18   **2.** 18   **3.** $(x - 5)(x + 5)$ **4.** $(x - 5)(x + 5)$
5. A common denominator   **6.** A common denominator
7. $\frac{a + b}{c}$ **8.** $\frac{a - b}{c}$ **9.** 30   **11.** 102   **13.** $18a^2$
15. $50x^2(x - 1)$ **17.** $(x - 5)(x + 1)^2$
19. $(x + y)(x - y)$ **21.** $\frac{5}{7}$ **23.** $\frac{7}{4}$ **25.** $-\frac{1}{5}$ **27.** $\frac{11}{8}$
29. $\frac{4}{x}$ **31.** $\frac{1 - x}{x^2 - 4}$ **33.** $\frac{9}{x^2}$ **35.** $-\frac{3}{xy}$ **37.** 1   **39.** 1
41. $\frac{r}{t^2}$ **43.** $\frac{1}{t - 3}$ **45.** $\frac{4b}{15a}$ **47.** $\frac{n + 4}{(n - 4)(n - 2)}$

49. $\frac{-5x - 4}{x(x + 4)}$ **51.** $\frac{-4x^2 + x + 2}{x^2}$ **53.** $\frac{x^2 + 5x - 34}{(x - 5)(x - 3)}$
55. $-\frac{4(n + 6)}{(n - 3)(n + 3)}$ **57.** $\frac{x(5x + 16)}{(x - 3)(x + 3)}$ **59.** $-\frac{1}{2}$
61. $\frac{6x^2 - 1}{(x - 5)(3x - 1)}$ **63.** $\frac{4x^2 + 4xy - 9x + 9y}{(x - y)(x + y)}$
65. $\frac{4x^2 - x + 3}{(x - 2)(x - 1)(x + 1)}$ **67.** $\frac{x + 15}{(x - 3)(x + 2)(x + 3)}$
69. $\frac{4x - 7}{(x - 2)(x - 1)^2}$ **71.** $\frac{3x^2 - 2x + 3}{(x - 1)^2(x + 3)}$
73. $\frac{-2a^2 + 3b^2 + 4c^2}{abc}$ **75.** $\frac{5n^2 + 3n - 168}{(n - 6)(n + 6)}$
77. $\frac{-2(x^2 - 4x + 2)}{(x - 5)(x - 3)}$ **79.** $\frac{x^2 + x + 5}{(x + 1)(2x - 3)}$
81. $\frac{3}{(x - 1)(x + 1)}$ **83.** $\frac{2(a^2 + b^2)}{(a + b)(a - b)}$ **85.** $1; \frac{1 - x}{x + 1}$
87. $\frac{2x}{(x - 2)(x + 2)}; \frac{-4}{(x - 2)(x + 2)}$ **89.** 60 years
91. $\frac{1200}{19} \approx 63.2$ ohms   **93.** $S \approx 0.101$ foot or about
1.2 inches   **95.** $\frac{16}{d^2}$ watts per square meter

SECTION 6.4 (pp. 448–452)

1. Multiply each side by $x + 2$.   **2.** Multiply each side by
the LCD.   **3.** $\frac{1}{2}$ **4.** bc **5.** LCD   **6.** intersect   **7.** $5x$
9. $x^2 - 1$ **11.** $2(2x + 1)(x - 2)$ **13.** 1   **15.** 5
17. 4   **19.** $-\frac{7}{6}$ **21.** -3 **23.** 1   **25.** 6   **27.** No solutions
29. No solutions   **31.** $-\frac{1}{12}$ **33.** $1, -\frac{1}{2}$ **35.** $-1, 8$
37. 1   **39.** $-\frac{4}{15}, 3$ **41.** 3   **43.** -3 **45.** -10 **47.** $-\frac{1}{2}, \frac{1}{2}$
49. $\frac{a - b}{c}$ **51.** 1   **53.** 2   **55.** 3   **57.** $-3, 1$ **59.** 2.5
61. $-0.4, 0.67$ **63.** ± 1 **65.** 3   **67.** $-\frac{3}{2}, 1$
69. $-3.28, -0.90, 1.18$ **71.** $r = \frac{d}{t}$ **73.** $b = \frac{2A}{h}$
75. $a = \frac{b}{2}$ **77.** $R_1 = \frac{RR_2}{R_2 - R}$ **79.** $x = 15 - \frac{1}{T}$
81. $t = r - 1$ **83.** $b = a(r - 1)$ **85. (a)** About 54
(b) If cars arrive, on average, at 54 per hour, the line will
be, on average, 8 cars long.   **87. (a)** $\frac{x}{5} + \frac{x}{2} = 1$
(b) $\frac{10}{7}$ hours   **(c)** $\frac{10}{7} \approx 1.43$ hours   **89.** Winner: 10 miles
per hour; second place: 8 miles per hour   **91.** 6250 feet
93. 3 miles per hour   **95.** 250 miles per hour   **97.** 3 hr and
6 hr   **99.** 4 mph and 3 mph   **101.** 120 hr   **103.** Yes;
slightly greater than 2

CHECKING BASIC CONCEPTS 6.3 & 6.4 (p. 452)

1. (a) $\frac{1}{x - 1}$ **(b)** $-\frac{2(x - 3)}{x(x - 2)}$ **(c)** $\frac{3}{x(x + 1)(x - 1)}$
2. (a) 4   **(b)** 5   **(c)** $-\frac{1}{4}$ **3.** 8.4 minutes   **4.** $S = \frac{DF}{D - F}$

SECTION 6.5 (pp. 458–460)

1. $\frac{5}{7} \cdot \frac{11}{3} = \frac{55}{21}$ **2.** $\frac{a}{b} \cdot \frac{d}{c}$ **3.** Multiply numerator and
denominator by $x - 1$ (answers may vary).

4. A rational expression with fractions in its numerator, denominator, or both

5. $\dfrac{z + \frac{3}{4}}{z - \frac{3}{4}}$ **6.** $\dfrac{\frac{a}{b}}{\frac{a - b}{a + b}}$ **7.** $\frac{7}{20}$ **9.** 2   **11.** $\frac{32}{21}$ **13.** $\frac{2b}{3}$

15. $\frac{3}{4}$ **17.** $\dfrac{2(n - 1)}{n + 1}$ **19.** $\dfrac{2k + 3}{k - 4}$ **21.** $\frac{3}{2}$ **23.** $\dfrac{x}{x + 4}$

25. $\frac{1}{x}$ **27.** $-\dfrac{x}{2x + 3}$ **29.** $\dfrac{x + 2}{3x - 1}$ **31.** $\dfrac{3(x + 1)}{(x + 3)(2x - 7)}$

33. $\dfrac{4x(x + 5)}{(x - 5)(2x + 5)}$ **35.** $\dfrac{p + q}{q - p}$ **37.** $\dfrac{a + b}{a - b}$ **39.** $\dfrac{2x + 1}{x}$

41. $\frac{5}{27}$ **43.** $\dfrac{mn^2 - 2m^2}{m^2n^2 + 1}$ **45.** $\dfrac{n}{n + 1}$ **47.** $\dfrac{(x - 1)(x + 4)}{x^2 - 4}$

49. $\dfrac{P\left(1 + \frac{r}{12}\right)^{24} - P}{\frac{r}{12}}$ **51.** $R = \dfrac{R_1R_2}{R_1 + R_2}$

SECTION 6.6 (pp. 469–473)

1. A statement that two ratios are equal   **2.** $\frac{5}{6} = \frac{x}{7}$
3. It doubles.   **4.** It is reduced by half.   **5.** constant
6. constant   **7.** kxy **8.** kx^2y^3 **9.** Directly; if the number of people doubled, the food bill would double.
10. Inversely; increasing the number of painters would decrease the time needed to paint the building.
11. 10   **13.** 12   **15.** 72   **17.** $\frac{21}{20}$ **19.** $-\frac{5}{13}$ **21.** $-6, 6$
23. (a) $\frac{7}{9} = \frac{10}{x}$ (b) $x = \frac{90}{7}$ **25.** (a) $\frac{5}{3} = \frac{x}{6}$ (b) $x = 10$
27. (a) $\frac{78}{6} = \frac{x}{8}$ (b) $x = \$104$ **29.** (a) $\frac{2}{90} = \frac{5}{x}$
(b) $x = 225$ minutes   **31.** (a) $k = 2$ (b) $y = 14$
33. (a) $k = 2.5$ (b) $y = 17.5$ **35.** (a) $k = -7.5$
(b) $y = -52.5$ **37.** (a) $k = 20$ (b) $y = 2$
39. (a) $k = 50$ (b) $y = 5$ **41.** (a) $k = 400$
(b) $y = 40$ **43.** (a) $k = 0.25$ (b) $z = 8.75$
45. (a) $k = 11$ (b) $z = 385$ **47.** (a) $k = 10$
(b) $y = 350$
49. (a) Direct   (b) $y = 1.5x$
(c)

51. (a) Neither   (b) N/A   (c) N/A
53. (a) Neither   (b) N/A   (c) N/A
55. (a) Direct   (b) $y = -2bx$ **57.** Direct; $k = 1$
59. Neither   **61.** Direct; $k = 2$ **63.** About 23.1 ft
65. 1.375 inches   **67.** 2000   **69.** 75 ft

71. (a) Direct; the ratios $\frac{R}{W}$ always equal 0.012.
(b) $R = 0.012W$

(c) 38.4 pounds

73. (a) Direct; the ratios $\frac{G}{A}$ always equal 27.
(b) $G = 27A$

(c) For each square-inch increase in the cross-sectional area of the hose, the flow increases by 27 gallons/minute.

75. (a) $F = \dfrac{1200}{L}$ (b) 60 pounds   **77.** (a) Direct
(b) $y = -19x$ (c) Negative; for each 1-mile increase in altitude, the temperature decreases by $19°\text{F}$.   (d) $66.5°\text{F}$
decrease   **79.** About 1.43 ohms   **81.** $z = 0.5104x^2y^3$
83. About 133 pounds   **85.** About 35.2 pounds   **87.** 750

CHECKING BASIC CONCEPTS 6.5 & 6.6 (p. 473)

1. (a) $\dfrac{3x^2 - 1}{3x^2 + 1}$ (b) 1   **2.** (a) $k = 0.75$ (b) $y = 8.25$
3. (a) Direct; $y = 0.4x$ (b) Inverse; $y = \dfrac{120}{x}$

SECTION 6.7 (pp. 480–482)

1. term   **2.** $\frac{a}{c} + \frac{b}{c}$ **3.** 5; 4; 1   **4.** $3x - 5$; $x - 2$; -2
5. No; the divisor is not in the form $x - k$.   **6.** The last number in the third row   **7.** $2x - 3$ **9.** $2x^2 - 3$
11. $2 - \frac{1}{2x} + \frac{1}{2x^2}$ **13.** $3x^2 - 4x - 1$ **15.** $2a^2 - 3$
17. $\frac{4}{3}x^2 - 2$ **19.** $ab - 4 + b$ **21.** $2m^2n^2 + 1 - \dfrac{4}{m^2n^2}$
23. $3x - 7$ **25.** $x^2 - 1 + \dfrac{1}{2x + 3}$ **27.** $10x + 10 + \dfrac{5}{x - 1}$
29. $4x^2 - 1$ **31.** $x^2 - 4x + 19 - \dfrac{80}{x + 4}$
33. $x^2 + 3x - 6 + \dfrac{1}{3x - 1}$ **35.** $a^3 - a$ **37.** $3x + 4$
39. $x + 1 + \dfrac{1}{x^2 - 1}$ **41.** $2a^2 - a + 3 - \dfrac{5}{a^2 - a + 5}$
43. $a^3 - b^3 + 1$ **45.** $x + 4 + \dfrac{3}{x - 1}$ **47.** $3x - 1$
49. $x^2 + 3x + 2$ **51.** $2x^2 + 5x + 10 + \dfrac{19}{x - 2}$
53. $2x^3 - 4x^2 + 11x - 22 + \dfrac{40}{x + 2}$
55. $b^3 + b^2 + b + 1$ **57.** $3x + 5$; 29 ft   **59.** $x + 2$
61. (a) 0; 0   (b) 0; 0   (c) 1; 1   (d) 0; 0   (e) 35; 35
63. (a) 0; yes   (b) 0; yes   (c) -1; no   (d) 0; yes
(e) -9; no

CHECKING BASIC CONCEPTS 6.7 (p. 482)

1. (a) $\frac{2}{x} - 1$ **(b)** $2a - 3 + \frac{5}{a}$ **2.** $5x - 3 + \frac{7}{2x + 1}$

3. (a) $2x^2 - 3x - 3 - \frac{4}{x - 1}$

(b) $2x^2 - 9x + 18 - \frac{37}{x + 2}$

CHAPTER 6 REVIEW (pp. 487–491)

1. $f(x) = \frac{1}{x - 1}$ **2.** $f(x) = \frac{x - 3}{x}$

3. $\{x \mid x \neq -2\}$

4. $\frac{1}{8}; x = \pm 1$ **5.** $-3; 0.75$ **6.** Undefined; 1.2

7. $3; 1; x = 1$ **8.** $2;$ undefined; $x = -2$ **9.** 1   **10.** 2

11. No solutions   **12.** 2   **13. (a)** 12   **(b)** 27

14. (a) $x^2 - x$ **(b)** $x + 1$ **15.** $\frac{2}{3a^3}$ **16.** $\frac{x + 2}{x + 1}$

17. $x + 2$ **18.** $\frac{x - 7}{2x - 3}$ **19.** -1 **20.** 1   **21.** $\frac{y}{4}$

22. $\frac{x + 2}{x + 1}$ **23.** $\frac{x^2 + 1}{(x + 1)^2}$ **24.** $\frac{x + 1}{x - 3}$ **25.** $3y^3$ **26.** $\frac{2}{3}$

27. $\frac{x}{x - 5}$ **28.** $\frac{x + 5}{x + 3}$ **29.** $\frac{x(x + 2)}{(2x - 1)(x + 3)}$

30. $\frac{(x + 1)^2}{(x + 2)(x + 4)}$ **31.** 144   **32.** $4a^2b$ **33.** $18x^2y^3$

34. $(x - 1)(x + 2)$ **35.** $x(x - 3)(x + 3)$

36. $x^2(x - 3)^2$ **37.** $\frac{4}{x + 4}$ **38.** $\frac{x - 1}{x}$ **39.** $\frac{1 - x}{x + 1}$

40. $\frac{2x - 2}{x - 2}$ **41.** $\frac{t - 4}{t - 1}$ **42.** $\frac{8}{(y - 2)(y + 2)}$ **43.** $\frac{4b^3 - 3a^3}{a^2b^2c}$

44. $\frac{r^3 + t^3}{5r^2t^2}$ **45.** $-\frac{2(a - b - 2)}{(a - b)(a + b)}$ **46.** $\frac{a^2 + 2ab - b^2}{(a - b)(a + b)}$

47. $\frac{2x}{(x - 2)(x - 1)(x + 2)}$ **48.** $\frac{6}{(x - 3)(x - 2)(x + 3)}$

49. $\frac{-x^2 + x - 2}{(x - 2)(x + 2)}$ **50.** $\frac{2x - 2}{2x + 1}$ **51.** 3   **52.** 11

53. $-2, 1$ **54.** -2 **55.** $-2, \frac{1}{2}$ **56.** $-\frac{5}{2}$ **57.** 0

58. $0, 1$ **59.** -1 **60.** -1 **61.** 2   **62.** $-2, 3$

63. $y_2 = m(x_2 - x_1) + y_1$ **64.** $a = T(b + 2)$

65. $p = \frac{fq}{q - f}$ **66.** $b = \frac{2a}{aI - 3}$ **67.** $\frac{39}{50}$ **68.** $\frac{2c}{a}$

69. $\frac{4n^2 - 1}{3n^2}$ **70.** $x + y$ **71.** $\frac{2x + 3}{2x - 3}$ **72.** $\frac{2(x + 2)}{x - 8}$

73. $\frac{4 - 5x}{x + 1}$ **74.** $\frac{-3}{x - 9}$ **75.** $\frac{9}{5}$ **76.** $\frac{77}{5}$ **77.** $\frac{3}{2}$ **78.** $\frac{31}{3}$

79. $\frac{7}{3}$ **80.** $\frac{88}{7} \approx 12.6$ **81.** $y = 28$ **82.** $y = 2$

83. $k = 3$ **84.** $z = 720$ **85.** Inverse; $y = \frac{200}{x}$

86. Direct; $y = 3x$ **87.** Direct; $k = \frac{1}{2}$

88. Inverse; $k = 6$ **89.** $2x + 3$ **90.** $2x + 1$

91. $2x - \frac{1}{2} + \frac{1}{x}$ **92.** $\frac{2a}{b} - \frac{3}{a}$ **93.** $2x - 3 + \frac{1}{x + 1}$

94. $x^2 - x + 2 - \frac{3}{x + 1}$ **95.** $2x^2 - x + 1 + \frac{1}{3x - 2}$

96. $2x - 9 + \frac{25x - 39}{x^2 - 2}$ **97.** $2x - 5 - \frac{2}{x - 3}$

98. $3x^2 - 2x + 4 + \frac{3}{x + 4}$

99. (a) $D(0) = 166.\overline{6}$ feet, $D(0.1) = 242.\overline{42}$ feet;

about 75.8 feet   **(b)** $x = 0.05\overline{3}$ or $5.\overline{3}\%$

100. (a)

X	Y1
9	1
9.1	1.1111
9.2	1.25
9.3	1.4286
9.4	1.6667
9.5	2
9.6	2.5

Y1■1/(10−X)

(b) It increases; as vehicles arrive at a faster rate, the wait in line increases.   **101. (a)** About 13 cars   **(b)** As x increases, the number of cars in line increases; yes.

102. (a) 5; initially there were 5000 fish in the lake.

(b) $[0, 6, 1]$ by $[0, 6, 1]$ **(c)** It decreases.   **(d)** After 2 years

103. (a) $\frac{x}{2} + \frac{x}{3} = 1$ **(b)** $\frac{6}{5} = 1.2$ hr   **(c)** $\frac{6}{5} = 1.2$ hr

104. 4 miles per hour   **105.** About 44 minutes

106. About 43.3 feet

107. (a)   Inverse

(b) $R = \frac{12,100}{W}$; $k = 12,100$ **(c)** $R = 220$ ohms

108. (a) $D = 0.06W$; $k = 0.06$ **(b)** 0.42 inch

109. 53°F   **110. (a)** Direct   **(b)** $y = 3.5x$ **(c)** 8.05%

CHAPTER 6 TEST (pp. 492–493)

1. $f(x) = \frac{x}{x + 2}$ **2. (a)** $\frac{1}{15}$ **(b)** $\left\{x \mid x \neq \frac{1}{2}, x \neq -\frac{1}{2}\right\}$

3.

4. $\frac{a}{2}$ **5.** -1 **6.** $\frac{x-5}{2x-7}$ **7.** $\frac{x^2+4}{(x+2)^2}$ **8.** $2y^2$ **9.** $\frac{1}{x+5}$

10. $\frac{2x^2+3x+2}{(x-2)(x+2)}$ **11.** $\frac{5a^3-6b^4}{15ab}$ **12.** $\frac{x^3-2x^2+8}{x^2(x-2)}$

13. $\frac{x+1}{x-1}$ **14.** $\frac{4}{(z+4)^2}$ **15.** $\frac{3x+3}{x-17}$ **16.** $-\frac{2}{3}$ **17.** $-1, 2$

18. 5   **19.** $\frac{1}{2}$ **20.** $m = \frac{Er^2}{G}$ **21.** 0.47   **22.** $0; \frac{1}{x-1}$

23. $\frac{35}{3}$ **24.** $\frac{80}{23}$ **25.** Inverse; $y = \frac{100}{x}$ **26.** Direct; $y = 1.5x$

27. $2a^2 + 5$ **28.** $3x^2 - x + 2 - \frac{6}{x+2}$ **29.** 21.9 feet

30. (a) [0, 25, 5] by [0, 2, 0.5]

$x = 25$

(b) 24 vehicles per minute

31. (a) $\frac{x}{24} + \frac{x}{30} = 1$ **(b)** $\frac{40}{3} \approx 13.3$ hours   **32.** $41.75°$F

CHAPTERS 1–6 CUMULATIVE REVIEW
(pp. 494–496)

1. 9   **2.** 0   **3.** Natural: 1; whole: 0, 1; integer: $-\frac{12}{4}, 0, 1$;
rational: $-\frac{12}{4}, 0, 1, 2.\overline{11}, \frac{13}{2}$; irrational: $\sqrt{3}$ **4.** i

5. $\frac{6y^6}{x^4}$ **6.** $\frac{9d^6}{4c^4}$ **7.** 6.73×10^{10}

8. $D = \{-3, -1, 0, 4\}$
   $R = \{-2, 0, 1, 5\}$

9. $(-2, -7), (-1, -4),$
   $(0, -1), (1, 2), (2, 5)$

10. $(-2, 0), \left(-1, \frac{3}{2}\right), (0, 2),$
   $\left(1, \frac{3}{2}\right), (2, 0)$

11.

12. $\{x \mid x \neq 1\}$ **13.** $f(x) = 2x - 1$

14.

15. $-3; 2$ **16.** -3

17.

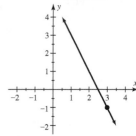

18. $y = -\frac{1}{2}x + 2$ **19.** $y = 2x + 2$ **20.** $y = -\frac{3}{2}x + 4$

21. 4   **22.** $-\frac{7}{29}$ **23.** 3   **24.** $\left(-\infty, -\frac{5}{6}\right]$ **25.** $(0, \infty)$
26. $(-3, 3]$

[number line from −5 to 5, open interval from −3 to 3]

27. $(-\infty, 2] \cup (4, \infty)$

[number line from −5 to 5]

28. $-30, -6$ **29.** $(-4, 7)$ **30.** $(-\infty, -1] \cup [11, \infty)$
31. $(-8, -1)$
32.

33. $\left(\frac{1}{2}, -\frac{1}{2}\right)$ **34.** $(6, 0)$ **35.** $R = 10$ **36.** $(1, 1, 2)$

37. $\begin{bmatrix} 1 & 1 & -1 & | & 4 \\ -1 & -1 & -1 & | & 0 \\ 1 & -2 & 1 & | & -9 \end{bmatrix}; (-1, 3, -2)$

38. 14   **39.** 8 in^2 **40.** $x = -1, y = 2$
41. $3x^5 + 15x^3 - 6x^2$ **42.** $2x^2 + x - 15$ **43.** $-2, 0$
44. $(3a - 1)(a^2 + 5)$ **45.** $(4x - 3)(x + 2)$
46. $3x(x - 2)(2x + 1)$ **47.** $(3a - 2b)(3a + 2b)$
48. $(4t + 3)(16t^2 - 12t + 9)$ **49.** $-\frac{1}{3}, 4$
50. $-5, 0, 6$ **51.** $\frac{x-2}{x+2}$ **52.** $x - 4$ **53.** $\frac{t-4}{t^2-4}$

54. $\frac{4a^2c + 3b^3}{3a^2b^2c}$ **55.** $-\frac{7}{2}$ **56.** -3 **57.** $z = \frac{y}{J-1}$

58. $\frac{4+x}{4-x}$ **59.** $\frac{1}{2}$ **60.** $x^2 - 2x + 6 - \frac{1}{x+2}$

61. 3 **62.** $x - 1$

63. (a) Linear

(b) $f(x) = \frac{5}{9}(x - 32)$ (answers may vary)   (c) $40°C$
64. 6, 6, and 10 inches   **65.** Stair climber: $\frac{1}{2}$ hr; stationary bicycle: 1 hr   **66.** 24 children, 6 adults   **67.** 11 by 15 ft
68. (a) After 2.75 seconds   (b) After 0.5 and 2.25 seconds
69. (a) $\frac{x}{15} + \frac{x}{10} = 1$ (b) 6 hours   **70.** 48 feet

CHAPTER 7: RADICAL EXPRESSIONS AND FUNCTIONS

SECTION 7.1 (pp. 507–509)

1. ± 3 **2.** 3   **3.** 2   **4.** Yes   **5.** b **6.** $x^{1/2}$ **7.** $a^{4/3}$
8. $\sqrt[n]{a}$ **9.** $(\sqrt[n]{a})^m$ or $\sqrt[n]{a^m}$ **10.** Yes   **11.** 3   **13.** 0.6
15. $\frac{4}{5}$ **17.** x **19.** 3   **21.** -4 **23.** $\frac{2}{3}$ **25.** $-x^3$
27. $4x^2$ **29.** 3   **31.** -3 **33.** Not possible   **35.** -2.24
37. 1.71   **39.** -1.48 **41.** 1.74   **43.** 1.71   **45.** 3.74
47. 0.55   **49.** $\sqrt{9}$; 3   **51.** $\sqrt[3]{8}$; 2   **53.** $\sqrt{\frac{4}{9}}$; $\frac{2}{3}$
55. $\sqrt[3]{(-8)^2}$ or $(\sqrt[3]{-8})^2$; 4   **57.** $\sqrt[3]{8}$; 2
59. $\frac{1}{\sqrt[4]{16^3}}$ or $\frac{1}{(\sqrt[4]{16})^3}$; $\frac{1}{8}$ **61.** $\frac{1}{(\sqrt[4]{4})^3}$; $\frac{1}{8}$ **63.** $\sqrt[4]{z}$
65. $\frac{1}{\sqrt[5]{y^2}}$ **67.** $\sqrt[3]{3x}$ **69.** $y^{1/2}$ **71.** x **73.** $2x^{2/3}$
75. $\frac{7}{x^{1/6}}$ **77.** b^3 **79.** x^3 **81.** xy^2 **83.** $\frac{y^2}{x}$
85. $y^{13/6}$ **87.** $\frac{x^4}{9}$ **89.** $\frac{y^3}{x}$ **91.** $y^{1/4}$ **93.** $\frac{1}{a^{2/3}}$
95. $\frac{1}{k^2}$ **97.** $b^{3/4}$ **99.** $p^2 + p$ **101.** $x^{5/6} - x$
103. 4   **105.** $|y|$ **107.** $|x - 5|$ **109.** $|x - 1|$
111. $|y|$ **113.** $|x^3|$ **115.** x **117.** $R \approx 1.17$ miles
119. About 1 step/sec   **121.** $A = 6$

SECTION 7.2 (pp. 515–517)

1. Yes   **2.** No   **3.** $\sqrt[3]{ab}$ **4.** $\frac{a}{b}$ **5.** $\frac{a}{b}$ **6.** $\frac{1}{3}$ **7.** No
8. Yes   **9.** No, since $1^3 \neq 3$ **10.** Yes; $4^3 = 64$
11. 3   **13.** 10   **15.** 4   **17.** $\frac{3}{5}$ **19.** $\frac{1}{4}$ **21.** $\frac{2}{3}$ **23.** x^3
25. $\frac{\sqrt[3]{7}}{3}$ **27.** $\frac{\sqrt[4]{x}}{3}$ **29.** $\frac{3}{2}$ **31.** $\frac{x}{4}$ **33.** 3   **35.** 4   **37.** 3
39. -2 **41.** a **43.** 3   **45.** $2x^2$ **47.** $-a^2\sqrt[3]{5}$
49. $2x\sqrt[4]{y}$ **51.** $6x$ **53.** $2x^2yz^3$ **55.** $\frac{3}{2}$ **57.** $\sqrt[3]{12ab}$

59. $5\sqrt{z}$ **61.** $\frac{1}{a}$ **63.** $\sqrt{x^2 - 16}$ **65.** $\sqrt[3]{a^3 + 1}$
67. $\sqrt{x + 1}$ **69.** 10   **71.** 2   **73.** 3   **75.** $10\sqrt{2}$
77. $3\sqrt[3]{3}$ **79.** $2\sqrt{2}$ **81.** $-2\sqrt[5]{2}$ **83.** $b^2\sqrt{b}$
85. $2n\sqrt{2n}$ **87.** $2ab^2\sqrt{3b}$ **89.** $-5xy\sqrt[3]{xy^2}$
91. $5\sqrt[3]{5t^2}$ **93.** $\frac{3t}{r\sqrt[4]{5r^3}}$ **95.** $\frac{3\sqrt[3]{x^2}}{y}$ **97.** $\frac{7a\sqrt{a}}{9}$
99. $\left(\sqrt[mn]{a^m b^m}\right)^n = (a^m b^m)^{n/mn}$
$= (a^m b^m)^{1/m}$
$= a^{m/m}b^{m/m}$
$= ab$
101. $\sqrt[6]{3^5}$ **103.** $2\sqrt[12]{2^5}$ **105.** $3\sqrt[12]{3^{11}}$ **107.** $x\sqrt[12]{x}$
109. $\sqrt[12]{r^{11}t^7}$ **111.** (a) 400 in^2 (b) $A = 100W^{2/3}$

CHECKING BASIC CONCEPTS 7.1 & 7.2 (p. 517)

1. (a) ± 7 (b) 7   **2.** (a) -2 (b) -3
3. (a) $\sqrt{x^3}$ or $(\sqrt{x})^3$ (b) $\sqrt[3]{x^2}$ or $(\sqrt[3]{x})^2$
(c) $\frac{1}{\sqrt[5]{x^2}}$ or $\frac{1}{(\sqrt[5]{x})^2}$ **4.** $|x - 1|$ **5.** (a) $\frac{1}{8}$ (b) 10
(c) $-2x\sqrt[3]{xy}$ (d) $\frac{4b^2}{5}$ **6.** $\sqrt[6]{7^5}$

SECTION 7.3 (pp. 527–528)

1. $2\sqrt{a}$ **2.** $3\sqrt[3]{b}$ **3.** like
4. Yes; $4\sqrt{15} - 3\sqrt{15} = \sqrt{15}$ **5.** No   **6.** $\frac{\sqrt{7}}{\sqrt{7}}$
7. $\sqrt{t} + 5$ **8.** $\frac{5 + \sqrt{2}}{5 + \sqrt{2}}$ **9.** Not possible
11. $\sqrt{7}, 2\sqrt{7}, 3\sqrt{7}$ **13.** $2\sqrt[3]{2}, -3\sqrt[3]{2}$
15. Not possible   **17.** $2\sqrt[3]{xy}, xy\sqrt[3]{xy}$ **19.** $9\sqrt{3}$
21. $6\sqrt[3]{5}$ **23.** Not possible   **25.** Not possible
27. Not possible   **29.** $5\sqrt[3]{2}$ **31.** $8\sqrt{2}$ **33.** $6\sqrt{11}$
35. $2\sqrt{x} - \sqrt{y}$ **37.** $2\sqrt[3]{z}$ **39.** $-5\sqrt[3]{6}$ **41.** $y^2 - y$
43. $9\sqrt{7}$ **45.** $6\sqrt[4]{3}$ **47.** $7\sqrt{x}$ **49.** $8\sqrt{2k}$
51. $-2\sqrt{11}$ **53.** $5\sqrt[3]{2} - \sqrt{2}$ **55.** $-\sqrt[3]{xy}$
57. $3\sqrt{x + 2}$ **59.** $4x\sqrt{x}$ **61.** $\frac{\sqrt[3]{7x}}{6}$ **63.** $\frac{3\sqrt{3}}{2}$
65. $\frac{71\sqrt{2}}{10}$ **67.** $2\sqrt{2}$ **69.** $(5x - 1)\sqrt[4]{x}$
71. $(8x + 2)\sqrt{x}$ or $2\sqrt{x}(4x + 1)$ **73.** $(3ab - 1)\sqrt[4]{ab}$
75. $(n - 2)\sqrt[3]{n}$ **77.** $x - \sqrt{x} - 6$ **79.** 2   **81.** 119
83. $x - 64$ **85.** $ab - c$ **87.** $x + \sqrt{x} - 56$ **89.** $\frac{\sqrt{7}}{7}$
91. $\frac{4\sqrt{3}}{3}$ **93.** $\frac{\sqrt{5}}{3}$ **95.** $\frac{\sqrt{3b}}{6}$ **97.** $\frac{t\sqrt{r}}{2r}$ **99.** $\frac{3 + \sqrt{2}}{7}$
101. $\sqrt{10} - 2\sqrt{2}$ **103.** $\frac{11 - 4\sqrt{7}}{3}$ **105.** $\sqrt{7} + \sqrt{6}$
107. $\frac{z + 3\sqrt{z}}{z - 9}$ **109.** $\frac{a + 2\sqrt{ab} + b}{a - b}$ **111.** $\sqrt{x + 1} + \sqrt{x}$
113. $\frac{3\sqrt[3]{x^2}}{x}$ **115.** $\frac{\sqrt[3]{x}}{x}$ **117.** $12\sqrt{3} \approx 20.8$ cm

SECTION 7.4 (pp. 537–540)

1.

2.

3. $\{x \mid x \geq 0\}$ **4.** All real numbers   **5.** $f(x) = x^p$, p is rational.   **6.** $f(x) = \sqrt[n]{x}$, where n is an integer greater than 1.   **7.** $\{x \mid x \geq 0\}$ **8.** All real numbers   **9.** 3, Not possible   **11.** $\sqrt{6}$, Not possible   **13.** $2\sqrt{5}$, $\sqrt{6}$ **15.** 1, 2   **17.** $-2, 1$ **19.** -1, $\sqrt[3]{-6}$ or $-\sqrt[3]{6}$ **21.** 4   **23.** 5

25.

x	$\sqrt{x}+1$
-1	—
0	1
1	2
4	3
9	4

27.

x	$\sqrt{3x}$
-1	—
0	0
$\frac{1}{3}$	1
$\frac{4}{3}$	2
3	3

29.

x	$2\sqrt[3]{x}$
-8	-4
-1	-2
0	0
1	2
8	4

31.

x	$\sqrt[3]{x-1}$
-7	-2
0	-1
1	0
2	1
9	2

33. $[-2, \infty)$ **35.** $[2, \infty)$ **37.** $[2, \infty)$ **39.** $(-\infty, 1]$
41. $\left(-\infty, \frac{8}{5}\right]$ **43.** $(-\infty, \infty)$ **45.** $\left(-\frac{1}{2}, \infty\right)$
47.

49.

Shifted 2 units left   Shifted 2 units upward
51.

Shifted 2 units left
53. $f(x) = \sqrt{x}$ **55.** $f(x) = \sqrt[3]{x^2}$ **57.** $f(x) = \frac{1}{\sqrt[5]{x}}$
59. 32; 55.90   **61.** $-\frac{1}{128} \approx -0.01$; 0.04
63. 4; Not possible   **65.** 4; 4
67. [0, 6, 1] by [0, 6, 1]   **69.** [0, 6, 1] by [0, 6, 1]

$g(x)$ $f(x)$
71. $x^p > x^q$ **73. (a)** 6   **(b)** $\sqrt{2x}$ **(c)** $4\,|\,x\,|$
(d) 2   **75.** b.   **77.** c.   **79.** 1 second
81. (a) 6 years   **(b)** The twin in the spaceship will be 4 years younger than the twin on Earth.
83. (a) [0, 5, 1] by [0, 0.5, 0.1]   **(b)** $k \approx 0.16$

(c) [0, 5, 1] by [0, 0.5, 0.1]; yes   **(d)** 0.295 m^2

(answers may vary)

85. (a) $k \approx 0.91$
(b) [0, 1.5, 0.1] by [0, 1, 0.1]

It increases.
(c) About 0.808 m   **(d)** About 0.788; a bird weighing 0.65 kg has a wing span of about 0.788 m.   **87.** 2877 in^2

CHECKING BASIC CONCEPTS 7.3 & 7.4 (p. 540)

1. (a) 6   **(b)** 3   **(c)** $6x^3$ **2. (a)** $7\sqrt{6} + \sqrt{7}$
(b) $5\sqrt[3]{x}$ **(c)** $\sqrt{x}$ **3. (a)** $(y - x)\sqrt[3]{xy}$ **(b)** 14
4. $\frac{\sqrt{6}}{2}$ **5.** $\frac{\sqrt{5}+1}{2}$
6. (a)   **(b)**

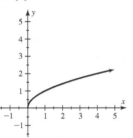

$f(-1)$ is undefined. $f(-1) = -1$
(c)

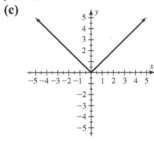

$f(-1) = 1$
7. 3.2   **8.** $[4, \infty)$

SECTION 7.5 (pp. 551–555)

1. Square each side.   **2.** Cube each side.   **3.** Yes
4. Check them.   **5.** Finding an unknown side of a right triangle (answers may vary)   **6.** 5
7. $d = \sqrt{(x_2 - x_1)^2 + (y_2 - y_1)^2}$ **8.** $x^{1/2} + x^{3/4} = 2$
9. 2   **11.** x **13.** $2x + 1$ **15.** $5x^2$ **17.** 64   **19.** 81
21. 6   **23.** 48   **25.** 6   **27.** 3   **29.** 27   **31.** -2
33. 15   **35.** $\frac{1}{2}$ **37.** 0, 1   **39.** 2   **41.** -4 **43.** 9
45. 9   **47.** ± 7 **49.** ± 10 **51.** $-5, 3$ **53.** $-3, 7$
55. 4   **57.** -4 **59.** 1   **61.** $\frac{7}{5}$ **63.** ± 2 **65.** $\sqrt[5]{12}$
67. $-5, 1$ **69.** 3   **71.** 1.88   **73.** $-1, 0.70$ **75.** 1.79
77. -0.47 **79.** 16   **81.** 11   **83.** $L = \frac{8T^2}{\pi^2}$ **85.** $A = \pi r^2$

87. Yes   **89.** Yes   **91.** Yes   **93.** No   **95.** $\sqrt{32} = 4\sqrt{2}$
97. 7   **99.** $c = 5$ **101.** $b = \sqrt{61}$ **103.** $a = 14$
105. $\sqrt{20} = 2\sqrt{5}$ **107.** $\sqrt{4000} = 20\sqrt{10}$ **109.** $\sqrt{89}$
111. 5   **113.** 4   **115.** 2, 122   **117.** $W = 8$ pounds
119. About 3 miles   **121.** About 269 feet
123. 19 inches   **125.** $h \approx 16.3$ inches, $d \approx 33.3$ inches
127. (a) 121 feet   **(b)** About 336 feet
129. (a) About 38 miles per hour; the vehicle involved in the accident was traveling about 38 miles per hour.
(b) About 453 feet   **131. (a)** It increases by a factor of 8.
(b) $v = \sqrt[3]{\frac{W}{3.8}}$ **(c)** 20 mph   **133.** $a\sqrt{2}$

SECTION 7.6 (pp. 562–563)

1. $2 + 3i$ (answers may vary)   **2.** No; any real number a can be written as $a + 0i$.   **3.** i **4.** -1 **5.** $i\sqrt{a}$
6. $10 - 7i$ **7.** $a + bi$ **8.** $1 + 2i$ **9.** 4   **10.** -5
11. 0   **12.** pure   **13.** $i\sqrt{5}$ **15.** $10i$ **17.** $12i$
19. $2i\sqrt{3}$ **21.** $3i\sqrt{2}$ **23.** 3   **25.** $-8 + 7i$
27. $1 - 9i$ **29.** $-10 + 7i$ **31.** $-13 + 13i$
33. $20 - 12i$ **35.** 41   **37.** 20   **39.** $1 + 5i$
41. $3 + 4i$ **43.** $-2 - 6i$ **45.** -2 **47.** $a^2 + 9b^2$
49. $-i$ **51.** i **53.** -1 **55.** 1   **57.** $3 - 4i$ **59.** $6i$
61. $5 + 4i$ **63.** -1 **65.** $1 - i$ **67.** $-\frac{6}{29} + \frac{15}{29}i$
69. $2 + i$ **71.** $-1 + 6i$ **73.** $-1 - 2i$ **75.** $-\frac{3}{2}i$
77. $-\frac{1}{2} + \frac{3}{2}i$ **79.** $\frac{290}{13} + \frac{20}{13}i$

CHECKING BASIC CONCEPTS 7.5 & 7.6 (p. 563)

1. (a) 4   **(b)** 28   **(c)** 3   **2.** 13   **3.** 9.6 inches   **4.** $-3, 1$
5. (a) $8i$ **(b)** $i\sqrt{17}$ **6. (a)** $3 - 4i$ **(b)** $-2 + 3i$
(c) $5 + i$ **(d)** $\frac{3}{4} + \frac{3}{4}i$

CHAPTER 7 REVIEW (pp. 567–570)

1. 2   **2.** 6   **3.** $3|x|$ **4.** $|x - 1|$ **5.** -4
6. -5 **7.** x^2 **8.** $3x$ **9.** 2   **10.** -1 **11.** x^2
12. $x + 1$ **13.** $\sqrt{14}$ **14.** $\sqrt[3]{-5}$ **15.** $\left(\sqrt{\frac{x}{y}}\right)^3$ or $\sqrt{\left(\frac{x}{y}\right)^3}$
16. $\frac{1}{\sqrt[3]{(xy)^2}}$ or $\frac{1}{(\sqrt[3]{xy})^2}$ **17.** 9   **18.** 2   **19.** 64   **20.** 27
21. z^2 **22.** xy^2 **23.** $\frac{x^3}{y^9}$ **24.** $\frac{y^2}{x}$ **25.** 8   **26.** -2
27. x^2 **28.** 2   **29.** $-\frac{\sqrt[3]{x}}{2}$ **30.** $\frac{1}{3}$ **31.** $4\sqrt{3}$ **32.** $3\sqrt{6}$
33. $\frac{3}{x}$ **34.** $4ab\sqrt{2a}$ **35.** $9xy$ **36.** $5z\sqrt[3]{z}$ **37.** $x + 1$
38. $\frac{2a\sqrt[4]{a}}{b}$ **39.** $2\sqrt[6]{x^5}$ **40.** $\sqrt[6]{r^5 t^8}$ or $t\sqrt[6]{r^5 t^2}$ **41.** $4\sqrt{3}$
42. $3\sqrt[3]{x}$ **43.** $-3\sqrt[3]{5}$ **44.** $-\sqrt[4]{y}$ **45.** $11\sqrt{3}$
46. $7\sqrt{2}$ **47.** $13\sqrt[3]{2}$ **48.** $3\sqrt{x + 1}$ **49.** $(2x - 1)\sqrt{x}$
50. $(b + 2a)\sqrt[3]{ab}$ **51.** $5 + 4\sqrt{2}$
52. $7 + 7\sqrt{3} - \sqrt{5} - \sqrt{15}$ **53.** 3   **54.** 95

55. $a - 2b$ **56.** $xy + \sqrt{xy} - 2$ **57.** $\frac{4\sqrt{5}}{5}$ **58.** $\frac{r\sqrt{t}}{2t}$

59. $\frac{3 - \sqrt{2}}{7}$ **60.** $\frac{5 + \sqrt{7}}{9}$ **61.** $\sqrt{8} + \sqrt{7}$

62. $\frac{a - 2\sqrt{ab} + b}{a - b}$

63. **64.**

65. $f(x) = \sqrt{x}; 2$ **66.** $f(x) = \sqrt[3]{x^2}; \sqrt[3]{16}$

67. **68.**

Shifted 2 units downward   Shifted 1 unit to the right

69. $[1, \infty)$ **70.** $(-\infty, 3]$ **71.** $(-\infty, \infty)$ **72.** $(-2, \infty)$

73. 2 **74.** 4 **75.** 9 **76.** 9 **77.** 8 **78.** $\frac{1}{4}$ **79.** 4.5

80. 1.62 **81.** $c = \sqrt{65}$ **82.** $b = \sqrt{39}$ **83.** $\sqrt{41}$

84. $\sqrt{52} = 2\sqrt{13}$ **85.** ± 11 **86.** ± 4 **87.** $-3, 5$

88. 4 **89.** 3 **90.** 2 **91.** ± 4 **92.** -1 **93.** 1

94. $-2, 0$ **95.** -2 **96.** $-2 + 4i$ **97.** $5 + i$

98. $1 + 2i$ **99.** $-\frac{14}{13} + \frac{5}{13}i$ **100.** $2 - 2i$

101. About 85 feet **102.** $\sqrt{16{,}200} = 90\sqrt{2} \approx 127.3$ feet
103. About 0.79 second **104.** **(a)** 5 square units
(b) $5\sqrt{5}$ cubic units **(c)** $\sqrt{10}$ units **(d)** $\sqrt{15}$ units
105. About 0.82 foot **106.** About 0.13 foot; it is shorter.
107. $r = \sqrt[210]{\frac{281}{4}} - 1 \approx 0.02$; from 1790 through 2000 the
average annual percentage growth rate was about 2%.
108. **(a)** About 43 miles per hour **(b)** About 34 miles per
hour; a steeper bank allows for a higher speed limit; yes
109. $\sqrt{7} \approx 2.65$ feet **110.** About 2108 square inches
111. **(a)** $0.5 = \frac{1}{2}$ **(b)** About 0.09, or $\frac{9}{100}$

CHAPTER 7 TEST (pp. 570–571)

1. -3 **2.** $|z + 1|$ **3.** $5x^2$ **4.** $2z^2$ **5.** $2xy\sqrt[4]{y}$

6. 1 **7.** $\sqrt[5]{7^2}$ or $(\sqrt[5]{7})^2$ **8.** $\sqrt[3]{\left(\frac{y}{x}\right)^2}$ or $\left(\sqrt[3]{\frac{y}{x}}\right)^2$ **9.** 16

10. $\frac{1}{216}$ **11.** $x^{4/3}$ **12.** $x^{7/10}$ **13.** $(-\infty, 4]$

14.

15. $8z^{3/2}$ **16.** $\frac{z}{y^{2/3}}$ **17.** 9 **18.** $\frac{y}{2}$ **19.** $4\sqrt{7} + \sqrt{5}$

20. $6\sqrt[3]{x}$ **21.** $14\sqrt{2}$ **22.** 2 **23.** **(a)** 27 **(b)** 7

(c) 3 **(d)** 17 **24.** **(a)** $\frac{2\sqrt{7}}{21}$ **(b)** $\frac{-1 + \sqrt{5}}{4}$ **25.** 2.63

26. $\sqrt{120} \approx 10.95$ **27.** $\sqrt{8} = 2\sqrt{2}$ **28.** $2 - 19i$

29. $-6 + 8i$ **30.** $\frac{5}{4}$ **31.** $\frac{4}{29} + \frac{10}{29}i$ **32.** **(a)** $r = \sqrt[3]{\frac{3V}{4\pi}}$

(b) About 2.29 inches **33.** 1.31 pounds

CHAPTERS 1–7 CUMULATIVE REVIEW (pp. 572–573)

1. 36π **2.** $D = \{-1, 0, 1\}, R = (2, 4\}$

3. **(a)** $\frac{1}{a^3 b^9}$ **(b)** $x^4 x^9$ **(c)** $r^8 t^5$ **4.** 4.3×10^{-4}

5. $3; x \neq 2$ **6.** All real numbers

7. **8.**

9.

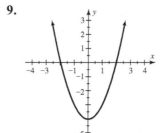

(a) D: all real numbers; $R: y \geq -4$ **(b)** 0 **(c)** $-2, 2$
(d) $-2, 2$ **10.** $y = \frac{1}{2}x + \frac{5}{2}$ **11.** $f(x) = 1 - 3x$
12.

13. $\frac{6}{11}$ **14.** $(-\infty, 3]$ **15.** $[-1, 5]$ **16.** $\left[-\frac{5}{2}, 1\right]$

17. (a) $(4, 4)$ **(b)** No solutions

18.

19. $(3, 2, 1)$ **20.** 4   **21.** $-4x^4 + 16x$ **22.** $x^2 - 16$

23. $5x^2 - 7x - 6$ **24.** $16x^2 + 72x + 81$

25. $(3x - 4)(3x + 4)$ **26.** $(x - 2)^2$ **27.** $3x^2(5x - 3)$

28. $(4x - 3)(3x + 1)$ **29.** $(r - 1)(r^2 + r + 1)$

30. $(x - 3)(x^2 + 5)$ **31.** $1, 2$ **32.** $-2, 0, 2$

33. $2(x + 2)$ **34.** $\frac{7x - 5}{x(x - 1)}$ **35.** $6x$ **36.** 4   **37.** $\frac{1}{64}$

38. 5   **39.** $4x$ **40.** $x^{3/4}$ or $\sqrt[4]{x^3}$ **41.** $2x$ **42.** $6\sqrt{3x}$

43. $2x^2 - \sqrt{3x} - 3$ **44.** $(-\infty, 1]$

45.

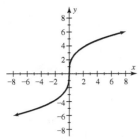

46. $\sqrt{10}$ **47.** $5 + i$ **48.** 13   **49.** 6   **50.** 28

51. $\frac{4}{9}, 4$ **52.** ± 3 **53.** 1.41   **54.** 4.06

55. Water is leaving the tank at 15 gal/min.

56.

57. $1300 at 5%, $700 at 4%   **58.** 8 in. by 8 in. by 4 in.

59. 22.4 feet   **60.** $45°, 55°, 80°$

CHAPTER 8: QUADRATIC FUNCTIONS AND EQUATIONS

SECTION 8.1 (pp. 586–590)

1. parabola   **2.** The vertex

3. axis of symmetry   **4.** $(0, 0)$

5.

6. $-\frac{b}{2a}$ **7.** narrower   **8.** reflected   **9.** $ax^2 + bx + c$ with $a \neq 0$ **10.** vertex   **11.** $0, -4$ **13.** $-2, -2$

15. $(1, -2)$; $x = 1$; upward; incr: $x \geq 1$; decr: $x \leq 1$

17. $(-2, 3)$; $x = -2$; downward; incr: $x \leq -2$; decr: $x \geq -2$

19. (a)

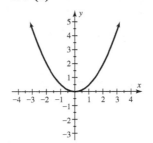

(b) $(0, 0)$; $x = 0$

(c) $2; 4.5$

21. (a)

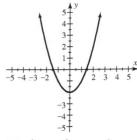

(b) $(0, -2)$; $x = 0$

(c) $2; 7$

23. (a)

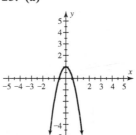

(b) $(0, 1)$; $x = 0$

(c) $-11; -26$

25. (a)

(b) $(1, 0)$; $x = 1$

(c) $9; 4$

27. (a)

(b) $(-2, 0)$; $x = -2$

(c) $0; -25$

29. (a)

(b) $(-0.5, -2.25)$; $x = -0.5$

(c) $0; 10$

31. (a)

(b) $(0, -3); x = 0$
(c) $5; 15$

35. (a)

(b) $(1, 1); x = 1$
(c) $-17; -7$
39. $(2, -6)$ **41.** $(-3, 4)$

47.

Reflected across the *x*-axis
51.

Wider

55. -2; incr: $x \geq -1$; decr: $x \leq -1$
57. $-\frac{25}{4}$; incr: $x \geq \frac{5}{2}$; decr: $x \leq \frac{5}{2}$

33. (a)

(b) $(1, 1); x = 1$
(c) $-8; -3$

37. (a)

(b) $(2, 4); x = 2$
(c) $8; 4.25$
43. $(0, 3)$ **45.** $(1, 1.4)$

49.

Narrower
53.

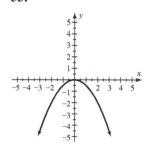

Reflected across the *x*-axis
and wider

59. $-\frac{7}{2}$; incr: $x \geq -\frac{1}{2}$; decr: $x \leq -\frac{1}{2}$
61. 6; incr: $x \leq 1$; decr: $x \geq 1$ **63.** 4; incr: $x \leq 2$;
decr: $x \geq 2$ **65.** $-\frac{39}{8}$; incr: $x \leq \frac{1}{4}$; decr: $x \geq \frac{1}{4}$
67. (a) Upward; wider
(b) $x = -1; (-1, -2)$
(c) *y*-int: $-\frac{3}{2}$; *x*-int: $-3, 1$
(d)

69. (a) Downward; the same
(b) $x = 1; (1, 1)$
(c) *y*-int: 0; *x*-int: $0, 2$
(d)

71. (a) Upward; narrower   **(b)** $x = -\frac{1}{2}; \left(-\frac{1}{2}, -\frac{9}{2}\right)$
(c) *y*-int: -4; *x*-int: $-2, 1$
(d)

73. $10, 10$ **75.** d.   **77.** a.   **79. (a)** 2 feet   **(b)** 2 seconds
(c) 66 feet   **81.** $\frac{66}{32} \approx 2$ seconds; about 74 feet
83. (a) The revenue increases when $x \leq 50$ and it
decreases when $x \geq 50$.   **(b)** $2500; 50$
(c) $f(x) = x(100 - x)$ **(d)** $2500; 50$
85. 300 feet by 600 feet
87. (a) [20, 40, 5] by [0, 30, 5]

(b) About $28.4°C$ **(c)** About $28.4°C$ **89.** 42 in.

SECTION 8.2 (pp. 598–600)

1. $x^2 + 2$ **2.** $(x - 2)^2$ **3.** $(1, 2)$ **4.** $(-1, -2)$
5. $f(x) = ax^2 + bx + c; f(x) = a(x - h)^2 + k$
6. $y = a(x - h)^2 + k; (h, k)$ **7.** downward   **8.** $-\frac{b}{2a}$

9. (a)

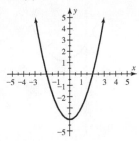

(b) $(0, -4)$
(c) Down 4 units

11. (a)

(b) $(0, 1)$
(c) Narrower and up 1 unit

25. (a)

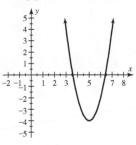

(b) $(5, -4)$
(c) Narrower, right 5 units and down 4 units

27. (a)

(b) $(-3, 1)$
(c) Wider, reflected across the x-axis, left 3 units and up 1 unit

13. (a)

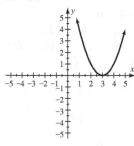

(b) $(3, 0)$
(c) Right 3 units

15. (a)

(b) $(0, 0)$
(c) Reflected across the x-axis

29. Translated 1 unit right, 2 units downward, and is wider

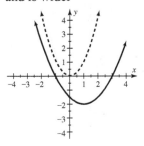

31. Translated 1 unit left, 3 units upward, opens downward, and is narrower

17. (a)

(b) $(0, 2)$
(c) Reflected across the x-axis and up 2 units

19. (a)

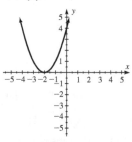

(b) $(-2, 0)$
(c) Left 2 units

33. $[-20, 20, 2]$ by $[-20, 20, 2]$

35. $y = 3(x - 3)^2 + 4; y = 3x^2 - 18x + 31$
37. $y = -\frac{1}{2}(x - 5)^2 - 2; y = -\frac{1}{2}x^2 + 5x - \frac{29}{2}$
39. $y = (x - 1)^2 + 2$ **41.** $y = -(x - 0)^2 - 3$
43. $y = (x - 0)^2 - 3$ **45.** $y = -(x + 1)^2 + 2$
47. $y = (x + 1)^2 - 4; (-1, -4)$
49. $y = (x - 2)^2 + 1; (2, 1)$
51. $y = \left(x + \frac{3}{2}\right)^2 - \frac{17}{4}; \left(-\frac{3}{2}, -\frac{17}{4}\right)$
53. $y = \left(x - \frac{7}{2}\right)^2 - \frac{45}{4}; \left(\frac{7}{2}, -\frac{45}{4}\right)$
55. $y = 3(x + 1)^2 - 4; (-1, -4)$
57. $y = 2\left(x - \frac{3}{4}\right)^2 - \frac{9}{8}; \left(\frac{3}{4}, -\frac{9}{8}\right)$
59. $y = -2(x + 2)^2 + 13; (-2, 13)$ **61.** $a = 2$
63. $a = 0.3$ **65.** $y = 2(x - 1)^2 - 3$
67. $y = 0.5(x - 1980)^2 + 6$

21. (a)

(b) $(-1, -2)$
(c) Left 1 unit and down 2 units

23. (a)

(b) $(1, 2)$
(c) Right 1 unit and up 2 units

69. (a)

(b) $D(x) = \frac{1}{12}x^2$

71. (a) $f(x) = 2(x - 1982)^2 + 1$ (answers may vary)
(b) 201 thousand (answers may vary)

CHECKING BASIC CONCEPTS 8.1 & 8.2 (p. 600)

1. (a)

(b)

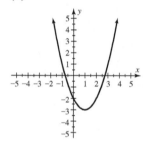

$(0, -2); x = 0$ $(1, -3); x = 1$
2. y_1 opens upward, whereas y_2 opens downward, y_1 is narrower than y_2. **3.** 7; incr: $x \le 2$; decr: $x \ge 2$
4. (a) **(b)**

1 unit right, 2 units up Reflected across the x-axis,
3 units left
5. (a) $y = (x + 7)^2 - 56$ **(b)** $y = 4(x + 1)^2 - 6$

SECTION 8.3 (pp. 610–613)

1. $x^2 + 3x - 2 = 0$ (answers may vary); it can have 0, 1, or 2 solutions **2.** Nonlinear **3.** Factoring, square root property, completing the square

4.

5.

(answers may vary) (answers may vary)
6. Two; the solutions are the x-intercepts. **7.** ± 8; the square root property (answers may vary) **8.** $\left(\frac{b}{2}\right)^2$ **9.** Yes
11. No **13.** Yes **15.** No **17. (a)** $3.65, -1.65$
(b) $1.32, -5.32$ **19. (a)** $1.32, -0.12$ **(b)** $-0.28, -0.83$
21. $-2, 1$ **23.** No real solutions **25.** $-2, 3$ **27.** -0.5
29. $-1, 5$ **31.** $-3, 1$ **33.** $-3, 3$ **35.** $-\frac{1}{2}, \frac{3}{2}$ **37.** -1
39. No real solutions **41.** $-7, 5$ **43.** $-\frac{1}{3}, \frac{1}{2}$ **45.** $1, \frac{3}{2}$
47. $-2, 7$ **49.** $\frac{6}{5}, \frac{3}{2}$ **51.** ± 12 **53.** $\pm\frac{8}{\sqrt{5}}$ or $\pm\frac{8\sqrt{5}}{5}$
55. $-6, 4$ **57.** $-7, 9$ **59.** $\frac{1 \pm \sqrt{5}}{2}$ **61.** $5 \pm \sqrt{5}$
63. 4 **65.** $\frac{25}{4}$ **67.** $16; (x - 4)^2$ **69.** $\frac{81}{4}; \left(x + \frac{9}{2}\right)^2$
71. $-4, 6$ **73.** $-3 \pm \sqrt{11}$ **75.** $\frac{3 \pm \sqrt{29}}{2}$ **77.** $\frac{5 \pm \sqrt{21}}{2}$
79. $1 \pm \sqrt{5}$ **81.** $\frac{3 \pm \sqrt{41}}{4}$ **83.** $\frac{2 \pm \sqrt{11}}{2}$
85. $\frac{-3 \pm \sqrt{5}}{12}$ **87.** $-6, 2$ **89.** $-2 \pm \sqrt{2}$ **91.** $\pm\sqrt{2}$
93. $-5, \frac{7}{3}$ **95.** $4 \pm \sqrt{14}$ **97.** $\pm\sqrt{\frac{c}{a}}$ **99.** $-3, 6$
101. $3, 5$ **103.** $5, 7$ **105.** $y = \pm\sqrt{x + 1}$
107. $v = \pm\sqrt{\frac{2K}{m}}$ **109.** $r = \pm\sqrt{\frac{k}{E}}$ **111.** $f = \pm\frac{1}{2\pi\sqrt{LC}}$
113. (a) 30 miles per hour **(b)** 40 miles per hour
115. About 1.9 seconds; no **117.** About 8 feet
119. 2 hours **121. (a)** $x^2 + 6x - 520 = 0$
(b) -26 or 20; 20 feet **123.** About 23°C and 34°C
125. (a) The rate of increase for each 20-year period is not constant. **(b)** $(1800, 5)$; in 1800 the population was 5 million. **(c)** 1910

SECTION 8.4 (pp. 623–626)

1. To solve quadratic equations that are written in the form $ax^2 + bx + c = 0$ **2.** Completing the square
3. $b^2 - 4ac$ **4.** One solution **5.** Factoring, square root property, completing the square, and the quadratic formula
6. No; not when $b^2 - 4ac < 0$ **7.** ± 2 **8.** $\pm 2i$
9. $-6, \frac{1}{2}$ **11.** 1 **13.** $-2, 8$ **15.** $\frac{1 \pm \sqrt{17}}{8}$
17. No real solutions **19.** $\frac{1}{2}$ **21.** $\frac{3 \pm \sqrt{13}}{2}$
23. $2 \pm \sqrt{3}$ **25.** $\frac{1 \pm \sqrt{37}}{6}$ **27.** $\frac{1 \pm \sqrt{15}}{2}$

29. $\dfrac{5 \pm \sqrt{10}}{3}$ **31. (a)** $a > 0$ **(b)** $-1, 2$ **(c)** Positive
33. (a) $a > 0$ **(b)** No real solutions   **(c)** Negative
35. (a) $a < 0$ **(b)** 2   **(c)** Zero   **37. (a)** 25   **(b)** 2
39. (a) 0   **(b)** 1   **41. (a)** $-\dfrac{7}{4}$ **(b)** 0   **43. (a)** 21
(b) 2   **45.** $1 \pm \sqrt{2}$ **47.** $-\dfrac{3}{2}, 1$ **49.** None   **51.** None
53. $\dfrac{-2 \pm \sqrt{10}}{3}$ **55.** $\pm 3i$ **57.** $\pm 4i\sqrt{5}$ **59.** $\pm \dfrac{1}{2}i$
61. $\pm \dfrac{3}{4}i$ **63.** $\pm i\sqrt{6}$ **65.** $\pm \sqrt{3}$ **67.** $\pm i\sqrt{2}$
69. $\dfrac{1}{2} \pm i\dfrac{\sqrt{7}}{2}$ **71.** $-\dfrac{3}{4} \pm i\dfrac{\sqrt{23}}{4}$ **73.** $2 \pm \sqrt{3}$
75. $-\dfrac{1}{2} \pm i\dfrac{\sqrt{7}}{2}$ **77.** $-\dfrac{1}{5} \pm i\dfrac{\sqrt{19}}{5}$ **79.** $-\dfrac{3}{4} \pm i\dfrac{\sqrt{23}}{4}$
81. $-\dfrac{1}{2} \pm i\dfrac{\sqrt{15}}{2}$ **83.** $\dfrac{1 \pm \sqrt{3}}{2}$ **85.** $\dfrac{1}{4} \pm i\dfrac{\sqrt{15}}{4}$
87. 1, 2   **89.** $-\dfrac{1}{2}, 4$ **91.** $\dfrac{5 \pm \sqrt{17}}{2}$ **93.** $-\dfrac{1}{4} \pm \dfrac{3}{4}i\sqrt{7}$
95. $\pm \dfrac{1}{2}$ **97.** $\pm i\sqrt{2}$ **99.** $\dfrac{1}{3}$ **101.** 9 miles per hour
103. 45 miles per hour   **105.** $x \approx 8.04$, or about 1992; this
agrees with the graph.   **107.** 30 mi, 40 mi   **109. (a)–(c)** 11 in.
by 14 in.   **111. (a)** The rate of change is not constant.
(b) 75 seconds (answers may vary)   **(c)** 75 seconds

CHECKING BASIC CONCEPTS 8.3 & 8.4 (p. 627)

1. $\dfrac{1}{2}, 3$ **2.** $\pm \sqrt{5}$ **3.** $2 \pm \sqrt{3}$ **4.** $y = \pm \sqrt{1 - x^2}$
5. (a) $\dfrac{3 \pm \sqrt{17}}{4}$ **(b)** $\dfrac{4}{3}$ **(c)** $-\dfrac{1}{2} \pm i\dfrac{\sqrt{7}}{2}$
6. (a) 5; two real solutions   **(b)** -7; no real solutions
(c) 0; one real solution

SECTION 8.5 (pp. 633–636)

1. It has an inequality symbol rather than an equals sign.
2. No, they often have infinitely many.   **3.** No   **4.** Yes
5. $-2 < x < 4$ **6.** $x < -3$ or $x > 1$ **7.** Yes   **9.** Yes
11. No   **13.** Yes   **15.** No   **17.** No   **19. (a)** $-3, 2$
(b) $-3 < x < 2$ **(c)** $x < -3$ or $x > 2$ **21. (a)** $-2, 2$
(b) $-2 < x < 2$ **(c)** $x < -2$ or $x > 2$ **23. (a)** $-10, 5$
(b) $x < -10$ or $x > 5$ **(c)** $-10 < x < 5$
25. (a) $-2, 2$ **(b)** $-2 < x < 2$ **(c)** $x < -2$ or $x > 2$
27. (a) $-4, 0$ **(b)** $-4 < x < 0$ **(c)** $x < -4$ or $x > 0$
29. $(-3, -1)$ **31.** $(-\infty, -2.5] \cup [3, \infty)$ **33.** $[-2, 2]$
35. $(-\infty, \infty)$ **37.** $(0, 3)$ **39.** No real solutions   **41.** 2
43. $(-\infty, -1) \cup (-1, \infty)$ **45.** $[-1, 2]$ **47. (a)** $-2, 2$
(b) $-2 < x < 2$ **(c)** $x < -2$ or $x > 2$
49. (a) $\dfrac{-1 \pm \sqrt{5}}{2}$ **(b)** $\dfrac{-1 - \sqrt{5}}{2} < x < \dfrac{-1 + \sqrt{5}}{2}$
(c) $x < \dfrac{-1 - \sqrt{5}}{2}$ or $x > \dfrac{-1 + \sqrt{5}}{2}$
51. $[-7, -3]$ **53.** $(-\infty, 1) \cup (2, \infty)$
55. $(-\sqrt{10}, \sqrt{10})$ **57.** $(-\infty, 0) \cup (6, \infty)$
59. $(-\infty, 2 - \sqrt{2}] \cup [2 + \sqrt{2}, \infty)$ **61.** $[-0.128, 0.679]$
63. (a) From 1131 feet to 3535 feet (approximately)
(b) Before 1131 feet or after 3535 feet (approximately)

65. (a) About 383; they agree (approx.).   **(b)** About 1969
or after   **(c)** About 1969 or after   **67.** From 11 feet to 20 feet

SECTION 8.6 (p. 640)

1. $\pm 1, \pm \sqrt{6}$ **3.** $-\sqrt[3]{2}, \sqrt[3]{\dfrac{5}{3}}$ **5.** $-\dfrac{4}{5}, -\dfrac{1}{3}$
7. $-3, 3$ **9.** $-\sqrt[3]{\dfrac{1}{3}}, \sqrt[3]{2}$ **11.** $-\dfrac{1}{8}, \dfrac{2}{5}$ **13.** 1
15. $1, 32^5 = 33{,}554{,}432$ **17.** 16, 81   **19.** 1
21. $-3, 6$ **23.** $-\sqrt{3}, \sqrt{3}$ **25.** $\pm 2, \pm 2i$ **27.** $0, \pm i$
29. $\pm \sqrt{2}, \pm i$ **31.** $-1 \pm i$ **33.** $\pm 2i$

CHECKING BASIC CONCEPTS 8.5 & 8.6 (p. 640)

1. $(-\infty, -2) \cup (3, \infty)$ **2.** $\left[-1, -\dfrac{2}{3}\right]$ **3.** $-2, \sqrt[3]{2}$
4. $-1, 8^3 = 512$ **5.** $\pm i$

CHAPTER 8 REVIEW (pp. 643–647)

1. $(-3, 4)$; $x = -3$; downward; incr: $x \le -3$;
decr: $x \ge -3$ **2.** $(1, 0)$; $x = 1$; upward; incr: $x \ge 1$;
decr: $x \le 1$

3. (a)

4. (a)

(b) $(0, -2)$; $x = 0$ **(b)** $(2, 1)$; $x = 2$
(c) -1 **(c)** 0

5. (a)

6. (a)

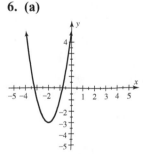

(b) $(1, 2)$; $x = 1$ **(b)** $(-2, -3)$; $x = -2$
(c) -2.5 **(c)** -1
7. $-\dfrac{7}{2}$ **8.** $-\dfrac{14}{3}$ **9.** $(2, -6)$ **10.** $(0, 5)$ **11.** $(2, 2)$
12. $(-1, 1)$

13. (a)

(b) Up 2 units

14. (a)

(b) Narrower

15. (a)

(b) Right 2 units

16. (a)

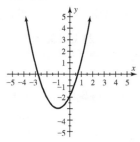

(b) Left 1 unit, down 3 units

17. (a)

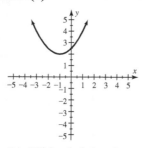

(b) Wider, left 1 unit, up 2 units

18. (a)

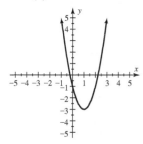

(b) Narrower, right 1 unit, down 3 units

19. $y = -4(x - 2)^2 - 5$ **20.** $y = -(x + 4)^2 + 6$

21. $y = (x + 2)^2 - 11; (-2, -11)$

22. $y = \left(x - \frac{7}{2}\right)^2 - \frac{45}{4}; \left(\frac{7}{2}, -\frac{45}{4}\right)$

23. $y = 2\left(x - \frac{3}{4}\right)^2 - \frac{73}{8}; \left(\frac{3}{4}, -\frac{73}{8}\right)$

24. $y = 3(x + 1)^2 - 5; (-1, -5)$ **25.** $a = 3$

26. $a = \frac{1}{4}$ **27.** $f(x) = -5x^2 + 30x - 41; -41$

28. $f(x) = 3x^2 + 12x + 8; 8$ **29.** $-2, 3$ **30.** -1

31. No real solutions **32.** $-4, 6$ **33.** $-10, 5$

34. $-0.5, 0.25$ **35.** $-5, 10$ **36.** $-3, 1$ **37.** $-4, 2$

38. $-1, 3$ **39.** $-5, 4$ **40.** $-8, -3$ **41.** $-\frac{2}{5}, \frac{2}{3}$

42. $\frac{4}{7}, 3$ **43.** ± 10 **44.** $\pm\frac{1}{3}$ **45.** $\pm\frac{\sqrt{6}}{2}$ **46.** No real

solutions **47.** $-3\pm\sqrt{7}$ **48.** $2 \pm \sqrt{10}$ **49.** $1 \pm \sqrt{6}$

50. $\frac{-3 \pm \sqrt{11}}{2}$ **51.** $R = -r \pm \sqrt{\frac{k}{F}}$

52. $y = \pm\sqrt{\frac{12 - 2x^2}{3}}$ **53.** $3, 6$ **54.** $11, 13$ **55.** $-\frac{1}{2}, \frac{1}{3}$

56. $\frac{5 \pm \sqrt{5}}{10}$ **57.** $4 \pm \sqrt{21}$ **58.** $\frac{3 \pm \sqrt{3}}{2}$

59. ± 2 **60.** $\pm\frac{1}{2}$ **61.** $\frac{5}{2}, 3$ **62.** $\frac{3}{2}, 5$ **63.** $\frac{3 \pm \sqrt{5}}{2}$

64. $\frac{1 \pm \sqrt{5}}{4}$ **65. (a)** $a > 0$ **(b)** $-2, 3$ **(c)** Positive

66. (a) $a > 0$ **(b)** 2 **(c)** Zero **67. (a)** $a < 0$

(b) No real solutions **(c)** Negative **68. (a)** $a < 0$

(b) $-4, 2$ **(c)** Positive **69. (a)** 1 **(b)** 2 **70. (a)** 144

(b) 2 **71. (a)** -23 **(b)** 0 **72. (a)** 0 **(b)** 1

73. $-\frac{1}{2} \pm i\frac{\sqrt{19}}{2}$ **74.** $\pm 2i$ **75.** $\frac{1}{4} \pm i\frac{\sqrt{7}}{4}$ **76.** $\frac{1}{7} \pm i\frac{\sqrt{34}}{7}$

77. (a) $-2, 6$ **(b)** $-2 < x < 6$ **(c)** $x < -2$ or $x > 6$

78. (a) $-2, 0$ **(b)** $x < -2$ or $x > 0$ **(c)** $-2 < x < 0$

79. (a) $-4, 4$ **(b)** $-4 < x < 4$ **(c)** $x < -4$ or $x > 4$

80. (a) $-2, 1$ **(b)** $-2 < x < 1$ **(c)** $x < -2$ or $x > 1$

81. (a) $-1, 3$ **(b)** $-1 < x < 3$ **(c)** $x < -1$ or $x > 3$

82. (a) $-\frac{3}{2}, 5$ **(b)** $-\frac{3}{2} \leq x \leq 5$ **(c)** $x \leq -\frac{3}{2}$ or $x \geq 5$

83. $[-3, -1]$ **84.** $\left(\frac{1}{5}, 3\right)$ **85.** $\left(-\infty, \frac{1}{6}\right) \cup (2, \infty)$

86. $(-\infty, -\sqrt{5}] \cup [\sqrt{5}, \infty)$ **87.** $(-\infty, \infty)$ **88.** No

solutions **89.** $\pm\sqrt{5}, \pm 3$ **90.** $-\frac{1}{4}, \frac{2}{7}$ **91.** $1, 512$ **92.** 0

93. $\pm i\frac{\sqrt{2}}{2}$ **94.** $2 \pm i\sqrt{2}$ **95. (a)** $f(x) = x(12 - 2x)$

(b) 6 inches by 3 inches **96. (a)** After 1 second and

1.75 seconds **(b)** 1.375 seconds; 34.25 feet

97. (a) $f(x) = x(90 - 3x)$

(b) [0, 30, 5] by [0, 800, 100]

(c) 10 or 20 rooms **(d)** 15 rooms

98. (a) 2.4; in 1999, there were 2.4 complaints per

100,000 passengers.

(b) [1997, 1999, 1] by [0.5, 3, 0.5]

Complaints have increased.

99. (a) $\sqrt{1728} \approx 41.6$ miles per hour **(b)** 60 miles per

hour **100. (a)** $x(x + 2) = 143$ **(b)** $x = -13$ or

$x = 11$; the numbers are -13 and -11 or 11 and 13.

101. (a) [1935, 1995, 10] by [0, 100, 10]

(b) Yes, the data are nearly linear.

(c) $f(x) = 1.04(x - 1940) + 25$ (answers may vary)

(d) 82%, 93%; answers may vary.

102. (a) (1950, 220); in 1950, the per capita consumption was at a low of 220 million Btu.

(b) [1950, 1970, 5] by [200, 350, 25]

It increased.

(c) $f(1996) = 749$; no; the trend represented by this model did not continue after 1970.

103. About 11.1 inches by 11.1 inches   **104.** 50 feet

105. About 1.5 feet   **106.** About 6.0 to 9.0 inches

CHAPTER 8 TEST (pp. 647–648)

1. $\left(1, \frac{3}{2}\right); x = 1; -3$ **2.** $-\frac{29}{4}$ **3.** $a = -\frac{1}{2}$

4.

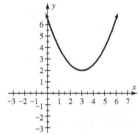

It is wider, shifted right 3 units and upward 2 units.

5. $y = (x - 3)^2 - 7; (3, -7); x = 3$ **6.** $-1, 2; 2$

7. $-4, \frac{1}{3}$ **8.** $-\frac{1}{2}, \frac{1}{2}$ **9.** $4 \pm \sqrt{17}$ **10.** $\frac{3 \pm \sqrt{17}}{4}$

11. $\pm\frac{4}{3}$ **12.** $m = \pm\sqrt{\frac{Fr^2}{G}}$ **13. (a)** $a < 0$ **(b)** $-3, 1$

(c) Positive   **14. (a)** -44 **(b)** No real solutions

(c) The graph of $y = -3x^2 + 4x - 5$ does not intersect the x-axis.   **15. (a)** $-1, 1$ **(b)** $-1 < x < 1$

(c) $x < -1$ or $x > 1$ **16. (a)** $-10, 20$

(b) $x < -10$ or $x > 20$ **(c)** $-10 < x < 20$

17. (a) $-\frac{1}{2}, \frac{3}{4}$ **(b)** $\left[-\frac{1}{2}, \frac{3}{4}\right]$ **(c)** $\left(-\infty, -\frac{1}{2}\right] \cup \left[\frac{3}{4}, \infty\right)$

18. $[-2, 0]$ **19.** $\sqrt[3]{2}, 1$ **20.** $-1 \pm i\frac{\sqrt{2}}{2}$

21. $-1.37, 0.69$ **22.** $\sqrt{2250} \approx 47.4$ miles per hour

23. (a) $f(x) = (x + 20)(90 - x)$ **(b)** 35

24. (a) [0, 6, 1] by [0, 150, 50]

Maximum
X=2.7499999 Y=129

(b) After about 5.6 seconds   **(c)** 2.75 seconds; 129 feet

CHAPTERS 1–8 CUMULATIVE REVIEW (pp. 651–652)

1. 1   **2.** Natural: $\sqrt[3]{8}$; whole: 0, $\sqrt[3]{8}$; integer: 0, -5, $\sqrt[3]{8}$;

rational: $0.\overline{4}, 0, -5, \sqrt[3]{8}, -\frac{4}{3}$; irrational: $\sqrt{7}$ **3. (a)** $x^{10}y^{12}$

(b) $\frac{x}{y^8}$ **(c)** $\frac{1}{b^{10}}$ **4.** 9.29×10^6 **5.** $2; x \le 2$ **6.** $(2, 5)$

7.

8.

9. $y = -\frac{3}{2}x + 5$ **10.** $x = -3$ **11.** -12

12. $\left(-\infty, \frac{7}{4}\right)$ **13.** $\left[\frac{1}{3}, 1\right]$ **14.** $(-1, 5]$ **15.** $(-1, 1)$

16.

17. $(2, 2, 1)$ **18.** $6x^2 + 17x - 14$ **19.** $3x^3y + 3xy^3$

20. $x - 9$ **21.** $x(x + 1)(x - 2)$ **22.** $(2x + 5)(2x - 5)$

23. $\pm\sqrt{3}$ **24.** 1   **25.** $\frac{1}{2}(x + 3)$ **26.** $-\frac{2}{x(x + 2)}$

27. $4x^3$ **28.** $\frac{1}{64}$ **29.** 3   **30.** $3\sqrt{2x}$

31.

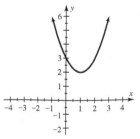

32. $\sqrt{26}$ **33.** $1 - i$ **34.** 3   **35.** 0.79

36.

(a) $(1, 2)$ **(b)** 6   **(c)** $x = 1$ **(d)** $x \ge 1$

37. $f(x) = 2(x - 1)^2 - 3$ **38.** Shifted 1 unit left, 2 units downward; narrower   **39.** $-3 \pm \sqrt{11}$ **40.** $\frac{3 \pm \sqrt{17}}{4}$

41. 1, 3   **42. (a)** $-2, 1$ **(b)** $-2 \le x \le 1$

43. $x < 1$ or $x > 2$ **44.** $\pm 4, \pm 4i$ **45.** c.   **46.** f.

47. g.   **48.** e.   **49.** d.   **50.** a.   **51.** b.   **52.** h.

53. (a) 300; initially, the tank holds 300 gal.
(b) 6; after 6 minutes the tank is empty.   **(c)** -50; water
is pumped out at 50 gal/min.   **(d)** $G(t) = 300 - 50t$
54. $2200 at 6%, $1200 at 5%, $600 at 4%
55. 125 ft by 125 ft   **56.** 33 feet

GLOSSARY

absolute value A real number a, written $|a|$, is equal to its distance from the origin on the number line.

absolute value equation An equation that contains an absolute value.

absolute value function The function defined by $f(x) = |x|$.

absolute value inequality An inequality that contains an absolute value.

addends In an addition problem, the two numbers that are added.

addition property of equality If a, b, and c are real numbers, then $a = b$ is equivalent to $a + c = b + c$.

additive identity The number 0.

additive inverse (opposite) The additive inverse or opposite of a real number a is $-a$.

adjacency matrix A matrix used to represent a map showing distances between cities.

algebraic expression An expression consisting of numbers, variables, arithmetic symbols, and grouping symbols, such as parentheses, brackets, and square roots.

annuity A sum of money from which regular payments are made.

approximately equal The symbol $\approx$ indicates that two quantities are nearly equal.

arithmetic sequence A linear function given by $a_n = dn + c$ whose domain is the set of natural numbers.

arithmetic series The sum of the terms of an arithmetic sequence.

associative property for addition For any real numbers a, b, and c, $(a + b) + c = a + (b + c)$.

associative property for multiplication For any real numbers a, b, and c, $(a \cdot b) \cdot c = a \cdot (b \cdot c)$.

asymptotes of a hyperbola The two lines determined by the diagonals of the hyperbola's fundamental rectangle.

augmented matrix A matrix used to represent a system of linear equations; a vertical line is positioned in the matrix where the equals signs occur in the system of equations.

average The result of adding up the numbers of a set and then dividing the sum by the number of elements in the set.

axis of symmetry of a parabola The line passing through the vertex of the parabola that divides the parabola into two symmetric parts.

base The value of a in the expression a^x.

basic principle of fractions When simplifying fractions, the principle which states $\frac{a \cdot c}{b \cdot c} = \frac{a}{b}$.

binomial A polynomial with two terms.

binomial coefficient The expression $_nC_r$ that can be used to calculate the numbers in Pascal's triangle.

binomial theorem A theorem that provides a formula to expand expressions of the form $(a + b)^n$.

branches A hyperbola has two branches, a left branch and a right branch, or an upper branch and a lower branch.

break-even point The point at which the cost of producing an item equals the revenue made from selling it.

byte A unit of computer memory, capable of storing one letter of the alphabet.

Cartesian coordinate system (xy-plane) The xy-plane used to plot points and visualize a relation; points are identified by ordered pairs.

center of a circle The point that is a fixed distance from all the points on a circle.

circle The set of points in a plane that are a constant distance from a fixed point called the center.

clearing fractions The process of multiplying both sides of an equation by a common denominator to eliminate the fractions.

coefficient The numeric constant in a monomial.

common denominator A number or expression that each denominator can divide into *evenly* (without a remainder).

common difference The value of d in an arithmetic sequence, $a_n = dn + c$.

common logarithmic function The function given by $f(x) = \log x$.

common logarithm of a positive number x Denoted $\log x$, it may be calculated as follows: if x is expressed as $x = 10^k$, then $\log x = k$, where k is a real number. That is, $\log 10^k = k$.

common ratio The value of r in a geometric sequence, $a_n = a_1(r)^{n-1}$.

commutative property for addition For any real numbers a and b, $a + b = b + a$.

commutative property for multiplication For any real numbers a and b, $a \cdot b = b \cdot a$.

completing the square An important technique in mathematics that involves adding a constant to a binomial so that a perfect square trinomial results.

complex conjugate The complex conjugate of $a + bi$ is $a - bi$.

complex fraction A rational expression that contains fractions in its numerator, denominator, or both.

complex number A complex number can be written in standard form as $a + bi$, where a and b are real numbers and i is the imaginary unit.

compound inequality Two inequalities joined by the words *and* or *or*.

conic section The curve formed by the intersection of a plane and a cone.

conjugate The conjugate of $a + b$ is $a - b$.

consistent system A system of linear equations with at least one solution.

constant function A linear function of the form $f(x) = b$, where b is a constant.

constant of proportionality (constant of variation) In the equation $y = kx$, the number k.

constraint In linear programming, an inequality that limits the objective function.

continuous growth Growth in a quantity that is directly proportional to the amount present.

contradiction An equation that is always false, regardless of the values of any variables.

Cramer's rule A method that uses determinants to solve linear systems of equations.

cubed Process of raising a number or variable to the third power.

cube root The number b is a cube root of a number a if $b^3 = a$.

cube root function The function defined by $g(x) = \sqrt[3]{x}$.

cubic polynomial A polynomial of degree 3 that can be written as $ax^3 + bx^2 + cx + d$, where $a \neq 0$.

decay factor The value of a in an exponential function, $f(x) = Ca^x$, where $0 < a < 1$.

degree of a monomial The sum of the exponents of the variables.

degree of a polynomial The degree of the monomial with highest degree.

dependent equations Equations in a linear system that have the same solution set.

dependent variable The variable that represents the output of a function.

determinant A real number associated with a square matrix.

diagrammatic representation A function represented by a diagram.

difference The answer to a subtraction problem.

difference of two cubes Expression in the form $a^3 - b^3$, which can be factored as $(a - b)(a^2 + ab + b^2)$.

difference of two squares Expression in the form $a^2 - b^2$, which can be factored as $(a - b)(a + b)$.

dimension of a matrix The size expressed in number of rows and columns. For example, if a matrix has m rows and n columns, its dimension is $m \times n$ (m by n).

directly proportional A quantity y is directly proportional to x if there is a nonzero number k such that $y = kx$.

discriminant The expression $b^2 - 4ac$ in the quadratic formula.

distance formula The distance between the points (x_1, y_1) and (x_2, y_2) in the xy-plane is $d = \sqrt{(x_2 - x_1)^2 + (y_2 - y_1)^2}$.

distributive properties For any real numbers a, b, and c, $a(b + c) = ab + ac$ and $a(b - c) = ab - ac$.

dividend In a division problem, the number being divided.

divisor In a division problem, the number being divided *into* another.

domain The set of all x-values of the ordered pairs in a relation.

element Each number in a matrix.

elimination (or addition) method A symbolic method used to solve a system of equations that is based on the property that "equals added to equals are equal."

ellipse The set of points in a plane, the sum of whose distances from two fixed points is constant.

equation A statement that two algebraic expressions are equal.

equivalent equations Two equations that have the same solution set.

even root The nth root, $\sqrt[n]{a}$, where n is even.

expansion of a determinant by minors A method of finding a 3×3 determinant by using determinants of 2×2 matrices.

exponent The value of a in the expression b^a.

exponential decay When $0 < a < 1$, the graph of $f(x) = Ca^x$ models exponential decay.

exponential equation An equation that has a variable as an exponent.

exponential expression An expression that has an exponent.

exponential function with base a and coefficient C A function represented by $f(x) = Ca^x$, where $a > 0$, $C > 0$, and $a \neq 1$.

exponential growth When $a > 1$, the graph of $f(x) = Ca^x$ models exponential growth.

extraneous solution A solution that does not satisfy the given equation.

factors In a multiplication problem, the two numbers multiplied.

factorial notation $n! = 1 \cdot 2 \cdot 3 \cdot \cdots \cdot n$ for any positive integer n.

factoring by grouping A technique that uses the distributive property by grouping four terms of a polynomial in such a way that the polynomial can be factored even though its greatest common factor is 1.

feasible solutions In linear programming, the set of solutions that satisfies the constraints.

finite sequence A function with domain $D = \{1, 2, 3, \ldots, n\}$ for some fixed natural number n.

finite series A series that contains a finite number of terms, and can be expressed in the form $a_1 + a_2 + a_3 + \cdots + a_n$ for some n.

focus (plural foci) A fixed point used to determine the points that form a parabola, an ellipse, or a hyperbola.

FOIL A method for multiplying two binomials $(A + B)$ and $(C + D)$. Multiply First terms AC, Outer terms AD, Inner terms BC, and Last terms BD; then combine like terms.

formula An equation that can be used to calculate one quantity by using a known value of another quantity.

function A relation where each element in the domain corresponds to exactly one element in the range.

function notation $y = f(x)$ is read "y equals f of x". This means that function f with input x produces output y.

fundamental rectangle of a hyperbola The rectangle whose four vertices are determined by either $(\pm a, \pm b)$ or $(\pm b, \pm a)$, where $\frac{x^2}{a^2} - \frac{y^2}{b^2} = 1$ or $\frac{y^2}{a^2} - \frac{x^2}{b^2} = 1$.

Gauss–Jordan elimination A numerical method used to solve a linear system in which matrix row transformations are used.

general term (nth term) of a sequence a_n where n is a natural number in the domain of a sequence $a_n = f(n)$.

geometric sequence A function given by $a_n = a_1(r)^{n-1}$ whose domain is the set of natural numbers.

graphical representation A graph of a function.

graphical solution A solution to an equation obtained by graphing.

greater than If a real number a is located to the right of a real number b on the number line, a is greater than b, or $a > b$.

greatest common factor (GCF) The term with the highest degree and largest coefficient that is a factor of all terms in the polynomial.

growth factor The value of a in the exponential function, $f(x) = Ca^x$, where $a > 1$.

half-life The time it takes for a radioactive sample to decay to half its original amount.

hyperbola The set of points in a plane, the difference of whose distances from two fixed points is constant.

identity An equation that is always true regardless of the values of any variables.

identity property of 1 If any number a is multiplied by 1, the result is a, that is, $a \cdot 1 = 1 \cdot a = a$.

identity property of 0 If 0 is added to any real number, a, the result is a, that is, $a + 0 = 0 + a = a$.

imaginary number A complex number $a + bi$ with $b \neq 0$.

imaginary part The value of b in the complex number $a + bi$.

imaginary unit A number denoted i whose properties are $i = \sqrt{-1}$ and $i^2 = -1$.

inconsistent system A system of linear equations that has no solution.

independent equations Equations in a linear system that have a unique solution.

independent variable The variable that represents the input of a function.

index The value of n in the expression $\sqrt[n]{a}$.

index of summation The variable k in the expression $\sum_{k=1}^{n}$.

inequality When the equals sign in an equation is replaced with any one of the symbols $<, \leq, >$, or $\geq$.

infinite sequence A function whose domain is the set of natural numbers.

input An element of the domain of a function.

integers A set I of numbers given by $I = \{\ldots, -3, -2, -1, 0, 1, 2, 3, \ldots\}$.

interval notation A notation for number line graphs that eliminates the need to draw the entire line. A **closed interval** is ex-

pressed by the endpoints in brackets, such as $[-2, 7]$; an **open interval** is expressed in parentheses, such as $(-2, 7)$, and indicates that the endpoints are not included in the solution. A **half-open interval** has a bracket and a parenthesis, such as $[-2, 7)$.

inversely proportional A quantity y is inversely proportional to x if there is a nonzero number k such that $y = k/x$.

irrational numbers Real numbers that cannot be expressed as fractions, such as π or $\sqrt{2}$.

joint variation A quantity z varies jointly as x and y if there is a nonzero number k such that $z = kxy$.

leading coefficient In a polynomial of one variable, the coefficient of the monomial with highest degree.

least common denominator (LCD) The common denominator with the fewest factors.

least common multiple (LCM) The smallest number that two or more numbers will divide into evenly.

less than If a real number a is located to the left of a real number b on the number line, we say that a is less than b, or $a < b$.

like radicals Radicals that have the same index and the same radicand.

like terms Two terms that contain the same variables raised to the same powers.

linear equation An equation that can be written in the form $ax + b = 0$, where $a \neq 0$.

linear function A function f represented by $f(x) = ax + b$, where a and b are constants.

linear inequality in one variable An inequality that can be written in the form $ax + b > 0$, where $a \neq 0$. (The symbol $>$ may be replaced with $\leq, <$, or $\geq$.)

linear inequality in two variables When the equals sign in a linear equation of two variables is replaced with $<, \leq, >$, or $\geq$, a linear inequality in two variables results.

linear polynomial A polynomial of degree 1 that can be written as $ax + b$, where $a \neq 0$.

line graph The graph resulting when consecutive data points in a scatterplot are connected with straight line segments.

linear programming problem A problem consisting of an objective function and a system of linear inequalities called constraints.

logarithm with base a of a positive number x Denoted $\log_a x$, it may be calculated as follows: if x can be expressed as $x = a^k$, then $\log_a x = k$, where $a > 0, a \neq 1$, and k is a real number. That is, $\log_a a^k = k$.

logarithmic function with base a The function represented by $f(x) = \log_a x$.

lower limit In summation notation, the number representing the subscript of the first term of the series.

main diagonal The elements $a_{11}, a_{22}, a_{33}, \ldots, a_{nn}$ in a matrix with n rows.

major axis The longest axis of an ellipse, which connects the vertices.

matrix A rectangular array of numbers.

minor axis The shortest axis of an ellipse.

monomial A term whose variables have only nonnegative integer exponents.

multiplication property of equality If a, b, and c are real numbers with $c \neq 0$, then $a = b$ is equivalent to $ac = bc$.

multiplicative identity The number 1.

multiplicative inverse (reciprocal) The multiplicative inverse of a nonzero number a is $1/a$.

natural exponential function The function represented by $f(x) = e^x$, where $e \approx 2.71828$.

natural logarithm The base-e logarithm, denoted either $\log_e x$ or $\ln x$.

natural numbers The set of numbers given by $N = \{1, 2, 3, 4, 5, 6, \ldots\}$.

negative number A number a such that $a < 0$.

negative slope On a graph, the slope of a line that falls from left to right.

negative square root The negative square root is denoted $-\sqrt{a}$.

nonlinear data If data points do not lie on a (straight) line, the data are nonlinear.

nonlinear system of equations Two or more equations, at least one of which is nonlinear.

nonlinear system of inequalities Two or more inequalities, at least one of which is nonlinear.

nth root The number b is an nth root of a if $b^n = a$, where n is a positive integer, and is denoted $\sqrt[n]{a} = b$.

nth term (general term) of a sequence Denoted $a_n = f(n)$.

numerical representation A table of values for a function.

numerical solution A solution often obtained by using a table of values.

objective function The given function in a linear programming problem.

odd root The nth root, $\sqrt[n]{a}$, where n is odd.

opposite (additive inverse) The opposite, or additive inverse, of a real number a is $-a$.

opposite of a polynomial The polynomial obtained by negating each term in a given polynomial.

optimal value In linear programming, the value that often results in maximum revenue or minimum cost.

ordered pair A pair of numbers written in parentheses (x, y), in which the order of the numbers is important.

ordered triple Can be expressed as (x, y, z), where x, y, and z are numbers.

origin On the number line, the point associated with the real number 0; in the xy-plane, the point $(0, 0)$.

output An element of the range of a function.

parabola The U-shaped graph of a quadratic function.

parallel lines Two or more lines in the same plane that never intersect.

Pascal's triangle A triangle made up of numbers in which there are 1s along the sides and each element inside the triangle is the sum of the two numbers above it.

perfect cube An integer with an integer cube root.

perfect nth power The value of a if there exists an integer b such that $b^n = a$.

perfect square An integer with an integer square root.

perfect square trinomial A trinomial that can be factored as the square of a binomial, for example, $a^2 + 2ab + b^2 = (a + b)^2$.

perpendicular lines Two lines in a plane that intersect to form a right (90°) angle.

pixels The tiny units that comprise screens for computer terminals or graphing calculators.

point–slope form The line with slope m passing through the point (x_1, y_1) given by the equation $y = m(x - x_1) + y_1$ or equivalently, $y - y_1 = m(x - x_1)$.

polynomial A monomial or a sum of monomials.

polynomials of one variable Polynomials that contain one variable.

positive number A number a such that $a > 0$.

positive slope On a graph, the slope of a line that rises from left to right.

power function A function that can be represented by $f(x) = x^p$, where p is a rational number.

principle square root The positive square root, denoted $\sqrt{a}$.

product The answer to a multiplication problem.

proportion A statement that two ratios are equal.

Pythagorean theorem If a right triangle has legs a and b with hypotenuse c, then $a^2 + b^2 = c^2$.

quadrants The four regions determined by a Cartesian coordinate system.

quadratic equation An equation that can be written as $ax^2 + bx + c = 0$, where a, b, and c are real numbers, with $a \neq 0$.

quadratic formula The solutions to the quadratic equation, $ax^2 + bx + c = 0$, $a \neq 0$, are $x = (-b \pm \sqrt{b^2 - 4ac})/(2a)$.

quadratic function A function f represented by the equation $f(x) = ax^2 + bx + c$, where a, b, and c are real numbers with $a \neq 0$.

quadratic inequality If the equals sign in a quadratic equation is replaced with $>$, $\geq$, $<$, or $\leq$, a quadratic inequality results.

quadratic polynomial A polynomial of degree 2 that can be written as $ax^2 + bx + c$ with $a \neq 0$.

quotient The answer to a division problem.

radical expression An expression that contains a radical sign.

radical sign The symbol $\sqrt{}$ or $\sqrt[n]{}$ for some positive integer n.

radicand The expression under the radical sign.

radius The fixed distance between the center and any point on the circle.

range The set of all y-values of the ordered pairs in a relation.

rate of change The value of a for the linear function given by $f(x) = ax + b$; slope can be interpreted as a rate of change.

rational equation An equation that involves a rational expression.

rational expression A polynomial divided by a nonzero polynomial.

rational function A function defined by $f(x) = p(x)/q(x)$, where $p(x)$ and $q(x)$ are polynomials and the domain of f includes all x-values such that $q(x) \neq 0$.

rational number Any number that can be expressed as the ratio of two integers p/q, where $q \neq 0$; a fraction.

rationalizing the denominator The process of removing radicals from a denominator so that the denominator contains only rational numbers.

real numbers All rational and irrational numbers; any number that can be written using decimals.

real part The value of a in a complex number $a + bi$.

reciprocal (multiplicative inverse) The reciprocal of a nonzero number a is $1/a$.

reduced row–echelon form A matrix form for representing a system of linear equations in which there are 1s on the main diagonal with 0s above and below each 1.

relation A set of ordered pairs.

rise The vertical change between two points on a line, that is, the change in the y-values.

root function In the power function, $f(x) = x^p$, if $p = 1/n$, where $n \geq 2$ is an integer, then f is also a root function, which is given by $f(x) = \sqrt[n]{x}$.

run The horizontal change between two points on a line, that is, the change in the x-values.

scatterplot A graph of distinct points plotted in the xy-plane.

scientific notation A real number a written as $b \times 10^n$, where $1 \leq |b| < 10$ and n is an integer.

set braces $\{\ \}$, used to enclose the elements of a set.

set-builder notation Notation to describe a set of numbers without having to list all of the elements. For example, $\{x \mid x > 5\}$ is read as "the set of all real numbers x such that x is greater than 5."

similar triangles Triangles that have equal corresponding angles and proportional corresponding sides.

slope The ratio of the change in y (rise) to the change in x (run) along a line. Slope m of a line equals $\frac{y_2 - y_1}{x_2 - x_1}$, where (x_1, y_1) and (x_2, y_2) are points on the line.

slope–intercept form The line with slope m and y-intercept b is given by $y = mx + b$.

solution A value for a variable that makes an equation a true statement.

solution set The set of all solutions to an equation.

squared The process of raising a number or variable to the second power.

square matrix A matrix in which the number of rows and the number of columns are equal.

square root The number b is a square root of a number a if $b^2 = a$.

square root function The function given by $f(x) = \sqrt{x}$, where $x \geq 0$.

square root property If k is a nonnegative number, then the solutions to the equation $x^2 = k$ are $x = \pm\sqrt{k}$. If $k < 0$, then this equation has no real solutions.

standard equation of a circle The standard equation of a circle with center (h, k) and radius r is $(x - h)^2 + (y - k)^2 = r^2$.

standard form of a complex number $a + bi$, where a and b are real numbers.

standard form of an equation for a line The form $ax + by = c$, where a, b, and c are constants with a and b not both 0.

standard viewing rectangle of a graphing calculator Xmin $= -10$, Xmax $= 10$, Xscl $= 1$, Ymin $= -10$, Ymax $= 10$, and Yscl $= 1$, denoted $[-10, 10, 1]$ by $[-10, 10, 1]$.

subscript The expression x_1 has a subscript of 1; it is read "x sub one" or "x one".

substitution method A symbolic method for solving a system of equations in which one equation is solved for one of the variables and then the result is substituted into the other equation.

sum The answer to an addition problem.

summation notation Notation in which the uppercase Greek letter sigma represents the sum, for example, $\sum_{k=1}^{n} k^2$.

sum of two cubes Expression in the form $a^3 + b^3$, which can be factored as $(a + b)(a^2 - ab + b^2)$.

symbolic representation Representing a function with a formula; for example, $f(x) = x^2 - 2x$.

symbolic solution A solution to an equation obtained by using properties of equations, and the resulting solution set is exact.

synthetic division A shortcut that can be used to divide $x - k$, where k is a number, into a polynomial.

system of two linear equations in two variables A system of two equations in which each equation can be written in the form $ax + by = c$; an ordered pair (x, y) is a solution to the system of equations if the values for x and y make *both* equations true.

system of linear inequalities Two or more linear inequalities to be solved at the same time, the solution to which must satisfy both inequalities.

table of values An organized way to display the inputs and outputs of a function; a numerical representation.

term A number, a variable, or a product of numbers and variables raised to powers.

terms of a sequence $a_1, a_2, a_3, \ldots, a_n, \ldots$ where the first term is $a_1 = f(1)$, the second term is $a_2 = f(2)$, and so on.

test value When graphing the solution set of a linear inequality, a point chosen to determine which region of the xy-plane to shade.

three-part inequality A compound inequality written in the form $a < x < b$.

translation The shifting of a graph upward, downward, to the right, or to the left in such a way that the shape of the graph stays the same.

transverse axis In a hyperbola, the line segment that connects the vertices.

trinomial A polynomial with three terms.

upper limit In summation notation, the number representing the subscript of the last term of the series.

variable A symbol, such as x, y, or t, used to represent any unknown number or quantity.

varies directly A quantity y varies directly with x if there is a nonzero number k such that $y = kx$.

varies inversely A quantity y varies inversely with x if there is a nonzero number k such that $y = k/x$.

varies jointly A quantity z varies jointly as x and y if there is a nonzero number k such that $z = kxy$.

verbal representation A description of what a function computes in words.

vertex The lowest point on the graph of a parabola that opens upward or the highest point on the graph of a parabola that opens downward.

vertex form of a parabola The vertex form of a parabola with vertex (h, k) is $y = a(x - h)^2 + k$, where $a \neq 0$ is a constant.

vertical asymptote A vertical asymptote typically occurs in the graph of a rational function when the denominator of the rational expression is 0, but the numerator is not 0; it can be represented by a vertical line in the graph of a rational function.

vertical line test If every vertical line intersects a graph at most once, then the graph represents a function.

vertices of an ellipse The endpoints of the major axis.

vertices of a hyperbola The endpoints of the transverse axis.

viewing rectangle (window) On a graphing calculator, the window that determines the x- and y-values shown in the graph.

whole numbers The set of numbers given by $W = \{0, 1, 2, 3, 4, 5, \ldots\}$.

x-axis The horizontal axis in a Cartesian coordinate system.

x-intercept The x-coordinate of a point where a graph intersects the x-axis.

Xmax Regarding the viewing rectangle of a graphing calculator, Xmax is the maximum x-value along the x-axis.

Xmin Regarding the viewing rectangle of a graphing calculator, Xmin is the minimum x-value along the x-axis.

Xscl The distance represented by consecutive tick marks on the x-axis.

y-axis The vertical axis in a Cartesian coordinate system.

y-intercept The y-coordinate of a point where a graph intersects the y-axis.

Ymax Regarding the viewing rectangle of a graphing calculator, Ymax is the maximum y-value along the y-axis.

Ymin Regarding the viewing rectangle of a graphing calculator, Ymin is the minimum y-value along the y-axis.

Yscl The distance represented by consecutive tick marks on the y-axis.

zero-product property If the product of two numbers is 0, then at least one of the numbers must equal 0, that is, $ab = 0$ implies $a = 0$ or $b = 0$.

zero of a polynomial An x-value that results in an output of 0 when it is substituted into a polynomial; for example, the zeros of $f(x) = x^2 - 4$ are 2 and -2.

BIBLIOGRAPHY

Baase, S. *Computer Algorithms: Introduction to Design and Analysis.* 2nd ed. Reading, Mass.: Addison-Wesley Publishing Company, 1988.

Baker, S., with B. Leak, "Math Will Rock Your World." *Business Week*, January 23, 2006.

Battan, L. *Weather in Your Life.* San Francisco: W. H. Freeman, 1983.

Beckmann, P. *A History of Pi.* New York: Barnes and Noble, Inc., 1993.

Brown, D., and P. Rothery. *Models in Biology: Mathematics, Statistics and Computing.* West Sussex, England: John Wiley and Sons Ltd, 1993.

Callas, D. *Snapshots of Applications in Mathematics.* Delhi, New York: State University College of Technology, 1994.

Carr, G. *Mechanics of Sport.* Champaign, Ill.: Human Kinetics, 1997.

Conquering the Sciences. Sharp Electronics Corporation, 1986.

Elton, C. S., and M. Nicholson. "The ten year cycle in numbers of lynx in Canada." *J. Anim. Ecol.* 11 (1942): 215–244.

Eves, H. *An Introduction to the History of Mathematics,* 5th ed. Philadelphia: Saunders College Publishing, 1983.

Freedman, B. *Environmental Ecology: The Ecological Effects of Pollution, Disturbance, and Other Stresses.* 2nd ed. San Diego: Academic Press, 1995.

Friedhoff, M., and W. Benzon. *The Second Computer Revolution: Visualization.* New York: W. H. Freeman, 1991.

Garber, N., and L. Hoel. *Traffic and Highway Engineering.* Boston, Mass.: PWS Publishing Co., 1997.

Grigg, D. *The World Food Problem.* Oxford: Blackwell Publishers, 1993.

Haefner, L. *Introduction to Transportation Systems.* New York: Holt, Rinehart and Winston, 1986.

Harrison, F., F. Hills, J. Paterson, and R. Saunders. "The measurement of liver blood flow in conscious calves." *Quarterly Journal of Experimental Physiology* 71: 235–247.

Historical Topics for the Mathematics Classroom, Thirty-first Yearbook. National Council of Teachers of Mathematics, 1969.

Horn, D. *Basic Electronics Theory.* Blue Ridge Summit, Penn.: TAB Books, 1989.

Howells, G. *Acid Rain and Acid Waters.* 2nd ed. New York: Ellis Horwood, 1995.

Karttunen, H., P. Kroger, H. Oja, M. Poutanen, K. Donner, eds. *Fundamental Astronomy.* 2nd ed. New York: Springer-Verlag, 1994.

Kincaid, D., and W. Cheney. *Numerical Analysis.* Pacific Grove, Calif.: Brooks/Cole Publishing Company, 1991.

Kraljic, M. *The Greenhouse Effect.* New York: The H. W. Wilson Company, 1992.

Lack, D. *The Life of a Robin.* London: Collins, 1965.

Lancaster, H. *Quantitative Methods in Biological and Medical Sciences: A Historical Essay.* New York: Springer-Verlag, 1994.

Mannering, F., and W. Kilareski. *Principles of Highway Engineering and Traffic Analysis.* New York: John Wiley and Sons, 1990.

Mar, J., and H. Liebowitz. *Structure Technology for Large Radio and Radar Telescope Systems.* Cambridge, Mass.: The MIT Press, 1969.

Meadows, D. *Beyond the Limits.* Post Mills, Vermont: Chelsea Green Publishing Co., 1992.

Miller, A., and J. Thompson. *Elements of Meteorology.* 2nd ed. Columbus, Ohio: Charles E. Merrill Publishing Company, 1975.

Miller, A., and R. Anthes. *Meteorology.* 5th ed. Columbus, Ohio: Charles E. Merrill Publishing Company, 1985.

Monroe, J. *Steffi Graf.* Mankato, Minn.: Crestwood House, 1988.

Motz, L., and J. Weaver. *The Story of Mathematics.* New York: Plenum Press, 1993.

Nemerow, N., and A. Dasgupta. *Industrial and Hazardous Waste Treatment.* New York: Van Nostrand Reinhold, 1991.

Nicholson, A. J. "An Outline of the dynamics of animal populations." *Austr. J. Zool.* 2 (1935): 9–65.

Nielson, G., and B. Shriver, eds. *Visualization in Scientific Computing.* Los Alamitos, Calif.: IEEE Computer Society Press, 1990.

Nilsson, A. *Greenhouse Earth.* New York: John Wiley and Sons, 1992.

Paetsch, M. *Mobile Communications in the U.S. and Europe: Regulation, Technology, and Markets.* Norwood, Mass.: Artech House, Inc., 1993.

Pearl, R., T. Edwards, and J. Miner. "The growth of *Cucumis melo* seedlings at different temperatures." *J. Gen. Physiol.* 17: 687–700.

Pennycuick, C. *Newton Rules Biology.* New York: Oxford University Press, 1992.

Pielou, E. *Population and Community Ecology: Principles and Methods.* New York: Gordon and Breach Science Publishers, 1974.

Pokorny, C., and C. Gerald. *Computer Graphics: The Principles behind the Art and Science.* Irvine, Calif.: Franklin, Beedle, and Associates, 1989.

Ronan, C. *The Natural History of the Universe.* New York: MacMillan Publishing Company, 1991.

Sharov, A., and I. Novikov. *Edwin Hubble, The Discoverer of the Big Bang Universe.* New York: Cambridge University Press, 1993.

Smith, C. *Practical Cellular and PCS Design.* New York: McGraw-Hill, 1998.

Stent, G. S. *Molecular Biology of Bacterial Viruses.* San Francisco: W. H. Freeman, 1963.

Taylor, J. *DVD Demystified.* New York: McGraw-Hill, 1998.

Taylor, W. *The Geometry of Computer Graphics.* Pacific Grove, Calif.: Wadsworth and Brooks/Cole, 1992.

Thomas, D. *Swimming Pool Operators Handbook.* National Swimming Pool Foundation of Washington, D.C., 1972.

Thomas, V. *Science and Sport.* London: Faber and Faber, 1970.

Thomson, W. *Introduction to Space Dynamics.* New York: John Wiley and Sons, 1961.

Toffler, A., and H. Toffler. *Creating a New Civilization: The Politics of the Third Wave.* Kansas City, Mo.: Turner Publications, 1995.

Triola, M. *Elementary Statistics.* 7th ed. Reading, Mass.: Addison-Wesley Publishing Company, 1998.

Tucker, A., A. Bernat, W. Bradley, R. Cupper, and G. Scragg. *Fundamentals of Computing I: Logic, Problem Solving, Programs, and Computers.* New York: McGraw-Hill, 1995.

Turner, R. K., D. Pierce, and I. Bateman. *Environmental Economics, An Elementary Approach.* Baltimore: The Johns Hopkins University Press, 1993.

Varley, G., and G. Gradwell. "Population models for the winter moth." *Symposium of the Royal Entomological Society of London* 4: 132–142.

Wang, T. *ASHRAE Trans.* 81, Part 1 (1975): 32.

Weidner, R., and R. Sells. *Elementary Classical Physics,* Vol. 2. Boston: Allyn and Bacon, Inc., 1965.

Wigner, E., "The Unreasonable Effectiveness of Mathematics in the Natural Sciences." *Communictions of Pure and Applied Mathematics,* Vol. 13, No. I, February, 1960.

Williams, J. *The Weather Almanac 1995.* New York: Vintage Books, 1994.

Wright, J. *The New York Times Almanac 1999.* New York: Penguin Group, 1998.

Zeilik, M., S. Gregory, and D. Smith. *Introductory Astronomy and Astrophysics.* 3rd ed. Philadelphia: Saunders College Publishers, 1992.

PHOTO CREDITS

1, Ingram Publishing/Getty Royalty Free   2, PhotoDisc Red   3, Blend Images/Getty Royalty Free
9, Thinkstock/Punchstock   18, Stockbyte Silver/Getty Royalty Free   23, PhotoDisc   24, Digital Vision
36, U.S. Department of Defense Visual Information Center   38, PhotoDisc Blue   40, Photographer's
Choice/PhotoDisc Red   47 (top), Blend Images/Getty Royalty Free   47 (bottom), Purestock/Getty
Royalty Free   49, PhotoDisc Blue   52, Corbis Royalty Free   58, Foodcollection/Getty Royalty Free
73, Andy Rain/epa/Corbis   74, Blend Images/Getty Royalty Free   77, Purestock/Getty Royalty Free
82, PhotoDisc   91, PhotoDisc Red   96, PhotoDisc Red   98, Photographer's Choice/Getty Royalty
Free   103, National Geographic Image Collection   104, Sara Piaseczynski   105, Photographer's
Choice/Getty Royalty Free   110, PhotoDisc Red   118, Corbis Royalty Free   119, PhotoDisc Red
135, Purestock/Getty Royalty Free   143, Glowimages/Getty Royalty Free   149, NOAA
150, PhotoDisc   157, Digital Vision   164, Stockdisk   169, Digital Vision   177, Corbis Royalty Free
190, PhotoDisc   201, Beth Anderson   227, Corbis Royalty Free   228, Corbis Royalty Free
233, PhotoDisc Blue   236, PhotoDisc Red   240, Getty Images Sport   241, NASA   248, PhotoDisc
Red   249, Photographer's Choice/Getty Royalty Free   250, PhotoDisc Red   253, PhotoDisc Red
256 (top), PhotoDisc   256 (bottom), PhotoDisc Red   266, Corbis   269, Corbis Royalty Free
274, PhotoDisc   276, Digital Vision   285, Digital Vision   287, PhotoDisc Red   298, Digital Vision
303, PhotoDisc   312, Image Source/Getty Royalty Free   319, Corbis   320, PhotoDisc   326, Beth
Anderson   328, Purestock/Getty Royalty Free   334, Kobal Collection   339, PhotoDisc Red
345, Getty Editorial   346, PhotoDisc Red   352, PhotoAlto/Getty Royalty Free   357 (left), Digital
Vision   357 (right), NASA   358, Corbis Royalty Free   363, PhotoDisc   368, Digital Vision
375, PhotoDisc Red   380, PhotoDisc   390, PhotoDisc Blue   397, Corbis Royalty Free   403, Digital
Vision   404, Digital Vision   428, PhotoDisc   440, Image Source/Getty Royalty Free   444, Corbis
Royalty Free   445, PhotoDisc Red   450, Blend Images/Getty Royalty Free   452, Stockbyte
Platinum/Getty Royalty Free   460, PhotoDisc   463, PhotoDisc   471, PhotoDisc Red   473, PhotoDisc
490, PhotoDisc Red   497, Stockbyte   498, Digital Vision   504, Digital Vision   508, Stockbyte/Getty
Royalty Free   509, PhotoDisc Red   529, Corbis   535, Stockbyte/Getty Royalty Free   539, Image
Source/Getty Royalty Free   541, Digital Vision   549, Sara Anderson   553, Stockbyte/Getty Royalty
Free   555, Corbis Royalty Free   573, Digital Vision   575, Corbis Royalty Free   576, Digital Vision
584, PhotoDisc   595, Digital Vision   601, DigitalStock   605, Westend61/Getty Royalty Free
608, Digital Vision   612, Digital Vision   627, Photographer's Choice Royalty Free/Getty Royalty Free
653, Purestock/Getty Royalty Free   654, PhotoDisc   669, PhotoDisc   674, Beth Anderson
680, PhotoDisc   693, NASA   699, The Image Bank/Getty Images   703, iStockphoto   706, PhotoDisc
723, PhotoDisc Blue   724, Space Telescope Science Institute   733, NASA Headquarters   736, NASA
738, NASA   761, PhotoDisc   763, Corbis   764, Westend61/Getty Royalty Free   772, PhotoDisc Red
777 (top), Digital Vision   777 (bottom), Getty Royalty Free   782, Getty Royalty Free   784, PhotoDisc
792, Getty Royalty Free

INDEX OF APPLICATIONS

INDEX

Portland Community College

MTH 95
and MTH 91/92
SUPPLEMENTAL
PROBLEM SETS

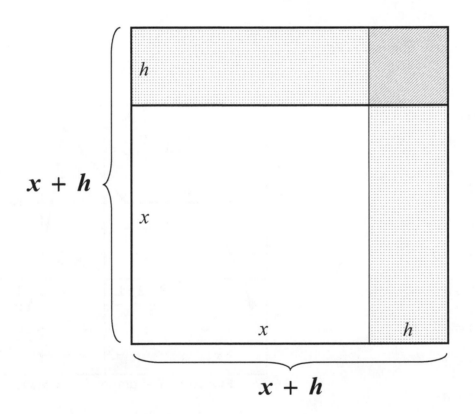

$$(x + h)^2 = x^2 + xh + xh + h^2$$
$$= x^2 + 2xh + h^2$$

SUPPLEMENT TO §2.1

EXERCISES:

1. Determine whether one quantity is a function of another within real life contexts by applying the definition of a function

   a. Is *height* a function of *age*?

   b. Is *age* a function of *height*?

   c. Is *name* a function of *G#* (i.e., PCC ID number)?

   d. Is *G#* a function of *name*?

   e. Is the *cost per person* a function of the *number of people sharing a $20 pizza*?

2. The function $y = p(x)$ graphed in Figure 1.

   a. Find $p(0)$.

   b. Find $p(1.5)$.

   c. Find $p(5)$.

   d. Find $p(-7)$.

   e. Find $p(2)$.

   f. Solve $p(x) = -2$.

   g. Solve $p(x) = 1$.

   h. Solve $p(x) = -4$.

   i. Solve $p(x) = 3$.

   j. Solve $p(x) = 0$.

   k. State the domain p in interval notation.

   l. State the range of p in interval notation.

   m. Find all x for which $p(x) > 1$.

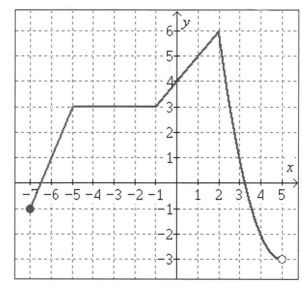

Figure 1: The graph of $y = p(x)$.

3. A group of rafters take a 15 day rafting trip down the Colorado River through the Grand Canyon. The distance in miles, $K(t)$, that the group has floated is a function of the number of days traveled, t. The table below gives some data about the trip.

t	0	1	2	3	4	5	6	7	8	9	10	11	12	13	14	15
$K(t)$	0	20	35	45	58	75	100	125	135	145	158	175	211	230	258	277

    a. Find and interpret $K(8)$. (Hint: After 8 days of rafting....)

    b. Find and interpret $K(35)$.

    c. Solve $K(t) = 125$ and interpret your answer.

    d. Find the average rate of change between $t = 11$ and $t = 13$. Explain your answer.

    e. Find and interpret the vertical intercept of the function K.

    f. What is the domain of the function K? Explain your answer.

    g. What is the range of the function K? Explain your answer.

4. The value of a computer, in dollars, is given by $c(t) = 600 - 150t$, where t is the number of years since the computer was purchased.

    a. Find and interpret the vertical intercept of the function c.

    b. Find and interpret the horizontal intercept of c.

    c. Find the domain and range of c. (Use interval notation.)

5. The historic Arlene Schnitzer Concert Hall originally opened in 1928 as the Portland Publix Theatre. The Theatre seated 2776 people and it cost 60 cents per ticket. Let $r(x)$ be the revenue, in dollars, from selling x tickets for an event at the Theatre.

    a. Find the algebraic formula for $r(x)$.

    b. Find the domain and range of r.

6. The recorded low temperature in Portland, in degrees Fahrenheit, is a function, f, of the number of days after January 1, 2009. Interpret $f(29) = 30$.

7. Consider the linear function $f(x) = 4 - 0.5x$.

   a. Find and simplify the expressions for $y = f(x + 6)$ and $y = f(x) + 6$.

   b. Graph $y = f(x)$, $y = f(x + 6)$, and $y = f(x) + 6$ on the same set of coordinate axes. Scale the axes and label each function on the graph. (Linear functions should be straight: use a ruler and graph paper.)

8. If $p(x) = x^2$, find and simplify expressions for $p(x + 2)$ and $p(x) + 2$. Are the resulting expressions equivalent?

9. Let $j(t) = 4 - t + 2t^2$. Find and simplify the expressions below.

   a. $j(3t)$

   b. $j(3 - t)$

   c. $3j(t)$

   d. $3 - j(t)$

10. Suppose that $y = g(x)$ is a linear function and that $g(0) = -150$ and $g(50) = 2000$. Find the algebraic formula for $g(x)$.

11. Suppose that $y = h(x)$ is a linear function and that $h(-5) = 2$ and $h(5) = 20$. Find an algebraic formula for $h(x)$.

12. Suppose that $y = j(t)$ is a linear function and that $j(-6) = 5$ and $j(10) = -1$. Find an algebraic formula for $j(x)$.

13. Figure 2 shows a graph of the total net income, y, in millions of dollars, x years after 1995 for Yahoo! Inc.

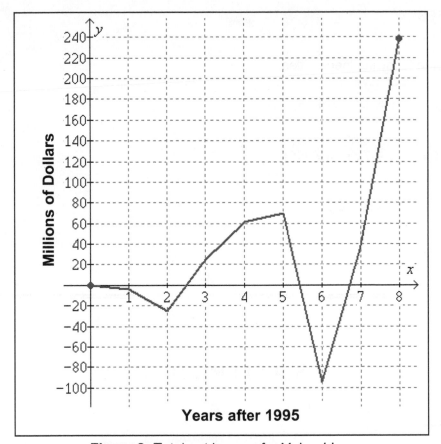

Figure 2: Total net income for Yahoo! Inc.

a. If $y = f(x)$ evaluate $f(6)$ and state the practical significance of this value.

b. Estimate a solution to the equation $f(x) = 120$ and state the practical significance of this solution.

c. Estimate the solutions to the equation $f(x) = 60$ and state the practical significance of this solution.

d. Estimate the solutions to the equation $f(x) = -100$ and state the practical significance of this solution.

SUPPLEMENT TO §3.3

EXERCISES:

1. Solve the following inequalities.

    a. $3(2x - 5) + 2x > 2(4x + 1)$.

    b. $-3(x - 7) + 7x \leq 4(x + 6)$.

    c. $2(3x + 9) < 6(3 + x)$.

SUPPLEMENT TO §3.4

EXERCISES:

1. The graph of $y = w(x)$ is given in Figure 3.

    a. Solve $w(x) < 1$.

    b. Solve $w(x) \geq -2$.

    c. Solve $-2 < w(x) \leq 6$.

    d. Solve $w(x) < -3$.

    e. Find the domain and range of w.
       (Use interval notation.)

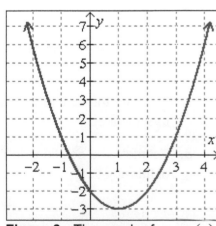

Figure 3: The graph of $y = w(x)$.

2. The graph of $y = f(x)$ is given in Figure 4.

a. Evaluate $f(-1)$.

b. Solve $f(x) = 0$.

c. Solve $f(x) > 0$.

d. Estimate solutions to $f(x) = 1$.

e. Find the domain and range of f.
(Use interval notation.)

Figure 4: The graph of $y = f(x)$.

3. The graph of $y = m(x)$ is given in Figure 5.

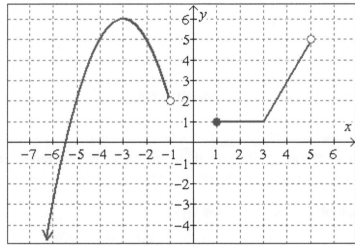

Figure 5: The graph of $y = m(x)$.

a. Evaluate $m(-5)$.   **b.** Evaluate $m(-1)$.

c. Evaluate $m(3)$.   **d.** Solve $m(x) = -3$.

e. Solve $m(x) = 2$.   **f.** Solve $m(x) = 3$.

g. Solve $m(x) = 6$.   **h.** Solve $m(x) \le -3$.

i. Solve $m(x) > 0$.   **j.** Solve $m(x) > 5$.

k. Find the domain and range of m. (Use interval notation.)

SPS 7

4. The graph of $y = F(x) = |x|$ is given in Figure 6.

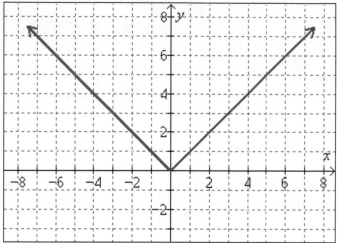

Figure 6: The graph of $y = F(x)$.

a. Find the domain and range of F. (Use interval notation.)

b. Solve the equation $F(x) = 4$.

c. Solve the inequality $F(x) < 5$. Express the solution in interval notation.

d. Solve the inequality $F(x) \geq 3$. Express the solution in interval notation.

e. Using a graphing calculator, graph $y = G(x) = |x - 3| + 2$ and then sketch the graph onto the grid in Figure 6 above. State the domain and range of G using interval notation. Do the graphs of F and G appear to be related? If so, explain.

f. Use your graph of $y = G(x)$ to solve $G(x) = 4$.

g. Use your graph of $y = G(x)$ to solve $G(x) = 1$.

h. Use your graph of $y = G(x)$ to solve $G(x) \leq 6$.

5. Let $Q(x) = x^3 + 7x^2 + 8x - 13$ and $P(x) = x + 2$. Use the graphing capabilities of your graphing calculator to solve the following:

a. $P(x) = Q(x)$

b. $P(x) < Q(x)$.

SUPPLEMENT TO §6.1

EXERCISES:

1. Find the domain and range of the functions graphed below. (Use interval notation.)

a.

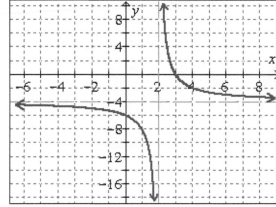

The graph of $y = k(x)$.

b.

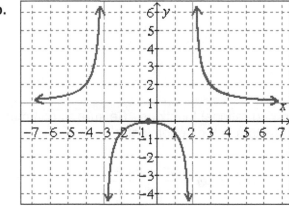

The graph of $y = j(x)$.

2. Let $f(x) = \dfrac{2x + 1}{5 - x}$. Simplify the expressions below.

    a. $f(x) + 2$ **b.** $f(x + 2)$

    c. $3f(x)$ **d.** $f(3x)$

SUPPLEMENT TO §6.2

When we simplify the algebraic formula for a function we can lose information about the domain. We need to communicate hidden domain restrictions after we cancel factors in the denominator.

EXAMPLE: Simplify the algebraic formula for $p(x) = \dfrac{3x+3}{4x^2 - 4x - 8}$.

$$p(x) = \frac{3x+3}{4x^2 - 4x - 8}$$

$$= \frac{3(x+1)}{4(x^2 - x - 2)}$$

$$= \frac{3(x+1)}{4(x+1)(x-2)}$$

$$= \frac{3\cancel{(x+1)}}{4\cancel{(x+1)}(x-2)}$$

$$= \frac{3}{4(x-2)}, \quad x \neq -1$$

(we write "$x \neq -1$" since we canceled the factor in the denominator that makes this restriction obvious)

EXERCISES:

1. Simplify the algebraic formulas for the following rational functions. Be sure to communicate domain restrictions hidden after you cancel factors in the denominator.

  a. $f(x) = \dfrac{2x^2 + 6x}{3x + 9}$

  b. $T(x) = \dfrac{x^2 + 6x + 9}{x^2 - 9}$

  c. $g(x) = \dfrac{2x^2 - x - 6}{x^2 + x - 6}$

  d. $L(x) = \dfrac{x^3 - 4x^2 - 5x}{2x^2 - 13x + 15}$

  e. $d(x) = \dfrac{x^2 - 16}{12 - 3x}$

  f. $A(x) = \dfrac{12x^2 - 23x + 10}{12x^2 - 23x + 10}$

SUPPLEMENT TO §6.3

EXERCISES:

1. Let $S(x) = \dfrac{x+1}{x-3}$ and $R(x) = \dfrac{2}{x+2}$.

    a. If $a(x) = S(x) + R(x)$, find a simplified expression for $a(x)$ and find the domain of a.

    b. If $b(x) = S(x) - R(x)$, find a simplified expression for $b(x)$ and find the domain of b.

    c. If $c(x) = S(x) \cdot R(x)$, find a simplified expression for $c(x)$ and find the domain of c.

    d. If $d(x) = \dfrac{S(x)}{R(x)}$, find a simplified expression for $d(x)$.

SUPPLEMENT TO §7.4

EXERCISES:

1. Let $Y(x) = \sqrt{x-5} + 3$.

    a. Find the domain of Y algebraically. (Use interval notation.)

    b. Create a graph of $y = Y(x)$ on your graphing calculator.

    c. Find the range of Y using your graph. (Use interval notation.)

2. Let $Z(x) = \sqrt{7-2x} - 5$.

    a. Find the domain of Z algebraically. (Use interval notation.)

    b. Create a graph of $y = Z(x)$ on your graphing calculator.

    c. Find the range of Z using your graph. (Use interval notation.)

3. Let $U(t) = 2 - \sqrt{3 + 2t}$.

    a. Find the domain of U algebraically. (Use interval notation.)

    b. Create a graph of $y = U(x)$ on your graphing calculator.

    c. Find the range of U using your graph. (Use interval notation.)

4. Let $V(x) = \sqrt[3]{x + 2}$.

    a. Find the domain of V algebraically. (Use interval notation.)

    b. Create a graph of $y = V(x)$ on your graphing calculator.

    c. Find the range of V using your graph. (Use interval notation.)

5. Let $T(k) = 3 - \sqrt[4]{3k - 7}$.

    a. Find the domain of T algebraically. (Use interval notation.)

    b. Create a graph of $y = T(k)$ on your graphing calculator.

    c. Find the range of T using your graph. (Use interval notation.)

SUPPLEMENT TO §7.5

EXERCISES:

1. Let $f(x) = \sqrt{8 - 4x}$.

    a. Evaluate $f(-2)$.

    b. State the domain of f using interval notation. (If you determine the domain algebraically, show these steps; if you determine the domain graphically, include a graph to justify your conclusion.)

    c. Solve $f(x) = 2$.

2. **a.** Solve the equation $1 + \sqrt{x} = \sqrt{3x - 3}$ algebraically.

    b. Now solve the equation $1 + \sqrt{x} = \sqrt{3x - 3}$ graphically using your calculator.

    c. Check the solutions you found in part (a) to eliminate extraneous solutions.

    d. What is the connection between what you found in parts **b** and **c**?

SUPPLEMENT TO §8.2

EXERCISES:

1. Use interval notation to express domain and range of the quadratic functions graphed below.

a.
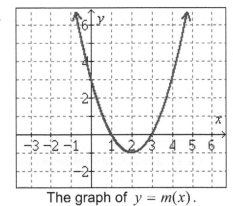
The graph of $y = m(x)$.

b.

The graph of $y = n(x)$.

2. Graph of the quadratic function $f(x) = -0.4x^2 + 5x + 15$ on your graphing calculator. Be sure to find a viewing window that allows you to see the vertex and all intercepts.

    a. Use either the min or max key to estimate the coordinates of the vertex of $y = f(x)$.

    b. Use function notation to compose an equation that communicates the information contained in the vertex.

    c. Use the zero/root key to estimate both horizontal intercepts of $y = f(x)$.

    d. Use the trace key and substitute $x = 0$ to find the vertical intercept of $y = f(x)$.

    e. Use interval notation to express the domain and range of f.

SPS 13

SUPPLEMENT TO §8.3

EXERCISES:

1. The function $F(t) = -t^2 + 2t + 3$ models the depth of water (in feet) in a large drainage ditch, where t is measured in hours and $t = 0$ corresponds to the moment that a summer storm has ended.

    a. Evaluate and interpret $F(2)$ in the context of the real world function.

    b. Write $F(t)$ in vertex form by completing the square.

    c. State and interpret the vertex of $y = F(t)$ as a maximum or minimum of the real life situation.

    d. Using the vertex form of $F(t)$ you found in part **b**, solve the equation $F(t) = 0$ using the square root method.

    e. What is the domain of the real world function F? Write your answer in interval notation. Explain your answer in a sentence.

    f. What is the range of the real world function $F(t)$? Write your answer in interval notation. Explain your answer in a sentence.

    g. At what time(s) will the water in the ditch be 1 foot deep? Round your solutions to three decimal places. Interpret your solutions in the context of the real world application.

    h. At what time(s) will the water in the ditch be 6 feet deep? Round your solutions to three decimal places. Interpret your solutions in the context of the real world application.

    I. Make a graph the parabola $y = F(t)$ **on its implied domain** without using your calculator. Scale and label your axes. (Start by plotting the vertex; then use what you learned in parts **a** – **h** to plot a few other points; finally, use the symmetry of a parabola to find at least one more point, and then connect all of your points.)

2. A television is launched with a trebuchet. Suppose that the function $h(d) = -\frac{1}{100}d^2 + \frac{6}{5}d + 28$ models the television's height above ground when its horizontal distance from the trebuchet is d feet.

    a. Find and interpret the vertical intercept.

    b. Find and interpret the horizontal intercept(s).

    c. Find and interpret the vertex.

    d. What is the horizontal distance at which the TV is 40 feet above the ground?

    e. What is the horizontal distance at which the TV is 75 feet above the ground?

    f. A six foot tall woman is positioned 130 feet from the trebuchet. How high above her head is the TV when it passes over her?

    g. What is the domain based on the context of the problem? Explain your reasoning.

    h. What is the range based on the context of the problem? Explain your reasoning.

ANSWERS

SUPPLEMENT TO §2.1:

1. **a.** Answers may vary. You could answer, "Yes," since, at a particular time, you can only be only one height. Or you could answer, "No," since, during a given year, you can grow and thus be more than one height at that age.

   b. No. You can be the same height for many years.

   c. Yes. Each G# is associated with only one name.

   d. No. There can be more than one person with the same name attending PCC, so there can more than one G# associated with a particular name.

   e. Yes, if you split the cost evenly. The cost per person, c, can be a function of the number of people splitting the pizza, n, given by $c = f(n) = \frac{20}{n}$. For each positive integer number, n, the cost c will be unique.

2. **a.** $p(0) = 4$.   **b.** $p(1.5) = 5.5$.

   c. $p(5)$ is undefined.   **d.** $p(-7) = -1$.

   e. $p(2) = 6$.   **f.** The solution set is $\{4\}$.

   g. The solution set is $\{-6, 3\}$.   **h.** There is no solution.

   i. The solution set is $\{x \mid -5 \le x \le -1 \text{ or } x \approx 2.5\}$.   **j.** The solution set is $\{x \mid x \approx -6.5 \text{ or } x \approx 3.2\}$.

   k. The domain is $[-7, 5)$.   **l.** The range is $(-3, 6]$.

   m. $\{x \mid -6 < x < 3\}$.

3. **a.** $K(8) = 135$. After 8 days of rafting, the group has floated 135 miles down the Colorado River.

   b. $K(35)$ is undefined. The rafting trip was finished after 15 days, so the group was no longer rafting 35 days after starting the trip.

   c. The solution to $K(t) = 125$ is $t = 7$ since the group had floated down 125 miles of the Colorado River 7 days after staring the trip.

   d. The average rate of change is 27.5 mi/day. This means that each day between days 11 and 13 the rafting group traveled an average of 27.5 mi.

   e. The vertical intercept is $(0, 0)$, so the vertical and horizontal intercepts are the same. This point means that after 0 days of rafting, the group had floated 0 miles down the Colorado River.

   f. The domain is $[0, 15]$. The input values for this function represent the number-of-days of the rafting trip and the trip was 15 days long, so all time periods between (and including) 0 and 15 days must be in the domain.

   g. The range is $[0, 277]$. The rafters floated all 277 miles of the Grand Canyon so at some moment during the 15 day trip, the rafters had floated each unique distance between (and including) 0 and 277 miles, so all of these values must be in the range.

4. **a.** $(0, 600)$ is the vertical intercept. It means that when the computer is brand new, it is worth $600.

   b. $(4, 0)$ is the horizontal intercept. It means that when the computer is 4 years old, it is worth nothing.

   c. Domain: $[0, 4]$.   Range: $[0, 600]$.

5. **a.** $r(x) = 0.6x$

   b. Domain: $\{0, 1, 2, ..., 2775, 2776\}$.
   Range: $\{0.00, 0.60, 1.20, 1.80, ... ,1664.40, 1665.00, 1665.60\}$.

6. $f(29) = 30$ means that on January 28, 2009, the recorded low temperature in Portland was $30°\,\text{F}$.

7. **a.** $y = f(x + 6) = 1 - 0.5x$ and $y = f(x) + 6 = 10 - 0.5x$

   b. Check your graph by graphing these functions on your graphing calculator.

SPS 17

8. $p(x + 2) = x^2 + 4x + 4$

$\left.\begin{array}{l}\\ \\ \\ \end{array}\right\}$ Not Equal

$p(x) + 2 = x^2 + 2$

9. a. $j(3t) = 18t^2 - 3t + 4$ **b.** $j(3 - t) = 2t^2 - 11t + 19$

c. $3j(t) = 6t^2 - 3t + 12$ **d.** $3 - j(t) = -2t^2 + t - 1$

10. $g(x) = 43x - 150$

11. $h(x) = \dfrac{9}{5}x + 11$

12. $j(x) = -\dfrac{3}{8}x + \dfrac{11}{4}$

13. a. $f(6) \approx -95$. This means that in 2001 Yahoo lost about 95 million dollars.

 b. The solution is approximately 7.5, which means that about 7.5 years after 1995, i.e., somewhere in the middle of 2002, Yahoo made 120 million dollars.

 c. A set of approximate solutions is $\{4, 5.1, 7.1\}$. These solutions mean that in 1999, 2000, and 2002 Yahoo made about 60 million dollars.

 d. $f(x) = -100$. There is no solution to this, which means that Yahoo has never lost 100 million dollars after 1995.

SUPPLEMENT TO §3.3:

1. a. No solution.

 b. The solution set is $(-\infty, \infty)$.

 c. No solution.

SUPPLEMENT TO §3.4:

1. **a.** The solution set is $(-1, 3)$.

   b. The solution set is $(-\infty, 0] \cup [2, \infty)$.

   c. The solution set is $[-2, 0) \cup (2, 4]$.

   d. No solution.

   e. Domain: $(-\infty, \infty)$.   Range: $[-3, \infty)$.

2. **a.** $f(-1) = -2$.

   b. The solution set is $\{-3, 0, 3\}$.

   c. The solution set is $(-\infty, -3) \cup (0, 1) \cup (1, 3)$.

   d. The solution set is $\{x \mid x \approx -3.2 \text{ or } x \approx 0.5 \text{ or } x \approx 2.8\}$.

   e. Domain: $(-\infty, 1) \cup (1, \infty)$.   Range: $(-\infty, \infty)$.

3. **a.** $m(-5) = 2$.

   b. $m(-1)$ is not defined.

   c. $m(3) = 1$.

   d. The solution set is $\{-6\}$.

   e. The solution set is $\{-5, 3.5\}$.

   f. The solution set is $\{x \mid x \approx -4.8 \text{ or } x \approx -1.3 \text{ or } x = 4\}$.

   g. The solution set is $\{-3\}$.

   h. The solution set is $(-\infty, -6]$.

   i. The solution set is $(-5.5, -1) \cup [1, 5)$.

   j. The solution set is $(-4, -2)$.

   k. Domain: $(-\infty, -1) \cup [1, 5)$.   Range: $(-\infty, 6]$.

4. a. Domain: $(-\infty, \infty)$.   Range: $[0, \infty)$.

b. The solution set is $\{-4, 4\}$.

c. The solution set is $(-5, 5)$.

d. The solution set is $(-\infty, -3] \cup [3, \infty)$.

e.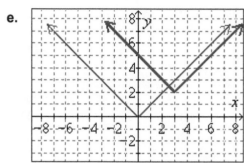

Domain: G $(-\infty, \infty)$.   Range: $[2, \infty)$.

Compared with the graph of $F(x) = |x|$, the graph of $G(x) = |x - 3| + 2$ appears to be shifted right 3 units and shifted up 2 units.

f. The solution set is $\{1, 5\}$.

g. No solution.

h. The solution set is $[-1, 7]$.

5. a. The solution set is $\{-5, -3, 1\}$.

b. The solution set is $(-5, -3) \cup (1, \infty)$.

SUPPLEMENT TO §6.1:

1. a. Domain: $(-\infty, 2) \cup (2, \infty)$.
Range: $(-\infty, -4) \cup (-4, \infty)$.

b. Domain: $(-\infty, -3) \cup (-3, 2) \cup (2, \infty)$.
Range: $(-\infty, 0] \cup (1, \infty)$.

2. a. $f(x) + 2 = \dfrac{11}{5 - x}$.

b. $f(x + 2) = \dfrac{2x + 5}{3 - x}$.

c. $3f(x) = \dfrac{6x + 3}{5 - x}$.

d. $f(3x) = \dfrac{6x + 1}{5 - 3x}$.

SUPPLEMENT TO §6.2:

1. a. $f(x) = \dfrac{2x^2 + 6x}{3x + 9}$

$= \dfrac{2x}{3}, \quad x \neq -3$

b. $T(x) = \dfrac{x^2 + 6x + 9}{x^2 - 9}$

$= \dfrac{x + 3}{x - 3}, \quad x \neq -3$

c. $g(x) = \dfrac{2x^2 - x - 6}{x^2 + x - 6}$

$= \dfrac{2x + 3}{x + 3}, \quad x \neq 2$

d. $L(x) = \dfrac{x^3 - 4x^2 - 5x}{2x^2 - 13x + 15}$

$= \dfrac{x(x + 1)}{2x - 3}, \quad x \neq 5$

e. $d(x) = \dfrac{x^2 - 16}{12 - 3x}$

$= -\dfrac{x + 4}{3}, \quad x \neq 4$

f. $A(x) = \dfrac{12x^2 - 23x + 10}{12x^2 - 23x + 10}$

$= 1, \quad x \neq \tfrac{5}{4}, x \neq \tfrac{2}{3}$

SUPPLEMENT TO §6.3:

1. a. $a(x) = \dfrac{x^2 + 5x - 4}{(x + 2)(x - 3)}$; Domain: $\left\{ x \mid x \neq -2 \text{ and } x \neq 3 \right\}$

b. $b(x) = \dfrac{x^2 + x + 8}{(x + 2)(x - 3)}$; Domain: $\left\{ x \mid x \neq -2 \text{ and } x \neq 3 \right\}$

c. $c(x) = \dfrac{2(x + 1)}{(x + 2)(x - 3)};$ Domain : $\{x \mid x \neq -2 \text{ and } x \neq 3\}$

d. $d(x) = \dfrac{(x + 1)(x + 2)}{2(x - 3)}$

SUPPLEMENT TO §7.4:

1. a. $[5, \infty)$

c. $[3, \infty)$

2. a. $\left(-\infty, \frac{7}{2}\right]$

c. $[-5, \infty)$

3. a. $\left[-\frac{3}{2}, \infty\right)$

c. $(-\infty, 2]$

4. a. $(-\infty, \infty)$

c. $(-\infty, \infty)$

5. a. $\left[\frac{7}{3}, \infty\right)$

c. $(-\infty, 3]$

SUPPLEMENT TO §7.5:

1. a. $f(-2) = 4$

b. $(-\infty, 2]$

c. $x = 1$

2. **a.** Algebraically, we get two solutions: $x = 1$, $x = 4$.

   b. Graphically, we get one solution: $x = 4$.

   c. $x = 1$ does not satisfy the original equation, leaving $x = 4$ as the only solution.

   d. We see that the algebraic solutions which do not work in the original equation also do not show up as solutions when solving graphically.

SUPPLEMENT TO §8.2:

1. **a.** Domain: $(-\infty, \infty)$. Range: $(-1, \infty)$.

   b. Domain: $(-\infty, \infty)$. Range: $(-\infty, 6]$.

2. **a.** The coordinates of the vertex are approximately $(-6.25, 30.625)$.

   b. $f(-6.25) = 30.625$.

   c. The horizontal intercepts are approximately $(-2.5, 0)$ and $(15, 0)$.

   d. The vertical intercept is $(0, 15)$.

   e. Domain: $(-\infty, \infty)$. Range: $(-\infty, 30.625]$.

SUPPLEMENT TO §8.3:

1. **a.** $F(2) = 3$. Two hours after the storm ended, the water in the ditch was 3 feet deep.

   b. $F(t) = -(t - 1)^2 + 4$.

   c. The vertex is $(1, 4)$. One hour after the storm ended, the water in the ditch reached its maximum depth of 4 feet.

   d. The solution set is $\{-1, 3\}$.

e. Domain: $[-1, 3]$. One hour before the storm ended the ditch was empty and 3 hours after the storm ended, the ditch was empty again, having drained completely, and between these two times there was always water in the ditch, so all values between (and including) -1 and 3 need to be in the domain.

f. Range: $[0, 4]$. The range represents all possible water depths in the ditch. Since the maximum depth is 4 feet and the minimum depth is 0 feet (when the ditch is dry), and since all depths between these are possible, all values between (and including) 0 and 4 need to be in the range.

g. The water in the ditch will be 1 foot deep at approximately 0.732 hours before the storm ended and approximately 2.732 hours after the storm ended.

h. The solution set contains only non-real solutions, which indicates that the water level is never 6 feet deep in the ditch.

i.

2. a. $(0, 28)$. The TV is launched from a height of 28 feet.

b. $(-20, 0)$ and $(140, 0)$. Only the second point makes sense in context. The TV lands 140 feet horizontally from where it was launched.

c. The vertex is $(60, 64)$. The TV reaches its maximum height of 64 feet when it is 60 feet horizontally from the trebuchet.

d. The TV is 40 feet above the ground when it is approximately 11.01 feet and approximately 108.99 feet horizontally away from the trebuchet.

e. The TV never gets 75 feet above the ground.

f. The TV is 9 feet above her head when it passes over her.

g. $[0, 140]$ because, at some point during its trip, the TV's horizontal distance was each unique value between (and including) 0 and 140 feet, so all of these values must be in the domain.

h. $[0, 64]$ because, at some point during its trip, the TV's height was each unique value between (and including) 0 and 64 feet, so all of these values must be in the range.

SPS 24

Formulas and Equations

$m = \dfrac{y_2 - y_1}{x_2 - x_1}$ Slope of a line

$ax + b = 0$ Linear equation

$y = mx + b$ Slope–intercept form

$y = m(x - x_1) + y_1$ Point–slope form

$x = h$ Vertical line

$y = b$ Horizontal line

$d = rt$ Distance, rate, and time

$s = 16t^2$ Distance for a falling object

$a^2 - b^2 = (a - b)(a + b)$ Difference of two squares

$\begin{aligned}(a + b)^2 &= a^2 + 2ab + b^2\\ (a - b)^2 &= a^2 - 2ab + b^2\end{aligned}$ Square of a binomial

$x = -\dfrac{b}{2a}$ Vertex formula (x-coordinate)

$y = a(x - h)^2 + k$ Vertex form

$ax^2 + bx + c = 0$ Quadratic equation

$x = \dfrac{-b \pm \sqrt{b^2 - 4ac}}{2a}$ Quadratic formula

$(x - h)^2 + (y - k)^2 = r^2$ Equation of a circle

$d = \sqrt{(x_2 - x_1)^2 + (y_2 - y_1)^2}$ Distance between two points

Geometry

Rectangle
$A = LW$
$P = 2L + 2W$

Triangle
$A = \frac{1}{2}bh$
$P = a + b + c$

Pythagorean Theorem
$c^2 = a^2 + b^2$

Circle
$C = 2\pi r$
$A = \pi r^2$

Rectangular (Parallelepiped) Box
$V = LWH$
$S = 2LW + 2LH + 2WH$

Cylinder
$V = \pi r^2 h$
$S = 2\pi rh + 2\pi r^2$

Sphere
$V = \frac{4}{3}\pi r^3$
$S = 4\pi r^2$

Cone
$V = \frac{1}{3}\pi r^2 h$
$S = \pi r^2 + \pi r\sqrt{r^2 + h^2}$

Library of Functions
Basic Functions

Several important functions are used in algebra. The following provides symbolic, numerical, and graphical representations for several of these basic functions.

Absolute Value Function: $f(x) = |x|$

x	-2	-1	0	1	2
$|x|$	2	1	0	1	2

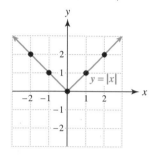

Domain: $(-\infty, \infty)$
Range: $[0, \infty)$

Square Function: $f(x) = x^2$

x	-2	-1	0	1	2
x^2	4	1	0	1	4

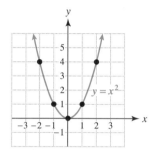

Domain: $(-\infty, \infty)$
Range: $[0, \infty)$

Cube Function: $f(x) = x^3$

x	-2	-1	0	1	2
x^3	-8	-1	0	1	8

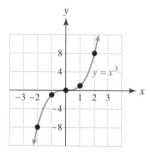

Domain: $(-\infty, \infty)$
Range: $(-\infty, \infty)$

Square Root Function: $f(x) = \sqrt{x}$

x	0	1	4	9
$\sqrt{x}$	0	1	2	3

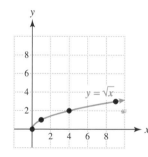

Domain: $[0, \infty)$
Range: $[0, \infty)$

Cube Root Function: $f(x) = \sqrt[3]{x}$

x	-8	-1	0	1	8
$\sqrt[3]{x}$	-2	-1	0	1	2

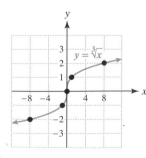

Domain: $(-\infty, \infty)$
Range: $(-\infty, \infty)$

Reciprocal Function: $f(x) = \dfrac{1}{x}$

x	-2	-1	0	1	2
$\dfrac{1}{x}$	$-\dfrac{1}{2}$	-1	—	1	$\dfrac{1}{2}$

Domain: $(-\infty, 0) \cup (0, \infty)$
Range: $(-\infty, 0) \cup (0, \infty)$